MW00368554

Applied Social and Political Philosophy

Elizabeth Smith

Ohio University

H. Gene Blocker

Ohio University

Prentice Hall, Upper Saddle River, New Jersey 07458

Library of Congress Cataloging-in-Publication Data

Applied social and political philosophy/[compiled by] Elizabeth
   Smith and H. Gene Blocker.
      p. cm.
   ISBN 0-13-816448-7
   1. Political science—Philosophy.   2. Civil rights.   3. Human
rights.   4. Social problems.   I. Smith, Elizabeth H., [date].
II. Blocker, H. Gene.
JA71.A65   1994
320.5—dc20   93-38376

Acquisitions editor: *Ted Bolen*
Editorial/production supervision: *Edie Riker*
Cover design: *Bruce Kenselaar*
Cover photo illustration: *George Bellows, "New York," 1911, (detail) Oil on canvas, 40 x 60". Collection
   of Mr. and Mrs. Paul Mellon © 1993 National Gallery of Art, Washington, D.C.*
Production Coordinator: *Peter Havens*
Assistant editor: *Nicole Gray*

© 1994 by Prentice-Hall, Inc.
A Pearson Education Company
Upper Saddle River, NJ 07458

All rights reserved. No part of this book may be
reproduced, in any form or by any means,
without permission in writing from the publisher.

Printed in the United States of America

10 9 8 7 6 5 4 3 2 1

ISBN   0-13-816448-7

Prentice-Hall International (UK) Limited, London
Prentice-Hall of Australia Pty. Limited, Sydney
Prentice-Hall Canada Inc., Toronto
Prentice-Hall Hispanoamericana, S.A., Mexico
Prentice-Hall of India Private Limited, New Delhi
Prentice-Hall of Japan, Inc., Tokyo
Pearson Education Asia Pte. Ltd., Singapore
Editoria Prentice-Hall do Brasil, Ltda., Rio De Janeiro

Peace

Is the temporary beautiful ignorance that War
Somewhere progresses.

Edna St. Vincent Millay

Contents

2. Enlightenment   49

3. Industrial Revolution   101

7. Human Rights   314

8. The Rights and Welfare of the Environment, Animals, and Future Generations 357

9. Discrimination 409

Preface for the Instructor

This is a book in "applied social and political philosophy," which is both an extension of and different from the now more familiar notion of "applied ethics." Just as social and political philosophy is different in significant ways from ethics, so applied social and political philosophy is in principle different from applied ethics. Recently the very active field of applied ethics has tended to absorb related discussions of social and political issues, such as preferential treatment, censorship, abortion legislation, and so forth. This may be why there has been a relative neglect in recent years of the application of social and political philosophy to the hard public policy decisions we face. We think the time is right and much is to be gained by making a separation and treating these issues and topics as social and political, rather than ethical, problems.

Of course, even before the days of "applied philosophy," ethics and social/political philosophy shared points of concern and overlapped in important areas. Both are concerned with normative human decisions, with right and wrong, good and bad, with duty and obligation. Surely one of the moral obligations of the individual is their prima facie obligation to obey the laws of the state in which they reside. In addition, state policies often raise moral concerns; for example, there are many ethical questions about a state policy of ethnic purification or, as it is called today, "ethnic cleansing." Nonetheless, the focus in ethics and in social and political philosophy is different. I may believe on moral grounds that abortion is wrong, but nonetheless for social and political reasons hold that governments should not interfere in a woman's choice whether to have an abortion or not. The first is a question of what an individual ought or ought not to do; the second is a question of what the state should do about it, if anything. An individual person, we might think, ought to pray before each meal, help a homeless person, abstain from addictive substances, prevent child abuse, avoid homosexual practices and pornographic stimulation—but it does not follow that that same person will vote for school prayer, welfare socialism, prohibition, anti-gay legislation, or censorship of pornography.

The question of what is morally right is not identical to the quite different, though often and confusingly related, question of how the state should intervene, if at all. What is the proper role of the state? What is the relation between the power of the state to command the obedience of its citizens and the freedom of the individual citizen to pursue their own individual interests? Economically, how much can and should the state do and who is going to pay for it? How can or should the state intervene in questions of moral or religious belief where there are deep divisions of opinion among the citizens? These essentially social and political questions cannot be answered solely by reference to our decisions about what is moral or ethical. The person voting for school prayer, welfare for the homeless, anti-gay legislation will therefore need good social and political reasons, and not just good moral (and possibly religious) grounds, for their decision.

Once we focus on the uniquely social and political nature of these issues, we find ourselves at once entangled in the nitty-gritty arena of some very "hard choices." Consider, for example, such current issues as hazardous waste disposal, forbidding logging to protect the spotted owl, and abortion. Not only are moral, religious, as well as political considerations involved in these contemporary issues, but also different and competing interest groups, each vying for protection of its special rights and privileges at the expense of everyone else. Add to that, the complicating problems of economics, scientific feasibility, environmental protection, health concerns—plus the fact that in many cases such issues are so urgent and pressing they cannot be endlessly debated, but for better or worse, must be decided now or very soon. Finally, although many people are affected, no one is in the position of an authoritative expert. The physicist can tell us how long nuclear waste takes to decay; health professionals can explain the health risks; geologists can predict the probability of seepage into underground water systems; economists can be called upon to speak to the economic impact of new waste disposal sites; biologists can help us understand the ecological dangers; and so on—but there is no one trained to put all these competing concerns together, weighing differently valued risks and benefits, to formulate a decision whether to allow the siting of a proposed nuclear waste disposal facility. "Applied social and political philosophy" is concerned with facilitating decision making in these very difficult, complex, and urgent matters in which everyone's interests are at stake and in which, at the same time, no one is or can be an "expert."

This collection of readings is designed to be used in a course on political, or social and political philosophy. Our main objective is to provide teaching materials for those wishing to develop courses in *applied* social/political philosophy. Theories cannot be applied until we know what those theories are. It is for this reason that we have divided the readings into two parts: Part I has a fairly complete selection of primary sources drawn from classical theorists in social and political philosophy, while Part II has a selection of attempts to apply social and political theories to pressing, concrete social problems.

One way to use this book is to divide the course, discussing the traditional philosophical theories in the first half, before turning in the second half, to the "applications." But this is not the *only* way this book can be fruitfully used. For those instructors who prefer a historical approach, encouraging students to dig deeply into the philosophical classics, we have included plenty of material to keep the brightest and most ambitious students well occupied for an entire quarter or semester. Those instructors who wish to focus on contemporary events may begin with Part II. This might also be the preferred option for an advanced class of students who have already read something of the history of social and political philosophy and who are now ready to tackle some of the knotty contemporary issues. An obvious variation on this last plan would be to start with one of the contemporary issues, referring back to the "classics" as the need arises. So, for example, several of the readings in Part II concerning distributive justice refer to the work of Nozick. Students unfamiliar with Nozick can backtrack and read that selection. And since Nozick discusses his theory in terms of Locke, students may find it helpful to turn to the selection from Locke as well.

Whatever option is adopted, we think this book contains enough relevant material for many different courses in social and political philosophy. And, of course, whatever option is chosen, some selection will have to be made among all the possible readings contained in this book. We do not imagine that readers of this book will sit down and read it from cover to cover, but rather that individual instructors will select the readings and the order and arrangement of these readings to suit their own particular interests, as well as the level and interests of their students. It is also for this reason that we have tried in our introductions not to summarize and assess the arguments put forward in the various readings but rather to provide some background understanding of relevant concepts, distinctions, and theories. In Part II, we have tried to select readings which represent the range of ongoing debates on sensitive contemporary social issues. We have also included readings which address contemporary political developments, such as the reemergence of fascism and nationalism. We have tried not to interfere with the student's primary task to come to terms with the readings, nor with the instructors' choice of approach to the issues raised in the readings. Our task in putting together this collection of readings, in other words, is not to construct what we consider the ideal university course in social and political philosophy but rather to provide in a single volume an adequate range of the materials from which different instructors with different interests and objectives can organize any number of different courses of their own design. The only course in social and political philosophy for which this book would *not* be suitable is one in which the instructor felt students simply could not master original philosophical texts and would therefore prefer a monograph written especially for beginning students. Otherwise we invite instructors to freely select and rearrange the material in our book to suit the needs of the particular course they plan to teach.

Introduction

We have always lived within social groupings. Biologically it is hard to imagine human beings surviving long without the protection of at least the nuclear or extended family, if not some larger community. This is part of what Aristotle meant when he said that "man is a social animal."

At the same time however, there does not appear to be any single universal, biologically innate or hereditary way in which this social grouping must occur. While some theorists argue that some very general social arrangements are biologically innate, for example, male dominance, a female role of child rearing and nurturing, there remains a wide range of more specific possibilities for social arrangements available to human groups to accomplish this. Anthropologists and historians have described dozens of quite different specific patterns of social arrangements—monogamous versus polygamous marital practices, secular versus nonsecular states, military versus priestly rule, hereditary versus elected rulers. Social arrangements are therefore, at least to some extent, a matter of convention. The human animal is also capable of consciously reflecting on and questioning the value of different human practices. Unlike other animals, human beings can therefore reflect on their social practices, evaluate them, and so to some extent work to change them. It is therefore natural for human beings to reflect on the ideal group dynamics and the correct relationship of the individual to the group. This is part of what Aristotle meant when he said that "man is a rational animal."

Although human beings have surely always reflected, questioned, and sought to change existing social patterns in which they found themselves, the first *written* evidence of such reflection occurs in the ancient period, of roughly 500 to 200 B.C. in Greece and also in other parts of the world. This written evidence is the beginning of social and political philosophy. Many of the issues raised at this early period have continued, up to the present, to be the most important pressing social and political questions. Examples are: Are there limits on the authority of the state? What are they and why? What is a just state, and what ought to be the relationship between the individual and the state?

In Western social and political thought theories have shifted back and forth between the tendency to put a primary emphasis on the welfare of the community, with the idea that the individual is better off in a properly functioning, healthy, unified community with which the individual identifies, and the tendency to put the primary emphasis on the freedom of the individual, with the idea that the community is better off if individuals are free to exercise individual autonomy.

Since social arrangements are open to change and rational negotiation, the question arises of how to *justify* proposed changes or whether to retain the status quo. Social and political philosophers have offered a number of bases for justifying one form of social organization over others, for example, on the basis of human rights, social utility, or as a means of perfecting our basic human nature.

Although people *in general* are free to choose particular forms of government, individuals are so molded by their society they often do not see the choices open to them. We may not even be aware of alternatives. Most of us tend to assume that the forms of social organization with which we have grown up are natural, obviously correct, and even the only choice. Part of the task of social and political philosophy is to make us more reflective about our own presuppositions and assumptions. In America in particular we tend to take for granted that governments exist to protect the freedom of individuals, that people should be treated equally, that individuals should be free from constraints to conform to the group, and particularly that minorities ought to be protected from conformity to the will of the majority. But it is important to realize this is a particular American view, based on our particular historical situation. The Bill of Rights, attached as the first amendments to the U.S. Constitution, appears to limit the power of the majority to act as they want. For example, polls indicate that most people want to ban flag burning, but the Supreme Court says doing so is unconstitutional, which limits majority rule. Even so, the Constitution, including the Bill of Rights, could legally be changed. And interpretations of the Constitution have changed over time. For example, slavery was once legal and suffrage not universal. In fact, Americans have legally changed voting practices over the years, gradually expanding voting rights from free, male, literate, property-owning adults to include uneducated, nonpropertied citizens, African Americans, women, and 18-year-olds.

Social and political philosophers have sought, not only to reflect on and become more aware of our internalized biases, but to construct viable theories of just social arrangements and to use those theories to correct perceived injustices and to improve social ordering. At first it may seem strange how philosophical "armchair" "ivory-tower" theories could have any practical application to real-life social and political issues. Philosophers are no more "experts" in these matters than are scientists, but philosophers are experienced in managing and seeking to resolve difficult and complex issues through reasoned debate. A study of social and political philosophy can, therefore, be useful first in identifying the issues, and second in introducing concepts and logical methods for reconciling conflicts among these competing issues. In Part I we will examine the main theories of social and political philosophy and in Part II we will look at some examples of attempts to apply these theories to real problems.

Part I
Classical Theories

1   Ancient and Medieval

The major tradition in Western philosophy has its roots in a form of analysis which began in Asia Minor around the eleventh century B.C. Fragments of philosophical works of early periods tell us that systematic philosophical theories were being debated, but it is not until Plato, an Athenian philosopher (ca. 428–348/7 B.C.) that an extensive body of written text survives. The first true institution of higher learning was begun by Plato (called the Academy), but prior to this time students studied on a more informal basis with persons who questioned the nature of society, mathematical relations, music, and the arts. Plato studied with Socrates (470–399 B.C.), the most famous of these informal philosophy teachers. No works written by Socrates are in existence, but he is the major character and the chief protagonist in almost all of Plato's *Dialogues*. Whether the views attributed to him in the *Dialogues* were his is debatable, but we do know that he was concerned with understanding what morally right actions are, the relationship between moral correctness and self-interest, and the nature of justice. Plato, on the other hand, we know was a critic of the Athenian government of his day, which was a form of direct democracy in which every citizen (limited to freeborn males) was expected to take part in the governance of the Athenian city-state by voting and speaking in the Assembly, sitting on juries, accepting election or appointment to office, and so forth. This system was easily dominated by powerful men, and it sometimes collapsed into an oligarchy in which a few powerful persons were able to subvert democratic rule. Other forms of government among Greek city-states were dictatorship and aristocracy. The Athenian city-state was only one of a number of Greek city-states. The Greek city-states had relationships with one another and with other political states which were sometimes friendly and sometimes warlike.

Aristotle (384–322 B.C.) entered Plato's Academy ca. 367 B.C. He was critical of much of Plato's thought and later began a new university of his own. He was tutor for the future Alexander the Great, who attempted to bring under one government the various Greek city-states, as well as such far flung places as Persia, India, and Egypt. By the time of the Roman rhetorician and statesman, Cicero (106–43 B.C.), Greek political power had waned, but Greek philosophy was still influential. A new political force was found in Rome which in time would attempt to unite in one political entity, under Roman domination, the Western world from Asia to Great Britain.

During the period of the Roman Empire (27 B.C.–A.D.284) the Christian faith began its rise to a position of intellectual and political power. By the medieval period the system of education was dominated by the Catholic church. St. Thomas Aquinas (1224–1274) was a

Catholic scholar and theoretician who attempted to reconcile some elements of Aristotle's thought with church doctrine.

A striking feature when we consider today the social and political thought of the ancient and medieval thinkers is the extent to which they focus on concerns which are still very real and immediate to us, even though much of their perspective is different. Some important differences should be noted. "Individualism," as we understand it, and particularly "individual rights," are modern concepts. Indeed, earlier thinkers were very concerned to determine which actions are right and to determine what makes an action right. But the concept of a person having a right vis-à-vis other persons had not yet evolved. The related notion of "equality" is impacted by this. The ancient and medieval thinkers are concerned with justice but equal treatment of all people is not the bedrock of their notion of what is just, in part because early Greek philosophers did not take it for granted that people were sufficiently alike to be treated equally.

READINGS

Plato's (428–348/7 B.C.) concerns in social and political philosophy are deep-seated and far-reaching. He searches for a definition of "justice" and seeks to distinguish it from self-interest. Justice, he argues, is a matter of balance in the individual soul between appetite, spirit, and reason, and in the state between parts of the community analogous to the parts of the soul, namely, craftsmen, auxiliaries, and rulers. In both cases, Plato's view is that the "best part" (reason and rulers) should be in control over the "worst parts." This is his basis for criticizing a democratic form of government, which he argues will result in chaos and ultimately tyranny. Instead, Plato favored an aristocracy, not an aristocracy of nobility, but an aristocracy of talented, knowledgeable people capable of knowing what is good and making wise political decisions. Plato's view is that a chief role of the state is to maintain a healthy moral environment to enable individuals to become virtuous by regulating expression, education, and the arts. Plato's account of the properly functioning state is utopian in nature.

Aristotle (384–322 B.C.) emphasizes the practical as opposed to utopian analysis of political arrangements. Man, he says, is a political or social creature whose nature is to form communities. Justice within a community he treats as a matter of proportion between individuals. Individuals who are alike should be treated alike. Aristotle, however, shares with Plato the view that not all people are alike in some respects and hence that freeborn Greek males form a natural aristocracy.

The extension of government from relatively small communities to vast continental areas during Alexander's Empire and continuing into the Roman Empire leads to the question of how to justify governing different peoples and societies by one set of laws and institutions. Cicero provides one answer in arguing, in counterdistiction to the early Greek view, that human nature is alike and that hence one set of standards pertains to everyone. These standards he calls "natural law" and he argues that these universal moral standards can be reasoned out by anyone and that they provide the basis of a just state.

St. Thomas Aquinas extends the conception of natural law and distinguishes it from other kinds of laws (positive or civil law, divine law, and eternal law). Aquinas argues that policies which are inconsistent with natural law are unjust and hence natural law becomes a test of the validity of civil law. Each individual is responsible for making their own determination about how to act and will be held individually responsible. This emphasis reflects the increased emphasis on individual accountability arising within Christian thought.

The Republic

Plato

I walked down to the Piraeus yesterday with Glaucon to make my prayers to the goddess....The prayers and the spectacle were over, and we were leaving to go back to the city, when from some way off Polemarchus...caught sight of us starting homewards....

Socrates, said Polemarchus, I do believe you are starting back to town and leaving us....Well, he said you see what a large party we are?...Unless you are more than a match for us, then, you must stay here....

Accordingly, we went home with Polemarchus....Polemarchus' father, Cephalus, was at home,...and it struck me that he had aged a good deal....As soon as he saw me, Cephalus greeted me. You don't often...visit us, Socrates, he said. But you ought to. If I still had the strength to walk to town easily, you would not have to come here....But, as things are, you really ought to come here oftener. I find...that in proportion as bodily pleasures lose their savour, my appetite for the things of the mind grows keener and I enjoy discussing them more than ever. So you must not disappoint me. Treat us like old friends, and come here often to have a talk with these young men.

To tell the truth, Cephalus, I answered, I enjoy talking with very old people. They have gone before us on a road by which we too may have to travel, and I think we do well to learn from them what it is like, easy or difficult, rough or smooth. And now that you have reached an age when your foot...is on the threshold, I should like to hear what report you can give and whether you find it a painful time of life.

All these troubles, Socrates,...have only one cause; and that is not old age, but a man's character. If you have a contented mind at peace with itself, age is no intolerable burden; without that, Socrates, age and youth will be equally painful....

I fancy, Cephalus, said I, most people will not accept that account; they imagine that it is not character that makes your burden light, but your wealth. The rich, they say, have many consolations.

That is true, he replied; they do not believe me; and there is something in their suggestion, though not so much as they suppose....If it is true that a good man will not find it easy to bear old age and poverty combined, no more will riches ever make a bad man contented and cheerful....

What do you take to be the greatest advantage you have got from being wealthy?

One that perhaps not many people would take my word for. I can tell you, Socrates, that, when the prospect of dying is near at hand, a man begins to feel some alarm about things that never troubled him before. He may have laughed at those stories they tell of another world and of punishments there for wrongdoing in this life; but now the soul is tormented by a doubt whether they may not be true....He begins thinking over the past: is there anyone he has wronged? If he finds that his life has been full of wrongdoing, he starts up from his sleep in terror like a child, and his life is haunted by dark forebodings....

Now in this, as I believe, lies the chief value of wealth....It can do much to save us from going to that other world in fear of having cheated or deceived anyone even unintentionally or of being in debt to some god for sacrifice or to some man for money....

You put your case admirably, Cephalus, said I. But take this matter of doing right: can we say that it really consists in nothing more nor less than

From *The Republic of Plato*, Francis Macdonald Cornford, trans. (New York: Oxford University Press, 1945). Reprinted by permission of Oxford University Press.

telling the truth and paying back anything we may have received? Are not these very actions sometimes right and sometimes wrong? Suppose, for example, a friend who had lent us a weapon were to go mad and then ask for it back, surely anyone would say we ought not to return it. It would not be 'right' to do so; nor yet to tell the truth without reserve to a madman.

No, it would not.

Right conduct, then, cannot be defined as telling the truth and restoring anything we have been trusted with.

Yes, it can, Polemarchus broke in, at least if we are to believe Simonides.

Well, well, said Cephalus, I will bequeath the argument to you. It is time for me to attend to the sacrifice.

Your part, then, said Polemarchus, will fall to me as your heir.

By all means, said Cephalus with a smile; and with that he left.

Then, said I,...tell me, what is this saying of Simonides about right conduct which you approve?

That it is just to render every man his due. That seems to me a fair statement....

What this saying means you may know, Polemarchus, but I do not. Obviously it does not mean...—returning something we have been entrusted with to the owner even when he has gone out of his mind. And yet surely it is his due, if he asks for it back?

Yes.

But it is out of the question to give it back when he has gone mad?

True.

Simonides, then, must have meant something different from that when he said it was just to render a man his due.

Certainly he did; his idea was that, as between friends, what one owes to another is to do him good, not harm.

I see, said I; to repay money entrusted to one is not to render what is due, if the two parties are friends and the repayment proves harmful to the lender. That is what you say Simonides meant?

Yes, certainly.

And what about enemies? Are we to render whatever is their due to them?

Yes certainly, what really is due to them; which means, I suppose, what is appropriate to an enemy—some sort of injury.

It seems, then, that Simonides was using words with a hidden meaning, as poets will. He really meant to define justice as rendering to everyone what is appropriate to him; only he called that his 'due.'...

Which do you mean by a man's friends and enemies—those whom he believes to be good honest people and the reverse, or those who really are, though they may not seem so?

Naturally, his loves and hates depend on what he believes.

But don't people often mistake an honest man for a rogue, or a rogue for an honest man; in which case they regard good people as enemies and bad people as friends?

No doubt.

But all the same, it will then be right for them to help the rogue and to injure the good man?

Apparently.

And yet a good man is one who is not given to doing wrong.

True.

According to your account, then, it is right to ill-treat a man who does no wrong.

No, no, Socrates; that can't be sound doctrine.

It must be the wrongdoers, then, that it is right to injure, and the honest that are to be helped.

That sounds better.

Then, Polemarchus, the conclusion will be that for a bad judge of character it will often be right to injure his friends, when they really are rogues, and to help his enemies, when they really are honest men—the exact opposite of what we took Simonides to mean.

That certainly does follow, he said. We must shift our ground. Perhaps our definition of friend and enemy was wrong.

What definition, Polemarchus?

We said a friend was one whom we believe to be an honest man.

And how are we to define him now?

As one who really is honest as well as seeming so. If he merely seems so, he will be only a seeming friend. And the same will apply to enemies.

On this showing, then, it is the good people that will be our friends, the wicked our enemies.

Yes.

You would have us, in fact, add something to our original definition of justice: it will not mean merely doing good to friends and harm to enemies, but doing good to friends who are good, and harm to enemies who are wicked.

Yes, I think that is all right.

Can it really be a just man's business to harm any human being?

Certainly; it is right for him to harm bad men who are his enemies.

But does not harming a horse or a dog mean making it a worse horse or dog, so that each will be a less perfect creature in its own special way?

Yes.

Isn't that also true of human beings—that to harm them means making them worse men by the standard of human excellence?

Yes.

And is not justice a peculiarly human excellence?

Undoubtedly.

To harm a man, then, must mean making him less just.

I suppose so....

Whereas the just man is to exercise his justice by making men unjust? Or, in more general terms, the good are to make men bad by exercising their virtue? Can that be so?

No, it cannot.

It can no more be the function of goodness to do harm than of heat to cool or of drought to produce moisture. So if the just man is good, the business of harming people, whether friends or not, must belong to his opposite, the unjust.

I think that is perfectly true, Socrates.

So it was not a wise saying that justice is giving every man his due, if that means that harm is due from the just man to his enemies, as well as help to his friends. That is not true; because we have found that it is never right to harm anyone....

All this time Thrasymachus had been trying more than once to break in upon our conversation; but his neighbours had restrained him, wishing to hear the argument to the end. In the pause after my last words he could keep quiet no longer; but gathering himself up like a wild beast he sprang at us as if he would tear us in pieces....

Listen,...Thrasymachus began. What I say is that 'just' or 'right' means nothing but what is to the interest of the stronger party. Well, where is your applause? You don't mean to give it me.

I will, as soon as I understand, I said. I don't see yet what you mean by right being the interest of the stronger party. For instance, Polydamas, the athlete, is stronger than we are, and it is to his interest to eat beef for the sake of his muscles; but surely you don't mean that the same diet would be good for weaker men and therefore be right for us?

You are trying to be funny, Socrates. It's a low trick to take my words in the sense you think will be most damaging.

No, no, I protested; but you must explain.

Don't you know, then, that a state may be ruled by a despot, or a democracy, or an aristocracy?

Of course.

And that the ruling element is always the strongest?

Yes.

Well then, in every case the laws are made by the ruling party in its own interest; a democracy makes democratic laws, a despot autocratic ones, and so on. By making these laws they define as 'right' for their subjects whatever is for their own interest, and they call anyone who breaks them a 'wrongdoer' and punish him accordingly. That is what I mean: in all states alike 'right' has the same meaning, namely what is for the interest of the party established in power, and that is the strongest. So the sound conclusion is that what is 'right' is the same everywhere: the interest of the stronger party.

Now I see what you mean, said I; whether it is true or not, I must try to make out....

We must find out whether your definition is true....

Go ahead, then.

I will. Tell me this. No doubt you also think it is right to obey the men in power?

I do.

Are they infallible in every type of state, or can they sometimes make a mistake?

Of course they can make a mistake.

In framing laws, then, they may do their work well or badly?

No doubt.

Well, that is to say, when the laws they make are to their own interest; badly, when they are not?

Yes.

But the subjects are to obey any law they lay down, and they will then be doing right?

Of course.

If so, by your account, it will be right to do what is not to the interest of the stronger party, as well as what is so.

What's that you are saying?

Just what you said, I believe; but let us look again. Haven't you admitted that the rulers, when they enjoin certain acts on their subjects, sometimes mistake their own best interests, and at the same time that it is right for the subjects to obey, whatever they may enjoin?

Yes, I suppose so.

Well, that amounts to admitting that it is right to do what is not to the interest of the rulers or the stronger party. They may unwittingly enjoin what is to their own disadvantage; and you say it is right for the others to do as they are told. In that case, their duty must be the opposite of what you said, because the weaker will have been ordered to do what is against the interest of the stronger. You with your intelligence must see how that follows.

Yes, Socrates, said Polemarchus, that is undeniable....

No, said Cleitophon; he meant whatever the stronger *believes* to be in his own interest. That is what the subject must do, and what Thrasymachus meant to define as right....

If Thrasymachus says so now, let us take him in that sense. Now, Thrasymachus, tell me, was that what you intended to say—that right means what the stronger thinks is to his interest, whether it really is so or not?

Most certainly not, he replied. Do you suppose I should speak of a man as 'stronger' or 'superior' at the very moment when he is making a mistake?

I did think you said as much when you admitted that rulers are not always infallible.

That is because you are a quibbler, Socrates. Would you say a man deserves to be called a physician at the moment when he makes a mistake in treating his patient and just in respect of that mistake; or a mathematician, when he does a sum wrong and just in so far as he gets a wrong result? Of course we do commonly speak of a physician or a mathematician or a scholar having made a mistake; but really none of these, I should say, is ever mistaken, in so far as he is worthy of the name we give him. So strictly speaking—and you are all for being precise—no one who practices a craft makes mistakes. A man is mistaken when his knowledge fails him; and at that moment he is no craftsman. And what is true of craftsmanship or any sort of skill is true of the ruler: he is never mistaken so long as he is acting as a ruler; though anyone might speak of a ruler making a mistake, just as he might of a physician. You must understand that I was talking in that loose way when I answered your question just now; but the precise statement is this. The ruler, in so far as he is acting as a ruler, makes no mistakes and consequently enjoins what is best for himself; and that is what the subject is to do. So, as I said at first, 'right' means doing what is to the interest of the stronger....

Now tell me about the physician in that strict sense you spoke of: is it his business to earn money or to treat his patients? Remember, I mean your physician who is worthy of the name.

To treat his patients.

And what of the ship's captain in the true sense? Is he a mere seaman or the commander of the crew?

The commander.

Yes, we shall not speak of him as a seaman just because he is on board a ship. That is not the point. He is called captain because of his skill and authority over the crew.

Quite true.

And each of these people has some special interest?

No doubt.

And the craft in question exists for the very purpose of discovering that interest and providing for it?

Yes.

Can it equally be said of any craft that it has an interest, other than its own greatest possible perfection?

What do you mean by that?

Here is an illustration. If you ask me whether it is sufficient for the human body just to be itself, with no need of help from without, I should say, Certainly not; it has weaknesses and defects, and its condition is not all that it might be. That is precisely why the art of medicine was invented: it was designed to help the body and provide for its interests. Would not that be true?

It would.

But now take the art of medicine itself....

Is it not true that no art needs to have its weaknesses remedied or its interests studied either by another art or by itself, because no art has in itself any weakness or fault, and the only interest it is required to serve is that of its subject-matter? In itself, an art is sound and flawless, so long as it is entirely true to its own nature as an art in the strictest sense—and it is the strict sense that I want you to keep in view. Is not that true?

So it appears.

Then, said I, the art of medicine does not study its own interest, but the needs of the body, just as a groom shows his skill by caring for horses, not for the art of grooming. And so every art seeks, not its own advantage—for it has no deficiencies—but the interest of the subject on which it is exercised.

It appears so.

But surely, Thrasymachus, every art has authority and superior power over its subject.

To this he agreed, though very reluctantly.

So far as arts are concerned, then, no art ever studies or enjoins the interest of the superior or stronger party, but always that of the weaker over which it has authority.

Thrasymachus assented to this at last, though he tried to put up a fight. I then went on:

So the physician, as such, studies only the patient's interest, not his own. For as we agreed, the business of the physician, in the strict sense, is not to make money for himself, but to exercise his power over the patient's body; and the ship's captain, again, considered strictly as no mere sailor, but in command of the crew, will study and enjoin the interest of his subordinates, not his own.

He agreed reluctantly.

And so with government of any kind: no ruler, in so far as he is acting as ruler, will study or enjoin what is for his own interest. All that he says and does will be said and done with a view to what is good and proper for the subject for whom he practices his art.

At this point, when everyone could see that Thrasymachus' definition of justice had been turned inside out, instead of making any reply, he said:

Socrates, have you a nurse?

Why do you ask such a question as that? I said. Wouldn't it be better to answer mine?

Because she lets you go about sniffling like a child whose nose wants wiping. She hasn't even taught you to know a shepherd when you see one, or his sheep either.

What makes you say that?

Why, you imagine that a herdsman studies the interests of his flocks or cattle, tending and fattening them up with some other end in view than his master's profit or his own; and so you don't see that, in politics, the genuine ruler regards his subjects exactly like sheep, and thinks of nothing else, night and day, but the good he can get out of them for himself. You are so far out in your notions of right and wrong, justice and injustice, as not to know that 'right' actually means what is good for someone else, and to be 'just' means serving the interest of the stronger who rules, at the cost of the subject who obeys; whereas injustice is just the reverse, asserting its authority over those innocents who are called just, so that they minister solely to their master's advantage and happiness, and not in the least degree to their own. Innocent as you are yourself, Socrates, you must see that a just man always has the worst of it. Take a private business: when a partnership is wound up, you will never find that the more honest of two partners comes off with the larger share; and in their relations to the state, when there are taxes to be paid, the honest man will pay more than the other on the same amount of property; or if there is money to be distributed, the dishonest will get it all. When either of them hold some public office, even if the just man loses in no other way, his private affairs at any rate will suffer from neglect, while his principles will not allow him to help himself from the public funds; not to mention the offence he will give to his friends and relations by refusing to sacrifice those principles to do them a good turn. Injustice has all the opposite advantages. I am speaking of the type I described just now, the man who can get the better of other people on a large scale: you must fix your eye on him, if you want to judge how much it is to one's own interest not to be just. You can see that best in the most consummate form of injustice, which rewards wrongdoing with supreme welfare and happiness and reduces its victims, if they won't retaliate in kind, to misery. That form is despotism, which uses force or fraud to plunder the goods of others, public or private, sacred or profane, and to do it in a wholesale way. If you are caught committing any one of these crimes on a small scale, you are punished and disgraced; they call it sacrilege, kidnapping, burglary, theft and brigandage. But if, besides taking their property, you turn all your countrymen into slaves, you will hear no more of those ugly names; your countrymen themselves will call you the happiest of men and bless your name, and so will everyone who hears of such a complete triumph of injustice; for when people denounce injustice, it is because they are afraid of suffering wrong, not of doing it. So true is it, Socrates, that injustice, on a grand enough scale, is superior to justice in strength and freedom and autocratic power; and 'right,' as I said at first, means simply what serves the interest of the stronger party; 'wrong' means what is for the interest and profit of oneself.

Having deluged our ears with this torrent of words, as the man at the baths might empty a bucket over one's head, Thrasymachus meant to take himself off; but the company obliged him to stay and defend his position. I was specially urgent in my entreaties.

My good Thrasymachus, said I, do you propose to fling a doctrine like that at our heads and then go away without explaining it properly or letting us point out to you whether it is true or not? I want you to stand by your own words; or, if you shift your ground, shift it openly and stop trying to hoodwink us as you are doing now. You see, Thrasymachus, to go back to your earlier argument, in speaking of the shepherd you did not think it necessary to keep to that strict sense you laid down when you defined the genuine physician. You represent him, in his character of shepherd, as feeding up his flock, not for their own sake but for the table or the market, as if he were out to make money as a caterer or a cattle-dealer, rather than a shepherd. Surely the sole concern of the shepherd's art is to do the best for the charges put under its care; its own best interest is sufficiently provided for, so long as it does not fall short of all that shepherding should imply. On that principle it followed, I thought, that any kind of authority, in the state or in private life, must, in its character of authority, consider solely what is best for those under its care. Now what is your opinion? Do you think that the men who govern states—I mean rulers in the strict sense—have no reluctance to hold office?

I don't think so, he replied; I know it.

Well, but haven't you noticed, Thrasymachus, that in other positions of authority no one is willing to act unless he is paid wages, which he demands on the assumption that all the benefit of his action will go to his charges? Tell me: Don't we always distinguish one form of skill from another by its power to effect some particular result? Do say what you really think, so that we may get on.

Yes, that is the distinction.

And also each brings us some benefit that is peculiar to it: medicine gives health, for example; the art of navigation, safety at sea; and so on.

Yes.

And wage-earning brings us wages; that is its distinctive product. Now, speaking with that precision which you proposed, you would not say that the art of navigation is the same as the art of medicine, merely on the ground that a ship's captain regained his health on a voyage, because the sea air was good for him. No more would you identify the practice of medicine with wage-earning because a man may keep his health while earning wages, or a physician attending a case may receive a fee.

No.

And, since we agreed that the benefit obtained by each form of skill is peculiar to it, any common benefit enjoyed alike by all these practitioners must come from some further practice common to them all?

It would seem so.

Yes, we must say that if they all earn wages, they get that benefit in so far as they are engaged in wage-earning as well as in practising their several arts.

He agreed reluctantly.

This benefit, then—the receipt of wages—does not come to a man from his special art. If we are to speak strictly, the physician, as such, produces health; the builder, a house; and then each, in his further capacity of wage-earner, gets his pay. Thus every art has its own function and benefits its proper subject. But suppose the practitioner is not paid; does he then get any benefit from his art?

Clearly not.

And is he doing no good to anyone either, when he works for nothing?

No, I suppose he does some good.

Well then, Thrasymachus, it is now clear that no form of skill or authority provides for its own benefit. As we were saying some time ago, it always studies and prescribes what is good for its subject—the interest of the weaker party, not of the stronger. And that, my friend, is why I said that no one is willing to be in a position of authority and undertake to set straight other men's troubles, without demanding to be paid; because, if he is to do his work well, he will never, in his capacity of ruler, do, or command others to do, what is best for himself, but only what is best for the subject. For that reason, if he is to consent, he must have his recompense....

However, I continued, we may return to that question later. Much more important is the position Thrasymachus is asserting now: that a life of injustice is to be preferred to a life of justice. Which side do you take, Glaucon? Where do you think the truth lies?

I should say that the just life is the better worth having.

You heard Thrasymachus' catalogue of all the good things in store for injustice?

I did, but I am not convinced.

Shall we try to convert him, then, supposing we can find some way to prove him wrong?

By all means....

Come then, Thrasymachus, said I, let us start afresh with our questions. You say that injustice pays better than justice, when both are carried to the furthest point?

I do, he replied; and I have told you why.

And how would you describe them? I suppose you would call one of them an excellence and the other a defect?

Of course.

Justice an excellence, and injustice a defect?

Now is that likely, when I am telling you that injustice pays, and justice does not?

Then what do you say?

The opposite.

That justice is a defect?

No; rather the mark of a good-natured simpleton.

Injustice, then, implies being ill-natured?

No; I should call it good policy.

Do you think the unjust are positively superior in character and intelligence, Thrasymachus?

Yes, if they are the sort that can carry injustice to perfection and make themselves masters of whole cities and nations. Perhaps you think I was talking of pickpockets. There is profit even in that trade, if you can escape detection; but it doesn't come to much as compared with the gains I was describing.

I understand you now on that point, I replied. What astonished me was that you should class injustice with superior character and intelligence and justice with the reverse.

Well, I do, he rejoined.

That is a much more stubborn position, my friend; and it is not so easy to see how to assail it. If you would admit that injustice, however well it pays, is nevertheless, as some people think, a defect and a discreditable thing, then we could argue on generally accepted principles. But now that you have gone so far as to rank it with superior character and intelligence, obviously you will say it is an admirable thing as well as a source of strength, and has all the other qualities we have attributed to justice.

You read my thoughts like a book, he replied.

However, I went on, it is no good shirking; I must go through with the argument, so long as I can be sure you are really speaking your mind. I do believe you are not playing with us now, Thrasymachus, but stating the truth as you conceive it....

Would you agree that a state may be unjust and may try to enslave other states or to hold a number of others in subjection unjustly?

Of course it may, he said; above all if it is the best sort of state, which carries injustice to perfection.

I understand, said I; that was your view. But I am wondering whether a state can do without justice when it is asserting its superior power over another in that way.

Not if you are right, that justice implies intelligence; but if I am right, injustice will be needed....

Thank you. Please add to your kindness by telling me whether any set of men—a state or an army or a band of robbers or thieves—who were acting together for some unjust purpose would be likely to succeed; if they were always trying to injure one another. Wouldn't they do better, if they did not?

Yes, they would.

Because, of course, such injuries must set them quarrelling and hating each other. Only fair treatment can make men friendly and of one mind.

Be it so, he said; I don't want to differ from you.

Thank you once more, I replied. But don't you agree that, if injustice has this effect of implanting hatred wherever it exists, it must make any set of people, whether freemen or slaves, split into factions, at feud with one another and incapable of any joint action?

Yes.

And so with any two individuals: injustice will set them at variance and make them enemies to each other as well as to everyone who is just.

It will.

And will it not keep its character and have the same effect, if it exists in a single person?

Let us suppose so.

The effect being, apparently, wherever it occurs—in a state or a family or an army or anywhere else—to make united action impossible because of factions and quarrels, and moreover to set whatever it resides in at enmity with itself as well as with any opponent and with all who are just.

Yes, certainly.

Then I suppose it will produce the same natural results in an individual. He will have a divided mind and be incapable of action, for lack of singleness of purpose; and he will be at enmity with all who are just as well as with himself?

Yes....

I thought that, with these words, I was quit of the discussion; but it seems this was only a prelude. Glaucon, undaunted as ever, was not content to let Thrasymachus abandon the field.

Socrates, he broke out, you have made a show of proving that justice is better than injustice in every way. Is that enough, or do you want us to be really convinced?

Certainly I do, if it rests with me.

Then you are not going the right way about it. I want to know how you classify the things we call good. Are there not some which we should wish to have, not for their consequences, but just for their own sake, such as harmless pleasures and enjoyments that have no further result beyond the satisfaction of the moment?

Yes, I think there are good things of that description.

And also some that we value both for their own sake and for their consequences—things like knowledge and health and the use of our eyes?

Yes.

And a third class which would include physical training, medical treatment, earning one's bread as a doctor or otherwise—useful, but burdensome things, which we want only for the sake of the profit or other benefit they bring.

Yes, there is that third class. What then?

In which class do you place justice?

I should say, in the highest, as a thing which anyone who is to gain happiness must value both for itself and for its results.

Well, that is not the common opinion. Most people would say it was one of those things, tiresome and disagreeable in themselves, which we cannot avoid practising for the sake of reward or a good reputation.

I know, said I; that is why Thrasymachus has been finding fault with it all this time and praising injustice. But I seem to be slow in seeing his point.

Listen to me, then, and see if you agree with mine. There was no need, I think, for Thrasymachus to yield so readily, like a snake you had charmed into submission; and nothing so far said about justice and injustice has been established to my satisfaction. I want to be told what each of them really is, and what effect each has, in itself, on the soul that harbours it, when all rewards and consequences are left out of account. So here is my plan, if you approve. I shall revive Thrasymachus' theory. First, I will state what is commonly held about the nature of justice and its origin; secondly, I shall maintain that it is always practised with reluctance, not as good in itself, but as a thing one cannot do without; and thirdly, that this reluctance is reasonable, because the life of injustice is much the better life of the two—so people say. That is not what I think myself, Socrates; only I am bewildered by all that Thrasymachus and ever so many others have dinned into my ears; and I have never yet heard the case for justice stated as I wish to hear it. You, I believe, if anyone, can tell me what is to be said in praise of justice in and for itself; that is what I want. Accordingly, I shall set you an example by glorifying the life of injustice with all the energy that I hope you will show later in denouncing it and exalting justice in its stead. Will that plan suit you?

Nothing could be better, I replied....

Good, said Glaucon. Listen then, and I will begin with my first point: the nature and origin of justice.

What people say is that to do wrong is, in itself, a desirable thing; on the other hand, it is not at all desirable to suffer wrong, and the harm to the sufferer outweighs the advantage to the doer. Consequently, when men have had a taste of both, those who have not the power to seize the advantage and escape the harm decide that they would be better off if they made a compact neither to do wrong nor to suffer it. Hence they began to make laws and covenants with one another; and whatever the law prescribed they called lawful and right. That is what right or justice is and how it came into existence; it stands half-way between the best thing of all—to do wrong with impunity—and the worst, which is to suffer wrong without the power to retaliate. So justice is accepted as a compromise, and valued, not as good in itself, but for lack of power to do wrong; no man worthy of the name, who had that power, would ever enter into such a compact with anyone; he would be made if he did. That, Socrates, is the nature of justice according to this account, and such the circumstances in which it arose.

The next point is that men practise it against the grain, for lack of power to do wrong. How true that is, we shall best see if we imagine two men, one just, the other unjust, given full licence to do whatever they like, and then follow them to observe where each will be led by his desires. We shall catch the just man taking the same road as the unjust; he will be moved by self-interest, the end which it is natural to every creature to pursue as good, until forcibly turned aside by law and custom to respect the principle of equality.

Now, the easiest way to give them that complete liberty of action would be to imagine them possessed of the talisman found by Gyges....The story tells how he was a shepherd in the King's service. One day there was a great storm, and the ground where his flock was feeding was rent by an earthquake. Astonished at the sight, he went down into the chasm and saw, among other wonders of which the story tells, a brazen horse, hollow, with windows in its sides. Peering in, he saw a dead body, which seemed to be of more than human size. It was naked save for a gold ring, which he took from the finger and made his way out. When the shepherds met, as they did every month, to send an account to the King of the state of his flocks, Gyges came wearing the ring. As he was sitting with the others, he happened to turn the bezel of the ring inside his hand. At once he became invisible, and his companions, to his surprise, began to speak of him as if he had left them. Then, as he was fingering the ring, he turned the bezel outwards and became visible again. With that, he set about testing the

ring to see if it really had this power, and always with the same result: according as he turned the bezel inside or out he vanished and reappeared. After this discovery he contrived to be one of the messengers sent to the court. There he seduced the Queen, and with her help murdered the King and seized the throne.

Now suppose there were two such magic rings, and one were given to the just man, the other to the unjust. No one, it is commonly believed, would have such iron strength of mind as to stand fast in doing right or keep his hands off other men's goods, when he could go to the market-place and fearlessly help himself to anything he wanted, enter houses and sleep with any woman he chose, set prisoners free and kill men at his pleasure, and in a word go about among men with the powers of a god. He would behave no better than the other; both would take the same course. Surely this would be strong proof that men do right only under compulsion; no individual thinks of it as good for him personally, since he does wrong whenever he finds he has the power. Every man believes that wrongdoing pays him personally much better, and, according to this theory, that is the truth. Granted full licence to do as he liked, people would think him a miserable fool if they found him refusing to wrong his neighbours or to touch their belongings, though in public they would keep up a pretence of praising his conduct, for fear of being wronged themselves. So much for that.

Finally, if we are really to judge between the two lives, the only way is to contrast the extremes of justice and injustice. We can best do that by imagining our two men to be perfect types, and crediting both to the full with the qualities they need for their respective ways of life. To begin with the unjust man: he must be like any consummate master of a craft, a physician or a captain, who, knowing just what his art can do, never tries to do more, and can always retrieve a false step. The unjust man, if he is to reach perfection, must be equally discreet in his criminal attempts, and he must not be found out, or we shall think him a bungler; for the highest pitch of injustice is to seem just when you are not. So we must endow our man with the full complement of injustice; we must allow him to have secured a spotless reputation for virtue while committing the blackest crimes; he must be able to retrieve any mistake, to defend himself with convincing eloquence if his misdeeds are denounced, and, when force is required, to bear down all opposition by his courage and strength and by his command of friends and money.

Now set beside this paragon the just man in his simplicity and nobleness, one who...'would be, not seem, the best.' There must, indeed, be no such seeming; for if his character were apparent, his reputation would bring him honours and rewards, and then we should not know whether it was for their sake that he was just or for justice's sake alone. He must be stripped of everything but justice, and denied every advantage the other enjoyed. Doing no wrong, he must have the worst reputation for wrong-doing, to test whether his virtue is proof against all that comes of having a bad name; and under this lifelong imputation of wickedness, let him hold on his course of justice unwavering to the point of death. And so, when the two men have carried their justice and injustice to the last extreme, we may judge which is the happier.

My dear Glaucon, I exclaimed, how vigorously you scour these two characters clean for inspection, as if you were burnishing a couple of statues!

I am doing my best, he answered. Well, given two such characters, it is not hard, I fancy, to describe the sort of life that each of them may expect; and if the description sounds rather coarse, take it as coming from those who cry up the merits of injustice rather than from me. They will tell you that our just man will be thrown into prison, scourged and racked, will have his eyes burnt out, and, after every kind of torment, be impaled. That will teach him how much better it is to seem virtuous than to be so....With his reputation for virtue, he will hold offices of state, ally himself by marriage to any family he may choose, become a partner in any business, and, having no scruples about being dishonest, turn all these advantages to profit. If he is involved in a lawsuit, public or private, he will get the better of his opponents, grow rich on the proceeds, and be able to help his friends and harm his enemies. Finally, he can make sacrifices to the gods and dedicate offerings with due magnificence, and, being in a much better position than the just man to serve the gods as well as his chosen friends, he may reasonably hope to stand higher in the favour of heaven. So much better, they say, Socrates, is the life prepared for the unjust by gods and men.

Here Glaucon ended, and I was meditating a reply, when his brother Adeimantus exclaimed:...

What reason, then, remains for preferring justice to the extreme of injustice, when common belief and the best authorities promise us the fulfillment of our desires in this life and the next, if only we conceal our ill-doing under a veneer of decent behaviour? The upshot is, Socrates, that no man possessed of superior powers of mind or person or rank or wealth will set any value on justice; he is more likely to laugh when he hears it praised....

What lies at the bottom of all this is nothing but the fact from which Glaucon, as well as I, started upon this long discourse. We put it to you, Socrates, with all respect, in this way. All you who profess to sing the praises of right conduct, from the ancient heroes whose legends have survived down to the men of the present day, have never denounced injustice or praised justice apart from the reputation, honours, and rewards they bring; but what effect either of them in itself has upon its possessor when it dwells in his soul unseen of gods or men, no poet or ordinary man has ever yet explained. No one has proved that a soul can harbour no worse evil than injustice, no greater good than justice. Had all of you said that from the first and tried to convince us from our youth up, we should not be keeping watch upon our neighbours to prevent them from doing wrong to us, but everyone would keep a far more effectual watch over himself, for fear lest by wronging others he should open his doors to the worst of all evils.

That, Socrates, is the view of justice and injustice which Thrasymachus and, no doubt, others would state, perhaps in even stronger words. For myself, I believe it to be a gross perversion of their true worth and effect; but, as I must frankly confess, I have put the case with all the force I could muster because I want to hear the other side from you. You must not be content with proving that justice is superior to injustice; you must make clear what good or what harm each of them does to its possessor, taking it simply in itself and, as Glaucon required, leaving out of account the reputation it bears....You have agreed that justice belongs to that highest class of good things which are worth having not only for their consequences, but much more for their own sakes—things like sight and hearing, knowledge, and health, whose value is genuine and intrinsic, not dependent on opinion. So I want you, in commending justice, to consider only how justice, in itself, benefits a man who has it in him, and how injustice harms him, leaving rewards and reputation out of account....

Glaucon and the others begged me to step into the breach and carry through our inquiry into the real nature of justice and injustice, and the truth about their respective advantages. So I...will make a suggestion as to how we should proceed. Imagine a rather short-sighted person told to read an inscription in small letters from some way off. He would think it a godsend if someone pointed out that the same inscription was written up elsewhere on a bigger scale, so that he could first read the larger characters and then make out whether the smaller ones were the same.

No doubt, said Adeimantus; but what analogy do you see in that to our inquiry?

I will tell you. We think of justice as a quality that may exist in a whole community as well as in an individual, and the community is the bigger of the two. Possibly, then, we may find justice there in larger proportions, easier to make out. So I suggest that we should begin by inquiring what justice means in a state. Then we can go on to look for its counterpart on a smaller scale in the individual.

That seems a good plan, he agreed.

Well then, I continued, suppose we imagine a state coming into being before our eyes. We might then be able to watch the growth of justice or of injustice within it....

Now let us build up our imaginary state from the beginning. Apparently, it will owe its existence to our needs, the first and greatest need being the provision of food to keep us alive. Next we shall want a house; and thirdly, such things as clothing.

True.

How will our state be able to supply all these demands? We shall need at least one man to be a farmer, another a builder, and a third a weaver. Will that do, or shall we add a shoemaker and one or two more to provide for our personal wants?

By all means.

The minimum state, then, will consist of four or five men.

Apparently.

Now here is a further point. Is each one of them to bring the product of his work into a common stock? Should our one farmer, for example, provide food enough for four people and spend the whole of his working time in producing corn, so as to share with the rest; or should he take no notice of them and spend only a quarter of his time on growing just enough corn for himself, and divide the other three-quarters between building his house, weaving his clothes, and making his shoes, so as to save the trouble of sharing with others and attend himself to all his own concerns?

The first plan might be the easier, replied Adeimantus.

That may very well be so, said I; for, as you spoke, it occurred to me, for one thing, that no two people are born exactly alike. There are innate differences which fit them for different occupations.

I agree.

And will a man do better working at many trades, or keeping to one only?

Keeping to one.

And there is another point: obviously work may be ruined, if you let the right time go by. The workman must wait upon the work; it will not wait upon his leisure and allow itself to be done in a spare moment. So the conclusion is that more things will be produced and the work be more easily and better done, when every man is set free from all other occupations to do, at the right time, the one thing for which he is naturally fitted.

That is certainly true.

We shall need more than four citizens, then, to supply all those necessaries we mentioned. You see, Adeimantus, if the farmer is to have a good plough and spade and other tools, he will not make them himself. No more will the builder and weaver and shoemaker make all the many implements they need. So quite a number of carpenters and smiths and other craftsmen must be enlisted. Our miniature state is beginning to grow....Still, it will not be very large, even when we have added cowherds and shepherds to provide the farmers....

No; but it will not be so very small either.

And yet, again, it will be next to impossible to plant our city in a territory where it will need no imports. So there will have to be still another set of people, to fetch what it needs from other countries....

Moreover, if these agents take with them nothing that those other countries require in exchange, they will return as empty-handed as they went. So, besides everything wanted for consumption at home, we must produce enough goods of the right kind for the foreigners whom we depend on to supply us....

And then, there are...merchants, as we call them. We must have them; and if they are to do business overseas, we shall need quite a number of ship-owners and others who know about that branch of trading.

We shall....

Obviously, they must buy and sell.

That will mean having a market-place, and a currency to serve as a token for purposes of exchange.

Certainly....

That, then, is the reason why our city must include a class of shopkeepers—so we call these people who sit still in the market-place to buy and sell, in contrast with merchants who travel to other countries.

Quite so.

There are also the services of yet another class, who have the physical strength for heavy work, though on intellectual grounds they are hardly worth including in our society—hired labourers, as we call them, because they sell the use of their strength for wages. They will go to make up our population.

Yes.

Well, Adeimantus, has our state now grown to its full size?

Perhaps.

Then, where in it shall we find justice or injustice? If they have come in with one of the elements we have been considering, can you say with which one?

I have no idea, Socrates; unless it be somewhere in their dealings with one another.

You may be right, I answered....

Let us begin, then, with a picture of our citizens' manner of life, with the provision we have made for them. They will be producing corn and wine, and making clothes and shoes. When they have built their houses, they will mostly work without their coats or shoes in summer, and in winter be well shod and clothed. For their food, they will prepare flour and barley-meal for kneading and baking, and set out a grand spread of loaves and cakes on rushes or fresh leaves. Then they will lie on beds of myrtle-boughs and bryony and make merry with their children, drinking their wine after the feast with garlands on their heads and singing the praises of the gods. So they will live pleasantly together; and a prudent fear of poverty or war will keep them from begetting children beyond their means.

Here Glaucon interrupted me: You seem to expect your citizens to feast on dry bread.

True, I said; I forgot that they will have something to give it a relish, salt, no doubt, and olives, and cheese, and country stews of roots and vegetables. And for dessert we will give them figs and peas and beans; and they shall roast myrtle-berries and acorns at the fire, while they sip their wine. Leading such a healthy life in peace, they will naturally come to a good old age, and leave their children to live after them in the same manner.

That is just the sort of provender you would supply, Socrates, if you were founding a community of pigs.

Well, how are they to live, then, Glaucon?

With the ordinary comforts. Let them lie on couches and dine off tables on such dishes and sweets as we have nowadays.

Ah, I see, said I; we are to study the growth, not just of a state, but of a luxurious one. Well, there may be no harm in that; the consideration of luxury may help us to discover how justice and injustice take root in society. The community I have described seems to me the ideal one, in sound health as it were: but if you want to see one suffering from inflammation, there is nothing to hinder us. So some people, it seems, will not be satisfied to live in this simple way; they must have couches and tables and furniture of all sorts; and delicacies too, perfumes, unguents, courtesans, sweetmeats, all in plentiful variety. And besides, we must not limit ourselves now to those bare necessaries of house and clothes and shoes; we shall have to set going the arts of embroidery and painting, and collect rich materials, like gold and ivory.

Yes.

Then we must once more enlarge our community. The healthy one will not be big enough now; it must be swollen up with a whole multitude of callings not ministering to any bare necessity....

The country, too, which was large enough to support the original inhabitants, will now be too small. If we are to have enough pasture and plough land, we shall have to cut off a slice of our neighbours' territory; and if they too are not content with necessaries, but give themselves up to getting unlimited wealth, they will want a slice of ours.

That is inevitable, Socrates.

So the next thing will be, Glaucon, that we shall be at war.

No doubt.

We need not say yet whether war does good or harm, but only that we have discovered its origin in desires which are the most fruitful source of evils both to individuals and to states

Quite true.

This will mean a considerable addition to our community—a whole army, to go out to battle with any invader, in defence of all this property and of the citizens we have been describing.

Why so? Can't they defend themselves?

Not if the principle was right, which we all accepted in framing our society. You remember we agreed that no one man can practise many trades or arts satisfactorily.

True....

Now in no form of work is efficiency so important as in war; and fighting is not so easy a business that a man can follow another trade, such as farming or shoemaking, and also be an efficient soldier....These guardians of our state, then, inasmuch as their work is the most important of all, will need the most complete freedom from other occupations and the greatest amount of skill and practice....So it is our business to define, if we can, the natural gifts that fit men to be guardians of a commonwealth, and to select them accordingly. It will certainly be a formidable task; but we must grapple with it to the best of our power.

Yes....

How are these Guardians to be brought up and educated?...Perhaps we shall hardly invent a system better than the one which long experience has worked out, with its two branches for the cultivation of the mind and of the body. And I suppose we shall begin with the mind, before we start physical training.

Naturally.

Under that head will come stories; and of these there are two kinds: some are true, others fictitious. Both must come in, but we shall begin our education with the fictitious kind.

I don't understand, he said.

Don't you understand, I replied, that we begin by telling children stories, which, taken as a whole, are fiction, though they contain some truth? Such story-telling begins at an earlier age than physical training; that is why I said we should start with the mind.

You are right.

And the beginning, as you know, is always the most important part, especially in dealing with anything young and tender. That is the time when the character is being moulded and easily takes any impress one may wish to stamp on it.

Quite true.

Then shall we simply allow our children to listen to any stories that anyone happens to make up, and so receive into their minds ideas often the very opposite of those we shall think they ought to have when they are grown up?

No, certainly not.

It seems, then, our first business will be to supervise the making of fables and legends, rejecting all which are unsatisfactory; and we shall induce nurses and mothers to tell their children only those which we have approved, and to think more of moulding their souls with these stories than they now do of rubbing their limbs to make them strong and shapely. Most of the stories now in use must be discarded....If a poet writes of the gods in this way, we shall be angry and refuse him the means to produce his play. Nor shall we allow such poetry to be used in educating the young, if we mean our Guardians to be godfearing and to reproduce the divine nature in themselves so far as man may.

I entirely agree with your principles, he said, and I would have them observed as laws....

Yes, he said; and I believe we have settled right.

We also want them to be brave. So the stories they hear should be such as to make them unafraid of death. A man with that fear in his heart cannot be brave, can he?

Surely not.

And can a man be free from that fear and prefer death in battle to defeat and slavery, if he believes in a world below which is full of terrors?

No....

Again, our Guardians ought not to be overmuch given to laughter. Violent laughter tends to provoke an equally violent reaction. We must not allow poets to describe men of worth being overcome by it; still less should Homer speak of the gods giving way to 'unquenchable laughter.'...

Again, a high value must be set upon truthfulness. If we were right in saying that gods have no use for falsehood and it is useful to mankind only in the way of a medicine, obviously a medicine should be handled by no one but a physician.

Obviously.

If anyone, then, is to practise deception, either on the country's enemies or on its citizens, it must be the Rulers of the commonwealth, acting for its benefit; no one else may meddle with this privilege....

Next, our young men will need self-control; and for the mass of mankind that chiefly means obeying their governors, and themselves governing their appetite for the pleasures of eating and drinking and sex....

I agree.

Whereas we shall allow the poets to represent any examples of self-control and fortitude on the part of famous men....

Nor again must these men of ours be lovers of money, or ready to take bribes. They must not hear that 'gods and great princes may be won by gifts.'...

Then we must not only compel our poets, on pain of expulsion, to make their poetry the express image of noble character; we must also supervise craftsmen of every kind and forbid them to leave the stamp of baseness, licence, meanness, unseemliness, on painting and sculpture, or building, or any other work of their hands; and anyone who cannot obey shall not practise his art in our commonwealth. We would not have our Guardians grow up among representations of moral deformity, as in some foul pasture where, day after day, feeding on every poisonous weed they would, little by little, gather insensibly a mass of corruption in their very souls. Rather we must seek out those craftsmen whose instinct guides them to whatsoever is lovely and gracious; so that our young men, dwelling in a wholesome climate, may drink in good from every quarter

There could be no better upbringing than that....

Good, said I; and what is the next point to be settled? Is it not the question, which of these Guardians are to be rulers and which are to obey?

No doubt.

Well, it is obvious that the elder must have authority over the young, and that the rulers must be the best.

Yes.

And as among farmers the best are those with a natural turn for farming, so, if we want the best among our Guardians, we must take those naturally fitted to watch over a commonwealth. They must have the right sort of intelligence and ability; and also they must look upon the commonwealth as their special concern—the sort of concern that is felt for something so closely bound up with oneself that its interests and fortunes, for good or ill, are held to be identical with one's own.

Exactly.

So the kind of men we must choose from among the Guardians will be those who, when we look at the whole course of their lives, are found to be full of zeal to do whatever they believe is for the good of the commonwealth and never willing to act against its interest.

Yes, they will be the men we want.

We must watch them, I think, at every age and see whether they are capable of preserving this conviction that they must do what is best for the community, never forgetting it or allowing themselves to be either forced or bewitched into throwing it over....

Now, said I, can we devise something in the way of those convenient fictions we spoke of earlier, a single bold flight of invention, which we may induce the community in general, and if possible the Rulers themselves, to accept?

What kind of fiction?...

I shall try to convince, first the Rulers and the soldiers, and then the whole community, that all that nurture and education which we gave them was only something they seemed to experience as it were in a dream. In reality they were the whole time down inside the earth, being moulded and fostered while their arms and all their equipment were being fashioned also; and at last, when they were complete, the earth sent them up from her womb into the light of day. So now they must think of the land they dwell in as a mother and nurse, whom they must take thought for and defend against any attack, and of their fellow citizens as brothers born of the same soil.

You might well be bashful about coming out with your fiction.

No doubt; but still you must hear the rest of the story. It is true, we shall tell our people in this fable, that all of you in this land are brothers; but the god who fashioned you mixed gold in the composition of those among you who are fit to rule so that they are of the most precious quality; and he put silver in the Auxiliaries and iron and brass in the farmers and craftsmen. Now, since you are all of one stock, although your children will generally be like their parents, sometimes a golden parent may have a silver child or a silver parent a golden one, and so on with all the other combinations. So the first and chief injunction laid by heaven upon the Rulers is that, among all the things of which they must show themselves good guardians, there is none that needs to be so carefully watched as the mixture of metals in the souls of the children. If a child of their own is born with an alloy of iron or brass, they must, without the smallest pity, assign him the station proper to his nature and thrust him out among the craftsmen or the farmers. If, on the contrary, these classes produce a child with gold or silver in his composition, they will promote him, according to his value, to be a Guardian or an Auxiliary. They will appeal to a prophecy that ruin will come upon the state when it passes into the keeping of a man of iron or brass. Such is the story; can you think of any device to make them believe it?

Not in the first generation; but their sons and descendants might believe it, and finally the rest of mankind.

Well, said I, even so it might have a good effect in making them care more for the commonwealth and for one another; for I think I see what you mean....

True.

With that end in view, let us consider how the Guardians should live and be housed. First, none of them must possess any private property beyond the barest necessaries. Next, no one is to have any dwelling or store-house that is not open for all to enter at will. Their food, in the quantities required by men of temperance and courage who are in training for war, they will receive from the other citizens as the wages of their guardianship, fixed so that there shall be just enough for the year with nothing over; and they will have meals in common and all live together like soldiers in a camp. Gold and silver, we shall tell them, they will not need, having the divine counterparts of those metals always in their souls as a god-given possession, whose purity it is not lawful to sully by the acqui-

sition of that mortal dross, current among mankind, which has been the occasion of so many unholy deeds. They alone of all the citizens are forbidden to touch and handle silver or gold, or to come under the same roof with them, or wear them as ornaments, or drink from vessels made of them. This manner of life will be their salvation and make them the saviours of the commonwealth. If ever they should come to possess land of their own and houses and money, they will give up their guardianship for the management of their farms and households and become tyrants at enmity with their fellow citizens instead of allies. And so they will pass all their lives in hating and being hated, plotting and being plotted against, in much greater fear of their enemies at home than of any foreign foe, and fast heading for the destruction that will soon overwhelm their country with themselves. For all these reasons let us say that this is how our Guardians are to be housed and otherwise provided for, and let us make laws accordingly.

By all means, said Glaucon.

Here Adeimantus interposed. Socrates, he said, how would you meet the objection that you are not making these people particularly happy?...

We shall say that, though it would not be surprising if even these people were perfectly happy under such conditions, our aim in founding the commonwealth was not to make any one class specially happy, but to secure the greatest possible happiness for the community as a whole....

So now at last, son of Ariston, said I, your commonwealth is established. The next thing is to bring to bear upon it all the light you can get from any quarter, with the help of your brother and Polemarchus and all the rest, in the hope that we may see where justice is to be found in it and where injustice, how they differ, and which of the two will bring happiness to its possessor, no matter whether gods and men see that he has it or not....

I take it that our state, having been founded and built up on the right lines, is good in the complete sense of the word.

It must be.

Obviously, then, it is wise, brave, temperate, and just....

To begin then: the first quality to come into view in our state seems to be its wisdom; and there appears to be something odd about this quality.

What is there odd about it?

I think the state we have described really has wisdom; for it will be prudent in counsel, won't it?

Yes....

And where does it reside?

It is precisely that art of guardianship which resides in those Rulers whom we just now called Guardians in the full sense....

If a state is constituted on natural principles, the wisdom it possesses as a whole will be due to the knowledge residing in the smallest part, the one which takes the lead and governs the rest. Such knowledge is the only kind that deserves the name of wisdom, and it appears to be ordained by nature that the class privileged to possess it should be the smallest of all.

Quite true.

Next there is courage. It is not hard to discern that quality or the part of the community in which it resides so as to entitle the whole to be called brave.

Why do you say so?

Because anyone who speaks of a state as either brave or cowardly can only be thinking of that part of it which takes the field and fights in its defence; the reason being, I imagine, that the character of the state is not determined by the bravery or cowardice of the other parts.

No....

Two qualities, I went on, still remain to be made out in our state, temperance and the object of our whole inquiry, justice....At first sight, temperance seems more like some sort of concord or harmony than the other qualities did.

How so?

Temperance surely means a kind of orderliness, a control of certain pleasures and appetites. People use the expression, 'master of oneself,' whatever that means, and various other phrases that point the same way....

I think, however, the phrase means that within the man himself, in his soul, there is a better part and a worse; and that he is his own master when the part which is better by nature has the worse under its control....

So we were not wrong in divining a resemblance between temperance and some kind of harmony. Temperance is not like courage and wisdom, which made the state wise and brave by residing each in one particular part. Temperance works in a different way; it extends throughout the whole gamut of the state, producing a consonance of all its elements from the weakest to the strongest as measured by any standard you like to take—wisdom, bodily strength, numbers, or wealth. So we are entirely justified in identifying with temperance this unanimity or harmonious agreement between the naturally superior and inferior elements on the question which of the two should govern, whether in the state or in the individual.

I fully agree.

Good, said I. We have discovered in our commonwealth three out of our four qualities, to the best of our present judgment. What is the remaining one, required to make up its full complement of goodness? For clearly this will be justice.

Clearly....

Really, I said, we have been extremely stupid. All this time the thing has been under our very noses from the start, and we never saw it. We have been as absurd as a person who hunts for something he has all the time got in his hand. Instead of looking at the thing, we have been staring into the distance. No doubt that is why it escaped us.

What do you mean?

I believe we have been talking about the thing all this while without ever understanding that we were giving some sort of account of it.

Do come to the point. I am all ears.

Listen, then, and judge whether I am right. You remember how, when we first began to establish our commonwealth and several times since, we have laid down, as a universal principle, that everyone ought to perform the one function in the community for which his nature best suited him. Well, I believe that that principle, or some form of it, is justice....Justice admittedly means that a man should possess and concern himself with what properly belongs to him.

True.

Again, do you agree with me that no great harm would be done to the community by a general interchange of most forms of work, the carpenter and the cobbler exchanging their positions and their tools and taking on each other's jobs, or even the same man undertaking both?

Yes, there would not be much harm in that.

But I think you will also agree that another kind of interchange would be disastrous. Suppose, for instance, someone whom nature designed to be an artisan or tradesman should be emboldened by some advantage, such as wealth or command of votes or bodily strength, to try to enter the order of fighting men; or some member of that order should aspire, beyond his merits, to a seat in the council-chamber of the Guardians. Such interference and exchange of social positions and tools, or the attempt to combine all these forms of work in the same person, would be fatal to the commonwealth.

Most certainly.

Where there are three orders, then, any plurality of functions or shifting from one order to another is not merely utterly harmful to the community, but one might fairly call it the extreme of wrongdoing. And you will agree that to do the greatest of wrongs to one's own community is injustice.

Surely.

This, then, is injustice. And, conversely, let us repeat that when each order—tradesman, Auxiliary, Guardian—keeps to its own proper business in the commonwealth and does its own work, that is justice and what makes a just society.

I entirely agree.

We must not be too positive yet, said I. If we find that this same quality when it exists in the individual can equally be identified with justice, then we can at once give our assent; there will be no more to be said; otherwise, we shall have to look further. For the moment, we had better finish the inquiry which we began with the idea that it would be easier to make out the nature of justice in the individual if we first tried to study it in something on a larger scale. That larger thing we took to be a state, and so we set about constructing the best one we could, being sure of finding justice in a state that was good. The discovery we made there must now be applied to the individual. If it is confirmed, all will be well....

True.

Accordingly, my friend, if we are to be justified in attributing those same virtues to the individual, we shall expect to find that the individual soul contains the same three elements and that they are affected in the same way as are the corresponding types in society.

That follows.

Here, then, we have stumbled upon another little problem: Does the soul contain these three elements or not?...

Surely, I began, we must admit that the same elements and characters that appear in the state

must exist in every one of us; where else could they have come from?...

Let us approach the problem whether these elements are distinct or identical in this way. It is clear that the same thing cannot act in two opposite ways or be in two opposite states at the same time, with respect to the same part of itself, and in relation to the same object. So if we find such contradictory actions or states among the elements concerned, we shall know that more than one must have been involved.

Very well....

Now, would you class such things as assent and dissent, striving after something and refusing it, attraction and repulsion, as pairs of opposite actions or states of mind—no matter which?

Yes, they are opposites....

The soul of a thirsty man, just in so far as he is thirsty, has no other wish than to drink. That is the object of its craving, and towards that it is impelled.

That is clear.

Now if there is ever something which at the same time pulls it the opposite way, that something must be an element in the soul other than the one which is thirsting and driving it like a beast to drink; in accordance with our principle that the same thing cannot behave in two opposite ways at the same time and towards the same object with the same part of itself. It is like an archer drawing the bow: it is not accurate to say that his hands are at the same time both pushing and pulling it. One hand does the pushing, the other the pulling.

Exactly.

Now, is it sometimes true that people are thirsty and yet unwilling to drink?

Yes, often.

What, then, can one say of them, if not that their soul contains something which urges them to drink and something which holds them back, and that this latter is a distinct thing and overpowers the other?

I agree.

And is it not true that the intervention of this inhibiting principle in such cases always has its origin in reflection; whereas the impulses driving and dragging the soul are engendered by external influences and abnormal conditions?

Evidently.

We shall have good reason, then, to assert that they are two distinct principles. We may call that part of the soul whereby it reflects, rational; and the other, with which it feels hunger and thirst and is distracted by sexual passion and all the other desires, we will call irrational appetite, associated with pleasure in the replenishment of certain wants.

Yes, there is good ground for that view.

Let us take it, then, that we have now distinguished two elements in the soul. What of that passionate element which makes us feel angry and indignant? Is that a third, or identical in nature with one of those two?...Anger is sometimes in conflict with appetite, as if they were two distinct principles. Do we not often find a man whose desires would force him to go against his reason, reviling himself and indignant with this part of his nature which is trying to put constraint on him? It is like a struggle between two factions, in which indignation takes the side of reason....

And so, after a stormy passage, we have reached the land. We are fairly agreed that the same three elements exist alike in the state and in the individual soul....

That must be true.

Then it applies to justice: we shall conclude that a man is just in the same way that a state was just. And we have surely not forgotten that justice in the state meant that each of the three orders in it was doing its own proper work. So we may henceforth bear in mind that each one of us likewise will be a just person, fulfilling his proper function, only if the several parts of our nature fulfil theirs.

Certainly.

And it will be the business of reason to rule with wisdom and forethought on behalf of the entire soul; while the spirited element ought to act as its subordinate and ally. The two will be brought into accord, as we said earlier, by that combination of mental and bodily training which will tune up one-string of the instrument and relax the other, nourishing the reasoning part on the study of noble literature and allaying the other's wildness by harmony and rhythm. When both have been thus nurtured and trained to know their own true functions, they must be set in command over the appetites, which form the greater part of each man's soul and are by nature insatiably covetous. They must keep watch lest this part, by battening on the pleasures that are called bodily, should grow so great and powerful that it will no longer keep to its

own work, but will try to enslave the others and usurp a dominion to which it has no right, thus turning the whole of life upside down. At the same time, those two together will be the best of guardians for the entire soul and for the body against all enemies from without: the one will take counsel, while the other will do battle, following its ruler's commands and by its own bravery giving effect to the ruler's designs.

Yes, that is all true.

And so we call an individual brave in virtue of this spirited part of his nature, when, in spite of pain or pleasure, it holds fast to the injunctions of reason about what he ought or ought not to be afraid of.

True.

And wise in virtue of that small part which rules and issues these injunctions, possessing as it does the knowledge of what is good for each of the three elements and for all of them in common.

Certainly.

And, again, temperate by reason of the unanimity and concord of all three, when there is no internal conflict between the ruling element and its two subjects, but all are agreed that reason should be ruler.

Yes, that is an exact account of temperance, whether in the state or in the individual.

Finally, a man will be just by observing the principle we have so often stated.

Necessarily....

So be it, said I. Next, I suppose, we have to consider injustice.

Evidently.

This must surely be a sort of civil strife among the three elements, whereby they usurp and encroach upon one another's functions and some one part of the soul rises up in rebellion against the whole, claiming a supremacy to which it has no right because its nature fits it only to be the servant of the ruling principle. Such turmoil and aberration we shall, I think, identify with injustice, intemperance, cowardice, ignorance, and in a word with all wickedness.

Exactly....

How do you mean?

Plainly, they are exactly analogous to those wholesome and unwholesome activities which respectively produce a healthy or unhealthy condition in the body; in the same way just and unjust conduct produce a just or unjust character. Justice is produced in the soul, like health in the body, by establishing the elements concerned in their natural relations of control and subordination, whereas injustice is like disease and means that this natural order is inverted.

Quite so.

It appears, then, that virtue is as it were the health and comeliness and well-being of the soul, as wickedness is disease, deformity, and weakness.

True.

And also that virtue and wickedness are brought about by one's way of life, honourable or disgraceful.

That follows.

So now it only remains to consider which is the more profitable course: to do right and live honourably and be just, whether or not anyone knows what manner of man you are, or to do wrong and be unjust, provided that you can escape the chastisement which might make you a better man.

But really, Socrates, it seems to me ridiculous to ask that question now that the nature of justice and injustice has been brought to light. People think that all the luxury and wealth and power in the world cannot make life worth living when the bodily constitution is going to rack and ruin; and are we to believe that, when the very principle whereby we live is deranged and corrupted, life will be worth living so long as a man can do as he will, and wills to do anything rather than to free himself from vice and wrongdoing and to win justice and virtue?

Yes, I replied, it is a ridiculous question....

Go on.

Unless either philosophers become kings in their countries or those who are now called kings and rulers come to be sufficiently inspired with a genuine desire for wisdom; unless, that is to say, political power and philosophy meet together, while the many natures who now go their several ways in the one or the other direction are forcibly debarred from doing so, there can be no rest from troubles, my dear Glaucon, for states, nor yet, as I believe, for all mankind; nor can this commonwealth which we have imagined ever till then see the light of day and grow to its full stature....

Here is a parable to illustrate the degrees in which our nature may be enlightened or unenlightened. Imagine the condition of men living in a sort of cavernous chamber underground, with an entrance open to the light and a long passage all down the cave. Here they have been from childhood, chained by the leg and also by the neck, so that they cannot move and can see only what is in front of them, because the chains will not let them turn their heads. At some distance higher up is the light of a fire burning behind them; and between the prisoners and the fire is a track with a parapet built along it, like the screen at a puppet-show, which hides the performers while they show their puppets over the top.

Now behind this parapet imagine persons carrying along various artificial objects, including figures of men and animals in wood or stone or other materials, which project above the parapet. Naturally, some of these persons will be talking, others silent.

It is a strange picture, he said, and a strange sort of prisoners.

Like ourselves, I replied; for in the first place prisoners so confined would have seen nothing of themselves or of one another, except the shadows thrown by the fire-light on the wall of the Cave facing them, would they?

Not if all their lives they had been prevented from moving their heads.

And they would have seen as little of the objects carried past.

Of course.

Now, if they could talk to one another, would they not suppose that their words referred only to those passing shadows which they saw?

Necessarily.

And suppose their prison had an echo from the wall facing them? When one of the people crossing behind them spoke, they could only suppose that the sound came from the shadow passing before their eyes.

No doubt.

In every way, then, such prisoners would recognize as reality nothing but the shadows of those artificial objects.

Inevitably.

Now consider what would happen if their release from the chains and the healing of their unwisdom should come about in this way. Suppose one of them set free and forced suddenly to stand up, turn his head, and walk with eyes lifted to the light; all these movements would be painful, and he would be too dazzled to make out the objects whose shadows he had been used to see. What do you think he would say, if someone told him that what he had formerly seen was meaningless illusion, but now, being somewhat nearer to reality and turned towards more real objects, he was getting a truer view? Suppose further that he were shown the various objects being carried by and were made to say, in reply to questions, what each of them was. Would he not be perplexed and believe the objects now shown him to be not so real as what he formerly saw?

Yes, not nearly so real.

And if he were forced to look at the fire-light itself, would not his eyes ache, so that he would try to escape and turn back to the things which he could see distinctly, convinced that they really were clearer than these other objects now being shown to him?

Yes.

And suppose someone were to drag him away forcibly up the steep and rugged ascent and not let him go until he had hauled him out into the sunlight, would he not suffer pain and vexation at such treatment, and, when he had come out into the light, find his eyes so full of its radiance that he could not see a single one of the things that he was now told were real?

Certainly he would not see them all at once.

He would need, then, to grow accustomed before he could see things in that upper world. At first it would be easiest to make out shadows, and then the images of men and things reflected in water, and later on the things themselves. After that, it would be easier to watch the heavenly bodies and the sky itself by night, looking at the light of the moon and stars rather than the Sun and the Sun's light in the day-time.

Yes, surely.

Last of all, he would be able to look at the Sun and contemplate its nature, not as it appears when reflected in water or any alien medium, but as it is in itself in its own domain.

No doubt.

And now he would begin to draw the conclusion that it is the Sun that produces the seasons and the course of the year and controls everything in the visible world, and moreover is in a way the cause of all that he and his companions used to see.

Clearly he would come at last to that conclusion.

Then if he called to mind his fellow prisoners and what passed for wisdom in his former dwelling-place, he would surely think himself happy in the change and be sorry for them. They may have had a practice of honouring and commending one another, with prizes for the man who had the keenest eye for the passing shadows and the best memory for the order in which they followed or accompanied one another, so that he could make a good guess as to which was going to come next. Would our released prisoner be likely to covet those prizes or to envy the men exalted to honour and power in the Cave? Would he not feel…that he would far sooner 'be on earth as a hired servant in the house of a landless man' or endure anything rather than go back to his old beliefs and live in the old way?

Yes, he would prefer any fate to such a life.

Now imagine what would happen if he went down again to take his former seat in the Cave. Coming suddenly out of the sunlight, his eyes would be filled with darkness. He might be required once more to deliver his opinion on those shadows, in competition with the prisoners who had never been released, while his eyesight was still dim and unsteady; and it might take some time to become used to the darkness. They would laugh at him and say that he had gone up only to come back with his sight ruined; it was worth no one's while even to attempt the ascent. If they could lay hands on the man who was trying to set them free and lead them up, they would kill him.

Yes, they would.

This parable, my dear Glaucon, corresponds to the region revealed to us through the sense of sight, and the fire-light within it to the power of the Sun. The ascent to see the things in the upper world you may take as standing for the upward journey of the soul into the region of the intelligible; then you will be in possession of what I surmise, since that is what you wish to be told. Heaven knows whether it is true; but this, at any rate, is how it appears to me. In the world of knowledge, the last thing to be perceived and only with great difficulty is the essential Form of Goodness. Once it is perceived, the conclusion must follow that, for all things, this is the cause of whatever is right and good; in the visible world it gives birth to light and to the lord of light, while it is itself sovereign in the intelligible world and the parent of intelligence and truth.

Without having had a vision of this Form no one can act with wisdom, either in his own life or in matters of state.

So far as I can understand, I share your belief.

Then you may also agree that it is no wonder if those who have reached this height are reluctant to manage the affairs of men. Their souls long to spend all their time in that upper world—naturally enough, if here once more our parable holds true. Nor, again, is it at all strange that one who comes from the contemplation of divine things to the miseries of human life should appear awkward and ridiculous when, with eyes still dazed and not yet accustomed to the darkness, he is compelled, in a law-court or elsewhere, to dispute about the shadows of justice or the images that cast those shadows, and to wrangle over the notions of what is right in the minds of men who have never beheld Justice itself.

It is not at all strange.

No; a sensible man will remember that the eyes may be confused in two ways—by a change from light to darkness or from darkness to light; and he will recognize that the same thing happens to the soul. When he sees it troubled and unable to discern anything clearly, instead of laughing thoughtlessly, he will ask whether, coming from a brighter existence, its unaccustomed vision is obscured by the darkness, in which case he will think its condition enviable and its life a happy one; or whether, emerging from the depths of ignorance, it is dazzled by excess of light. If so, he will rather feel sorry for it; or, if he were inclined to laugh, that would be less ridiculous than to laugh at the soul which has come down from the light.

That is a fair statement.

If this is true, then, we must conclude that education is not what it is said to be by some, who profess to put knowledge into a soul which does not possess it, as if they could put sight into blind eyes. On the contrary, our own account signifies that the soul of every man does possess the power of learning the truth and the organ to see it with; and that, just as one might have to turn the whole body round in order that the eye should see light instead of darkness, so the entire soul must be turned away from this changing world, until its eye can bear to contemplate reality and that supreme splendour which we have called the Good. Hence there may well be an art whose aim would be to

effect this very thing, the conversion of the soul, in the readiest way; not to put the power of sight into the soul's eye, which already has it, but to ensure that, instead of looking in the wrong direction, it is turned the way it ought to be.

Yes, it may well be so.

It looks, then, as though wisdom were different from those ordinary virtues, as they are called, which are not far removed from bodily qualities, in that they can be produced by habituation and exercise in a soul which has not possessed them from the first. Wisdom, it seems, is certainly the virtue of some diviner faculty, which never loses its power, though its use for good or harm depends on the direction towards which it is turned. You must have noticed in dishonest men with a reputation for sagacity the shrewd glance of a narrow intelligence piercing the objects to which it is directed. There is nothing wrong with their power of vision, but it has been forced into the service of evil, so that the keener its sight, the more harm it works.

Quite true.

And yet if the growth of a nature like this had been pruned from earliest childhood, cleared of those clinging overgrowths which come of gluttony and all luxurious pleasure and, like leaden weights charged with affinity to this mortal world, hang upon the soul, bending its vision downwards; if, freed from these, the soul were turned round towards true reality, then this same power in these very men would see the truth as keenly as the objects it is turned to now.

Yes, very likely.

Is it not also likely, or indeed certain after what has been said, that a state can never be properly governed either by the uneducated who know nothing of truth or by men who are allowed to spend all their days in the pursuit of culture?...

It is for us, then, as founders of a commonwealth, to bring compulsion to bear on the noblest natures. They must be made to climb the ascent to the vision of Goodness, which we called the highest object of knowledge; and, when they have looked upon it long enough, they must not be allowed, as they now are, to remain on the heights, refusing to come down again to the prisoners or to take any part in their labours and rewards, however much or little these may be worth.

Shall we not be doing them an injustice, if we force on them a worse life than they might have?

You have forgotten again, my friend, that the law is not concerned to make any one class specially happy, but to ensure the welfare of the commonwealth as a whole. By persuasion or constraint it will unite the citizens in harmony, making them share whatever benefits each class can contribute to the common good; and its purpose in forming men of that spirit was not that each should be left to go his own way, but that they should be instrumental in binding the community into one.

True, I had forgotten.

You will see, then, Glaucon, that there will be no real injustice in compelling our philosophers to watch over and care for the other citizens....

Yes, my friend; for the truth is that you can have a well-governed society only if you can discover for your future rulers a better way of life than being in office; then only will power be in the hands of men who are rich, not in gold, but in the wealth that brings happiness, a good and wise life. All goes wrong when, starved for lack of anything good in their own lives, men turn to public affairs hoping to snatch from thence the happiness they hunger for. They set about fighting for power, and this internecine conflict ruins them and their country. The life of true philosophy is the only one that looks down upon offices of state; and access to power must be confined to men who are not in love with it; otherwise rivals will start fighting. So whom else can you compel to undertake the guardianship of the commonwealth, if not those who, besides understanding best the principles of government, enjoy a nobler life than the politician's and look for rewards of a different kind?

There is indeed no other choice...

We may finally answer the question how pure justice and pure injustice stand in respect of the happiness or misery they bring, and so decide to pursue the one or the other, according as we listen to Thrasymachus or to the argument we are now developing.

Yes, that is the next thing to be done.

When we were studying moral qualities earlier, we began with the state, because they stood out more clearly there than in the individual. On the same principle we had better now take, in each case, the constitution first, and then, in the light of our results, examine the corresponding character. We shall start with the constitution dominated by motives of ambition—it has no name in common

use that I know of; let us call it timarchy or timocracy—and then go on to oligarchy and democracy, and lastly visit a state under despotic government and look into the despot's soul. We ought then to be in a position to decide the question before us.

Yes, such a systematic review should give us the materials for judgement.

Come then, let us try to explain how the government of the best might give place to a timocracy. Is it not a simple fact that in any form of government revolution always starts from the outbreak of internal dissension in the ruling class? The constitution cannot be upset so long as that class is of one mind, however small it may be.

That is true.

Then how, Glaucon, will trouble' begin in our commonwealth?...

The rulers you have bred for your commonwealth, wise as they are, will not be able, by observation and reckoning, to hit upon the times propitious or otherwise for birth; some day the moment will slip by and they will beget children out of due season....When your Guardians, from ignorance...bring together brides and bridegrooms out of season, their children will not be well-endowed or fortunate. The best of these may be appointed by the elder generation; but when they succeed to their fathers' authority as Guardians, being unworthy, they will begin to neglect us and to think too lightly first of the cultivation of the mind, and then of bodily training, so that your young men will come to be worse educated. Then Rulers appointed from among them will fail in their duty as Guardians to try the mettle of your citizens, those breeds of gold and silver, brass and iron that Hesiod told of; and when the silver is alloyed with iron and the gold with brass, diversity, inequality, and disharmony will beget, as they always must, enmity and war. Such, everywhere, is the birth and lineage of civil strife.'

Yes, we will take that as a true answer to our question....

Once civil strife is born, the two parties begin to pull different ways: the breed of iron and brass towards money-making and the possession of house and land, silver and gold; while the other two, wanting no other wealth than the gold and silver in the composition of their souls, try to draw them towards virtue and the ancient ways. But the violence of their contention ends in a compromise:

they agree to distribute land and houses for private ownership; they enslave their own people who formerly lived as free men under their guardianship and gave them maintenance; and, holding them as serfs and menials, devote themselves to war and to keeping these subjects under watch and ward.

I agree: that is how the transition begins.

And this form of government will be midway between the rule of the best and oligarchy, will it not?

Yes.

Such being the transition, how will the state be governed after the change? Obviously, as intermediate between the earlier constitution and oligarchy, it will resemble each of these in some respects and have some features of its own.

True.

It will be like the earlier constitution in several ways. Authority will be respected; the fighting class will abstain from any form of business, farming, or handicrafts; they will keep up their common meals and give their time to physical training and martial exercises.

Yes.

On the other hand, it will have some peculiar characteristics. It will be afraid to admit intellectuals to office. The men of that quality now at its disposal will no longer be single-minded and sincere; it will prefer simpler characters with plenty of spirit, better suited for war than for peace. War will be its constant occupation, and military tricks and stratagems will be greatly admired.

Yes.

At the same time, men of this kind will resemble the ruling class of an oligarchy in being avaricious, cherishing furtively a passionate regard for gold and silver; for they will now have private homes where they can hoard their treasure in secret and live ensconced in a nest of their own, lavishing their riches on their women or whom they please. They will also be miserly, prizing the money they may not openly acquire, though prodigal enough of other people's wealth for the satisfaction of their desires. They will enjoy their pleasures in secret, like truant children, in defiance of the law; because they have been educated not by gentle influence but under compulsion, cultivating the body in preference to the mind and caring nothing for the spirit of genuine culture which seeks truth by the discourse of reason.

The society you describe is certainly a mixture of good and evil.

Yes, it is a mixture; but, thanks to the predominance of the spirited part of our nature, it has one most conspicuous feature: ambition and the passion to excel.

Quite so.

Such, then, is the origin and character of this form of government....

True.

And now what of the corresponding individual? How does he come into being, and what is he like?

I imagine, said Adeimantus, his desire to excel, so far as that goes, would make him rather like Glaucon.

Perhaps, said I; but in other ways the likeness fails. He must be more self-willed than Glaucon and rather uncultivated, though fond of music; one who will listen readily, but is no speaker. Not having a properly educated man's consciousness of superiority to slaves, he will treat them harshly; though he will be civil to free men, and very obedient to those in authority. Ambitious for office, he will base his claims, not on any gifts of speech, but on his exploits in war and the soldierly qualities he has acquired through his devotion to athletics and hunting. In his youth he will despise money, but the older he grows the more he will care for it, because of the touch of avarice in his nature; and besides his character is not thoroughly sound, for lack of the only safeguard that can preserve it throughout life, a thoughtful and cultivated mind.

Quite true....

Shall we go on then?...

By all means.

Then I suppose the next type of constitution will be oligarchy.

What sort of régime do you mean?

The one which is based on a property qualification, where the rich are in power and the poor man cannot hold office.

I see.

We must start, then, by describing the transition from timocracy to oligarchy. No one could fail to see how that happens. The downfall of timocracy is due to the flow of gold into those private stores we spoke of. In finding new ways of spending their money, men begin by stretching the law for that purpose, until they and their wives obey it no longer. Then, as each keeps an envious eye on his neighbour, their rivalry infects the great mass of them; and as they go to further lengths in the pursuit of riches, the more they value money and the less they care for virtue. Virtue and wealth are balanced against one another in the scales; as the rich rise in social esteem, the virtuous sink. These changes of valuation, moreover, are always reflected in practice. So at last the competitive spirit of ambition in these men gives way to the passion for gain; they despise the poor man and promote to power the rich, who wins all their praise and admiration. At this point they fix by statute the qualification for privilege in an oligarchy, an amount of wealth which varies with the strength of the oligarchical principle; no one may hold office whose property falls below the prescribed sum. This measure is carried through by armed force, unless they have already set up their constitution by terrorism. That, then, is how an oligarchy comes to be established.

Yes, said Adeimantus; but what is the character of this régime, and what are the defects we said it would have?

In the first place, I replied, the principle on which it limits privilege. How would it be, if the captain of a ship were appointed on a property qualification, and a poor man could never get a command, though he might know much more about seamanship?

The voyage would be likely to end in disaster.

Is not the same true of any position of authority? Or is the government of a state an exception?

Anything but an exception, inasmuch as a state is the hardest thing to govern and the most important.

So this is one serious fault of oligarchy.

Evidently.

Is it any less serious that such a state must lose its unity and become two, one of the poor, the other of the rich, living together and always plotting against each other?

Quite as serious.

Another thing to its discredit is that they may well be unable to carry on a war. Either they must call out the common people or not. If they do, they will have more to fear from the armed multitude than from the enemy; and if they do not, in the day of battle these oligarchs will find themselves only too literally a government of the few. Also, their avarice will make them unwilling to pay war-taxes.

True.

And again, is it right that the same persons should combine many occupations, agriculture, business, and soldiering? We condemned that practice some time ago.

No, not at all right.

Worst of all, a man is allowed to sell all he has to another and then to go on living in a community where he plays no part as tradesman or artisan or as a soldier capable of providing his own equipment; he is only what they call a pauper. This is an evil which first becomes possible under an oligarchy, or at least there is nothing to prevent it; otherwise there would not be some men excessively wealthy and others destitute.

True.

Now think of this pauper in his earlier days when he was well off. By spending his money, was he doing any more good to the community in those useful ways I mentioned? He seemed to belong to the ruling class, but really he was neither ruling the state nor serving it; he was a mere consumer of goods. His house might be compared to one of those cells in the honeycomb where a drone is bred to be the plague of the hive. Some drones can fly, and these were all created without stings; others, which cannot fly, are of two sorts: some have formidable stings, the rest have none. In society, the stingless drones end as beggars in their old age; the ones which have stings become what is known as the criminal class. It follows that, in any community where beggars are to be seen, there are also thieves and pickpockets and temple-robbers and other such artists in crime concealed somewhere about the place. And you will certainly see beggars in any state governed by an oligarchy.

Yes, nearly everywhere, outside the ruling class.

Then we may assume that there are also plenty of drones with stings, criminals whom the government takes care to hold down by force; and we shall conclude that they are bred by lack of education, bad upbringing, and a vicious form of government.

Yes.

Such, then, is the character of a state ruled by an oligarchy. It has all these evils and perhaps more.

Very likely.

We have finished, then, with the constitution known as oligarchy, where power is held on a property qualification, and we may turn now to the history and character of the corresponding individual.

Yes, let us do so.

The transition from the timocratic type to the oligarchical happens somewhat in this way....Reason, whose thought is now confined to calculating how money may breed more money, and Ambition; suffered to admire and value nothing but wealth and its possessors and to excel in nothing but the struggle to gain money by any and every means....

Is this, then, our oligarchical type?

Well, at any rate, the type from which he has developed corresponded to the constitution from which oligarchy arose.

Let us see, then, whether he will not have the same sort of character. The first point of resemblance is that he values wealth above everything. Another is that he is niggardly and a worker who satisfies only his necessary wants and will go to no further expense; his other desires he keeps in subjection as leading nowhere. There is something squalid about him, with his way of always expecting to make a profit and add to his hoard—the sort of person who is much admired by the vulgar. Surely there is a likeness here to the state under an oligarchy?

I think there is, especially in the way that money is valued above everything.

Because, I suspect, he has never thought of cultivating his mind.

Never; or he would not have promoted the blind god of Wealth to lead the dance.

Good; and here is another point. As a consequence of his lack of education, appetites will spring up in him, comparable to those drones in society whom we classified as either beggars or criminals, though his habitual carefulness will keep them in check. If you want to see his criminal tendencies at work, you must look to any occasions, such as the guardianship of orphans, where he has a chance to be dishonest without risk. It will then be clear that in his other business relations, where his apparent honesty gives him a good reputation, he is only exercising a sort of enforced moderation. The base desires are there, not tamed by a reasonable conviction that it is wrong to gratify them, but only held down under stress of fear, which makes him tremble for the safety of his

whole fortune. Moreover, you may generally be sure of discovering these drone-like appetites whenever men of this sort have other people's money to spend.

That is very true.

Such a man, then, will not be single-minded but torn in two by internal conflict, though his better desires will usually keep the upper hand over the worse. Hence he presents a more decent appearance than many; but the genuine virtue of a soul in peace and harmony with itself will be utterly beyond his reach.

I agree.

Further, his stinginess weakens him as a competitor for any personal success or honourable distinction. He is unwilling to spend his money in a struggle for that sort of renown, being afraid to stir up his expensive desires by calling upon them to second his ambition. So, like a true oligarch, fighting with only a small part of his forces, he is usually beaten and remains a rich man.

Quite so.

Have we any further doubts, then, about the likeness between a state under an oligarchy and this parsimonious money-getter?

None at all.

Democracy, I suppose, should come next. A study of its rise and character should help us to recognize the democratic type of man and set him beside the others for judgement.

Certainly that course would fit in with our plan.

If the aim of life in an oligarchy is to become as rich as possible, that insatiable craving would bring about the transition to democracy. In this way: since the power of the ruling class is due to its wealth, they will not want to have laws restraining prodigal young men from ruining themselves by extravagance. They will hope to lend these spendthrifts money on their property and buy it up, so as to become richer and more influential than ever. We can see at once that a society cannot hold wealth in honour and at the same time establish a proper self-control in its citizens. One or the other must be sacrificed.

Yes, that is fairly obvious.

In an oligarchy, then, this neglect to curb riotous living sometimes reduces to poverty men of a not ungenerous nature. They settle down in idleness, some of them burdened with debt, some disfranchised, some both at once; and these drones are armed and can sting. Hating the men who have acquired their property and conspiring against them and the rest of society, they long for a revolution. Meanwhile the usurers, intent upon their own business, seem unaware of their existence; they are too busy planting their own stings into any fresh victim who offers them an opening to inject the poison of their money; and while they multiply their capital by usury, they are also multiplying the drones and the paupers. When the danger threatens to break out, they will do nothing to quench the flames, either in the way we mentioned, by forbidding a man to do what he likes with his own, or by the next best remedy, which would be a law enforcing a respect for right conduct. If it were enacted that, in general, voluntary contracts for a loan should be made at the lender's risk, there would be less of this shameless pursuit of wealth and a scantier crop of those evils I have just described.

Quite true.

But, as things are, this is the plight to which the rulers of an oligarchy, for all these reasons, reduce their subjects. As for themselves, luxurious indolence of body and mind makes their young men too lazy and effeminate to resist pleasure or to endure pain; and the fathers, neglecting everything but money, have no higher ideals in life than the poor. Such being the condition of rulers and subjects, what will happen when they are thrown together,…and can observe one another's demeanour in a moment of danger? The rich will have no chance to feel superior to the poor. On the contrary, the poor man, lean and sunburnt, may find himself posted in battle beside one who, thanks to his wealth and indoor life, is panting under his burden of fat and showing every mark of distress. 'Such men,' he will think, 'are rich because we are cowards'; and when he and his friends meet in private, the word will go round: 'These men are no good: they are at our mercy.'

Yes, that is sure to happen.

This state, then, is in the same precarious condition as a person so unhealthy that the least shock from outside will upset the balance or, even without that, internal disorder will break out. It falls sick and is at war with itself on the slightest occasion, as soon as one party or the other calls in allies from a neighbouring oligarchy or democracy; and sometimes civil war begins with no help from without.

Quite true.

And when the poor win, the result is a democracy. They kill some of the opposite party, banish others, and grant the rest an equal share in civil rights and government, officials being usually appointed by lot.

Yes, that is how a democracy comes to be established, whether by force of arms or because the other party is terrorized into giving way.

Now what is the character of this new régime? Obviously the way they govern themselves will throw light on the democratic type of man.

No doubt.

First of all, they are free. Liberty and free speech are rife everywhere; anyone is allowed to do what he likes.

Yes, so we are told.

That being so, every man will arrange his own manner of life to suit his pleasure. The result will be a greater variety of individuals than under any other constitution. So it may be the finest of all, with its variegated pattern of all sorts of characters. Many people may think it the best, just as women and children might admire a mixture of colours of every shade in the pattern of a dress. At any rate if we are in search of a constitution, here is a good place to look for one. A democracy is so free that it contains a sample of every kind; and perhaps anyone who intends to found a state, as we have been doing, ought first to visit this emporium of constitutions and choose the model he likes best.

He will find plenty to choose from.

Here, too, you are not obliged to be in authority, however competent you may be, or to submit to authority, if you do not like it; you need not fight when your fellow citizens are at war, nor remain at peace when they do, unless you want peace; and though you may have no legal right to hold office or sit on juries, you will do so all the same if the fancy takes you. A wonderfully pleasant life, surely, for the moment.

For the moment, no doubt….A democracy,…with a magnificent indifference to the sort of life a man has led before he enters politics,…will promote to honour anyone who merely calls himself the people's friend.

Magnificent indeed.

These then, and such as these, are the features of a democracy, an agreeable form of anarchy with plenty of variety and an equality of a peculiar kind for equals and unequals alike.

All that is notoriously true.

Now consider the corresponding individual character....

Yes.

I imagine him as the son of our miserly oligarch, brought up under his father's eye and in his father's ways. So he too will enforce a firm control over all such pleasures as lead to expense rather than profit—unnecessary pleasures, as they have been called....When a young man, bred, as we were saying, in a stingy and uncultivated home, has once tasted the honey of the drones and keeps company with those dangerous and cunning creatures, who know how to purvey pleasures in all their multitudinous variety, then the oligarchical constitution of his soul begins to turn into a democracy. Knowledge, right principles, true thoughts, are not at their post; and the place lies open to the assault of false and presumptuous notions. So he turns again to those lotus-eaters and now throws in his lot with them openly. If his family send reinforcements to the support of his thrifty instincts, the impostors who have seized the royal fortress shut the gates upon them, and will not even come to parley with the fatherly counsels of individual friends. In the internal conflict they gain the day; modesty and self-control, dishonoured and insulted as the weaknesses of an unmanly fool, are thrust out into exile; and the whole crew of unprofitable desires take a hand in banishing moderation and frugality, which, as they will have it, are nothing but churlish meanness. So they take possession of the soul which they have swept clean, as if purified for initiation into higher mysteries; and nothing remains but to marshal the great procession bringing home Insolence, Anarchy, Waste, and Impudence, those resplendent divinities crowned with garlands, whose praises they sing under flattering names: Insolence they call good breeding, Anarchy freedom, Waste magnificence, and Impudence a manly spirit. Is not that a fair account of the revolution which gives free rein to unnecessary and harmful pleasures in a young man brought up in the satisfaction only of the necessary desires?

Yes, it is a vivid description....

When he is told that some pleasures should be sought and valued as arising from desires of a higher order, others chastised and enslaved because the desires are base, he will shut the gates of the citadel against the messengers of truth, shaking his head and declaring that one appetite is as good as another and all must have their equal rights. So he spends his days indulging the pleasure of the moment, now intoxicated with wine and music, and then taking to a spare diet and drinking nothing but water; one day in hard training, the next doing nothing at all, the third apparently immersed in study. Every now and then he takes a part in politics, leaping to his feet to say or do whatever comes into his head. Or he will set out to rival someone he admires, a soldier it may be, or, if the fancy takes him, a man of business. His life is subject to no order or restraint, and he has no wish to change an existence which he calls pleasant, free, and happy.

That well describes the life of one whose motto is liberty and equality.

Yes, and his character contains the same fine variety of pattern that we found in the democratic state; it is as multifarious as that epitome of all types of constitution. Many a man, and many a woman too, will find in it something to envy. So we may see in him the counterpart of democracy, and call him the democratic man.

We may.

Now there remains only the most admired of all constitutions and characters—despotism and the despot. How does despotism arise? That it comes out of democracy is fairly clear. Does the change take place in the same sort of way as the change from oligarchy to democracy? Oligarchy was established by men with a certain aim in life: the good they sought was wealth, and it was the insatiable appetite for money-making to the neglect of everything else that proved its undoing. Is democracy likewise ruined by greed for what it conceives to be the supreme good?

What good do you mean?

Liberty. In a democratic country you will be told that liberty is its noblest possession, which makes it the only fit place for a free spirit to live in.

True; that is often said.

Well then, as I was saying, perhaps the insatiable desire for this good to the neglect of everything else may transform a democracy and lead to a demand for despotism. A democratic state may fall under the influence of unprincipled leaders, ready to minister to its thirst for liberty with too deep draughts of this heady wine; and then, if its rulers are not complaisant enough to give it unstinted freedom, they will be arraigned as accursed oligarchs and punished. Law-abiding citizens will be insulted as nonentities who hug their chains; and all praise and honour will be bestowed, both publicly and in private, on rulers who behave like subjects and subjects who behave like rulers. In such a state the spirit of liberty is bound to go to all lengths.

Inevitably.

It will make its way into the home, until at last the very animals catch the infection of anarchy. The parent falls into the habit of behaving like the child, and the child like the parent: the father is afraid of his sons, and they show no fear or respect for their parents, in order to assert their freedom. Citizens, resident aliens, and strangers from abroad are all on an equal footing. To descend to smaller matters, the schoolmaster timidly flatters his pupils, and the pupils make light of their masters as well as of their attendants. Generally speaking, the young copy their elders, argue with them, and will not do as they are told; while the old, anxious not to be thought disagreeable tyrants, imitate the young and condescend to enter into their jokes and amusements. The full measure of popular liberty is reached when the slaves of both sexes are quite as free as the owners who paid for them; and I had almost forgotten to mention the spirit of freedom and equality in the mutual relations of men and women....

Putting all these items together, you can see the result: the citizens become so sensitive that they resent the slightest application of control as intolerable tyranny, and in their resolve to have no master they end by disregarding even the law, written or unwritten.

Yes, I know that only too well.

Such then, I should say, is the seed, so full of fair promise, from which springs despotism.

Promising indeed. But what is the next stage?

The same disease that destroyed oligarchy breaks out again here, with all the more force because of the prevailing licence, and enslaves democracy. The truth is that, in the constitution of society, quite as much as in the weather or in plants and animals, any excess brings about an equally violent reaction. So the only outcome of too much freedom is likely to be excessive subjection, in the

state or in the individual; which means that the culmination of liberty in democracy is precisely what prepares the way for the cruellest extreme of servitude under a despot. But I think you were asking rather about the nature of that disease which afflicts democracy in common with oligarchy and reduces it to slavery.

Yes, I was.

What I had in mind was that set of idle spendthrifts, among whom the bolder spirits take the lead. We compared these leaders, if you remember, to drones armed with stings, the stingless drones being their less enterprising followers. In any society where these two groups appear they create disorder, as phlegm and bile do in the body. Hence the lawgiver, as a good physician of the body politic, should take measures in advance, no less than the prudent bee-keeper who tries to forestall the appearance of drones, or, failing that, cuts them out, cells and all, as quickly as he can.

Quite true.

Then, to gain a clearer view of our problem, let us suppose the democratic commonwealth to be divided into three parts, as in fact it is. One consists of the drones we have just described. Bred by the spirit of licence, in a democracy this class is no less numerous and much more energetic than in an oligarchy, where it is despised and kept out of office and so remains weak for lack of exercise. But in a democracy it furnishes all the leaders, with a few exceptions; its keenest members make the speeches and transact the business, while the other drones settle on the benches round, humming applause to drown any opposition. Thus nearly the whole management of the commonwealth is in its hands.

Quite true.

Meanwhile, a second group is constantly emerging from the mass. Where everyone is bent upon making money, the steadiest characters tend to amass the greatest wealth. Here is a very convenient source from which the drones can draw an abundance of honey.

No doubt; they cannot squeeze any out of men of small means.

'The rich,' I believe, is what they call this class which provides provender for the drones.

Yes.

The third class will be the 'people,' comprising all the peasantry who work their own farms, with few possessions and no interest in politics. In a democracy this is the largest class and, when once assembled, its power is supreme.

Yes, but it will not often meet, unless it gets some share of the honey.

Well, it always does get its share, when the leaders are distributing to the people what they have taken from the well-to-do, always provided they can keep the lion's share for themselves. The plundered rich are driven to defend themselves in debate before the Assembly and by any measures they can compass; and then, even if they have no revolutionary designs, the other party accuse them of plotting against the people and of being reactionary oligarchs. At last, when they see the people unwittingly misled by such denunciation into attempts to treat them unjustly, then, whether they wish it or not, they become reactionaries in good earnest. There is no help for it; the poison is injected by the sting of those drones we spoke of. Then follow impeachments and trials, in which each party arraigns the other.

Quite so.

And the people always put forward a single champion of their interests, whom they nurse to greatness. Here, plainly enough, is the root from which despotism invariably springs.

Yes.

How does the transformation of the people's champion into a despot begin? You have heard the legend they tell of the shrine of Lycaean Zeus in Arcadia: how one who tastes a single piece of human flesh mixed in with the flesh of the sacrificial victims is fated to be changed into a wolf. In the same way the people's champion, finding himself in full control of the mob, may not scruple to shed a brother's blood; dragging him before a tribunal with the usual unjust charges, he may foully murder him, blotting out a man's life and tasting kindred blood with unhallowed tongue and lips; he may send men to death or exile with hinted promises of debts to be cancelled and estates to be redistributed. Is it not thenceforth his inevitable fate either to be destroyed by his enemies or to seize absolute power and be transformed from a human being into a wolf?

It is.

Here, then, we have the party-leader in the civil war against property. If he is banished, and then returns from exile in despite of his enemies, he will come back a finished despot. If they cannot procure his banishment or death by denouncing him to the state, they will conspire to assassinate him. Then comes the notorious device of all who have reached this stage in the despot's career, the request for a bodyguard to keep the people's champion safe for them. The request is granted, because the people, in their alarm on his account, have no fear for themselves.

Quite true.

This is a terrifying sight for the man of property, who is charged with being not merely rich but the people's enemy....

And now shall we describe the happy condition of the man and of the country which harbours a creature of this stamp?

By all means.

In the early days he has a smile and a greeting for everyone he meets; disclaims any absolute power; makes large promises to his friends and to the public; sets about the relief of debtors and the distribution of land to the people and to his supporters; and assumes a mild and gracious air towards everybody. But as soon as he has disembarrassed himself of his exiled enemies by coming to terms with some and destroying others, he begins stirring up one war after another, in order that the people may feel their need of a leader, and also be so impoverished by taxation that they will be forced to think of nothing but winning their daily bread, instead of plotting against him. Moreover, if he suspects some of cherishing thoughts of freedom and not submitting to his rule, he will find a pretext for putting them at the enemy's mercy and so making away with them. For all these reasons a despot must be constantly provoking wars.

He must.

This course will lead to his being hated by his countrymen more and more. Also, the bolder spirits among those who have helped him to power and now hold positions of influence will begin to speak their mind to him and among themselves and to criticize his policy. If the despot is to maintain his rule, he must gradually make away with all these malcontents, until he has not a friend or an enemy left who is of any account. He will need to keep a sharp eye open for anyone who is courageous or high-minded or intelligent or rich; it is his happy fate to be at war with all such, whether he likes it or not, and to lay his plans against them until he has purged the commonwealth.

A fine sort of purgation!

Yes, the exact opposite of the medical procedure, which removes the worst elements in the bodily condition and leaves the best.

There seems to be no choice, if he is to hold his power.

No; he is confined to the happy alternatives of living with people most of whom are good for nothing and who hate him into the bargain, or not living at all. And the greater the loathing these actions inspire in his countrymen, the more he will need trustworthy recruits to strengthen his bodyguard. Where will he turn to find men on whom he can rely?

They will come flocking of their own accord, if he offers enough pay.

Foreigners of all sorts, you mean—yet another swarm of drones. But why not draw upon the home supply? He could rob the citizens of their slaves, emancipate them, and enroll them in his bodyguard.

No doubt they would be the most faithful adherents he could find.

What an enviable condition for the despot, to put his trust in such friends as these, when he has made away with his earlier supporters! He will, of course, be the admiration of all this band of new-made citizens, whose company he will enjoy when every decent person shuns him with loathing....

Let us go back to the despot's army. How is he to maintain this fine, ever-shifting array of nondescripts?

No doubt he will spend any treasure there may be in the temples, so long as it will last, as well as the property of his victims, thus lightening the war-taxes imposed on the people.

And when that source fails?

Clearly he will support himself, with his boon-companions, minions, and mistresses, from his parent's estate.

I understand: the despot and his comrades will be maintained by the common people which gave him birth.

Inevitably.

But how if the people resent this and say it is not right for the father to support his grown-up son—it ought to be the other way about; they did

not bring him into being and set him up in order that, when he had grown great, they should be the slaves of their own slaves and support them together with their master and the rest of his rabble; he was to be the champion to set them free from the rich and the so-called upper class. Suppose they now order him and his partisans to leave the country, as a father might drive his son out of the house along with his riotous friends?

Then, to be sure, the people will learn what sort of a creature it has bred and nursed to greatness in its bosom, until now the child is too strong for the parent to drive out.

Do you mean that the despot will dare to lay violent hands on this father of his and beat him if he resists?

Yes, when once he has disarmed him.

So the despot is a parricide, with no pity for the weakness of age. Here, it seems, is absolutism openly avowed. The people, as they say, have escaped the smoke only to fall into the fire, exchanging service to free men for the tyranny of slaves. Than freedom which knew no bounds must now put on the livery of the most harsh and bitter servitude, where the slave has become the master.

Yes, that is what happens.

May we say, then, that we have now sufficiently described the transition from democracy to despotism, and what despotism is like when once established?

Yes, quite sufficiently.

Last comes the man of despotic character. It remains to ask how he develops from the democratic type, what he is like, and whether his life is one of happiness or of misery.

Yes.

Here I feel the need to define, more fully than we have so far done, the number and nature of the appetites. Otherwise it will not be so easy to see our way to a conclusion.

Well, it is not too late.

Quite so. Now, about the appetites, here is the point I want to make plain. Among the unnecessary pleasures and desires, some, I should say, are unlawful. Probably they are innate in everyone; but when they are disciplined by law and by the higher desires with the aid of reason, they can in some people be got rid of entirely, or at least left few and feeble, although in others they will be comparatively strong and numerous....

Remember, then, our account of the democratic man, how his character was shaped by his early training under a parsimonious father, who respected only the businesslike desires, dismissing the unnecessary ones as concerned with frivolous embellishments. Then, associating with more sophisticated people who were a prey to those lawless appetites we have just described, he fell into their ways, and hatred of his father's miserliness drove him into every sort of extravagance. But, having a better disposition than his corrupters, he came to a compromise between the two conflicting ways of life, making the best of both with what he called moderation and avoiding alike the meanness of the one and the licence of the other. So the oligarchical man was transformed into the democratic type.

Yes, I hold by that description.

Now imagine him grown old in his turn, with a young son bred in his ways, who is exposed to the same influences, drawn towards the utter lawlessness which his seducers call perfect freedom, while on the other side his father and friends lend their support to the compromise. When those terrible wizards who would conjure up an absolute ruler in the young man's soul begin to doubt the power of their spells, in the last resort they contrive to engender in him a master passion, to champion the mob of idle appetites which are for dividing among themselves all available plunder—a passion that can only be compared to a great winged drone. Like a swarm buzzing round this creature, the other desires come laden with incense and perfumes, garlands and wine, feeding its growth to the full on the pleasures of a dissolute life, until they have implanted the sting of a longing that cannot be satisfied. Then at last this passion, as leader of the soul, takes madness for the captain of its guard and breaks out in frenzy; if it can lay hold upon any thoughts or desires that are of good report and still capable of shame, it kills them or drives them forth, until it has purged the soul of all sobriety and called in the partisans of madness to fill the vacant place.

That is a complete picture of how the despotic character develops.

Is not this the reason why lust has long since been called a tyrant? A drunken man, too, has something of this tyrannical spirit; and so has the lunatic who dreams that he can lord it over all mankind and heaven besides. Thus, when nature or habit or both have combined the traits of drunkenness, lust, and lunacy, then you have the perfect specimen of the despotic man.

Quite true.

Such, then, being his origin and character, what will his life be like?

I give it up. You must tell me.

I will. When a master passion is enthroned in absolute dominion over every part of the soul, feasting and revelling with courtesans and all such delights will become the order of the day. And every day and night a formidable crop of fresh appetites springs up, whose numerous demands quickly consume whatever income there may be. Soon he will be borrowing and trenching on his capital; and when all resources fail, the lusty brood of appetites will crowd about him clamouring. Goaded on to frenzy by them and above all by that ruling passion to which they serve as a sort of bodyguard, he will look out for any man of property whom he can rob by fraud or violence. Money he must have, no matter how, if he is not to suffer torments.

All that is inevitable....

If there are a few such characters in a country where most men are law-abiding, they will go elsewhere to join some despot's bodyguard or serve as mercenaries in any war that is toward. In quiet times of peace, they stay at home and commit crimes on a small scale, as thieves, burglars, pickpockets, temple-robbers, kidnappers; or, if they have a ready tongue, they may take to selling their services as informers and false witnesses.

Such crimes will be a small matter, you mean, so long as the criminals are few in number.

Small is a relative term; and all of them put together do not, as they say, come within sight of the degradation and misery of society under a despot. When the number of such criminals and their hangers-on increases and they become aware of their strength, then it is they who, helped by the folly of the common people, create the despot out of that one among their number whose soul is itself under the most tyrannical despotism.

Yes, such a state of mind would naturally be his best qualification.

All goes smoothly if men are ready to submit. But the country may resist; and then, just as he began by calling his father and mother to order, so now he will discipline his once loved fatherland, or motherland,...and see that it shall live in subjection to the new-found partisans he has called in to enslave it. So this man's desires come to their fulfilment.

Yes, that is true.

In private life, before they gain power, men of this stamp either consort with none but parasites ready to do them any service, or, if they have a favour to beg, they will not hesitate themselves to cringe and posture in simulated friendliness, which soon cools off when their end is gained. So, throughout life, the despotic character has not a friend in the world; he is sometimes master, sometimes slave, but never knows true friendship or freedom. There is no faithfulness in him; and, if we were right in our notion of justice, he is the perfect example of the unjust man.

Certainly.

To sum up, then: this worst type of man is he who behaves in waking life as we said men do in their dreams. The born despot who gains absolute power must come to this, and the longer he lives as a tyrant, the more this character grows upon him.

Inevitably, said Glaucon, who now took his turn to answer.

Now shall we find that the lowest depth of wickedness goes with the lowest depth of unhappiness, and that the misery of the despot is really in proportion to the extent and duration of his power, though the mass of mankind may hold many different opinions?

Yes, that much is certain.

It is true, is it not? That each type of individual—the despotic, the democratic, and so on—resembles the state with the corresponding type of constitution, and will be good and happy in a corresponding degree.

Yes, of course.

In point of excellence, then, how does a state under a despotism compare with the one governed by kings, such as we first described?

They are at opposite extremes: the best and the worst.

I shall not ask which is which, for that is obvious. Is your estimate the same with respect to their degrees of happiness or misery?...

From every point of view, then, whether of pleasure or reputation or advantage, one who praises justice speaks the truth; he who disparages it does not know what it is that he idly condemns....

The Nicomachean Ethics

Aristotle

It seems that both "justice" and "injustice" have several senses, but, as the different things covered by the common name are very closely related, the fact that they are different escapes notice and does not strike us, as it does when there is a great disparity—a great difference, say, in outward appearance....

Let us then ascertain in how many different senses we call a man unjust.

Firstly, he who breaks the laws is considered unjust, and, secondly, he who takes more than his share, or the unfair man.

Plainly, then, a just man will mean (1) a law-abiding and (2) a fair man.

A just thing then will be (1) that which is in accordance with the law, (2) that which is fair; and the unjust thing will be (1) that which is contrary to law, (2) that which is unfair.

From *The Nicomachean Ethics of Aristotle*, 9th ed., F. H. Peters, trans. (London: Kegan Paul, Trench, Trübner & Co., Ltd., 1904).

But since the unjust man, in one of the two senses of the word, takes more than his share, the sphere of his action will be good things—not all good things, but those with which good and ill fortune are concerned, which are always good in themselves, but not always good for us—the things that we men pray for and pursue, whereas we ought rather to pray that what is good in itself may be good for us, while we choose that which is good for us....

We found that the law-breaker is unjust, and the law-abiding man is just. Hence it follows that whatever is according to law is just in one sense of the word. And this, we see, is in fact the case; for what the legislator prescribes is according to law, and is always said to be just.

Now, the laws prescribe about all manner of things, aiming at the common interest of all, or of the best men, or of those who are supreme in the state (position in the state being determined by reference to personal excellence, or to some other such standard); and so in one sense we apply the term just to whatever tends to produce and preserve the happiness of the community, and the several elements of that happiness. The law bids us display courage (as not to leave our ranks, or run, or throw away our arms), and temperance (as not to commit adultery or outrage), and gentleness (as not to strike or revile our neighbours), and so on with all the other virtues and vices, enjoining acts and forbidding them, rightly when it is a good law, not so rightly when it is a hastily improvised one.

Justice, then, in this sense of the word, is complete virtue, with the addition that it is displayed towards others. On this account it is often spoken of as the chief of the virtues, and such that "neither evening nor morning star is so lovely;" and the saying has become proverbial, "Justice sums up all virtues in itself."

It is complete virtue, first of all, because it is the exhibition of complete virtue: it is also complete because he that has it is able to exhibit virtue in dealing with his neighbours, and not merely in his private affairs; for there are many who can be virtuous enough at home, but fail in dealing with their neighbours.

This, too, is the reason why justice alone of all the virtues is thought to be another's good, as implying this relation to others; for it is another's interest that justice aims at—the interest, namely, of the ruler or of our fellow-citizens.

While then the worst man is he who displays vice both in his own affairs and in his dealings with his friends, the best man is not he who displays virtue in his own affairs merely, but he who displays virtue towards others; for this is the hard thing to do.

Justice, then, in this sense of the word, is not a part of virtue, but the whole of it; and the injustice which is opposed to it is not a part of vice, but the whole of it.

How virtue differs from justice in this sense is plain from what we have said; it is one and the same character differently viewed: viewed in relation to others, this character is justice; viewed simply as a certain character, it is virtue.

We have now to examine justice in that sense in which it is a part of virtue—for we maintain that there is such a justice—and also the corresponding kind of injustice.

That the word is so used is easily shown. In the case of the other kinds of badness, the man who displays them, though he acts unjustly [in one sense of the word], yet does not take more than his share: for instance, when a man throws away his shield through cowardice, or reviles another through ill temper, or through illiberality refuses to help another with money. But when he takes more than his share, he displays perhaps no one of these vices, nor does he display them all, yet he displays a kind of badness (for we blame him), namely, injustice in the second sense of the word.

We see, then, that there is another sense of the word injustice, in which it stands for a part of that injustice which is coextensive with badness, and another sense of the word unjust, in which it is applied to a part only of those things to which it is applied in the former sense of "contrary to law."...

It is plain than that, besides the injustice which is coextensive with vice, there is a second kind of injustice, which is a particular kind of vice, bearing the same name as the first, because the same generic conception forms the basis of its definition; *i.e.*, both display themselves in dealings with others, but the sphere of the second is limited to such things as honour, wealth, security (perhaps some one name might be found to include all this class), and its motive is the pleasure of gain, while the sphere of the first is coextensive with the sphere of the good man's action.

We have ascertained, then, that there are more kinds of justice than one, and that there is another kind besides that which is identical with complete virtue; we now have to find what it is, and what are its characteristics.

We have already distinguished two senses in which we speak of things as unjust, viz. (1) contrary to law, (2) unfair; and two senses in which we speak of things as just, viz. (1) according to law, (2) fair.

The injustice which we have already considered corresponds to unlawful.

But since unfair is not the same as unlawful, but differs from it as the part from the whole (for unfair is always unlawful, but unlawful is not always unfair), unjust and injustice in the sense corresponding to unfair will not be the same as unjust and injustice in the sense corresponding to unlawful, but different as the part from the whole; for this injustice is a part of complete injustice, and the corresponding justice is a part of complete justice. We must therefore speak of justice and injustice, and of that which is just and that which is unjust, in this limited sense....

But of justice as a part of virtue, and of that which is just in the corresponding sense, one kind is that which has to do with the distribution of honour, wealth, and the other things that are divided among the members of the body politic (for in these circumstances it is possible for one man's share to be unfair or fair as compared with another's); and another kind is that which has to give redress in private transactions.

The latter kind is again subdivided; for private transactions are (1) voluntary, (2) involuntary.

"Voluntary transactions or contracts" are such as selling, buying, lending at interest, pledging, lending without interest, depositing, hiring: these are called "voluntary contracts," because the parties enter into them of their own will.

"Involuntary transactions," again, are of two kinds: one involving secrecy, such as theft, adultery, poisoning, procuring, corruption of slaves, assassination, false witness; the other involving open violence, such as assault, seizure of the person, murder, rape, maiming, slander, contumely.

The unjust man in this limited sense of the word, we say, is unfair, and that which is unjust is unfair.

Now, it is plain that there must be a mean which lies between what is unfair on this side and on that. And this is that which is fair or equal; for any act that admits of a too much and a too little admits also of that which is fair.

If then that which is unjust be unfair, that which is just will be fair, which indeed is admitted by all without further proof.

But since that which is fair or equal is a mean between two extremes, it follows that what is just will be a mean.

But equality or fairness implies two terms at least.

It follows, then, that that which is just is both a mean quantity and also a fair amount relatively to something else and to certain persons—in other words, that, on the one hand, as a mean quantity it implies certain other quantities, *i.e.*, a more and a less; and, on the other hand, as an equal or fair amount it involves two quantities, and as a just amount it involves certain persons.

That which is just, then, implies four terms at least: two persons to whom justice is done, and two things.

And there must be the same "equality" (*i.e.*, the same ratio) between the persons and the things: as the things are to one another, so must the persons be. For if the persons be not equal, their shares will not be equal; and this is the source of disputes and accusations, when persons who are equal do not receive equal shares, or when persons who are not equal receive equal shares.

This is also plainly indicated by the common phrase "according to merit." For in distribution all men allow that what is just must be according to merit or worth of some kind, but they do not all adopt the same standard of worth; in democratic states they take free birth as the standard, in oligarchic states they take wealth, in others noble birth, and in the true aristocratic state virtue or personal merit....

This then is one form of that which is just.

It remains to treat of the other form, viz. that which is just in the way of redress, the sphere of which is private transactions, whether voluntary or involuntary.

This differs in kind from the former.

For that which is just in the distribution of a common stock of good things is always in accordance with the proportion above specified (even when it is a common fund that has to be divided, the sums which the several participants take must bear the same ratio to one another as the sums they have put in), and that which is unjust in the corresponding sense is that which violates this proportion.

But that which is just in private transactions is indeed fair or equal in some sort, and that which is unjust is unfair or unequal; but the proportion to be observed here is not a geometrical proportion as above, but an arithmetical one.

For it makes no difference whether a good man defrauds a bad one, or a bad man a good one, nor whether a man who commits an adultery be a good or a bad man; the law looks only to the difference created by the injury, treating the parties themselves as equal, and only asking whether the one has done, and the other suffered, injury or damage.

That which is unjust, then, is here something unequal [or unfair] which the judge tries to make equal [or fair]. For even when one party is struck and the other strikes, or one kills and the other is killed, that which is suffered and that which is done may be said to be unequally or unfairly divided; the judge then tries to restore equality by the penalty or loss which he inflicts upon the offender, subtracting it from his gain.

For in such cases, though the terms are not always quite appropriate, we generally talk of the doer's "gain" (*e.g.*, the striker's) and the sufferer's "loss;" but when the suffering has been assessed by the court, what the doer gets is called "loss" or penalty, and what the sufferer gets is called "gain."

What is fair or equal, then, is a mean between more or too much and less or too little; but gain and loss are both more or too much and less or too little in opposite ways, *i.e.*, gain is more or too much good and less or too little evil, and loss the opposite of this.

And in the mean between them, as we found, lies that which is equal or fair, which we say is just.

That which is just in the way of redress, then, is the mean between loss and gain.

When disputes arise, therefore, men appeal to the judge and an appeal to the judge is an appeal to that which is just; for the judge is intended to be as it were a living embodiment of that which is just; and men require of a judge that he shall be moderate or observe the mean, and sometimes even call judges "mediators," signifying that if they get the mean they will get that which is just.

That which is just, then, must be a sort of mean, if the judge be a "mediator."

But the judge restores equality; it is as if he found a line divided into two unequal parts, and were to cut off from the greater that by which it exceeds the half, and to add this to the less.

But when the whole is equally divided, the parties are said to have their own, each now receiving an equal or fair amount.

But the equal or fair amount is here the *arithmetic* mean between the more or too much and the less or too little....

The Politics

Aristotle

Seeing that every State is a sort of association and every association is formed for the attainment of some Good—for some presumed Good is the end of all action—it is evident that, as some Good is the object of all associations, so in the highest degree is the supreme Good the object of that association which is supreme and embraces all the rest, in other words, of the State or political association....

From *The Politics of Aristotle*, J.E.C. Welldon, trans. (London: Macmillan and Co., 1883).

Here, as elsewhere, the best system of examination will be to begin at the beginning and observe things in their growth.

There are certain primary essential combinations of those who cannot exist independently one of another. Thus male and female must combine in order to the procreation of children, nor is there anything deliberate or arbitrary in their so doing; on the contrary, the desire of leaving an offspring like oneself is natural to man as to the whole animal and vegetable world. Again, natural rulers and subjects combine for safety—*and when I say "natural,"* I mean that there are some persons qualified intellectually to form projects, and these are natural rulers or natural masters; while there are others qualified physically to carry them out, and these are subjects or natural slaves, so that the interests of master and slave are coincident....

Thus the association naturally formed for the supply of everyday wants is a household....

Again, the simplest association of several households for something more than ephemeral purposes is a village. It seems that the village in its most natural form is derived from the household, including all the children of certain parents and the children's children....

This is the reason why States were originally governed by kings as is still the case with uncivilized peoples; they were composed of units accustomed to this form of government. For as each household is under the kingly government of its eldest member, so were also the offshoot-households as comprising none but blood-relations....This patriarchal government was universal in primitive times; in fact the reason why all nations represent the polity of the Gods as monarchical is that such originally was, if it is not still, their own polity, and men assimilate the lives no less than the bodily forms of the Gods to their own.

Lastly, the association composed of several villages in its complete form is the State, in which the goal of full independence may be said to be first attained. For as the State was formed to make life possible, so it exists to make life good. Consequently if it be allowed that the simple associations, *i.e., the household and the village,* have a natural existence, so has the State in all cases; for in the State they attain complete development, and Nature implies complete development, as the nature of anything, e.g., of a man, a house or a horse, may be defined to be its condition when the process of production is complete. Or *the naturalness of the State may be proved in another way:* the object proposed or the complete development of a thing is its highest Good; but independence *which is first attained in the State* is a complete development or the highest Good *and is therefore natural.*

Thus we see that the State is a natural institution, that Man is naturally a political animal and that one who is not a citizen of any State, if the cause of his isolation be natural and not accidental, is either a superhuman being or low *in the scale of civilization.*...Also that Man is a political animal in a higher sense than a bee or any other gregarious creature is evident from the fact that Nature, as we are fond of asserting, creates nothing without a purpose and Man is the only animal endowed with speech. Now mere sounds serve to indicate sensations of pain and pleasure and are therefore assigned to other animals as well as to Man; for their nature does not advance beyond the point of perceiving pain and pleasure and signifying these perceptions to one another. The object of speech on the other hand is to indicate advantage and disadvantage and therefore also justice and injustice. For the special characteristic which distinguishes Man from all other animals is that he alone enjoys perception of good and evil, justice and injustice and the like. But these are the principles of that association which constitutes a household or a State.

Again, in the order of Nature the State is prior to the household or the individual. For the whole must needs be prior to its part. For instance, if you take away *the body which is* the whole, there will not remain any such thing as a foot or a hand, unless we use the same word in a different sense as when we speak of a stone hand as a hand. For a hand separated from the body will be a disabled hand; whereas it is the function or faculty of a thing which makes it what it is, and therefore when things lose their function or faculty it is not correct to call them the same things but rather homonymous, *i.e., different things having the same name.*

We see then that the State is a natural institution, and also that it is prior to the individual. For if the individual as a separate unit is not independent, he must be a part and must bear the same relation to the State as other parts to their wholes; and one who is incapable of association with others or is inde-

pendent and has no need of such association is no
member of a State, in other words he is either a
brute or a God. Now the impulse to political association is innate in all men. Nevertheless the author
of the first combination whoever he was was a
great benefactor of human kind. For man, as in his
condition of complete development, *i.e., in the
State*, he is the noblest of all animals, so apart from
law and justice he is the vilest of all. For injustice
is always most formidable when it is armed; and
Nature has endowed Man with arms which are
intended to subserve the purposes of prudence and
virtue but are capable of being wholly turned to
contrary ends. Hence if Man be devoid of virtue,
no animal is so unscrupulous or savage, none so
sensual, none so gluttonous. Just action on the
other hand is bound up with the existence of a
State; for the administration of justice is an ordinance of the political association and the administration of justice is nothing else than the decision
of what is just....

There are, as we have seen, three branches of
Domestic Economy, viz. the relations of a slave-
master to his slaves,...the relations of a father to
his children, and thirdly the relations of a husband
to his wife. *I distinguish the paternal from the
marital form of rule*; for although the head of the
family rules both his wife and children and rules
them in both cases as free persons, yet the kind of
rule is different, being constitutional in the wife's
case, while in the children's it is regal. *The justification of these forms of rule lies in the fact* that
males are by Nature better qualified to command
than females, wherever the union is not unnaturally
constituted, and those who are elder and more
mature than those who are younger and immature.
It is true that in most cases of political or constitutional rule there is an interchange of the functions
of rulers and subject, as it is assumed that they are
naturally equal and indistinguishable. Nevertheless at any particular time an effort is made to
distinguish the rulers from the subjects by insiguia
of office, forms of address and acts of respect....Now the relation *which rulers in a constitutional country bear during their term of office to
their subjects is* the relation which the male at all
times bears to the female. The rule of a father over
his children on the other hand is like that of a king
over his subjects; for the parental rule rests upon
affection and respect, and this is precisely the

character of kingly rule....For the ideal of a king is
that he should be distinct from his subjects in
nature but one with them in race; and this is exactly
the relation of a senior to a junior or of a parent to
his child....

Let us take then the sum of the functions *of a
State* as a test which will serve to elucidate the
matter. The first requisite of a State then is food;
next arts, as there are various instruments, *which
are made by the arts*, necessary to human existence; thirdly arms, for the members of the political
association require arms at home to enforce their
authority against recalcitrant persons as well as to
defeat the attempts of enemies to inflict injury upon
the State from without; next a tolerable supply of
money for purposes both domestic and military;
fifthly the due worship of the Gods or ritual, as it
is termed; and sixthly, but most necessary of all,
the means of deciding questions of policy and of
justice between man and man. Such are the functions generally indispensable to a State. For a State
according to our definition does not consist of any
chance population but of one that is able to lead an
independent life; and if any of these functions is
wanting, the association in question cannot be absolutely independent. It follows that all these processes must enter into the composition of a State.
There must be in a State then a number of husbandmen who supply the food, artisans, an army, a
propertied class, a priesthood and judges of questions of justice and policy.

Having now determined the functions of the
citizens, we have still to consider the question
whether all the citizens are to share them all—for
it is possible that the same persons should be all at
one and the same time husbandmen, artisans and
deliberative and judicial functionaries—or we are
to assume the existence of a separate class of
citizens for each of the functions specified, or again
some necessarily belong to a special class, while
others are necessarily open to all the citizens....But
as we are engaged in a consideration of the best
polity, and this is the polity under which our State
will attain the *maximum* of happiness, and happiness, as has been already remarked, cannot exist
apart from virtue, it is evident from these considerations that in a State, in which the polity is perfect
and the citizens are just men in an absolute sense
and not merely in reference to the assumed principle *of the polity*, the citizens ought not to lead a

mechanical or commercial life; for such a life is ignoble and opposed to virtue. Nor again must the persons who are to be our citizens be husbandmen, as leisure *which is impossible in an agricultural life* is equally essential to the culture of virtue and to political action. But as besides these there exists in the State a military class and a class whose function it is to deliberate on questions of policy and to decide questions of justice, and these are evidently in the strictest sense parts of the State, *the question arises*. Are these functions too to be distinguished or both to be assigned to the same persons? And here again it is obvious that in one sense they must be assigned to the same and in another to different persons—to different persons in so far as the two functions are severally suited to a different prime of life, and the one requires prudence while the other requires physical strength, but to the same in so far as it is an impossibility that persons who possess the power of compulsion and prevention should put up with a permanent state of subjection; for the classes which have arms in their hands have in their hands also the continuance or dissolution of the polity. It remains then that in our polity both these functions should be assigned to the same persons, not simultaneously however but according to the plan of Nature by which physical strength resides in the younger and wisdom in the elder generation. This method of distribution then among the two is expedient and just, as the division is one which preserves the principle of desert. And further the landed estates should be in the hands of these classes, as affluence is a necessary qualification of our citizens, and these and these alone possess the citizenship. For neither the mechanics nor any other members of the State who do not cultivate virtue are entitled to political rights, as in fact is evident from our fundamental principle; for happiness, as we said, can exist only in union with virtue and, when we speak of a State as happy, it is right that we should regard not a single particular part of it but the citizens collectively....

Further, a State is virtuous only when all the citizens who enjoy political rights are virtuous, and political rights are universal among the citizens of our State. The point to be considered therefore is the means by which a man becomes virtuous. For even if we admit the possibility of the citizens being virtuous collectively without each individual being so, still it is better that the individuals should be virtuous, as the virtue of all is a consequence of the virtue of each. But there are three means by which a person becomes good and virtuous viz. nature, habit and reason. He must in the first place possess a certain nature e.g., the nature of a human being rather than of some other animal, and similarly certain natural qualities of body and soul. There are some points however in which natural disposition is of no value, as they are altered by habituation, for there are certain qualities which are naturally ambiguous but directed by habit to a lower or a higher end. And hence the need that nature and habit should be harmonious. Now while all animals except Man live principally according to the impulses of their nature and only in some cases and to a slight extent by habit, Man as being the only rational animal lives also by reason. For it often happens that our reason leads us to act contrary to our training and nature, if we are convinced of the advantage of a different course....

As every political association is composed of rulers and subjects, the question we now have to consider is whether the rulers and subjects are to be different *at different times* or the same for life; for it is evident that their education will necessarily vary according as the distinction is permanent or temporary.

If then there should be a class of persons as far superior to all others as are the Gods and heroes in our conception to human beings, having a vast preeminence first of all in bodily stature and then secondly in the qualities of the soul, so that the superiority of the rulers to the subjects was indisputable and self-evident, in that case it would doubtless be desirable that the same persons should be respectively rulers and subjects once and always. But as this is a state of things hard to realize and it is not the case, as Scylax describes among the Indians, that the kings display this eminent superiority to their subjects, it is evident that there are many reasons why all the citizens must alike participate in an alternation of rule and subjection. For among persons who are similar, equality consists in identity *of power*, and a polity which is framed in defiance of justice can hardly be of a permanent character. *Its peril is the greater* inasmuch as on the side of the subject citizens, *who have been excluded from power*, are all the *unenfranchised* inhabitants of the land ready for revolt. It is an impossibility that the members of the governing class should be so numerous as to be stronger than the two together. On the other hand that the rulers should be superior to the subjects is indisputable. The means of arriving at this result and of giving all the citizens a share in rule and subjection are matters for the consideration of the legislator. Or rather the point is one which has been already discussed. Nature has herself supplied the distinction we need, in that those who are in actual race the same she has made some junior and others senior, and to the former a position of subjection and to the latter one of rule is appropriate. Nobody feels indignant or fancies himself superior to his place, if the ground of his subjection is simply his youth, especially when he is sure to enjoy this privilege *of rule* in his turn, as soon as he has reached the proper age. Our conclusion then is that the rulers and subjects are in one sense the same and in another different. And from this it follows that their education too must be in one sense the same and in another different. *The point of identity and of difference is the fact* that nobody, as it is said, can be a good ruler without having first been a subject....

The Republic and Laws

Cicero

True law is right reason in agreement with nature; it is of universal application, unchanging and ever-lasting; it summons to duty by its commands, and averts from wrongdoing by its prohibitions. And it does not lay its commands or prohibitions upon good men in vain, though neither have any effect on the wicked. It is a sin to try to alter this law, nor is it allowable to attempt to repeal any part of it, and it is impossible to abolish it entirely. We cannot be freed from its obligations by senate or people, and we need not look outside ourselves for an expounder or interpreter of it. And there will not be different laws at Rome and at Athens, or differ-ent laws now and in the future, but one eternal and unchangeable law will be valid for all nations and all times, and there will be one master and ruler, that is, God, over us all, for he is the author of this law, its promulgator, and its enforcing judge. Who-ever is disobedient is fleeing from himself and denying his human nature, and by reason of this very fact he will suffer the worst penalties, even if he escapes what is commonly considered punish-ment....But in our present investigation we intend to cover the whole range of universal Justice and Law in such a way that our own civil law, as it is called, will be confined to a small and narrow corner. For we must explain the nature of Justice, and this must be sought for in the nature of man; we must also consider the laws by which States ought to be governed; then we must deal with the enactments and decrees of nations which are al-ready formulated and put in writing; and among these the civil law, as it is called....

Well then, the most learned men have determined to begin with Law, and it would seem that they are right, if, according to their definition, Law is the highest reason, implanted in Nature, which com-mands what ought to be done and forbids the oppo-site. This reason, when firmly fixed and fully developed in the human mind, is Law. And so they believe that Law is intelligence, whose natural func-tion it is to command right conduct and forbid wrongdoing....For as they have attributed the idea of fairness to the word law, so we have given it that

From *Cicero*, *De Republica*, *De Legibus*, Clinton Walker Keyes, trans. (Cambridge, MA: Harvard University Press, 1928). Reprinted by permission of the publishers.

of selection, though both ideas properly belong to
Law. Now if this is correct, as I think it to be in
general, then the origin of Justice is to be found in
Law, for Law is a natural force; it is the mind and
reason of the intelligent man, the standard by which
Justice and Injustice are measured. But since our
whole discussion has to do with the reasoning of the
populace, it will sometimes be necessary to speak in
the popular manner, and give the name of law to that
which in written form decrees whatever it wishes,
either by command or prohibition. For such is the
crowd's definition of law. But in determining what
Justice is, let us begin with that supreme Law which
had its origin ages before any written law existed or
any State had been established....

That animal which we call man, endowed with
foresight and quick intelligence, complex, keen,
possessing memory, full of reason and prudence,
has been given a certain distinguished status by
the supreme God who created him; for he is the
only one among so many different kinds and varieties of living beings who has a share in reason
and thought, while all the rest are deprived of it.
But what is more divine, I will not say in man only,
but in all heaven and earth, than reason? And
reason, when it is full grown and perfected, is
rightly called wisdom. Therefore, since there is
nothing better than reason, and since it exists both
in man and God, the first common possession of
man and God is reason. But those who have reason
in common must also have right reason in common. And since right reason is Law, we must
believe that men have Law also in common with
the gods. Further, those who share Law must also
share Justice; and those who share these are to be
regarded as members of the same commonwealth.
If indeed they obey the same authorities and powers, this is true in a far greater degree; but as a
matter of fact they do obey this celestial system,
the divine mind, and the God of transcendent
power. Hence we must now conceive of this whole
universe as one commonwealth of which both
gods and men are members....

Moreover, virtue exists in man and God alike,
but in no other creature besides; virtue, however,
is nothing else than Nature perfected and developed to its highest point; therefore there is a likeness between man and God....

Out of all the material of the philosophers'
discussions, surely there comes nothing more valu-

able than the full realization that we are born for
Justice, and that right is based, not upon men's
opinions, but upon Nature. This fact will immediately be plain if you once get a clear conception of
man's fellowship and union with his fellow-men.
For no single thing is so like another, so exactly its
counterpart, as all of us are to one another. Nay, if
bad habits and false beliefs did not twist the weaker
minds and turn them in whatever direction they are
inclined, no one would be so like his own self as
all men would be like all others. And so, however
we may define man, a single definition will apply
to all. This is a sufficient proof that there is no
difference in kind between man and man; for if
there were, one definition could not be applicable
to all men: and indeed reason, which alone raises
us above the level of the beasts and enables us to
draw inferences, to prove and disprove, to discuss
and solve problems, and to come to conclusions, is
certainly common to us all, and, though varying in
what it learns, at least in the capacity to learn it is
invariable. For the same things are invariably perceived by the senses, and those things which stimulate the senses, stimulate them in the same way in
all men; and those rudimentary beginnings of intelligence to which I have referred, which are imprinted on our minds, are imprinted on all minds
alike; and speech, the mind's interpreter, though
differing in the choice of words, agrees in the
sentiments expressed. In fact, there is no human
being of any race who, if he finds a guide, cannot
attain to virtue.

The similarity of the human race is clearly
marked in its evil tendencies as well as in its
goodness. For pleasure also attracts all men; and
even though it is an enticement to vice, yet it has
some likeness to what is naturally good. For it
delights us by its lightness and agreeableness; and
for this reason, by an error of thought, it is embraced as something wholesome. It is through a
similar misconception that we shun death as
though it were a dissolution of nature, and cling to
life because it keeps us in the sphere in which we
were born; and that we look upon pain as one of
the greatest of evils, not only because of its cruelty,
but also because it seems to lead to the destruction
of nature. In the same way, on account of the
similarity between moral worth and renown, those
who are publicly honoured are considered happy,
while those who do not attain fame are thought

miserable. Troubles, joys, desires, and fears haunt the minds of all men without distinction, and even if different men have different beliefs, that does not prove, for example, that it is not the same quality of superstition that besets those races which worship dogs and cats as gods, as that which torments other races. But what nation does not love courtesy, kindliness, gratitude, and remembrance of favours bestowed? What people does not hate and despise the haughty, the wicked, the cruel, and the ungrateful? Inasmuch as these considerations prove to us that the whole human race is bound together in unity, it follows, finally, that knowledge of the principles of right living is what makes men better....

The next point, then, is that we are so constituted by Nature as to share the sense of Justice with one another and to pass it on to all men. And in this whole discussion I want it understood that what I shall call Nature is [that which is implanted in us by Nature]; that, however, the corruption caused by bad habits is so great that the sparks of fire, so to speak, which Nature has kindled in us are extinguished by this corruption, and the vices which are their opposites spring up and are established. But if the judgments of men were in agreement with Nature, so that, as the poet says, they considered "nothing alien to them which concerns mankind," then Justice would be equally observed by all. For those creatures who have received the gift of reason from Nature have also received right reason, and therefore they have also received the gift of Law, which is right reason applied to command and prohibition. And if they have received Law, they have received Justice also. Now all men have received reason; therefore all men have received Justice. Consequently Socrates was right when he cursed, as he often did, the man who first separated utility from Justice; for this separation, he complained, is the source of all mischief....

For Justice is one; it binds all human society, and is based on one Law, which is right reason applied to command and prohibition. Whoever knows not this Law, whether it has been recorded in writing anywhere or not, is without Justice.

But if Justice is conformity to written laws and national customs, and if, as the same persons claim, everything is to be tested by the standard of utility, then anyone who thinks it will be profitable to him will, if he is able, disregard and violate the laws. It follows that Justice does not exist at all, if it does not exist in Nature, and if that form of it which is based on utility can be overthrown by that very utility itself. And if Nature is not to be considered the foundation of Justice, that will mean the destruction [of the virtues on which human society depends]. For where then will there be a place for generosity, or love of country, or loyalty, or the inclination to be of service to others or to show gratitude for favours received? For these virtues originate in our natural inclination to love our fellow-men, and this is the foundation of Justice. Otherwise not merely consideration for men but also rites and pious observances in honour of the gods are done away with; for I think that these ought to be maintained, not through fear, but on account of the close relationship which exists between man and God....But in fact we can perceive the difference between good laws and bad by referring them to no other standard than Nature; indeed, it is not merely Justice and Injustice which are distinguished by Nature, but also and without exception things which are honourable and dishonourable. For since an intelligence common to us all makes things known to us and formulates them in our minds, honourable actions are ascribed by us to virtue, and dishonourable actions to vice; and only a madman would conclude that these judgments are matters of opinion, and not fixed by Nature....

Treatise on Law

Thomas Aquinas

Concerning law, we must consider—(1) Law itself in general; (2) its parts. Concerning law in general three points offer themselves for our consideration: (1) Its essence; (2) The different kinds of law; (3) The effects of law.

Under the first head there are four points of inquiry: (1) Whether law is something pertaining to reason? (2) Concerning the end of law; (3) Its cause; (4) The promulgation of law.

It belongs to the law to command and to forbid. But it belongs to reason to command....Therefore law is something pertaining to reason.

Law is a rule and measure of acts, whereby man is induced to act or is restrained from acting: for *lex* (law) is derived from *ligare* (to bind), because it binds one to act. Now the rule and measure of human acts is the reason, which is the first principle of human acts;...since it belongs to the reason to direct to the end, which is the first principle in all matters of action....

Since law is a kind of rule and measure, it may be in something in two ways. First, as in that which measures and rules: and since this is proper to reason, it follows that, in this way, law is in the reason alone.—Secondly, as in that which is measured and ruled. In this way, law is in all those things that are inclined to something by reason of some law....

Reason has its power of moving from the will,...for it is due to the fact that one wills the end, that the reason issues its commands as regards things ordained to the end. But in order that the volition of what is commanded may have the nature of law, it needs to be in accord with some rule of reason. And in this sense is to be understood the saying that the will of the sovereign has the force of law; otherwise the sovereign's will would savor of lawlessness rather than of law.

The law belongs to that which is a principle of human acts, because it is their rule and measure. Now as reason is a principle of human acts, so in reason itself there is something which is the principle in respect of all the rest: wherefore to this principle chiefly and mainly law must needs be referred.—Now the first principle in practical matters, which are the object of the practical reason, is the last end: and the last end of human life is bliss or happiness....Consequently the law must needs regard principally the relationship to happiness. Moreover, since every part is ordained to the whole, as imperfect to perfect; and since one man is a part of the perfect community, the law must needs regard properly the relationship to universal happiness....Since the law is chiefly ordained to the common good, any other precept in regard to some individual work, must needs be devoid of the nature of a law, save in so far as it regards the common good. Therefore every law is ordained to the common good....

A law, properly speaking, regards first and foremost the order to the common good. Now to order anything to the common good, belongs either to the whole people, or to someone who is the viceregent of the whole people. And therefore the making of a law belongs either to the whole people or to a public personage who has care of the whole people: since in all other matters the directing of anything to the end concerns him to whom the end belongs....

A law is imposed on others by way of a rule and measure. Now a rule or measure is imposed by being applied to those who are to be ruled and measured by it. Wherefore, in order that a law obtain the binding force which is proper to a law, it must needs be applied to the men who have to be ruled by it. Such application is made by its being

From *St. Thomas Aquinas: Summa Theologica*, Fathers of the English Dominican Province, trans. (New York: Benziger Brothers, Inc., 1947).

notified to them by promulgation. Wherefore promulgation is necessary for the law to obtain its force.

Thus,...the definition of law may be gathered; and it is nothing else than an ordinance of reason for the common good, made by him who has care of the community, and promulgated....We must now consider the various kinds of law: under which head there are six points of inquiry: (1) Whether there is an eternal law? (2) Whether there is a natural law? (3) Whether there is a human law? (4) Whether there is a Divine law? (5) Whether there is one Divine law, or several? (6) Whether there is a law of sin?

Law is nothing else but a dictate of practical reason emanating from the ruler who governs a perfect community. Now it is evident, granted that the world is ruled by Divine Providence, ...that the whole community of the universe is governed by Divine Reason. Wherefore the very Idea of the government of things in God the Ruler of the universe, has the nature of a law. And since the Divine Reason's conception of things is not subject to time but is eternal,...therefore it is that this kind of law must be called eternal.

Law, being a rule and measure, can be in a person in two ways: in one way, as in him that rules and measures; in another way, as in that which is ruled and measured, since a thing is ruled and measured, in so far as it partakes of the rule or measure. Wherefore, since all things subject to Divine providence are ruled and measured by the eternal law,...it is evident that all things partake somewhat of the eternal law, in so far as, namely, from its being imprinted on them, they derive their respective inclinations to their proper acts and ends. Now among all others, the rational creature is subject to Divine providence in the most excellent way, in so far as it partakes of a share of providence, by being provident both for itself and for others. Wherefore it has a share of the Eternal Reason, whereby it has a natural inclination to its proper act and end: and this participation of the eternal law in the rational creature is called the natural law....

A law is a dictate of the practical reason. Now it is to be observed that the same procedure takes place in the practical and in the speculative reason: for each proceeds from principles to conclusions....Accordingly we conclude that just as, in

the speculative reason, from naturally known indemonstrable principles, we draw the conclusions of the various sciences, the knowledge of which is not imparted to us by nature, but acquired by the efforts of reason, so too it is from the precepts of the natural law, as from general and indemonstrable principles, that the human reason needs to proceed to the more particular determination of certain matters. These particular determinations, devised by human reason, are called human laws, provided the other essential conditions of law be observed....

Besides the natural and the human law it was necessary for the directing of human conduct to have a Divine law. And this for four reasons. First, because it is by law that man is directed how to perform his proper acts in view of his last end. And indeed if man were ordained to no other end than that which is proportionate to his natural faculty, there would be no need for man to have any further direction on the part of his reason, besides the natural law and human law which is derived from it. But since man is ordained to an end of eternal happiness which is inproportionate to man's natural faculty,...therefore it was necessary that, besides the natural and the human law, man should be directed to his end by a law given by God.

Secondly, because, on account of the uncertainty of human judgment, especially on contingent and particular matters, different people form different judgments on human acts; whence also different and contrary laws result. In order, therefore, that man may know without any doubt what he ought to do and what he ought to avoid, it was necessary for man to be directed in his proper acts by a law given by God, for it is certain that such a law cannot err.

Thirdly, because man can make laws in those matters of which he is competent to judge. But man is not competent to judge of interior movements, that are hidden, but only of exterior acts which appear: and yet for the perfection of virtue it is necessary for man to conduct himself aright in both kinds of acts. Consequently human law could not sufficiently curb and direct interior acts; and it was necessary for this purpose that a Divine law should supervene.

Fourthly, because, as Augustine says...human law cannot punish or forbid all evil deeds: since while aiming at doing away with all evils, it would do away with many good things, and would hinder the advance of the common good, which is necessary for human intercourse. In order, therefore, that no evil might remain unforbidden and unpunished, it was necessary for the Divine law to supervene, whereby all sins are forbidden....

A thing may be known in two ways: first, in itself; secondly, in its effect, wherein some likeness of that thing is found: thus someone not seeing the sun in its substance, may know it by its rays. So then no one can know the eternal law, as it is in itself, except the blessed who see God in His Essence. But every rational creature knows it in its reflection, greater or less. For every knowledge of truth is a kind of reflection and participation of the eternal law, which is the unchangeable truth....

Now all men know the truth to a certain extent, at least as to the common principles of the natural law: and as to the others, they partake of the knowledge of truth, some more, some less; and in this respect are more or less cognizant of the eternal law....

We must now consider the natural law; concerning which there are six points of inquiry: (1) What is the natural law? (2) What are the precepts of the natural law? (3) Whether all acts of virtue are prescribed by the natural law? (4) Whether the natural law is the same in all? (5) Whether it is changeable? (6) Whether it can be abolished from the heart of man?...

The precepts of the natural law are to the practical reason, what the first principles of demonstrations are to the speculative reason; because both are self-evident principles. Now a thing is said to be self-evident in two ways: first, in itself; secondly, in relation to us. Any proposition is said to be self-evident in itself, if its predicate is contained in the notion of the subject: although, to one who knows not the definition of the subject, it happens that such a proposition is not self-evident. For instance, this proposition, *Man is a rational being*, is, in its very nature, self-evident, since who says *man*, says *a rational being*: and yet to one who knows not what a man is, this proposition is not self-evident. Hence it is that,...certain axioms or propositions are universally self-evident to all; and such are those propositions whose terms are known to all, as, *Every whole is greater than its part, and, Things equal to one and the same are equal to one another*. But some propositions are self-evident only to the wise, who understand the meaning of the terms of such propositions: thus to one who understands that an angel is not a body, it is self-evident that an angel is not circumscriptively in a place: but this is not evident to the unlearned, for they cannot grasp it.

Good is the first thing that falls under the apprehension of the practical reason, which is directed to action: since every agent acts for an end under the aspect of good. Consequently the first principle in the practical reason is one founded on the notion of good, viz., that *good is that which all things seek after*. Hence this is the first precept of law, that *good is to be done and pursued, and evil is to be avoided*. All other precepts of the natural law are based upon this: so that whatever the practical reason naturally apprehends as man's good (or evil) belongs to the precepts of the natural law as something to be done or avoided.

Since, however, good has the nature of an end, and evil, the nature of a contrary, hence it is that all those things to which man has a natural inclination, are naturally apprehended by reason as being good, and consequently as objects of pursuit, and their contraries as evil, and objects of avoidance....

To the natural law belongs those things to which a man is inclined naturally: and among these it is proper to man to be inclined to act according to reason. Now the process of reason is from the common to the proper....The speculative reason, however, is differently situated in this matter, from the practical reason. For, since the speculative reason is busied chiefly with necessary things, which cannot be otherwise than they are, its proper conclusions, like the universal principles, contain the truth without fail. The practical reason, on the other hand, is busied with contingent matters, about which human actions are concerned: and consequently, although there is necessity in the general principles, the more we descend to matters of detail, the more frequently we encounter defects. Accordingly then in speculative matters truth is the same in all men, both as to principles and as to conclusions: although the truth is not known to all as regards the conclusions, but only as regards the principles which are called common notions. But in matters of action, truth or practical rectitude is not the same for all, as to matters of detail, but only as to the general principles: and where there is the same rectitude in matters of detail, it is not equally known to all.

It is therefore evident that, as regards the general principles whether of speculative or of practical reason, truth or rectitude is the same for all, and is equally known by all. As to the proper conclusions of the speculative reason, the truth is the same for all, but is not equally known to all: thus it is true for all that the three angles of a triangle are together equal to two right angles, although it is not known to all. But as to the proper conclusions of the practical reason, neither is the truth or rectitude the same for all, nor, where it is the same, is it equally known by all. Thus it is right and true for all to act according to reason: and from this principle it follows as a proper conclusion, that goods entrusted to another should be restored to their owner. Now this is true for the majority of cases: but it may happen in a particular case that it would be injurious, and therefore unreasonable, to restore goods held in trust; for instance if they are claimed for the purpose of fighting against one's country. And this principle will be found to fail the more, according as we descend further into detail, *e.g.*, if one were to say that goods held in trust should be restored with such and such a guarantee, or in such and such a way; because the greater the number of conditions added, the greater the number of ways in which the principle may fail, so that it be not right to restore or not to restore.

Consequently we must say that the natural law, as to general principles, is the same for all, both as to rectitude and as to knowledge. But as to certain matters of detail, which are conclusions, as it were, of those general principles, it is the same for all in the majority of cases, both as to rectitude and as to knowledge; and yet in some few cases it may fail, both as to rectitude, by reason of certain obstacles (just as natures subject to generation and corruption fail in some few cases on account of some obstacle), and as to knowledge, since in some the reason is perverted by passion, or evil habit, or an evil disposition of nature....

A change in the natural law may be understood by way of subtraction, so that what previously was according to the natural law, ceases to be so. In this sense, the natural law is altogether unchangeable in its first principles: but in its secondary principles, which, as we have said...are certain detailed proximate conclusions drawn from the first princi-

ples, the natural law is not changed so that what it prescribes be not right in most cases. But it may be changed in some particular cases of rare occurrence, through some special causes hindering the observance of such precepts, as stated above....We must now consider human law; and (1) this law considered in itself; (2) its power; (3) its mutability. Under the first head there are four points of inquiry: (1) Its utility. (2) Its origin. (3) Its quality. (4) Its division.

Man has a natural aptitude for virtue; but the perfection of virtue must be acquired by man by means of some kind of training. Thus we observe that man is helped by industry in his necessities, for instance, in food and clothing. Certain beginnings of these he has from nature, viz., his reason and his hands; but he has not the full complement, as other animals have, to whom nature has given sufficiency of clothing and food. Now it is difficult to see how man could suffice for himself in the matter of this training: since the perfection of virtue consists chiefly in withdrawing man from undue pleasures, to which above all man is inclined, and especially the young, who are more capable of being trained. Consequently a man needs to receive this training from another, whereby to arrive at the perfection of virtue. And as to those young people who are inclined to acts of virtue, by their good natural disposition, or by custom, or rather by the gift of God, paternal training suffices, which is by admonitions. But since some are found to be depraved, and prone to vice, and not easily amenable to words, it was necessary for such to be restrained from evil by force and fear, in order that, at least, they might desist from evil-doing, and leave others in peace, and that they themselves, by being habituated in this way, might be brought to do willingly what hitherto they did from fear, and thus become virtuous. Now this kind of training, which compels through fear of punishment, is the discipline of laws. Therefore, in order that man might have peace and virtue, it was necessary for laws to be framed....

That which is not just seems to be no law at all: wherefore the force of a law depends on the extent of its justice. Now in human affairs a thing is said to be just, from being right, according to the rule of reason. But the first rule of reason is the law of nature, as is clear from what has been stated above....Consequently every human law has just so much of the nature of law, as it is derived from the law of nature. But if in any point it deflects from the law of nature, it is no longer a law but a perversion of law....

Laws framed by man are either just or unjust. If they be just, they have the power of binding in conscience, from the eternal law whence they are derived....Now laws are said to be just, both from the end, when, to wit, they are ordained to the common good,—and from their author, that is to say, when the law that is made does not exceed the power of the lawgiver,—and from their form, when, to wit, burdens are laid on the subjects, according to an equality of proportion and with a view to the common good. For, since one man is a part of the community, each man in all that he is and has, belongs to the community; just as a part, in all that it is, belongs to the whole; wherefore

nature inflicts a loss on the part, in order to save the whole: so that on this account, such laws as these, which impose proportionate burdens, are just and binding in conscience, and are legal laws.

On the other hand laws may be unjust in two ways: first, by being contrary to human good, through being opposed to the things mentioned above:—either in respect of the end, as when an authority imposes on his subjects burdensome laws, conducive, not to the common good, but rather to his own cupidity or vainglory;—or in respect of the author, as when a man makes a law that goes beyond the power committed to him;—or in respect of the form, as when burdens are imposed unequally on the community, although with a view to the common good....Wherefore such laws do not bind in conscience, except perhaps in order to avoid scandal or disturbance....

2 ENLIGHTENMENT

Two important developments distinguish ancient and medieval thought from that of the early modern period (sixteenth to eighteenth centuries) which is referred to as the "Enlightenment." In the medieval period the Catholic church had preserved and extended the intellectual heritage of the Greeks and Romans by building great institutions of higher learning. However, these institutions were open to only a few persons studying primarily law and theology. Formal attempts to understand the natural and social world were largely confined to a few elite scholars working within a theoretical scholastic-Aristotelean non-empirical tradition. Gradually the idea that everyone could engage in this dialogue became more accepted.

Curiosity about the physical world, and an attempt to study and classify it, had begun with Aristotle but did not progress for centuries and had only reemerged several centuries earlier in the Renaissance, when direct investigation of nature by inventors and engineers, working with their hands, rather than from their armchairs, began. This, along with the greater availability of books in print, enabled more people to gain knowledge outside the confines of the religiously dominated universities. Many of the leading thinkers of this period were not university teacher-scholars, but individuals working on their own. This period is sometimes referred to as the Age of Reason as a reflection of the demand that access to the tools of reasoning become more widespread. This, together with the Reformation, loosened the monopoly on education held by the church.

The second development was that empirical science began to rival faith as a way of understanding the world. Advances in medicine, astronomy, and physics enabled us to develop new techniques and technologies. The idea of "progress," the idea that we could reshape our world, both natural and social, took root. This encouraged greater confidence in the ability of human beings, using their own rational faculties, to learn about the world and to develop ways to change it for the better—downplaying reliance on supernatural sources.

Along with these changes in perspective, new political and social developments occurred. The breakdown of the feudal system, in which individuals were limited to precise functions or roles in society depending on heredity—families of rulers, peasant-farmers, craftsmen, and so on—began. Most people were either aristocratic noble rulers, clergy, or peasant-farmers. But gradually the small class of craftspeople escaped to cities (London or Paris, for example) where they were free from their feudal obligations to the nobility to pursue their own business interests. Many of these people became very wealthy, creating a new "middle class" which eventually became the *dominant* class, overpowering even the nobility. These monumental changes necessitated changes in forms of government and social organization and therefore new ways of *thinking* about government and social organization. As Karl Marx later argued, much of the new political thinking defended the rights and privileges of the new middle class, both against their aristocratic rivals and against the claims of the poor worker-peasant class. Members of the new middle class had certain rights (to property, to live where they chose, to educate themselves, to engage in whatever business they preferred, to determine their government democratically , and so on), and the justification for government came increasingly to be seen as designed to serve the interests of the new middle class. As this occurred, people began a process of identifying themselves as full and equal members of a wider political community, rather than the small feudal community, as before. This was a step in the direction of modern nationalism and provided the basis for the emerging nation-states.

This shift in power relations did not occur quickly or easily. The royal families struggled for power and engaged in various alliances and schemes to preserve position and power. They warred with one another. England in the sixteenth century, for example, was nearly always in chaos. Charles I was put to death; Cromwell was made Protector, and the crown was restored to Charles II. The emerging middle class began to seek a basis for a better, more stable social order in which the interests of ordinary people would be shown consideration.

READINGS

It was in this social context that Thomas Hobbes, an English philosopher (1588–1679), began to think about the basis and justification of government. Born prematurely when his mother heard of the approaching Spanish Armada, Hobbes said of himself that "fear and I were born twins." The chaotic political conditions in England were an important part of Hobbes's personal life since he was a tutor to Charles II, and these conditions doubtless influenced his approach to political philosophy. Another influence on his work was his materialist, determinist, and very mechanistic approach to the physical world, in keeping with the "new science" of his time.

Hobbes raised the interesting question of what human beings would be like if there were no civil authority. He characterized this situation as being a "state of nature." Hobbes viewed human nature as being egoistic, so that in the state of nature each of us would attempt to better our own condition even at the expense of others. In Hobbes's view, in the state of nature each of us has a "natural right" to whatever we can do or obtain. These natural rights are more or less natural "mights" or abilities to exercise our autonomy, rather than "rights" understood as entitlements. In Hobbes's analysis of the state of nature, it would be a state of continual warfare within which human life would be "nasty, brutish and short."

However, human reason is capable of discovering a "natural law," he thought, which would tell us to seek peace. He argues this can be done by forming a social contract with a sovereign by each of us handing to the sovereign virtually all of our natural rights. The sovereign becomes an authority capable of maintaining social order but has no limitations on exercising that authority, short of failing to keep the peace.

The ideas of a social contract and natural rights are used by the later English philosopher John Locke (1632–1704) in very different ways. For Locke, natural law consists of moral law which most people would conform to in the state of nature. But the state of nature is inconvenient because there is no formal mechanism for dealing with those who violate natural law. His idea is that we therefore form a social contract with each other, not with a sovereign, each agreeing to be members of a social union and to abide by the civil authority.

Natural rights, which Locke identifies as the rights to life, liberty, and property, must be protected by the civil authority, and the failure to do so invalidates the contract and justifies rebellion against it. Locke advocated a form of democratic rule and a separation of powers between branches of the government as well as a separation of church and state. Clearly, Locke's work was an important influence on the leaders of the American Revolution.

Yet another application of these concepts can be found in the work of Jean-Jacques Rousseau (1712–1778), a Swiss philosopher, novelist, and musician. As Rousseau describes the social contract, it is an agreement of individual people to give up their individual freedom to the collective sovereignty of the people as a whole. Sovereignty for Rousseau resides in the "general will" of the people, but this does not necessarily coincide with the will of the majority of the citizens, as expressed in an actual election, for example. Individual citizens, even a majority, may not know or fully understand what they really want or need. Individuals do not really exist apart from their participation in the larger "general will" or life of the society as a whole. The whole is greater than the sum of its parts. The state as a body of many people has an existence and therefore a life and a will of its own over and above the aggregate sum of each citizen added together.

David Hume (1711–1776) was a Scottish historian and philosopher who was a critic of the social contract, natural law, and natural rights tradition. The basis for Hume's analysis of morality is utility. What is useful varies with societal conditions; hence, Hume argues that standards of justice are conventional and not based on universal natural law or natural rights. When and where, he asks, could we form the social contract? We are born into a particular conventional social arrangement and the conditions within that arrangement are just if they prove to be useful.

The Leviathan

Thomas Hobbes

Nature, the art whereby God hath made and governs the world, is by the *art* of man, as in many other things, so in this also imitated, that it can make an artificial animal. For seeing life is but a motion of limbs, the beginning whereof is in some principal part within; why may we not say, that all *automata* (engines that move themselves by springs and wheels as doth a watch) have an artificial life? For what is the *heart*, but a *spring*; and the *nerves*, but so many *strings*; and the *joints*, but so many *wheels*, giving motion to the whole body, such as was intended by the artificer? *Art* goes yet further, imitating that rational and most excellent work of nature, *man*. For by art is created that great LEVIATHAN called a COMMONWEALTH, or STATE,...which is but an artificial man; though of greater stature and strength than the natural, for whose protection and defence it was intended; and in which the *sovereignty* is an artificial *soul*, as giving life and motion to the whole body; the *magistrates*, and other *officers* of judica-

---

From *The Leviathan*, Vol. 3, Sir William Molesworth, ed. (London: John Bohn, 1839).

ture and execution, artificial *joints*; *reward* and *punishment*, by which fastened to the seat of the sovereignty every joint and member is moved to perform his duty, are the *nerves*, that do the same in the body natural; the *wealth* and *riches* of all the particular members, are the *strength*;...the *people's safety*, its *business*; *counsellors*, by whom all things needful for it to know are suggested unto it, are the *memory*; *equity*, and *laws*, an artificial *reason* and *will*; *concord, health*; *sedition, sickness*; and *civil war, death*. Lastly, the *pacts* and *covenants*, by which the parts of this body politic were at first made, set together, and united, resemble that *fiat*, or the *let us make man*, pronounced by God in the creation....

There be in animals, two sorts of *motions* peculiar to them: one called *vital*; begun in generation, and continued without interruption through their whole life; such as are the *course* of the *blood*, the *pulse*, the *breathing*, the *concoction, nutrition, excretion*, &c. to which motions there needs no help of imagination: the other is *animal motion*, otherwise called *voluntary motion*; as to *go*, to *speak*, to *move* any of our limbs, in such manner as is first fancied in our minds. ...Sense is motion in the organs and interior parts of man's body, caused by the action of the things we see, hear, &c.; and...fancy is but the relics of the same motion, remaining after sense,. ...And because *going, speaking*, and the like voluntary motions, depend always upon a precedent thought of *whither, which way*, and *what*; it is evident, that the imagination is the first internal beginning of all voluntary motion. ...These small beginnings of motion, within the body of man, before they appear in walking, speaking, striking, and other visible actions, are commonly called ENDEAVOUR.

This endeavour, when it is toward something which causes it, is called APPETITE, or DESIRE. ...And when the endeavour is fromward something, it is generally called AVERSION. These words, *appetite* and *aversion*,...both of them signify the motions, one of approaching, the other of retiring. ...

That which men desire, they are also said to LOVE: and to HATE those things for which they have aversion. So that desire and love are the same thing; save that by desire, we always signify the absence of the object; by love, most commonly the presence of the same. So also by aversion, we signify the absence; and by hate, the presence of the object.

Of appetites and aversions, some are born with men; as appetite of food, appetite of excretion, and exoneration. ...The rest, which are appetites of particular things, proceed from experience, and trial of their effects upon themselves or other men. For of things we know not at all, or believe not to be, we can have no further desire, than to taste and try. But aversion we have for things, not only which we know have hurt us, but also that we do not know whether they will hurt us, or not.

Those things which we neither desire, nor hate, we are said to contemn; CONTEMPT being nothing else but an immobility,...in resisting the action of certain things; and proceeding from that the heart is already moved otherwise, by other more potent objects; or from want of experience of them.

And because the constitution of a man's body is in continual mutation, it is impossible that all the same things should always cause in him the same appetites, and aversions: much less can all men consent, in the desire of almost any one and the same object.

But whatsoever is the object of any man's appetite or desire, that is it which he for his part calleth good: and the object of his hate and aversion, evil; and of his contempt, vile and inconsiderable. For these words of good, evil, and contemptible, are ever used with relation to the person that useth them: there being nothing simply and absolutely so; nor any common rule of good and evil, to be taken from the nature of the objects themselves; but from the person of the man, where there is no commonwealth; or, in a commonwealth, from the person that representeth it; or from an arbitrator or judge, whom men disagreeing shall by consent set up, and make his sentence the rule thereof. ...

When in the mind of man, appetites, and aversions, hopes, and fears, concerning one and the same thing, arise alternately; and divers good and evil consequences of the doing, or omitting the thing propounded, come successively into our thoughts; so that sometimes we have an appetite to it; sometimes an aversion from it; sometimes hope to be able to do it; sometimes despair, or fear to attempt it; the whole sum of desires, aversions, hopes and fears continued till the thing be either done, or thought impossible, is that we call DELIBERATION.

Therefore of things past, there is no *deliberation*; because manifestly impossible to be changed: nor of things known to be impossible, or thought so; because men know, or think such deliberation vain. But of things impossible, which we think possible, we may deliberate; not knowing it is in vain. And it is called *deliberation*; because it is a putting an end to the *liberty* we had of doing, or omitting, according to our own appetite, or aversion.

This alternate succession of appetites, aversions, hopes and fears, is no less in other living creatures than in man: and therefore beasts also deliberate.

Every *deliberation* is then said to *end*, when that whereof they deliberate, is either done, or thought impossible; because till then we retain the liberty of doing, or omitting; according to our appetite, or aversion.

In *deliberation*, the last appetite, or aversion, immediately adhering to the action, or to the omission thereof, is that we call the WILL; the act, not the faculty, of *willing*. And beasts that have *deliberation*, must necessarily also have *will*. ...

Nature hath made men so equal, in the faculties of the body, and mind; as that though there be found one man sometimes manifestly stronger in body, or of quicker mind than another; yet when all is reckoned together, the difference between man, and man, is not so considerable, as that one man can thereupon claim to himself any benefit, to which another may not pretend, as well as he. For as to the strength of body, the weakest has strength enough to kill the strongest, either by secret machination, or by confederacy with others, that are in the same danger with himself.

And as to the faculties of the mind, setting aside the arts grounded upon words, and especially that skill of proceeding upon general, and infallible rules, called science. ...I find yet a greater equality amongst men, than that of strength. For prudence, is but experience; which equal time, equally bestows on all men, in those things they equally apply themselves unto. That which may perhaps make such equality incredible, is but a vain conceit of one's own wisdom, which almost all men think they have in a greater degree, than the vulgar; that is, than all men but themselves, and a few others, whom by fame, or for concurring with themselves, they approve. For such is the nature of men, that howsoever they may acknowledge many others to

be more witty, or more eloquent, or more learned; yet they will hardly believe there be many so wise as themselves; for they see their own wit at hand, and other men's at a distance. But this proveth rather that men are in that point equal, than unequal. For there is not ordinarily a greater sign of the equal distribution of any thing, than that every man is contented with his share.

From this equality of ability, ariseth equality of hope in the attaining of our ends. And therefore if any two men desire the same thing, which nevertheless they cannot both enjoy, they become enemies; and in the way to their end, which is principally their own conservation, and sometimes their delectation only, endeavour to destroy, or subdue one another. And from hence it comes to pass, that where an invader hath no more to fear, than another man's single power; if one plant, sow, build, or possess a convenient seat, others may probably be expected to come prepared with forces united, to dispossess, and deprive him, not only of the fruit of his labour, but also of his life, or liberty. And the invader again is in the like danger of another.

And from this diffidence of one another, there is no way for any man to secure himself, so reasonable, as anticipation; that is, by force, or wiles, to master the persons of all men he can, so long, till he see no other power great enough to endanger him: and this is no more than his own conservation requireth, and is generally allowed. Also because there be some, that taking pleasure in contemplating their own power in the acts of conquest, which they pursue farther than their security requires; if others, that otherwise would be glad to be at ease within modest bounds, should not by invasion increase their power, they would not be able, long time, by standing only on their defence, to subsist. And by consequence, such augmentation of dominion over men being necessary to a man's conservation, it ought to be allowed him.

Again, men have no pleasure, but on the contrary a great deal of grief, in keeping company, where there is no power able to over-awe them all. For every man looketh that his companion should value him, at the same rate he sets upon himself; and upon all signs of contempt, or undervaluing, naturally endeavours, as far as he dares, (which amongst them that have no common power to keep them in quiet, is far enough to make them destroy each other), to extort a greater value from his contemners, by damage; and from others, by the example.

So that in the nature of man, we find three principal causes of quarrel. First, competition; secondly, diffidence; thirdly, glory.

The first, maketh men invade for gain; the second, for safety; and the third, for reputation. The first use violence, to make themselves masters of other men's persons, wives, children, and cattle; the second, to defend them; the third, for trifles, as a word, a smile, a different opinion, and any other sign of undervalue, either direct in their persons, or by reflection in their kindred, their friends, their nation, their profession, or their name.

Hereby it is manifest, that during the time men live without a common power to keep them all in awe, they are in that condition which is called war; and such a war, as is of every man, against every man. For WAR, consisteth not in battle only, or the act of fighting; but in a tract of time, wherein the will to contend by battle is sufficiently known: and therefore the notion of *time*, is to be considered in the nature of war; as it is in the nature of weather. For as the nature of foul weather, lieth not in a shower or two of rain; but in an inclination thereto of many days together: so the nature of war, consisteth not in actual fighting; but in the known disposition thereto, during all the time there is no assurance to the contrary. All other time is PEACE.

Whatsoever therefore is consequent to a time of war, where every man is enemy to every man; the same is consequent to the time, wherein men live without other security, than what their own strength; and their own invention shall furnish them withal. In such condition, there is no place for industry; because the fruit thereof is uncertain: and consequently no culture of the earth; no navigation, nor use of the commodities that may be imported by sea; no commodious building; no instruments of moving, and removing, such things as require much force; no knowledge of the face of the earth; no account of time; no arts; no letters; no society; and which is worst of all, continual fear, and danger of violent death; and the life of man, solitary, poor, nasty, brutish, and short.

It may seem strange to some man, that has not well weighed these things; that nature should thus dissociate, and render men apt to invade, and destroy one another: and he may therefore, not trust-ing to this inference, made from the passions, desire perhaps to have the same confirmed by experience. Let him therefore consider with himself, when taking a journey, he arms himself, and seeks to go well accompanied; when going to sleep, he locks his doors; when even in his house he locks his chests; and this when he knows there be laws, and public officers, armed, to revenge all injuries shall be done him; what opinion he has of his fellow-subjects, when he rides armed; of his fellow citizens, when he locks his doors; and of his children, and servants, when he locks his chests. Does he not there as much accuse mankind by his actions, as I do by my words? But neither of us accuse man's nature in it. The desires, and other passions of man, are in themselves no sin. No more are the actions, that proceed from those passions, till they know a law that forbids them: which till laws be made they cannot know: nor can any law be made, till they have agreed upon the person that shall make it.

It may peradventure be thought, there was never such a time, nor condition of war as this; and I believe it was never generally so, over all the world: but there are many places, where they live so now. For the savage people in many places of America, except the government of small families, the concord whereof dependeth on natural lust, have no government at all; and live at this day in that brutish manner, as I said before. Howsoever, it may be perceived what manner of life there would be, where there were no common power to fear, by the manner of life, which men that have formerly lived under a peaceful government, use to degenerate into, in a civil war.

But though there had never been any time, wherein particular men were in a condition of war one against another; yet in all times, kings, and persons of sovereign authority, because of their independency, are in continual jealousies, and in the state and posture of gladiators; having their weapons pointing, and their eyes fixed on one another; that is, their forts, garrisons, and guns upon the frontiers of their kingdoms; and continual spies upon their neighbours; which is a posture of war. But because they uphold thereby the industry of their subjects; there does not follow from it, that misery, which accompanies the liberty of particular men.

To this war of every man, against every man, this also is consequent; that nothing can be unjust. The notions of right and wrong, justice and injustice have there no place. Where there is no common power, there is no law: where no law, no injustice. Force, and fraud, are in war the two cardinal virtues. Justice, and injustice are none of the faculties neither of the body, nor mind. If they were, they might be in a man that were alone in the world, as well as his senses, and passions. They are qualities, that relate to men in society, not in solitude. It is consequent also to the same condition, that there be no propriety, no dominion, no *mine* and *thine* distinct; but only that to be every man's, that he can get; and for so long, as he can keep it. And thus much for the ill condition, which man by mere nature is actually placed in; though with a possibility to come out of it, consisting partly in the passions, partly in his reason.

The passions that incline men to peace, are fear of death; desire of such things as are necessary to commodious living; and a hope by their industry to obtain them. And reason suggesteth convenient articles of peace, upon which men may be drawn to agreement. These articles, are they, which otherwise are called the Laws of Nature. ...The right of nature...is the liberty each man hath, to use his own power, as he will himself, for the preservation of his own nature; that is to say, of his own life; and consequently, of doing any thing, which in his own judgment, and reason, he shall conceive to be the aptest means thereunto.

By LIBERTY, is understood, according to the proper signification of the word, the absence of external impediments: which impediments, may oft take away part of a man's power to do what he would; but cannot hinder him from using the power left him, according as his judgment, and reason shall dictate to him.

A LAW OF NATURE...is a precept or general rule, found out by reason, by which a man is forbidden to do that, which is destructive of his life, or taketh away the means of preserving the same; and to omit that, by which he thinketh it may be best preserved. For though they that speak of this subject, use to confound *right* and *law*: yet they ought to be distinguished; because RIGHT, consisteth in liberty to do, or to forbear: whereas LAW, determineth, and bindeth to one of them: so that law, and right, differ

as much, as obligation, and liberty; which in one and the same matter are inconsistent.

And because the condition of man...is a condition of war of every one against every one: in which case every one is governed by his own reason; and there is nothing he can make use of, that may not be a help unto him, in preserving his life against his enemies; it followeth, that in such a condition, every man has a right to every thing; even to one another's body. And therefore, as long as this natural right of every man to every thing endureth, there can be no security to any man, how strong or wise soever he be, of living out the time, which nature ordinarily alloweth men to live. And consequently it is a precept, or general rule of reason, *that every man, ought to endeavour peace, as far as he has hope of obtaining it; and when he cannot obtain it, that he may seek, and use, all helps, and advantages of war.* The first branch of which rule, containeth the first, and fundamental law of nature; which is, *to seek peace, and follow it.* The second, the sum of the right of nature; which is, *by all means we can, to defend ourselves.*

From this fundamental law of nature, by which men are commanded to endeavour peace, is derived this second law; *that a man be willing, when others are so too, as far-forth, as for peace, and defence of himself he shall think it necessary, to lay down this right to all things; and be contented with so much liberty against other men, as he would allow other men against himself.* For as long as every man holdeth this right, of doing any thing he liketh; so long are all men in the condition of war. But if other men will not lay down their right, as well as he; then there is no reason for any one, to divest himself of his: for that were to expose himself to prey, which no man is bound to, rather than to dispose himself to peace. ...

To *lay down* a man's *right* to any thing, is to *divest* himself of the *liberty*, of hindering another of the benefit of his own right to the same. For he that renounceth, or passeth away his right, giveth not to any other man a right which he had not before; because there is nothing to which every man had not right by nature: but only standeth out of his way, that he may enjoy his own original right, without hindrance from him; not without hindrance from another. So that the effect which redoundeth to one man, by another man's defect of right, is but so much diminution of impediments to the use of his own right original.

Right is laid aside, either by simply renouncing it; or by transferring it to another. By *simply* RE-NOUNCING; when he cares not to whom the benefit thereof redoundeth. By TRANSFERRING; when he intendeth the benefit thereof to some certain person, or persons. And when a man hath in either manner abandoned, or granted away his right; then is he said to be OBLIGED, or BOUND, not to hinder those, to whom such right is granted, or abandoned, from the benefit of it: and that he *ought*, and it is his DUTY, not to make void that voluntary act of his own: and that such hindrance is INJUSTICE, and INJURY.

So that *injury*, or *injustice*, in the controversies of the world, is somewhat like to that, which in the disputations of scholars is called *absurdity*. For as it is there called an absurdity, to contradict what one maintained in the beginning: so in the world, it is called injustice, and injury, voluntarily to undo that, which from the beginning he had voluntarily done. The way by which a man either simply renounceth, or transferreth his right, is a declaration, or signification, by some voluntary and sufficient sign, or signs, that he doth so renounce, or transfer; or hath so renounced, or transferred the same, to him that accepteth it. And these signs are either words only, or actions only; or, as it happeneth most often, both words, and actions. And the same are the BONDS, by which men are bound, and obliged: bonds, that have their strength, not from their own nature, for nothing is more easily broken than a man's word, but from fear of some evil consequence upon the rupture.

Whensoever a man transferreth his right, or renounceth it; it is either in consideration of some right reciprocally transferred to himself; or for some other good he hopeth for thereby. For it is a voluntary act: and of the voluntary acts of every man, the object is some *good to himself*. And therefore there be some rights, which no man can be understood by any words, or other signs, to have abandoned, or transferred. As first a man cannot lay down the right of resisting them, that assault him by force, to take away his life; because he cannot be understood to aim thereby, at any good to himself. The same may be said of wounds, and chains, and imprisonment; both because there is no benefit consequent to such patience; as there is to

the patience of suffering another to be wounded, or imprisoned: as also because a man cannot tell, when he seeth men proceed against him by violence, whether they intend his death or not. And lastly the motive, and end for which this renouncing, and transferring of right is introduced, is nothing else but the security of a man's person, in his life, and in the means of so preserving life, as not to be weary of it. And therefore if a man by words, or other signs, seem to despoil himself of the end, for which those signs were intended; he is not to be understood as if he meant it, or that it was his will; but that he was ignorant of how such words and actions were to be interpreted.

The mutual transferring of right, is that which men call CONTRACT. ...

If a covenant be made, wherein neither of the parties perform presently, but trust one another; in the condition of mere nature, which is a condition of war of every man against every man, upon any reasonable suspicion, it is void: but if there be a common power set over them both, with right and force sufficient to compel performance, it is not void. For he that performeth first, has no assurance the other will perform after; because the bonds of words are too weak to bridle men's ambition, avarice, anger, and other passions, without the fear of some coercive power; which in the condition of mere nature, where all men are equal, and judges of the justness of their own fears, cannot possibly be supposed. And therefore he which performeth first, does but betray himself to his enemy; contrary to the right, he can never abandon, of defending his life, and means of living.

But in a civil estate, where there is a power set up to constrain those that would otherwise violate their faith, that fear is no more reasonable; and for that cause, he which by the covenant is to perform first, is obliged so to do. ...

He that transferreth any right, transferreth the means of enjoying it, as far as lieth in his power. As he that selleth land, is understood to transfer the herbage, and whatsoever grows upon it: nor can he that sells a mill turn away the stream that drives it. And they that give to a man the right of government in sovereignty, are understood to give him the right of levying money to maintain soldiers; and of appointing magistrates for the administration of justice. ...

The final cause, end, or design of men, who naturally love liberty, and dominion over others, in the introduction of that restraint upon themselves, in which we see them live in commonwealths, is the foresight of their own preservation, and of a more contented life thereby; that is to say, of getting themselves out from that miserable condition of war, which is necessarily consequent...to the natural passions of men, when there is no visible power to keep them in awe, and tie them by fear of punishment to the performance of their covenants, and observation of the laws of nature. ...

For the laws of nature, as *justice, equity, modesty, mercy*, and, in sum, *doing to others, as we would be done to*, of themselves, without the terror of some power, to cause them to be observed, are contrary to our natural passions, that carry us to partiality, pride, revenge, and the like. And covenants, without the sword, are but words, and of no strength to secure a man at all. Therefore notwithstanding the laws of nature, which every one hath then kept, when he has the will to keep them, when he can do it safely, if there be no power erected, or not great enough for our security; every man will, and may lawfully rely on his own strength and art, for caution against all other men. And in all places, where men have lived by small families, to rob and spoil one another, has been a trade, and so far from being reputed against the law of nature, that the greater spoils they gained, the greater was their honour; and men observed no other laws therein, but the laws of honour; that is, to abstain from cruelty, leaving to men their lives, and instruments of husbandry. And as small families did then; so now do cities and kingdoms which are but greater families, for their own security, enlarge their dominions, upon all pretences of danger, and fear of invasion, or assistance that may be given to invaders, and endeavour as much as they can, to subdue, or weaken their neighbours, by open force, and secret arts, for want of other caution, justly; and are remembered for it in after ages with honour. ...

Nor is it enough for the security, which men desire should last all the time of their life, that they be governed, and directed by one judgment, for a limited time; as in one battle, or one war. For though they obtain a victory by their unanimous endeavour against a foreign enemy; yet afterwards, when either they have no common enemy, or he that by one part is held for an enemy, is by another part held for a friend, they must needs by the difference of their interests dissolve, and fall again into a war amongst themselves.

It is true, that certain living creatures, as bees, and ants, live sociably one with another, which are therefore by Aristotle numbered amongst political creatures; and yet have no other direction, than their particular judgments and appetites; nor speech, whereby one of them can signify to another, what he thinks expedient for the common benefit: and therefore some man may perhaps desire to know, why mankind cannot do the same. To which I answer,

First, that men are continually in competition for honour and dignity, which these creatures are not; and consequently amongst men there ariseth on that ground, envy and hatred, and finally war; but amongst these not so.

Secondly, that amongst these creatures, the common good differeth not from the private; and being by nature inclined to their private, they procure thereby the common benefit. But man, whose joy consisteth in comparing himself with other men, can relish nothing but what is eminent.

Thirdly, that these creatures, having not, as man, the use of reason, do not see, nor think they see any fault, in the administration of their common business; whereas amongst men, there are very many, that think themselves wiser, and abler to govern the public, better than the rest; and these strive to reform and innovate, one this way, another that way; and thereby bring it into distraction and civil war.

Fourthly, that these creatures, though they have some use of voice, in making known to one another their desires, and other affections; yet they want that art of words, by which some men can represent to others, that which is good, in the likeness of evil; and evil, in the likeness of good; and augment, or diminish the apparent greatness of good and evil; discontenting men, and troubling their peace at their pleasure.

Fifthly, irrational creatures cannot distinguish between *injury*, and *damage*; and therefore as long as they be at ease, they are not offended with their fellows: whereas man is then most troublesome, when he is most at ease: for then it is that he loves to shew his wisdom, and control the actions of them that govern the commonwealth.

Lastly, the agreement of these creatures is natural; that of men, is by covenant only, which is artificial: and therefore it is no wonder if there be somewhat else required, besides covenant, to make their agreement constant and lasting; which is a common power, to keep them in awe, and to direct their actions to the common benefit.

The only way to erect such a common power, as may be able to defend them from the invasion of foreigners, and the injuries of one another, and thereby to secure them in such sort, as that by their own industry, and by the fruits of the earth, they may nourish themselves and live contentedly; is, to confer all their power and strength upon one man, or upon one assembly of men, that may reduce all their wills, by plurality of voices, unto one will: which is as much as to say, to appoint one man, or assembly of men, to bear their person; and every one to own, and acknowledge himself to be author of whatsoever he that so beareth their person, shall act, or cause to be acted, in those things which concern the common peace and safety; and therein to submit their wills, every one to his will, and their judgments, to his judgment. This is more than consent, or concord; it is a real unity of them all, in one and the same person, made by covenant of every man with every man, in such manner, as if every man should say to every man, *I authorise and give up my right of governing myself, to this man, or to this assembly of men, on this condition, that thou give up thy right to him, and authorize all his actions in like manner*. This done, the multitude so united in one person, is called a COMMONWEALTH. …This is the generation of that great LEVIATHAN, or rather, to speak more reverently, of that *mortal god*, to which we owe under the *immortal God*, our peace and defence. For by this authority, given him by every particular man in the commonwealth, he hath the use of so much power and strength conferred on him, that by terror thereof, he is enabled to perform the wills of them all, to peace at home, and mutual aid against their enemies abroad. And in him consisteth the essence of the commonwealth; which, to define it, is *one person, of whose acts a great multitude, by mutual covenants one with another, have made themselves every one the author, to the end he may use the strength and means of them all, as he shall think expedient, for their peace and common defence*

And he that carrieth this person, is called SOVEREIGN, and said to have *sovereign power*; and every one besides, his SUBJECT.

The attaining to this sovereign power, is by two ways. One, by natural force; as when a man maketh his children, to submit themselves, and their children to his government, as being able to destroy them if they refuse; or by war subdueth his enemies to his will, giving them their lives on that condition. The other, is when men agree amongst themselves, to submit to some man, or assembly of men, voluntarily, on confidence to be protected by him against all others. This latter, may be called a political commonwealth, or commonwealth by *institution*; and the former, a commonwealth by *acquisition*. And first, I shall speak of a commonwealth by institution.

A *commonwealth* is said to be *instituted*, when a *multitude* of men do agree, and *covenant, every one, with every one*, that to whatsoever *man*, or *assembly of men*, shall be given by the major part, the *right* to *present* the person of them all, that is to say, to be their *representative*; every one, as well he that *voted for it*, as he that *voted against it*, shall *authorize* all the actions and judgments, of that man, or assembly of men, in the same manner, as if they were his own, to the end, to live peaceably amongst themselves, and be protected against other men.

From this institution of a commonwealth are derived all the *rights*, and *faculties* of him, or them, on whom sovereign power is conferred by the consent of the people assembled.

First, because they covenant, it is to be understood, they are not obliged by former covenant to anything repugnant hereunto. And consequently they that have already instituted a commonwealth, being thereby bound by covenant, to own the actions, and judgments of one, cannot lawfully make a new covenant, amongst themselves, to be obedient to any other, in any thing whatsoever, without his permission. And therefore, they that are subjects to a monarch, cannot without his leave cast off monarchy, and return to the confusion of a disunited multitude; nor transfer their person from him that beareth it, to another man, or other assembly of men: for they are bound, every man to every man, to own, and be reputed author of all, that he that already is their sovereign, shall do, and judge fit to be done: so that any one man dissenting, all the rest should break their covenant made to that man, which is injustice: and they have also every man given the sovereignty to him that beareth their person; and therefore if they depose him, they take from him that which is his own, and so again it is injustice. Besides, if he that attempteth to depose his sovereign, be killed, or punished by him for such attempt, he is author of his own punishment, as being by the institution, author of all his sovereign shall do: and because it is injustice for a man to do anything, for which he may be punished by his own authority, he is also upon that title, unjust. And whereas some men have pretended for their disobedience to their sovereign, a new covenant, made, not with men, but with God; this also is unjust: for there is no covenant with God, but by mediation of somebody that representeth God's person; which none doth but God's lieutenant, who hath the sovereignty under God. But this pretence of covenant with God, is so evident a lie, even in the pretenders' own consciences, that it is not only an act of an unjust, but also of a vile, and unmanly disposition.

Secondly, because the right of bearing the person of them all, is given to him they make sovereign, by covenant only of one to another, and not of him to any of them; there can happen no breach of covenant on the part of the sovereign; and consequently none of his subjects, by any pretence of forfeiture, can be freed from his subjection. That he which is made sovereign maketh no covenant with his subjects beforehand, is manifest; because either he must make it with the whole multitude, as one party to the covenant; or he must make a several covenant with every man. With the whole, as one party, it is impossible; because as yet they are not one person: and if he make so many several covenants as there be men, those covenants after he hath the sovereignty are void; because what act soever can be pretended by any one of them for breach thereof, is the act both of himself, and of all the rest, because done in the person, and by the right of every one of them in particular. Besides, if any one, or more of them, pretend a breach of the covenant made by the sovereign at his institution; and others, or one other of his subjects, or himself alone, pretend there was no such breach, there is in this case, no judge to decide the controversy; it returns therefore to the sword again; and every man recovereth the right of protecting himself by his own strength, contrary to the design they had in the institution. …

Thirdly, because the major part hath by consenting voices declared a sovereign; he that dissented must now consent with the rest; that is, be contented to avow all the actions he shall do, or else justly be destroyed by the rest. For if he voluntarily entered into the congregation of them that were assembled, he sufficiently declared thereby his will, and therefore tacitly covenanted, to stand to what the major part should ordain: and therefore if he refuse to stand thereto, or make protestation against any of their decrees, he does contrary to his covenant, and therefore unjustly. And whether he be of the congregation, or not; and whether his consent be asked, or not, he must either submit to their decrees, or be left in the condition of war he was in before; wherein he might without injustice be destroyed by any man whatsoever.

Fourthly, because every subject is by this institution author of all the actions, and judgments of the sovereign instituted; it follows, that whatsoever he doth, it can be no injury to any of his subjects; nor ought he to be by any of them accused of injustice. For he that doth anything by authority from another, doth therein no injury to him by whose authority he acteth: but by this institution of a commonwealth, every particular man is author of all the sovereign doth: and consequently he that complaineth of injury from his sovereign, complaineth of that whereof he himself is author; and therefore ought not to accuse any man but himself; no nor himself of injury; because to do injury to one's self, is impossible. It is true that they that have sovereign power may commit iniquity; but not injustice, or injury in the proper signification.

Fifthly, and consequently to that which was said last, no man that hath sovereign power can justly be put to death, or otherwise in any manner by his subjects punished. For seeing every subject is author of the actions of his sovereign; he punisheth another for the actions committed by himself.

And because the end of this institution, is the peace and defence of them all; and whosoever has right to the end, has right to the means; it belongeth of right, to whatsoever man, or assembly that hath the sovereignty, to be judge both of the means of peace and defence, and also of the hindrances, and disturbances of the same; and to do whatsoever he shall think necessary to be done, both beforehand, for the preserving of peace and security, by prevention of discord at home, and hostility from abroad; and, when peace and security are lost, for the recovery of the same. And therefore,

Sixthly, it is annexed to the sovereignty, to be judge of what opinions and doctrines are averse, and what conducing to peace; and consequently, on what occasions, how far, and what men are to be trusted withal, in speaking to multitudes of people; and who shall examine the doctrines of all books before they be published. For the actions of men proceed from their opinions; and in the well-governing of opinions, consisteth the well-governing of men's actions, in order to their peace, and concord. And though in matter of doctrine, nothing ought to be regarded but the truth; yet this is not repugnant to regulating the same by peace. For doctrine repugnant to peace, can no more be true, than peace and concord can be against the law of nature. It is true, that in a commonwealth, where by the negligence, or unskillfulness of governors, and teachers, false doctrines are by time generally received; the contrary truths may be generally offensive. Yet the most sudden, and rough bursting in of a new truth, that can be, does never break the peace, but only sometimes awake the war. For those men that are so remissly governed, that they dare take up arms to defend, or introduce an opinion, are still in war; and their condition not peace, but only a cessation of arms for fear of one another; and they live, as it were, in the precincts of battle continually. It belongeth therefore to him that hath the sovereign power, to be judge, or constitute all judges of opinions and doctrines, as a thing necessary to peace; thereby to prevent discord and civil war.

Seventhly, is annexed to the sovereignty, the whole power of prescribing the rules, whereby every man may know, what goods he may enjoy, and what actions he may do, without being molested by any of his fellow-subjects; and this is it men call *propriety*. ...

Eighthly, is annexed to the sovereignty, the right of judicature; that is to say, of hearing and deciding all controversies, which may arise concerning law, either civil, or natural; or concerning fact. For without the decision of controversies, there is no protection of one subject, against the injuries of another. ...

Ninthly, is annexed to the sovereignty, the right of making war and peace with other nations, and commonwealths; that is to say, of judging when it is for the public good, and how great forces are to be assembled, armed, and paid for that end; and to levy money upon the subjects, to defray the expenses thereof. For the power by which the people are to be defended, consisteth in their armies; and the strength of an army, in the union of their strength under one command; which command the sovereign instituted, therefore hath; because the command of the *militia*, without other institution, maketh him that hath it sovereign. And therefore whosoever, is made general of an army, he that hath the sovereign power is always generalissimo.

Tenthly, is annexed to the sovereignty, the choosing of all counsellors, ministers, magistrates, and officers, both in peace, and war. For seeing the sovereign is charged with the end, which is the common peace and defence, he is understood to have power to use such means, as he shall think most fit for his discharge.

Eleventhly, to the sovereign is committed the power of rewarding with riches, or honour, and of punishing with corporal or pecuniary punishment, or with ignominy, every subject according to the law he hath formerly made; or if there be no law made, according as he shall judge most to conduce to the encouraging of men to serve the commonwealth, or deterring of them from doing disservice to the same. ...

LIBERTY, or FREEDOM, signifieth, properly, the absence of opposition. ...And according to this proper, and generally received meaning of the word, a FREEMAN, *is he, that in those things, which by his strength and wit he is able to do, is not hindered to do what he has a will to.* ...

But as men, for the attaining of peace, and conservation of themselves thereby, have made an artificial man, which we call a commonwealth; so also have they made artificial chains, called *civil laws*, which they themselves, by mutual covenants, have fastened at one end, to the lips of that man, or assembly, to whom they have given the sovereign power; and at the other end to their own ears. These bonds, in their own nature but weak, may nevertheless be made to hold, by the danger; though not by the difficulty of breaking them.

In relation to these bonds only it is, that I am to speak now, of the *liberty* of *subjects*. For seeing there is no commonwealth in the world, wherein there be rules enough set down, for the regulating of all the actions, and words of men; as being a thing impossible: it followeth necessarily, that in all kinds of actions by the laws permitted, men have the liberty, of doing what their own reasons shall suggest, for the most profitable to themselves. For if we take liberty in the proper sense, for corporal liberty; that is to say, freedom from chains and prison; it were very absurd for men to clamour as they do, for the liberty they so manifestly enjoy. Again, if we take liberty, for an exemption from laws, it is it no less absurd, for men to demand as they do, that liberty, by which all other men may be masters of their lives. And yet, as absurd as it is, this is it they demand; not knowing that the laws are of no power to protect them, without a sword in the hands of a man, or men, to cause those laws to be put in execution. The liberty of a subject, lieth therefore only in those things, which in regulating their actions, the sovereign hath permitted: such as is the liberty to buy, and sell, and otherwise contract with one another; to choose their own abode, their own diet, their own trade of life, and institute their children as they themselves think fit; and the like.

Nevertheless we are not to understand, that by such liberty, the sovereign power of life and death, is either abolished, or limited. For it has been already shown, that nothing the sovereign representative can do to a subject, on what pretence soever, can properly be called injustice, or injury; because every subject is author of every act the sovereign doth; so that he never wanteth right to anything, otherwise, than as he himself is the subject of God, and bound thereby to observe the laws of nature. And therefore it may, and doth often happen in commonwealths, that a subject may be put to death, by the command of the sovereign power; and yet neither do the other wrong. ...

"An Essay Concerning the True Original, Extent and End of Civil Government"

John Locke

To understand political power aright, and derive it from its original, we must consider what state all men are naturally in, and that is a state of perfect freedom to order their actions and dispose of their possessions and persons as they think fit, within the bounds of the law of nature, without asking leave, or depending upon the will of any other man.

A state also of equality, wherein all the power and jurisdiction is reciprocal, no one having more than another; there being nothing more evident than that creatures of the same species and rank, promiscuously born to all the same advantages of nature, and the use of the same faculties, should also be equal one amongst another without subordination or subjection, unless the Lord and Master of them all should by any manifest declaration of His will set one above another, and confer on him by an evident and clear appointment an undoubted right to dominion and sovereignty. ...

But though this be a state of liberty, yet it is not a state of license; though man in that state have an uncontrollable liberty to dispose of his person or possessions, yet he has not liberty to destroy himself, or so much as any creature in his possession, but where some nobler use than its bare preservation calls for it. The state of nature has a law of nature to govern it, which obliges everyone; and reason, which is that law, teaches all mankind who

From *Two Treatises on Government*, from *The Works of John Locke*, Vol. 5 (London: Thomas Tegg, W. Sharpe and Son; G. Offor; G. and J. Robinson; J. Evans and Co., 1823).

will but consult it, that, being all equal and independent, no one ought to harm another in his life, health, liberty, or possessions. ...Everyone, as he is bound to preserve himself, and not to quit his station willfully, so, by the like reason, when his own preservation comes not in competition, ought he, as much as he can, to preserve the rest of mankind, and not, unless it be to do justice on an offender, take away or impair the life, or what tends to the preservation of the life, the liberty, health, limb, or goods of another.

And that all men may be restrained from invading others' rights, and from doing hurt to one another, and the law of nature be observed, which willeth the peace and preservation of all mankind, the execution of the law of nature is in that state put into every man's hand, whereby everyone has a right to punish the transgressors of that law to such a degree as may hinder its violation. For the law of nature would, as all other laws that concern men in this world, be in vain if there were nobody that, in the state of nature, had a power to execute that law, and thereby preserve the innocent and restrain offenders. And if anyone in the state of nature may punish another for any evil he has done, everyone may do so. For in that state of perfect equality, where naturally there is no superiority or jurisdiction of one over another, what any may do in prosecution of that law, everyone must needs have a right to do.

And thus in the state of nature one man comes by a power over another; but yet no absolute or arbitrary power, to use a criminal, when he has got him in his hands, according to the passionate heats or boundless extravagance of his own will; but only to retribute to him so far as calm reason and conscience dictate what is proportionate to his transgression, which is so much as may serve for reparation and restraint. For these two are the only reasons why one man may lawfully do harm to another, which is that we call punishment. In transgressing the law of nature, the offender declares himself to live by another rule than that of common reason and equity, which is that measure God has set to the actions of men, for their mutual security; and so he becomes dangerous to mankind, the tie which is to secure them from injury and violence being slighted and broken by him. Which, being a trespass against the whole species, and the peace and safety of it, provided for by the law of nature,

every man upon this score, by the right he hath to preserve mankind in general, may restrain, or, where it is necessary, destroy things noxious to them, and so may bring such evil on anyone who hath transgressed that law, as may make him repent the doing of it, and thereby deter him, and by his example others, from doing the like mischief. And in this case, and upon this ground, every man hath a right to punish the offender, and be executioner of the law of nature. ...

And thus it is that every man in the state of nature has a power to kill a murderer, both to deter others from doing the like injury, which no reparation can compensate, by the example of the punishment that attends it from everybody, and also to secure men from the attempts of a criminal who having renounced reason, the common rule and measure God hath given to mankind, hath by the unjust violence and slaughter he hath committed upon one, declared war against all mankind, and therefore may be destroyed as a lion or a tiger. ...

'Tis often asked as a mighty objection, Where are, or ever were there, any men in such a state of nature? To which it may suffice as an answer at present: That since all princes and rulers of independent governments all through the world are in a state of nature, 'tis plain the world never was, nor ever will be, without numbers of men in that state. I have named all governors of independent communities, whether they are or are not in league with others. For 'tis not every compact that puts an end to the state of nature between men, but only this one of agreeing together mutually to enter into one community, and make one body politic; other promises and compacts men may make one with another, and yet still be in the state of nature. The promises and bargains for truck, etc., between the two men in Soldania, in or between a Swiss and an Indian, in the woods of America, are binding to them, though they are perfectly in a state of nature in reference to one another. For truth and keeping of faith belong to men as men, and not as members of society.

To those that say there were never any men in the state of nature, I...moreover affirm that all men are naturally in that state, and remain so, till by their own consents they make themselves members of some politic society; and I doubt not, in the sequel of this discourse, to make it very clear.

The state of war is a state of enmity and destruction; and therefore declaring by word or action, not a passionate and hasty, but a sedate, settled design upon another man's life, puts him in a state of war with him against whom he has declared such an intention, and so has exposed his life to the other's power to be taken away by him, or anyone that joins with him in his defense and espouses his quarrel; it being reasonable and just I should have a right to destroy that which threatens me with destruction. For by the fundamental law of nature, man being to be preserved as much as possible, when all cannot be preserved, the safety of the innocent is to be preferred; and one may destroy a man who makes war upon him, or has discovered an enmity to his being, for the same reason that he may kill a wolf or a lion; because they are not under the ties of the common law of reason, have no other rule but that of force and violence, and so may be treated as a beast of prey, those dangerous and noxious creatures that will be sure to destroy him whenever he falls into their power.

And hence it is that he who attempts to get another man into his absolute power does thereby put himself into a state of war with him; it being to be understood as a declaration of a design upon his life. For I have reason to conclude that he who would get me into his power without my consent, would use me as he pleased when he had got me there, and destroy me too, when he had a fancy to it; for nobody can desire to have me in his absolute power, unless it be to compel me by force to that which is against the right of my freedom, *i.e.*, make me a slave. To be free from such force is the only security of my preservation; and reason bids me look on him as an enemy to my preservation who would take away that freedom which is the fence to it; so that he who makes an attempt to enslave me, thereby puts himself into a state of war with me. He that in the state of nature would take away the freedom that belongs to any one in that state, must necessarily be supposed to have a design to take away everything else, that freedom being the foundation of all the rest; as he that in the state of society would take away the freedom belonging to those of that society or commonwealth, must be supposed to design to take away from them everything else, and so be looked on as in a state of war.

This makes it lawful for a man to kill a thief who has not in the least hurt him, nor declared any design upon his life, any farther than by the use of force, so to get him in his power as to take away his money, or what he pleases, from him; because using force, where he has no right to get me into his power, let his pretense be what it will, I have no reason to suppose that he who would take away my liberty would not, when he had me in his power, take away everything else. And, therefore, it is lawful for me to treat him as one who has put himself into a state of war with me—i.e., kill him if I can; for to that hazard does he justly expose himself whoever introduces a state of war, and is aggressor in it. ...

The natural liberty of man is to be free from any superior power on earth, and not to be under the will or legislative authority of man, but to have only the law of nature for his rule. The liberty of man in society is to be under no other legislative power but that established by consent in the commonwealth; nor under the dominion of any will or restraint of any law, but what that legislative shall enact according to the trust put in it. Freedom then is not what Sir Robert Filmer tells us,..."a liberty for everyone to do what he lists, to live as he pleases, and not to be tied by any laws." But freedom of men under government is to have a standing rule to live by, common to everyone of that society, and made by the legislative power erected in it; a liberty to follow my own will in all things, where that rule prescribes not; and not to be subject to the inconstant, uncertain, unknown, arbitrary will of another man: as freedom of nature is to be under no other restraint but the law of nature.

This freedom from absolute arbitrary power is so necessary to, and closely joined with, a man's preservation, that he cannot part with it but by what forfeits his preservation and life together. For a man not having the power of his own life cannot by compact, or his own consent, enslave himself to anyone, nor put himself under the absolute arbitrary power of another to take away his life when he pleases. Nobody can give more power than he has himself; and he that cannot take away his own life, cannot give another power over it. Indeed, having by his fault forfeited his own life by some act that deserves death, he to whom he has forfeited it may (when he has him in his power) delay to take it, and make use of him to his own service; and he does him no injury by it. For whenever he finds the hardship of his slavery outweigh the value of his life, 'tis in his power by resisting the will of his master to draw on himself the death he desires.

This is the perfect condition of slavery, which is nothing else but the state of war continued between a lawful conqueror and a captive, for if once compact enter between them, and make an agreement for a limited power on the one side, and obedience on the other, the state of war and slavery ceases as long as the compact endures; for, as has been said, no man can by agreement pass over to another that which he hath not in himself—a power over his own life. ...

God, who hath given the world to men in common, hath also given them reason to make use of it to the best advantage of life and convenience. The earth and all that is therein is given to men for the support and comfort of their being. And though all the fruits it naturally produces, and beasts it feeds, belong to mankind in common, as they are produced by the spontaneous hand of nature; and nobody has originally a private dominion exclusive of the rest of mankind in any of them as they are thus in their natural state; yet being given for the use of men, there must of necessity be a means to appropriate them some way or other before they can be of any use or at all beneficial to any particular man. ...

Though the earth and all inferior creatures be common to all men, yet every man has a property in his own person; this nobody has any right to but himself. The labor of his body and the work of his hands we may say are properly his. Whatsoever, then, he removes out of the state that nature hath provided and left it in, he hath mixed his labor with, and joined to it something that is his own, and thereby makes it his property. It being by him removed from the common state nature placed it in, it hath by this labor something annexed to it that excludes the common right of other men. For this labor being the unquestionable property of the laborer, no man but he can have a right to what that is once joined to, at least where there is enough, and as good left in common for others.

He that is nourished by the acorns he picked up under an oak, or the apples he gathered from the trees in the wood, has certainly appropriated them to himself. Nobody can deny but the nourishment is his. I ask, then, When did they begin to be his—when he digested, or when he ate, or when he boiled, or when he brought them home, or when he picked them up? And 'tis plain if the first gathering made them not his, nothing else could. That labor put a distinction between them and common; that added something to them more than nature, the common mother of all, had done, and so they became his private right. And will anyone say he had no right to those acorns or apples he thus appropriated, because he had not the consent of all mankind to make them his? Was it a robbery thus to assume to himself what belonged to all in common? If such a consent as that was necessary, man had starved, notwithstanding the plenty God had given him. We see in commons which remain so by compact that 'tis the taking any part of what is common and removing it out of the state nature leaves it in, which begins the property; without which the common is of no use. And the taking of this or that part does not depend on the express consent of all the commoners. Thus the grass my horse has bit, the turfs my servant has cut, and the ore I have dug in any place where I have a right to them in common with others, become my property without the assignation or consent of anybody. The labor that was mine removing them out of that common state they were in, hath fixed my property in them. ...

It will perhaps be objected to this, that if gathering the acorns, or other fruits of the earth, etc., makes a right to them, then anyone may engross as much as he will. To which I answer, Not so. The same law of nature that does by this means give us property, does also bound that property too. "God has given us all things richly"...is the voice of reason confirmed by inspiration. But how far has He given it us? To enjoy. As much as anyone can make use of to any advantage of life before it spoils, so much he may by his labor fix a property in; whatever is beyond this, is more than his share, and belongs to others. Nothing was made by God for man to spoil or destroy. And thus considering the plenty of natural provisions there was a long time in the world, and the few spenders, and to how small a part of that provision the industry of one man could extend itself, and engross it to the prejudice of others—especially keeping within the bounds, set by reason, of what might serve for his use—there could be then little room for quarrels or contentions about property so established.

But the chief matter of property being now not the fruits of the earth, and the beasts that subsist on it, but the earth itself, as that which takes in and carries with it all the rest, I think it is plain that property in that, too, is acquired as the former. As much land as a man tills, plants, improves, cultivates, and can use the product of, so much is his property. He by his labor does as it were enclose it from the common. Nor will it invalidate his right to say, everybody else has an equal title to it; and therefore he cannot appropriate, he cannot enclose, without the consent of all his fellow-commoners, all mankind. ...

Nor was this appropriation of any parcel of land, by improving it, any prejudice to any other man, since there was still enough and as good left; and more than the yet unprovided could use. So that in effect there was never the less left for others because of his enclosure for himself. For he that leaves as much as another can make use of, does as good as take nothing at all. Nobody could think himself injured by the drinking of another man, though he took a good draught, who had a whole river of the same water left him to quench his thirst; and the case of land and water, where there is enough of both, is perfectly the same. ...

This is certain, that in the beginning, before the desire of having more than man needed had altered the intrinsic value of things, which depends only on their usefulness to the life of man; or had agreed that a little piece of yellow metal which would keep without wasting or decay should be worth a great piece of flesh or a whole heap of corn, though men had a right to appropriate by their labor, each one to himself, as much of the things of nature as he could use, yet this could not be much, nor to the prejudice of others, where the same plenty was still left to those who would use the same industry. ...

For it is labor indeed that puts the difference of value on everything; and let anyone consider what the difference is between an acre of land planted with tobacco or sugar, sown with wheat or barley, and an acre of the same land lying in common without any husbandry upon it, and he will find that the improvement of labor makes the far greater part of the value. ...

To make this a little clearer, let us but trace some of the ordinary provisions of life, through their several progresses, before they come to our use, and see how much they receive of their value from human industry. Bread, wine, and cloth are things of daily use and great plenty; yet, notwithstanding, acorns, water, and leaves or skins, must be our bread, drink, and clothing, did not labor furnish us with these more useful commodities. For whatever bread is more worth than acorns, wine than water, and cloth or silk than leaves, skins, or moss, that is wholly owing to labor and industry. ...

Thus labor, in the beginning, gave a right of property, wherever anyone was pleased to employ it upon what was common, which remained a long while the far greater part, and is yet more than mankind makes use of. Men at first, for the most part, contented themselves with what unassisted nature offered to their necessities; and though afterwards, in some parts of the world (where the increase of people and stock, with the use of money, had made land scarce, and so of some value), the several communities settled the bounds of their distinct territories, and, bylaws within themselves, regulated the properties of the private men of their society, and so, by compact and agreement, settled the property which labor and industry began—and the leagues that have been made between several states and kingdoms, either expressly or tacitly disowning all claim and right to the land in the other's possession have, by common consent, given up their pretenses to their natural common right, which originally they had to those countries; and so have, by positive agreement, settled a property amongst themselves in distinct parts of the world—yet there are still great tracts of ground to be found which, the inhabitants thereof not having joined with the rest of mankind in the consent of the use of their common money, lie waste, and are more than the people who dwell on it do or can make use of, and so still lie in common; though this can scarce happen amongst that part of mankind that have consented to the use of money...some lasting thing that men might keep without spoiling, and that, by mutual consent, men would take in exchange for the truly useful but perishable supports of life. ...

But since gold and silver, being little useful to the life of man in proportion to food, raiment, and carriage, has its value only from the consent of men, whereof labor yet makes, in great part, the measure, it is plain that the consent of men have agreed to a disproportionate and unequal possession of the earth—I mean out of the bounds of society and compact; for in governments the laws regulate it; they having, by consent, found out and agreed in a way how a man may rightfully and without injury possess more than he himself can make use of by receiving gold and silver, which may continue long in a man's possession, without decaying for the overplus, and agreeing those metals should have a value. ...

Man being born, as has been proved, with a title to perfect freedom, and an uncontrolled enjoyment of all the rights and privileges of the law of nature equally with any other man or number of men in the world, hath by nature a power not only to preserve his property—that is, his life, liberty, and estate—against the injuries and attempts of other men, but to judge of and punish the breaches of that law in others as he is persuaded the offense deserves, even with death itself, in crimes where the heinousness of the fact in his opinion requires it. But because no political society can be nor subsist without having in itself the power to preserve the property, and, in order thereunto, punish the offenses of all those of that society, there, and there only, is political society, where every one of the members hath quitted this natural power, resigned it up into the hands of the community in all cases that exclude him not from appealing for protection to the law established by it; and thus all private judgment of every particular member being excluded, the community comes to be umpire; and by understanding indifferent rules and men authorized by the community for their execution, decides all the differences that may happen between any members of that society concerning any matter of right, and punishes those offenses which any member hath committed against the society with such penalties as the law has established; whereby it is easy to discern who are and who are not in political society together. Those who are united into one body, and have a common established law and judicature to appeal to, with authority to decide controversies between them and punish offenders, are in civil society one with another; but those who have no such common appeal—I mean on earth—are still in the state of nature, each being, where there is no other, judge for himself and executioner, which is, as I have before shown it, the perfect state of nature.

And thus the commonwealth comes by a power to set down what punishment shall belong to the several transgressions which they think worthy of it committed amongst the members of that society, which is the power of making laws, as well as it has the power to punish any injury done unto any of its members by anyone that is not of it, which is the power of war and peace; and all this for the preservation of the property of all the members of that society as far as is possible. But though every man entered into civil society, has quitted his power to punish offenses against the law of nature in prosecution of his own private judgment, yet with the judgment of offenses, which he has given up to the legislative in all cases where he can appeal to the magistrate, he has given a right to the commonwealth to employ his force for the execution of the judgments of the commonwealth whenever he shall be called to it; which, indeed, are his own judgments, they being made by himself or his representative. And herein we have the original of the legislative and executive power of civil society, which is to judge by standing laws how far offenses are to be punished when committed within the commonwealth, and also by occasional judgments founded on the present circumstances of the fact, how far injuries from without are to be vindicated; and in both these to employ all the force of all the members when there shall be need.

Wherever, therefore, any number of men so unite into one society, as to quit everyone his executive power of the law of nature, and to resign it to the public, there, and there only, is a political, or civil society. And this is done wherever any number of men, in the state of nature, enter into society to make one people, one body politic, under one supreme government, or else when anyone joins himself to, and incorporates with, any government already made. For hereby he authorises the society, or, which is all one, the legislative thereof, to make laws for him, as the public good of the society shall require, to the execution whereof his own assistance (as to his own decrees) is due. And this puts men out of a state of nature into that of a commonwealth, by setting up a judge on earth with authority to determine all the controversies and redress the injuries that may happen to any member of the commonwealth; which judge is the legislative, or magistrates appointed by it. And wherever there are any number of men, however associated, that have no such decisive power to appeal to, there they are still in the state of nature.

Hence it is evident that absolute monarchy, which by some men is counted the only government in the world, is indeed inconsistent with civil society, and so can be no form of civil government at all. For the end of civil society being to avoid and remedy those inconveniences of the state of nature which necessarily follow from every man's being judge in his own case, by setting up a known authority to which everyone of that society may appeal upon any injury received or controversy that may arise, and which every one of the society ought to obey; wherever any persons are who have not such an authority to appeal to and decide any difference between them there, those persons are still in the state of nature. And so is every absolute prince, in respect of those who are under his dominion.

For he being supposed to have all, both legislative and executive power in himself alone, there is no judge to be found; no appeal lies open to anyone who may fairly and indifferently and with authority decide, and from whence relief and address may be expected of any injury or inconvenience that may be suffered from or by his order; so that such a man, however entitled—Czar, or Grand Seignior, or how you please—is as much in the state of nature, with all under his dominion, as he is with the rest of mankind. For wherever any two men are, who have no standing rule and common judge to appeal to on earth for the determination of controversies of right betwixt them, there they are still in the state of nature, and under all the inconveniences of it, with only this woful difference to the subject, or rather slave, of an absolute prince: that, whereas in the ordinary state of nature he has a liberty to judge of his right, and according to the best of his power to maintain it, now, whenever his property is invaded by the will and order of his monarch, he has not only no appeal, as those in the society ought to have, but, as if he were degraded from the common state of rational creatures, is denied a liberty to judge of or to defend his right; and so is exposed to all the misery and inconveniences that a man can fear from one who, being in the unrestrained state of nature, is yet corrupted with flattery, and armed with power. ...

Men being, as has been said, by nature all free, equal, and independent, no one can be put out of this estate, and subjected to the political power of another, without his own consent, which is done by agreeing with other men to join and unite into a community for their comfortable, safe, and peaceable living one amongst another, in a secure enjoyment of their properties, and a greater security against any that are not of it. This any number of men may do, because it injures not the freedom of the rest; they are left as they were in the liberty of the state of nature. When any number of men have so consented to make one community or government, they are thereby presently incorporated, and make one body politic, wherein the majority have a right to act and conclude the rest.

For when any number of men have, by the consent of every individual, made a community, they have thereby made that community one body, with a power to act as one body, which is only by the will and determination of the majority. For that which acts any community being: only the consent of the individuals of it, and it being one body must move one way, it is necessary the body should move that way whither the greater force carries it, which is the consent of the majority; or else it is impossible it should act or continue one body, one community which the consent of every individual that united into it agreed: that it should; and so everyone is bound by that consent to be concluded by the majority. And therefore we see that in assemblies empowered to act by positive laws, where no number is set by that positive law which empowers them, the act of the majority passes for the act of the whole, and of course determines, as having by the law of nature and reason the power of the whole.

And thus every man, by consenting with others to make one body politic under one government, puts himself under an obligation to every one of that society, to submit to the determination of the majority, and to be concluded by it; or else this original compact, whereby he with others incorporates into one society, would signify nothing, and be no compact, if he be left free and under no other ties than he was in before in the state of nature. For what appearance would there be of any compact? What new engagement if he were no farther tied by any decrees of the society, than he himself thought fit, and did actually consent to? This would be still as great a liberty as he himself had before his compact, or anyone else in the state of nature hath, who may submit himself and consent to any acts of it if he thinks fit.

For if the consent of the majority shall not in reason be received as the act of the whole and conclude every individual, nothing but the consent of every individual can make anything to be the act of the whole, which considering the infirmities of health and avocations of business, which in a number, though much less than that of a commonwealth, will necessarily keep many away from the public assembly, and the variety of opinions, and contrariety of interest, which unavoidably happen in all collections of men, 'tis next to impossible ever to be had. ...Such a constitution as this would make the mighty leviathan of a shorter duration than the feeblest creatures, and not let it outlast the day it was born in; which cannot be supposed till we can think that rational creatures should desire and constitute societies only to be dissolved. For where the majority cannot conclude the rest, there they cannot act as one body, and consequently will be immediately dissolved again.

Whosoever therefore out of a state of nature unite into a community must be understood to give up all the power necessary to the ends for which they unite into society, to the majority of the community, unless they expressly agreed in any number greater than the majority. And this is done by barely agreeing to unite into one political society, which is all the compact that is, or needs be, between the individuals that enter into or make up a commonwealth. And thus that which begins and actually constitutes any political society is nothing but the consent of any number of freemen capable of a majority to unite and incorporate into such a society. And this is that, and that only, which did or could give beginning to any lawful government in the world.

To this I find two objections made.

First: That there are no instances to be found in story of a company of men independent, and equal one amongst another, that met together and in this way began and set up a government.

Secondly: 'Tis impossible of right that men should do so, because all men being born under government, they are to submit to that, and are not at liberty to begin a new one.

To the first there is this to answer—That it is not at all to be wondered that history gives us but a very little account of men that lived together in the state of nature. The inconveniences of that condition, and the love and want of society, no sooner brought any number of them together, but they presently united and incorporated if they designed to continue together. And if we may not suppose men ever to have been in the state of nature, because we hear not much of them in such a state, we may as well suppose the armies of Salmanasser or Xerxes were never children, because we hear little of them till they were men, and embodied in armies. Government is everywhere antecedent to records, and letters seldom come in amongst a people, till a long continuation of civil society has, by other more necessary arts, provided for their safety, ease, and plenty. And then they begin to look after the history of their founders, and search into their original, when they have outlived the memory of it. ...

"All men," say they, "are born under government, and therefore they cannot be at liberty to begin a new one. Everyone is born a subject to his father, or his prince, and is therefore under the perpetual tie of subjection and allegiance." It is plain mankind never owned nor considered any such natural subjection that they were born in, to one or to the other that tied them without their own consents, to a subjection to them and their heirs.

For there are no examples so frequent in history, both sacred and profane, as those of men withdrawing themselves and their obedience from the jurisdiction they were born under, and the family or community they were bred up in, and setting up new governments in other places. ..

Every man being, as has been shown, naturally free, and nothing being able to put him into subjection to any earthly power but only his own consent, it is to be considered what shall be understood to be sufficient declaration of a man's consent to make him subject to the laws of any government. There is a common distinction of an express and a tacit consent, which will concern our present case. Nobody doubts but an express consent of any man entering into any society makes him a perfect member of that society, a subject of that government. The difficulty is, what ought to be looked upon as a tacit consent, and how far it binds, i.e., how far anyone shall be looked on to have consented, and thereby submitted to any government where he has made no expressions of it at all. And to this I say that every man that hath any possession or enjoyment of any part of the dominions of any government doth thereby give his tacit consent, and is as far forth obliged to obedience to the laws of that government during such enjoyment as anyone under it; whether this his possession be of land to him and his heirs for ever, or a lodging only for a week; or whether it be barely traveling freely on the highway; and in effect it reaches as far as the very being of anyone within the territories of that government. ...

But submitting to the laws of any country, living quietly and enjoying privileges and protection under them makes not a man a member of that society. This is only a local protection and homage due to and from all those who, not being in the state of war, come within the territories belonging to any government to all parts whereof the force of its law extends. But this no more makes a man a member of that society a perpetual subject of that commonwealth, than it would make a man a subject to another in whose family he found it convenient to abide for some time; though whilst he continued in it he were obliged to comply with the laws, and submit to the government he found there. And thus we see, that foreigners by living all their lives under another government, and enjoying the privileges and protection of it, though they are bound even in conscience to submit to its administration as far forth as any denizen, yet do not thereby come to be subjects or members of that commonwealth. Nothing can make any man so, but his actually entering into it by positive engagement, and express promise and compact. This is that, which I think, concerning the beginning of political societies, and that consent which makes anyone a member of any commonwealth.

If man in the state of nature be so free, as has been said, if he be absolute lord of his own person and possessions, equal to the greatest, and subject to nobody, why will he part with his freedom, this empire, and subject himself to the dominion and control of any other power? To which, it is obvious to answer, that though in the state of nature he hath such a right, yet the enjoyment of it is very uncertain, and constantly exposed to the invasions of others. For all being kings as much as he, every man his equal, and the greater part no strict observers of equity and justice, the enjoyment of the property he has in this state is very unsafe, very unsecure. This makes him willing to quit this condition, which, however free, is full of fears and continual dangers; and it is not without reason that he seeks out and is willing to join in society with others, who are already united, or have a mind to unite, for the mutual preservation of their lives, liberties, and estates, which I call by the general name, property.

The great and chief end, therefore, of men's uniting into commonwealths, and putting themselves under government, is the preservation of their property; to which in the state of nature there are many things wanting.

First, There wants an established, settled, known law, received and allowed by common consent to be the standard of right and wrong, and the common measure to decide all controversies between them. For though the law of nature be plain and intelligible to all rational creatures; yet men, being biased by their interest, as well as ignorant for want of study of it, are not apt to allow of it as a law binding to them in the application of it to their particular cases.

Secondly, In the state of nature there wants a known and indifferent judge, with authority to determine all differences according to the established law. For everyone in that state, being both judge and executioner of the law of nature, men being partial to themselves, passion and revenge is very apt to carry them too far, and with too much heat in their own cases, as well as negligence and unconcernedness, to make them too remiss in other men's.

Thirdly, In the state of nature there often wants power to back and support the sentence when right, and to give it due execution. They who by any injustice offend, will seldom fail, where they are able by force to make good their injustice; such resistance many times makes the punishment dangerous, and frequently destructive to those who attempt it.

Thus mankind, notwithstanding all the privileges of the state of nature, being but in an ill condition, while they remain in it, are quickly driven into society. Hence it comes to pass that we seldom find any number of men live any time together in this state. The inconveniences that they are therein exposed to by the irregular and uncertain exercise of the power every man has of punishing the transgressions of others, make them take sanctuary under the established laws of government, and therein seek the preservation of their property. It is this makes them so willingly give up everyone his single power of punishing, to be exercised by such alone, as shall be appointed to it amongst them; and by such rules as the community, or those authorized by them to that purpose, shall agree on. And in this we have the original right and rise of both the legislative and executive power, as well as of the governments and societies themselves.

For in the state of nature, to omit the liberty he has of innocent delights, a man has two powers.

The first is to do whatsoever he thinks fit for the preservation of himself, and others within the permission of the law of nature, by which law, common to them all, he and all the rest of mankind are of one community, make up one society, distinct from all other creatures. And were it not for the corruption and viciousness of degenerate men there would be no need of any other, no necessity that men should separate from this great and natural community, and associate into lesser combinations.

The other power a man has in the state of nature is the power to punish the crimes committed against that law. Both these he gives up when he joins in a private, if I may so call it, or particular political society, and incorporates into any commonwealth separate from the rest of mankind.

The first power, viz., of doing whatsoever he thought fit for the preservation of himself and the rest of mankind, he gives up to be regulated by laws made by the society, so far forth as the preservation of himself and the rest of that society shall require; which laws of the society in many things confine the liberty he had by the law of nature.

Secondly, The power of punishing he wholly gives up, and engages his natural force (which he might before employ in the execution of the law of nature, by his own single authority as he thought fit), to assist the executive power of the society, as the law thereof shall require. For being now in a new state, wherein he is to enjoy many conveniences, from the labor, assistance, and society of others in the same community, as well as protection from its whole strength; he has to part also with as much of his natural liberty, in providing for himself, as the good, prosperity and safety of the society shall require; which is not only necessary but just, since the other members of the society do, the like.

But though men when they enter into society give up the equality, liberty and executive power

they had in the state of nature into the hands of the society, to be so far disposed of by the legislative as the good of the society shall require; yet it being only with an intention in everyone the better to preserve himself, his liberty and property (for no rational creature can be supposed to change his condition with an intention to be worse), the power of the society, or legislative constituted by them, can never be supposed to extend farther than the common good, but is obliged to secure everyone's property by providing against those three defects above-mentioned that made the state of nature so unsafe and uneasy. And so whoever has the legislative or supreme power of any commonwealth is bound to govern by established standing laws, promulgated and known to the people, and not by extemporary decrees; by indifferent and upright judges, who are to decide controversies by those laws; and to employ the force of the community at home only in the execution of such laws, or abroad, to prevent or redress foreign injuries, and secure the community from inroads and invasion. And all this to be directed to no other end but the peace, safety, and public good of the people.

The majority having, as has been shown, upon men's first uniting into society, the whole power of the community, naturally in them, may employ all that power in making laws for the community from time to time, and executing those laws by officers of their own appointing: and then the form of the government is a perfect democracy; or else may put the power of making laws into the hands of a few select men, and their heirs or successors, and then it is an oligarchy; or else into the hands of one man and then it is a monarchy; if to him and his heirs, it is an hereditary monarchy; if to him only for life, but upon his death the power only of nominating a successor to return to them, an elective monarchy. And so accordingly of these, the community may make compounded and mixed forms of government, as they think good. And if the legislative power be at first given by the majority to one or more persons only for their lives, or any limited time, and then the supreme power to revert to them again; when it is so reverted, the community may dispose of it again anew into what hands they please, and so constitute a new form of government. For the form of government depending upon the placing of the supreme power, which is the legislative, it is being impossible to conceive that an inferior power should prescribe to a superior, or any but the supreme make laws, according as the power of making laws is placed, such is the form of the commonwealth.

The great end of men's entering into society being the enjoyment of their properties in peace and safety, and the great instrument and means of that being the laws established in that society: the first and fundamental positive law of all commonwealths, is the establishing of the legislative power; as the first and fundamental natural law, which is to govern even the legislative itself, is the preservation of the society, and (as far as will consist with the public good) of every person in it. This legislative is not only the supreme power of the commonwealth, but sacred and unalterable in the hands where the community have once placed it; nor can any edict of anybody else, in what form soever conceived, or by what power soever backed, have the force and obligation of a law, which has not its sanction from that legislative which the public has chosen and appointed. For without this the law could not have that, which is absolutely necessary to its being a law, the consent of the society over whom nobody can have a power to make laws; but by their own consent, and by authority received from them; and therefore all the obedience, which by the most solemn ties anyone can be obliged to pay, ultimately terminates in this supreme power, and is directed by those laws which it enacts; nor can any oaths to any foreign power whatsoever, or any domestic subordinate power discharge any member of the society from his obedience to the legislative, acting pursuant to their trust; nor oblige him to any obedience contrary to the laws so enacted, or farther than they do allow; it being ridiculous to imagine one can be tied ultimately to obey any power in the society which is not the supreme.

Though the legislative, whether placed in one or more, whether it be always in being, or only by intervals, though it be the supreme power in every commonwealth, yet,

First, It is not nor can possibly be absolutely arbitrary over the lives and fortunes of the people. For it being but the joint power of every member of the society given up to that person, or assembly, which is legislator; it can be no more than those persons had in a state of nature before they entered into society, and gave it up to the community. For nobody can transfer to another more power than he has in himself; and nobody has an absolute arbitrary power over himself, or over any other to destroy his own life, or take away the life or property of another. A man as has been proved cannot subject himself to the arbitrary power of another; and having in the state of nature no arbitrary power over the life, liberty, or possession of another, but only so much as the law of nature gave him for the preservation of himself, and the rest of mankind; this is all he doth, or can give up to the commonwealth, and by it to the legislative power, so that the legislative can have no more than this. Their power in the utmost bounds of it, is limited to the public good of the society. It is a power that hath no other end but preservation, and therefore can never have a right to destroy, enslave, or designedly to impoverish the subjects. The obligations of the law of nature cease not in society, but only in many cases are drawn closer, and have by human laws known penalties annexed to them to enforce their observation. Thus the law of nature stands as an eternal rule to all men, legislators as well as others. The rules that they make for other men's actions must, as well as their own, and other men's actions be conformable to the law of nature, i.e., to the will of God, of which that is a declaration, and the fundamental law of nature being the preservation of mankind, no human sanction can be good or valid against it.

Secondly, The legislative, or supreme authority, cannot assume to itself a power to rule by extemporary arbitrary decrees, but is bound to dispense justice, and decide the rights of the subject by promulgated standing laws, and known authorized judges. For the law of nature being unwritten, and so nowhere to be found but in the minds of men, they who through passion or interest shall miscite or misapply it, cannot so easily be convinced of their mistake where there is no established judge. And so it serves not, as it ought, to determine the rights, and fence the properties of those that live under it, especially where everyone is judge, interpreter, and executioner of it too, and that in his own case; and he that has right on his side, having ordinarily but his own single strength hath not force enough to defend himself from injuries, or punish delinquents. To avoid these inconveniences, which disorder men's properties in the state of nature, men unite into societies that they may have the united strength of the whole society to secure and defend their properties, and may have standing rules to bound it, by which everyone may know what is his. To this end it is that men give up all their natural power to the society which they enter into, and the community put the legislative power into such hands as they think fit, with this trust, that they shall be governed by declared laws, or else their peace, quiet, and property, will still be at the same uncertainty as it was in the state of nature.

Absolute arbitrary power, or governing without settled standing laws, can neither of them consist with the ends of society and government, which men would not quit the freedom of the state of nature for, and tie themselves up under, were it not to preserve their lives, liberties, and fortunes; and by stated rules of right and property to secure their peace and quiet. It cannot be supposed that they should intend, had they a power so to do, to give to anyone, or more, an absolute arbitrary power over their persons and estates, and put a force into the magistrate's hand to execute his unlimited will arbitrarily upon them. This were to put themselves into a worse condition than the state of nature, wherein they had a liberty to defend their right against the injuries of others, and were upon equal terms of force to maintain it, whether invaded by a single man or many in combination. Whereas, by supposing they have given up themselves to the absolute arbitrary power and will of a legislator, they have disarmed themselves, and armed him, to make prey of them when he pleases. He being in a much worse condition that is exposed to the arbitrary power of one man who has the command of 100,000, than he that is exposed to the arbitrary power of 100,000 single men; nobody being secure that his will, who hath such a command, is better than that of other men, though his force be 100,000 times stronger. And, therefore, whatever form the commonwealth is under, the ruling power ought to govern by declared and received laws, and not by extemporary dictates and undetermined resolutions. For then mankind will be in a far worse condition than in the state of nature, if they shall have armed one, or a few men, with the joint power of a multitude to force them to obey at pleasure the exorbitant and unlimited decrees of their sudden thoughts, or unrestrained, and, till that moment, unknown wills, without having any measures set

down which may guide and justify their actions. For all the power the government has, being only for the good of the society, as it ought not to be arbitrary and at pleasure, so it ought to be exercised by established and promulgated laws; that both the people may know their duty and be safe and secure within the limits of the law; and the rulers too kept within their due bounds, and not be tempted by the power they have in their hands to employ it to such purposes, and by such measures, as they would not have known, and own not willingly.

Thirdly, The supreme power cannot take from any man any part of his property without his own consent. For the preservation of property being the end of government, and that for which men enter into society, it necessarily supposes and requires that the people should have property, without which they must be supposed to lose that by entering into society, which was the end for which they entered into it, too gross an absurdity for any man to own. Men, therefore, in society having property, they have such a right to the goods which by the law of the community are theirs, that nobody hath a right to take them or any part of them from them, without their own consent; without this they have no property at all. For I have truly no property in that which another can by right take from me when he pleases, against my consent. Hence it is a mistake to think that the supreme or legislative power of any commonwealth can do what it will, and dispose of the estates of the subjects arbitrarily, or take any part of them at pleasure. This is not much to be feared in governments where the legislative consists wholly, or in part, in assemblies which are variable, whose members, upon the dissolution of the assembly, are subjects under the common laws of their country, equally with the rest. But in governments where the legislative is in one lasting assembly, always in being, or in one man, as in absolute monarchies, there is danger still, that they will think themselves to have a distinct interest from the rest of the community, and so will be apt to increase their own riches and power by taking what they think fit from the people. For a man's property is not at all secure, though there be good and equitable laws to set the bounds of it between him and his fellow subjects, if he who commands those subjects have power to take from any private man what part he pleases of his property, and use and dispose of it as he thinks good.

But government, into whosesoever hands it is put, being, as I have before shown, entrusted with this condition, and for this end, that men might have and secure their properties, the prince, or senate, however it may have power to make laws for the regulating of property between the subjects one amongst another, yet can never have a power to take to themselves the whole or any part of the subject's property without their own consent. For this would be in effect to leave them no property at all. And to let us see that even absolute power, where it is necessary, is not arbitrary by being absolute, but is still limited by that reason, and confined to those ends which required it in some cases to be absolute, we need look no farther than the common practice of martial discipline. For the preservation of the army, and in it the whole commonwealth, requires an absolute obedience to the command of every superior officer, and it is justly death to disobey or dispute the most dangerous or unreasonable of them; but yet we see that neither the sergeant, that could command a soldier to march up to the mouth of a cannon, or stand in a breach, where he is almost sure to perish, can command that soldier to give him one penny of his money; nor the general, that can condemn him to death for deserting his post, or not obeying the most desperate orders, cannot yet, with all his absolute power of life and death, dispose of one farthing of that soldier's estate, or seize one jot of his goods, whom yet he can command anything, and hang for the least disobedience. Because such a blind obedience is necessary to that end for which the commander has his power, viz., the preservation of the rest; but the disposing of his goods has nothing to do with it.

'Tis true governments cannot be supported without great charge, and it is fit everyone who enjoys a share of the protection should pay out of his estate his proportion for the maintenance of it. But still it must be with his own consent, i.e., the consent of the majority giving it either by themselves or their representatives chosen by them. For if anyone shall claim a power to lay and levy taxes on the people, by his own authority, and without such consent of the people, he thereby invades the fundamental law of property, and subverts the end of government. For what property have I in that which another may by right take when he pleases to himself?

Fourthly, The legislative cannot transfer the power of making laws to any other hands; for it being but a delegated power from the people, they who have it cannot pass it over to others. The people alone can appoint the form of the commonwealth, which is by constituting the legislative, and appointing in whose hands that shall be. And when the people have said we will submit to rules, and be governed by laws made by such men, and in such forms, nobody else can say other men shall make laws for them; nor can the people be bound by any laws but such as are enacted by those whom they have chosen and authorized to make laws for them. ...

The legislative power is that which has a right to direct how the force of the commonwealth shall be employed for preserving the community and the members of it. Because those laws which are constantly to be executed, and whose force is always to continue, may be made in a little time, therefore there is no need that the legislative should be always in being, not having always business to do; and because it may be too great a temptation to human frailty, apt to grasp at power for the same persons, who have the power of making laws, to have also in their hands the power to execute them, whereby they exempt themselves from obedience to the laws they make, and suit the law, both in its making and execution to their own private advantage, and thereby come to have a distinct interest from the rest of the community, contrary to the end of society and government. Therefore, in well-ordered commonwealths, where the good of the whole is so considered as it ought, the legislative power is put into the hands of diverse persons who duly assembled, have by themselves or jointly with others a power to make laws, which when they have done, being separated again, they are themselves subject to the laws they have made; which is a new and near tie upon them, to take care that they make them for the public good. ...

He that will with any clearness speak of the dissolution of government ought, in the first place, to distinguish between the dissolution of the society and the dissolution of the government. That which makes the community, and brings men out of the loose state of nature into one politic society, is the agreement which everyone has with the rest to incorporate and act as one body, and so be one distinct commonwealth. The usual and almost only way whereby this union is dissolved, is the inroad of foreign force making a conquest upon them. For in that case (not being able to maintain and support themselves as one entire and independent body) the union belonging to that body which consisted therein must necessarily cease, and so everyone return to the state he was in before, with a liberty to shift for himself and provide for his own safety as he thinks fit in some other society. Whenever the society is dissolved, it is certain the government of that society cannot remain. Thus conquerors' swords often cut up governments by the roots, and mangle societies to pieces. ...

Besides this overturning from without, governments are dissolved from within. ...

First, That when such a single person or prince sets up his own arbitrary will in place of the laws which are the will of the society, declared by the legislative, then the legislative is changed. For that being in effect the legislative whose rules and laws are put in execution and required to be obeyed when other laws are set up, and other rules pretended and enforced, than what the legislative constituted by the society have enacted, it is plain that the legislative is changed. Whoever introduces new laws, not being thereunto authorized by the fundamental appointment of the society, or subverts the old, disowns and overturns the power by which they were made, and so sets up a new legislative.

Secondly, When the prince hinders the legislative from assembling in its due time, or from acting freely, pursuant to those ends for which it was constituted, the legislative is altered. For it is not a certain number of men, no, nor their meeting, unless they have also freedom of debating and leisure of perfecting what is for the good of the society, wherein the legislative consists. When these are taken away or altered so as to deprive the society of the due exercise of their power, the legislative is truly altered. For it is not names that constitute governments, but the use and exercise of those powers that were intended to accompany them; so that he who takes away the freedom, or hinders the acting of the legislative in its due seasons, in effect takes away the legislative, and puts an end to the government.

Thirdly, When, by the arbitrary power of the prince, the electors or ways of elections are altered, without the consent and contrary to the common interest of the people, there also the legislative is altered. For if others than those whom the society hath authorized thereunto, do choose, or in another way than what the society hath prescribed, those chosen are not the legislative appointed by the people.

Fourthly, The delivery also of the people into the subjection of foreign power, either by the prince, or by the legislative, is certainly a change of the legislative, and so a dissolution of the government. For the end why people entered into society being to be preserved one entire, free, independent society, to be governed by its own laws, this is lost whenever they are given up into the power of another. ...

There is one way more whereby such a government may be dissolved, and that is, when he who has the supreme executive power neglects and abandons that charge, so that the laws already made can no longer be put in execution. This is demonstratively to reduce all to anarchy, and so effectually to dissolve the government. For laws not being made for themselves, but to be by their execution the bonds of the society, to keep every part of the body politic, in its due place and function, when that totally ceases, the government visibly ceases, and the people become a confused multitude without order or connection. Where there is no longer the administration of justice, for the securing of men's rights, nor any remaining power within the community to direct the force, or provide for the necessities of the public, there certainly is no government left. Where the laws cannot be executed, it is all one as if there were no laws; and a government without laws is, I suppose, a mystery in politics, inconceivable to human capacity, and inconsistent with human society.

In these and the like cases, when the government is dissolved, the people are at liberty to provide for themselves by erecting a new legislative, differing from the other, by the change of persons, or form, or both, as they shall find it most for their safety and good. For the society can never, by the fault of another, lose the native and original right it has to preserve itself, which can only be done by a settled legislative, and a fair and impartial execution of the laws made by it. But the state of mankind is not so miserable that they are not capable of using this remedy, till it be too late to look for any. To tell people they may provide for themselves by erecting a new legislative, when by oppression, artifice, or being delivered over to a foreign power, their old one is gone, is only to tell them they may expect relief when it is too late, and the evil is past cure. This is in effect no more than to bid them first be slaves, and then to take care of their liberty; and when their chains are on tell them they may act like free men. This, if barely so, is rather mockery than relief; and men can never be secure from tyranny if there be no means to escape it till they are perfectly under it. And therefore it is that they have not only a right to get out of it, but to prevent it.

There is therefore secondly another way whereby governments are dissolved, and that is when the legislative or the prince, either of them, act contrary to their trust.

First, The legislative acts against the trust reposed in them when they endeavor to invade the property of the subject, and to make themselves or any part of the community masters or arbitrary disposers of the lives, liberties, or fortunes of the people.

The reason why men enter into society is the preservation of their property; and the end why they choose and authorize a legislative is that there may be laws made, and rules set, as guards and fences to the properties of all the members of the society to limit the power and moderate the dominion of every part and member of the society. For since it can never be supposed to be the will of the society that the legislative should have a power to destroy that which everyone designs secure by entering into society, and for which the people submitted themselves to legislators of their own making, whenever the legislators endeavor to take away and destroy the property of the people, or to reduce them to slavery under arbitrary power, they put themselves into a state of war with the people, who are thereupon absolved from any further obedience, and are left to the common refuge which God hath provided for all men against force and violence. Whensoever, therefore, the legislative shall transgress this fundamental rule of society, and either by ambition, fear, folly, or corruption, endeavor to grasp themselves or put into the hands of any other an absolute power over the lives, liberties, and estates of the people, by this breach of trust they forfeit the power the people had put into their hands, for quite contrary ends, and it devolves to the people, who have a right to resume

their original liberty, and by the establishment of the new legislative (such as they shall think fit) provide for their own safety and security, which is the end for which they are in society. ...

But it will be said, this hypothesis lays a ferment for frequent rebellion. To which I answer:

First, no more than any other hypothesis. For when the people are made miserable, and find themselves exposed to the ill-usage of arbitrary power, cry up their governors as much as you will for sons of Jupiter, let them be sacred and divine, descended, or authorized from heaven, give them out for whom or what you please, the same will happen. The people generally ill-treated, and contrary to right, will be ready upon any occasion to ease themselves of a burden that sits heavy upon them. They will wish and seek for the opportunity, which in the change, weakness, and accidents of human affairs seldom delays long to offer itself. He must have lived but a little while in the world who has not seen examples of this in his time, and he must have read very little who cannot produce examples of it in all sorts of governments in the world.

Secondly, I answer, such revolutions happen not upon every little mismanagement in public affairs. Great mistakes in the ruling part, many wrong and inconvenient laws, and all the slips of human frailty will be borne by the people without mutiny or murmur. But if a long train of abuses, prevarications and artifices, all tending the same way, make the design visible to the people—and they cannot but feel what they lie under, and see whither they are going—it is not to be wondered that they should then rouse themselves and endeavor to put the rule into such hands which may secure to them the ends for which government was at first erected, and without which ancient names and specious forms are so far from being better that they are much worse than the state of nature or pure anarchy; the inconveniences being all as great and as near, but the remedy farther off and more difficult.

Thirdly, I answer that this power in the people of providing for their safety anew by a new legislative when their legislators have acted contrary to their trust by invading their property, is the best fence against rebellion, and the probablest means to hinder it. For rebellion being an opposition, not to persons, but authority, which is founded only in the constitutions and laws of the government, those whoever they be who by force break through, and by force justify their violation of them, are truly and properly rebels. For when men by entering into society and civil government have excluded force, and introduced laws for the preservation of property, peace, and unity amongst themselves, those who set up force again in opposition to the laws do *rebellare*—that is, bring back again the state of war—and are properly rebels; which they who are in power (by the pretense they have to authority, the temptation of force they have in their hands, and the flattery of those about them) being likeliest to do, the properest way to prevent the evil is to show them the danger and injustice of it who are under the greatest temptation to run into it.

In both the forementioned cases, when either the legislative is changed or the legislators act contrary to the end for which they were constituted, those who are guilty are guilty of rebellion. For if anyone by force takes away the established legislative of any society, and the laws by them made pursuant to their trust, he thereby takes away the umpirage which everyone had consented to for a peaceable decision of all their controversies, and a bar to the state of war amongst them. They who remove or change the legislative, take away this decisive power, which nobody can have but by the appointment and consent of the people, and so destroying the authority which the people did, and nobody else can, set up; and introducing a power which the people hath not authorized, actually introduce a state of war which is that of force without authority. And thus by removing the legislative established by the society (in whose decisions the people acquiesced and united as to that of their own will), they untie the knot and expose the people anew to the state of war. And if those who by force take away the legislative are rebels, the

legislators themselves, as has been shown, can be no less esteemed so, when they who were set up for the protection and preservation of the people, their liberties and properties, shall by force invade and endeavor to take them away; and so they, putting themselves into a state of war with those who made them the protectors and guardians of their peace, are properly and with the greatest aggravation *rebellantes* (rebels).

But if they who say it lays a foundation for rebellion mean that it may occasion civil wars or intestine broils, to tell the people they are absolved from obedience when illegal attempts are made upon their liberties or properties, and may oppose the unlawful violence of those who were their magistrates when they invade their properties contrary to the trust put in them and that therefore this doctrine is not to be allowed, being so destructive to the peace of the world: they may as well say upon the same ground that honest men may not oppose robbers or pirates because this may occasion disorder or bloodshed. If any mischief come in such cases, it is not to be charged upon him who defends his own right, but on him that invades his neighbor's. If the innocent honest man must quietly quit all he has for peace's sake to him who will lay violent hands upon it, I desire it may be considered what a kind of peace there will be in the world which consists only in violence and rapine, and which is to be maintained only for the benefit of robbers and oppressors. ...

The end of government is the good of mankind, and which is best for mankind, that the people should be always exposed to the boundless will of tyranny, or that the rulers should be sometimes liable to be opposed when they grow exorbitant in the use of their power, and employ it for the destruction and not the preservation of the properties of their people?

The Social Contract

Jean-Jacques Rousseau

Man is born free, and yet we see him everywhere in chains. Those who believe themselves the masters of others cease not to be even greater slaves than the people they govern. How this happens I am ignorant; but, if I am asked what renders it justifiable, I believe it may be in my power to resolve the question.

If I were only to consider force, and the effects of it, I should say, "When a people is constrained to obey, and does obey, it does well; but as soon as it can throw off its yoke, and does throw it off, it does better: for a people may certainly use, for the recovery of their liberty, the same right that was employed to deprive them of it: it was either justifiably recovered, or unjustifiably torn from them." But the social order is a sacred right which serves for the basis of all others. Yet this right comes not from nature; it is therefore founded on conventions. The question is, what those conventions are. But, before I come to that point, I must establish the principles which I have just asserted.

The earliest and the only natural societies are families: yet the children remain attached to the father no longer than they have need for his protection. As soon as that need ceases, the bond of nature is dissolved. The child, exempt from the obedience he owed the father, and the father, from the duties he owed the child, return equally to independence. If they continue to remain together, it is not in consequence of a natural, but a voluntary union; and the family itself is maintained only by a convention.

This common liberty is a consequence of the nature of man. His first law is that of self-preservation, his first cares those which he owes to himself; and as soon as he has attained the age of reason, being the only judge of the means proper to preserve himself, he becomes at once his own master.

It appears therefore that families are the first models of political societies: the chief represents the father of the family, the children the people; and being all born equal, and all free, they in either case only alienate their liberty in order to obtain what is more useful. All the difference between the two societies is that, in the family, the gratification which paternal tenderness derives from a consciousness of benefiting those who are the objects of it makes a full amends to the father for the care he bestows on the children; while, in the State, the pleasure of commanding takes the place of that love which the chief does not feel for his people. ...

Aristotle had said, before any of them, that men are not naturally equal, but that some are born for slavery and others for dominion.

Aristotle was right; but he mistook the effect for the cause. Nothing is more certain than that all men who are born in slavery are born for slavery. Slaves become so debased by their chains as to lose even the desire of breaking from them; they love their servitude, even as the companions of Ulysses loved their brutishness. If there are some who are slaves by nature, the reason is that men were made slaves against nature. Force made the first slaves, and slavery, by degrading and corrupting its victims, perpetuated their bondage. ...

The strongest are still never sufficiently strong to ensure them continual mastership, unless they find means of transforming force into right, and obedience into duty. Hence the right of the strongest—a right which seems ironical in appearance, but is really established as a principle. But shall we never have an explanation of this term? Force is a physical power; I do not see what morality can result from its effects. To yield to force is an act of necessity, not of inclination; or it is at best only an act of prudence. In what sense then can it be a duty?

From *The Social Contract*, Charles Frankel, trans. (New York: Hafner Publishing Co., 1947). Reprinted by permission of Macmillan Publishing Company.

Let us suppose for a moment the existence of this pretended right. I see nothing that can arise from it but inexplicable nonsense. For, if we admit that force constitutes right, the effect changes with the cause: all force which overcomes the first succeeds to its right. As soon as men can disobey with impunity, they can do so justifiably; and because the strongest is always in the right, strength is the only thing men should seek to acquire. But what sort of right is that which perishes with the force that gave it existence? If it is necessary to obey by force, there can be no occasion to obey from duty; and when force is no more, all obligation ceases with it. We see, therefore, that this word "right" adds nothing to force, but is indeed an unmeaning term. ...

Since no man has any natural authority over his fellows, and since force produces no right to any, all justifiable authority among men must be established on the basis of conventions.

If an individual, says Grotius, can alienate his liberty, and become the slave of a master, why may not a whole people alienate theirs, and become the subject of a king? There are some equivocal words in this sentence, which require an explanation; but I will confine myself to the word "alienate." To alienate is to give or sell. But a man who becomes the slave of another, cannot give but must sell himself, at least for a subsistence. But for what do a people sell themselves? A king, so far from furnishing his subjects with subsistence, draws his own from them. ...

We are told that a despot ensures civil tranquility for his subjects. Be it so; but what do his subjects gain if the wars which his ambition draws them into, if his insatiable avarice, and the vexations of his administration, desolate the country even more than civil dissensions? What do they gain if this very tranquility is one of their miseries? We find tranquility also in dungeons; but is that enough to make them enjoyable?. ...

If each individual could alienate himself, he could not alienate his descendants; for, being born men and free, their liberty is their own, and no person can dispose of it but they themselves. ...

To renounce our liberty is to renounce our quality of man, and with it all the rights and duties of humanity. No adequate compensation can possibly be made for a sacrifice so complete. Such a renunciation is incompatible with the nature of man;

whose actions, when once he is deprived of his free will, must be destitute of all morality. Finally, a convention which stipulates absolute authority on one side, and unlimited obedience on the other, must be considered as vain and contradictory. Is it not clear that there can be no obligation to a person from whom everything may be justly required? And does not the single circumstance of there being no equivalence and no exchange also annul the act?. ...

There will always be a great difference between subduing a multitude and governing a society. When unorganized men are successively subjugated by one individual, whatever number there may be of them, they appear to me only as a master and slaves; I cannot regard them as a people and their chief; they are, if you please, an *aggregation*, but they are not as yet an *association*; for there is neither public property, nor a political body, among them. A man may have enslaved half the world, and yet continue only a private individual; his interest is separate from that of others, and confined to himself alone. When such a man falls, his empire remains unconnected and without any bond of union, as an oak dissolves and becomes a mass of ashes when consumed by fire.

"A people," says Grotius, "can give themselves to a king." According to Grotius, then, they are a people before they give themselves to a king. The donation itself is a civil act, and supposes a public consultation. It would therefore be better before we examine the act by which they elected a king, to enquire into that by which they became a people; for that act, being necessarily anterior to the other, is the true foundation of society.

In fact, if there was no prior convention, where would be—unless the election was unanimous—the obligation which should bind the minority to submit to the choice of the majority? And whence would a hundred men, who wish to submit to a master, derive the right of binding by their votes ten other men who were not disposed to acknowledge any chief? The law which gives the majority of votes the power of deciding for the whole body can only be established by a convention, and proves that there must have been unanimity at one time at least.

I will suppose that men in the state of nature are arrived at that crisis when the strength of each individual is insufficient to overcome the resistance of the obstacles to his preservation. This primitive state can therefore subsist no longer; and the human race would perish unless it changed its manner of life.

As men cannot create for themselves new forces, but merely unite and direct those which already exist, the only means they can employ for their preservation is to form by aggregation an assemblage of forces that may be able to overcome the resistance, to be put in motion as one body, and to act in concert.

This assemblage of forces must be produced by the concurrence of many; but as the force and the liberty of each man are the chief instruments of his preservation, how can he engage them elsewhere without danger to himself, and without neglecting the care which is due himself? This difficulty, which leads directly to my subject, may be expressed in these words:

"Where shall we find a form of association which will defend and protect with the whole common force the person and the property of each associate, and by which every person, while uniting himself with all, shall obey only himself and remain as free as before?" Such is the fundamental problem of which the Social Contract gives the solution.

The articles of this contract are so unalterably fixed by the nature of the act that the least modification renders them vain and of no effect; so that they are the same everywhere, and are everywhere tacitly understood and admitted, even though they may never have been formally announced; until, the social compact being violated, each individual is restored to his original rights, and resumes his native liberty, while losing the conventional liberty for which he renounced it.

The articles of the social contract will, when clearly understood, be found reducible to this single point: the total alienation of each associate, and all his rights, to the whole community; for, in the first place, as every individual gives himself up entirely, the condition of every person is alike; and being so, it would not be to the interest of any one to render that condition offensive to others.

Nay, more than this, the alienation being made without any reserve, the union is as complete as it can be, and no associate has any further claim to anything: for if any individual retained rights not enjoyed in general by all, as there would be no common superior to decide between him and the public, each person being in some points his own judge, would soon pretend to be so in everything; and thus would the state of nature be continued and the association necessarily become tyrannical or be annihilated.

Finally, each person gives himself to all, and so not to any one individual; and as there is no one associate over whom the same right is not acquired which is ceded to him by others, each gains an equivalent for what he loses, and finds his force increased for preserving that which he possesses.

If, therefore, we exclude from the social compact all that is not essential, we shall find it reduced to the following terms:

Each of us places in common his person and all his power under the supreme direction of the general will; and as one body we all receive each member as an indivisible part of the whole.

From that moment, instead of as many separate persons as there are contracting parties, this act of association produces a moral and collective body, composed of as many members as there are votes in the assembly, which from this act receives its unity, its common self, its life, and its will. This public person, which is thus formed by the union of all other persons, took formerly the name of "city," and now takes that of "republic" or "body politic." It is called by its members "State" when it is passive, "Sovereign" when in activity, and, whenever it is compared with other bodies of a similar kind, it is denominated "power." The associates take collectively the name of "people," and separately, that of "citizens," as participating in the sovereign authority, and of "subjects," because they are subjected to the laws of the State. But these terms are frequently confounded and used one for the other; and it is enough that a man understands how to distinguish them when they are employed in all their precision.

It appears from this formula that the act of association contains a reciprocal engagement between the public and individuals, and that each individual, contracting, as it were, with himself, is engaged under a double character; that is, as a member of the Sovereign engaging with individuals, and as a member of the State engaged with the Sovereign. But we cannot apply here the maxim of civil right, that no person is bound by any engagement which he makes with himself; for there is a material difference between an obligation to oneself individually, and an obligation to a collective body of which oneself constitutes a part.

It is necessary to observe here that public deliberation, which can bind all the subjects to the Sovereign, in consequence of the double character under which the members of that body appear, cannot, for the opposite reason, bind the Sovereign to itself; and consequently that it is against the nature of the body politic for the sovereign power to impose on itself any law which it cannot break. Being able to consider itself as acting under one character only, it is in the situation of an individual forming a contract with himself; and we see therefore that there neither is nor can be any kind of fundamental law obligatory for the body of the people, not even the social contract itself. But this does not mean that this body could not very well engage itself to others in any manner which would not derogate from the contract; for, with respect to what is external to it, it becomes a simple being, an individual. But the body politic, or the Sovereign, which derives its existence from the sacredness of the contract, can never bind itself, even towards outsiders, in anything that would derogate from the original act, such as alienating any portion of itself, or submitting to another Sovereign. To violate the contract by which it exists would be to annihilate itself; and that which is nothing can produce nothing.

As soon as this multitude is united in one body, you cannot offend one of its members without attacking the body; much less can you offend the body without incurring the resentment of all the members. Thus duty and interest equally oblige the two contracting parties to lend aid to each other; and the same men must endeavour to unite under this double character all the advantages which attend it.

Further, the Sovereign, being formed only of the individuals who compose it, neither has, nor can have, any interest contrary to theirs; consequently, the sovereign power need give no guarantee to its subjects, because it is impossible that the body should seek to injure all its members; and we shall see presently that it can do no injury to any individual in particular. The Sovereign, by its nature, is always everything it ought to be.

But this is not so with the relation of subjects towards the Sovereign, which, notwithstanding the common interest, has nothing to make them responsible for the performance of their engagements if some means is not found of ensuring their fidelity.

In fact, each individual may, as a man, have a private will, dissimilar or contrary to the general will which he has as a citizen. His own private interest may dictate to him very differently from the common interest; his absolute and naturally independent existence may make him regard what he owes to the common cause as a gratuitous contribution, the omission of which would be less injurious to others than the payment would be burdensome to himself; and considering the moral person which constitutes the State as a creature of the imagination, because it is not a man, he may wish to enjoy the rights of a citizen without being disposed to fulfil the duties of a subject. Such an injustice would in its progress cause the ruin of the body politic.

In order, therefore, to prevent the social compact from becoming an empty formula, it tacitly comprehends the engagement, which alone can give effect to the others—that whoever refuses to obey the general will shall be compelled to it by the whole body: this in fact only forces him to be free; for this is the condition which, by giving each citizen to his country, guarantees his absolute personal independence, a condition which gives motion and effect to the political machine. This alone renders all civil engagements justifiable, and without it they would be absurd, tyrannical, and subject to the most enormous abuses.

The passing from the state of nature to the civil state produces in man a very remarkable change, by substituting justice for instinct in his conduct, and giving to his actions a moral character which they lacked before. It is then only that the voice of duty succeeds to physical impulse, and a sense of what is right, to the incitements of appetite. Man, who had till then regarded none but himself, perceives that he must act on other principles, and learns to consult his reason before he listens to his inclinations. Although he is deprived in this new state of many advantages which he enjoyed from nature, he gains in return others so great, his faculties so unfold themselves by being exercised, his ideas are so extended, his sentiments so exalted, and his whole mind so enlarged and refined, that if, by abusing his new condition, he did not sometimes degrade it even below that from which he emerged, he ought to bless continually the happy moment that snatched him forever from it, and transformed him from a circumscribed and stupid animal to an intelligent being and a man.

In order to draw a balance between the advantages and disadvantages attending his new situation, let us state them in such a manner that they may be easily compared. Man loses by the social contract his *natural* liberty, and an unlimited right to all which tempts him, and which he can obtain; in return he acquires *civil* liberty, and proprietorship of all he possesses. That we may not be deceived in the value of these compensations, we must distinguish natural liberty, which knows no bounds but the power of the individual, from civil liberty, which is limited by the general will; and between possession, which is only the effect of force or of the right of the first occupant, from property, which must be founded on a positive title. In addition we might add to the other acquisitions of the civil state that of moral liberty, which alone renders a man master of himself; for it is *slavery* to be under the impulse of mere appetite, and *freedom* to obey a law which we prescribe for ourselves. ...

Each member of the community, at the moment of its formation, gives himself up to it just as he is: himself and all his forces, of which his wealth forms a part. By this act, however, possession does not change in nature when it changes its master, and become property when it falls into the hands of the Sovereign; but as the forces of the city are infinitely greater than those of an individual, it is better secured when it becomes a public possession, without being more justifiable, at least with respect to foreigners. As to its members, the State is made master of all their wealth by the social contract, which within the State serves as the basis of all rights; but with regard to other powers, it claims only under the title of first occupancy, which it derives from individuals.

The right of the first occupant, though more substantial than that of the strongest, does not become a real right, until after the right of property is established. All men have naturally a right to whatever is necessary for them; but the act which renders a man the positive proprietor of any property excludes him from everything else. This being

accomplished, the possessor must confine himself to what is thus made his own, and he can claim no right beyond it against the community. It is by this means that the right of the first occupant, so weak in the state of nature, is respected by every man in civil society. In this right we respect less what is another's than what is not our own.

The following conditions are in general necessary to give validity to the right founded on first occupancy in any domain whatever. In the first place, the land must not yet be inhabited by any person; secondly, the party must not occupy more land than is sufficient to supply him with subsistence; thirdly, he must take possession, not by a vain ceremony, but by labour and cultivation, as they are the only proofs of a man's being a proprietor, which, in default of a legal title, deserve to be respected by others. ...

In accepting the property of individuals, the community is far from despoiling them, and only ensures them justifiable possession, changes usurpation into a true right, and enjoyment into property. By this means, the possessors being considered as depositaries of the public good, their rights are respected by all the members of the State, and protected with all their force against foreigners. So that by a resignation, advantageous to the public, and still more so to the resigners, they may be justly said to have acquired all that they gave up: a paradox which will be easily explained by distinguishing, as I shall do hereafter, between the rights which the Sovereign and the proprietors have in the same property.

It may also happen that men begin to associate before they have any possessions, and that, spreading afterwards over a country sufficient for them all, they may either enjoy it in common, or part it between them equally, or in such proportions as the Sovereign shall direct. In whatever manner the acquisition is made, the right which each individual has over his own property is always subordinate to the right which the community has over all; without which there would be no solidity in the social bond, nor any real force in the exercise of sovereignty. ...Instead of destroying the natural equality of mankind, the fundamental compact substitutes, on the contrary, a moral and legal equality for that physical inequality which nature placed among men, and that, let men be ever so unequal in strength or in genius, they are all equalized by convention and legal right.

The first and most important consequence of the principles already established is that the general will alone can direct the forces of the State agreeably to the end of its institution, which is the common good; for if the clashing of private interests has rendered the establishing of societies necessary, the agreement of the same interests has made such establishments possible. It is what is common in these different interests that forms the social bond; and if there was not some point in which they all unanimously centered, no society could exist. It is on the basis of this common interest alone that society must be governed.

I say, therefore, that sovereignty, being only the exercise of the general will, can never alienate itself, and that the Sovereign, which is only a collective being, cannot be represented but by itself: the *power* may well be transmitted but not the *will*.

Indeed, if it is not impossible that a private will should accord on some point with the general will, it is at least impossible that such agreement should be regular and lasting; for the private will is inclined by its nature to partiality, and the general will to impartiality. It is even more impossible to guarantee the continuance of this agreement, even if we were to see it always exist; because that existence must be owing not to art but to chance. ...If, therefore, the people promise unconditionally to obey, the act of making such a promise dissolves their existence, and they lose their quality of a people; for at the moment that there is a master, there is no longer a Sovereign, and from that moment the body politic is destroyed. ...

For the same reason that sovereignty is inalienable, it is indivisible. For the will is general or it is not; it is either the will of the whole body of the people, or only of a part. In the first case, this declared will is an act of sovereignty and constitutes law; in the second, it is but a private will or an act of magistracy, and is at most but a decree.

But our political thinkers, not being able to divide sovereignty in principle, have divided it in its object: into force and will; legislative power and executive power; the rights of levying taxes, of administering justice, and making war; the internal government and the power of treating with foreigners. But by sometimes confounding all these parts,

and sometimes separating them, they make of the sovereign power a fantastical being composed of related pieces; as if man were composed of several bodies, one with eyes, another with arms, another with feet, but none with anything more. ...

This error arises from our not having formed exact ideas of the sovereign authority, and from our taking for parts of that authority what are only its emanations. For example, the acts of declaring war and making peace are considered as acts of sovereignty, when in fact they are not so, because neither of these acts is a law, but only the application of the law, a particular act which determines the application of the law, as we shall clearly perceive when the idea attached to the word "law" is fixed.

By tracing in the same manner the other divisions, we should find that whenever we suppose sovereignty divided we deceive ourselves; that the rights which we take for a part of that sovereignty are all subordinate to it, and always suppose supreme wills of which they only sanction the execution. ...

It follows from what has been said that the general will is always right and tends always to the public advantage; but it does not follow that the deliberations of the people have always the same rectitude. Our will always seeks our own good, but we do not always perceive what it is. The people are never corrupted, but they are often deceived, and only then do they seem to will what is bad.

There is frequently much difference between the *will of all* and the *general will*. The latter regards only the common interest; the former regards private interest, and is indeed but a sum of private wills: but remove from these same wills the pluses and minuses that cancel each other, and then the general will remains as the sum of the differences.

If, when the people, sufficiently informed, deliberated, there was to be no communication among them, from the grand total of trifling differences the general will would always result, and their resolutions be always good. But when cabals and partial associations are formed at the expense of the great association, the will of each such association, though *general* with regard to its members, is *private* with regard to the State: it can then be said no longer that there are as many voters as men, but only as many as there are associations. By this means the differences being less numerous, they produce a result less general. Finally, when one of these associations becomes so large that it prevails over all the rest, you have no longer the sum of many opinions dissenting in a small degree from each other, but one great dictating dissentient; from that moment there is no longer a general will, and the predominating opinion is only an individual one.

It is therefore of the utmost importance for obtaining the expression of the general will, that no partial society should be formed in the State, and that every citizen should speak his opinion entirely from himself. ...If the state or city is only a moral person, the existence of which consists in the union of its members, and if its most important care is that of preserving itself, there is a necessity for its possessing a universally compulsive power, for moving and disposing each part in the manner most convenient to the whole. As nature gives to every man absolute command over all his members, the social compact gives to the body politic absolute command over the members of which it is formed; and it is this power, when directed by the general will, that bears, as I have said before, the name of "sovereignty."

But, besides the public person, we have to consider the private persons who compose it, and whose lives and liberty are naturally independent of it. The point here is to distinguish properly between the respective rights of the citizens and the Sovereign, and between the duties which the former have to fulfil in quality of subjects, and the natural rights which they ought to enjoy in quality of men.

It is granted that all which an individual alienates by the social compact is only that part of his power, his property, and his liberty, the use of which is important to the community; but we must also grant that the Sovereign is the only judge of what is important to the community.

All the services which a citizen can render to the State ought to be rendered as soon as the Sovereign demands them; but the Sovereign cannot, on its side, impose any burden on the subject useless to the community; it cannot even have the inclination to do so; for, under the law of reason, nothing is done without a cause, any more than under the law of nature.

The engagements which bind us to the social body are only obligatory because they are mutual; and their nature is such that in fulfilling them we cannot labour for others without labouring at the same time for ourselves. Wherefore is the general will always right, and wherefore do all the wills invariably seek the happiness of every individual among them, if it is not that there is no person who does not appropriate the word "each" to himself, and who does not think of himself when he is voting for all? This proves that the equality of right, and the idea of justice which it inspires, is derived from the preference which each gives to himself, and consequently from the nature of man; that the general will, to be truly such, ought to be so in its object, as well as its essence: that it ought to come from all, if we are to apply it to all; and that it loses its natural rectitude when it tends towards any one individual and determinate object, because then, judging of what is external to us, we have no true principle of equity to guide us.

In fact, as soon as it is a matter of an individual fact or right, on any point which has not been previously regulated by a general convention, the affair becomes contentious. It is a process wherein the persons interested are one of the parties, and the public the other, but where I do not see any law that must be followed, or any judge who ought to decide. It would be ridiculous in such a case to bring the question to an express decision of the general will, which could only be the conclusion of one party, and consequently, which would be, with respect to the other party, but an external and private will, hurried on that occasion into injustice, and subject to error. Thus, in the same manner as a private will cannot represent the general will, the general will, in its turn, changes its nature if its object is private, and cannot, as the general will, pronounce either on a man or a fact. ...This will appear contradictory to common ideas; but I must have time to unfold mine.

We should perceive by this that the generality of the will depends less on the number of voters than on the common interest which unites them; for, in this institution, each necessarily submits to the conditions which he imposes on others—an admirable union of interest and justice, which gives to the common deliberations a character of equity that vanishes in the discussion of all private affairs for want of a common interest to combine and identify the ruling of the judge with that of the party.

By whatever path we return to our principle, we always arrive at the same conclusion—that is, that the social compact establishes among citizens such an equality that they are all engaged under the same conditions, and should all enjoy the same rights. Thus, by the nature of the compact all acts of sovereignty, that is to say, all authentic acts of the general will, oblige or favour all citizens alike in such a manner as evinces that the Sovereign knows no person but the body of the nation, and does not make any distinction among the individuals who compose it. What, therefore, is properly an act of sovereignty? It is not a convention between a superior and an inferior, but a convention of the body with each of its members—a justifiable convention because it has the social contract for its basis; equitable, because it is common to all; beneficial, because it can have no other object but the general good; and solid, because it is guaranteed by the public force and the supreme power. While subjects are under the governance of such conventions only, they obey no one but only their own will: and to enquire how far the respective rights of the Sovereign and citizens extend is to ask how far the citizens can engage with themselves, each towards all, and all towards each.

We see by this that the sovereign power, all absolute, all sacred, all inviolable as it is, neither will, nor can, exceed the bounds of general conventions; and that every man may fully dispose of what is left to him of his property and his liberty by these conventions; so that the Sovereign never has any right to lay a greater charge on one subject than on another, because then the affair would become personal, and in such cases the power of the Sovereign is no longer competent.

These distinctions once admitted, it is evidently false that individuals have made any real renunciation by the social contract. On the contrary, they find their situation, by the effect of that contract, really rendered preferable to what it was before. Instead of making any alienation they have only made an advantageous transition from a mode of living unsettled and precarious to one better and more secure, from a state of natural independence to one of liberty, from possessing the power of injuring others to security for themselves, and from their strength, which others might, by the employment of theirs, overcome, to a right which social union renders invincible. Even their lives, which they have devoted to the State, are continually protected by it; and when they are exposed in its

defence, what is it but restoring that which they have received from it? What do they do but what they would do more frequently, and with more danger, in the state of nature, when, living in continual and unavoidable conflicts, they would have to defend at the peril of their lives what was necessary to the preservation of life? All, it is true, must fight for their country when their service is requisite; but then no person has occasion to fight for himself as an individual. And is it not gaining a great advantage to be obliged, for the protection of that to which we owe our security, to incur occasionally only a part of that danger to which we must be again exposed as individuals as soon as we were deprived of it?. ...

The end of the social treaty is the preservation of the contracting parties. Whoever wants to enjoy the end must will the means, and some risks, and even some dangers, are inseparable from these means. The man who would preserve his life at the expense of the lives of others ought in turn to expose his own for their protection when it is necessary. The citizen is not a judge of the peril to which the law may expose him; and when the prince says to him, "It is expedient for the State that thou shouldst die," he ought to die, because it is only on that condition that he has enjoyed his security up to that moment, and because his life is not to be considered simply as the boon of nature, but as a conditional gift from the State.

The punishment of death inflicted on criminals may be considered from the same point of view: it is to secure himself from being the victim of assassins that a man consents to die if he becomes an assassin. In this treaty the parties are so far from disposing of their own lives that they think only of guarding them, and it is not to be supposed that, at the time of contracting, any of the contracting parties intends to deserve the gallows.

Further, every malefactor, by attacking the social right, becomes by his crimes a rebel and a traitor to his country; by violating its laws, he ceases to be a member of it and, in fact, makes war upon it. The existence of the State then becomes incompatible with his; one of the two must therefore perish; and when the criminal is executed he suffers less as a citizen than as an enemy. The proceedings against him, and the judgment pronounced in consequence, are the proofs and the declaration that he has broken the social treaty, and, consequently, that he is no longer a member of the State. But, as he is still considered as such at least while he sojourns there, he must be either removed by exile, as a violator of the pact, or by death, as a public enemy; for such an enemy is not a moral person, he is simply a man: and it is then that it is the right of war to kill the vanquished. ...

By the social compact we have given existence and life to the body politic; it now remains to give it motion and will by legislation. For the original act by which the body is formed and united determines none of the measures that ought to be taken for its preservation.

What is good, and conformable to order, is so from the nature of things, and independently of human conventions. ...This justice is undoubtedly universal and emanates from reason alone; but this justice, to be admitted among us, must be reciprocal. Humanly speaking, the laws of justice, when they have no natural sanction, are vain among men; they are only injurious to the just and advantageous to the wicked part of mankind, for the just man invariably adheres to its rules with respect to everyone, but no one adheres to them towards him. There must therefore be conventions and laws to combine our duties and our rights, and to direct justice to its end. In the state of nature, where everything is in common, I owe nothing to those to whom I have promised nothing; and I do not acknowledge that anything, but what I do not wish to use, can be the property of another person. It is not so in the civil order, where every right is determined by law.

But what, in fine, is a law? While men content themselves with affixing none but metaphysical ideas to this word, they must continue to reason without understanding one another; and when they have said what a law of nature is, they will still be no less ignorant of what a law of the State is.

I have already said that there can be no general will directed towards a private object. ...But when the whole people determines for the whole people, it considers only itself; and if a relation is then formed it is only a relation of the whole object from one point of view to the whole object from another point of view, and the whole itself is not divided. Then the affair on which they enact is general, as is the will that enacts. It is this act that I call a "law."

When I say that the object of the laws is always general, I mean that the law views its subjects collectively and their actions abstractly, never a man as individual or an action as private. Thus the law may enact that there shall be certain privileges, but it cannot name the persons who are to enjoy them; the law may divide the citizens into several classes, and specify the qualifications which shall give a right of admission to each class; but it cannot direct such or such a person to be admitted; the law can establish a monarchical government and an hereditary succession, but it cannot elect a king or name a royal family. In a word, all those functions which relate to any individual object pertain not to the legislative power.

Under this idea, we perceive at once how unnecessary it would be to enquire to whom the function of making laws belongs, because the laws are but the acts of the general will; neither need we ask whether the prince is above the laws, since he is a member of the State; nor whether the law can be unjust, as no one is unjust towards himself; nor how we can be free while subjected to the laws, since they are but the registers of our own wills.

We see also that, since the law unites universality of will with universality of object, whatever is ordered of his own accord by any man, whoever he may be, is not law; nay, even that which the Sovereign orders relative to a private object is not a law but a decree; neither is it an act of sovereignty but of magistracy.

I therefore denominate every State a "republic" which is governed by laws, under whatever form of administration it may be; for then only the public interest governs, and the affairs of the public obtain a due regard. All justifiable governments are republican; and I will hereafter explain what government is.

The laws are properly but the conditions of civil association. The people submit themselves to the laws, and ought to enjoy the right of making them; it pertains only to those who associate to regulate the terms of the society. But how do they regulate them? Is it by a common agreement, by a sudden inspiration? Has the body politic an organ for declaring its will? Who gives to that body the necessary foresight to form these acts and publish them beforehand? Or how are they declared at the moment of need? How can an unenlightened multitude, which often does not know what it wants, since it so seldom knows what is good for it, execute, of itself, so great, so difficult an enterprise as a system of legislation? Of themselves the people always will the good, but of themselves they do not always see in what it consists. The general will is always right, but the judgment that guides it is not always enlightened. It is therefore necessary to make the people see things as they are, and sometimes as they ought to appear, to point out to them the right path which they are seeking, to guard them from the seducing voice of private wills, and, helping them to see how times and places are connected, to induce them to balance the attraction of immediate and sensible advantage against the apprehension of unknown and distant evil. Individuals see the good they reject; the public wills the good it does not see. All have equally need for guidance. Some must have their wills made conformable to their reason, and others must be taught what it is they will. From this increase of public knowledge would result the union of judgment and will in the social body; from that union comes the harmony of the parties and the highest power of the whole. From thence is born the necessity of a legislator.

To discover those happy rules of government which would agree with every nation could only be the work of some superior intelligence, acquainted with all the passions of men, but liable to none of them; who, without bearing any affinity to our nature, knew it perfectly; whose happiness was independent of ours, but who still condescended to make us the object of his care; and who having persevered through a long course of years in the pursuit of distant glory, could enjoy in other ages the reward of his unwearied zeal. In short, gods would be required to give laws to mankind. ...

Those who dare to undertake the institution of a people must feel themselves capable, as it were, of changing human nature, of transforming each individual, who by himself is a perfect and solitary whole, into a part of a much greater whole, from which he in some measure receives his being and his life; of altering the constitution of man for the purpose of strengthening it; of substituting a moral and partial existence instead of the physical and independent existence which we have all received from nature. They must, in a word, remove from man his own proper energies to bestow upon him those which are strange to him, and which he cannot employ without the assistance of others. The more those natural powers are annihilated, the more august and permanent are those which he acquires, and the more solid and perfect is the institution: so that if each citizen is nothing and can do nothing but when combined with all the other citizens, and the force acquired by the whole from this combination is equal or superior to the sum of all the natural forces of all these individuals, it may be said that legislation is at the highest point of perfection which human talents can attain.

The legislator is in every sense a most extraordinary man in the State. If he must be so from his genius, he is no less so from his employment, which is neither magistracy nor sovereignty. This employment, which constitutes the republic, enters not into its constitution; it is a particular and superior function, which has nothing in common with human empire; because, if he who commands men must not preside over the laws, he who presides over the laws must not have the command over men: otherwise his laws, employed as the ministers of his passions, would frequently merely perpetuate his injustices; and it would be impossible to prevent private aims from defiling the sanctity of his work. ...

He who compiles the laws, therefore, has not, nor ought he to have, any right to legislate, and the people cannot, even if they should be inclined, deprive themselves of that incommunicable right, because, according to the fundamental compact, it is only the general will that can compel individuals, and it can never be known whether a private will is conformable to the general will until it has been submitted to the free vote of the people. ...

Every free act must be produced by the concurrence of two causes: the one moral, that is to say, the will which must resolve upon the act, the other physical, that is to say, the power which must execute it. When I go towards an object, it is necessary, in the first place, that I should will to go; and, secondly, that my feet should bear me. If a paralytic person should will to go, and an active man should not will, both would remain where they were. The body politic has the same moving forces: and we find equally in it, as in the natural body, both force and will; the latter distinguished by the name of "legislative power," and the former by that of "executive power." Nothing is or should be done without their concurrence.

We have seen that the legislative power belongs to the people, and can belong to that body only. It is easy to see, on the contrary, by the principles already established, that the executive power cannot belong to the generality as legislator or Sovereign, because that power consists only in individual acts, which are not to be performed by the law, and consequently neither by the Sovereign, all whose acts must be laws.

It is therefore necessary that the public force should have an agent of its own which shall unite and apply that force according to the direction of the general will, to serve as the means of communication between the State and the Sovereign, and to form a sort of public person, in which, as in a man, the union of mind and body should be found. This is the reason why the government in a State is generally, and very improperly, confounded with the Sovereign, of which it is but the minister.

What then is that government? An intermediate body established between the subjects and the Sovereign, for their mutual correspondence, charged with the execution of the laws, and the maintenance of both civil and political liberty.

The members of this body are denominated "magistrates" or "kings," that is to say, "governors"; and the body collectively takes the name of "prince." Thus those who think that the act by which a people submit themselves to their chiefs is not a contract have good foundation for their opinion. That act is certainly no more than a commission, an employment, under which, simply as officers of the Sovereign, the members of government exercise in the name of the Sovereign the power delegated to them, and which may be limited, modified, or recalled at the pleasure of the Sovereign, the alienation of such a right being incompatible with the nature of the social body, and contrary to the end of association.

I therefore give the name of "government" or "supreme administration" to the justifiable exercise of the executive power; and "prince" or "magistrate" to the man or body charged with that administration.

It is in government that those intermediate powers are found whose connections constitute that of the whole with the whole, or of the Sovereign with the State. One can represent this last relation as that between the extreme terms of a continuous proportion of which the mean proportional is government. The government receives from the Sovereign the orders which it transmits to the people; and, to hold the State in proper balance, it is necessary, when everything is considered, to keep upon an equality the power of the government, taken in itself, and the power of the citizens, who are sovereigns in one view and subjects in another.

Further, not one of these three states can be altered without instantly destroying the proportion. If the Sovereign wants to govern, or if the magistrate wants to make laws, or if the subjects refuse to obey, disorder succeeds regularity; and, as force and will can then no longer act in concert, the State is dissolved, and must of course fall into despotism or anarchy. Finally, as there can be but one mean proportional between each relation, there cannot possibly be more than one good government in a State. But, as a thousand events may change the relations of a people, not only may different systems of government be good for different peoples, but for the same people at different periods. ...

The less the private wills are related to the general will, that is, manners and morals to laws, the more the restraining power should be augmented. Therefore, the government, that it may be adequate to the duty required from it, should be made strong in proportion to the number of the people.

On the other hand, as the increasing size of the State presents to the depositaries of the public authority greater temptation and opportunity to abuse their power, the greater force it is necessary to give the government for the purpose of controlling the people, the more should the power of the Sovereign be augmented, that it may control the government. ...

There is this essential difference between the State and the government: the former is self-existent, and the existence of the latter depends entirely on the Sovereign. Thus the ruling will of the prince neither is nor ought to be anything more than the general will or the law; his force is only the public force concentrated in his hands: if he attempts to execute on his own authority any absolute and independent act, the chain which combines the whole relaxes immediately. And if at last the private will of the prince is more active than the will of the Sovereign, and the public force in his hands is employed to enforce obedience to this private will, so that there are in effect two sovereigns, the one by right, and the other in fact, at that moment the social union ceases, and the body politic is dissolved.

It is, however, necessary that the government should so far have a real existence and life as to be distinguishable from the body of the State; in order that all its members should be able to act in concert and work for the end for which it was instituted, it must have a particular *self*, a sensibility common to its members, and a force and will sufficient for its preservation. This distinct existence supposes assemblies and councils, a power to deliberate and resolve, rights, titles, and privileges which belong to the prince alone, and which render the situation of a magistrate more honourable in proportion as it is more laborious. The great difficulty of forming a body of government lies in ordering this subaltern whole within the whole in such a manner that the general constitution may not be altered by giving too much strength to this part; that the particular force necessary for preserving itself may be kept distinct from the public force which is necessary to preserve the State; and in fine, that on every occasion the government may be sacrificed to the people, and not the people to the government. ...

So long as several men unite and consider themselves as one body, they have but one will, which is to promote the common safety and general wellbeing. While this union continues, all the springs of the State will be vigorous and simple, the maxims by which they are regulated will be clear and comprehensible; and there will be no jarring, opposing interests; the common good will then be everywhere evident, and nothing will be necessary but a sound understanding to perceive it. ...

A State thus governed requires but very few laws; and whenever it becomes necessary to promulgate new ones, the necessity is perceived universally. He who proposes them only says what all have already felt, and neither faction nor eloquence is required to obtain the passage of a measure which each person has already resolved to adopt, as soon as he is sure that the others will act with him. ...

But when the social bond once begins to relax and the State to grow weak, when private interests begin to take the lead, and smaller societies have an influence on the greater, the common interest changes and finds many opposers: there is no longer unanimity of opinion; the general will is no longer the will of all; everything is contested; and the best advice is never adopted without much dispute and opposition.

Finally, when a State upon the brink of ruin supports only a vain illusory form and the social bond no longer unites the hearts of the people, and when the sacred name of public good is made use of to cover the basest interest, then the general will is silenced; and every one, being directed by secret motives, no more gives an opinion as a citizen than if the State had never existed; decrees which have no other object but private interest are then passed, to which the name of laws is falsely given.

But does it follow that the general will is annihilated or corrupted? No: it will remain always constant, unalterable, and pure; but it is rendered subordinate to other wills, which domineer over it. In this state of affairs, though each individual detaches his interest from the common interest, yet he finds it impossible to separate them entirely; but his part of the common ill appears trifling to him when balanced against some private advantage which he has in view. This particular object only excepted, he is in every point as solicitous as any other member to promote the general welfare on his own account. Even by selling his vote for money he does not destroy his own general will, he only eludes it. The fault which such a man commits is that of changing the state of the question, and answering something else than what he was asked: instead of saying by his vote, "It is advantageous to the State," he says, "It is advantageous to such a man, or to such a party, that such a motion should pass." Thus the law for regulating public assemblies is not so much intended to maintain there the general will as to enforce the full and clear repetition of the question on which that will is to determine. ...

The manner of conducting general affairs is the best criterion by which to judge of the morality and health of the body politic. In proportion to the degree of concord which reigns in the assemblies, that is, the nearer opinion approaches unanimity, the more the general will predominates; while tumults, dissensions, and long debates declare the ascendancy of private interests and the declining situation of the State. ...

There is one law only which, by its nature, requires unanimous consent; I mean the social compact: for civil association is the most voluntary of all acts; every man being born free and master of himself, no person can under any pretense whatever subject him without his consent. To affirm that the son of a slave is born a slave is to pronounce that he is not born a man.

Should there be any men who oppose the social compact, their opposition will not invalidate it, but only hinder their being included: they are foreigners among citizens. When the State is instituted, residence constitutes consent; to inhabit a territory is to submit to the sovereignty.

Except in this original contract, a majority of votes is sufficient to bind all the others. This is a consequence of the contract itself. But it may be asked how a man can be free and yet forced to conform to the will of others. How are the opposers free when they are in submission to laws to which they have never consented?

I answer that the question is not fairly stated. The citizen consents to all the laws, to those which are passed in spite of his opposition, and even to those which sentence him to punishment if he violates any one of them. The constant will of all the members of the State is the general will; it is by that they are citizens and free. When any law is proposed in the assembly of the people, the ques-tion is not precisely to enquire whether they approve the proposition or reject it, but if it is conformable or not to the general will, which is their will. Each citizen, in giving his suffrage, states his mind on that question; and the general will is found by counting the votes. When, therefore, the motion which I opposed carries, it only proves to me that I was mistaken, and that what I believed to be the general will was not so. If my particular opinion had prevailed, I should have done what I was not willing to do, and, consequently, I should not have been in a state of freedom. ...

In the same manner as the general will is declared by the law, the public judgment is declared by the censorship; public opinion is the kind of law of which the censor is the minister, and which he only causes to be applied to particular cases, after the example of the prince.

The censors are so far from being the arbiters of the people's opinion, that their business is only to declare it, and whenever they cease to do so faithfully, their decisions are vain and of no effect. ...

"Of Justice"

David Hume

That Justice is useful to society, and consequently that *part* of its merit, at least, must arise from that consideration, it would be a superfluous undertaking to prove. That public utility is the *sole* origin of justice, and that reflections on the beneficial consequences of this virtue are the *sole* foundation of its merit; this proposition, being more curious and important, will better deserve our examination and enquiry

Let us suppose that nature has bestowed on the human race such profuse *abundance* of all *external* conveniencies, that, without any uncertainty in the event, without any care or industry on our part, every individual finds himself fully provided with whatever his most voracious appetites can want, or luxurious imagination wish or desire. His natural beauty, we shall suppose, surpasses all acquired ornaments: the perpetual clemency of the seasons renders useless all clothes or covering: the raw herbage affords him the most delicious fare; the clear fountain, the richest beverage. No laborious occupation required: no tillage: no navigation. Music, poetry, and contemplation form his sole business: conversation, mirth, and friendship his sole amusement.

From *An Enquiry Concerning the Principles of Morals* (London: A. Millar, 1751).

It seems evident that, in such a happy state, every other social virtue would flourish, and receive tenfold increase; but the cautious, jealous virtue of justice would never once have been dreamed of. For what purpose make a partition of goods, where every one has already more than enough? Why give rise to property, where there cannot possibly be any injury? Why call this object *mine*, when upon the seizure of it by another, I need but stretch out my hand to possess myself of what is equally valuable? Justice, in that case, being totally useless, would be an idle ceremonial, and could never possibly have place in the catalogue of virtues.

We see, even in the present necessitous condition of mankind, that, wherever any benefit is bestowed by nature in an unlimited abundance, we leave it always in common among the whole human race, and make no subdivisions of right and property. Water and air, though the most necessary of all objects, are not challenged by [sic] of individuals; nor can any man commit injustice by the most lavish use and enjoyment of these blessings. In fertile extensive countries, with few inhabitants, land is regarded on the same footing. And no topic is so much insisted on by those, who defend the liberty of the seas, as the unexhausted use of them in navigation. Were the advantages, procured by navigation, as inexhaustible, these reasoners had never had any adversaries to refute; nor had any claims ever been advanced of a separate, exclusive dominion over the ocean.

It may happen in some countries, at some periods, that there be established a property in water, none in land; if the latter be in greater abundance than can be used by the inhabitants, and the former be found, with difficulty, and in very small quantities.

Again; suppose, that, though the necessities of human race continue the same as at present, yet the mind is so enlarged, and so replete with friendship and generosity, that every man has the utmost tenderness for every man, and feels no more concern for his own interest than for that of his fellow; it seems evident, that the use of justice would, in this case, be suspended by such an extensive benevolence, nor would the divisions and barriers of property and obligation have ever been thought of. Why should I bind another, by a deed or promise, to do me any good office, when I know that he is

beforehand prompted, by the strongest inclination, to seek my happiness, and would, of himself, perform the desired service; except the hurt, he thereby receives, be greater than the benefit accruing to me? In which case, he knows, that, from my innate humanity and friendship, I should be the first to oppose myself to his imprudent generosity. Why raise landmarks between my neighbour's field and mine, when my heart has made no division between our interests; but shares all his joys and sorrows with the same force and vivacity as if originally my own? Every man, upon this supposition, being a second self to another, would trust all his interests to the discretion of every man; without jealousy, without partition, without distinction. And the whole human race of mankind would form only one family; where all would lie in common, and was used freely, without regard to property; but cautiously too, with as entire regard to the necessities of each individual, as if our own interests were most intimately concerned.

In the present disposition of the human heart, it would, perhaps, be difficult to find complete instances of such enlarged affections; but still we may observe, that the case of families approaches towards it; and the stronger is the mutual benevolence among the individuals, the nearer it approaches; till all distinction of property be, in a great measure, lost and confounded among them. Between married persons, the cement of friendship is by the laws supposed so strong as to abolish all division of possessions; and has often, in reality, the force ascribed to it. And it is observable, that, during the ardour of new enthusiasms, when every principle is inflamed into extravagance, the community of goods has frequently been attempted; and nothing but experience of its inconveniencies, from the returning or disguised selfishness of men, could make the imprudent fanatics adopt anew the ideas of justice and of separate property. So true is it, that that virtue derives its existence altogether from its necessary *use* to the intercourse and social state of mankind.

To make this truth more evident, let us reverse the foregoing suppositions; and carrying everything to the opposite extreme, consider what would be the effect of these new situations. Suppose a society to fall into such want of all common necessaries, that the utmost frugality and industry cannot preserve the greater number from suffering;

it will readily, I believe, be admitted, that the strict laws of justice are suspended, in such a pressing emergency, and give place to the stronger motives of necessity and self-preservation. Is it any crime, after a shipwreck, to seize whatever means or instrument of safety one can lay hold of, without regard to former limitations of property? Or if a city besieged were dying with hunger; can we imagine, that men will see any means of life before them, and perish from a scrupulous regard to what, in other situations, would be the rules of equity and justice? The use and tendency of that virtue is to procure happiness and security, by preserving order in society: but where the society is ready to perish from extreme necessity, no greater evil can be dreaded from violence and injustice; and every man may now provide for himself by all the means, which prudence can dictate, or humanity permit. The public, even in less urgent necessities, opens granaries, without the consent of proprietors; as justly supposing, that the authority of magistracy may, consistent with equity, extend so far: but were any number of men to assemble, without the tie of laws or civil jurisdiction; would an equal partition of bread in a famine, even without the proprietor's consent, be regarded as criminal or injurious?

Suppose also, that it should be a virtuous man's fate to fall into the society of ruffians, remote from the protection of laws and government; what conduct must he embrace in that melancholy situation? He sees such a desperate rapaciousness prevail; such a disregard to equity, such contempt of order, such stupid blindness to future consequences, as must immediately have the most tragical conclusion, and must terminate in destruction to the greater number, and in a total dissolution of society to the rest. He, meanwhile, can have no other expedient than to arm himself, to whomever the sword he seizes, or the buckler, may belong: make provision of all means of defence and security: And his particular regard to justice being no longer of use to his own safety or that of others, he must consult the dictates of self-preservation, without concern for those who no longer merit his care and attention.

When any man, even in political society, renders himself, by his crimes, obnoxious to the public, he is punished by the laws in his goods and person; that is, the ordinary rules of justice are, with regard to him, suspended for a moment, and it becomes equitable to inflict on him, for the *benefit* of society, what, otherwise, he could not suffer without wrong or injury.

The rage and violence of public war; what is it but a suspension of justice among the warring parties, who perceive, that that virtue is now no longer of any *use* or *advantage* to them? The laws of war, which then succeed to those of equity and justice, are rules calculated for the *advantage* and *utility* of that particular state, in which men are now placed. And were a civilized nation engaged with barbarians, who observed no rules even of war, the former must also suspend their observance of them, where they no longer serve to any purpose; and must render every action or encounter as bloody and pernicious as possible to the first aggressors.

Thus, the rules of equity or justice depend entirely on the particular state and condition, in which men are placed, and owe their origin and existence to that utility, which results to the public from their strict and regular observance. Reverse, in any considerable circumstance, the condition of men: Produce extreme abundance or extreme necessity: Implant in the human breast perfect moderation and humanity, or perfect rapaciousness and malice: By rendering justice totally *useless*, you thereby totally destroy its essence, and suspend its obligation upon mankind. ...

The more we vary our views of human life, and the newer and more unusual the lights are, in which we survey it, the more shall we be convinced, that the origin here assigned for the virtue of justice is real and satisfactory.

Were there a species of creatures intermingled with men, which, though rational, were possessed of such inferior strength, both of body and mind, that they were incapable of all resistance, and could never, upon the highest provocation, make us feel the effects of their resentment; the necessary consequence, I think, is that we should be bound by the laws of humanity, to give gentle usage to these creatures, but should not, properly speaking, lie under any restraint of justice with regard to them, nor could they possess any right or property, exclusive of such arbitrary lords. Our intercourse with them could not be called society, which supposes a degree of equality; but absolute command on the one side, and servile obedience on the other. Whatever we covet, they must instantly resign: Our permission is the only tenure, by which they hold their possessions: Our compassion and kindness the only check, by which they curb our lawless will: And as no inconvenience ever results from the exercise of a power, so firmly established in nature, the restraints of justice and property, being totally *useless*, would never have place in so unequal a confederacy.

This is plainly the situation of men, with regard to animals; and how far these may be said to possess reason, I leave it to others to determine. The great superiority of civilized Europeans above barbarous Indians, tempted us to imagine ourselves on the same footing with regard to them, and made us throw off all restraints of justice, and even of humanity, in our treatment of them. In many nations, the female sex are reduced to like slavery, and are rendered incapable of all property, in opposition to their lordly masters. But though the males, when united, have in all countries, bodily force sufficient to maintain this severe tyranny, yet such are the insinuation, address, and charms of their fair companions, that they are commonly able to break the confederacy, and share with the superior sex in all the rights and privileges of society.

Were the human species so framed by nature as that each individual possessed within himself every faculty, requisite both for his own preservation and for the propagation of his kind: Were all society and intercourse cut off between man and man, by the primary intention of the supreme Creator: It seems evident, that so solitary a being would be as much incapable of justice, as of social discourse and conversation. Where mutual regards and forbearance serve no manner of purpose, they would never direct the conduct of any reasonable man. The headlong course of the passions would be checked by no reflection on future consequences. And as each man is here supposed to love himself alone, and to depend only on himself and his own activity for safety and happiness, he would, on every occasion, to the utmost of his power, challenge the preference above every other being, to none of which he is bound by any ties, either of nature or of interest.

But suppose the conjunction of the sexes to be established in nature, a family immediately arises; and particular rules being found requisite for its subsistence, these are immediately embraced; though without comprehending the rest of mankind within their prescriptions. Suppose that several families unite together into one society, which is totally disjoined from all others, the rules, which preserve peace and order, enlarge themselves to the utmost extent of that society; but being entirely useless, lose their force when carried one step farther. But again suppose, that several distinct societies maintain a kind of intercourse for mutual convenience and advantage, the boundaries of justice still grow larger and larger, in proportion to the largeness of men's views, and the force of their mutual connexions. History, experience, reason sufficiently instruct us in this natural progress of human sentiments, and in the gradual increase of our regards to property and justice, in proportion as we become acquainted with the extensive utility of that virtue.

If we examine the *particular* laws, by which justice is directed, and property determined; we shall still be presented with the same conclusion. The good of mankind is the only object of all these laws and regulations. Not only it is requisite, for the peace and interest of society, that men's possessions should be separated; but the rules, which we follow in making the separation, are such as can best be contrived to serve farther the interests of society.

We shall suppose that a creature, possessed of reason, but unacquainted with human nature, deliberates with himself what rules of justice or property would best promote public interest, and establish peace and security among mankind: His most obvious thought would be, to assign the largest possessions to the most extensive virtue, and give every one the power of doing good, proportioned to his inclination. In a perfect theocracy, where a being, infinitely intelligent, governs by particular volitions, this rule would certainly have place, and might serve to the wisest purposes: But were mankind to execute such a law; (so great is the uncertainty of merit, both from its natural obscurity, and from the self-conceit of each individual) that no determinate rule of conduct would ever result from it; and the total dissolution of society must be the immediate consequence. Fanatics may suppose, *that dominion is founded in grace,* and *that saints alone inherit the earth*; but the civil magistrate very justly puts these sublime theorists on the same footing with common robbers, and teaches them, by the severest discipline, that a rule, which, in speculation, may seem the most advantageous to society, may yet be found, in practice, totally pernicious and destructive. ...

It must, indeed, be confessed, that nature is so liberal to mankind, that were all her presents equally divided among the species, and improved by art and industry, every individual would enjoy all the necessaries, and even most of the comforts of life; nor would ever be liable to any ills, but such as might accidentally arise from the sickly frame and constitution of his body. It must also be confessed, that, wherever we depart from this equality, we rob the poor of more satisfaction than we add to the rich, and that the slight gratification of a frivolous vanity, in one individual, frequently costs more than bread to many families, and even provinces. It may appear withal, that the rule of equality, as it would be highly *useful*, is not altogether *impracticable*; but has taken place, at least in an imperfect degree, in some republics; particularly that of Sparta; where it was attended, it is said, with the most beneficial consequences. Not to mention that the Agrarian laws, so frequently claimed in Rome, and carried into execution in many Greek cities, proceeded, all of them, from a general idea of the utility of this principle.

But historians, and even common sense, may inform us, that, however specious these ideas of *perfect* equality may seem, they are really, at bottom, *impracticable*; and were they not so, would be extremely *pernicious* to human society. Render possessions of men ever so equal, their different degrees of art, care, and industry will immediately break that equality. Or if you check these virtues, you reduce society to the extremest indigence; and instead of preventing want and beggary in a few, render it unavoidable to the whole community. The most rigorous inquisition too, is requisite to watch every inequality on its first appearance; and the most severe jurisdiction, to punish and redress it. But besides, that so much authority must soon degenerate into tyranny, and be exerted with great partialities; who can possibly be possessed of it, in such a situation as is here supposed? Perfect equality of possessions, destroying all subordination, weakens extremely the authority of magistracy, and must reduce all power nearly to a level, as well as property.

We may conclude, therefore, that, in order to establish law for the regulation of property, we must be acquainted with the nature and situation of man; must reject appearances, which may be false, though specious; and must search for those rules, which are, on the whole, most *useful* and *beneficial*. Vulgar sense and slight experience are sufficient for this purpose; where men give not way to too selfish avidity, or too extensive enthusiasm. ...

These reflections are far from weakening the obligations of justice, or diminishing anything from the most sacred attention to property. On the contrary, such sentiments must acquire new force from the present reasoning. For what stronger foundation can be desired or conceived for any duty than to observe, that human society, or even human nature, could not subsist, without the establishment of it, and will still arrive at greater degrees of happiness and perfection, the more inviolable the regard is, which is paid to that duty?

Thus we seem, upon the whole, to have attained a knowledge of the force of that principle here insisted on, and can determine what degree of esteem or moral approbation may result from reflections on public interest and utility. The necessity of justice to the support of society is the *sole* foundation of that virtue; and since no moral excellence is more highly esteemed, we may conclude that this circumstance of usefulness has, in general, the strongest energy, and most entire command over our sentiments. It must, therefore, be the source of a considerable part of the merit, ascribed to humanity, benevolence, friendship, public spirit, and other social virtues of that stamp; as it is the *sole* source of the moral approbation paid to fidelity, justice, veracity, integrity, and those other estimable and useful qualities and principles.

A Treatise of Human Nature

David Hume

There are three different species of goods, which we are possess'd of; the internal satisfaction of our minds, the external advantages of our body, and the enjoyment of such possessions as we have acquir'd by our industry and good fortune. We are perfectly secure in the enjoyment of the first. The second may be ravish'd from us, but can be of no advantage to him who deprives us of them. The last only are both expos'd to the violence of others, and may be transferr'd without suffering any loss or alteration; while at the same time, there is not a sufficient quantity of them to supply every one's desires and necessities. As the improvement, therefore, of these goods is the chief advantage of society, so the *instability* of their possession, along with their *scarcity*, is the chief impediment.

In vain shou'd we expect to find, in *uncultivated nature*, a remedy to this inconvenience; or hope for any inartificial principle of the human mind, which might controul those partial affections, and make us overcome the temptations arising from our circumstances. The idea of justice can never serve to this purpose, or be taken for a natural principle, capable of inspiring men with an equitable conduct towards each other. That virtue, as it is now understood, wou'd never have been dream'd of among rude and savage men. For the notion of injury or injustice implies an immorality or vice committed against some other person: And as every immorality is deriv'd from some defect or unsoundness of the passions, and as this defect must be judg'd of, in a great measure, from the ordinary course of nature in the constitution of the mind; 'twill be easy to know, whether we be guilty of any immorality, with regard to others, by considering the natural, and usual force of those several affections, which are directed towards them. Now it appears, that in the original frame of our mind, our strongest attention is confin'd to ourselves; our next is extended to our relations and acquaintance; and 'tis only the weakest which reaches to strangers and indifferent persons. This partiality, then, and unequal affection, must not only have an influence on our behaviour and conduct in society, but even on our ideas of vice and virtue; so as to make us regard any remarkable transgression of such a degree of partiality, either by too great an enlargement, or contraction of the affections, as vicious and immoral. This we may observe in our common judgments concerning actions, where we blame a person, who either centers all his affections in his family, or is so regardless of them, as, in any opposition of interest, to give the preference to a stranger, or mere chance acquaintance. From all which it follows, that our natural uncultivated ideas of morality, instead of providing a remedy for the partiality of our affections, do rather conform themselves to that partiality, and give it an additional force and influence.

The remedy, then, is not deriv'd from nature, but from *artifice*; or more properly speaking, nature provides a remedy in the judgment and understanding, for what is irregular and incommodious in the affections. For when men, from their early education in society, have become sensible of the infinite advantages that result from it, and have besides acquir'd a new affection to company and conversation; and when they have observ'd, that the principal disturbance in society arises from those goods, which we call external, and from their looseness and easy transition from one person to another; they must seek for a remedy, by putting these goods, as far as possible, on the same footing with the fix'd and constant advantages of the mind

From *A Treatise of Human Nature*, L. A. Selby-Bigge, ed. (Oxford: Clarendon Press, 1888).

and body. This can be done after no other manner, than by a convention enter'd into by all the members of the society to bestow stability on the possession of those external goods, and leave every one in the peaceable enjoyment of what he may acquire by his fortune and industry. By this means, every one knows what he may safely possess; and the passions are restrain'd in their partial and contradictory motions. Nor is such a restraint contrary to these passions; for if so, it cou'd never be enter'd into, nor maintain'd; but it is only contrary to their heedless and impetuous movement. Instead of departing from our own interest, or from that of our nearest friends, by abstaining from the possessions of others, we cannot better consult both these interests, than by such a convention; because it is by that means we maintain society, which is so necessary to their well-being and subsistence, as well as to our own. ...

It is only a general sense of common interest; which sense all the members of the society express to one another, and which induces them to regulate their conduct by certain rules. I observe, that it will be for my interest to leave another in the possession of his goods, *provided* he will act in the same manner with regard to me. He is sensible of a like interest in the regulation of his conduct. When this common sense of interest is mutually express'd, and is known to both, it produces a suitable resolution and behaviour. And this may properly enough be call'd a convention or agreement betwixt us, tho' without the interposition of a promise; since the actions of each of us have a reference to those of the other, and are perform'd upon the supposition, that something is to be perform'd on the other part. Two men, who pull the oars of a boat, do it by an agreement or convention, tho' they have never given promises to each other. Nor is the rule concerning the stability of possession the less deriv'd from human conventions, that it arises gradually, and acquires force by a slow progression, and by our repeated experience of the inconveniences of transgressing it. On the contrary, this experience assures us still more, that the sense of interest has become common to all our fellows, and gives us a confidence of the future regularity of their conduct: And 'tis only on the expectation of this, that our moderation and abstinence are founded. In like manner are languages gradually establish'd by human conventions without any

promise. In like manner do gold and silver become the common measures of exchange, and are esteem'd sufficient payment for what is of a hundred times their value.

After this convention, concerning abstinence from the possessions of others, is enter'd into, and every one has acquir'd a stability in his possessions, there immediately arise the ideas of justice and injustice; as also those of *property, right*, and *obligation*. The latter are altogether unintelligible without first understanding the former. Our property is nothing but those goods, whose constant possession is establish'd by the laws of society, that is, by the laws of justice. Those, therefore, who make use of the words *property*, or *right*, or *obligation*, before they have explain'd the origin of justice, or even make use of them in that explication, are guilty of a very gross fallacy, and can never reason upon any solid foundation. A man's property is some object related to him. This relation is not natural, but moral, and founded on justice. 'Tis very preposterous, therefore, to imagine, that we can have any idea of property, without fully comprehending the nature of justice, and shewing its origin in the artifice and contrivance of men. The origin of justice explains that of property. The same artifice gives rise to both. As our first and most natural sentiment of morals is founded on the nature of our passions, and gives the preference to ourselves and friends, above strangers; 'tis impossible there can be naturally any such thing as a fix'd right or property, while the opposite passions of men impel them in contrary directions, and are not restrain'd by any convention or agreement.

No one can doubt, that the convention for the distinction of property, and for the stability of possession, is of all circumstances the most necessary to the establishment of human society, and that after the agreement for the fixing and observing of this rule, there remains little or nothing to be done towards settling a perfect harmony and concord. All the other passions, beside this of interest, are either easily restrain'd, or are not of such pernicious consequence, when indulg'd. *Vanity* is rather to be esteem'd a social passion, and a bond of union among men. *Pity* and *love* are to be consider'd in the same light. And as to *envy* and *revenge*, tho' pernicious, they operate only by intervals, and are directed against particular persons, whom we consider as our superiors or enemies. This avidity alone, of acquiring goods and possessions for ourselves and our nearest friends, is insatiable, perpetual, universal, and directly destructive of society. There scarce is any one, who is not actuated by it; and there is no one, who has not reason to fear from it, when it acts without any restraint, and gives way to its first and most natural movements. So that upon the whole, we are to esteem the difficulties in the establishment of society, to be greater or less, according to those we encounter in regulating and restraining this passion.

'Tis certain, that no affection of the human mind has both a sufficient force, and a proper direction to counter-balance the love of gain, and render men fit members of society, by making them abstain from the possessions of others. Benevolence to strangers is too weak for this purpose; and as to the other passions, they rather inflame this avidity, when we observe, that the larger our possessions are, the more ability we have of gratifying all our appetites. There is no passion, therefore, capable of controlling the interested affection, but the very affection itself, by an alteration of its direction. Now this alteration must necessarily take place upon the least reflection; since 'tis evident, that the passion is much better satisfy'd by its restraint, than by its liberty, and that in preserving society, we make much greater advances in the acquiring possessions, than in the solitary and forlorn condition, which must follow upon violence and an universal licence. The question, therefore, concerning the wickedness or goodness of human nature, enters not in the least into that other question concerning the origin of society; nor is there any thing to be consider'd but the degrees of men's sagacity or folly. For whether the passion of self-interest be esteemed vicious or virtuous, 'tis all a case; since itself alone restrains it: So that if it be virtuous, men become social by their virtue; if vicious, their vice has the same effect.

Now as 'tis by establishing the rule for the stability of possession, that this passion restrains itself; if that rule be very abstruse, and of difficult invention; society must be esteem'd, in a manner, accidental, and the effect of many ages. But if it be found, that nothing can be more simple and obvious than that rule; that every parent, in order to preserve peace among his children, must establish it; and that these first rudiments of justice must every day be improv'd, as the society enlarges: If

all this appear evident, as it certainly must, we may conclude, that 'tis utterly impossible for men to remain any considerable time in that savage condition, which precedes society; but that his very first state and situation may justly be esteem'd social. This, however, hinders not, but that philosophers may, if they please, extend their reasoning to the suppos'd *state of nature*; provided they allow it to be a mere philosophical fiction, which never had, and never cou'd have any reality. Human nature being compos'd of two principal parts, which are requisite in all its actions, the affections and understanding; 'tis certain, that the blind motions of the former, without the direction of the latter, incapacitate men for society: And it may be allow'd us to consider separately the effects, that result from the separate operations of these two component parts of the mind. The same liberty may be permitted to moral, which is allow'd to natural philosophers; and 'tis very usual with the latter to consider any motion as compounded and consisting of two parts separate from each other, tho' at the same time they acknowledge it to be in itself uncompounded and inseparable.

This *state of nature*, therefore, is to be regarded as a mere fiction, not unlike that of the *golden age*, which poets have invented; only with this difference, that the former is describ'd as full of war, violence and injustice; whereas the latter is painted out to us, as the most charming and most peaceable condition, that can possibly be imagin'd. ...

A single act of justice is frequently contrary to *public interest*; and were it to stand alone, without being follow'd by other acts, may, in itself, be very prejudicial to society. When a man of merit, of a beneficent disposition, restores a great fortune to a miser, or a seditious bigot, he has acted justly and laudably, but the public is a real sufferer. Nor is every single act of justice, consider'd apart, more conducive to private interest, than to public; and 'tis easily conceiv'd how a man may impoverish himself by a signal instance of integrity, and have reason to wish, that with regard to that single act, the laws of justice were for a moment suspended in the universe. But however single acts of justice may be contrary, either to public or private interest, 'tis certain, that the whole plan or scheme is highly conducive, or indeed absolutely requisite, both to the support of society, and the well-being of every individual. 'Tis impossible to separate the good from the ill. Property must be stable, and must be fix'd by general rules. Tho' in one instance the public be a sufferer, this momentary ill is amply compensated by the steady prosecution of the rule, and by the peace and order, which it establishes in society. And even every individual person must find himself a gainer, on balancing the account; since, without justice, society must immediately dissolve, and every one must fall into that savage and solitary condition, which is infinitely worse than the worst situation that can possibly be suppos'd in society. When therefore men have had experience enough to observe, that whatever may be the consequence of any single act of justice, perform'd by a single person, yet the whole system of actions, concurr'd in by the whole society, is infinitely advantageous to the whole, and to every part; it is not long before justice and property take place. Every member of society is sensible of this interest: Every one expresses this sense to his fellows, along with the resolution he has taken of squaring his actions by it, on condition that others will do the same. No more is requisite to induce any one of them to perform an act of justice, who has the first opportunity. This becomes an example to others. And thus justice establishes itself by a kind of convention or agreement; that is, by a sense of interest, suppos'd to be common to all, and where every single act is perform'd in expectation that others are to perform the like. Without such a convention, no one wou'd ever have dream'd, that there was such a virtue as justice, or have been induc'd to conform his actions to it. Taking any single act, my justice may be pernicious in every respect; and 'tis only upon the supposition, that others are to imitate my example, that I can be induc'd to embrace that virtue; since nothing but this combination can render justice advantageous, or afford me any motives to conform my self to its rules.

We come now to the *second* question we propos'd, *viz. Why we annex the idea of virtue to justice, and of vice to injustice.* ...After men have found by experience, that their selfishness and confin'd generosity, acting at their liberty, totally incapacitate them for society; and at the same time have observ'd, that society is necessary to the satisfaction of those very passions, they are naturally induc'd to lay themselves under the restraint of such rules, as may render their commerce more safe and commodious. To the imposition then, and observance of these rules, both in general, and in every particular instance, they are at first induc'd only by a regard to interest; and this motive, on the first formation of society, is sufficiently strong and forcible. But when society has become numerous, and has encreas'd to a tribe or nation, this interest is more remote; nor do men so readily perceive, that disorder and confusion follow upon every breach of these rules, as in a more narrow and contracted society. But tho' in our own actions we may frequently lose sight of that interest, which we have in maintaining order, and may follow a lesser and more present interest, we never fail to observe the prejudice we receive, either mediately or immediately, from the injustice of others; as not being in that case either blinded by passion, or byass'd by any contrary temptation. Nay when the injustice is so distant from us, as no way to affect our interest, it still displeases us; because we consider it as prejudicial to human society, and pernicious to every one that approaches the person guilty of it. We partake of their uneasiness by *sympathy*; and as every thing, which gives uneasiness in human actions, upon the general survey, is call'd Vice, and whatever produces satisfaction, in the same manner, is denominated Virtue; this is the reason why the sense of moral good and evil follows upon justice and injustice. And tho' this sense, in the present case, be deriv'd only from contemplating the actions of others, yet we fail not to extend it even to our own actions. The *general rule* reaches beyond those instances, from which it arose; while at the same time we naturally *sympathize* with others in the sentiments they entertain of us. *Thus self-interest is the original motive to the* establishment *of justice*: but a sympathy *with public interest is the source of the* moral approbation, *which attends that virtue.*

Tho' this progress of the sentiments be *natural*, and even necessary, 'tis certain, that it is here forwarded by the artifice of politicians, who, in order to govern men more easily, and preserve peace in human society, have endeavour'd to produce an esteem for justice, and an abhorrence of injustice. ...

As publick praise and blame encrease our esteem for justice; so private education and instruction contribute to the same effect. ...What farther contributes to encrease their solidity, is the interest of our reputation, after the opinion, *that a merit or demerit attends justice or injustice,* is once firmly establish'd among mankind. There is nothing, which touches us more nearly than our reputation, and nothing on which our reputation more depends than our conduct, with relation to the property of others. For this reason, every one, who has any regard to his character, or who intends to live on good terms with mankind, must fix an inviolable law to himself, never, by any temptation, to be induc'd to violate those principles, which are essential to a man of probity and honour.

I shall make only one observation before I leave this subject, *viz.* that tho' I assert, that in the *state of nature*, or that imaginary state, which preceded society, there be neither justice nor injustice, yet I assert not, that it was allowable, in such a state, to violate the property of others. I only maintain, that there was no such thing as property; and consequently cou'd be no such thing as justice or injustice. ...

Tho' the establishment of the rule, concerning the stability of possession, be not only useful, but even absolutely necessary to human society, it can never serve to any purpose, while it remains in such general terms. Some method must be shewn, by which we may distinguish what particular goods are to be assign'd to each particular person, while the rest of mankind are excluded from their possession and enjoyment. Our next business, then, must be to discover the reasons which modify this general rule, and fit it to the common use and practice of the world.

'Tis obvious, that those reasons are not deriv'd from any utility or advantage, which either the *particular* person or the public may reap from his enjoyment of any *particular* goods, beyond what wou'd result from the possession of them by any other person. 'Twere better, no doubt, that every one were possess'd of what is most suitable to him, and proper for his use: But besides, that this relation of fitness may be common to several at once, 'tis liable to so many controversies, and men are so partial and passionate in judging of these controversies, that such a loose and uncertain rule wou'd be absolutely incompatible with the peace of human society. The convention concerning the stability of possession is enter'd into, in order to cut off all occasions of discord and contention; and this end wou'd never be attain'd, were we allow'd to apply this rule differently in every particular case, according to every particular utility, which might be discover'd in such an application. Justice, in her decisions, never regards the fitness or unfitness of objects to particular persons, but conducts herself by more extensive views. Whether a man be generous, or a miser, he is equally well receiv'd by her, and obtains with the same facility a decision in his favour, even for what is entirely useless to him.

It follows, therefore, that the general rule, *that possession must be stable*, is not apply'd by particular judgments, but by other general rules, which must extend to the whole society, and be inflexible either by spite or favour. To illustrate this, I propose the following instance. I first consider men in their savage and solitary condition; and suppose, that being sensible of the misery of that state, and foreseeing the advantages that wou'd result from society, they seek each other's company, and make an offer of mutual protection and assistance. I also suppose, that they are endow'd with such sagacity as immediately to perceive, that the chief impediment to this project of society and partnership lies in the avidity and selfishness of their natural temper; to remedy which, they enter into a convention for the stability of possession, and for mutual restraint and forbearance. ...

'Tis evident, then, that their first difficulty, in this situation, after the general convention for the establishment of society, and for the constancy of possession, is, how to separate their possessions, and assign to each his particular portion, which he must for the future inalterably enjoy. This difficulty will not detain them long; but it must immediately occur to them, as the most natural expedient, that every one continue to enjoy what he is at present master of, and that property or constant possession be conjoin'd to the immediate possession. Such is the effect of custom, that it not only reconciles us to any thing we have long enjoy'd, but even gives us an affection for it, and makes us prefer it to other objects, which may be more valuable, but are less known to us. What has long lain under our eye, and has often been employ'd to our advantage, *that* we are always the most unwilling to part with; but can easily live without possessions, which we never have enjoy'd, and are not accustom'd to. 'Tis evident, therefore, that men wou'd easily acquiesce in this expedient, *that every one continue to enjoy what he is at present possess'd of*; and this is the reason, why they wou'd so naturally agree in preferring it. ...

But we may observe, that tho' the rule of the assignment of property to the present possessor be natural, and by that means useful, yet its utility extends not beyond the first formation of society; nor wou'd any thing be more pernicious, than the constant observance of it; by which restitution wou'd be excluded, and every injustice wou'd be authoriz'd and rewarded. We must, therefore, seek for some other circumstance, that may give rise to property after society is once establish'd; and of this kind, I find four most considerable, *viz.* Occupation, Prescription, Accession, and Succession. We shall briefly examine each of these, beginning with *Occupation.*

The possession of all external goods is changeable and uncertain; which is one of the most considerable impediments to the establishment of society, and is the reason why, by universal agreement, express or tacite, men restrain themselves by what we now call the rules of justice and equity. The misery of the condition, which precedes this restraint, is the cause why we submit to that remedy as quickly as possible; and this affords us an easy reason, why we annex the idea of property to the first possession, or to *occupation.* Men are unwilling to leave property in suspence, even for the shortest time, or open the least door to violence and disorder. To which we may add, that the first possession always engages the attention most; and did we neglect it, there wou'd be no colour of reason for assigning property to any succeeding possession.

There remains nothing, but to determine exactly, what is meant by possession; and this is not so easy as may at first sight be imagin'd. We are said to be in possession of any thing, not only when we immediately touch it, but also when we are so situated with respect to it, as to have it in our power to use it; and may move, alter, or destroy it, according to our present pleasure or advantage. This relation, then, is a species of cause and effect; and as property is nothing but a stable possession, deriv'd from the rules of justice, or the conventions of men, 'tis to be consider'd as the same species of relation. But here we may observe, that as the power of using any object becomes more or less certain, according as the interruptions we may meet with are more or less probable; and as this probability may increase by insensible degrees; 'tis in many cases impossible to determine when possession begins or ends; nor is there any certain standard, by which we can decide such controversies. ...

But it often happens, that the title of first possession becomes obscure thro' time; and that 'tis impossible to determine many controversies, which may arise concerning it. In that case long possession or *prescription* naturally takes place, and gives a person a sufficient property in any thing he enjoys. The nature of human society admits not of any great accuracy; nor can we always remount to the first origin of things, in order to determine their present condition. Any considerable space of time sets objects at such a distance, that they seem, in a manner, to lose their reality, and have as little influence on the mind, as if they never had been in being. A man's title, that is clear and certain at present, will seem obscure and doubtful fifty years hence, even tho' the facts, on which it is founded, shou'd be prov'd with the greatest evidence and certainty. The same facts have not the same influence after so long an interval of time. And this may be receiv'd as a convincing argument for our preceding doctrine with regard to property and justice. Possession during a long tract of time conveys a title to any object. But as 'tis certain, that, however every thing be produc'd in time, there is nothing real, that is produc'd by time; it follows, that property being produc'd by time, is not any thing real in the objects, but is the offspring of the sentiments, on which alone time is found to have any influence.

We acquire the property of objects by *accession,* when they are connected in an intimate manner with objects that are already our property, and at the same time are inferior to them. Thus the fruits of our garden, the offspring of our cattle, and the work of our slaves, are all of them esteem'd our property, even before possession. Where objects are connected together in the imagination, they are apt to be put on the same footing, and are commonly suppos'd to be endow'd with the same qualities. We readily pass from one to the other, and make no difference in our judgments concerning them; especially if the latter be inferior to the former.

The right of *succession* is a very natural one, from the presum'd consent of the parent or near relation, and from the general interest of mankind, which requires, that men's possessions shou'd pass to those, who are dearest to them, in order to render them more industrious and frugal. Perhaps these causes are seconded by the influence of *relation*, or the association of ideas, by which we are naturally directed to consider the son after the parent's decease, and ascribe to him a title to his father's possessions. Those goods must become the property of some body: But *of whom* is the question. Here 'tis evident the persons children naturally present themselves to the mind; and being already connected to those possessions by means of their deceas'd parent, we are apt to connect them still farther by the relation of property. Of this there are many parallel instances.

However useful, or even necessary, the stability of possession may be to human society, 'tis attended with very considerable inconveniences. The relation of fitness or suitableness ought never to enter into consideration, in distributing the properties of mankind; but we must govern ourselves by rules, which are more general in their application, and more free from doubt and uncertainty. Of this kind is *present* possession upon the first establishment of society; and afterwards *occupation, prescription, accession*, and *succession*. As these depend very much on chance, they must frequently prove contradictory both to men's wants and de-

sires; and persons and possessions must often be very ill adjusted. This is a grand inconvenience, which calls for a remedy. To apply one directly, and allow every man to seize by violence what he judges to be fit for him, wou'd destroy society; and therefore the rules of justice seek some medium betwixt a rigid stability, and this changeable and uncertain adjustment. But there is no medium better than that obvious one, that possession and property shou'd always be stable, except when the proprietor consents to bestow them on some other person. This rule can have no ill consequence, in occasioning wars and dissentions; since the proprietor's consent, who alone is concern'd, is taken along in the alienation: And it may serve to many good purposes in adjusting property to persons. Different parts of the earth produce different commodities; and not only so, but different men both are by nature fitted for different employments, and attain to greater perfection in any one, when they confine themselves to it alone. All this requires a mutual exchange and commerce; for which reason the translation of property by consent is founded on a law of nature, as well as its stability without such a consent. ...

3 Industrial Revolution

In the nineteenth-century Industrial Revolution a series of technological innovations in the methods of production and economic distribution occurred which profoundly affected social organization in Europe and North America. Before the Industrial Revolution most Europeans were either farmers living in the countryside or small-scale craftsmen and tradesmen living in the cities. With the invention of steam and later electric-driven machines and assembly-line production, more and more people left the farms to work for wages in large factories run by major industrialists, replacing the small-scale farmer and craftsperson working largely by hand. Because the new factories were more efficient, enormous profits were made. But these profits were not evenly distributed among everyone participating in the production. Those who owned the factories became enormously rich while those who worked in the factories earned barely enough to stay alive. Once farmers had left their farms to work in the factories in the city, they had no means of livelihood except to hire themselves out as wage workers, and since there were many workers competing for available jobs, workers had little choice but to accept the extremely low wages offered them.

It is difficult to imagine today what working conditions would have been like in a woolen mill in Pennsylvania or England in the mid-1800s. With no minimum wage or minimum age; without labor unions or government regulations on health and safety conditions in the factories or pollution controls of any kind; in the absence of unemployment compensation, social security, and so forth, vast disparities quickly began to develop between the wealthy factory owners and the workers in those factories.

It was out of these new social conditions that philosophers began to be concerned with the need for governments to put restraints on business and to regulate working conditions.

READINGS

Jeremy Bentham (1748–1832) was an English legal theorist much concerned with reforming the English legal system. He was witness to both the American and the French revolutions. The supporters of both these revolutions attempted to justify them by appealing to natural law and natural or human rights which they claimed were being unjustly denied. Advocates of both revolutions claimed rebellion is justified when government violates these rights. While Bentham shared with the natural law–natural rights advocates a desire for a fair society, he thought the bloody and totalitarian outcome of the French Revolution showed that rebellion is not the way to secure justice.

Moreover, Bentham's analysis of the nature of law led him to reject the concept of natural law. According to Bentham, real laws have to be enacted and enforced. Rights are created when the legal system imposes an obligation on someone. For example, the traffic law that obligates me to stop at a red light gives you the right to expect me to stop when your light is green and makes me subject to penalty if I proceed through the intersection. But slave owners in slave-owning states face no such penalty. Hence, in Bentham's reasoning, the slave has no right to freedom.

However, he strove to show that the slave *ought* to have the legal right to freedom because it would be to everyone's advantage to change the law and penalize slavery. Bentham held that governments should enact by law whatever rights are useful to the well-being of the society as determined by the utilitarian calculation of the average increase or decrease of pleasure or well-being of all the citizens. This puts the criteria for legislating rights on an empirical, factual basis, rather some unverifiable, metaphysical supposition about innate rights. Nothing could be more certain and transparently clear, Bentham argues, than that people seek pleasure and avoid pain. In the absence of metaphysical or religious certainty concerning the ultimate "good of mankind," he asks, why not give people what will make them happy and act according to the utilitarian principle and produce the greatest amount of happiness for the greatest number of people? The good of the whole community, Bentham argues, is equal to the sum of each individual's happiness.

The great spokesperson for the modern notion of the freedom of the individual is John Stuart Mill (1806–1873), an English philosopher who accepted Bentham's utilitarianism. Like Bentham, Mill rejects the notion of inherent natural rights and argues on utilitarian grounds for the social utility of individual freedom as a justification for having a government which acts to protect and not to abridge those freedoms. Mill's "On Liberty" remains the classic and still controversial statement of the position known as "liberalism." Mill argues that it is socially useful for individuals to be free to do as they please as long as they do not "harm" others, and that the state should not intervene "paternalistically" even to prevent people from harming themselves, either physically or morally. Mill traces the history of various attempts to curb the political power of the ruling elite, for example, limiting the power of the king by the Magna Carta, until finally political power resides in "the people" themselves. He argues that there is a threat that majority rule could impose a tyranny over nonconforming individuals which can be avoided by limiting majority rule to those cases where an individual's behavior actually "harms" others.

According to the German idealist philosopher, Georg Hegel (1770–1831), the state is not a mere summation of the wills of individual members of the community; it is an organic whole with a general will of its own. It is an all-embracing spiritual being, having a mental life and character of its own over and above the life of its individual citizens. For Hegel, the state is not an intellectual abstraction but a real conscious entity evolving toward greater and greater self-awareness, especially as this manifests itself in the attitudes and aspirations of the middle class. Unlike Bentham's view, in which the individual is the building block of society, Hegel argues that the existence of the individual is only possible in a relationship with others. The state is no mere collection of "atomic" individuals because individuals only exist within the state. Individuals do not make the state; rather the state makes the individuals, so the opinions of ordinary citizens are politically important only when they reflect the overriding consciousness of the state as a whole. Actual majority opinion may not reflect the real consciousness of "the people" (i.e., the state) because the individual citizens, even a majority, may not understand their own historical destiny. Only a great man, Hegel says, can interpret what the general will really is. The social arrangements are not negotiated rationally or created conventionally as Enlightenment thinkers said; instead they must reflect the already existing spiritual will of the people at a particular stage of spiritual evolution.

Pierre Kropotkin (1842–1921), a Russian prince and geographer, held an anarchist position that the state is not necessary and is indeed a hindrance to human good. Indeed, insofar as a government's use of force cannot be justified, that force is immoral and deserves to be resisted. Of course, Kropotkin is not suggesting that human beings can exist without some form of social order, but he denies the need for any formal state bureaucracy beyond the traditional system of village or clan mores which exist in all societies however ancient or simple.

Karl Marx (1818–1883) was a German philosopher who collaborated with Friedrich Engels (1820–1895), an industrialist, in developing a socialist analysis of the growth of society based on historical or "scientific" grounds. Marx held that ideas do not cause social change but rather the driving force is economic relations and technology. The change in the means of production during the Industrial Revolution caused capitalism and a capitalist ethic to emerge.

According to Marx, all theories about people are unconsciously designed to support those in power. When small business people at the end of the feudal period wanted to break away from their feudal lords to establish themselves independently in commercial centers, like Paris and London, they developed a theory which defended their new interests—namely, that they had a "right" to be free to move where they wanted, to engage in whatever businesses they saw fit, and to keep whatever money they made. Thus, values, virtues, and truths are relative to the particular society of which they are an integral part.

Marx and Engels developed a powerful critique of capitalism arguing that it led to exploitation of labor, economic chaos, and increasingly severe depressions and imperialism. They thought it inevitable that capitalism would collapse into socialism. They envisioned a socialist state in which the working class would dictate policy and everyone would have their needs met. The last economic stage would be communism during which the state would become unnecessary. Just as the physical world is governed by inexorable laws of nature, so social history is strictly determined by economic inevitability. When Marx predicts the downfall of capitalism, he is not issuing a moral plea that this is what *ought* to happen or what justice demands; he is simply working out in great detail what, according to scientific laws of economic necessity, must surely and inevitably happen. Even philosophical theories, including presumably Marx's own, are the byproduct of historical necessity. One of the lasting legacies of Marx, whether one accepts his theory or not, is the heightened consciousness, after Marx, of the wider social context in which theories arise.

"A Critical Examination of the Declaration of Rights"

Jeremy Bentham

PRELIMINARY OBSERVATIONS

THE Declaration of Rights—I mean the paper published under that name by the French National Assembly in 1791—assumes for its subject-matter a field of disquisition as unbounded in point of extent as it is important in its nature. But the more ample the extent given to any proposition or string of propositions, the more difficult it is to keep the import of it confined without deviation, within the bounds of truth and reason....

The revolution, which threw the government into the hands of the penners and adopters of this declaration, having been the effect of insurrection, the grand object evidently is to justify the cause. But by justifying it, they invite it: in justifying past insurrection, they plant and cultivate a propensity to perpetual insurrection in time future; they sow the seeds of anarchy broad-cast: in justifying the demolition of existing authorities, they undermine all future ones, their own consequently in the number. Shallow and reckless vanity!—They imitate in their conduct the author of that fabled law, according to which the assassination of the prince upon the throne gave to the assassin a title to succeed him. "*People, behold your rights! If a single article of them be violated, insurrection is not your right only, but the most sacred of your duties.*" Such is the constant language, for such is the professed object of this source and model of all laws—this self-consecrated oracle of all nations.

The more *abstract*—that is, the more *extensive* the proposition is, the more liable is it to involve a fallacy. Of fallacies, one of the most natural modifications is that which is called *begging the question*—the abuse of making the abstract proposition resorted to for proof, a lever for introducing, in the company of *other* propositions that are nothing to the purpose, the very proposition which is admitted to stand in need of proof.

Is the provision in question fit in point of expediency to be passed into a law for the government of the French nation?...

Instead of that, as often as the utility of a provision appeared (by reason of the wideness of its extent, for instance) of a doubtful nature, the way taken to clear the doubt was to assert it to be a provision fit to be made law for all men—for all Frenchmen—and for all Englishmen, for example, into the bargain. This medium of proof was the more alluring, inasmuch as to the advantage of removing opposition, was added the pleasure, the sort of titillation so exquisite to the nerve of vanity in a French heart—the satisfaction, to use a homely, but not the less opposite proverb, of teaching grandmothers to suck eggs. Hark! ye citizens of the other side of the water! Can you tell us what rights you have belonging to you? No, that you can't. It's *we* that understand rights: not our own only, but yours into the bargain; while you, poor simple souls! know nothing about the matter. ...

The great enemies of public peace are the selfish and dissocial passions:—necessary as they are— the one to the very existence of each individual, the other to his security. On the part of these affections, a deficiency in point of strength is never to be apprehended: all that is to be apprehended in respect of them, is to be apprehended on the side of their excess. Society is held together only by the sacrifices that men can be induced to make of the gratifications they demand: to obtain these sacrifices is the great difficulty, the great task of government. What has been the object, the perpetual and palpable object, of this declaration of pretended rights? To add as much force as possible to

---

From *The Works of Jeremy Bentham*, Vol. 2, John Bowring, ed. (Edinburgh, 1838–43).

these passions, already but too strong,—to burst the cords that hold them in,—to say to the selfish passions, there—everywhere—is your prey!—to the angry passions, there—everywhere—is your enemy....

The logic of it is of a piece with its morality:—a perpetual vein of nonsense, flowing from a perpetual abuse of words,—words having a variety of meanings, where words with single meanings were equally at hand—the same words used in a variety of meanings in the same page,—words used in meanings not their own, where proper words were equally at hand,—words and propositions of the most unbounded signification, turned loose without any of those exceptions or modifications which are so necessary on every occasion to reduce their import within the compass, not only of right reason, but even of the design in hand, of whatever nature it may be;—the same inaccuracy, the same inattention in the penning of this cluster of truths on which the fare of nations was to hang, as if it had been an oriental tale, or an allegory for a magazine:—stale epigrams, instead of necessary distinctions,—figurative expressions preferred to simple ones,—sentimental conceits, as trite as they are unmeaning, preferred to apt and precise expressions,—frippery ornament preferred to the majestic simplicity of good sound sense,—and the acts of the senate loaded and disfigured by the tinsel of the playhouse.

In a play or a novel, an improper word is but a word: and the impropriety, whether noticed or not, is attended with no consequences. In a body of laws—especially of laws given as constitutional and fundamental ones—an improper word may be a national calamity:—and civil war may be the consequence of it. Out of one foolish word may start a thousand daggers.....

In running over the several articles, I shall on the occasion of each article point out, in the first place, the errors it contains in theory; and then, in the second place, the mischiefs it is pregnant with in practice.

The criticism is verbal:—true, but what else can it be? Words—words without a meaning, or with a meaning too flatly false to be maintained by anybody, are the stuff it is made of. Look to the letter, you find nonsense—look beyond the letter, you find nothing.

Article I

Men [all men] are born and remain free, and equal in respect of rights. Social distinctions cannot be founded, but upon common utility.

In this article are contained, grammatically speaking, two distinct sentences. The first is full of error, the other of ambiguity.

In the first are contained four distinguishable propositions, all of them false—all of them notoriously and undeniably false:

1. That all men are born free.
2. That all men remain free.
3. That all men are born equal in rights.
4. That all men remain (*i.e.*, remain for ever, for the proposition is indefinite and unlimited) equal in rights.

All men are born free? All men remain free? No, not a single man: not a single man that ever was, or is, or will be. All men, on the contrary, are born in subjection, and the most absolute subjection—the subjection of a helpless child to the parents on whom he depends every moment for his existence. In this subjection every man is born—in this subjection he continues for years—for a great number of years—and the existence of the individual and of the species depends upon his so doing.

What is the state of things to which the supposed existence of these supposed rights is meant to bear reference?—a state of things prior to the existence of government, or a state of things subsequent to the existence of government? If to a state prior to the existence of government, what would the existence of such rights as these be to the purpose, even if it were true, in any country where there is such a thing as government? If to a state of things subsequent to the formation of government—if in a country where there is a government, in what single instance—in the instance of what single government, is it true? Setting aside the case of parent and child, let any man name that single government under which any such equality is recognised.

All men born free? Absurd and miserable nonsense! When the great complaint—a complaint made perhaps by the very same people at the same time, is—that so many men are born slaves. Oh! but when we acknowledge them to be born slaves, we refer to the laws in being; which laws being void, as being contrary to those laws of nature which are the efficient causes of those rights of man that we are declaring, the men in question are free in one sense, though slaves in another;—slaves, and free, at the same time:—free in respect of the laws of nature—slaves in respect of the pretended human laws, which, though called laws, are no laws at all, as being contrary to the laws of nature. For such is the difference—the great and perpetual difference, between the good subject, the rational censor of the laws, and the anarchist—between the moderate man and the man of violence. The rational censor, acknowledging the existence of the law he disapproves, proposes the repeal of it: the anarchist, setting up his will and fancy for a law before which all mankind are called upon to bow down at the first word—the anarchist, trampling on truth and decency, denies the validity of the law in question,—denies the existence of it in the character of a law, and calls upon all mankind to rise up in a mass, and resist the execution of it....

All men are born equal in rights. The rights of the heir of the most indigent family equal to the rights of the heir of the most wealthy? In what case is this true? I say nothing of hereditary dignities and powers. Inequalities such as these being proscribed under and by the French government in France, are consequently proscribed by that government under every other government, and consequently have no existence anywhere....

All men (i. e. all human creatures of both sexes) *remain equal in rights.* All men, meaning doubtless all human creatures. The apprentice, then, is equal in rights to his master; he has as much liberty with relation to the master, as the master has with relation to him; he has as much right to command and to punish him; he is as much owner and master of the master's house, as the master himself. The case is the same as between ward and guardian. So again as between wife and husband. The madman has as good a right to confine anybody else, as anybody else has to confine him. The idiot has as much right to govern everybody, as anybody can have to govern him. The physician and the nurse, when called in by the next friend of a sick man seized with a delirium, have no more right to prevent his throwing himself out of the window, than he has to throw them out of it. All this is plainly and incontestably included in this article of the Declaration of Rights: in the very words of it,

and in the meaning—if it have any meaning. Was this the meaning of the authors of it?—or did they mean to admit this explanation as to some of the instances, and to explain the article away as to the rest?...

So, again, in the case of husband and wife. Amongst the other abuses which the oracle was meant to put an end to, may, for aught I can pretend to say, have been the institution of marriage. For what is the subjection of a small and limited number of years, in comparison of the subjection of a whole life? Yet without subjection and inequality, no such institution can by any possibility take place; for of two contradictory wills, both cannot take effect at the same time.

The same doubts apply to the case of master and hired servant. Better a man should starve than hire himself;—better half the species starve, than hire itself out to service. For, where is the compatibility between liberty and servitude?...

Sentence 2. Social distinctions cannot be founded but upon common utility.—This proposition has two or three meanings. According to one of them, the proposition is notoriously false: according to another, it is in contradiction to the four propositions that preceded it in the same sentence.

What is meant by *social distinctions*? what is meant by *can*? what is meant by *founded*?

What is meant by *social distinctions*?—Distinctions not respecting equality?—then these are nothing to the purpose. Distinctions in respect of equality?—then, consistently with the preceding propositions in this same article, they can have no existence: not existing, they cannot be founded upon anything. The distinctions above exemplified, are they in the number of the social distinctions here intended? Not one of them (as we have been seeing,) but has subjection—not one of them, but has inequality for its very essence.

What is meant by *can*—can not be founded but upon common utility? Is it meant to speak of what is established, or of what *ought to be established*? Does it mean that no social distinctions, but those which it approves as having the foundation in question, are established anywhere? or simply that none such *ought to be* established anywhere? or that, if the establishment or maintenance of such dispositions by the laws be attempted anywhere, such laws ought to be treated as void, and the attempt to execute them to be resisted? For such is the venom that lurks under such words as *can* and *can not*, when set up as a check upon the laws,—they contain all these three so perfectly distinct and widely different meanings. In the first, the proposition they are inserted into refers to practice, and makes appeal to observation—to the observation of other men, in regard to a matter of fact: in the second, it is an appeal to the approving faculty of others, in regard to the same matter of fact: in the third, it is no appeal to anything, or to anybody, but a vio-action on the part of others, by the terrors of anarchical despotism, rising up in opposition to the laws: it is an attempt to lift the dagger of the assassin against all individuals who presume to hold an opinion different from that of the orator or the writer, and against all governments which presume to support any such individuals in any such presumption. In the first of these imports, the proposition is perfectly harmless: but it is commonly so untrue, so glaringly untrue, so palpably untrue, even to drivelling, that it must be plain to everybody it can never have been the meaning that was intended.

In the second of these imports, the proposition may be true or not, as it may happen, and at any rate is equally innocent: but it is such as will not answer the purpose; for an opinion that leaves others at liberty to be of a contrary one, will never answer the purpose of the passions: and if this had been the meaning intended, not this ambiguous phraseology, but a clear and simple one, presenting this meaning and no other, would have been employed. The third, which may not improperly be termed the *ruffian-like* or threatening import, is the meaning intended to be presented to the weak and timid, while the two innocent ones, of which one may even be reasonable, are held up before it as a veil to blind the eyes of the discerning reader, and screen from him the mischief that lurks beneath.....

Look where I will, I see but too many laws, the alteration or abolition of which, would in my poor judgment be a public blessing. I can conceive some,—to put extreme and scarcely exampled cases,—to which I might be inclined to oppose resistance, with a prospect of support such as promised to be effectual. But to talk of what the law, the supreme legislature of the country, acknowledged as such, *can* not do!—to talk of a *void* law as you would of a *void* order or a *void* judgment!—The very act of bringing such words into conjunction is either the

vilest of nonsense, or the worst of treasons:—treason, not against one branch of the sovereignty, but against the whole: treason, not against this or that government, but against *all* governments.

Article II

> The end in view of every political association is the preservation of the natural and imprescriptible rights of man. These rights are liberty, property, security, and resistance to oppression.

Sentence 1. The end in view of every political association, is the preservation of the natural and imprescriptible rights of man.

More confusion—more nonsense,—and the nonsense, as usual, dangerous nonsense. The words can scarcely be said to have a meaning: but if they have, or rather if they had a meaning, these would be the propositions either asserted or implied:—

1. That there are such things as rights anterior to the establishment of governments: for natural, as applied to rights, if it mean anything, is meant to stand in opposition to legal—to such rights as are acknowledged to owe their existence to government, and are consequently posterior in their date to the establishment of government.

2. That these rights *can not* be abrogated by government: for *can not* is implied in the form of the word imprescriptible, and the sense it wears when so applied, is the cut-throat sense above explained.

3. That the governments that exist derive their origin from formal associations, or what are now called *conventions*: associations entered into by a partnership contract, with all the members for partners,—entered into at a day prefixed, for a predetermined purpose, the formation of a new government where there was none before (for as to formal meetings holden under the control of an existing government, they are evidently out of question here) in which it seems again to be implied in the way of inference, though a necessary and an unavoidable inference, that all governments (that is, self-called governments, knots of persons exercising the powers of government) that have had any other origin than an association of the above description, are illegal, that is, no governments at all; resistance to them, and subversion of them, lawful and commendable; and so on.

Such are the notions implied in this first part of the article. How stands the truth of things? That there are no such things as natural rights—no such things as rights anterior to the establishment of government—no such things as natural rights opposed to, in contradistinction to, legal: that the expression is merely figurative; that when used, in the moment you attempt to give it a literal meaning it leads to error, and to that sort of error that leads to mischief—to the extremity of mischief.

We know what it is for men to live without government—and living without government, to live without rights: we know what it is for men to live without government, for we see instances of such a way of life—we see it in many savage nations, or rather races of mankind; for instance, among the savages of New South Wales, whose way of living is so well known to us: no habit of obedience, and thence no government—no government, and thence no laws—no laws, and thence no such things as rights—no security—no property:—liberty, as against regular control, the control of laws and government—perfect; but as against all irregular control, the mandates of stronger individuals, none. In this state, at a time earlier than the commencement of history—in this same state, judging from analogy, we, the inhabitants of the part of the globe we call Europe, were;—no government, consequently no rights: no rights, consequently no property—no legal security—no legal liberty: security not more than belongs to beasts—forecast and sense of insecurity keener—consequently in point of happiness below the level of the brutal race.

In proportion to the want of happiness resulting from the want of rights, a reason exists for wishing that there were such things as rights. But reasons for wishing there were such things as rights, are not rights;—a reason for wishing that a certain right were established, is not that right—want is not supply—hunger is not bread.

That which has no existence cannot be destroyed—that which cannot be destroyed cannot require anything to preserve it from destruction. *Natural rights* is simple nonsense: natural and imprescriptible rights, rhetorical nonsense,—nonsense upon stilts. But this rhetorical nonsense ends in the old strain of mischievous nonsense: for immediately a list of these pretended natural rights is given, and those are so expressed as to present

to view legal rights. And of these rights, whatever they are, there is not, it seems, any one of which any government *can*, upon any occasion whatever, abrogate the smallest particle.

So much for terrorist language. What is the language of reason and plain sense upon this same subject? That in proportion as it is *right* or *proper*, *i. e.* advantageous to the society in question, that this or that right—a right to this or that effect—should be established and maintained, in that same proportion it is *wrong* that it should be abrogated: but that as there is no *right*, which ought not to be maintained so long as it is upon the whole advantageous to the society that it should be maintained, so there is no right which, when the abolition of it is advantageous to society, should not be abolished. To know whether it would be more for the advantage of society that this or that right should be maintained or abolished, the time at which the question about maintaining or abolishing is proposed, must be given, and the circumstances under which it is proposed to maintain or abolish it; the right itself must be specifically described, not jumbled with an undistinguishable heap of others, under any such vague general terms as property, liberty, and the like.

One thing, in the midst of all this confusion, is but too plain. They know not of what they are talking under the name of natural rights, and yet they would have them imprescriptible—proof against all the power of the laws—pregnant with occasions summoning the members of the community to rise up in resistance against the laws. What, then, was their object in declaring the existence of imprescriptible rights, and without specifying a single one by any such mark as it could be known by? This and no other—to excite and keep up a spirit of resistance to all laws—a spirit of insurrection against all governments...

The origination of governments from a contract is a pure fiction, or in other words, a falsehood. It never has been known to be true in any instance; the allegation of it does mischief, by involving the subject in error and confusion, and is neither necessary nor useful to any good purpose.

All governments that we have any account of have been gradually established by habit, after having been formed by force; unless in the instance of governments formed by individuals who have been emancipated, or have emancipated themselves, from governments already formed, the governments under which they were born—a rare case, and from which nothing follows with regard to the rest....

Whence is it, but from government, that contracts derive their binding force? Contracts came from government, not government from contracts. It is from the habit of enforcing contracts, and seeing them enforced, that governments are chiefly indebted for whatever disposition they have to observe them.

Sentence 2. These rights [these imprescriptible as well as natural rights,] are liberty, property, security, and resistance to oppression.

Observe the extent of these pretended rights, each of them belonging to every man, and all of them without bounds. Unbounded liberty; that is, amongst other things, the liberty of doing or not doing on every occasion whatever each man pleases:—Unbounded property; that is, the right of doing with everything around him (with every *thing* at least, if not with every person,) whatsoever he pleases; communicating that right to anybody, and withholding it from anybody:—Unbounded security; that is, security for such his liberty, for such his property, and for his person, against every defalcation that can be called for on any account in respect of any of them:—Unbounded resistance to oppression; that is, unbounded exercise of the faculty of guarding himself against whatever unpleasant circumstance may present itself to his imagination or his passions under that name. Nature, say some of the interpreters of the pretended law of nature—nature gave to each man a right to everything; which is, in effect, but another way of saying—nature has given no such right to anybody; for in regard to most rights, it is as true that what is every man's right is no man's right, as that what is every man's business is no man's business....

In vain would it be said, that though no bounds are here assigned to any of these rights, yet it is to be understood as taken for granted, and tacitly admitted and assumed, that they are to have bounds; viz. such bounds as it is understood will be set them by the laws. Vain, I say, would be this apology; for the supposition would be contradictory to the express declaration of the article itself, and would defeat the very object which the whole declaration has in view. It would be self-contradic-

tory, because these rights are, in the same breath in which their existence is declared, declared to be imprescriptible; and imprescriptible, or, as we in England should say, indefeasible, means nothing unless it exclude the interference of the laws....

So much for all these pretended indefeasible rights in the lump: their inconsistency with each other, as well as the inconsistency of them in the character of indefeasible rights with the existence of government and all peaceable society, will appear still more plainly when we examine them one by one.

1. *Liberty*, then, is imprescriptible—incapable of being taken away—out of the power of any government ever to take away: liberty,—that is, every branch of liberty—every individual exercise of liberty; for no line is drawn—no distinction—no exception made. What these instructors as well as governors of mankind appear not to know, is, that all rights are made at the expense of liberty—all laws by which rights are created or confirmed. No right without a correspondent obligation. Liberty, as against the coercion of the law, may, it is true, be given by the simple removal of the obligation by which that coercion was applied—by the simple repeal of the coercing law. But as against the coercion applicable by individual to individual, no liberty can be given to one man but in proportion as it is taken from another. All coercive laws, therefore (that is, all laws but constitutional laws, and laws repealing or modifying coercive laws,) and in particular all laws creative of liberty, are, as far as they go, abrogative of liberty. Not here and there a law only—not this or that possible law, but almost all laws, are therefore repugnant to these natural and imprescriptible rights: consequently null and void, calling for resistance and insurrection, and so on, as before.

Laws creative of rights of property are also struck at by the same anathema. How is property given? By restraining liberty; that is, by taking it away so far as is necessary for the purpose. How is your house made yours? By debarring every one else from the liberty of entering it without your leave. But

2. *Property*. Property stands second on the list,—proprietary rights are in the number of the natural and imprescriptible rights of man—of the rights which a man is not indebted for to the laws, and which cannot be taken from him by the laws.

Men—that is, every man (for a general expression given without exception is an universal one) has a right to property, to proprietary rights, *a right which* cannot be taken away from him by the laws. To proprietary rights. Good: but in relation to what subject? for as to proprietary rights—without a subject to which they are referable—without a subject in or in relation to which they can be exercised—they will hardly be of much value, they will hardly be worth taking care of, with so much solemnity. In vain would all the laws in the world have ascertained that I have a right to something. If this be all they have done for me—if there be no specific subject in relation to which my proprietary rights are established, I must either take what I want without right, or starve. As there is no such subject specified with relation to each man, or to any man (indeed how could there be?) the necessary inference (taking the passage literally) is, that every man has all manner of proprietary rights with relation to every subject of property without exception: in a word, that every man has a right to every thing. Unfortunately, in most matters of property, what is every man's right is no man's right; so that the effect of this part of the oracle, if observed, would be, not to establish property, but to extinguish it—to render it impossible ever to be revived: and this is one of the rights declared to be imprescriptible.

It will probably be acknowledged, that according to this construction, the clause in question is equally ruinous and absurd:—and hence the inference may be, that this was not the construction—this was not the meaning in view. But by the same rule, every possible construction which the words employed can admit of, might be proved not to have been the meaning in view: nor is this clause a whit more absurd or ruinous than all that goes before it, and a great deal of what comes after it. And, in short, if this be not the meaning of it, what is? Give it a sense—give it any sense whatever,—it is mischievous:—to save it from that imputation, there is but one course to take, which is to acknowledge it to be nonsense.

Thus much would be clear, if anything were clear in it, that according to this clause, whatever proprietary rights, whatever property a man once has, no matter how, being imprescriptible, can never be taken away from him by any law: or of what use or meaning is the clause? So that the

moment it is acknowledged in relation to any article, that such article is my property, no matter how or when it became so, that moment it is acknowledged that it can never be taken away from me: therefore, for example, all laws and all judgments, whereby anything is taken away from me without my free consent—all taxes, for example, and all fines—are void, and, as such, call for resistance and insurrection, and so forth, as before.

3. *Security.* Security stands the third on the list of these natural and imprescriptible rights which laws did not give, and which laws are not in any degree to be suffered to take away. Under the head of security, liberty might have been included, so likewise property: since security for liberty, or the enjoyment of liberty, may be spoken of as a branch of security:—security for property, or the enjoyment of proprietary rights, as another. Security for person is the branch that seems here to have been understood:—security for each man's person, as against all those hurtful or disagreeable impressions (exclusive of those which consist in the mere disturbance of the enjoyment of liberty,) by which a man is affected in his person; loss of life—loss of limbs—loss of the use of limbs—wounds, bruises, and the like. All laws are null and void, then, which on any account or in any manner seek to expose the person of any man to any risk—which appoint capital or other corporal punishment—which expose a man to personal hazard in the service of the military power against foreign enemies, or in that of the judicial power against delinquents:—all laws which, to preserve the country from pestilence, authorize the immediate execution of a suspected person, in the event of his transgressing certain bounds.

4. *Resistance to oppression.* Fourth and last in the list of natural and imprescriptible rights, resistance to oppression—meaning, I suppose, the right to resist oppression. What is oppression? Power misapplied to the prejudice of some individual. What is it that a man has in view when he speaks of oppression? Some exertion of power which he looks upon as misapplied to the prejudice of some individual—to the producing on the part of such individual some suffering, to which (whether as forbidden by the laws or otherwise) we conceive he ought not to have been subjected. But against everything that can come under the name of oppression, provision has been already made, in the

manner we have seen, by the recognition of the three preceding rights; since no oppression can fall upon a man which is not an infringement of his rights in relation to liberty, rights in relation to property, or rights in relation to security, as above described. Where, then, is the difference?—to what purpose this fourth clause after the three first? To this purpose: the mischief they seek to prevent, the rights they seek to establish, are the same; the difference lies in the nature of the remedy endeavoured to be applied. To prevent the mischief in question, the endeavour of the three former clauses is, to tie the hand of the legislator and his subordinates, by the fear of nullity, and the remote apprehension of general resistance and insurrection. The aim of this fourth clause is to raise the hand of the individual concerned to prevent the apprehended infraction of his rights at the moment when he looks upon it as about to take place.

Whenever you are about to be oppressed, you have a right to resist oppression: whenever you conceive yourself to be oppressed, conceive yourself to have a right to make resistance, and act accordingly. In proportion as a law of any kind—any act of power, supreme or subordinate, legislative, administrative, or judicial, is unpleasant to a man, especially if, in consideration of such its unpleasantness, his opinion is, that such act of power ought not to have been exercised, he of course looks upon it as oppression: as often as anything of this sort happens to a man—as often as anything happens to a man to inflame his passions,—this article, for fear his passions should not be sufficiently inflamed of themselves, sets itself to work to blow the flame, and urges him to resistance. Submit not to any decree or other act of power, of the justice of which you are not yourself perfectly convinced. If a constable call upon you to serve in the militia, shoot the constable and not the enemy;—if the commander of a press-gang trouble you, push him into the sea—if a bailiff, throw him out of the window. If a judge sentence you to be imprisoned or put to death, have a dagger ready, and take a stroke first at the judge....

"An Introduction to the Principles of Morals and Legislation"

Jeremy Bentham

Nature has placed mankind under the governance of two sovereign masters, *pain and pleasure*. It is for them alone to point out what we ought to do, as well as to determine what we shall do. On the one hand the standard of right and wrong, on the other the chain of causes and effects, are fastened to their throne. They govern us in all we do, in all we say, in all we think: every effort we can make to throw off our subjection, will serve but to demonstrate and confirm it. In words a man may pretend to abjure their empire: but in reality he will remain subject to it all the while. The *principle of utility* recognises this subjection, and assumes it for the foundation of that system, the object of which is to rear the fabric of felicity by the hands of reason and of law...

The principle of utility is the foundation of the present work: it will be proper therefore at the outset to give an explicit and determinate account of what is meant by it. By the principle of utility is meant that principle which approves or disapproves of every action whatsoever, according to

From *The Works of Jeremy Bentham*, Vol. 1, John Bowring, ed. (Edinburgh, 1839–43).

the tendency which it appears to have to augment or diminish the happiness of the party whose interest is in question: or, what is the same thing in other words, to promote or to oppose that happiness. I say of every action whatsoever; and therefore not only of every action of a private individual, but of every measure of government.

By utility is meant that property in any object, whereby it tends to produce benefit, advantage, pleasure, good, or happiness (all this in the present case comes to the same thing), or (what comes again to the same thing) to prevent the happening of mischief, pain, evil, or unhappiness to the party whose interest is considered: if that party be the community in general, then the happiness of the community: if a particular individual, then the happiness of that individual.

The interest of the community is one of the most general expressions that can occur in the phraseology of morals: no wonder that the meaning of it is often lost. When it has a meaning, it is this. The community is a fictitious *body*, composed of the individual persons who are considered as constituting as it were its *members*. The interest of the community then is, what?—the sum of the interests of the several members who compose it.

It is in vain to talk of the interest of the community, without understanding what is the interest of the individual. A thing is said to promote the interest, or to be *for* the interest, of an individual, when it tends to add to the sum total of his pleasures: or, what comes to the same thing, to diminish the sum total of his pains.

An action then may be said to be conformable to the principle of utility, or, for shortness sake, to utility (meaning with respect to the community at large), when the tendency it has to augment the happiness of the community is greater than any it has to diminish it.

A measure of government (which is but a particular kind of action, performed by a particular person or persons) may be said to be conformable to or dictated by the principle of utility, when in like manner the tendency which it has to augment the happiness of the community is greater than any which it has to diminish it.

When an action, or in particular a measure of government, is supposed by a man to be conformable to the principle of utility, it may be convenient, for the purposes of discourse, to imagine a kind of law or dictate, called a law or dictate of utility: and to speak of the action in question, as being conformable to such law or dictate....

Of an action that is conformable to the principle of utility, one may always say either that it is one that ought to be done, or at least that it is not one that ought not to be done. One may say also, that it is right it should be done; at least that it is not wrong it should be done: that it is a right action; at least that it is not a wrong action. When thus interpreted, the words *ought*, and *right* and *wrong*, and others of that stamp, have a meaning: when otherwise, they have none.

Has the rectitude of this principle been ever formally contested? It should seem that it had, by those who have not known what they have been meaning. Is it susceptible of any direct proof? It should seem not: for that which is used to prove every thing else, cannot itself be proved: a chain of proofs must have their commencement somewhere. To give such proof is as impossible as it is needless.

Not that there is or ever has been that human creature breathing, however stupid or perverse, who has not on many, perhaps on most occasions of his life, deferred to it. By the natural constitution of the human frame, on most occasions of their lives men in general embrace this principle, without thinking of it: if not for the ordering of their own actions, yet for the trying of their own actions, as well as of those of other men. There have been, at the same time, not many, perhaps, even of the most intelligent, who have been disposed to embrace it purely and without reserve. There are even few who have not taken some occasion or other to quarrel with it, either on account of their not understanding always how to apply it, or on account of some prejudice or other which they were afraid to examine into, or could not bear to part with. For such is the stuff that man is made of: in principle and in practice, in a right track and in a wrong one, the rarest of all human qualities is consistency....

Pleasures then, and the avoidance of pains are the *ends* which the legislator has in view; it behoves him therefore to understand their *value*. Pleasures and pains are the *instruments* he has to work with: it behoves him therefore to understand their force, which is again, in another point of view, their value.

To a person considered *by himself*, the value of a pleasure or pain considered *by itself*, will be greater or less, according to the four following circumstances:

1. Its *intensity*.
2. Its *duration*.
3. Its *certainty* or *uncertainty*.
4. Is *propinquity* or *remoteness*.

These are the circumstances which are to be considered in estimating a pleasure or a pain considered each of them by itself. But when the value of any pleasure or pain is considered for the purpose of estimating the tendency of any act by which it is produced, there are two other circumstances to be taken into the account; these are,

5. Its *fecundity*, or the chance it has of being followed by sensations of the *same* kind: that is, pleasures, if it be a pleasure: pains, if it be a pain.

6. Its *purity*, or the chance it has of *not* being followed by sensations of the *opposite* kind: that is, pains, if it be a pleasure: pleasures, if it be a pain.

And one other; to wit:

7. Its *extent*; that is, the number of persons to whom it *extends*; or (in other words) who are affected by it.

To take an exact account, then, of the general tendency of any act, by which the interests of a community are affected, proceed as follows. Begin with any one person of those whose interests seem most immediately to be affected by it: and take an account,

1. Of the value of each distinguishable *pleasure* which appears to be produced by it in the *first* instance.

2. Of the value of each *pain* which appears to be produced by it in the *first* instance.

3. Of the value of each pleasure which appears to be produced by it *after* the first. This constitutes the *fecundity* of the first *pleasure* and the impurity of the first *pain*.

4. Of the value of each *pain* which appears to be produced by it after the first. This constitutes the *fecundity* of the first *pain*, and the *impurity* of the first pleasure.

5. Sum up all the values of all the *pleasures* on the one side, and those of all the pains on the other. The balance, if it be on the side of pleasure, will give the *good* tendency of the act upon the whole, with respect to the interests of that *individual* person; if on the side of pain, the *bad* tendency of it upon the whole.

6. Take an account of the *number* of persons whose interests appear to be concerned; and repeat the above process with respect to each. *Sum up* the numbers expressive of the degrees of *good* tendency, which the act has, with respect to each individual, in regard to whom the tendency of it is *good* upon the whole: do this again with respect to each individual, in regard to whom the tendency of it is *good* upon the whole: do this again with respect to each individual, in regard to whom the tendency of it is *bad* upon the whole. Take the *balance*; which, if on the side of *pleasure*, will give the general *good tendency* of the act, with respect to the total number or community of individuals concerned; if on the side of pain, the general *evil tendency*, with respect to the same community.

It is not to be expected that this process should be strictly pursued previously to every moral judgment, or to every legislative or judicial operation. It may, however, be always kept in view: and as near as the process actually pursued on these occasions approaches to it, so near will such process approach to the character of an exact one....

"A Fragment on Government"

Jeremy Bentham

In regard to a government that is *free*, and one that is *despotic*, wherein is it, then, that the difference consists? Is it that those persons in whose hands that power is lodged which is acknowledged to be supreme, have less power in the one than in the other, when it is from custom that they derive it? By no means. It is not that the power of one, any more than of the other, has any certain bounds to it. The distinction turns upon circumstances of a very different complexion:—on the *manner* in which the whole mass of power, which, taken together, is supreme, is, in a free state, *distributed* among the several ranks of persons that are sharers in it:—on the source from whence their titles to it are successively derived:—on the frequent and easy *changes* of condition between govern*ors* and govern*ed*; whereby the interests of the one class are more or less indistinguishably blended with those of the other:—on the *responsibility* of the governors; or the right which a subject has of having the reasons publicly assigned and canvassed of every act of power that is exerted over him:—on the *liberty of the press*; or the security with which every man, be he of the one class or the other, may make known his complaints and remonstrances to the whole community:—on the *liberty of public association*; or the security with which malcontents may communicate their sentiments, concert their plans, and practice every mode of opposition short of actual revolt, before the executive power can be legally justified in disturbing them....

Let us avow then, in short, steadily but calmly, what our Author hazards with anxiety and agitation, that the authority of the supreme body cannot, *unless where limited by express convention*, be said to have any assignable, any certain bounds.—That to say there is any act they *cannot* do,—to speak of any thing of their's as being *illegal*,—as being *void*;—to speak of their exceeding their *authority* (whatever be the phrase)—their *power*,—their *right*,—is, however common, an abuse of language....

From *The Works of Jeremy Bentham*, Vol. 1, John Bowring, ed. (Edinburgh, 1838–43).

On Liberty

John Stuart Mill

The subject of this Essay is...Civil, or Social Liberty: the nature and limits of the power which can be legitimately exercised by society over the individual....

The struggle between Liberty and Authority is the most conspicuous feature in the portions of history with which we are earliest familiar, particularly in that of Greece, Rome, and England. But in old times this contest was between subjects, or some classes of subjects, and the government. By liberty, was meant protection against the tyranny of the political rulers. The rulers were conceived (except in some of the popular governments of Greece) as in a necessarily antagonistic position to the people whom they ruled. They consisted of a governing One, or a governing tribe or caste, who derived their authority from inheritance or conquest, who, at all events, did not hold it at the pleasure of the governed, and whose supremacy men did not venture, perhaps did not desire, to contest, whatever precautions might be taken against its oppressive exercise. Their power was regarded as necessary, but also as highly dangerous; as a weapon which they would attempt to use against their subjects, no less than against external enemies....The aim, therefore, of patriots, was to set limits to the power which the ruler should be suffered to exercise over the community; and this limitation was what they meant by liberty. It was attempted in two ways. First, by obtaining a recognition of certain immunities, called political liberties or rights, which it was to be regarded as a breach of duty in the ruler to infringe, and which if he did infringe, specific resistance, or general rebellion, was held to be justifiable. A second, and generally a later expedient, was the establishment of constitutional checks; by which the consent of the community, or of a body of some sort, supposed to represent its interests, was made a necessary condition to some of the more important acts of the governing power. To the first of these modes of limitation, the ruling power, in most European countries, was compelled, more or less, to submit. It was not so with the second; and to attain this, or when already in some degree possessed, to attain it more completely, became everywhere the principal object of the lovers of liberty....

A time, however, came, in the progress of human affairs, when men ceased to think it a necessity of nature that their governors should be an independent power, opposed in interest to themselves. It appeared to them much better that the various magistrates of the State should be their tenants or delegates, revocable at their pleasure. In that way alone, it seemed, could they have complete security that the powers of government would never be abused to their disadvantage. By degrees, this new demand for elective and temporary rulers became the prominent object of the exertions of the popular party, wherever any such party existed; and superseded, to a considerable extent, the previous efforts to limit the power of rulers. As the struggle proceeded for making the ruling power emanate from the periodical choice of the ruled, some persons began to think that too much importance had been attached to the limitation of the power itself. *That* (it might seem) was a resource against rulers whose interests were habitually opposed to those of the people. What was now wanted was, that the rulers should be identified with the people; that their interest and will should be the interest and will of the nation. The nation did not need to be protected against its own will. There was no fear of its tyrannizing over itself....

From *On Liberty* (London: J. W. Parker and Sons, 1859).

But, in political and philosophical theories, as well as in persons, success discloses faults and infirmities which failure might have concealed from observation. The notion, that the people have no need to limit their power over themselves, might seem axiomatic, when popular government was a thing only dreamed about, or read of as having existed at some distant period of the past. Neither was that notion necessarily disturbed by such temporary aberrations as those of the French Revolution, the worst of which were the work of a usurping few, and which, in any case, belonged, not to the permanent working of popular institutions, but to a sudden and convulsive outbreak against monarchical and aristocratic despotism. In time, however, a democratic republic came to occupy a large portion of the earth's surface, and made itself felt as one of the most powerful members of the community of nations; and elective and responsible government became subject to the observations and criticisms which wait upon a great existing fact. It was now perceived that such phrases as "self-government", and "the power of the people over themselves", do not express the true state of the case. The "people" who exercise the power, are not always the same people with those over whom it is exercised; and the "self-government" spoken of, is not the government of each by himself, but of each by all the rest. The will of the people, moreover, practically means, the will of the most numerous or the most active *part* of the people; the majority, or those who succeed in making themselves accepted as the majority: the people, consequently, *may* desire to oppress a part of their number; and precautions are as much needed against this, as against any other abuse of power. The limitation, therefore, of the power of government over individuals, loses none of its importance when the holders of power are regularly accountable to the community, that is, to the strongest party therein. This view of things, recommending itself equally to the intelligence of thinkers and to the inclination of those important classes in European society to whose real or supposed interests democracy is adverse, has had no difficulty in establishing itself; and in political speculations "the tyranny of the majority" is now generally included among the evils against which society requires to be on its guard.

Like other tyrannies, the tyranny of the majority was at first, and is still vulgarly, held in dread, chiefly as operating through the acts of the public authorities. But reflecting persons perceived that when society is itself the tyrant—society collectively, over the separate individuals who compose it—its means of tyrannizing are not restricted to the acts which it may do by the hands of its political functionaries. Society can and does execute its own mandates: and if it issues wrong mandates instead of right, or any mandates at all in things with which it ought not to meddle, it practises a social tyranny more formidable than many kinds of political oppression, since, though not usually upheld by such extreme penalties, it leaves fewer means of escape, penetrating much more deeply into the details of life, and enslaving the soul itself. Protection, therefore, against the tyranny of the magistrate is not enough: there needs protection also against the tyranny of the prevailing opinion and feeling; against the tendency of society to impose, by other means than civil penalties, its own ideas and practices as rules of conduct on those who dissent from them; to fetter the development, and, if possible, prevent the formation, of any individuality not in harmony with its ways, and compel all characters to fashion themselves upon the model of its own. There is a limit to the legitimate interference of collective opinion with individual independence: and to find that limit, and maintain it against encroachment, is as indispensable to a good condition of human affairs, as protection against political despotism.

But though this proposition is not likely to be contested in general terms, the practical question, where to place the limit—how to make the fitting adjustment between individual independence and social control—is a subject on which nearly everything remains to be done. All that makes existence valuable to anyone, depends on the enforcement of restraints upon the actions of other people. Some rules of conduct, therefore, must be imposed, by law in the first place, and by opinion on many things which are not fit subjects for the operation of law. What these rules should be, is the principal question in human affairs; but if we except a few of the most obvious cases, it is one of those which least progress has been made in resolving. No two ages, and scarcely any two countries, have decided it alike; and the decision of one age or country is a wonder to another. Yet the people of any given age and country no more suspect any difficulty in it, than if it were a subject on which mankind had always been agreed. The rules which obtain among themselves appear to them self-evident and self-justifying. This all but universal illusion is one of the examples of the magical influence of custom....The practical principle which guides them to their opinions on the regulation of human conduct, is the feeling in each person's mind that everybody should be required to act as he, and those with whom he sympathizes, would like them to act. No one, indeed, acknowledges to himself that his standard of judgment is his own liking; but an opinion on a point of conduct, not supported by reasons, can only count as one person's preference; and if the reasons, when given, are a mere appeal to a similar preference felt by other people, it is still only many people's liking instead of one....

Those who first broke the yoke of what called itself the Universal Church, were in general as little willing to permit difference of religious opinion as that church itself. But when the heat of the conflict was over, without giving a complete victory to any party, and each church or sect was reduced to limit its hopes to retaining possession of the ground it already occupied; minorities, seeing that they had no chance of becoming majorities, were under the necessity of pleading to those whom they could not convert, for permission to differ. It is accordingly on this battlefield, almost solely, that the rights of the individual against society have been asserted on broad grounds of principle, and the claim of society to exercise authority over dissentients, openly controverted. The great writers to whom the world owes what religious liberty it possesses, have mostly asserted freedom of conscience as an indefeasible right, and denied absolutely that a human being is accountable to others for his religious belief. Yet so natural to mankind is intolerance in whatever they really care about, that religious freedom has hardly anywhere been practically realized, except where religious indifference, which dislikes to have its peace disturbed by theological quarrels, has added its weight to the scale. In the minds of almost all religious persons, even in the most tolerant countries, the duty of toleration is admitted with tacit reserves....

In England, there is a considerable amount of feeling ready to be called forth against any attempt of the law to control individuals in things in which they have not hitherto been accustomed to be controlled by it; and this with very little discrimination as to whether the matter is, or is not, within the legitimate sphere of legal control; insomuch that the feeling, highly salutary on the whole, is perhaps quite as often misplaced as well grounded in the particular instances of its application. There is, in fact, no recognized principle by which the propriety or impropriety of government interference is customarily tested. People decide according to their personal preferences. Some, whenever they see any good to be done, or evil to be remedied, would willingly instigate the government to undertake the business; while others prefer to bear almost any amount of social evil, rather than add one to the departments of human interests amenable to governmental control....

The object of this Essay is to assert one very simple principle, as entitled to govern absolutely the dealings of society with the individual in the way of compulsion and control, whether the means used be physical force in the form of legal penalties, or the moral coercion of public opinion. That principle is, that the sole end for which mankind are warranted, individually or collectively, in interfering with the liberty of action of any of their number, is self-protection. That the only purpose for which power can be rightfully exercised over any member of a civilized community, against his will, is to prevent harm to others. His own good, either physical or moral, is not a sufficient warrant. He cannot rightfully be compelled to do or forbear because it will be better for him to do so, because it will make him happier, because, in the opinions of others, to do so would be wise, or even right. These are good reasons for remonstrating with him, or reasoning with him, or persuading him, or entreating him, but not for compelling him, or visiting him with any evil in case he do otherwise. To justify that, the conduct from which it is desired to deter him, must be calculated to produce evil to someone else. The only part of the conduct of anyone, for which he is amenable to society, is that which concerns others. In the part which merely concerns himself, his independence is, of right, absolute. Over himself, over his own body and mind, the individual is sovereign.

It is, perhaps, hardly necessary to say that this doctrine is meant to apply only to human beings in the maturity of their faculties. We are not speaking of children, or of young persons below the age which the law may fix as that of manhood or womanhood. Those who are still in a state to require being taken care of by others, must be protected against their own actions as well as against external injury. For the same reason, we may leave out of consideration those backward states of society in which the race itself may be considered as in its nonage. The early difficulties in the way of spontaneous progress are so great, that there is seldom any choice of means for overcoming them; and a ruler full of the spirit of improvement is warranted in the use of any expedients that will attain an end, perhaps otherwise unattainable. Despotism is a legitimate mode of government in dealing with barbarians, provided the end be their improvement, and the means justified by actually effecting that end. Liberty, as a principle, has no application to any state of things anterior to the time when mankind have become capable of being improved by free and equal discussion. Until then, there is nothing for them but implicit obedience to an Akbar or a Charlemagne, if they are so fortunate as to find one. But as soon as mankind have attained the capacity of being guided to their own improvement by conviction or persuasion (a period long since reached in all nations with whom we need here concern ourselves), compulsion, either in the direct form or in that of pains and penalties for non-compliance, is no longer admissible as a means to their own good, and justifiable only for the security of others.

It is proper to state that I forgo any advantage which could be derived to my argument from the idea of abstract right, as a thing independent of utility. I regard utility as the ultimate appeal on all ethical questions; but it must be utility in the largest sense, grounded on the permanent interests of man as a progressive being. Those interests, I contend, authorize the subjection of individual spontaneity to external control, only in respect to those actions of each, which concern the interest of other people. If anyone does an act hurtful to others, there is a *prima facie* case for punishing him, by law, or, where legal penalties are not safely applicable, by general disapprobation. There are also many positive acts for the benefit of others, which he may rightfully be compelled to perform; such as, to give evidence in a court of justice; to bear his fair share in the common defence, or in any other joint work necessary to the interest of the society of which he enjoys the protection; and to perform certain acts of individual beneficence, such as saving a fellow creature's life, or interposing to protect the defenceless against ill usage, things which whenever it is obviously a man's duty to do, he may rightfully be made responsible to society for not doing. A person may cause evil to others not only by his actions but by his inaction, and in either case he is justly accountable to them for the injury. The latter case, it is true, requires a much more cautious exercise of compulsion than the former. To make anyone answerable for doing evil to others, is the rule; to make him answerable for not preventing evil, is, comparatively speaking, the exception. Yet there are many cases clear enough and grave enough to justify that exception. In all things which regard the external relations of the individual, he is *de jure* amenable to those whose interests are concerned, and if need be, to society as their protector. There are often good reasons for not holding him to the responsibility; but these reasons must arise from the special expediencies of the case: either because it is a kind of case in which he is on the whole likely to act better, when left to his own discretion, than when controlled in any way in which society have it in their power to control him; or because the attempt to exercise control would produce other evils, greater than those which it would prevent. When such reasons as these preclude the enforcement of responsibility, the conscience of the agent himself should step into the vacant judgment seat, and protect those interests of others which have no external protection; judging himself all the more rigidly, because the case does not admit of his being made accountable to the judgment of his fellow creatures.

But there is a sphere of action in which society, as distinguished from the individual, has, if any, only an indirect interest; comprehending all that portion of a person's life and conduct which affects only himself, or if it also affects others, only with their free, voluntary, and undeceived consent and participation. When I say only himself, I mean directly, and in the first instance: for whatever affects himself, may affect others *through* himself; and the objection which may be grounded on this contingency, will receive consideration in the sequel. This, then, is the appropriate region of human liberty. It comprises, first, the inward domain of consciousness; demanding liberty of conscience, in the most comprehensive sense; liberty of thought and feeling; absolute freedom of opinion and sentiment on all subjects, practical or speculative, scientific, moral, or theological. The liberty of expressing and publishing opinions may seem to fall under a different principle, since it belongs to that part of the conduct of an individual which concerns other people; but, being almost of as much importance as the liberty of thought itself, and resting in great part on the same reasons, is practically inseparable from it. Secondly, the principle requires liberty of tastes and pursuits; of framing the plan of our life to suit our own character; of doing as we like, subject to such consequences as may follow: without impediment from our fellow creatures, so long as what we do does not harm them, even though they should think our conduct foolish, perverse, or wrong. Thirdly, from this liberty of each individual, follows the liberty, within the same limits, of combination among individuals; freedom to unite, for any purpose not involving harm to others: the persons combining being supposed to be of full age, and not forced or deceived.

No society in which these liberties are not, on the whole, respected, is free, whatever may be its form of government; and none is completely free in which they do not exist absolute and unqualified. The only freedom which deserves the name, is that of pursuing our own good in our own way, so long as we do not attempt to deprive others of theirs, or impede their efforts to obtain it. Each is the proper guardian of his own health, whether bodily, or mental and spiritual. Mankind are greater gainers by suffering each other to live as seems good to themselves, than by compelling each to live as seems good to the rest.

Though this doctrine is anything but new, and, to some persons, may have the air of a truism, there is no doctrine which stands more directly opposed to the general tendency of existing opinion and practice. Society has expended fully as much effort in the attempt (according to its lights) to compel people to conform to its notions of personal, as of social excellence. The ancient commonwealths thought themselves entitled to practise, and the ancient philosophers countenanced, the regulation of every part of private conduct by public authority, on the ground that the State had a deep interest in the whole bodily and mental discipline of every one of its citizens....

Apart from the peculiar tenets of individual thinkers, there is also in the world at large an increasing inclination to stretch unduly the powers of society over the individual, both by the force of opinion and even by that of legislation: and as the tendency of all the changes taking place in the world is to strengthen society, and diminish the power of the individual, this encroachment is not one of the evils which tend spontaneously to disappear, but, on the contrary, to grow more and more formidable. The disposition of mankind, whether as rulers or as fellow citizens, to impose their own opinions and inclinations as a rule of conduct on others, is so energetically supported by some of the best and by some of the worst feelings incident to human nature, that it is hardly ever kept under restraint by anything but want of power; and as the power is not declining, but growing, unless a strong barrier of moral conviction can be raised against the mischief, we must expect, in the present circumstances of the world, to see it increase....

The time, it is to be hoped, is gone by, when any defence would be necessary of the "liberty of the press" as one of the securities against corrupt or tyrannical government. No argument, we may suppose, can now be needed, against permitting a legislature or an executive, not identified in interest with the people, to prescribe opinions to them, and determine what doctrines or what arguments they shall be allowed to hear. This aspect of the question, besides, has been so often and so triumphantly enforced by preceding writers, that it needs not be specially insisted on in this place....Speaking generally, it is not, in constitutional countries, to be apprehended, that the government, whether completely responsible to the people or not, will often attempt to control the expression of opinion, except when in doing so it makes itself the organ of the general intolerance of the public. Let us suppose, therefore, that the government is entirely at one with the people, and never thinks of exerting any power of coercion unless in agreement with what it conceives to be their voice. But I deny the right of the people to exercise such coercion, either by themselves or by their government. The power itself is illegitimate. The best government has no more title to it than the worst. It is as noxious, or more noxious, when exerted in accordance with public opinion, than when in opposition to it. If all mankind minus one, were of one opinion, and only one person were of the contrary opinion, mankind would be no more justified in silencing that one person, than he, if he had the power, would be justified in silencing mankind. Were an opinion a personal possession of no value except to the owner; if to be obstructed in the enjoyment of it were simply a private injury, it would make some difference whether the injury was inflicted only on a few persons or on many. But the peculiar evil of silencing the expression of an opinion is, that it is robbing the human race; posterity as well as the existing generation; those who dissent from the opinion, still more than those who hold it. If the opinion is right, they are deprived of the opportunity of exchanging error for truth: if wrong, they lose, what is almost as great a benefit, the clearer perception and livelier impression of truth, produced by its collision with error.

It is necessary to consider separately these two hypotheses, each of which has a distinct branch of the argument corresponding to it. We can never be sure that the opinion we are endeavouring to stifle is a false opinion; and if we were sure, stifling it would be an evil still.

First: the opinion which it is attempted to suppress by authority may possibly be true. Those who desire to suppress it, of course deny its truth; but they are not infallible. They have no authority to decide the question for all mankind, and exclude every other person from the means of judging. To refuse a hearing to an opinion, because they are sure that it is false, is to assume that *their* certainty is the same thing as *absolute* certainty. All silencing of discussion is an assumption of infallibility. Its condemnation may be allowed to rest on this common argument, not the worse for being common.

Unfortunately for the good sense of mankind, the fact of their fallibility is far from carrying the weight in their practical judgment, which is always allowed to it in theory; for while everyone well knows himself to be fallible, few think it necessary to take any precautions against their own fallibility, or admit the supposition that any opinion, of which they feel very certain, may be one of the examples of the error to which they acknowledge themselves to be liable.... Ages are no more infallible than individuals; every age having held many opinions which subsequent ages have deemed not only false but absurd; and it is as certain that many opinions,

now general, will be rejected by future ages, as it is that many, once general, are rejected by the present.

The objection likely to be made to this argument, would probably take some such form as the following. There is no greater assumption of infallibility in forbidding the propagation of error, than in any other thing which is done by public authority on its own judgment and responsibility. Judgment is given to men that they may use it. Because it may be used erroneously, are men to be told that they ought not to use it at all? To prohibit what they think pernicious, is not claiming exemption from error, but fulfilling the duty incumbent on them, although fallible, of acting on their conscientious conviction. If we were never to act on our opinions, because those opinions may be wrong, we should leave all our interests uncared for, and all our duties unperformed....There is no such thing as absolute certainty, but there is assurance sufficient for the purposes of human life. We may, and must, assume our opinion to be true for the guidance of our own conduct: and it is assuming no more when we forbid bad men to pervert society by the propagation of opinions which we regard as false and pernicious.

I answer, that it is assuming very much more. There is the greatest difference between presuming an opinion to be true, because, with every opportunity for contesting it, it has not been refuted, and assuming its truth for the purpose of not permitting its refutation. Complete liberty of contradicting and disproving our opinion, is the very condition which justifies us in assuming its truth for purposes of action; and on no other terms can a being with human faculties have any rational assurance of being right.

When we consider either the history of opinion, or the ordinary conduct of human life, to what is it to be ascribed that the one and the other are no worse than they are? Not certainly to the inherent force of the human understanding; for, on any matter not self-evident, there are ninety-nine persons totally incapable of judging of it, for one who is capable; and the capacity of the hundredth person is only comparative; for the majority of the eminent men of every past generation held many opinions now known to be erroneous, and did or approved numerous things which no one will now justify. Why is it, then, that there is on the whole a preponderance among mankind of rational opinions and rational conduct? If there really is this preponderance—which there must be, unless human affairs are, and have always been, in an almost desperate state—it is owing to a quality of the human mind, the source of everything respectable in man either as an intellectual or as a moral being, namely, that his errors are corrigible. He is capable of rectifying his mistakes, by discussion and experience. Not by experience alone. There must be discussion, to show how experience is to be interpreted....The steady habit of correcting and completing his own opinion by collating it with those of others, so far from causing doubt and hesitation in carrying it into practice, is the only stable foundation for a just reliance on it: for, being cognizant of all that can, at least obviously, be said against him, and having taken up his position against all gainsayers—knowing that he has sought for objections and difficulties, instead of avoiding them, and has shut out no light which can be thrown upon the subject from any quarter—he has a right to think his judgment better than that of any person, or any multitude, who have not gone through a similar process...

In the present age—which has been described as "destitute of faith, but terrified at scepticism"—in which people feel sure, not so much that their opinions are true, as that they should not know what to do without them—the claims of an opinion to be protected from public attack are rested not so much on its truth, as on its importance to society. There are, it is alleged, certain beliefs, so useful, not to say indispensable to well-being, that it is as much the duty of governments to uphold those beliefs, as to protect any other of the interests of society. In a case of such necessity, and so directly in the line of their duty, something less than infallibility may, it is maintained, warrant, and even bind, governments, to act on their own opinion, confirmed by the general opinion of mankind. It is also often argued, and still oftener thought, that none but bad men would desire to weaken these salutary beliefs; and there can be nothing wrong, it is thought, in restraining bad men, and prohibiting what only such men would wish to practise. This mode of thinking makes the justification of restraints on discussion not a question of the truth of doctrines, but of their usefulness; and flatters itself by that means to escape the responsibility of claiming to be an infallible judge of opinions. But those who thus satisfy themselves, do not perceive that the assumption of infallibility is merely shifted from one point to another. The usefulness of an opinion is itself matter of opinion: as disputable, as open to discussion, and requiring discussion as much, as the opinion itself. There is the same need of an infallible judge of opinions to decide an opinion to be noxious, as to decide it to be false, unless the opinion condemned has full opportunity of defending itself. And it will not do to say that the heretic may be allowed to maintain the utility or harmlessness of his opinion, though forbidden to maintain its truth. The truth of an opinion is part of its utility....

Our merely social intolerance kills no one, roots out no opinions, but induces men to disguise them, or to abstain from any active effort for their diffusion. With us, heretical opinions do not perceptibly gain, or even lose, ground in each decade or generation: they never blaze out far and wide, but continue to smoulder in the narrow circles of thinking and studious persons among whom they originate, without ever lighting up the general affairs of mankind with either a true or a deceptive light. And thus is kept up a state of things very satisfactory to some minds, because, without the unpleasant process of fining or imprisoning anybody, it maintains all prevailing opinions outwardly undisturbed, while it does not absolutely interdict the exercise of reason by dissentients afflicted with the malady of thought. A convenient plan for having peace in the intellectual world, and keeping all things going on therein very much as they do already. But the price paid for this sort of intellectual pacification, is the sacrifice of the entire moral courage of the human mind. A state of things in which a large portion of the most active and inquiring intellects find it advisable to keep the genuine principles and grounds of their convictions within their own breasts, and attempt, in what they address to the public, to fit as much as they can of their own conclusions to premises which they have internally renounced, cannot send forth the open, fearless characters, and logical, consistent intellects who once adorned the thinking world....

Those in whose eyes this reticence on the part of heretics is no evil, should consider in the first place, that in consequence of it there is never any fair and thorough discussion of heretical opinions;

and that such of them as could not stand such a discussion, though they may be prevented from spreading, do not disappear. But it is not the minds of heretics that are deteriorated most, by the ban placed on all inquiry which does not end in the orthodox conclusions. The greatest harm done is to those who are not heretics, and whose whole mental development is cramped, and their reason cowed, by the fear of heresy. Who can compute what the world loses in the multitude of promising intellects combined with timid characters, who dare not follow out any bold, vigorous, independent train of thought, lest it should land them in something which would admit of being considered irreligious or immoral?...

No one can be a great thinker who does not recognize, that as a thinker it is his first duty to follow his intellect to whatever conclusions it may lead. Truth gains more even by the errors of one who, with due study and preparation, thinks for himself, than by the true opinions of those who only hold them because they do not suffer themselves to think. Not that it is solely, or chiefly, to form great thinkers, that freedom of thinking is required. On the contrary, it is as much, and even more indispensable, to enable average human beings to attain the mental stature which they are capable of. There have been, and may again be, great individual thinkers, in a general atmosphere of mental slavery. But there never has been, nor ever will be, in that atmosphere, an intellectually active people....

Let us now pass to the second division of the argument, and dismissing the supposition that any of the received opinions may be false, let us assume them to be true, and examine into the worth of the manner in which they are likely to be held, when their truth is not freely and openly canvassed. However unwillingly a person who has a strong opinion may admit the possibility that his opinion may be false, he ought to be moved by the consideration that however true it may be, if it is not fully, frequently, and fearlessly discussed, it will be held as a dead dogma, not a living truth.

There is a class of persons (happily not quite so numerous as formerly) who think it enough if a person assents undoubtingly to what they think true, though he has no knowledge whatever of the grounds of the opinion, and could not make a tenable defence of it against the most superficial objections. Such persons, if they can once get their creed taught from authority, naturally think that no good, and some harm, comes of its being allowed to be questioned....This is not the way in which truth ought to be held by a rational being. This is not knowing the truth. Truth, thus held, is but one superstition the more, accidentally clinging to the words which enunciate a truth.

If the cultivation of the understanding consists in one thing more than in another, it is surely in learning the grounds of one's own opinions. Whatever people believe, on subjects on which it is of the first importance to believe rightly, they ought to be able to defend against at least the common objections. But, someone may say, "Let them be *taught* the grounds of their opinions. It does not follow that opinions must be merely parroted because they are never heard controverted. Persons who learn geometry do not simply commit the theorems to memory, but understand and learn likewise the demonstrations; and it would be absurd to say that they remain ignorant of the grounds of geometrical truths, because they never hear anyone deny, and attempt to disprove them." Undoubtedly: and such teaching suffices on a subject like mathematics, where there is nothing at all to be said on the wrong side of the question. The peculiarity of the evidence of mathematical truths is, that all the argument is on one side. There are no objections, and no answers to objections. But on every subject on which difference of opinion is possible, the truth depends on a balance to be struck between two sets of conflicting reasons....

He who knows only his own side of the case, knows little of that. His reasons may be good, and no one may have been able to refute them. But if he is equally unable to refute the reasons on the opposite side; if he does not so much as know what they are, he has no ground for preferring either opinion. The rational position for him would be suspension of judgment, and unless he contents himself with that, he is either led by authority, or adopts, like the generality of the world, the side to which he feels most inclination. Nor is it enough that he should hear the arguments of adversaries from his own teachers, presented as they state them, and accompanied by what they offer as refutations. That is not the way to do justice to the arguments, or bring them into real contact with his own mind He must be able to hear them from persons who actually believe them: who defend them in earnest, and do their very utmost for them. He must know them in their most plausible and persuasive form; he must feel the whole force of the difficulty which the true view of the subject has to encounter and dispose of; else he will never really possess himself of the portion of truth which meets and removes that difficulty.... So essential is this discipline to a real understanding of moral and human subjects, that if opponents of all important truths do not exist, it is indispensable to imagine them, and supply them with the strongest arguments which the most skilful devil's advocate can conjure up.

If, however, the mischievous operation of the absence of free discussion, when the received opinions are true, were confined to leaving men ignorant of the grounds of those opinions, it might be thought that this, if an intellectual, is no moral evil, and does not affect the worth of the opinions, regarded in their influence on the character. The fact, however, is, that not only the grounds of the opinion are forgotten in the absence of discussion, but too often the meaning of the opinion itself. The words which convey it, cease to suggest ideas, or suggest only a small portion of those they were originally employed to communicate. Instead of a vivid conception and a living belief, there remain only a few phrases retained by rote; or, if any part, the shell and husk only of the meaning is retained, the finer essence being lost.

The same thing holds true, generally speaking, of all traditional doctrines—those of prudence and knowledge of life as well as of morals or religion.... As mankind improve, the number of doctrines which are no longer disputed or doubted will be constantly on the increase: and the well-being of mankind may almost be measured by the number and gravity of the truths which have reached the point of being uncontested. The cessation, on one question after another, of serious controversy, is one of the necessary incidents of the consolidation of opinion; a consolidation as salutary in the case of true opinions, as it is dangerous and noxious when the opinions are erroneous. But though this gradual narrowing of the bounds of diversity of opinion is necessary in both senses of the term, being at once inevitable and indispensable, we are not therefore obliged to conclude that all its consequences must be beneficial. The loss of so impor-

tant an aid to the intelligent and living apprehension of a truth, as is afforded by the necessity of explaining it to, or defending it against, opponents, though not sufficient to outweigh, is no trifling drawback from, the benefit of its universal recognition. Where this advantage can no longer be had, I confess I should like to see the teachers of mankind endeavouring to provide a substitute for it; some contrivance for making the difficulties of the question as present to the learner's consciousness, as if they were pressed upon him by a dissentient champion, eager for his conversion....

A person who derives all his instruction from teachers or books, even if he escape the besetting temptation of contenting himself with cram, is under no compulsion to hear both sides; accordingly it is far from a frequent accomplishment, even among thinkers, to know both sides; and the weakest part of what everybody says in defence of his opinion, is what he intends as a reply to antagonists. It is the fashion of the present time to disparage negative logic—that which points out weaknesses in theory or errors in practice, without establishing positive truths. Such negative criticism would indeed be poor enough as an ultimate result; but as a means to attaining any positive knowledge or conviction worthy the name, it cannot be valued too highly;...

It still remains to speak of one of the principal causes which make diversity of opinion advantageous, and will continue to do so until mankind shall have entered a stage of intellectual advancement which at present seems at an incalculable distance. We have hitherto considered only two possibilities: that the received opinion may be false, and some other opinion, consequently, true; or that, the received opinion being true, a conflict with the opposite error is essential to a clear apprehension and deep feeling of its truth. But there is a commoner case than either of these; when the conflicting doctrines, instead of being one true and the other false, share the truth between them; and the nonconforming opinion is needed to supply the remainder of the truth, of which the received doctrine embodies only a part. Popular opinions, on subjects not palpable to sense, are often true, but seldom or never the whole truth. They are a part of the truth; sometimes a greater, sometimes a smaller part, but exaggerated, distorted, and disjoined from the truths by which they ought to be accompanied and limited. Heretical opinions, on the other hand, are generally some of these suppressed and neglected truths, bursting the bonds which kept them down, and either seeking reconciliation with the truth contained in the common opinion, or fronting it as enemies, and setting themselves up, with similar exclusiveness, as the whole truth. The latter case is hitherto the most frequent, as, in the human mind, one-sidedness has always been the rule, and many-sidedness the exception....

In politics, again, it is almost a commonplace, that a party of order or stability, and a party of progress or reform, are both necessary elements of a healthy state of political life; until the one or the other shall have so enlarged its mental grasp as to be a party equally of order and of progress, knowing and distinguishing what is fit to be preserved from what ought to be swept away. Each of these modes of thinking derives its utility from the deficiencies of the other; but it is in a great measure the opposition of the other that keeps each within the limits of reason and sanity. Unless opinions favourable to democracy and to aristocracy, to property and to equality, to co-operation and to competition, to luxury and to abstinence, to sociality and individuality, to liberty and discipline, and all the other standing antagonisms of practical life, are expressed with equal freedom, and enforced and defended with equal talent and energy, there is no chance of both elements obtaining their due; one scale is sure to go up, and the other down. Truth, in the great practical concerns of life, is so much a question of the reconciling and combining of opposites, that very few have minds sufficiently capacious and impartial to make the adjustment with an approach to correctness, and it has to be made by the rough process of a struggle between combatants fighting under hostile banners. On any of the great open questions just enumerated, if either of the two opinions has a better claim than the other, not merely to be tolerated, but to be encouraged and countenanced, it is the one which happens at the particular time and place to be in a minority...

We have now recognized the necessity to the mental well-being of mankind (on which all their other well-being depends) of freedom of opinion, and freedom of the expression of opinion, on four distinct grounds: which we will now briefly recapitulate.

First, if any opinion is compelled to silence, that opinion may, for aught we can certainly know, be true. To deny this is to assume our own infallibility.

Secondly, though the silenced opinion be an error, it may, and very commonly does, contain a portion of truth; and since the general or prevailing opinion on any subject is rarely or never the whole truth, it is only by the collision of adverse opinions that the remainder of the truth has any chance of being supplied.

Thirdly, even if the received opinion be not only true, but the whole truth; unless it is suffered to be, and actually is, vigorously and earnestly contested, it will, by most of those who receive it, be held in the manner of a prejudice, with little comprehension or feeling of its rational grounds. And not only this, but, fourthly, the meaning of the doctrine itself will be in danger of being lost, or enfeebled, and deprived of its vital effect on the character and conduct: the dogma becoming a mere formal profession, inefficacious for good, but cumbering the ground, and preventing the growth of any real and heartfelt conviction, from reason or personal experience....

Such being the reasons which make it imperative that human beings should be free to form opinions, and to express their opinions without reserve; and such the baneful consequences to the intellectual, and through that to the moral nature of man, unless this liberty is either conceded, or asserted in spite of prohibition; let us next examine whether the same reasons do not require that men should be free to act upon their opinions—to carry these out in their lives, without hindrance, either physical or moral, from their fellow men, so long as it is at their own risk and peril. This last proviso is of course indispensable. No one pretends that actions should be as free as opinions. On the contrary, even opinions lose their immunity, when the circumstances in which they are expressed are such as to constitute their expression a positive instigation to some mischievous act. An opinion that corn-dealers are starvers of the poor, or that private property is robbery, ought to be unmolested when simply circulated through the press, but may justly incur punishment when delivered orally to an excited mob assembled before the house of a corn-dealer, or when handed about among the same mob in the form of a placard. Acts, of whatever kind, which, without justifiable cause, do harm to others, may be, and in the more important cases absolutely require to be, controlled by the unfavourable sentiments, and, when needful, by the active interference of mankind. The liberty of the individual must be thus far limited; he must not make himself a nuisance to other people. But if he refrains from molesting others in what concerns them, and merely acts according to his own inclination and judgment in things which concern himself, the same reasons which show that opinion should be free, prove also that he should be allowed, without molestation, to carry his opinions into practice at his own cost. That mankind are not infallible; that their truths, for the most part, are only half-truths; that unity of opinion, unless resulting from the fullest and freest comparison of opposite opinions, is not desirable, and diversity not an evil, but a good, until mankind are much more capable than at present of recognizing all sides of the truth, are principles applicable to men's modes of action, not less than to their opinions. As it is useful that while mankind are imperfect there should be different opinions, so is it that there should be different experiments of living; that free scope should be given to varieties of character, short of injury to others; and that the worth of different modes of life should be proved practically, when anyone thinks fit to try them. It is desirable, in short, that in things which do not primarily concern others, individuality should assert itself. Where, not the person's own character, but the traditions or customs of other people are the rule of conduct, there is wanting one of the principal ingredients of human happiness, and quite the chief ingredient of individual and social progress.

In maintaining this principle, the greatest difficulty to be encountered does not lie in the appreciation of means towards an acknowledged end, but in the indifference of persons in general to the end itself. If it were felt that the free development of individuality is one of the leading essentials of well-being; that it is not only a co-ordinate element with all that is designated by the terms civilization, instruction, education, culture, but is itself a necessary part and condition of all those things; there would be no danger that liberty should be undervalued, and the adjustment of the boundaries between it and social control would present no extraordinary difficulty. But the evil is, that individual spontaneity is hardly recognized by the common modes of thinking, as having any intrinsic worth, or deserving any regard on its own account. The majority, being satisfied with the ways of mankind as they now are (for it is they who make them what they are), cannot comprehend why those ways should not be good enough for everybody; and what is more, spontaneity forms no part of the ideal of the majority of moral and social reformers, but is rather looked on with jealousy, as a troublesome and perhaps rebellious obstruction to the general acceptance of what these reformers, in their own judgment, think would be best for mankind....The question, one must nevertheless think, can only be one of degree. No one's idea of excellence in conduct is that people should do absolutely nothing but copy one another. No one would assert that people ought not to put into their mode of life, and into the conduct of their concerns, any impress whatever of their own judgment, or of their own individual character. On the other hand, it would be absurd to pretend that people ought to live as if nothing whatever had been known in the world before they came into it; as if experience had as yet done nothing towards showing that one mode of existence, or of conduct, is preferable to another. Nobody denies that people should be so taught and trained in youth, as to know and benefit by the ascertained results of human experience. But it is the privilege and proper condition of a human being, arrived at the maturity of his faculties, to use and interpret experience in his own way. It is for him to find out what part of recorded experience is properly applicable to his own circumstances and character....

He who lets the world, or his own portion of it, choose his plan of life for him, has no need of any other faculty than the ape-like one of imitation. He who chooses his plan for himself, employs all his faculties. He must use observation to see, reasoning and judgment to foresee, activity to gather materials for decision, discrimination to decide, and when he has decided, firmness and self-control to hold to his deliberate decision. And these qualities he requires and exercises exactly in proportion as the part of his conduct which he determines according to his own judgment and feelings is a large one. It is possible that he might be guided in some good path, and kept out of harm's way, without any of these things. But what will be his comparative worth as a human being? It really is of importance, not only what men do, but also what manner of men they are that do it. Among the works of man, which human life is rightly employed in perfecting and beautifying, the first in importance surely is man himself. Supposing it were possible to get houses built, corn grown, battles fought, causes tried, and even churches erected and prayers said, by machinery—by automatons in human form—it would be a considerable loss to exchange for these automatons even the men and women who at present inhabit the more civilized parts of the world, and who assuredly are but starved specimens of what nature can and will produce. Human nature is not a machine to be built after a model, and set to do exactly the work prescribed for it, but a tree, which requires to grow and develop itself on all sides, according to the tendency of the inward forces which make it a living thing....

There has been a time when the element of spontaneity and individuality was in excess, and the social principle had a hard struggle with it. The difficulty then was, to induce men of strong bodies or minds to pay obedience to any rules which required them to control their impulses....But society has now fairly got the better of individuality; and the danger which threatens human nature is not the excess, but the deficiency, of personal impulses and preferences. Things are vastly changed, since the passions of those who were strong by station or by personal endowment were in a state of habitual rebellion against laws and ordinances, and required to be rigorously chained up to enable the persons within their reach to enjoy any particle of security. In our times, from the highest class of society down to the lowest, everyone lives as under the eye of a hostile and dreaded censorship. Not only in what concerns others, but in what concerns only themselves, the individual, or the family, do not ask themselves—what do I prefer? or, what would suit my character and disposition? or, what would allow the best and highest in me to have fair play, and enable it to grow and thrive? They ask themselves, what is suitable to my position? what is usually done by persons of my station and pecuniary circumstances? or (worse still) what is usually done by persons of a station and circumstances superior to mine? I do not mean that they choose what is customary, in preference to what suits their own inclination. It does not occur to them to have any inclination, except for what is customary....

It is not by wearing down into uniformity all that is individual in themselves, but by cultivating it and calling it forth, within the limits imposed by the rights and interests of others, that human beings become a noble and beautiful object of contemplation; and as the works partake the character of those who do them, by the same process human life also becomes rich, diversified, and animating, furnishing more abundant aliment to high thoughts and elevating feelings, and strengthening the tie which binds every individual to the race, by making the race infinitely better worth belonging to. In proportion to the development of his individuality, each person becomes more valuable to himself, and is therefore capable of being more valuable to others. There is a greater fullness of life about his own existence, and when there is more life in the units there is more in the mass which is composed of them. As much compression as is necessary to prevent the stronger specimens of human nature from encroaching on the rights of others, cannot be dispensed with; but for this there is ample compensation even in the point of view of human development. The means of development which the individual loses by being prevented from gratifying his inclinations to the injury of others, are chiefly obtained at the expense of the development of other people. And even to himself there is a full equivalent in the better development of the social part of his nature, rendered possible by the restraint put upon the selfish part. To be held to rigid rules of justice for the sake of others, develops the feelings and capacities which have the good of others for their object. But to be restrained in things not affecting their good, by their mere displeasure, develops nothing valuable, except such force of character as may unfold itself in resisting the restraint. If acquiesced in, it dulls and blunts the whole nature. To give any fair play to the nature of each, it is essential that different persons should be allowed to lead different lives....

Having said that individuality is the same thing with development, and that it is only the cultivation of individuality which produces, or can produce, well-developed human beings, I might here close the argument; for what more or better can be said of any condition of human affairs, than that it brings human beings themselves nearer to the best thing they can be? or what worse can be said of any obstruction to good, than that it prevents this?

Doubtless, however, these considerations will not suffice to convince those who most need convincing; and it is necessary further to show, that these developed human beings are of some use to the undeveloped—to point out to those who do not desire liberty, and would not avail themselves of it, that they may be in some intelligible manner rewarded for allowing other people to make use of it without hindrance.

In the first place, then, I would suggest that they might possibly learn something from them. It will not be denied by anybody, that originality is a valuable element in human affairs. There is always need of persons not only to discover new truths, and point out when what were once truths are true no longer, but also to commence new practices, and set the example of more enlightened conduct, and better taste and sense in human life....

I insist thus emphatically on the importance of genius, and the necessity of allowing it to unfold itself freely both in thought and in practice, being well aware that no one will deny the position in theory, but knowing also that almost everyone, in reality, is totally indifferent to it. People think genius a fine thing if it enables a man to write an exciting poem, or paint a picture. But in its true sense, that of originality in thought and action, though no one says that it is not a thing to be admired, nearly all, at heart, think that they can do very well without it. Unhappily this is too natural to be wondered at. Originality is the one thing which unoriginal minds cannot feel the use of. They cannot see what it is to do for them: how should they? If they could see what it would do for them, it would not be originality. The first service which originality has to render them, is that of opening their eyes; which being once fully done, they would have a chance of being themselves original. Meanwhile, recollecting that nothing was ever yet done which someone was not the first to do, and that all good things which exist are the fruits of originality, let them be modest enough to believe that there is something still left for it to accomplish, and assure themselves that they are more in need of originality, the less they are conscious of the want.

In sober truth, whatever homage may be professed, or even paid, to real or supposed mental superiority, the general tendency of things throughout the world is to render mediocrity the ascendant power among mankind. In ancient history, in the middle ages, and in a diminishing degree through the long transition from feudality to the present time, the individual was a power in himself; and if he had either great talents or a high social position, he was a considerable power. At present individuals are lost in the crowd. In politics it is almost a triviality to say that public opinion now rules the world. The only power deserving the name is that of masses, and of governments while they make themselves the organ of the tendencies and instincts of masses. This is as true in the moral and social relations of private life as in public transactions....Their thinking is done for them by men much like themselves, addressing them or speaking in their name, on the spur of the moment, through the newspapers. I am not complaining of all this. I do not assert that anything better is compatible, as a general rule, with the present low state of the human mind. But that does not hinder the government of mediocrity from being mediocre government....It does seem, however, that when the opinions of masses of merely average men are everywhere become or becoming the dominant power, the counterpoise and corrective to that tendency would be, the more and more pronounced individuality of those who stand on the higher eminences of thought. It is in these circumstances most especially, that exceptional individuals, instead of being deterred, should be encouraged in acting differently from the mass. In other times there was no advantage in their doing so, unless they acted not only differently, but better. In this age the mere example of non-conformity, the mere refusal to bend the knee to custom, is itself a service. Precisely because the tyranny of opinion is such as to make eccentricity a reproach, it is desirable, in order to break through that tyranny, that people should be eccentric. Eccentricity has always abounded when and where strength of character has abounded; and the amount of eccentricity in a society has generally been proportional to the amount of genius, mental vigour, and moral courage which it contained. That so few now dare to be eccentric, marks the chief danger of the time.

I have said that it is important to give the freest scope possible to uncustomary things, in order that it may in time appear which of these are fit to be converted into customs. But independence of action, and disregard of custom are not solely deserving of encouragement for the chance they afford that better modes of action, and customs more worthy of general adoption, may be struck out; nor is it only persons of decided mental superiority who have a just claim to carry on their lives in their own way. There is no reason that all human existences should be constructed on some one, or some small number of patterns. If a person possesses any tolerable amount of common sense and experience, his own mode of laying out his existence is the best, not because it is the best in itself, but because it is his own mode....

There is one characteristic of the present direction of public opinion, peculiarly calculated to make it intolerant of any marked demonstration of individuality. The general average of mankind are not only moderate in intellect, but also moderate in inclinations: they have no tastes or wishes strong enough to incline them to do anything unusual, and they consequently do not understand those who have, and class all such with the wild and intemperate whom they are accustomed to look down upon. Now, in addition to this fact which is general, we have only to suppose that a strong movement has set in towards the improvement of morals, and it is evident what we have to expect. In these days such a movement has set in; much has actually been effected in the way of increased regularity of conduct, and discouragement of excesses; and there is a philanthropic spirit abroad, for the exercise of which there is no more inviting field than the moral and prudential improvement of our fellow creatures. These tendencies of the times cause the public to be more disposed than at most former periods to prescribe general rules of conduct, and endeavour to make everyone conform to the approved standard. And that standard, express or tacit, is to desire nothing strongly. Its ideal of character is to be without any marked character: to maim by compression, like a Chinese lady's foot, every part of human nature which stands out prominently, and tends to make the person markedly dissimilar in outline to commonplace humanity.

The despotism of custom is everywhere the standing hindrance to human advancement, being in unceasing antagonism to that disposition to aim at something better than customary, which is called, according to circumstances, the spirit of liberty, or that of progress or improvement. The spirit of improvement is not always a spirit of liberty, for it may aim at forcing improvements on an unwilling people; and the spirit of liberty, in so far as it resists such attempts, may ally itself locally and temporarily with the opponents of improvement; but the only unfailing and permanent source of improvement is liberty, since by it there are as many possible independent centres of improvement as there are individuals. The progressive principle, however, in either shape, whether as the love of liberty or of improvement, is antagonistic to the sway of Custom, involving at least emancipation from that yoke; and the contest between the two constitutes the chief interest of the history of mankind. The greater part of the world has, properly speaking, no history, because the despotism of Custom is complete....

What has made the European family of nations an improving, instead of a stationary portion of mankind? Not any superior excellence in them, which, when it exists, exists as the effect, not as the cause; but their remarkable diversity of character and culture. Individuals, classes, nations, have been extremely unlike one another: they have struck out a great variety of paths, each leading to something valuable; and although at every period those who travelled in different paths have been intolerant of one another, and each would have thought it an excellent thing if all the rest could have been compelled to travel his road, their attempts to thwart each other's development have rarely had any permanent success, and each has in time endured to receive the good which the others have offered. Europe is, in my judgment, wholly indebted to this plurality of paths for its progressive and many-sided development. But it already begins to possess this benefit in a considerably less degree....

What, then, is the rightful limit to the sovereignty of the individual over himself? Where does the authority of society begin? How much of human life should be assigned to individuality, and how much to society?

Each will receive its proper share, if each has that which more particularly concerns it. To individuality should belong the part of life in which it is chiefly the individual that is interested; to society, the part which chiefly interests society.

Though society is not founded on a contract, and though no good purpose is answered by inventing a contract in order to deduce social obligations from it, everyone who receives the protection of society owes a return for the benefit, and the fact of living in society renders it indispensable that each should be bound to observe a certain line of conduct towards the rest. This conduct consists, first, in not injuring the interests of one another; or rather certain interests, which, either by express legal provision or by tacit understanding, ought to be considered as rights; and secondly, in each person's bearing his share (to be fixed on some equitable principle) of the labours and sacrifices incurred for defending the society or its members from injury and molestation. These conditions society is justified in enforcing, at all costs to those who endeavour to withhold fulfillment. Nor is this all that society may do. The acts of an individual may be hurtful to others, or wanting in due consideration for their welfare, without going the length of violating any of their constituted rights. The offender may then be justly punished by opinion, though not by law. As soon as any part of a person's conduct affects prejudicially the interests of others, society has jurisdiction over it, and the question whether the general welfare will or will not be promoted by interfering with it, becomes open to discussion. But there is no room for entertaining any such question when a person's conduct affects the interests of no persons besides himself, or needs not affect them unless they like (all the persons concerned being of full age, and the ordinary amount of understanding). In all such cases there should be perfect freedom, legal and social, to do the action and stand the consequences.

It would be a great misunderstanding of this doctrine, to suppose that it is one of selfish indifference, which pretends that human beings have no business with each other's conduct in life, and that they should not concern themselves about the well-doing or well-being of one another, unless their own interest is involved. Instead of any diminution, there is need of a great increase of disinterested exertion to promote the good of others. But disinterested benevolence can find other instruments to persuade people to their good, than whips and scourges, either of the literal or the metaphorical sort. I am the last person to undervalue the self-regarding virtues; they are only second in importance, if even second, to the social. It is equally the business of education to cultivate both. But

even education works by conviction and persuasion as well as by compulsion, and it is by the former only that, when the period of education is past, the self-regarding virtues should be inculcated. Human beings owe to each other help to distinguish the better from the worse, and encouragement to choose the former and avoid the latter. They should be forever stimulating each other to increased exercise of their higher faculties, and increased direction of their feelings and aims towards wise instead of foolish, elevating instead of degrading, objects and contemplations. But neither one person, nor any number of persons, is warranted in saying to another human creature of ripe years, that he shall not do with his life for his own benefit what he chooses to do with it. He is the person most interested in his own well-being: the interest which any other person, except in cases of strong personal attachment, can have in it, is trifling, compared with that which he himself has; the interest which society has in him individually (except as to his conduct to others) is fractional, and altogether indirect; while, with respect to his own feelings and circumstances, the most ordinary man or woman has means of knowledge immeasurably surpassing those that can be possessed by anyone else. The interference of society to overrule his judgment and purposes in what only regards himself, must be grounded on general presumptions; which may be altogether wrong, and even if right, are as likely as not to be misapplied to individual cases, by persons no better acquainted with the circumstances of such cases than those are who look at them merely from without. In this department, therefore, of human affairs, individuality has its proper field of action. In the conduct of human beings towards one another, it is necessary that general rules should for the most part be observed, in order that people may know what they have to expect; but in each person's own concerns, his individual spontaneity is entitled to free exercise. Considerations to aid his judgment, exhortations to strengthen his will, may be offered to him, even obtruded on him, by others; but he himself is the final judge. All errors which he is likely to commit against advice and warning, are far outweighed by the evil of allowing others to constrain him to what they deem his good.

I do not mean that the feelings with which a person is regarded by others, ought not to be in any way affected by his self-regarding qualities or deficiencies. This is neither possible nor desirable. If he is eminent in any of the qualities which conduce to his own good, he is, so far, a proper object of admiration. He is so much the nearer to the ideal perfection of human nature. If he is grossly deficient in those qualities, a sentiment the opposite of admiration will follow. There is a degree of folly, and a degree of what may be called (though the phrase is not unobjectionable) lowness or depravation of taste, which, though it cannot justify doing harm to the person who manifests it, renders him necessarily and properly a subject of distaste, or, in extreme cases, even of contempt: a person could not have the opposite qualities in due strength without entertaining these feelings. Though doing no wrong to anyone, a person may so act as to compel us to judge him, and feel to him, as a fool, or as a being of an inferior order: and since this judgment and feeling are a fact which he would prefer to avoid, it is doing him a service to warn him of it beforehand, as of any other disagreeable consequence to which he exposes himself. It would be well, indeed, if this good office were much more freely rendered than the common notions of politeness at present permit, and if one person could honestly point out to another that he thinks him in fault, without being considered unmannerly or presuming. We have a right, also, in various ways, to act upon our unfavourable opinion of anyone, not to the oppression of his individuality, but in the exercise of ours. We are not bound, for example, to seek his society; we have a right to avoid it (though not to parade the avoidance), for we have a right to choose the society most acceptable to us. We have a right, and it may be our duty, to caution others against him, if we think his example or conversation likely to have a pernicious effect on those with whom he associates. We may give others a preference over him in optional good offices, except those which tend to his improvement. In these various modes a person may suffer very severe penalties at the hands of others, for faults which directly concern only himself; but he suffers these penalties only in so far as they are the natural, and, as it were, the spontaneous consequences of the faults themselves, not because they are purposely inflicted on him for the sake of punishment. A person who shows rashness, obstinacy, self-conceit—who cannot live within moderate means—

who cannot restrain himself from hurtful indulgences—who pursues animal pleasures at the expense of those of feeling and intellect—must expect to be lowered in the opinion of others, and to have a less share of their favourable sentiments; but of this he has no right to complain, unless he has merited their favour by special excellence in his social relations, and has thus established a title to their good offices, which is not affected by his demerits towards himself.

What I contend for is, that the inconveniences which are strictly inseparable from the unfavourable judgment of others, are the only ones to which a person should ever be subjected for that portion of his conduct and character which concerns his own good, but which does not affect the interests of others in their relations with him. Acts injurious to others require a totally different treatment. Encroachment on their rights; infliction on them of any loss or damage not justified by his own rights; falsehood or duplicity in dealing with them; unfair or ungenerous use of advantages over them; even selfish abstinence from defending them against injury—these are fit objects of moral reprobation, and, in grave cases, of moral retribution and punishment....

The distinction between the loss of consideration which a person may rightly incur by defect of prudence or of personal dignity, and the reprobation which is due to him for an offence against the rights of others, is not a merely nominal distinction. It makes a vast difference both in our feelings and in our conduct towards him, whether he displeases us in things in which we think we have a right to control him, or in things in which we know that we have not. If he displeases us, we may express our distaste, and we may stand aloof from a person as well as from a thing that displeases us; but we shall not therefore feel called on to make his life uncomfortable. We shall reflect that he already bears, or will bear, the whole penalty of his error; if he spoils his life by mismanagement, we shall not, for that reason, desire to spoil it still further,...otherwise if he has infringed the rules necessary for the protection of his fellow creatures, individually or collectively. The evil consequences of his acts do not then fall on himself, but on others; and society, as the protector of all its members, must retaliate on him; must inflict pain on him for the express purpose of punishment, and must take care that it be sufficiently severe. In the one case, he is an offender at our bar, and we are called on not only to sit in judgment on him, but, in one shape or another, to execute our own sentence: in the other case, it is not our part to inflict any suffering on him, except what may incidentally follow from our using the same liberty in the regulation of our own affairs, which we allow to him in his.

The distinction here pointed out between the part of a person's life which concerns only himself, and that which concerns others, many persons will refuse to admit. How (it may be asked) can any part of the conduct of a member of society be a matter of indifference to the other members? No person is an entirely isolated being; it is impossible for a person to do anything seriously or permanently hurtful to himself, without mischief reaching at least to his near connections, and often far beyond them. If he injures his property, he does harm to those who directly or indirectly derived support from it, and usually diminishes, by a greater or less amount, the general resources of the community. If he deteriorates his bodily or mental faculties, he not only brings evil upon all who depended on him for any portion of their happiness, but disqualifies himself for rendering the services which he owes to his fellow creatures generally; perhaps becomes a burden on their affection or benevolence; and if such conduct were very frequent, hardly any offence that is committed would detract more from the general sum of good. Finally, if by his vices or follies a person does no direct harm to others, he is nevertheless (it may be said) injurious by his example; and ought to be compelled to control himself, for the sake of those whom the sight or knowledge of his conduct might corrupt or mislead.

And even (it will be added) if the consequences of misconduct could be confined to the vicious or thoughtless individual, ought society to abandon to their own guidance those who are manifestly unfit for it? If protection against themselves is confessedly due to children and persons under age, is not society equally bound to afford it to persons of mature years who are equally incapable of self-government? If gambling, or drunkenness, or incontinence, or idleness, or uncleanliness, are as injurious to happiness, and as great a hindrance to improvement, as many or most of the acts prohibited by law, why (it may be asked) should not law,

so far as is consistent with practicability and social convenience, endeavour to repress these also? And as a supplement to the unavoidable imperfections of law, ought not opinion at least to organize a powerful police against these vices, and visit rigidly with social penalties those who are known to practice them? There is no question here (it may be said) about restricting individuality, or impeding the trial of new and original experiments in living. The only things it is sought to prevent are things which have been tried and condemned from the beginning of the world until now; things which experience has shown not to be useful or suitable to any person's individuality. There must be some length of time and amount of experience, after which a moral or prudential truth may be regarded as established: and it is merely desired to prevent generation after generation from falling over the same precipice which has been fatal to their predecessors.

I fully admit that the mischief which a person does to himself, may seriously affect, both through their sympathies and their interests, those nearly connected with him, and in a minor degree, society at large. When, by conduct of this sort, a person is led to violate a distinct and assignable obligation to any other person or persons, the case is taken out of the self-regarding class, and becomes amenable to moral disapprobation in the proper sense of the term. If, for example, a man, through intemperance or extravagance, becomes unable to pay his debts, or, having undertaken the moral responsibility of a family, becomes from the same cause incapable of supporting or educating them, he is deservedly reprobated, and might be justly punished; but it is for the breach of duty to his family or creditors, not for the extravagance. If the resources which ought to have been devoted to them, had been diverted from them for the most prudent investment, the moral culpability would have been the same.....In like manner, when a person disables himself, by conduct purely self-regarding, from the performance of some definite duty incumbent on him to the public, he is guilty of a social offence. No person ought to be punished simply for being drunk; but a soldier or a policeman should be punished for being drunk on duty. Whenever, in short, there is a definite damage, or a definite risk of damage, either to an individual or to the public, the case is taken out of the province of liberty, and placed in that of mortality or law.

But with regard to the merely contingent, or, as it may be called, constructive injury which a person causes to society, by conduct which neither violates any specific duty to the public, nor occasions perceptible hurt to any assignable individual except himself; the inconvenience is one which society can afford to bear, for the sake of the greater good of human freedom. If grown persons are to be punished for not taking proper care of themselves, I would rather it were for their own sake, than under pretence of preventing them from impairing their capacity of rendering to society benefits which society does not pretend it has a right to exact. But I cannot consent to argue the point as if society had no means of bringing its weaker members up to its ordinary standard of rational conduct, except waiting till they do something irrational, and then punishing them, legally or morally, for it. Society has had absolute power over them during all the early portion of their existence: it has had the whole period of childhood and nonage in which to try whether it could make them capable of rational conduct in life. The existing generation is master both of the training and the entire circumstances of the generation to come; it cannot indeed make them perfectly wise and good, because it is itself so lamentably deficient in goodness and wisdom; and its best efforts are not always, in individual cases, its most successful ones; but it is perfectly well able to make the rising generation, as a whole, as good as, and a little better than, itself. If society lets any considerable number of its members grow up mere children, incapable of being acted on by rational consideration of distant motives, society has itself to blame for the consequences. Nor is there anything which tends more to discredit and frustrate the better means of influencing conduct, than a resort to the worse. If there be among those whom it is attempted to coerce into prudence or temperance, any of the material of which vigorous and independent characters are made, they will infallibly rebel against the yoke. No such person will ever feel that others have a right to control him in his concerns, such as they have to prevent him from injuring them in theirs; and it easily comes to be considered a mark of spirit and courage to fly in the face of such usurped authority, and do with ostentation the exact opposite of what it enjoins....

But the strongest of all the arguments against the interference of the public with purely personal conduct, is that when it does interfere, the odds are

that it interferes wrongly, and in the wrong place. On questions of social morality, of duty to others, the opinion of the public, that is, of an overruling majority, though often wrong, is likely to be still oftener right; because on such questions they are only required to judge of their own interests; of the manner in which some mode of conduct, if allowed to be practiced, would affect themselves. But the opinion of a similar majority, imposed as a law on the minority, on questions of self-regarding conduct, is quite as likely to be wrong as right; for in these cases public opinion means, at the best, some people's opinion of what is good or bad for other people; while very often it does not even mean that; the public, with the most perfect indifference, passing over the pleasure or convenience of those whose conduct they censure, and considering only their own preference. There are many who consider as an injury to themselves any conduct which they have a distaste for, and resent it as an outrage to their feelings; as a religious bigot, when charged with disregarding the religious feelings of others, has been known to retort that they disregard his feelings, by persisting in their abominable worship or creed....In its interferences with personal conduct it is seldom thinking of anything but the enormity of acting or feeling differently from itself; and this standard of judgment, thinly disguised, is held up to mankind as the dictate of religion and philosophy, by nine-tenths of all moralists and speculative writers....

The principles asserted in these pages must be more generally admitted as the basis for discussion of details, before a consistent application of them to all the various departments of government and morals can be attempted with any prospect of advantage. The few observations I propose to make on questions of detail, are designed to illustrate the principles, rather than to follow them out to their consequences. I offer, not so much applications, as specimens of application; which may serve to bring into greater clearness the meaning and limits of the two maxims which together form the entire doctrine of this Essay, and to assist the judgment in holding the balance between them, in the cases where it appears doubtful which of them is applicable to the case.

The maxims are, first, that the individual is not accountable to society for his actions, in so far as these concern the interests of no person but himself. Advice, instruction, persuasion, and avoidance by other people if thought necessary by them for their own good, are the only measures by which society can justifiably express its dislike or disapprobation of his conduct. Secondly, that for such actions as are prejudicial to the interests of others, the individual is accountable, and may be subjected either to social or to legal punishments, if society is of opinion that the one or the other is requisite for its protection.

In the first place, it must by no means be supposed, because damage, or probability of damage, to the interests of others, can alone justify the interference of society, that therefore it always does justify such interference. In many cases, an individual, in pursuing a legitimate object, necessarily and therefore legitimately causes pain or loss to others, or intercepts a good which they had a reasonable hope of obtaining. Such oppositions of interest between individuals often arise from bad social institutions, but are unavoidable while those institutions last; and some would be unavoidable under any institutions. Whoever succeeds in an overcrowded profession, or in a competitive examination; whoever is preferred to another in any contest for an object which both desire, reaps benefit from the loss of others, from their wasted exertion and their disappointment. But it is, by common admission, better for the general interest of mankind, that persons should pursue their objects undeterred by this sort of consequences. In other words, society admits no right, either legal or moral, in the disappointed competitors, to immunity from this kind of suffering; and feels called on to interfere, only when means of success have been employed which it is contrary to the general interest to permit—namely, fraud or treachery, and force.

Again, trade is a social act. Whoever undertakes to sell any description of goods to the public, does what affects the interest of other persons, and of society in general; and thus his conduct, in principle, comes within the jurisdiction of society: accordingly, it was once held to be the duty of governments, in all cases which were considered of importance, to fix prices, and regulate the processes of manufacture. But it is now recognized, though not till after a long struggle, that both the cheapness and the good quality of commodities are most effectually provided for by leaving the producers and sellers perfectly free, under the sole check of equal freedom to the buyers for supplying themselves elsewhere. This is the so-called doctrine of Free Trade, which rests on grounds different from, though equally solid with, the principle of individual liberty asserted in this Essay. Restrictions on trade, or on production for purposes of trade, are indeed restraints; and all restraint, *qua* restraint, is an evil: but the restraints in question affect only that part of conduct which society is competent to restrain, and are wrong solely because they do not really produce the results which it is desired to produce by them. As the principle of individual liberty is not involved in the doctrine of Free Trade, so neither is it in most of the questions which arise respecting the limits of that doctrine: as for example, what amount of public control is admissible for the prevention of fraud by adulteration; how far sanitary precautions, or arrangements to protect workpeople employed in dangerous occupations, should be enforced on employers. Such questions involve considerations of liberty, only in so far as leaving people to themselves is always better, *caeteris paribus*, than controlling them: but that they may be legitimately controlled for these ends, is in principle undeniable. On the other hand, there are questions relating to interference with trade, which are essentially questions of liberty; such as the...prohibition of the importation of opium into China; the restriction of the sale of poisons; all cases, in short, where the object of the interference is to make it impossible or difficult to obtain a particular commodity. These interferences are objectionable, not as infringements on the liberty of the producer or seller, but on that of the buyer.

One of these examples, that of the sale of poisons, opens a new question; the proper limits of what may be called the functions of police; how far liberty may legitimately be invaded for the prevention of crime, or of accident. It is one of the undisputed functions of government to take precautions against crime before it has been committed, as well as to detect and punish it afterwards. The preventive function of government, however, is far more liable to be abused, to the prejudice of liberty, than the punitory function; for there is hardly any part of the legitimate freedom of action of a human being which would not admit of being represented, and fairly too, as increasing the facilities for some form or other of delinquency. Nevertheless, if a public authority, or even a private person, sees anyone evidently preparing to commit a crime, they are not bound to look on inactive until the crime is committed, but may interfere to prevent it. If poisons were never bought or used for any purpose except the commission of murder, it would be right to prohibit their manufacture and sale. They may, however, be wanted not only for innocent but for useful purposes, and restrictions cannot be imposed in the one case without operating in the other. Again, it is a proper office of public authority to guard against accidents. If either a public officer or anyone else saw a person attempting to cross a bridge which had been ascertained to be unsafe, and there were no time to warn him of his danger, they might seize him and turn him back, without any real infringement of his liberty; for liberty consists in doing what one desires, and he does not desire to fall into the river. Nevertheless, when there is not a certainty, but only a danger of mischief, no one but the person himself can judge of the sufficiency of the motive which may prompt him to incur the risk: in this case, therefore (unless he is a child, or delirious, or in some state of excitement or absorption incompatible with the full use of the reflecting faculty), he ought, I conceive, to be only warned of the danger; not forcibly prevented from exposing himself to it. Similar considerations, applied to such a question as the sale of poisons, may enable us to decide which among the possible modes of regulation are or are not contrary to principle. Such a precaution, for example, as that of labelling the drug with some word expressive of its dangerous character, may be enforced without violation of liberty: the buyer cannot wish not to know that the thing he possesses has poisonous qualities. But to require in all cases the certificate of a medical practitioner, would make it sometimes impossible, always expensive, to obtain the article for legitimate uses. The only mode apparent to me, in which difficulties may be thrown in the way of crime committed through this means, without any infringement, worth taking into account, upon the liberty of those who desire the poisonous substance for other purposes, consists in providing what, in the apt language of Bentham, is called "preappointed evidence". This provision is familiar to everyone in the case of contracts. It is usual and right that the law, when a

contract is entered into, should require as the condition of its enforcing performance, that certain formalities should be observed, such as signatures, attestation of witnesses, and the like, in order that in case of subsequent dispute, there may be evidence to prove that the contract was really entered into, and that there was nothing in the circumstances to render it legally invalid: the effect being, to throw great obstacles in the way of fictitious contracts, or contracts made in circumstances which, if known, would destroy their validity. Precautions of a similar nature might be enforced in the sale of articles adapted to be instruments of crime. The seller, for example, might be required to enter in a register the exact time of the transaction, the name and address of the buyer, the precise quality and quantity sold; to ask the purpose for which it was wanted, and record the answer he received. When there was no medical prescription, the presence of some third person might be required, to bring home the fact to the purchaser, in case there should afterwards be reason to believe that the article had been applied to criminal purposes. Such regulations would in general be no material impediment to obtaining the article, but a very considerable one to making an improper use of it without detection.

The right inherent in society, to ward off crimes against itself by antecedent precautions, suggests the obvious limitations to the maxim, that purely self-regarding misconduct cannot properly be meddled with in the way of prevention or punishment. Drunkenness, for example, in ordinary cases, is not a fit subject for legislative interference; but I should deem it perfectly legitimate that a person, who had once been convicted of any act of violence to others under the influence of drink, should be placed under a special legal restriction, personal to himself; that if he were afterwards found drunk, he should be liable to a penalty, and that if when in that state he committed another offence, the punishment to which he would be liable for that other offence should be increased in severity. The making himself drunk, in a person whom drunkenness excites to do harm to others, is a crime against others. So, again, idleness, except in a person receiving support from the public, or except when it constitutes a breach of contract, cannot without tyranny be made a subject of legal punishment; but if either from idleness or from any other avoidable cause, a man fails to perform his legal duties to others, as for instance to support his children, it is no tyranny to force him to fulfil that obligation, by compulsory labour, if no other means are available.

Again, there are many acts which, being directly injurious only to the agents themselves, ought not to be legally interdicted, but which, if done publicly, are a violation of good manners, and coming thus within the category of offences against others, may rightfully be prohibited....

There is another question to which an answer must be found, consistent with the principles which have been laid down. In cases of personal conduct supposed to be blameable, but which respect for liberty precludes society from preventing or punishing, because the evil directly resulting falls wholly on the agent; what the agent is free to do, ought other persons to be equally free to counsel or instigate? This question is not free from difficulty. The case of a person who solicits another to do an act, is not strictly a case of self-regarding conduct. To give advice or offer inducements to anyone, is a social act, and may therefore, like actions in general which affect others, be supposed amenable to social control. But a little reflection corrects the first impression, by showing that if the case is not strictly within the definition of individual liberty, yet the reasons on which the principle of individual liberty is grounded, are applicable to it. If people must be allowed, in whatever concerns only themselves, to act as seems best to themselves at their own peril, they must equally be free to consult with one another about what is fit to be so done; to exchange opinions, and give and receive suggestions. Whatever it is permitted to do, it must be permitted to advise to do. The question is doubtful, only when the instigator derives a personal benefit from his advice; when he makes it his occupation, for subsistence or pecuniary gain, to promote what society and the state consider to be an evil. Then, indeed, a new element of complication is introduced; namely, the existence of classes of persons with an interest opposed to what is considered as the public weal, and whose mode of living is grounded on the counteraction of it. Ought this to be interfered with, or not? Fornication, for example, must be tolerated, and so must gambling; but should a person be free to be a pimp, or to keep a gambling-house? The case is one of those which lie on the exact boundary line between two princi-

ples, and it is not at once apparent to which of the two it properly belongs. There are arguments on both sides. On the side of toleration it may be said, that the fact of following anything as an occupation, and living or profiting by the practice of it, cannot make that criminal which would otherwise be admissible; that the act should either be consistently permitted or consistently prohibited; that if the principles which we have hitherto defended are true, society has no business, *as* society, to decide anything to be wrong which concerns only the individual; that it cannot go beyond dissuasion, and that one person should be as free to persuade, as another to dissuade. In opposition to this it may be contended, that although the public, or the State, are not warranted in authoritatively deciding, for purposes of repression or punishment, that such or such conduct affecting only the interests of the individual is good or bad, they are fully justified in assuming, if they regard it as bad, that its being so or not is at least a disputable question: That, this being supposed, they cannot be acting wrongly in endeavouring to exclude the influence of solicitations which are not disinterested, of instigators who cannot possibly be impartial—who have a direct personal interest on one side, and that side the one which the State believes to be wrong, and who confessedly promote it for personal objects only. There can surely, it may be urged, be nothing lost, no sacrifice of good, by so ordering matters that persons shall make their election, either wisely or foolishly, on their own prompting, as free as possible from the arts of persons who stimulate their inclinations for interested purposes of their own. Thus (it may be said) though the statutes respecting unlawful games are utterly indefensible—though all persons should be free to gamble in their own or each other's houses, or in any place of meeting established by their own subscriptions, and open only to the members and their visitors—yet public gambling-houses should not be permitted. It is true that the prohibition is never effectual, and that whatever amount of tyrannical power is given to the police, gambling-houses can always be maintained under other pretences; but they may be compelled to conduct their operations with a certain degree of secrecy and mystery, so that nobody knows anything about them but those who seek them; and more than this, society ought not to aim at. There is considerable force in these arguments; I will not venture to decide whether they are sufficient to justify the moral anomaly of punishing the accessary, when the principal is (and must be) allowed to go free; of fining or imprisoning the procurer, but not the fornicator, the gambling-house keeper, but not the gambler. Still less ought the common operations of buying and selling to be interfered with on analogous grounds. Almost every article which is bought and sold may be used in excess, and the sellers have a pecuniary interest in encouraging that excess;...because the class of dealers in strong drinks, though interested in their abuse, are indispensably required for the sake of their legitimate use. The interest, however, of these dealers in promoting intemperance is a real evil, and justifies the State in imposing restrictions and requiring guarantees, which but for that justification would be infringements of legitimate liberty.

A further question is, whether the State, while it permits, should nevertheless indirectly discourage conduct which it deems contrary to the best interests of the agent; whether, for example, it should take measures to render the means of drunkenness more costly, or add to the difficulty of procuring them, by limiting the number of the places of sale. On this as on most other practical questions, many distinctions require to be made. To tax stimulants for the sole purpose of making them more difficult to be obtained, is a measure differing only in degree from their entire prohibition; and would be justifiable only if that were justifiable. Every increase of cost is a prohibition, to those whose means do not come up to the augmented price; and to those who do, it is a penalty laid on them for gratifying a particular taste. Their choice of pleasures, and their mode of expending their income, after satisfying their legal and moral obligations to the State and to individuals, are their own concern, and must rest with their own judgment. These considerations may seem at first sight to condemn the selection of stimulants as special subjects of taxation for purposes of revenue. But it must be remembered that taxation for fiscal purposes is absolutely inevitable; that in most countries it is necessary that a considerable part of that taxation should be indirect; that the State, therefore, cannot help imposing penalties, which to some persons may be prohibitory, on the use of some articles of consumption. It is hence the duty of the State to consider, in the imposition of

taxes, what commodities the consumers can best spare; and *a fortiori*, to select in preference those of which it deems the use, beyond a very moderate quantity, to be positively injurious. Taxation, therefore, of stimulants, up to the point which produces the largest amount of revenue (supposing that the State needs all the revenue which it yields) is not only admissible, but to be approved of.

The question of making the sale of these commodities a more or less exclusive privilege, must be answered differently, according to the purposes to which the restriction is intended to be subservient. All places of public resort require the restraint of a police, and places of this kind peculiarly, because offences against society are especially apt to originate there. It is, therefore, fit to confine the power of selling these commodities (at least for consumption on the spot) to persons of known or vouched-for respectability of conduct; to make such regulations respecting hours of opening and closing as may be requisite for public surveillance, and to withdraw the licence if breaches of the peace repeatedly take place through the connivance or incapacity of the keeper of the house, or if it becomes a rendezvous for concocting and preparing offences against the law. Any further restriction I do not conceive to be, in principle, justifiable. The limitation in number, for instance, of beer and spirit-houses, for the express purpose of rendering them more difficult of access, and diminishing the occasions of temptation, not only exposes all to an inconvenience because there are some by whom the facility would be abused, but is suited only to a state of society in which the labouring classes are avowedly treated as children or savages, and placed under an education of restraint, to fit them for future admission to the privileges of freedom. This is not the principle on which the labouring classes are professedly governed in any free country; and no person who sets due value on freedom will give his adhesion to their being so governed, unless after all efforts have been exhausted to educate them for freedom and govern them as freemen, and it has been definitively proved that they can only be governed as children....

It was pointed out in an early part of this Essay, that the liberty of the individual, in things wherein the individual is alone concerned, implies a corresponding liberty in any number of individuals to regulate by mutual agreement such things as regard them jointly, and regard no persons but themselves. This question presents no difficulty, so long as the will of all the persons implicated remains unaltered; but since that will may change, it is often necessary, even in things in which they alone are concerned, that they should enter into engagements with one another; and when they do, it is fit, as a general rule, that those engagements should be kept. Yet in the laws, probably, of every country, this general rule has some exceptions. Not only persons are not held to engagements which violate the rights of third parties, but it is sometimes considered a sufficient reason for releasing them from an engagement, that it is injurious to themselves. In this and most other civilized countries, for example, an engagement by which a person should sell himself, or allow himself to be sold, as a slave, would be null and void; neither enforced by law nor by opinion. The ground for thus limiting his power of voluntarily disposing of his own lot in life, is apparent, and is very clearly seen in this extreme case. The reason for not interfering, unless for the sake of others, with a person's voluntary acts, is consideration for his liberty. His voluntary choice is evidence that what he so chooses is desirable, or at the least endurable, to him, and his good is on the whole best provided for by allowing him to take his own means of pursuing it. But by selling himself for a slave, he abdicates his liberty: he forgoes any future use of it, beyond that single act. He therefore defeats, in his own case, the very purpose which is the justification of allowing him to dispose of himself. He is no longer free; but is thenceforth in a position which has no longer the presumption in its favour, that would be afforded by his voluntarily remaining in it. The principle of freedom cannot require that he should be free not to be free. It is not freedom, to be allowed to alienate his freedom. These reasons, the force of which is so conspicuous in this peculiar case, are evidently of far wider application; yet a limit is everywhere set to them by the necessities of life, which continually require, not indeed that we should resign our freedom, but that we should consent to this and the other limitation of it. The principle, however, which demands uncontrolled freedom of action in all that concerns only the agents themselves, requires that those who have become bound to one another, in things which concern no third party, should be able to release

one another from the engagement; and even without such voluntary release, there are perhaps no contracts or engagements, except those that relate to money or money's worth, of which one can venture to say that there ought to be no liberty whatever of retraction.... When a person, either by express promise or by conduct, has encouraged another to rely upon his continuing to act in a certain way—to build expectations and calculations, and stake any part of his plan of life upon that supposition—a new series of moral obligations arises on his part towards that person, which may possibly be overruled, but cannot be ignored. And again, if the relation between two contracting parties has been followed by consequences to others; if it has placed third parties in any peculiar position, or, as in the case of marriage, has even called third parties into existence, obligations arise on the part of both the contracting parties towards those third persons, the fulfilment of which, or at all events the mode of fulfilment, must be greatly affected by the continuance or disruption of the relation between the original parties to the contract. It does not follow, nor can I admit, that these obligations extend to requiring the fulfilment of the contract at all costs to the happiness of the reluctant party; but they are a necessary element in the question; and even if,...they ought to make no difference in the *legal* freedom of the parties to release themselves from the engagement (and I also hold that they ought not to make *much* difference), they necessarily make a great difference in the *moral* freedom. A person is bound to take all these circumstances into account, before resolving on a step which may affect such important interests of others; and if he does not allow proper weight to those interests, he is morally responsible for the wrong....

I have already observed that, owing to the absence of any recognized general principles, liberty is often granted where it should be withheld, as well as withheld where it should be granted; and one of the cases in which, in the modern European world, the sentiment of liberty is the strongest, is a case where, in my view, it is altogether misplaced. A person should be free to do as he likes in his own concerns; but he ought not to be free to do as he likes in acting for another, under the pretext that the affairs of another are his own affairs. The State, while it respects the liberty of each in what specially regards himself, is bound to maintain a vigilant control over his exercise of any power which it allows him to possess over others. This obligation is almost entirely disregarded in the case of the family relations, a case, in its direct influence on human happiness, more important than all others taken together. The almost despotic power of husbands over wives needs not be enlarged upon here, because nothing more is needed for the complete removal of the evil, than that wives should have the same rights, and should receive the protection of law in the same manner, as all other persons; and because, on this subject, the defenders of established injustice do not avail themselves of the plea of liberty, but stand forth openly as the champions of power. It is in the case of children, that misapplied notions of liberty are a real obstacle to the fulfilment by the State of its duties. One would almost think that a man's children were supposed to be literally, and not metaphorically, a part of himself, so jealous is opinion of the smallest interference of law with his absolute and exclusive control over them; more jealous than of almost any interference with his own freedom of action: so much less do the generality of mankind value liberty than power....

I have reserved for the last place a large class of questions respecting the limits of government interference, which, though closely connected with the subject of this Essay, do not, in strictness, belong to it. These are cases in which the reasons against interference do not turn upon the principle of liberty; the question is not about restraining the actions of individuals, but about helping them: it is asked whether the government should do, or cause to be done, something for their benefit, instead of leaving it to be done by themselves, individually, or in voluntary combination.

The objections to government interference, when it is not such as to involve infringement of liberty, may be of three kinds.

The first is, when the thing to be done is likely to be better done by individuals than by the government. Speaking generally, there is no one so fit to conduct any business, or to determine how or by whom it shall be conducted, as those who are personally interested in it. This principle condemns the interferences, once so common, of the legislature, or the officers of government, with the ordinary processes of industry....

In many cases, though individuals may not do the particular thing so well, on the average, as the officers of government, it is nevertheless desirable that it should be done by them, rather than by the government, as a means to their own mental education—a mode of strengthening their active faculties, exercising their judgment, and giving them a familiar knowledge of the subjects with which they are thus left to deal. This is a principal, though not the sole, recommendation of jury trial (in cases not political); of free and popular local and municipal institutions; of the conduct of industrial and philanthropic enterprises by voluntary associations. These are not questions of liberty, and are connected with that subject only by remote tendencies; but they are questions of development,...as parts of national education; as being, in truth, the peculiar training of a citizen, the practical part of the political education of a free people, taking them out of the narrow circle of personal and family selfishness, and accustoming them to the comprehension of joint interests, the management of joint concerns—habituating them to act from public or semi-public motives, and guide their conduct by aims which unite instead of isolating them from one another. Without these habits and powers, a free constitution can neither be worked nor preserved, as is exemplified by the too-often transitory nature of political freedom in countries where it does not rest upon a sufficient basis of local liberties. The management of purely local business by the localities, and of the great enterprises of industry by the union of those who voluntarily supply the pecuniary means, is further recommended by all the advantages which have been set forth in this Essay as belonging to individuality of development, and diversity of modes of action. Government operations tend to be everywhere alike. With individuals and voluntary associations, on the contrary, there are varied experiments, and endless diversity of experience. What the State can usefully do, is to make itself a central depository, and active circulator and diffuser, of the experience resulting from many trials. Its business is to enable each experimentalist to benefit by the experiments of others, instead of tolerating no experiments but its own.

The third, and most cogent reason for restricting the interference of government, is the great evil of adding unnecessarily to its power. Every function superadded to those already exercised by the government, causes its influence over hopes and fears to be more widely diffused, and converts, more and more, the active and ambitious part of the public into hangers-on of the government, or of some party which aims at becoming the government. If the roads, the railways, the banks, the insurance offices, the great joint-stock companies, the universities, and the public charities, were all of them branches of the government; if, in addition, the municipal corporations and local boards, with all that now devolves on them, became departments of the central administration; if the employees of all these different enterprises were appointed and paid by the government, and looked to the government for every rise in life; not all the freedom of the press and popular constitution of the legislature would make this or any other country free otherwise than in name. And the evil would be greater, the more efficiently and scientifically the administrative machinery was constructed—the more skilful the arrangements for obtaining the best qualified hands and heads with which to work it....

If every part of the business of society which required organized concert, or large and comprehensive views, were in the hands of the government, and if government offices were universally filled by the ablest men, all the enlarged culture and practised intelligence in the country, except the purely speculative, would be concentrated in a numerous bureaucracy, to whom alone the rest of the community would look for all things: the multitude for direction and dictation in all they had to do; the able and aspiring for personal advancement. To be admitted into the ranks of this bureaucracy, and when admitted, to rise therein, would be the sole objects of ambition. Under this régime, not only is the outside public ill-qualified, for want of practical experience, to criticize or check the mode of operation of the bureaucracy, but even if the accidents of despotic or the natural working of popular institutions occasionally raise to the summit a ruler or rulers of reforming inclinations, no reform can be effected which is contrary to the interest of the bureaucracy....

It is not, also, to be forgotten, that the absorption of all the principal ability of the country into the governing body is fatal, sooner or later, to the mental activity and progressiveness of the body itself. Banded together as they are—working a system which, like all systems, necessarily proceeds in a great measure by fixed rules—the official body are under the constant temptation of sinking into indolent routine, or, if they now and then desert that mill-horse round, of rushing into some half-examined crudity which has struck the fancy of some leading member of the corps: and the sole check to these closely allied, though seemingly opposite, tendencies, the only stimulus which can keep the ability of the body itself up to a high standard, is liability to the watchful criticism of equal ability outside the body. It is indispensable, therefore, that the means should exist, independently of the government, of forming such ability, and furnishing it with the opportunities and experience necessary for a correct judgment of great practical affairs. If we would possess permanently a skilful and efficient body of functionaries—above all, a body able to originate and willing to adopt improvements; if we would not have our bureaucracy degenerate into a pedantocracy, this body must not engross all the occupations which form and cultivate the faculties required for the government of mankind.

To determine the point at which evils, so formidable to human freedom and advancement, begin, or rather at which they begin to predominate over the benefits attending the collective application of the force of society, under its recognized chiefs, for the removal of the obstacles which stand in the way of its well-being; to secure as much of the advantages of centralized power and intelligence, as can be had without turning into governmental channels too great a proportion of the general activity, is one of the most difficult and complicated questions in the art of government. It is, in a great measure, a question of detail, in which many and various considerations must be kept in view, and no absolute rule can be laid down. But I believe that the practical principle in which safety resides, the ideal to be kept in view, the standard by which to test all arrangements intended for overcoming the difficulty, may be conveyed in these words: the greatest dissemination of power consistent with efficiency; but the greatest possible centralization of information, and diffusion of it from the centre....

A government cannot have too much of the kind of activity which does not impede, but aids and stimulates, individual exertion and development. The mischief begins when, instead of calling forth the activity and powers of individuals and bodies, it substitutes its own activity for theirs; when, instead of informing, advising, and, upon occasion, denouncing, it makes them work in fetters, or bids them stand aside and does their work instead of them. The worth of a State, in the long run, is the worth of the individuals composing it; and a State which postpones the interests of *their* mental expansion and elevation, to a little more of administrative skill, or of that semblance of it which practice gives, in the details of business; a State which dwarfs its men, in order that they may be more docile instruments in its hands even for beneficial purposes, will find that with small men no great thing can really be accomplished; and that the perfection of machinery to which it has sacrificed everything, will in the end avail it nothing, for want of the vital power which, in order that the machine might work more smoothly, it has preferred to banish.

Philosophy of Right

G. W. F. Hegel

The state is the realized ethical idea or ethical spirit. It is the will which manifests itself, makes itself clear and visible, substantiates itself. It is the will which thinks and knows itself, and carries out what it knows, and in so far as it knows. The state finds in ethical custom its direct and unreflected existence, and its indirect and reflected existence in the self-consciousness of the individual and in his knowledge and activity. Self-consciousness in the form of social disposition has its substantive freedom in the state, as the essence, purpose, and product of its activity....

The state as a completed reality is the ethical whole and the actualization of freedom. It is the absolute purpose of reason that freedom should be actualized. The state is the spirit, which abides in the world and there realizes itself consciously; while in nature it is realized only as the other of itself or the sleeping spirit. Only when it is present in consciousness, knowing itself as an existing object, is it the state....The state is the march of God in the world; its ground or cause is the power of reason realizing itself as will. When thinking of the idea of the state, we must not have in our mind any particular state, or particular institution, but must rather contemplate the idea, this actual God, by itself....But as it is more easy to detect shortcomings than to grasp the positive meaning, one easily falls into the mistake of dwelling so much upon special aspects of the state as to overlook its inner organic being. The state is not a work of art. It is in the world, in the sphere of caprice, accident, and error. Evil behaviour can doubtless disfigure it in many ways, but the ugliest man, the criminal, the invalid, the cripple, are living men. The positive thing, the life, is present in spite of defects, and it is with this affirmative that we have here to deal....

Everything depends on the union of universality and particularity in the state. In the ancient states the subjective end was out-and-out one with the volition of the state. In modern times, on the contrary, we demand an individual view, and individual will and conscience. Of these things the ancients had none in the same sense. For them the final thing was the will of the state. While in Asiatic despotisms the individual had no inner nature, and no self-justification, in the modern world man's inner self is honoured. The conjunction of duty and right has the twofold aspect that what the state demands as duty should forthwith be the right of individuality, since the state's demand is nothing

From *Philosophy of Right*, S. W. Dyde, trans. (London: George Bell and Sons, 1896).

other than the organization of the conception of freedom. The prevailing characters of the individual will are by the state brought into objective reality, and in this way first attain to their truth and realization. The state is the sole and essential condition of the attainment of the particular end and good.... Political sentiment, as a mere appearance, is also to be distinguished from what men truly will. They will in fact the real matter, but they hold fast to bits, and delight in the vanity of making improvements. Men trust in the stability of the state, and suppose that in it only the particular interest can come into being. But custom makes invisible that upon which our whole existence turns. If any one goes safe through the streets at night, it does not occur to him that it could be otherwise. The habit of feeling secure has become a second nature, and we do not reflect that it is first brought about by the agency of special institutions. Often it is imagined that force holds the state together, but the binding cord is nothing else than the deep-seated feeling of order, which is possessed by all

The state is an organism or the development of the idea into its differences. These different sides are the different functions, affairs and activities of state by means of which the universal unceasingly produces itself by a necessary process. At the same time it is self-contained, since it is presupposed in its own productive activity. This organism is the political constitution. It proceeds eternally out of the state, just as the state in turn is self-contained by means of the constitution. If these two things fall apart, and make the different aspects independent, the unity produced by the constitution is no longer established. The true relation is illustrated by the fable of the belly and the limbs. Although the parts of an organism do not constitute an identity, yet it is of such a nature that, if one of its parts makes itself independent, all must be harmed. We cannot by means of predicates, propositions, etc., reach any right estimate of the state, which should be apprehended as an organism....

The state is real. Its reality consists in its realizing the interest of the whole in particular ends. Actuality is always the unity of universality and particularity. Universality exists piecemeal in particularity. Each side appears as if self-sufficient, although it is upheld and sustained only in the whole. In so far as this unity is absent, the thing is unrealized, even though existence may be predicated of it. A bad state is one which merely exists. A sick body also exists, but it has no true reality. A hand, which is cut off, still looks like a hand and exists, though it is not real. True reality is necessity. What is real is in itself necessary....

To the complete state essentially belong consciousness and thought. Hence the state knows what it wills, and knows it as something thought....

It yet remains essentially distinguished from religion in that its commands are a legal duty, it being a matter of indifference in what spirit the duty is performed, while the empire of religion, on the contrary, is the internal. Just as the state, if it were to make such a claim as religion makes, would endanger the right of the inner mind, so the church degenerates into a tyrannical religion, if it acts as a state and imposes punishments....

The expression, "The pious are subject to no law," is nothing more than the decree of fanaticism. Piety, when it replaces the state, cannot tolerate that which is definitely constituted and destroys it. A kindred type of mind is shown by him who permits conscience or internality to judge, and does not decide on general grounds. This internality does not in its development proceed to principles, and gives itself no justification. If piety is counted as the reality of the state, all laws are cast to the winds, and subjective feeling legislates. This feeling may be nothing but caprice, and yet this cannot be ascertained except by its acts. But in so far as it becomes acts or commands, it assumes the shape of laws, and is directly opposed to subjective feeling. God, who is the object of this feeling, may also be regarded as a being who determines. But God is the universal idea, and is in feeling the undetermined, which is not mature enough to determine what actually exists in a developed form in the state. The fact that everything in the state is firm and secure is a bulwark against caprice and positive opinion. So religion, as such, ought not to rule.

The political constitution is...the organization of the state and the process of its organic life in reference to its own self. In this process the state distinguishes within itself its elements, and unfolds them into self-subsistence.

The constitution is rational in so far as the active working divisions of the state are in accord with the nature of the conception....

Who shall frame the constitution? This question seems intelligible at first glance, but on closer examination turns out to be meaningless. It presupposes that no constitution exists, but merely a collection of atomic individuals. How a heap of individuals is to obtain a constitution, whether by its own efforts or by means of others, whether by goodness, thought, or force, must be left to itself to decide, for with a mere mass the conception has nothing to do. If the question, however, takes for granted the existence of an actual constitution, then to make a constitution means only to modify it, the previous existence of the constitution implying that any change must be made constitutionally. But it is strictly essential that the constitution, though it is begotten in time, should not be contemplated as made. It is rather to be thought of as above and beyond what is made, as self-begotten and self-centred, as divine and perpetual.

The principle of the modern world as a whole is freedom of subjectivity, the principle that all essential aspects of the spiritual whole should attain their right by self-development. From this standpoint one can hardly raise the idle question, as to which form is the better, monarchy or democracy. We venture to reply simply that the forms of all constitutions of the state are one-sided, if they are not able to contain the principle of free subjectivity, and do not know how to correspond to completed reason.

Spirit is real only in what it knows itself to be. The state, which is the nation's spirit, is the law which permeates all its relations, ethical observances, and the consciousness of its individuals. Hence the constitution of a people depends mainly on the kind and character of its self-consciousness. In it are found both its subjective freedom and the actuality of the constitution.

To think of giving to a people a constitution *a priori* is a whim, overlooking precisely that element which renders a constitution something more than a product of thought. Every nation, therefore, has the constitution which suits it and belongs to it.

The state must in its constitution penetrate all its aspects....A constitution is not a mere manufacture, but the work of centuries. It is the idea and the consciousness of what is reasonable, in so far as it is developed in a people. Hence no constitution is merely created....

Because sovereignty is the ideality of all particular powers, it easily gives rise to the common misconception; which takes it to be mere force, empty wilfulness, and a synonym for despotism. But despotism is a condition of lawlessness, in which the particular will, whether of monarch or people (ochlocracy) counts as law, or rather instead of law. Sovereignty, on the contrary, constitutes the element of the ideality of particular spheres and offices, in a condition which is lawful and constitutional.....

But the sovereignty of the people is usually in modern times opposed to the sovereignty of the monarch. This view of the sovereignty of the people may be traced to a confused idea of what is meant by "the people." The people apart from their monarch, and the common membership necessarily and directly associated with him, is a formless mass. It is no longer a state. In it occur none of the characteristic features of an equipped whole, such as sovereignty, government, law-courts, magistrates, professions, etc., etc. When these elements of an organized national life make their appearance in a people, it ceases to be that undefined abstraction, which is indicated by the mere general notion "people."...

The state must be regarded as a great architectonic building, or the hieroglyph of reason, presenting itself in actuality. Everything referring merely to utility, externality, etc., must be excluded from a philosophic treatment. It is easy for one to grasp the notion that the state is the self-determining and completely sovereign will, whose judgment is final. It is more difficult to apprehend this "I will" as a person. By this is not meant that the monarch can be wilful in his acts. Rather is he bound to the concrete content of the advice of his councillors, and, when the constitution is established, he has often nothing to do but sign his name....

A monarch is not remarkable for bodily strength or intellect, and yet millions permit themselves to be ruled by him. To say that men permit themselves to be governed contrary to their interests, ends, and intentions is preposterous, since men are not so stupid. It is their need and the inner power of the idea which urge them to this in opposition to their seeming consciousness, and retain them in this relation.

The main point which crops up in connection with the executive is the division of offices. This division is concerned with the transition from the universal to the particular and singular; and the business is to be divided according to the different branches. The difficulty is that the different functions, the inferior and superior, must work in harmony....For some time past the chief task has been that of organization carried on from above: while the lower and bulky part of the whole was readily left more or less unorganized. Yet it is of high importance that it also should be organized, because only as an organism is it a power or force. Otherwise it is a mere heap or mass of broken bits. An authoritative power is found only in the organic condition of the particular spheres....

The public service requires the sacrifice of independent self-satisfaction at one's pleasure, and grants the right of finding satisfaction in the performance of duty, but nowhere else. Here is found the conjunction of universal and particular interests, a union which constitutes the conception and the internal stability of the state....

The members of the executive and the state officials constitute the main part of the middle class, in which are found the educated intelligence and the consciousness of right of the mass of a people. The institutions of sovereignty operating from above and the rights of corporations from below prevent this class from occupying the position of an exclusive aristocracy and using their education and skill wilfully and despotically.

The state's consciousness and the most conspicuous education are found in the middle class, to which the state officials belong. The members of this class, therefore, form the pillars of the state in regard to rectitude and intelligence. The state, if it has no middle class, is still at a low stage of development...

The legislature interprets the laws and also those internal affairs of the state whose content is universal. This function is itself a part of the constitution. In it the constitution is presupposed, and so far lies absolutely beyond direct delimitation. Yet it receives development in the improvement of the laws, and the progressive character of the universal affairs of government.

The constitution must unquestionably be the solid ground, on which the legislature stands. Hence, the prime essential is not to set to work to make a constitution. It exists, but yet it radically becomes, that is, it is formed progressively. This progress is an alteration which is not noticed, and has not the form of an alteration. For example,...the emperor was formerly judge, and travelled about in his kingdom giving the law. Through the merely seeming or external progress of civilization, it has become necessary that the emperor should more and more delegate this office of judge to others. Thus the judicial function passed from the person of the prince to colleagues. So the progress of any condition of things is a seemingly calm and unnoticed one. In the lapse of time a constitution attains a position quite other than it had before....

In the legislative function in its totality are active both the monarchical element and the executive. The monarchical gives the final decision, and the executive element advises. The executive element has concrete knowledge and oversight of the whole in its many sides and in the actual principles firmly rooted in them. It has also acquaintance with the wants of the offices of state. In the legislature are at last represented the different classes or estates.

The expression "The Many"...characterizes the empirical universality better than the word "All," which is in current use. Under this "all," children, women, etc., are manifestly not meant to be included. Manifestly, therefore, the definite term "all" should not be employed, when, it may be, some quite indefinite thing is being discussed.

There are found in current opinion so unspeakably many perverted and false notions and sayings concerning the people, the constitution, and the classes, that it would be a vain task to specify, explain, and correct them. When it is argued that an assembly of estates is necessary and advantageous, it is meant that the people's deputies, or, indeed, the people itself, must best understand their own interest, and that it has undoubtedly the truest desire to secure this interest. But it is rather true that the people, in so far as this term signifies a special part of the citizens, does not know what it wills. To know what we will, and further what the absolute will, namely reason, wills, is the fruit of deep knowledge and insight, and is therefore not the property of the people....

As for the conspicuously good will, which is said to be shown by the classes towards the general interest,…the masses, who in general adopt a negative standpoint, take for granted that the will of the government is evil or but little good….

The attitude of the government to the classes must not be in its essence hostile. The belief in the necessity of this hostile relation is a sad mistake. The government is not one party which stands over against another, in such a way that each is seeking to wrest something from the other. If the state should find itself in such a situation, it must be regarded as a misfortune and not as a sign of health. Further, the taxes, to which the classes give their consent, are not to be looked upon as a gift to the state, but are contributed for the interest of the contributors. The peculiar significance of the classes or estates is this, that through them the state enters into and begins to share in the subjective consciousness of the people….

Since the private class is in the legislature exalted to participation in the universal business, it must appear in the form of individuals, be it that representatives are chosen for this purpose, or that every person shall exercise a voice. But even in the family this abstract atomic view is no longer to be found, nor in the civic community, in both of which the individual makes his appearance only as a member of a universal. As to the state, it is essentially an organization, whose members are independent spheres, and in it no phase shall show itself as an unorganized multitude. The many, as individuals, whom we are prone to call the people, are indeed a collective whole, but merely as a multitude or formless mass, whose movement and action would be elemental, void of reason, violent, and terrible…

The concrete state is the whole, articulated into its particular circles, and the member of the state is the member of a circle or class. Only his objective character can be recognized in the state. His general character contains the twofold element, private person and thinking person, and thinking is the consciousness and willing of the universal. But consciousness and will cease to be empty only when they are filled with particularity, and by particularity is meant the characteristic of a particular class. The individual is species, let us say, but has his intrinsic general actuality in the species next above it. He attains actual and vital contact with the universal in the sphere of the corporations and societies. It remains open to him by means of

his skill to make his way into any class, for which he has the capacity, including the universal class….

Public opinion is the unorganized means through which what a people wills and thinks is made known. That which is effective in the state must indeed be in organic relation to it; and in the constitution this is the case. But at all times public opinion has been a great power, and it is especially so in our time, when the principle of subjective freedom has such importance and significance. What now shall be confirmed is confirmed no longer through force, and but little through use and wont, but mainly by insight and reasons.

Public opinion contains therefore the eternal substantive principles of justice, the true content and result of the whole constitution, of legislation, and of the universal condition in general. It exists in the form of sound human understanding, that is, of an ethical principle which in the shape of prepossessions runs through everything. It contains the true wants and right tendencies of actuality…. A great mind has publicly raised the question, whether it be permitted to deceive a people. We must answer that a people does not allow itself to be deceived in regard to its substantive basis, or the essence and definite character of its spirit; but in regard to the way in which it knows this, and judges of its acts and phases, it deceives itself….

Public opinion deserves, therefore, to be esteemed and despised; to be despised in its concrete consciousness and expression, to be esteemed in its essential basis. At best, its inner nature makes merely an appearance in its concrete expression, and that, too, in a more or less troubled shape. Since it has not within itself the means of drawing distinctions, nor the capacity to raise its substantive side into definite knowledge, independence of it is the first formal condition of anything great and reasonable, whether in actuality or in science. Of any reasonable end we may be sure that public opinion will ultimately be pleased with it, recognize it, and constitute it one of its prepossessions.

In public opinion all is false and true, but to find out the truth in it is the affair of the great man. He who tells the time what it wills and means, and then brings it to completion, is the great man of the time. In his act the inner significance and essence of the time is actualized. Who does not learn to despise public opinion, which is one thing in one place and another in another, will never produce anything great.

The liberty of taking part in state affairs, the pricking impulse to say and to have said one's opinion, is directly secured by police laws and regulations, which, however, hinder and punish the excess of this liberty. Indirect security is based upon the government's strength, which lies mainly in the rationality of its constitution and the stability of its measures, but partly also in the publicity given to the assemblies of the classes. Security is guaranteed by publicity in so far as the assemblies voice the mature and educated insight into the interests of the state, and pass over to others what is less significant, especially if they are disabused of the idea that the utterances of these others are peculiarly important and efficacious. Besides, a broad guarantee is found in the general indifference and contempt, with which shallow and malicious utterances are quickly and effectually visited.

One means of freely and widely participating in public affairs is the press, which, in its more extended range, is superior to speech, although inferior in vivacity. To define the liberty of the press as the liberty to speak and write what one pleases is parallel to the definition of liberty in general, as liberty to do what one pleases. These views belong to the undeveloped crudity and superficiality of fanciful theorizing.... And this was to be expected, because the object is here the most transient, accidental, and particular in the whole range of opinion.

The element in which public opinion finds utterance and becomes an overt and tangible act is, as we have already observed, the intelligence, principles, and opinions of others. It is this element which determines the peculiar effect of these acts or the danger of them to individuals, the community or the state, just as a spark, if thrown upon a heap of gunpowder, is much more dangerous than if thrown on the ground, where it goes out and leaves no trace....

Property and life, not to speak of opinions and the ordinary routine of existence, they must sacrifice, if necessary, in order to preserve the substantive individuality, independence, and sovereignty of the state. It is a very distorted account of the matter when the state, in demanding sacrifices from the citizens, is taken to be simply the civic community, whose object is merely the security of life and property. Security cannot possibly be obtained by the sacrifice of what is to be secured.

Herein is to be found the ethical element in war. War is not to be regarded as an absolute evil. It is not a merely external accident, having its accidental ground in the passions of powerful individuals or nations, in acts of injustice, or in anything which ought not to be....

The military class is the class of universality. To it are assigned the defence of the state and the duty of bringing into existence the ideality implicit in itself. In other words it must sacrifice itself. Bravery is, it is true, of different sorts. The courage of the animal, or the robber, the bravery due to a sense of honour, the bravery of chivalry, are not yet the true forms of it. True bravery in civilized peoples consists in a readiness to offer up one-self in the service of the state, so that the individual counts only as one amongst many. Not personal fearlessness, but the taking of one's place in a universal cause, is the valuable feature of it....

Just as the individual person is not real unless related to others,...so the state is not really individual unless related to other states....The legitimate province of a state in its foreign relations, and more especially of the princely function, is on one side wholly internal; a state shall not meddle with the internal affairs of another state. Yet, on the other side, it is essential for its completeness that it be recognized by others. But this recognition demands as a guarantee that it shall recognize those who recognize it, and will have respect for their independence. Therefore they cannot be indifferent to its internal affairs....

When the particular wills of states can come to no agreement, the controversy can be settled only by war. Owing to the wide field and the varied relations of the citizens of different states to one another, injuries occur easily and frequently. What of these injuries is to be viewed as a specific breach of a treaty or as a violation of formal recognition and honour remains from the nature of the case indefinite. A state may introduce its infinitude and honour into every one of its separate compartments. It is all the more tempted to make or seek some occasion for a display of irritability, if the individuality within it has been strengthened by long internal rest, and desires an outlet for its pent-up activity....

The nations of Europe form a family by virtue of the universal principle of their legislation, their ethical observances, and their civilization....The relation of one state to another fluctuates; no judge is present to compose differences; the higher judge is simply the universal and absolute spirit, the spirit of the world.

As states are particular, there is manifested in their relation to one another a shifting play of internal particularity of passions, interests, aims, talents, virtues, force, wrong, vice, and external contingency on the very largest scale. In this play even the ethical whole, national independence, is exposed to chance. The spirit of a nation is an existing individual having in particularity its objective actuality and self-consciousness. Because of this particularity it is limited. The destinies and deeds of states in their connection with one another are the visible dialectic of the finite nature of these spirits. Out of this dialectic the universal spirit, the spirit of the world, the unlimited spirit, produces itself. It has the highest right of all, and exercises its right upon the lower spirits in world-history. The history of the world is the world's court of judgment....

Law and Authority

Pierre Kropotkin

"When ignorance reigns in society and disorder in the minds of men, laws are multiplied, legislation is expected to do everything, and each fresh law being a fresh miscalculation, men are continually led to demand from it what can proceed only from themselves, from their own education and their own morality." It is no revolutionist who says this, nor even a reformer. It is the jurist, Dalloy, author of the Collection of French law known as "Repertoire de la Legislation." And yet, though these lines were written by a man who was himself a maker and admirer of law, they perfectly represent the abnormal condition of our society.

In existing States a fresh law is looked upon as a remedy for evil. Instead of themselves altering what is bad, people begin by demanding a *law* to alter it. If the road between two villages is impassable, the peasant says:—"There should be a law about parish roads." If a park-keeper takes advantage of the want of spirit in those who follow him with servile observance and insults one of them, the insulted man says "There should be a law to enjoin more politeness upon park-keepers." If there is stagnation in agriculture or commerce, the husbandman, cattle-breeder, or corn speculator argues, "It is protective legislation that we require." Down to the old clothesman there is not one who does not demand a law to protect his own little trade. If the employer lowers wages or increases the hours of labour, the politician in embryo exclaims, "We must have a law to put all that to rights," instead of telling the workers that there are other, and much more effectual means of settling these things straight; namely, recovering from the employer the wealth of which he has been despoiling the workmen for generations. In short, a law everywhere and for everything! A law about fashions, a law about mad dogs, a law about virtue, a law to put a stop to all the vices and all the evils which result from human indolence and cowardice.

We are so perverted by an education which from infancy seeks to kill in us the spirit of revolt, and to develop that of submission to authority; we are so perverted by this existence under the ferule of a

From *Law and Authority* (London: Freedom Press, 1886).

law, which regulates every event in life—our birth, our education, our development, our love, our friendship—that, if this state of things continues, we shall lose all initiative, all habit of thinking for ourselves. Our society seems no longer able to understand that it is possible to exist otherwise than under the reign of Law, elaborated by a representative government and administered by a handful of rulers....

Indeed, for some thousands of years, those who govern us have done nothing but ring the changes upon "Respect for law, obedience to authority." This is the moral atmosphere in which parents bring up their children, and school only serves to confirm the impression. Cleverly assorted scraps of spurious science are inculcated upon the children to prove necessity of law; obedience to the law is made a religion; moral goodness and the law of the masters are fused into one and the same divinity. The historical hero of the schoolroom is the man who obeys the law, and defends it against rebels....

The confused mass of rules of conduct called Law, which has been bequeathed to us by slavery, serfdom, feudalism, and royalty, has taken the place of those stone monsters before whom human victims used to be immolated, and whom slavish savages dared not even touch lest they should be slain by the thunder-bolts of heaven....

To understand this, we must transport ourselves in imagination into the eighteenth century. Our hearts must have ached at the story of the atrocities committed by the all-powerful nobles of that time upon the men and women of the people, before we can understand what must have been the magic influence upon the peasant's mind of the words, "Equality before the law, obedience to the law without distinction of birth or fortune." He, who until then, had been treated more cruelly than a beast, he who had never had any rights, he who had never obtained justice against the most revolting actions on the part of a noble, unless in revenge he killed him and was hanged—he saw himself recognised by this maxim, at least in theory, at least with regard to his personal rights, as the equal of his lord. Whatever this law might be, it promised to affect lord and peasant alike; it proclaimed the equality of rich and poor before the judge. The promise was a lie, and to-day we know it; but at that period it was an advance, a homage to justice,

as hypocrisy is a homage rendered to truth. This is the reason that when the saviours of the menaced middle-class (the Robespierres and the Dantons) took their stand upon the writings of the Rousseaus and the Voltaires, and proclaimed "Respect for law, the same for every man," the people accepted the compromise; for their revolutionary impetus had already spent its force in the contest with a foe whose ranks drew closer day by day. They bowed the neck beneath the yoke of law to save themselves from the arbitrary power of their lords.

The Middle-Class has ever since continued to make the most of this maxim, which, with another principle, that of representative government, sums up the whole philosophy of the bourgeois age, the XIX century. It has preached this doctrine in its schools, it has propagated it in its writings, it has moulded its art and science to the same purpose, it has thrust its beliefs into every hole and corner—like a pious Englishwoman, who slips tracts under the door,—and it has done all this so successfully, that to-day we behold the issue in the detestable fact, that, at the very moment when the spirit of turbulent criticism as re-awakening, men who long for freedom begin the attempt to obtain it by entreating their masters to be kind enough to protect them by modifying the laws which these masters themselves have created!

But times and tempers are changed since a hundred years ago. Rebels are everywhere to be found, who no longer wish to obey the law without knowing whence it comes, what are its uses, and whither arises the obligation to submit to it, and the reverence with which it is encompassed. The rebels of our day are criticising the very foundations of Society, which have hitherto been held sacred, and first and foremost amongst them that fetish, law. Just for this reason, the upheaval which is at hand, is no mere insurrection, it is a *Revolution*.

The critics analise the sources of law, and find there, either a god, product of the terrors of the savage, and stupid, paltry, and malicious as the priests who vouch for its supernatural origin, or else, bloodshed, conquest by fire and sword. They study the characteristics of law, and instead of perpetual growth corresponding to that of the human race, they find its distinctive trait to be immobility, a tendency to crystalise what should be modified and developed day by day. They ask how law has been maintained, and in its service they see the atrocities of Byzantinism, the cruelties of the Inquisition, the tortures of the Middle Ages, living flesh torn by the lash of the executioner, chains, clubs, axes, the gloomy dungeons of prisons, agony, curses and tears. In our own days they see, as before, the axe, the cord, the rifle, the prison; on the one hand, the brutalised prisoner, reduced to the condition of a caged beast by the debasement of his whole moral being, and on the other, the judge, stripped of every feeling which does honor to human nature, living like a visionary in a world of legal fictions, revelling in the inflection of imprisonment and death, without even suspecting, in the cold malignity of his madness, the abyss of degradation into which he has himself fallen before the eyes of those whom he condemns.

They see a race of law-makers legislating without knowing what their laws are about; to-day voting a law on the sanitation of towns, without the faintest notion of hygiene, tomorrow making regulations for the armament of troops, without so much as understanding a gun; making laws about teaching and education without ever having given a lesson of any sort, or even an honest education to their own children; legislating at random in all directions, but never forgetting the penalties to be meted out to ragamuffins, the prison and the galleys, which are to be the portion of men a thousand times less immoral than these legislators themselves.

Finally, they see the gaoler on the way to lose all human feeling, the detective trained as a bloodhound, the police spy despising himself; "informing," metamorphosed into a virtue; corruption, erected into a system; all the vices, all the evil qualities of mankind countenanced and cultivated to insure the triumph of law.

All this we see, and, therefore, instead of inanely repeating the old formula, "Respect the law," we say, "Despise law and all its attributes!" In place of the cowardly phrase "Obey the law," our cry is "Revolt against all laws!"

Only compare the misdeeds accomplished in the name of each law, with the good it has been able to effect, and weigh carefully both good and evil, and you will see if we are right.

Relatively speaking, law is a product of modern times. For ages and ages mankind lived without any written law, even that graved in symbols upon the entrance stones of a temple. During that period, human relations were simply regulated by customs, habits and usages, made sacred by constant repetition, and acquired by each person in childhood, exactly as he learned how to obtain his food by hunting, cattle-rearing, or agriculture.

All human societies have passed through this primitive phase, and to this day a large proportion of mankind have no written law. Every tribe has its own manners and customs; customary law, as the jurists say. It has social habits, and that suffices to maintain cordial relations between the inhabitants of the village, the members of the tribe or community. Even amongst ourselves—the "civilised" nations—when we leave large towns, and go into the country, we see that there the mutual relations of the inhabitants are still regulated according to ancient and generally accepted customs, and not according to the written law of the legislators....

Two distinctly marked currents of custom are revealed by analysis of the usages of primitive people.

As man does not live in a solitary state, habits and feelings develop within him which are useful for the preservation of society and the propagation of the race. Without social feelings and usages, life in common would have been absolutely impossible. It is not law which has established them; they are anterior to all law. Neither is it religion which has ordained them; they are anterior to all religions. They are found amongst all animals living in society. They are spontaneously developed by the very nature of things, like those habits in animals which men call instinct. They spring from a process of evolution, which is useful, and, indeed, necessary, to keep society together in the struggle it is forced to maintain for existence. Savages end by no longer eating one another, because they find it in the long-run more advantageous to devote themselves to some sort of cultivation, than to enjoy the pleasure of feasting upon the flesh of an aged relative once a year. Many travellers have depicted the manners of absolutely independent tribes, where laws and chiefs are unknown, but where the members of the tribe have given up stabbing one another in every dispute, because the habit of living in society has ended by developing certain feelings of fraternity and oneness of interest, and they prefer appealing to a third person to settle their differences. The hospitality of primitive peoples, respect for human life, the sense of reciprocal obligation, compassion for the weak, courage, extending even to the sacrifice of self for others, which is first learnt for the sake of children and friends, and later, for that of members of the same community—all these qualities are developed in man anterior to all law, independently of all religion, as in the case of the social animals. Such feelings and practices are the inevitable results of social life. Without being, as say priests and metaphysicians, inherent in man, such qualities are the consequence of life in common.

But side by side with these customs, necessary to the life of societies and the preservation of the race, other desires, other passions, and therefore other habits and customs, are evolved in human associations. The desire to dominate others and impose one's own will upon them; the desire to seize upon the products of the labour of a neighbouring tribe; the desire to surround oneself with comforts, without producing anything, whilst slaves provide their master with the means of procuring every sort of pleasure and luxury—these selfish, personal desires give rise to another current of habits and customs. The priest and the warrior, the charlatan who makes a profit out of superstition, and after freeing himself from the fear of the devil, cultivates it in others; and the bully, who procures the invasion and pillage of his neighbours, that he may return laden with booty, and followed by slaves; these two, hand in hand, have succeeded in imposing upon primitive society customs advantageous to both of them, but tending to perpetuate their domination of the masses.

For this purpose, they have made use, in the first place, of that tendency to run in a groove, so highly developed in mankind. In children and all savages it attains striking proportions, and it may also be observed in animals. Man, when he is at all superstitious, is always afraid to introduce any sort of change into existing conditions; he generally venerates what is ancient. "Our fathers did so and so; they got on pretty well; they brought you up; they were not unhappy; do the same!" the old say to the young, every time the latter wish to alter things. The unknown frightens them, they prefer to cling to the past, even when that past represents poverty, oppression, and slavery. It may even be said that the more miserable a man is, the more he dreads every sort of change, lest it may make him more wretched still. Some ray of hope, a few scraps of comfort, must penetrate his gloomy abode before he can begin to desire better things, to criticise the

old ways of living, and prepare to imperil them for the sake of bringing about a change. So long as he is not imbued with hope, so long as he is not freed from the tutelage of those who utilise his superstition and his fears, he prefers remaining in his former position. If the young desire any change, the old raise a cry of alarm against the innovators. Some savages would rather die than transgress the customs of their country, because they have been told from childhood that the least infraction of established routine would bring ill-luck, and ruin the whole tribe. Even in the present day, what numbers of politicians, economists, and would-be revolutionists act under the same impression, and cling to a vanishing past. How many care only to seek for precedents. How many fiery innovators are mere copyists of bygone revolutions.

This spirit of routine, originating in superstition, indolence, and cowardice, has in all times been the mainstay of oppression. In primitive human societies, it was cleverly turned to account by priests and military chiefs, They perpetuated customs useful only to themselves, and succeeded in imposing them on the whole tribe. So long as this conservative spirit could be exploited so as to assure the chief in his encroachments upon individual liberty, so long as the only inequalities between men were the work of nature, and these were not increased a hundred-fold by the concentration of power and wealth, there was no need for law, and the formidable paraphernalia of tribunals and ever-augmenting penalties to enforce it.

But as society became more and more divided into two hostile classes, one seeking to establish its domination, the other struggling to escape, the strife began. Now the conqueror was in a hurry to secure the results of his actions in a permanent form, he tried to place them beyond question, to make them holy and venerable by every means in his power. Law made its appearance under the sanction of the priest, and the warrior's club was placed at its service. Its office was to render immutable such customs as were to the advantage of the dominant minority. Military authority undertook to ensure obedience. This new function was a fresh guarantee to the power of the warrior; now he had not only mere brute force at his service; he was the defender of law.

If law, however, presented nothing but a collection of prescriptions serviceable to rulers, it would find some difficulty in insuring acceptance and obedience. Well, the legislators confounded in one code the two currents of custom, of which we have just been speaking, the maxims which represent principles of morality and social union wrought out as a result of life in common, and the mandates, which are meant to ensure eternal existence to inequality. Customs, absolutely essential to the very being of society, are, in the code, cleverly intermingled with usages imposed by the ruling caste, and both claim equal respect from the crowd. "Do not kill," says the code, and hastens to add, "And pay tithes to the priest." "Do not steal," says the code, and immediately after, "He who refuses to pay taxes, shall have his hand struck off."

Such was law; and it has maintained its twofold character to this day. Its origin is the desire of the ruling class to give permanence to customs imposed by themselves for their own advantage. Its character is the skilful co-mingling of customs useful to society, customs which have no need of law to ensure respect, with other customs useful only to rulers, injurious to the mass of the people, and maintained only by the fear of punishment.

Like individual capital, which was born of fraud and violence, and developed under the auspices of authority, law has no title to the respect of men. Born of violence and superstition, and established in the interests of consumer, priest and rich exploiter, it must be utterly destroyed on the day when the people desire to break their chains....

The great Revolution began the demolition of this framework of law, bequeathed to us by feudalism and royalty. But after having demolished some portions of the ancient edifice, the Revolution delivered over the power of law-making to the bourgeoisie, who, in their turn, began to raise a fresh framework of laws intended to maintain and perpetuate middle-class domination amongst the masses. Their Parliament makes laws right and left, and mountains of law accumulate with frightful rapidity. But what *are* all these laws at bottom?

The major portion have but one object—to protect private property, *i.e.*, wealth acquired by the exploitation of man by man. Their aim is to open out to capital fresh fields for exploitation, and to sanction the new forms which that exploitation continually assumes, as capital swallows up another branch of human activity, railways, telegraphs, electric light, chemical industries, the

expression of man's thought in literature and science, &c. The object of the rest of these laws is fundamentally the same. They exist to keep up the machinery of government, which serves to secure to capital the exploitation and monopoly of the wealth produced. Magistrature, police, army, public instruction, finance, all serve one God—capital; all have but one object—to facilitate the exploitation of the worker by the capitalist. Analyse all the laws passed for the last eighty years, and you will find nothing but this. The protection of the person, which is put forward as the true mission of law, occupies an imperceptible space amongst them, for, in existing society, assaults upon the person, directly dictated by hatred and brutality, lend to disappear. Now-a-days, if anyone is murdered, it is generally for the sake of robbing him; rarely from personal vengeance. But if this class of crimes and misdemeanours is continually diminishing, we certainly do not owe the change to legislation. It is due to the growth of humanitarianism in our societies, to our increasingly social habits rather than to the prescriptions of our laws. Repeal to-morrow every law dealing with the protection of the person, and to-morrow stop all proceedings for assault, and the number of attempts, dictated by personal vengeance and by brutality, would not be augmented by one single instance.

It will, perhaps, be objected that, during the last fifty years, a good many liberal laws have been enacted. But, if these laws are analysed, it will be discovered that this liberal legislation consists in the repeal of the laws bequeathed to us by the barbarism of preceding centuries. Every liberal law, every radical programme, may be summed up in these words, abolition of laws grown irksome to the middle-class itself, and return and extension to all citizens of liberties enjoyed by the townships of the twelfth century....

Thus, the protection of exploitation, directly by laws on property, and indirectly by the maintenance of the State, is both the spirit and the substance of our modern codes, and the one function of our costly legislative machinery. But it is time we gave up being satisfied with mere phrases, and learned to appreciate their real signification. The law, which on its first appearance presented itself as a compendium of customs useful for the preservation of society, is now perceived to be nothing but an instrument for the maintenance of exploitation, and the domination of the toiling masses by rich idlers. At the present day its civilising mission is *nil*; it has but one object, to bolster up exploitation.

This is what is told us by history as to the development of law. Is it in virtue of this history that we are called upon to respect it? Certainly not. It has no more title to respect than capital, the fruit of pillage; and the first duty of the revolutionists of the nineteenth century will be to make a bonfire of all existing laws, as they will of all titles to property.

The millions of laws which exist for the regulation of humanity, appear upon investigation to be divided into three principal categories—protection of property, protection of persons, protection of government. And by analysing each of these three categories, we arrive at the same logical and necessary conclusion: *the uselessness and hurtfulness of law.*

Socialists know what is meant by protection of property. Laws on property are not made to guarantee either to the individual or to society the enjoyment of the produce of their own labor. On the contrary, they are made to rob the producer of a part of what he has created, and to secure to certain other people that portion of the produce which they have stolen either from the producer or from society as a whole. When, for example, the law establishes Mr. So-and-So's right to a house, it is not establishing his right to a cottage he has built for himself, or to a house he has erected with the help of some of his friends. In that case no one would have disputed his right. On the contrary, the law is establishing his right to a house which is *not* the product of his labor; first of all, because he has had it built for him by others, to whom he has not paid the full value of their work; and next, because that house represents a social value, which he could not have produced for himself. The law is establishing his right to what belongs to everybody in general and to nobody in particular. The same house built in the midst of Siberia would not have the value it possesses in a large town, and, as we know, that value arises from the labor of something like fifty generations of men who have built the town, beautified it, supplied it with water and gas, fine promenades, colleges, theatres, shops, railways, and roads leading in all directions. Thus, by recognising the right of Mr. So-and-So to a particular house in Paris, London, or Rouen, the law is unjustly appropriating to him a certain portion of the produce of the labour of mankind in general. And it is precisely because this appropriation and all other forms of property bearing the same character, are a crying injustice, that a whole arsenal of laws, and a whole army of soldiers, policemen, and judges are needed to maintain it against the good sense and just feeling inherent in humanity.

Well, half our laws, the civil code in each country, serves no other purpose than to maintain this appropriation, this monopoly for the benefit of certain individuals against the whole of mankind. Three-fourths of the causes decided by the tribunals are nothing but quarrels between monopolists—two robbers disputing over their booty. And a great many of our criminal laws have the same object in view, their end being to keep the workman in a subordinate position towards his employer, and thus afford security to exploitation.

As for guaranteeing the product of his labour to the producer, there are no laws which even attempt such a thing. It is so simple and natural, so much a part of the manners and customs of mankind, that law has not given it so much as a thought....Neither does one workman ever come and dispute the produce of his labour with another. If they have a misunderstanding they settle it by calling in a third person, without having recourse to law. The only person who exacts from another what that other has produced, is the proprietor, who comes in and deducts the lion's share. As for humanity in general, it everywhere respects the right of each to what he has created, without the interposition of any special laws.

As all the laws about property, which make up thick volumes of codes, and are the delight of our lawyers, have no other object than to protect the unjust appropriation of human labour by certain monopolists, there is no reason for their existence, and, on the day of the Revolution, social revolutionists are thoroughly determined to put an end to them. Indeed, a bonfire might be made with perfect justice of all laws bearing upon the so-called "rights of property," all title-deeds, all registers, in a word, of all that is in any way connected with an institution which will soon be looked upon as a blot in the history of humanity, as humiliating as the slavery and serfdom of past ages.

The remarks just made upon laws concerning property are quite as applicable to the second category of laws; those for the maintenance of government *i.e.*, Constitutional Law.

It again is a complete arsenal of laws, decrees, ordinances, orders in council, and what not, all serving to protect the diverse forms of representative government, delegated or usurped, beneath which humanity is writhing. We know very well—Anarchists have often enough pointed out in their perpetual criticism of the various forms of government—that the mission of all governments, monarchical, constitutional, or republican, is to protect and maintain by force the privileges of the classes in possession, the aristocracy, clergy, and traders. A good third of our laws—and each country possesses some tens of thousands of them—the fundamental laws on taxes, excise duties, the organization of ministerial departments and their offices, of the army, the police, the Church, &c., have no other end than to maintain, patch up, and develop the administrative machine. And this machine in its turn serves almost entirely to protect the privileges of the possessing classes. Analyse all these laws, observe them in action day by day, and you will discover that not one is worth preserving.

About such laws there can be no two opinions. Not only Anarchists, but more or less revolutionary radicals also, are agreed that the only use to be made of laws concerning the organization of government is to fling them into the fire.

The third category of law still remains to be considered, that relating to the protection of the person and the detection and prevention of "crime." This is the most important, because most prejudices attach to it; because, if law enjoys a certain amount of consideration, it is in consequence of the belief that this species of law is absolutely indispensable to the maintenance of security in our societies. These are laws developed from the nucleus of customs useful to human communities, which have been turned to account by rulers to sanctify their own domination. The authority of the chiefs of tribes, of rich families in towns, and of the king, depended upon their judicial functions, and even down to the present day, whenever the necessity of government is spoken of, its function as supreme judge is the thing implied. "Without a government men would tear one another to pieces," argues the village orator. "The ultimate end of all government is to secure twelve honest jurymen to every accused person," said Burke.

Well, in spite of all the prejudices existing on this subject, it is quite time that Anarchists should boldly declare this category of laws as useless and injurious as the preceding ones.

First of all, as to so-called "crimes"—assaults upon persons—it is well-known that two-thirds, and often as many as three-fourths, of such "crimes" are instigated by the desire to obtain possession of someone's wealth. This immense class of so-called "crimes and misdemeanours" will disappear on the day on which private property ceases to exist. "But," it will be said, "there will always be brutes who will attempt the lives of their fellow-citizens, who will lay their hands to a knife in every quarrel, and revenge the slightest offence by murder, if there are no laws to restrain and punishments to withhold them." This refrain is repeated every time the right of society *to punish* is called in question....

It is also a well-known fact that the fear of punishment has never stopped a single murderer. He who kills his neighbour from revenge or misery does not reason much about consequences; and there have been few murderers who were not firmly convinced that they should escape prosecution.

Without speaking of a society in which a man will receive a better education, in which the development of all his faculties, and the possibility of exercising them, will procure him so many enjoyments, that he will not seek to poison them by remorse—without speaking of the society of the future—even in our society, even with those sad products of misery, whom we see to-day in the public-houses of great cities—on the day when no punishment is inflicted upon murderers, the number of murders will not augment by a single case; and it is extremely probable that it will be, on the contrary, diminished by all those cases which are due at present to habitual criminals, who have been brutalised in prisons.

We are continually being told of the benefits conferred by law, and the beneficial effect of penalties, but have the speakers ever attempted to strike a balance between the benefits attributed to laws and penalties, and the degrading effect of these penalties upon humanity? Only calculate all the evil passions awakened in mankind by the atrocious punishments formerly inflicted in our streets! Man is the cruellest animal upon earth; and who has pampered and developed the cruel instincts unknown, even amongst monkeys, if it is not the king, the judge, and the priest, armed with law, who caused flesh to be torn off in strips boiling pitch to be poured into wounds, limbs to be dislocated, bones to be crushed, men to be sawn asunder to maintain their authority?...

Only go into the gaols and study what man becomes when he is deprived of freedom and shut up with other depraved beings, steeped in the vice and corruption which oozes from the very walls of our existing prisons. Only remember that the more these prisons are reformed, the more detestable they become; our model modern penitentiaries are a hundred-fold more abominable than the dungeons of the middle ages. Finally, consider what corruption, what depravity of mind, is kept up amongst men by the idea of obedience, the very essence of law; of chastisement; of authority having the right to punish, to judge irrespective of our conscience and the esteem of our friends; of the necessity for executioners, gaolers, and informers—in a word, by all the attributes of law and authority. Consider all this, and you will assuredly agree with us in saying that a law inflicting penalties is an abomination which should cease to exist.

Peoples without political organization, and therefore less depraved than ourselves, have perfectly understood that the man who is called "criminal" is simply unfortunate; that the remedy is not to flog him, to chain him up, or to kill him on the scaffold or in prison, but to relieve him by the most brotherly care, by treatment based on equality, by the usages of life amongst honest men. In the next revolution we hope that this cry will go forth:

"Burn the guillotines; demolish the prisons; drive away the judges, policemen, and informers— the impurest race upon the face of the earth; treat as a brother the man who has been led by passion to do ill to his fellow; above all, take from the ignoble products of middle-class idleness the possibility of displaying their vices in attractive colours; and be sure that but few crimes will mar our society."...

No more laws! No more judges! Liberty, equality, and practical human sympathy are the only effectual barriers we can oppose to the anti-social instincts of certain amongst us.

"Alienated Labour"

Karl Marx

We have now to grasp the real connection between this whole system of alienation—private property, acquisitiveness, the separation of labour, capital and land, exchange and competition, value and the devaluation of man, monopoly and competition— and the system of *money*.

Let us not begin our explanation, as does the economist, from a legendary primordial condition.

Such a primordial condition does not explain anything; it merely removes the question into a grey and nebulous distance....

We shall begin from a *contemporary* economic fact. The worker becomes poorer the more wealth he produces and the more his production increases in power and extent. The worker becomes an ever cheaper commodity the more goods he creates. The

From *Karl Marx: Early Writings*, T. B. Bottomore, trans. and ed. (New York: McGraw Hill, 1964). Reprinted by permission of the publisher.

devaluation of the human world increases in direct relation with the *increase in value* of the world of things. Labour does not only create goods; it also produces itself and the worker as a *commodity*, and indeed in the same proportion as it produces goods.

This fact simply implies that the object produced by labour, its product, now stands opposed to it as an *alien being*, as a *power independent* of the producer. The product of labour is labour which has been embodied in an object and turned into a physical thing; this product is an *objectification* of labour. The performance of work is at the same time its objectification. The performance of work appears in the sphere of political economy as a *vitiation* of the worker, objectification as a *loss* and as *servitude to the object*, and appropriation as *alienation*.

So much does the performance of work appear as vitiation that the worker is vitiated to the point of starvation. So much does objectification appear as loss of the object that the worker is deprived of the most essential things not only of life but also of work. Labour itself becomes an object which he can acquire only by the greatest effort and with unpredictable interruptions. So much does the appropriation of the object appear as alienation that the more objects the worker produces the fewer he can possess and the more he falls under the domination of his product, of capital.

All these consequences follow from the fact that the worker is related to the *product of his labour* as to an *alien* object. For it is clear on this presupposition that the more the worker expends himself in work the more powerful becomes the world of objects which he creates in face of himself, the poorer he becomes in his inner life, and the less he belongs to himself. It is just the same as in religion. The more of himself man attributes to God the less he has left in himself. The worker puts his life into the object, and his life then belongs no longer to himself but to the object. The greater his activity, therefore, the less he possesses. What is embodied in the product of his labour is no longer his own. The greater this product is, therefore, the more he is diminished. The *alienation* of the worker in his product means not only that his labour becomes an object, assumes an *external* existence, but that it exists independently, *outside himself*, and alien to him, and that it stands opposed to him as an autonomous power. The life which he has given to the

object sets itself against him as an alien and hostile force.

Let us now examine more closely the phenomenon of *objectification*; the worker's production and the *alienation* and *loss* of the object it produces, which is involved in it. The worker can create nothing without *nature*, without the *sensuous external world*. The latter is the material in which his labour is realized, in which it is active, out of which and through which it produces things.

But just as nature affords the *means of existence* of labour, in the sense that labour cannot *live* without objects upon which it can be exercised, so also it provides the *means of existence* in a narrower sense; namely the means of physical existence for the *worker* himself. Thus, the more the worker *appropriates* the external world of sensuous nature by his labour the more he deprives himself of *means of existence*, in two respects: first, that the sensuous external world becomes progressively less an object belonging to his labour or a means of existence of his labour, and secondly, that it becomes progressively less a means of existence in the direct sense, a means for the physical subsistence of the worker.

In both respects, therefore, the worker becomes a slave of the object; first, in that he receives an *object of work*, i.e., receives *work*, and secondly, in that he receives *means of subsistence*. Thus the object enables him to exist, first as a *worker* and secondly, as a *physical subject*. The culmination of this enslavement is that he can only maintain himself as a *physical subject* so far as he is a *worker*, and that it is only as a *physical subject* that he is a worker.

(The alienation of the worker in his object is expressed as follows in the laws of political economy: the more the worker produces the less he has to consume; the more value he creates the more worthless he becomes; the more refined his product the more crude and misshapen the worker; the more civilized the product the more barbarous the worker; the more powerful the work the more feeble the worker; the more the work manifests intelligence the more the worker declines in intelligence and becomes a slave of nature.)

Political economy conceals the alienation in the nature of labour in so far as it does not examine the direct relationship between the worker (work) and production. Labour certainly produces marvels for the rich but it produces privation for the worker. It produces palaces, but hovels for the worker. It produces beauty, but deformity for the worker. It replaces labour by machinery, but it casts some of the workers back into a barbarous kind of work and turns the others into machines. It produces intelligence, but also stupidity and cretinism for the workers....

So far we have considered the alienation of the worker only from one aspect; namely, *his relationship with the products of his labour.* However, alienation appears not merely in the result but also in the *process* of *production,* within *productive activity* itself. How could the worker stand in an alien relationship to the product of his activity if he did not alienate himself in the act of production itself? The product is indeed only the *résumé* of activity, of production. Consequently, if the product of labour is alienation, production itself must be active alienation—the alienation of activity and the activity of alienation. The alienation of the object of labour merely summarizes the alienation in the work activity itself.

What constitutes the alienation of labour? First, that the work is *external* to the worker, that it is not part of his nature; and that, consequently, he does not fulfil himself in his work but denies himself, has a feeling of misery rather than well-being, does not develop freely his mental and physical energies but is physically exhausted and mentally debased. The worker, therefore, feels himself at home only during his leisure time, whereas at work he feels homeless. His work is not voluntary but imposed, *forced labour.* It is not the satisfaction of a need, but only a *means* for satisfying other needs. Its alien character is clearly shown by the fact that as soon as there is no physical or other compulsion it is avoided like the plague. External labour, labour in which man alienates himself, is a labour of self-sacrifice, of mortification. Finally, the external character of work for the worker is shown by the fact that it is not his own work but work for someone else, that in work he does not belong to himself but to another person....

We began with an economic fact, the alienation of the worker and his production. We have expressed this fact in conceptual terms as *alienated labour,* and in analyzing the concept we have merely analyzed an economic fact.

Let us now examine further how this concept of alienated labour must express and reveal itself in reality. If the product of labour is alien to me and confronts me as an alien power, to whom does it belong? If my own activity does not belong to me but is an alien, forced activity, to whom does it belong? To a being *other* than myself. And who is this being?...

The *alien* being to whom labour and the product of labour belong, to whose service labour is devoted, and to whose enjoyment the product of labour goes, can only be *man* himself. If the product of labour does not belong to the worker, but confronts him as an alien power, this can only be because it belongs to *a man other than the worker.* If his activity is a torment to him it must be a source of *enjoyment* and pleasure to another....

Thus, through alienated labour the worker creates the relation of another man, who does not work and is outside the work process, to this labour. The relation of the worker to work also produces the relation of the capitalist (or whatever one likes to call the lord of labour) to work. *Private property* is, therefore, the product, the necessary result, of *alienated labour,* of the external relation of the worker to nature and to himself.

Private property is thus derived from the analysis of the concept of *alienated labour;* that is, alienated man, alienated labour, alienated life, and estranged man.

We have, of course, derived the concept of *alienated labour* (*alienated life*) from political economy, from an analysis of the *movement of private property.* But the analysis of this concept shows that although private property appears to be the basis and cause of alienated labour, it is rather a consequence of the latter, just as the gods are *fundamentally* not the cause but the product of confusions of human reason. At a later stage, however, there is a reciprocal influence.

Only in the final stage of the development of private property is its secret revealed, namely, that it is on one hand the *product* of alienated labour, and on the other hand the *means* by which labour is alienated, *the realization of this alienation....*

"Socialism: Utopian and Scientific"

Friedrich Engels

The more strongly...earlier socialism denounced the exploitation of the working class, inevitable under capitalism, the less able was it clearly to show in what this exploitation consisted and how it arose. But for this it was necessary—(1) to present the capitalistic method of production in its historical connection and its inevitableness during a particular historical period, and therefore, also, to present its inevitable downfall; and (2) to lay bare its essential character, which was still a secret. This was done by the discovery of *surplus value*. It was shown that the appropriation of unpaid labour is the basis of the capitalist mode of production and of the exploitation of the worker that occurs under it; that even if the capitalist buys the labour power of his labourer at its full value as a commodity on the market, he yet extracts more value from it than he paid for; and that in the ultimate analysis this surplus value forms those sums of value from which are heaped up the constantly increasing masses of capital in the hands of the possessing classes....

These two great discoveries, the materialistic conception of history and the revelation of the secret of capitalistic production through surplus value, we owe to Marx. With these discoveries socialism became a science. The next thing was to work out all its details and relations.

The materialist conception of history starts from the proposition that the production of the means to support human life and, next to production, the exchange of things produced, is the basis of all social structure; that in every society that has appeared in history, the manner in which wealth is distributed and society divided into classes or orders is dependent upon what is produced, how it is produced, and how the products are exchanged. From this point of view the final causes of all social changes and political revolutions are to be sought, not in men's brains, not in men's better insight into eternal truth and justice, but in changes in the modes of production and exchange. They are to be sought not in the *philosophy*, but in the *economics* of each particular epoch. The growing perception that existing social institutions are unreasonable and unjust, that reason has become unreason and right wrong, is only proof that in the modes of production and exchange changes have silently taken place with which the social order, adapted to earlier economic conditions, is no longer in keeping. From this it also follows that the means of getting rid of the incongruities that have been brought to light must also be present, in a more or less developed condition, within the changed modes of production themselves. These means are not to be invented by deduction from fundamental principles, but are to be discovered in the stubborn facts of the existing system of production.

What is, then, the position of modern socialism in this connection?

The present structure of society—this is now pretty generally conceded—is the creation of the ruling class of today, of the bourgeoisie. The mode of production peculiar to the bourgeoisie, known, since Marx, as the capitalist mode of production, was incompatible with the feudal system, with the privileges it conferred upon individuals, entire social ranks and local corporations, as well as with the hereditary ties of subordination which constituted the framework of its social organisation. The bourgeoisie broke up the feudal system and built upon its ruins the capitalist order of society, the kingdom of free competition, of personal liberty, of the equality, before the law, of all commodity owners, of all the rest of the capitalist blessings. Thenceforward the capitalist mode of production

From *Karl Marx and Frederick Engels: Selected Works*, Vol 2 (Moscow· Foreign Languages Publishing House, 1962)

could develop in freedom. Since steam, machinery, and the making of machines by machinery transformed the older manufacture into modern industry, the productive forces evolved under the guidance of the bourgeoisie developed with a rapidity and in a degree unheard of before. But just as the older manufacture, in its time, and handicraft, becoming more developed under its influence, had come into collision with the feudal trammels of the guilds, so now modern industry, in its more complete development, comes into collision with the bounds within which the capitalistic mode of production holds it confined. The new productive forces have already outgrown the capitalistic mode of using them. And this conflict between productive forces and modes of production is not a conflict engendered in the mind of man, like that between original sin and divine justice. It exists, in fact, objectively, outside us, independently of the will and actions even of the men that have brought it on. Modern socialism is nothing but the reflex, in thought, of this conflict in fact; its ideal reflection in the minds, first, of the class directly suffering under it, the working class.

Now, in what does this conflict consist?

Before capitalistic production, i.e., in the Middle Ages, the system of petty industry obtained generally, based upon the private property of the labourers in their means of production; in the country, the agriculture of the small peasant, freeman or serf; in the towns, the handicrafts organised in guilds. The instruments of labour—land, agricultural implements, the workshop, the tool—were the instruments of labour of single individuals, adapted for the use of one worker, and, therefore, of necessity, small, dwarfish, circumscribed. But, for this very reason they belonged, as a rule, to the producer himself. To concentrate these scattered, limited means of production, to enlarge them, to turn them into the powerful levers of production of the present day—this was precisely the historic role of capitalist production and of its upholder, the bourgeoisie. In the fourth section of *Capital* Marx has explained in detail, how since the fifteenth century this has been historically worked out through the three phases of simple co-operation, manufacture and modern industry. But the bourgeoisie, as is also shown there, could not transform these puny means of production into mighty productive forces without transforming them, at the same time, from means of production of the individual into *social* means of production only workable by a collectivity of men. The spinning-wheel, the hand-loom, the blacksmith's hammer, were replaced by the spinning-machine, the power-loom, the steam-hammer; the individual workshop, by the factory implying the co-operation of hundreds and thousands of workmen. In like manner, production itself changed from a series of individual into a series of social acts, and the products from individual to social products. The yarn, the cloth, the metal articles that now came out of the factory, were the joint product of many workers, through whose hands they had successively to pass before they were ready. No one person could say of them: "I made that; this is *my* product."

But where, in a given society, the fundamental form of production is that spontaneous division of labour which creeps in gradually and not upon any preconceived plan, there the products take on the form of *commodities*, whose mutual exchange, buying and selling, enable the individual producers to satisfy their manifold wants. And this was the case in the Middle Ages. The peasant, e.g., sold to the artisan agricultural products and bought from him the products of handicraft. Into this society of individual producers, of commodity producers, the new mode of production thrust itself. In the midst of the old division of labour, grown up spontaneously and upon *no definite plan*, which had governed the whole of society, now arose division of labour upon a *definite plan*, as organised in the factory; side by side with *individual* production appeared *social* production. The products of both were sold in the same market, and, therefore, at prices at least approximately equal. But organisation upon a definite plan was stronger than spontaneous division of labour. The factories working with the combined social forces of a collectivity of individuals produced their commodities far more cheaply than the individual small producers. Individual production succumbed in one department after another. Socialised production revolutionised all the old methods of production. But its revolutionary character was, at the same time, so little recognised that it was, on the contrary, introduced as a means of increasing and developing the production of commodities. When it arose, it found ready-made, and made liberal use of, certain machinery for the production and exchange of commodities: merchants' capital, handicraft, wage-labour. Socialised production thus introducing itself as a new form of the production of commodities, it was a matter of course that under it the old forms of appropriation remained in full swing, and were applied to its products as well.

In the mediaeval stage of evolution of the production of commodities, the question as to the owner of the product of labour could not arise. The individual producer, as a rule, had, from raw material belonging to himself, and generally his own handiwork, produced it with his own tools, by the labour of his own hands or of his family. There was no need for him to appropriate the new product. It belonged wholly to him, as a matter of course. His property in the product was, therefore, based *upon his own labour*. Even where external help was used, this was, as a rule, of little importance, and very generally was compensated by something other than wages. The apprentices and journeymen of the guilds worked less for board and wages than for education, in order that they might become master craftsmen themselves.

Then came the concentration of the means of production and of the producers in large workshops and manufactories, their transformation into actual socialised means of production and socialised producers. But the socialised producers and means of production and their products were still treated, after this change, just as they had been before, i.e., as the means of production and the products of individuals. Hitherto, the owner of the instruments of labour had himself appropriated the product, because, as a rule, it was his own product and the assistance of others was the exception. Now the owner of the instruments of labour always appropriated to himself the product, although it was no longer *his* product but exclusively the product of the *labour of others*. Thus, the products now produced socially were not appropriated by those who had actually set in motion the means of production and actually produced the commodities, but by the *capitalists*. The means of production, and production itself, had become in essence socialised. But they were subjected to a form of appropriation which presupposes the private production of individuals, under which, therefore, everyone owns his own product and brings it to market. The mode of production is subjected to this form of appropriation, although it abolishes the conditions upon which the latter rests.

This contradiction, which gives to the new mode of production its capitalistic character, *contains the germ of the whole of the social antagonisms of today*. The greater the mastery obtained by the new mode of production over all important fields of production and in all manufacturing countries; the more it reduced individual production to an insignificant residuum, *the more clearly was brought out the incompatibility of socialised production with capitalistic appropriation*.

The first capitalists found, as we have said, alongside of other forms of labour, wage-labour ready-made for them on the market. But it was exceptional, complementary, accessory, transitory wage-labour. The agricultural labourer, though, upon occasion, he hired himself out by the day, had a few acres of his own land on which he could at all events live at a pinch. The guilds were so organised that the journeyman of today became the master of tomorrow. But all this changed, as soon as the means of production became socialised and concentrated in the hands of capitalists. The means of production, as well as the product, of the individual producer became more and more worthless; there was nothing left for him but to turn wageworker under the capitalist. Wage-labour, aforetime the exception and accessory, now became the rule and basis of all production; aforetime complementary, it now became the sole remaining function of the worker. The wage-worker for a time became a wage-worker for life. The number of these permanent wage-workers was further enormously increased by the breaking-up of the feudal system that occurred at the same time, by the disbanding of the retainers of the feudal lords, the eviction of the peasants from their homesteads, etc. The separation was made complete between the means of production concentrated in the hands of the capitalists, on the one side, and the producers, possessing nothing but their labour-power, on the other. *The contradiction between socialised production and capitalistic appropriation manifested itself as the antagonism of proletariat and bourgeoisie.*

We have seen that the capitalistic mode of production thrust its way into a society of commodity-producers, of individual producers, whose social bond was the exchange of their products. But every society based upon the production of commodities has this peculiarity: that the producers have lost control over their own social interrelations. Each man produces for himself with such means of production as he may happen to have, and for such exchange as he may require to satisfy his remaining wants. No one knows how much of his particular article is coming on the market, nor how much of it will be wanted. No one knows whether his individual product will meet an actual demand, whether he will be able to make good his costs of production or even to sell his commodity at all. Anarchy reigns in socialised production.

But the production of commodities, like every other form of production, has its peculiar, inherent laws inseparable from it; and these laws work, despite anarchy, in and through anarchy. They reveal themselves in the only persistent form of social interrelations, i.e., in exchange, and here they affect the individual producers as compulsory laws of competition. They are, at first, unknown to these producers themselves, and have to be discovered by them gradually and as the result of experience. They work themselves out, therefore, independently of the producers, and in antagonism to them, as inexorable natural laws of their particular form of production. The product governs the producers.

In mediaeval society, especially in the earlier centuries, production was essentially directed towards satisfying the wants of the individual. It satisfied, in the main, only the wants of the producer and his family. Where relations of personal dependence existed, as in the country, it also helped to satisfy the wants of the feudal lord. In all this there was, therefore, no exchange; the products, consequently, did not assume the character of commodities. The family of the peasant produced almost everything they wanted: clothes and furniture, as well as means of subsistence. Only when it began to produce more than was sufficient to supply its own wants and the payments in kind to the feudal lord, only then did it also produce commodities. This surplus, thrown into socialised exchange and offered for sale, became commodities.

The artisans of the towns, it is true, had from the first to produce for exchange. But they, also, themselves supplied the greatest part of their own individual wants. They had gardens and plots of land. They turned their cattle out into the communal forest, which, also, yielded them timber and firing. The women spun flax, wool, and so forth. Production for the purpose of exchange, production of commodities, was only in its infancy. Hence, exchange was restricted, the market narrow, the methods of production stable.....

But with the extension of the production of commodities, and especially with the introduction of the capitalist mode of production, the laws of commodity production, hitherto latent, came into action more openly and with greater force. The old bonds were loosened, the old exclusive limits broken through, the producers were more and more turned into independent, isolated producers of commodities. It became apparent that the production of society at large was ruled by absence of plan, by accident, by anarchy; and this anarchy grew to greater and greater height. But the chief means by aid of which the capitalist mode of production intensified this anarchy of socialised production was the exact opposite of anarchy. It was the increasing organisation of production, upon a social basis, in every individual productive establishment. By this, the old, peaceful, stable condition of things was ended. Wherever this organisation of production was introduced into a branch of industry, it brooked no other method of production by its side. The field of labour became a battle-ground. The great geographical discoveries, and the colonisation following upon them, multiplied markets and quickened the transformation of handicraft into manufacture. The war did not simply break out between the individual producers of particular localities. The local struggles begot in their turn national conflicts, the commercial wars of the seventeenth and the eighteenth centuries.

Finally, modern industry and the opening of the world market made the struggle universal, and at the same time gave it an unheard-of virulence. Advantages in natural or artificial conditions of production now decide the existence or non-existence of individual capitalists, as well as of whole industries and countries. He that falls is remorselessly cast aside. It is the Darwinian struggle of the individual for existence transferred from Nature to society with intensified violence. The conditions of existence natural to the animal appear as the final term of human development. The contradiction between socialised production and capitalistic appropriation now presents itself as *an antagonism between the organisation of production in the in-*

dividual workshop and the anarchy of production in society generally.

The capitalistic mode of production moves in these two forms of the antagonism immanent to it from its very origin. It is never able to get out of that "vicious circle" which Fourier had already discovered. What Fourier could not, indeed, see in his time is that this circle is gradually narrowing; that the movement becomes more and more a spiral, and must come to an end, like the movement of the planets, by collision with the centre. It is the compelling force of anarchy in the production of society at large that more and more completely turns the great majority of men into proletarians; and it is the masses of the proletariat again who will finally put an end to anarchy in production. It is the compelling force of anarchy in social production that turns the limitless perfectibility of machinery under modern industry into a compulsory law by which every individual industrial capitalist must perfect his machinery more and more, under penalty of ruin.

But the perfecting of machinery is making human labour superfluous. If the introduction and increase of machinery means the displacement of millions of manual by a few machine-workers, improvement in machinery means the displacement of more and more of the machine-workers themselves. It means, in the last instance, the production of a number of available wage-workers in excess of the average needs of capital, the formation of a complete industrial reserve army,...available at the times when industry is working at high pressure, to be cast out upon the street when the inevitable crash comes, a constant dead weight upon the limbs of the working class in its struggle for existence with capital, a regulator for the keeping of wages down to the low level that suits the interests of capital. Thus it comes about, to quote Marx, that machinery becomes the most powerful weapon in the war of capital against the working class; that the instruments of labour constantly tear the means of subsistence out of the hands of the labourer; that the very product of the worker is turned into an instrument for his subjugation. Thus it comes about that the economising of the instruments of labour becomes at the same time, from the outset, the most reckless waste of labour power, and robbery based upon the normal conditions under which labour functions; that machinery, "the

most powerful instrument for shortening labour time, becomes the most unfailing means for placing every moment of the labourer's time and that of his family at the disposal of the capitalist for the purpose of expanding the value of his capital."...Thus it comes about that the overwork of some becomes the preliminary condition for the idleness of others, and that modern industry, which hunts after new consumers over the whole world, forces the consumption of the masses at home down to a starvation minimum, and in doing thus destroys its own home market....And to expect any other division of the products from the capitalistic mode of production is the same as expecting the electrodes of a battery not to decompose acidulated water, not to liberate oxygen at the positive, hydrogen at the negative pole, so long as they are connected with the battery.

We have seen that the ever-increasing perfectibility of modern machinery is, by the anarchy of social production, turned into a compulsory law that forces the individual industrial capitalist always to improve his machinery, always to increase its productive force. The bare possibility of extending the field of production is transformed for him into a similar compulsory law. The enormous expansive force of modern industry, compared with which that of gases is mere child's play, appears to us now as a *necessity* for expansion, both qualitative and quantitative, that laughs at all resistance. Such resistance is offered by consumption, by sales, by the markets for the products of modern industry. But the capacity for extension, extensive and intensive, of the markets is primarily governed by quite different laws that work much less energetically. The extension of the markets cannot keep pace with the extension of production. The collision becomes inevitable, and as this cannot produce any real solution so long as it does not break in pieces the capitalist mode of production, the collisions become periodic. Capitalist production has begotten another "vicious circle."

As a matter of fact, since 1825, when the first general crisis broke out, the whole industrial and commercial world, production and exchange among all civilised peoples and their more or less barbaric hangers-on, are thrown out of joint about once every ten years. Commerce is at a standstill, the markets are glutted, products accumulate, as multitudinous as they are unsaleable, hard cash disappears, credit vanishes, factories are closed, the mass of the workers are in want of the means of subsistence, because they have produced too much of the means of subsistence; bankruptcy follows upon bankruptcy, execution upon execution. The stagnation lasts for years; productive forces and products are wasted and destroyed wholesale, until the accumulated mass of commodities finally filters off, more or less depreciated in value, until production and exchange gradually begin to move again. Little by little the pace quickens. It becomes a trot. The industrial trot breaks into a canter, the canter in turn grows into the headlong gallop of a perfect steeplechase of industry, commercial credit, and speculation which finally, after breakneck leaps, ends where it began—in the ditch of a crisis. And so over and over again. We have now, since the year 1825, gone through this five times, and at the present moment (1877) we are going through it for the sixth time. And the character of these crises is so clearly defined that Fourier hit all of them off when he described the first as a crisis from plethora.

In these crises, the contradiction between socialised production and capitalist appropriation ends in a violent explosion. The circulation of commodities is, for the time being, stopped. Money, the means of circulation, becomes a hindrance to circulation. All the laws of production and circulation of commodities are turned upside down. The economic collision has reached its apogee. *The mode of production is in rebellion against the mode of exchange.*

The fact that the socialised organisation of production within the factory has developed so far that it has become incompatible with the anarchy of production in society, which exists side by side with and dominates it, is brought home to the capitalists themselves by the violent concentration of capital that occurs during crises, through the ruin of many large, and a still greater number of small, capitalists. The whole mechanism of the capitalist mode of production breaks down under the pressure of the productive forces, its own creations. It is no longer able to turn all this mass of means of production into capital. They lie fallow, and for that very reason the industrial reserve army must also lie fallow. Means of production, means of subsistence, available labourers, all the elements of production and of general wealth, are present in abundance. But "abundance becomes the source of

distress and want" (Fourier), because it is the very thing that prevents the transformation of the means of production and subsistence into capital. For in capitalistic society the means of production can only function when they have undergone a preliminary transformation into capital, into the means of exploiting human labour power. The necessity of this transformation into capital of the means of production and subsistence stands like a ghost between these and the workers. It alone prevents the coming together of the material and personal levers of production; it alone forbids the means of production to function, the workers to work and live. On the one hand, therefore, the capitalistic mode of production stands convicted of its own incapacity to further direct these productive forces. On the other, these productive forces themselves, with increasing energy, press forward to the removal of the existing contradiction, to the abolition of their quality as capital, to the *practical recognition of their character as social productive forces*.

This rebellion of the productive forces, as they grow more and more powerful, against their quality as capital, this stronger and stronger command that their social character shall be recognised, forces the capitalist class itself to treat them more and more as social productive forces, so far as this is possible under capitalist conditions. The period of industrial high pressure, with its unbounded inflation of credit, not less than the crash itself, by the collapse of great capitalist establishments, tends to bring about that form of the socialisation of great masses of means of production which we meet with in the different kinds of joint-stock companies. Many of these means of production and of distribution are, from the outset, so colossal that, like the railways, they exclude all other forms of capitalistic exploitation. At a further stage of evolution this form also becomes insufficient. The producers on a large scale in a particular branch of industry in a particular country unite in a trust, a union for the purpose of regulating production. They determine the total amount to be produced, parcel it out among themselves, and thus enforce the selling price fixed beforehand. But trusts of this kind, as soon as business becomes bad, are generally liable to break up, and on this very account compel a yet greater concentration of association. The whole of the particular industry is turned into one gigantic joint-stock company; internal competition gives place to the internal monopoly of this one company.

In the trusts, freedom of competition changes into its very opposite—into monopoly; and the production without any definite plan of capitalistic society capitulates to the production upon a definite plan of the invading socialistic society. Certainly this is so far still to the benefit and advantage of the capitalists. But in this case the exploitation is so palpable that it must break down. No nation will put up with production conducted by trusts, with so barefaced an exploitation of the community by a small band of dividend-mongers.

In any case, with trusts or without, the official representative of capitalist society—the state—will ultimately have to undertake the direction of production. This necessity for conversion into state property is felt first in the great institutions for intercourse and communication—the post office, the telegraphs, the railways.

If the crises demonstrate the incapacity of the bourgeoisie for managing any longer modern productive forces, the transformation of the great establishments for production and distribution into joint-stock companies, trusts and state property shows how unnecessary the bourgeoisie are for that purpose. All the social functions of the capitalist are now performed by salaried employees. The capitalist has no further social function than that of pocketing dividends, tearing off coupons, and gambling on the Stock Exchange, where the different capitalists despoil one another of their capital. At first the capitalistic mode of production forces out the workers. Now it forces out the capitalists, and reduces them, just as it reduced the workers, to the ranks of the surplus population, although not immediately into those of the industrial reserve army.

But the transformation, either into joint-stock companies and trusts, or into state ownership, does not do away with the capitalistic nature of the productive forces. In the joint-stock companies and trusts this is obvious. And the modern state, again, is only the organisation that bourgeois society takes on in order to support the external conditions of the capitalist mode of production against the encroachments as well of the workers as of individual capitalists. The modern state, no matter what its form, is essentially a capitalist machine, the state of the capitalists, the ideal personification

of the total national capital. The more it proceeds to the taking over of productive forces, the more does it actually become the national capitalist, the more citizens does it exploit. The workers remain wage-workers—proletarians. The capitalist relation is not done away with. It is rather brought to a head. But, brought to a head, it topples over. State ownership of the productive forces is not the solution of the conflict, but concealed within it are the technical conditions that form the elements of that solution.

This solution can only consist in the practical recognition of the social nature of the modern forces of production, and therefore in the harmonising of the modes of production, appropriation, and exchange with the socialised character of the means of production. And this can only come about by society openly and directly taking possession of the productive forces which have outgrown all control except that of society as a whole. The social character of the means of production and of the products today reacts against the producers, periodically disrupts all production and exchange, acts only like a law of Nature working blindly, forcibly, destructively. But with the taking over by society of the productive forces, the social character of the means of production and of the products will be utilised by the producers with a perfect understanding of its nature, and instead of being a source of disturbance and periodical collapse, will become the most powerful lever of production itself.

Active social forces work exactly like natural forces: blindly, forcibly, destructively, so long as we do not understand, and reckon with them. But when once we understand them, when once we grasp their action, their direction, their effects, it depends only upon ourselves to subject them more and more to our own will, and by means of them to reach our own ends. And this holds quite especially of the mighty productive forces of today. As long as we obstinately refuse to understand the nature and the character of these social means of action—and this understanding goes against the grain of the capitalist mode of production and its defenders—so long these forces are at work in spite of us, in opposition to us, so long they master us, as we have shown above in detail.

But when once their nature is understood, they can, in the hands of the producers working together, be transformed from master demons into willing servants. The difference is as that between the destructive force of electricity in the lightning of the storm, and electricity under command in the telegraph and the voltaic arc; the difference between a conflagration, and fire working in the service of man. With this recognition, at last, of the real nature of the productive forces of today, the social anarchy of production gives place to a social regulation of production upon a definite plan, according to the needs of the community and of each individual. Then the capitalist mode of appropriation, in which the product enslaves first the producer and then the appropriator, is replaced by the mode of appropriation of the products that is based upon the nature of the modern means of production; upon the one hand, direct social appropriation, as means to the maintenance and extension of production—on the other, direct individual appropriation, as means of subsistence and of enjoyment.

Whilst the capitalist mode of production more and more completely transforms the great majority of the population into proletarians, it creates the power which, under penalty of its own destruction, is forced to accomplish this revolution. Whilst it forces on more and more the transformation of the vast means of production, already socialised, into state property, it shows itself the way to accomplishing this revolution. *The proletariat seizes political power and turns the means of production into state property.*

But in doing this, it abolishes itself as proletariat, abolishes all class distinctions and class antagonisms, abolishes also the state as state. Society thus far, based upon class antagonisms, had need of the state. That is, of an organisation of the particular class which was *pro tempore* the exploiting class, an organisation for the purpose of preventing any interference from without with the existing conditions of production, and, therefore, especially, for the purpose of forcibly keeping the exploited classes in the condition of oppression corresponding with the given mode of production (slavery, serfdom, wage-labour). The state was the official representative of society as a whole; the gathering of it together into a visible embodiment. But it was this only in so far as it was the state of that class which itself represented, for the time being, society as a whole: in ancient times, the state of slaveowning citizens; in the Middle Ages, the feudal lords; in our own time, the bourgeoisie. When at last it

becomes the real representative of the whole of society, it renders itself unnecessary. As soon as there is no longer any social class to be held in subjection; as soon as class rule, and the individual struggle for existence based upon our present anarchy in production, with the collisions and excesses arising from these, are removed, nothing more remains to be repressed, and a special repressive force, a state, is no longer necessary. The first act by virtue of which the state really constitutes itself the representative of the whole of society—the taking possession of the means of production in the name of society—this is, at the same time, its last independent act as a state. State interference in social relations becomes, in one domain after another, superfluous, and then dies out of itself; the government of persons is replaced by the administration of things, and by the conduct of processes of production. The state is not "abolished." *It dies out.* This gives the measure of the value of the phrase *"a free state,"* both as to its justifiable use at times by agitators, and as to its ultimate scientific insufficiency; and also of the demands of the so-called anarchists for the abolition of the state out of hand.

Since the historical appearance of the capitalist mode of production, the appropriation by society of all the means of production has often been dreamed of, more or less vaguely, by individuals, as well as by sects, as the ideal of the future. But it could become possible, could become a historical necessity, only when the actual conditions for its realisation were there. Like every other social advance, it becomes practicable, not by men understanding that the existence of classes is in contradiction to justice, equality, etc., not by the mere willingness to abolish these classes, but by virtue of certain new economic conditions. The separation of society into an exploiting and an exploited class, a ruling and an oppressed class, was the necessary consequence of the deficient and restricted development of production in former times. So long as the total social labour only yields a produce which but slightly exceeds that barely necessary for the existence of all; so long, therefore, as labour engages all or almost all the time of the great majority of the members of society—so long, of necessity, this society is divided into classes. Side by side with the great majority, exclusively bond slaves to labour, arises a class freed from directly productive labour, which looks after the general affairs of society: the direction of labour, state business, law, science, art, etc. It is, therefore, the law of division of labour that lies at the basis of the division into classes. But this does not prevent this division into classes from being carried out by means of violence and robbery, trickery and fraud. It does not prevent the ruling class, once having the upper hand, from consolidating its power at the expense of the working class, from turning its social leadership into an intensified exploitation, of the masses.

But if, upon this showing, division into classes has a certain historical justification, it has this only for a given period, only under given social conditions. It was based upon the insufficiency of production. It will be swept away by the complete development of modern productive forces. And, in fact, the abolition of classes in society presupposes a degree of historical evolution at which the existence, not simply of this or that particular ruling class, but of any ruling class at all, and, therefore, the existence of class distinction itself has become an obsolete anachronism. It presupposes, therefore, the development of production carried out to a degree at which appropriation of the means of production and of the products, and, with this, of political domination, of the monopoly of culture, and of intellectual leadership by a particular class of society, has become not only superfluous but economically, politically, intellectually, a hindrance to development.

This point is now reached. Their political and intellectual bankruptcy is scarcely any longer a secret to the bourgeoisie themselves. Their economic bankruptcy recurs regularly every ten years. In every crisis, society is suffocated beneath the weight of its own productive forces and products, which it cannot use, and stands helpless, face to face with the absurd contradiction that the producers have nothing to consume, because consumers are wanting. The expansive force of the means of production bursts the bonds that the capitalist mode of production had imposed upon them. Their deliverance from these bonds is the one precondition for an unbroken, constantly accelerated development of the productive forces, and therewith for a practically unlimited increase of production itself. Nor is this all. The socialised appropriation of the means of production does away, not only with the present artificial restrictions upon production, but also with the positive waste and devastation of productive forces and products that are at the present time the inevitable concomitants of production, and that reach their height in the crises. Further, it sets free for the community at large a mass of means of production and of products, by doing away with the senseless extravagance of the ruling classes of today and their political representatives. The possibility of securing for every member of society, by means of socialised production, an existence not only fully sufficient materially, and becoming day by day more full, but an existence guaranteeing to all the free development and exercise of their physical and mental faculties—this possibility is now for the first time here, but *it is here.*

With the seizing of the means of production by society, production of commodities is done away with, and, simultaneously, the mastery of the product over the producer. Anarchy in social production is replaced by systematic, definite organisation. The struggle for individual existence disappears. Then for the first time man, in a certain sense, is finally marked off from the rest of the animal kingdom, and emerges from mere animal conditions of existence into really human ones. The whole sphere of the conditions of life which environ-man, and which have hitherto ruled man, now comes under the dominion and control of man, who for the first time becomes the real, conscious lord of Nature, because he has now become master of his own social organisation. The laws of his own social action, hitherto standing face to face with man as laws of Nature foreign to, and dominating him, will then be used with full understanding, and so mastered by him. Man's own social organisation, hitherto confronting him as a necessity imposed by Nature and history, now becomes the result of his own free action. The extraneous objective forces that have hitherto governed history pass under the control of man himself. Only from that time will man himself, more and more consciously, make his own history—only from that time will the social causes set in movement by him have, in the main and in a constantly growing measure, the results intended by him. It is the ascent of man from the kingdom of necessity to the kingdom of freedom....

Manifesto of the Communist Party

Karl Marx and Friedrich Engels

Proletarians and Communists

In what relation do the Communists stand to the proletarians as a whole?

The Communists do not form a separate party opposed to other working-class parties.

They have no interests separate and apart from those of the proletariat as a whole.

They do not set up any sectarian principles of their own, by which to shape and mould the proletarian movement.

The Communists are distinguished from the other working-class parties by this only: 1. In the national struggles of the proletarians of the different countries, they point out and bring to the front the common interests of the entire proletariat, independently of all nationality. 2. In the various stages of development which the struggle of the working class against the bourgeoisie has to pass through, they always and everywhere represent the interests of the movement as a whole.

The Communists, therefore, are on the one hand, practically, the most advanced and resolute section of the working-class parties of every country, that section which pushes forward all others; on the other hand, theoretically, they have over the great mass of the proletariat the advantage of clearly understanding the line of march, the conditions, and the ultimate general results of the proletarian movement.

The immediate aim of the Communists is the same as that of all the other proletarian parties: formation of the proletariat into a class, overthrow of the bourgeois supremacy, conquest of political power by the proletariat.

The theoretical conclusions of the Communists are in no way based on ideas or principles that have been invented, or discovered by this or that would-be universal reformer.

They merely express, in general terms, actual relations springing from an existing class struggle, from a historical movement going on under our very eyes. The abolition of existing property relations is not at all a distinctive feature of Communism.

All property relations in the past have continually been subject to historical change consequent upon the change in historical conditions.

The French Revolution, for example, abolished feudal property in favour of bourgeois property.

The distinguishing feature of Communism is not the abolition of property generally, but the abolition of bourgeois property. But modern bourgeois private property is the final and most complete expression of the system of producing and appropriating products, that is based on class antagonisms, on the exploitation of the many by the few.

In this sense, the theory of the Communists may be summed up in the single sentence: Abolition of private property.

We Communists have been reproached with the desire of abolishing the right of personally acquiring property as the fruit of a man's own labour, which property is alleged to be the ground work of all personal freedom, activity and independence.

Hard-won, self-acquired, self-earned property! Do you mean the property of the petty artisan and of the small peasant, a form of property that preceded the bourgeois form? There is no need to abolish that; the development of industry has to a great extent already destroyed it, and is still destroying it daily.

Or do you mean modern bourgeois private property?

From *Manifesto of the Communist Party* (Moscow: Progress Publishers, 1971).

But does wage labour create any property for the labourer? Not a bit. It creates capital, *i.e.*, that kind of property which exploits wage labour, and which cannot increase except upon condition of begetting a new supply of wage labour for fresh exploitation. Property, in its present form, is based on the antagonism of capital and wage labour. Let us examine both sides of this antagonism.

To be a capitalist, is to have not only a purely personal, but a social *status* in production. Capital is a collective product, and only by the united action of many members, nay, in the last resort, only by the united action of all members of society, can it be set in motion.

Capital is, therefore, not a personal, it is a social power. When, therefore, capital is converted into common property, into the property of all members of society, personal property is not thereby transformed into social property. It is only the social character of the property that is changed. It loses its class character.

Let us now take wage labour.

The average price of wage labour is the minimum wage, *i.e.*, that quantum of the means of subsistence, which is absolutely requisite to keep the labourer in bare existence as a labourer. What, therefore, the wage-labourer appropriates by means of his labour, merely suffices to prolong and reproduce a bare existence. We by no means intend to abolish this personal appropriation of the products of labour, an appropriation that is made for the maintenance and reproduction of human life, and that leaves no surplus wherewith to command the labour of others. All that we want to do away with is the miserable character of this appropriation, under which the labourer lives merely to increase capital, and is allowed to live only in so far as the interest of the ruling class requires it.

In bourgeois society, living labour is but a means to increase accumulated labour. In Communist society, accumulated labour is but a means to widen, to enrich, to promote the existence of the labourer.

In bourgeois society, therefore, the past dominates the present; in Communist society, the present dominates the past. In bourgeois society capital is independent and has individuality, while the living person is dependent and has no individuality.

And the abolition of this state of things is called by the bourgeois, abolition of individuality and freedom! And rightly so. The abolition of bourgeois individuality, bourgeois independence, and bourgeois freedom is undoubtedly aimed at.

By freedom is meant, under the present bourgeois conditions of production, free trade, free selling and buying.

But if selling and buying disappears, free selling and buying disappears also. This talk about free selling and buying, and all the other "brave words" of our bourgeoisie about freedom in general, have a meaning, if any, only in contrast with restricted selling and buying, with the fettered traders of the Middle Ages, but have no meaning when opposed to the Communistic abolition of buying and selling, of the bourgeois conditions of production, and of the bourgeoisie itself.

You are horrified at our intending to do away with private property. But in your existing society, private property is already done away with for nine-tenths of the population; its existence for the few is solely due to its non-existence in the hands of those nine-tenths. You reproach us, therefore, with intending to do away with a form of property, the necessary condition for whose existence is, the non-existence of any property for the immense majority of society.

In one word, you reproach us with intending to do away with your property. Precisely so; that is just what we intend.

From the moment when labour can no longer be converted into capital, money, or rent, into a social power capable of being monopolised, *i.e.*, from the moment when individual property can no longer be transformed into bourgeois property, into capital, from that moment, you say, individuality vanishes.

You must, therefore, confess that by "individual" you mean no other person than the bourgeois, than the middle-class owner of property. This person must, indeed, be swept out of the way, and made impossible.

Communism deprives no man of the power to appropriate the products of society; all that it does is to deprive him of the power to subjugate the labour of others by means of such appropriation.

It has been objected that upon the abolition of private property all work will cease, and universal laziness will overtake us.

According to this, bourgeois society ought long ago to have gone to the dogs through sheer idleness; for those of its members who work, acquire nothing, and those who acquire anything, do not work. The whole of this objection is but another expression of the tautology: that there can no longer be any wage labour when there is no longer any capital.

All objections urged against the Communistic mode of producing and appropriating material products, have, in the same way, been urged against the Communistic modes of producing and appropriating intellectual products. Just as, to the bourgeois, the disappearance of class property is the disappearance of production itself, so the disappearance of class culture is to him identical with the disappearance of all culture.

That culture, the loss of which he laments, is, for the enormous majority, a mere training to act as a machine.

But don't wrangle with us so long as you apply, to our intended abolition of bourgeois property, the standard of your bourgeois notions of freedom, culture, law, &c. Your very ideas are but the outgrowth of the conditions of your bourgeois production and bourgeois property, just as your jurisprudence is but the will of your class made into a law for all, a will, whose essential character and direction are determined by the economical conditions of existence of your class.

The selfish misconception that induces you to transform into eternal laws of nature and of reason, the social forms springing from your present mode of production and form of property—historical relations that rise and disappear in the progress of production—this misconception you share with every ruling class that has preceded you. What you see clearly in the case of ancient property, what you admit in the case of feudal property, you are of course forbidden to admit in the case of your own bourgeois form of property.

Abolition of the family! Even the most radical flare up at this infamous proposal of the Communists.

On what foundation is the present family, the bourgeois family, based? On capital, on private gain. In its completely developed form this family exists only among the bourgeoisie. But this state of things finds its complement in the practical absence of the family among the proletarians, and in public prostitution.

The bourgeois family will vanish as a matter of course when its complement vanishes, and both will vanish with the vanishing of capital

Do you charge us with wanting to stop the exploitation of children by their parents? To this crime we plead guilty.

But, you will say, we destroy the most hallowed of relations, when we replace home education by social.

And your education! Is not that also social, and determined by the social conditions under which you educate, by the intervention, direct or indirect, of society, by means of schools, &c.?

The Communists have not invented the intervention of society in education; they do but seek to alter the character of that intervention, and to rescue education from the influence of the ruling class.

The bourgeois clap-trap about the family and education, about the hallowed co-relation of parent and child, becomes all the more disgusting, the more, by the action of Modern Industry, all family ties among the proletarians are torn asunder, and their children transformed into simple articles of commerce and instruments of labour.

But you Communists would introduce community of women, screams the whole bourgeoisie in chorus.

The bourgeois sees in his wife a mere instrument of production. He hears that the instruments of production are to be exploited in common, and, naturally, can come to no other conclusion than that the lot of being common to all will likewise fall to the women.

He has not even a suspicion that the real point aimed at is to do away with the status of women as mere instruments of production.

For the rest, nothing is more ridiculous than the virtuous indignation of our bourgeois at the community of women which, they pretend, is to be openly and officially established by the Communists. The Communists have no need to introduce community of women; it has existed almost from time immemorial.

Our bourgeois, not content with having the wives and daughters of their proletarians at their disposal, not to speak of common prostitutes, take the greatest pleasure in seducing each other's wives.

Bourgeois marriage is in reality a system of wives in common and thus, at the most, what the Communists might possibly be reproached with, is that they desire to introduce, in substitution for a hypocritically concealed, an openly legalised community of women. For the rest, it is self-evident that the abolition of the present system of production must bring with it the abolition of the community of women springing from that system, *i.e.*, of prostitution both public and private.

The Communists are further reproached with desiring to abolish countries and nationality.

The working men have no country. We cannot take from them what they have not got. Since the proletariat must first of all acquire political supremacy, must rise to be the leading class of the nation, must constitute itself *the* nation, it is, so far, itself national, though not in the bourgeois sense of the word.

National differences and antagonisms between peoples are daily more and more vanishing, owing to the development of the bourgeoisie, to freedom of commerce, to the world market, to uniformity in the mode of production and in the conditions of life corresponding thereto.

The supremacy of the proletariat will cause them to vanish still faster. United action, of the leading civilised countries at least, is one of the first conditions for the emancipation of the proletariat.

In proportion as the exploitation of one individual by another is put an end to, the exploitation of one nation by another will also be put an end to. In proportion as the antagonism between classes within the nation vanishes, the hostility of one nation to another will come to an end.

The charges against Communism made from a religious, a philosophical, and, generally, from an ideological standpoint, are not deserving of serious examination.

Does it require deep intuition to comprehend that man's ideas, views and conceptions, in one word, man's consciousness, changes with every change in the conditions of his material existence, in his social relations and in his social life?

What else does the history of ideas prove, than that intellectual production changes its character in proportion as material production is changed? The ruling ideas of each age have ever been the ideas of its ruling class.

When people speak of ideas that revolutionise society, they do but express the fact, that within the old society, the elements of a new one have been created, and that the dissolution of the old ideas keeps even pace with the dissolution of the old conditions of existence.

When the ancient world was in its last throes, the ancient religions were overcome by Christianity. When Christian ideas succumbed in the 18th century to rationalist ideas, feudal society fought its death battle with the then revolutionary bourgeoisie. The ideas of religious liberty and freedom of conscience, merely gave expression to the sway of free competition within the domain of knowledge.

"Undoubtedly," it will be said "religious, moral, philosophical and juridical ideas have been modified in the course of historical development. But religion, morality, philosophy, political science, and law, constantly survived this change."

"There are, besides, eternal truths, such as Freedom Justice, etc., that are common to all states of society. But Communism abolishes eternal truths, it abolishes all religion and all morality, instead of constituting them on a new basis; it therefore acts in contradiction to all past historical experience."

What does this accusation reduce itself to? The history of all past society has consisted in the development of class antagonisms, antagonisms that assumed different forms at different epochs.

But whatever form they may have taken, one fact is common to all past ages, *viz.*, the exploitation of one part of society by the other. No wonder, then, that the social consciousness of past ages, despite all the multiplicity and variety it displays, moves within certain common forms, or general ideas, which cannot completely vanish except with the total disappearance of class antagonisms.

The Communist revolution is the most radical rupture with traditional property relations; no wonder that its development involves the most radical rupture with traditional ideas.

But let us have done with the bourgeois objections to Communism.

We have seen above, that the first step in the revolution by the working class, is to raise the proletariat to the position of ruling class, to win the battle of democracy.

The proletariat will use its political supremacy to wrest, by degrees, all capital from the bourgeoisie, to centralise all instruments of production in the hands of the State, *i.e.*, of the proletariat organised as the ruling class; and to increase the total of productive forces as rapidly as possible.

Of course, in the beginning, this cannot be effected except by means of despotic inroads on the rights of property, and on the conditions of bourgeois production; by means of measures, therefore, which appear economically insufficient and untenable, but which, in the course of the movement, outstrip themselves, necessitate further inroads upon the old social order, and are unavoidable as a means of entirely revolutionising the mode of production.

These measures will of course be different in different countries.

Nevertheless in the most advanced countries, the following will be pretty generally applicable:

1. Abolition of property in land and application of all rents of land to public purposes.

2. A heavy progressive or graduated income tax.

3. Abolition of all right of inheritance.

4. Confiscation of the property of all emigrants and rebels.

5. Centralisation of credit in the hands of the State, by means of a national bank with State capital and an exclusive monopoly.

6. Centralisation of the means of communication and transport in the hands of the State.

7. Extension of factories and instruments of production owned by the State; the bringing into cultivation of waste-lands, and the improvement of the soil generally in accordance with a common plan.

8. Equal liability of all to labour. Establishment of industrial armies, especially for agriculture.

9. Combination of agriculture with manufacturing industries; gradual abolition of the distinction between town and country, by a more equable distribution of the population over the country.

10. Free education for all children in public schools. Abolition of children's factory labour in its present form. Combination of education with industrial production, &c., &c.

When, in the course of development, class distinctions have disappeared, and all production has been concentrated in the hands of a vast association of the whole nation, the public power will lose its political character. Political power, properly so called, is merely the organised power of one class for oppressing another. If the proletariat during its contest with the bourgeoisie is compelled, by the force of circumstances, to organise itself as a class, if, by means of a revolution, it makes itself the ruling class, and, as such, sweeps away by force the old conditions of production, then it will, along with these conditions, have swept away the conditions for the existence of class antagonisms and of classes generally, and will thereby have abolished its own supremacy as a class.

In place of the old bourgeois society, with its classes and class antagonisms, we shall have an association, in which the free development of each is the condition for the free development of all.

4 Communism and Fascism

The Industrial Revolution brought technological changes which made it possible and advantageous for the powerful industrial nations of Europe and North America to dominate the less powerful countries that had not enjoyed the benefits of the Industrial Revolution. The developed nations achieved this first by exploiting the natural resources of undeveloped nations for industrial production and second by developing them as new markets for the products produced. Since the undeveloped nations were unable to resist the military might of the developed nations, the developed nations assumed the right to rule and control the undeveloped areas in a system known as "colonialism," or "imperialism." This arrangement has had a major impact on historical developments in the twentieth century.

One major impact that colonialism and imperialism had was to create artificial national entities which did not reflect ethnic or religious identities. Britain and France, for example, at the very end of the nineteenth century divided up between them most of West Africa into colonial "nation-states" which they ruled. In the process people of different ethnic and religious identities were geographically lumped together within the same colonial nation-state, while people of the same ethnic group were geographically separated by artificial national boundaries. For example, Nigeria is today composed of dozens of different ethnic and religious groups, and one ethnic group, the Yoruba, are divided between French-speaking Benin Republic and English-speaking Nigeria. The problem this has created is that even today Nigerians may identify themselves primarily with the ethnic group and not the country of Nigeria. At the same time, the cultural pride of the ethnic group and its desire for self-determination have been undermined.

Europe also did not escape the creation of artificial boundaries. Over the course of the many centuries between the time of Alexander the Great and the collapse of the Austria-Hungarian Empire the various empires which arose and then fell left behind political boundaries that did not reflect the national or religious identities of the inhabitants. For example, ethnic Germans were artificially divided into many different nation-states including Austria, Hungary, Poland, and parts of France. On the other hand, some ethnic groups like the Armenians, Lithuanians, and Serbs had long lost political autonomy and for centuries had been forced to be part of other nations which they deeply resented. The twentieth century saw the reassertion of demands for political expression of national identity.

Another source of ethnic tension concerned the settlement of Jews in Europe dating as far back as the Diaspora following the sack of Jerusalem by the Roman Army in the first century A.D. In the medieval period Jews were allowed to live in German-speaking regions, for example, but only in restricted areas known as ghettos, and only as "resident aliens," not as full citizens. The Napoleonic forces which occupied these Germanic areas in the early part of the nineteenth century insisted that everyone living in what is now Germany, including Jews, gypsies, Slavs, and others, be accorded full human rights as outlined in the French Declaration of the Universal Rights of Man—the late eighteenth-century Enlightenment concept that all human beings were possessors of inalienable basic human, or natural, rights simply by virtue of their being human beings. Under this Enlightenment concept of universal human rights, Jews were allowed out of the ghettos, to speak German, and to participate in German culture (in music, education, scientific research, business, and so on) as full citizens of the state. During the early and middle nineteenth century many German-Jews embraced German culture, identifying themselves as Germans first and Jews second, and successfully competed for positions of prominence in areas of the arts, science, business, and the legal profession. But increasingly in the late nineteenth and early twentieth centuries non-Jewish Germans refused to accept Jews as Germans. Rather, Jews continued to be regarded by many Germans as outsiders, even though many Jewish families had lived in German-speaking areas of Europe for centuries. Whenever social problems arose, some of these Germans blamed the Jews, often attacking them in periodic anti-semitic "pogroms."

The demand for ethnic self-determination was the immediate cause of World War I, a brutal war which only heightened the already existing tensions. The war ended in 1918 with the Treaty of Versailles, a peace treaty which punished and humiliated the Germans by taking away economic and political power and forcing them to pay reparations.

In 1929 a series of world-wide financial collapses began triggering the Great Depression. Though unemployment and financial hardship extended throughout all the developed world, Germany was particularly affected since it had not yet recovered from the effects of World War I.

It seemed to many people that the world was spinning out of control and that drastic measures were needed. It appeared as though democracy was a poorly suited instrument to address the difficult times because its emphasis on individualism and majority rule was inconsistent with the need for strong centralized planning, and in fact it seemed to some that democracy and individualism might even be the cause of much of the difficulty. A demand arose for a new approach which could promise both political and economic stability. Various political solutions were suggested, ranging from anarchism to different forms of social engineering. The most important new ideologies were communism and fascism.

The shape of events was different in the non-industrialized countries of Russia and China. Neither had achieved democracy and both had changed little since the eighteenth century. Rich in natural resources, Russia and China had an unrealized development potential and their large populations still lived largely on the land and engaged in primitive agriculture. Politically they were authoritarian states ruled by hereditary monarchs who were out of touch with their people. When the czar of Russia was overthrown in the Russian Revolution of 1917, the political organization which took power was the Communist party led by V. I. Lenin.

China, which was anxious to modernize, saw great promise in the Russian Revolution. Here seemed a model of a backward nation for whom communism provided a means of rapidly making great strides forward. During the 1920s and 1930s the Chinese Communist party, led by Mao Tse-tung, struggled for power against the Kuomintang (Nationalist) forces of Chiang Kai-shek. Internationally Mao was supported by the Soviet Union, while Chiang Kai-shek was supported by the United States and the European democracies. Since those nations which supported democracy were also capitalist nations principally responsible for colonialism and other forms of imperialism, there was a widespread perception that the Soviet Union opposed and the Western democracies supported colonialism and other forms of imperialism. During the Second World War, which in China was primarily the attempt of the Chinese to repel the Japanese invasion of their country, Mao and Chiang joined forces. But once the war was over the two turned on each other in a bloody civil war which ended in 1949 with the retreat of Chiang's forces to Taiwan Island and the complete victory of Mao's Communists on the mainland of China.

Along with all this political turmoil, two major social-political philosophies were developed and used as justifications for political events. They were communism and fascism. Though they were very different political theories, they shared some common ground. Both demanded a strong centralized government which would engage in economic and social planning. Both refused to allow demands for individual freedom to produce gridlock and paralyze the functioning of the state. They also both emphasized, indeed glorified, individual sacrifice for the greater good of the community as a whole. Another common theme was the idea that the individual can only be fulfilled by becoming an integral part of the state.

READINGS

Communist ideology was first politically implemented by V. I. Lenin. Lenin (1870–1924) was a Russian political theorist who had been influenced by the work of Karl Marx and who reinterpreted Marxian thought to provide a theory on which to develop a new Russian political organization. Marx had argued that socialism would develop from the clash between the workers and the capitalists and that a dictatorship of the working class, called "the proletariat," would be a first step in the inevitable evolution to communism. This dictatorship would be necessary in order to prevent the reemergence of the once powerful capitalists. Lenin applied this reasoning as support for defending the Soviet dictatorship in which coercion was used to suppress anti-communists. He insisted on the need for deliberate planning of state policies by governmental councils (soviets) elected by the workers. This, he argued, was the only means to fulfill the promise of a better society by the revolution, rather than relying on the forces of history as Marx's theory had done.

Following the lead of Lenin, and later Stalin in the Soviet Union, Mao Tse-tung (1893–1976) defended the right of the Communist party to establish what Marx had earlier called the "dictatorship of the proletariat." For Mao, the Communist party represented the working class, and the working class represented, as he said, "the people." The dictatorship was necessary, he argued, to prevent the reemergence of the "capitalists," that is, the once powerful rich landlords and traditional local rulers, who had supported Chiang and who hoped to regain power. Critics of both Russian and Chinese Communist governments claim that these communist dictatorships were not really dictatorships of the working-class people but ordinary dictatorships of a small new elite class—those belonging to the Communist party.

Fascism arose first in Italy, shortly followed by the rise of the Nazi party of Germany. Benito Mussolini (1883–1945) and his followers criticized liberal democracy as encouraging materialistic, pleasure-seeking, selfish, secular individuals uprooted from spiritual, societal values, and endlessly, fruitlessly debating social issues from different and competing self-interested perspectives. Instead, Fascists glorified the idea that individuals define themselves by service and sacrifice to the state. The ethnic identity Mussolini emphasized was primarily cultural and historical—the identification of the Italian people with the great civilization of the Roman Empire and the great Italian commercial and artistic centers during the Renaissance. Like the communists, Mussolini emphasized the need for ruthless suppression of the liberal and democratic foes of fascism.

In the 1930s Adolf Hitler (1889–1945) came to power in Germany on a political platform modeled partly on the Fascist party of Mussolini. But whereas Mussolini had emphasized the nationalistic identification of the Italian people in their glorious military and cultural history, Hitler stressed the racial identity of the German people as pure Aryans, as opposed to Slavs, Mediterranean peoples, gypsies, and Jews. Hitler's Nazi party promised the German people strong, central government actively engaged in social engineering, including racial purification, to correct Germany's economic depression and to restore ethnic pride in the German people—whatever the cost to the rights of individuals and non-Aryan ethnic minorities.

To enforce his policy of a racially pure Germany, Hitler devised a plan, which he called "the Final Solution" to the "Jewish Problem," whereby Germany would be rid of Jews (and gypsies and Slavs) forever—they would all be rounded up in concentration camps and systematically killed, as indeed were six million European Jews during World War II (1944–1949). After the war many of the Nazi leaders were tried and convicted of war crimes, and many people around the world felt that the Nazi atrocities were merely an aberration by a handful of truly insane individuals which could "never happen again." Today, however, as we witness the "ethnic cleansing" in the former Yugoslavia, in India, and in other areas of the world, it seems more likely that violent solutions to ethnic tensions arise out of a more deep-seated, fundamental human sense of group identity to the exclusion of others.

"The Immediate Tasks of the Soviet Government"

V. I. Lenin

The resolution adopted by the recent Moscow Congress of Soviets advanced as the primary task of the moment the establishment of a "harmonious organization", and the tightening of discipline. Everyone now readily "votes for" and "subscribes to" resolutions of this kind; but usually people do not think over the fact that the application of such resolutions calls for coercion—coercion precisely in the form of dictatorship. And yet it would be extremely stupid and absurdly utopian to assume that the transition from capitalism to socialism is possible without coercion and without dictatorship. Marx's theory very definitely opposed this petty-bourgeois-democratic and anarchist absurdity long ago. And Russia of 1917-18 confirms the correctness of Marx's theory in this respect so strikingly, palpably and imposingly that only those who are hopelessly dull or who have obstinately decided to turn their backs on the

truth can be under any misapprehension concerning this. Either the dictatorship of Kornilov (if we take him as the Russian type of bourgeois Cavaignac), or the dictatorship of the proletariat—any other choice is out of the question for a country which is developing at an extremely rapid rate with extremely sharp turns and amidst desperate ruin created by one of the most horrible wars in history. Every solution that offers a middle path is either a deception of the people by the bourgeoisie—...who chatter about the unity of democracy, the dictatorship of democracy, the general democratic front, and similar nonsense. Those whom even the progress of the Russian Revolution of 1917-18 has not taught that a middle course is impossible, must be given up for lost.

On the other hand, it is not difficult to see that during every transition from capitalism to socialism, dictatorship is necessary for two main reasons,

From *On Soviet Socialist Democracy* (Moscow: Progress Publishers, 1962).

or along two main channels. Firstly, capitalism cannot be defeated and eradicated without the ruthless suppression of the resistance of the exploiters, who cannot at once be deprived of their wealth, of their advantages of organization and knowledge, and consequently for a fairly long period will inevitably try to overthrow the hated rule of the poor; secondly, every great revolution, and a socialist revolution in particular, even if there is no external war, is inconceivable without internal war, i.e., civil war, which is even more devastating than external war, and involves thousands and millions of cases of wavering and desertion from one side to another, implies a state of extreme indefiniteness, lack of equilibrium and chaos. And of course, all the elements of disintegration of the old society, which are inevitably very numerous and connected mainly with the petty bourgeoisie (because it is the petty bourgeoisie that every war and every crisis ruins and destroys first), are bound to "reveal themselves" during such a profound revolution. And these elements of disintegration *cannot* "reveal themselves" otherwise than in an increase of crime, hooliganism, corruption, profiteering and outrages of every kind. To put these down requires time and *requires an iron hand*.

There has not been a single great revolution in history in which the people did not instinctively realize this and did not show salutary firmness by shooting thieves on the spot. The misfortune of previous revolutions was that the revolutionary enthusiasm of the people, which sustained them in their state of tension and gave them the strength to suppress ruthlessly the elements of disintegration, did not last long. The social, i.e., the class, reason for this instability of the revolutionary enthusiasm of the people was the weakness of the proletariat, which alone is able (if it is sufficiently numerous, class-conscious and disciplined) to win over to its side the majority of the working and exploited people (the majority of the poor, to speak more simply and popularly) and retain power sufficiently long to suppress completely all the exploiters as well as all the elements of disintegration.

It was this historical experience of all revolutions, it was this world-historic—economic and political—lesson that Marx summed up when he gave his short, sharp, concise and expressive formula: dictatorship of the proletariat. And the fact that the Russian-revolution has been correct in its approach to this world-historic task *has been proved* by the victorious progress of the Soviet form of organization among all the peoples and tongues of Russia. For Soviet power is nothing but an organizational form of the dictatorship of the proletariat, the dictatorship of the advanced class, which raises to a new democracy and to independent participation in the administration of the state tens upon tens of millions of working and exploited people, who by their own experience learn to regard the disciplined and class-conscious vanguard of the proletariat as their most reliable leader.

Dictatorship, however, is a big word, and big words should not be thrown about carelessly. Dictatorship is iron rule, government that is revolutionary bold, swift and ruthless in suppressing both exploiters and hooligans. But our government is excessively mild, very often it resembles jelly more than iron....The nearer we approach the complete military suppression of the bourgeoisie, the more dangerous does the element of petty-bourgeois anarchy become. And the fight against this element cannot be waged solely with the aid of propaganda and agitation, solely by organizing competition and by selecting organizers. The struggle must also be waged by means of coercion....

It is not yet sufficiently realized that the courts are an organ which enlists precisely the poor, every one of them, in the work of state administration (for the work of the courts is one of the functions of state administration), that the courts are an *organ of the power* of the proletariat and of the poor peasants, that the courts are an instrument *for inculcating discipline*. There is not yet sufficient appreciation of the simple and obvious fact that if the principal misfortunes of Russia at the present time are hunger and unemployment, these misfortunes cannot be overcome by spurts, but only by comprehensive, all-embracing, country-wide organization and discipline in order to increase the output of bread for the people and bread for industry (fuel), to transport these in good time to the places where they are required, and to distribute them properly; and it is not fully appreciated that, consequently, it is *those* who violate labour discipline at any factory, in any undertaking, in any matter, who are *responsible* for the sufferings caused by the famine and unemployment, that we must know how to find the guilty ones, to bring them to trial and ruthlessly punish them. Where the petty-bourgeois anarchy against which we must now wage a most persistent struggle makes itself felt is in the failure to appreciate the economic and political connection between famine and unemployment, on the one hand, and general laxity in matters of organization and discipline, on the other....

Here and there, among Left Socialist-Revolutionaries, a positively hooligan agitation, i.e., agitation appealing to the base instincts and to the small proprietor's urge to "grab all he can", has been developed against the dictatorship decree. The question has become one of really enormous significance. Firstly, the question of principle, namely, is the appointment of individuals, dictators with unlimited powers, in general compatible with the fundamental principles of Soviet government? Secondly, what relation has this case—this precedent, if you will—to the special tasks of government in the present concrete situation? We must deal very thoroughly with both these questions.

That in the history of revolutionary movements the dictatorship of individuals was very often the expression, the vehicle, the channel of the dictatorship of the revolutionary classes has been shown by the irrefutable experience of history. Undoubtedly, the dictatorship of individuals was compatible with bourgeois democracy. On this point, however, the bourgeois denigrators of the Soviet system, as well as their petty-bourgeois henchmen, always display sleight of hand: on the one hand, they declare the Soviet system to be something absurd, anarchistic and savage, and carefully pass over in silence all our historical examples and theoretical arguments which prove that the Soviets are a higher form of democracy, and what is more, the beginning of a *socialist* form of democracy; on the other hand, they demand of us a higher democracy than bourgeois democracy and say: personal dictatorship is absolutely incompatible with your, Bolshevik (i.e., not bourgeois, *but socialist*), Soviet democracy.

These are exceedingly poor arguments. If we are not anarchists, we must admit that the state, *that is, coercion*, is necessary for the transition from capitalism to socialism. The form of coercion is determined by the degree of development of the given revolutionary class, and also by special circumstances, such as, for example, the legacy of a long and reactionary war and the forms of resistance put up by the bourgeoisie and the petty bourgeoisie. There is, therefore, absolutely *no* contradiction in principle between Soviet (*that is*, socialist) democracy and the exercise of dictatorial powers by individuals. The difference between proletarian dictatorship and bourgeois dictatorship is that the former strikes at the exploiting minority in the interests of the exploited majority, and that it is exercised—*also through individuals*—not only by the working and exploited people, but also by organizations which are built in such a way as to rouse these people to history-making activity. (The Soviet organizations are organizations of this kind.)

In regard to the second question, concerning the significance of individual dictatorial powers from the point of view of the specific tasks of the present moment, it must be said that large-scale machine industry—which is precisely the material source, the productive source, the foundation of socialism—calls for absolute and strict *unity of will*, which directs the joint labours of hundreds, thousands and tens of thousands of people. The technical, economic and historical necessity of this is obvious, and all those who have thought about socialism have always regarded it as one of the conditions of socialism. But how can strict unity of will be ensured? By thousands subordinating their will to the will of one.

Given ideal class-consciousness and discipline on the part of those participating in the common work, this subordination would be something like the mild leadership of a conductor of an orchestra. It may assume the sharp forms of a dictatorship if ideal discipline and class-consciousness are lacking. But be that as it may, *unquestioning subordination* to a single will is absolutely necessary for the success of processes organized on the pattern of large-scale machine industry....

We have successfully fulfilled the first task of the revolution; we have seen how the mass of working people evolved in themselves the fundamental condition for its success: they united their efforts against the exploiters in order to overthrow them....

We have successfully fulfilled the second task of the revolution: to awaken, to raise those very "lower ranks" of society whom the exploiters had pushed down, and who only after October 25, 1917, obtained complete freedom to overthrow the exploiters and to begin to take stock of things and arrange life in their own way. The airing of questions at public meetings by the most oppressed and downtrodden, by the least educated mass of working people, their coming over to the side of the Bolsheviks, their setting up everywhere of their own Soviet organizations—this was the second great stage of the revolution.

The third stage is now beginning. We must consolidate what we ourselves have won, what we ourselves have decreed, made law, discussed, planned—consolidate all this in stable forms of *everyday labour discipline*. This is the most difficult, but the most gratifying task, because only its fulfillment will give us a socialist system. We must learn to combine the "public meeting" democracy of the working people—turbulent, surging, overflowing its banks like a spring flood—with *iron* discipline while at work, with *unquestioning obedience* to the will of a single person, the Soviet leader, while at work....

We must work unremittingly to develop the organization of the Soviets and of the Soviet government. There is a petty-bourgeois tendency to transform the members of the Soviets into "parliamentarians", or else into bureaucrats. We must combat this by drawing *all* the members of the Soviets into the practical work of administration. In many places the departments of the Soviets are gradually merging with the Commissariats. Our aim is to draw *the whole of the poor* into the practical work of administration, and all steps that are taken in this direction—the more varied they are, the better—should be carefully recorded, studied, systematized, tested by wider experience and embodied in law. Our aim is to ensure that *every* toiler, having finished his eight hours' "task" in productive labour, shall perform state duties *without pay*; the transition to this is particularly difficult, but this transition alone can guarantee the final consolidation of socialism. Naturally, the novelty and difficulty of the change lead to an abundance of steps being taken, as it were, gropingly, to an abundance of mistakes, vacillation—without this, any marked progress is impossible. The reason why the present position seems peculiar to many of those who would like to be regarded as socialists is that they have been accustomed to contrasting capitalism with socialism abstractly, and that they profoundly put between the two the word "leap" (some of them, recalling fragments of what they have read of Engels's writings, still more profoundly add the phrase "leap from the realm of necessity into the realm of freedom")....

The fight against the bureaucratic distortion of the Soviet form of organization is assured by the firmness of the connection between the Soviets and the "people", meaning by that the working and exploited people, and by the flexibility and elasticity of this connection. Even in the most democratic capitalist republics in the world, the poor never regard the bourgeois parliament as "their" institution. But the Soviets are "theirs" and not alien institutions to the mass of workers and peasants....

It is the closeness of the Soviets to the "people", to the working people, that creates the special forms of recall and other means of control from below which must be most zealously developed now. The more resolutely we now have to stand for a ruthlessly firm government, for the dictatorship of individuals *in definite processes of work*, in definite aspects of *purely executive* functions, the more varied must be the forms and methods of control from below in order to counteract every shadow of a possibility of distorting the principles of Soviet government, in order repeatedly and tirelessly to weed out bureaucracy.

"On the People's Democratic Dictatorship"

Mao Tse-tung

The first of July 1949 marks the fact that the Communist Party of China has already lived through twenty-eight years. Like a man, a political party has its childhood, youth, manhood and old age. TheThe Communist Party of China is no longer a child or a lad in his teens but has become an adult. When a man reaches old age, he will die; the same is true of a party. When classes disappear, all instruments of class struggle—parties and the state machinery—will lose their function, cease to be necessary, therefore gradually wither away and end their historical mission; and human society will move to a higher stage. We are the opposite of the political parties of the bourgeoisie. They are afraid to speak of the extinction of classes, state power and parties. We, on the contrary, declare openly that we are striving hard to create the very conditions which will bring about their extinction. The leadership of the Communist Party and the state power of the people's dictatorship are such conditions. Anyone who does not recognize this truth is no communist....Understand that the road to the abolition of classes, to the abolition of state power and to the abolition of parties is the road all mankind must take; it is only a question of time and conditions. Communists the world over are wiser than the bourgeoisie, they understand the laws governing the existence and development of things, they understand dialectics and they can see farther. The bourgeoisie does not welcome this truth because it does not want to be overthrown. To be overthrown is painful and is unbearable to contemplate for those overthrown....But for the working class, the labouring people and the Communist Party the question is not one of being overthrown, but of working hard to create the conditions in which classes, state power and political parties will die out very naturally and mankind will enter the realm of Great Harmony.[1]...

As everyone knows, our Party passed through these twenty-eight years not in peace but amid hardships, for we had to fight enemies, both foreign and domestic, both inside and outside the Party. We thank Marx, Engels, Lenin and Stalin for giving us a weapon. This weapon is not a machine-gun, but Marxism-Leninism.

Only after several decades of hardship and suffering did the Russians find Marxism. Many things in China were the same as, or similar to, those in Russia before the October Revolution. There was the same feudal oppression. There was similar economic and cultural backwardness. Both countries were backward, China even more so. In both countries alike, for the sake of national regeneration progressives braved hard and bitter struggles in their quest for revolutionary truth.

From the time of China's defeat in the Opium War of 1840, Chinese progressives went through untold hardships in their quest for truth from the Western countries....Chinese who then sought progress would read any book containing the new knowledge from the West....

In my youth, I too engaged in such studies. They represented the culture of Western bourgeois democracy, including the social theories and natural sciences of that period, and they were called "the new learning" in contrast to Chinese feudal culture, which was called "the old learning." For quite a long time, those who had acquired the new learning felt confident that it would save China, and very few of them had any doubts on this score, as the adherents of the old learning had. Only modernization could save China, only learning from foreign countries could modernize China. Among the foreign countries, only the Western capitalist countries were then progressive, as they had successfully built modern bourgeois states. The Japanese

From Mao Tse-tung and Lin Piao, *Post Revolutionary Writings*, K. Fan,ed. (New York: Anchor Books, 1972). Reprinted by permission of the publisher.

177

had been successful in learning from the West, and the Chinese also wished to learn from the Japanese. The Chinese in those days regarded Russia as backward, and few wanted to learn from her....

Imperialist aggression shattered the fond dreams of the Chinese about learning from the West. It was very odd—why were the teachers always committing aggression against their pupil? The Chinese learned a good deal from the West, but they could not make it work and were never able to realize their ideals. Their repeated struggles,...all ended in failure. Day by day, conditions in the country got worse, and life was made impossible. Doubts arose, increased and deepened. World War I shook the whole globe. The Russians made the October Revolution and created the world's first socialist state. Under the leadership of Lenin and Stalin, the revolutionary energy of the great proletariat and labouring people of Russia, hitherto latent and unseen by foreigners, suddenly erupted like a volcano, and the Chinese and all mankind began to see the Russians in a new light. Then, and only then, did the Chinese enter an entirely new era in their thinking and their life. They found Marxism-Leninism, the universally applicable truth, and the face of China began to change....

The Communist Party of China has made tremendous advances both in theory and practice and has radically changed the face of China. Up to now the principal and fundamental experience the Chinese people have gained is twofold:

(1) Internally, arouse the masses of the people. That is, unite the working class, the peasantry, the urban petty bourgeoisie and the national bourgeoisie, form a domestic united front under the leadership of the working class, and advance from this to the establishment of a state which is a people's democratic dictatorship under the leadership of the working class and based on the alliance of workers and peasants.

(2) Externally, unite in a common struggle with those nations of the world which treat us as equals and with the peoples of all countries. That is, ally ourselves with the Soviet Union, with the People's Democracies and with the proletariat and the broad masses of the people in all other countries, and form an international united front.

"You are leaning to one side." Exactly....All Chinese without exception must lean either to the side of imperialism or to the side of socialism. Sitting on the fence will not do, nor is there a third road....

"You are too irritating." We are talking about how to deal with domestic and foreign reactionaries, the imperialists and their running dogs, not about how to deal with anyone else. With regard to such reactionaries, the question of irritating them or not does not arise. Irritated or not irritated, they will remain the same because they are reactionaries. Only if we draw a clear line between reactionaries and revolutionaries, expose the intrigues and plots of the reactionaries, arouse the vigilance and attention of the revolutionary ranks, heighten our will to fight and crush the enemy's arrogance can we isolate the reactionaries, vanquish them or supersede them. We must not show the slightest timidity before a wild beast. We must learn from Wu Sung....

As Wu Sung saw it, the tiger on Chingyang Ridge was a man-eater, whether irritated or not. Either kill the tiger or be eaten by him—one or the other.

"We want to do business." Quite right, business will be done. We are against no one except the domestic and foreign reactionaries who hinder us from doing business. Everybody should know that it is none other than the imperialists and their running dogs, who hinder us from doing business and also from establishing diplomatic relations with foreign countries. When we have beaten the internal and external reactionaries by uniting all domestic and international forces, we shall be able to do business and establish diplomatic relations with all foreign countries on the basis of equality, mutual benefit and mutual respect for territorial integrity and sovereignty.

"Victory is possible even without international help." This is a mistaken idea. In the epoch in which imperialism exists, it is impossible for a genuine people's revolution to win victory in any country without various forms of help from the international revolutionary forces, and even if victory were won, it could not be consolidated....

"You are dictatorial." My dear sirs, you are right, that is just what we are. All the experience the Chinese people have accumulated through several decades teaches us to enforce the people's democratic dictatorship, that is, to deprive the reactionaries of the right to speak and let the people alone have that right.

Who are the people? At the present stage in China, they are the working class, the peasantry, the urban petty bourgeoisie and the national bourgeoisie. These classes, led by the working class and the Communist Party, unite to form their own state and elect their own government; they enforce their dictatorship over the running dogs of imperialism—the landlord class and bureaucrat-bourgeoisie, as well as the representatives of those classes,…reactionaries and their accomplices—suppress them, allow them only to behave themselves and not to be unruly in word or deed. If they speak or act in an unruly way, they will be promptly stopped and punished. Democracy is practised within the ranks of the people, who enjoy the rights of freedom of speech, assembly, association and so on. The right to vote belongs only to the people, not to the reactionaries. The combination of these two aspects, democracy for the people and dictatorship over the reactionaries, is the people's democratic dictatorship.

Why must things be done this way? The reason is quite clear to everybody. If things were not done this way, the revolution would fail, the people would suffer, the country would be conquered.

"Don't you want to abolish state power?" Yes, we do, but not right now; we cannot do it yet. Why? Because imperialism still exists, because domestic reaction still exists, because classes still exist in our country. Our present task is to strengthen the people's state apparatus—mainly the people's army, the people's police and the people's courts—in order to consolidate national defence and protect the people's interests. Given this condition, China can develop steadily, under the leadership of the working class and the Communist Party, from an agricultural into an industrial country and from a new-democratic into a socialist and communist society, can abolish classes and realize the Great Harmony. The state apparatus, including the army, the police and the courts, is the instrument by which one class oppresses another. It is an instrument for the oppression of antagonistic classes; it is violence and not "benevolence." "You are not benevolent!" Quite so. We definitely do not apply a policy of benevolence to the reactionaries and towards the reactionary activities of the reactionary classes. Our policy of benevolence is applied only within the ranks of the people, not beyond them to the reactionaries or to the reactionary activities of reactionary classes.

The people's state protects the people. Only when the people have such a state can they educate and remould themselves by democratic methods on a country-wide scale, with everyone taking part, and shake off the influence of domestic and foreign reactionaries (which is still very strong, will survive for a long time and cannot be quickly destroyed), rid themselves of the bad habits and ideas acquired in the old society, not allow themselves to be led astray by the reactionaries, and continue to advance—to advance towards a socialist and communist society.

Here, the method we employ is democratic, the method of persuasion, not of compulsion. When anyone among the people breaks the law, he too should be punished, imprisoned or even sentenced to death; but this is a matter of a few individual cases, and it differs in principle from the dictatorship exercised over the reactionaries as a class.

As for the members of the reactionary classes and individual reactionaries, so long as they do not rebel, sabotage or create trouble after their political power has been overthrown, land and work will be given to them as well in order to allow them to live and remould themselves through labour into new people. If they are not willing to work, the people's state will compel them to work. Propaganda and educational work will be done among them too and will be done, moreover, with as much care and thoroughness as among the captured army officers in the past. This, too, may be called a "policy of benevolence" if you like, but it is imposed by us on the members of the enemy classes and cannot be mentioned in the same breath with the work of self-education which we carry on within the ranks of the revolutionary people.

Such remoulding of members of the reactionary classes can be accomplished only by a state of the people's democratic dictatorship under the leadership of the Communist Party. When it is well done, China's major exploiting classes, the landlord class and the bureaucrat-bourgeoisie (the monopoly capitalist class), will be eliminated for good. There remain the national bourgeoisie; at the present stage, we can already do a good deal of suitable educational work with many of them. When the time comes to realize socialism, that is, to nationalize private enterprise, we shall carry the work of educating and remoulding them a step further. The people have a powerful state apparatus in their hands—there is no need to fear rebellion by the national bourgeoisie....

The foreign reactionaries who accuse us of practising "dictatorship" or "totalitarianism" are the very persons who practise it. They practise the dictatorship or totalitarianism of one class, the bourgeoisie, over the proletariat and the rest of the people...."Deal with a man as he deals with you." This is just what we do; we deal with the imperialists and their running dogs, the Chiang Kai-shek reactionaries, as they deal with us. That is all there is to it!...

The people's democratic dictatorship is based on the alliance of the working class, the peasantry and the urban petty bourgeoisie, and mainly on the alliance of the workers and the peasants, because these two classes comprise 80 to 90 per cent of China's population. These two classes are the main force in overthrowing imperialism....The transition from New Democracy to socialism also depends mainly upon their alliance.

The people's democratic dictatorship needs the leadership of the working class. For it is only the working class that is most far-sighted, most selfless and most thoroughly revolutionary. The entire history of revolution proves that without the leadership of the working class revolution fails and that with the leadership of the working class revolution triumphs. In the epoch of imperialism, in no country can any other class lead any genuine revolution to victory. This is clearly proved by the fact that the many revolutions led by China's petty bourgeoisie and national bourgeoisie all failed.

The national bourgeoisie at the present stage is of great importance. Imperialism, a most ferocious enemy, is still standing alongside us....China must utilize all the factors of urban and rural capitalism that are beneficial and not harmful to the national economy and the people's livelihood; and we must unite with the national bourgeoisie in common struggle. Our present policy is to regulate capitalism, not to destroy it. But the national bourgeoisie cannot be the leader of the revolution, nor should it have the chief role in state power. The reason it cannot be the leader of the revolution and should not have the chief role in state power is that the social and economic position of the national bourgeoisie determines its weakness; it lacks foresight and sufficient courage and many of its members are afraid of the masses....

To sum up our experience and concentrate it into one point, it is: the people's democratic dictatorship under the leadership of the working class (through the Communist Party) and based upon the alliance of workers and peasants. This dictatorship must unite as one with the international revolutionary forces. This is our formula, our principal experience, our main programme....

NOTES

1. Also known as the world of Great Harmony. It refers to a society based on public ownership, free from class exploitation and oppression—a lofty ideal long cherished by the Chinese people. Here the realm of Great Harmony means communist society.

Fascism: Doctrine and Institutions

Benito Mussolini

Like all sound political conceptions, Fascism is action and it is thought; action in which doctrine is immanent, and doctrine arising from a given system of historical forces in which it is inserted, and working on them from within.3It has therefore a form correlated to contingencies of time and space; but it has also an ideal content which makes it an expression of truth in the higher region of the history of thought. There is no way of exercising a spiritual influence in the world as a human will dominating the will of others, unless one has a conception both of the transient and the specific reality on which that action is to be exercised, and of the permanent and universal reality in which the transient dwells and has its being. To know men one must know man; and to know man one must be acquainted with reality and its laws. There can be no conception of the State which is not fundamentally a conception of life: philosophy or intuition, system of ideas evolving within the framework of logic or concentrated in a vision or a faith, but always, at least potentially, an organic conception of the world.

Thus many of the practical expressions of Fascism—such as party organisation, system of education, discipline—can only be understood when considered in relation to its general attitude toward life. A spiritual attitude. Fascism sees in the world not only those superficial, material aspects in which man appears as an individual, standing by himself, self-centred, subject to natural law which instinctively urges him toward a life of selfish momentary pleasure; it sees not only the individual but the nation and the country; individuals and generations bound together by a moral law, with common traditions and a mission which suppressing the instinct for life closed in a brief circle of pleasure, builds up a higher life, founded on duty, a life free from the limitations of time and space, in which the individual, by self-sacrifice, the renunciation of self-interest, by death itself, can achieve that purely spiritual existence in which his value as a man consists.

The conception is therefore a spiritual one, arising from the general reaction of the century against the flacid materialistic positivism of the XIXth century. Anti-positivistic but positive; neither sceptical nor agnostic; neither pessimistic nor supinely optimistic as are, generally speaking, the doctrines (all negative) which place the centre of life outside man; whereas, by the exercise of his free will, man can and must create his own world.

Fascism wants man to be active and to engage in action with all his energies; it wants him to be manfully aware of the difficulties besetting him and ready to face them. It conceives of life as a struggle in which it behoves a man to win for himself a really worthy place, first of all by fitting himself (physically, morally, intellectually) to become the implement required for winning it. As for the individual, so for the nation, and so for mankind. Hence the high value of culture in all its forms (artistic, religious, scientific), and the outstanding importance of education. Hence also the essential value of work, by which man subjugates nature and creates the human world (economic, political, ethical, intellectual).

This positive conception of life is obviously an ethical one. It invests the whole field of reality as well as the human activities which master it. No action is exempt from moral judgement; no activity can be despoiled of the value which a moral purpose confers on all things. Therefore life, as conceived of by the Fascist, is serious, austere, religious; all its manifestations are poised in a world sustained by moral forces and subject to spiritual responsibilities. The Fascist disdains an "easy" life.

From Fascism: *Doctrines and Institutions* (New York: Howard Fertig, 1968).

The Fascist conception of life is a religious one, in which man is viewed in his immanent relation to a higher law, endowed with an objective will transcending the individual and raising him to conscious membership of a spiritual society. Those who perceive nothing beyond opportunistic considerations in the religious policy of the Fascist régime fail to realise that Fascism is not only a system of government but also and above all a system of thought.

In the Fascist conception of history, man is man only by virtue of the spiritual process to which he contributes as a member of the family, the social group, the nation, and in function of history to which all nations bring their contribution. Hence the great value of tradition in records, in language, in customs, in the rules of social life. Outside history man is a nonentity. Fascism is therefore opposed to all individualistic abstractions based on eighteenth century materialism....It does not believe in the possibility of "happiness" on earth as conceived by the economistic literature of the XVIIIth century, and it therefore rejects the teleological notion that at some future time the human family will secure a final settlement of all its difficulties. This notion runs counter to experience which teaches that life is in continual flux and in process of evolution. In politics Fascism aims at realism; in practice it desires to deal only with those problems which are the spontaneous product of historic conditions and which find or suggest their own solutions. Only by entering in to the process of reality and taking possession of the forces at work within it, can man act on man and on nature.

Anti-individualistic, the Fascist conception of life stresses the importance of the State and accepts the individual only in so far as his interests coincide with those of the State, which stands for the conscience and the universal will of man as a historic entity. It is opposed to classical liberalism which arose as a reaction to absolutism and exhausted its historical function when the State became the expression of the conscience and will of the people. Liberalism denied the State in the name of the individual; Fascism reasserts the rights of the State as expressing the real essence of the individual. And if liberty is to be the attribute of living men and not of abstract dummies invented by individualistic liberalism, then Fascism stands for liberty, and for the only liberty worth having, the liberty of the State and of the individual within the State. The Fascist conception of the State is all-embracing; outside of it no human or spiritual values can exist, much less have value. Thus understood, Fascism, is totalitarian, and the Fascist State—a synthesis and a unit inclusive of all values—interprets, develops, and potentiates the whole life of a people.

No individuals or groups (political parties, cultural associations, economic unions, social classes) outside the State. Fascism is therefore opposed to Socialism to which unity within the State (which amalgamates classes into a single economic and ethical reality) is unknown, and which sees in history nothing but the class struggle. Fascism is likewise opposed to trade-unionism as a class weapon. But when brought within the orbit of the State, Fascism recognises the real needs which gave rise to socialism and trade-unionism, giving them due weight in the guild or corporative system in which divergent interests are coordinated and harmonised in the unity of the State.

Grouped according to their several interests, individuals form classes; they form trade-unions when organised according to their several economic activities; but first and foremost they form the State, which is no mere matter of numbers, the sum of the individuals forming the majority. Fascism is therefore opposed to that form of democracy which equates a nation to the majority, lowering it to the level of the largest number; but it is the purest form of democracy if the nation be considered—as it should be—from the point of view of quality rather than quantity, as an idea, the mightiest because the most ethical, the most coherent, the truest, expressing itself in a people as the conscience and will of the few, if not, indeed, of one, and ending to express itself in the conscience and the will of the mass, of the whole group ethnically moulded by natural and historical conditions into a nation, advancing, as one conscience and one will, along the self-same line of development and spiritual formation. Not a race, nor a geographically defined region, but a people, historically perpetuating itself; a multitude unified by an idea and imbued with the will to live, the will to power, self-consciousness, personality.

In so far as it is embodied in a State, this higher personality becomes a nation. It is not the nation which generates the State; that is an antiquated naturalistic concept which afforded a basis for

XIXth century publicity in favor of national governments. Rather is it the State which creates the nation, conferring volition and therefore real life on a people made aware of their moral unity.

The right to national independence does not arise from any merely literary and idealistic form of self-consciousness; still less from a more or less passive and unconscious *de facto* situation, but from an active, self-conscious, political will expressing itself in action and ready to prove its rights. It arises, in short, from the existence, at least *in fieri*, of a State. Indeed, it is the State which, as the expression of a universal ethical will, creates the right to national independence.

A nation, as expressed in the State, is a living, ethical entity only in so far as it is progressive. Inactivity is death. Therefore the State is not only Authority which governs and confers legal form and spiritual value on individual wills, but it is also Power which makes its will felt and respected beyond its own frontiers, thus affording practical proof of the universal character of the decisions necessary to ensure its development. This implies organisation and expansion, potential if not actual. Thus the State equates itself to the will of man, whose development cannot be checked by obstacles and which, by achieving self-expression, demonstrates its own infinity.

The Fascist State, as a higher and more powerful expression of personality, is a force, but a spiritual one. It sums up all the manifestations of the moral and intellectual life of man. Its functions cannot therefore be limited to those of enforcing order and keeping the peace, as the liberal doctrine had it. It is no mere mechanical device for defining the sphere within which the individual may duly exercise his supposed rights. The Fascist State is an inwardly accepted standard and rule of conduct, a discipline of the whole person; it permeates the will no less than the intellect. It stands for a principle which becomes the central motive of man as a member of civilised society, sinking deep down into his personality; it dwells in the heart of the man of action and of the thinker, of the artist and of the man of science: soul of the soul.

Fascism, in short, is not only a law-giver and a founder of institutions, but an educator and a promoter of spiritual life. It aims at refashioning not only the forms of life but their content—man, his character, and his faith. To achieve this purpose it enforces discipline and uses authority, entering into the soul and ruling with undisputed sway....

Mein Kampf

Adolf Hitler

Even the most superficial observation shows, as an almost brazen basic principle of all the countless forms of expression of Nature's will to live, her limited form of propagation and increase, limited in itself. Every animal mates only with a representative of the same species....Any crossing between two beings of not quite the same high standard produces a medium between the standards of the parents. That means: the young one will probably be on a higher level than the racially lower parent, but not as high as the higher one. Consequently, it will succumb later on in the fight against the higher level. But such a mating contradicts Nature's will to breed life as a whole towards a higher level. The presumption for this does not lie in blending the superior with the inferior, but

From *Mein Kampf* (New York: Reynal and Hitchcock, 1939). Reprinted by permission of Houghton Mifflin Company.

rather in a complete victory of the former. The stronger has to rule and he is not to amalgamate with the weaker one, that he may not sacrifice his own greatness. Only the born weakling can consider this as cruel, but at that he is only a weak and limited human being; for, if this law were not dominating, all conceivable development towards a higher level, on the part of all organically living beings, would be unthinkable for man.

Just as little as Nature desires a mating between weaker individuals and stronger ones, far less she desires the mixing of a higher race with a lower one, as in this case her entire work of higher breeding, which has perhaps taken hundreds of thousands of years, would tumble at one blow.

Historical experience offers countless proofs of this. It shows with terrible clarity that with any mixing of the blood of the Aryan with lower races the result was the end of the culture-bearer....

But quite apart from the fact that so far man has never conquered Nature in any affair, but that at the most he gets hold of and tries to lift a flap of her enormous, gigantic veil of eternal riddles and secrets, that in reality he does not 'invent' anything but only discovers everything, that he does not dominate Nature, but that, based on the knowledge of a few laws and secrets of Nature, he has risen to the position of master of those other living beings lacking this knowledge. Without men there is no human idea in this world; thus the idea is always caused by the presence of men, and, with it, of all those laws which created the presumptions for this existence....

Everything that today we admire on this earth—science and art, technique and inventions—is only the creative product of a few peoples and perhaps originally of *one* race. On them now depends also the existence of this entire culture. If they perish, then the beauty of this earth sinks into the grave with them.

No matter how much the soil, for instance, is able to influence the people, the result will always be a different one, according to the races under consideration. The scanty fertility of a living space may instigate one race towards the highest achievements, while with another race this may only become the cause for the most dire poverty and ultimate malnutrition with all its consequences. The inner disposition of the peoples is always decisive for the way in which outward influences

work themselves out. What leads one people to starvation, trains the other for hard work.

All great cultures of the past perished only because the originally creative race died off through blood-poisoning.

The ultimate cause of such a decline was always the forgetting that all culture depends on men and not the reverse; that means, that in order to save a certain culture the man who created it has to be saved. But the preservation is bound to the brazen law of necessity and of the right of the victory of the best and the strongest in this world....

He who wants to live should fight, therefore, and he who does not want to battle in this world of eternal struggle does not deserve to be alive.

Even if this were hard, this is the way things are. But it is certain that by far the hardest fate is the fate which meets that man who believes he can 'conquer' Nature, and yet, in truth, only seems to mock her. Misery, distress, and diseases are then her answer!

The man who misjudges and disdains the laws of race actually forfeits the happiness that seems destined to be his. He prevents the victorious march of the best race and with it also the presumption for all human progress, and in consequence he will remain in the domain of the animal's helpless misery, burdened with the sensibility of man....

What we see before us of human culture today, the results of art, science, and techniques, is almost exclusively the creative product of the Aryan. But just this fact admits of the not unfounded conclusion that he alone was the founder of higher humanity as a whole, thus the prototype of what we understand by the word 'man.' He is the Prometheus of mankind, out of whose bright forehead springs the divine spark of genius at all times, forever rekindling that fire which in the form of knowledge lightened up the night of silent secrets and thus made man climb the path towards the position of master of the other beings on this earth. Exclude him—and deep darkness will again fall upon the earth, perhaps even, after a few thousand years, human culture would perish and the world would turn into a desert.

If one were to divide mankind into three groups: culture-founders, culture-bearers, and culture-destroyers, then, as representative of the first kind, only the Aryan would come in question. It is from him that the foundation and the walls of all human creations originate, and only the external form and color depend on the characteristics of the various peoples involved. He furnishes the gigantic building-stones and also the plans for all human progress, and only the execution corresponds to the character of the people and races in the various instances....

In general even Nature has the habit of making certain corrective decisions about the racial purity of mortal beings. Nature likes bastards only little. Especially the first products of such cross-breeding, say in the third, fourth or fifth generation, have to suffer bitterly. Not only the importance of the originally highest constituent of the cross-breeding is taken from them, but they lack, with the deficient unity of the blood, also the unity of will power and determination for life as a whole. In all critical moments, when the racially uniform being makes correct decisions, and consistent decisions at that, the racially torn will become uncertain, that means he will arrive at half measures. Taking both facts together, this means not only a certain inferiority of the racially unstable as compared with the racially uniform, but in practice also the possibility of a quicker decline. *In countless cases where the race holds out the bastard breaks down.* In this must be seen the correction of Nature. Frequently it goes even farther. It limits the possibility of propagation. By this Nature limits the fertility of remote crossings as a whole and thus makes them die off.

If, for example, a single individual of a certain race were to enter into a union with a racially lower individual, the result would be, first, a lowering of the standard in itself; further it would mean a weakening of the offspring as compared with the surroundings which remained racially unmixed. With the complete prevention of a further blood influx on the part of the highest race, the bastards, with continued mutual crossing, would either die off because of Nature's wisely reducing their ability of resistance, or in the course of thousands of years they would form a new mixture in which the original individual elements, in consequence of a thousandfold crossing, are completely mixed and no longer recognizable. Thus a new nationality with a certain herd-like resistibility would have been formed, but compared with the highest race which helped in forming the first cross-breed, it would be considerably reduced in its spiritual and cultural importance. But also, in this case, the product of the crossing would succumb in the mutual struggle for life, as long as there exists a higher race, that remained unmixed, as opponent. Any herd-like inner completeness of this new national body, formed in the course of a thousand years, would nevertheless, in consequence of the general lowering of the race standard and the diminishing of mental elasticity and creative ability, conditioned by it, not suffice for overcoming victoriously the struggle with an equally uniform but spiritually and culturally superior race.

Thus one can establish the following valid conclusion: *Every race-crossing leads necessarily sooner or later to the decline of the mixed product, as long as the higher part of this crossing still exists in some racially pure unity.* The danger for the mixed product is abolished only in the moment of the bastardization of the last higher, racially pure element.

In this is rooted a slow yet natural process of regeneration which gradually eliminates racial poisonings, as long as there still exists a basic stock of racially pure elements and no further bastardization takes place....

There is only one most sacred human right, and this right is at the same time the most sacred obligation, namely: to see to it that the blood is preserved pure, so that by the preservation of the best human material a possibility is given for a more noble development of these human beings.

Thus a folkish State primarily will have to lift marriage out of the level of a permanent race degradation in order to give it the consecration of that institution which is called upon to beget images of the Lord and not deformities half man and half ape....The folkish State has to make up for what is today neglected in this field in all directions. It has to put the race into the center of life in general. It has to care for its preservation in purity. It has to make the child the most precious possession of a people. It has to take care that only the healthy beget children; that there is only one disgrace: to be sick and to bring children into the world despite one's own deficiencies; but one highest honor: to renounce this. Further, on the other hand this has to be looked upon as objectionable: to keep healthy children from the nation. Thereby the State has to appear as the guardian of a thousand years' future, in the face of which the wish and the egoism of the individual appears as nothing and has to submit. It has to put the most modern medical means at the service of this knowledge. It has to declare unfit for propagation everybody who is visibly ill and has inherited a disease and it has to carry this out in practice. On the other hand, it has to care that the fertility of the healthy woman is not limited by the financial mismanagement of a State régime which makes children a curse for the parents. It has to do away with that foul, nay criminal, indifference with which today the social presumptions of a family with many children is treated, and in its place it has to consider itself the guardian of this precious blessing of a people. Its care belongs more to the child than to the adult.

He who is not physically and mentally healthy and worthy must not perpetuate his misery in the body of his child. Here the folkish State has to achieve the most enormous work of education. Some day it will appear as a greater deed than the most victorious wars of our present bourgeois era. By education it has to teach the individual that it is not a disgrace but only a regrettable misfortune to be sick and weakly, but that it is a crime and therefore at the same time a disgrace to dishonor this misfortune by one's egoism by burdening it again upon an innocent being; that in the face of this it gives proof of a nobility of the highest mind and of most admirable humaneness if the innocently sick, by renouncing his own child, gives his love and tenderness to an unknown, poor young descendant of his nationality, whose health promises that one day he will become a vigorous member of a powerful community. With this work of education the State has to render the purely spiritual supplement of its practical activity. Without considering understanding or non-understanding, approval or disapproval, it has to act in this sense....

If as the State's first task in the service and for the welfare of its nationality we recognize the preservation, care and development of the racially best elements, it is natural that this care has to extend not only to the time of birth of the young member of people and race, but that it has to educate the young offspring towards becoming a valuable member in view of later propagation.

Just as in general the presumption for spiritual achievements lies in the racial quality of the given human material, thus also the individual's education has to focus upon and to promote first of all physical health; for, within the masses, a healthy, vigorous spirit will be found only in a healthy and powerful body. The fact that geniuses are sometimes physically badly formed, even sick beings, is no objection. They are the exceptions which—as everywhere—prove the rule. But if the mass of a people consists of physical degenerates, then out of this swamp a really great spirit will arise only very rarely. His activity will in no case be rewarded with great success. The degraded rabble will either not understand him at all, or it will be so weakened in its will power that it will be unable to follow the soaring flight of such an eagle.

The folkish State, through this realization, has to direct its entire education primarily not at pumping in mere knowledge, but at the breeding of absolutely healthy bodies. Of secondary importance is the training of the mental abilities. But here again first of all the development of the character, especially the promotion of will power and determination, connected with education for joyfully assuming responsibility, and only as the last thing, scientific schooling.

Thereby the folkish State has to start from the presumption that a man, though scientifically little educated but physically healthy, who has a sound, firm character, filled with joyful determination and will power, is of greater value to the national community than an ingenious weakling. A people of scholars, when they are physically degenerated, irresolute and cowardly pacifists, will not conquer heaven, nay it will not even be able to assure its existence on this globe....

Loyalty, willingness to sacrifice, and silence are virtues which a great people urgently needs, and their inculcation by education and training in school is more important than many of the things which now fill our curriculum. Also the elimination by education of tearful complaining, of lamenting, etc., belongs in this field....

Of highest importance is the training of will power and determination, as well as the cultivation of joy in taking responsibility.

The parliamentary principle of decision by majority, by denying the authority of the person and placing in its stead the number of the crowd in question, sins against the aristocratic basic idea of Nature, whose opinion of aristocracy, however, need in no way be represented by the present-day decadence of our Upper Ten Thousand.

The reader of Jewish newspapers can hardly imagine the devastation which results from this institution of modern democratic parliamentary rule, unless he has learned to think and examine for himself. It is above all the cause of the terrible flooding of the entire political life with the most inferior products of our time. No matter how far the true leader withdraws from political activity, which to a great extent does not consist of creative work and achievement, but rather of bargaining and haggling for the favor of a majority, this very activity, however, will agree with and attract the people of low mentality.

The more dwarfish the mentality and the abilities of such a present-day leather merchant are, the more clearly his knowledge makes him conscious of the wretchedness of his actual appearance, the more will he praise a system that does not demand of him the strength and the genius of a giant, but rather which calls for the cunning of a village chief or which even prefers this kind of wisdom to that of a Pericles. Such a simpleton need never worry about the responsibility of his actions. He is relieved of this care for the reason that he knows, no matter what the result of his 'statesmanlike' bungling may be, that his end has long been predicted by the stars; some day he will have to make room for another, an equally great mind. It is, among other things, a symptom of such a decline that the number of great statesmen increases in the measure in which the competence of the individual one decreases. With increasing dependence on parliamentary majorities, he is bound to shrink, for great minds will refuse to serve as bailiff for stupid good-for-nothings and babblers, and on the other hand, the representatives of the majority, that is, of stupidity, hate nothing more ardently than a superior mind.

For such an assembly of wise men of Gotham, it is always a comforting feeling to know that they are headed by a leader whose wisdom corresponds to the mentality of the assembly; for, is it not pleasant to let one's intellect flash forth from time to time, and finally, if Smith can be master, why not Jones also?

This invention of democracy most closely conforms to a quality which lately has developed into a crying shame, that is, the cowardice of a great part of our so-called 'leaders.' How fortunate to be able to hide, whenever decisions of importance are involved, behind the coat-tails of a so-called majority!...

With the victorious march of German technical skill and industry, with the rising successes of German trade, the knowledge was gradually lost that all this was only possible on the basis of a strong State. On the contrary, in many circles one went so far as to have the opinion that the State itself owed its existence only to these developments, that the State itself represented only an economic institution, that it was to be ruled according to economic rules, and that therefore it depended in its makeup on economics, a condition which was then looked upon and praised as by far the soundest and most natural.

But the State has nothing whatsoever to do with a definite conception of economics or development of economics.

The State is not an assembly of commercial parties in a certain prescribed space for the fulfillment of economic tasks, but the organization of a community of physically and mentally equal human beings for the better possibility of the furtherance of their species as well as for the fulfillment of the goal of their existence assigned to them by Providence. This, and nothing else, is the purpose and the meaning of a State. Economy is, therefore, only one of the many auxiliary means necessary for reaching this goal. But it is never the cause or the purpose of a State, provided the latter is not based from the start on a foundation that is wrong because it is unnatural. Only thus can it be explained that the State, as such, need not even have a territorial limitation as its assumption. This will be necessary only with those nations which for their own part want to secure the maintenance of their fellow men; that means that they are ready to fight the struggle for existence by their own work. Nations which are able to sneak their way into the rest of mankind like drones, in order to make them work for them under all kinds of pretexts, are able to form States without any certain limited living area of their own. This may be said primarily of that people under the parasitism of which, especially today, the entire honest mankind has to suffer: the Jews.

The Jewish State was never spatially limited in itself; it was universally unlimited in respect to space, but it was restricted to the collectivity of a race. This is the reason why this people always forms a State within other States. It was one of the most ingenious tricks that was ever invented to let this State sail under the flag of 'religion,' thus securing for it the tolerance that the Aryan is always ready to grant to a religious denomination. Actually the Mosaic religion is nothing but a doctrine of the preservation of the Jewish race. Therefore, it comprises also nearly all sociological, political, and economic fields of knowledge which could ever come into question.

The instinct of preserving the species is the first cause of the formation of human communities. But the State is a folk organism and not an economic organization. A difference that is as great as it remains incomprehensible to the so-called 'statesmen,' especially of today. They believe, therefore, that they can build up the State by economy, whereas in reality it is always the result of the activity of those qualities which lie in line with the will to preserve the species and the race. But these are always heroic virtues and never commercial egoism, since the preservation of the existence of a species presupposes the individual's willingness to sacrifice itself....The sacrifice of the personal existence is necessary in order to guarantee the preservation of the species. Thus the most essential supposition for the formation and preservation of a State is the presence of a certain feeling of homogeneity on the basis of the same entity and the same species, as well as the readiness to risk one's life for this with all means, something that will lead nations on their own soil to the creation of heroic virtues, but parasites to mendacious hypocrisy and malicious cruelty; that is, these qualities must be present as the supposition for their existence which varies in the various State forms. But the formation of a State will always be brought about by at least originally risking these qualities, whereby in the struggle of self-preservation those people will be defeated—that means be subject to enslavement and thus, sooner or later, die out—who, in the mutual battle, call the smallest share of heroic virtues their own, or which are not adequate to the mendacious ruse of the hostile parasite. But in this case also this is due not so much to a lack of cleverness as to a lack of determination and courage that tries to conceal itself under the cloak of a humanitarian attitude

However, how little the qualities forming and preserving a State are connected with economy is shown most clearly by the fact that the inner strength of a State coincides only in the very rarest cases with the so-called economic zenith, but that this usually announces in so many examples the already approaching decay of the State. If one had to ascribe the formation of human communities first of all to economic forces or impulses, then the highest economic development should at the same time indicate the greatest strength of the State, and not *vice versa*....

Whenever in Germany an upswing of political power took place, economy also began to rise; but thereafter, whenever economy was made the sole content of our people's life, thus suffocating the ideal virtues, the State collapsed again, and after a certain time it pulled economy down with it into the grave.

But if one asks oneself the question what the forces forming or otherwise preserving a State are in reality, it can be summed up with one single characterization: the individual's ability and willingness to sacrifice himself for the community. But that these virtues have really nothing whatsoever to do with economics is shown by the simple realization that man never sacrifices himself for them; that means: one does not die for business, but for ideals....

The transformation of an ideal conception of highest veracity, based upon a general view of life, into a definitely limited, tightly organized political community of believers and fighters, uniform in spirit and will power, is the most significant achievement, as solely on its fortunate solution the possibility of a victory of the idea depends. Therefore, out of the host of sometimes millions of people, who individually more or less clearly and distinctly guess this truth, partly perhaps understand it, *one man* must step forward in order to form, with apodictic force, out of the wavering world of imagination of the great masses, granite principles, and to take up the fight for their sole correctness, until out of the playing waves of a free world of thought a brazen rock of uniform combination of form and will arises.

The general right for such an activity is based on its necessity, the personal right, in success.

If we try to extract from the word 'folkish' the innermost nucleus, representing its meaning, we come to the following fact:

Our present current political conception of life is generally based upon the conception that one can ascribe to the State in itself a creative culture-forming force, but that it has nothing to do with racial presumptions, and that it is rather a product of economic necessities, but at best the natural result of the political urge for power. This fundamental view, in its further logical and consequent development, leads not only to a mistaken recognition of racial original forces, but also to an undervaluation of the individual. For the negation of the difference of the several races as regards their general culture-creating forces, must necessarily also transfer this greatest error to the judgment of the individual person. The belief in the equality of the races will then become the basis of an equal manner of observation of the peoples and further for the individual man. Therefore Marxism itself is nothing but the transmission, carried out by the Jew Karl Marx, of a long existing attitude and conception, conditioned by a view of life, to the form of a definite political creed: international Marxism. Without the basis of such a general, previously existing poisoning, the astounding political success of this doctrine would never have been possible. Karl Marx was really the only *one* among millions who, in the swamp of a gradually decomposing world, recognized, with the keen eye of the prophet, the most essential poison elements, took them out, in order to render them, like a magician of the black arts, into a concentrated solution for the quicker destruction of the independent existence of the free nations of this earth. But all this in the service of his race.

The Marxist doctrine is the brief spiritual extract of the view of life that is generally valid today. Merely for this reason every fight by our so-called *bourgeois* world against it is impossible, even ridiculous, as this *bourgeois* world also is essentially interspersed with all these poison elements, and worships a view of life which in general is distinguished from the Marxian view only by degrees or persons. The *bourgeois* world is Marxist, but it believes in the possibility of a domination of certain human groups (*bourgeoisie*), while Marxism itself plans to transmit the world systematically into the hands of Jewry.

In opposition to this, the 'folkish' view recognizes the importance of mankind in its racially innate elements. In principle, it sees in the State only a means to an end, and as its end it considers the preservation of the racial existence of men. Thus it by no means believes in an equality of the races, but with their differences it also recognizes their superior and inferior values, and by this recognition it feels the obligation in accordance with the Eternal Will that dominates this universe to promote the victory of the better and stronger, and to demand the submission of the worse and the weaker. Thus in principle it favors also the fundamental aristocratic thought of nature and believes in the validity of this law down to the last individual. It sees not only the different values of the races, but also the different values of individual man. In its opinion, out of the masses emerges the importance of the person, but by this it has an organizing effect, as contrasted with disorganizing Marxism. It believes in the necessity of idealizing mankind, as, in turn, it sees in this the only presumption for the existence of mankind. But it cannot grant the right of existence to an ethical idea, if this idea represents a danger for the racial life of the bearers of higher ethics; for in a hybridized and negrified world all conceptions of the humanly beautiful and sublime, as well as all conceptions of an idealized future of our mankind, would be lost forever.

In this world human culture and civilization are inseparably bound up with the existence of the Aryan. His dying-off or his decline would again lower upon this earth the dark veils of a time without culture.

The undermining of the existence of human culture by destroying its supporters appears, in a folkish view of life, as the most execrable crime. He who dares to lay hand upon the highest image of the Lord sins against the benevolent Creator of this miracle and helps in the expulsion from Paradise.

With this the folkish view of life corresponds to the innermost will of nature, as nature restores that free play of the forces which is bound to lead to a permanent mutual higher breeding, until finally the best of mankind, having acquired the possession of this earth, is given a free road for activity in domains which will lie partly above, partly outside it.

We all sense that in the distant future problems could approach man for the conquest of which only a highest race, as the master nation, based upon the means and the possibilities of an entire globe, will be called upon....

The *folkish State* divides its inhabitants into three classes: State citizens, State subjects, and aliens.

In principle, only birth confers the status of subject. Being a State subject as such does not entitle one to hold public offices, to exercise political activity in the sense of participation in elections, be it actively or passively. In principle, every State subject's race and nationality have to be ascertained. Every State subject is free at any time to abandon his status and to become a State citizen in that country the nationality of which corresponds to his own. The *alien* is distinguished from the State subject only by the fact that he is a State subject of an alien State....

5   Liberalism and Its Critics

The dominant political ideology of the modern period, especially in the Western world, has been some form of liberalism, though liberalism has not been without critics, even from within the tradition itself.

Liberalism begins with a defense of the rights of the individual from undue governmental interference. Its most fundamental tenet is that there are limits on what a government, indeed, a society, can ask of individual members of the community and that these limits ought to be respected. Inherent difficulties in this position began to be appreciated only after the conception had firmly taken root and had been instituted as policy in the democratic governments of Europe and North America. Two main areas of concern arose. First, the idea that there are limits on what can be asked of the individual has as a flip side, the consequence that there are limits on majority rule.

Where those limits should be drawn is not agreed upon by liberal theorists. The general issue arises in many areas of social-political debate. However, none has proven to be as fundamental and difficult to resolve as the disagreement about what should "give" when promoting the interest of one individual can be accomplished only by abridging the freedom of others.

Consider the right of individuals to speech or political participation. These rights can be extended universally because when I exercise my right to speak it does not deprive you of your right to speak. If we all speak at once it might get noisy, but no one's freedom has been abridged. Rights such as these have sometimes been called "negative" rights since they are rights that create areas of action in which individuals are protected *against* interference.

But after these rights were instituted by democratic governments, two problems became clear. First, one can be fully endowed with these rights and yet be trapped in a life so devoid of those social and economic goods, such as housing, medical care, and adequate food, that life itself is without dignity. Second, in such a life, the rights one has cannot be exercised in any meaningful way. That a street person has a right to hold elective office means little.

Two different philosophical responses to these difficulties have dominated the discussion of these problems. It seems to some that we have not only "negative" rights but also the "positive" right to adequate social and economic goods. On the other hand, utilitarian thinkers often come to a similar conclusion but by a different route. They argue that society as a whole would benefit and the welfare of everyone would be enhanced if we would adopt policies which would provide a more equitable distribution of social and economic goods.

In the first account individuals have the right to an equitable share of economic and social goods even if the majority fails to recognize that fact. In the utilitarian account, the majority ought to act to secure equity when it determines it is useful to do so.

Both these views clash with the view of those theorists who put a primary value on the right to own and privately dispose of one's own property since a more equitable distribution of social and economic goods can be achieved only by taking away from those who have more to give to those who have less.

In the United States this clash was at the root of the Civil War. Abolitionists insisted that slaves should enjoy the same rights and liberties as others while slave owners perceived this demand as one to relinquish control of their property. More recently, some liberals have argued that the underprivileged are entitled to a larger cut of the economic pie and have supported programs, such as food stamps, affirmative action, which aim to redistribute the wealth. Other liberals perceive this as an attack on property rights, since in order to accomplish these goals government must take from some to give to others. If we stress the individual's freedom to dispose of their property as they see fit, then any attempt of the state to redistribute that wealth against their wishes will inevitably be seen as a violation of liberalism's insistence on individual rights and freedoms. But if we stress the individual's right to dignity and respect, then we tend to see liberalism as demanding that the state arrange its affairs so that social goods are distributed equitably even if this means taking from the rich to give to the poor. The debate about this issue is sometimes characterized as a clash between liberty and equality.

In fact *both* sides in the debate claim to be "liberals" and both have a right to their claim. Since liberals have long been pulled in both directions, two forms of liberalism have emerged today: "libertarian liberals," who emphasize property rights, and "egalitarian liberals," who emphasize the right of every individual to equal respect and dignity.

The second area of tension in Western liberal thought focuses on the extent to which the individual can be conceived as and identified as an atomic entity independent of the community in which the individual is embedded. Some versions of liberalism start with fully formed individuals having values and rights and use this concept as a basis for constructing a social order. Others argue that this is distorted thinking since individuals really exist only as persons with values and rights within an already existing community. Liberals in general will not go as far as Rousseau, Hegel, Mussolini, or Hitler in glorifying the state and suggesting that the individual becomes real only by identifying with the greater good of the community, but those liberals who identify themselves as "communitarians" argue that other liberals have gone too far in isolating the individual from the community.

READINGS

The first three readings in this chapter address the first issue described above and the rest of the chapter addresses the second issue. John Rawls, a Harvard University philosophy professor, takes the primary problem to be addressed by social and political philosophy to be that of justice or fairness. The difficulty is how to decide what social arrangements are just. Rawls's suggestion is that we construct a decision-making model within which we are forced to make equitable decisions. Conceiving of ourselves in "an original position" in which a "veil of ignorance" prevents us from knowing particular information about ourselves while at the same time we try to make decisions which will be in our own best interest, he argues, will have the effect of forcing us to be fair to everyone. Under such conditions he argues we would make decisions on the basis of the "maxi-min" principle drawn from game theory. This principle would lead us to chose the best-worst outcome. It is Rawls's position that use of this principle would force us to adopt a democracy within which we all have equal amounts of basic rights (voting, speech, participating in the political process, etc.) but one which would require us to distribute social and economic goods (health care, respect, housing, etc.) so that the most disadvantaged would have more of those goods than they would have under any other distribution. On this account, differences in shares in economic goods could be justified only if they enhanced the condition of everyone. Hence, Rawls regards economic goods as communal property to be divided fairly and not on the basis of prior ownership, and he envisions an expansive role for government in making distributions.

It is this to which Robert Nozick, Rawls's colleague at Harvard, strongly objects. Nozick's position is that if a person's property and wealth has been acquired fairly, then they have fair title to it. Hence its use and dispensation ought not to be decided as a matter of public policy. In his view the most minimal state having the fewest possible functions and interfering with individual decision making as little as possible is the most extensive state which can be justified.

On the other hand, Kai Nielson, a contemporary philosopher at the University of Calgary, Canada, argues for an egalitarian conception of justice even more radical than the one suggested by Rawls. He says that "we should seek a 'republic of equals' where there will be a fundamental equality of social condition for everyone."

Addressing the other theme which has concerned contemporary liberals, Elizabeth Wolgast, philosophy professor at California State University at Hayward, questions whether human beings are really the "social atoms" some liberal views make them appear to be and whether the assumption that they are has led to many of the social problems of alienation and selfishness which we face today. She traces the history of atomistic accounts of the individual, finding evidence of it in writings from Descartes to Nozick and Rawls and attempts to show how such a conception has both aided and hindered our attempts to understand ourselves and our society.

Marilyn Friedman of the philosophy department of Washington University in St. Louis finds a connection between contemporary critiques of social atomism and elements of feminist thought. She argues that the emphasis on conflict and competition found in many political and social theories is replaced in feminist thought by an emphasis on basic human relationships. However, she finds some communitarian analyses to be leading in a direction which feminists should resist since we should continue to question the relationships within our community and not assume them to be inevitable or desirable. Communitarian notions of community often covertly champion the enforcement of traditional and often inhibiting roles for women, whereas the feminism she supports is one which encourages the freedom to associate with and form communities with whomever we choose. We should strive for "communities of choice, supplementing, if not displacing the communities and attachments which are merely found."

Another critic of communitarianism, Michael Walzer of the Princeton Institute for Advanced Study, argues that communitarians contradict themselves when they argue that we are not social atoms and at the same time trace our current problems to having come to think of ourselves as social atoms. If we are not social atoms, then problems resulting from our being social atoms obviously cannot arise. He further argues that both the emphasis on the individual at the expense of the community and the alternative communitarian theory are views that periodically challenge and correct one another. In his analysis it is not so much that one is right and the other wrong but that each needs to challenge the other.

A Theory of Justice

John Rawls

I shall begin by considering the role of the principles of justice.1Let us assume, to fix ideas, that a society is a more or less self-sufficient association of persons who in their relations to one another recognize certain rules of conduct as binding and who for the most part act in accordance with them. Suppose further that these rules specify a system of cooperation designed to advance the good of those taking part in it. Then, although a society is a cooperative venture for mutual advantage, it is typically marked by a conflict as well as by an identity of interests. There is an identity of interests since social cooperation makes possible a better life for all than any would have if each were to live solely by his own efforts. There is a conflict of interests since persons are not indifferent as to how the greater benefits produced by their collaboration are distributed, for in order to pursue their ends they each prefer a larger to a lesser share. A set of principles is required for choosing among the various social arrangements which determine this division of advantages and for underwriting an agreement on the proper distributive shares. These principles are the principles of social justice: they provide a way of assigning rights and duties in the basic institutions of society and they define the appropriate distribution of the benefits and burdens of social cooperation....

Men disagree about which principles should define the basic terms of their association. Yet we may still say, despite this disagreement, that they each have a conception of justice. That is, they understand the need for, and they are prepared to affirm, a characteristic set of principles for assigning basic rights and duties and for determining what they take to be the proper distribution of the benefits and burdens of social cooperation. Thus it seems natural to think of the concept of justice as distinct from the various conceptions of justice and as being specified by the role which these different sets of principles, these different conceptions, have in common. Those who hold different conceptions of justice can, then, still agree that institutions are just when no arbitrary distinctions are made between persons in the assigning of basic rights and duties and when the rules determine a proper balance between competing claims to the advantages of social life....

Some measure of agreement in conceptions of justice is, however, not the only prerequisite for a viable human community. There are other fundamental social problems, in particular those of coordination, efficiency, and stability. Thus the plans of individuals need to be fitted together so that their activities are compatible with one another and they can all be carried through without anyone's legitimate expectations being severely disappointed. Moreover, the execution of these plans should lead to the achievement of social ends in ways that are efficient and consistent with justice. And finally, the scheme of social cooperation must be stable: it must be more or less regularly complied with and its basic rules willingly acted upon; and when infractions occur, stabilizing forces should exist that prevent further violations and tend to restore the arrangement. Now it is evident that these three problems are connected with that of justice. In the absence of a certain measure of agreement on what is just and unjust, it is clearly more difficult for individuals to coordinate their plans efficiently in order to insure that mutually beneficial arrangements are maintained. Distrust and resentment corrode the ties of civility, and suspicion and hostility tempt men to act in ways they would otherwise avoid. So while the distinctive role of conceptions of justice is to specify basic rights and duties and

From A Theory of Justice (Cambridge, MA: Harvard University Press, 1971). Reprinted by permission of the publisher.

to determine the appropriate distributive shares, the way in which a conception does this is bound to affect the problems of efficiency, coordination, and stability. We cannot, in general, assess a conception of justice by its distributive role alone, however useful this role may be in identifying the concept of justice. We must take into account its wider connections; for even though justice has a certain priority, being the most important virtue of institutions, it is still true that, other things equal, one conception of justice is preferable to another when its broader consequences are more desirable....

For us the primary subject of justice is the basic structure of society, or more exactly, the way in which the major social institutions distribute fundamental rights and duties and determine the division of advantages from social cooperation. By major institutions I understand the political constitution and the principal economic and social arrangements. Thus the legal protection of freedom of thought and liberty of conscience, competitive markets, private property in the means of production, and the monogamous family are examples of major social institutions. Taken together as one scheme, the major institutions define men's rights and duties and influence their life-prospects, what they can expect to be and how well they can hope to do. The basic structure is the primary subject of justice because its effects are so profound and present from the start. The intuitive notion here is that this structure contains various social positions and that men born into different positions have different expectations of life determined, in part, by the political system as well as by economic and social circumstances. In this way the institutions of society favor certain starting places over others. These are especially deep inequalities. Not only are they pervasive, but they affect men's initial chances in life; yet they cannot possibly be justified by an appeal to the notions of merit or desert. It is these inequalities, presumably inevitable in the basic structure of any society, to which the principles of social justice must in the first instance apply. These principles, then, regulate the choice of a political constitution and the main elements of the economic and social system. The justice of a social scheme depends essentially on how fundamental rights and duties are assigned and on the economic opportunities and social conditions in the various sectors of society....

My aim is to present a conception of justice which generalizes and carries to a higher level of abstraction the familiar theory of the social contract as found, say, in Locke, Rousseau, and Kant. In order to do this we are not to think of the original contract as one to enter a particular society or to set up a particular form of government. Rather, the guiding idea is that the principles of justice for the basic structure of society are the object of the original agreement. They are the principles that free and rational persons concerned to further their own interests would accept in an initial position of equality as defining the fundamental terms of their association. These principles are to regulate all further agreements; they specify the kinds of social cooperation that can be entered into and the forms of government that can be established. This way of regarding the principles of justice I shall call justice as fairness.

Thus we are to imagine that those who engage in social cooperation choose together, in one joint act, the principles which are to assign basic rights and duties and to determine the division of social benefits. Men are to decide in advance how they are to regulate their claims against one another and what is to be the foundation charter of their society. Just as each person must decide by rational reflection what constitutes his good, that is, the system of ends which it is rational for him to pursue, so a group of persons must decide once and for all what is to count among them as just and unjust. The choice which rational men would make in this hypothetical situation of equal liberty, assuming for the present that this choice problem has a solution, determines the principles of justice.

In justice as fairness the original position of equality corresponds to the state of nature in the traditional theory of the social contract. This original position is not, of course, thought of as an actual historical state of affairs, much less as a primitive condition of culture. It is understood as a purely hypothetical situation characterized so as to lead to a certain conception of justice. Among the essential features of this situation is that no one knows his place in society, his class position or social status, nor does any one know his fortune in the distribution of natural assets and abilities, his intelligence, strength, and the like. I shall even assume that the parties do not know their conceptions of the good or their special psychological propensities. The principles of justice are chosen behind a veil of ignorance. This ensures that no one is advantaged or disadvantaged in the choice of principles by the outcome of natural chance or the contingency of social circumstances. Since all are similarly situated and no one is able to design principles to favor his particular condition, the principles of justice are the result of a fair agreement or bargain. For given the circumstances of the original position, the symmetry of everyone's relations to each other, this initial situation is fair between individuals as moral persons, that is, as rational beings with their own ends and capable, I shall assume, of a sense of justice. The original position is, one might say, the appropriate initial status quo, and thus the fundamental agreements reached in it are fair. This explains the propriety of the name "justice as fairness": it conveys the idea that the principles of justice are agreed to in an initial situation that is fair....

Justice as fairness begins, as I have said, with one of the most general of all choices which persons might make together, namely, with the choice of the first principles of a conception of justice which is to regulate all subsequent criticism and reform of institutions. Then, having chosen a conception of justice, we can suppose that they are to choose a constitution and a legislature to enact laws, and so on, all in accordance with the principles of justice initially agreed upon. Our social situation is just if it is such that by this sequence of hypothetical agreements we would have contracted into the general system of rules which defines it. Moreover, assuming that the original position does determine a set of principles (that is, that a particular conception of justice would be chosen), it will then be true that whenever social institutions satisfy these principles those engaged in them can say to one another that they are cooperating on terms to which they would agree if they were free and equal persons whose relations with respect to one another were fair. They could all view their arrangements as meeting the stipulations which they would acknowledge in an initial situation that embodies widely accepted and reasonable constraints on the choice of principles. The general recognition of this fact would provide the basis for a public acceptance of the corresponding principles of justice. No society can, of course, be a scheme of cooperation which men enter voluntarily in a literal sense; each person finds himself placed at birth in some particular position in some particular society, and the nature of this position materially affects his life prospects. Yet a society satisfying the principles of justice as fairness comes as close as a society can to being a voluntary scheme, for it meets the principles which free and equal persons would assent to under circumstances that are fair. In this sense its members are autonomous and the obligations they recognize self-imposed.

One feature of justice as fairness is to think of the parties in the initial situation as rational and mutually disinterested. This does not mean that the parties are egoists, that is, individuals with only certain kinds of interests, say in wealth, prestige, and domination. But they are conceived as not taking an interest in one another's interests. They are to presume that even their spiritual aims may be opposed, in the way that the aims of those of different religions may be opposed. Moreover, the concept of rationality must be interpreted as far as possible in the narrow sense, standard in economic theory, of taking the most effective means to given ends....

In working out the conception of justice as fairness one main task clearly is to determine which principles of justice would be chosen in the original position. To do this we must describe this situation in some detail and formulate with care the problem of choice which it presents....It may be observed, however, that once the principles of justice are thought of as arising from an original agreement in a situation of equality, it is an open question whether the principle of utility would be acknowledged. Offhand it hardly seems likely that persons who view themselves as equals, entitled to press their claims upon one another, would agree to a principle which may require lesser life prospects for some simply for the sake of a greater sum of advantages enjoyed by others. Since each desires to protect his interests, his capacity to advance his conception of the good, no one has a reason to acquiesce in an enduring loss for himself in order to bring about a greater net balance of satisfaction. In the absence of strong and lasting benevolent impulses, a rational man would not accept a basic structure merely because it maximized the algebraic sum of advantages irrespective of its permanent effects on his own basic rights and interests. Thus it seems that the principle of utility is incompatible with the conception of social cooperation among equals for mutual advantage. It appears to be inconsistent with the idea of reciprocity implicit in the notion of a well-ordered society....

I shall maintain instead that the persons in the initial situation would choose two rather different principles: the first requires equality in the assignment of basic rights and duties, while the second holds that social and economic inequalities, for example inequalities of wealth and authority, are just only if they result in compensating benefits for everyone, and in particular for the least advantaged members of society. These principles rule out justifying institutions on the grounds that the hardships of some are offset by a greater good in the aggregate. It may be expedient but it is not just that some should have less in order that others may prosper. But there is no injustice in the greater benefits earned by a few provided that the situation of persons not so fortunate is thereby improved. The intuitive idea is that since everyone's well-being depends upon a scheme of cooperation without which no one could have a satisfactory life, the division of advantages should be such as to draw forth the willing cooperation of everyone taking part in it, including those less well situated. Yet this can be expected only if reasonable terms are proposed. The two principles mentioned seem to be a fair agreement on the basis of which those better endowed, or more fortunate in their social position, neither of which we can be said to deserve, could expect the willing cooperation of others when some workable scheme is a necessary condition of the welfare of all. Once we decide to look for a conception of justice that nullifies the accidents of natural endowment and the contingencies of social circumstance as counters in quest for political and economic advantage, we are led to these principles. They express the result of leaving aside those aspects of the social world that seem arbitrary from a moral point of view....

Justice as fairness is an example of what I have called a contract theory. The merit of the contract terminology is that it conveys the idea that principles of justice may be conceived as principles that would be chosen by rational persons, and that in this way conceptions of justice may be explained and justified....Furthermore, principles of justice deal with conflicting claims upon the advantages won by social cooperation; they apply to the relations among several persons or groups. The word

"contract" suggests this plurality as well as the condition that the appropriate division of advantages must be in accordance with principles acceptable to all parties. The condition of publicity for principles of justice is also connoted by the contract phraseology. Thus, if these principles are the outcome of an agreement, citizens have a knowledge of the principles that others follow....

I have said that the original position is the appropriate initial status quo which insures that the fundamental agreements reached in it are fair. This fact yields the name "justice as fairness." It is clear, then, that I want to say that one conception of justice is more reasonable than another, or justifiable with respect to it, if rational persons in the initial situation would choose its principles over those of the other for the role of justice. Conceptions of justice are to be ranked by their acceptability to persons so circumstanced. Understood in this way the question of justification is settled by working out a problem of deliberation: we have to ascertain which principles it would be rational to adopt given the contractual situation. This connects the theory of justice with the theory of rational choice....

One should not be misled...by the somewhat unusual conditions which characterize the original position. The idea here is simply to make vivid to ourselves the restrictions that it seems reasonable to impose on arguments for principles of justice, and therefore on these principles themselves. Thus it seems reasonable and generally acceptable that no one should be advantaged or disadvantaged by natural fortune or social circumstances in the choice of principles. It also seems widely agreed that it should be impossible to tailor principles to the circumstances of one's own case. We should insure further that particular inclinations and aspirations, and persons' conceptions of their good do not affect the principles adopted. The aim is to rule out those principles that it would be rational to propose for acceptance, however little the chance of success, only if one knew certain things that are irrelevant from the standpoint of justice. For example, if a man knew that he was wealthy, he might find it rational to advance the principle that various taxes for welfare measures be counted unjust; if he knew that he was poor, he would most likely propose the contrary principle. To represent the desired restrictions one imagines a situation in which everyone is deprived of this sort of information. One excludes the knowledge of those contingencies which sets men at odds and allows them to be guided by their prejudices. In this manner the veil of ignorance is arrived at in a natural way. This concept should cause no difficulty if we keep in mind the constraints on arguments that it is meant to express. At any time we can enter the original position, so to speak, simply by following a certain procedure, namely, by arguing for principles of justice in accordance with these restrictions.

It seems reasonable to suppose that the parties in the original position are equal. That is, all have the same rights in the procedure for choosing principles; each can make proposals, submit reasons for their acceptance, and so on. Obviously the purpose of these conditions is to represent equality between human beings as moral persons, as creatures having a conception of their good and capable of a sense of justice. The basis of equality is taken to be similarity in these two respects. Systems of ends are not ranked in value; and each man is presumed to have the requisite ability to understand and to act upon whatever principles are adopted. Together with the veil of ignorance, these conditions define the principles of justice as those which rational persons concerned to advance their interests would consent to as equals when none are known to be advantaged or disadvantaged by social and natural contingencies.

There is, however, another side to justifying a particular description of the original position. This is to see if the principles which would be chosen match our considered convictions of justice or extend them in an acceptable way. We can note whether applying these principles would lead us to make the same judgments about the basic structure of society which we now make intuitively and in which we have the greatest confidence; or whether, in cases where our present judgments are in doubt and given with hesitation, these principles offer a resolution which we can affirm on reflection. There are questions which we feel sure must be answered in a certain way. For example, we are confident that religious intolerance and racial discrimination are unjust. We think that we have examined these things with care and have reached what we believe is an impartial judgment not likely to be distorted by an excessive attention to our own interests. These convictions are provisional fixed points which we presume any conception of justice must fit. But we have much less assurance as to what is the correct distribution of wealth and authority. Here we may be looking for a way to remove our doubts. We can check an interpretation of the initial situation, then, by the capacity of its principles to accommodate our firmest convictions and to provide guidance where guidance is needed....

I shall now state in a provisional form the two principles of justice that I believe would be chosen in the original position....

The first statement of the two principles reads as follows.

First: each person is to have an equal right to the most extensive basic liberty compatible with a similar liberty for others.

Second: social and economic inequalities are to be arranged so that they are both (a) reasonably expected to be to everyone's advantage, and (b) attached to positions and offices open to all....

By way of general comment, these principles primarily apply, as I have said, to the basic structure of society. They are to govern the assignment of rights and duties and to regulate the distribution of social and economic advantages. As their formulation suggests, these principles presuppose that the social structure can be divided into two more or less distinct parts, the first principle applying to the one, the second to the other. They distinguish between those aspects of the social system that define and secure the equal liberties of citizenship and those that specify and establish social and economic inequalities. The basic liberties of citizens are, roughly speaking, political liberty (the right to vote and to be eligible for public office) together with freedom of speech and assembly; liberty of conscience and freedom of thought; freedom of the person along with the right to hold (personal) property; and freedom from arbitrary arrest and seizure as defined by the concept of the rule of law. These liberties are all required to be equal by the first principle, since citizens of a just society are to have the same basic rights.

The second principle applies, in the first approximation, to the distribution of income and wealth and to the design of organizations that make use of differences in authority and responsibility, or chains of command. While the distribution of wealth and income need not be equal, it must be to everyone's advantage, and at the same time, positions of authority and offices of command must be accessible to all. One applies the second principle by holding positions open, and then, subject to this constraint, arranges social and economic inequalities so that everyone benefits.

These principles are to be arranged in a serial order with the first principle prior to the second. This ordering means that a departure from the institutions of equal liberty required by the first principle cannot be justified by, or compensated for, by greater social and economic advantages. The distribution of wealth and income, and the hierarchies of authority, must be consistent with both the liberties of equal citizenship and equality of opportunity.

Suppose that the basic structure of society distributes certain primary goods, that is, things that every rational man is presumed to want. These goods normally have a use whatever a person's rational plan of life. For simplicity, assume that the chief primary goods at the disposition of society are rights and liberties, powers and opportunities, income and wealth....These are the social primary goods. Other primary goods such as health and vigor, intelligence and imagination, are natural goods; although their possession is influenced by the basic structure, they are not so directly under its control. Imagine, then, a hypothetical initial arrangement in which all the social primary goods are equally distributed: everyone has similar rights and duties, and income and wealth are evenly shared. This state of affairs provides a benchmark for judging improvements. If certain inequalities of wealth and organizational powers would make everyone better off than in this hypothetical starting situation, then they accord with the general conception.

Now it is possible, at least theoretically, that by giving up some of their fundamental liberties men are sufficiently compensated by the resulting social and economic gains. The general conception of justice imposes no restrictions on what sort of inequalities are permissible; it only requires that everyone's position be improved. We need not suppose anything so drastic as consenting to a condition of slavery. Imagine instead that men forego certain political rights when the economic returns are significant and their capacity to influence the course of policy by the exercise of these rights would be marginal in any case. It is this kind of exchange which the two principles as stated rule out; being arranged in serial order they do not permit exchanges between basic liberties and economic and social gains. The serial ordering of principles expresses an underlying preference among primary social goods. When this preference is rational so likewise is the choice of these principles in this order....

The fact that the two principles apply to institutions has certain consequences. Several points illustrate this. First of all, the rights and liberties referred to by these principles are those which are defined by the public rules of the basic structure. Whether men are free is determined by the rights and duties established by the major institutions of society. Liberty is a certain pattern of social forms. The first principle simply requires that certain sorts of rules, those defining basic liberties, apply to everyone equally and that they allow the most extensive liberty compatible with a like liberty for all. The only reason for circumscribing the rights defining liberty and making men's freedom less extensive than it might otherwise be is that these equal rights as institutionally defined would interfere with one another....

Now the second principle insists that each person benefit from permissible inequalities in the basic structure. This means that it must be reasonable for each relevant representative man defined by this structure, when he views it as a going concern, to prefer his prospects with the inequality to his prospects without it. One is not allowed to justify differences in income or organizational powers on the ground that the disadvantages of those in one position are outweighed by the greater advantages of those in another. Much less can infringements of liberty be counterbalanced in this way. Applied to the basic structure, the principle of utility would have us maximize the sum of expectations of representative men (weighted by the number of persons they represent, on the classical view); and this would permit us to compensate for the losses of some by the gains of others. Instead, the two principles require that everyone benefit from economic and social inequalities. It is obvious, however, that there are indefinitely many ways in which all may be advantaged when the initial arrangement of equality is taken as a benchmark. How then are we to choose among these possibilities? The principles must be specified so that they yield a determinate conclusion. I now turn to this problem....

In a basic structure with n relevant representatives, first maximize the welfare of the worst off representative man; second, for equal welfare of the worst-off representative, maximize the welfare of the second worst-off representative man, and so on until the last case which is, for equal welfare of all the preceding n-1 representatives, maximize the welfare of the best-off representative man. We may think of this as the lexical difference principle. However, I shall always use the difference principle in the simpler form. And therefore,...

the second principle is to read as follows. Social and economic inequalities are to be arranged so that they are both (a) to the greatest benefit of the least advantaged and (b) attached to offices and positions open to all under conditions of fair equality of opportunity....

The idea of the original position is to set up a fair procedure so that any principles agreed to will be just. The aim is to use the notion of pure procedural justice as a basis of theory. Somehow we must nullify the effects of specific contingencies which put men at odds and tempt them to exploit social and natural circumstances to their own advantage. Now in order to do this I assume that the parties are situated behind a veil of ignorance. They do not know how the various alternatives will affect their own particular case and they are obliged to evaluate principles solely on the basis of general considerations.

It is assumed, then, that the parties do not know certain kinds of particular facts. First of all, no one knows his place in society, his class position or social status; nor does he know his fortune in the distribution of natural assets and abilities, his intelligence and strength, and the like. Nor, again, does anyone know his conception of the good, the particulars of his rational plan of life, or even the special features of his psychology such as his aversion to risk or liability to optimism or pessimism. More than this, I assume that the parties do not know the particular circumstances of their own society. That is, they do not know its economic or political situation, or the level of civilization and culture it has been able to achieve. The persons in the original position have no informa-

tion as to which generation they belong....In order to carry through the idea of the original position, the parties must not know the contingencies that set them in opposition. They must choose principles the consequences of which they are prepared to live with whatever generation they turn out to belong to.

As far as possible, then, the only particular facts which the parties know is that their society is subject to the circumstances of justice and whatever this implies. It is taken for granted, however, that they know the general facts about human society. They understand political affairs and the principles of economic theory; they know the basis of social organization and the laws of human psychology. Indeed, the parties are presumed to know whatever general facts affect the choice of the principles of justice. There are no limitations on general information, that is, on general laws and theories, since conceptions of justice must be adjusted to the characteristics of the systems of social cooperation which they are to regulate, and there is no reason to rule out these facts....

The original position is not to be thought of as a general assembly which includes at one moment everyone who will live at some time; or, much less, as an assembly of everyone who could live at some time. It is not a gathering of all actual or possible persons. To conceive of the original position in either of these ways is to stretch fantasy too far; the conception would cease to be a natural guide to intuition. In any case, it is important that the original position be interpreted so that one can at any time adopt its perspective. It must make no difference when one takes up this viewpoint, or who does so: the restrictions must be such that the same principles are always chosen. The veil of ignorance is a key condition in meeting this requirement. It insures not only that the information available is relevant, but that it is at all times the same....

Thus there follows the very important consequence that the parties have no basis for bargaining in the usual sense. No one knows his situation in society nor his natural assets, and therefore no one is in a position to tailor principles to his advantage. We might imagine that one of the contractees threatens to hold out unless the others agree to principles favorable to him. But how does one know which principles are especially in his interests?...

I have assumed throughout that the persons in the original position are rational. In choosing between principles each tries as best he can to advance his interests. But I have also assumed that the parties do not know their conception of the good. This means that while they know that they have some rational plan of life, they do not know the details of this plan, the particular ends and interests which it is calculated to promote. How, then, can they decide which conceptions of justice are most to their advantage? Or must we suppose that they are reduced to mere guessing? To meet this difficulty, I postulate that...they assume that they would prefer more primary social goods rather than less. Of course, it may turn out, once the veil of ignorance is removed, that some of them for religious or other reasons may not, in fact, want more of these goods.

But from the standpoint of the original position, it is rational for the parties to suppose that they do want a larger share, since in any case they are not compelled to accept more if they do not wish to, nor does a person suffer from a greater liberty. Thus even though the parties are deprived of information about their particular ends, they have enough knowledge to rank the alternatives. They know that in general they must try to protect their liberties, widen their opportunities, and enlarge their means for promoting their aims whatever these are....

The assumption of mutually disinterested rationality, then, comes to this: the persons in the original position try to acknowledge principles which advance their system of ends as far as possible. They do this by attempting to win for themselves the highest index of primary social goods, since this enables them to promote their conception of the good most effectively whatever it turns out to be. The parties do not seek to confer benefits or to impose injuries on one another; they are not moved by affection or rancor. Nor do they try to gain relative to each other; they are not envious or vain....

It seems clear...that the two principles are at least a plausible conception of justice. The question, though, is how one is to argue for them more systematically. Now there are several things to do. One can work out their consequences for institutions and note their implications for fundamental social policy. In this way they are tested by a comparison with our considered judgments of jus-

tice....But one can also try to find arguments in their favor that are decisive from the standpoint of the original position. In order to see how this might be done, it is useful as a heuristic device to think of the two principles as the maximin solution to the problem of social justice. There is an analogy between the two principles and the maximin rule for choice under uncertainty. This is evident from the fact that the two principles are those a person would choose for the design of a society in which his enemy is to assign him his place. The maximin rule tells us to rank alternatives by their worst possible outcomes: we are to adopt the alternative the worst outcome of which is superior to the worst outcomes of the others....The term "maximin" means the *maximum minimorum*; and the rule directs our attention to the worst that can happen under any proposed course of action, and to decide in the light of that....

The veil of ignorance excludes all but the vaguest knowledge of likelihoods. The parties have no basis for determining the probable nature of their society, or their place in it. Thus they have strong reasons for being wary of probability calculations if any other course is open to them. They must also take into account the fact that their choice of principles should seem reasonable to others, in particular their descendants, whose rights will be deeply affected by it....

In this section my aim is to use the conditions of publicity and finality to give some of the main arguments for the two principles of justice. I shall rely upon the fact that for an agreement to be valid, the parties must be able to honor it under all relevant and foreseeable circumstances. There must be a rational assurance that one can carry through. The arguments I shall adduce fit under the heuristic schema suggested by the reasons for following the maximin rule. That is, they help to show that the two principles are an adequate minimum conception of justice in a situation of great uncertainty. Any further advantages that might be won by the principle of utility, or whatever, are highly problematical, whereas the hardship if things turn out badly are intolerable. It is at this point that the concept of a contract has a definite role: it suggests the condition of publicity and sets limits upon what can be agreed to. Thus justice as fairness uses the concept of contract to a greater extent than the discussion so far might suggest.

The first confirming ground for the two principles can be explained in terms of what I earlier referred to as the strains of commitment. I said...that the parties have a capacity for justice in the sense that they can be assured that their undertaking is not in vain. Assuming that they have taken everything into account, including the general facts of moral psychology, they can rely on one another to adhere to the principles adopted. Thus they consider the strains of commitment. They cannot enter into agreements that may have consequences they cannot accept. They will avoid those that they can adhere to only with great difficulty. Since the original agreement is final and made in perpetuity, there is no second chance. In view of the serious nature of the possible consequences, the question of the burden of commitment is especially acute. A person is choosing once and for all the standards which are to govern his life prospects. Moreover, when we enter an agreement we must be able to honor it even should the worst possibilities prove to be the case. Otherwise we have not acted in good faith. Thus the parties must weigh with care whether they will be able to stick by their commitment in all circumstances. Of course, in answering this question they have only a general knowledge of human psychology to go on. But this information is enough to tell which conception of justice involves the greater stress.

In this respect the two principles of justice have a definite advantage. Not only do the parties protect their basic rights but they insure themselves against the worst eventualities. They run no chance of having to acquiesce in a loss of freedom over the course of their life for the sake of a greater good enjoyed by others, an undertaking that in actual circumstances they might not be able to keep....The principle of utility seems to require a greater identification with the interests of others than the two principles of justice. Thus the latter will be a more stable conception to the extent that this identification is difficult to achieve. When the two principles are satisfied, each person's liberties are secured and there is a sense defined by the difference principle in which everyone is benefited by social cooperation. Therefore we can explain the acceptance of the social system and the principles it satisfies by the psychological law that persons tend to love, cherish, and support whatever affirms their own good. Since everyone's good is affirmed, all acquire inclinations to uphold the scheme.

When the principle of utility is satisfied, however, there is no such assurance that everyone benefits. Allegiance to the social system may demand that some should forgo advantages for the sake of the greater good of the whole. Thus the scheme will not be stable unless those who must make sacrifices strongly identify with interests broader than their own....

A desirable feature of a conception of justice is that it should publicly express men's respect for one another. In this way they insure a sense of their own value. Now the two principles achieve this end. For when society follows these principles, everyone's good is included in a scheme of mutual benefit and this public affirmation in institutions of each man's endeavors supports men's self-esteem. The establishment of equal liberty and the operation of the difference principle are bound to have this effect. The two principles are equivalent, as I have remarked, to an undertaking to regard the distribution of natural abilities as a collective asset so that the more fortunate are to benefit only in ways that help those who have lost out....

It is evident that some sort of framework is needed to simplify the application of the two principles of justice. For consider three kinds of judgments that a citizen has to make. First of all, he must judge the justice of legislation and social policies. But he also knows that his opinions will not always coincide with those of others, since men's judgments and beliefs are likely to differ especially when their interests are engaged. Therefore secondly, a citizen must decide which constitutional arrangements are just for reconciling conflicting opinions of justice. We may think of the political process as a machine which makes social decisions when the views of representatives and their constituents are fed into it. A citizen will regard some ways of designing this machine as more just than others. So a complete conception of justice is not only able to assess laws and policies but it can also rank procedures for selecting which political opinion is to be enacted into law. There is still a third problem. The citizen accepts a certain constitution as just, and he thinks that certain traditional procedures are appropriate, for example, the procedure of majority rule duly circumscribed.

Yet since the political process is at best one of imperfect procedural justice, he must ascertain when the enactments of the majority are to be complied with and when they can be rejected as no longer binding. In short, he must be able to determine the grounds and limits of political duty and obligation. Thus a theory of justice has to deal with at least three types of questions, and this indicates that it may be useful to think of the principles as applied in a several-stage sequence....

Thus I suppose that after the parties have adopted the principles of justice in the original position, they move to a constitutional convention. Here they are to decide upon the justice of political forms and choose a constitution: they are delegates, so to speak, to such a convention. Subject to the constraints of the principles of justice already chosen, they are to design a system for the constitutional powers of government and the basic rights of citizens. It is at this stage that they weigh the justice of procedures for coping with diverse political views. Since the appropriate conception of justice has been agreed upon, the veil of ignorance is partially lifted. The persons in the convention have, of course, no information about particular individuals: they do not know their own social position, their place in the distribution of natural attributes, or their conception of the good. But in addition to an understanding of the principles of social theory, they now know the relevant general facts about their society, that is, its natural circumstances and resources, its level of economic advance and political culture, and so on. They are no longer limited to the information implicit in the circumstances of justice. Given their theoretical knowledge and the appropriate general facts about their society, they are to choose the most effective just constitution, the constitution that satisfies the principles of justice and is best calculated to lead to just and effective legislation....

The liberties of equal citizenship must be incorporated into and protected by the constitution. These liberties include those of liberty of conscience and freedom of thought, liberty of the person, and equal political rights. The political system, which I assume to be some form of constitutional democracy, would not be a just procedure if it did not embody these liberties.

Clearly any feasible political procedure may yield an unjust outcome. In fact, there is no scheme of procedural political rules which guarantees that unjust legislation will not be enacted. In the case of a constitutional regime, or indeed of any political form, the ideal of perfect procedural justice cannot be realized. The best attainable scheme is one of imperfect procedural justice. Nevertheless some schemes have a greater tendency than others to result in unjust laws....

Now the question whether legislation is just or unjust, especially in connection with economic and social policies, is commonly subject to reasonable differences of opinion. In these cases judgment frequently depends upon speculative political and economic doctrines and upon social theory generally. Often the best that we can say of a law or policy is that it is at least not clearly unjust. The application of the difference principle in a precise way normally requires more information than we can expect to have and, in any case, more than the application of the first principle. It is often perfectly plain and evident when the equal liberties are violated. These violations are not only unjust but can be clearly seen to be unjust: the injustice is manifest in the public structure of institutions. But this state of affairs is comparatively rare with social and economic policies regulated by the difference principle.

I imagine then a division of labor between stages in which each deals with different questions of social justice. This division roughly corresponds to the two parts of the basic structure. The first principle of equal liberty is the primary standard for the constitutional convention. Its main requirements are that the fundamental liberties of the person and liberty of conscience and freedom of thought be protected and that the political process as a whole be a just procedure. Thus the constitution establishes a secure common status of equal citizenship and realizes political justice. The second principle comes into play at the stage of the legislature. It dictates that social and economic policies be aimed at maximizing the long-term expectations of the least advantaged under conditions of fair equality of opportunity, subject to the equal liberties being maintained. At this point the full range of general economic and social facts is brought to bear. The second part of the basic structure contains the distinctions and hierarchies of political, economic, and social forms which are necessary for efficient and mutually beneficial social cooperation. Thus the priority of the first principle of justice to the second is reflected in the priority of the constitutional convention to the legislative stage.

The last stage is that of the application of rules to particular cases by judges and administrators, and the following of rules by citizens generally. At this stage everyone has complete access to all the facts. No limits on knowledge remain since the full system of rules has now been adopted and applies to persons in virtue of their characteristics and circumstances....

The availability of knowledge in the four-stage sequence is roughly as follows. Let us distinguish between three kinds of facts: the first principles of social theory (and other theories when relevant) and their consequences; general facts about society, such as its size and level of economic advance, its institutional structure and natural environment, and so on; and finally, particular facts about individuals such as their social position, natural attributes, and peculiar interests. In the original position the only particular facts known to the parties are those that can be inferred from the circumstances of justice. While they know the first principles of social theory, the course of history is closed to them; they have no information about how often society has taken this or that form, or which kinds of societies presently exist. In the next stages, however, the general facts about their society are made available to them but not the particularities of their own condition. Limitations on knowledge can be relaxed since the principles of justice are already chosen. The flow of information is determined at each stage by what is required in order to apply these principles intelligently to the kind of question of justice at hand, while at the same time any knowledge that is likely to give rise to bias and distortion and to set men against one another is ruled out. The notion of the rational and impartial application of principles defines the kind of knowledge that is admissible. At the last stage, clearly, there are no reasons for the veil of ignorance in any form, and all restrictions are lifted.

It is essential to keep in mind that the four-stage sequence is a device for applying the principles of justice. This scheme is part of the theory of justice as fairness and not an account of how constitutional conventions and legislatures actually proceed. It sets out a series of points of view from which the different problems of justice are to be settled, each point of view inheriting the constraints adopted at the preceding stages. Thus a just constitution is one that rational delegates subject to the restrictions of the second stage would adopt for their society. And similarly just laws and policies are those that would be enacted at the legislative stage. Of course, this test is often indeterminate: it is not always clear which of several constitutions, or economic and social arrangements, would be chosen. But when this is so, justice is to that extent likewise indeterminate. Institutions within the permitted range are equally just, meaning that they could be chosen; they are compatible with all the constraints of the theory. Thus on many questions of social and economic policy we must fall back upon a notion of quasi-pure procedural justice: laws and policies are just provided that they lie within the allowed range, and the legislature, in ways authorized by a just constitution, has in fact enacted them. This indeterminacy in the theory of justice is not in itself a defect. It is what we should expect. Justice as fairness will prove a worthwhile theory if it defines the range of justice more in accordance with our considered judgments than do existing theories, and if it singles out with greater sharpness the graver wrongs a society should avoid....

Political justice has two aspects arising from the fact that a just constitution is a case of imperfect procedural justice. First, the constitution is to be a just procedure satisfying the requirements of equal liberty; and second, it is to be framed so that of all the feasible just arrangements, it is the one more likely than any other to result in a just and effective system of legislation. The justice of the constitution is to be assessed under both headings in the light of what circumstances permit, these assessments being made from the standpoint of the constitutional convention.

The principle of equal liberty, when applied to the political procedure defined by the constitution, I shall refer to as the principle of (equal) participation. It requires that all citizens are to have an equal right to take part in, and to determine the outcome of, the constitutional process that establishes the laws with which they are to comply. Justice as fairness begins with the idea that where common principles are necessary and to everyone's advantage, they are to be worked out from the viewpoint of a suitably defined initial situation of equality in which each person is fairly represented. The principle of participation transfers this notion from the original position to the constitution as the highest-order system of social rules for making rules. If the state is to exercise a final and coercive authority over a certain territory, and if it is in this way to affect permanently men's prospects in life, then the constitutional process should preserve the equal representation of the original position to the degree that this is practicable....

All sane adults, with certain generally recognized exceptions, have the right to take part in political affairs, and the precept one elector one vote is honored as far as possible. Elections are fair and free, and regularly held. Sporadic and unpredictable tests of public sentiment by plebiscite or other means, or at such times as may suit the convenience of those in office, do not suffice for a representative regime. There are firm constitutional protections for certain liberties, particularly freedom of speech and assembly, and liberty to form political associations. The principle of loyal opposition is recognized, the clash of political beliefs, and of the interests and attitudes that are likely to influence them, are accepted as a normal condition of human life....

The principle of participation also holds that all citizens are to have an equal access, at least in the formal sense, to public office. Each is eligible to join political parties, to run for elective positions, and to hold places of authority. To be sure, there may be qualifications of age, residency, and so on. But these are to be reasonably related to the tasks of office; presumably these restrictions are in the common interest and do not discriminate unfairly among persons or groups in the sense that they fall evenly on everyone in the normal course of life.

The second point concerning equal political liberty is its extent. How broadly are these liberties to be defined? Offhand it is not clear what extent means here. Each of the political liberties can be more or less widely defined. Somewhat arbitrarily, but nevertheless in accordance with tradition, I shall assume that the main variation in the extent of equal political liberty lies in the degree to which the constitution is majoritarian. The definition of the other liberties I take to be more or less fixed. Thus the most extensive political liberty is established by a constitution that uses the procedure of so-called bare majority rule (the procedure in which a minority can neither override nor check a majority) for all significant political decisions unimpeded by any constitutional constraints. Whenever the constitution limits the scope and authority of majorities, either by requiring a greater plurality for certain types of measures, or by a bill of rights restricting the powers of the legislature, and the like, equal political liberty is less extensive....

Turning now to the worth of political liberty, the constitution must take steps to enhance the value of the equal rights of participation for all members of society. It must underwrite a fair opportunity to take part in and to influence the political process....Ideally, those similarly endowed and motivated should have roughly the same chance of attaining positions of political authority irrespective of their economic and social class. But how is this fair value of these liberties to be secured?

Compensating steps must...be taken to preserve the fair value for all of the equal political liberties. A variety of devices can be used. For example, in a society allowing private ownership of the means of production, property and wealth must be kept widely distributed and government monies provided on a regular basis to encourage free public discussion. In addition, political parties are to be made independent from private economic interests by allotting them sufficient tax revenues to play their part in the constitutional scheme....

What is necessary is that political parties be autonomous with respect to private demands, that is, demands not expressed in the public forum and argued for openly by reference to a conception of the public good. If society does not bear the costs of organization, and party funds need to be solicited from the more advantaged social and economic interests, the pleadings of these groups are bound to receive excessive attention. And this is all the more likely when the less favored members of society, having been effectively prevented by their lack of means from exercising their fair degree of influence, withdraw into apathy and resentment.

Historically one of the main defects of constitutional government has been the failure to insure the fair value of political liberty. The necessary corrective steps have not been taken, indeed, they never seem to have been seriously entertained. Disparities in the distribution of property and wealth that far exceed what is compatible with political equality have generally been tolerated by the legal system. Public resources have not been devoted to maintaining the institutions required for the fair value of political liberty. Essentially the fault lies in the fact that the democratic political process is at best regulated rivalry; it does not even in theory have the desirable properties that price theory ascribes to truly competitive markets. Moreover, the effects of injustices in the political system are much more grave and long lasting than market imperfections. Political power rapidly accumulates and becomes unequal; and making use of the coercive apparatus of the state and its law, those who gain the advantage can often assure themselves of a favored position. Thus inequities in the economic and social system may soon undermine whatever political equality might have existed under fortunate historical conditions. Universal suffrage is an insufficient counterpoise; for when parties and elections are financed not by public funds but by private contributions, the political forum is so constrained by the wishes of the dominant interests that the basic measures needed to establish just constitutional rule are seldom properly presented....

An economic system regulates what things are produced and by what means, who receives them and in return for which contributions, and how large a fraction of social resources is devoted to saving and to the provision of public goods. Ideally all of these matters should be arranged in ways that satisfy the two principles of justice. But we have to ask whether this is possible and what in particular these principles require....

A...feature of the public sector is the proportion of total social resources devoted to public goods....A public good has two characteristic features, indivisibility and publicness. That is, there are many individuals, a public so to speak, who want more or less of this good, but if they are to enjoy it at all must each enjoy the same amount. The quantity produced cannot be divided up as private goods can and purchased by individuals according to their preferences for more and less....

Where the public is large and includes many individuals, there is a temptation for each person to try to avoid doing his share. This is because whatever one man does his action will not significantly affect the amount produced. He regards the collective action of others as already given one way or the other. If the public good is produced his enjoyment of it is not decreased by his not making a contribution. If it is not produced his action would not have changed the situation anyway. A citizen receives the same protection from foreign invasion regardless of whether he has paid his taxes. Therefore in the polar case trade and voluntary agreements cannot be expected to develop.

It follows that arranging for and financing public goods must be taken over by the state and some binding rule requiring payment must be enforced. Even if all citizens were willing to pay their share, they would presumably do so only when they are assured that others will pay theirs as well. Thus once citizens have agreed to act collectively and not as isolated individuals taking the actions of the others as given, there is still the task of tying down the agreement. The sense of justice leads us to promote just schemes and to do our share in them when we believe that others, or sufficiently many of them, will do theirs. But in normal circumstances a reasonable assurance in this regard can only be given if there is a binding rule effectively enforced. Assuming that the public good is to everyone's advantage, and one that all would agree to arrange for, the use of coercion is perfectly rational from each man's point of view. Many of the traditional activities of government, insofar as they can be justified, can be accounted for in this way.

I should like to conclude with a few comments about the extent to which economic arrangements may rely upon a system of markets in which prices are freely determined by supply and demand. Several cases need to be distinguished. All regimes will normally use the market to ration out the consumption goods actually produced. Any other procedure is administratively cumbersome, and rationing and other devices will be resorted to only in special cases. But in a free market system the output of commodities is also guided as to kind and quantity by the preferences of households as shown by their purchases on the market. Goods fetching a greater than normal profit will be produced in larger amounts until the excess is reduced. In a socialist regime planners' preferences or collective decisions often have a larger part in determining the direction of production. Both private-property and socialist systems normally allow for the free choice of occupation and of one's place of work. It is only under command systems of either kind that this freedom is overtly interfered with.

Finally, a basic feature is the extent to which the market is used to decide the rate of saving and the direction of investment, as well as the fraction of national wealth devoted to conservation and to the elimination of irremediable injuries to the welfare of future generations. Here there are a number of possibilities. A collective decision may determine the rate of saving while the direction of investment is left largely to individual firms competing for funds. In both a private-property as well as in a socialist society great concern may be expressed for preventing irreversible damages and for husbanding natural resources and preserving the environment. But again either one may do rather badly.

It is evident, then, that there is no essential tie between the use of free markets and private ownership of the instruments of production. The idea that competitive prices under normal conditions are just or fair goes back at least to medieval times. While the notion that a market economy is in some sense the best scheme has been most carefully investigated by so-called bourgeois economists, this connection is a historical contingency in that, theoretically at least, a socialist regime can avail itself of the advantages of this system. One of these advantages is efficiency. Under certain conditions competitive prices select the goods to be produced and allocate resources to their production in such a manner that there is no way to improve upon either the choice of productive methods by firms, or the distribution of goods that arises from the purchases of households. There exists no rearrangement of the resulting economic configuration that makes one household better off (in view of its preferences) without making another worse off. No further mutually advantageous trades are possible; nor are there any feasible productive processes that will yield more of some desired commodity without requiring a cutback in another. For if this were not so, the situation of some individuals could be made more advantageous without a loss for anyone else. The theory of general equilibrium explains how, given the appropriate conditions, the information supplied by prices leads economic agents to act in ways that sum up to achieve this outcome. Perfect competition is a perfect procedure with respect to efficiency. Of course, the requisite conditions are highly special ones and they are seldom if ever fully satisfied in the real world Moreover,

market failures and imperfections are often serious, and compensating adjustments must be made by the allocation branch....Monopolistic restrictions, lack of information, external economies and diseconomies, and the like must be recognized and corrected. And the market fails altogether in the case of public goods....

A further and more significant advantage of a market system is that, given the requisite background institutions, it is consistent with equal liberties and fair equality of opportunity. Citizens have a free choice of careers and occupations. There is no reason at all for the forced and central direction of labor. Indeed, in the absence of some differences in earnings as these arise in a competitive scheme, it is hard to see how, under ordinary circumstances anyway, certain aspects of a command society inconsistent with liberty can be avoided. Moreover, a system of markets decentralizes the exercise of economic power. Whatever the internal nature of firms, whether they are privately or state owned, or whether they are run by entrepreneurs or by managers elected by workers, they take the prices of outputs and inputs as given and draw up their plans accordingly. When markets are truly competitive, firms do not engage in price wars or other contests for market power. In conformity with political decisions reached democratically, the government regulates the economic climate by adjusting certain elements under its control, such as the overall amount of investment, the rate of interest, and the quantity of money, and so on. There is no necessity for comprehensive direct planning. Individual households and firms are free to make their decisions independently, subject to the general conditions of the economy....

The main problem of distributive justice is the choice of a social system. The principles of justice apply to the basic structure and regulate how its major institutions are combined into one scheme. Now, as we have seen, the idea of justice as fairness is to use the notion of pure procedural justice to handle the contingencies of particular situations. The social system is to be designed so that the resulting distribution is just however things turn out. To achieve this end it is necessary to set the social and economic process within the surroundings of suitable political and legal institutions. Without an appropriate scheme of these background institutions the outcome of the distributive process will not be just

I shall give a brief description of these supporting institutions as they might exist in a properly organized democratic state that allows private ownership of capital and natural resources....

First of all, I assume that the basic structure is regulated by a just constitution that secures the liberties of equal citizenship (as described in the preceding chapter). Liberty of conscience and freedom of thought are taken for granted, and the fair value of political liberty is maintained. The political process is conducted, as far as circumstances permit, as a just procedure for choosing between governments and for enacting just legislation. I assume also that there is fair (as opposed to formal) equality of opportunity. This means that in addition to maintaining the usual kinds of social overhead capital, the government tries to insure equal chances of education and culture for persons similarly endowed and motivated either by subsidizing private schools or by establishing a public school system. It also enforces and underwrites equality of opportunity in economic activities and in the free choice of occupation. This is achieved by policing the conduct of firms and private associations and by preventing the establishment of monopolistic restrictions and barriers to the more desirable positions. Finally, the government guarantees a social minimum either by family allowances and special payments for sickness and employment, or more systematically by such devices as a graded income supplement (a so-called negative income tax).

In establishing these background institutions the government may be thought of as divided into four branches. Each branch consists of various agencies, or activities thereof, charged with preserving certain social and economic conditions. These divisions do not overlap with the usual organization of government but are to be understood as different functions. The allocation branch, for example, is to keep the price system workably competitive and to prevent the formation of unreasonable market power. Such power does not exist as long as markets cannot be made more competitive consistent with the requirements of efficiency and the facts of geography and the preferences of households. The allocation branch is also charged with identifying and correcting, say by suitable taxes and subsidies and by changes in the definition of property rights, the more obvious departures

from efficiency caused by the failure of prices to measure accurately social benefits and costs. To this end suitable taxes and subsidies may be used, or the scope and definition of property rights may be revised. The stabilization branch, on the other hand, strives to bring about reasonably full employment in the sense that those who want work can find it and the free choice of occupation and the deployment of finance are supported by strong effective demand. These two branches together are to maintain the efficiency of the market economy generally.

The social minimum is the responsibility of the transfer branch....The essential idea is that the workings of this branch take needs into account and assign them an appropriate weight with respect to other claims. A competitive price system gives no consideration to needs and therefore it cannot be the sole device of distribution. There must be a division of labor between the parts of the social system in answering to the common sense precepts of justice. Different institutions meet different claims. Competitive markets properly regulated secure free choice of occupation and lead to an efficient use of resources and allocation of commodities to households. They set a weight on the conventional precepts associated with wages and earning, whereas the transfer branch guarantees a certain level of well-being and honors the claims of need....

It is clear that the justice of distributive shares depends on the background institutions and how they allocate total income, wages and other income plus transfers. There is with reason strong objection to the competitive determination of total income, since this ignores the claims of need and an appropriate standard of life. From the standpoint of the legislative stage it is rational to insure oneself and one's descendants against these contingencies of the market. Indeed, the difference principle presumably requires this. But once a suitable minimum is provided by transfers, it may be perfectly fair that the rest of total income be settled by the price system, assuming that it is moderately efficient and free from monopolistic restrictions, and unreasonable externalities have been eliminated. Moreover, this way of dealing with the claims of need would appear to be more effective than trying to regulate income by minimum wage standards, and the like. It is better to assign to each branch only such tasks as are compatible with one another. Since the market is not suited to answer the claims of need, these should be met by a separate arrangement. Whether the principles of justice are satisfied, then, turns on whether the total income of the least advantaged (wages plus transfers) is such as to maximize their long-run expectations (consistent with the constraints of equal liberty and fair equality of opportunity).

Finally, there is a distribution branch. Its task is to preserve an approximate justice in distributive shares by means of taxation and the necessary adjustments in the rights of property. Two aspects of this branch may be distinguished. First of all, it imposes a number of inheritance and gift taxes, and sets restrictions on the rights of bequest. The purpose of these levies and regulations is not to raise revenue (release resources to government) but gradually and continually to correct the distribution of wealth and to prevent concentrations of power detrimental to the fair value of political liberty and fair equality of opportunity....

The unequal inheritance of wealth is no more inherently unjust than the unequal inheritance of intelligence. It is true that the former is presumably more easily subject to social control; but the essential thing is that as far as possible inequalities founded on either should satisfy the difference principle. Thus inheritance is permissible provided that the resulting inequalities are to the advantage of the least fortunate and compatible with liberty and fair equality of opportunity. As earlier defined, fair equality of opportunity means a certain set of institutions that assures similar chances of education and culture for persons similarly motivated and keeps positions and offices open to all on the basis of qualities and efforts reasonably related to the relevant duties and tasks. It is these institutions that are put in jeopardy when inequalities of wealth exceed a certain limit; and political liberty likewise tends to lose its value, and representative government to become such in appearance only. The taxes and enactments of the distribution branch are to prevent this limit from being exceeded. Naturally, where this limit lies is a matter of political judgment guided by theory, good sense, and plain hunch, at least within a wide range. On this sort of question the theory of justice has nothing specific to say. Its aim is to formulate the principles that are to regulate the background institutions.

The second part of the distribution branch is a scheme of taxation to raise the revenues that justice requires. Social resources must be released to the government so that it can provide for the public goods and make the transfer payments necessary to satisfy the difference principle. This problem belongs to the distribution branch since the burden of taxation is to be justly shared and it aims at establishing just arrangements. Leaving aside many complications, it is worth noting that a proportional expenditure tax may be part of the best tax scheme. For one thing, it is preferable to an income tax (of any kind) at the level of common sense precepts of justice, since it imposes a levy according to how much a person takes out of the common store of goods and not according to how much he contributes (assuming here that income is fairly earned). Again, a proportional tax on total consumption (for each year say) can contain the usual exemptions for dependents, and so on; and it treats everyone in a uniform way (still assuming that income is fairly earned). It may be better, therefore, to use progressive rates only when they are necessary to preserve the justice of the basic structure with respect to the first principle of justice and fair equality of opportunity, and so to forestall accumulations of property and power likely to undermine the corresponding institutions. Following this rule might help to signal an important distinction in questions of policy. And if proportional taxes should also prove more efficient, say because they interfere less with incentives, this might make the case for them decisive if a feasible scheme could be worked out....

The two parts of the distribution branch derive from the two principles of justice. The taxation of inheritance and income at progressive rates (when necessary), and the legal definition of property rights, are to secure the institutions of equal liberty in a property-owning democracy and the fair value of the rights they establish. Proportional expenditure (or income) taxes are to provide revenue for public goods, the transfer branch and the establishment of fair equality of opportunity in education, and the like, so as to carry out the second principle. No mention has been made at any point of the traditional criteria of taxation such as that taxes are to be levied according to benefits received or the ability to pay....

So far I have assumed that the aim of the branches of government is to establish a democratic regime in which land and capital are widely though not presumably equally held. Society is not so divided that one fairly small sector controls the preponderance of productive resources. When this is achieved and distributive shares satisfy the principles of justice, many socialist criticisms of the market economy are met. But it is clear that, in theory anyway, a liberal socialist regime can also answer to the two principles of justice. We have only to suppose that the means of production are publicly owned and that firms are managed by workers' councils say, or by agents appointed by them. Collective decisions made democratically under the constitution determine the general features of the economy, such as the rate of saving and the proportion of society's production devoted to essential public goods. Given the resulting economic environment, firms regulated by market forces conduct themselves much as before. Although the background institutions will take a different form, especially in the case of the distribution branch, there is no reason in principle why just distributive shares cannot be achieved. The theory of justice does not by itself favor either form of regime. As we have seen, the decision as to which system is best for a given people depends upon their circumstances, institutions, and historical traditions....

Anarchy, State, and Utopia

Robert Nozick

The minimal state is the most extensive state that can be justified. Any state more extensive violates people's rights. Yet many persons have put forth reasons purporting to justify a more extensive state. It is impossible...to examine all the reasons that have been put forth. Therefore, I shall focus upon those generally acknowledged to be most weighty and influential, to see precisely wherein they fail....We consider the claim that a more extensive state is justified, because necessary (or the best instrument) to achieve distributive justice....The term "distributive justice" is not a neutral one. Hearing the term "distribution," most people presume that some thing or mechanism uses some principle or criterion to give out a supply of things. Into this process of distributing shares some error may have crept. So it is an open question, at least, whether redistribution should take place; whether we should do again what has already been done once, though poorly. However, we are not in the position of children who have been given portions of pie by someone who now makes last minute adjustments to rectify careless cutting. There is no central distribution, no person or group entitled to control all the resources, jointly deciding how they are to be doled out. What each person gets, he gets from others who give to him in exchange for something, or as a gift. In a free society, diverse persons control different resources, and new holdings arise out of the voluntary exchanges and actions of persons. There is no more a distributing or distribution of shares than there is a distributing of mates in a society in which persons choose whom they shall marry. The total result is the product of many individual decisions which the different individuals involved are entitled to make....

From *Anarchy, State, and Utopia* (New York: Basic Books, 1974), Reprinted by permission of the publisher.

The subject of justice in holdings consists of three major topics. The first is the *original acquisition of holdings*, the appropriation of unheld things. This includes the issues of how unheld things may come to be held, the process, or processes, by which unheld things may come to be held, the things that may come to be held by these processes, the extent of what comes to be held by a particular process, and so on. We shall refer to the complicated truth about this topic as the principle of justice in acquisition. The second topic concerns the *transfer of holdings* from one person to another. By what processes may a person transfer holdings to another? How may a person acquire a holding from another who holds it? Under this topic come general descriptions of voluntary exchange, and gift and (on the other hand) fraud, as well as reference to particular conventional details fixed upon in a given society. The complicated truth about this subject...we shall call the principle of justice in transfer. (And we shall suppose it also includes principles governing how a person may divest himself of a holding, passing it into an unheld state.)

If the world were wholly just, the following inductive definition would exhaustively cover the subject of justice in holdings.

1. A person who acquires a holding in accordance with the principle of justice in acquisition is entitled to that holding.
2. A person who acquires a holding in accordance with the principle of justice in transfer, from someone else entitled to the holding, is entitled to the holding.
3. No one is entitled to a holding except by (repeated) applications of 1 and 2.

The complete principle of distributive justice would say simply that a distribution is just if everyone is entitled to the holdings they possess under the distribution.

A distribution is just if it arises from another just distribution by legitimate means. The legitimate means of moving from one distribution to another are specified by the principle of justice in transfer. The legitimate first "moves" are specified by the principle of justice in acquisition. Whatever arises from a just situation by just steps is itself just. The means of change specified by the principle of justice in transfer preserve justice....

Not all actual situations are generated in accordance with the two principles of justice in holdings: the principle of justice in acquisition and the principle of justice in transfer. Some people steal from others, or defraud them, or enslave them, seizing their product and preventing them from living as they choose, or forcibly exclude others from competing in exchanges. None of these are permissible modes of transition from one situation to another. And some persons acquire holdings by means not sanctioned by the principle of justice in acquisition. The existence of past injustice (previous violations of the first two principles of justice in holdings) raises the third major topic under justice in holdings: the rectification of injustice in holdings. If past injustice has shaped present holdings in various ways, some identifiable and some not, what now, if anything, ought to be done to rectify these injustices? What obligations do the performers of injustice have toward those whose position is worse than it would have been had the injustice not been done? Or, than it would have been had compensation been paid promptly? How, if at all, do things change if the beneficiaries and those made worse off are not the direct parties in the act of injustice, but, for example, their descendants? Is an injustice done to someone whose holding was itself based upon an unrectified injustice? How far back must one go in wiping clean the historical slate of injustices? What may victims of injustice permissibly do in order to rectify the injustices being done to them, including the many injustices done by persons acting through their government? I do not know of a thorough or theoretically sophisticated treatment of such issues. Idealizing greatly, let us suppose theoretical investigation will produce a principle of rectification. This principle uses historical information about previous situations and injustices done in them (as defined by the first two principles of justice and rights against interference), and information about the actual course of events that flowed from these injustices, until the present, and it yields a description (or descriptions) of holdings in the society. The principle of rectification presumably will make use of its best estimate of subjunctive information about what would have occurred (or a probability distribution over what might have occurred, using the expected value) if the injustice had not taken place....

The general outlines of the theory of justice in holdings are that the holdings of a person are just if he is entitled to them by the principles of justice in acquisition and transfer, or by the principle of rectification of injustice (as specified by the first two principles). If each person's holdings are just, then the total set (distribution) of holdings is just. To turn these general outlines into a specific theory we would have to specify the details of each of the three principles of justice in holdings: the principle of acquisition of holdings, the principle of transfer of holdings, and the principle of rectification of violations of the first two principles. I shall not attempt that task here....

The general outlines of the entitlement theory illuminate the nature and defects of other conceptions of distributive justice. The entitlement theory of justice in distribution is *historical*; whether a distribution is just depends upon how it came about. In contrast, *current time-slice principles* of justice hold that the justice of a distribution is determined by how things are distributed (who has what) as judged by some *structural* principle(s) of just distribution. A utilitarian who judges between any two distributions by seeing which has the greater sum of utility and, if the sums tie, applies some fixed equality criterion to choose the more equal distribution, would hold a current time-slice principle of justice. As would someone who had a fixed schedule of trade-offs between the sum of happiness and equality. According to a current time-slice principle, all that needs to be looked at, in judging the justice of a distribution, is who ends up with what; in comparing any two distributions one need look only at the matrix presenting the distributions. No further information need be fed into a principle of justice. It is a consequence of such principles of justice that any two structurally identical distributions are equally just....Welfare economics is the theory of current time-slice principles of justice. The subject is conceived as operating on matrices representing only current information about distribution. This, as well as some of the usual conditions (for example, the choice of distribution is invariant under relabeling of columns), guarantees that welfare economics will be a current time-slice theory, with all of its inadequacies.

Most persons do not accept current time-slice principles as constituting the whole story about distributive shares. They think it relevant in assessing the justice of a situation to consider not only the distribution it embodies, but also how that distribution came about. If some persons are in prison for murder or war crimes, we do not say that to assess the justice of the distribution in the society we must look only at what this person has, and that person has, and that person has,...at the current time. We think it relevant to ask whether someone did something so that he *deserved* to be punished, deserved to have a lower share. Most will agree to the relevance of further information with regard to punishments and penalties. Consider also desired things. One traditional socialist view is that workers are entitled to the product and full fruits of their labor; they have earned it; a distribution is unjust if it does not give the workers what they are entitled to. Such entitlements are based upon some past history. No socialist holding this view would find it comforting to be told that because the actual distribution A happens to coincide structurally with the one he desires D, A therefore is no less just than D; it differs only in that the "parasitic" owners of capital receive under A what the workers are entitled to under D, and the workers receive under A what the owners are entitled to under D, namely very little. This socialist rightly, in my view, holds onto the notions of earning, producing, entitlement, desert, and so forth, and he rejects current time-slice principles that look only to the structure of the resulting set of holdings....His mistake lies in his view of what entitlements arise out of what sorts of productive processes....Henceforth, we shall refer to such unhistorical principles of distributive justice, including the current time-slice principles, as *end-result principles* or *end-state principles*.

In contrast to end-result principles of justice, *historical principles* of justice hold that past circumstances or actions of people can create differential entitlements or differential deserts to things. An injustice can be worked by moving from one distribution to another structurally identical one, for the second, in profile the same, may violate people's entitlements or deserts; it may not fit the actual history.

The entitlement principles of justice in holdings that we have sketched are historical principles of justice. To better understand their precise character, we shall distinguish them from another subclass of the historical principles. Consider, as an example, the principle of distribution according to moral merit. This principle requires that total distributive shares vary directly with moral merit; no person should have a greater share than anyone whose moral merit is greater....Or consider the principle that results by substituting "usefulness to society" for "moral merit" in the previous principle. Or instead of "distribute according to moral merit," or "distribute according to usefulness to society," we might consider "distribute according to the weighted sum of moral merit, usefulness to society, and need," with the weights of the different dimensions equal. Let us call a principle of distribution *patterned* if it specifies that a distribution is to vary along with some natural dimension, weighted sum of natural dimensions, or lexicographic ordering of natural dimensions. And let us say a distribution is patterned if it accords with some patterned principle....The principle of distribution in accordance with moral merit is a patterned historical principle, which specifies a patterned distribution. "Distribute according to I.Q." is a patterned principle that looks to information not contained in distributional matrices. It is not historical, however, in that it does not look to any past actions creating differential entitlements to evaluate a distribution; it requires only distributional matrices whose columns are labeled by I.Q. scores....

Almost every suggested principle of distributive justice is patterned: to each according to his moral merit, or needs, or marginal product, or how hard he tries, or the weighted sum of the foregoing, and so on. The principle of entitlement we have sketched is *not* patterned....

To think that the task of a theory of distributive justice is to fill in the blank in "to each according to his _____" is to be predisposed to search for a pattern; and the separate treatment of "from each according to his _____" treats production and distribution as two separate and independent issues. On an entitlement view these are *not* two separate and independent issues. On an entitlement view these are *not* two separate questions. Whoever makes something, having bought or contracted for all other held resources used in the process (transferring some of his holdings for these cooperating factors), is entitled to it. The situation is *not* one of something's getting made, and there being an open

question of who is to get it. Things come into the world already attached to people having entitlements over them. From the point of view of the historical entitlement conception of justice in holdings, those who start afresh to complete "to each according to his _____" treat objects as if they appeared from nowhere, out of nothing....

It is not clear how those holding alternative conceptions of distributive justice can reject the entitlement conception of justice in holdings. For suppose a distribution favored by one of these nonentitlement conceptions is realized. Let us suppose it is your favorite one and let us call this distribution D_1; perhaps everyone has an equal share, perhaps shares vary in accordance with some dimension you treasure. Now suppose that Wilt Chamberlain is greatly in demand by basketball teams, being a great gate attraction. (Also suppose contracts run only for a year, with players being free agents.) He signs the following sort of contract with a team: In each home game, twenty-five cents from the price of each ticket of admission goes to him. (We ignore the question of whether he is "gouging" the owners, letting them look out for themselves.) The season starts, and people cheerfully attend his team's games; they buy their tickets, each time dropping a separate twenty-five cents of their admission price into a special box with Chamberlain's name on it. They are excited about seeing him play; it is worth the total admission price to them. Let us suppose that in one season one million persons attend his home games, and Wilt Chamberlain winds up with $250,000, a much larger sum than the average income and larger even than anyone else has. Is he entitled to this income? Is this new distribution D_2, unjust? If so, why? There is *no* question about whether each of the people was entitled to the control over the resources they held in D_1; because that was the distribution (your favorite) that (for the purposes of argument) we assumed was acceptable. Each of these persons *chose* to give twenty-five cents of their money to Chamberlain. They could have spent it on going to the movies, or on candy bars, or on copies of *Dissent* magazine, or of *Monthly Review*. But they all, at least one million of them, converged on giving it to Wilt Chamberlain in exchange for watching him play basketball. If D_1 was a just distribution, and people voluntarily moved from it to D_2, transferring parts of their shares they were given under D_1, (what was it for if not to do something with?), isn't D_2 also just? If the people were entitled to dispose of the resources to which they were entitled (under D_1), didn't this include their being entitled to give it to, or exchange it with, Wilt Chamberlain? Can anyone else complain on grounds of justice? Each other person already has his legitimate share under D_1. Under D_1, there is nothing that anyone has that anyone else has a claim of justice against. After someone transfers something to Wilt Chamberlain, third parties *still* have their legitimate shares; *their* shares are not changed. By what process could such a transfer among two persons give rise to a legitimate claim of distributive justice on a portion of what was transferred, by a third party who had no claim of justice on any holding of the others *before* the transfer?...

The general point illustrated by the Wilt Chamberlain example...is that no end-state principle or distributional patterned principle of justice can be continuously realized without continuous interference with people's lives. Any favored pattern would be transformed into one unfavored by the principle, by people choosing to act in various ways; for example, by people exchanging goods and services with other people, or giving things to other people, things the transferrers are entitled to under the favored distributional pattern. To maintain a pattern one must either continually interfere to stop people from transferring resources as they wish to, or continually (or periodically) interfere to take from some persons resources that others for some reason chose to transfer to them. (But if some time limit is to be set on how long people may keep resources others voluntarily transfer to them, why let them keep these resources for *any* period of time? Why not have immediate confiscation?)...

Apparently, patterned principles allow people to choose to expend upon themselves, but not upon others, those resources they are entitled to (or rather, receive) under some favored distributional pattern D_1. For if each of several persons chooses to expend some of his D_1 resources upon one other person, then that other person will receive more than his D_1 share, disturbing the favored distributional pattern. Maintaining a distributional pattern is individualism with a vengeance! Patterned distributional principles do not give people what entitlement principles do, only better distributed. For

they do not give the right to choose what to do with what one has; they do not give the right to choose to pursue an end involving (intrinsically, or as a means) the enhancement of another's position. To such views, families are disturbing; for within a family occur transfers that upset the favored distributional pattern. Either families themselves become units to which distribution takes place, the column occupiers (on what rationale?), or loving behavior is forbidden. We should note in passing the ambivalent position of radicals toward the family. Its loving relationships are seen as a model to be emulated and extended across the whole society, at the same time that it is denounced as a suffocating institution to be broken and condemned as a focus of parochial concerns that interfere with achieving radical goals....

Proponents of patterned principles of distributive justice focus upon criteria for determining who is to receive holdings; they consider the reasons for which someone should have something, and also the total picture of holdings. Whether or not it is better to give than to receive, proponents of patterned principles ignore giving altogether. In considering the distribution of goods, income, and so forth, their theories are theories of recipient justice; they completely ignore any right a person might have to give something to someone. Even in exchanges where each party is simultaneously giver and recipient, patterned principles of justice focus only upon the recipient role and its supposed rights. Thus discussions tend to focus on whether people (should) have a right to inherit, rather than on whether people (should) have a right to bequeath or on whether persons who have a right to hold also have a right to choose that others hold in their place. I lack a good explanation of why the usual theories of distributive justice are so recipient oriented; ignoring givers and transferrers and their rights is of a piece with ignoring producers and their entitlements. But why is it *all* ignored?

Patterned principles of distributive justice necessitate *re*distributive activities. The likelihood is small that any actual freely-arrived-at set of holdings fits a given pattern; and the likelihood is nil that it will continue to fit the pattern as people exchange and give. From the point of view of an entitlement theory, redistribution is a serious matter indeed, involving, as it does, the violation of people's rights. (An exception is those takings that fall under the principle of the rectification of injustices.) From other points of view, also, it is serious.

Taxation of earnings from labor is on a par with forced labor. Some persons find this claim obviously true: taking the earnings of n hours labor is like taking *n* hours from the person; it is like forcing the person to work *n* hours for another's purpose. Others find the claim absurd. But even these, *if* they object to forced labor, would oppose forcing unemployed hippies to work for the benefit of the needy. And they would also object to forcing each person to work five extra hours each week for the benefit of the needy. And they would also object to forcing each person to work five extra hours each week for the benefit of the needy. But a system that takes five hours' wages in taxes does not seem to them like one that forces someone to work five hours, since it offers the person forced a wider range of choice in activities than does taxation in kind with the particular labor specified. (But we can imagine a gradation of systems of forced labor, from one that specifies a particular activity, to one that gives a choice among two activities, to...; and so on up.) Furthermore, people envisage a system with something like a proportional tax on everything above the amount necessary for basic needs. Some think this does not force someone to work extra hours, since there is no fixed number of extra hours he is forced to work, and since he can avoid the tax entirely by earning only enough to cover his basic needs. This is a very uncharacteristic view of forcing for those who *also* think people are forced to do something *whenever* the alternatives they face are considerably worse. However, *neither* view is correct. The fact that others intentionally intervene, in violation of a side constraint against aggression, to threaten force to limit the alternatives, in this case to paying taxes or (presumably the worse alternative) bare subsistence, makes the taxation system one of forced labor and distinguishes it from other cases of limited choices which are not forcings....

What sort of right over others does a legally institutionalized end-state pattern give one? The central core of the notion of a property right in *X*, relative to which other parts of the notion are to be explained, is the right to determine what shall be done with *X*; the right to choose which of the constrained set of options concerning *X* shall be

realized or attempted. The constraints are set by other principles or laws operating in the society; in our theory, by the Lockean rights people possess (under the minimal state). My property rights in my knife allow me to leave it where I will, but not in your chest. I may choose which of the acceptable options involving the knife is to be realized. This notion of property helps us to understand why earlier theorists spoke of people as having property in themselves and their labor. They viewed each person as having a right to decide what would become of himself and what he would do, and as having a right to reap the benefits of what he did....

When end-result principles of distributive justice are built into the legal structure of a society, they (as do most patterned principles) give each citizen an enforceable claim to some portion of the total social product; that is, to some portion of the sum total of the individually and jointly made products. This total product is produced by individuals laboring, using means of production others have saved to bring into existence, by people organizing production or creating means to produce new things or things in a new way. It is on this batch of individual activities that patterned distributional principles give each individual an enforceable claim. Each person has a claim to the activities and the products of other persons, independently of whether the other persons enter into particular relationships that give rise to these claims, and independently of whether they voluntarily take these claims upon themselves, in charity or in exchange for something.

Whether it is done through taxation on wages or on wages over a certain amount, or through seizure of profits, or through there being a big *social pot* so that it's not clear what's coming from where and what's going where, patterned principles of distributive justice involve appropriating the actions of other persons. Seizing the results of someone's labor is equivalent to seizing hours from him and directing him to carry on various activities. If people force you to do certain work, or unrewarded work, for a certain period of time, they decide what you are to do and what purposes your work is to serve apart from your decisions. This process whereby they take this decision from you makes them a *part-owner* of you; it gives them a property right in you. Just as having such partial control and power of decision, by right, over an animal or inanimate object would be to have a property right in it.

End-state and most patterned principles of distributive justice institute (partial) ownership by others of people and their actions and labor. These principles involve a shift from the classical liberals' notion of self-ownership to a notion of (partial) property rights in *other* people.

Considerations such as these confront end-state and other patterned conceptions of justice with the question of whether the actions necessary to achieve the selected pattern don't themselves violate moral side constraints. Any view holding that there are moral side constraints on actions, that not all moral considerations can be built into end states that are to be achieved,…must face the possibility that some of its goals are not achievable by any morally permissible available means. An entitlement theorist will face such conflicts in a society that deviates from the principles of justice for the generation of holdings, if and only if the only actions available to realize the principles themselves violate some moral constraints. Since deviation from the first two principles of justice (in acquisition and transfer) will involve other persons' direct and aggressive intervention to violate rights, and since moral constraints will not exclude defensive or retributive action in such cases, the entitlement theorist's problem rarely will be pressing. And whatever difficulties he has in applying the principle of rectification to persons who did not themselves violate the first two principles are difficulties in balancing the conflicting considerations so as correctly to formulate the complex principle of rectification itself; he will not violate moral side constraints by applying the principle. Proponents of patterned conceptions of justice, however, often will face head-on clashes (and poignant ones if they cherish each party to the clash) between moral side constraints on how individuals may be treated and their patterned conception of justice that presents an end state or other pattern that *must* be realized.…

Locke views property rights in an unowned object as originating through someone's mixing his labor with it. This gives rise to many questions. What are the boundaries of what labor is mixed with? If a private astronaut clears a place on Mars, has he mixed his labor with (so that he comes to own) the whole planet, the whole uninhabited universe, or just a particular plot? Which plot does an act bring under ownership? The minimal (possibly disconnected) area such that an act decreases entropy in that area, and not elsewhere? Can virgin land (for the purposes of ecological investigation by high-flying airplane) come under ownership by a Lockean process? Building a fence around a territory presumably would make one the owner of only the fence (and the land immediately underneath it).

Why does mixing one's labor with something make one the owner of it? Perhaps because one owns one's labor, and so one comes to own a previously unowned thing that becomes permeated with what one owns. Ownership seeps over into the rest. But why isn't mixing what I own with what I don't own a way of losing what I own rather than a way of gaining what I don't? If I own a can of tomato juice and spill it in the sea so that its molecules (made radioactive, so I can check this) mingle evenly throughout the sea, do I thereby come to own the sea, or have I foolishly dissipated my tomato juice? Perhaps the idea, instead, is that laboring on something improves it and makes it more valuable; and anyone is entitled to own a thing whose value he has created.…Ignore the fact that laboring on something may make it less valuable (spraying pink enamel paint on a piece of driftwood that you have found). Why should one's entitlement extend to the whole object rather than just to the *added value* one's labor has produced?…

It will be implausible to view improving an object as giving full ownership to it, if the stock of unowned objects that might be improved is limited. For an object's coming under one person's ownership changes the situation of all others. Whereas previously they were at liberty…to use the object, they now no longer are. This change in the situation of others (by removing their liberty to act on a previously unowned object) need not worsen their situation. If I appropriate a grain of sand from Coney Island, no one else may now do as they will with that grain of sand. But there are plenty of other grains of sand left for them to do the same with. Or if not grains of sand, then other things. Alternatively, the things I do with the grain of sand I appropriate might improve the position of others, counterbalancing their loss of the liberty to use that grain. The crucial point is whether appropriation of an unowned object worsens the situation of others.

Locke's proviso that there be "enough and as good left in common for others" (sect. 27) is meant to ensure that the situation of others is not worsened. (If this proviso is met is there any motivation for his further condition of nonwaste?) It is often said that this proviso once held but now no longer does. But there appears to be an argument for the conclusion that if the proviso no longer holds, then it cannot ever have held so as to yield permanent and inheritable property rights. Consider the first person Z for whom there is not enough and as good left to appropriate. The last person Y to appropriate left Z without his previous liberty to act on an object, and so worsened Z's situation. So Y's appropriation is not allowed under Locke's proviso. Therefore the next to last person X to appropriate left Y in a worse position, for X's act ended permissible appropriation. Therefore X's appropriation wasn't permissible. But then the appropriator two from last, W, ended permissible appropriation and so, since it worsened X's position, W's appropriation wasn't permissible. And so on back to the first person A to appropriate a permanent property right.

This argument, however, proceeds too quickly. Someone may be made worse off by another's appropriation in two ways: first, by losing the opportunity to improve his situation by a particular appropriation or any one; and second, by no longer being able to use freely (without appropriation) what he previously could. A stringent requirement that another not be made worse off by an appropriation would exclude the first way if nothing else counterbalances the diminution in opportunity, as well as the second. A weaker requirement would exclude the second way, though not the first. With the weaker requirement, we cannot zip back so quickly from Z to A, as in the above argument; for though person Z can no longer appropriate, there may remain some for him to use as before. In this case Y's appropriation would not violate the weaker Lockean condition. (With less remaining that people are at liberty to use, users might face more inconvenience, crowding, and so on; in that way the situation of others might be worsened, unless appropriation stopped far short of such a point.) It is arguable that no one legitimately can complain if the weaker provi-

sion is satisfied. However, since this is less clear than in the case of the more stringent proviso, Locke may have intended this stringent proviso by "enough and as good" remaining, and perhaps he meant the non-waste condition to delay the end point from which the argument zips back.

Is the situation of persons who are unable to appropriate (there being no more accessible and useful unowned objects) worsened by a system allowing appropriation and permanent property? Here enter the various familiar social considerations favoring private property: it increases the social product by putting means of production in the hands of those who can use them most efficiently (profitably); experimentation is encouraged, because with separate persons controlling resources, there is no one person or small group whom someone with a new idea must convince to try it out; private property enables people to decide on the pattern and types of risks they wish to bear, leading to specialized types of risk bearing; private property protects future persons by leading some to hold back resources from current consumption for future markets; it provides alternate sources of employment for unpopular persons who don't have to convince any one person or small group to hire them, and so on. These considerations enter a Lockean theory to support the claim that appropriation of private property satisfies the intent behind the "enough and as good left over" proviso, *not* as a utilitarian justification of property. They enter to rebut the claim that because the proviso is violated no natural right to private property can arise by a Lockean process. The difficulty in working such an argument to show that the proviso is satisfied is in fixing the appropriate base line for comparison. Lockean appropriation makes people no worse off than they would be *how*? This question of fixing the baseline needs more detailed investigation than we are able to give it here. It would be desirable to have an estimate of the general economic importance of original appropriation in order to see how much leeway there is for differing theories of appropriation and of the location of the baseline. Perhaps this importance can be measured by the percentage of all income that is based upon untransformed raw materials and given resources (rather than upon human actions), mainly rental income representing the unimproved value of land, and the price of raw material *in situ*, and by the percentage of current wealth which represents such income in the past....

Whether or not Locke's particular theory of appropriation can be spelled out so as to handle various difficulties, I assume that any adequate theory of justice in acquisition will contain a proviso similar to the weaker of the ones we have attributed to Locke. A process normally giving rise to a permanent bequeathable property right in a previously unowned thing will not do so if the position of others no longer at liberty to use the thing is thereby worsened....

A theory which includes this proviso in its principle of justice in acquisition must also contain a more complex principle of justice in transfer. Some reflection of the proviso about appropriation constrains later actions. If my appropriating all of a certain substance violates the Lockean proviso, then so does my appropriating some and purchasing all the rest from others who obtained it without otherwise violating the Lockean proviso. If the proviso excludes someone's appropriating all the drinkable water in the world, it also excludes his purchasing it all....

Each owner's title to his holding includes the historical shadow of the Lockean proviso on appropriation. This excludes his transferring it into an agglomeration that does violate the Lockean proviso and excludes his using it in a way, in coordination with others or independently of them, so as to violate the proviso by making the situation of others worse than their baseline situation. Once it is known that someone's ownership runs afoul of the Lockean proviso, there are stringent limits on what he may do with (what it is difficult any longer unreservedly to call) "his property." Thus a person may not appropriate the only water hole in a desert and charge what he will. Nor may he charge what he will if he possesses one, and unfortunately it happens that all the water holes in the desert dry up, except for his. This unfortunate circumstance, admittedly no fault of his, brings into operation the Lockean proviso and limits his property rights. Similarly, an owner's property right in the only island in an area does not allow him to order a castaway from a shipwreck off his island as a trespasser, for this would violate the Lockean proviso.

Notice that the theory does not say that owners do have these rights, but that the rights are overridden to avoid some catastrophe. (Overridden rights do not disappear; they leave a trace of a sort absent in the cases under discussion.) There is no such external (and *ad hoc?*) overriding. Considerations internal to the theory of property itself, to its theory of acquisition and appropriation, provide the means for handling such cases....

The fact that someone owns the total supply of something necessary for others to stay alive does *not* entail that his (or anyone's) appropriation of anything left some people (immediately or later) in a situation worse than the baseline one. A medical researcher who synthesizes a new substance that effectively treats a certain disease and who refuses to sell except on his terms does not worsen the situation of others by depriving them of whatever he has appropriated. The others easily can possess the same materials he appropriated; the researcher's appropriation or purchase of chemicals didn't make those chemicals scarce in a way so as to violate the Lockean proviso. Nor would someone else's purchasing the total supply of the synthesized substance from the medical researcher. The fact that the medical researcher uses easily available chemicals to synthesize the drug no more violates the Lockean proviso than does the fact that the only surgeon able to perform a particular operation eats easily obtainable food in order to stay alive and to have the energy to work. This shows that the Lockean proviso is not an "end-state principle"; it focuses on a particular way that appropriative actions affect others, and not on the structure of the situation that results.

Intermediate between someone who takes all of the public supply and someone who makes the total supply out of easily obtainable substances is someone who appropriates the total supply of something in a way that does not deprive the others of it. For example, someone finds a new substance in an out-of-the-way place. He discovers that it effectively treats a certain disease and appropriates the total supply. He does not worsen the situation of others; if he did not stumble upon the substance no one else would have, and the others would remain without it. However, as time passes, the likelihood increases that others would have come across the substance; upon this fact might be based a limit to his property right in the substance so that others are not below their baseline position; for example, its bequest might be limited. The theme of someone worsening another's situation by depriving him of something he otherwise would possess may also illuminate the example of patents. An inventor's patent does not deprive others of an object which would not exist if not for the inventor. Yet patents would have this effect on others who independently invent the object. Therefore, these independent inventors, upon whom the burden of proving independent discovery may rest, should not be excluded from utilizing their own invention as they wish (including selling it to others). Furthermore, a known inventor drastically lessens the chances of actual independent invention. For persons who know of an invention usually will not try to reinvent it, and the notion of independent discovery here would be murky at best. Yet we may assume that in the absence of the original invention, sometime later someone else would have come up with it. This suggests placing a time limit on patents, as a rough rule of thumb to approximate how long it would have taken, in the absence of knowledge of the invention, for independent discovery.

I believe that the free operation of a market system will not actually run afoul of the Lockean proviso....If this is correct, the proviso will not play a very important role in the activities of protective agencies and will not provide a significant opportunity for future state action. Indeed, were it not for the effects of previous *illegitimate* state action, people would not think the possibility of the proviso's being violated as of more interest than any other logical possibility. (Here I make an empirical historical claim; as does someone who disagrees with this.)...

"Impediments to Radical Egalitarianism"

Kai Nielsen

I have elsewhere explicated and defended a radical egalitarian conception of justice. In deliberate contrast with Rawls' account, I have argued for two radical egalitarian principles of social justice and a conception of social justice I call *justice as equality*.3I have attempted, against conventional wisdom and the mainstream of philosophical opinion, to argue that a radical egalitarianism is not only coherent it is also reasonable. It is not the case, I have argued, that Rawls' account of justice is the most egalitarian account that can reasonably be defended. Justice in society as a whole ought to be understood as a complete equality of the overall level of benefits and burdens of each member of that society. What we should aim at is a structuring of the institutions of society so that each person can, to the fullest extent compatible with all other people doing likewise, satisfy his/her needs. We should seek a "republic of equals" where there will be a fundamental equality of social condition for everyone. The two principles which should govern that conception of justice as equality are the following:

1. Each person is to have an equal right to the most extensive total system of equal basic liberties and opportunities (including equal opportunities for meaningful work, for self-determination and political participation) compatible with a similar treatment of all. (This principle gives expression to a commitment to attain and/or sustain equal moral autonomy and equal self-respect.)
2. After provisions are made for common social (community) values, for capital overhead to preserve the society's productive capacity and allowances are

From "Impediments to Radical Egalitarianism," *American Philosophical Quarterly*, Vol. 18, (1981). Reprinted by permission of the publisher.

made for differing unmanipulated needs and preferences, the income and wealth (the common stock of means) is to be so divided that each person will have a right to an equal share. The necessary burdens requisite to enhance well-being are also to be equally shared, subject, of course, to limitations by differing abilities and differing situations (natural environment, not class position).

In asking about justice as equality three questions readily spring to mind: (1) Why is a greater equality in the conditions of life desirable? (2) Is anything like my radical egalitarianism something that could actually be achieved or even be reasonably approximated? (3) Given the steep inequalities we actually have, if they (or at least most of them) are eradicable, are they only so at an unacceptable cost? In short is the cost of equality too high?

There is no complete answer to (1), (2) and (3) which is entirely independent. There is, that is to say, reason for not considering them in utter isolation. In the essays mentioned above, I try to give an extended answer to (1). But the short answer to (1)—an answer I would be prepared to defend—is that a greater equality is desirable because it brings with it greater moral autonomy and greater self-respect for more people. It isn't, as some conservative critics assume, equality *per se* which is so desirable but what it brings in the way of human flourishing, though there is in such egalitarian thinking the assumption that the most extensive equal realization of that is an end devoutly to be desired. What I argued for in the essays previously mentioned, I shall assume here, namely that equality, if its costs are not too high, is desirable. That is (1), I shall assume, has a positive answer at least when it is not considered in relation to (2) and (3). But, as (3) asks, are the costs of this equality, after all, just too high? Many a conservative critic claims that they are. I shall, before I turn to (2), consider (3), as it is more closely linked to (1).

It is pointed out by conservative critics that we cannot in our assessments of what is just and what is unjust start from scratch. Goods to be distributed do not come down, like manna from heaven, they come with entitlements. Certain people have produced them, bought them, been given them, inherited them, found them, struggled to make them and

to preserve them. To think that we can override their entitlements in setting our ideal distributive patterns is to fail to respect people. It is to be willing to run over their rights in redistributing goods, but this is to treat some people as means only. A society in which a state or a class can take from people what is rightfully theirs cannot be a just society. The ideals of equality and the ideals of justice are different ideals. Equality is a forward-looking virtue concerned with making and keeping everyone's condition, in some appropriate sense, equal. Justice, by contrast, is a backward-looking virtue, concerned, some conservative theorists claim, with seeing that it is the case that people have their various and not infrequently unequal entitlements. Justice will be done in a society when people have what they are entitled to. The idea isn't to establish a certain distributive pattern, but to protect people's entitlements. Because this is what justice really is, rather than anything about equality, it will sometimes be the case that an individual, a family or even a class will quite justly achieve certain advantages on which the rest of the society can have no proper claim. Our maxim for justice should not be "Holdings ought to be equal unless there is a weighty moral reason they ought to be unequal," where the burden of proof is always to justify unequal treatment. Rather our maxim should be "People are entitled to keep whatever they happen to have unless there is a weighty moral reason why they ought to give it up." The burden of proof has now shifted to the redistributivist to justify a redistribution. The normal situation will be that people will be entitled to what they have properly acquired. These entitlements are rooted in the particular situations and activities of people. They cannot in the typical situation be equal. Fairness doesn't come to distributing things equally, even with allowance for differing needs, but to not taking from people what they are entitled to. Particular entitlements can be challenged, but if any one with a passion for justice sets out "systematically and at a stroke to devalue the lot, in the interests of a new strictly forward-looking distribution, he is by this move abandoning the whole notion of justice in favour of another alternative ideal".

I shall return to this objection in a moment. However, even if it is the case, that some distinction between social justice and individual justice or justice in acquisition and justice in distribution should show this criticism to be mistaken, there are still two related objections that remain in place and again have to do with the value of individual autonomy. (It is the three together which seem to me to constitute a formidable cluster of objections.) Firstly, it is claimed that if we treat social justice as equality, we will repeatedly have to use state intervention to keep the pattern of distribution at the requisite level of equality, for people in their ordinary transactions will continually upset the pattern. But such continual intervention constitutes an intolerable interference in the lives of people. No one who cares about individual liberty and moral autonomy could support that. Secondly, in a democratic society, people would not support with their votes a redistributive policy that was egalitarian, let alone the radical egalitarianism that I propose. It would have to be imposed from above by some dictatorial elite. It will not be accepted in a democratic society. Again its costs would be too high because it could only be achieved by abandoning democracy.

I shall start with the last objection for that one seems to me the weakest. It seems to me that it is not at all a question of imposing or trying to impose egalitarianism on anyone. In the first place, it is unrealistic because it cannot be done, but, even if it could and such a procedure were not self-undermining, it still would be undesirable. Justice as equality is set out as an ideal of social justice which, radical egalitarians argue, best captures what is fundamental to the very idea of justice. The thing is, by moral argumentation in "the public sphere," to use Habermas' conception, to convince people of it. There is no question at all of imposing it or of an "Egalitarian clerisy" indoctrinating people. Whatever the morality of it, it is impractical to try in such circumstances to impose equality or such an understanding of justice. The only road here is through patient and careful social argumentation to make the case for egalitarianism.

Socialists are well aware that the consciousness industry will be turned against radical egalitarianism and that there will be a barrage of propaganda directed against it, some (depending on the audience) subtle and some unsubtle. It will not get a fair hearing, but there is nothing else to be expected from a class society in the hands of a class who must be

deeply opposed to egalitarianism. But this is just a specific application of the general political problem of how social change can be achieved in an increasingly managed class society. This is one of the deep and intractable social problems of our time—one of the problems Horkheimer and Adorno anguished over—and, particularly for those of us in developed capitalist societies, it is a very puzzling and intractable problem indeed. But whatever we should say and do here, it will not be the case, that we intelligentsia should try to impose egalitarian ideals on an unwilling working class. Until the working class—the vast majority of people—sees fit to set about the construction of a genuinely egalitarian society, the role of the intellectual can, and should be, that of, through argumentation, to engage in critical analysis in an attempt at consciousness raising. (This is also perfectly compatible with an unflinching search for truth.)

I want now to consider the second objection, namely the claim that any patterned distribution, and most particularly the patterned distributions of radical egalitarianism, would require such continuous and massive state intervention that it would undermine individual liberty and the moral autonomy essential for the good of self-respect.

This objection uncritically makes all the background assumptions of *laissez-faire* capitalism—a social order which has not existed for a long time and probably could not exist in our contemporary world. But, a society committed to radical egalitarianism would also be a genuinely socialist society and would have very different background conditions. The objection just unrealistically assumes a genuinely free market society where people are busy possessive individualists devoted to accumulating and bargaining and are concerned very centrally with protecting their private property. It simply assumes that human beings, independently of the particular type of socialization they have been subject to, have very little sense of or feeling for community or cooperativeness, except in the form of bargaining (again the free market being the model). But a society in which radical egalitarianism could flourish would be an advanced socialist society under conditions of moderate abundance. People would not have a market orientation. They would not be accumulators or possessive individualists and the aim of their economic organization would not be profit maximization but the satisfaction of the human needs of everyone. The more pressing problems of scarcity would have been overcome. Everyone would have a secure life, their basic needs would be met and their level of education, and hence their critical consciousness, would be much higher than it is now, such that, in their situation, they would not be committed to Gomper's dictum of "more." Furthermore, the society would be thoroughly democratic and this would mean industrial democracy as well as political democracy. That would mean that working people, where every able bodied adult would be a worker, would control—collectively control in a fair democratic manner—their own work: that is the production relations would be in their hands as well as the governmental functions of the society, which in this changed environment would have become essentially administrative functions. In fine the institutions of the society and the psychological motivations of people would be very different than those implicitly appealed to in the objection. Under these conditions, the state, if that is the best thing still to call it, would not be the instrument of class oppression and management that it now is. People would democratically manage their own lives and the design of their society in a genuine *gemeinschaft* so that there would not be the question of an instrument of class domination interfering with people's liberties. People would be their own masters with a psychology that thinks in terms of "we" and not just, and most fundamentally, in terms of 'I', where the protection of my rights is the crucial thing. Moreover, now the society would be so organized that cooperation made sense and was not just to avoid the "state of nature." The society would be a secure society of relative abundance. (Communism and radical egalitarianism are unthinkable in any other situation.) It would be a society in which their needs were met. Since the society would be geared, within the limits of reasonable growth, to maximize for everyone, and as equally as possible, the satisfaction of their needs, a roughly egalitarian pattern would be in a steady state. It would not have to be constantly tinkered with to maintain the pattern. People would not, in such a secure situation have such a possessive hankering to acquire things or to pass them on. Such acquisitiveness would no longer be such a major feature of our psychologies. Moreover,

given the productive wealth of the society, there would be no need to worry, if in practice distributions sometimes swayed a little from the norm of equality. Everyone would have plenty and have security; people would not be possessive individualists bent on accumulating and obsessively concerned with mine and thine. There would, moreover, be no way for anyone to become a capitalist and exploit others and indeed there would be precious little motivation to do so.

If in spite of this an elite did show signs of forming, there would be, firmly in place, democratic institutions sufficient to bring about the demise of such deviations from the norm. This should not be pictured as an impersonal dictatorial state interfering with people's liberties, but as the people, acting collectively, to protect their liberties against practices which would undermine them. Yet that things like this would actually happen—that such elitist practices would evolve—in such a situation of abundance and cooperation is rather unlikely. In such circumstances the pattern of distribution of justice as equality would be stable and, when it did require adjustment, it would be done by a democratic government functioning to protect and further the interests of everyone. This patterning would not upset liberty and undermine moral autonomy and self-respect.

I will now turn to the first objection—the objection that justice is entitlement and not anything even like equality. It may be that justice as entitlement is that part of justice which is concerned with justice in initial acquisition and in transfer of what is initially justly acquired and is not distributive justice at all, the justice in social schemes of cooperation. It may be that these are two different species of justice that need capturing in some larger overall theory, but, be that as it may, the challenge of justice as entitlement seems, at least on the surface, to be a very real one. Entitlement theorists certainly have a hold of something that is an essential part of justice.

On some other occasion, I hope to be able to sort these issues out, but here I believe, I can give a "practical answer" which will show that such a challenge is not a threat to justice as equality. In doing this I want to show how such a conception of justice can do justice to the rights of entitlement. Recall that a radical egalitarian will also be a socialist. He will be concerned with justice in the distribution of products but he will be centrally concerned as well with justice in production. His concern with the justice to be obtained in production will come, most essentially, to a concern with transforming society from a society of private ownership and control of the means of production to one of a social ownership and control of the means of production, such that each worker—in a world of workers—will have an equal say in the disposition and rationale of work. (Control here seems to me the key notion. In such new production relations, the very idea of ownership may not have any unproblematic meaning.) It will, that is, be work which is democratically controlled. The aim will be to end class society and a society with an elite managerial stratum which runs society. Justice as equality most essentially requires a society with no bosses. The demand for equality is most fundamentally a demand to end that state of affairs and to attain a situation of equal moral autonomy and equal self-respect.

These considerations are directly relevant when we consider that entitlement conceptions of justice are most at home in situations where a person has mixed his labor and care with something, say built and lovingly cared for a house or built up a family farm. It would, *ceteris paribus*, be wrong, plainly unjust, to take those possessions away from that person and give them to someone else. But a radical egalitarian is not challenging entitlements of this type. Socialists do not want to take people's houses or family farms from them. In a Communist society there are consumer durables. The private property socialists seek to eliminate is private ownership and control of the major means of production. This is the private property that is the source and sustainer of class divisions, not private ownership of things like cars, houses, family farms, a fishing boat and the like. It is ownership and control over the major means of production that is the source of the great power of one person over another and the great advantages of one group over another....

The entitlement theorist will surely respond by saying 'If the person who builds a house or works a farm up out of a wilderness is entitled to it, why isn't a capitalist who, through his own initiative, creativeness and dogged determination, creates an industrial empire entitled to keep his property as well?' They both are the effect of something we prize in human nature, namely we see here human

beings not merely as satisfiers of desires but as exercisors of opportunities. At least in some cases, though less and less typically now, they can be his hard-earned and creatively-struggled-for holdings.

This creates a presumption of entitlement, but only a presumption. (Alternatively, we can say it creates an entitlement but a defeasible one that is rightly overridden.) We, as we do not in the case of the house or the family farm, have very good grounds indeed for overriding this presumption and requiring a redistribution. Remember the conservative principle was "People are entitled to keep whatever they happen to have, unless there is a weighty moral reason why they should relinquish it." Well, in this situation, there are weighty moral reasons, entirely absent in cases like that of the fishing boat, family farm or house. First, in our historical circumstances such capitalist ownership and control of the means of production causes extensive misery and impoverishment that could otherwise be avoided. Secondly, it gives capitalists and a small managerial elite (who are also often capitalists themselves) control over people's lives in such a way as to lessen their effective equal citizenship and undermine their self-respect and moral autonomy. Moreover, these are not inevitabilities of human life but the special and inescapable features of a class society, where there must be a dominant capitalist class who owns and controls the means of production. But they are not inescapable features of the human condition and they have not been shown simply to be something that must come with industrial society.

Someone determined to defend *laissez-faire* capitalism and an entitlement theory of justice might tough it out and claim that the error in the above entitlement theorist's conduct of his case is in stating his account in such a conditional way, namely that "people are entitled to keep whatever they happen to have, unless there is a (weighty) moral reason why they ought to relinquish it." It should instead be stated as "People are entitled to their holdings if the initial acquisition was just and any transfer from it just; the initial acquisition, in turn, was just if it accords with the Lockean proviso that it was taken from unclaimed land and if the initial appropriation left enough in kind for everyone else." This principle of justice is designed, in the way the first entitlement account was not, to normatively block any attempt, by the state or any group of people, to justifiably compel any transfer, under any circumstances, not specified in the above formulation, of any holdings to satisfy any redistributive scheme. Any person, quite categorically, may justifiably and justly hold on to whatever he initially justly acquired, not matter what the consequences. There is the obvious point that we do not know how to go about ascertaining whether in fact the patterns of holdings now in effect result from just acquisitions via just transfers. But this obvious point aside, such a categorical entitlement account has plain defects. To take such a right of property to be a moral absolute is to unduly narrow even a rights-based moral theory. A society organized with that as its fundamental moral principle— a principle of justice which could never rightly be overridden—would lead to the degradation of large numbers of people. They would, in circumstances such as our own, have the *formal* right to acquire property but in actuality they would have little or no property and their impoverishment and loss of autonomy and self-respect would be very great indeed. To hold on to an unqualified right to property in those circumstances would be not only arbitrary and morally one-sided, it would be morally callous as well. Moreover, it is not a commitment that clearheadedness and a devotion to rationality dictates. What such a one-valued absolutism neglects is that we are morally obliged to respond to suffering. On such an entitlement theory we would not be obliged to relieve the suffering of another even when we could do so without serious loss to ourselves. What it gains here in categoricalness, it *loses* in moral coherence....Sometimes we are morally compelled to redistribute. Anything else would be grossly unjust and immoral. Whether we feel compassion or not, the relief of human misery, where this is reasonably within our capacities, is something that is morally required of us. What we otherwise would be entitled to, we can hardly be entitled to when we could, by sharing it, save the life of another and (to put it concessively and minimally) not cause any great distress to ourselves. My last remark can easily be misunderstood. It is not so much demands placed on individuals within an unjust social system that are crucial but a commitment on the part of individuals to alter the social system. In a period of political stagnation, to demand of a tolerably well off suburbanite that he greatly diminish his holdings and

send a not inconsiderable sum of money to India comes too close to requiring him to be a Don Quixote. What needs to be altered is the social system. To maintain that severe sacrifices are required of individuals when there is little prospect of turning the society around is to ask them to be martyrs if, by so acting, there is not a chance for significant social change. Still, morally speaking, there has to be redistribution and where we genuinely could relieve misery to not acknowledge that such a *sharing* is required of us is to fail to grasp something very essential to morality. Failure here is as much a moral failing as an intellectual one and no amount of cleverness can get around that.

I want now to turn to the second general problem about radical egalitarianism, I mentioned at the beginning of this article. Some critics of egalitarianism maintain that however abstractly desirable egalitarianism may be it still is an impossible ideal for it is impossible to achieve or even reasonably to approximate. Such a criticism would apply doubly to my radical form of egalitarianism. We must just come to recognize, so the criticism goes, that inequality is inevitable and erect our account of justice in the light of this inevitability.

Are there any basic features or functional prerequisites of society or human nature that make inequality inevitable in all societies or at least in all industrial societies? I shall limit my answer to remarks about industrial societies and consider the claims that classes, bureaucracies (with their hierarchical social relations) and social stratification are inevitable. The inevitability of any of them would ensure that any future industrial society would also be to some degree a status society with a ranking of people, and not just a society with differentiations, according to social roles. With these inequalities in status there would be the differences in power and authority that have plagued societies in the past and continue to plague our societies.

It has been claimed that inequalities are functionally necessary to any industrial society. There will be a division of labour and a differentiation of social roles in those societies. Since certain social roles are functionally more important than others—being a doctor at the Crisis Centre is functionally more important than being a ski instructor—and since suitable performance in these more important roles requires, in a world where such talent is scarce, suitable training and discipline, it is necessary to induce with adequate rewards those with the appropriate talents to delay gratification and take on the required training—the long years of struggle in medical school, graduate school or law school. This is done by assuring them that at the end of their training they will be rewarded more highly for their sacrifice in taking on that training. This requires the inequalities of differential incentives. People, the argument goes, simply will not make the sacrifice of going to medical school or going to law school unless they have very good reason to believe that they will make much more money than they would by selling cars or running a little shop. To stream people into these functionally necessary occupations, there must be differential rewards and with those rewards social stratification with its concomitant inequalities in prestige, power and authority. Moreover, we must do this to make sure that the most talented people will continue to occupy the most functionally important positions and to work at their maximal capacity. The very good of the society requires it.

The first thing to note is that all this, even if sound, does not add up to an inevitability. Still, some might say that it is all the same a 'rational inevitability', given that it is a functional prerequisite for the proper functioning of an industrial society. But is it actually a functional prerequisite? Again, like some of the previous criticisms of egalitarianism we have examined, it simply uncritically assumes something like contemporary capitalism as being the norm for how any industrial society must operate, but there is no reason why the additional training should be a form of sacrifice or even be regarded as a sacrifice. It too much takes the ideology of the present as an accurate depiction of social reality. In an egalitarian society, by contrast, everyone would be materially secure and there would be no material loss in remaining in medical school, law school, or graduate school. Once that becomes so and once the pace is slowed down, as it really could be, so that students are not rushed through at great stress and strain, it would be, for many people at least, far less of a sacrifice to go through medical school than to be a bank-teller, rug salesman or assembly line workman all day. For many people, perhaps for most people of normal intelligence, the work both during their school years and afterwards would be more re-

warding and challenging than the routine jobs. There is no need to provide special incentives, given other suitable changes in society, changes which are quite feasible if we do not continue to take a capitalist organization of society as normative....

I now turn to what I, at least, take to be the most troubling arguments about the inevitability of inequality in industrial societies. They turn on the claim that the empirical evidence, when linked to reasonable theories and arguments, shows that a status society is inevitable under the conditions of modern life. There is no way of making industrial societies free of bureaucracy with the cluster of privileges and differential power and authority which go with such inegalitarian structures.

It is reasonable to argue that there are, when we look at the various modern societies (including Russia, China, Cuba and Yugoslavia), no classless societies or, what is more relevant, no societies which are clearly tending in the direction of classless societies. Given this, isn't radical egalitarianism implausible? Would it not be better, given these empirical facts, to opt for a more modest egalitarianism with principles something like Rawls'? We must not tell ourselves Marxist fairy tales!

The above argument rests on reasonable empirical data....It is certainly anything but clear that there are any complex societies which are moving in the direction of classlessness....Rather than put all, or even most, of one's eggs in that historical basket, it is theoretically more useful, I believe, to note certain general facts, and on the basis of them to develop a theoretical argument.

First the facts. We have not had any proletarian revolutions yet, though we have had revolutions made in the name of a very small and undeveloped proletariat. We have yet to have a dictatorship of the proletariat—a society controlled by the proletariat and run principally in its own interests. The state socialist societies that exist are not socialist societies that developed in the conditions that Marx said were propitious for the development of socialism but...in economically backward societies that had yet to experience a bourgeois revolution. It is also a fact that these socialist societies are surrounded by strong Capitalist societies which are, naturally enough, implacably hostile to socialism.

If these are the facts, as I believe they are, then it is very unlikely that a classless society will begin to emerge out of these societies until those empirical situations radically change. There is a further fact that should be noted. In the bourgeois democracies there is not yet good evidence of a rising class consciousness. In North America it is almost nonexistent. It is slightly stronger in Europe....Again, in these circumstances, a movement in the direction of classlessness is hardly evident....

If the instability of monopoly capitalism increases and if the third world remains unpacified, conditions in the industrially developed capitalist countries may change. A militancy and a sense of class may arise and class conflict may no longer be merely a muted and disguised reality. That could lead to the first social transformation by an actual proletarian class, a class developed enough, educated enough, numerous enough and strong enough to democratically run things in its own interests and to pave the way for a society organized in the interests of everyone, namely a classless society. I do not maintain that we have good grounds for saying that it will happen. I say only that that scenario is a coherent possibility. Minimally I do not believe that anyone has shown this to be a mere dream, a fantastic bit of utopianism. If it is also, as I believe it to be, everything considered a desirable possibility it is something to be struggled for with all the class conflict that that will involve....

"A World of Social Atoms"

Elizabeth H. Wolgast

We call on the ideas of social atomism when we reason about political and ethical issues, but, perhaps because they are so familiar, we don't often examine them critically. Here we look at the logic and interconnections of ideas of social atomism and at some of their historical sources.

In the seventeenth century a new fashion in thought appeared, one whose motivation was to challenge traditional authorities in a variety of dimensions. René Descartes, for instance, challenged the church's claim to authority on matters concerning God, the soul, and the world God presumably made. Thomas Hobbes and John Locke challenged the traditional grounds given for political authority. In that enlightened time government could not be based on divine right or on natural heredity or paternalism; it needed some more rational basis. David Hume, Thomas Reid, and Immanuel Kant in turn took up the question of the foundation of morality; why should we accept what anyone says about what is right and morally justifiable?

Standing against the old authorities required a secure point, an Archimedean point from which to strike. So it happened that in a variety of fields—science, theology, political theory, morality—such a point was located in the autonomous, unconnected, rational human individual. Starting with this person and his or her inherent abilities, requirements, and values, one got a neutral and detached perspective on any claim to authority. Thus a new kind of moral, political, and epistemological justification came into being, one that derived from the natural, free, rational, and morally autonomous individual. It was an unbinding of the inquiring spirit; it

From *The Grammar of Justice* (Ithaca, NY: Cornell University Press, 1987). Reprinted by permission of the publisher.

was a new premise for shedding a critical light on old orthodoxies.

Contemporary American social and moral theories and our political arguments bear the mark of this bold anti-authoritarianism. The new ideas of the Enlightenment became unshakable American principles. Nonetheless, new problems followed upon this advance, and we face them still.

Descartes's anti-authoritarianism appears in his claim that men are equal in their reason. No one is distinguished by intelligence, rather "good sense is of all things in the world the most equally distributed...[and] the power of forming a good judgment and distinguishing the true from the false...is naturally equal in all men." One finds it astonishing that an indisputable and not very modest genius should say such a thing if one neglects its importance for the challenge he took up in theology and science. For if all people are alike in their ability to learn and know, and there are no experts, then a person who wants to understand God or the soul or the universe doesn't need anyone else. We can all figure it out for ourselves.

Along with this intellectual individualism Descartes proposed a method for investigating problems, a method universally applicable to theology, mathematics, physiology, morals, and every other subject. Its use, he proposed, would guarantee that all attainable human knowledge would be within the reach of everyone....Deductive demonstrations require nothing from outside a person, they do not call on a specialized knowledge....This was something new, a do-it-yourself science and theology. Thus in the end it is Descartes's egalitarianism that provides the power that drives his rational anti-authoritarianism.

Descartes's English contemporary Thomas Hobbes used the autonomous individual in a very different way—to give a novel justification for government. From the Archimedean point of such individuals Hobbes believed he could justify the existence of government—of any form—in a way that anyone would have to accept. His justification would not appeal to natural, divine, or hereditary right but only to human nature and human rationality. A government comes into existence through a contract, he proposed, a covenant that free and independent individuals make with one another. The resulting government is then a kind of artifact.

Before there was government, Hobbes's theory said, people managed to exist, but not well and not peacefully. For in that presocial state men separately governed their activities, that is to say, each pursued his own interest and depended entirely upon himself for protection. People in this condition were roughly equal, Hobbes held....Equality of people both mentally and physically, combined with desires and motives of self-interest, yielded competition as a natural way of life, competition that was unrelenting, harsh, deadly....This natural state was consequently barren of the goods of civilization:..."no Arts; no Letters; no Society; and which is worst of all, continuall fear, and danger of violent death; And the life of man, solitary, poor, nasty, brutish, and short."

In Hobbes's picture of equal autonomous agents, people can be likened to molecules of gas bouncing around inside a container. Each molecule proceeds independently, is free to go its own way, although it occasionally bumps into others in its path. As molecules have their energy, people are driven by their passions, and their relations with one another reflect both their "love [of] Liberty, and [love of] Dominion over others." No atom helps or moves aside for another; that wouldn't make sense. They are a collection of unrelated units. This fundamental picture I call "social atomism," for it shows society as a simple collection of independent, self-motivated units.

In Hobbes's view, government is justified as an instrument by which people further their security and thus their self-interest. It is the people's creation, and its irreplaceable function is to create a state of peace and security in which the human atoms can pursue their interests without fear. That function and that alone justifies government's existence; therefore it cannot have interests that are not ultimately reducible to the interests of its members. So Hobbes reserved for citizens the right to disobey their government in the face of threats to their lives or security. Insofar as government was a creation of the people who were to live under it, this was a do-it-yourself political theory.

Atomism need not be associated with such a dismal account of human nature as Hobbes's. Another social atomist of this period, John Locke, held a more generous view. For him people are generally sociable and not naturally at war; only a few create problems....Human nature did not generally need restraint by government, and the value people placed on liberty, property, and political equality needed to be respected by government. Still the autonomous, independent individual is the central motif....Individuals have the power to keep or give away authority over them. Therefore at bottom of political authority is the idea of individual independence and autonomy: the authority one has over oneself....

For Locke a contract is optional rather than a matter of survival, and any number of people may contract with one another to join together while leaving the rest in the state of nature. When they do so contract, they have formed a community....

While Hobbes's and Locke's views of men's nature and the form of government that's "natural" for them differ, their views of the contract on which government is based are similar. Both see it as being made voluntarily and rationally, out of people's natural, self-oriented desires and their recognition of their limitations; and should people be thrown into the state of nature again, both see the rational course as being to make another contract of the same kind. Without claiming to represent the historical origins of society, this conception came to have a profound effect on the understanding Americans have of the relation holding between government and citizens.

In the following century another form of atomism was developed by Kant, Hume, Shaftesbury, and Reid: its concern was morality. These philosophers held that the source of moral authority lay in the individual—in one's conscience, moral sense, or reason. This conception of moral autonomy sets the stage for the proper treatment of others, and it gives force to the idea that political authority must have its moral source in such individuals. For these philosophers, the justification of moral precepts must derive from an individual conceived without the imprint of society. The single individual is the ground of moral principles. This is do-it-yourself moral theory.

Ethical atomism combined with Hobbes's and Locke's social atomism supplies some of the most important and characteristic features of American political theory, and the imprint of these ideas is evident and fixed in the Constitution. It is from Hobbes, for example, that we derive the idea that no one should be forced to give evidence against himself and threaten his own security—the essence of the Fifth Amendment. From Locke we have a picture of man as a solid citizen, conscientious and property-owning, and the right of such citizens to monitor the actions of their government. From him, too, we have emphasis on the sanctity of property. From the ethical atomists we derive the need to respect expressions of conscience, since conscience is tied to moral autonomy; it follows that the authority of government must be qualified by the moral authority of the governed.

Such timeless theoretical foundations give Americans a vocabulary and a framework for discussing social problems, and at the same time they define avenues for addressing such problems. If its implications fail to square with our moral judgment, then—by ethical atomism's own premise of individual authority—it is subject to serious criticism.

In form, social atomism appears scientific, and its analogues in science are easy to recognize. For we understand what physical compounds are when we know what they're made of. A wall of bricks is understood as an assemblage of separate bricks. A molecule of water is made up of separable atoms, and to understand what water is you must know about those atoms. Often we talk about compounds in terms of their parts; why not apply the same method to a society? Thus we can understand a society if we know what it's made of. The resulting theory of society can then claim a truth that is abstracted from historical contexts, can claim the lasting and objective validity of physics or chemistry. It will include the features that a society not only has but must of necessity have. In giving social theory this foundation, Hobbes became one of the founders of political and social "science."

In contemporary political thought the idea is expressed by Robert Nozick, who says that although the political realm can be "understood" by various means, a nonpolitical explanation is the only means that "promises full understanding"....A complete understanding of the political requires us to begin with the nonpolitical, and Nozick's starting point, like Hobbes's and Locke's, is the single human individual. This is their Archimedean point....

It may seem self-evident that one way to understand a thing is to take it apart, but notice what this idea assumes. It assumes that a part will be a discrete thing with its own nature, and that if we know the component parts, we will understand the whole. But not every compound or complex thing can be understood by this means. Take a machine: it is not just a collection of parts, but a collection of parts assembled in accordance with a particular design and in a particular order. If we have only the assorted parts or a list of them, we may altogether fail to understand how the assembled parts function. We still need a diagram or design, a conception of how the machine works, maybe an idea of its eventual purpose. Then are the design and purpose *parts* of the machine? Hardly. But if the machine is not understandable without the design and can't be assembled without it, how can the machine be understood in terms of parts? Or take a cake: it's a collection of ingredients, but not ingredients assembled any which way. It needs a method or recipe, or else it can't be accounted for, putting the same ingredients together at random may yield a disaster. Then is the recipe *part of* the cake? No. Nonetheless, the cake cannot be understood in terms solely of its parts or ingredients.

Consider the following argument, then. Some things cannot be understood in terms of simple units, units that exist originally in isolation; an understanding even of the parts may depend on their being in an appropriate context and related within a whole. Take part of a flower, a pistil, for instance. What is it? It's part of a particular flower, with a function in the life of the plant and the generation of new plants, a function in a whole pattern of the plant's growth and its relation to other things. It is the pistil of that flower, functioning with respect to it; that is what it is. The same problem applies to some parts of machines. Think of finding an odd-looking piece of metal in the road; how does one describe or identify it? Most commonly, perhaps, as a part of some kind of machine, a piece that has a characteristic place and function in various mechanisms. Some fairly standard parts—bolts, screws, wheels—are describable individually because, like atoms and bricks and marbles, they are interchangeable and their functions standardized. But in any case they are identified as things with a certain function in a larger whole. Therefore while an atomistic approach works to explain some things, we can't assume it will provide an adequate understanding of society, though it will certainly press out a crisp and simple theory.

Among those who have held anti-atomistic views were the ancient Greeks. Aristotle, for instance, believed that a man is a particular individual only in the context of his community. To understand the individual, then, we must begin with the community he or she belongs to....Moreover, without a state, a man is without family, heritage, and home, for these things have reality only within a political community....The community is the right place for a person, and humans need to be seen in that context if we want to understand them.

For Aristotle a person *is* the legal child of So-and-so, the husband of So-and-so, the father of So-and-so, the owner of such land, the person who trades in such goods, the one who holds such office and votes under such-and-such name. These social properties and relationships define a person. They do so by referring to other people, some of them closely related, others more distant, others who are fellow citizens, and eventually to the community itself. The individual is nothing without these relationships, has no importance, is nobody; for it is in this framework that he is credited and counts as an individual. The whole makes the part comprehensible.

Not everyone accepts atomism's assumption that separate units provide understanding of a compound....Such views encourage the suspicion that atomism may not be the only or best way to understand human society. Whether it is even a reasonable one needs reflection as well, for insofar as we take a theory of society seriously, our choice of a model is crucial.

The question of what a society is made up seems to many to have an obvious answer: It's made up of individual people, as bricks in a wall, as molecules in a substance. What else is there besides individuals?

To explain a community in terms of these units is to imply that people are complete in themselves, that they are self-contained, independent, self-motivated, energized from within—by passions and desires, Hobbes would say. They are complete and real, each in him- or herself, and their autonomy is related to a certain independence....

Starting with these units, we naturally see society as deriving from their individual interests. In its favor is Occam's razor, which says that you should make only the minimum assumptions, nothing more. Social atomism needs nothing besides the individual units with their individual interests. It needs no glue to bind people together; self-interest will account for the society in what Nozick calls an "invisible hand" explanation, accounting for laws and institutions as the natural result of individual choices. Rationality enters here, for on this account we are rational if we recognize our self-interest and act accordingly. Because it is formed to serve people's self-interests, government can be seen as just; it represents only what the people *chose*.

Given the starting point of separate and self-interested individuals, it is clear that those individuals must be equal. They must be equal to satisfy the anti-authoritarian mission of the theory, but also because this analysis is meant to derive a just society from a universal theory of human nature, a theory that represents humans as alike. People's distinguishing characteristics, the superior talents and skills of some, differences of personality, age, sex, and ability to contribute to the community—all these elements must drop out if the analysis is to work. The atoms must be equal....

Bricks are interchangeable and so are molecules of water; interchangeability goes with our understanding of such units. But in fact people are in many ways not alike, and then how can it be fair to treat them as interchangeable?...

The theoretical role of the interchangeability principle is clear, but its application is not; in particular its application to differences of sex is problematic. How it can be just to treat people alike when their needs and situations differ?

Answers to this question are notoriously involved and difficult. Some people say that justice presupposes equality, but equality doesn't mean similarity; people can be treated equally but differently. People's equality is something more general, a matter of meriting equal respect, and not any specific treatment or specific rights. Others have called a prejudice our tendency to characterize *any* fair arrangement as one of equality....

How can the model's egalitarianism be squared with a society that accords respect to different kinds of individuals? Perhaps the most ingenious answer is John Rawls's conception of an "original position" and the "veil of ignorance" that characterizes it. Rawls believes that the basic principles of a fair society can be founded upon a kind of blind

egalitarianism, a philosophical starting point at which people are ignorant of their own characteristics and therefore of what would serve their advantage. In this position one would not know one's sex, financial situation, education, talents, weaknesses, abnormalities. Not to know these things is not to know whether one is in a strong or weak position vis-à-vis others who are parties to the contract. Thus in the original position one will be careful to accept only principles that *will not* be prejudicial to oneself if one's real position turns out to be weak. For it is assumed that people will take advantage of one another *unless* they imagine themselves similarly vulnerable. From this position, Rawls believes, people will come to agree on principles that are fair to everyone.

The original position is a philosophical device whose purpose is to make plausible the adoption of fair principles as people move from an unorganized existence to membership in a community. The resulting community, moreover, is one in which their conflicts of interest are resolved through a commonly accepted conception of justice. What guarantees people's agreement to a single conception is that each will look at his own position in terms of all the possible positions, which will include those of others as well as his own, and come to a decision that will be both his own and hypothetically that of others.

It is important to distinguish the sense in which Rawls means a person to "put himself in the place of another" and the sense in which a white person, for instance, may "put himself in the place of" a black person when he considers racial issues. The latter projection is an exercise in sympathy with the lot of others. But Rawls's original position doesn't depend on sympathy or feeling of humanity. It doesn't ask the original parties imaginatively to take the point of view of others, projecting sympathy or empathy in the manner of Butler or Shaftesbury while they know that their own positions are secure. On the contrary: to evaluate the justice of a principle, one needs to look at its implications from a self-interested point of view, to consider all possible situations *as if they might really be one's own*. Thus self-interest serves to define for Rawls a *dis*interested point of view; and such a view he considers the key to justice.

Rawls's derivation of a just state from self-interest is part of a long, ongoing tradition of attempts to derive moral rules or principles of justice from self-interest, of attempts to show that being moral must in some way be reducible to doing what is to one's benefit. What I attempt here is to understand why such projects seem plausible.

In a container of gas all molecules are free to move where they want. But the freedom they enjoy is to move randomly in space; what does the metaphor mean as applied to human beings? If we ask whether people act freely in a real community, the answer is most certainly no. Most of them, adults and children, act a good deal of the time according to fixed rules and responsibilities, according to promises and needs, not to mention the constraints of laws. What does it mean to say that nonetheless they are free? This remark signifies that we are looking through the grid of the model. Just as one cannot imagine molecules being restricted by invisible bonds, people must be free and independent, for only in this way can they satisfy the features of the model.

Autonomy, Rawls emphasizes, is closely connected with freedom, since everyone needs "equal liberty to pursue whatever plan of life he pleases" within broad limits.…But what does this mean for a real human life: from what position does one make his or her long-range plans? Is there an absolute beginning from which all possible life plans can be arrayed? Our real beginnings seem full of influences and training, and our plans change all the time. Is there undue interference with our free choice? And is it really so bad that some plans are frustrated while others fall of their own defects? Making and fulfilling our long-range plans might be crucial for happiness if happiness depended on our plan's fulfillment, and if we knew at some very early age what would make us happy and what kind of life we wanted. But these are large qualifications.

The autonomy of individuals and their self-interest are connected with the use of contract to explain human connections and institutions. Consider the explanation of marriage as a contract made by two parties for their mutual self-interest. A sensible person has to wonder: a contract for what and concerning what? A contract involves specific conditions, and failure to carry out any one of them breaches the contract. Imagine, then, that a couple at their wedding are making a legally enforceable agreement regarding the exchange of goods or services, some kind of fair agreement based on mutual self-interest. What are the conditions of the contract? Does one promise to love and honor? The first is impossible to promise, the second is demeaning to free, autonomous agents. Other conditions mentioned are to stay together for better or worse, for richer or poorer, in sickness and in health—eventualities as risky as they are vague. And how long does the contract run? Until death. Besides the wonder that any rational being would engage in such a deal, there is the fact that such a contract could not be validly enforced. No performances are specified, no term is mentioned, much is specifically left to chance; how could such a contract be binding? And of course such "contracts" aren't enforced.

Marriage *is* a legal relationship, voluntarily entered into, and in that way it is like a contract. But the commitment to weather unknown exigencies is a feature that no contract can tolerate. On the other side, if marriage had to be construed as a contract, one might argue that there would be nothing resembling marriage at all.

The reduction of such human relationships to contracts is forced upon us by a picture, the picture of atomism, and the problems it creates suggest that the picture cannot be right.

Nonetheless, society was also thought to rest on a contract. As Ronald Dworkin observes, the "contract device" is one that "supposes each individual to pursue his own interest and gives each a veto on the collective decision.…It is designed to produce the distribution that each individual deems in his own best interest, given his knowledge under [the contract]." Dworkin believes, however, that the relation of man in the state of nature to his role as citizen needs more explication. The claim that a society founded on a contract will be just is not self-evident; other fundamental requirements are needed, in particular the theory of natural rights. Thus he argues that "the deep theory behind the original position…must be a theory that is based on the concept of rights that are *natural*, in the sense that they are not the product of any legislation, or convention, or hypothetical contract."

My claim is that the "deep theory" here goes even deeper than a theory of natural rights. At bottom is a theory of people's natural discreteness, and from this theory an account of their relations to one another and to society has somehow to be derived. In that picture society arises only from some individual-based reason. For such creatures communal life has to result from rational self-interest, and even then the adjustments required may be awkward and uncomfortable....In this tradition the individual always *was* at the center—his freedom to act, to express himself and pursue his interests entail his reluctance to be governed at all. He is at heart an anarchist and accepts government as a necessary evil.

Connected with individual freedom is the importance of competition. Just as molecules in a container bounce around in their competition for space, so the social molecules compete for the satisfaction of their needs and desires. In the state of nature competition was perfectly free but threatening; in a society it can be made orderly and peaceful, and thus it becomes the normal mode of human interaction.

But when this picture is applied to society, anomalies appear. In such a society the elderly and frail must compete with the young and strong, men compete with their childbearing wives, the handicapped compete with the well endowed. Correspondingly, the economy of the community is seen as an *n*-person game in which each player plays against all others to maximize his advantage. The problems of this picture have not deterred social and economic thinkers from using it, even though it is at center a picture of ruthless egoism and unconcern for others.

Through Hobbes and Locke the political implications of the model profoundly influenced the framers of the Constitution, who sharply appreciated its anti-authoritarian force. They viewed the founding of a new constitutional government as a new beginning, a chance to follow and act out the tenets of the contract theory, and as they were no longer united with England, they could assume the role of a collection of people who could choose and form their government as they wanted. Insofar as all the colonies had to ratify it, the Constitution could be thought of as a voluntary contract among all the people.

Much of the language of the Constitution, and the constitutions of the states, comes from social contract philosophers, especially Locke. The constitution of Virginia states, for example, "that all men are by nature equally free and independent, and have certain inherent rights, of which, when

they enter into a state of society, they cannot by any compact deprive or divest their posterity: namely, the enjoyment of life and liberty, with the means of acquiring and possessing property, and pursuing and obtaining happiness and safety." The Alabama Declaration of Rights declares "that all *freemen*, when they form a social compact, are equal in rights." And the Connecticut Declaration of Rights pronounces "that all men, when they form a social compact, are equal in rights, and that no man or set of men are entitled to exclusive public emoluments or privileges from the community." Sometimes it was the states rather than individuals that were viewed as the independent parties to the contract. But throughout the early American state papers appears language suggesting that a contract is the proper foundation for government.

The model's claim to be scientific was also an important virtue. The framers did not, however, adopt Hobbes's materialism and its deterministic consequences....The emphasis on a human's ability to reason and so to understand himself became associated later with the philosophy of John Locke.

Man was not to be seen only in terms of intellect and animal functions; he also had a moral side. But how could a moral nature be reconciled with the self-interest of atomism? The moral philosophers Francis Hutcheson, Thomas Reid, and Anthony Shaftesbury gave answers that showed man as a divided creature, a creature who was on one side moral, and who, regardless of intellect and education, was endowed with a moral sense....

Both Reid and Hutcheson picture a moral egalitarianism, a moral democracy in which each person is competent to make good judgments and to be fully responsible for decisions. This vision had a profound influence on Jefferson, among others....

Although the state is founded on contract, Jefferson believes justice has its source in men's moral sense. But can these two views be made consistent? The social contract made voluntarily by all parties seems to have implicit justification; it was chosen freely....But if every individual has a moral sense, justice ought to relate to that sense. Both of these conceptions of justice cannot be right. Nonetheless both belong to our tradition, and the tension between social contract theory and a moral view of human nature is reflected in the history of our political theory. It is a conflict that cannot be resolved..

The atomistic model has important virtues. It founds the values of the community on private values; it encourages criticism of government and requires any government to answer to its original justification; it limits government's powers, as they may threaten to interfere with the needs of atomistic units. It gives us assumptions about the nature of man and the composition of society to start our reasoning, gives us a common ground in the values of freedom, autonomy, respect, equality, and the sanctity of desires. It thus frames a multitude of important political disputes, holds them together, shapes them, and sheds a clear, unequivocal theoretical light on them.

But it leaves a great deal out, as we have seen. In it one cannot picture human connections or responsibilities. We cannot locate friendliness or sympathy in it any more than we can imagine one molecule or atom moving aside for or assisting another; to do so would make a joke of the model....The atomistic person is an unfortunate myth....On a number of grounds the model needs challenging. A larger picture of human life needs to be considered, one that allows a firmer juncture between the moral and political realms, between the grammar of good and the grammar of justice. Or, what may amount to the same thing, we need to loosen the hold that the atomistic picture has on our thinking, and recognize the importance that theory has on our judgments and our moral condition.

"Feminism and Modern Friendship"

Marilyn Friedman

A predominant theme of much recent feminist thought is the critique of the abstract individualism which underlies some important versions of liberal political theory. Abstract individualism considers individual human beings as social atoms, -stracted from their social contexts, and disregards the role of social relationships and human community in constituting the very identity and nature of individual human beings. Sometimes the individuals of abstract individualism are posited as rationally self-interested utility-maximizers. Sometimes, also, they are theorized to form communities based fundamentally on competition and conflict among persons vying for scarce resources, communities which represent no deeper social bond than that of instrumental relations based on calculated self-interest.

Against this abstractive individualist view of the self and of human community, many feminists have asserted a conception of what might be called the "social self." This conception acknowledges the fundamental role of social relationships and human community in constituting both self-identity and the nature and meaning of the particulars of individual lives. The modified conception of the self has carried with it an altered conception of community. Conflict and competition are no longer considered to be the basic human relationships; instead they are being replaced by alternative visions of the foundation of human society derived from nurturance, caring attachment, and mutual interestedness. Some feminists, for example, recommend that the mother-child relationship be viewed as central to human society, and they

From "Feminism and Modern Friendship: Dislocating the Community," *Ethics*, Vol. 99 (1989). Reprinted by permission of The University of Chicago project major changes in moral theory from such a revised focus.

Some of these anti-individualist developments emerging from feminist thought are strikingly similar to other theoretical developments which are not specifically feminist. Thus, the "new communitarians," to borrow political theorist Amy Gutmann's term, have also reacted critically to various aspects of modern liberal thought, including abstract individualism, rational egoism, and an instrumental conception of social relationships. The communitarian self, or subject, is also not a social atom but is instead a being constituted and defined by its attachments, including the particularities of its social relationships, community ties, and historical context. Its identity cannot be abstracted from community or social relationships.

With the recent feminist attention to values of care, nurturance, and relatedness—values that psychologists call "communal" and which have been amply associated with women and women's moral reasoning—one might anticipate that communitarian theory would offer important insights for feminist reflection. There is considerable power to the model of the self as deriving its identity and nature from its social relationships, from the way it is intersubjectively apprehended, from the norms of the community in which it is embedded.

However, communitarian philosophy as a whole is a perilous ally for feminist theory. Communitarians invoke a model of community which is focused particularly on families, neighborhoods, and nations. These sorts of communities have harbored social roles and structures which have been highly oppressive for women, as recent feminist critiques have shown. But communitarians seem oblivious to those difficulties and manifest a troubling complacency about the moral authority claimed or presupposed by these communities in regard to their members. By building on uncritical references to those sorts of communities, communitarian philosophy can lead in directions which feminists should not wish to follow.

This article is an effort to redirect communitarian thought so as to avoid some of the pitfalls which it poses, in its present form, for feminist theory and feminist practice. In the first part of the article, I develop some feminist-inspired criticisms of communitarian philosophy as it is found in writings by Michael Sandel and Alasdair MacIntyre....

Communitarians share with most feminist theorists a rejection of the abstractly individualist conception of self and society so prominent in modern liberal thought. This self—atomistic, pre-social, empty of all metaphysical content except abstract reason and will—is allegedly able to stand back from all the contingent moral commitments and norms of its particular historical context and assess each one of them in the light of impartial and universal criteria of reason. The self who achieves a substantial measure of such reflective reconsideration of the moral particulars of her life has achieved "autonomy," a widely esteemed liberal value.

In contrast to this vision of the self, the new communitarians pose the conception of a self whose identity and nature are defined by her contingent and particular social attachments. Communitarians extol the communities and social relationships, including family and nation, which comprise the typical social context in which the self emerges to self-consciousness. Thus, Michael Sandel speaks warmly of:

> those loyalties and convictions whose moral force consists partly in the fact that living by them is inseparable from understanding ourselves as the particular persons we are—as members of this family or community or nation or people, as bearers of this history, as sons and daughters of that revolution, as citizens of this republic.

Sandel continues:

> Allegiances such as these are more than values I happen to have or aims I "espouse at any given time." They go beyond the obligations I voluntarily incur and the "natural duties" I owe to human beings as such. They allow that to some I owe more than justice requires or even permits, not by reason of agreements I have made but instead in virtue of those more or less enduring attachments and commitments which taken together partly *define the person I am*.

Voicing similar sentiments, Alasdair MacIntyre writes:

> We all approach our own circumstances as bearers of a particular social identity. I am someone's son or daugh-

ter, someone else's cousin or uncle; I am a citizen of this or that city, a member of this or that guild or profession; I belong to this clan, that tribe, this nation. Hence what is good for me has to be the good for one who inhabits these roles. As such, I inherit from the past of my family, my city, my tribe, my nation, a variety of debts, inheritances, rightful expectations and obligations. These constitute the given of my life, my moral starting point. This is in part what gives my life its own moral particularity.

For communitarians, these social relationships and communities have a kind of morally normative legitimacy; they define the "moral starting points," to use MacIntyre's phrase, of each individual life. The traditions, practices, and conventions of our communities have at least a *prima facie* legitimate moral claim upon us. MacIntyre does qualify the latter point by conceding that

the fact that the self has to find its moral identity in and through its membership in communities such as those of the family, the neighborhood, the city and the tribe does not entail that the self has to accept the moral limitations of the particularity of those forms of community.

Nevertheless, according to MacIntyre, one's moral quests must begin by "moving forward from such particularity" for it "can never be simply left behind or obliterated."

Despite feminist sympathy toward a social conception of the self and an emphasis on the importance of social relationships, at least three features of the communitarian version of these notions are troubling from a feminist standpoint....

First, the communitarian's metaphysical conception of the social self will not support feminist critiques of ruggedly individualist personality or its associated attributes: the avoidance of intimacy, non-nurturance, social distancing, aggression, or violence. Feminist theorists have often been interested in developing a critique of the norm of the highly individualistic, competitive, aggressive personality type, seeing that personality type as more characteristically male than female and as an important part of the foundation for patriarchy.

Many feminists have theorized that the processes of psycho-gender development, in a society in which early infant care is the primary responsibility of women but not men, result in a radical distinction between the genders in the extent to which the self is constituted by, and self-identifies

with, its relational connections to others. Males are theorized to seek and value autonomy, individuation, separation, and the moral ideals of rights and justice which are thought to depend on a highly individuated conception of persons. By contrast, females are theorized to seek and value connection, sociality, inclusion, and moral ideals of care and nurturance.

From this perspective, highly individuated selves have been viewed as a problem. They are seen as: incapable of human attachments based on mutuality and trust, unresponsive to human needs, approaching social relationships merely as rationally self-interested utility maximizers, thriving on separation and competition, and creating social institutions which tolerate, even legitimize, violence and aggression.

However, a metaphysical view that all human selves are constituted by their social and communal relationships does not itself entail a critique of these highly individualistic selves, or yield any indication of what degree of psychological attachment to others is desirable. On metaphysical grounds alone, there is no reason to suppose that caring, nurturant, relational, sociable selves are better than more autonomous, individualistic, and independent selves. All would be equivalently socially constituted at a metaphysical level. Abstract individualism's failure would be not that it has produced asocial selves, for, on the communitarian view, such beings are metaphysically impossible, but, rather, that it has simply failed theoretically to acknowledge that selves are inherently social. And autonomy, independence, and separateness would become just a different way of being socially constituted, no worse nor better than heteronomy, dependence, or connectedness.

The communitarian conception of the social self, if it were simply a metaphysical view about the constitution of the self (which is what it seems to be), thus provides no basis for regarding nurturant, relational selves as morally superior to those who are highly individualistic. For that reason, it appears to be of no assistance to feminist theorists seeking a normative account of what might be wrong or excessive about competitive self-seeking behaviors or other seeming manifestations of an individualistic perspective. The communitarian "social self," as a metaphysical account of the self, is largely irrelevant to the array of normative tasks which many feminist thinkers have set for a conception of the self.

My second concern about communitarian philosophy has to do with the legitimacy of the communal norms and traditions which are supposed to define the moral starting points of community members. As a matter of moral psychology, it is common for persons to take for granted the moral legitimacy of the norms, traditions, and practices of their communities. However, this point about moral psychology does not entail that those norms and practices really are morally legitimate. It leaves open the question of whether, and to what extent, those claims might "really" be morally binding. Unfortunately, the new communitarians seem sometimes to go beyond the point of moral psychology to a stronger view, namely that the moral claims of communities really are morally binding, at least as "moral starting points." MacIntyre refers to the "debts, inheritances, *rightful* expectations and obligations" which we "inherit" from family, nation and so forth.

But such inheritances are enormously varied. In light of this variety, MacIntyre's normative complacency is quite troubling. Many communities practice the exclusion and suppression of non-group members, especially outsiders defined by ethnicity and sexual orientation. Aren't there "rightful expectations and obligations" *across* community lines? Don't whites, for example, have debts to Blacks and native Americans for histories of exploitation? Didn't Jews, Gypsies, Poles, Czeckoslovakians, and others have "rightful expectations" that Germany would not practice military conquest and unimaginable genocide? Didn't Germany owe reparations to non-Germans for those same genocidal practices? If the new communitarians do not recognize legitimate "debts, inheritances, rightful expectations and obligations" across community lines, then their views have little relevance for our radically heterogeneous modern society. If there are such inter-community obligations which override communal norms and practices, then moral particularity is not accounted for by communal norms alone. In that case, "the" community as such, that is, the relatively bounded and local network of relationships which forms a subject's primary social setting, would not singularly determine the legitimate

moral values or requirements which rightfully constitute the self's moral commitments or self-definition.

Besides excluding or suppressing outsiders, the practices and traditions of numerous communities are exploitative and oppressive toward many of their own members. This problem is of special relevance to women. Feminist theory is rooted in a recognition of the need for change in all the traditions and practices which show gender differentiation; many of these are located in just the sorts of communities invoked by communitarians, for example, family practices and national political traditions. The communitarian emphasis on communities unfortunately dovetails too well with the current popular emphasis on "the family," and seems to harken back to the repressive world, of what some sociologists call communities of "place," the world of family, neighborhood, school, and church, which so intimately enclosed women in oppressive gender politics—the peculiar politics which it has been feminism's distinctive contribution to uncover. Any political theory which appears to support the hegemony of such communities, and which appears to restore them to a position of unquestioned moral authority must be viewed with grave suspicion. I will come back to this issue when I turn to my third objection to communitarian philosophy.

Thus, while admitting into our notion of the self the important constitutive role played by social and communal relationships, we, from a standpoint independent of some particular subject, are not forced to accept as binding on that subject, the moral claims made by the social and communal relationships in which that subject is embedded or by which she is identified. Nor are we required to say that any particular subject is herself morally obliged to accept as binding the moral claims made on her by any of the communities which constitute or define her. To evaluate the moral identities conferred by communities on their members, we need a theory of communities, of their interrelationships, of the structures of power, dominance, and oppression within and among them. Only such a theory would allow us to assess the legitimacy of the claims made by communities upon their members by way of their traditions, practices, and conventions of "debts, inheritances,…expectations, and obligations."

The communitarian approach suggests an attitude of celebrating the attachments which one finds oneself unavoidably to have, the familial ties, and so forth. But some relationships compete with others, and some relationships provide standpoints from which other relationships appear threatening or dangerous to oneself, one's integrity, or one's well-being. In such cases, simple formulas about the value of community provide no guidance. The problem is not simply to appreciate community *per se*, but rather to reconcile the conflicting claims, demands, and identity-defining influences of the variety of communities of which one is a part.

It is worth recalling that liberalism has always condemned, in principle if not in practice, the norms of social hierarchy and political subordination based on inherited or ascribed status. Where liberals historically have applied this tenet at best only to the public realm of civic relationships, feminism seeks to extend it more radically to the "private" realm of family and other communities of place. Those norms and claims of local communities which sustain gender hierarchies have no intrinsic legitimacy from a feminist standpoint. A feminist interest in community must certainly aim for social institutions and relational structures which diminish and, finally, erase gender subordination.

Reflections such as these characterize the concerns of the modern self, the self who acknowledges no *a priori* loyalty to any feature of situation or role, and who claims the right to question the moral legitimacy of any contingent moral claim. We can agree with the communitarians that it would be impossible for the self to question all her contingencies at once, yet at the same time, unlike the communitarians, still emphasize the critical importance of morally questioning various particular communal norms and circumstances....

A third problem with communitarian philosophy has to do with the sorts of communities evidently endorsed by communitarian theorists. Human beings participate in a variety of communities and social relationships, not only across time, but at any one time. However, when people think of "community," it is common for them to think of certain particular social networks, namely, those formed primarily out of family, neighborhood, school, and church....

MacIntyre and Sandel both emphasize family specifically. MacIntyre cites neighborhood along with clan, tribe, city, and nation, while Sandel includes "nation or people,...bearers of this history,...sons and daughters of that revolution,...citizens of this republic."

But where, one might ask, is the International Ladies Garment Workers' Union, the Teamsters, the Democratic Party, Alcoholics Anonymous, or the Committee in Solidarity with the People of El Salvador? Although MacIntyre does mention professions and, rather archaically, "guilds," these references are anomolous in his work, which, for the most part, ignores such communities as trade unions, political action groups, associations of hobbiests, and so forth.

Some of the communities cited by MacIntyre and Sandel will resonate with the historical experiences of women, especially the inclusive communities of family and neighborhood. However, political communities form a particularly suspect class from a feminist standpoint. We all recall how political communities have, until only recently, excluded the legitimate participation of women. It would seem to follow that they have accordingly *not* historically constituted the identities of women in profound ways. As "daughters" of an American revolution spawned parthenogenically by the "fathers" of our country, we find our political community to have denied us the self-identifying heritage of our cultural *mothers*. In general, the contribution made to the identities of various groups of people by political communities is quite uneven, given that they are communities to which many are subject, but in which far fewer actively participate.

At any rate, there is an underlying commonality to most of the communities which MacIntyre and Sandel cite as constitutive of self-identity and definitive of our moral starting points. Sandel himself explicates this commonality when he writes that, for people "bound by a sense of community," the notion of community describes:

> not a relationship they choose (as in a voluntary association) but an attachment they discover, not merely an attribute but a constituent of their identity. (italics mine.)

Not voluntary but "discovered" relationships and communities are what Sandel takes to define subjective identity for those who are bound by a "sense of community." It is the communities to which we are involuntarily bound to which Sandel accords metaphysical pride of place in the constitution of subjectivity. What are important are not simply the "associations" in which people "cooperate," but the "communities" in which people "participate," for these latter:

> describe a form of life in which the members find themselves commonly situated "to begin with," their commonality consisting less in relationships they have entered than in attachments they have found.

Thus, the social relationships which one finds, the attachments which are discovered and not chosen, become the points of reference for self-definition by the communitarian subject.

For the child maturing to self-consciousness in her community of origin, typically a complex of family, neighborhood, school, and church, it seems uncontroversial that "the" community is found, not entered: discovered, not created. But this need not be true of an adult's communities of mature self-identification. Many communities are, for at least some of their members, communities of choice to a significant extent: labor unions, philanthropic associations, political coalitions, and, if one has ever moved or migrated, even the communities of neighborhood, church, city, or nation-state might have been chosen to an important extent. One need not have simply discovered oneself to be embedded in them in order that one's identity or the moral particulars of one's life be defined by them. Sandel is right to indicate the role of found communities in constituting the unreflective, "given" identity which the self discovers when first beginning to reflect on herself. But for mature self-identity, we should also recognize a legitimate role for communities of choice, supplementing, if not displacing, the communities and attachments which are merely found....

Thus, the commitments and loyalties of our found communities, our communities of origin, may harbor ambiguities, ambivalences, contradictions, and oppressions which complicate as well as constitute identity, and which have to be sorted out, critically scrutinized. In these undertakings, we are likely to utilize resources and skills derived from various communities and relationships, both those which are chosen or created, as well as those which are found or discovered. Thus, our theories of community should recognize that resources and skills derived from communities which are not merely found or discovered may equally well contribute to the constitution of identity. The constitution of identity and moral particularity, for the modern self, may well require the contribution of radically different communities from those invoked by communitarians.

The whole tenor of communitarian thinking would change once we opened up the conception of the social self to encompass chosen communities, especially those which lie beyond the typical original community of family-neighborhood-school-church. No longer would communitarian thought present a seemingly conservative complacency about the private and local communities of place which have so effectively circumscribed, in particular, the lives of most women....

My goals are twofold: to retain the communitarian insights about the contribution of community and social relationship to self-identity, yet open up for critical reflection the moral particulars imparted by those communities, and identify the sorts of communities which will provide nonoppressive and enriched lives for women.

Toward this end, it will be helpful to consider models of human relationship and community which contrast with those cited by communitarians. I believe that modern friendship and urban community can offer us crucial insights into the social nature of the modern self. It is in moving forward from these relationships that we have the best chance of reconciling the communitarian conception of the social self with the longed-for communities of feminist aspiration.

Both modern friendship and the stereotypical urban community share an important feature which is either neglected or deliberately avoided in communitarian conceptions of human relationship. From a liberal, or Enlightenment, or modernist standpoint, this feature would be characterized as voluntariness: those relationships are based partly on choice.

Let's first consider friendship as it is understood in this culture. Friends are supposed to be people whom one chooses on one's own to share activities and intimacies. No particular people are assigned by custom or tradition to be a person's friends.

From among the larger number of one's acquaintances, one moves toward closer and more friendlike relationships with some of them, motivated by one's own needs, values, and attractions. No consanguineal or legal connections establish or maintain ties of friendship. As this relationship is widely understood in our culture, its basis lies in voluntary choice.

In this context, "voluntary choice" refers to motivations arising out of one's own needs, desires, interests, values, and attractions, in contrast to motivations arising from what is socially assigned, ascribed, expected, or demanded. Because of its basis in voluntary choice, friendship is more likely than many other relationships, such as those of family and neighborhood, to be grounded and sustained by shared interests and values, mutual affection, and possibilities for generating reciprocal respect and esteem.

In general friendship has had an obvious importance to feminist aspirations as the basis of the bond which is (ironically) called "sisterhood." Friendship among women has been the cement not only of the various historical waves of the feminist movement, but as well of numerous communities of women throughout history who defied the local conventions for their gender and lived lives of creative disorder. In all these cases, women moved out of their given or found communities into new attachments with other women by their own choice, that is, motivated by their own needs, desires, attractions, and fears, rather than, and often in opposition to, the expectations and ascribed roles of their found communities.

Like friendship, many urban relationships are also based more on choice than on socially ascribed roles, biological connections or other nonvoluntary ties. Urban communities include numerous voluntary associations such as political action groups, support groups, associations of co-hobbiests, and so on. But while friendship is almost universally extolled, urban communities and relationships have been theorized in wildly contradictory ways. Cities have sometimes been taken as "harbingers" of modern culture *per se*, and have been particularly associated with the major social trends of modern life, such as industrialization and bureaucratization. The results of these trends are often thought to have been a fragmentation of "real" community, and the widely-lamented alienation of modern urban life: people seldom know their neighbors; population concentration generates massive psychic overload; fear and mutual distrust, even outright hostility, generated by the dangers of urban life, may dominate most daily associations. Under such circumstances, meaningful relationships are often theorized to be rare, if at all possible.

But is this image a complete portrait of urban life? It is probably true, in urban areas, that communities of *place* are diminished in importance; neighborhood plays a far less significant role in constituting community than it does in nonurban areas. But this does not mean that the social networks and communities of urban dwellers are inferior to those of non-urban residents.

Much evidence suggests that urban settings do not, as commonly stereotyped, promote only alienation, isolation, and psychic breakdown. The communities available to urban dwellers are different from those available to non-urban dwellers, but not necessarily less gratifying or fulfilling. Communities of place are relatively non-voluntary; for example, one's extended family of origin is given or ascribed, and the relationships found as one grows. Sociological research has shown that urban dwellers tend to form their social networks, their communities, out of people who are brought together for reasons other than geographical proximity....

As the sociologist, Claude Fischer, has stated it, in urban areas, "population concentration stimulates allegiances to subcultures based on more significant social traits" than common locality or neighborhood. Communities of place, centered around family-neighborhood-church-school are more likely, for urban dwellers, to be supplanted by other sorts of communities, resulting in what the sociologist Melvin Webber has called "community without propinquity." But most importantly for our purposes, these are still often genuine communities, and not the cesspools of "Rum, Romanism, and Rebellion" sometimes depicted by anti-urbanists.

Literature reveals that women writers have been both repelled and inspired by urban communities. The city, as a concentrated center of male political and economic power, seems to exclude women altogether. However, as literary critic Susan Merrill Squier points out, the city can provide women with jobs, education, and the cultural tools with which to escape imposed gender roles, familial demands, and domestic servitude. The city can also bring women together, in work or in leisure, and lay the basis for bonds of sisterhood. The quests of women who journey to cities leaving behind men, home, and family, are subversive, writes literary critic Blanche Gelfant, and may well be perceived by others "as assaults upon society." Cities open up for women possibilities of supplanting communities of place with relationships and communities of choice. Thus, urban communities of choice can provide the resources for women to surmount the moral particularities of family and place which define and limit their moral starting points.

Social theorists have long decried the interpersonal estrangement of urban life, an observation which seems predominantly inspired by the public world of conflict between various subcultural groups. Urbanism does not create interpersonal estrangement *within* subcultures but, rather, tends to promote social involvement. This is especially true for people with special backgrounds and interests, for people who are members of small minorities, and for ethnic groups. Fischer has found that social relationships in urban centers are more:

culturally specialized: urbanites were relatively involved with associates in the social world they considered most important and relatively uninvolved with associates, if any, in other worlds.

As Fischer summarizes it, "Urbanism...fosters social involvement in the subculture(s) of *choice*, rather than the subculture(s) of circumstances." This is doubtless reinforced by the recent more militant expression of group values and group demands for rights and respect on the parts of urban subcultural minorities.

We might describe urban relationships as being characteristically "modern" to signal their relatively greater voluntary basis. We find, in these relationships and the social networks formed of them, not a loss of community, but an increase in importance of community of a different sort from that of family-neighborhood-church-school complexes. Yet these more voluntary communities

may be as deeply constitutive of the identities and particulars of the individuals who participate in them as are the communities of place so warmly invoked by communitarians....

To be sure, non-voluntary communities of place are not without value. Most lives contain mixtures of relationships and communities, some given/found/discovered, and some chosen/created. Most people probably are, to some extent, ineradicably constituted by their communities of place, their original families, neighborhoods, schools, churches, or nations. It is noteworthy that dependent children, elderly persons, and all other individuals whose lives and well-being are at great risk, need the support of communities whose other members do not or cannot choose arbitrarily to leave. Recent philosophical reflection on communities and relationships not founded or sustained by choice has brought out the importance of these social networks for the constitution of social life. But these insights should not obscure the additional need for communities of choice to counter oppressive and abusive relational structures in those non-voluntary communities by providing models of alternative social relationships and standpoints for critical reflection on self and community.

Having attained a critically reflective stance toward one's communities of origin, one's community of place, toward family, neighborhood, church, school, and nation, one has probably at the same time already begun to question and distance oneself from aspects of one's "identity" in that community, and, therefore, to have embarked on the path of personal redefinition. From such a perspective, the communities of place uncritically invoked by the communitarians appear deeply problematic. We can concede the influence of those communities without having unreflectively to endorse it. We must develop communitarian thought beyond its complacent regard for the communities in which we once found ourselves toward (and beyond) an awareness of the crucial importance of "dislocated" communities, communities of choice.

"The Communitarian Critique of Liberalism"

Michael Walzer

Intellectual fashions are notoriously short-lived, very much like fashions in popular music, art, or dress. But there are certain fashions that seem regularly to reappear. Like pleated trousers or short skirts, they are inconstant features of a larger and more steadily prevailing phenomenon—in this case, a certain way of dressing. They have brief but recurrent lives; we know their transience and expect their return. Needless to say, there is no afterlife in which trousers will be permanently pleated or skirts forever short. Recurrence is all.

Although it operates at a much higher level (an infinitely higher level?) of cultural significance, the communitarian critique of liberalism is like the pleating of trousers: transient but certain to return. It is a consistently intermittent feature of liberal politics and social organization. No liberal success will make it permanently unattractive. At the same time, no communitarian critique, however penetrating, will ever be anything more than an inconstant feature of liberalism. Someday, perhaps, there will be a larger transformation, like the shift from aristocratic knee-breeches to plebian pants, rendering liberalism and its critics alike irrelevant. But I see no present signs of anything like that, nor am I sure that we should look forward to it. For now, there is much to be said for a recurrent critique, whose protagonists hope only for small victories, partial incorporations, and when they are rebuffed or dismissed or coopted, fade away for a time only to return.

Communitarianism is usefully contrasted with social democracy, which has succeeded in establishing a permanent presence alongside of and sometimes conjoined with liberal politics. Social democracy has its own intermittently fashionable critics, largely anarchist and libertarian in character. Since it sponsors certain sorts of communal identification, it is less subject to communitarian criticism than liberalism is. But it can never escape such criticism entirely, for liberals and social democrats alike share a commitment to economic growth and cope (although in different ways) with the deracinated social forms that growth produces. Community itself is largely an ideological presence in modern society; it has no recurrent critics of its own. It is intermittently fashionable only because it no longer exists in anything like full strength, and it is criticized only when it is fashionable.

The communitarian critique is nonetheless a powerful one; it would not recur if it were not capable of engaging our minds and feelings. In this essay, I want to investigate the power of its current American versions and then offer a version of my own—less powerful, perhaps, than the ones with which I shall begin, but more available for incorporation within liberal (or social democratic) politics. I do not mean (I hardly have the capacity) to lay communitarianism to rest, although I would willingly wait for its reappearance in a form more coherent and incisive than that in which it currently appears. The problem with communitarian criticism today—I am not the first to notice this—is that it suggests two different, and deeply contradictory, arguments against liberalism. One of these arguments is aimed primarily at liberal practice, the other primarily at liberal theory, but they cannot both be right. It is possible that each one is partly right—indeed, I shall insist on just this partial validity—but each of the arguments is right in a way that undercuts the value of the other.

The first argument holds that liberal political theory accurately represents liberal social practice. As if the Marxist account of ideological reflection were literally true, and exemplified here, contem-

From "The Communitarian Critique of Liberalism," *Political Theory*, Vol. 18 (1990). Reprinted by permission of the publisher

porary Western societies (American society especially) are taken to be the home of radically isolated individuals, rational egotists, and existential agents, men and women protected and divided by their inalienable rights. Liberalism tells the truth about the asocial society that liberals create—not, in fact, *ex nihilo* as their theory suggests, but in a struggle against traditions and communities and authorities that are forgotten as soon as they are escaped, so that liberal practices seem to have no history. The struggle itself is ritually celebrated but rarely reflected on. The members of liberal society share no political or religious traditions; they can tell only one story about themselves and that is the story of *ex nihilo* creation, which begins in the state of nature or the original position. Each individual imagines himself absolutely free, unencumbered, and on his own—and enters society, accepting its obligations, only in order to minimize his risks. His goal is security, and security is, as Marx wrote, "the assurance of his egoism."…

The writings of the young Marx represent one of the early appearances of communitarian criticism, and his argument, first made in the 1840s, is powerfully present today. Alastair MacIntyre's description of the incoherence of modern intellectual and cultural life and the loss of narrative capacity makes a similar point in updated, state-of-the-art, theoretical language. But the only theory that is necessary to the communitarian critique of liberalism is liberalism itself. All that the critics have to do, so they say is to take liberal theory seriously. The self-portrait of the individual constituted only by his willfulness, liberated from all connection, without common values, binding ties, customs, or traditions—sans eyes, sans teeth, sans taste, sans everything—need only be evoked in order to be devalued: It is already the concrete absence of value. What can the real life of such a person be like? Imagine him maximizing his utilities, and society is turned into a war of all against all, the familiar rat race, in which, as Hobbes wrote, there is "no other goal, nor other garland, but being foremost." Imagine him enjoying his rights, and society is reduced to the coexistence of isolated selves.…They are concretely expressed in separation, divorce, withdrawal, solitude, privacy, and political apathy. And finally, the very fact that individual life can be described in these two philosophical languages, the language of utilities and

the language of rights, is a further mark, says MacIntyre, of its incoherence: Men and women in liberal society no longer have access to a single moral culture within which they can learn how they ought to live. There is no consensus, no public meeting-of-minds, on the nature of the good life, hence the triumph of private caprice, revealed, for example, in Sartrean existentialism, the ideological reflection of everyday capriciousness.

We liberals are free to choose, and we have a right to chose, but we have no criteria to govern our choices except our own wayward understanding of our wayward interests and desires. And so our choices lack the qualities of cohesion and consecutiveness. We can hardly remember what we did yesterday; we cannot with any assurance predict what we will do tomorrow. We cannot give a proper account of ourselves. We cannot sit together and tell comprehensible stories, and we recognize ourselves in the stories we read only when these are fragmented narratives, without plots, the literary equivalent of atonal music and nonrepresentational art.

Liberal society, seen in the light of this first communitarian critique, is fragmentation in practice; and community is the exact opposite, the home of coherence, connection, and narrative capacity. But I am less concerned here with the different accounts that might be provided of this lost Eden than I am with the repeated insistence on the reality of fragmentation after the loss. This is the common theme of all contemporary communitarianisms: neoconservative lamentation, neo-Marxist indictment, and neoclassical or republican hand-wringing. (The need for the prefix "neo" suggests again the intermittent or recurrent character of communitarian criticism.) I should think it would be an awkward theme, for if the sociological argument of liberal theory is right, if society is actually decomposed, without residue, into the problematic coexistence of individuals, then we might well assume that liberal politics is the best way to deal with the problems of decomposition. If we have to create an artificial and a historical union out of a multitude of isolated selves, why not take the state of nature or the original position as our conceptual starting point? Why not accept, in standard liberal fashion, the priority of procedural justice over substantive conceptions of the good, since we can hardly expect, given our fragmentation, to agree about the good? Michael Sandel asks whether a community of those who put justice first can ever be more than a community of strangers. The question is a good one, but its reverse form is more immediately relevant: If we really are a community of strangers, how can we do anything else but put justice first?

We are saved from this entirely plausible line of argument by the second communitarian critique of liberalism. The second critique holds that liberal theory radically misrepresents real life. The world is not like that nor could it be. Men and women cut loose from all social ties, literally unencumbered, each one the one and only inventor of his or her own life, with no criteria, no common standards, to guide the invention—these are mythical figures. How can any group of people be strangers to one another when each member of the group is born with parents, and when these parents have friends, relatives, neighbors, comrades at work, coreligionists, and fellow citizens—connections, in fact, which are not so much chosen as passed on and inherited? Liberalism may well enhance the significance of purely contractual ties, but it is obviously false to suggest, as Hobbes sometimes seemed to do, that all our connections are mere "market friendships," voluntarist and self-interested in character, which cannot outlast the advantages they bring. It is in the very nature of a human society that individuals bred within it will find themselves caught up in patterns of relationship, networks of power, and communities of meaning. That quality of being caught up is what makes them persons of a certain sort. And only then can they make themselves persons of a (marginally) different sort by reflecting on what they are and by acting in more or less distinctive ways within the patterns, networks, and communities that are willy-nilly theirs.

The burden of the second critique is that the deep structure even of liberal society is in fact communitarian. Liberal theory distorts this reality and, insofar as we adopt the theory, deprives us of any ready access to our own experience of communal embeddedness. The rhetoric of liberalism—this is the argument of the authors of *Habits of the Heart*—limits our understanding of our own heart's habits, and gives us no way to formulate the convictions that hold us together as persons and that bind persons together into a community. The

assumption here is that we are in fact persons and that we are in fact bound together. The liberal ideology of separatism cannot take personhood and bondedness away from us. What it does take away is the *sense* of our personhood and bondedness, and this deprivation is then reflected in liberal politics. It explains our inability to form cohesive solidarities, stable movements and parties, that might make our deep convictions visible and effective in the world. It also explains our radical dependence (brilliantly foreshadowed in Hobbes's *Leviathan*) on the central state.

But how are we to understand this extraordinary disjunction between communal experience and liberal ideology, between personal conviction and public rhetoric, and between social bondedness and political isolation? That question is not addressed by communitarian critics of the second sort. If the first critique depends on a vulgar Marxist theory of reflection, the second critique requires an equally vulgar idealism. Liberal theory now seems to have a power over and against real life that has been granted to few theories in human history. Plainly, it has not been granted to communitarian theory, which cannot, on the first argument, overcome the reality of liberal separatism and cannot, on the second argument, evoke the already existing structures of social connection. In any case, the two critical arguments are mutually inconsistent; they cannot both be true. Liberal separatism either represents or misrepresents the conditions of everyday life. It might, of course, do a little of each—the usual muddle—but that is not a satisfactory conclusion from a communitarian standpoint. For if the account of dissociation and separatism is even partly right, then we have to raise questions about the depth, so to speak, of the deep structure. And if we are all to some degree communitarians under the skin, then the portrait of social incoherence loses its critical force.

But each of the two critical arguments is partly right. I will try to say what is right about each, and then ask if something plausible can be made of the parts. First, then, there cannot be much doubt that we (in the United States) live in a society where individuals are relatively dissociated and separated from one another, or better, where they are continually separating from one another—continually in motion, often in solitary and apparently random motion, as if in imitation of what physicists call

Brownian movement. Hence we live in a profoundly unsettled society. We can best see the forms of unsettlement if we track the most important moves. So, consider (imitating the Chinese style) the Four Mobilities:

1. *Geographic mobility*. Americans apparently change their residence more often than any people in history, at least since the barbarian migrations, excluding only nomadic tribes and families caught up in civil or foreign wars. Moving people and their possessions from one city or town to another is a major industry in the United States, even though many people manage to move themselves. In another sense, of course, we are all self-moved, not refugees but voluntary migrants. The sense of place must be greatly weakened by this extensive geographic mobility, although I find it hard to say whether it is superseded by mere insensitivity or by a new sense of many places. Either way, communitarian feeling seems likely to decline in importance. Communities are more than just locations, but they are most often successful when they are permanently located.

2. *Social mobility*. This article will not address the arguments about how best to describe social standing or how to measure changes, whether by income, education, class membership, or rank in the status hierarchy. It is enough to say that fewer Americans stand exactly where their parents stood or do what they did than in any society for which we have comparable knowledge. Americans may inherit many things from their parents, but the extent to which they make a different life, if only by making a different living, means that the inheritance of community, that is, the passing on of beliefs and customary ways, is uncertain at best. Whether or not children are thereby robbed of narrative capacity, they seem likely to tell different stories than their parents told.

3. *Marital mobility*. Rates of separation, divorce, and remarriage are higher today than they have ever been in our own society and probably higher than they have ever been in any other (except perhaps among Roman aristocrats, although I know of no statistics from that time, only anecdotes). The first two mobilities, geographic and social, also disrupt family life, so that siblings, for example, often live at great distances from one another, and later as uncles and aunts, they are far removed from nephews and nieces. But what we call "broken homes" are the product of marital breaks, of husbands or wives moving out— and then, commonly, moving on to new partners. Insofar as home is the first community and the first school of ethnic identity and religious conviction, this kind of breakage must have countercommuni-

tarian consequences. It means that children often do not hear continuous or identical stories from the adults with whom they live. (Did the greater number of children ever hear such stories? The death of one spouse and the remarriage of the other may once have been as common as divorce and remarriage are today. But, then, other sorts of mobility have to be considered: Both men and women are more likely today to marry across class, ethnic, and religious lines; remarriage will therefore often produce extraordinarily complex and socially diverse families—which probably are without historical precedent.)

4. *Political mobility*. Loyalty to leaders, movements, parties, clubs, and urban machines seems to decline rapidly as place and social standing and family membership become less central in the shaping of personal identity. Liberal citizens stand outside all political organizations and then choose the one that best serves their ideals or interests. They are, ideally, independent voters, that is, people who move around; they choose for themselves rather than voting as their parents did, and they choose freshly each time rather than repeating themselves. As their numbers increase, they make for a volatile electorate and hence for institutional instability, particularly at the local level where political organization once served to reinforce communal ties.

The effects of the Four Mobilities are intensified in a variety of ways by other social developments which we are likely to talk about in the common metaphor of movement: the advance of knowledge, technological progress, and so on. But I am concerned here only with the actual movement of individuals. Liberalism is, most simply, the theoretical endorsement and justification of this movement. In the liberal view, then, the Four Mobilities represent the enactment of liberty, and the pursuit of (private or personal) happiness. And it has to be said that, conceived in this way, liberalism is a genuinely popular creed. Any effort to curtail mobility in the four areas described here would require a massive and harsh application of state power. Nevertheless, this popularity has an underside of sadness and discontent that are intermittently articulated, and communitarianism is, most simply, the intermittent articulation of these feelings. It reflects a sense of loss, and the loss is real. People do not always leave their old neighborhoods or hometowns willingly or happily. Moving may be a personal adventure in our standard cultural mythologies, but it is often a family trauma in real life. The same thing is true of social mobility, which carries people down as well as up and requires adjustments that are never easy to manage. Marital breaks may sometimes give rise to new and stronger unions, but they also pile up what we might think of as family fragments: single-parent households, separated and lonely men and women, and abandoned children. And independence in politics is often a not-so-splendid isolation: Individuals with opinions are cut loose from groups with programs. The result is a decline in "the sense of efficacy," with accompanying effects on commitment and morale.

All in all, we liberals probably know one another less well, and with less assurance, than people once did, although we may see more aspects of the other than they saw, and recognize in him or her a wider range of possibilities (including the possibility of moving on). We are more often alone than people once were, being without neighbors we can count on, relatives who live nearby or with whom we are close, or comrades at work or in the movement. This is the truth of the first communitarian argument. We must now fix the limits of this truth by seeking what is true in the second argument.

In its easiest version, the second argument— that we are really, at bottom, creatures of community—is certainly true but of uncertain significance. The ties of place, class or status, family, and even politics survive the Four Mobilities to a remarkable extent. To take just one example, from the last of the Four: It remains true, even today in this most liberal and mobile of societies, that the best predictor of how people will vote is our knowledge of how their parents voted....But we do not know to what extent inheritances of this sort are a dwindling communal resource; it may be that each generation passes on less than it received. The full liberalization of the social order, the production and reproduction of self-inventing individuals, may take a long time, much longer, indeed, than liberals themselves expected. There is not much comfort here for communitarian critics, however, while they can recognize and value the survival of older ways of life, they cannot count on, and they must have anxieties about, the vitality of those ways.

But there is another approach to the truth of the second critical argument. Whatever the extent of the Four Mobilities, they do not seem to move us so far apart that we can no longer talk with one another. We often disagree, of course, but we disagree in mutually comprehensible ways. I should think it fairly obvious that the philosophical controversies that MacIntyre laments are not in fact a mark of social incoherence. Where there are philosophers, there will be controversies, just as where there are knights, there will be tournaments. But these are highly ritualized activities, which bear witness to the connection, not the disconnection, of their protagonists. Even political conflict in liberal societies rarely takes forms so extreme as to set its protagonists beyond negotiation and compromise, procedural justice, and the very possibility of speech. The American civil rights struggle is a nice example of a conflict for which our moral/political language was and is entirely adequate. The fact that the struggle has had only partial success does not reflect linguistic inadequacy but rather political failures and defeats.

Martin Luther King's speeches evoked a palpable tradition, a set of common values such that public disagreement could focus only on how (or how quickly) they might best be realized. But this is not, so to speak, a traditionalist tradition, a *Gemeinschaft* tradition, a survival of the preliberal past. It is a liberal tradition modified, no doubt, by survivals of different sorts. The modifications are most obviously Protestant and republican in character, though by no means exclusively so: The years of mass immigration have brought a great variety of ethnic and religious memories to bear on American politics. What all of them bear on, however, is liberalism. The language of individual rights—voluntary association, pluralism, toleration, separation, privacy, free speech, the career open to talents, and so on—is simply inescapable. Who among us seriously attempts to escape? If we really are situated selves, as the second communitarian critique holds, then our situation is largely captured by that vocabulary. This is the truth of the second critique. Does it make any sense then to argue that liberalism prevents us from understanding or maintaining the ties that bind us together?

It makes some sense, because liberalism is a strange doctrine, which seems continually to undercut itself, to disdain its own traditions, and to produce in each generation renewed hopes for a more absolute freedom from history and society alike. Much of liberal political theory, from Locke to Rawls, is an effort to fix and stabilize the doctrine in order to end the endlessness of liberal liberation....

Liberalism is a self-subverting doctrine; for that reason, it really does require periodic communitarian correction. But it is not a particularly helpful form of correction to suggest that liberalism is literally incoherent or that it can be replaced by some preliberal or antiliberal community waiting somehow just beneath the surface or just beyond the horizon. Nothing is waiting; American communitarians have to recognize that there is no one out there but separated, rights-bearing, voluntarily associating, freely speaking, liberal selves. It would be a good thing, though, if we could teach those selves to know themselves as social beings, the historical products of, and in part the embodiments of, liberal values. For the communitarian correction of liberalism cannot be anything other than a selective reinforcement of those same values or, to appropriate the well-known phrase of Michael Oakeshott, a pursuit of the intimations of community within them.

The place to begin the pursuit is with the liberal idea of voluntary association, which is not well-understood, it seems to me, either among liberals or among their communitarian critics. In both its theory and its practice, liberalism expresses strong associative tendencies alongside its dissociative tendencies: Its protagonists form groups as well as split off from the groups they form; they join up and resign, marry and divorce. Nevertheless, it is a mistake, and a characterically liberal mistake, to think that the existing patterns of association are entirely or even largely voluntary and contractual, that is, the product of will alone. In a liberal society, as in every other society, people are born into very important sorts of groups, born with identities, male or female, for example, working class, Catholic or Jewish, black, democrat, and so on. Many of their subsequent associations (like their subsequent careers) merely express these underlying identities, which, again, are not so much chosen as enacted. Liberalism is distinguished less by the freedom to form groups on the basis of these identities than the freedom to leave the groups and sometimes even the identities behind. Association is always at risk in a liberal society. The boundaries

of the group are not policed; people come and go, or they just fade into the distance without ever quite acknowledging that they have left. That is why liberalism is plagued by free-rider problems—by people who continue to enjoy the benefits of membership and identity while no longer participating in the activities that produce those benefits. Communitarianism, by contrast, is the dream of a perfect free-riderlessness.

At its best, the liberal society is the social union of social unions that John Rawls described: a pluralism of groups bonded by shared ideas of toleration and democracy. But if all the groups are precarious, continually on the brink of dissolution or abandonment, then the larger union must also be weak and vulnerable. Or, alternatively, its leaders and officials will be driven to compensate for the failures of association elsewhere by strengthening their own union, that is, the central state, beyond the limits that liberalism has established. These limits are best expressed in terms of individual rights and civil liberties, but they also include a prescription for state neutrality. The good life is pursued by individuals, sponsored by groups; the state presides over the pursuit and the sponsorship but does not participate in either. Presiding is singular in character; pursuing and sponsoring are plural. Hence it is a critical question for liberal theory and practice whether the associative passions and energies of ordinary people are likely over the long haul to survive the Four Mobilities and prove themselves sufficient to the requirements of pluralism. There is at least some evidence that they will not prove sufficient—without a little help. But, to repeat an old question, whence cometh our help? A few of the existing social unions live in the expectation of divine assistance. For the rest, we can only help one another, and the agency through which help of that sort comes most expeditiously is the state. But what kind of a state is it that fosters associative activities? What kind of a social union is it that includes without incorporating a great and discordant variety of social unions?

Obviously, it is a liberal state and social union; any other kind is too dangerous for communities and individuals alike. It would be an odd enterprise to argue in the name of communitarianism for an alternative state, for that would be to argue against our own political traditions and to repudiate whatever community we already have. But the communitarian correction does require a liberal state of a certain sort, conceptually though not historically unusual: a state that is, at least over some part of the terrain of sovereignty, deliberately nonneutral. The standard liberal argument for neutrality is an induction from social fragmentation. Since dissociated individuals will never agree on the good life, the state must allow them to live as they think best, subject only to John Stuart Mill's harm principle, without endorsing or sponsoring any particular understanding of what "best" means. But there is a problem here: The more dissociated individuals are, the stronger the state is likely to be, since it will be the only or the most important social union. And then membership in the state, the only good that is shared by all individuals, may well come to seem the good that is "best."

This is only to repeat the first communitarian critique, and it invites a response like the second critique: that the state is not in fact the only or even, for ordinary people in their everyday lives, the most important social union. All sorts of other groups continue to exist and to give shape and purpose to the lives of their members, despite the triumph of individual rights, the Four Mobilities in which that triumph is manifest, and the free-riding that it makes possible. But these groups are continually at risk. And so the state, if it is to remain a liberal state, must endorse and sponsor some of them, namely, those that seem most likely to provide shapes and purposes congenial to the shared values of a liberal society....

Let me give three relatively familiar examples of state behavior of this kind. First, the Wagner Act of the 1930s: This was not a standard liberal law, hindering the hindrances to union organization, for it actively fostered union organization, and it did so precisely by solving the free-rider problem. By requiring collective bargaining whenever there was majority support (but not necessarily unanimous support) for the union, and then by allowing union shops, the Wagner Act sponsored the creation of strong unions capable, at least to some degree, of determining the shape of industrial relations....

The second example is the use of tax exemptions and matching grants of tax money to enable different religious groups to run extensive systems of day-care centers, nursing homes, hospitals, and

so on—welfare societies inside the welfare state. I do not pretend that these private and pluralist societies compensate for the shoddiness of the American welfare state. But they do improve the delivery of services by making it a more immediate function of communal solidarity....The liberal response is that the social union of social unions must always operate at two levels: A welfare system run entirely by private, nonprofit associations would be dangerously inadequate and inequitable in its coverage; and a totally nationalized system would deny expression to local and particularist solidarities.

The third example is the passage of plant-closing laws designed to afford some protection to local communities of work and residence. Inhabitants are insulated, although only for a time, against market pressure to move out of their old neighborhoods and search for work elsewhere. Although the market "needs" a highly mobile work force, the state takes other needs into account, not only in a welfarist way (through unemployment insurance and job retraining programs) but also in a communitarian way. But the state is not similarly committed to the preservation of every neighborhood community. It is entirely neutral toward communities of ethnicity and residence, offering no protection against strangers who want to move in. Here, geographic mobility remains a positive value, one of the rights of citizens.

Unions, religious organizations, and neighborhoods each draw on feelings and beliefs that, in principle if not always in history, predate the emergence of the liberal state...communal feeling and belief seem considerably more stable than we once thought they would be, and the proliferation of secondary associations in liberal society is remarkable—even if many of them have short lives and transient memberships. One has a sense of people working together and trying to cope, and not, as the first communitarian critique suggests, just getting by on their own, by themselves, one by one....

I have avoided until now what is often taken to be the central issue between liberals and their communitarian critics—the constitution of the self. Liberalism, it is commonly said, is founded on the idea of a presocial self, a solitary and sometimes heroic individual confronting society, who is fully formed before the confrontation begins. Communitarian critics then argue, first, that instability and dissociation are the actual and disheartening achievement of individuals of this sort and, second, that there really cannot be individuals of this sort. The critics are commonly said in turn to believe in a radically socialized self that can never "confront" society because it is, from the beginning, entangled in society, itself the embodiment of social values. The disagreement seems sharp enough, but in fact, in practice, it is not sharp at all—for neither of these views can be sustained for long by anyone who goes beyond staking out a position and tries to elaborate an argument. Nor does liberal or communitarian theory require views of this sort. Contemporary liberals are not committed to a presocial self, but only to a self capable of reflecting critically on the values that have governed its socialization; and communitarian critics, who are doing exactly that, can hardly go on to claim that socialization is everything. The philosophical and psychological issues here go very deep, but so far as politics is concerned, there is little to be won on this battlefield; concessions from the other side come too easily to count as victories.

The central issue for political theory is not the constitution of the self but the connection of constituted selves, the pattern of social relations. Liberalism is best understood as a theory of relationship, which has voluntary association at its center and which understands voluntariness as the right of rupture or withdrawal. What makes a marriage voluntary is the permanent possibility of divorce. What makes any identity or affiliation voluntary is the easy availability of alternative identities and affiliations. But the easier this easiness is, the less stable all our relationships are likely to become. The Four Mobilities take hold and society seems to be in perpetual motion, so that the actual subject of liberal practice, it might be said, is not a presocial but a postsocial self, free at last from all but the most temporary and limited alliances. Now, the liberal self reflects the fragmentation of liberal society: It is radically undetermined and divided, forced to invent itself anew for every public occasion. Some liberals celebrate this freedom and self-invention; all communitarians lament its arrival, even while insisting that it is not a possible human condition.

I have argued that insofar as liberalism tends toward instability and dissociation, it requires periodic communitarian correction....

There is no strong or permanent remedy for communal attenuation short of an antiliberal curtailment of the Four Mobilities and the rights of rupture and divorce on which they rest. Communitarians sometimes dream of such a curtailment, but they rarely advocate it. The only community that most of them actually know, after all, is just this liberal union of unions, always precarious and always at risk. They cannot triumph over this liberalism; they can only, sometimes, reinforce its internal associative capacities. The reinforcement is only temporary, because the capacity for dissociation is also strongly internalized and highly valued. That is why communitarianism criticism is doomed—it probably is not a terrible fate—to eternal recurrence.

6   The Extent of Personal Liberty

A society is always made up of different individuals with different temperaments and person-alities. For these different individuals to come together as a society there must be some cohesive forces which bind individual people together. In some communities these cohesive forces come mainly through custom, tradition, religion, and the like. However, over most of the world today, state power is the primary agency used to ensure stability of the community by enforcing standards of behavior. The least controversial behavior is that which directly and tangibly harms other people. Few would question the need to prohibit rape, robbery, or murder. A society which tolerated that sort of behavior would not continue to long exist. But there are three areas concerning control of the individual about which reasonable persons can and do disagree.

The first issue concerns whether society, through state action, ought to strive to achieve the well-being of its citizens, even if this requires restrictions on individuals which they themselves oppose. Plato contended that one of the most important functions of a state is to enact legislation which will contribute to the moral virtue of the citizenry. This led him to justify state censorship of all literary and artistic productions since he thought that being exposed to certain art forms could arouse emotions and encourage undisciplined behavior. John Stuart Mill, on the other hand, argued that it is wrong for anyone, including the state, to interfere with another's behavior in order to prevent him from harming himself either morally or physically.

While one form of paternalism is to force an individual to conform to our set of values for their own good, not all paternalism is moral paternalism. Helmet and seat-belt laws are examples in which it is not the *moral* well-being of the individual which is at stake but rather their *physical* well-being. Increasingly citizens demand paternalistic legislation, such as consumer protection laws. Other examples of nonmoral paternalism are usuary laws which prevent us from borrowing at a high interest rate even if we wish to (or feel we must), as well as social security legislation which forces us to save for our old age even if we would rather spend the money now. The implication here is interesting—the more we *need* to do something which may be bad for us the less able we are to decide for ourselves freely and voluntarily. The more financially desperate I am, the less voluntary is my consent to loans at extremely high interest rates and therefore the more I need to be protected from myself. Suppose we want to test possibly dangerous new drugs on humans before putting them on the market. Those in our experiment must give their "free and informed consent." So we offer homeless "street people" in a northern city in the middle of winter six weeks' free room and board with hot showers and clean sheets if they will volunteer for our drug testing program. Are the participants who sign our consent forms really "freely" consenting or do they need to be protected from themselves?

Consider another example. Johnson Controls, Inc., a Milwaukee battery manufacturer, banned "women with childbearing capacity" from work involving high lead exposure even when the women involved did not intend to become pregnant. Charged with sex discrimination, the company replied that they were only trying to protect the unborn fetus. An appeals court upheld the ban, saying that women might "discount this clear risk" to the fetus out of a desire to keep their jobs, and so needed to be protected from themselves. Appeals court justice Frank Easterbrook dissented, arguing that "no legal or ethical principle allows Johnson to assume that women are less able than men to make intelligent decisions about the welfare of the next generation." On the surface the Johnson case may not look like a case of paternalism, but some considerations may lead us to think that it is. It might be argued that the court is trying to protect the fetus from harm by the woman. In fact, however, the ban is not against lead exposure to pregnant women, but women of "child bearing age." Do unborn and even unconceived people have rights or interests which require protection? How can they if they do not exist? Also, there are many other occupations which pose possible risks for the fetus of pregnant women workers. Men also present risks to their offspring from the same exposure to lead and other hazards faced by women. Finally, women might argue that the actual and potential risks to their children from poverty outweigh other risks. In any case, who should decide, the women or a paternalistic state acting in what it decides is the women's best interests?

The second area of disagreement is about the moral environment of the society itself. Today we object to those who dump trash, even if it is in their own front yard, because the practice degrades the community in which we live. In the same way, there are those who argue that a society has a responsibility to maintain the moral climate of the community by protecting the values of the community. The issue here is whether the society itself has interests, *over and above* those of individuals, which must be promoted and protected by legal enactments designed to protect the community.

The third area of contention is the one about which there is the most disagreement. Even Mill agrees that behavior which harms others might require limitation to protect those who would be injured. However, it is not clear what should count as harm. The "harm principle" articulated by Mill says "the only purpose for which power can be rightfully exercised over any member of a civilized community, against his will, is to prevent harm to others. His own good, either physical or moral, is not a sufficient warrant." But even Mill understood that there is very little conduct which does not affect others in some way. Mill cites as an example the person who works hard to succeed in a crowded profession and thereby diminishes the chances of other less hard-working individuals. For this reason Mill adopts a strict notion of harm in which harm must accrue to a specific person and be "perceptible." This is intended to rule out claims of harm to society as a whole and the claim that one is harmed by being offended.

But it is not easy to determine the nature of harm. The person who fails to wear a seat belt and is seriously injured costs society in increased health insurance and emergency services. Is this economic harm sufficient to outweigh the interest of individuals acting as they please? Does pornography harm women by degrading them and leading men to have distorted ideas of feminine sexuality? Does it lead men to sexually abuse women? If so, should this "speech" be restricted?

Is public, or even private, behavior which the majority finds offensive "harmful"? We have a right to expect a certain quality of life in our immediate environment. We choose communities to live in partly on the basis of atmosphere. We adopt zoning laws which require people to keep the grass mowed, signs out of their yards, and their houses painted. Why? Members of a community have certain minimal standards on which they insist. Uncut grass may not be harmful, but it is offensive. In the same way, we would be offended if our neighbor went to the pound every day, got a puppy, and in the privacy of his own home tortured the poor thing to death. Why should the offensiveness of the act justify restraining it? In this case, it might be argued that the revulsion experienced is so universal, so strong, and so uncontrollable that we do need to have protection from having to experience such feelings on a daily basis. But what if we don't know it is going on? After all, I can avoid snooping in my neighbor's house and thus avoid being offended.

Many would argue that the only possible explanation why someone would torture a puppy to death every day is that the torturer is truly wicked. This practice is just plain wrong. And just as we have a right to expect certain minimal standards of home maintenance, so also do we have a right to expect that certain minimal standards of decency will be maintained in our community—a right to protect the moral atmosphere of the place in which we live. It is this kind of claim which is usually pointed to in justifying laws prohibiting homosexual acts. Discreet homosexuality can offend only the nosy, but some question whether society must tolerate conduct which some people consider immoral just because it is hidden.

Problematic cases are not just hypothetical. On June 11, 1990, the Supreme Court ruled (for the second time) that a law prohibiting flag burning was unconstitutional because flag burning is a way of making a political statement and as such is protected speech. And yet a poll in *USA Today* (June 12, 1990) showed that 69 percent of Americans support passing a constitutional amendment to ban flag burning. Clearly, the content of the message of flag burning depends on the ability of the flag to symbolize values which are dear to many people, which is precisely why flag burning is attractive to the dissident and repugnant to the majority. Several years ago a grand jury indicted the director of the Cincinnati Contemporary Art Center on obscenity charges for allowing an exhibition of Robert Mapplethorpe's photographs, some of which depicted images of a gay life style. Charges of obscenity have also been leveled against members of 2 Live Crew, whose lyrics contain graphic depictions of sexual acts and especially sexual violence to women. More recently Ice-T's song "Body Count" was removed from his album after a public outcry that it advocated killing policemen.

It is not hard to establish that people are deeply offended in these cases, but it is hard to prove that listening to "Body Count" will cause people to go out and kill policemen or hearing 2 Live Crew's lyrics will make people sexually violent. On the other hand, there is the case of the children who watched a TV program about a rape performed with a broomstick and went out and reproduced the crime. In August 1992, a confessed "serial killer" of young women claimed to have gotten ideas for his brutal murders from watching sexual violence on film and TV. By using evidence of this sort, it has been argued that offensive behavior can affect individuals very personally.

In 1989 a student at the University of Michigan said that he thought homosexuality is a disease treatable by therapy. The student was charged with violating the university's regulation against speech which victimizes individuals on the basis of "sexual orientation." As in many other American universities, the University of Michigan's regulation was provoked by a number of ugly incidents which have occurred on college campuses. At the University of Connecticut in December 1987, Asian-American students were spat upon and called "Oriental faggots" by football players singing "we all live in a yellow submarine." At Arizona State University in 1989 a black student was called a "coon, nigger and porch-monkey." On the one hand, how can students thrive in an environment in which slurs about their race, gender, and so forth, are allowed? But, on the other hand, how can they be protected without denying freedom of expression to others? Mill would argue that the remedy would be *more* rather than *less* speech "Speak out against the bigots," he would say. But is that really enough?

Other issues also raise legitimate concern. The depiction of children in explicit sex acts and "snuff films" which film actual murders are examples of speech some would argue should be banned. Civil libertarians point out that the *production* of such material is already illegal and hence that there is no need to censor speech. But what of materials already produced? Should they be available to those who choose to view them? An alternative would be better enforcement of existing laws against murder and child abuse. But is this feasible?

These cases show us that there are very real conflicting interests that must be weighed in resolving these issues. An additional factor which influences the contemporary debate on allowable limits on personal liberty is the institution of majority rule. In a democracy the minority must accede to the wishes of the majority. Mill argues on utilitarian grounds, however, that when an action is self-regarding the majority should not tyrannize the minority by forcing its values on individuals who do not share them. In the United States, the Bill of Rights appears to set limits on the majority by guaranteeing freedom of speech, religion, and so forth. Nonetheless, such rights are not inviolable. The majority can, after all, change the Constitution and courts can interpret the Bill of Rights in ways which set limits on existing rights. But this does not resolve the issue of whether the majority should be able to impose its will on the minority.

READINGS

Patrick Devlin, an English jurist, takes the position that Mill was wrong in asserting that there is an area of privacy of the individual over which the majority has no right to interfere. Devlin argues that what makes a community is shared values which a community has a right, even a duty, to protect in much the same way as it has a duty to protect the state from treason. In his view, there is no area of self-regarding actions in which an individual can act privately. Devlin further argues that the natural consequence of majority rule is that the majority can set whatever standards it wishes.

Devlin distinguishes two kinds of harm not found in Mill. Tangible harm to society is done by individuals who indulge in such activities as taking drugs and drinking to excess, even if they take care not to harm particular individuals. This tangible harm is produced because the indulgent individual is not giving as much to society as otherwise might be the case. Intangible harm to society is the damage that weakens the value system which establishes and maintains a community. Devlin argues that this damage is intolerable because it threatens the very existence of the community.

H. L. A. Hart, a distinguished British legal theorist, rejects the assumption that society is an entity over and above the individuals which compose it. He attacks Devlin's disintegration thesis and asks for empirical evidence that a common morality is necessary for the existence of a society. He argues that areas of moral pluralism do not threaten the existence of society. If the attitudes and values of these individuals change over time, as is often the case, then the society will change. This does not *destroy* the society; it is merely a sign that, like all other things, societies *change* over time. Individuals living at one time in history therefore have no right to prevent future changes in the name of protecting society.

Joel Feinberg of the University of Arizona explores at length cases which make the application of Mill's "harm principle" problematic, and he explores other possible principles, such as the offense principle, legal paternalism, legal moralism, and the welfare principle, and concludes that there are some modifications of the harm principle which even Mill would approve.

United States Senator Gordon Humphrey of New Hampshire, speaking before the Senate concerning proposed legislation to ban flag-burning, argued that "except to insure public safety and protect the rights of others, speech must never be restricted" and hence that flag burning, just as other offensive uses of the flag such as making slippers out of it, must be protected

In the same proceedings, Judge Robert Bork, then of the American Enterprise Institute and later a nominee for the Supreme Court, argues that the courts should look to community standards to determine what conduct constitutes indecent behavior.

Gerald Dworkin of the University of Illinois at Chicago analyses the issues inherent in Mill's discussion of paternalism and points out that paternalistic legislation is far more widespread today than Mill could have imagined. Dworkin makes an important distinction between paternalistic legislation which enforces values not shared by the individual and legislation which paternalistically promotes what the individual does value.

The special problem of pornography is addressed by Elizabeth Wolgast of California State University, Hayward, who argues that the traditional defense of free speech found in Mill depends, in part, on viewing individuals in society as social atoms whose conduct is self-regarding. Contrary to this view, Wolgast argues that pornography is demeaning to women and that Mill "who argued passionately for women's rights and equal worth and dignity, would find it intolerable to have his views invoked to protect pornography as they have been." Her suggestion is that we search for a "middle way between broad and oppressive controls and reckless liberty."

Catharine MacKinnon, a professor of law at the University of Michigan, argues that pornography is *not* a protected right of speech but rather the *violation* of a right of women to dignity and respect. There is a causal link, she argues, between obscenity and violent sexual attacks on women and that obscenity is therefore a form of sex discrimination. It causes not only violence, she argues, but also the devaluation of women in society as a whole. She and other feminists have proposed antipornographic legislation which would consider pornography a violation of the civil liberties of women or anyone who is hurt by it on the basis of their sex.

Ronald Dworkin, a legal theorist who teaches at both New York University and Oxford University, uses the classic discussion by Isaiah Berlin of two concepts of liberty, one conceived as negative liberty and the other as positive liberty, as a foil for addressing the problems presented by pornography. He specifically addresses the legislation proposed by MacKinnon but argues that while pornography "is often grotesquely offensive...not only to women but to men as well" that cannot be a sufficient reason for banning it.

The Enforcement of Morals

Patrick Devlin

The report of the Committee on Homosexual Offences and Prostitution, generally known as the Wolfenden Report, is recognized to be an excellent study of two very difficult legal and social problems. But it has also a particular claim to the respect of those interested in jurisprudence; it does what law reformers so rarely do; it sets out clearly and carefully what in relation to its subjects it

From *The Enforcement of Morals* (Oxford: Oxford University Press, 1965). Reprinted by permission of the publisher.

considers the function of the law to be. Statutory additions to the criminal law are too often made on the simple principle that 'there ought to be a law against it'. The greater part of the law relating to sexual offences is the creation of statute and it is difficult to ascertain any logical relationship between it and the moral ideas which most of us uphold. Adultery, fornication, and prostitution are not, as the Report points out, criminal offences: homosexuality between males is a criminal offence, but between females it is not. Incest was not an offence until it was declared so by statute only fifty years ago. Does the legislature select these offences haphazardly or are there some principles which can be used to determine what part of the moral law should be embodied in the criminal?...What is the connection between crime and sin and to what extent, if at all, should the criminal law of England concern itself with the enforcement of morals and punish sin or immorality as such?

The statements of principle in the Wolfenden Report provide an admirable and modern starting-point for such an inquiry...

Early in the Report the Committee put forward

our own formulation of the function of the criminal law so far as it concerns the subjects of this inquiry. In this field, its function, as we see it, is to preserve public order and decency, to protect the citizen from what is offensive or injurious, and to provide sufficient safeguards against exploitation and corruption of others, particularly those who are specially vulnerable because they are young, weak in body or mind, inexperienced, or in a state of special physical, official or economic dependence.

It is not, in our view, the function of the law to intervene in the private lives of citizens, or to seek to enforce any particular pattern of behavior, further than is necessary to carry out the purposes we have outlined.

The Committee preface their most important recommendation

that homosexual behavior between consenting adults in private should no longer be a criminal offence, [by stating the argument] which we believe to be decisive, namely, the importance which society and the law ought to give to individual freedom of choice and action in matters of private morality. Unless a deliberate attempt is to be made by society, acting through the agency of the law, to equate the sphere of crime with that of sin, there must remain a realm of private morality and im-

morality which is, in brief and crude terms, not the law's business. To say this is not to condone or encourage private immorality.

Similar statements of principle are set out in the chapters of the Report which deal with prostitution. No case can be sustained, the Report says, for attempting to make prostitution itself illegal. The Committee refer to the general reasons already given and add: 'We are agreed that private immorality should not be the concern of the criminal law except in the special circumstances therein mentioned.' They quote with approval the report of the Street Offences Committee, which says: 'As a general proposition it will be universally accepted that the law is not concerned with private morals or with ethical sanctions.' It will be observed that the emphasis is on *private* immorality. By this is meant immorality which is not offensive or injurious to the public in the ways defined or described in the first passage which I quoted. In other words, no act of immorality should be made a criminal offence unless it is accompanied by some other feature such as indecency, corruption, or exploitation. This is clearly brought out in relation to prostitution: 'It is not the duty of the law to concern itself with immorality as such...it should confine itself to those activities which offend against public order and decency or expose the ordinary citizen to what is offensive or injurious.'

These statements of principle are naturally restricted to the subject-matter of the Report. But they are made in general terms and there seems to be no reason why, if they are valid, they should not be applied to the criminal law in general. They separate very decisively crime from sin, the divine law from the secular, and the moral from the criminal. They do not signify any lack of support for the law, moral or criminal, and they do not represent an attitude that can be called either religious or irreligious. There are many schools of thought among those who may think that morals are not the law's business. There is first of all the agnostic or free-thinker. He does not of course disbelieve in morals, nor in sin if it be given the wider of the two meanings assigned to it in the *Oxford English Dictionary* where it is defined as 'transgression against divine law or the principles of morality'. He cannot accept the divine law; that does not mean that he might not view with suspicion any departure from moral principles that have for generations been accepted by the society in which he lives; but in the end he judges for himself. Then there is the deeply religious person who feels that the criminal law is sometimes more of a hindrance than a help in the sphere of morality, and that the reform of the sinner—at any rate when he injures only himself—should be a spiritual rather than a temporal work. Then there is the man who without any strong feeling cannot see why, where there is freedom in religious belief, there should not logically be freedom in morality as well. All these are powerfully allied against the equating of crime with sin.

I must disclose at the outset that I have as a judge an interest in the result of the inquiry which I am seeking to make as a jurisprudent....

I think it is clear that the criminal law as we know it is based upon moral principle. In a number of crimes its function is simply to enforce a moral principle and nothing else. The law, both criminal and civil, claims to be able to speak about morality and immorality generally. Where does it get its authority to do this and how does it settle the moral principles which it enforces? Undoubtedly, as a matter of history, it derived both from Christian teaching. But I think that the strict logician is right when he says that the law can no longer rely on doctrines in which citizens are entitled to disbelieve. It is necessary therefore to look for some other source.

In jurisprudence...everything is thrown open to discussion and, in the belief that they cover the whole field, I have framed three interrogatories addressed to myself to answer:

1. Has society the right to pass judgment at all on matters of morals? Ought there, in other words, to be a public morality, or are morals always a matter for private judgment?
2. If society has the right to pass judgment, has it also the right to use the weapon of the law to enforce it?
3. If so, ought it to use that weapon in all cases or only in some; and if only in some, on what principles should it distinguish?

I shall begin with the first interrogatory and consider what is meant by the right of society to pass a moral judgment, that is, a judgment about what is good and what is evil. The fact that a majority of people may disapprove of a practice does not of itself make it a matter for society as a whole. Nine men out of ten may disapprove of what the tenth man is doing and still say that it is not their business. There is a case for a collective judgment (as distinct from a large number of individual opinions which sensible people may even refrain from pronouncing at all if it is upon somebody else's private affairs) only if society is affected. Without a collective judgment there can be no case at all for intervention. Let me take as an illustration the Englishman's attitude to religion as it is now and as it has been in the past. His attitude now is that a man's religion is his private affair; he may think of another man's religion that it is right or wrong, true or untrue, but not that it is good or bad. In earlier times that was not so; a man was denied the right to practice what was thought of as heresy, and heresy was thought of as destructive of society.

The...Wolfenden Report suggests the view that there ought not to be a collective judgment about immorality *per se*. Is this what is meant by 'private morality' and 'individual freedom of choice and action'? Some people sincerely believe that homosexuality is neither immoral nor unnatural. Is the 'freedom of choice and action' that is offered to the individual, freedom to decide for himself what is moral or immoral, society remaining neutral; or is it freedom to be immoral if he wants to be? The language of the Report may be open to question, but the conclusions at which the Committee arrive answer this question unambiguously. If society is not prepared to say that homosexuality is morally wrong, there would be no basis for a law protecting youth from 'corruption' or punishing a man for living on the 'immoral' earnings of a homosexual prostitute, as the Report recommends. This attitude the Committee make even clearer when they come to deal with prostitution. In truth, the Report takes it for granted that there is in existence a public morality which condemns homosexuality and prostitution. What the Report seems to mean by private morality might perhaps be better described as private behavior in matters of morals.

This view—that there is such a thing as public morality—can also be justified by *a priori* argument. What makes a society of any sort is community of ideas, not only political ideas but also ideas about the way its members should behave and govern their lives; these latter ideas are its morals. Every society has a moral structure as well as a political one: or rather, since that might suggest two independent systems, I should say that the structure of every society is made up both of politics and morals. Take, for example, the institution of marriage. Whether a man should be allowed to take more than one wife is something about which every society has to make up its mind one way or the other. In England we believe in the Christian idea of marriage and therefore adopt monogamy as a moral principle. Consequently the Christian institution of marriage has become the basis of family life and so part of the structure of our society. It is there not because it is Christian. It has got there because it is Christian, but it remains there because it is built into the house in which we live and could not be removed without bringing it down. The great majority of those who live in this country accept it because it is the Christian idea of marriage and for them the only true one. But a non-Christian is bound by it, not because it is part of Christianity but because, rightly or wrongly, it has been adopted by the society in which he lives. It would be useless for him to stage a debate designed to prove that polygamy was theologically more correct and socially preferable; if he wants to live in the house, he must accept it as built in the way in which it is.

We see this more clearly if we think of ideas or institutions that are purely political. Society cannot tolerate rebellion; it will not allow argument about the rightness of the cause. Historians a century later may say that the rebels were right and the Government was wrong and a percipient and conscientious subject of the State may think so at the time. But it is not a matter which can be left to individual judgment.

The institution of marriage is a good example for my purpose because it bridges the division, if there is one, between politics and morals. Marriage is part of the structure of our society and it is also the basis of a moral code which condemns fornication and adultery. The institution of marriage would be gravely threatened if individual judgments were permitted about the morality of adultery; on these points there must be a public morality. But public morality is not to be confined to those moral principles which support institutions such as marriage. People do not think of monogamy as something which has to be sup-

ported because our society has chosen to organize itself upon it; they think of it as something that is good in itself and offering a good way of life and that it is for that reason that our society has adopted it. I return to the statement that I have already made, that society means a community of ideas; without shared ideas on politics, morals, and ethics no society can exist. Each one of us has ideas about what is good and what is evil; they cannot be kept private from the society in which we live. If men and women try to create a society in which there is no fundamental agreement about good and evil they will fail; if, having based it on common agreement, the agreement goes, the society will disintegrate. For society is not something that is kept together physically; it is held by the invisible bonds of common thought. If the bonds were too far relaxed the members would drift apart. A common morality is part of the bondage. The bondage is part of the price of society; and mankind, which needs society, must pay its price....

You may think that I have taken far too long in contending that there is such a thing as public morality, a proposition which most people would readily accept, and may have left myself too little time to discuss the next question which to many minds may cause greater difficulty: to what extent should society use the law to enforce its moral judgments? But I believe that the answer to the first question determines the way in which the second should be approached and may indeed very nearly dictate the answer to the second question. If society has no right to make judgments on morals, the law must find some special justification for entering the field of morality: if homosexuality and prostitution are not in themselves wrong, then the onus is very clearly on the lawgiver who wants to frame a law against certain aspects of them to justify the exceptional treatment. But if society has the right to make a judgment and has it on the basis that a recognized morality is as necessary to society as, say, a recognized government, then society may use the law to preserve morality in the same way as it uses it to safeguard anything else that is essential to its existence. If therefore the first proposition is securely established with all its implications, society has a *prima facie* right to legislate against immorality as such....

I think, therefore, that it is not possible to set theoretical limits to the power of the State to legislate against immorality. It is not possible to settle in advance exceptions to the general rule or to define inflexibly areas of morality into which the law is in no circumstances to be allowed to enter. Society is entitled by means of its laws to protect itself from dangers, whether from within or without. Here again I think that the political parallel is legitimate. The law of treason is directed against aiding the king's enemies and against sedition from within. The justification for this is that established government is necessary for the existence of society and therefore its safety against violent overthrow must be secured. But an established morality is as necessary as good government to the welfare of society. Societies disintegrate from within more frequently than they are broken up by external pressures. There is disintegration when no common morality is observed and history shows that the loosening of moral bonds is often the first stage of disintegration, so that society is justified in taking the same steps to preserve its moral code as it does to preserve its government and other essential institutions. The suppression of vice is as much the law's business as the suppression of subversive activities; it is no more possible to define a sphere of private morality than it is to define one of private subversive activity. It is wrong to talk of private morality or of the law not being concerned with immorality as such or to try to set rigid bounds to the part which the law may play in the suppression of vice. There are no theoretical limits to the power of the State to legislate against treason and sedition, and likewise I think there can be no theoretical limits to legislation against immorality. You may argue that if a man's sins affect only himself it cannot be the concern of society. If he chooses to get drunk every night in the privacy of his own home, is any one except himself the worse for it? But suppose a quarter or a half of the population got drunk every night, what sort of society would it be? You cannot set a theoretical limit to the number of people who can get drunk before society is entitled to legislate against drunkenness. The same may be said of gambling. The Royal Commission on Betting, Lotteries, and Gaming took as their test the character of the citizen as a member of society. They said: 'Our concern with the ethical significance of gambling is confined to the effect which it may have on the character of the gambler as a member of society. If we were convinced that whatever the degree of gambling this effect must be harmful we should be inclined to think that it was the duty of the state to restrict gambling to the greatest extent practicable.'

In what circumstances the State should exercise its power is the third of the interrogatories I have framed. But before I get to it I must raise a point which might have been brought up in any one of the three. How are the moral judgments of society to be ascertained? By leaving it until now, I can ask it in the more limited form that is now sufficient for my purpose. How is the law-maker to ascertain the moral judgments of society? It is surely not enough that they should be reached by the opinion of the majority; it would be too much to require the individual assent of every citizen. English law has evolved and regularly uses a standard which does not depend on the counting of heads. It is that of the reasonable man. He is not to be confused with the rational man. He is not expected to reason about anything and his judgment may be largely a matter of feeling. It is the viewpoint of the man in the street—or to use an archaism familiar to all lawyers—the man in the Clapham omnibus. He might also be called the right-minded man. For my purpose I should like to call him the man in the jury box, for the moral judgment of society must be something about which any twelve men or women drawn at random might after discussion be expected to be unanimous....

Immorality then, for the purpose of the law, is what every right-minded person is presumed to consider to be immoral. Any immorality is capable of affecting society injuriously and in effect to a greater or lesser extent it usually does; this is what gives the law its *locus standi*. It cannot be shut out. But—and this brings me to the third question—the individual has a *locus standi* too; he cannot be expected to surrender to the judgment of society the whole conduct of his life. It is the old and familiar question of striking a balance between the rights and interests of society and those of the individual. This is something which the law is constantly doing in matters large and small. To take a very down-to-earth example, let me consider the right of the individual whose house adjoins the highway to have access to it; that means in these days the right to have vehicles stationary in the highway, sometimes for a considerable time if there is a lot of loading or unloading. There are many cases in which the courts have had to balance the private right of access against the public right to use the highway without obstruction. It cannot be done by carving up the highway into public and private areas. It is done by recognizing that each have rights over the whole; that if each were to exercise their rights to the full, they would come into conflict; and therefore that the rights of each must be curtailed so as to ensure as far as possible that the essential needs of each are safeguarded.

I do not think that one can talk sensibly of a public and private morality any more than one can of a public or private highway. Morality is a sphere in which there is a public interest and a private interest, often in conflict, and the problem is to reconcile the two. This does not mean that it is impossible to put forward any general statements about how in our society the balance ought to be struck. Such statements cannot of their nature be rigid or precise....Nothing should be punished by the law that does not lie beyond the limits of tolerance; it is not nearly enough to say that a majority dislike a practice; there must be a real feeling of reprobation. Those who are dissatisfied with the present law on homosexuality often say that the opponents of reform are swayed simply by disgust. If that were so it would be wrong, but I do not think one can ignore disgust if it is deeply felt and not manufactured. Its presence is a good indication that the bounds of toleration are being reached. Not everything is to be tolerated. No society can do without intolerance, indignation, and disgust; they are the forces behind the moral law, and indeed it can be argued that if they or something like them are not present, the feelings of society cannot be weighty enough to deprive the individual of freedom of choice. I suppose that there is hardly anyone nowadays who would not be disgusted by the thought of deliberate cruelty to animals. No one proposes to relegate that or any other form of sadism to the realm of private morality or to allow it to be practiced in public or in private. It would be possible no doubt to point out that until a comparatively short while ago nobody thought very much of cruelty to animals and also that pity and kindliness and the unwillingness to inflict pain are virtues more generally esteemed now than they have ever been in the past. But matters of this sort are not determined by rational argument. Every moral judgment, unless it claims a divine source, is simply a feeling that no right-minded man could behave in any other way without admitting that he was doing wrong. It is the power of a common sense and not the power of reason that is behind the judgments of society. But before a society can put a practice beyond the limits of tolerance there must be a deliberate judgment that the practice is injurious to society. There is, for example, a general abhorrence of homosexuality. We should ask ourselves in the first instance whether, looking at it calmly and dispassionately, we regard it as a vice so abominable that its mere presence is an offence. If that is the genuine feeling of the society in which we live, I do not see how society can be denied the right to eradicate it. Our feeling may not be so intense as that. We may feel about it that, if confined, it is tolerable, but that if it spread it might be gravely injurious; it is in this way that most societies look upon fornication, seeing it as a natural weakness which must be kept within bounds but which cannot be rooted out. It becomes then a question of balance, the danger to society in one scale and the extent of the restriction in the other....

The limits of tolerance shift. This is supplementary to what I have been saying but of sufficient importance in itself to deserve statement as a separate principle which law-makers have to bear in mind. I suppose that moral standards do not shift; so far as they come from divine revelation they do not, and I am willing to assume that the moral judgments made by a society always remain good for that society. But the extent to which society will tolerate—I mean tolerate, not approve—departures from moral standards varies from generation to generation. It may be that over-all tolerance is always increasing. The pressure of the human mind, always seeking greater freedom of thought, is outwards against the bonds of society forcing their gradual relaxation. It may be that history is a tale of contraction and expansion and that all developed societies are on their way to dissolution. I must not speak of things I do not know; and anyway as a practical matter no society is willing to make provision for its own decay. I return therefore to the simple and observable fact that in matters of morals the limits of tolerance shift. Laws, especially those which are based on morals, are less easily moved. It follows as another good working principle that in any new matter of morals the law should be slow to act. By the next generation the swell of indignation may have abated and the law be left without the strong backing which it needs. But it is then difficult to alter the law without giving the impression that moral judgment is being weakened. This is now one of the factors that is strongly militating against any alteration to the law on homosexuality....

It is that as far as possible privacy should be respected. This is not an idea that has ever been made explicit in the criminal law. Acts or words done or said in public or in private are all brought within its scope without distinction in principle. But there goes with this a strong reluctance on the part of judges and legislators to sanction invasions of privacy in the detection of crime. The police have no more right to trespass than the ordinary citizen has; there is no general right of search; to this extent an Englishman's home is still his castle. The Government is extremely careful in the exercise even of those powers which it claims to be undisputed. Telephone tapping and interference with the mails afford a good illustration of this....

The part that the jury plays in the enforcement of the criminal law, the fact that no grave offence against morals is punishable without their verdict, these are of great importance in relation to the statements of principle that I have been making. They turn what might otherwise be pure exhortation to the legislature into something like rules that the law-makers cannot safely ignore. The man in the jury box is not just an expression; he is an active reality. It will not in the long run work to make laws about morality that are not acceptable to him.

This then is how I believe my third interrogatory should be answered—not by the formulation of hard and fast rules, but by a judgement in each case taking into account the sort of factors I have been mentioning....

The true principle is that the law exists for the protection of society. It does not discharge its function by protecting the individual from injury, annoyance, corruption, and exploitation; the law must protect also the institutions and the community of ideas, political and moral, without which people cannot live together. Society cannot ignore the morality of the individual any more than it can his loyalty; it flourishes on both and without either it dies.

I have said that the morals which underlay the law must be derived from the sense of right and wrong which resides in the community as a whole; it does not matter whence the community of thought comes, whether from one body of doctrine or another or from the knowledge of good and evil which no man is without. If the reasonable man believes that a practice is immoral and believes also—no matter whether the belief is right or wrong, so be it that it is honest and dispassionate—that no right-minded member of his society could think otherwise, then for the purpose of the law it is immoral. This, you may say, makes immorality a question of fact—what the law would consider as self-evident fact no doubt, but still with no higher authority than any other doctrine of public policy. I think that that is so, and indeed the law does not distinguish between an act that is immoral and one that is contrary to public policy. But the law has never yet had occasion to inquire into the differences between Christian morals and those which every right-minded member of society is expected to hold. The inquiry would, I believe, be academic. Moralists would find differences; indeed they would find them between different branches of the Christian faith on subjects such as divorce and birth-control. But for the purpose of the limited entry which the law makes into the field of morals, there is no practical difference. It seems to me therefore that the free-thinker and the non-Christian can accept, without offence to his convictions, the fact that Christian morals are the basis of the criminal law and that he can recognize, also without taking offence, that without the support of the churches the moral order, which has its origin in and takes its strength from Christian beliefs, would collapse....

I return now to the main thread of my argument and summarize it. Society cannot live without morals. Its morals are those standards of conduct which the reasonable man approves. A rational man, who is also a good man, may have other standards. If he has no standards at all he is not a good man and need not be further considered. If he has standards, they may be very different; he may, for example, not disapprove of homosexuality or abortion. In that case he will not share in the common morality; but that should not make him deny that it is a social necessity. A rebel may be rational in thinking that he is right but he is irrational if he thinks that society can leave him free to rebel.

A man who concedes that morality is necessary to society must support the use of those instruments without which morality cannot be maintained. The two instruments are those of teaching, which is doctrine, and of enforcement, which is the law....

Freedom is not a good in itself. We believe it to be good because out of freedom there comes more good than bad. If a free society is better than a disciplined one, it is because—and this certainly was Mill's view—it is better for a man himself that he should be free to seek his own good in his own way and better too for the society to which he belongs, since thereby a way may be found to a greater good for all. But no good can come from a man doing what he acknowledges to be evil. The freedom that is worth having is freedom to do what you think to be good notwithstanding that others think it to be bad. Freedom to do what you know to be bad is worthless....

Granted then that the law can play some part in the war against vice, ought it to be excluded for the reason that private vice cannot do any harm to society? I think that it is capable of doing both physical harm and spiritual harm. Tangible and intangible may be better words; body and soul a better simile.

Let me consider first the tangible harm. It is obvious that an individual may by unrestricted indulgence in vice so weaken himself that he ceases to be a useful member of society. It is obvious also that if a sufficient number of individuals so weaken themselves, society will thereby be weakened. That is what I mean by tangible harm to society. If the proportion grows sufficiently large, society will succumb either to its own disease or to external pressure. A nation of debauchees would not in 1940 have responded satisfactorily to Winston Churchill's call to blood and toil and sweat and tears. I doubt if any of this would be denied. The answer that is made to it is that the danger, if private immorality were tolerated, of vice spreading to such an extent as to affect society as a whole is negligible and in a free society ought to be ignored....

In the same way, while a few people getting drunk in private cause no problem at all, widespread drunkenness, whether in private or public, would create a social problem. The line between drunkenness that creates a social problem of sufficient magnitude to justify the intervention of the law and that which does not, cannot be drawn on the distinction between private indulgence and public sobriety. It is a practical one, based on an estimate of what can safely be tolerated whether in public or in private, and shifting from time to time as circumstances change. The licensing laws coupled with high taxation may be all that is needed. But if more be needed there is no doctrinal answer even to complete prohibition. It cannot be said that so much is the law's business but more is not.

I move now to the consideration of intangible harm to society and begin by noting a significant distinction. When considering tangible damage to society we are concerned chiefly with immoral activity. Moral belief is relevant only in so far as the lack of it contributes to immoral activity. A vicious minority diminishes the physical strength of society even if all its members believe themselves to be sinning. But if they all believed that, they would not diminish the common belief in right and wrong which is the intangible property of society. When considering intangible injury to society it is moral belief that matters; immoral activity is relevant only in so far as it promotes disbelief.

It is generally accepted that some shared morality, that is, some common agreement about what is right and what is wrong, is an essential element in the constitution of any society. Without it there would be no cohesion. But polygamy can be as cohesive as monogamy and I am prepared to believe that a society based on free love and a community of children could be just as strong (though according to our ideas it could not be as good) as one based on the family. What is important is not the quality of the creed but the strength of the belief in it. The enemy of society is not error but indifference.

On this reasoning there is nothing inherently objectionable about the change of an old morality for a new one. Why then is the law used to guard existing moral beliefs? It is because an old morality cannot be changed for a new morality as an old coat for a new one. The old belief must be driven out by disbelief....

It can be said in general terms, and often is, that law-makers are bound to legislate for the common good. The common good is perhaps a useful and compendious, if vague, description of all the things law-makers should have in mind when they legislate. But it does not constitute a clear limitation on the right to legislate. There may be a difference of opinion about what is for the common good which can be solved only by a judgement upon the conflicting values. Society alone can make that judgement and if it makes it honestly, it is a judgement that cannot be impugned.

Can then the judgement of society sanction every invasion of a man's privacy, however extreme? Theoretically that must be so; there is no theoretical limitation. Society must be the judge of what is necessary to its own integrity if only because there is no other tribunal to which the question can be submitted. In a free society the understanding that men have with each other is that each shall retain for himself the greatest measure of personal freedom that is compatible with the integrity and good government of his society. In a free society men must trust each other and each man must put his trust in his fellows that they will not interfere with him unless in their honest judgement it is necessary to do so. Furthermore, in a free

society checks are usually put upon the government, both the executive and the legislature, so that it is difficult for them to enact and enforce a law that takes away another's freedom unless in the honest judgement of society it is necessary to do so. One sort of check consists in the safeguarding of certain specific freedoms by the articles of a constitution; another consists in trial by jury. But the only certain security is the understanding in the heart of every man that he must not condemn what another does unless he honestly considers that it is a threat to the integrity or good government of their society.

If one man practices what he calls virtue and the others call vice and if he fails to convince the others that they are wrong, he has the right to make a further appeal. He has, in a free society, a right to claim that however much the others dislike and deplore what he does, they should allow him to do it unless they are genuinely convinced that it threatens the integrity of society. If the others reject that appeal, constitutionally that is the end. He must either submit or reject society....

"Social Solidarity and the Enforcement of Morality"

H. L. A. Hart

It is possible to extract from Plato's *Republic* and *Laws*...the following thesis about the role of law in relation to the enforcement of morality: the law of the city state exists not merely to secure that men have the opportunity to lead a morally good life, but to see that they do. According to this thesis not only may the law be used to punish men for doing what morally it is wrong for them to do, but it should be so used; for the promotion of moral virtue by these means and by others is one of the Ends or Purposes of a society complex enough to

have developed a legal system....I shall call this theory "the classical thesis" and not discuss it further.

From the classical thesis there is to be distinguished what I shall call "the disintegration thesis." This inverts the order of instrumentality between society on the one hand and morality on the other as it appears in the classical thesis; for in this thesis society is not the instrument of the moral life; rather morality is valued as the cement of society, the bond, or one of the bonds, without which men

---

From "Social Solidarity and the Enforcement of Morality," *University of Chicago Law Review*, vol. 35 (1967). Reprinted by permission of the publisher.

would not cohere in society....It is not the quality of the morality but its cohesive power which matters. "What is important is not the quality of the creed but the strength of the belief in it. The enemy of society is not error but indifference." The case for the enforcement of morality on this view is that its maintenance is necessary to prevent the disintegration of society.

The disintegration thesis, under pressure of the request for empirical evidence to substantiate the claim that the maintenance of morality is in fact necessary for the existence of society, often collapses into another thesis which I shall call "the conservative thesis." This is the claim that society has a right to enforce its morality by law because the majority have the right to follow their own moral convictions that their moral environment is a thing of value to be defended from change.

The topic of this article is the disintegration thesis, but I shall discharge in relation to it only a very limited set of tasks. What I shall mainly do is attempt to discover what, when the ambiguities are stripped away, is the empirical claim which the thesis makes and in what directions is it conceivable that a search for evidence to substantiate this claim would be rewarding. But even these tasks I shall discharge only partially.

The disintegration thesis is a central part of the case presented by Lord Devlin justifying the legal enforcement of morality at points where followers of John Stuart Mill and other latter day liberals would consider this an unjustifiable extension of the scope of the criminal law. The morality, the enforcement of which is justified according to Lord Devlin, is variously described as "the moral structure" of society, "a public morality," "a common morality," "shared ideas on politics, morals, and ethics," "fundamental agreement about good and evil," and "a recognized morality." This is said to be part of "the invisible bonds of common thought" which hold society together; and "if the bonds were too far relaxed the members would drift apart." It is part of "the bondage...of society" and is "as necessary to society as, say, a recognized government." The justification for the enforcement of this recognized morality is simply that the law may be used to preserve anything essential to society's existence. "There is disintegration when no common morality is observed and history shows that the loosening of moral bonds is often the first stage

of disintegration." If we consider these formulations they seem to constitute a highly ambitious empirical generalization about a necessary condition for the existence or continued existence of a society and so give us a sufficient condition for the disintegration of society. Apart from the one general statement that "history shows that the loosening of moral bonds is often the first stage of disintegration," no evidence is given in support of the argument and no indication is given of the kind of evidence that would support it, nor is any sensitivity betrayed to the need for evidence.

In disputing with Lord Devlin, I offered him the alternative of supplementing his contentions with evidence, or accepting that his statements about the necessity of a common morality for the existence of society were not empirical statements at all but were disguised tautologies or necessary truths depending entirely on the meaning given to the expressions "society," "existence," or "continued existence" of society. If the continued existence of a society meant living according to some specific shared moral code, then the preservation of a moral code is logically and not causally or contingently necessary to the continued existence of society and this seems too unexciting a theme to be worth ventilating. Yet at points Lord Devlin adopts a definition of society ("a society *means* a community of ideas") which seems to suggest that he intended his statements about the necessity of a morality to society's existence as a definitional truth. Of course, very often the expressions "society," "existence of society," and "the same society" are used in this way: that is, they refer to a form or type of social life individuated by a certain morality or moral code or by distinctive legal, political, or economic institutions. A society in the sense of a form or type of social life can change, disappear, or be succeeded by different forms of society without any phenomenon describable as "disintegration" or "members drifting apart." In this sense of "society," post-feudal England was a different society from feudal England. But if we express this simple fact by saying that *the same English society* was at one time a feudal society and at another time not, we make use of another sense of society with different criteria of individuation and continued identity. It is plain that if the threat of disintegration or "members drifting apart" is to have any reality, or if the claim that a common morality is "as necessary to society as, say, a recognized government" is taken to be part of an argument for the enforcement of morality, definitional truths dependent upon the identification of society with its shared morality are quite irrelevant. Just as it would be no reply to an anarchist who wished to preserve society to tell him that government is necessary to an organized society, if it turned out that by "organized society" we merely meant a society with a government, so it is empty to argue against one who considers that the preservation of society's code of morality is not the law's business, that the maintenance of the moral code is necessary to the existence of society, if it turns out that by society is meant a society living according to this moral code.

The short point is that if we *mean* by "society ceasing to exist" not "disintegration" nor "the drifting apart" of its members but a radical change in its common morality, then the case for using the law to preserve morality must rest not on any disintegration thesis but on some variant of the claim that when groups of men have developed a common form of life rich enough to include a common morality, this is something which ought to be preserved. One very obvious form of this claim is the conservative thesis that the majority have a right in these circumstances to defend their existing moral environment from change. But this is no longer an empirical claim.

Views not dissimilar from Lord Devlin's, and in some cases hovering in a similar way between the disintegration thesis and the conservative thesis, can be found in much contemporary sociological theory of the structural and functional prerequisites of society....I shall select from the literature of sociology Durkheim's elaboration of a form of the disintegration theory....

Durkheim distinguishes two forms of what he calls "solidarity" or factors tending to unify men or lead them to cohere in discriminable and enduring societies. The minimum meaning attached to society here is that of a group of men which we can distinguish from other similar groups and can recognize as being the same group persisting through a period of time though its constituent members have been replaced during that time by others. One of the forms of solidarity, "mechanical solidarity," springs from men's resemblances and the other, "organic solidarity," from their differences. Me-

chanical solidarity depends on, or perhaps indeed consists in, sharing of common beliefs about matters of fact and common standards of behavior among which is a common morality. This blend of common belief and common standards constitutes the *"conscience collective,"* which draws upon all the ambiguities of the French word *conscience* as between consciousness or knowledge and conscience. The point of the use of this terminology of *conscience* is largely that the beliefs and subscription to the common standards become internalized as part of the personality or character of the members of society.

Organic solidarity by contrast depends on the dissimilarities of human beings and their mutual need to be complemented by association in various forms with others who are unlike themselves. The most prominent aspect of this interdependence of dissimilars is the division of labour, but Durkheim warns us that we must not think of the importance of this as a unifying element of society as residing simply in its economic payoff. "[T]he economic services that it [the division of labour] can render are picayune compared to the moral effect that it produces, and its true function is to create in two or more persons a feeling of solidarity." Generally, mechanical solidarity is the dominant form of solidarity in simple societies and diminishes in importance, though apparently it is never eliminated altogether as a unifying factor, as organic solidarity develops in more complex societies. According to Durkheim the law presents a faithful mirror of both forms of solidarity, and can be used as a gauge of the relative importance at any time of the two forms. The criminal law, with its repressive sanctions, reflects mechanical solidarity; the civil law reflects organic solidarity, since it upholds the typical instruments of interdependence, *e.g.*, the institution of contract, and generally provides not for repressive sanctions, but for restitution and compensation.

Somewhat fantastically Durkheim thinks that the law can be used as a measuring instrument. We have merely to count the number of rules which at any time constitute the criminal law and the number of rules which constitute the civil law expressing the division of labour, and then we know what fraction to assign to the relative importance of the two forms of solidarity. This fantasy opens formidable problems concerning the individuation and countability of legal rules which occupied Bentham a good deal, but perhaps need not detain us here. What is of great interest, however, is Durkheim's view of the role of the criminal law in relation to a shared morality. Durkheim is much concerned to show the hollowness of rationalistic and utilitarian accounts of the institution of criminal punishment. For him, as for his English judicial counterpart, utilitarian theory fails as an explanatory theory for it distorts the character of crime and punishment and considered as a normative theory would lead to disturbing results. Durkheim therefore provides fresh definitions of both crime and punishment. For him a crime is essentially (though in developed societies there are secondary senses of crime to which this definition does not apply directly) a serious offense against the collective conscience—the common morality which holds men together at points where its sentiments are both strong and precise. Such an act is not condemned by that morality because it is independently a crime or wrong, it is a crime or wrong because it is so condemned. Above all, to be wrong or a crime an act need not be, nor even be believed to be, harmful to anyone or to society in any sense other than that it runs counter to the common morality at points where its sentiments are strong and precise. These features of Durkheim's theory are striking analogues of Lord Devlin's observation that it is not the quality of the morality that matters but the strength of the belief in it and its consequent cohesive power and his stipulation that the morality to be enforced must be up to what may be called concert pitch: it must be marked by "intolerance, indignation, and disgust."

What, then, on this view, is punishment? Why punish? And how severely? Punishment for Durkheim is essentially the hostility excited by violations of the common morality which may be either diffused throughout society or administered by official action when it will usually have the form of specifically graduated measures. His definition, therefore, is that punishment is "a passionate reaction of graduated intensity" to offences against the collective conscience. The hollowness of utilitarian theory as an explanation of criminal punishment is evident if we look at the way that, even in contemporary society, criminal punishments are graduated. They are adapted not to the utilitarian aim of preventing what would be ordinarily de-

scribed as harmful conduct, but to the appropriate expression of the degree of feeling excited by the offence, on the footing that such appropriate expression of feeling is a means of sustaining the belief in the collective morality. Many legal phenomena bear this out. We punish a robber, even if he is likely to offend again, less severely than a murderer whom we have every reason to think will not offend again. We adopt the principle that ignorance of the law is no excuse in criminal matters and, he might have added, we punish attempts less severely than completed offences thereby reflecting a difference in the resentment generated for the completed as compared with the uncompleted crime.

Hence, to the question "Why punish?" Durkheim's answer is that we do so primarily as a symbolic expression of the outraged common morality the maintenance of which is the condition of cohesion resulting from men's likenesses. Punishing the offender is required to maintain social cohesion because the common conscience, violated by the offence, "would necessarily lose its energy if an emotional reaction of the community [in the form of punishment] did not come to compensate its loss, and it would result in a breakdown of social solidarity."

This thumbnail sketch of Durkheim's theory presents its essentials, but there are two complexities of importance, as there are also in Lord Devlin's case. Both have to do with the possibilities of change in the common morality. Both theorists seem to envisage a spontaneous or natural change and warn us in different ways that the enforcement of morality must allow for this. Thus Lord Devlin issues prudential warnings to the legislator that "[t]he limits of tolerance shift" and that we should not make criminal offences out of moral opinion which is likely soon to change and leave the law high, and, so to speak, morally dry. Durkheim similarly says that his theory does not mean that it is necessary to conserve a penal rule because it once corresponded to the collective sentiments, but only if the sentiment is still "living and energetic." If it has disappeared or enfeebled, nothing is worse than trying to keep it alive artificially by the law. This means that we must distinguish a natural or nonmalignant change in the social morality or a natural "shift in its limits of tolerance" from a malignant form of change against which society is to be protected and which is the result of individual deviation from its morality. It is, however, a further complexity in these theories that the function of punishment, or rather the mechanism by which punishment operates in preserving a social morality from malignant change, differs as between Durkheim and Lord Devlin. For Lord Devlin punishment protects the existing morality by repressing or diminishing the number of immoral actions which in themselves are considered "to threaten" or weaken the common morality. For Durkheim, however, punishment sustains the common morality, not mainly by repressing the immoral conduct, but principally by giving satisfactory vent to a sense of outrage because if the vent were closed the common conscience would "lose its energy" and the cohesive morality would weaken.

If we ask in relation to theories such as Lord Devlin's and Durkheim's precisely what empirical claim they make concerning the connection between the maintenance of a common morality and the existence of society, some further disentangling of knots has to be done.

It seems a very natural objection to such theories that if they are to be taken seriously as variants of the disintegration thesis, the justification which they attempt to give for the enforcement of social morality is far too general. It is surely both possible and good sense to discriminate between those parts of a society's moral code (assuming it has a single moral code) which are essential for the existence of a society and those which are not. Prima facie, at least, the need for such a discrimination seems obvious even if we assume that the moral code is only to be enforced where it is supported by "sentiments which are strong and precise" (Durkheim) or by "intolerance, indignation and disgust" (Devlin). For the decay of all moral restraint or the free use of violence or deception would not only cause individual harm but would jeopardise the existence of a society since it would remove the main conditions which make it possible and worthwhile for men to live together in close proximity to each other. On the other hand the decay of moral restraint on, say, extramarital intercourse, or a general change of sexual morality in a permissive direction seems to be quite another matter and not obviously to entail any such consequences as "disintegration" or "men drifting apart."

It seems, therefore, worthwhile pausing to consider two possible ways of discriminating within a social morality the parts which are to be considered essential.

(i) The first possibility is that the common morality which is essential to society, and which is to be preserved by legal enforcement, is that part of its social morality which contains only those restraints and prohibitions that are essential to the existence of any society of human beings whatever. Hobbes and Hume have supplied us with general characterisations of this moral minimum essential for social life: they include rules restraining the free use of violence and minimal forms of rules regarding honesty, promise keeping, fair dealing, and property. It is, however, quite clear that neither Devlin nor Durkheim means that only these elements, which are to be found in common morality, are to be enforced by law, since any utilitarian or supporter of the Wolfenden Report would agree to that. Quite clearly the argument of both Lord Devlin and Durkheim concerns moral rules which may differ from society to society. Durkheim actually insists that the common morality, violations of which are to be punished by the criminal law, may have no relation to utility: "It was not at all useful for them [these prohibitions] to be born, but once they have endured, it becomes necessary that they persist in spite of their irrationality." The morality to be punished includes much that relates "neither to vital interests of society nor to a minimum of justice."

(ii) The second possibility is this: the morality to be enforced, while not coextensive with every jot and title of an existent moral code, includes not only the restraints and prohibitions such as those relating to the use of violence or deception which are necessary to any society whatever, but also what is essential for a particular society. The guiding thought here is that for any society there is to be found, among the provisions of its code of morality, a central core of rules or principles which constitutes its pervasive and distinctive style of life. Lord Devlin frequently speaks in this way of what he calls monogamy adopted "as a moral principle," and of course this does deeply pervade our society in two principal ways. First, marriage is a *legal* institution and the recognition of monogamy as the sole legal form of marriage carries implications for the law related to wide areas of conduct:

the custody and education of children, the rules relating to inheritance and distribution of property, etc. Second, the principle of monogamy is also morally pervasive: monogamous marriage is at the heart of our conception of family life, and with the aid of the law has become part of the structure of society. Its disappearance would carry with it vast changes throughout society so that without exaggeration we might say that it had changed its character.

On this view the morality which is necessary to the existence of society is neither the moral minimum required in all societies (Lord Devlin himself says that the polygamous marriage in a polygamous society may be an equally cohesive force as monogamy is in ours), nor is it every jot and tittle of a society's moral code. What is essential and is to be preserved is the central core. On this footing it would be an open and empirical question whether any particular moral rule or veto, *e.g.*, on homosexuality, adultery, or fornication, is so organically connected with the central core that its maintenance and preservation is required as a vital outwork or bastion. There are perhaps traces of some of these ideas in Lord Devlin but not in Durkheim. But even if we take this to be the position, we are still not really confronted with an empirical claim concerning the connection of the maintenance of a common morality and the prevention of disintegration or "drifting apart." Apart from the point about whether a particular rule is a vital outwork or bastion of the central core, we may still be confronted only with the unexciting tautology depending now on the identification of society, not with the whole of its morality but only with its central core or "character" and this is not the disintegration thesis.

What is required to convert the last mentioned position into the disintegration thesis? It must be the theory that the maintenance of the core elements in a particular society's moral life is in fact necessary to prevent disintegration, because the withering or malignant decay of the central morality is a disintegrating factor. But even if we have got thus far in identifying an empirical claim, there would of course be very many questions to be settled before anything empirically testable could be formulated. What are the criteria in a complex society for determining the existence of a single recognised morality or its central core? What is

"disintegration" and "drifting apart" under modern conditions? I shall not investigate these difficulties but I shall attempt to describe in outline the types of evidence that might conceivably be relevant to the issue if and when these difficulties are settled. They seem to be the following:

(a) Crude historical evidence in which societies—not individuals—are the units. The suggestion is that we should examine societies which have disintegrated and enquire whether their disintegration was preceded by a malignant change in their common morality. This done, we should then have to address ourselves to the possibility of a causal connection between decay of a common morality and disintegration. But of course all the familiar difficulties involved in macroscopic generalisations about society would meet us at this point, and anyone who has attempted to extract generalisations from what is called the decline and fall of the Roman Empire would know that they are formidable. To take only one such difficulty: suppose that all our evidence was drawn from simple tribal societies or closely knit agrarian societies (which would seem to be the most favourable application of Durkheim's theory of mechanical solidarity). We should not, I take it, have much confidence in applying any conclusions drawn from these to modern industrial societies. Or, if we had, it would be because we had some well developed and well evidenced theory to show us that the differences between simple societies and our own were irrelevant to these issues as the differences in the size of a laboratory can safely be ignored as irrelevant to the scope of the generalisations tested by laboratory experiments. Durkheim, it may be said, is peculiarly obscure on just this point, since it is not really clear from his book whether he means that in advanced societies characterized by extensive division of labour the mechanical solidarity which would still be reflected in its criminal law could be disregarded or not.

(b) The alternative type of evidence must be drawn presumably from social psychology and must break down into at least two sub-forms according to the way in which we conceive the alternatives to the maintenance of a common morality. One alternative is general uniform *permissiveness* in the area of conduct previously covered by the common morality. The lapse, for example, of the conception that the choices between two wives or one, heterosexuality of homosexuality, are more than matters of personal taste. This (the alternative of permissiveness) is what Lord Devlin seems to envisage or to fear when he says: "The enemy of society is not error but indifference," and "Whether the new belief is better or worse than the old, it is the interregnum of disbelief that is perilous." On the other hand the alternative may be not permissiveness but *moral pluralism* involving divergent submoralities in relation to the same area of conduct.

To get off the ground with the investigation of the questions that either of these two alternatives opens up, it would be reasonable to abandon any general criteria for the disintegration of society in favour of something sufficiently close to satisfy the general spirit of the disintegration thesis. It would be no doubt sufficient if our evidence were to show that malignant change in a common morality led to a general increase in such forms of antisocial behaviour as would infringe what seem the minimum essentials: the prohibitions and restraints of violence, disrespect for property, and dishonesty. We should then require some account of the conceivable psychological mechanisms supposed to connect the malignant decay of a social morality with the increase in such forms of behavior. Here there would no doubt be signal differences between the alternatives of permissiveness and moral pluralism. On the permissiveness alternative, the theory to be tested would presumably be that in the "interregnum conditions," without the discipline involved in the submission of one area of life, *e.g.*, the sexual, to the requirements of a common morality, there would necessarily be a weakening of the general capacity of individuals for self control. So, with permissiveness in the area formally covered by restrictive sexual morality, there would come increases in violence and dishonesty and a general lapse of those restraints which are essential for any form of social life. This is the view that the

morality of the individual constitutes a seamless web. There is a hint that this, in the last resort, is Lord Devlin's view of the way in which the "interregnum" constitutes a danger to the existence of society: for he replied to my charge that he had assumed without evidence that morality was a seamless web by saying that though "[s]eamlessness presses the simile rather hard," "most men take their morality as a whole." But surely this assumption cannot be regarded as obviously true. The contrary view seems at least equally plausible: permissiveness in certain areas of life (even if it has come about through the disregard of a previously firmly established social morality) might make it easier for men to submit to restraints on violence which are essential for social life.

If we conceive the successor to the "common morality" to be not permissiveness but moral pluralism in some area of conduct once covered by a sexual morality which has decayed through the flouting of its restrictions, the thesis to be tested would presumably be that where moral pluralism develops in this way quarrels over the differences generated by divergent moralities must eventually destroy the minimal forms of restraints necessary for social cohesion. The counter-thesis would be that plural moralities in the conditions of modern large scale societies might perfectly well be mutually tolerant. To many indeed it might seem that the counter-thesis is the more cogent of the two, and that over wide areas of modern life, sometimes hiding behind lip service to an older common morality, there actually are divergent moralities living in peace.

I have done no more than to sketch in outline the type of evidence required to substantiate the disintegration thesis. Till psychologists and sociologists provide such evidence, supporters of the enforcement of morality would do better to rest their case candidly on the conservative rather than on the disintegration thesis.

"Grounds for Coercion: Hard Cases for the Harm Principle"

Joel Feinberg

Whatever else we believe about freedom, most of us believe it is something to be praised, or so luminously a Thing of Value that it is beyond praise. What is it that makes freedom a good thing? Some say that freedom is good in itself quite apart from its consequences. On the other hand, James Fitzjames Stephen wrote that "...the question whether liberty is a good or a bad thing appears as irrational as the question whether fire is a good or a bad thing." Freedom, according to Stephen, is good (when it is good) only because of what it does, not because of what it is.

It would be impossible to demonstrate that freedom is good for its own sake, and indeed, this proposition is far from self-evident. Still, Stephen's analogy to fire seems an injustice to freedom. Fire has no constant and virtually invariant effects that tend to make it, on balance, a good thing whenever and wherever it occurs, and bad only when its subsequent remoter effects are so evil as to counterbalance its direct and immediate ones. Thus, a fire in one's bed while one is sleeping is dreadful because its effects are evil, but a fire under the pot on the stove is splendid because it makes possible a hot cup of coffee when one wants it. The direct effect of fire in these and all other cases is to oxidize material objects and raise the temperature in its immediate environment; but *these* effects, from the point of view of human interests, and considered just in themselves, are neither good nor bad.

Freedom has seemed to most writers quite different in this respect. When a free man violates his neighbor's interests, then his freedom, having been put to bad use, was, on balance, a bad thing, but unlike the fire in the bed, it was not an unalloyed

evil. Whatever the harmful consequences of freedom in a given case, there is always a direct effect on the person of its possessor which must be counted a positive good. Coercion may prevent great evils, and be wholly justified on that account, but it always has its price. Coercion may be on balance a great gain, but its direct effects always, or nearly always, constitute a definite loss. If this is true, there is always a *presumption* in favor of freedom, even though it can in some cases be overridden by more powerful reasons on the other side.

The presumption in favor of freedom is usually said to rest on freedom's essential role in the development of traits of intellect and character which constitute the good of individuals and are centrally important means to the progress of societies. One consensus argument,...and many others, goes roughly as follows. The highest good for man is neither enjoyment nor passive contentment, but rather a dynamic process of growth and self-realization. This can be called "happiness" if we mean by that term what the Greeks did, namely, "The exercise of vital powers along lines of excellence in a life affording them scope." The highest social good is then the greatest possible amount of individual self-realization and (assuming that different persons are inclined by their natures in different ways) the resultant diversity and fullness of life. Self-realization consists in the actualization of certain uniquely human potentialities, the bringing to full development of certain powers and abilities. This in turn requires constant practice in making difficult choices among alternative hypotheses, policies, and actions—and the more difficult the better. John Stuart Mill explained why:

From *Social Philosophy* (Englewood Cliffs, NJ: Prentice Hall, 1973). Reprinted by permission of the publisher.

The human faculties of perception, judgment, discriminative feeling, mental activity, and even moral preference are exercised only in making a choice. He who does anything because it is the custom makes no choice. He gains no practice either in discerning or in desiring what is best. The mental and moral, like the muscular, powers are improved only by being used.

In short, one does not realize what is best in oneself when social pressures to conform to custom lead one mindlessly along. Even more clearly, one's growth will be stunted when one is given no choice in the first place, either because of being kept in ignorance or because one is terrorized by the wielders of bayonets.

Freedom to decide on one's own while fully informed of the facts thus tends to promote the good of the person who exercises it, even if it permits him to make foolish or dangerous mistakes. Mill added to this argument the citation of numerous social benefits that redound indirectly but uniformly to those who grant freedom as well as those who exercise it. We all profit from the fruits of genius, he maintained, and genius, since it often involves doggedness and eccentricity, is likely to flourish only where coercive pressures toward conformity are absent. Moreover, social progress is more likely to occur where there is free criticism of prevailing ways and adventurous experiments in living. Finally, true understanding of human nature requires freedom, since without liberty there will be little diversity, and without diversity *all* aspects of the human condition will be ascribed to fixed nature rather than to the workings of a particular culture.

Such are the grounds for holding that there is always a presumption in favor of freedom, that whenever we are faced with an option between forcing a person to do something and letting him decide on his own whether or not to do it, other things being equal, we should always opt for the latter. If a strong general presumption for freedom has been established, the burden of proof rests on the shoulders of the advocate of coercion, and the philosopher's task will be to state the conditions under which the presumption can be overridden....

If social and political coercion is a harm-causing evil, then one way to justify it is to show that it is necessary for the prevention of even greater evils. That is the generating insight of the "harm to others principle" (henceforth called simply "the

harm principle") which permits society to restrict the liberty of some persons in order to prevent harm to others. Two versions of this principle can be distinguished. The first would justify restriction of one person's liberty to prevent injury to other specific individuals, and can therefore be called "the private harm principle." The second can be invoked to justify coercion on the distinct ground that it is necessary to prevent impairment of institutional practices and regulatory systems that are in the public interest; thus it can be called "the public harm principle." That the private harm principle (whose chief advocate was J. S. Mill) states at least one of the acceptable grounds for coercion is virtually beyond controversy. Hardly anyone would deny the state the right to make criminal such directly injurious conduct as willful homicide, assault and battery, and robbery. Mill often wrote as if prevention of private harm is the *sole* valid ground for state coercion, but this must not have been his considered intention. He would not have wiped from the books such crimes as tax evasion, smuggling, and contempt of court, which need not injure any specific individuals, except insofar as they weaken public institutions in whose health we all have a stake. I shall assume that Mill held both the public and private versions of the harm principle.

In its simplest formulations, the harm principle is still a long way from being a precise guide to the ideal legislator, especially in those difficult cases where harms of different orders, magnitudes, and probabilities must be balanced against one another. Even when made fully explicit and qualified in appropriate ways, however, the unsupplemented harm principle cannot be fairly assessed until it is known precisely what is meant by "harm."

It has become common, especially in legal writings, to take the object of harm always to be an *interest*....

Legal writers classify interests in various ways. One of the more common lists "Interests of Personality," "Interests of Property," "Interest in Reputation," "Interest in Domestic Relations," and "Interest in Privacy," among others. A humanly inflicted harm is conceived as the violation of one of a person's interests, an injury to something in which he has a genuine stake. In the lawyer's usage, an interest is something a person always possesses in some condition, something that can grow and flourish or diminish and decay, but which can rarely be totally lost. Other persons can be said to promote or hinder an individual's interest in bodily health, or in the avoidance of damaging or offensive physical contacts, or in the safety and security of his person, his family, his friends, and his property. One advantage of this mode of speaking is that it permits us to appraise harms by distinguishing between more and less important interests, and between those interests which are, and those which are not, worthy of legal recognition and/or protection.

Is it true that "what a person doesn't know can't *harm* him"? For most cases, this maxim certainly does *not* apply, and it is one of the merits of the "interest" analysis of harm that it explains why. Typically, having one's interests violated is one thing, and knowing that one's interests have been violated is another. The rich man is harmed at the time his home is burgled, even though he may not discover the harm for months; similarly, a soldier is harmed the moment he is wounded, though in the heat of the battle he may not discover even his serious wounds for some time....

The distinction between hurt and (generic) harm raises one additional question. We must include in the category of "hurts" not only physical pains but also forms of mental distress. Our question is whether, in applying the harm principle, we should permit coercion designed to prevent mental distress when the distress is not likely to be followed by hurt or harm of any other kind. Some forms of mental distress (e.g., "hurt feelings") can be ruled out simply on the ground that they are too minor or trivial to warrant interference. Others are so severe that they can lead to mental breakdowns. In such cases, however, it is the consequential harm to mental health and not the mere fact of distress that clearly warrants interference on the ground of harmfulness. Thus, a convenient criterion for determining whether a hurt is sufficiently harmful to justify preventive coercion on that ground suggests itself: the hurt is serious enough if and only if it is either a symptom of a prior or concurrent harm of another order (as a pain in an arm may be the result and sign of a broken bone), or is in itself the cause of a consequential harm (e.g., mental breakdown) of another order.

The relation of offensiveness to harmfulness can be treated in much the same way as that of hurtfulness to harmfulness. The following points can be made of both:

1. Some harms do not offend (as some do not hurt).
2. All offenses (like all hurts) are harms, inasmuch as all men have an interest in not being offended or hurt.
3. Some offenses (like some hurts) are symptoms or consequences of prior or concurrent harms.
4. Some offenses (like some hurts) are causes of subsequent harms: in the case of extreme hurt, harm to health; in the case of extreme offense, harm from provoked ill will or violence. These subsequent harms are harms of a different order, i.e., violations of interests other than the interest in not being hurt or offended.
5. Some offenses, like some hurts, are "harmless," i.e., do not lead to any *further* harm (violations of any interests other than the interest in not being hurt or offended).
6. Although offense and hurt are in themselves harms, they are harms of a relatively trivial kind (unless they are of sufficient magnitude to violate interests in health and peace).

Partly because of points 5 and 6, many writers use the word "harm" in a sense that is much narrower than "the invasion of any interest." In this narrower sense, harm is distinguished from and even contrasted with "mere offense." Some distinguish "harm to one's interests" from "offense to one's feelings" (as if there were no interest in unoffended feelings). This is a permissible, even useful, way of talking, if we agree that offensiveness as such is strictly speaking a kind of harm, but harm of such a trivial kind that it cannot by itself ever counterbalance the direct and immediate harm caused by coercion. One should appreciate how radical the harm principle is when interpreted in the strict and narrow way that excludes mere offensiveness as a relevant sort of harm. Both the British Wolfenden Report and the American Model Penal Code, for example, recognize "harmless" offensiveness as a ground for preventive coercion in some circumstances....For clarity and convenience only, I shall stipulate then that "offensiveness as such" is a proposed ground for coercion distinct from harm of the sort required by the harm principle (narrowly interpreted), so that "the offense principle" can be treated as an independent principle in its own right.

Offensive behavior is such in virtue of its capacity to induce in others any of a large miscellany of mental states that have little in common except that they are unpleasant, uncomfortable, or disliked. These states do not necessarily "hurt," as do sorrow and distress. Rather the relation between them and hurt is analogous to that between physical unpleasantness and pain, for there is also a great miscellany of unpleasant but not painful bodily states—itches, shocks, and discomforts—that have little in common except that they don't hurt but are nevertheless universally disliked. Among the main sorts of "harmless but disliked" *mental* states are irritating sensations (e.g., bad smells, cacophony, clashing colors), disgust, shocked moral sensibilities, and shameful embarrassment.

When the harm principle is unsupplemented by any other accepted ground for coercion, it decrees that state power may not be used against one person to *benefit* another, but only to prevent harm to another. One way of coercing citizens is to force them to pay taxes in support of various state activities. A partisan of the harm principle might be expected to cast a suspicious eye on all such schemes of involuntary support. Indeed, he might argue that taxing some to educate others is to coerce some merely to benefit others, or that taxing some to provide libraries, museums, theatres, or concert halls for others is to coerce some merely to amuse, inspire, or edify others, and is therefore unjustified. On the other hand, an advocate of the harm principle could with consistency *deny* the foregoing propositions if he had a different way of construing the harm-nonbenefit distinction....

Promising correlations, at first sight, are those between harms and unmet *needs* and between benefits and unneeded goods. We harm a man when we deny or deprive him of something he needs; we fail to benefit him (merely) when we deny or deprive him of some good he does not need. An unneeded good is something a person wants which is not necessary for his welfare, something he can do without. To receive something one wants but does not need is to benefit or profit, but not to the point where loss of the gain would be a harm. Thus, if I have an annual salary of one hundred thousand dollars, and my employer gives me a fifty thousand dollar raise, I benefit substan-

tially from his largesse. If he fails to give me a raise, I am not so benefited, but surely not harmed either (given my needs). If he reduces me to five thousand or fires me, however, he not merely fails to benefit me, he causes me harm by withholding money I *need.* These examples suggest that a statesman or legislator who is committed to an unsupplemented harm principle must have means for distinguishing authentic human needs from mere wants, and that his problem is little different in principle from that of the ordinary householder who must often distinguish between "luxuries" and "necessities" when he plans his household budget.

The problem is more complex, however, than these homey examples suggest. The "unmet need" analysis of harm would imply, for example, that a rich man is not harmed by a minor larceny, a conclusion we have already rejected. Still another distinction can be helpful at this point: that between *being in a harmful condition* (whatever its cause or origin) and undergoing *a change in one's condition in a harmful direction.* To deprive even a rich man of money is to damage his interests, that is, to change his condition for the worse, even though not yet to the state of actual injury. Thus, it is to "harm" him in one sense, but not in another. At best, the "unmet need" criterion is a test for determining when a damaged interest has reached the threshold of "actual injury," rather than a weathervane-indicator of harmful directions. Let us stipulate at this point, for the sake of clarity and convenience, that the harm principle be interpreted in such a way that changes in the condition of a protectable interest in harmful directions, even short of the stage of "actual injury" (unmet need), count as a kind of harm, the prevention of which, in some circumstances, may justify coercion. However, when harms have to be ranked and balanced in a given application of the harm principle, an actually injurious condition should outweigh a mere change in a harmful direction.

Arguments against Mill's unsupplemented harm principle (his claim that the private and public harm principles state the *only* grounds for justified interference with liberty) have been mainly of two different kinds. Many have argued that the harm principle justifies too much social and political interference in the affairs of individuals. Others allow that the prevention of individual and social harm is always a ground for interference, but insist that it is by no means the only ground.

Mill maintained in *On Liberty* that social interference is never justified in those of a man's affairs that concern himself only. But no man's affairs have effects on himself alone. There are a thousand subtle and indirect ways in which every individual act, no matter how private and solitary, affects others. It would therefore seem that society has a right, on Mill's own principles, to interfere in every department of human life. Mill anticipated this objection and took certain steps to disarm it. Let it be allowed that no human conduct is entirely, exclusively, and to the last degree self-regarding. Still, Mill insisted, we can distinguish between actions that are plainly other-regarding and those that are "directly," "chiefly," or "primarily" self-regarding. There will be a twilight area of cases difficult to classify, but that is true of many other workable distinctions, including that between night and day.

It is essential to Mill's theory that we make a distinction between two different kinds of consequences of human actions: the consequences *directly* affecting the interests of others, and those of primarily self-regarding behavior which only *indirectly* or *remotely* affect the interests of others. "No person ought to be punished simply for being drunk," Mill wrote, "but a soldier or policeman should be punished for being drunk on duty." A drunk policeman directly harms the interests of others. His conduct gives opportunities to criminals and thus creates grave risk of harm to other citizens. It brings the police into disrepute, and makes the work of his colleagues more dangerous. Finally, it may lead to loss of the policeman's job, with serious consequences for his wife and children.

Consider, on the other hand, a hard working bachelor who habitually spends his evening hours drinking himself into a stupor, which he then sleeps off, rising fresh in the morning to put in another hard day's work. His drinking does not *directly* affect others in any of the ways of the drunk policeman's conduct. He has no family; he drinks alone and sets no direct example; he is not prevented from discharging any of his public duties; he creates no substantial risk of harm to the interests of other individuals. Although even his private conduct will have some effects on the interests of others, these are precisely the sorts of effects Mill would call "indi-

rect" and "remote." First, in spending his evenings the way he does, our solitary tippler is *not* doing any number of other things that might be of greater utility to others. In not earning and spending more money, he is failing to stimulate the economy (except for the liquor industry) as much as he might. Second, he fails to spend his evening time improving his talents and making himself a better person. Perhaps he has a considerable native talent for painting or poetry, and his wastefulness is depriving the world of some valuable art. Third, he may make those of his colleagues who like him sad on his behalf. Finally, to those who know of his habits, he is a "bad example." All of these "indirect harms" together, Mill maintained, do not outweigh the direct and serious harm that would result from social or legal coercion.

Mill's critics have never been entirely satisfied by this. Many have pointed out that Mill is concerned not only with political coercion and legal punishment but also with purely social coercion—moral pressure, social avoidance, ostracism. No responsible critic would wish the state to punish the solitary tippler, but social coercion is another matter. We can't prevent people from disapproving of an individual for his self-regarding faults or from expressing that disapproval to others, without undue restriction on *their* freedom. Such expressions, in Mill's view, are inevitably coercive, constituting a "milder form of punishment." Hence "social punishment" of individuals for conduct that directly concerns only themselves—the argument concludes—is both inevitable and, according to Mill's own principles, proper.

Mill anticipated this objection, too, and tried to cope with it by making a distinction between types of social responses. We cannot help but lower in our estimation a person with serious self-regarding faults. We will think ill of him, judge him to be at fault, and make him the inevitable and proper object of our disapproval, distaste, even contempt. We may warn others about him, avoid his company, and withhold gratuitous benefits from him— "not to the oppression of his individuality but in the exercise of ours." Mill concedes that all of these social responses can function as "penalties"—but they are suffered "only in so far as they are the natural and, as it were, the spontaneous consequences of the faults themselves, not because they are purposely inflicted on him for the sake of punishment" Other responses, on the other hand, add something to the "natural penalties"—pointed snubbing, economic reprisals, gossip campaigns, and so on. The added penalties, according to Mill, are precisely the ones that are never justified as responses to merely self-regarding flaws—"if he displeases us, we may express our distaste; and we may stand aloof from a person as well as from a thing that displeases us, but we shall not therefore feel called on to make his life uncomfortable."

The distinction between self-regarding and other-regarding behavior, as Mill intended it to be understood, does seem at least roughly serviceable, and unlikely to invite massive social interference in private affairs. I think most critics of Mill would grant that, but reject the harm principle on the opposite ground that it doesn't permit enough interference. These writers would allow at least one, and as many as five or more, additional valid grounds for coercion. Each of these proposed grounds is stated in a principle listed below. One might hold that restriction of one person's liberty can be justified:

1. To prevent harm to others, either
   a. injury to individual persons (*The Private Harm Principle*),
      or
   b. impairment of institutional practices that are in the public interest (*The Public Harm Principle*);
2. To prevent offense to others (*The Offense Principle*);
3. To prevent harm to self (*Legal Paternalism*);
4. To prevent or punish sin, i.e., to "enforce morality as such" (*Legal Moralism*);
5. To benefit the self (*Extreme Paternalism*);
6. To benefit others (*The Welfare Principle*).

The liberty-limiting principles on this list are best understood as stating neither necessary nor sufficient conditions for justified coercion, but rather specifications of the *kinds* of reasons that are always relevant or acceptable in support of proposed coercion, even though in a given case they may not be conclusive. Each principle states that interference might be permissible *if* (but not *only if*) a certain condition is satisfied. Hence the principles are not mutually exclusive; it is possible to hold two or more of them at once, even all of them together, and it is possible to deny all of them. Moreover, the principles cannot be construed as

stating sufficient conditions for legitimate interference with liberty, for even though the principle is satisfied in a given case, the general presumption against coercion might not be outweighed. The harm principle, for example, does not justify state interference to prevent a tiny bit of inconsequential harm. Prevention of minor harm always counts in favor of proposals (as in a legislature) to restrict liberty, but in a given instance it might not count *enough* to outweigh the general presumption against interference, or it might be outweighed by the prospect of practical difficulties in enforcing the law, excessive costs, and forfeitures of privacy. A liberty-limiting principle states considerations that are always good reasons for coercion, though neither exclusively nor, in every case, decisively good reasons....

Immoral conduct is no trivial thing, and we should hardly expect societies to tolerate it; yet if men are *forced* to refrain from immorality, their own choices will play very little role in what they do, so that they can hardly develop critical judgment and moral traits of a genuinely praiseworthy kind. Thus legal enforcement of morality seems to pose a dilemma. The problem does not arise if we assume that all immoral conduct is socially harmful, for immoral conduct will then be prohibited by law not just to punish sin or to "force men to be moral," but rather to prevent harm to others. If, however, there are forms of immorality that do not necessarily cause harm, "the problem of the enforcement of morality" becomes especially acute.

The central problem cases are those criminal actions generally called "morals offenses." Offenses against morality and decency have long constituted a category of crimes (as distinct from offenses against the person, offenses against property, and so on). These have included mainly sex offenses, such as adultery, fornication, sodomy, incest, and prostitution, but also a miscellany of nonsexual offenses, including cruelty to animals, desecration of the flag or other venerated symbols, and mistreatment of corpses....Louis B. Schwartz maintains that what sets these crimes off as a class is not their special relation to morality (murder is also an offense against morality, but it is not a "morals offense") but the lack of an essential connection between them and social harm. In particular, their suppression is not required by the public security. Some morals offenses may harm the perpetrators themselves, but the risk of harm of this sort has usually been consented to in advance by the actors. Offense to other parties, when it occurs, is usually a consequence of perpetration of the offenses *in public*, and can be prevented by statutes against "open lewdness," or "solicitation" in public places. That still leaves "morals offenses" committed by consenting adults in private. Should they really be crimes?

In addition to the general presumption against coercion, other arguments against legislation prohibiting private and harmless sexual practices are drawn from the harm principle itself; laws governing private affairs are extremely awkward and expensive to enforce, and have side effects that are invariably harmful. Laws against homosexuality, for example, can only be occasionally and randomly enforced, and this leads to the inequities of selective enforcement and opportunities for blackmail and private vengeance. Moreover, "the pursuit of homosexuals involves policemen in degrading entrapment practices, and diverts attention and effort" from more serious (harmful) crimes of aggression, fraud, and corruption.

These considerations have led some to argue against statutes that prohibit private immorality, but, not surprisingly, it has encouraged others to abandon their exclusive reliance on the harm and/or offense principles, at least in the case of morals offenses. The alternative principle of "legal moralism" has several forms. In its more moderate version it is commonly associated with the views of Patrick Devlin, whose theory, as I understand it, is really an application of the public harm principle. The proper aim of criminal law, he agrees, is the prevention of harm, not merely to individuals, but also (and primarily) to society itself....

The second version of legal moralism is the pure version, not some other principle in disguise. Enforcement of morality as such and the attendant punishment of sin are not justified as means to some further social aim (such as preservation of social cohesiveness) but are ends in themselves. Perhaps J. F. Stephen was expressing this pure moralism when he wrote that "there are acts of wickedness so gross and outrageous that...[protection of others apart], they must be prevented at any cost to the offender and punished if they occur with exemplary severity." From his examples it is clear that Stephen had in mind the very acts that are called "morals offenses" in the law.

It is sometimes said in support of pure legal moralism that the world as a whole would be a better place without morally ugly, even "harmlessly immoral," conduct, and that our actual universe is intrinsically worse for having such conduct in it. The threat of punishment, the argument continues, deters such conduct. Actual instances of punishment not only back up the threat, and thus help keep future moral weeds out of the universe's garden, they also erase past evils from the universe's temporal record by "nullifying" them, or making it as if they never were. Thus punishment, it is said, contributes to the intrinsic value of the universe in two ways: by canceling out past sins and preventing future ones.

There is some plausibility in this view when it is applied to ordinary harmful crimes, especially those involving duplicity or cruelty, which really do seem to "set the universe out of joint." It is natural enough to think of repentance, apology, or forgiveness as "setting things straight," and of punishment as a kind of "payment" or a wiping clean of the moral slate. But in cases where it is natural to resort to such analogies, there is not only a rule infraction, there is also a *victim*—some person or society of persons who have been harmed. Where there is no victim—and especially where there is no profit at the expense of another—"setting things straight" has no clear intuitive content.

Punishment may yet play its role in discouraging harmless private immoralities for the sake of "the universe's moral record." But if fear of punishment is to keep people from illicit intercourse (or from desecrating flags, or mistreating corpses) in the privacy of their own rooms, then morality shall have to be enforced with a fearsome efficiency that shows no respect for individual privacy. If private immoralities are to be deterred by threat of punishment, the detecting authorities must be able to look into the hidden chambers and locked rooms of anyone's private domicile. When we put this massive forfeiture of privacy into the balance along with the usual costs of coercion—loss of spontaneity, stunting of rational powers, anxiety, hypocrisy, and the rest—the price of securing mere outward conformity to the community's moral standards (for that is all that can be achieved by the penal law) is exorbitant.

Perhaps the most interesting of the nonsexual morals offenses, and the most challenging case for application of liberty-limiting principles, is cruelty to animals. Suppose that John Doe is an intelligent, sensitive person with one very severe neurotic trait—he loves to see living things suffer pain. Fortunately, he never has occasion to torture human beings (he would genuinely regret that), for he can always find an animal for the purpose. For a period he locks himself in his room every night, draws the blind, and then beats and tortures a dog to death. The sounds of shrieks and moans, which are music to his ears, are nuisances to his neighbors, and when his landlady discovers what he has been doing she is so shocked she has to be hospitalized. Distressed that he has caused harm to human beings, Doe leaves the rooming house, buys a five hundred acre ranch, and moves into a house in the remote, unpopulated center of his own property. There, in the perfect privacy of his own home, he spends every evening maiming, torturing, and beating to death his own animals.

What are we to say of Doe's bizarre behavior? We have three alternatives. First we can say that it is perfectly permissible since it consists simply in a man's destruction of his own property. How a man disposes in private of his own property is no concern of anyone else providing he causes no nuisance such as loud noises and evil smells. Second, we can say that this behavior is patently immoral even though it causes no harm to the interests of anyone other than the actor; further, since it obviously should *not* be permitted by the law, this is a case where the harm principle is inadequate and must be supplemented by legal moralism. Third, we can extend the harm principle to animals, and argue that the law can interfere with the private enjoyment of property not to enforce "morality as such," but rather to prevent harm to the animals. The third alternative is the most inviting, but not without its difficulties. We *must* control animal movements, exploit animal labor, and, in many cases, deliberately slaughter animals. All these forms of treatment would be "harm" if inflicted on human beings, but cannot be allowed to count as harm to animals if the harm principle is to be extended to them in a realistic way. The best compromise is to recognize one supreme interest of animals, namely the interest in freedom from

cruelly or wantonly inflicted pain, and to count as "harm" all and only invasions of *that* interest.

Up to this point we have considered the harm and offense principles together in order to determine whether between them they are sufficient to regulate conventional immoralities, or whether they need help from a further independent principle, legal moralism. Morals offenses were treated as essentially private so that the offense principle could not be stretched to apply to them. Obscene literature and pornographic displays would appear to be quite different in this respect. Both are materials deliberately published for the eyes of others, and their existence can bring partisans of the unsupplemented harm principle into direct conflict with those who endorse *both* the harm and offense principles.

In its untechnical, prelegal sense, the word "obscenity" refers to material dealing with nudity, sex, or excretion in an offensive manner. Such material becomes obscene in the legal sense when, because of its offensiveness or for some other reason [this question had best be left open in the definition], it is or ought to be without legal protection. The legal definition then incorporates the everyday sense, and essential to both is the requirement that the material be *offensive*. An item may offend one person and not another. "Obscenity," if it is to avoid this subjective relativity, must involve an interpersonal objective sense of "offensive." Material must be offensive by prevailing community standards that are public and well known, or be such that it is apt to offend virtually everyone.

Not all material that is generally offensive need also be harmful in any sense recognized by the harm principle. It is partly an empirical question whether reading or witnessing obscene material causes social harm; reliable evidence, even of a statistical kind, of causal connections between obscenity and antisocial behavior is extremely hard to find. In the absence of clear and decisive evidence of harmfulness, the American Civil Liberties Union insists that the offensiveness of obscene material cannot be a sufficient ground for its repression:

the question in a case involving obscenity, just as in every case involving an attempted restriction upon free speech, is whether the words or pictures are used in such circumstances and are of such a nature as to create a clear and present danger that they will bring about a substantial evil that the state has a right to prevent....We believe that under the current state of knowledge, there is grossly insufficient evidence to show that obscenity brings about *any* substantive evil.

The A.C.L.U. argument employs *only* the harm principle among liberty-limiting principles, and treats literature, drama, and painting as forms of expression subject to the same rules as expressions of opinion. In respect to both types of expression, "every act of deciding what should be barred carries with it a danger to the community." The suppression itself is an evil to the author who is squelched. The power to censor and punish involves risks that socially valuable material will be repressed along with the "filth." The overall effect of suppression, the A.C.L.U. concludes, is almost certainly to discourage nonconformist and eccentric expression generally. In order to override these serious risks, there must be in a given case an even more clear and present danger that the obscene material, if not squelched, will cause even greater harm; such countervailing evidence is never forthcoming. (If such evidence were to accumulate, the A.C.L.U. would be perfectly willing to change its position on obscenity.)

The A.C.L.U. stand on obscenity seems clearly to be the position dictated by the unsupplemented harm principle and its corollary, the clear and present danger test. Is there any reason at this point to introduce the offense principle into the discussion? Unhappily, we may be forced to if we are to do justice to all of our particular intuitions in the most harmonious way. Consider an example suggested by Professor Schwartz. By the provisions of the new Model Penal Code, he writes, "a rich homosexual may not use a billboard on Times Square to promulgate to the general populace the techniques and pleasures of sodomy." If the notion of "harm" is restricted to its narrow sense, that is, contrasted with "offense," it will be hard to reconstruct a rationale for this prohibition based on the harm principle. There is unlikely to be evidence that a lurid and obscene public poster in Times Square would create a clear and present danger of injury to those who fail to avert their eyes in time as they come blinking out of the subway stations. Yet it will be surpassingly difficult for even the most dedicated liberal to advocate freedom of expression in a case of this kind. Hence, if we are to justify coercion in this case, we will likely be driven, however reluctantly, to the offense principle.

There is good reason to be "reluctant" to embrace the offense principle until driven to it by an example like the above. People take perfectly genuine offense at many socially useful or harmless activities, from commercial advertisements to inane chatter. Moreover, widespread irrational prejudices can lead people to be disgusted, shocked, even morally repelled by perfectly innocent activities, and we should be loath to permit their groundless repugnance to override the innocence. The offense principle, therefore, must be formulated very precisely and applied in accordance with carefully formulated standards so as not to open the door to wholesale and intuitively unwarranted repression. At the very least we should require that the prohibited conduct or material be of the sort apt to offend almost everybody, and not just some shifting majority or special interest group.

It is instructive to note that a strictly drawn offense principle would not only justify prohibition of conduct and pictured conduct that is in its inherent character repellent, but also conduct and pictured conduct that is inoffensive in itself but offensive in inappropriate circumstances. I have in mind so-called indecencies such as public nudity. One can imagine an advocate of the unsupplemented harm principle arguing against the public nudity prohibition on the grounds that the sight of a naked body does no one any harm, and the state has no right to impose standards of dress or undress on private citizens. How one chooses to dress, after all, is a form of self-expression. If we do not permit the state to bar clashing colors or bizarre hair styles, by what right does it prohibit total undress? Perhaps the sight of naked people could at first lead to riots or other forms of antisocial behavior, but that is precisely the sort of contingency for which we have police. If we don't take away a person's right of free speech for the reason that its exercise may lead others to misbehave, we cannot in consistency deny his right to dress or undress as he chooses for the same reason.

There may be no answering this challenge on its own ground, but the offense principle provides a ready rationale for the nudity prohibition. The sight of nude bodies in public places is for almost everyone acutely *embarrassing*. Part of the explanation no doubt rests on the fact that nudity has an irresistible power to draw the eye and focus the thoughts on matters that are normally repressed. The conflict between these attracting and repressing forces is exciting, upsetting, and anxiety-producing. In some persons it will create at best a kind of painful turmoil, and at worst that experience…which is called *shame*.…The result is not mere "offense," but a kind of psychic jolt that in many normal people can be a painful wound. Even those of us who are better able to control our feelings might well resent the *nuisance* of having to do so.

If we are to accept the offense principle as a supplement to the harm principle, we must accept two corollaries which stand in relation to it similarly to the way in which the clear and present danger test stands to the harm principle. The first, the *standard of universality*, has already been touched upon. For the offensiveness (disgust, embarrassment, outraged sensibilities, or shame) to be sufficient to warrant coercion, it should be the reaction that could be expected from almost any person chosen at random from the nation as a whole, regardless of sect, faction, race, age, or sex. The second is the *standard of reasonable avoidability*. No one has a right to protection from the state against offensive experiences if he can effectively avoid those experiences with no unreasonable effort or inconvenience. If a nude person enters a public bus and takes a seat near the front, there may be no effective way for other patrons to avoid intensely shameful embarrassment (or other insupportable feelings) short of leaving the bus, which would be an unreasonable inconvenience. Similarly, obscene remarks over a loudspeaker, homosexual billboards in Times Square, and pornographic handbills thrust into the hands of passing pedestrians all fail to be reasonably avoidable.

On the other hand, the offense principle, properly qualified, can give no warrant to the suppression of *books* on the grounds of obscenity. When printed words hide decorously behind covers of books sitting passively on bookstore shelves, their offensiveness is easily avoided. The contrary view is no doubt encouraged by the common comparison of obscenity with "smut," "filth," or "dirt." This in turn suggests an analogy to nuisance law, which governs cases where certain activities create loud noises or terrible odors offensive to neighbors.…There is, however, one vitiating disanalogy in this comparison. In the case of "dirty books" the offense is easily avoidable. There is nothing like the evil smell of rancid garbage oozing right out through the covers

of a book. When an "obscene" book sits on a shelf, who is there to be offended? Those who want to read it for the sake of erotic stimulation presumably will not be offended (or else they wouldn't read it), and those who choose not to read it will have no experience by which to be offended. If its covers are too decorous, some innocents may browse through it by mistake and be offended by what they find, but they need only close the book to escape the offense. Even this offense, minimal as it is, could be completely avoided by prior consultation of trusted book reviewers. I conclude that there are no sufficient grounds derived either from the harm or offense principles for suppressing obscene literature, unless that ground be the protection of children; but I can think of no reason why restrictions on sales to children cannot work as well for printed materials as they do for cigarettes and whiskey.

The liberty-limiting principle called legal paternalism justifies state coercion to protect individuals from self-inflicted harm, or, in its extreme version, to guide them, whether they like it or not, toward their own good. Parents can be expected to justify interference in the lives of their children (e.g., telling them what they must eat and when they must sleep) on the ground that "daddy knows best." Legal paternalism seems to imply that, since the state often perceives the interests of individual citizens better than do the citizens themselves, it stands as a permanent guardian of those interests *in loco parentis*. Put this bluntly, paternalism seems a preposterous doctrine. If adults are treated as children they will come in time to be like children. Deprived of the right to choose for themselves, they will soon lose the power of rational judgment and decision. Even children, after a certain point, had better not be "treated as children," or they will never acquire the outlook and capability of responsible adults.

Yet if we reject paternalism entirely, and deny that a person's own good is ever a valid ground for coercing him, we seem to fly in the face both of common sense and long-established customs and laws. In the criminal law, for example, a prospective victim's freely granted consent is no defense to the charge of mayhem or homicide. The state simply refuses to permit anyone to agree to his own disablement or killing. The law of contracts similarly refuses to recognize as valid contracts to sell oneself into slavery, or to become a mistress, or a second wife. Any ordinary citizen is legally justified in using reasonable force to prevent another from mutilating himself or committing suicide. No one is allowed to purchase certain drugs even for therapeutic purposes without a physician's prescription (doctor knows best). The use of other drugs, such as heroin, for mere pleasure is not permitted under any circumstances. It is hard to find any convincing rationale for all such restrictions apart from the argument that beatings, mutilations, death, concubinage, slavery, and bigamy are always bad for a person whether he or she knows it or not, and that antibiotics are too dangerous for any nonexpert, and narcotics for anyone at all, to take on his own initiative.

The trick is stopping short once one undertakes this path, unless we wish to ban whiskey, cigarettes, and fried foods, which tend to be bad for people, too. We must somehow reconcile our general repugnance for paternalism with the apparent necessity, or at least reasonableness, of some paternalistic regulations. The way to do this is to find mediating maxims or standards of application for the paternalistic principle which restrict its use in a way analogous to that in which the universality and reasonable avoidance tests delimit the offense principle. Let us begin by rejecting the views that the protection of a person from himself is *always* a valid ground for interference and that it is *never* a valid ground. It follows that it is a valid ground only under certain conditions, which we must now try to state.

It will be useful to make some preliminary distinctions. The first is between those cases in which a person directly produces harm to himself (where the harm is the certain and desired end of his conduct), and those cases in which a person simply creates a *risk* of harm to himself in the course of activities directed toward other ends. The man who knowingly swallows a lethal dose of arsenic will certainly die, and death must be imputed as his goal. Another man is offended by the sight of his left hand, so he grasps an ax in his right hand and chops his left hand off. He does not thereby "endanger" his interest in the physical integrity of his limbs, or "risk" the loss of his hand; he brings about the loss directly and deliberately. On the other hand, to smoke cigarettes or to drive at excessive speeds is not to harm oneself directly, but rather to increase beyond a normal level the probability that harm to oneself will result.

The second distinction is that between reasonable and unreasonable risks. There is no form of activity (or inactivity, for that matter) that does not involve some risks. On some occasions we have a choice between more and less risky actions, and prudence dictates that we take the less risky course. However, what is called "prudence" is not always reasonable. Sometimes it is more reasonable to assume a great risk for a great gain than to play it safe and forfeit a unique opportunity. Thus, it is not necessarily more reasonable for a coronary patient to increase his life expectancy by living a life of quiet inactivity than to continue working hard at his career in the hope of achieving something important, even at the risk of a sudden fatal heart attack. Although there is no simple mathematical formula to guide one in making such decisions or for judging them "reasonable" or "unreasonable," there are some decisions that are manifestly unreasonable. It is unreasonable to drive at sixty miles an hour through a twenty mile an hour zone in order to arrive at a party on time, but it may be reasonable to drive fifty miles an hour to get a pregnant wife to the maternity ward. It is foolish to resist an armed robber in an effort to protect one's wallet, but it may be worth a desperate lunge to protect one's very life.

All of these cases involve a number of distinct considerations. If there is time to deliberate one should consider: (1) the degree of probability that harm to oneself will result from a given course of action, (2) the seriousness of the harm being risked, i.e., "the value or importance of that which is exposed to the risk," (3) the degree of probability that the goal inclining one to shoulder the risk will in fact result from the course of action, (4) the value or importance of achieving that goal, that is, just how worthwhile it is to one (this is the intimately personal factor, requiring a decision about one's own preferences, that makes it so difficult for the outsider to judge the reasonableness of a risk), and (5) the necessity of the risk, that is, the availability or absence of alternative, less risky, means to the desired goal.

Certain judgments about the reasonableness of risk assumptions are quite uncontroversial. We can say, for example, that the greater are considerations 1 and 2, the less reasonable the risk, and the greater are considerations 3, 4, and 5, the more reasonable the risk. But in a given difficult case, even where questions of "probability" are meaningful and beyond dispute, and where all the relevant facts are known, the risk decision may defy objective assessment because of its component personal value judgments. In any case, if the state is to be given the right to prevent a person from risking harm to himself (and only himself), it must not be on the ground that the prohibited action is risky, or even extremely risky, but rather that the risk is extreme and, in respect to its objectively assessable components, manifestly unreasonable. There are sometimes very good reasons for regarding even a person's judgment of personal worthwhileness (consideration 4) to be "manifestly unreasonable," but it remains to be seen whether (or when) that kind of unreasonableness can be sufficient grounds for interference.

The third and final distinction is between fully voluntary and not fully voluntary assumptions of a risk. One assumes a risk in a fully voluntary way when one shoulders it while informed of all relevant facts and contingencies, and in the absence of all coercive pressure or compulsion. To whatever extent there is neurotic compulsion, misinformation, excitement or impetuousness, clouded judgment (as, e.g., from alcohol), or immature or defective faculties of reasoning, the choice falls short of perfect voluntariness. Voluntariness, then, is a matter of degree. One's "choice" is *completely involuntary* when it is no choice at all, properly speaking—when one lacks all muscular control of one's movements, or is knocked down or sent reeling by a blow or an explosion—or when, through ignorance, one chooses something other than what one means to choose, as when one thinks the arsenic powder is table salt and sprinkles it on one's scrambled eggs. Most harmful choices, as most choices generally, fall somewhere between the extremes of perfect voluntariness and complete involuntariness.

The central thesis of Mill and other individualists about paternalism is that the fully voluntary choice or consent (to another's doing) of a mature and rational human being concerning matters that directly affect only his own interests is so precious that no one else (especially the state) has a right to interfere with it simply for the person's "own good." No doubt this thesis was also meant to apply to almost-but-not-quite fully voluntary choices as well, and probably even to some substantially nonvoluntary ones (e.g., a neurotic person's choice of a wife who will satisfy his neurotic needs, but only at the price of great unhappiness, eventual divorce,

and exacerbated guilt). However, it is not probable that the individualist thesis was meant to apply to choices near the bottom of the voluntariness scale, and Mill himself left no doubt that he did not intend it to apply to completely involuntary "choices." Neither should we expect antipaternalistic individualism to deny protection to a person from his own nonvoluntary choices, for insofar as the choices are not voluntary they are just as alien to him as the choices of someone else.

Thus Mill would permit the state to protect a man from his own ignorance, at least in circumstances that create a strong presumption that his uninformed or misinformed choice would not correspond to his eventual enlightened one.

> If either a public officer or anyone else saw a person attempting to cross a bridge which had been ascertained to be unsafe, and there were no time to warn him of his danger, they might seize him and turn him back, without any real infringement of his liberty; for liberty consists in doing what one desires, and he does not desire to fall into the river.

Of course, for all the public officer may know, the man on the bridge does desire to fall into the river, or to take the risk of falling for other purposes. Then, Mill argues, if the person is fully warned of the danger and wishes to proceed anyway, that is his business alone, despite the advance presumption that most people do not wish to run such risks. Hence the officer was justified, Mill would argue, in his original interference.

On other occasions a person may need to be protected from some other condition that may render his informed choice substantially less than voluntary. He may be "a child, or delirious, or in some state of excitement or absorption incompatible with the full use of the reflecting faculty." Mill would not permit any such person to cross an objectively unsafe bridge. On the other hand, there is no reason why a child, or an excited person, or a drunkard, or a mentally ill person should not be allowed to proceed on his way home across a perfectly safe thoroughfare. Even substantially nonvoluntary choices deserve protection unless there is good reason to judge them dangerous.

For all we can know, the behavior of a drunk or an emotionally upset person would be exactly the same even if he were sober and calm. But when the behavior seems patently self-damaging and is of a sort in which most calm and normal persons would not engage, then there are strong grounds, if only of a statistical sort, for inferring the opposite; these grounds, on Mill's principle, would justify interference. It may be that there is no kind of action of which it can be said, "No mentally competent adult in a calm, attentive mood, fully informed, and so on, would ever choose (or consent to) that." Nevertheless, there are some actions that create a powerful presumption that an actor in his right mind would not choose them. The point of calling this hypothesis a "presumption" is to require that it be completely overridden before legal permission be given to a person who has already been interfered with to go on as before. For example, if a policeman (or anyone else) sees John Doe about to chop off his hand with an ax, he is perfectly justified in using force to prevent him, because of the presumption that no one could voluntarily choose to do such a thing. The presumption, however, should always be taken as rebuttable in principle; it will be up to Doe to prove before an official tribunal that he is calm, competent, and free, and still wishes to chop off his hand. Perhaps this is too great a burden to expect Doe himself to "prove," but the tribunal should require that the presumption against voluntariness be overturned by evidence from some source or other. The existence of the presumption should require that an objective determination be made, whether by the usual adversary procedures of law courts, or simply by a collective investigation by the tribunal into the available facts. The greater the presumption to be overridden, the more elaborate and fastidious should be the legal paraphernalia required, and the stricter the standards of evidence. The point of the procedure would not be to evaluate the wisdom or worthiness of a person's choice, but rather to determine whether the choice really is his.

This seems to lead us to a form of paternalism so weak and innocuous that it could be accepted even by Mill, namely, that the state has the right to prevent self-regarding harmful conduct only when it is substantially nonvoluntary, or when temporary intervention is necessary to establish whether it is voluntary or not. A strong presumption that no normal person would voluntarily choose or consent to the kind of conduct in question should be a proper ground for detaining the person until the voluntary character of his choice can be estab-

lished. We can use the phrase "the standard of voluntariness" as a label for considerations that mediate application of the principle that a person can be protected from his own folly.

Consider some typical hard cases for the application of the voluntariness standard. First take the problem of harmful drugs. Suppose that Richard Roe requests a prescription of drug X from Dr. Doe, and the following discussion ensues:

DR. DOE: I cannot prescribe drug X to you because it will do you physical harm.

MR. ROE: But you are mistaken. It will not cause me physical harm.

In a case like this, the state, of course, backs the doctor, since it deems medical questions to be technical matters subject to expert opinions. If a layman disagrees with a physician on a question of medical fact, the layman is presumed wrong, and if he nevertheless chooses to act on his factually mistaken belief, his action will be substantially less than fully voluntary. That is, the action of *ingesting a substance which will in fact harm him* is not the action he voluntarily chooses to do (because he does not believe that it is harmful). Hence the state intervenes to protect him not from his own free and voluntary choices, but from his own ignorance.

Suppose however that the exchange goes as follows:

DR. DOE: I cannot prescribe drug X to you because it will do you physical harm.

MR. ROE: Exactly. That's just what I want. I want to harm myself.

In this case Roe is properly apprised of the facts; he suffers from no delusions or misconceptions. Yet his choice is so odd that there exists a reasonable presumption that he has been deprived of the "full use of his reflecting faculty." It is because we know that the overwhelming majority of choices to inflict injury for its own sake on oneself are not fully voluntary that we are entitled to presume that the present choice is not fully voluntary. If no further evidence of derangement, illness, severe depression, or unsettling excitation can be discovered, however, and the patient can convince an objective panel that his choice is voluntary (unlikely event!), then our "voluntariness standard" would permit no further state constraint.

Now consider the third possibility:

DR. DOE: I cannot prescribe drug X to you because it is very likely to do you physical harm.

MR. ROE: I don't care if it causes me physical harm. I'll get a lot of pleasure first, so much pleasure, in fact, that it is well worth running the risk of physical harm. If I must pay a price for my pleasure I am willing to do so.

This is perhaps the most troublesome case. Roe's choice is not patently irrational on its face. A well thought-out philosophical hedonism may be one of his profoundest convictions, involving a fundamental decision of principle to commit himself to the intensely pleasurable, even if brief, life. If no third party interests are directly involved, the state can hardly be permitted to declare his philosophical convictions unsound or "sick" and prevent him from practicing them, without assuming powers that it will inevitably misuse.

On the other hand, this case may be quite similar to the preceding one, depending on what the exact facts are. If the drug is known to give only an hour's mild euphoria and then cause an immediate, violently painful death, then the risks appear so unreasonable as to create a powerful presumption of nonvoluntariness. The desire to commit suicide must always be presumed to be both nonvoluntary and harmful to others until shown otherwise. (Of course, in some cases it can be shown otherwise.) Alternatively, drug X may be harmful in the way nicotine is now known to be harmful; twenty or thirty years of heavy use may create a grave risk of lung cancer or heart disease. Using the drug for pleasure when the risks are of this kind may be to run unreasonable risks, but that is no strong evidence of nonvoluntariness. Many perfectly normal, rational persons voluntarily choose to run precisely these risks for whatever pleasures they find in smoking. To assure itself that such practices are truly voluntary, the state should continually confront smokers with the ugly medical facts so that there is no escaping the knowledge of the exact medical risks to health. Constant reminders of the hazards should be at every hand, with no softening of the gory details. The state might even be justified in using its taxing, regulatory, and persuasive powers to make smoking (and similar drug usage) more difficult or less attractive; but to prohibit it outright would be to tell the voluntary risk-taker that his informed judgments of what is worthwhile are less reasonable than those of the state, and therefore he may not act on them. This is paternalism of the strong kind, unmediated by the voluntariness standard. As a principle of public policy it has an acrid moral flavor, and creates serious risks of governmental tyranny....

U.S. Senate Hearings on Flag Desecration

Senator Gordon Humphrey of New Hampshire and Judge Robert H. Bork

---

**Opening Statement
of Senator Humphrey**

Thank you, Mr. Chairman....Clearly, the Founders meant for the Constitution to be amendable. But amending must always be viewed as a radical remedy. There have been radical wrongs that demanded such a radical remedy: for example, slavery; for example, denial of equal protection of the law; for example, denial of the right to vote on account of race, color, or previous condition of servitude; for example, denial of the right to vote on account of sex; for example, denial of the right

---

From U.S. Senate Committee on Flag Desecration *Hearings*, 101st Cong., 1st Sess., 1989. U.S. Government Y4, J89/2:s, 4KR9, 101-355.

vote by reason of failure to pay any poll tax or other tax. These were radical wrongs demanding a radical remedy.

But does the comparatively rare desecration of our flag merit the radical remedy of amending the Constitution? Further, does this rare act of desecration merit amending of the first amendment—that precious bedrock of our freedom? Not in my view. It does not even come close.

Judging by the hyperactivity of politicians from the President, to Members of Congress, to State legislators, to members of city councils, you would think that American was aflame with burning flags. That is not the case. Americans revere our flag. Every day there are millions—literally millions—of acts of reverence for our flag. School children salute our flag and pledge their allegiance in thousands of classrooms every day. Citizens raise the flag at their homes and their places of business. The flag is displayed at ceremonies of every kind by every kind of group. These are everyday acts that number in the millions every day. They number in the billions every year. Measure that against an occasional burning of the flag. How many cases of desecration are there? Ten or twenty in a year? So few that no one bothers to keep count. In fact, the Department of Justice so far has only found one person presently incarcerated under the Federal flag statute.

So I say enough hyperactivity. Enough breast-beating. Enough political one-upsmanship. Amending the Constitution is serious business, not a ploy for gaining an advantage in the next election....Burning the flag is distasteful. Showing disrespect of any kind toward the flag is disgusting and highly offensive to nearly every American Citizen, including this one. And if the majority rules, the majority in society rules in this case, we shall have a new law or a new provision of the Constitution. A new law will not last, it seems to me. And while it does last, for those few years, Congress will be engaged in an endless struggle defining by statute and redefining by statute just what constitutes desecration.

May I have that bag, please?

I view this constitutes desecration, making footwear, slippers out of the American flag. I mean, there it is. It is unmistakable, stars on a field of blue, red and white stripes, that President and Mrs. Reagan are sitting in the slippers is incidental. That is also an act of disrespect, but it pales in comparison to what has

been done to this flag. Making footwear out of the American flag, that seems to me to be desecration.

If we are going to get into this kind of arcane minutia, I do not know where it will all end. I think it will be an endless riddle, paper flags worn as caps or patches on trousers, it will be endless. But in any event, I think such a law will not last very long at all.

So returning to the matter of a constitutional amendment, Mr. Chairman, the framers of the Bill of Rights, in effect, withdrew from the legislature authority to legislate in a way that would limit free speech. Of course, the right of free speech is not absolute, nor was it meant to be. No one has a right to endanger public safety by means of intemperate speech. No one has a right to injure another through slander or libel. No one has the right to injure or destroy the property of another while expressing himself under the first amendment.

But apart from these restrictions, based upon the upholding of the rights of others, there are no restrictions on our right to free speech, nor should there be. Of course, some will remind me of the laws on pornography. But I hope we are not going to define political debate and political expression, or some of it, as pornography. Some might think it is, but I hope we are not going to define it as thus for the law.

Except to ensure public safety and to protect the rights of others, speech must never be restricted, simply because the majority want it restricted. The right to free speech must always be just as broad and far reaching as the rights of others will permit. However obnoxious and offensive flag burning might be, it does not constitute the grounds for restricting the right to free speech. It does not constitute the grounds for amending the first amendment.

The Republic is in no danger from the isolated few, often demented, who burn the flag. Their tiny sparks of hatred are quickly extinguished by a vast ocean of love for our flag. Those who dishonor the flag are but specks in the huge throngs of Americans who honor and uphold our flag every day.

The Republic can be endangered, however, by political opportunism. It can be endangered by those who might be tempted to use the flag controversy for partisan purposes, and, therefore, I appeal to Republicans and Democrats alike, from the White House to the city halls across America, for the sake of our country, for the sake of the Bill of Rights, for the sake of all that the flag represents, let us not throw the gasoline of partisan politics onto this red hot controversy....

Statement of Hon. Robert H. Bork, American Enterprise Institute

Thank you, Mr. Chairman....There is no need to begin with a tribute to the flag. Reverence for the flag is why we are here. But it is not merely that Americans revere the flag that makes this subject so important. If a multitude of individuals are also to be a community, they must have symbols by which they live, symbols that express their identity as a community. The United States is a large and increasingly diverse and pluralistic society. In that there is always the danger of divisiveness and fragmentation, which makes all the more crucial the preservation of the one symbol we share as an expression of our Nation and our community, the American flag....It is repeatedly said that we should not tamper with the Constitution. But the fact is that this amendment would not alter but would rather restore the first amendment to the Constitution. It is wholly unrealistic to suppose that every decision of the Supreme Court, no matter how wrong, represents the real Constitution. *Texas* v. *Johnson*, the flag burning decision, is a decision that probably no other Supreme Court in our history would have reached. Given that fact, the constitutional amendment before you would not tamper with the historic Constitution but merely with a decision that a switch in one vote would have caused to go the other way.

Johnson holds that flag burning is a mode of expression protected by the first amendment's guarantee of the freedom of speech. The majority's analysis, however, does not support that conclusion.

The first proposition relied upon by the five-Justice majority in *Johnson* was this:

If there is a bedrock principle underlying the First Amendment, it is that government may not prohibit the expression of an idea simply because society finds the idea itself offensive or disagreeable.

The difficulty is that this bedrock principle had no application to the question before the Court. The Texas statute in question did not suppress any idea at all. Johnson's idea, if it deserves to be called that rather than a venting of spleen, was simply the hatred of the United States. He was and is entirely free to

hate the United States and to express his hatred in a hundred ways other than by burning the flag.

In fact, he and his fellow demonstrators did just that by chanting "America, the red, white, and blue, we spit on you," while the flag burned. He was not prosecuted for that chant and no one suggests that he could be. The first amendment guarantees his freedom to speak in that manner. Under the Texas statute, Johnson was free to engage in any form of rhetoric about the flag and the Republic it represents, to use any form of insulting words or gestures he cared to. He was simply not free to desecrate the flag physically.

While the first amendment allows the expression of any opinion or emotion, it has never been interpreted to allow any and all means of expressing opinions or emotions. Even after the *Johnson* decision, one supposes, the Federal Government or a State government could punish such things as delivering a political message over television in obscenities, or expressing a political viewpoint from a sound truck at 2 o'clock in the morning in a residential neighborhood, or making a point by engaging in indecent public behavior. Yet if the rationale of the *Johnson* decision were consistently applied, none of these actions could be punished.

They are all powerful methods of expressing an attitude. Why does the first amendment allow them to be punished? Simply because the community finds them extremely offensive methods of making points that could be made in hundreds of other ways. Simply because putting out of bounds a few means of expressions like that in no way threatens the American system of freedom of speech.

We know that the physical desecration of the flag is like the use of obscenities or of indecent behavior to express an idea. We know that because of the wave of public outrage that followed the Supreme Court's decision in *Johnson*. We know that because 48 States and the United States had enacted laws prohibiting the physical desecration of the flag.

The other proposition upon which the Supreme Court majority rested fares no better. That proposition was the familiar slippery slope argument. But there was no slippery slope here.

The majority opinion stated:

To conclude that the government may permit designated symbols to be used to communicate only a limited set of messages would be to enter territory having no discernible or defensible boundaries. Could the government on this theory, prohibit the burning of state flags, of copies of the Presidential seal, of the Constitution? In evaluating those choices under the first amendment, how would we decide which symbols were sufficiently special to warrant this unique status? To do so, we would be forced to consult our own political preferences, and impose them on the citizenry in the very way that the first amendment forbids us to do.

That argument is wide of the mark. The Justices need not have consulted their own political preferences to decide that the flag is a unique symbol any more than they need to consult their own preferences to decide that the Government may punish expression through indecent behavior. The community's standards decide the question for the court in both instances, and there are objective means for determining those standards.

No other object even remotely resembles the flag as the symbol of our identity as a Nation. Forty-eight States and the United States have not enacted statutes prohibiting the burning of copies of the Constitution. Copies of the Constitution do not fly over public buildings and are not lowered to half mast when a national leader dies. Nobody salutes the Presidential seal. Nobody pledges allegiance to the Presidential seal. Marines did not fight their way across Iwo Jima and up Mount Suribachi to raise the President seal, a copy of the Constitution, or the flag of the State of New Jersey.

"Paternalism"

Gerald Dworkin

Neither one person, nor any number of persons, is warranted in saying to another human creature of ripe years, that he shall not do with his life for his own benefit what he chooses to do with it. [Mill]

I do not want to go along with a volunteer basis. I think a fellow should be compelled to become better and not let him use his discretion whether he wants to get smarter, more healthy or more honest. [General Hershey]

I take as my starting point the "one very simple principle" proclaimed by Mill *On Liberty...*

That principle is, that the sole end for which mankind are warranted, individually or collectively, in interfering with the liberty of action of any of their number, is self-protection. That the only purpose for which power can be rightfully exercised over any member of a civilized community, against his will, is to prevent harm to others. He cannot rightfully be compelled to do or forbear because it will be better for him to do so, because it will make him happier, because, in the opinion of others, to do so would be wise, or even right.

This principle is neither "one" nor "very simple." It is at least two principles; one asserting that self-protection or the prevention of harm to others is sometimes a sufficient warrant and the other claiming that the individual's own good is *never* a sufficient warrant for the exercise of compulsion either by the society as a whole or by its individual members. I assume that no one, with the possible exception of extreme pacifists or anarchists, questions the correctness of the first half of the principle. This essay is an examination of the negative claim embodied in Mill's principle—the objection to paternalistic interferences with a man's liberty.

From *Morality and the Law*, Richard A. Wasserstrom, ed. (Belmont, CA: Wadsworth Publishing Co., 1971). Reprinted by permission of the publisher and the author

By paternalism I shall understand roughly the interference with a person's liberty of action justified by reasons referring exclusively to the welfare, good, happiness, needs, interests or values of the person being coerced. One is always well-advised to illustrate one's definitions by examples but it is not easy to find "pure" examples of paternalistic interferences. For almost any piece of legislation is justified by several different kinds of reasons and even if historically a piece of legislation can be shown to have been introduced for purely paternalistic motives, it may be that advocates of the legislation with an antipaternalistic outlook can find sufficient reasons justifying the legislation without appealing to the reasons which were originally adduced to support it. Thus, for example, it may be that the original legislation requiring motorcyclists to wear safety helmets was introduced for purely paternalistic reasons. But the Rhode Island Supreme Court recently upheld such legislation on the grounds that it was "not persuaded that the legislature is powerless to prohibit individuals from pursuing a course of conduct which could conceivably result in their becoming public charges," thus clearly introducing reasons of a quite different kind. Now I regard this decision as being based on reasoning of a very dubious nature but it illustrates the kind of problem one has in finding examples. The following is a list of the kinds of interferences I have in mind as being paternalistic.

1. Laws requiring motorcyclists to wear safety helmets when operating their machines.
2. Laws forbidding persons from swimming at a public beach when lifeguards are not on duty.
3. Laws making suicide a criminal offense.
4. Laws making it illegal for women and children to work at certain types of jobs.
5. Laws regulating certain kinds of sexual conduct, for example, homosexuality among consenting adults in private.
6. Laws regulating the use of certain drugs which may have harmful consequences to the user but do not lead to antisocial conduct.
7. Laws requiring a license to engage in certain professions with those not receiving a license subject to fine or jail sentence if they do engage in the practice.
8. Laws compelling people to spend a specified fraction of their income on the purchase of retirement annuities (Social Security).
9. Laws forbidding various forms of gambling (often justified on the grounds that the poor are more likely to throw away their money on such activities than the rich who can afford to).
10. Laws regulating the maximum rates of interest for loans.
11. Laws against duelling.

In addition to laws which attach criminal or civil penalties to certain kinds of action there are laws, rules, regulations, decrees which make it either difficult or impossible for people to carry out their plans and which are also justified on paternalistic grounds. Examples of this are:

1. Laws regulating the types of contracts which will be upheld as valid by the courts, for example,…no man may make a valid contract for perpetual involuntary servitude.
2. Not allowing assumption of risk as a defense to an action based on the violation of a safety statute.
3. Not allowing as a defense to a charge of murder or assault the consent of the victim.
4. Requiring members of certain religious sects to have compulsory blood transfusions. This is made possible by not allowing the patient to have recourse to civil suits for assault and battery and by means of injunctions.
5. Civil commitment procedures when these are specifically justified on the basis of preventing the person being committed from harming himself. The D.C. Hospitalization of the Mentally Ill Act provides for involuntary hospitalization of a person who "is mentally ill, and because of that illness, is likely to injure himself or others if allowed to remain at liberty." The term injure in this context applies to unintentional as well as intentional injuries.

All of my examples are of existing restrictions on the liberty of individuals. Obviously one can think of interferences which have not yet been imposed. Thus one might ban the sale of cigarettes….

Bearing these examples in mind, let me return to a characterization of paternalism. I said earlier that I meant by the term, roughly, interference with a person's liberty for his own good. But, as some of the examples show, the class of persons whose good is involved is not always identical with the class of persons whose freedom is restricted. Thus, in the case of professional licensing it is the practitioner who is directly interfered with but it is the would-be patient whose interests are presumably being served. Not allowing the consent of the victim to be a defense to certain types of crime primarily affects the would-be aggressor but it is the interests of the willing victim that we are trying to protect. Sometimes a person may fall into both classes as would be the case if we banned the manufacture and sale of cigarettes and a given manufacturer happened to be a smoker as well.

Thus we may first divide paternalistic interferences into "pure" and "impure" cases. In "pure" paternalism the class of persons whose freedom is restricted is identical with the class of persons whose benefit is intended to be promoted by such restrictions. Examples: the making of suicide a crime, requiring passengers in automobiles to wear seat belts, requiring a Christian Scientist to receive a blood transfusion. In the case of "impure" paternalism in trying to protect the welfare of a class of persons we find that the only way to do so will involve restricting the freedom of other persons besides those who are benefitted. Now it might be thought that there are no cases of "impure" paternalism since any such case could always be justified on nonpaternalistic grounds, that is, in terms of preventing harm to others. Thus we might ban cigarette manufacturers from continuing to manufacture their product on the grounds that we are preventing them from causing illness to others in the same way that we prevent other manufacturers from releasing pollutants into the atmosphere, thereby causing danger to the members of the community. The difference is, however, that in the former but not the latter case the harm is of such a nature that it could be avoided by those individuals affected if they so chose. The incurring of the harm requires, so to speak, the active cooperation of the victim. It would be mistaken theoretically and hypocritical in practice to assert that our interference in such cases is just like our interference in standard cases of protecting others from harm. At the very least someone interfered with in this way can reply that no one is complaining about his activities. It may be that impure paternalism requires arguments or reasons of a stronger kind in order to be justified, since there are persons who are losing a portion of their liberty and they do not even have the solace of having it be done "in their own interest." Of course in some sense, if paternalistic justifications are ever correct, then we are protecting others, we are preventing some from

injuring others, but it is important to see the differences between this and the standard case.

Paternalism then will always involve limitations on the liberty of some individuals in their own interest but it may also extend to interferences with the liberty of parties whose interests are not in question.

Finally, by way of some more preliminary analysis, I want to distinguish paternalistic interference with liberty from a related type with which it is often confused. Consider, for example, legislation which forbids employees to work more than, say, forty hours per week. It is sometimes argued that such legislation is paternalistic for if employees desired such a restriction on their hours of work they could agree among themselves to impose it voluntarily. But because they do not the society impose its own conception of their best interests upon them by the use of coercion. Hence this is paternalism.

Now it may be that some legislation of this nature is, in fact, paternalistically motivated. I am not denying that. All I want to point out is that there is another possible way of justifying such measures which is not paternalistic in nature. It is not paternalistic because, as Mill puts it in a similar context, such measures are "required not to overrule the judgment of individuals respecting their own interest, but to give effect to that judgment: they being unable to give effect to it except by concert, which concert again cannot be effectual unless it receives validity and sanction from the law." (*Principles of Political Economy*).

The line of reasoning here is a familiar one first found in Hobbes and developed with great sophistication by contemporary economists in the last decade or so. There are restrictions which are in the interests of a class of persons taken collectively but are such that the immediate interest of each individual is furthered by his violating the rule when others adhere to it. In such cases the individuals involved may need the use of compulsion to give effect to their collective judgment of their own interest by guaranteeing each individual compliance by the others. In these cases compulsion is not used to achieve some benefit which is not recognized to be a benefit by those concerned, but rather because it is the only feasible means of achieving some benefit which *is* recognized as such by all concerned. This way of viewing matters provides us with another characterization of paternalism in general. Paternalism might be thought of as the use of coercion to achieve a good which is not recognized as such by those persons for whom the good is intended. Again while this formulation captures the heart of the matter—it is surely what Mill is objecting to in *On Liberty*—the matter is not always quite like that. For example, when we force motorcyclists to wear helmets we are trying to promote a good—the protection of the person from injury—which is surely recognized by most of the individuals concerned. It is not that a cyclist doesn't value his bodily integrity; rather, as a supporter of such legislation would put it, he either places, perhaps irrationally, another value or good (freedom from wearing a helmet) above that of physical well-being or, perhaps, while recognizing the danger in the abstract, he either does not fully appreciate it or he underestimates the likelihood of its occurring. But now we are approaching the question of possible justifications of paternalistic measures and the rest of this essay will be devoted to that question.

I shall begin for dialectical purposes by discussing Mill's objections to paternalism and then go on to discuss more positive proposals.

An initial feature that strikes one is the absolute nature of Mill's prohibitions against paternalism. It is so unlike the carefully qualified admonitions of Mill and his fellow utilitarians on other moral issues. He speaks of self-protection as the *sole* end warranting coercion, of the individual's own goals as *never* being a sufficient warrant. Contrast this with his discussion of the prohibition against lying in *Utilitarianism*:

Yet that even this rule, sacred as it is, admits of possible exception, is acknowledged by all moralists, the chief of which is where the with-holding of some fact...would save an individual...from great and unmerited evil.

The same tentativeness is present when he deals with justice:

It is confessedly unjust to break faith with any one: to violate an engagement, either express or implied, or disappoint expectations raised by our own conduct, at least if we have raised these expectations knowingly and

voluntarily. Like all the other obligations of justice already spoken of, this one is not regarded as absolute, but as capable of being overruled by a stronger obligation of justice on the other side.

This anomaly calls for some explanation. The structure of Mill's argument is as follows:

1. Since restraint is an evil the burden of proof is on those who propose such restraint.
2. Since the conduct which is being considered is purely self-regarding, the normal appeal to the protection of the interests of others is not available.
3. Therefore we have to consider whether reasons involving reference to the individual's own good, happiness, welfare, or interests are sufficient to overcome the burden of justification.
4. We either cannot advance the interests of the individual by compulsion, or the attempt to do so involves evils which outweigh the good done.
5. Hence the promotion of the individual's own interests does not provide a sufficient warrant for the use of compulsion.

Clearly the operative premise here is (4), and it is bolstered by claims about the status of the individual as judge and appraiser of his welfare, interests, needs, et cetera:

With respect to his own feelings and circumstances, the most ordinary man or woman has means of knowledge immeasurably surpassing those that can be possessed by any one else.

He is the man most interested in his own well-being: the interest which any other person, except in cases of strong personal attachment, can have in it is trifling, compared to that which he himself has.

These claims are used to support the following generalizations concerning the utility of compulsion for paternalistic purposes.

The interferences of society to overrule his judgment and purposes in what only regards himself must be grounded on general presumptions; which may be altogether wrong, and even if right, are as likely as not to be misapplied to individual cases.

But the strongest of all the arguments against the interference of the public with purely personal conduct is that when it does interfere, the odds are that it interferes wrongly and in the wrong place.

All errors which the individual is likely to commit against advice and warning are far outweighed by the evil of allowing others to constrain him to what they deem his good.

Performing the utilitarian calculation by balancing the advantages and disadvantages, we find that: "Mankind are greater gainers by suffering each other to live as seems good to themselves, than by compelling each other to live as seems good to the rest." Ergo, (4).

This classical case of a utilitarian argument with all the premises spelled out is not the only line of reasoning present in Mill's discussion. There are asides, and more than asides, which look quite different and I shall deal with them later. But this is clearly the main channel of Mill's thought and it is one which has been subjected to vigorous attack from the moment it appeared—most often by fellow utilitarians. The link that they have usually seized on is, as Fitzjames Stephen put it in *Liberty, Equality, Fraternity*, the absence of proof that the "mass of adults are so well acquainted with their own interests and so much disposed to pursue them that no compulsion or restraint put upon them by any others for the purpose of promoting their interest can really promote them." Even so sympathetic a critic as H. L. A. Hart is forced to the conclusion that:

In Chapter 5 of his essay [On Liberty] Mill carried his protests against paternalism to lengths that may now appear to us as fantastic....No doubt if we no longer sympathise with this criticism this is due, in part, to a general decline in the belief that individuals know their own interest best.

Mill endows the average individual with "too much of the psychology of a middle-aged man whose desires are relatively fixed, not liable to be artificially stimulated by external influences; who knows what he wants and what gives him satisfaction or happiness; and who pursues these things when he can."

Now it is interesting to note that Mill himself was aware of some of the limitations on the doctrine that the individual is the best judge of his own interests. In his discussion of government intervention in general (even where the intervention does not interfere with liberty but provides alternative institutions to those of the market) after making claims which are parallel to those just discussed, for example, "People understand their own business and their own interests better, and care for them more, than the government does, or can be expected to do," he goes on to an intelligent discussion of the "very large and conspicuous exceptions" to the maxim that:

Most persons take a juster and more intelligent view of their own interest, and of the means of promoting it than can either be prescribed to them by a general enactment of the legislature, or pointed out in the particular case by a public functionary.

Thus there are things

of which the utility does not consist in ministering to inclinations, nor in serving the daily uses of life, and the want of which is least felt where the need is greatest. This is peculiarly true of those things which are chiefly useful as tending to raise the character of human beings. The uncultivated cannot be competent judges of cultivation. Those who most need to be made wiser and better, usually desire it least, and, if they desire it, would be incapable of finding the way to it by their own lights.

...A second exception to the doctrine that individuals are the best judges of their own interest, is when an individual attempts to decide irrevocably now what will be best for his interest at some future and distant time. The presumption in favor of individual judgment is only legitimate, where the judgment is grounded on actual, and especially on present, personal experience; not where it is formed antecedently to experience, and not suffered to be reversed even after experience has condemned it.

The upshot of these exceptions is that Mill does not declare that there should never be government interference with the economy but rather that

...in every instance, the burden of making out a strong case should be thrown not on those who resist but those who recommend government interference. Letting alone, in short, should be the general practice; every departure from it, unless required by some great good, is a certain evil.

In short, we get a presumption, not an absolute prohibition. The question is why doesn't the argument against paternalism go the same way?

I suggest that the answer lies in seeing that in addition to a purely utilitarian argument Mill uses another as well. As a utilitarian, Mill has to show, in Fitzjames Stephen's words, that: "Self-protection apart, no good object can be attained by any compulsion which is not in itself a greater evil than the absence of the object which the compulsion obtains." To show this is impossible, one reason being that it is isn't true. Preventing a man from selling himself into slavery (a paternalistic measure which Mill himself accepts as legitimate), or from taking heroin, or from driving a car without wearing seat belts may constitute a lesser evil than allowing him to do any of these things. A consistent utilitarian can only argue against paternalism on the grounds that it (as a matter of fact) does not maximize the good. It is always a contingent question that may be returned by the evidence. But there is also a non-contingent argument which runs through *On Liberty*. When Mill states that "there is a part of the life of every person who has come to years of discretion, within which the individuality of that person ought to reign uncontrolled either by any other person or by the public collectively," he is saying something about what it means to be a person, an autonomous agent. It is because coercing a person for his own good denies this status as an independent entity that Mill objects to it so strongly and in such absolute terms. To be able to choose is a good that is independent of the wisdom of what is chosen. A man's "mode of laying out his existence is the best, not because it is the best in itself, but because it is his own mode." It is the privilege and proper condition of a human being, arrived at the maturity of his faculties, to use and interpret experience in his own way.

As further evidence of this line of reasoning in Mill, consider the one exception to his prohibition against paternalism.

In this and most civilized countries, for example, an engagement by which a person should sell himself, or allow himself to be sold, as a slave, would be null and void; neither enforced by law nor by opinion. The ground for thus limiting his power of voluntarily disposing of his own lot in life, is apparent, and is very clearly seen in this extreme case. The reason for not interfering, unless for the sake of others, with a person's voluntary acts, is consideration for his liberty. His voluntary choice is evidence that what he so chooses is desirable, or at least endurable, to him, and his good is on the whole best provided for by allowing him to take his own means of pursuing it. But by selling himself for a slave, he abdicates his liberty; he foregoes any future use of it beyond that single act. He therefore defeats, in his own case, the very purpose which is the justification of allowing him to dispose of himself. He is no longer free; but is thenceforth in a position which has no longer the presumption

in its favour, that would be afforded by his voluntarily remaining in it. The principle of freedom cannot require that he should be free not to be free. It is not freedom to be allowed to alienate his freedom.

Now leaving aside the fudging on the meaning of freedom in the last line, it is clear that part of this argument is incorrect. While it is true that *future* choices of the slave are not reasons for thinking that what he chooses then is desirable for him, what is at issue is limiting his immediate choice; and since this choice is made freely, the individual may be correct in thinking that his interests are best provided for by entering such a contract. But the main consideration for not allowing such a contract is the need to preserve the liberty of the person to make future choices. This gives us a principle—a very narrow one—by which to justify some paternalistic interferences. Paternalism is justified only to preserve a wider range of freedom for the individual in question. How far this principle could be extended, whether it can justify all the cases in which we are inclined upon reflection to think paternalistic measures justified, remains to be discussed. What I have tried to show so far is that there are two strains of argument in Mill—one a straightforward utilitarian mode of reasoning and one which relies not on the goods which free choice leads to but on the absolute value of the choice itself. The first cannot establish any absolute prohibition but at most a presumption and indeed a fairly weak one given some fairly plausible assumptions about human psychology; the second, while a stronger line of argument, seems to me to allow on its own grounds a wider range of paternalism than might be suspected. I turn now to a consideration of these matters.

We might begin looking for principles governing the acceptable use of paternalistic power in cases where it is generally agreed that it is legitimate. Even Mill intends his principles to be applicable only to mature individuals, not those in what he calls "non-age." What is it that justifies us in interfering with children? The fact that they lack some of the emotional and cognitive capacities required in order to make fully rational decisions. It is an empirical question to just what extent children have an adequate conception of their own present and future interests but there is not much doubt that there are many deficiencies. For example, it is very difficult for a child to defer gratification for any considerable period of time. Given these deficiencies and given the very real and permanent dangers that may befall the child, it becomes not only permissible but even a duty of the parent to restrict the child's freedom in various ways. There is however an important moral limitation on the exercise of such parental power which is provided by the notion of the child eventually coming to see the correctness of his parent's interventions. Parental paternalism may be thought of as a wager by the parent on the child's subsequent recognition of the wisdom of the restrictions. There is an emphasis on what could be called future-oriented consent—on what the child will come to welcome, rather than on what he does welcome.

The essence of this idea has been incorporated by idealist philosophers into various types of "real-will" theory as applied to fully adult persons. Extensions of paternalism are argued for by claiming that in various respects, chronologically mature individuals share the same deficiencies in knowledge, capacity to think rationally, and the ability to carry out decisions that children possess. Hence in interfering with such people we are in effect doing what they would do if they were fully rational. Hence we are not really opposing their will, hence we are not really interfering with their freedom....Still the basic notion of consent is important and seems to me the only acceptable way of trying to delimit an area of justified paternalism.

Let me start by considering a case where the consent is not hypothetical in nature. Under certain conditions it is rational for an individual to agree that others should force him to act in ways which, at the time of action, the individual may not see as desirable. If, for example, a man knows that he is subject to breaking his resolves when temptation is present, he may ask a friend to refuse to entertain his requests at some later stage.

A classical example is given in the Odyssey when Odysseus commands his men to tie him to the mast and refuse all future orders to be set free, because he knows the power of the Sirens to enchant men with their songs. Here we are on relatively sound ground in later refusing Odysseus' request to be set free. He may even claim to have changed his mind but, since it is *just* such changes that he wished to guard against we are entitled to ignore them.

A process analogous to this may take place on a social rather than individual basis. An electorate may mandate its representatives to pass legislation which when it comes time to "pay the price" may be unpalatable. I may believe that a tax increase is necessary to halt inflation though I may resent the lower pay check each month. However in both this case and that of Odysseus, the measure to be enforced is specifically requested by the party involved and at some point in time there is genuine consent and agreement on the part of those persons whose liberty is infringed. Such is not the case for the paternalistic measures we have been speaking about. What must be involved here is not consent to specific measures but rather consent to a system of government, run by elected representatives, with an understanding that they may act to safeguard our interests in certain limited ways.

I suggest that since we are all aware of our irrational propensities, deficiencies in cognitive and emotional capacities, and avoidable and unavoidable ignorance, it is rational and prudent for us to in effect take out "social insurance policies." We may argue for and against proposed paternalistic measures in terms of what fully rational individuals would accept as forms of protection. Now clearly, since the initial agreement is not about specific measures we are dealing with a more-or-less blank check and therefore there have to be carefully defined limits. What I am looking for are certain kinds of conditions which make it plausible to suppose that rational men could reach agreement to limit their liberty even when other men's interest are not affected.

Of course as in any kind of agreement schema there are great difficulties in deciding what rational individuals would or would not accept. Particularly in sensitive areas of personal liberty, there is always a danger of the dispute over agreement and rationality being a disguised version of evaluative and normative disagreement.

Let me suggest types of situations in which it seems plausible to suppose that fully rational individuals would agree to having paternalistic restrictions imposed upon them. It is reasonable to suppose that there are "goods" such as health which any person would want to have in order to pursue his own good—no matter how that good is conceived. This is an argument used in connection with compulsory education for children but it seems to me that it can be extended to other goods which have this character. Then one could agree that the attainment of such goods should be promoted even when not recognized to be such, at the moment, by the individuals concerned.

An immediate difficulty arises from the fact that men are always faced with competing goods and that there may be reasons why even a value such as health—or indeed life—may be overridden by competing values. Thus the problem with the Christian Scientist and blood transfusions. It may be more important for him to reject "impure substances" than to go on living. The difficult problem that must be faced is whether one can give sense to the notion of a person irrationally attaching weights to competing values.

Consider a person who knows the statistical data on the probability of being injured when not wearing seat belts in an automobile and knows the types and gravity of the various injuries. He also insists that the inconvenience attached to fastening the belt every time he gets in and out of the car outweighs for him the possible risks to himself. I am inclined in this case to think that such a weighing is irrational. Given his life plans, which we are assuming are those of the average person, his interests and commitments already undertaken, I think it is safe to predict that we can find inconsistencies in his calculations at some point. I am assuming that this is not a man who for some conscious or unconscious reasons is trying to injure himself nor is he a man who just likes to "live dangerously." I am assuming that he is like us in all the relevant respects but just puts an enormously high negative value on inconvenience—one which does not seem comprehensible or reasonable.

It is always possible, of course, to assimilate this person to creatures like myself. I, also, neglect to fasten my seat belt and I concede such behavior is not rational but not because I weigh the inconvenience differently from those who fasten the belts. It is just that having made (roughly) the same calculation as everybody else, I ignore it in my actions....A plausible explanation for this deplorable habit is that although I know in some intellectual sense what the probabilities and risks are I do not fully appreciate them in an emotionally genuine manner.

We have two distinct types of situation in which a man acts in a nonrational fashion. In one case he attaches incorrect weights to some of his values; in the other he neglects to act in accordance with his actual preferences and desires. Clearly there is a stronger and more persuasive argument for paternalism in the latter situation. Here we are really not—by assumption—imposing a good on another person. But why may we not extend our interference to what we might call evaluative delusions? After all, in the case of cognitive delusions we are prepared, often, to act against the expressed will of the person involved. If a man believes that when he jumps out the window he will float upwards—Robert Nozick's example—would not we detain him, forcibly if necessary? The reply will be that this man doesn't wish to be injured and if we could convince him that he is mistaken as to the consequences of his action, he would not wish to perform the action. But part of what is involved in claiming that the man who doesn't fasten his seat-belts is attaching an incorrect weight to the inconvenience of fastening them is that if he were to be involved in an accident and severely injured he would look back and admit that the inconvenience wasn't as bad as all that. So there is a sense in which, if I could convince him of the consequences of his action, he also would not wish to continue his present course of action. Now the notion of consequences being used here is covering a lot of ground. In one case it's being used to indicate what will or can happen as a result of a course of action and in the other it's making a prediction about the future evaluation of the consequences—in the first sense—of a course of action. And whatever the difference between facts and values—whether it be hard and fast or soft and slow—we are genuinely more reluctant to consent to interferences where evaluative differences are the issue. Let me now consider another factor which comes into play in some of these situations which may make an important difference in our willingness to consent to paternalistic restrictions.

Some of the decisions we make are of such a character that they produce changes which are in one or another way irreversible. Situations are created in which it is difficult or impossible to return to anything like the initial stage at which the decision was made. In particular, some of these changes will make it impossible to continue to make reasoned choices in the future. I am thinking specifically of decisions which involve taking drugs that are physically or psychologically addictive and those which are destructive of one's mental and physical capacities.

I suggest we think of the imposition of paternalistic interferences in situations of this kind as being a kind of insurance policy which we take out against making decisions which are far-reaching, potentially dangerous and irreversible. Each of these factors is important. Clearly there are many decisions we make that are relatively irreversible. In deciding to learn to play chess, I could predict in view of my general interest in games that some portion of my free time was going to be preempted and that it would not be easy to give up the game once I acquired a certain competence. But my whole life style was not going to be jeopardized in an extreme manner. Further it might be argued that even with addictive drugs such as heroin one's normal life plans would not be seriously interfered with if an inexpensive and adequate supply were readily available. So this type of argument might have a much narrower scope than appears to be the case at first.

A second class of cases concerns decisions which are made under extreme psychological and sociological pressures. I am not thinking here of the making of the decision as being something one is pressured into—for example, a good reason for making duelling illegal is that unless this is done many people might have to manifest their courage and integrity in ways in which they would rather not do so—but rather of decisions, such as that to commit suicide, which are usually made at a point where the individual is not thinking clearly and calmly about the nature of his decision. In addition, of course, this comes under the previous heading of all-too-irrevocable decisions. Now there are practical steps which a society could take if it wanted to decrease the possibility of suicide—for example not paying social security benefits to the survivors or, as religious institutions do, not allowing persons to be buried with the same status as natural deaths. I think we may count these as interferences with the liberty of persons to attempt suicide and the question is whether they are justifiable.

Using my argument schema the question is whether rational individuals would consent to such limitations. I see no reason for them to consent to an absolute prohibition but I do think it is reasonable for them to agree to some kind of enforced

waiting period. Since we are all aware of the possibility of temporary states, such as great fear of depression, that are inimical to the making of well-informed and rational decisions, it would be prudent for all of us if there were some kind of institutional arrangement whereby we were restrained from making a decision which is so irreversible. What this would be like in practice is difficult to envisage and it may be that if no practical arrangements were feasible we would have to conclude that there should be no restriction at all on this kind of action. But we might have a "cooling off" period, in much the same way that we now require couples who file for divorce to go through a waiting period. Or, more far-fetched, we might imagine a Suicide Board composed of a psychologist and another member picked by the applicant. The Board would be required to meet and talk with the person proposing to take his life, though its approval would not be required.

A third class of decisions—these classes are not supposed to be disjoint—involves dangers which are either not sufficiently understood or appreciated correctly by the persons involved. Let me illustrate, using the example of cigarette smoking, a number of possible cases.

1. A man may not know the facts—for example, smoking between one and two packs a day shortens life expectancy 6.2 years, the costs and pain of the illness caused by smoking, et cetera.
2. A man may know the facts, wish to stop smoking, but not have the requisite will-power.
3. A man may know the facts but not have them play the correct role in his calculation because, say, he discounts the danger psychologically since it is remote in time and/or inflates the attractiveness of other consequences of his decision which he regards as beneficial.

In case 1 what is called for is education, the posting of warnings, et cetera. In case 2 there is no theoretical problem. We are not imposing a good on someone who rejects it. We are simply using coercion to enable people to carry out their own goals. (Note: There obviously is a difficulty in that only a subclass of the individuals affected wish to be prevented from doing what they are doing.) In case 3 there is a sense in which we are imposing a good on someone in that given his current appraisal of the facts he doesn't wish to be restricted. But in another sense we are not imposing a good since what is being claimed—and what must be shown or at least argued for—is that an accurate accounting on his part would lead him to reject his current course of action. Now we all know that such cases exist, that we are prone to disregarding dangers that are only possibilities, that immediate pleasures are often magnified and distorted.

If in addition the dangers are severe and far-reaching, we could agree to allow the state a certain degree of power to intervene in such situations. The difficulty is in specifying in advance, even vaguely, the class of cases in which intervention will be legitimate.

A related difficulty is that of drawing a line so that it is not the case that all ultra-hazardous activities are ruled out, for example, mountain-climbing, bull-fighting, sports-car racing, et cetera. There are some risks—even very great ones—which a person is entitled to take with his life.

A good deal depends on the nature of the deprivation—for example, does it prevent the person from engaging in the activity completely or merely limit his participation—and how important to the nature of the activity is the absence of restriction when this is weighed against the role that the activity plays in the life of the person. In the case of automobile seat belts, for example, the restriction is trivial in nature, interferes not at all with the use or enjoyment of the activity, and does, I am assuming, considerably reduce a high risk of serious injury. Whereas, for example, making mountain-climbing illegal completely prevents a person from engaging in an activity which may play an important role in his life and his conception of the person he is.

In general, the easiest cases to handle are those which can be argued about in the terms which Mill thought to be so important—a concern not just for the happiness or welfare, in some broad sense, of the individual but rather a concern for the autonomy and freedom of the person. I suggest that we would be most likely to consent to paternalism in those instances in which it preserves and enhances for the individual his ability to rationally consider and carry out his own decisions.

I have suggested in this essay a number of types of situations in which it seems plausible that rational men would agree to granting the legislative powers of a society the right to impose restrictions on what Mill calls "self-regarding" conduct. However, rational men knowing something about the resources of ignorance, ill-will and stupidity available to the lawmakers of a society—a good case in point is the history of drug legislation in the United States—will be concerned to limit such intervention to a minimum. I suggest in closing two principles designed to achieve this end.

In all cases of paternalistic legislation there must be a heavy and clear burden of proof placed on the authorities to demonstrate the exact nature of the harmful effects (or beneficial consequences) to be avoided (or achieved) and the probability of their occurrence. The burden of proof here is two-fold—what lawyers distinguish as the burden of going forward and the burden of persuasion. That the authorities have the burden of going forward means that it is up to them to raise the question and bring forward evidence of the evils to be avoided. Unlike the case of new drugs, where the manufacturer must produce some evidence that the drug has been tested and found not harmful, no citizen has to show with respect to self-regarding conduct that it is not harmful or promotes his best interest. In addition the nature and cogency of the evidence for the harmfulness of the course of action must be set at a high level. To paraphrase a formulation of the burden of proof for criminal proceedings—better ten men ruin themselves than one man be unjustly deprived of liberty.

Finally, I suggest a principle of the least restrictive alternative. If there is an alternative way of accomplishing the desired end without restricting liberty although it may involve great expense, inconvenience, et cetera, the society must adopt it.

"Pornography and the Tyranny of the Majority"

Elizabeth H. Wolgast

The respect that atomism accords individuals justifies the maximum degree of freedom of expression, and that freedom protects pornography from public control. But many objectors to pornography, righteously indignant, also emphasize individual respect, particularly the respect due to women as sexual partners. Thus conflicting views, on both sides fervent and moralistic, draw their support from a single atomistic root. Where does such conflict lead us?

"If all mankind minus one were of one opinion," John Stuart Mill wrote, "mankind would be no more justified in silencing that one person than he, if he had the power, would be justified in silencing mankind." No matter how great the majority, the very power to control opinion and expression is illegitimate, he argued. Worse, such power "is robbing the human race" of the chance to hear different sides of a question whether right or wrong, and thus does injury to the whole community.

Society has no right to demand conformity to a set of beliefs, to "maim by compression, like a Chinese lady's foot, every part of human nature which stands out prominently, and tends to make the person markedly dissimilar in outline to commonplace humanity." A person needs opportunity to live as he chooses, to take up causes passionately, make mistakes, change his or her mind. Only in this way can anyone develop to the fullest potential. "Human nature is not a machine to be built after a model, and set to do exactly the work prescribed for it, but a tree, which requires to grow and develop itself on all sides, according to the tendency of the inward forces which make it a living thing." Society will itself benefit when people have liberty to experiment in ideas and ways of living, Mill believed, for it is innovators, not conformists, who advance culture.

Truth also is advanced when people are allowed to express all opinions and to debate every question. And who is it argues against a popular view but a minority of dissenters? They are the ones, then, who need the most protection: "On any of the great open questions...if either of the two opinions has a better claim than the other, not merely to be tolerated but to be encouraged...it is the one which happens at the particular time and place to be in a minority. That is the one which for the time being represents the neglected interests, the side of human well-being which is in danger of obtaining less than its share."

Even in the gentler form of custom, majority tyranny is as much to be feared as political tyranny, Mill believes, and maybe more. His criterion for interference is that only if harm or injury to someone results should people be restrained from acting and living as they please. There is a presumption that in the absence of proof of injury, individuals should be left alone.

I quote extensively from Mill because his language is echoed in modern discussions of free speech, particularly those related to control of pornography. Control is seen as a simple case of the majority forcing others into conformity with their (puritanical) moral standard without argument. It appears a clear case of social compression, what Mill would call a "Calvinistic" demand for "Christian self-denial," aimed at stifling the virtue of "Pagan self-assertion." Similarly Joel Feinberg refers to control as "moralistic paternalism." Other writers echo Mill's attitude.

For Americans this is a powerful and seductive argument against restrictions on any published material, including pornography. All the libertarian or the nonconformist minority asks of the majority is tolerance of its curious ways. What problem is

From *The Grammar of Justice* (Ithaca, NY: Cornell University Press, 1987). Reprinted by permission of the publisher.

there in that? Others don't have to look or buy; one person should be free to enjoy pornography even though others prefer not to, just as they are free to accept or reject escargots or dandelion wine. Passionate tastes are not a bad thing, Mill argued; they are the very "raw material of human nature," capable of both more good and more evil than ordinary feelings. "Strong impulses are but another name for energy. A person whose desires and impulses are his own—are the expression of his own nature—...is said to have a character." And society needs people of strong character: that is the romantic message.

To understand the role of Mill's argument, it is important to recognize that he wrote long after the Bill of Rights became law, and that his view of freedom was not the one that prompted the First Amendment, or even one shared by the early Americans. The idea that truth depends on a "marketplace of ideas," that freedom of expression advances the universal search for truth, that self-expression is an essential part of a person's self-development, that—most important—the only restriction rightly placed on a person's freedom is the injunction not to injure others—such ideas are those of Mill's time, not of Jefferson's. They originated with romantic philosophers of the nineteenth century, not with the political and moral thinkers of seventeenth-century England and eighteenth-century America, who stressed individual responsibility, restraint, and self-governance. Such virtues Mill would probably find much too straitlaced. It is therefore a wild anachronism to use Mill's *On Liberty* as a gloss on the First Amendment. But my argument does not turn on this point. I will argue that one kind of moral issue raised by pornography overshadows and requires us to re-evaluate the free-speech issue. Further, once the argument against protecting pornography is spelled out, I believe Mill can be rallied to its support instead of to the libertarian side.

Two points about "harm" should be made. First, the language of injury and harm are no part of the First Amendment. The framers of that amendment did not suggest that if someone's practice of religion, for example, were to cause injury in some vague sense, the right of religious practice is restrictable. One might conclude from their terse statement that on the contrary, the right to practice religion should be very difficult to restrict. The

"injury" proviso, which may originate with utilitarians, is therefore a gauntlet I do not propose to pick up. Second, Mill's single proviso that a person's exercise of freedom should not harm others places a heavy burden of proof on anyone defending pornography's restriction, and sets the presumption that freedom should prevail. How can injury be shown? How can it even be understood here? Who is injured when pornography is aimed at adult customers, free to decide whether they are interested in it?

To answer these questions we appear to need both a specific conception of harm and persuasive evidence of a causal connection, both of which various critics have shown to be problematic. I will argue, on the contrary, that to accept this burden of proof—that harm or injury to an individual has been caused—is an error of strategy. It is to accept a difficult or even impossible challenge when a more direct and powerful moral argument is available.

Freedom of speech and press are commonly connected with democratic government and seen as essential to it. Tocqueville, for instance, wrote: "In the countries in which the doctrine of the sovereignty of the people ostensibly prevails, the censorship of the press is not only dangerous, but it is absurd." It was a connection not lost on the framers of the Constitution, who were on their guard against the danger that government might seek to impose its will on reluctant citizens. We don't need to doubt the connection here. The question is: Does protection of free expression legitimately protect pornography?

A reasonable statement on this point is made by Ronald Dworkin, who argues that the right to have an equal voice in the political process is not denied when a person "is forbidden to circulate photographs of genitals to the public at large, or denied his right to listen to argument when he is forbidden to consider these photographs at his leisure." Some other basis for protection is needed, according to him.

The Supreme Court argued along similar lines in *Roth v. United States*. What the amendment protects, it says, is the "unfettered interchange of ideas for the bringing about of political and social changes desired by the people." And pornography is "no essential part of any exposition of ideas."

In my view the distinction set forth in *Roth* is important and should have been developed. But instead of developing it, the Court went on to give another reason not to protect pornography, namely, that a "social interest in order and morality" clearly "outweighed" pornography's right to protection. Such a move was plainly hazardous: if other "social interests" can "outweigh" the right to free expression, then the protection of the First Amendment has been greatly diluted. The better argument would follow along the original lines, saying that pornography isn't in the category of "expression" meant to be protected.

A knotty problem arises, however, when pornography is excluded from protection: the amendment speaks of freedom of the *press*. So from one angle it looks as if the amendment was meant to protect not citizens who want to read but publishers in the business of selling printed matter of whatever kind. And pornography certainly belongs in this large domain.

Were the framers trying to protect one kind of business while refusing to protect others? We are helped here by remembering that the First Amendment also dealt with freedom of worship and the right to congregate. The rights to worship and congregate in public rest on the respect of one's need to commune with God on the one hand and with one's fellow citizens on the other. The latter right has something to do with the role citizens play in the whole process of government, their sense that the government is there to serve them and it is their job to monitor it. None of this suggests why publishers should be protected by a fundamental constitutional right, rather than cobblers or hotelkeepers. The more plausible connection is that between protecting the press and protecting citizens from oppression through censorship. The citizens have a need to know and hear printed opinions, just as they have a need to get together and talk, if they are to do their civic duty and live by their consciences. However, this ambiguity in the language of the First Amendment, this way of speaking of the press as if publishers per se are protected and not the free exchange of opinion, seems never to have been cogently dealt with by the courts, and it perennially causes problems, as it does in the present case.

The main point here is that if the amendment is understood to protect publishers as a special form of business protection, then it has no particular moral weight; business protections and trade restrictions may change with the times and do, and a business may seek protection for some political reason or other without invoking the First Amendment or any basic constitutional values.

Another problem with the *Roth* argument is that it invites the comparison of pornography with art, thereby suggesting that good art is more entitled to protection than bad. Good art presumably should survive lack of social value; bad art shouldn't. But what validity is there in this idea? It invites the comment that the degree of badness is relative and may well be a matter of taste, that history has shown...and so on. A more important point is that bad literature—bad essays on politics, appealing to weak and unworthy motives of a reader—*are* surely protected by the First Amendment. And bad political art too. Then why not the poor-quality stuff called pornography? The case made in *Roth* for restricting pornography is worse than unconvincing: it provides ground for a kind of moral repression that both the Constitution's framers and Mill would abhor. We still have to explain what is bad about pornography that is not bad about bad literature and bad art in general.

Joel Feinberg's use of "pornography," he says, is "purely descriptive"; he uses the term to refer to "sexually explicit writing and pictures designed entirely and plausibly to induce sexual excitement in the reader or observer." According to this definition, pornography is a genre of materials of an erotic sort, some of which may be objectionable while the rest is not. Some Japanese prints or Indian murals could be described as pornographic and still appreciated as art by this characterization, for "pornography" is used in a morally neutral way. But since we are not concerned at the moment with erotic materials that are not offensive, I propose to use "pornography" as a pejorative term, which is to say in the way Feinberg would speak of *offensive* pornography. In response to the objection that the word is (most) commonly used in a descriptive and neutral way, I suggest that many ordinary people, including many feminists, commonly use it in a pejorative way, and that in much ordinary speech to call something pornographic is to say that it is offensive. That is sufficient justification for using the term in this way.

It needs to be pointed out that to say that pornography is objectionable is not to demonstrate that it should be controlled. Many things that people do and say are acknowledged to be bad, including being unfaithful to one's spouse, misusing and deceiving friends, neglecting elderly parents, and lying. But we don't have laws against these things. As Feinberg says, in many respects "the Court has interpreted [the Constitution]...to permit responsible adults to go to Hell morally in their own way provided only they don't drag others unwillingly along with them." Such interpretations constitute a formidable defense against controls.

Though pornography may be objectionable in various dimensions (and I believe it is), I will focus on only one kind of objection that I claim to have moral weight. I will substantiate the claim that there *is* such an objection by citing expressions of it. Then I will defend the claim that this kind of objection should carry enough legal weight to justify the control of the objectionable materials. Last, I will argue that such control is quite compatible with the Constitution and the First Amendment and, finally, John Stuart Mill.

The objections I focus on are those expressed by women against certain representations of women in sexual situations: objections against representations of women "being raped, beaten or killed for sexual stimulation," and women enjoying brutal sexual treatment, usually at the hands of men. One pornography model demands censorship of "all pornography which portrays torture, murder, and bondage for erotic stimulation and pleasure." What is objectionable is not just the representations but the lack of a context in which they are understood to be reprehensible and condemnable. Without some such context, the representations carry the message that such treatment of women is all right. This is one kind of objection.

Another model protests against the circulation of any representation "that reduces women to passive objects to be abused, degraded, and used in violence against women, because now every woman is for sale to the lowest bidder and to all men." She adds that a government that protects this kind of image making expresses "an ideology of women as sexual objects and nothing else." A related criticism was made by Gloria Steinem: "[Pornography's] message is violence, dominance, and conquest....If we are to feel anything, we must identify with conqueror or victim." It is a poor choice for women: "we can only experience pleas-

ure through the adoption of some degree of sadism or masochism....We may feel diminished by the role of conqueror, or enraged, humiliated, and vengeful by sharing identity with the victim."

These quotations illustrate one general kind of objection made to pornography. That it is objectionable in these respects is an inference I make from the facts that (1) people do make vehement objections to it and (2) they see the offense as a moral one, concerning the respect due any individual.

I emphasize that although I take it for granted that pornography deals with human sexuality, I am not defining it, although many writers consider a definition crucial for a coherent argument. There is a variety of erotic material that could be called pornographic, and whether we call something pornographic or not will depend in part on whether people find it seriously objectionable. But my argument isn't meant to fit all varieties of such material. I am testing only one dimension of objectionability against the First Amendment defense with the claim that it has moral weight.

My partial characterization is this: some pornography is objectionable because it is perceived as seriously degrading and demeaning to women as a group. This characterization draws on the fact that the materials are perceived by women as representing them as inferior or less-than-human beings to be used by others in sexual and sadistic ways.

Now, why should we take this complaint seriously, so seriously as to control a class of printed and pictorial materials? I hold that such complaints are the stuff of a serious moral issue.

Let us see how the reasoning works. Where is the moral problem? Who is to blame that the speaker was a pornography model? Presumably she chose to be one and her choice—*volenti*, as Feinberg argues—applies to her as well as to the consumers. But this answer is not clearly adequate. The complaint is against the role in which women are portrayed, not against the working conditions, as it were.

The perception that one is being demeaned and that sanction is given to one's mistreatment—to mistreatment as a means to sexual satisfaction here—is a complaint that touches an important moral nerve. It offends basic moral ideas, in particular the Kantian one that everyone should be treated with dignity and respect and not used as a means to another's end. The complaint or objection needs therefore to be taken seriously. That is the first inference.

But several questions leap to mind. First, what determines that this complaint justifies—or lays the foundation for justifying—control of the objectionable materials? Does just any group have the license to insist that laws be changed to improve that group's image? How is the line to be drawn so as to prevent censuring of political caricatures, for instance?

The answer to this question is complicated but contains a general point. If respect for individuals is an important community value, then complaints by any group that their members are demeaned by some vehicle or other *must* have some weight. Such complaints must be addressed by the community seriously, for otherwise the value of respect is immediately and automatically undermined. The message conveyed that it doesn't matter if these people—members of this group—are demeaned suggests that some people are less important than others.

Therefore the answer to the question whose complaints count is that *any* complaint by *any* group that its members are not treated with respect deserves and needs to be treated seriously. To treat such complaints seriously isn't to concede automatically that the complainers *are* treated with disrespect, or that the changes they want should be made. But at issue is not which is the right and which the wrong side of the question; justice doesn't have to be conceived in this way. The issue is the need to deal seriously with the complaint, the need to discuss it in a serious way and then either answer it or act upon it. Ignoring it, laughing at it, and dismissing it are self-incriminating responses that tend to undermine the trust that the emphasis on respect helps to guard.

An underlying theme here is that *if* respect is valued and presumed to prevail in the society, then the respect given one group cannot be casually evaluated by the perception of other groups. What respect for all others amounts to cannot be defined by a single authoritative group, say the group of the majority; the relation of this point to the pornography issue is explored below. Therefore if a number of members of some group perceive their treatment as demeaning, that is prima facie evidence that there is a problem. And given the seriousness of the matter, the rest of the community must take it seriously either by answering it or by making changes.

I conclude that although there may be different ways of responding to pornography and alternatives to control of such materials, this kind of complaint cannot be lightly dismissed. It needs to be handled in terms of the respect felt to be accorded the complainants by the rest of the community. One way the complaint against pornography by women is *not* addressed is by reference to the First Amendment and the possible "slippery slope" of censorship.

Granted that there is a prima facie reason to think women are demeaned by pornographic materials, how does censorship become justified? Isn't some other means to deal with it available and wouldn't that be preferable? The answer is that of course it's possible and other means may be preferable, for there certainly are dangers in permitting one group to control what others may read or see. It is not my thesis that censorship of pornography is the only answer to the moral complaint or that it should be invoked lightly. In fact, it might be invoked as a last resort when such moral protests are raised. But censorship is one answer, and my aim is to show that the justification for using it is not rebutted by an appeal to the First Amendment. Whatever answer is given, that answer needs to address the moral objection to the way treatment of women is represented. The establishment of guidelines for sexual representations might be a solution. Must we decide in general which kind of response is best? I propose rather that there is no theoretical and final answer, but that an acceptable response will take serious account of the perceptions of the objecting group.

One has to ask, however, whether there isn't a danger in appealing to the moral standards of any one group when laws are formulated. As Mill suggests, shouldn't anyone have the right to live anyway he wishes? Isn't experimentation generally a good and not a bad thing?

One kind of answer to the libertarian would relate a society to a "moral community," showing that morals and laws must be joined together. Harry Clor and Patrick Devlin each defend such views, the former defending a restrained use of censorship, the latter a freer use. The problem with such views is that they are too broad. What is the "moral community" and where is it to be found? Is it represented by the majority? If so, then surely moral constraints are worse than paternalistic: they are downright tyrannical, as Mill said.

Even though the complaint of women against pornography cannot be dismissed by appeals to freedom of the press, why shouldn't Mill's argument for freedom apply here? Why shouldn't the objection still hold that if women don't want to look at pornographic pictures or film, they shouldn't look? So long as there is "reasonable avoidability" and people can avoid pornography if they want to, where, as Feinberg argues, is the offense? "When the 'obscene' book sits on a shelf, who is there to be offended?" If pornography lies between "decorous covers," no one need look at it who doesn't want to. It is only when pornography produces an offense on a par with "shame, or disgust, or noisome stenches" (however they would translate in this case) that the law may justifiably interfere. That is to say, pornography should be restricted only when it becomes a nuisance difficult to avoid. To restrict it on other grounds would be to engage in moral paternalism. It would be to set standards for those who enjoy pornography in order to save them from themselves.

This protest, however, misses the point. The felt insult and indignity that women protest is not like a noise or bad odor, for these are group-neutral and may offend anyone, while pornography is felt to single women out as objects of insulting attention. There is a clear division in the community here, unlike the division between people who mind an odor very much and others who can ignore it. The question of how the rest of the community should respond to the perceived debasement that women feel is not analogous to the way the community should treat people particularly sensitive to and offended by certain smells. There is a democracy with respect to smells but with pornography there is a felt hostile discrimination.

One way to deal with objections to pornography has been to appeal to a typical member of the community, an "average man" who can judge as a representative of the rest whether some material is sufficiently objectionable to warrant restriction.

But there is an internal logical difficulty in this appeal. The "average man" is understood not to be a woman, as is clear from the way the perceptions of the average man are viewed. *Roth*, for instance, speaks of the "appeal to prurient interests"; but such interests are surely interests predominantly of men, not of women. Feinberg, too, speaks to public nudity in terms of "the conflict between these attracting and repressing forces, between allure and disgust," and

again leaves the impression that he is speaking of general human reactions while those he describes are characteristically male reactions. Other writers refer carelessly to the "effects" of pornography—sexual arousal or even criminal behavior—in such a way as to suggest that *all* people are included when in fact the effects referred to are specifically effects that pornography has on men.

The premise is essential to my argument that pornographic materials may be seen differently by one group than by another. They may be felt as insulting by one group but inoffensive to another, as seriously demeaning by one and silly by another. An analogy can be drawn with the different perceptions of blacks and whites, or of Jews and Gentiles, regarding certain materials: blacks may find demeaning an image that others think innocuous. It is crucial for my argument that such differences in perception be acknowledged as a social reality, and that our understanding of what it is to treat everyone with respect allow for such differences in the *perception* of respect. It is important, in short, that we do not assume that there is one. Everyman view, with the only question being which view that is. Only by respecting different perceptions about what is demeaning will we see that there may be a reason to limit materials that some group—even the largest—finds unobjectionable.

There is a further curious twist in the idea that there is an "average man" who can judge whether some materials are offensive and obscene, a man such as the "rational man" of English law or the "man in the jury box," as Devlin calls him, someone who expresses "the view" of the society. For presumably when such a person is called upon to judge the offending material, he is to judge it from his own character and conscience. And of course his character will influence what he finds: a man of very strong character may find pornography only mildly or not at all objectionable, a man of weaker character will find it has an influence on him but not in consequence call it objectionable, an "average man" will fall somewhere in between. So sound judgment is difficult to come by.

But not only does a man's character influence his perception; the perception he expresses—his judgment as to the offensiveness of lewd materials—reflects back upon his character. Suppose he says that some materials are very provocative and could lead a viewer to do wicked things. He is testifying not only against the materials but also about his own susceptibility, and thus indirectly incriminating himself. We are told something about his own weakness if he sees pornography as dangerous. He is testifying about his character.

The result is that a bias is built into the testimony of the "average man" and particularly of the "right-minded man" regarding the offensiveness of pornography. A man—even a right-minded one—cannot judge that materials are "corrupting" without revealing his own corruptibility. And so there is pressure both on men who are strong and on men who are not so strong to find pornography harmless. On the other side, a person who objects to it is likely to be characterized as "often...emotionally disturbed," "propelled by [his] own neurosis," or a "Comstock."

Given that there is a connection between a man's testimony about pornography and his character, should men who are weak and susceptible be consulted? That would be paradoxical: such people can hardly be counted on to give any reliable testimony. But a particularly upright and conscientious man (say a respected judge) is not qualified either, for he may be unable to see any problem. And the ordinarily upright but susceptible man may be reluctant to reveal his weakness. Then whose judgment should be given weight? Given the lack of any "objective" or authoritative spokesman for the whole society, there's only one sensible answer.

If blacks are in a position to say what is demeaning to them, why shouldn't women's voices be heard on the pornography issue? Not because they are truly "disinterested" parties and therefore qualified as authorities. On the contrary; I have been arguing that there are no disinterested authorities, no "objective" representatives of the moral community. And if one group were acknowledged to be completely disinterested in regard to sex or disinterested in regard to heterosexuality, *that* would be no qualification but the contrary. The objectionability of pornography cannot be assessed in this way; there is no analogue here to the "average consumer" who might represent the whole community in judging a retailing policy.

The reason that women should be viewed as particularly qualified is their charge that pornography is an offense against *them*. That charge puts them in a morally authoritative position, just as blacks are in such a position in regard to racial

insults and Jews in regard to anti-Semitic humiliations. Then we need only to add that a complaint of this kind demands to be addressed somehow. It does not follow what we should do.

What lies behind our invocation of an "average man" in regard to such issues is a powerful tendency to treat pornography—and other ethically colored issues—in androgynous terms. But common sense tells us that where sexuality is central, an androgynous point of view, even if there were one, would be irrelevant. Without sexuality and sexual difference, sexual attraction and sexual polarity, no pornography issue would ever arise. Therefore to treat the issue in terms of universal principles that hold objectively—atomistically—for all beings alike is to perpetrate a kind of legal comedy.

Feinberg questions Justice William Brennan's argument in *Roth* by asking, "What is the alleged 'state interest' that makes the unobtrusive and willing enjoyment of pornographic materials the state's business to control and prevent?" What is the positive ground for interference?

This demand is legitimate and it needs to be answered in full. Even if a moral argument such as I have outlined can be made for control of pornography, how can the moral argument be translated into constitutional terms? If controls are justified, their justification should answer Feinberg's question. The need to protect respect may be clear but the means for protecting it are not. Is there an analogy or a precedent to guide us.?

I will argue at a common-sense level, not meaning to interpret the notion of "state interest" in its technical legal sense. Given that respect for persons is an important constitutional value, I propose to show a strategy that connects respect with controls on pornography, to show that the means, the logical path, is there already and has no need to be newly cut. The connection between respect and constitutional action has been made already.

What we need here is reasoning somewhat like that in *Brown* v. *Board of Education*. There the Court decided that educational facilities—equal "with respect to buildings, curricula...and other 'tangible' factors"—might nevertheless be unequal in an important sense. And one of the reasons they might be counted unequal was (as one summary puts it) that "to separate [children] from others...solely because of their race generates a feeling of inferiority as to their status in the community that may affect their hearts and minds in a way unlikely ever to be undone." Such an institution with the "sanction of law" which thus produces the sense of inferiority of one race is unconstitutional. Respect is not to be measured in the specifics of equipment or curriculum but in the felt implication of inferiority.

In rejecting the justice of "separate but equal" facilities, the Court specifically rejected the protest that any "badge of inferiority" supposed to be implied by segregation exists "not by reason of anything found in the act, but solely because the colored race chooses to put that construction upon it." The insult perceived by blacks has priority over protests of innocence by those charged with offending. It is not crucial that *they* see the offense in the same way. Thus the Court answered by analogy the parallel argument in the pornography issue, that women shouldn't be so sensitive about pornography, for, since no one intends to demean them by it, there is nothing demeaning in it. The parallel answer is that whether there was intent to demean or not is irrelevant.

The argument in *Brown* exemplifies the general form of reasoning we need: an institution that perceptibly demeans some group and represents its members as inferior impugns the claim to equality of those members; in doing so it violates the Constitution's provisions; thus it shouldn't be protected by the federal government. There is no reference here to interpretations of other provisions of the Constitution. Of course the production of pornography isn't an institution; yet insofar as pornography is felt to demean women, its protection by the government under the First Amendment cannot be easily argued.

A caveat is needed here. This argument does not imply that if some group feels demeaned—say, by advertising or institutional arrangements—then censorship is automatically justified. Considerations other than the offense taken are often relevant, some of which may also be moral, and these considerations may over-balance the initial concern for respect. Nonetheless, if what is needed is a line of reasoning that can be used to support control of pornographic materials in the face of First Amendment protections, then such a line is clearly available.

In its general conception this approach accords with Ronald Dworkin's view that absolute princi-

ples are not what is needed in much legal reasoning. Instead we often need to balance one kind of claim or principle against others. That's the case here. The First Amendment is terribly important to us as a democracy; there's no dispute about that. But it doesn't give the last word on the question "What may a printer print and what may a store sell?" While this approach shows a way to defeat the absolutist claim of the First Amendment and open the possibility of censorship, I have no desire to insist that this course be taken. Other solutions may be preferable.

A number of features of the pornography issue are illuminated by its analogy with race discrimination. For one thing, it would be irrelevant to argue that the demeaning of blacks causes no "injury" and therefore is harmless. What it causes is not the issue: the harm and the offense lie in the practices themselves, and the felt implications for people's status, the light cast upon them as citizens, and the like. Second, just as it would be bizarre to appeal to a group of whites to determine whether racial inferiority is part of the message of segregation, it is curious to consult only men about the offense of pornography. Third, the protest that not all blacks were offended would be taken as specious. Even if many blacks denied that they felt offended, we might still acknowledge the vigorous complaints of others. The same holds for women; if some are not offended by pornography, it remains true that many are, and that they see the offense as one against women as a group.

But imagine that the Commission on Obscenity were to make the following argument: If we do nothing in the way of controls, we shall at least be doing nothing wrong. And in such a doubtful matter, with something as important as First Amendment protection at issue, it is better to do nothing. The answer to this argument contains a point often overlooked. When a powerful plea for respectful treatment is addressed by some group to the government, no "neutral" or safe response is possible. Inaction is a kind of action; it signifies toleration of the practice and thus condones it, and in condoning endorses it. Thus to respond to discrimination by arguing that the rights of states and communities are sacred matters, and that one risks a slide down a "slippery slope" if one interferes with them, would be hollow and disingenuous and recognized as such. Similarly I propose that there is also no "neutral" and safe response against pornography's demeaning of women. The issue demands to be addressed by a government that wants *not* to give sanction to the message carried by the images. A state that wants to ensure an atmosphere of respect for all persons has to face the issue in more decisive terms than protection of the First Amendment.

The Constitution does not lead us to believe that our first duty is to protect the First Amendment, as if its application needed no justification, as if it stood above other values, including that of respect for all persons. On the contrary, the rights of free speech, religion, and assembly are protected *because* of the respect due to citizens and their consequent need to be free of government control in certain ways. Freedom of speech is not a fundamental right of a certain kind of enterprise—namely, the press—but stems from a view of humans as morally autonomous.

Therefore it is curious that the Court and libertarian writers show such dedication to freedom of the press as an abstraction, as a principle taken by itself. They deal with it, so it seems to me, as with an ikon of a faith whose main tenets they have forgotten. In this respect theirs is less than a high moral stand. Remarking the irony of this liberal position, one writer comments that "women may rightly ask why the Constitution must be read to value the pornographer's first amendment claim to individual dignity and choice over women's equal rights claim to their own dignity and choice." It is a curious turn of thinking that asks citizens to lay down their claim to respect at the feet of this idol.

Mill warned us about the threat presented by people who think they have the "right" moral perspective and therefore the only "right" answers to serious questions. I agree; we need to beware of all sorts of tyranny, however righteous, well-meaning, and scholarly. For on its side the protection of pornography also may represent a kind of tyranny of opinion, a libertarian tyranny that treats would-be censors as neurotic, misguided zealots and dismisses the moral complaint altogether.

Looked at from the perspective of women, the tolerance of pornography is hard to understand. Equally hard to understand is a point of view that sees the offense of pornography only in terms of its impact on and significance to men, as if the women of the society were irrelevant or invisible. And a more political point can be added. In the light of women's increasing protests against pornogra-

phy and the proliferation of defenses of it, the issue carries the hazard of generating conflict between two definable groups, roughly between libertarian men on the one hand and outraged women on the other. Given these dimensions, it seems imperative to straighten the arguments and the issue out.

I wish to say something more about the claim that a definition of pornography is needed for the present argument. My argument has followed the tactic of considering certain objections to pornography without a definition of pornography or a criterion as to what objections are valid. While it focuses on objections of a certain kind, those imputing a demeaning character to pornography, it doesn't specify what kinds of things are legitimately objected to or what is really objectionable.

Where could we get a definition of pornography suitable to the role I give it, the role of materials to which a certain vague kind of objection is made? Who should define it authoritatively? Common sense does not endorse the view that legal authorities should set standards for the rest of the community, should decide about the inherent rightness or wrongness of certain pictures, for example; for there might be no strong moral objection to pictures the community calls pornographic, and in the absence of such objection the pictures are not, on my view, pornographic at all. My argument says only that the law *might* justifiably restrict materials that are found insulting in a sexual way, as some materials are by women.

Because the argument is so vague, however, it arouses concern. How will pornographic pictures be distinguished from sexy art, and pornography distinguished from sexy literature—Lawrence's portrayal of Constance Chatterly, for instance? The answer is that the lack of a sharp line is precisely what I allow for, as I allow for changing attitudes. If a public work of art is found insulting by some part of the community that has to look at it, then that is a reason—though only one—for restricting it in some way. If no one objects, then a definition that makes it objectionable would be superfluous and really beside the point.

The terms of the issue as I frame it require only the value of individual respect, which is part of our moral heritage, and the perceptions by members of the community about how they are respected. They therefore allow for changes in customs and tastes, allow that what is demeaning in one time may not be found so in another. When pornography is defined in terms of what is *perceptibly* demeaning, not what is permanently and abstractly so, there is no force to the protest that since "Grandpa was excited even by bare ankles, dad by flesh above the knee, grandson only by flimsy bikinis," no standards can be set. As fashions change, their moral implications change too. So if what was found demeaning once is not found so any longer, any problem regarding it has vanished. It is better not to define pornography for all time, or to define it at all.

One important problem involving the First Amendment still needs to be considered. Suppose we are considering a work that asserts and argues that women are inferior to men, more animal than men, and that they enjoy brutal and sadistic treatment. Imagine such a work: it *asserts* that there is evidence to show that women enjoy a subservient animal, victimized role, and that this is a correct and proper way to treat women, particularly with regard to sex. Some evidence or other is cited, and it is argued that "equality" is simply inappropriate for beings of this kind, belonging to an inferior level of sensibility or whatever. To be sure, these ideas run directly against the moral idea that an individual, qua individual, has worth; nonetheless, we believe in free pursuit of all manner of debate, moral, scientific, and political, without government interference. So would such a work, purporting to be a scientific study, come under the protections of the First Amendment, or may it be treated like pornography and restricted on the same grounds? Does it differ from the case of hard pornographic pictures and films, and if so how?

On this question I side with the libertarians, for the difference between pornographic pictures and such a report is a signal one for us and for the First Amendment. Mill also would recognize the difference, for he based the freedom of circulation of opinion on the possibility of refuting an opinion that is false and criticizing one that's poorly founded. In his vision an opinion or argument is at continual risk of being refuted, and so it cannot endanger a community where reason and truth are valued. We can draw the distinction by saying that the materials that say nothing are beyond this risk of refutation, and therefore by protecting them we give them an immunity to criticism that expressions of opinion do not enjoy. The argument of a work may be objectionable but, like all arguments,

it is vulnerable to criticism, while pornography lacks such vulnerability.

This distinction is one I believe the framers of the Constitution would also have recognized. The need for opinions to be circulated freely is part of the respect for citizens which prompted the Bill of Rights. But protection of opinion could be distinguished then as well as now from protection of the press to print what it likes, including offensive pictures.

Defenses of pornography have often turned on leaving this distinction obscure, arguing, for example, "that pornography is intended not as a statement of fact, but as an opinion or fantasy about male and female sexuality." Taken this way, it cannot be prohibited on the ground of being false. At the same time, however, one hears that "correction of opinion depends…'on the competition of other ideas.' " It is a catch-22. Critics of pornography who are told that they should "compete in the marketplace of ideas with their own views of sexuality" while pornography doesn't *present* ideas are placed in an impossible situation. The pictures don't argue for a demeaning attitude toward women in regard to sex or present a view of sexuality; at the same time they *are* demeaning. They don't argue that women enjoy being brutally handled; they show brutality and insinuate the victims' pleasure. While an author would be correct in saying that pornography carries an *implied* message that brutal treatment of women is acceptable, the fact that it is implied rather than explicit is important.

With this argument I believe Mill would concur, for he consistently maintained the need for respect of differences, including different points of view, and here the difference is one relating to the two sex groups. Respect for persons in all their variety was at the heart of both his libertarianism and his ethical philosophy. However difficult they may be to understand in terms of one's own principles, people are worthy of respect: that was his repeated theme. "Man is not a machine," he wrote, and he surely did not think women are machines for sex. To demean women in the way pornography is felt to do is to treat them as possessions or as servants. So in the end I think that Mill, who argued passionately for women's rights and equal worth and dignity, would find it intolerable to have his views invoked to protect pornography, as they have been.

Although the libertarian case against controls seemed clear-cut and irrefutable, appeal to atomistic ideas cannot solve such a powerfully felt moral issue. If respect for people really exists, it will appear in the way complaints of insult are handled and not only in the propositions used to rebut them.

What is needed is not a vision of justice, a simple doctrinaire solution, but a carefully plotted middle way between broad and oppressive controls and reckless liberty. Such an approach will go beyond atomism and deal with injustice in a different and less theoretical way....

"Pornography and the Rights of Women"

Catharine A. MacKinnon

Sometimes, when people are tortured and violated, it is seen as torture and violation. In the prisons of South and Central America, when people are imprisoned and abducted, when they are hung up, confined, tortured with cattle prods, when they are disappeared, the atrocity is acknowledged,—at least, it is here and now. In South Africa, when the same things are done to Black people; in Auschwitz and in Dachau, when they were done to Jews and others; in the American south, when they were done to Black people under slavery, the atrocity is now acknowledged. It is understood that some people have been selected for torture and violation on the basis of who they are, their group status— and within that group selected essentially at random—and that this is a very effective method of terrorizing and controlling that group.

Torture because of who you are is understood as a method of keeping people in submission, acquiescent, terrorized, and compliant, although they also resist. In the incidents that I have mentioned, the force, at least now, is acknowledged. And rights— civil liberties—are recognized to be violated. At times other than when it happens, and in other places and by other people, there is another recognized feature about systematic torture: the inequality of which it is a part is seen to be pervasive and acknowledged as political. It is understood that it is possible to do *these* things to *these* people, even though there may even be laws against doing them, because of an unequal social context which gives permission for *these* people to be stigmatized, singled out and tortured on the basis of a condition of birth. Even though people lack a final answer, still, to the agonizing ultimate question of why things like this happen, not having that answer does not lead most people to think that the atrocities should be allowed to go on and on and on.

But when these same acts are done in this country today, in basements or in studios, by men holding cameras to women, the atrocity is denied. It is not considered torture; it is considered sex. By many, it is even considered freedom, equality, and love. It forms an eight-billion-dollar industry in entertainment. It is enjoyed; it is considered fun; it is a consumer choice. Its relation to social inequality is denied or minimized. When it is done through pictures and words, it is passionately defended by the ACLU. It is allowing those to whom it is done to *do* something about it that is seen as the civil liberties violation.

When the denial of what is really being done is stripped away from pornography, what we see, very simply, is women being bound, battered, tortured, humiliated, and sometimes killed. Or, to be fair to what is termed the soft core, merely being

---

Based on an invited lecture before a Meeting of the American Civil Liberties Union, Ann Arbor, MI, May 1985. Used by Permission of Catharine MacKinnon.

taken and used. This is being done to real women right now. In hundreds and thousands of magazines, pictures, films, and so-called books now available in this country, women's legs are splayed, presented in postures of sexual submission, display and access—those that *Newsweek* recently wryly referred to as the gynecological shots. We see women becoming pussy, beaver, chick, cunt, named after parts of our bodies or animals, cut up into parts of our bodies or mated with animals. We are told this is a natural woman's sexuality, but as women who tell us about being in it know, it is elaborately contrived. The photographs are retouched, but even when they are not, often the bodies are.

We see children presented as adult women, adult women presented as children. We see so-called lesbian material, which is how men imagine women touch each other when men are not around, so men can enjoy watching. Pornography is a major medium for the sexualization of racial hatred; every racial stereotype is used. Black women are presented as animalistic bitches, bound, bruised, bleeding and struggling; Asian women are presented as so passive, so bound, they cannot be recognized to be human. You cannot tell if they are dead or alive. They are hanging from light fixtures and trees and clothes pegs in closets. We see amputees, sick people, the disabled, their illness or disability sexually fetishized. In some pornography, women and/or children are actually tortured to death, murdered, in fact, to make a sex film.

This is all being done for a reason. The reason is that it gives sexual pleasure to its consumers and therefore profits to its providers. When you look at a system like this, it becomes clear that some people matter and some people do not. Those who want the profits—in which I include the money and the pleasure—they matter. What they like and want is called a constitutional right. But to the women and children who are the victims of its making or use, that constitutional right means being bound, battered, tortured, humiliated or killed, or merely taken and used, and used, and used until you are used up or you can get out. Because someone with more power than you, someone who matters gets pleasure from seeing it done to you, or doing it to you, or seeing it as a form of doing it.

Since Andrea Dworkin first started talking about the harm of pornography to women, joined later by the rest of us, we have been deluged by evidence and documentation. In the hearings on our proposed law against pornography, we heard testimony that it does take coercion to make some pornography. We have come to think of those women as our "disappeared." We heard how pornography is forced on women and children in ways that give them no choice about viewing the pornography or performing the sex. We heard about the use of pornography to break women's self-esteem, to train them to sexual submission, to season them to forced sex, to intimidate them out of job opportunities, to blackmail them into prostitution and keep them there, to terrorize and humiliate them in to sexual compliance and to silence their dissent.

In private, we have heard from thousands of women in whispers, in desperation, remembering the camera, describing the pictures, remembering every detail of how the knots were tied according to the magazine, what the expression on their face should be according to the film, how they were forced to re-enact the photographs, how the abuse was created with the pornography as the man's main instrument of arousal, inspiration, energy and technical advice. We have heard about women who have been raped every way with every object and device that will fit and many that will not, by animals, and all of that filmed and the photographs of the rapes now being sold as protected speech. We have heard transgenerational stories of mother-daughter abuse premised on pornography and in which pornography is centrally used. We have heard of *Playboy* and *Penthouse* rapes of children—boys and girls in which the children are first shown the materials and then raped, or told to emulate the pictures they are shown while being raped,—we have heard of hundreds of women being violated, used on one end of the pornography or another. We have heard how pornography stimulates and condones all of those acts it took the feminist movement so much effort to discover and make public and break silence on: the rape, the battery, the sexual harassment, the child sexual abuse and the forced prostitution, not to mention the rest of the just plain denigration and discrimination.

We observed how the pornography contains all these abuses. All these acts of sexual violence are presented in the pornography, not as rape but as sex, not as battery but as sex, not as sexual harassment but as sex, not the sexual abuse of children, but the sexual fulfillment and expression of children. The forced prostitution is presented, of course, as consent. We have come to think that the sex-violence distinction so central to the way many people have thought about this question is false: that violence is sex when it is practiced as sex. What we have found here is a whole world of sexual abuse, silenced previously.

Because the pleasure pornography gives is sexual, it has been considered exempt from scrutiny and repressive to question. Because it is considered speech—because it is done at some point through words and pictures—it has been considered repressive to do anything about it, even to question, because it is thought that all speech is somehow at stake. I want to suggest to you that because the pornography is sexual, and works *as* sex, it is not even like the "literature" of other inequalities. It works differently. It works as a direct behavioral stimulus, conditioner and reinforcer of a very specific, compelling, and distinguishable kind. It is unique. What it does, and nothing else does, is makes orgasm a response to bigotry. Thus dominance and subordination, the daily dynamic of sexual inequality, is enjoyed and practiced as well as learned in the male body.

You know already that sexism is a lot of things. It is profitable; it is pervasive. I am suggesting you face the fact that it is also sexy, and that pornography is a big part of what makes it that way.

On the basis of this analysis, Andrea Dworkin and I have proposed that pornography—not abstractly, but in particular forms that is it practiced, and harms it does—should be considered a violation of the civil liberties of women and children primarily, but of anyone who is hurt by it on the basis of their sex. Pornography is a major institution of a subhuman, victimized, and second-class status for women. We think this is inconsistent with any serious legal mandate of sex equality and with the reasons speech is protected.

As to why our ordinance is constitutional, I am not going to argue existing law of speech to you, although it supports us, because many of you disagree with it. Instead I want to talk about why you should agree with us, why you should want our proposed ordinance to make the harm pornography does actionable as sex discrimination.

Our ordinance defines 'pornography' as the graphic sexually explicit subordination of women through pictures or words that also includes women presented dehumanized as sexual objects who enjoy pain, humiliation or rape—I am truncating it slightly—women bound, mutilated, dismembered or tortured, in postures of servility or submission or display, being penetrated by objects or animals. Men, children or transsexuals, all of whom are sometimes violated like women are, in and through pornography, can sue for similar treatment.

The term 'sexually explicit' is an existing term with a legal and social meaning that has never before been considered vague or problematic. It refers to sex being explicitly shown. Sex exists objectively in the world, unlike, for instance, obscenity's sex term 'prurient interest' (Miller Test). Subordination is a term that is often used politically when the people who are being put down or in a position of loss of power are considered real and fully human. It refers to *actively* placing someone in an unequal position. Presumably, people know that to be a subordinate is not the same as being an equal. When we say that pornography is the graphic sexually explicit subordination of women through pictures or words, it means the subordination must be able to be proven to be *done*, either through the making or use of the materials, or it does not fit the definition.

This definition is not actionable in itself. There are four harms through which, and only through which, it is actionable. Our civil rights law allows victims of four activities only—coercion, force, assault, and trafficking—to sue those who hurt them. 'Coercion' means someone is coerced into acts to make pornography. 'Force' means somebody has pornography forced on them. 'Assault' means someone can show that they were assaulted in a way that is directly caused by a specific piece of pornography. 'Trafficking' covers production, sale, exhibition or distribution—the activity of saturating a community, of pushing, of purveying pornography in the world. Coercion, force, assault and trafficking are not ideas. They are not fantasies. None of them, as such, are speech.

I understand that this organization is on record in opposition to all four harms of pornography being actionable to their victims. I am going to talk primarily about the trafficking provision though, because I also understand it gives most of you the most trouble.

Our hearings in Minneapolis produced overwhelming evidence of the harm of pornography. This evidence has changed and magnified and grown the more we have talked about pornography in public, the less silence the pornography has been able to impose, the more we have heard about its effects. In addition to the testimony that I mentioned before, we have heard from researchers and clinicians documenting the conclusion that women know from life: that pornography increases attitudes and behaviors of aggression and other discrimination, principally by men against women, and that this relation is causal. This evidence is better, more, and much more direct than existing exceptions to the First Amendment—although I recognize you may not care. It is also far better than correlations many people live by, like the smoking/cancer correlation, or the data on drinking and driving. We have social studies as well as lab studies and other expert testimony documenting the laboratory predictions of increased aggression toward women. It does happen, both in real life and in the laboratory, by men who use these materials.

The most accurate thing I can say about the state of the research on the broad social harm we have here, is that we may or may not be able to predict what particular individuals will do to what other particular individuals, although we *can* do that to some degree. But we *do* know that if men in a population consume pornography, more and more acts of sexual aggression and discrimination against women will occur, and less and less will be done about them, because those acts will be experienced sexually as more and more enjoyable and less and less violating. We know that so long as the pornography exists as it does now, women and children will be used and abused to make it, as they are now, and it will be used to abuse them, as it is now.

Those of you who want us to "go after the acts and not the speech," and don't consider that coercion, force, assault are acts, consider that the so-called speech can be the predicate for the acts. Someone rapes so they can take a picture of it. As to the much-loved causal connection between pornography and harm, between the acts and the speech, how about: *they did the act so they could make the speech.* Is that causal enough? If it hadn't been for making the "speech," *this* rape would not have happened. Is that a strong enough connection for you?

Those of you who want us to "enforce existing law" against these acts, I would like *you* to try to explain to *me* the difference between the real rape rate, the real child abuse rate, the real sexual harassment rate and the reported rates, and the prosecution rates, and the conviction rates. Tell us why we should use or rely on the system that produced them. *Why* are those laws not enforced? Why it is, for instance, that *the* most taboo thing, one of the most illegal things in virtually any society, the sexual abuse of children, it is also the most done, the most common? Maybe one reason is that those with power don't see those acts as a very big problem. We think that the ways women are used and presented in pornography, creating legitimacy for sexual abuse, may have something to do with why so little is done here and why we are making so little progress in getting real sex equality.

I hope you have observed that our law is not an obscenity law. Pornography does harm, unlike obscenity, for which no evidence of harm has ever been available or, in fact, required. Obscenity doctrine has never defined a harm, although it has been looking for one for a long time. The closest it could come was "offensiveness" (Miller test). Offensiveness is not our harm; *sex discrimination* is our harm. It is not our fault that obscenity law is vague; it is not our fault that it is available to and for police state repression. It is not our fault that it is anti-gay. It is not our fault that when legislatures and courts look at women being used and hurt, the most they have been able to see is sex they don't want to say they want to see. And finally it is not our fault that civil libertarians move to enact stricter obscenity laws, your policy against them notwithstanding, and move to get stricter enforcement of them by the police, in other words move to police-state repression, the minute something effective—our law—might be able to be done about the real pornography, which obscenity law never gets near. It is not our fault that the police crack down on those who are least responsible, and on those who are most vulnerable, and that the pornography and its real harm goes on and on.

There *is* an issue of speech here. I want to speak briefly about the silence of those on whose inequality First Amendment jurisprudence—and with all respect, the ACLU's policies—has been based. The First Amendment was written by those who had speech. They also had slaves, many of them, and a lot of them owned white women as well. They made sure, in their design of the Constitution, to keep their speech from what threatened it, the federal government. You first have to *have* speech before keeping the state from taking it away from you becomes your problem. Knowing that they have the speech and every other form of slaver's power, the pornographers have taken the position that they are the political rebels; they are the disenfranchised and the hated. But they are the practitioners of a ruling ideology of misogyny and racism and sexualized bigotry: It is ludicrous to say that something that is consumed more than *Time* and *Newsweek* is hated and outcast. It is ridiculous to say that an industry is disenfranchised that makes ten billion dollars a year—some of which they give to this organization, which makes sure they have a voice.

I wonder if the screams of the victims, of the tortured, are inaudible to you, or if they are sex to you. I wonder if you will continue to side with these pimps, so that an entire class of women will continue to exist who will be treated in the ways I have described, so that these pimps can have access to what they have sold to you as freedom of speech. Freedom meaning their *free* access to women, their *free* use of women, and speech meaning our bodies as the medium for their expression, saying what they want them to say.

Only once have I heard the term 'human being' defined when it did not come off reductive or abstract or sentimental or meaningless. In a recent speech Bishop Tutu said, "We just want the white people in South Africa to recognize that we're human beings, you know?" I couldn't believe he was going to have a second sentence, because no one ever does. He said, "I mean, when you scratch us, we bleed; when you tickle us, we laugh." In pornography, when you scratch us, we get turned on; when you tickle us, we start to come; and when you kill us, we orgasm until death. I know some of you are on our side and I hope that the rest of you will think about it.

"Liberty and Pornography"

Ronald Dworkin

Political philosophy thrives as a mature industry; it dominates many distinguished philosophy departments and attracts a large share of the best graduate students almost everywhere.

Berlin's lecture, "Two Concepts of Liberty," played an important and distinctive role in this renaissance. It provoked immediate, continuing, heated, and mainly illuminating controversy....

But chiefly, or so I think, its importance lay in the force of its central argument....

I must try to describe two central features of his argument....The first is the celebrated distinction described in the lecture's title: between two (closely allied) senses of liberty. Negative liberty...means not being obstructed by others in doing what one might wish to do. We count some negative liberties—like the freedom to speak our minds without censorship—as very important and others—like driving at very fast speeds—as trivial. But they are both instances of negative freedom,

From "Liberty and Pornography," *New York Review*, vol. 38, no. 14 (August 15, 1991). Reprinted by permission of the publisher.

and though a state may be justified in imposing speed limits, for example, on grounds of safety and convenience, that is nevertheless an instance of restricting negative liberty.

Positive liberty, on the other hand, is the power to control or participate in public decisions, including the decision how far to curtail negative liberty. In an ideal democracy—whatever that is—the people govern themselves. Each is master to the same degree, and positive liberty is secured for all....Berlin described the historical corruption of the idea of positive liberty, a corruption that began in the idea that someone's true liberty lies in control by his rational self rather than his empirical self, that is, in control that aims at securing goals other than those the person himself recognizes. Freedom, on that conception, is possible only when people are governed, ruthlessly if necessary, by rulers who know their true, metaphysical, will. Only then are people truly free, albeit against their will. That deeply confused and dangerous, but nevertheless potent, chain of argument had in many parts of the world turned positive liberty into the most terrible tyranny. Of course, by calling attention to this corruption of positive liberty, Berlin did not mean that negative liberty was an unalloyed blessing, and should be protected in all its forms in all circumstances at all costs. He said, later, that on the contrary the vices of excessive and indiscriminate negative liberty were so evident, particularly in the form of savage economic inequality, that he had not thought it necessary to describe them in much detail.

The second feature of Berlin's argument that I have in mind is a theme repeated throughout his writing on political topics. He insists on the complexity of political value, and the fallacy of supposing that all the political virtues that are attractive in themselves can be realized in a single political structure. The ancient Platonic ideal of some master accommodation of all attractive virtues and goals, combined in institutions satisfying each in the right proportion and sacrificing none, is in Berlin's view, for all its imaginative power and historical influence, only a seductive myth. He later summed this up:

One freedom may abort another; one freedom may obstruct or fail to create conditions which make other freedoms, or a larger degree of freedom, or freedom for more persons, possible: positive and negative freedom may collide: the freedom of the individual or the group may not be fully compatible with a full degree of participation in a common life, with its demands for cooperation, solidarity fraternity. But beyond all these there is an acuter issue: the paramount need to satisfy the claims of other, no less ultimate, values: justice, happiness, love, the realization of capacities to create new things and experiences and ideas, the discovery of the truth. Nothing is gained by identifying freedom proper, in either of its senses, with these values, or with the conditions of freedom, or by confounding types of freedom with one another.

Berlin's warnings about conflating positive and negative liberty, and liberty itself, with other values, seemed,...to provide important lessons about authoritarian regimes in other times and places. Though cherished liberties were very much under attack in both America and Britain in that decade, the attack was not grounded in or defended through either form of confusion. The enemies of negative liberty were powerful, but they were also crude and undisguised. Joseph McCarthy and his allies did not rely on any Kantian or Hegelian or Marxist concept of metaphysical selves to justify censorship or blacklists. They distinguished liberty not from itself, but from security; they claimed that too much free speech made us vulnerable to spies and intellectual saboteurs and ultimately to conquest.

In both Britain and America, in spite of limited reforms, the state still sought to enforce conventional sexual morality about pornography, contraception, prostitution, and homosexuality. Conservatives who defended these invasions of negative liberty appealed not to some higher or different sense of freedom, however, but to values that were plainly distinct from, and in conflict with, freedom: religion, true morality, and traditional and proper family values. The wars over liberty were fought, or so it seemed, by clearly divided armies. Liberals were for liberty, except, in some circumstances, for the negative liberty of economic entrepreneurs. Conservatives were for that liberty, but against other forms when these collided with security or their view of decency and morality.

But now the political maps have radically changed and some forms of negative liberty have acquired new opponents....Conflicts over race and gender have transformed old alliances and divisions. Speech that expresses racial hatred, or a degrading attitude toward women, has come to seem intolerable to many people whose convictions are otherwise traditionally liberal. It is hardly surprising that they should try to reduce the conflict between their old liberal ideals and their new acceptance of censorship by adopting some new definition of what liberty, properly understood, really is. It is hardly surprising, but the result is dangerous confusion, and Berlin's warnings, framed with different problems in mind, are directly in point.

I shall try to illustrate that point with a single example: a lawsuit arising out of the attempt by certain feminist groups in America to outlaw what they consider a particularly objectionable form of pornography. I select this example not because pornography is more important or dangerous or objectionable than racist invective or other highly distasteful kinds of speech, but because the debate over pornography has been the subject of the fullest and most comprehensive scholarly discussion.

Through the efforts of Catharine MacKinnon…and other prominent feminists, Indianapolis, Indiana, enacted an antipornography ordinance. The ordinance defined pornography as "the graphic sexually explicit subordination of women, whether in pictures or words…" and it specified, as among pornographic materials falling within that definition, those that present women as enjoying pain or humiliation or rape, or as degraded or tortured or filthy, bruised or bleeding, or in postures of servility or submission or display. It included no exception for literary or artistic value, and opponents claimed that applied literally it would outlaw James Joyce's *Ulysses*, John Cleland's *Memoirs of a Woman of Pleasure*, various works of D. H. Lawrence, and even Yeats's "Leda and the Swan." But the groups who sponsored the ordinance were anxious to establish that their objection was not to obscenity or indecency as such, but to the consequences for women of a particular kind of pornography, and they presumably thought that an exception for artistic value would undermine that claim.

The ordinance did not simply regulate the display of pornography so defined, or restrict its sale or distribution to particular areas, or guard against the exhibition of pornography to children. Regulation for those purposes does restrain negative liberty, but if reasonable it does so in a way compatible with free speech. Zoning and display regulations may make pornography more expensive or inconvenient to obtain, but they do not offend the principle that no one must be prevented from publishing or reading what he or she wishes on the ground that its content is immoral or offensive. The Indianapolis ordinance, on the other hand, prohibited any "production, sale, exhibition, or distribution" whatever of the material it defined as pornographic.

Publishers and members of the public who claimed a desire to read the banned material arranged a prompt constitutional challenge. The federal district court held that the ordinance was unconstitutional because it violated the First Amendment to the United States Constitution, which guarantees the negative liberty of free speech. The Circuit Court for the Seventh Circuit upheld the district court's decision, and the Supreme Court of the United States declined to review that holding. The Circuit Court's decision, in an opinion by Judge Easterbrook, noticed that the ordinance did not outlaw obscene or indecent material generally but only material reflecting the opinion that women are submissive, or enjoy being dominated, or should be treated as if they did. Easterbrook said that the central point of the First Amendment was exactly to protect speech from content-based regulation of that sort. Censorship may on some occasions be permitted if it aims to prohibit directly dangerous speech—crying fire in a crowded theater or inciting a crowd to violence, for example—or speech particularly and unnecessarily inconvenient—broadcasting from sound trucks patrolling residential streets at night, for instance. But nothing must be censored, Easterbrook wrote, because the message it seeks to deliver is a bad one, or because it expresses ideas that should not be heard at all.

It is by no means universally agreed that censorship should never be based on content. The British Race Relations Act, for example, forbids speech of racial hatred, not only when it is likely to lead to violence, but generally, on the grounds that members of minority races should be protected from racial insults. In America, however, it is a fixed principle of constitutional law that such regulation is unconstitutional unless some compelling necessity, not just official or majority disapproval of the message, requires it. Pornography is often grotesquely offensive; it is insulting, not only to women but to men as well. But we cannot consider that a sufficient reason for banning it without destroying the principle that the speech we hate is as much entitled to protection as any other. The essence of negative liberty is freedom to offend, and that applies to the tawdry as well as the heroic.

Lawyers who defend the Indianapolis ordinance argue that society does have a further justification for outlawing pornography: that it causes great harm as well as offense to women. But their arguments mix together claims about different types or kinds of harm, and it is necessary to distinguish these. They argue, first, that some forms of pornography significantly increase the danger that women will be raped or physically assaulted. If that were true, and the danger were clear and present, then it would indeed justify censorship of those forms, unless less stringent methods of control, such as restricting pornography's audience, would be feasible, appropriate, and effective. In fact, however, though there is some evidence that exposure to pornography weakens people's critical attitudes toward sexual violence, there is no persuasive evidence that it causes more actual incidents of assault. The Seventh Circuit cited a variety of studies...all of which concluded, the court said, "that it is not possible to demonstrate a direct link between obscenity and rape...." A recent report based on a year's research in Britain said: "The evidence does not point to pornography as a cause of deviant sexual orientation in offenders. Rather, it seems to be used as part of that deviant sexual orientation."

Some feminist groups argue, however, that pornography causes not just physical violence but a more general and endemic subordination of women. In that way, they say, pornography makes for inequality. But even if it could be shown, as a matter of causal connection, that pornography is in part responsible for the economic structure in which few women attain top jobs or equal pay for the same work, that would not justify censorship under the Constitution. It would plainly be unconstitutional to ban speech directly *advocating* that women occupy inferior roles, or none at all, in commerce and the professions, even if that speech fell on willing male ears and achieved its goals. So it cannot be a reason for banning pornography that it contributes to an unequal economic or social structure, even if we think that it does.

But the most imaginative feminist literature for censorship makes a further and different argument: that negative liberty for pornographers conflicts not just with equality but with positive liberty as well, because pornography leads to women's *political* as well as economic or social subordination. Of course pornography does not take the vote from women, or somehow make their votes count less. But it produces a climate according to this argument, in which women cannot have genuine political power or authority because they are perceived and understood unauthentically—that is, they are made over by male fantasy into people very different from, and of much less consequence than, the people they really are. Consider, for example, these remarks from the work of the principal sponsor of the Indianapolis ordinance. "[Pornography] institutionalizes the sexuality of male supremacy, fusing the eroticization of dominance and submission with the social construction of male and female....Men treat women as who they see women as being. Pornography constructs who that is. Men's power over women means that the way men see women defines who women can be."

Pornography, on this view, denies the positive liberty of women; it denies them the right to be their own masters by recreating them, for politics and society, in the shapes of male fantasy. That is a powerful argument, even in constitutional terms, because it asserts a conflict not just between liberty and equality but within liberty itself, that is, a conflict that cannot be resolved simply on the ground that liberty must be sovereign. What shall we make of the argument understood that way? We must notice, first, that it remains a causal argument. It claims not that pornography is a consequence or symbol or symptom of how the identity of women has been reconstructed by men, but an important cause or vehicle of that reconstruction.

That seems strikingly implausible. Sadistic pornography is revolting, but it is not in general circulation, except for its milder, soft-porn manifestations. It seems unlikely that it has remotely the influence over how women's sexuality or character or talents are conceived by men, and indeed by women, that commercial advertising and soap operas have. Television and other parts of popular culture use sexual display and sexual innuendo to sell virtually everything, and they often show women as experts in domestic detail and unreasoned intuition, and nothing else. The images they create are subtle and ubiquitous, and it would not be surprising to learn, through whatever research might establish this, that they indeed do great damage to the way women are understood and allowed to be influential in politics. Sadistic pornography, though much more offensive and disturbing, is greatly overshadowed by these dismal cultural influences as a causal force.

Judge Easterbrook's opinion…assumed, for the sake of argument, however, that pornography did have the consequences the defenders of the ordinance claimed. He said that the argument nevertheless failed because the point of free speech is precisely to allow ideas to have whatever consequences follow from their dissemination, including undesirable consequences for positive liberty. "Under the First Amendment," he said, "the government must leave to the people the evaluation of ideas. Bold or subtle, an idea is as powerful as the audience allows it to be.…[The assumed result] simply demonstrates the power of pornography as speech. All of these unhappy effects depend on mental intermediation."

That is right as a matter of American constitutional law. The Ku Klux Klan and the American Nazi Party are allowed to propagate their ideas in America, and the British Race Relations Act, so far as it forbids abstract speech of racial hatred, would be unconstitutional in the US. But does the American attitude represent the kind of Platonic absolutism Berlin warned against? No, because there is an important difference between the idea he thinks absurd, that all ideals attractive in themselves can be perfectly reconciled within a single utopian political order, and the different idea he thought essential, that we must, as individuals and nations, choose, among possible combinations of ideals, a coherent, even though inevitably and regrettably limited, set of these to define our own individual or national way of life. Freedom of speech, conceived and protected as a fundamental negative liberty, is the core of the choice modern democracies have made, a choice we must now honor in finding our own ways to combat the shaming inequalities women still suffer.

This reply depends, however, on seeing the alleged conflict within liberty as a conflict between the negative and positive senses of that virtue. We must consider yet another argument which, if successful, could not be met in the same way, because it claims that pornography presents a conflict within the negative liberty of speech itself. Berlin said that the character, at least, of negative liberty was reasonably clear, that although excessive claims of negative liberty were dangerous, they could at least always be seen for what they were. But the argument I have in mind, which has been offered by, among others, Frank Michelman of the Harvard Law School, expands the idea of negative liberty in an unanticipated way. He argues that some speech, including pornography, may be itself "silencing," so that its effect is to prevent other people from exercising their negative freedom to speak.

Of course it is fully recognized in First Amendment jurisprudence that some speech has the effect of silencing others. Government must indeed balance negative liberties when it prevents heckling or other demonstrative speech designed to stop others from speaking or being heard. But Michelman has something different in mind. He says that a woman's speech may be silenced not just by noise intended to drown her out but also by argument and images that change her audience's perceptions of her character, needs, desires, and standing, and also, perhaps, change her own sense of who she is and what she wants. Speech with that consequence silences her, Michelman supposes, by making it impossible for her effectively to contribute to the process Judge Easterbrook said the First Amendment protected, the process through which ideas battle for the public's favor. "[It] is a highly plausible claim," Michelman writes, "[that] pornography [is] a cause of women's subordination and silencing.…It is a fair and obvious question why our society's openess to challange does not need protection against repressive private as well as public action."

He argues that if our commitment to negative freedom of speech is consequentialist—if we want free speech in order to have a society in which no idea is barred from entry, then we must censor some ideas in order to make entry possible for other ones. He protests that the distinction that American constitutional law makes between the suppression of ideas by the effect of public criminal law and by the consequences of private speech is arbitrary, and that a sound concern for openness would be equally worried about both forms of control. But the distinction the law makes is not between public and private power as such, but between negative liberty and other virtues, including positive liberty. It would indeed be contradictory for a constitution to prohibit official censorship while also protecting the right of private citizens physically to prevent other citizens from publishing or broadcasting specified ideas. That would allow private citizens to violate the negative liberty of other citizens by preventing them from saying what they wish.

But there is no contradiction in insisting that every idea must be allowed to be heard, even those whose consequence is that other ideas will be misunderstood, or given little consideration, or even not be spoken at all because those who might speak them are not in control of their own public identities and therefore cannot be understood as they wish to be. These are very bad consequences, and they must be resisted by whatever means our Constitution permits. But acts that have these consequences do not, for that reason, deprive others of their negative liberty to speak, and the distinction, as Berlin insisted, is very far from arbitrary or inconsequential.

It is of course understandable why Michelman and others should want to expand the idea of negative liberty in the way they try to do. Only by characterizing certain ideas as themselves "silencing" ideas—only by supposing that censoring pornography is the same thing as stopping people from drowning out other speakers—can they hope to justify censorship within the constitutional scheme that assigns a preeminent place to free speech. But the assimilation is nevertheless a confusion, exactly the kind of confusion Berlin warned against in his original lecture, because it obscures the true political choice that must be made. I return to Berlin's lecture, which put the point with that striking combination of clarity and sweep I have been celebrating:

I should be guilt-stricken, and rightly so, if I were not, in some circumstances, ready to make [some] sacrifice [of freedom]. But a sacrifice is not an increase in what is being sacrificed, namely freedom, however great the moral need or the compensation for it. Everything is what it is: liberty is liberty, not equality or fairness or justice or culture, or human happiness or a quiet conscience.

7 Human Rights

In 1215 the English barons forced King John to agree that they had rights which could not be overridden by the king. This was the first step in a gradual process in which the idea of human rights grew and developed. By the eighteenth century the idea had crystallized into the doctrine of natural rights. It was argued that there are certain rights which are so basic that they are rights that everyone has. The Enlightenment philosophers, Hobbes, Locke, Rousseau, and so forth, argued that we each have certain basic rights which do not depend upon any conditions which are unique to our own position in society. It was this position which Jefferson cited in the Declaration of Independence when he said it is "self-evident that all men are created equal and endowed by their creator with certain inalienable rights, among which are life, liberty and the pursuit of happiness."

Jefferson's list of natural rights differs from the list given by Locke which included life, liberty, and property, and both differ from versions articulated by other natural rights proponents. One question which might occur to us as we reflect on natural rights theory is, why, if these rights are self-evident, should we not be able to agree on which rights are natural?

Further, even as Jefferson penned those famous words, there was an unwillingness to even consider the issue of exactly *who* possessed those rights and why. Historical evidence clearly demonstrates that while the rhetoric spoke of "all men" Jefferson and his comrades did not extend the natural right of liberty to their slaves. Abigail Adams chided her husband about the less than equal status of women, but a serious political discussion of the issue would not occur for another hundred years. Once one begins to question the issues, a number of conceptual issues emerge.

The doctrine of natural rights might amount to saying that there are rights we possess simply because we are human, but there is a difficulty in attributing to human beings even the most basic inherent rights. There is no empirical evidence that people are born with rights, while at the same time there is considerable empirical evidence that some people enjoy rights which other people do *not* enjoy, namely, those rights which have been legislated in certain countries but not in others. There is no question that there are *legal* rights, rights, that is, which have been passed into law by particular legislatures. Nor is there any question that some people have *special* rights by virtue of their own special circumstances. If I promise to mow your grass, you acquire a right which others do not possess. Special rights arise out of the many, various special roles and relationships we have with others.

If Enlightenment philosophers were correct and there are rights which are not specific to a particular situation or role but are basic and general, who possesses them? Intuitively, we want to say, "human beings." But we have already noticed that when the idea of these rights originated it was hardly contemplated that all human beings shared these rights. To be sure, the evolution of the idea of human rights has moved us to a point at which many of us do think of human rights as extending to all, or at least virtually all, human beings. But problematic cases still puzzle us. Ought we to say that a fetus, an infant, or a person in a vegetative state has the same rights to life and liberty as the rest of us? Or on the other hand, should we extend the notion of basic rights to other species, perhaps E.T., Klingons, or maybe the other primates?

The issue at stake is the basis on which we make the claim that we have these fundamental rights. What is it about ourselves that makes us right-bearers? What is it, which all people have in common and which no nonhumans have, which entitles them all to certain "basic" rights not shared by any nonhuman groups or individuals? The answer which is most often offered, going back to the Greek and Roman philosophers, is that all human beings are "rational," that is, capable of making rational decisions, deciding things on the basis of reason. But is that really true of all people? What about very young children and mentally handicapped or severely retarded individuals? If we weaken the criterion for what is to count as making a "rational" decision to include children and retarded individuals, then "rationality" no longer seems *unique* to human beings but to be shared to some extent by *other* animals. Perhaps the human characteristic we are looking for is the ability to carry out a plan of action, that is, to think of what one wants to do in life and try to do it—whether rationally or not. But, again, are *all* human beings capable of this? What about autistic or catatonic individuals?

READINGS

Even if we could agree that all human beings are born with basic "inalienable," or "natural" rights, it is not clear how extensive that list of rights is. Some of the social contractarians considered basic, natural human rights to be very limited indeed. The American Bill of Rights contains a longer but still very circumscribed list. The Declaration of the Rights of Man and of Citizens issued by the National Assembly of France during the French Revolution is more extensive. The latest attempt to list these rights was by United Nations 1948 Universal Declaration of Human Rights, which includes virtually everything which anyone has ever claimed human beings have a right to, including an extensive list of economic and social goods and even the right to a two-week annual paid vacation!

As we begin to think about these issues, notice that the concept of "a right" needs to be clarified. H. J. McCloskey, asks two questions: 1) What is a right? and 2) Who or what may possess rights? Rejecting the analysis of rights as powers or claims, he concludes that rights are entitlements to do, have, enjoy, or have done. He further distinguishes four concepts of moral rights—negative, positive, welfare, and special. The question of who or what can possess rights leads McCloskey to argue that there is a crucial link between possessing rights and having interests the violation of which is, ought to be, or would be of concern to the possessor. On this basis McCloskey concludes that inanimate objects and animals do not possess rights. The same reasoning leads him to the same conclusion with respect to infants, lunatics, and idiots—though it may be a "useful lie" to ignore this fact.

Douglas Husak of Rutgers University argues that the concept of a human right is conceived as a "moral trump" to protect every human being from the kind of utilitarian reasoning which might be supposed to justify eliminating or enslaving some persons or group of persons because it would make life much better for most of us. The problem Husak finds with human rights is that no one has found a morally relevant characteristic possessed by all human beings to provide a basis for the claim all humans have the same rights. Husak distinguishes between biological human beings and persons. Some human beings, for example someone in a vegetative state, are nonpersons. How we should be permitted to treat human nonpersons is a moral question yet to be answered, as is their moral status, but in Husak's view they cannot be protected by an appeal to ungrounded human rights or to the rights of persons.

In 1963 a debate raged over the Interstate Public Accomodations Act which, if passed, would outlaw the practice of refusing service and lodging to blacks. While Robert Bork, a federal judge nominated for the Supreme Court in the 1980s, opposed racial discrimination and favored ending legally required segregation, he opposed legislating an end to discrimination. Bork argues that the person who does not wish to do business with a person of another race is claiming a human right to deal with persons of their own choosing. The refusal of another individual to associate or deal with that person is, in Bork's view, insufficient to outweigh this right. The proposed legislation, he argues, would limit freedom and impose moral standards on those who do not share them. Individuals ought to be free to deal and associate with whom they please. Bork's position shows us that equality and freedom may conflict, since ending discrimination also limits the freedom to choose.

Ronald Dworkin, professor of law at Harvard and Oxford Universities, argues that the fundamental tension in weighting equality against liberty, which seems to some to be inherent in liberalism, is an illusion. He supports the idea that individuals have fundamental moral rights against government. He argues that the right to be treated as equal to other community members is fundamental but that there is no general right to liberty. Rights to special liberties, such as freedom of speech, arise when the right to treatment as an equal requires them.

Henry Shue of Cornell University is an example of a philosopher who interprets rights very broadly to include the right of everyone to have their basic housing, health, and nutritional needs met. Shue argues that the same grounds supporting the most basic rights to liberty and self-protection apply equally to the right to a minimum level of food, clothing, and shelter. Freedom is considered a right, even by minimalists like Bork, because it is necessary in order to carry out any plan of action, and the ability to carry out our plans is universally seen as one of the most important values in life. But Shue argues that adequate food, clothing, and shelter are just as necessary as is freedom to our being able to carry out any of our plans. I can no more move to a more prosperous part of the country in search of a job because I am starving or freezing to death than if I were enslaved or in jail.

Declaration of the Rights of Man and of Citizens

"Universal Declaration of Human Rights," adopted by The National Assembly of France, 1791

The representatives of the people of France, *formed into a* National Assembly, considering that ignorance, neglect, or contempt of human rights, are the sole causes of public misfortunes and corruptions of government, have resolved to set forth in a solemn declaration, these natural imprescriptible, and unalienable rights: that this declaration, being constantly present to the minds of the members of the body social, they may be ever kept attentive to their rights and their duties: that the acts of the legislative and executive powers of government, being capable of being every moment compared with the end of political institutions, may be more respected: and also, that the future claims of the citizens, being directed by simple and incontestible principles, may always tend to the maintenance of the Constitution, and the general happiness.

"For these reasons the National Assembly doth recognize and declare, in the presence of the Supreme Being, and with the hope of His blessing and favor, the following *sacred* rights of men and of citizens:

"I. *Men are born, and always continue, free, and equal in respect of their rights. Civil distinctions, therefore, can be founded only on public utility.*

"II. *The end of all political associations, is, the preservation of the natural and imprescriptible rights of man; and these rights are liberty, property, security, and resistance of oppression.*

"III. *The nation is essentially the source of all sovereignty; nor can any* individual, *or any body of men, be entitled to any authority which is not expressly derived from it.*

"IV. Political liberty consists in the power of doing whatever does not injure another. The exercise of the natural rights of every man has no other limits than those which are necessary to secure to every *other* man the free exercise of the same rights; and these limits are determinable only by the law.

"V. The law ought to prohibit only actions hurtful to society. What is not prohibited by the law, should not be hindered; nor should any one be compelled to that which the law does not require.

"VI. The law is an expression of the will of the community. All citizens have a right to concur, either personally, or by their representatives, in its formation. It should be the same to all, whether it protects or punishes; and *all being equal in its sight, are equally eligible to all honors, places, and employments, according to their different abilities, without any other distinction than that created by their virtues and talents.*

"VII. No man should be accused, arrested, or held in confinement, except in cases determined by the law, and according to the forms which it has prescribed. All who promote, solicit, execute, or cause to be executed, arbitrary orders, ought to be punished; and every citizen called upon or apprehended by virtue of the law, ought immediately to obey, and renders himself culpable by resistance.

"VIII. The law ought to impose no other penalties but such as are absolutely and evidently necessary: and no one ought to be punished, but in virtue of a law promulgated before the offense, and legally applied.

"IX. Every man being presumed innocent till he has been convicted, whenever his detention becomes indispensable, all rigor to him, more than is

"Declaration of the Rights of Man and of Citizens," adopted by the National Assembly of France (Thomas Paine, trans.)

necessary to secure his person, ought to be provided against by the law.

"X. No man ought to be molested on account of his opinions, not even on account of his *religious* opinions, provided his avowal of them does not disturb the public order established by the law.

"XI. The unrestrained communication of thoughts and opinions being one of the most precious rights of man, every citizen may speak, write, and publish freely, provided he is responsible for the abuse of this liberty in cases determined by the law.

"XII. A public force being necessary to give security to the rights of men and of citizens, that force is instituted for the benefit of the community, and not for the particular benefit of the persons with whom it is intrusted.

"XIII. A common contribution being necessary for the support of the public force, and for defraying the other expenses of government, it ought to be divided equally among the members of the community, according to their abilities.

"XIV. Every citizen has a right, either by himself or his representative, to a free voice in determining the necessity of public contributions, the appropriation of them, and their amount, mode of assessment, and duration.

"XV. Every community has a right to demand of all its agents, an account of their conduct.

"XVI. Every community in which a separation of powers and a security of rights is not provided for, wants a constitution.

"XVII. The rights to property being inviolable and sacred, no one ought to be deprived of it, except in cases of evident public necessity, legally ascertained, and on condition of a previous just indemnity."

Universal Declaration of Human Rights

United Nations, 1948

Preamble

WHEREAS recognition of the inherent dignity and of the equal and inalienable rights of all members of the human family is the foundation of freedom, justice and peace in the world,

WHEREAS disregard and contempt for human rights have resulted in barbarous acts which have outraged the conscience of mankind, and the advent of a world in which human beings shall enjoy freedom of speech and belief and freedom from fear and want has been proclaimed as the highest aspiration of the common people,

WHEREAS it is essential, if man is not to be compelled to have recourse, as a last resort, to rebellion against tyranny and oppression, that human rights should be protected by the rule of law,

WHEREAS it is essential to promote the development of friendly relations between nations,

WHEREAS the people of the United Nations have in the Charter reaffirmed their faith in fundamental human rights, in the dignity and worth of the human person and in the equal rights of men and women and have determined to promote social progress and better standards of life in larger freedom, the United Nations, the promotion of universal respect for and observance of human rights and fundamental freedoms,

WHEREAS a common understanding of these rights and freedoms is of the greatest importance for the full realisation of this pledge,

NOW, THEREFORE, THE GENERAL ASSEMBLY, PROCLAIM

this Universal Declaration of Human Rights as a common standard of achievement for all peoples and all nations, to the end that every individual and every organ of society, keeping this Declaration constantly in mind, shall strive by teaching and education to promote respect for these rights and freedoms and by progressive measures, national and international, to secure their universal and effective recognition and observance, both among the people of Member States themselves and among the people of territories under their jurisdiction.

Article 1

All human beings are born free and equal in dignity and rights. They are endowed with reason and conscience and should act towards one another in a spirit of brotherhood.

Article 2

1. Everyone is entitled to all the rights and freedoms set forth in this Declaration, without distinction of any kind, such as race, colour, sex, language, religion, political or other opinion, national or social origin, property, birth or other status.
2. Furthermore, no distinction shall be made on the basis of the political, jurisdictional or international status of the country or territory to which a person belongs, whether it be independent, trust, non-self governing or under any other limitation of sovereignty.

Article 3

Everyone has the right to life, liberty and security of person.

Article 4

No one shall be held in slavery or servitude; slavery and the slave trade shall be prohibited in all their forms.

Article 5

No one shall be subjected to torture or to cruel, inhuman or degrading treatment or punishment.

Article 6

Everyone has the right to recognition everywhere as a person before the law.

Article 7

All are equal before the law and are entitled without any discrimination to equal protection of the law. All are entitled to equal protection against any discrimination, in violation of this Declaration and against any incitement to such discrimination.

Article 8

Everyone has the right to an effective remedy by the competent national tribunals for acts violating the fundamental rights granted him by the constitution or by law.

Article 9

No one shall be subjected to arbitrary arrest, detention or exile.

Article 10

Everyone is entitled in full equality to a fair and public hearing by an independent and impartial tribunal, in the determination of his rights and obligations and of any criminal charge against him.

Article 11

1. Everyone charged with a penal offence has the right to be presumed innocent until proved guilty according to law in a public trial at which he has had all the guarantees necessary for his defence.
2. No one shall be held guilty of any penal offence on account of any act or omission which did not constitute a penal offence, under national or international law, at the time when it was committed. Nor shall a heavier penalty be imposed than the one that was applicable at the time the penal offence was committed.

Article 12

No one shall be subjected to arbitrary interference with his privacy, family, home or correspondence, nor to attacks upon his honour and reputation. Everyone has the right to the protection of the law against such interference or attacks.

Article 13

1. Everyone has the right to freedom of movement and residence within the borders of each State.
2. Everyone has the right to leave any country, including his own, and to return to his country.

Article 14

1. Everyone has the right to seek and to enjoy in other countries asylum from persecution.
2. This right may not be invoked in the case of prosecutions genuinely arising from non-political crimes or from acts contrary to the purposes and principles of the United Nations.

Article 15

1. Everyone has the right to a nationality.
2. No one shall be arbitrarily deprived of his nationality nor denied the right to change his nationality.

Article 16

1. Men and women of full age, without any limitation due to race, nationality or religion, have the right to marry and to found a family. They are entitled to equal rights as to marriage, during marriage and at its dissolution.
2. Marriage shall be entered into only with the free and full consent of the intending spouses.
3. The family is the natural and fundamental group unit of society and is entitled to protection by society and the State.

Article 17

1. Everyone has the right to own property alone as well as in association with others.
2. No one shall be arbitrarily deprived of his property.

Article 18

Everyone has the right to freedom of thought, conscience and religion; this right includes freedom to change his religion or belief, and freedom, either alone or in community with others and in public or private, to manifest his religion or belief in teaching practice, worship and observance.

Article 19

Everyone has the right to freedom of opinion and expression; this right includes freedom to hold opinions without interference and to seek, receive and impart information and ideas through any media and regardless of frontiers.

Article 20

1. Everyone has the right to freedom of peaceful assembly and association.
2. No one may be compelled to belong to an association.

Article 21

1. Everyone has the right to take part in the government of his country, directly or through freely chosen representatives.
2. Everyone has the right of equal access to public service in his country.
3. The will of the people shall be the basis of the authority of government; this will shall be expressed in periodic and genuine elections which shall be by universal and equal suffrage and shall be held by secret vote or by equivalent free voting procedures.

Article 22

Everyone, as a member of society, has the right to social security and is entitled to realisation, through national effort and international co-operation and in accordance with the organisation and resources of each State, of the economic, social and cultural rights indispensable for his dignity and the free development of his personality.

Article 23

1. Everyone has the right to work, to free choice of employment, to just and favourable conditions of work and to protection against unemployment.
2. Everyone, without any discrimination, has the right to equal pay for equal work.
3. Everyone who works has the right to just and favourable remuneration ensuring for himself and his family an existence worthy of human dignity, and supplemented, if necessary, by other means of social protection.
4. Everyone has the right to form and to join trade unions for the protection of his interests.

Article 24

Everyone has the right to rest and leisure, including reasonable limitation of working hours and periodic holidays with pay.

Article 25

1. Everyone has the right to a standard of living adequate for the health and well-being of himself and of his family, including food, clothing, housing and medical care and necessary social services, and the right to security in the event of unemployment, sickness, disability, widowhood, old age or other lack of livelihood in circumstances beyond his control.

2. Motherhood and childhood are entitled to special care and assistance. All children, whether born in or out of wedlock, shall enjoy the same social protection.

Article 26

1. Everyone has the right to education. Education shall be free, at least in the elementary and fundamental stages. Elementary education shall be compulsory. Technical and Professional education shall be made generally available and higher education shall be equally accessible to all on the basis of merit.
2. Education shall be directed to the full development of the human personality and to the strengthening of respect for human rights and fundamental freedoms. It shall promote understanding, tolerance and friendship among all nations, racial or religious groups, and shall further the activities of the United Nations for the maintenance of peace.
3. Parents have a prior right to choose the kind of education that shall be given to their children.

Article 27

1. Everyone has the right freely to participate in the cultural life of the community, to enjoy the arts and to share in scientific advancement and its benefits.
2. Everyone has the right to the protection of the moral and material interests resulting from any scientific, literary or artistic production of which he is the author.

Article 28

Everyone is entitled to a social and international order in which the rights and freedoms set forth in this Declaration can be fully realised.

Article 29

1. Everyone has duties to the community in which alone the free and full development of his personality is possible.
2. In the exercise of his rights and freedoms, everyone shall be subject only to such limitations as are determined by law solely for the purpose of securing due recognition and respect for the rights and freedoms of others and of meeting the just requirements of morality, public order and the general welfare in a democratic society.
3. These rights and freedoms may in no case be exercised contrary to the purposes and principles of the United Nations.

Article 30

Nothing in this Declaration may be interpreted as implying for any State, group or person any right to engage in any activity or to perform any act aimed at the destruction of any of the rights and freedoms set forth herein.

"Rights"

H. J. McCloskey

I propose to consider two questions:…What is a right? Who or what may possess rights? A moral right is commonly explained as being some sort of *claim* or *power* which ought to be recognized. D. G. Ritchie, for instance, observes that a moral right may be defined as "*the claim* of an individual upon others recognized by society, irrespective of its recognition by the State." Ryan and Boland, explaining the Catholic (Thomist) view of rights, state: "A right in the moral sense of the term may be defined as an inviolable moral *claim* to some personal good. When this claim is created as it

From "Rights," *Philosophical Quarterly*, vol. 15 (1965). Reprinted by permission of the author and the publisher.

sometimes is, by civil authority, it is a positive or legal right; when it is derived from man's rational nature it is a natural right." T. H. Green, on the other hand, argues: "A right is a power of acting for his own ends,—for what he conceives to be his good,—secured to an individual by the community on the supposition that its exercise contributes to the good of the community." Plamenatz follows Green in explaining rights in terms of powers, but in other respects his definition differs substantially from that of Green. Plamenatz states: "A right is a power which a creature ought to possess because its exercise by him is itself good, or else because it is a means to what is good, and in the exercise of which all rational beings ought to protect him." There are obvious grounds for rejecting such accounts of the concept of a right, whether it be a legal, moral, social, or institutional right. To consider first rights other than moral rights.

To have a *legal right* is not to have a power conferred or recognized by law, nor is it a power which ought to be recognized by law or by official administering the law. I may have a legal right to drive a car but lack the power to do so because temporarily paralysed or because too poor to buy or rent a car....The laws giving me the right to marry, divorce, or to make a will, are not conferring powers on me; yet they are clearly conferring legal rights. Similarly, criminal laws deny me legal rights but they do not interfere with my powers. Nor are legal rights powers recognized by the state, for legal rights may exist where there is no power to exercise the right. Similarly, a legal right does not amount to a claim upon others recognized by the state, although a right may provide a ground for such a claim. My legal right to marry consists primarily in the recognition of my entitlement to marry and to have my act recognized. It indirectly gives rise to claims on others nor to prevent me so acting, but it does not primarily consist in these claims. I am legally entitled under our legal system to do whatever is not forbidden by the law. Thus I have a legal right to grow roses in my garden. This legal right is not simply a claim I can make under the law that others not interfere with me when selecting plants for my garden. It is essentially an entitlement to act as I please. It may give rise to derivative entitlements, and claims on others and the state.

With *institutional rights,* e.g., rights as a member of a religious organization or a social club, the possession of a right does not consist in some sort of power or claim. A right to vote in the election of the elders of the Church is an entitlement to take part in the election; and an entitlement is very different from a power, whether it be a power conferred, recognized, or which ought to be recognized. To have the right to vote is not simply or necessarily to have the power to vote, nor is it a power to act which has been conferred or recognized or which ought to be recognized. In a laxly policed election non-members may have the power but not the right to vote. Similarly, the right does not consist primarily in claims on others. Consider the right of the Church member to partake of Holy Communion. The right and the power are clearly distinct, and the right is related to claims only in that, besides entitling the member to partake of Holy Communion, it also entitles him to resist any official or member of the Church who seeks to prevent him partaking. So too with rights as a member of a social club. My right to use the club—its writing room, library, bar—is an entitlement. I may lack the power to exercise this right, and still possess it; and I may enjoy it without making claims on others—e.g., if it were a small, self-service club with no staff. The right equally exists for the member who is unable to get to the club, i.e., who cannot make claims on others, and for the member who admits himself to the club building and who makes no claims on others.

Rights also figure in *games*, although of course they are rights of a conceptually different kind from moral rights such as the right to liberty. However, the essence of rights in games as elsewhere consists in their being entitlements. In Australian Rules football players have the right to place-kick after a mark or free kick; and it is clearly meaningful and correct to assert that the player who doesn't know how to place-kick, and the player who never marks the ball nor receives a free kick, enjoy the right as fully as the skillful place-kick who receives many free kicks. The right consists in an entitlement, which, if denied, would provide the player with grounds for making demands and claims on others, viz., the umpire, which may or may not succeed. It is to misconstrue rights in games to construe them as the claims to which they may or may not give rise....

If we look at *moral rights*, in particular at what we intend to claim when we claim a right, we find here too that a right is an entitlement. It may be an entitlement to do, to demand, to enjoy, to be, to have done for us. Rights may be rights to act, to exist, to enjoy, to demand. We speak of rights as being *possessed, exercised*, and *enjoyed*. In these respects there is an affinity between our talk about rights and our talk about capacities, powers, and the like, and a distinct contrast with talk about claims, for we *make* claims but do not possess, exercise, or enjoy them. But, since a right may exist and be possessed in the absence of the relevant power or capacity, rights are distinct from powers. I possess the rights to life, liberty and happiness; my possession of these rights means that I am entitled to live, to act freely without interference, and be unimpeded in my search for happiness.

It is often argued that rights are conceptually linked with *rules*. Benn and Peters, for instance, state: "To say that X has a right to £5 is to imply that there is a rule which, when applied to the case of X and some other person Y, imposes on Y a duty to pay X £5 if X so chooses. Without the possibility of the correlative duty resting somewhere, the attribution of the right to X would be meaningless." Our foregoing consideration of legal rights suggests that this is not the case. We have legal rights in the absence of legal rules, and the way in which rules are relevant to legal rights varies. Sometimes the rule explicitly denies a right, other rules confer rights, other rules sustain rights which are rule-grounded only in the very weakened sense that 'what is not forbidden in our legal system is permitted' may be said to be itself a rule of sorts. However, it is not a rule in the same sense or senses of rule as that in which criminal and power-conferring laws are rules. With rights as members of organizations, rules figure prominently, but rights may nonetheless exist which are not grounded on rules. There may be no rule concerning private worship in the church building on weekdays, but in the absence of a rule forbidding it, and even in the absence of a general rule stating that what is not forbidden is permitted, the member may reasonably claim the right to worship privately in the church each day. He could offer good reasons, not in terms of some rule, but in terms of the purpose of the building and the character of the religious organization. The same is true of moral rights. We do not always have to point to a rule of some sort to show that we have a moral right. A claim to a

right such as the right to life may be supported by a large variety of kinds of reasons. Indeed, the characteristic reasons appropriate as reasons in support of moral rights seem not to be reasons in terms of rules.

We speak of our rights as being *rights to*—as in the rights to life, liberty and happiness—not as *rights against*, as has so often mistakenly been claimed. Special rights are sometimes against specific individuals or institutions—e.g., rights created by promises, contracts, etc. The wife has rights against the husband, the creditor against the debtor, but these are special, nongeneral rights which differ from the characteristic cases of general rights, where the right is simply a right to (i.e., an entitlement to)—e.g., of the man to marry the woman of his choice. It is strangely artificial to suggest that this is a right against someone or some thing. Against whom or what is it a right? My right to life is not a right against anyone. It is *my* right and by virtue of it, it is normally permissible for me to sustain my life in the face of obstacles. It does give rise to rights against others *in the sense* that others have or may come to have duties to refrain from killing me, but it is essentially a right of mine, not an infinite list of claims, hypothetical and actual, against an infinite number of actual, potential, and as yet nonexistent human beings. Even non-moral rights such as legal rights, rights as a member of a club, rights in games, are not typically rights against but rights to have, to do, to be, to have done for us. My legal right to drive a car, having passed a test for a licence and paid the appropriate fee, is a right to do certain things, not a right against the police, magistrates, and other officials. Similarly, the right of the tennis club member to play on the club courts is a right to play, not a right against some vague group of potential or possible obstructors. Similarly, the right of the football player to place-kick if he so chooses is a right to do just that. It is not a right against his opponent or against the umpire. And if it is a right by virtue of his having taken a mark it is especially hard to see against whom it might be said to be.

Rights are entitlements to do, have, enjoy or have done. That it is a serious error to construe general rights as rights against rather than rights to or as entitlements, is confirmed by consideration of people who live in isolation. It is meaningful to speak of the hermit on an isolated island as having rights to do or have certain things, but it would be strange to speak of him as having rights against others. His rights may give rise to rights against others, but the right—e.g., to live—is not primarily against others. The infliction of avoidable suffering on animals is obviously *prima facie* wrong, but the fact that a person possesses the right to life, whether he be a hermit or not, justifies him in killing animals—and in the process causing them to suffer—in order to sustain himself. His right to life is inaptly described in such a situation as a right against the animals he kills. Many, although not myself, would wish to argue that there is no right to suicide. Clearly it is not *prima facie* absurd so to argue. Yet if there is no such right, the hermit would not be entitled to take his own life, although he would have rights to do other things.

The difficulties of "rights against" talk, and of any attempt to write into the concept of a right, that it must be against someone, are evident if we consider the extreme case of the last person in the universe, who alone survives the nuclear war. Imagine that the last person is a woman capable of reproducing by artificial insemination, a large sperm bank having also survived. I suggest that talk about rights would have real application in such a situation. Suppose the woman had good reason to believe that if she reproduced, her offspring would be monsters, defectives, imbeciles, doomed to life-long suffering. In such a case she would have to conclude that she did not possess the right to reproduce. If she had every reason to believe that her offspring would be healthy, she would conclude that she had the right to reproduce, unless of course she regarded artificial insemination as wrong. This suggests that the actual existence of other human beings is irrelevant to whether rights may or may not be possessed. Clearly *the possible existence* of other human beings is more than adequate as a basis for talk about rights to have point. And, as I argued earlier, even this seems not to be necessary....

So far I have spoken of rights, whether they be legal, moral, social, institutional, or in games, as essentially entitlements of some sort; yet obviously they are different sorts of entitlements, such that we should describe them as being conceptually different from one another. The concept of a legal right is a different concept from that of a right in a game, and both are different from rights which are created by membership of a club. Similarly, although all moral rights are entitlements, there are conceptual differences between various of the rights which may be characterized as moral rights, which makes it desirable to distinguish different *concepts* of moral rights, and to speak of legal, moral, social, etc. rights as rights of different *kinds*....In fact, if we look at the sorts of rights that are claimed as moral rights, at actual theories about rights, and at ordinary discourse, we find that there are at least four distinct concepts of moral rights, all of which are to be explained as entitlements.

(*a*) There is *the negative concept* of a right apparent in some of Locke's arguments for rights, particularly for the rights to life and liberty. To have a negative right to X is for it not to be wrong for us to do or have X and for other people to lack the right or have a duty not to interfere; and here the duty is obviously not a duty against us. For example, to have a right to life of this kind, would be for it to be right (or not wrong) for us to sustain ourselves, and for others to be obliged not to take our lives or at least not to be entitled to deprive us of our lives. This concept of a right lends itself most easily to modification to permit talk about animal rights, but it will be argued later that such modification is not in order as animals cannot be possessors of rights. Negative rights are not simply rights by analogy, nor are negative rights, rights in a sense parasitic on some other concept of a right. It is logically possible that all rights be of this negative character. A community which conceived of all rights as being of this kind would obviously be said to have grasped the concept of a right, although it would not have grasped the richest and fullest concept of a right. (It is still possible to speak of such negative rights as being possessed, but the sense of 'possessed' is weaker than in the other cases.)

(*b*) There is also *the positive concept* of a right such that to have a right is to have a moral authority or entitlement to act in a certain way. This concept is often elucidated in terms of legitimate claims on others, but such accounts obviously will not do, for we explain and justify our claim on others in terms of having a right, i.e., in terms of our having a positive moral entitlement to act in a certain way. It is this that entitles us to demand freedom from interference. The rights for which Thomists argue on the basis of the natural law are of this kind, e.g., rights to seek the truth, to rear one's offspring, to preserve oneself.

(*c*) There is a more positive, fuller concept which we may characterize as *the welfare concept of a right* such that a right is not merely a moral entitlement to do or to have, but also an entitlement to the efforts of others or to make demands on others to aid and promote our seeking after or enjoyment of some good. Thus, in terms of this welfare concept of a right, it is written into the concept that the conditions for its enjoyment be promoted. Such a concept underlies many arguments for welfare legislation, for many such arguments proceed by maintaining that respect for human rights, involves removing not simply *man-made* obstacles but also *natural* hindrances and impediments to the enjoyment of some power or good. For example, many demands for conditions to promote the enjoyment of the rights to health, life, etc., proceed from such a welfare concept of a right. Indeed, if such a concept is denied significance, a great deal of controversy about rights in this century becomes meaningless.

(*d*) There are also *special rights* noted above as admitting of being described as rights against, and which spring from duties to particular individuals. The right of the creditor to repayment of his loan on the due date is a right or entitlement of this kind.

The above distinctions between different concepts of rights are obviously relevant to the vexed question of the relation between *rights and duties*. And, of course, the question of the relation between rights and duties raises many important issues, not the least that concerning who or what may be the possessor of rights. It is commonly argued that there is a close conceptual connexion between rights and duties. To consider in what respects this is so. (i) Where the right is of type (*a*), its existence depends in part on there being a duty on others not to interfere *or* on others lacking a right of type (*b*) to interfere. Where the right is of type (*b*) A's right creates actual and potential duties for others and for potential and hypothetical others. To explain: My right to liberty creates no duty for the Hottentot or the Eskimo, for they cannot interfere with me and do not know of my existence. If they could come to interfere, my right would constitute a ground for the duty not to interfere. Similarly with infants. My rights do not create duties for them unless and until they become full moral agents and

have some relationship or connexion with me, when my right causes them to have duties not to interfere. Similarly with those as yet unborn. (ii) Rights of type (*c*) obviously give rise to duties and to potential duties. If the blind man whose sight can be restored has a right to sight (as part of the right to health) he has a right to our efforts on his behalf; and we have a duty to make the relevant effort. Such rights seem also to be possessed by those who are not full moral agents, for instance, by infants, curable lunatics, idiots, etc. If a minimal I.Q. idiot could be cured by a pill as cheap as an aspirin, it would be reasonable to claim that he has a right to the necessary treatment and that we have a duty to see that it is made available to him. (iii) Where the right is of type (*d*), i.e., a special right against another, the right implies a duty in the person against whom it is held. The husband of the wife who has promised to obey him has a right to her obedience, and she the duty to obey. In this case the duty is primary. It springs from the wife's promise and the right is created by the promise and the duty to keep the promise. (iv) Duties and rights. To have a duty is to have a right. One has the right to do what is necessary for the fulfillment of one's duty. But to have a duty is not necessarily for another to have a right. Ross notes the case of duties to animals, and other duties could be cited. For example, the duty to perfect one's talents is not a duty against oneself, nor is it a duty to one's self. It is simply a duty and creates no rights in others. Similarly with the duty to maximize good. The last person in the universe would have the duty to maximize good and to produce other human beings if this were a means to or part of maximizing good; but there would be no one with a right resulting from the duty. The duty of the artist to produce good and not slovenly paintings does not give to others the right to demand of the artist that he produce the best paintings of which he is capable. Again, I may have a duty to the state, e.g., to pay my income tax; but the sense in which the state might be said to have a right to my tax is distinct from the sense of 'right' in which we speak of moral rights as possessed by individuals. The state cannot be the possessor of the sorts of rights human beings may possess. Yet it may be the object of duties. Further, not all duties to the state or to other institutions create these rights in the institutions. It does not follow that, because the Church member has a duty to give generously to his Church, the Church has a right to his gifts. In brief: When a right is attributed, we cannot always significantly ask 'Who has the corresponding duties?' And, when a duty is postulated, we cannot always find someone who possesses a corresponding right.

The issue as to who or what may be a possessor of rights is not simply a matter of academic, conceptual interest. Obviously, important conclusions follow from any answer. If, for instance, it is determined that gravely mentally defective human beings and monsters born of human parents are not the kinds of beings who may possess rights, this bears on how we may treat them. It does not settle such questions as to whether it is right to kill them if they are a burden or if they are enduring pointless suffering, but it does bear in an important way on such questions. Even if such beings cannot be possessors of rights it might still be wrong to kill them, but the case against killing those who endure pain is obviously easier to set out if they can be shown to be capable of possessing rights and in fact possess rights. Similarly, important conclusions follow from the question as to whether animals have rights. If they do,…it would seem an illegitimate invasion of animal rights to kill and eat them, if, as seems to be the case, we can sustain ourselves without killing animals. If animals have rights, the case of vegetarianism is *prima facie* very strong, and is comparable with the case against cannibalism.

These issues, then, are not without importance, but they present very considerable difficulties. If we follow our unreflective moral consciousness we find ourselves drawn strongly to conclusions which seem radically inconsistent with one another; yet if we attempt to reason to a conclusion it is extremely difficult even to begin to set out an argument, let alone develop a carefully worked out, convincing argument in favour of one conclusion rather than another. And, whilst our analysis of the concept of a right takes us some way—it excludes some possibilities and some arguments—it seems on the face of it to leave open a very large number of possibilities.

Although an important and difficult problem, this is one to which few theorists have applied themselves with the attention and critical scrutiny which might be expected in such an important issue.…

T. H. Green does address himself to the problem to the extent of claiming that we have rights only as members of a community, that rights involve mutual recognition, and that they can therefore only be possessed by moral persons, i.e., rational beings. However, he offers only very general, sketchy arguments for these contentions, and seems to fail to realize that besides excluding animals as possible possessors of rights, they exclude infants, imbeciles, and other mentally defective human beings. Ritchie perhaps comes closest to offering an argument when he notes the difficultes which arise if animals are attributed rights. If animals have rights, the cat invades the right of the mouse, the tiger of the cow, etc. Should we restrict the liberty of the cat and of the tiger out of respect for the rights of the mouse and the cow? And should we, out of respect for the rights of animals, allow parasites to continue to inhabit us if they do not have seriously deleterious effects on our health? Plamenatz seeks a way out of such difficulties, whilst at the same time allowing that animals have rights, by claiming that rights are *rights against rational beings*, hence the cow has no rights against the tiger but only against human beings. This obviously will not do, for the reasons noted above, namely, that rights are not primarily rights against but rights to. They may rationally be demanded only of rational beings, for the obvious reason that only rational beings are capable of complying with the demands, but this does not mean that the tiger is not invading the rights of the cow when he kills it. The absurdity of the conclusions which follow from the admission of animal rights may, as Ritchie claims, *suggest* that animals cannot be possessors of rights, but it does not *establish* that this is so.

The general tendency has been to maintain that free agents and potential free agents have rights, with idiots, and all born of human parents being treated as potentially free agents, although many are obviously not such. Those who have claimed that animals have rights have rarely explained whether they mean all animals; equally seriously, they seem not to explain why they think some or all sentient beings have rights, and why not all animate objects and even perhaps things. The unspoken premiss seems to be either that where there is a possibility of "action" of some sort there is the possibility of rights, or that where there is a possibility of pain, there is the possibility of possession of rights. But the reasons underlying the assumption are not evident. Clearly, if lower animals, especially parasitic animals such as the flea, are allowed to be capable of possessing rights, argument is needed to show why such animals, and not all animate objects, e.g., a beautiful oak or mountain ash, can possess rights. If it were allowed that all sentient beings and all animate objects possess some rights—e.g., to life—why, it might be asked, should rights be denied of inanimate things? Might not beautiful works of art, paintings of Raphael and Leonardo da Vinci also have a right to continued existence? Argument is needed here, yet argument is notably lacking. Where it is to be found, it is of the very unconvincing kind offered by Thomists, that rational beings, being subject to the natural law, have rights, since rights are grounded on the natural law; that infants, lunatics, idiots have rights and are subject to natural law since they are rational beings. Obviously, even if the theory of natural law could be established—and this I should wish to deny—infants, lunatics and idiots are not subject to it as rational agents any more than is an intelligent dog or ape. The natural law is law, and is binding on men because and in so far as it is promulgated through reason. It is not promulgated to infants, idiots and certain lunatics. And, whilst it might be argued that it is promulgated potentially to infants, and hypothetically to idiots, potential and hypothetical promulgation are not promulgation, and to be a potential or a hypothetical possessor of rights is not to be a possessor of potential or hypothetical rights, nor of actual rights....

Moral rights can be possessed by beings who can claim them, and by those who can have them claimed on their behalf by others and whose interests are violated or disregarded if the rights are not respected. The concept of interests which is so important here is an obscure and elusive one. Interests are distinct from welfare and are more inclusive in certain respects—usually what is dictated by concern for a man's welfare is in his interests. However, interests suggest much more than that which is indicated by the person's welfare. They suggest that which is or ought to be or which would be of *concern* to the person/being. It is partly for this reason—because the concept of interests has this evaluative-prescriptive overtone—that we decline to speak of the interests of animals, and speak rather of their welfare.

That the possibility of possessing rights is limited in this way is confirmed by the very fact that we speak of rights as being *possessed and enjoyed*. A right cannot not be possessed by someone; hence, only beings which can possess things can possess rights. My right to life is mine; I possess it. It is as much mine as any of my possessions—indeed more so—for I possess them by virtue of my rights. It is true that I may possess rights and not know or enjoy my possession of them. Thus, whilst rights must be possessed by a possessor, they need not be enjoyed. All we can say is that they may admit of enjoyment by their possessors.

All these considerations seem to exclude the lower animals in a decisive way, and the higher animals in a less decisive but still fairly conclusive way as possible possessors of rights. (Consider 'possess' in its literal use. Can a horse possess anything, e.g., its stable, its rug, in a literal sense of 'possess'?) It might, however, be argued that animals can possess special rights, e.g., rights arising out of relations such as the owner's "debt of gratitude" to the animal for special services. Consider the blind man and his guide dog who repeatedly saves his life. The difficulty that rights are possessed and that animals cannot possess things remains; and, in any case, the animal's special services are more naturally described as creating special duties rather than as giving rise to entitlements in the animal.

It would seem to follow from all this that monsters born of human parents whose level of existence falls far short of that of the highest animals would also seem not to be possible possessors of rights. However, two qualifications may usefully be made here. Animals, or at least the higher animals, may usefully be said to have *rights by analogy*. We have duties involving them, and these duties might be said to create rights by analogy....

With those born of human parents, even the most inferior beings, it may be *a useful lie* to attribute rights where they are not and cannot be possessed, since to deny the very inferior beings born of human parents rights, opens the way to a dangerous slide. But whether useful or not, it is a lie or a mistake to attribute rights or the possibility of rights to such beings. More difficult are the cases of the infant, lunatic, etc. As indicated earlier, we do attribute rights and interests to infants, lunatics, and even to incurable lunatics. Part of the reason for this is the thought that such beings, unlike the

congenital idiot, etc., are possibly potential possessors of interests. Hence, until it is clear that they
can never really be said to have interests, we treat
them as if they do. Also relevant is the fact that
even a mentally defective human being—e.g., an

imbecile, or a lunatic with periods of sanity—may
literally demand some rights and possess others
and generally be attributed interests in a literal
sense....

"Why There Are No Human Rights"

Douglas Husak

There are no *human* rights. The chief difficulty in
defending this thesis is not in providing a sound
argument in its favor. Such an argument...has in
fact been familiar to philosophers for some time.
Instead, the difficulty is in offering an explanation
of why so few theorists have been persuaded by
this argument. An attack on human rights is bound
to give rise to misunderstandings I am anxious to
dispell. My purpose is not to discredit the noble
purposes to which human rights have been put, but
to suggest that these purposes are better served
without the highly problematic contention that all
human beings share rights. Thus my central project
is to undermine the philosophical motivation for
believing that human rights must exist. Once the
obstacles to rejecting human rights have been identified and removed, my thesis will be found much
more palatable.

A preliminary difficulty is to characterize what
human rights *are*. Otherwise it is unclear whether
philosophers who debate about the existence of
human rights are in genuine agreement or disagreement. Unfortunately, there is no consensus about
the definition of human rights. I will borrow from
philosophers sympathetic to human rights, first, an
account of what makes a right a *human* right, and
second, a theory of *rights*.

All philosophers agree that a right cannot be a
human right unless it is possessed (a) *by all human*

beings. But apart from this first condition, there are
two others that may or may not be necessary for a
right to qualify as a human right. Some philosophers insist that the right must be possessed (b)
only by human beings....The doctrine of human
rights I will attack includes the first condition but
rejects the second; thus, if a given right is shared
by nonhumans, it is not thereby disqualified as a
human right....Hence my attack upon human
rights construes them weakly, including only the
first condition. If I can show that there are no rights
possessed by all human beings, any stronger doctrine of human rights will have been refuted as
well.

Differences among philosophers about what
makes a right a *human* right account for only a
small part of the controversy about the existence,
basis, and content of human rights. Of far greater
significance is the fact that philosophers are unclear about what *rights* are. Human rights are,
presumably, a kind of right, and any confusion
about rights is bound to create uncertainty about
human rights. Once again, it is fair to conclude that
there is no consensus among philosophers about
the role played by rights in moral theory. How, if
at all, would a moral theory without a concept of
rights differ from one in which rights were included? Though there is much room for controversy here, I will assume the truth of a theory about

---

From "Why There Are No Human Rights," *Social Theory and Practice*, vol. 10 (1984).
Reprinted by permission of the publisher.

rights that has gained a substantial following among several of the most distinguished moral and political philosophers to have addressed these questions.

According to this theory, rights function to protect their possessors from being subjected to treatment solely in accordance with the outcomes of utilitarian calculations. In many circumstances, acts are justified—even when coercive and contrary to some person's interests—when they produce a net balance of benefits over harms. But when a *right* of such a person is violated, this utilitarian rationale is insufficient to justify the act in question. Thus it is sometimes said that rights "trump" countervailing utilitarian considerations. Many philosophers contend that the chief difficulty with utilitarianism is that it provides a defective account of rights. Hence a moral theory that did not include rights would be vulnerable to many of the difficulties urged against utilitarianism—it would allow the unjust sacrifice of one person's welfare for the greater good, and thus would exhibit disrespect for persons....

If the above theory of rights is juxtaposed with the earlier description of what makes a right a human right, the following account results. Human rights are those moral considerations that protect each and every human being from being subjected to treatment solely in accordance with the outcomes of utilitarian calculations. If they did not protect *every* human being, they would not be *human* rights; if they did not afford protection from being subjected to the outcomes of utilitarian calculations, they would not be *rights*.

I will adopt the terminology gaining currency among philosophers primarily concerned with the morality of abortion and distinguish between *human beings* and *persons*. The former designates a biological class; criteria for membership are specified by scientists. Membership in the class of persons, however, is determined by moral criteria. By definition, persons possess a higher moral status (perhaps conferred by the enjoyment of rights) than that of nonpersons. This distinction is useful in allowing the possibility that some persons may not be human beings, or, more importantly for present purposes, that some human beings may not be persons. An argument against the existence of human rights will almost certainly attempt to show that some human beings are not persons.

With this account in mind, we can envisage what a moral theory that did not countenance any human rights would be like. The thesis that there are no human rights denies that there is a single right possessed by all human beings. Some human beings either would possess *no* moral rights whatever, *or* different moral rights from those possessed by persons. Though these disjuncts express distinct theses, the former is almost certain to be affirmed by anyone who denies the existence of human rights. There is little motivation to believe that nonpersons have rights, though their rights are entirely distinct from any enjoyed by persons. Thus I will assume that anyone who denies the existence of human rights believes that some human beings are without moral rights. He would hold that at least some human beings—let us call them nonpersons—would properly be subject to treatment solely in accordance with the outcomes of utilitarian calculations. Whether or not this result is plausible is difficult to assess, for it is notoriously problematic to identify what specific treatment utilitarianism would prescribe in any but a few clear cases. But if my thesis that there are no human rights is to be persuasive, I must attempt to show that this result is not as unacceptable as it may first appear....

The argument against the existence of human rights is familiar, but only because champions of human rights regard its appeal as a challenge to be overcome rather than as an insight to be accommodated. The key premise in the argument is that no morally relevant characteristic(s) that could provide the basis or ground of such rights is possessed by all human beings. Whatever property (or properties) is adduced as a possible foundation for such rights is defective in one or both of two respects. Either it is not shared by each and every human being or it provides no reason for believing that its possessor enjoys rights. In other words, each proposed foundation of human rights fails what might be called the *universality* or *relevancy* tests. I would not make an original contribution to the voluminous literature on human rights by showing in detail how each of the several candidates put forth as a basis or ground of human rights—e.g., rationality, the ability to use language, reciprocity, the capacity to conform to moral requirements, self-motivated activity, self-consciousness, etc.— fails either or both of these tests. My central project is not to defend this argument so much as to explain why so many sensible moral and political philosophers have gone to such extraordinary and desperate lengths to resist it.

Which human beings are members of the class of nonpersons? Fortunately, I need not propose a definitive answer to this vexing question and commit myself to criteria of personhood. For *some* human beings fail *any* empirical test used to distinguish persons from nonpersons. Some human beings are neither rational, nor able to communicate, nor capable of reciprocity, nor able to conform to the requirements of morality, nor self-motivated, nor self-conscious, etc. Some philosophers have used this result to argue that abortion is morally permissible. The chief difficulty in drawing this conclusion is that most human fetuses possess the *potential* to satisfy the various criteria of personhood. Here I need not decide whether or to what extent the potential to become a person is morally relevant, for the least controversial examples of human nonpersons *lack* the potential to acquire any of the above characteristics. Karen Quinlan is a familiar example of a human member of the class of nonpersons.

It must be conceded that the above argument does not express a deductive proof that human rights cannot exist. I do not contend that human rights *cannot* exist: there is no contradiction in countenancing human rights. There remains the possibility that some ingenious philosopher will identify one or more characteristics that satisfy the universality and relevancy tests, and thus provide the basis or ground of human rights....My only evidence for remaining skeptical that such a defense will be provided is the inductive reason that no such characteristic(s) has yet been identified. There is little reason for optimism that any increased understanding of human beings we might gain will call such a characteristic(s) to our attention.

Some human rights theorists are likely to respond by claiming that I am attacking a straw man. They will admit that some human beings are nonpersons, but will insist that this concession is compatible with their conviction that some rights are human rights. They will deny, in other words, that they employ a purely biological criterion of humanity. The problem with this retort is that it runs squarely into a difficulty human rights theorists had hoped to avoid, and threatens to undermine

what is largely believed to be attractive about the concept of human rights. These theorists have aspired to show that *all* human beings possess rights, regardless of whatever contingent properties they might happen to have. If they now admit that some biological human beings *lack* rights *because* of their characteristics, they must abandon their claim that all such contingent properties are irrelevant to ascriptions of human rights. Human rights theorists like to emphasize that there are two fundamentally distinct kinds of ideologies about rights—those that extend rights to all of humanity and those that withhold rights from some subclass of mankind. But on this retort, the human rights movement is exposed as merely another instance of the latter ideology from which it had hoped to differentiate itself. Human rights theorists, like their adversaries, attribute or withhold rights from human beings on the basis of contingent properties some human beings possess and others lack. Thus champions of human rights should be uncomfortable about this response....

Not all philosophers confront this fundamental problem of specifying the foundation of human rights. Some simply provide a list of what are contended to be human rights. There are heated exchanges about whether, e.g., there is a human right to employment or medical care. Obviously, these debates will not impress one who is skeptical about whether there are any human rights at all. Unless the skeptic is to be dismissed without argument—as is too often the case—he is owed a reply.

Recent technological innovation has increased our need for such a reply. Many human rights theorists conveniently ignore the fact that some human beings lack the characteristic(s) on which they purport to base or ground human rights. But there are at least two reasons why the class of human nonpersons can no longer be safely ignored. First, the class continues to grow in number. Our medical science is now able to sustain the lives of many human beings with serious mental handicaps who would have died only a decade ago. The increasing size of this group indicates that it will continue to place greater demands in the competitive struggle for scarce medical resources. Thus it is crucial to determine how our obligations to this group are similar to or different from those owed to persons. Second and even more importantly, technology now offers the promise that nonpersons will become increasingly useful to us. Until recently, the suggestion that this group could constitute a benefit rather than a burden to mankind was dismissed as science fiction. There is some indication, however, that transplants of healthy brain tissue from nonpersons to persons will soon become a reality. Some groups have already begun to protest the ethics of such proposals, and they too are owed a reply.

Only two kinds of strategies are available to those who seek the basis or ground of human rights. The first is to show that the search for such a foundation is somehow misguided, and the second is to defend some basis or another. Among contemporary theorists, Joel Feinberg pursues the first strategy, while Alan Gewirth pursues the second. Despite their painful familiarity with the argument to the contrary, these philosophers remain staunch defenders of human rights. I critically examine their arguments here because the difficulties they encounter are typical of problems that any theorist who works within their frameworks should anticipate. Of course, particular problems are peculiar to theorists who explicate the details of these strategies differently. I do not propose to address each and every defense of human rights. My main purpose is to substantiate the description of defenses of human rights as implausible and somewhat desperate, so that philosophers will be more inclined to reexamine without prejudice the thesis that no human rights exist.

Joel Feinberg [*Social Philosophy*] describes the burden to be met by philosophers who seek the foundation of human rights: "If two things or two persons have the same worth, they must have in common some other characteristic—a nonvalue characteristic—that is the basis of their equal worth." But what might this common characteristic be? He notes that "philosophical champions of human rights have replied to this legitimate query with a bewildering variety of answers, almost all of them inadequate." In the course of rejecting a number of unsatisfactory attempts to ground human rights. Feinberg shrewdly observes that several " 'explain' human worth only be renaming that which is to be explained." The claims that all human beings are "ends in themselves," or "sacred," or "of infinite value" are themselves in need of a foundation and thus lead to circularity or regress when employed to base human rights. Fein-

berg concludes that such reasoning should not convince one who professes skepticism about human rights.

It is unclear, however, why Feinberg believes that his own solution should satisfy the skeptic. He maintains that "universal 'respect' for human beings is, in a sense, 'groundless'—a kind of ultimate attitude not itself justifiable in more ultimate terms." He continues: " 'Human worth' itself is best understood to name no property in the way that 'strength' names strength and 'redness' names redness. In attributing human worth to everyone we may be ascribing no property or set of qualities, but rather expressing an attitude—the attitude of respect—toward the humanity in each man's person." Though the search for a foundation of human rights was initially described as "legitimate," the enterprise is ultimately rejected as misguided: "If none of this convinces the skeptic, we should turn our backs on him to examine more important problems."

But the skeptic should not be dismissed as stubborn or unreasonable if he is not persuaded so easily. Among other difficulties, Feinberg's "argument" proves too much. It is equally convincing as a defense of universal *dis*respect. I hope it is not uncharitable to Feinberg to summarize his solution as urging philosophers to embrace human rights as an article of faith. Human rights exist but we cannot understand why. This approach does not even attempt to satisfy the relevancy condition. Silence awaits the skeptic who inquires why we should share the attitude of respect toward the Karen Quinlans of the world.

Alan Gewirth [*Reason and Morality*] employs the capacity for purposive agency as the ground for countenancing human rights. Agents consider their own purposes as "good" and thus, Gewirth argues, are committed to accepting as good the "necessary conditions" which make both action and the achievement of purposes possible. According to Gewirth, freedom and well-being comprise the necessary conditions for purposive action. A need for freedom and well-being, when expressed by the purposive agent himself, is prescriptive and thus contains the normative element necessary to transform these necessary goods into "prudential rights." These rights become human rights through the principle of universalizability; since purposive agency is a sufficient justification for having a right to freedom and well-being for the agent himself, all other purposive agents are equally deserving of these rights.

Gewirth's strategy is plagued with difficulties. One might well wonder how the alleged human rights of freedom and well-being could be necessary conditions for purposive agency. Presumably a great part of the world's population is without these rights; is it therefore logically impossible for them to act—or to attain any of their purposes? Moreover, the notion of "prudential rights" is curious and requires much more detailed elaboration. But conceding *arguendo* that purposive agency provides an adequate foundation for the moral rights of persons, it is crucial to determine whether such rights could qualify as *human* rights, as Gewirth alleges. Does his proposed foundation satisfy the universality condition?

It is difficult to understand how agency can serve as the basis of human rights when, as Gewirth admits, capacities of agency vary among individuals. Gewirth suggests that agency—although possessed by human beings in varying degrees—nonetheless provides a justification for human rights since those with less capacity for agency are to be granted "proportionately less" rights. He claims: "The degree to which different groups approach having the generic features and abilities of action determines the degree to which they have or approach having the generic rights." Gewirth might have anticipated a number of difficulties had he compared his definition of human rights with his project of grounding such rights in purposive agency. He begins: "We may assume, as true by definition, that human rights are rights that all persons have simply insofar as they are human." But it is evident on his account that we do not possess human rights simply in virtue of our humanity, but rather in virtue of our capacity for purposive agency. This discrepancy should have alerted Gewirth to problems that derive from the unfortunate fact that some creatures possessed of humanity are devoid of any capacity for purposive agency.

Gewirth's argument is defective for two reasons. Since Karen Quinlan is not a purposive agent in any ordinary sense, agency could not provide a foundation for the rights of *all* human beings unless the capacity for purposive agency is given a most peculiar interpretation. Moreover, even if it were the case that all human beings were purposive agents in some limited sense, to grant rights in proportion to agency is not merely to grant varying degrees of the same human right; it is tantamount to countenancing different rights with distinct duties. The conclusion that human beings share a number of given rights, but to different extents, is suspiciously similar to the admission that some of us do not have the same rights after all. Champions of human rights cannot be happy with this result. It allows possessors of "full" human rights to dominate those with "lesser" rights, which is the very sort of exploitation human rights were designed to prevent. If some human beings are to receive proportionately less rights than others, then those genuinely human rights which exist could be no greater than those possessed by the individual with the least capacity for agency. Thus purposive agency, while arguably an adequate foundation for the rights of persons, cannot ground *human* rights.

Suppose, e.g., that both Karen Quinlan and (what I have been calling) a person are in need of a life-saving transfusion and there is only enough blood available to save one. Suppose further that all factors that might influence priority (e.g., ownership of the blood, a first-come, first-served policy, etc.) are equal. Human rights theorists could hardly deny that both human beings possess the right to life. Is it therefore a matter of moral indifference who is saved? This result does not seem compelling. Human rights theorists might therefore "fudge" and claim that the right of the (acknowledged) person is more weighty, or more stringent, or overrides that of the (alleged) nonperson. If so, however, it seems hollow to insist that they both possess the *same* right.

These difficulties are reflected in Gewirth's ambivalence toward those human beings who lack a fully developed capacity for purposive agency. The rights of infants, fetuses, and the mentally defective are "watered down" to the point where it becomes evident that they share little in common with the rights of persons. Finally, Gewirth all but contradicts any promise that his rights apply universally to all human beings: "This absoluteness in having the generic rights applies even to a certain degree of human brain damage, so long as there remains the possibility of recovery." Apparently, then, human beings with no prospects of recovery do not possess human rights.

Difficulties and inconsistencies in the work of contemporary theorists who address the ground or basis of human rights do not provide the only reason for skepticism. Belief in the existence of human rights leads to results that should strike philosophers as highly counterintuitive. Much of the extensive literature on the so-called rights of (nonhuman) animals begins with the unsupported premise that there are human rights. Many defenders of animal rights then point out that whatever characteristic(s) provides the foundation of these rights is shared by some animals, who must therefore enjoy the same human rights as persons. The suggestion that some animals possess the same rights as persons would be treated as an absurdity were it not for the fact that human rights theorists can find little fault with the above reasoning. The rejection of human rights undercuts such arguments in favor of the "equal rights for animals" movement and allows us to escape charges of injustice and arbitrariness in many of our discriminations between persons and animals.

Nonhuman animals do not provide the only source of difficulty for human rights theorists. Suppose that a group of living Neanderthals (or even more primitive evolutionary forerunners of modern *homo sapiens*) were discovered. Would human rights theorists insist that they be afforded full human rights, unless shown to be biologically nonhuman? Neither alternative seems plausible. There must be have come a time in our evolutionary development when our ancestors required whatever characteristic(s) grounds our human rights, so there must also have been a time before they possessed such a characteristic(s). This transition into personhood need not have coincided with (and may have been subsequent to) our ascendancy into biological humanity.

Finally we come to the crux of the matter. If there is no sound argument establishing the existence of human rights, and numerous difficulties in any attempt to defend them, why have moral philosophers not abandoned them? A mere lapse of critical faculties does not explain why good philosophers are persuaded by bad arguments. More typically they are convinced of a conclusion not because of the arguments they marshall in its support, but for independent reasons not explicitly identified. I conjecture that they countenance human rights because of the allegedly devastating implications of the contrary supposition, and therefore reason that if a belief in human rights must be correct, then there must be some good arguments in favor of so believing. Thus they are less likely to be critical of unsound arguments, convinced as they are that *some* good arguments must be available.

This conjecture explains why virtually all defenses of human rights share a similar tone. Typically philosophers begin with the conviction that there are human rights and define their project as "providing an account" of them. Few philosophers seem to approach this area without prejudice, allowing themselves to be carried wherever their arguments might take them. The ground of their antecedent conviction is rarely identified for critical scrutiny. It is this lacuna I now attempt to fill by speculating about (and then undermining) a number of reasons why so few philosophers exhibit skepticism about the existence of human rights.

What are the allegedly devastating consequences that follow from a repudiation of human rights? In what follows I identify three such fears, and argue either that the consequences, though unacceptable, are not genuine implications of my thesis, or that the consequences, though genuine implications of my thesis, are not unacceptable.

1. A philosopher who abandons human rights places himself squarely within a tradition with highly dubious historical credentials. He is understandably uncomfortable to join company with Nazis, racists, and sexists. This is not simply a "guilt by association" objection. The undeniable fact is that repudiations of human rights have frequently been employed by warped theorists to promote pernicious ideologies. Too much bad political theory has traded upon an "us persons versus those nonpersons" mentality. Much of the resistance to skepticism about human rights is an overreaction to such misguided political theories. The claim that some human beings are nonpersons is certain to earn the scorn of well-intentioned philosophers who will remind me of this disastrous legacy.

But these past exclusions of some human beings from the class of persons were unjust because they were arbitrary—no morally relevant characteristic(s) differentiated these unfortunate victims from the class of persons. But if a morally relevant ground for distinguishing between persons and nonpersons is identified, discriminatory treatment based upon it need not be unjust. Everyone, including human rights theorists, is committed to drawing the boundary between persons and nonpersons *somewhere*. Though admittedly much mischief has been done when this line has been drawn to exclude some human beings, the sad but incontrovertible fact is that some human beings do not (and will not) possess whatever characteristic(s) is used for locating this boundary. We should not overreact to the past tendency to cast the net of personhood too narrowly by casting it too broadly.

2. A study of the primary use to which human rights have been put suggests a second reason why philosophers have been largely uncritical of them. Human rights have been a cornerstone of American foreign policy, and function as an effective tool for denouncing political regimes which show a callous disregard for them. Torture, denials of religious freedoms, and racial discrimination are only a small sample of the widespread atrocities that evoke criticism in the name of human rights. If human rights do not exist, this humanitarian movement might have to be reinterpreted as shallow propaganda. The alternative to human rights might be thought to be a kind of relativism, where the only moral rights possessed by persons are products of their particular social, political and legal systems. Thus a useful device for comparing and contrasting such systems would be lost.

Such fears, however, are grossly exaggerated. Nearly all the criticisms made about human rights violations throughout the world involve the maltreatment of persons. The victims of torture and religious oppression quite obviously satisfy the criteria of personhood, whatever they might be. Only occasionally do politicians decry the treatment of human beings who fall outside the ambit of personhood—the Karen Quinlans of the Soviet Union or South Africa rarely if ever attract our attention and sympathy. We can and should continue to protest the unjust treatment of persons, and to evaluate various social, political and legal systems to the extent that they exhibit respect for persons. But the existence of *human* rights is not required for this noble purpose. The crucial point is that the vast majority of sensible criticisms of unjust political systems can be preserved as intelligible even if it is conceded that no human rights exist.

3. Perhaps the most compelling reason for countenancing human rights is the fear of how it would be permissible to treat human nonpersons in the event that they are held to be without rights. Though it may be controversial whether human nonpersons are entitled to the same concern and respect as persons, the alternative that would treat them as mere things, to be used for our convenience and amusement, seems even more repellent. Does anyone seriously suggest that it would be permissible to breed and eat human nonpersons, provided that the public should develop a taste for their flesh? If not, how can such creatures be without rights?

There is admittedly something appealing in the conception of the moral universe as neatly divided into persons, who have rights and a high moral status, and nonpersons, who have neither. But this picture is an extreme oversimplification. There are any number of living (or extinct) creatures whose moral status is somewhere between persons and inanimate objects with no moral status whatever. Few philosophers have seriously undertaken to map these unchartered waters. There have been persistent attempts to fit intermediate cases into one or the other familiar category, as though the conclusion that Karen Quinlan is not a *person* with rights somehow entails that it is permissible to treat her in any way we wish. But our unwillingness to allow her to be eaten should not convince us that she must therefore be a person. Though she may lack rights altogether, she nonetheless occupies an intermediate category philosophers have seldom been willing to acknowledge, let alone to describe our obligations toward.

We must only be reminded of the earlier theory of rights to appreciate the moral limitations on the treatment of human nonpersons. Because creatures without rights lack the "trumps" of persons, it does not follow that they may be treated in any way we wish. Utilitarianism may be inadequate to govern our behavior toward persons, but it surely imposes *some* limitations on treatment apart from whether or not rights are violated. The supposition that an act cannot be wrongful unless it violates a right grossly exaggerates the role of rights in moral theory. Rights are multiplied indefinitely by the unwarranted assumption that all wrongful conduct necessarily violates one or more rights. A moral theory without rights may be impoverished, but it would not pronounce all actions permissible.

Is utilitarianism adequate to govern our moral relations with nonpersons, human or otherwise? Insofar as the outcomes of utilitarian calculations can be specified with any confidence, the results do not seem especially counterintuitive. The familiar counterexamples to utilitarianism urged by rights theorists all demonstrate (at most) the injustice of subjecting *persons* to utilitarian treatment. If nonpersons are substituted for persons in these hypotheticals, it is arguable that most or all the injustice vanishes.

Let us examine some of these hypotheticals. One familiar example supposes that an innocent patient, in a hospital for a routine examination, is carved up by well-intentioned surgeons in order to distribute his various organs to five patients who will die unless these transplants are performed. We are supposed to recoil in horror at this disregard for the rights of the single patient, even though a net saving of lives is achieved. Let us alter this scenario so that sheep rather than human beings are involved. To avoid complications, suppose that the sheep are unowned, or that all have the same owner. (If one believes that sheep have rights, the example may be amended so that trees rather than sheep are involved.) Presumably in this case the fact that a net saving of lives is achieved is an excellent reason for killing the single sheep and distributing his organs. My argument is, admittedly, solely on an intuitive level. My point is that utilitarianism seems to provide a plausible account of our considered moral judgments in those cases in which no persons or rights are involved.

In short, numbers are decisive in our considered moral judgments about the proper treatment of nonpersons. It is sensible to burn a few trees in order to prevent the spread of a fire that would otherwise kill greater numbers. Presumably we would oppose an analogous practice if persons rather than trees were involved, for the rights of persons protect us from being sacrificed to the greater good. Of course, the permissibility of burning a few trees for the sake of greater numbers hardly entails that trees may be destroyed for no good reason. Utilitarianism, construed (*ex hypothesi*) as a moral theory without rights, does not condone the wanton killing of sentient creatures.

Though trees may not have rights, it does not follow that they have no moral status whatever.

Now there may be little sympathy for believing that sheep or trees have rights, but the leap from sheep or trees to human nonpersons is certain to raise objections from human rights theorists. If the right to life is a human right, it should make no difference in these sorts of hypotheticals whether Karen Quinlan or (what I have been calling) a person is the single human whose organs are needed to save five persons. The transplants required to achieve a net saving of lives would violate her right to life, and thus would "trump" countervailing utilitarian considerations. It is only a slight exaggeration to suggest that the resolution of this hypothetical is the decisive basis on which the acceptance or rejection of my thesis depends. If one is willing to allow Karen Quinlan to be sacrificed to achieve a net saving of lives, while resisting that result when it is unquestionable that a *person* is involved, one has come a long way toward acceptance of the thesis that there are no human rights.

The suggestion that the above hypothetical represents a decisive test of my thesis is a slight exaggeration, primarily because of the uncertainty in predicting the outcomes of utilitarian calculations. Some utilitarians have claimed that the sacrifice of an innocent person to achieve a net saving of lives is impermissible *without* appeals to rights, and might make similar claims when Karen Quinlan is involved. Their reservations should be familiar to moral philosophers. They caution, e.g., that the sacrifice of innocent human beings sets a dangerous precedent for policies that promote disutility, or that no officials could be trusted to make such difficult determinations, etc. But *whatever* the outcomes of utilitarian calculations in such cases may be, my thesis (when coupled with the above theory of rights) requires that human nonpersons be treated accordingly. Thus my thesis does *not* relegate human nonpersons to the category of mere "things," with no moral status whatever. Their status is highly problematical, but no progress is made in this difficult determination by consulting treatises on human rights, which (at best) apply only to persons.

Philosophers have dreamed of specifying rights which human beings share regardless of their race, religion, sex or nationality. This dream is noble;

most discriminations between human beings based on the above differences are unquestionably unjust. But when such philosophers attempted to answer the question of why all human beings possessed rights by specifying their ground or basis, they identified a characteristic(s) that is not shared by all human beings. Thus their projects are better understood as defenses of the rights of *persons* rather than of *human beings.* As so construed, their projects remain interesting and important. I have tried to show why philosophers should not lament the passing of *human* rights....

"Civil Rights—a Challenge"

Robert Bork

Passions are running so high over racial discrimination that the various proposals to legislate its manifestations out of existence seem likely to become textbook examples of the maxim that great and urgent issues are rarely discussed in terms of the principles they necessarily involve. In this case, the danger is that justifiable abhorrence of racial discrimination will result in legislation by which the morals of the majority are self-righteously imposed upon a minority. That has happened before in the United States—Prohibition being the most notorious instance—but whenever it happens it is likely to be subversive of free institutions.

Instead of a discussion of the merits of legislation, of which the proposed Interstate Public Accommodations Act outlawing discrimination in business facilities serving the public may be taken as the prototype, we are treated to debate whether it is more or less cynical to pass the law under the commerce power or the Fourteenth Amendment, and whether the Supreme Court is more likely to hold it Constitutional one way or the other. Heretical, though it may sound to the constitutional sages, neither the Constitution nor the Supreme Court qualifies as a first principle. The discussion we ought to hear is of the cost in freedom that must be paid for such legislation, the morality of enforcing morals through law, and the likely consequences for law enforcement of trying to do so.

Few proponents of legislation such as the Interstate Public Accommodations Act seem willing to discuss either the cost in freedom which must accompany it or why this particular departure from freedom of the individual to choose with whom he will deal is justified....

There seems to be a strong disposition on the part of proponents of the legislation simply to ignore the fact that it means a loss in a vital area of personal liberty. That it does is apparent. The legislature would inform a substantial body of the citizenry that in order to continue to carry on the trades in which they are established they must deal with and serve persons with whom they do not wish to associate. In part the willingness to overlook that loss of freedom arises from the feeling that it is irrational to choose associates on the basis of racial characteristics. Behind that judgment, however, lies an unexpressed natural-law view that some personal preferences are rational, that others are irrational, and that a majority may impose upon a minority its scale of preferences. The fact that the coerced scale of preferences is said to be rooted in a moral order does not alter the impact upon freedom. In a society that purports to value freedom as an end in itself, the simple argument from morality

From "Civil Rights—a Challenge," *The New Republic,* August 31, 1963. Reprinted by permission of the publisher.

to law can be a dangerous non sequitur: Professor Mark DeWolf Howe, in supporting the proposed legislation, describes southern opposition to "the nation's objective" as an effort "to preserve ugly customs of a stubborn people." So it is. Of the ugliness of racial discrimination there need be no argument (though there may be some presumption in identifying one's own hotly controverted aims with the objective of the nation). But it is one thing when stubborn people express their racial antipathies in laws which prevent individuals, whether white or Negro, from dealing with those who are willing to deal with them, and quite another to tell them that even as individuals they may not act on their racial preferences in particular areas of life. The principle of such legislation is that if I find your behavior ugly by my standards, moral or aesthetic, and if you prove stubborn about adopting my view of the situation, I am justified in having the state coerce you into more righteous paths. That is itself a principle of unsurpassed ugliness.

Freedom is a value of very high priority and the occasions upon which it is sacrificed ought to be kept to a minimum. It is necessary that the police protect a man from assault or theft but it is a long leap from that to protection from the insult implied by the refusal of another individual to associate or deal with him. The latter involves a principle whose logical reach is difficult to limit. If it is permissible to tell a barber or a rooming house owner that he must deal with all who come to him regardless of race or religion, then it is impossible to see why a doctor, lawyer, accountant, or any other professional or business man should have the right to discriminate. Indeed, it would be unfair discrimination to leave anybody engaged in any commercial activity with that right. Nor does it seem fair or rational, given the basic premise, to confine the principle to equal treatment of Negroes as customers. Why should the law not require not merely fair hiring of Negroes in subordinate positions but the choice of partners or associates in a variety of business and professional endeavors without regard to race or creed? Though such a law might presently be unenforceable, there is no distinction in principle between it and what is proposed. It is difficult to see an end to the principle of enforcing fair treatment by private individuals. It certainly need not be confined to racial or commercial matters. The best way to demonstrate the expansiveness of the principle behind the proposed legislation is to examine the arguments which are used to justify it.

Perhaps the most common popular justification of such a law is based on a crude notion of waivers: insistence that barbers, lunch counter operators, and similar businessmen serve all comers does not infringe their freedom because they "hold themselves out to serve the public." The statement is so obviously a fiction that it scarcely survives articulation. The very reason for the proposed legislation is precisely that some individuals have made it as clear as they can that they do not hold themselves out to serve the public.

A second popular argument, usually heard in connection with laws proposed to be laid under the Fourteenth Amendment, is that the rationale which required the voiding of laws enforcing segregation also requires the prohibition of racial discrimination by business licensed by any governmental unit because "state action" is involved. The only legitimate thrust of the "state action" characterization, however, is to enable courts to see through governmental use of private organizations to enforce an official policy of segregation. There is a fundamental difference between saying that the state cannot turn over its primary election process, which is actually the only election that matters, to the "private" and all-white Democratic Party and saying that a chiropodist cannot refuse a Negro patient because a state board has examined him and certified his competence. The "state action" concept must be confined to discerning state enforcement of policy through a nominally private agency or else it becomes possible to discern the hand of the state in every private action.

One of the shabbiest forms of "argument" is that endorsed by James Reston when he described the contest over the public accommodations bill as one between "human rights" and "property rights." Presumably no one of "liberal" views has any difficulty deciding the question when so concisely put. One wishes nonetheless, that Mr. Reston would explain just who has rights with respect to property other than humans. If A demands to deal with B and B insists that for reasons sufficient to himself he wants nothing to do with A, I suppose even Reston would agree that both are claiming "human rights" and that this is in no way changed if one of the humans is colored and the other white.

How does the situation change if we stipulate that they are standing on opposite sides of a barber chair and that B owns it?

A number of people seem to draw a distinction between commercial relationships and all others. They feel justified, somehow, in compelling a rooming house owner or the proprietor of a lunch counter to deal with all comers without regard to race but would not legislate acceptance of Negroes into private clubs or homes. The rationale appears to be that one relationship is highly personal and the other is just business. Under any system which allows the individual to determine his own values that distinction is unsound. It is, moreover, patently fallacious as a description of reality. The very bitterness of the resistance to the demand for enforced integration arises because owners of many places of business do in fact care a great deal about whom they serve. The real meaning of the distinction is simply that some people do not think others ought to care that much about that particular aspect of their freedom....

Though the basic objection is to the law's impact upon individual liberty, it is also appropriate to question the practicality of enforcing a law which runs contrary to the customs, indeed the moral beliefs, of a large portion of the country. Of what value is a law which compels service to Negroes without close surveillance to make sure the service is on the same terms given to whites? It is not difficult to imagine many ways in which barbers, landlords, lunch counter operators, and the like can nominally comply with the law but effectively discourage Negro patrons. Must federal law enforcement agencies become in effect public utility commissions charged with the supervision of the nation's business establishments or will the law become an unenforceable symbol of hypocritical righteousness?

It is sad to have to defend the principle of freedom in this context, but the task ought not to be left to those southern politicians who only a short while ago were defending laws that enforced racial segregation. There seem to be few who favor racial equality who also perceive or are willing to give primacy to the value of freedom in this struggle. A short while back the majority of the nation's moral and intellectual leaders opposed all the manifestations of "McCarthyism" and quite correctly assured the nation that the issue was not whether communism was good or evil but whether men ought to be free to think and talk as they pleased. Those same leaders seem to be running with the other pack this time. Yet the issue is the same. It is not whether racial prejudice or preference is a good thing but whether individual men ought to be free to deal and associate with whom they please for whatever reasons appeal to them. This time "stubborn people" with "ugly customs" are under attack rather than intellectuals and academicians; but that sort of personal comparison surely ought not to make the difference.

The trouble with freedom is that it will be used in ways we abhor. It then takes great self restraint to avoid sacrificing it, just this once, to another end. One may agree that it is immoral to treat a man according to his race or religion and yet question whether that moral preference deserves elevation to the level of the principle of individual freedom and self-determination. If, every time an intensely-felt moral principle is involved, we spend freedom, we will run short of it.

Civil Rights—a Reply

The New Republic editors

The New Republic's commentary on civil rights over the years should make it obvious that the editors disagree emphatically with Mr. Bork's thesis. Yet his fears about the proposed legislation are shared by many Americans, including many readers of the *New Republic*, so they deserve both a forum and an answer.

In discussing the law we share Justice Holmes' preference for appeals to experience rather than logic. In the light of recent American experience Mr. Bork's argument seems to have several defects.

First, Mr. Bork speaks about the "freedom of the individual" as if the owners of hotels, motels, restaurants and other public accommodations were today legally free to serve whomever they please. This, as everyone knows, is seldom the case. For centuries English common law obligated innkeepers to accommodate any well-behaved traveller, and his horses. Most states have today embodied this tradition in public accommodation statutes. In the North, these statutes generally require a restaurant, hotel or motel to accept all sober and orderly comers, regardless of race. In the South, Jim Crow legislation enacted at the end of the nineteenth century until recently required the owners of public establishments to segregate their facilities. The Supreme Court has now declared the Jim Crow statutes unconstitutional, but even today the owner who wants to serve both Negroes and whites is likely to have difficulty exercising his newly acquired "right" in many areas. Mr. Bork would presumably deplore the whole tradition that "public accommodations" must provide public service as well as private profit. But he cannot maintain that new legislation in this field would mean a sudden increase of government intervention in private affairs. The Administration's civil rights bill would simply extend to the national level principles and practices long employed locally.

Experience also argues against Bork's equation between the distress caused by having to serve a Negro and the distress caused by refusing to serve him. Both exist, and both deserve consideration, but no amount of rhetoric about freedom can give them equal weight. Despite what Mr. Bork says, the "loss of freedom" caused by having to serve Negroes is in most cases pecuniary, not personal. If personal freedom were to be protected we would need legislation allowing individual waitresses, hotel clerks and charwomen to decide whom they would serve and whom they would not. The fact is, however, that such people must serve whomever their employer tells them to serve, and refuse whomever he tells them to refuse. The right to segregate is, as everyone but Mr. Bork admits, a right deriving solely from title to property. It is neither more nor less sacrosanct than other economic privileges. It can be regulated in the same way that the right to build a restaurant on one's residential property is regulated.

There are, of course, some owners of public establishments who have personal contact with the clients—the much debated case of Mrs. Murphy's boarding house. Perhaps such establishments should be exempt from the proposed public accommodations law. But even here the claims of private freedom must be weighed against the claims of public convenience.

Government without principle ends in shipwreck; but government according to any single principle, to the exclusion of all other, ends in madness. Mr. Bork's principle of private liberty is important, and his distrust of public authority often justified. But to apply this principle in disregard of all others would today require the repeal of the industrial revolution. Perhaps, however, that is what Mr. Bork wants.

From *The New Republic* Editors, August 31, 1963. Reprinted by permission of the publisher.

Taking Rights Seriously

Ronald Dworkin

The language of rights now dominates political debate in the United States. Does the Government respect the moral and political rights of its citizens? Or does the Government's foreign policy, or its race policy, fly in the face of these rights? Do the minorities whose rights have been violated have the right to violate the law in return? Or does the silent majority itself have rights, including the right that those who break the law be punished? It is not surprising that these questions are now prominent. The concept of rights, and particularly the concept of rights against the Government, has its most natural use when a political society is divided, and appeals to co-operation or a common goal are pointless....

It is much in dispute, of course, what *particular* rights citizens have. Does the acknowledged right to free speech, for example, include the right to participate in nuisance demonstrations? In practice the Government will have the last word on what an individual's rights are, because its police will do what its officials and courts say. But that does not mean that the Government's view is necessarily the correct one; anyone who thinks it does must believe that men and women have only such moral rights as Government chooses to grant, which means that they have no moral rights at all.

All this is sometimes obscured in the United States by the constitutional system. The American Constitution provides a set of individual *legal* rights in the First Amendment, and in the due process, equal protection, and similar clauses. Under present legal practice the Supreme Court has the power to declare an act of Congress or of a state legislature void if the Court finds that the act offends these provisions. This practice has led some commentators to suppose that individual moral rights are fully protected by this system, but that is hardly so, nor could it be so.

The Constitution fuses legal and moral issues, by making the validity of a law depend on the answer to complex moral problems, like the problem of whether a particular statute respects the inherent equality of all men. This fusion has important consequences for the debates about civil disobedience....

Does an American ever have the moral right to break a law? Suppose someone admits a law is valid; does he therefore have a duty to obey it? Those who try to give an answer seem to fall into two camps. The conservatives, as I shall call them, seem to disapprove of any act of disobedience; they appear satisfied when such acts are prosecuted and disappointed when convictions are reversed. The other group, the liberals, are much more sympathetic to at least some cases of disobedience; they sometimes disapprove of prosecutions and celebrate acquittals. If we look beyond these emotional reactions, however, and pay attention to the arguments the two parties use, we discover an astounding fact. Both groups give essentially the same answer to the question of principle that supposedly divides them.

The answer that both parties give is this. In a democracy, or at least a democracy that in principle respects individual rights, each citizen has a general moral duty to obey all the laws, even, though he would like some of them changed. He owes that duty to his fellow citizens, who obey laws that they do not like, to his benefit. But this general duty cannot be an absolute duty, because even a society that is in principle just may produce unjust laws and policies, and a man has duties other than his duties to the State. A man must honour his duties

From *Taking Rights Seriously* (Cambridge MA: Harvard University Press, 1977). Reprinted by permission of the publisher and the author.

to his God and to his conscience, and if these conflict with his duty to the State, then he is entitled, in the end, to do what he judges to be right. If he decides that he must break the law, however, then he must submit to the judgment and punishment that the State imposes, in recognition of the fact that his duty to his fellow citizens was overwhelmed but not extinguished by his religious or moral obligation...

But there seems to be a monstrous contradiction here. If a man has a right to do what his conscience tells him he must, then how can the State be justified in discouraging him from doing it? Is it not wicked for a state to forbid and punish what it acknowledges that men have a right to do?...

In order to explain this, I must call attention to the fact, familiar to philosophers, but often ignored in political debate, that the word 'right' has different force in different contexts. In most cases when we say that someone has 'right' to do something, we imply that it would be wrong to interfere with his doing it, or at least that some special grounds are needed for justifying any interference. I use this strong sense of right when I say that you have the right to spend your money gambling, if you wish, though you ought to spend it in a more worthwhile way. I mean that it would be wrong for anyone to interfere with you even though you propose to spend your money in a way that I think is wrong.

There is a clear difference between saying that someone has a right to do something in this sense and saying that it is the 'right' thing for him to do, or that he does no 'wrong' in doing it. Someone may have the right to do something that is the wrong thing for him to do, as might be the case with gambling. Conversely, something may be the right thing for him to do and yet he may have no right to do it, in the sense that it would not be wrong for someone to interfere with his trying. If our army captures an enemy soldier, we might say that the right thing for him to do is to try to escape, but it would not follow that it is wrong for us to try to stop him. We might admire him for trying to escape, and perhaps even think less of him if he did not. But there is no suggestion here that it is wrong of us to stand in his way; on the contrary, if we think our cause is just, we think it right for us to do all we can to stop him.

Ordinarily this distinction, between the issues of whether a man has a right to do something and

whether it is the right thing for him to do, causes no trouble. But sometimes it does, because sometimes we say that a man has a right to do something when we mean only to deny that it is the wrong thing for him to do. Thus we say that the captured soldier has a 'right' to try to escape when we mean, not that we do wrong to stop him, but that he has no duty not to make the attempt. We use 'right' this way when we speak of someone having the 'right' to act on his own principles, or the 'right' to follow his own conscience. We mean that he does no wrong to proceed on his honest convictions, even though we disagree with these convictions, and even though, for policy or other reasons, we must force him to act contrary to them.

Suppose a man believes that welfare payments to the poor are profoundly wrong, because they sap enterprise, and so declares his full income-tax each year but declines to pay half of it. We might say that he has a right to refuse to pay, if he wishes, but that the Government has a right to proceed against him for the full tax, and to fine or jail him for late payment if that is necessary to keep the collection system working efficiently. We do not take this line in most cases; we do not say that the ordinary thief has a right to steal, if he wishes, so long as he pays the penalty. We say a man has the right to break the law, even though the State has a right to punish him, only when we think that, because of his convictions, he does no wrong in doing so.

These distinctions enable us to see an ambiguity in the orthodox question: Does a man ever have a right to break the law? Does that question mean to ask whether he ever has a right to break the law in the strong sense, so that the Government would do wrong to stop him, by arresting and prosecuting him? Or does it mean to ask whether he ever does the right thing to break the law, so that we should all respect him even though the Government should jail him?...

I said that in the United States citizens are supposed to have certain fundamental rights against their Government, certain moral rights made into legal rights by the Constitution. If this idea is significant, and worth bragging about, then these rights must be rights in the strong sense I just described. The claim that citizens have a right to free speech must imply that it would be wrong for the Government to stop them from speaking, even when the Government believes that what they will say will cause more harm than good. The claim cannot mean, on the prisoner-of-war analogy, only that citizens do no wrong in speaking their minds, though the Government reserves the right to prevent them from doing so.

This is a crucial point, and I want to labour it. Of course a responsible government must be ready to justify anything it does, particularly when it limits the liberty of its citizens. But normally it is a sufficient justification, even for an act that limits liberty, that the act is calculated to increase what the philosophers call general utility—that it is calculated to produce more over-all benefit than harm. So, though the New York City government needs a justification for forbidding motorists to drive up Lexington Avenue, it is sufficient justification if the proper officials believe, on sound evidence, that the gain to the many will outweigh the inconvenience to the few. When individual citizens are said to have rights against the Government, however, like the right of free speech, that must mean that this sort of justification is not enough. Otherwise the claim would not argue that individuals have special protection against the law when their rights are in play, and that is just the point of the claim.

Not all legal rights, or even Constitutional rights, represent moral rights against the Government. I now have the legal right to drive either way on Fifty-seventh Street, but the Government would do no wrong to make that street one-way if it thought it in the general interest to do so. I have a Constitutional right to vote for a congressman every two years, but the national and state governments would do no wrong if, following the amendment procedure, they made a congressman's term four years instead of two, again on the basis of a judgment that this would be for the general good.

But those Constitutional rights that we call fundamental like the right of free speech, are supposed to represent rights against the Government in the strong sense; that is the point of the boast that our legal system respects the fundamental rights of the citizen. If citizens have a moral right of free speech, then governments would do wrong to repeal the First Amendment that guarantees it, even if they were persuaded that the majority would be better off if speech were curtailed.

I must not overstate the point. Someone who claims that citizens have a right against the Gov-

ernment need not go so far as to say that the State is *never* justified in overriding that right. He might say, for example, that although citizens have a right to free speech, the Government may override that right when necessary to protect the rights of others, or to prevent a catastrophe, or even to obtain a clear and major public benefit (though if he acknowledged this last as a possible justification he would be treating the right in question as not among the most important or fundamental). What he cannot do is to say that the Government is justified in overriding a right on the minimal grounds that would be sufficient if no such right existed. He cannot say that the Government is entitled to act on no more than a judgment that its act is likely to produce, overall, a benefit to the community. That admission would make his claim of a right pointless, and would show him to be using some sense of 'right' other than the strong sense necessary to give his claim the political importance it is normally taken to have....

The argument so far has been hypothetical: if a man has a particular moral right against the Government, that right survives contrary legislation or adjudication. But this does not tell us what rights he has, and it is notorious that reasonable men disagree about that. There is wide agreement on certain clearcut cases; almost everyone who believes in rights at all would admit, for example, that a man has a moral right to speak his mind in a non-provocative way on matters of political concern, and that this is an important right that the State must go to great pains to protect. But there is great controversy as to the limits of such paradigm rights....How should the different departments of government go about defining moral rights?

They should begin with a sense that whatever they decide might be wrong. History and their descendants may judge that they acted unjustly when they thought they were right. If they take their duty seriously, they must try to limit their mistakes, and they must therefore try to discover where the dangers of mistake lie....

The institution of rights against the Government is not a gift of God, or an ancient ritual, or a national sport. It is a complex and troublesome practice that makes the Government's job of securing the general benefit more difficult and more expensive, and it would be a frivolous and wrongful practice unless it served some point. Anyone who professes to take rights seriously, and who praises our Government for respecting them, must have some sense of what that point is. He must accept, at the minimum, one or both of two important ideas. The first is the vague but powerful idea of human dignity. This idea, associated with Kant, but defended by philosophers of different schools, supposes that there are ways of treating a man that are inconsistent with recognizing him as a full member of the human community, and holds that such treatment is profoundly unjust.

The second is the more familiar idea of political equality. This supposes that the weaker members of a political community are entitled to the same concern and respect of their government as the more powerful members have secured for themselves, so that if some men have freedom of decision whatever the effect on the general good, then all men must have the same freedom. I do not want to defend or elaborate these ideas here, but only to insist that anyone who claims that citizens have rights must accept ideas very close to these.

It makes sense to say that a man has a fundamental right against the Government, in the strong sense, like free speech, if that right is necessary to protect his dignity, or his standing as equally entitled to concern and respect, or some other personal value of like consequence. It does not make sense otherwise.

So if rights make sense at all, then the invasion of a relatively important right must be a very serious matter. It means treating a man as less than a man, or as less worthy of concern than other men. The institution of rights rests on the conviction that this is a grave injustice, and that it is worth paying the incremental cost in social policy or efficiency that is necessary to prevent it. But then it must be wrong to say that inflating rights is as serious as invading them....

Do we have a right to liberty? Thomas Jefferson thought so, and since his day the right to liberty has received more play than the competing rights he mentioned to life and the pursuit of happiness. Liberty gave its name to the most influential political movement of the last century, and many of those who now despise liberals do so on the ground that they are not sufficiently libertarian. Of course, almost everyone concedes that the right to liberty is not the only political right, and that therefore claims to freedom must be limited, for example, by restraints that protect the security or property of others. Nevertheless the consensus in favor of some right to liberty is a vast one, though it is, I shall argue, misguided.

The right to liberty is popular all over this political spectrum. The rhetoric of liberty fuels every radical movement from international wars of liberation to campaigns for sexual freedom and women's liberation. But liberty has been even more prominent in conservative service. Even the mild social reorganizations of the anti-trust and unionization movements, and of the early New Deal, were opposed on the grounds that they infringed the right to liberty, and just now efforts to achieve some racial justice in America through techniques like the busing of black and white schoolchildren, and social justice in Britain through constraints in private education are bitterly opposed on that ground.

It has become common, indeed, to describe the great social issues of domestic politics, and in particular the racial issue, as presenting a conflict between the demands of liberty and equality. It may be, it is said, that the poor and the black and the uneducated and the unskilled have an abstract right to equality, but the prosperous and the whites and the educated and the able have a right to liberty as well and any efforts at social reorganization in aid of the first set of rights must reckon with and respect the second. Everyone except extremists recognizes, therefore, the need to compromise between equality and liberty. Every piece of important social legislation, from tax policy to integration plans, is shaped by the supposed tension between these two goals.

I have this supposed conflict between equality and liberty in mind when I ask whether we have a *right* to liberty, as Jefferson and everyone else has supposed. That is a crucial question. If freedom to choose one's schools, or employees, or neighborhood is simply something that we all want, like air conditioning or lobsters, then we are not entitled to hang on to these freedoms in the face of what we concede to be the rights of others to an equal share of respect and resources. But if we can say, not simply that we want these freedoms, but that we are ourselves entitled to them, then we have established at least a basis for demanding a compromise.

There is now a movement, for example, in favor of a proposed amendment to the constitution of the

United States that would guarantee every school child the legal right to attend a 'neighborhood school' and thus outlaw busing. The suggestion, that neighborhood schools somehow rank with jury trials as constitutional values, would seem silly but for the sense many Americans have that forcing school children into buses is somehow as much an interference with the fundamental right to liberty as segregated schooling was an insult to equality. But that seems to me absurd; indeed it seems to me absurd to suppose that men and women have any general right to liberty at all, at least as liberty has traditionally been conceived by its champions.

I have in mind the traditional definition of liberty as the absence of constraints placed by a government upon what a man might do if he wants to. Isaiah Berlin, in the most famous modern essay on liberty, put the matter this way: 'The sense of freedom, in which I use this term, entails not simply the absence of frustration but the absence of obstacles to possible choices and activities—absence of obstructions on roads along which a man can decide to walk.' This conception of liberty as license is neutral amongst the various activities a man might pursue, the various roads he might wish to walk. It diminishes a man's liberty when we prevent him from talking or making love as he wishes, but it also diminishes his liberty when we prevent him from murdering or defaming others. These latter constraints may be justifiable, but only because they are compromises necessary to protect the liberty or security of others, and not because they do not, in themselves, infringe the independent value of liberty. Bentham said that any law whatsoever is an 'infraction' of liberty, and though some such infractions might be necessary, it is obscurantist to pretend that they are not infractions after all. In this neutral, all embracing sense of liberty as license, liberty and equality are plainly in competition. Laws are needed to protect equality, and laws are inevitably compromises of liberty.

Liberals like Berlin are content with this neutral sense of liberty, because it seems to encourage clear thinking. It allows us to identify just what is lost, though perhaps unavoidably, when men accept constraints on their actions for some other goal or value. It would be an intolerable muddle, on this view, to use the concept of liberty or freedom in such a way that we counted a loss of freedom only when men were prevented from doing something that we thought they ought to do. It would allow totalitarian governments to masquerade as liberal, simply by arguing that they prevent men from doing only what is wrong. Worse, it would obscure the most distinctive point of the liberal tradition, which is that interfering with a man's free choice to do what he might want to do is in and of itself an insult to humanity, a wrong that may be justified but can never be wiped away by competing considerations. For a true liberal, any constraint upon freedom is something that a decent government must regret, and keep to the minimum necessary to accommodate the other rights of its constituents.

In spite of this tradition, however, the neutral sense of liberty seems to me to have caused more confusion than it has cured, particularly when it is joined to the popular and inspiring idea that men and women have a right to liberty. For we can maintain that idea only by so watering down the idea of a right that the right to liberty is something hardly worth having at all.

The term 'right' is used in politics and philosophy in many different senses, some of which I have tried to disentangle elsewhere. In order sensibly to ask whether we have a right to liberty in the neutral sense, we must fix on some one meaning of 'right'. It would not be difficult to find a sense of that term in which we could say with some confidence that men have a right to liberty. We might say, for example, that someone has a right to liberty if it is in his interest to have liberty, that is, if he either wants it or if it would be good for him to have it. In this sense, I would be prepared to concede that citizens have a right to liberty. But in this sense I would also have to concede that they have a right, at least generally, to vanilla ice cream. My concession about liberty, moreover, would have very little value in political debate. I should want to claim, for example, that people have a right to equality in a much stronger sense, that they do not simply want equality but that they are entitled to it, and I would therefore not recognize the claim that some men and women want liberty as requiring any compromise in the efforts that I believe are necessary to give other men and women the equality to which they are entitled.

If the right to liberty is to play the role cut out for it in political debate, therefore, it must be a right in a much stronger sense....I defined a strong sense of right that seems to me to capture the claims men mean to make when they appeal to political and moral rights....A successful claim of right, in the strong sense I described, has this consequence. If someone has a right to something, then it is wrong for the government to deny it to him even though it would be in the general interest to do so. This sense of a right (which might be called the anti-utilitarian concept of a right) seems to me very close to the sense of right principally used in political and legal writing and argument in recent years. It marks the distinctive concept of an individual right against the State which is the heart, for example, of constitutional theory in the United States.

I do not think that the right to liberty would come to very much, or have much power in political argument, if it relied on any sense of the right any weaker than that. If we settle on this concept of a right, however, then it seems plain that there exists no general right to liberty as such. I have no political right to drive up Lexington Avenue. If the government chooses to make Lexington Avenue one-way down town, it is a sufficient justification that this would be in the general interest, and it would be ridiculous for me to argue that for some reason it would nevertheless be wrong. The vast bulk of the laws which diminish my liberty are justified on utilitarian grounds, as being in the general interest or for the general welfare; if, as Bentham supposes, each of these laws diminishes my liberty, they nevertheless do not take away from me any thing that I have a right to have. It will not do, in the one-way street case, to say that although I have a right to drive up Lexington Avenue, nevertheless the government for special reasons is justified in overriding that right. That seems silly because the government needs no special justification—but only *a* justification—for this sort of legislation. So I can have a political right to liberty, such that every act of constraint diminishes or infringes that right, only in such a weak sense of right that the so called right to liberty is not competitive with strong rights, like the right to equality, at all. In any strong sense of right, which would be competitive with the right to equality, there exists no general right to liberty at all.

It may now be said that I have misunderstood the claim that there is a right to liberty. It does not mean to argue, it will be said, that there is a right to all liberty, but simply to important or basic liberties. Every law is, as Bentham said; an infraction of liberty, but we have a right to be protected against only fundamental or serious infractions. If the constraint on liberty is serious or severe enough, then it is indeed true that the government is not entitled to impose that constraint simply because that would be in the general interest; the government is not entitled to constrain liberty of speech, for example, whenever it thinks that would improve the general welfare. So there is, after all, a general right to liberty as such, provided that that right is restricted to important liberties or serious deprivations. This qualification does not affect the political arguments I described earlier, it will be said, because the rights to liberty that stand in the way of full equality are rights to basic liberties like, for example, the right to attend a school of one's choice.

But this qualification raises an issue of great importance for liberal theory, which those who argue for a right to liberty do not face. What does it mean to say that the right to liberty is limited to basic liberties, or that it offers protection only against serious infractions of liberty? That claim might be spelled out in two different ways, with very different theoretical and practical consequences. Let us suppose two cases in which government constrains a citizen from doing what he might want to do: the government prevents him from speaking his mind on political issues; from driving his car uptown on Lexington Avenue. What is the connection between these two cases, and the difference between them, such that though they are both cases in which a citizen is constrained and deprived of liberty, his right to liberty is infringed only in the first, and not in the second?

On the first of the two theories we might consider, the citizen is deprived of the same commodity, namely liberty, in both cases, but the difference is that in the first case the amount of that commodity taken away from him is, for some reason, either greater in amount or greater in its impact than in the second. But that seems bizarre. It is very difficult to think of liberty as a commodity. If we do try to give liberty some operational sense, such that we can measure the relative diminution of liberty occasioned by different sorts of laws or constraints, then the result is unlikely to match our intuitive sense of what are basic liberties and what are not.

Suppose, for example, we measure a diminution in liberty by calculating the extent of frustration that it induces. We shall then have to face the fact that laws against theft, and even traffic laws, impose constraints that are felt more keenly by most men than constraints on political speech would be. We might take a different tack, and measure the degree of loss of liberty by the impact that a particular constraint has on future choices. But we should then have to admit that the ordinary criminal code reduces choice for most men more than laws which forbid fringe political activity. So the first theory—that the difference between cases covered and those not covered by our supposed right to liberty is a matter of degree—must fail.

The second theory argues that the difference between the two cases has to do, not with the degree of liberty involved, but with the special character of the liberty involved in the case covered by the right. On this theory, the offense involved in a law that limits free speech is of a different character, and not just different in degree, from a law that prevents a man from driving up Lexington Avenue. That sounds plausible, though as we shall see it is not easy to state what this difference in character comes to, or why it argues for a right in some cases though not in others. My present point, however, is that if the distinction between basic liberties and other liberties is defended in this way, then the notion of a general right to liberty as such has been entirely abandoned. If we have a right to basic liberties not because they are cases in which the commodity of liberty is somehow especially at stake, but because an assault on basic liberties injures us or demeans us in some way that goes beyond its impact on liberty, then what we have a right to is not liberty at all, but to the values or interests or standing that this particular constraint defeats.

This is not simply a question of terminology. The idea of a right to liberty is a misconceived concept that does a dis-service to political thought in at least two ways. First, the idea creates a false sense of a necessary conflict between liberty and other values when social regulation, like the busing program, is proposed. Second, the idea provides too easy an answer to the question of why we regard certain kinds of restraints, like the restraint on free speech or the exercise of religion, as especially unjust. The idea of a right to liberty allows us to say that these constraints are unjust because they have a special impact on liberty as such. Once we recognize that this answer is spurious, then we shall have to face the difficult question of what is indeed at stake in these cases.

I should like to turn at once to that question. If there is no general right to liberty, then why do citizens in a democracy have rights to any specific kind of liberty, like freedom of speech or religion or political activity? It is no answer to say that if individuals have these rights, then the community will be better off in the long run as a whole. This idea—that individual rights may lead to overall utility—may or may not be true, but it is irrelevant to the defence of rights as such, because when we say that someone has a right to speak his mind freely, in the relevant political sense, we mean that he is entitled to do so even if this would not be in the general interest. If we want to defend individual rights in the sense in which we claim them, then we must try to discover something beyond utility that argues for these rights.

I mentioned one possibility earlier. We might be able to make out a case that individuals suffer some special damage when the traditional rights are invaded. On this argument, there is something about the liberty to speak out on political issues such that if that liberty is denied the individual suffers a special kind of damage which makes it wrong to inflict that damage upon him even though the community as a whole would benefit. This line of argument will appeal to those who themselves would feel special deprivation at the loss of their political and civil liberties, but it is nevertheless a difficult argument to pursue for two reasons.

First, there are a great many men and women and they undoubtedly form the majority even in democracies like Britain and the United States, who do not exercise political liberties that they have, and who would not count the loss of these liberties as especially grievous. Second, we lack a psychological theory which would justify and explain the idea that the loss of civil liberties, or any particular liberties, involves inevitable or even likely psychological damage. On the contrary, there is now a lively tradition in psychology, led by psychologists like Ronald Laing, who argue that a good deal of mental instability in modern societies may be traced to the demand for too much liberty rather than too little. In their account, the need to choose, which follows from liberty, is an unnecessary source of destructive tension. These theories are not necessarily persuasive, but until we can be confident that they are wrong, we cannot assume that psychology demonstrates the opposite, however appealing that might be on political grounds.

If we want to argue for a right to certain liberties, therefore, we must find another ground. We must argue on grounds of political morality that it is wrong to deprive individuals of these liberties, for some reason, apart from direct psychological damage, in spite of the fact that the common interest would be served by doing so. I put the matter this vaguely because there is no reason to assume, in advance, that only one kind of reason would support that moral position. It might be that a just society would recognize a variety of individual rights, some grounded on very different sorts of moral considerations from others....I shall try to describe only one possible ground for rights. It does not follow that men and women in civil society have only the rights that the argument I shall make would support; but it does follow that they have at least these rights, and that is important enough.

The central concept of my argument will be the concept not of liberty but of equality. I presume that we all accept the following postulates of political morality. Government must treat those whom it governs with concern, that is, as human beings who are capable of suffering and frustration, and with respect, that is, as human beings who are capable of forming and acting on intelligent conceptions of how their lives should be lived. Government must not only treat people with concern and respect, but with equal concern and respect. It must not distribute goods or opportunities unequally on the ground that some citizens are entitled to more because they are worthy of more concern. It must not constrain liberty on the ground that one citizen's conception of the good life of one group is nobler or superior to another's. These postulates, taken together, state what might be called the liberal conception of equality; but it is a conception of equality, not of liberty as license, that they state.

The sovereign question of political theory, within a state supposed to be governed by the liberal conception of equality, is the question of what inequalities in goods, opportunities and liberties are permitted in such a state, and why. The beginning of an answer lies in the following distinction. Citizens governed by the liberal conception of equality each have a right to equal concern and respect. But there are two different rights that might be comprehended by that abstract right. The first is the right to equal treatment, that is, to the same distribution of goods or opportunities as anyone else has or is given. The Supreme Court, in the Reapportionment Cases, held that citizens have a right to equal treatment in the distribution of voting power; it held that one man must be given one vote in spite of the fact that a different distribution of votes might in fact work for the general benefit. The second is the right to treatment as an equal. This is the right, not to an equal distribution of some good or opportunity, but the right to equal concern and respect in the political decision about how these goods and opportunities are to be distributed. Suppose the question is raised whether an economic policy that injures long-term bondholders is in the general interest. Those who will be injured have a right that their prospective loss be taken into account in deciding whether the general interest is served by the policy. They may not simply be ignored in that calculation. But when their interest is taken into account it may nevertheless be outweighed by the interests of others who will gain from the policy, and in that case their right to equal concern and respect, so defined, would provide no objection. In the case of economic policy, therefore, we might wish to say that those who will be injured if inflation is permitted have a right to treatment as equals in the decision whether that policy would serve the general interest, but no right to equal treatment that would outlaw the policy even if it passed that test.

I propose that the right to treatment as an equal must be taken to be fundamental under the liberal conception of equality, and that the more restrictive right to equal treatment holds only in those special circumstances in which, for some special reason, it follows from the more fundamental right, as perhaps it does in the special circumstance of the Reapportionment Cases. I also propose that individual rights to distinct liberties must be recognized only when the fundamental right to treatment as an equal can be shown to require these rights. If this is correct, then the right to distinct liberties does not conflict with any supposed competing right to equality, but on the contrary follows from a conception of equality conceded to be more fundamental.

I must now show, however, how the familiar rights to distinct liberties—those established, for example, in the United States constitution—might be thought to be required by that fundamental conception of equality. I shall try to do this,...only by providing a skeleton of the more elaborate argument that would have to be made to defend any particular liberty on this basis, and then show why it would be plausible to expect that the more familiar political and civil liberties would be supported by such an argument if it were in fact made.

A government that respects the liberal conception of equality may properly constrain liberty only on certain very limited types of justification. I shall adopt, for purposes of making this point, the following crude typology of political justifications. There are, first, arguments of principle, which support a particular constraint on liberty on the argument that the constraint is required to protect the distinct right of some individual who will be injured by the exercise of the liberty. There are, second, arguments of policy, which support constraints on the different ground that such constraints are required to reach some overall political goal, that is, to realize some state of affairs in which the community as a whole, and not just certain individuals, are better off by virtue of the constraint. Arguments of policy might be further subdivided in this way. Utilitarian arguments of policy argue that the community as a whole will be better off because (to put the point roughly) more of its citizens will have more of what they want overall, even though some of them will have less. Ideal arguments of policy, on the other hand, argue that the community will be better off, not because more of its members will have more of what they want, but because the community will be in some way closer to an ideal community, whether its members desire the improvement in question or not.

The liberal conception of equality sharply limits the extent to which ideal arguments of policy may be used to justify any constraint on liberty. Such arguments cannot be used if the idea in question is itself controversial within the community. Constraints cannot be defended, for example, directly on the ground that they contribute to a culturally sophisticated community, whether the community wants the sophistication or not, because that argument would violate the canon of the liberal conception of equality that prohibits a government from relying on the claim that certain forms of life are inherently more valuable than others.

Utilitarian arguments of policy, however, would seem secure from that objection. They do not suppose that any form of life is inherently more valuable than any other, but instead base their claim, that constraints on liberty are necessary to advance some collective goal of the community, just on the fact that that goal happens to be desired more widely or more deeply than any other. Utilitarian arguments of policy, therefore, seem not to oppose but on the contrary to embody the fundamental right of equal concern and respect, because they treat the wishes of each member of the community on a par with the wishes of any other, with no bonus or discount reflecting the view that that member is more or less worthy of concern, or his views more or less worthy of respect, than any other.

This appearance of egalitarianism has, I think, been the principal source of the great appeal that utilitarianism has had, as a general political philosophy, over the last century....The egalitarian character of a utilitarian argument is often an illusion....

Utilitarian arguments fix on the fact that a particular constraint on liberty will make more people happier, or satisfy more of their preferences, depending upon whether psychological or preference utilitarianism is in play. But people's overall preference for one policy rather than another may be seen to include, on further analysis, both preferences that are *personal*, because they state a preference for the assignment of one set of goods or opportunities to him and preferences that are *external*, because they state a preference for one assignment of goods or opportunities to others. But a utilitarian argument that assigns critical weight to the external preferences of members of the community will not be egalitarian in the sense under consideration. It will not respect the right of everyone to be treated with equal concern and respect.

Suppose, for example, that a number of individuals in the community holds racist rather than utilitarian political theories. They believe, not that each man is to count for one and no one for more than one in the distribution of goods, but rather that a black man is to count for less and a white man therefore to count for more than one. That is an external preference, but it is nevertheless a genuine preference for one policy rather than another, the satisfaction of which will bring pleasure. Nevertheless if this preference or pleasure is given the normal weight in a utilitarian calculation, and blacks suffer accordingly, then their own assignment of goods and opportunities will depend, not simply on the competition among personal preferences that abstract statements of utilitarianism suggest, but precisely on the fact that they are thought less worthy of concern and respect than others are.

Suppose, to take a different case, that many members of the community disapprove on moral grounds of homosexuality, or contraception, or pornography, or expressions of adherence to the Communist party. They prefer not only that they themselves do not indulge in these activities, but that no one else does so either, and they believe that a community that permits rather than prohibits these acts is inherently a worse community. These are external preferences, but, once again, they are no less genuine, nor less a source of pleasure when satisfied and displeasure when ignored, than purely personal preferences. Once again, however, if these external preferences are counted, so as to justify a constraint on liberty, then those constrained suffer, not simply because their personal preferences have lost in a competition for scarce resources with the personal preferences of others, but precisely because their conception of a proper or desirable form of life is despised by others.

These arguments justify the following important conclusion. If utilitarian arguments of policy are to be used to justify constraints on liberty, then care must be taken to insure that the utilitarian calculations on which the argument is based fix only on personal and ignore external preferences. That is an important conclusion for political theory because it shows, for example, why the arguments of John Stuart Mill in *On Liberty* are not counter-utilitarian but, on the contrary, arguments in service of the only defensible form of utilitarianism.

Important as that conclusion is at the level of political philosophy, however, it is in itself of limited practical significance, because it will be impossible to devise political procedures that will accurately discriminate between personal and external preferences. Representative democracy is widely thought to be the institutional structure most suited, in a complex and diverse society, to the identification and achievement of utilitarian policies. It works imperfectly at this, for the familiar reason that majoritarianism cannot sufficiently take account of the intensity, as distinct from the number, of particular preferences, and because techniques of political persuasion, backed by money, may corrupt the accuracy with which votes represent the genuine preferences of those who have voted. Nevertheless democracy seems to enforce utilitarianism more satisfactorily, in spite of these imperfections, than any alternative general political scheme would.

But democracy cannot discriminate, within the overall preferences imperfectly revealed by voting, distinct personal and external components, so as to provide a method for enforcing the former while ignoring the latter. An actual vote in an election or referendum must be taken to represent an overall preference rather than some component of the preference that a skillful cross-examination of the individual voter, if time and expense permitted, would reveal. Personal and external preferences are sometimes so inextricably combined, moreover, that the discrimination is psychologically as well as institutionally impossible. That will be true, for example, in the case of the associational preferences that many people have for members of one race, or people of one talent or quality, rather than another, for this is a personal preference so parasitic upon external preferences that it is impossible to say, even as a matter of introspection, what personal preferences would remain if the underlying external preference were removed. It is also true of certain self-denying preferences that many individuals have; that is preferences for less of a certain good on the assumption, or rather proviso, that other people will have more. That is also a preference, however noble, that is parasitic upon external preferences, in the shape of political and moral theories, and they may no more be counted in a defensible utilitarian argument than less attractive preferences rooted in prejudice rather than altruism.

I wish now to propose the following general theory of rights. The concept of an individual political right, in the strong anti-utilitarian sense I distinguished earlier, is a response to the philosophical defects of a utilitarianism that counts external preferences and the practical impossibility of a utilitarianism that does not. It allows us to enjoy the institutions of political democracy, which enforce overall or unrefined utilitarianism, and yet protect the fundamental right of citizens to equal concern and respect by prohibiting decisions that seem, antecedently, likely to have been reached by virtue of the external components of the preferences democracy reveals.

It should be plain how this theory of rights might be used to support the idea,...that we have distinct rights to certain liberties like the liberty of free expression and of free choice in personal and sexual relations. It might be shown that any utilitarian constraint on these liberties must be based on overall preferences in the community that we know, from our general knowledge of society, are likely to contain large components of external preferences, in the shape of political or moral theories, which the political process cannot discriminate and eliminate....

Basic Rights

Henry Shue

A moral right provides (1) the rational basis for a justified demand (2) that the actual enjoyment of a substance be (3) socially guaranteed against standard threats. Since this is a somewhat complicated account of rights, each of its elements deserves a brief introductory explanation. The significance of the general structure of a moral right is, however, best seen in concrete cases of rights, to which we will quickly turn.

A right provides the rational basis for a justified demand. If a person has a particular right, the demand that the enjoyment of the substance of the right be socially guaranteed is justified by good reasons, and the guarantees ought, therefore, to be provided....To have a right is to be in a position to make demands of others, and to be in such a position is, among other things, for one's situation to fall under general principles that are good reasons why one's demands ought to be granted. A person who has a right has especially compelling reasons—especially deep principles—on his or her side. People can of course have rights without being able to explain them—without being able to articulate the principles that apply to their cases and serve as the reasons for their demands....Because a right is the basis for a justified demand, people not only may, but ought to, insist. Those who deny rights do so at their own peril. This does not mean that efforts to secure the fulfillment of the demand constituting a right ought not to observe certain constraints. It does mean that those who deny rights can have no complaint when their denial, especially if it is part of a systematic pattern of deprivation, is resisted. Exactly which countermeasures are justified by which sorts of deprivations of rights would require a separate discussion....Rights do not justify merely requests, pleas, petitions. It is only because rights may lead to demands and not something weaker that having rights is tied as closely as it is to human dignity....

That a right provides the rational basis for a justified demand for actual enjoyment is the most neglected element of many rights. A right does not yield a demand that it should be said that people are entitled to enjoy something, or that people should be promised that they will enjoy something. A proclamation of a right is not the fulfillment of a right, any more than an airplane schedule is a

From *Basic Rights* (Princeton, NJ: Princeton University Press, 1980). Reprinted by permission of the publisher.

flight. A proclamation may or may not be an initial step toward the fulfillment of the rights listed. It is frequently the substitute of the promise in the place of the fulfillment.

The substance of a right is whatever the right is a right to. A right is not a right to enjoy a right—it is a right to enjoy something else, like food or liberty. We do sometimes speak simply of someone's "enjoying a right," but I take this to be an elliptical way of saying that the person is enjoying something or other, which is the substance of a right, and, probably, enjoying it *as* a right. Enjoying a right to, for example, liberty normally means enjoying liberty. It may also mean enjoying liberty in the consciousness that liberty is a right. Being a right is a status that various subjects of enjoyment have. Simply to enjoy the right itself, the status, rather than to enjoy the subject of the right would have to mean something like taking satisfaction that there is such a status and that something has that status. But ordinarily when we say someone is enjoying a right, we mean the person is enjoying the substance of the right.

Being socially guaranteed is probably the single most important aspect of a standard right, because it is the aspect that necessitates correlative duties. A right is ordinarily a justified demand that some other people make some arrangements so that one will still be able to enjoy the substance of the right even if—actually, *especially* if—it is not within one's own power to arrange on one's own to enjoy the substance of the right. Suppose people have a right to physical security. Some of them may nevertheless choose to hire their own private guards, as if they had no right to social guarantees. But they would be justified, and everyone else is justified, in demanding that somebody somewhere make some effective arrangements to establish and maintain security. Whether the arrangements should be governmental or non-governmental; local, national, or international; participatory or non-participatory, are all difficult questions to which I may or may not be able to give definitive or conclusive answers here. But it is essential to a right that it is a demand upon others, however difficult it is to specify exactly which others.

And a right has been guaranteed only when arrangements have been made for people with the right to enjoy it. It is not enough that at the moment it happens that no one is violating the right. Just as

a proclamation of a right is not the fulfillment of a right and may in fact be either a step toward or away from actually fulfilling the right, an undertaking to create social guarantees for the enjoyment of various subjects of rights is by no means itself the guaranteeing and may or may not lead to real guarantees. But a right has not been fulfilled until arrangements are in fact in place for people to enjoy whatever it is to which they have the right. Usually, perhaps, the arrangements will take the form of law, making the rights legal as well as moral ones. But in other cases well-entrenched customs, backed by taboos, might serve better than laws—certainly better than unenforced laws....

I am not suggesting the absurd standard that a right has been fulfilled only if it is impossible for anyone to be deprived of it or only if no one is ever deprived of it. The standard can only be some reasonable level of guarantee. But if people who walk alone after dark are likely to be assaulted, or if infant mortality is 60 per 1000 live births, we would hardly say that enjoyment of, respectively, security or subsistence had yet been socially guaranteed. It is for the more precise specification of the reasonable level of social guarantees that we need the final element in the general structure of moral rights: the notion of a standard threat....

That a right involves a rationally justified demand for social guarantees against standard threats means, in effect, that the relevant other people have a duty to create, if they do not exist, or, if they do, to preserve effective institutions for the enjoyment of what people have rights to enjoy. From no theory like the present one is it possible to deduce precisely what sort of institutions are needed, and I have no reason to think that the same institutions would be most effective in all places and at all times. On its face, such universality of social institutions is most improbable, although some threats are indeed standard. What is universal, however, is a duty to make and keep effective arrangements, and...arrangements must serve at least the functions of avoiding depriving people of the substances of their rights, protecting them against deprivation, and aiding them if they are nevertheless deprived of rights....

One of the chief purposes of morality in general, and certainly of conceptions of rights, and of basic rights above all, is indeed to provide some minimal protection against utter helplessness to those too weak to protect themselves. Basic rights are a shield for the defenseless against at least some of the more devastating and more common of life's threats, which include, as we shall see, loss of security and loss of subsistence. Basic rights are a restraint upon economic and political forces that would otherwise be too strong to be resisted. They are social guarantees against actual and threatened deprivations of at least some basic needs. Basic rights are an attempt to give to the powerless a veto over some of the forces that would otherwise harm them the most.

Basic rights are the morality of the depths. They specify the line beneath which no one is to be allowed to sink. This is part of the reason that basic rights are tied so closely to self-respect....

And it is not surprising that what is in an important respect the essentially negative goal of preventing or alleviating helplessness is a central purpose of something as important as conceptions of basic rights. For everyone healthy adulthood is bordered on each side by helplessness, and it is vulnerable to interruption by helplessness, temporary or permanent, at any time. And many of the people in the world now have very little control over their fates, even over such urgent matters as whether their own children live through infancy. Nor is it surprising that although the goal is negative, the duties correlative to rights will turn out to include positive actions. The infant and the aged do not need to be assaulted in order to be deprived of health, life, or the capacity to enjoy active rights. The classic liberal's main prescription for the good life—do not interfere with thy neighbor—is the only poison they need. To be helpless they need only to be left alone....

Basic rights, then, are everyone's minimum reasonable demands upon the rest of humanity. They are the rational basis for justified demands the denial of which no self-respecting person can reasonably be expected to accept. Why should anything be so important? The reason is that rights are basic in the sense used here only if enjoyment of them is essential to the enjoyment of all other rights. This is what is distinctive about a basic right. When a right is genuinely basic, any attempt to enjoy any other right by sacrificing the basic right would be quite literally self-defeating, cutting the ground from beneath itself. Therefore, if a right is basic, other, non-basic rights may be sacrificed, if necessary, in order to secure the basic right. But the protection of a basic right may not be sacrificed in order to secure the enjoyment of a non-basic right. It may not be sacrificed because it cannot be sacrificed successfully. If the right sacrificed is indeed basic, then no right for which it might be sacrificed can actually be enjoyed in the absence of the basic right. The sacrifice would have proven self-defeating.

In practice, what this priority for basic rights usually means is that basic rights need to be established securely before other rights can be secured. The point is that people should be able to *enjoy*, or *exercise*, their other rights. The point is simple but vital. It is not merely that people should "have" their other rights in some merely legalistic or otherwise abstract sense compatible with being unable to make any use of the substance of the right. For example, if people have rights to free association, they ought not merely to "have" the rights to free association but also to enjoy their free association itself. Their freedom of association ought to be provided for by the relevant social institutions....

What is not meant by saying that a right is basic is that the right is more valuable or intrinsically more satisfying to enjoy than some other rights. For example, I...suggest that rights to physical security, such as the right not to be assaulted, are basic, and I shall not include the right to publicly supported education as basic. But I do not mean by this to deny that enjoyment of the right to education is much greater and richer—more distinctively human, perhaps—than merely going through life without ever being assaulted. I mean only that, if a choice must be made, the prevention of assault ought to supersede the provision of education. Whether a right is basic is independent of whether its enjoyment is also valuable in itself. Intrinsically valuable rights may or may not also be basic rights, but intrinsically valuable rights can be enjoyed only when basic rights are enjoyed. Clearly few rights could be basic in this precise sense.

Our first project will be to see why people have a basic right to physical security—a right that is basic not to be subjected to murder, torture, mayhem, rape, or assault. The purpose in raising the questions why there are rights to physical security and why they are basic is not that very many people would seriously doubt either that there are rights to physical security or that they are basic. Although it is not unusual in practice for members of at least one ethnic group in a society to be physically insecure—to be, for example, much more likely than other people to be beaten by the police if arrested—few, if any, people would be prepared to defend in principle the contention that anyone lacks a basic right to physical security....

If we had to justify our belief that people have a basic right to physical security to someone who challenged this fundamental conviction, we could in fact give a strong argument that shows that if there are any rights (basic or not basic) at all, there are basic rights to physical security:

No one can fully enjoy any right that is supposedly protected by society if someone can credibly threaten him or her with murder, rape, beating, etc., when he or she tries to enjoy the alleged right. Such threats to physical security are among the most serious and—in much of the world—the most widespread hindrances to the enjoyment of any right. If any right is to be exercised except at great risk, physical security must be protected. In the absence of physical security people are unable to use any other rights that society may be said to be protecting without being liable to encounter many of the worst dangers they would encounter if society were not protecting the rights....

A person could, of course, always try to enjoy some other right even if no social provision were made to protect his or her physical safety during attempts to exercise the right. Suppose there is a right to peaceful assembly but it is not unusual for peaceful assemblies to be broken up and some of the participants beaten. Whether any given assembly is actually broken up depends largely on whether anyone else (in or out of government is sufficiently opposed to it to bother to arrange an attack. People could still try to assemble, and they might sometimes assemble safely. But it would obviously be misleading to say that they are protected in their right to assemble if they are as vulnerable as ever to one of the most serious and general threats to enjoyment of the right, namely physical violence by other people. If they are as helpless against physical threats with the right "protected" as they would have been without the supposed protection, society is not actually protecting their exercise of the right to assembly.

So anyone who is entitled to anything as a right must be entitled to physical security as a basic right so that threats to his or her physical security cannot be used to thwart the enjoyment of the other right. This argument has two critical premises. The first is that everyone is entitled to enjoy something as a right. The second, which further explains the first, is that everyone is entitled to the removal of the most serious and general conditions that would prevent or severely interfere with the exercise of whatever rights the person has. I take this second premise to be part of what is meant in saving that everyone is entitled to enjoy something as a right....Since this argument applies to everyone, it establishes a right that is universal.

The main reason for discussing security rights, which are not very controversial, was to make explicit the basic assumptions that support the usual judgment that security rights are basic rights. Now that we have available an argument that supports them, we are in a position to consider whether matters other than physical security should, according to the same argument, also be basic rights. It will emerge that subsistence, or minimal economic security, which is more controversial than physical security, can also be shown to be as well justified for treatment as a basic right as physical security is—and for the same reasons.

By minimal economic security, or subsistence, I mean unpolluted air, unpolluted water, adequate food, adequate clothing, adequate shelter, and minimal preventive public health care. Many complications about exactly how to specify the boundaries of what is necessary for subsistence would be interesting to explore. But the basic idea is to have available for consumption what is needed for a decent chance at a reasonably healthy and active life of more or less normal length, barring tragic interventions. This central idea is clear enough to work with, even though disputes can occur over exactly where to draw its outer boundaries. A right to subsistence would not mean, at one extreme, that every baby born with a need for open-heart surgery has a right to have it, but it also would not count as adequate food a diet that produces a life expectancy of 35 years of fever-laden, parasite-ridden listlessness.

By a "right to subsistence" I shall always mean a right to at least subsistence. People may or may not have economic rights that go beyond subsistence rights, and I do not want to prejudge that question here. But people may have rights to subsistence even if they do not have any strict rights to economic well-being extending beyond subsistence. Subsistence rights and broader economic rights are separate questions, and I want to focus here on subsistence.

I also do not want to prejudge the issue of whether healthy adults are entitled to be provided with subsistence *only* if they cannot provide subsistence for themselves. Most of the world's malnourished, for example, are probably also diseased, since malnutrition lowers resistance to disease, and hunger and infestation normally form a tight vicious circle. Hundreds of millions of the malnourished are very young children. A large percentage of the adults, besides being ill and hungry, are also chronically unemployed, so the issue of policy toward healthy adults who refuse to work is largely irrelevant. By a "right to subsistence," then, I shall mean a right to subsistence that includes the provision of subsistence at least to those who cannot provide for themselves. I do not assume that no one else is also entitled to receive subsistence—I simply do not discuss cases of healthy adults who could support themselves but refuse to do so. If there is a right to subsistence in the sense discussed here, at least the people who cannot provide for themselves, including the children, are entitled to receive at least subsistence. Nothing follows one way or the other about anyone else.

It makes no difference whether the legally enforced system of property where a given person lives is private, state, communal, or one of the many more typical mixtures and variants. Under all systems of property people are prohibited from simply taking even what they need for survival. Whatever the property institutions and the economic system are, the question about rights to subsistence remains: if persons are forbidden by law from taking what they need to survive and they are unable within existing economic institutions and policies to provide for their own survival (and the survival of dependents for whose welfare they are responsible), are they entitled, as a last resort, to receive the essentials for survival from the remainder of humanity whose lives are not threatened?

The same considerations that support the conclusion that physical security is a basic right support the conclusion that subsistence is a basic right. Since the argument is now familiar, it can be given fairly briefly.

It is quite obvious why, if we still assume that there are some rights that society ought to protect and still mean by this the removal of the most serious and general hindrances to the actual enjoyment of the rights, subsistence ought to be protected as a basic right:

No one can fully, if at all, enjoy any right that is supposedly protected by society if he or she lacks the essentials for a reasonably healthy and active life. Deficiencies in the means of subsistence can be just as fatal, incapacitating, or painful as violations of physical security. The resulting damage or death can at least as decisively prevent the enjoyment of any right as can the effects of security violations. Any form of malnutrition, or fever due to exposure, that causes severe and irreversible brain damage, for example, can effectively prevent the exercise of any right requiring clear thought and may, like brain injuries caused by assault, profoundly disturb personality. And, obviously, any fatal deficiencies end all possibility of the enjoyment of rights as firmly as an arbitrary execution.

Indeed, prevention of deficiencies in the essentials for survival is, if anything, more basic than prevention of violations of physical security. People who lack protection against violations of their physical security can, if they are free, fight back against their attackers or flee, but people who lack essentials, such as food, because of forces beyond their control, often can do nothing and are on their own utterly helpless.

The scope of subsistence rights must not be taken to be broader than it is....Many causes of death and illness are outside the control of society, and many deaths and illnesses are the result of very particular conjunctions of circumstances that general social policies cannot control. But it is not impractical to expect some level of social organization to protect the minimal cleanliness of air and water and to oversee the adequate production, or import, and the proper distribution of minimal food, clothing, shelter, and elementary health care. It is not impractical, in short, to expect effective management, when necessary, of the supplies of the essentials of life. So the argument is: when death and serious illness could be prevented by different social policies regarding the essentials of life, the protection of any human right involves avoidance of fatal or debilitating deficiencies in these essential commodities. And this means fulfilling subsistence rights as basic rights. This is society's business because the problems are serious and general. This is a basic right because failure to deal with it would hinder the enjoyment of all other rights.

Thus, the same considerations that establish that security rights are basic for everyone also support the conclusion that subsistence rights are basic for everyone. It is not being claimed or assumed that security and subsistence are parallel in all, or even very many, respects. The only parallel being relied upon is that guarantees of security and guarantees of subsistence are equally essential to providing for the actual exercise of any other rights. As long as security and subsistence are parallel in this respect, the argument applies equally to both cases, and other respects in which security and subsistence are not parallel are irrelevant.

It is not enough that people merely happen to be secure or happen to be subsisting. They must have a right to security and a right to subsistence—the continued enjoyment of the security and the subsistence must be socially guaranteed. Otherwise a person is readily open to coercion and intimidation through threats of the deprivation of one or the other, and credible threats can paralyze a person and prevent the exercise of any other right as surely as actual beatings and actual protein/calorie deficiencies can. Credible threats can be reduced only by the actual establishment of social arrangements that will bring assistance to those confronted by forces that they themselves cannot handle....

Guarantees of security and subsistence are not added advantages over and above enjoyment of the right to assemble. They are essential parts of it. For this reason it would be misleading to construe security or subsistence—or the substance of any other basic right—merely as means to the enjoyment of all other rights. The enjoyment of security and subsistence is an essential part of the enjoyment of all other rights. Part of what it means to enjoy any other right is to be able to exercise that right without, as a consequence, suffering the actual or threatened loss of one's physical security or one's subsistence. And part of what it means to be able to enjoy any other right is not to be prevented from exercising it by lack of security or of subsistence. To claim to guarantee people a right that they are in fact unable to exercise is fraudulent, like furnishing people with meal tickets but providing no food....

I do not intend to say merely that enjoying security is a means to enjoying assembly. I intend to say that part of the meaning of the enjoyment of a right of assembly is that one can assemble in physical security. Being secure is an essential component of enjoying a right of assembly, so that there is no such thing as a situation in which people do have social guarantees for assembly and do not have social guarantees for security. If they do not have guarantees that they can assemble in security, they have not been provided with assembly as a right. They must assemble and merely hope for the best, because a standard threat to assembling securely has not been dealt with. The fundamental argument is that when one fully grasps what an ordinary right is, and especially which duties are correlative to a right, one can see that the guarantee of certain things (as basic rights) is part of—is a constituent of—is an essential component of—the establishment of the conditions in which the right can actually be enjoyed....

The structure of the argument that a specific right is basic may be outlined as follows, provided we are careful about what is meant by "necessary":

1. Everyone has a right to something.
2. Some other things are necessary for enjoying the first thing as a right, whatever the first thing is.
3. Therefore, everyone also has rights to the other things that are necessary for enjoying the first as a right.

Since this argument abstracts from the substance of the right assumed in the first premise, it is based upon what it normally means for anything to be a right or, in other words, upon the concept of a right. So, if the argument to establish the substances of basic rights is summarized by saying that these substances are the "other things...necessary" for enjoying any other right, it is essential to interpret "necessary" in the restricted sense of "made essential by the very concept of a right." The "other things" include not whatever would be convenient or useful, but only what is indispensable to anything else's being enjoyed as a right. Nothing will turn out to be necessary, in this sense, for the enjoyment of any right unless it is also necessary for the enjoyment of every right and is, for precisely this reason, qualified to be the substance of a basic right....

People are neither entitled to social guarantees against every conceivable threat, nor entitled to guarantees against ineradicable threats like eventual serious illness, accident, or death. Another way to indicate the restricted scope of the argument, then, is as follows. The argument rests upon what might be called a transitivity principle for rights: If everyone has a right to y, and the enjoyment of x is necessary for the enjoyment of y, then everyone also has a right to x. But the necessity in question is analytic. People also have rights—according to this argument—only to the additional substances made necessary by the paired concepts of a right and its correlative duties. It is analytically necessary that if people are to be provided with a right, their enjoyment of the substance of the right must be protected against the typical major threats. If people are as helpless against ordinary threats as they would be on their own, duties correlative to a right are not being performed. Precisely what those threats are, and which it is feasible to counter, are of course largely empirical questions, and the answers to both questions will change as the situation changes. In the argument for acknowledging security and subsistence as basic rights I have taken it to be fairly evident that the erosion of the enjoyment of any assumed right by deficiencies in subsistence is as common, as serious, and as remediable at present as the destruction of the enjoyment of any assumed right by assaults upon security.

What is, for example, eradicable changes, of course, over time. Today, we have very little excuse for allowing so many poor people to die of malaria and more excuse probably for allowing people to die of cancer. Later perhaps we will have equally little excuse to allow deaths by many kinds of cancer, or perhaps not. In any case, the measure is a realistic, not a utopian, one, and what is realistic can change....One fundamental purpose served by acknowledging basic rights at all is, in Camus' phrase, that we "take the victim's side," and the side of the potential victims. The honoring of basic rights is an active alliance with those who would otherwise be helpless against natural and social forces too strong for them. A basic right has, accordingly, not been honored until people have been provided rather firm protection—what I am calling "social guarantees"—for enjoying the substance of

their basic rights. What I am now stressing is that this protection need neither be ironclad nor include the prevention of every imaginable threat.

But the opposite extreme is to offer such weak social guarantees that people are virtually as vulnerable with their basic rights "fulfilled" as they are without them. The social guarantees that are part of any typical right need not provide impregnable protection against every imaginable threat, but they must provide effective defenses against predictable remediable threats. To try to count a situation of unrelieved vulnerability to standard threats as the enjoyment of basic rights by their bearers or the fulfillment of these rights by the bearers of the correlative duties is to engage in double-speak, or to try to behave as if concepts have no boundaries at all. To allow such practices to continue is to acquiesce in not only the violation of rights but also the destruction of the concept of rights.

Insofar as it is true that moral rights generally, and not basic rights only, include justified demands for social guarantees against standard threats, we have an interesting theoretical result. The fulfillment of both basic and non-basic moral rights consists of effective, but not infallible, social arrangements to guard against standard threats like threats to physical security and threats to economic security or subsistence. One way to characterize the substances of basic rights, which ties the account of basic rights tightly to the account of the structure of moral rights generally, is this: the substance of a basic right is something the deprivation of which is one standard threat to rights generally. The fulfillment of a basic right is a successful defense against a standard threat to rights generally. This is precisely why basic rights are basic. That to which they are rights is needed for the fulfillment of all other rights. If the substance of a basic right is not socially guaranteed, attempts actually to enjoy the substance of other rights remain open to a standard threat like the deprivation of security or subsistence. The social guarantees against standard threats that are part of moral rights generally *are the same as* the fulfillment of basic rights. This is why giving less priority to any basic right than to normal non-basic rights is literally impossible....

8 The Rights and Welfare of the Environment, Animals, and Future Generations

We encounter many difficulties in attempting to justify the claim that human beings all have equal rights, determining the criterion on which that claim is based, and deciding just what rights are so basic that they should be considered as human rights possessed by all persons. But most proposed criteria for grounding such rights raise the question of selecting too narrow or too wide a class of right-holders. For example, if the ability to reason is cited as the basis for having human rights, then what do we say about infants or the mentally retarded? Don't our intuitions tell us these are the very ones who need the concept of human rights as a protection? But on the other hand, are there not other animals who exercise reasoning abilities, and why should they not be considered to be right-bearers?

The problem with talking about *nonhuman* rights is that the concept of "rights" has traditionally been tied to the concept of a person. The supposition is that there is some defining trait of human beings which they all share but which is not shared by other beings, such as the capacity for reason, having conscious desires and interests, the ability to carry out a plan of action, and so on. This provides the theoretical justification for both "natural law" and "natural rights." But if so, then there would seem to be no justification for talking about the rights of trees or rivers, other animals, aliens, and so forth. On the other hand, there is some legal precedent for considering the rights of such nonhuman entities as corporations and for the state's claiming rights on behalf of entities, such as an infant or comatose patient, which they themselves cannot assert. If the infant cannot now reason, it has the potential to do so in the future. The same can be said of future generations of human beings. In this way there is some precedent for extending the list of right-bearers beyond living adult persons. The question is whether we can legitimately extend the list still farther, and if so how far?

The "politics" of nonhuman rights is essentially the same as that for human rights. Those who think that the need for sweeping legislation protecting animals or the environment is terribly urgent will argue that refusal to act on such legislation not only leads to undesirable consequences but is also a violation of fundamental rights, while those who put primary value on promoting the immediate needs and interests of human beings will urge a more gradual approach.

READINGS

Rene Descartes (1596–1650) identifies as a crucial difference between human beings and other animals the fact that we think and use language and they do not. Animals, he argues, have no reasoning ability at all and their actions are analogous to those of a clock "composed of wheels and weights." David Hume (1711–1776) takes it as equally self-evident that animals are "endow'd with thought and reason as well as men" and that their actions can be accounted for in the same way as human actions.

Jeremy Bentham (1748–1832) suggests that there may come a day when rights are extended to animals just as they have been to slaves. The issue is, he says, not whether animals can reason or talk but whether they can suffer.

David G. Ritchie (1853–1903) points to the conceptual difficulties we would encounter if we were to attempt to extend the concept of rights to animals and argues that the interest of human society is the ultimate criterion of right and wrong.

Joel Feinberg of the University of Arizona supports protecting our environment now out of respect for the rights of future generations of human beings. He argues that the sorts of things which can possess rights are those things which have or can have interests (or "goods") of their own. Animals, infants, fetuses, and generations yet unborn, as opposed to say, the Taj Mahal, are possible right-bearers. Surely, he says, "we owe it to future generations to pass on a world that is not a used up garbage heap."

R. G. Frey, a philosophy professor at Bowling Green University, also takes the view that the capacity to have interests is the basis for having rights. While he agrees that other animals have interests in that they can be harmed or benefited, he argues that this sense of "interest" is not the morally important one since even inanimate objects can have those sorts of interest. It is having a want which can be satisfied or left unsatisfied which is the basis of rights, and Frey argues that animals do not have *these* interests. Animals cannot have desires because they cannot have beliefs since beliefs are affirmations that a proposition is true or false. Propositions are elements of language and animals do not speak a language. For this reason animals cannot have beliefs and so cannot have desires and interests of a morally relevant sort.

Tom Regan of North Carolina State University presents a much more demanding view. Animals, he reasons, can and do experience pain. Pain is an intrinsic evil, an evil which is just as profound when experienced by an animal as by a human being. The practice of raising, keeping, and using animals for food produces undeserved pain for the animals. Regan denies that this pain is outweighed by the amount of pleasure human beings get from eating meat. The onus is on the nonvegetarian to show how eating meat can be justified.

Christopher D. Stone, law professor at the University of Southern California, takes a different tack. The Taj Mahal or a river do not have interests of their own, but they are things we ought to care about and respect. While our traditional moral and legal systems have at their center the notion of a person and begin to stretch out when we notice similarities between persons and other beings having interests of their own, Stone suggests a moral pluralism in which less importance is placed on having moral or legal rights and in which there is an increased emphasis on what should have legal or moral recognition. This idea he calls "legal considerateness." For example, a lake "is considerate within a legal system if the system's rules have as their immediate object to affect (as to preserve) some condition of the lake...without any further need to demonstrate anyone else's interest in or claims touching the lake."

"The Difference between Men and Animals"

Rene Descartes

The body is regarded as a machine which, having been made by the hands of God, is incomparably better arranged, and possesses in itself movements which are much more admirable, than any of those which can be invented by man. Here I specially stopped to show that if there had been such machines, possessing the organs and outward form of a monkey or some other animal without reason, we should not have had any means of ascertaining that they were not of the same nature as those animals. On the other hand, if there were machines which bore a resemblance to our body and imitated our actions as far as it was morally possible to do so, we should always have two very certain tests by which to recognise that, for all that, they were not real men. The first is, that they could never use speech or other signs as we do when placing our thoughts on record for the benefit of others. For we can easily understand a machine's being constituted so that it can utter words, and even emit some responses to action on it of a corporeal kind, which brings about a change in its organs; for instance, if it is touched in a particular part it may ask what we wish to say to it; if in another part it may exclaim that it is being hurt, and so on. But it never happens that it arranges its speech in various ways, in order to reply appropriately to everything that may be said in its presence, as even the lowest type of man can do. And the second difference is, that although machines can perform certain things as well as or perhaps better than any of us can do, they infallibly fall short in others, by the which means we may discover that they did not act from knowledge, but only from the disposition of their organs. For while reason is a universal instrument which can serve for all contingencies, these organs have need of some special adaptation for every particular action. From this it follows that it is morally impossible that there should be sufficient diversity in any machine to allow it to act in all the events of life in the same way as our reason causes us to act.

By these two methods we may also recognize the difference that exists between men and brutes. For it is a very remarkable fact that there are none so depraved and stupid, without even excepting idiots, that they cannot arrange different words together, forming of them a statement by which they make known their thoughts; while, on the other hand, there is no other animal, however perfect and fortunately circumstanced it may be, which can do the same. It is not the want of organs that brings this to pass, for it is evident that magpies and parrots are able to utter words just like ourselves; and yet they cannot speak as we do, that is, so as to give evidence that they think of what they say. On the other hand, men who, being born deaf and dumb, are in the same degree, or even more than the brutes, destitute of the organs which serve the others for talking, are in the habit of themselves inventing certain signs by which they make themselves understood by those who, being usually in their company, have leisure to learn their language. And this does not merely show that the brutes have less reason than men, but that they have none at all, since it is clear that very little is required in order to be able to talk. And when we notice the inequality that exists between animals of the same species, as well as between men, and observe that some are more capable of receiving instruction than others, it is not credible that a monkey or a parrot, selected as the most perfect of its species, should not in these matters equal the stupidest child to be found,

From "Discourse on the Method of Rightly Conducting the Reason and Seeking for Truth in the Sciences," *Philosophical Works of Descartes*, Vol. 1, (Cambridge: Cambridge University Press, 1967). Elizabeth Haldane and G. R. T. Ross, trans. Reprinted by permission of the publisher.

or at least a child whose mind is clouded, unless in the case of the brute the soul were of an entirely different nature from ours. And we ought not to confound speech with natural movements which betray passions and may be imitated by machines as well as be manifested by animals; nor must we think, as did some of the ancients, that brutes talk, although we do not understand their language. For if this were true, since they have many organs which are allied to our own, they could communicate their thoughts to us just as easily as to those of their own race. It is also a very remarkable fact that although there are many animals which exhibit more dexterity than we do in some of their actions, we at the same time observe that they do not manifest any dexterity at all in many others. Hence the fact that they do better than we do, does not prove that they are endowed with mind, for in this case they would have more reason than any of us, and would surpass us in all other things. It rather shows that they have no reason at all, and that it is nature which acts in them according to the disposition of their organs, just as a clock, which is only composed of wheels and weights is able to tell the hours and measure the time more correctly than we can do with all our wisdom.

"Of the Reason of Animals"

David Hume

No truth appears to me more evident, than that beasts are endow'd with thought and reason as well as men. The arguments are in this case so obvious, that they never escape the most stupid and ignorant.

We are conscious, that we ourselves, in adapting means to ends, are guided by reason and design, and that 'tis not ignorantly nor casually we perform those actions, which tend to self-preservation, to the obtaining pleasure, and avoiding pain. When therefore we see other creatures, in millions of instances, perform like actions, and direct them to like ends, all our principles of reason and probability carry us with an invincible force to believe the existence of a like cause. 'Tis needless in my opinion to illustrate this argument by the enumeration of particulars. The smallest attention will supply us with more than are requisite. The resemblance betwixt the actions of animals and those of men is so entire in this respect, that the very first action of the first animal we shall please to pitch on, will afford us an incontestable argument for the present doctrine.

This doctrine is as useful as it is obvious, and furnishes us with a kind of touchstone, by which we may try every system in this species of philosophy. 'Tis from the resemblance of the external actions of animals to those we ourselves perform, that we judge their internal likewise to resemble ours; and the same principle of reasoning, carry'd one step farther, will make us conclude that since our internal actions resemble each other, the causes, from which they are deriv'd, must also be resembling. When any hypothesis, therefore, is advanc'd to explain a mental operation, which is common to men and beasts, we must apply the same hypothesis to both; and as every true hypothesis will abide this trial, so I may venture to affirm, that no false one will ever be able to endure it. The common defect of those systems, which philosophers have employ'd to account for the actions of the mind, is, that they suppose such a subtility and refinement of thought, as not only exceeds the capacity of mere animals, but even of

From *A Treatise of Human Nature*, Part 1, Section 16, L. A. Selby-Bigge, ed. (Oxford: Clarendon Press, 1960). Reprinted with permission of the publisher.

children and the common people in our own species; who are notwithstanding susceptible of the same emotions and affections as persons of the most accomplish'd genius and understanding. Such a subtility is a clear proof of the falsehood, as the contrary simplicity of the truth, of any system.

Let us therefore put our present system concerning the nature of the understanding to this decisive trial, and see whether it will equally account for the reasonings of beasts as for these of the human species.

Here we must make a distinction betwixt those actions of animals, which are of a vulgar nature, and seem to be on a level with their common capacities, and those more extraordinary instances of sagacity, which they sometimes discover for their own preservation, and the propagation of their species. A dog, that avoids fire and precipices, that shuns strangers, and caresses his master, affords us an instance of the first kind. A bird, that chooses with such care and nicety the place and materials of her nest, and sits upon her eggs for a due time, and in a suitable season, with all the precaution that a chymist is capable of in the most delicate projection, furnishes us with a lively instance of the second.

As to the former actions, I assert they proceed from a reasoning, that is not in itself different, nor founded on different principles, from that which appears in human nature. 'Tis necessary in the first place, that there be some impression immediately present to their memory or senses, in order to be the foundation of their judgment. From the tone of voice the dog infers his master's anger, and foresees his own punishment. From a certain sensation affecting his smell, he judges his game not to be far distant from him.

Secondly, the inference he draws from the present impression is built on experience, and on his observation of the conjunction of objects in past instances. As you vary this experience, he varies his reasoning. Make a beating follow upon one sign or motion for some time, and afterwards upon another; and he will successively draw different conclusions according to his most recent experience....

Nothing shews more the force of habit in reconciling us to any phenomenon, than this, that men are not astonish'd at the operations of their own reason, at the same time, that they admire the *instinct* of animals, and find a difficulty in explaining it, merely because it cannot be reduc'd to the very same principles. To consider the matter aright, reason is nothing but a wonderful and unintelligible instinct in our souls, which carries us along a certain train of ideas, and endows them with particular qualities, according to their particular situations and relations. This instinct, 'tis true, arises from past observation and experience; but can any one give the ultimate reason, why past experience and observation produces such an effect, any more than why nature alone shou'd produce it? Nature may certainly produce whatever can arise from habit: Nay, habit is nothing but one of the principles of nature, and derives all its force from that origin.

Interests of the Inferior Animals

Jeremy Bentham

Interests of the inferior animals improperly neglected in legislation.... The laws that are have been the work of mutual fear; a sentiment which the less rational animals have not had the same means as man has of turning to account. Why ought they not? No reason can be given. If the being eaten

---

From *An Introduction to the Principles of Morals and Legislation*, 1823 edition.

were all, there is very good reason why we should be suffered to eat such of them as we like to eat: we are the better for it, and they are never the worse. They have none of those long-protracted anticipations of future misery which we have. The death they suffer in our hands commonly is, and always may be, a speedier, and by that means a less painful one, than that which would await them in the inevitable course of nature. If the being killed were all, there is very good reason why we should be suffered to kill such as molest us: we should be the worse for their living, and they are never the worse for being dead. But is there any reason why we should be suffered to torment them? Not any that I can see. Are there any why we should not be suffered to torment them? Yes, several....The day has been, I grieve to say in many places it is *not* yet past, in which the greater part of the species, under the denomination of slaves, have been treated by the law exactly upon the same footing as, in England for example, the inferior races of animals are still. The day may come, when the rest of the animal creation may acquire those rights which never could have been withholden from them but by the hand of tyranny. The French have already discovered that the blackness of the skin is no reason why a human being should be abandoned without redress to the caprice of a tormentor....It may come one day to be recognized, that the number of the legs, the villosity of the skin, or the termination of the *os sacrum*, are reasons equally insufficient for abandoning a sensitive being to the same fate. What else is it that should trace the insuperable line? Is it the faculty of reason, or, perhaps, the faculty of discourse? But a full-grown horse or dog is beyond comparison a more rational, as well as a more conversable animal, than an infant of a day, or a week, or even a month, old. But suppose the case were otherwise, what would it avail? the question is not, Can they *reason*? nor, Can they *talk*? but, Can they *suffer*?...

"Only Humans Have Rights"

David G. Ritchie

If rights are determined solely by reference to human society, it follows that the lower animals, not being members of human society, cannot have rights. This conclusion is resented by many modern humanitarians who, feeling that in some sense or other we may be said to have duties towards the lower animals, or at least duties in respect of our conduct towards them, conclude that the animals in their turn must have rights against us. If a utilitarian theory be based on a consideration of the pleasures of all sentient existence, then, whether or not the phraseology of natural rights be used, all animals must be taken into account in our judgments of right and wrong. Very difficult questions...will, indeed, arise because of the difference in grades of sentience; and the undoubted difference in degree of acuteness of feeling among human beings ought most assuredly to be taken account of also. If the recognition of Animal Rights is compatible with the kindly use of a horse as a beast of burden, would not a kindly negro-slavery be also perfectly compatible with the recognition of Natural Rights generally? And if we discriminate between what may be rightly done to the mollusc from what may be rightly done to the mammal, on grounds of different grades of sentience, should we not also—if sentience be our sole guiding principle—discriminate between what

---

From *Natural Rights* (London: George Allen and Unwin, 1894).

may be rightly done to lower and higher races among mankind—the lower and less civilised being undoubtedly less capable of acute feeling? An ethical theory which is based on the social nature of man is not directly troubled by these difficulties, though in the details of practical conduct these grades of sentience do enter in as one of the factors determining our moral judgments.

The most recent English book of which I know on the subject of *Animals' Rights* is that of Mr. H. S. Salt. "Have the lower animals 'rights'?" he asks, and answers his question, "Undoubtedly—if men have." But the question whether and in what sense men have rights, Mr. Salt refuses to discuss. He takes for granted that in some sense they have rights, and treats the controversy about rights as "little else than an academic battle over words...." Mr. Salt's justification for his assertion, that animals have rights if men have, must be discovered incidentally. First of all, I note that he appeals to the actual state of the law in England. "It is scarcely possible, in the face of this legislation [for the prevention of cruelty to animals], to maintain that 'rights' are a privilege with which none but human beings can be invested; for if *some* animals are already included within the pale of protection, why should not more and more be so included in the future?" Because a work of art or some ancient monument is protected by law from injury, do we speak of the "rights" of pictures or stones? Further, are animals capable of being parties to a lawsuit? It might be answered, they are on the same footing permanently on which human "infants" are temporarily (*i.e.*, until they attain full age). But if there are rights, there are correlative duties. And whereas infants may be tried on a criminal charge, I do not know, apart from a *cause cèlèbre* in Aristophanes, of any such trial of animals in any advanced legal system. Thus it will hardly do to appeal to existing law in proof that animals have rights in any *legal* sense. Again, I note that Mr. Salt quotes with approbation the maxim of the "Buddhist and Pythagorean canons"—"Not to kill or injure any innocent animal," and the words of Bentham: "We have begun by attending to the condition of slaves; we shall finish by softening that of all the animals which assist our labours or supply our wants." Why these limitations of the *jus animalium*? If the animal as such has rights, who are we to pronounce judgment, according to our own human conven-

ience, on his "innocence"? What is the "guilt" from the tiger's point of view of her raid on a human village? Why do we commend a cat that kills mice and punish her if she attacks a tame bird?...

It may be admitted, however, that towards the lower animals we must always stand in the relation of despots; but it may be urged that our despotism ought to be guided by a recognition of their rights. Well, then, in our exercise of our power and in our guardianship of the rights of animals, must we not protect the weak among them against the strong? Must we not put to death blackbirds and thrushes because they feed on worms, or (if capital punishment offends our humanitarianism) starve them slowly by permanent captivity and vegetarian diet? What becomes of the "return to nature" if we must prevent the cat's nocturnal wanderings, lest she should wickedly slay a mouse? Are we not to vindicate the rights of the persecuted prey of the stronger? or is our declaration of the rights of every creeping thing to remain a mere hypocritical formula to gratify pug-loving sentimentalists, who prate about a nature they will not take the trouble to understand—a nature whose genuine students they are ready to persecute? Mr. Salt injures a needed protest against certain barbarities of "sport," and against the habitual callousness of the ignorant in their treatment of animals, by his attacks on men of science and his opposition to the use of animal food. If all the world were Jews, it has been well said, there would be no pigs in existence; and if all the world were vegetarians, would there be any sheep or cattle, well cared for and guarded against starvation? Perhaps a stray specimen in a zoological garden: turnips being all needed for human food. Cruelty to animals is rightly supposed to be an offence against *humanitarian* feeling. Our duty to the animals is a duty to human society. It is an offence against civilised life to cause any unnecessary suffering, or to do any unnecessary damage—"unnecessary" meaning, as it means even in Mr. Salt's theory, unnecessary for *human* well-being. This consideration will explain also why we regard cruelty to domestic animals, especially to pets, with more horror than cruelty to wild animals—especially to dangerous or injurious wild animals. We have admitted certain animals to a sort of honorary membership of our society; and we come to think of them as standing in a quasi-human relation to ourselves, especially when we give them names of their own, as if they were persons. Of Schopenhauer, that poodle-loving hater of man, it might almost be said that he and his dog (the reigning sovereign for the time) formed society by themselves. In a metaphorical sense we may be said to have duties towards these honorary human beings.

Pain is in itself an evil, not in the special moral sense of the term "evil," but in the sense that it is an impediment to the maintenance and development of life: it is an impediment which every normal sentient being "naturally," *i.e.*, by mere instinct, strives to escape, and this instinct is kept alert by natural selection. The growth of sympathy and of imagination makes it possible for human beings to feel mental pain at the sufferings of other human beings, even of those not specially connected with them, and of other animals, in a manner and to an extent impossible in a more primitive stage of existence....And thus the avoidance of pain for other beings capable of feeling it, as well as for oneself, comes to be thought of as a duty, except when the infliction of such pain is necessary and unavoidable in the interests of human society and human progress. Thus we may be said to have duties of *kindness towards* the animals; but it is incorrect to represent these as strictly *duties towards* the animals themselves, as if they had rights against us. If the animals had in any proper sense rights, we should no more be entitled to put them to death without a fair trial, unless in strict self-defence, than to torture them for our amusement. It is our duty to put animals to death as painlessly as possible, when we wish their death for any human end; and similarly, in experiments on living animals for scientific purposes, it is right to prefer the less highly organised animal to the more highly organised, wherever the lower type is clearly sufficient for the purposes of the experiment. It is a duty also not to cause any suffering which is unnecessary for the properly scientific purpose of the experiment....I have already suggested the difficulties which would be involved in any consistent attempt to recognise in animals equal rights with human beings: on the other hand, to fix a scale of unequal rights solely from the point of view of human convenience is practically to give up basing ethics on the mere fact of sentience, and implicitly to recognise the interests of human society as our ultimate criterion of right and wrong....

"The Rights of Animals and Unborn Generations"

Joel Feinberg

Every philosophical paper must begin with an unproved assumption. Mine is the assumption that there will still be a world five hundred years from now, and that it will contain human beings who are very much like us. We have it within our power now, clearly, to affect the lives of these creatures for better or worse by contributing to the conservation or corruption of the environment in which they must live. I shall assume furthermore that it is psychologically possible for us to care about our remote descendants, that many of us in fact do care, and indeed that we ought to care. My main concern then will be to show that it makes sense to speak of the rights of unborn generations against us, and that given the moral judgment that we ought to conserve our environmental inheritance for them, and its grounds, we might well say that future generations do have rights correlative to our pre-

From "The Rights of Animals and Unborn Generations," *Philosophy and Environmental Crisis*, Terrell Hall, ed. (Athens: University of Georgia Press, 1974). Reprinted by permission of the publisher.

sent duties toward them. Protecting our environment now is also a matter of elementary prudence, and insofar as we do it for the next generation already here in the persons of our children, it is a matter of love. But from the perspective of our remote descendants it is basically a matter of justice, of respect for their rights. My main concern here will be to examine the concept of a right to better understand how that can be.

To have a right is to have a claim *to* something and *against* someone, the recognition of which is called for by legal rules or, in the case of moral rights, by the principles of an enlightened conscience. In the familiar cases of rights, the claimant is a competent adult human being, and the claimee is an officeholder in an institution or else a private individual, in either case, another competent adult human being. Normal adult human beings, then, are obviously the sorts of beings of whom rights can meaningfully be predicated. Everyone would agree to that, even extreme misanthropes who deny that anyone in fact has rights. On the other hand, it is absurd to say that rocks can have rights, not because rocks are morally inferior things unworthy of rights (that statement makes no sense either), but because rocks belong to a category of entities of whom rights cannot be meaningfully predicated. That is not to say that there are no circumstances in which we ought to treat rocks carefully, but only that the rocks themselves cannot validly claim good treatment from us. In between the clear cases of rocks and normal human beings, however, is a spectrum of less obvious cases, including some bewildering borderline ones. Is it meaningful or conceptually possible to ascribe rights to our dead ancestors? to individual animals? to whole species of animals? to plants? to idiots and madmen? to fetuses? to generations yet unborn? Until we know how to settle these puzzling cases, we cannot claim fully to grasp the concept of a right, or to know the shape of its logical boundaries.

One way to approach these riddles is to turn one's attention first to the most familiar and unproblematic instances of rights, note their most salient characteristics, and then compare the borderline cases with them, measuring as closely as possible the points of similarity and difference. In the end, the way we classify the borderline cases may depend on whether we are more impressed with the similarities or the differences between

them and the cases in which we have the most confidence.

It will be useful to consider the problem of individual animals first because....When we understand precisely what *is* at issue in the debate over animal rights, I think we will have the key to the solution of all the other riddles about rights.

Almost all modern writers agree that we ought to be kind to animals, but that is quite another thing from holding that animals can claim kind treatment from us as their due. Statutes making cruelty to animals a crime are now very common, and these, of course, impose legal duties on people not to mistreat animals; but that still leaves open the question whether the animals, as beneficiaries of those duties, possess rights correlative to them. We may very well have duties *regarding* animals that are not at the same time duties *to* animals, just as we may have duties regarding rocks, or buildings, or lawns, that are not duties *to* the rocks, buildings, or lawns. Some legal writers have taken the still more extreme position that animals themselves are not even the directly intended beneficiaries of statutes prohibiting cruelty to animals. During the nineteenth century, for example, it was commonly said that such statutes were designed to protect human beings by preventing the growth of cruel habits that could later threaten human beings with harm too. Prof. Louis B. Schwartz finds the rationale of the cruelty-to-animals prohibition in its protection of animal lovers from affronts to their sensibilities. "It is not the mistreated dog who is the ultimate object of concern," he writes. "Our concern is for the feelings of other human beings, a large proportion of whom, although accustomed to the slaughter of animals for food, readily identify themselves with a tortured dog or horse and respond with great sensitivity to its sufferings." This seems to me to be factitious. How much more natural it is to say with John Chipman Gray that the true purpose of cruelty-to-animals statutes is "to preserve the dumb brutes from suffering." The very people whose sensibilities are invoked in the alternative explanation, a group that no doubt now includes most of us, are precisely those who would insist that the protection belongs primarily to the animals themselves, not merely to their own tender feelings. Indeed, it would be difficult even to account for the existence of such feelings in the absence of a belief that the animals deserve the protection in their own right and for their own sakes.

Even if we allow, as I think we must, that animals are the intended direct beneficiaries of legislation forbidding cruelty to animals, it does not follow directly that animals have legal rights, and Gray himself, for one, refused to draw this further inference. Animals cannot have rights, he thought, for the same reason they cannot have duties, namely, that they are not genuine "moral agents." Now, it is relatively easy to see why animals cannot have duties, and this matter is largely beyond controversy. Animals cannot be "reasoned with" or instructed in their responsibilities; they are inflexible and unadaptable to future contingencies; they are subject to fits of instinctive passion which they are incapable of repressing or controlling, postponing or sublimating. Hence, they cannot enter into contractual agreements, or make promises; they cannot be trusted; and they cannot (except within very narrow limits and for purposes of conditioning) be blamed for what would be called "moral failures" in a human being. They are therefore incapable of being moral subjects, of acting rightly or wrongly in the moral sense, of having, discharging, or breeching duties and obligations.

But what is there about the intellectual incompetence of animals (which admittedly disqualifies them for duties) that makes them logically unsuitable for rights? The most common reply to this question is that animals are incapable of *claiming* rights on their own. They cannot make motion, on their own, to courts to have their claims recognized or enforced; they cannot initiate, on their own, any kind of legal proceedings; nor are they capable of even understanding when their rights are being violated, of distinguishing harm from wrongful injury, and responding with indignation and an outraged sense of justice instead of mere anger or fear.

No one can deny any of these allegations, but to the claim that they are the grounds for disqualification of rights of animals, philosophers on the other side of this controversy have made convincing rejoinders. It is simply not true, says W. D. Lamont, that the ability to understand what a right is and the ability to set legal machinery in motion by one's own initiative are necessary for the possession of rights. If that were the case, then neither human idiots nor wee babies would have any legal rights at all. Yet it is manifest that both of these classes of intellectual incompetents have legal rights recognized and easily enforced by the courts. Children and idiots start legal proceedings, not on their own direct initiative, but rather through the actions of proxies or attorneys who are empowered to speak in their names. If there is no conceptual absurdity in this situation, why should there be in the case where a proxy makes a claim on behalf of an animal? People commonly enough make wills leaving money to trustees for the care of animals. Is it not natural to speak of the animal's right to his inheritance in cases of this kind? If a trustee embezzles money from the animal's account, and a proxy speaking in the dumb brute's behalf presses the animal's claim, can he not be described as asserting the animal's *rights*? More exactly, the animal itself claims its rights through the vicarious actions of a human proxy speaking in its name and in its behalf. There appears to be no reason why we should require the animal to understand what is going on...as a condition for regarding it as a possessor of rights.

Some writers protest at this point that the legal relation between a principal and an agent cannot hold between animals and human beings. Between humans, the relation of agency can take two very different forms, depending upon the degree of discretion granted to the agent, and there is a continuum of combinations between the extremes. On the one hand, there is the agent who is the mere "mouthpiece" of his principal. He is a "tool" in much the same sense as is a typewriter or telephone; he simply transmits the instructions of his principal. Human beings could hardly be the agents or representatives of animals in this sense, since the dumb brutes could no more use human "tools" than mechanical ones. On the other hand, an agent may be some sort of expert hired to exercise his professional judgment on behalf of, and in the name of, the principal. He may be given, within some limited area of expertise, complete independence to act as he deems best, binding his principal to all the beneficial or detrimental consequences. This is the role played by trustees, lawyers, and ghost-writers. This type of representation requires that the agent have great skill, but makes little or no demand upon the principal, who may leave everything to the judgment of his agent. Hence, there appears, at first, to be no reason why an animal cannot be a totally passive principal in this second kind of agency relationship.

There are still some important dissimilarities, however. In the typical instance of representation by an agent, even of the second, highly discretionary kind, the agent is hired by a principal who enters into an agreement or contract with him; the principal tells his agent that within certain carefully specified boundaries "You may speak for me," subject always to the principal's approval, his right to give new directions, or to cancel the whole arrangement. No dog or cat could possibly do any of those things. Moreover, if it is the assigned task of the agent to defend the principal's rights, the principal may often decide to release his claimee, or to waive his own rights, and instruct his agent accordingly. Again, no mute cow or horse can do that. But although the possibility of hiring, agreeing, contracting, approving, directing, canceling, releasing, waiving, and instructing is present in the typical (all-human) case of agency representation, there appears to be no reason of a logical or conceptual kind why that *must* be so, and indeed there are some special examples involving human principals where it is not in fact so. I have in mind legal rules, for example, that require that a defendant be represented at his trial by an attorney, and impose a state-appointed attorney upon reluctant defendants, or upon those tried *in absentia*, whether they like it or not. Moreover, small children and mentally deficient and deranged adults are commonly represented by trustees and attorneys, even though they are incapable of granting their own consent to the representation, or of entering into contracts, of giving directions, or waiving their rights. It may be that it is unwise to permit agents to represent principals without the latters' knowledge or consent. If so, then no one should ever be permitted to speak for an animal, at least in a legally binding way. But that is quite another thing than saying that such representation is logically incoherent or conceptually incongruous—the contention that is at issue.

H. J. McCloskey, I believe, accepts the argument up to this point, but he presents a new and different reason for denying that animals can have legal rights. The ability to make claims, whether directly or through a representative, he implies, is essential to the possession of rights. Animals obviously cannot press their claims on their own, and

so if they have rights, these rights must be assertable by agents. Animals, however, cannot be represented, McCloskey contends, and not for any of the reasons already discussed, but rather because representation, in the requisite sense, is always of interests, and animals...are incapable of having interests.

Now, there is a very important insight expressed in the requirement that a being have interests if he is to be a logically proper subject of rights. This can be appreciated if we consider just why it is that mere things cannot have rights. Consider a very precious "mere thing"—a beautiful natural wilderness, or a complex and ornamental artifact, like the Taj Mahal. Such things ought to be cared for, because they would sink into decay if neglected, depriving some human beings, or perhaps even all human beings, of something of great value. Certain persons may even have as their own special job the care and protection of these valuable objects. But we are not tempted in these cases to speak of "thing-rights" correlative to custodial duties, because, try as we might, we cannot think of mere things as possessing interests of their own. Some people may have a duty to preserve, maintain, or improve the Taj Mahal, but they can hardly have a duty to help or hurt it, benefit or aid it, succor or relieve it. Custodians may protect it for the sake of a nation's pride and art lovers' fancy; but they don't keep it in good repair for "its own sake," or for "its own true welfare," or "well-being." A mere thing, however valuable to others, has no good of its own. The explanation of that fact, I suspect, consists in the fact that mere things have no conative life: no conscious wishes, desires, and hopes; or urges and impulses; or unconscious drives, aims, and goals; or latent tendencies, direction of growth, and natural fulfillments. Interests must be compounded somehow out of conations; hence mere things have no interests. *A fortiori*, they have no interests to be protected by legal or moral rules. Without interests a creature can have no "good" of its own, the achievement of which can be its due. Mere things are not loci of value in their own right, but rather their value consists entirely in their being objects of other beings' interests.

So far McCloskey is on solid ground, but one can quarrel with his denial that any animals but humans have interests. I should think that the trustee of funds willed to a dog or cat is more than a mere custodian of the animal he protects. Rather his job is to look out for the interests of the animal and make sure no one denies it its due. The animal itself is the beneficiary of his dutiful services. Many of the higher animals at least have appetites, conative urges, and rudimentary purposes, the integrated satisfaction of which constitutes their welfare or good. We can, of course, with consistency treat animals as mere pests and deny that they have any rights; for most animals, especially those of the lower orders, we have no choice but to do so. But it seems to me, nevertheless, that in general, animals *are* among the sorts of beings of whom rights can meaningfully be predicated and denied.

Now, if a person agrees with the conclusion of the argument thus far, that animals are the sorts of beings that *can* have rights, and further, if he accepts the moral judgment that we ought to be kind to animals, only one further premise is needed to yield the conclusion that some animals do in fact have rights. We must now ask ourselves for whose sake ought we to treat (some) animals with consideration and humaneness? If we conceive our duty to be one of obedience to authority, or to one's own conscience merely, or one of consideration for tender human sensibilities only, then we might still deny that animals have rights, even though we admit that they are the kinds of beings that *can* have rights. But if we hold not only that we ought to treat animals humanely but also that we should do so for the animals' own sake, that such treatment is something we owe animals as their due, something that can be claimed for them, something the withholding of which would be an injustice and a wrong, and not merely a harm, then it follows that we do ascribe rights to animals. I suspect that the moral judgments most of us make about animals do pass these phenomenological tests, so that most of us do believe that animals have right, but are reluctant to say so because of the conceptual confusions about the notion of a right that I have attempted to dispel above.

Now we can extract from our discussion of animal rights a crucial principle for tentative use in the resolution of the other riddles about the applicability of the concept of a right, namely, that the sorts of beings who *can* have rights are precisely those who have (or can have) interests. I have come to this tentative conclusion for two reasons: (1) because a right holder must be capable of being represented and it is impossible to represent a being that has no interests, and (2) because a right holder must be capable of being a beneficiary in his own person, and a being without interests is a being that is incapable of being harmed or benefitted, having no good or "sake" of its own. Thus, a being without interests has no "behalf" to act in, and no "sake" to act for. My strategy now will be to apply the "interest principle," as we can call it, to the other puzzles about rights, while being prepared to modify it where necessary (but as little as possible), in the hope of separating in a consistent and intuitively satisfactory fashion the beings who can have rights from those which cannot.

It is clear that we ought not to mistreat certain plants, and indeed there are rules and regulations imposing duties on persons not to misbehave in respect to certain members of the vegetable kingdom. It is forbidden, for example, to pick wildflowers in the mountainous tundra areas of national parks, or to endanger trees by starting fires in dry forest areas. Members of Congress introduce bills designed, as they say, to "protect" rare redwood trees from commercial pillage. Given this background, it is surprising that no one speaks of plants as having rights. Plants, after all, are not "mere things"; they are vital objects with inherited biological propensities determining their natural growth. Moreover, we do say that certain conditions are "good" or "bad" for plants, thereby suggesting that plants, unlike rocks, are capable of having a "good."...Finally, we are capable of feeling a kind of affection for particular plants, though we rarely personalize them, as we do in the case of animals, by giving them proper names.

Still, all are agreed that plants are not the kinds of beings that can have rights. Plants are never plausibly understood to be the direct intended beneficiaries of rules designed to "protect" them. We wish to keep redwood groves in existence for the sake of human beings who can enjoy their serene beauty, and for the sake of generations of human beings yet unborn. Trees are not the sorts of beings who have their "own sakes," despite the fact that they have biological propensities. Having no conscious wants or goals of their own, trees cannot know satisfaction or frustration, pleasure or pain. Hence, there is no possibility of kind or cruel treatment of trees. In these morally crucial respects, trees differ from the higher species of animals.

Yet trees are not mere things like rocks. They grow and develop according to the laws of their own nature. Aristotle and Aquinas both took trees to have their own "natural ends." Why then do I deny them the status of beings with interests of their own? The reason is that an interest, however the concept is finally to be analyzed, presupposes at least rudimentary cognitive equipment. Interests are compounded out of *desires* and *aims*, both of which presuppose something like *belief*, or cognitive awareness. A desiring creature may want X because he seeks anything that is Ø, and X appears to be Ø to him; or he may be seeking Y, and he believes, or expects, or hopes that X will be a means to Y. If he desires X in order to get Y, this implies that he believes that X will bring Y about, or at least that he has some sort of brute expectation that is a primitive correlate of belief. But what of the desire for Ø (or for Y) itself? Perhaps a creature has such a "desire" as an ultimate set, as if he had come into existence all "wound up" to pursue Ø-ness or Y-ness, and his not to reason why. Such a propensity, I think, would not qualify as a desire. Mere brute longings unmediated by beliefs—longings for one knows not what—might perhaps be a primitive form of consciousness (I don't want to beg that question) but they are altogether different from the sort of thing we mean by "desire," especially when we speak of human beings.

If some such account as the above is correct, we can never have any grounds for attributing a desire or a want to a creature known to be incapable even of rudimentary beliefs; and if desires or wants are the materials interests are made of, mindless creatures have no interests of their own. The law, therefore, cannot have as its intention the protection of their interests, so that "protective legislation" has to be understood as legislation protecting the interests human beings may have in them.

Plant life might nevertheless be thought at first to constitute a hard case for the interest principle for two reasons. In the first place, plants no less than animals are said to have needs of their own. To be sure, we can speak even of mere things as having needs too, but such talk misleads no one into thinking of the need as belonging, in the final analysis, to the "mere thing" itself. If we were so deceived we would not be thinking of the mere thing as a "mere thing" after all. We say, for example, that John Doe's walls need painting, or that Richard Roe's car needs a washing, but we direct our attitudes of sympathy or reproach (as the case may be) to John and Richard, not to their possessions. It would be otherwise, if we observed that some child is in need of a good meal. Our sympathy and concern in that case would be directed at the child himself as the true possessor of the need in question.

The needs of plants might well seem closer to the needs of animals than to the pseudoneeds of mere things. An owner may need a plant (say, for its commercial value or as a potential meal), but the plant itself, it might appear, needs nutrition or cultivation. Our confusion about this matter may stem from language. It is a commonplace that the word *need* is ambiguous. To say that A needs X may be to say either: (1) X is necessary to the achievement of one of A's goals, or to the performance of one of its functions, or (2) X is good for A; its lack would harm A or be injurious or detrimental to him (or it). The first sort of need-statement is value-neutral, implying no comment on the value of the goal or function in question; whereas the second kind of statement about needs commits its maker to a value judgment about what is good or bad for A in the long run, that is, about what is in A's interests.

A being must have interests, therefore, to have needs in the second sense, but any kind of thing, vegetable or mineral, could have needs in the first sense. An automobile needs gas and oil to function, but it is no tragedy for it if it runs out—an empty tank does not hinder or retard its interests. Similarly, to say that a tree needs sunshine and water is to say that without them it cannot grow and survive; but unless the growth and survival of trees are matters of human concern, affecting human interests, practical or aesthetic, the needs of trees alone will not be the basis of any claim of what is "due" them in their own right. Plants may need things in order to discharge their functions, but their functions are assigned by human interests, not their own.

The second source of confusion derives from the fact that we commonly speak of plants as thriving and flourishing, or withering and languishing. One might be tempted to think of these states either as themselves consequences of the possession of interests so that even creatures without wants or beliefs can be said to have interests, or else as grounds independent of the possession of interests for the making of intelligible claims of rights. In either case, plants would be thought of as conceivable possessors of rights after all.

Consider what it means to speak of something as "flourishing." The verb *to flourish* apparently was applied originally and literally to plants only, and in its original sense it meant simply "to bear flowers: BLOSSOM"; but then by analogical extension of sense it came also to mean "to grow luxuriantly: increase, and enlarge," and then to "THRIVE" (generally), and finally, when extended to human beings, "to be prosperous," or to "increase in wealth, honor, comfort, happiness, or whatever is desirable." [*Webster's Third New International Dictionary*] Applied to human beings the term is, of course, a fixed metaphor. When a person flourishes, something happens to his interests analogous to what happens to a plant when it flowers, grows, and spreads. A person flourishes when his interests (whatever they may be) are progressing severally and collectively toward their harmonious fulfillment and spawning new interests along the way whose prospects are also good. To flourish is to glory in the advancement of one's interests, in short, to be happy....

To speak of thriving human interests as if they were flowers is to speak naturally and well, and to mislead no one. But then to think of the flowers or plants as if they were interests (or the signs of interests) is to bring the metaphor back full circle for no good reason and in the teeth of our actual beliefs. Some of our talk about flourishing plants reveals quite clearly that the interests that thrive when plants flourish are human not "plant interests." For example, we sometimes make a flowering bush flourish by "frustrating" its own primary propensities. We pinch off dead flowers before seeds have formed, thus "encouraging" the plant to make new flowers in an effort to produce more seeds. It is not the plant's own natural propensity (to produce seeds) that is advanced, but rather the gardener's interest in the production of new flowers and the spectator's pleasure in aesthetic form, color, or scent. What we mean in such cases by saying that the plant flourishes is that our interest in the plant, not its own, is thriving. It is not always so clear that that is what we mean, for on other occasions there is a correspondence between our interests and the plant's natural propensities, a coinciding of what we want from nature and nature's own "intention." But the exceptions to this correspondence provide the clue to our real sense in speaking of a plant's good or welfare. And even when there exists such a correspondence, it is often because we have actually remade the plant's nature

so that our interests in it will flourish more "naturally" and effectively.

The topic of whole species, whether of plants or animals, can be treated in much the same way as that of individual plants. A whole collection, as such, cannot have beliefs, expectations, wants, or desires, and can flourish or languish only in the human interest-related sense in which individual plants thrive and decay. Individual elephants can have interests, but the species elephant cannot. Even where individual elephants are not granted rights, human beings may have an interest—economic, scientific, or sentimental—in keeping the species from dying out, and *that* interest may be protected in various ways by law. But that is quite another matter from recognizing a right to survival belonging to the species itself. Still, the preservation of a whole species may quite properly seem to be a morally more important matter than the preservation of an individual animal. Individual animals can have rights but it is implausible to ascribe to them a right to life on the human model. Nor do we normally have duties to keep individual animals alive or even to abstain from killing them provided we do it humanely and nonwantonly in the promotion of legitimate human interests. On the other hand, we do have duties to protect threatened species, not duties to the species themselves as such, but rather duties to future human beings, duties derived from our housekeeping role as temporary inhabitants of this planet.

We commonly and very naturally speak of corporate entities, such as institutions, churches, and national states as having rights and duties, and an adequate analysis of the conditions for ownership of rights should account for that fact. A corporate entity, of course, is more than a mere collection of things that have some important traits in common. Unlike a biological species, an institution has a charter, or constitution, or bylaws, with rules defining offices and procedures, and it has human beings whose function it is to administer the rules and apply the procedures. When the institution has a duty to an outsider, there is always some determinant human being whose duty it is to do something for the outsider, and when the state, for example, has a right to collect taxes, there are always certain definite flesh and blood persons who have rights to demand tax money from other citizens. We have no reluctance to use the language of corporate rights and duties because we know that in the last analysis these are rights or duties of individual persons, acting in their "official capacities." And when individuals act in their official roles in accordance with valid empowering rules, their acts are imputable to the organization itself and become "acts of state." Thus, there is no need to posit any individual superperson named by the expression "the State" (or for that matter, "the company," "the club," or "the church.") Nor is there any reason to take the rights of corporate entities to be exceptions to the interest principle. The United States is not a superperson with wants and beliefs of its own, but it is a corporate entity with corporate interests that are, in turn, analyzable into the interests of its numerous flesh and blood members.

So far we have refined the interest principle but we have not had occasion to modify it. Applied to dead persons, however, it will have to be stretched to near the breaking point if it is to explain, how our duty to honor commitments to the dead can be thought to be linked to the rights of the dead against us. The case against ascribing rights to dead men can be made very simply: a dead man is a mere corpse, a piece of decaying organic matter. Mere inanimate things can have no interests, and what is incapable of having interests is incapable of having rights. If, nevertheless, we grant dead men rights against us, we would seem to be treating the interests they had while alive as somehow surviving their deaths. There is the sound of paradox in this way of talking, but it may be the least paradoxical way of describing our moral relations to our predecessors. And if the idea of an interest's surviving its possessor's death is a kind of fiction, it is a fiction that most living men have a real interest in preserving.

Most persons while still alive have certain desires about what is to happen to their bodies, their property, or their reputations after they are dead. For that reason, our legal system has developed procedures to enable persons while still alive to determine whether their bodies will be used for purposes of medical research or organic transplantation, and to whom their wealth (after taxes) is to be transferred. Living men also take out life insurance policies guaranteeing that the accumulated benefits be conferred upon beneficiaries of their own choice. They also make private agreements, both contractual and informal, in which they receive promises that certain things will be done after

their deaths in exchange for some present service or consideration. In all these cases promises are made to living persons that their wishes will be honored after they are dead. Like all other valid promises, they impose duties on the promisor and confer correlative rights on the promisee.

How does the situation change after the promisee has died? Surely the duties of the promisor do not suddenly become null and void. If that were the case, and known to be the case, there could be no confidence in promises regarding posthumous arrangements; no one would bother with wills or life insurance policies. Indeed the duties of courts and trustees to honor testamentary directions, and the duties of life insurance companies to pay benefits to survivors, are, in a sense, only conditional duties before a man dies. They come into existence as categorical demands for immediate action only upon the promisee's death. So the view that death renders them null and void has the truth exactly upside down.

The survival of the promisor's duty after the promisee's death does not prove that the promisee retains a right even after death, for we might prefer to conclude that there is one class of cases where duties to keep promises are not logically correlated with a promisee's right, namely, cases where the promisee has died. Still, a morally sensitive promisor is likely to think of his promised performance not only as a duty (i.e., a morally required action) but also as something owed to the deceased promisee as his due. Honoring such promises is a way of keeping faith with the dead. To be sure, the promisor will not think of his duty as something to be done for the promisee's "good," since the promisee, being dead, has no "good" of his own. We can think of certain of the deceased's interests, however, (including especially those enshrined in wills and protected by contracts and promises) as surviving their owner's death, and constituting claims against us that persist beyond the life of the claimant. Such claims can be represented by proxies just like the claims of animals. This way of speaking, I believe, reflects more accurately than any other an important fact about the human condition: we have an interest while alive that other interests of ours will continue to be recognized and served after we are dead. The whole practice of honoring wills and testaments, and the like, is thus for the sake of the living, just as a particular instance of it may be thought to be for the sake of one who is dead.

Conceptual sense, then, can be made of talk about dead men's rights; but it is still a wide open moral question whether dead men in fact have rights, and if so, what those rights are. In particular, commentators have disagreed over whether a man's interest in his reputation deserves to be protected from defamation even after his death. With only a few prominent exceptions, legal systems punish a libel on a dead man "only when its publication is in truth an attack upon the interests of living persons."...

This presupposes, however, that the whole point of guarding the reputations even of living men, is to protect them from hurt feelings, or to protect some other interests, for example, economic ones, that do not survive death. A moment's thought, I think, will show that our interests are more complicated than that. If someone spreads a libelous description of me, without my knowledge, among hundreds of persons in a remote part of the country, so that I am, still without my knowledge, an object of general scorn and mockery in that group, I have been injured, even though I never learn what has happened. That is because I have an interest, so I believe, in having a good reputation *simpliciter*, in addition to my interest in avoiding hurt feelings, embarrassment, and economic injury. In the example, I do not know what is being said and believed about me, so my feelings are not hurt; but clearly if I did know; I would be enormously distressed. The distress would be the natural consequence of my belief that an interest other than my interest in avoiding distress had been damaged. How else can I account for the distress? If I had no interest in a good reputation as such, I would respond to news of harm to my reputation with indifference.

While it is true that a dead man cannot have his feelings hurt, it does not follow, therefore, that his claim to be thought of no worse than he deserves cannot survive his death. Almost every living person, I should think, would wish to have this interest protected after his death, at least during the lifetimes of those persons who were his contemporaries. We can hardly expect the law to protect Julius Caesar from defamation in the history books. This might hamper historical research and restrict socially valuable forms of expression. Even interests that survive their owner's death are not immortal. Anyone should be permitted to say anything he wishes about George Washington or Abraham Lincoln, though perhaps not everything is morally permissible. Everyone ought to refrain from malicious lies even about Nero or King Tut, though not so much for those ancients' own sakes as for the sake of those who would now know the truth about the past. We owe it to the brothers Kennedy, however, as their due, not to tell damaging lies about them to those who were once their contemporaries. If the reader would deny that judgment, I can only urge him to ask himself whether he now wishes his own interest in reputation to be respected, along with his interest in determining the distribution of his wealth, after his death.

Mentally deficient and deranged human beings are hardly ever so handicapped intellectually that they do not compare favorably with even the highest of the lower animals, though they are commonly so incompetent that they cannot be assigned duties or be held responsible for what they do. Since animals can have rights, then, it follows that human idiots and madmen can too. It would make good sense, for example, to ascribe to them a right to be cured whenever effective therapy is available at reasonable cost, and even those incurables who have been consigned to a sanatorium for permanent "warehousing" can claim (through a proxy) their right to decent treatment.

Human beings suffering extreme cases of mental illness, however, may be so utterly disoriented or insensitive as to compare quite unfavorably with the brightest cats and dogs. Those suffering from catatonic schizophrenia may be barely distinguishable in respect to those traits presupposed by the possession of interests from the lowliest vegetables. So long as we regard these patients as potentially curable, we may think of them as human beings with interests in their own restoration and treat them as possessors of rights. We may think of the patient as a genuine human person inside the vegetable casing struggling to get out, just as in the old fairy tales a pumpkin could be thought of as a beautiful maiden under a magic spell waiting only the proper words to be restored to her true self. Perhaps it is reasonable never to lose hope that a patient can be cured, and therefore to regard him always as a person "under a spell" with a permanent interest in his own recovery that is entitled to recognition and protection.

What if, nevertheless, we think of the catatonic schizophrenic and the vegetating patient with irreversible brain damage as absolutely incurable? Can we think of them at the same time as possessed of interests and rights too, or is this combination of traits a conceptual impossibility? Shocking as it may at first seem, I am driven unavoidably to the latter view. If redwood trees and rosebushes cannot have rights, neither can incorrigible human vegetables. The trustees who are designated to administer funds for the care of these unfortunates are better understood as mere custodians than as representatives of their interests since these patients no longer have interests. It does not follow that they should not be kept alive as long as possible: that is an open moral question not foreclosed by conceptual analysis. Even if we have duties to keep human vegetables alive, however, they cannot be duties *to* them. We may be obliged to keep them alive to protect the sensibilities of others, or to foster humanitarian tendencies in ourselves, but we cannot keep them alive for their own good, for they are no longer capable of having a "good" of their own. Without awareness, expectation, belief, desire, aim, and purpose, a being can have no interests; without interests, he cannot be benefited; without the capacity to be a beneficiary, he can have no rights. But there may nevertheless be a dozen other reasons to treat him as if he did.

If the interest principle is to permit us to ascribe rights to infants, fetuses, and generations yet unborn, it can only be on the grounds that interests can exert a claim upon us even before their possessors actually come into being, just the reverse of the situation respecting dead men where interests are respected even after their possessors have ceased to be. Newly born infants are surely noisier than mere vegetables, but they are just barely brighter. They come into existence, as Aristotle said, with the capacity to acquire concepts and dispositions, but in the beginning we suppose that their consciousness of the world is a "blooming, buzzing confusion." They do have a capacity, no doubt from the very beginning, to feel pain, and this alone may be sufficient ground for ascribing both an interest and a right to them. Apart from that, however, during the first few hours of their lives, at least, they may well lack even the rudimentary intellectual equipment necessary to the possession of interests. Of course, this induces no moral reservations whatever in adults. Children grow and mature almost visibly in the first few months so that those future interests that are so rapidly emerging from the unformed chaos of their earliest days seem unquestionably to be the basis of their present rights. Thus, we say of a newborn infant that he has a right now to live and grow into his adulthood, even though he lacks the conceptual equipment at this very moment to have this or any other desire. A new infant, in short, lacks the traits necessary for the possession of interests, but he has the capacity to acquire those traits, and his inherited potentialities are moving quickly toward actualization even as we watch him. Those proxies who make claims in behalf of infants, then, are more than mere custodians: they are (or can be) genuine representatives of the child's emerging interests, which may need protection even now if they are to be allowed to come into existence at all.

The same principle may be extended to "unborn persons." After all, the situation of fetuses one day before birth is not strikingly different from that a few hours after birth. The rights our law confers on the unborn child, both proprietary and personal, are for the most part, placeholders or reservations for the rights he shall inherit when he becomes a full-fledged interested being. The law protects a potential interest in these cases before it has even grown into actuality, as a garden fence protects newly seeded flower beds long before blooming flowers have emerged from them. The unborn child's present right to property, for example, is a legal protection offered now to his future interest, contingent upon his birth, and instantly voidable if he dies before birth. As Coke put it: "The law in many cases hath consideration of him in respect of the apparent expectation of his birth"; but this is quite another thing than recognizing a right actually to be born. Assuming that the child will be born, the law seems to say, various interests that he will come to have after birth must be protected from damage that they can incur even before birth. Thus prenatal injuries of a negligently inflicted kind can give the newly born child a right to sue for damages which he can exercise through a proxy-attorney and in his own name any time *after* he is born.

There are numerous other places, however, where our law seems to imply an unconditional right to be born, and surprisingly no one seems ever to have found that idea conceptually absurd. One interesting example comes from an article given the following headline by the *New York Times*: "Unborn Child's Right Upheld Over Religion." A hospital patient in her eighth month of pregnancy refused to take a blood transfusion even though warned by her physician that "she might die at any minute and take the life of her child as well." The ground of her refusal was that blood transfusions are repugnant to the principles of her religion (Jehovah's Witnesses). The Supreme Court of New Jersey expressed uncertainty over the constitutional question of whether a nonpregnant adult might refuse on religious grounds a blood transfusion pronounced necessary to her own survival, but the court nevertheless ordered the patient in the present case to receive the transfusion on the grounds that "the unborn child is entitled to the law's protection."

It is important to reemphasize here that the questions of whether fetuses do or ought to have rights are substantive questions of law and morals open to argument and decision. The prior question of whether fetuses are the kind of beings that can have rights, however, is a conceptual, not a moral, question, amenable only to what is called "logical analysis," and irrelevant to moral judgment. The correct answer to the conceptual question, I believe, is that unborn children are among the sorts of beings of whom possession of rights can meaningfully be predicated, even though they are (temporarily) incapable of having interests, because their future interests can be protected now, and it does make sense to protect a potential interest even before it has grown into actuality. The interest principle, however, makes perplexing, at best, talk of a noncontingent fetal right to be born; for fetuses, lacking actual wants and beliefs, have no actual interest in being born, and it is difficult to think of any other reason for ascribing any rights to them other than on the assumption that they will in fact be born.

We have it in our power now to make the world a much less pleasant place for our descendants than the world we inherited from our ancestors. We can continue to proliferate in ever greater numbers, using up fertile soil at an even greater rate, dumping our wastes into rivers, lakes, and oceans, cutting down our forests, and polluting the atmosphere with noxious gases. All thoughtful people agree that we ought not to do these things. Most would say that we have a duty not to do these things, meaning not merely that conservation is morally required (as opposed to merely desirable) but also that it is something due our descendants, something to be done for their sakes. Surely we

owe it to future generations to pass on a world that is not a used up garbage heap. Our remote descendants are not yet present to claim a livable world as their right, but there are plenty of proxies to speak now in their behalf. These spokesmen, far from being mere custodians, are genuine representatives of future interests.

Why then deny that the human beings of the future have rights which can be claimed against us now in their behalf? Some are inclined to deny them present rights out of a fear of falling into obscure metaphysics, by granting rights to remote and unidentifiable beings who are not yet even in existence. Our unborn great-great-grandchildren are in some sense "potential" persons, but they are far more remotely potential, it may seem, than fetuses. This, however, is not the real difficulty. Unborn generations are more remotely potential than fetuses in one sense, but not in another. A much greater period of time with a far greater number of causally necessary and important events must pass before their potentiality can be actualized, it is true; but our collective posterity is just as certain to come into existence "in the normal course of events" as is any given fetus now in its mother's womb. In that sense the existence of the distant human future is no more remotely potential than that of a particular child already on its way.

The real difficulty is not that we doubt whether our descendants will ever be actual, but rather that we don't know who they will be. It is not their temporal remoteness that troubles us so much as their indeterminacy—their present facelessness and namelessness. Five centuries from now men and women will be living where we live now. Any given one of them will have an interest in living space, fertile soil, fresh air, and the like, but that arbitrarily selected one has no other qualities we can presently envision very clearly. We don't even know who his parents, grandparents, or great-grandparents are, or even whether he is related to us. Still, whoever these human beings may turn out to be, and whatever they might reasonably be expected to be like, they will have interests that we can affect, for better or worse, right now. That much we can and do know about them. The identity of the owners of these interests is now necessarily obscure, but the fact of their interest-ownership is crystal clear, and that is all that is necessary to certify the coherence of present talk about their rights. We can tell, sometimes, that shadowy forms in the spatial distance belong to human beings, though we know not who or how many they are; and this imposes a duty on us not to throw bombs, for example, in their direction. In like manner, the vagueness of the human future does not weaken its claim on us in light of the nearly certain knowledge that it will, after all, be human.

Doubts about the existence of a right to be born transfer neatly to the question of a similar right to come into existence ascribed to future generations. The rights that future generations certainly have against us are contingent rights: the interests they are sure to have when they come into being (assuming of course that they will come into being) cry out for protection from invasions that can take place now. Yet there are no actual interests, presently existent, that future generations, presently nonexistent, have now. Hence, there is no actual interest that they have in simply coming into being, and I am at a loss to think of any other reason for claiming that they have a right to come into existence (though there may well be such a reason). Suppose then that all human beings at a given time voluntarily form a compact never again to produce children, thus leading within a few decades to the end of our species. This of course is a wildly improbable hypothetical example but a rather crucial one for the position I have been tentatively considering. And we can imagine, say, that the whole world is converted to a strange ascetic religion which absolutely requires sexual abstinence for everyone. Would this arrangement violate the rights of anyone? No one can complain on behalf of presently nonexistent future generations that their future interests which give them a contingent right of protection have been violated since they will never come into existence to be wronged. My inclination then is to conclude that the suicide of our species would be deplorable, lamentable, and a deeply moving tragedy, but that it would violate no one's rights. Indeed if, contrary to fact, all human beings could ever agree to such a thing, that very agreement would be a symptom of our species' biological unsuitability for survival anyway.

For several centuries now human beings have run roughshod over the lands of our planet, just as if the animals who do live there and the generations of humans who will live there had no claims on them whatever. Philosophers have not helped matters by arguing that animals and future generations are not the kinds of beings who can have rights now, that they don't presently qualify for membership, even "auxiliary membership," in our moral community. I have tried in this essay to dispel the conceptual confusions that make such conclusions possible. To acknowledge their rights is the very least we can do for members of endangered species (including our own). But that is something.

"Rights, Interests, Desires and Beliefs"

R. G. Frey

The question of whether non-human animals possess moral rights is once again being widely argued. Doubtless the rise of ethology is partly responsible for this: as we learn more about the behavior of animals, it seems inevitable that we shall be led to focus upon the similarities between them and us, with the result that the extension of moral rights from human beings to non-human animals can appear, as the result of these similarities, to have a firm basis in nature....But the major impetus to

From R. G. Frey, "Rights, Interests, Desires and Beliefs," *American Philosophical Quarterly*, 16 (1979). Reprinted by permission of the publisher and the author.

renewed interest in the subject of animal rights almost certainly stems from a heightened and more critical awareness, among philosophers and non-philosophers alike, of the arguments for and against eating animals and using them in scientific research. For if animals *do* have moral rights, such as a right to live and to live free from unnecessary suffering, and if our present practices systematically tread upon these rights, then the case for eating and experimenting upon animals, especially when other alternatives are for the most part readily available, is going to have to be a powerful one indeed.

It is important, however, not to misconstrue the question: the question is not about which rights animals may or may not be thought to possess or about whether their alleged rights in a particular regard are on a par with the alleged rights of humans in this same regard but rather about the more fundamental issue of whether animals—or, in any event, the "higher" animals—are a kind of being which can be the logical subject of rights. It is this issue, and a particular position with respect to it, that I want critically to address here.

The position I have in mind is the widely influential one which links the possession of rights to the possession of interests. In his *System of Ethics*, Leonard Nelson is among the first, if not the first, to propound the view that all and only beings which have interests can have rights, a view which has attracted an increasingly wide following ever since. For example, in his paper "Rights," H. J. McCloskey embraces this view but goes on to deny that animals have interests; whereas Joel Feinberg, in his seminal paper "The Rights of Animals and Unborn Generations," likewise embraces the view but goes on to affirm that animals do have interests. Nelson himself is emphatic that animals as well as human beings are, as he puts it, "carriers of interests," and he concludes, accordingly, that animals possess rights, rights which both deserve and warrant our respect. For Nelson, then, it is because animals have interests that they can be the logical subject of rights, and his claim that animals *do have* interests forms the minor premiss, therefore, in an argument for the moral rights of animals:

All and only beings which (can) have interests (can) have moral rights; Animals as well as humans (can) have interests; Therefore, animals (can) have moral rights.

Both McCloskey and Feinberg accept the major premiss of this argument, which I shall dub the interest thesis, but disagree over the truth of the minor premiss; and it is apparent that the minor premiss is indeed the key to the whole matter. For given the truth of the major premiss, given, that is, that the possession of interests *is* a criterion for the possession of rights; it is nevertheless only the truth of the minor premiss that would result in the inclusion of creatures other than human beings within the class of right-holders. This premiss is doubtful, however, and the case against it a powerful one, or so I want to suggest.

This case is not that developed by McCloskey, whose position is not free of a rather obvious difficulty. He makes the issue of whether animals have interests turn upon their failure and/or inability to grasp and so behave in accordance with the prescriptive overtone which he takes talk of "*X* is in *A*'s interests" to have, when it is not obvious that expressions like "*X* is in *A*'s interests" do have a prescriptive overtone and certainly not obvious that a prescriptive overtone is part of the meaning of such expressions....

To say that "Good health is in John's interests" is not at all the same thing as to say that "John has an interest in good health." The former is intimately bound up with having a good or well-being to which good health is conducive, so that we could just as easily have said "Good health is conducive to John's good or well-being," whereas the latter— "John has an interest in good health"—is intimately bound up with wanting, with John's wanting good health. That these two notions of "interest" are logically distinct is readily apparent: good health may well be in John's interests, in the sense of being conducive to his good or well-being, even if John does not want good health, indeed, even if he wants to continue taking hard drugs, with the result that his health is irreparably damaged; and John may have an interest in taking drugs, in the sense of wanting to take them, even if it is apparent to him that it is not conducive to his good or well-being to continue to do so. In other words, something can be *in* John's interests without John's *having* an interest in it, and John can *have* an interest in something without its being *in* his interests.

If this is right, and there are these two logically distinct senses of "interest," we can go on to ask whether animals can have interests in either of these senses; and if they do, then perhaps the minor premiss of Nelson's argument for the moral rights of animals can be sustained.

Do animals, therefore, have interests in the first sense, in the sense of having a good or well-being which can be harmed or benefited? The answer, I think, is that they certainly do have interests in this sense; after all, it is plainly not good for a dog to be fed certain types of food or to be deprived of a certain amount of exercise. This answer, however, is of little use to the Nelsonian cause; for it yields the counter-intuitive result that manmade/manufactured objects and even things have interests, and, therefore, on the interest thesis, have or at least are candidates for having moral rights. For example, just as it is not good for a dog to be deprived of a certain amount of exercise, so it is not good for prehistoric cave drawings to be exposed to excessive amounts of carbon dioxide or for Rembrandt paintings to be exposed to excessive amounts of sunlight.

If, nevertheless, one is inclined to doubt that the notion of "not being good for" in the above examples shows that the object or thing in question "has a good," consider the case of tractors: anything, including tractors, can have a good, a well-being, I submit, if it is the sort of thing that can be good of its kind; and there are obviously good and bad tractors. A tractor which cannot perform certain tasks is not a good tractor, is not good of its kind; it falls short of those standards tractors must meet in order to be good ones. Thus, to say that it is in a tractor's interests to be well-oiled means only that it is conducive to the tractor's being a good one, good of its kind, if it is well-oiled. Just as John is good of his kind (i.e., human being) only if he is in health, so tractors are good of their kind only if they are well-oiled. Of course, farmers *have an interest* in their tractors being well-oiled; but this does not show that being well-oiled is not in a tractor's interest, in the sense of contributing to its being good of its kind. It *may* show that what makes good tractors good depends upon the purposes for which *we* make them; but the fact that we make them for certain purposes in no way shows that, once they are made, they cannot have a good of their own. Their good is being good of their kind, and being well-oiled is conducive to their being good of their kind and so, in this sense, in their interests. If this is right, if tractors do have interests, then on the

interest thesis they have or can have moral rights, and this is a counter-intuitive result.

It is tempting to object, I suppose, that tractors cannot be harmed and benefited and, therefore, cannot have interests. My earlier examples, however, suffice to meet this objection. Prehistoric cave drawings are (not benefited but) positively harmed by excessive amounts of carbon dioxide, and Rembrandt paintings are likewise certainly harmed through exposure to excessive amounts of sunlight. It must be emphasized that it is these objects themselves that are harmed, and that their owners are harmed only in so far as and to the extent that the objects themselves undergo harm. Accordingly, on the present objection, interests are present, and the interest thesis once again gives the result that objects or things have or can have moral rights. To accommodate those, should there be any, who just might feel that objects or things can have moral rights, when these objects or things are, e.g., significant works of art, the examples can be suitably altered, so that what is harmed is, e.g., a quite ordinary rug. But if drawings, paintings and rugs can be harmed, why not tractors? Surely a tractor is harmed by prolonged exposure to rain? And surely the harm the tractor's owner suffers comes through and is a function of the harm to the tractor itself?

In short, it cannot be in this first sense of "interest" that the case for animals and for the truth of Nelson's minor premiss is to be made; for though animals do have interests in this sense, so, too, do tractors, with awkward results.

Do animals, therefore, have interests in the second sense, in the sense of having wants which can be satisfied or left unsatisfied? In this sense, of course, it appears that tractors do not have interests; for though being well-oiled may be conducive to tractors being good of their kind, tractors do not *have an interest* in being well-oiled, since they cannot *want* to be well-oiled, cannot, in fact, have any wants whatever. But farmers can have wants, and they certainly have an interest in their tractors being well-oiled.

What, then, about animals? Can they have wants? By "wants," I understand a term that encompasses both needs and desires, and it is these that I shall consider.

If to ask whether animals can have wants is to ask whether they can have needs, then certainly animals have wants. A dog can need water. But *this* cannot be the sense of "want" on which having interests will depend, since it does not exclude things from the class of want-holders. Just as dogs need water in order to function normally, so tractors need oil in order to function normally; and just as dogs will die unless their need for water is satisfied, so trees and grass and a wide variety of plants and shrubs will die unless their need for water is satisfied. Though we should not give the fact undue weight, someone who in ordinary discourse says "The tractor wants oiling" certainly means the tractor needs oiling, if it is not to fall away from those standards which make tractors good of their kind. Dogs, too, need water, if they are not to fall away from the standards which make them good of their kind. It is perhaps worth emphasizing, moreover, as the cases of the tractor, trees, grass, etc., show, that needs do not require the presence either of consciousness or of knowledge of the lack which makes up the need. If, in sum, we are to agree that tractors, trees, grass, etc., do not have wants, and, therefore, interests, it cannot be the case that wants are to be construed as needs.

This, then, leaves desires, and the question of whether animals can have wants as desires. I may as well say at once that I do not think animals can have desires. My reasons for thinking this turn largely upon my doubts that animals can have beliefs, and my doubts in this regard turn partially, though in large part, upon the view that having beliefs is not compatible with the absence of language and linguistic ability. I realize that the claim that animals cannot have desires is a controversial one; but I think the case to be made in support of it, complex though it is, is persuasive....

Suppose I am a collector of rare books and desire to own a Gutenberg Bible: my desire to own this volume is *to be traced* to my belief that I do not now own such a work and that my rare book collection is deficient in this regard. By "to be traced" here, what I mean is this: if someone were to ask *how* my belief that my book collection lacks a Gutenberg Bible is connected with my desire to own such a Bible, what better or more direct reply could be given that that, without this belief, I would not have this desire? For if I believed that my rare book collection *did* contain a Gutenberg Bible and so was complete in this sense, then I would not desire a Gutenberg Bible in order to make up what I now believe to be a notable deficiency in my

collection. (Of course, I might desire to own more than one such Bible, but this contingency is not what is at issue here.)

Now what is it that I believe? I believe that my collection lacks a Gutenberg Bible; that is, I believe that the sentence "My collection lacks a Gutenberg Bible" is true. In constructions of the form "I believe that...," what follows upon the "that" is a declarative sentence; and *what* I believe is that that sentence is true. The same is the case with constructions of the form "He believes that...": what follows upon the "that" is a declarative sentence, and what the "he" in question believes is that that sentence is true. The difficulty in the case of animals should be apparent: if someone were to say, e.g., "The cat believes that the door is locked," then that person is holding, as I see it, that the cat holds the declarative sentence "The door is locked" to be true; and I can see no reason whatever for crediting the cat or any other creature which lacks language, including human infants, with entertaining declarative sentences and holding certain declarative sentences to be true.

Importantly, nothing whatever in this account is affected by changing the example, in order to rid it of sophisticated concepts like "door" and "locked," which in any event may be thought beyond cats, and to put in their place more rudimentary concepts. For the essence of this account is not about the relative sophistication of this or that concept but rather about the relationship between believing something and entertaining and regarding as true certain declarative sentences. If what is believed is that a certain declarative sentence is true, then no creature which lacks language can have beliefs; and without beliefs, a creature cannot have desires. And this is the case with animals, or so I suggest; and if I am right, not even in the sense, then, of wants as desires do animals have interests, which, to recall, is the minor premiss in the Nelsonian argument for the moral rights of animals.

But is what is believed that a certain declarative sentence is true? I think there are three arguments of sorts that shore up the claim that this *is* what is believed.

First, I do not see how a creature could have the concept of belief without being able to distinguish between true and false beliefs. When I believe that my collection of rare books lacks a Gutenberg Bible, I believe that it is true that my collection lacks a

Gutenberg Bible; put another way, I believe that it is false that my collection contains a Gutenberg Bible. I can distinguish, and do distinguish, between the sentences "My collection lacks a Gutenberg Bible" and "My collection contains a Gutenberg Bible," and it is only the former I hold to be true. According to my view, what I believe in this case is that this sentence is true; and sentences are the sorts of things we regard as or hold to be true. As for the cat, and leaving aside now all questions about the relative sophistication of concepts, I do not see how it could have the belief that the door is locked unless it could distinguish this true belief from the false belief that the door is unlocked. But what is true or false are not states of affairs which correspond to or reflect or pertain to these beliefs; states of affairs are not true or false but either are or are not the case, either do or do not obtain. If, then, one is going to credit cats with beliefs, and cats must be able to distinguish true from false beliefs, and states of affairs are not true or false, then what exactly is it that cats are being credited with distinguishing as true or false? Reflection on this question, I think, forces one to credit cats with language, in order for there to be something that can be true or false in belief; and it is precisely because they lack language that we cannot make this move.

Second, if in order to have the concept of belief a creature must be possessed of the difference between true and false belief, then in order for a creature to be able to distinguish true from false beliefs that creature must—simply must, as I see it—have some awareness of, to put the matter in the most general terms, how language connects with, links up with the world; and I see no reason to credit cats with such an awareness. My belief that my collection lacks a Gutenberg Bible is true if and only if my collection lacks a Gutenberg Bible; that is, the *truth* of this belief cannot be entertained by me without it being the case that I am aware that the truth of the sentence "My collection lacks a Gutenberg Bible" is *at the very least* partially a function of how the world is. However difficult to capture, it is this relationship between language and the world a grasp of which is necessary if a creature is to grasp the difference between true and false belief, a distinction which it must grasp, if it is to possess the concept of belief at all.

Third, I do not see how a creature could have an awareness or grasp of how language connects with, links up with the world, to leave the matter at its most general, unless that creature was itself possessed of language; and cats are not possessed of language. If it were to be suggested, for example, that the sounds that cats make do amount to a language, I should deny it. This matter is far too large and complex to be tackled here; but the general line of argument I should use to support my denial can be sketched in a very few words. Can cats lie? If they cannot, then they cannot assert anything; and if they lack assertion, I do not see how they could possess a language. And I should be strict: I do not suggest that, lacking assertion, cats possess a language in some attenuated or secondary sense; rather, I suggest that, lacking assertion, they do not possess a language *at all*.

It may be suggested, of course, that there might possibly be a class of desires—let us call them simple desires—which do not involve the intervention of belief, in order to have them, and which do not require that we credit animals with language. Such simple desires, for example, might be for some object or other, and we as language-users might try to capture these simple desires in the case of a dog by describing its behavior in such terms as "The dog simply desires the bone." (This position may have to be complicated, as the result of questions about whether the dog possesses the concept "bone" or even more general concepts such as "material object," "thing" and "thing in my visual field"; but these questions I shall leave aside here.) If all the dog's desires are simple desires, and this is the point, then my arguments to show that dogs lack beliefs may well be beside the point.

A subsidiary argument is required, therefore, in order to cover this possibility. Suppose, then, the dog simply desires the bone: is the dog aware that it has this simple desire or not? If it is alleged to have this desire but to be unaware that it has it, to want but to be unaware that it wants, then a problem arises. In the case of human beings, unconscious desire can be made sense of, but only because we first make sense of conscious desire; but where no desires are conscious ones, where the creature in question is alleged to have only unconscious desires, what cash value can the use of the term "desire" have in such a case? This question must be appreciated against the backdrop of what appears to ensue as a result of the present claim. On the strength of the dog's behavior, it is claimed that the dog simply desires the bone; the desire we claim for it is one which, if we concede that it has it, it is unaware that it has; and no distinction between conscious and unconscious desire is to be drawn in the dog's case. Consider, then, a rubber plant which shuns the dark and through a series of movements, seeks the light: by parity of reasoning with the dog's case, we can endow the plant with an unconscious desire for the light, and claim as we do so that it, too, is a type of creature for whom no distinction between conscious and unconscious desire is possible. In other words, without an awareness-condition of some sort, it would seem that the world can be populated with an enormous number of unconscious desires in this way, and it no longer remains clear what, if anything, the cash value of the term "desire" is in such cases. If, however, the dog is alleged to have a simple desire for the bone and to be aware that it has this desire, then the dog is aware that it simply desires the bone; it is, in other words, self-conscious. Now my objection to regarding the dog as self-conscious is not merely founded upon the view that self-consciousness presupposes the possession of language,...upon the fact that there is nothing the dog can do which can express the difference between desiring the bone and being aware of desiring the bone. Yet, the dog would have to be capable of expressing this difference in its behavior, if one is going to hold, *on the basis of that behavior*, that the dog is aware that it has a simple desire for the bone, aware that it simply desires the bone.

Even, then, if we concede for the sake of argument that there are simple desires, desires which do not involve the intervention of belief in order to have them, the suggestion that we can credit animals with these desires, without also having to credit them with language, is at best problematic.

I want, finally, to comment upon a contention that is not exactly an objection to my earlier remarks so much as a thesis which might be thought to serve as a possible rallying point for opponents.

In *Belief, Truth and Knowledge*, D. M. Armstrong proposes a way of interpreting "that"-clauses used of animals, such that the attribution of beliefs to animals in sentences of the form "The dog believes that..." remains intelligible but does not commit us to characterizing the exact content of animal beliefs. Briefly, Armstrong suggests that "that"-clauses used of animals be treated as referentially transparent (as opposed to opaque) con-

structions, so that, "in saying that the dog believes that his master is at the door we are, or should be, attributing to the dog a belief whose exact content we do not know but which can be obtained by substituting *salva veritate* in the proposition 'that his master is at the door.' " There are problems here, as Armstrong says, with the use of human concepts to describe the actual content of animal beliefs, and further problems, which Armstrong does not go into, about the actual categories of things which animals recognize; and these two clusters of problems together, I suspect, prove highly damaging to Armstrong's analysis. But at least his way of proceeding, he claims, "shows that we need not give up our natural inclination to attribute beliefs to animals just because the descriptions we give of the beliefs almost certainly do not fit the beliefs' actual content."

My problem with Armstrong's position is this: on the strength of the dog's behavior, we say "The dog believes that his master is at the door"; but our attributing this belief to the dog is not the same thing as showing that it actually has this belief. What we require, if we are to move from our saying "The dog believes that *p*" to holding that the dog actually has the belief *that p*, is some account of the connection, not between behavior and our attribution of belief, but between behavior and belief. Now if, as Armstrong, one allows belief to have any propositional content whatever, even propositional content that is to be regarded and treated as referentially transparent; and if, as Armstrong, one is prepared to concede that dogs do not possess language; then it must be the case, if one is going to claim that dogs actually do have beliefs, both that they have some grasp (a term which the reader is to interpret as liberally as he desires) of this propositional content and that non-linguistic behavior alone can suffice to show that they have such a grasp. I have two difficulties here. First, I do not understand how nonlinguistic behavior can *show* that a dog possesses the belief *that p* unless it is the case that nonlinguistic behavior is connected with the belief *that p* in such a way that same piece of non-linguistic behavior is not compatible with the belief *that q* or *that r* or *that s*. For if the dog's nonlinguistic behavior is compatible both with the belief *that p* and with these other beliefs, then I do not understand how it can be concluded on the basis of that behavior that it has the belief *that p* or that it has a grasp of the propositional content of the belief *that p*. For example, yesterday, my dog wagged its tail when its master was at the door, but it also wagged its tail when its lunch was about to be prepared and when the sun was being eclipsed by the moon. On all three occasions, it barked and jumped about. So far as I could see, its non-linguistic behavior was the same on the last two occasions as it was on the first, and I am not clear how on the basis of that behavior it can possibly be concluded that the dog *had* the belief that his master was at the door or that the dog *had* a grasp of the propositional content of the belief that its master was at the door. Second, I do not understand how a piece of non-linguistic behavior could be connected with the belief *that p* in such a way that we could conclude on the basis of the presence of that piece of behavior that the dog actually had the belief *that p* or had actually grasped the propositional content of the belief *that p* unless it were the case that there were some intrinsic connection between that piece of non-linguistic behavior and the proposition *that p* itself. The dog allegedly believes *that p*: according to Armstrong, *that p* is, even if in a referentially transparent fashion, what is believed, and *that p* is a proposition. In order to show that the dog grasps the proposition *that p*, its behavior must suffice; but if its behavior is in fact to show that it grasps just this particular proposition, just this proposition *that p*, then surely there must be some intrinsic connection between that behavior *and that proposition*? But there is no intrinsic connection between the dog's wagging its tail and its barking and jumping about and the proposition. "Its master is at the door," since that behavior is compatible with the widely different propositions "Lunch is about to be served" and "The sun is being eclipsed by the moon." We can describe the dog's behavior in

propositional terms, describe it as believing *that p* or as having a grasp of the propositional content of the belief *that p*; but the fact that the dog wags its tail, barks and jumps about does not show that the dog has grasped the proposition *that p* and *could not* show this, I think, unless wagging its tail, barking and jumping about were intrinsically connected with just that proposition, which they are not, any more than they are so connected with any other proposition.

Put succinctly, then, my complaint against Armstrong is that, even if his analysis of the use of "that"-clauses in respect of animals is correct, it still has not been shown *either* that the dog has a grasp of the proposition *that p* or the propositional content of the belief *that p* or that non-linguistic behavior alone can suffice to establish such a grasp. But it is precisely these things which must be shown, if we are to pass from merely attributing beliefs to animals on the strength of their behavior to concluding on the strength of their behavior that they actually have some beliefs.

I conclude, then, that the Nelsonian position on the moral rights of animals is not a sound one: the truth of the minor premiss in his argument—that animals have interests—is doubtful at best, and animals must have interests if, in accordance with the interest thesis, they are to be a logical subject of such rights. For animals either have interests in a sense which allows objects and things to have interests, and so, on the interest thesis, to have or to be candidates for having moral rights or they do not have interests at all, and so, on the interest thesis, do not have and are not candidates for having moral rights. I have reached this conclusion, moreover, without querying the correctness of the interest thesis itself, without querying, that is, whether the possession of interests *really is* a criterion for the possession of moral rights.

"The Moral Basis of Vegetarianism"

Tom Regan

Vegetarianism...might seem to represent a way of life where an excessive sentimentality has spilled over the edges of rational action.

I cannot accept such a view. My belief is that a vegetarian way of life can be seen, from the moral point of view, to have a rational foundation. This is what I shall try to show in what follows....

Descartes, as is well known, held the view that animals are like *automata* or machines: they have no mind (or incorporeal soul); they are unable to think; they are altogether lacking in consciousness. Like the motions of machines, animal behavior can be explained in purely mechanical terms. The fact that animals do some things better than we do, says Descartes, "does not prove that they are endowed with mind...(I)t is nature which acts in them according to the disposition of their organs, just as a clock, which is only composed of wheels and weights is able to tell the hours and measure the time more correctly than we can do with our wisdom."

All this is common knowledge. What perhaps is not so widely known is that Descartes was well aware of the practical implications of his view. On the matter of killing and eating animals, for example, Descartes, in a letter to More, observes that "my opinion is not so much cruel to animals as indulgent to men—at least to those who are not given over to the superstitions of Pythagoras (a vegetarian)—since it absolves them from any suspicion of crime when they eat or kill animals." Second, and relatedly, the view that animals do not feel pain might be expected to erase any moral qualms, any "suspicion of crime" we might have in using animals as subjects in scientific research. Descartes, himself, was an active participant in such research, as may be inferred from his discussion of the circulation of the blood in the *Discourse on Method*, and it is significant that the first champions of his views on the nature of animals...were physiologists. That Descartes was taken literally by these pioneers of science may be seen from a passage describing their work....

There was hardly a *solitaire* who didn't talk of automata....They administered beatings to dogs with perfect indifference, and made fun of those who pitied the creatures as if they felt pain. They said the animals were clocks; that the cries they emitted when struck, were only the noise of a little spring that had been touched, but that the whole body was without feeling. They nailed poor animals up on boards by their four paws to vivesect them and see the circulation of the blood which was a great subject of controversy....

Though, in this essay, I will confine my attention to defending the "superstitions" of Pythagoras and other vegetarians,...the argument that follows could be applied, with equal force, to the practice of using animals as subjects in "scientific" research.

Now, there can be no doubt that animals sometimes appear to be in pain. On this point, even Descartes would agree. In order for us to be rationally entitled to abandon the belief that they actually do experience pain, therefore, especially in view of the close physiological resemblances that often exist between them and us, we are in need of some rationally compelling argument that would demonstrate that this belief is erroneous. Descartes' principal argument...consists in the claim that, since animals cannot speak or use a language, they do not think, and since they do not think, they have no minds; lacking in these respects, therefore, they have no consciousness either. Thus, since a necessary condition of a creature's being able to experience pain is that it be a conscious being, it follows, given Descartes' reasoning, that animals do not experience pain.

From "The Moral Basis of Vegetarianism," *The Canadian Journal of Philosophy*, vol. 5 (1975). Reprinted by permission of the publisher.

There are two ways in which this argument can be challenged. First, one might dispute Descartes' claim that no animals can speak or use a language; second, one might dispute the view that being able to use a language is a necessary condition of being a conscious being. I think the second challenge is the stronger of the two....

Let us ask, then, whether Descartes is correct in holding that only a being who can use a language can experience pain. It seems he is not. Infants, for example, are not able to describe the location and character of their pains, and yet we do not, for all that, suppose that, when they fill the air with their piercing cries, they are not (or, stronger still, cannot possibly be) in pain. True, we can say of infants, what we may not be in a position to say of animals, that they have the *potential* to learn to use a language. But this cannot help the Cartesian. For when the infant screams for all he is worth, and when we find the diaper pin piercing his side, we do not say "My oh my, the lad certainly has a fine potential for feeling pain." We say he really is feeling it....

Whether or not a person is experiencing pain, in short, does not depend on his being able to perform one or another linguistic feat. Why, then, should it be any different in the case of animals? It would seem to be the height of human arrogance, rather than of Pythagorean "superstition," to erect a double standard here, requiring that animals meet a standard not set for humans. If humans can experience pain without being logically required to be able to say so, or in other ways to use a language, then the same standard should apply to animals as well.

Of course, none of this, by itself, settles the question "Do animals experience pain?"...Animals...certainly appear at times to be in pain. In order for us to be rationally justified in denying that they ever are in pain, therefore, we are in need of some rationally compelling argument that demonstrates that, though they may appear to suffer, they never really do so....Moreover, how animals who are physiologically similar to man behave in certain circumstances—for example, how muskrats behave when they try to free themselves from a trap—provides us with all the evidence we *could* have that they are in pain, given that they are not able to speak; in the case of the muskrats struggling to free themselves, that is, one wants to ask what *more* evidence could be rationally required to show that they are in pain in addition to their cries, their

whimpers, the straining of their bodies, the desperate look of their eyes, and so on. For my own part, I do not know what else could be required....If a person were of the opinion that this did not constitute enough evidence to show that the muskrats were in pain—I cannot see how any additional evidence would (or could) dissuade him of his scepticism. My position, therefore, is the "naive" one—namely, that animals can and do feel pain, and that, unless or until we are presented with an argument that shows that, all the appearances to the contrary, animals do not experience pain, we are rationally justified in continuing to believe that they do. And a similar line of argument can be given, I think, in support of the view that animals have experiences that are pleasant or enjoyable, experiences which, though they may be of a low level in comparison to, say, the joys of philosophy or the raptures of the beatific vision, are pleasurable nonetheless.

If, then, we are rationally entitled to believe that animals can and do experience both pleasure and pain, we are rationally compelled to regard animals as beings who count for something, when we attempt to determine what we morally ought or ought not to do. Bentham saw this clearly when he observed that the morally relevant question about animals is not "Can they *reason*? or Can they *talk*? but, Can they *suffer*?"...For if it is true that animals can and do experience pain; and if, furthermore, it is true, as I think it is, that pain is an intrinsic evil; then it must be true that the painful experience of an animal is, considered intrinsically, just as much of an evil as a comparable experience of a human being....

Now, an essential part of any enlightened morality is the principle of non-injury. What this principle declares is that we are not to inflict pain on, or otherwise bring about or contribute to the pain in, any being capable of experiencing it. This principle, moreover, is derivable from the more general principle of non-maleficence, which declares that we are not to do or cause evil, together with the value judgment that pain, considered in itself, is intrinsically evil. It is, I think, possible to hold that it is *always* wrong to cause pain, but the objections raised against this view, from Plato onward, seem to me to be decisive. The parent who causes pain to the child in the course of forcing him to take some essential medicine does cause pain, but does not do wrong; for the pain caused in this case is necessary if greater pain is to be avoided. More reasonable, then, is the view that causing pain is always *prima facie* wrong—that is, wrong in the absence of any other overriding moral consideration. Such a view leaves open the possibility that, in some actual or possible cases, a person can be morally justified in causing pain. At the same time, however, by insisting that to do so is always *prima facie* wrong, it has the important consequence of placing the onus of justification on anyone who is involved in causing pain. In other words, if, as a consequence of my actions, other creatures are made to suffer pain, then I am rationally obliged to show how it is that my failure to observe the principle of non-injury does not constitute any actual wrong doing on my part....It is clear that cases can arise in which the evil (pain) caused to animals is not compensated for by the good (pleasure) caused humans. The classical utilitarians...all were aware of this; nor did Mill, for one, flinch from insisting upon the conclusion which he thought utilitarianism required, given such a state of affairs. He writes:

> We (the utilitarians) are perfectly willing to stake the whole question on this one issue. Granted that any practice causes more pain to animals than it gives pleasure to 'man': is that practice moral or immoral. And if, exactly in proportion as human beings raise their heads out of the slough of selfishness, they do not with one voice answer "immoral," let the morality of the principle of utility be forever condemned....

What Mill does say shows that he is opposed to the view, endorsed by such diverse writers as St. Thomas and Kant, that we have no direct duties to animals....Kant...formulates the categorical imperative in such a way that it excludes any reference to non-human animals; we are to act in such a way that we treat humanity, both in our own person and in the person of every other, always as an end, never as a means merely....Of course, Kant, who rejected the Cartesian idea that animals lack the capacity even to feel pain, did not regard the matter of man's treatment of animals as one of moral indifference. It is wrong, he thinks, as does Aquinas, to be cruel to animals. But what makes it wrong, according to these thinkers, is not the fact that the animals suffer pain. What makes it wrong is that such treatment of animals tends to lead its perpetrators to treat human beings in a similar fashion....

Mill, quite rightly, will have none of this. His argument makes clear that he is sensitive to the implications of the view that pain is an intrinsic evil. For if, as Mill imagines, there be a practice which causes more pain to animals than it gives pleasure to man, then the practice is wrong, not *just* because or *only* if there be a rise in the nastiness of some men toward their fellows; it is wrong because of the unjustified pain felt by the animals. To suppose otherwise would do violence to the conception of pain as an intrinsic evil—an evil, that is, no matter when or where it exists, and no matter who experiences it....

Mill appears to me to be correct. And yet he does not go as far as he should....The case he considers is the one where a practice causes more undeserved pain to animals than it gives pleasure to man. This is just one among a number of possible cases of the comparative distribution of pleasure and pain....Consider...three others....(1) The case where the amount of undeserved pain caused to animals is equivalent to the amount of pleasure given to man; (2) the case where the amount of undeserved pain caused to animals is slightly exceeded by the amount of pleasure given to man; and (3) the case where the amount of pleasure greatly exceeds the amount of pain....

Let us begin here by first considering a conceivable practice that involves inflicting undeserved pain on human beings. Imagine, then, the following Swiftian possibility. Suppose that a practice develops whereby the severely mentally retarded among us are routinely sent to Human Farms, where they are made to live in incredibly crowded, unsanitary and confining conditions. Except for contact with one another, they have very little human contact. They are kept in stalls or in cages where they are fed by automated devices. Many of them are kept permanently indoors, and among those who are permitted outside, most of them are deprived of the ordinary means they might employ to secure enjoyment. And imagine, further, that the purpose of all this is to raise these human beings as a source of food for other human beings. At the end of a certain period of time, let us say, or after each has attained a certain weight, they are sold at public auction to the highest bidder and summarily carted off in loathsome vehicles to be "humanely" slaughtered....

Let us suppose that the following is true....The amount of undeserved pain caused to these human beings is exactly equivalent to the amount of pleasure other human beings secure as a result of the practice. The question is: would we say that this equality of pain and pleasure shows that there are no moral grounds for objecting to the practice in question? I do not think we would. I think we would want to say that this way of treating humans is not morally justified.

Consider, next, the following possibility. Imagine the same practice, only now imagine that the amount of pleasure other humans get from the practice slightly exceeds the amount of undeserved pain experienced by those who suffer. Would we say that, in this case, the practice is morally justified? Once again, I do not think we would. On the contrary, I think we would want to say here, as in the previous case, that the practice is immoral.

Now, if this is true of the two cases just imagined, why would not the same thing be true of cases where the practice imagined involves the treatment of animals? Let us suppose, that is, that there is a practice which involves treating animals in such a way that either (1) the amount of undeserved pain they experience is equal to the amount of pleasure human beings get from the practice or (2) the amount of pleasure humans receive slightly exceeds the amount of undeserved pain the animals suffer. And let us suppose that the pain suffered in either case is comparable to the pain suffered by the humans in the cases previously described....Why would the practice in question not be just as wrong in this case as in the case of the practice involving human beings? Well, certainly it cannot consistently be said that the intrinsic evil of an animal's pain counts for less than the intrinsic evil of a comparable human pain, and that that is why the practice involving the treatment of animals can be morally alright while the practice involving humans is not. For it has already been pointed out that the pain an animal feels is just as much pain, and just as much an intrinsic evil, as a comparable pain felt by a human being. So, if there is any rational basis for rendering conflicting judgments about the two practices, it must be looked for in some other direction.

The most likely and, on the face of it, the most plausible direction in which to look is in the direction of rights. "Humans," this line of reasoning goes, "have certain natural rights which animals lack, and that's what makes the two practices differ in a morally significant way. For in the case of the practice involving humans, their equal natural right to be spared undeserved pain is being violated, while in the case of the practice involving animals, since animals can have no rights, *their* rights are not being ignored. That's what makes the two cases differ. And that's what makes the practice involving humans an immoral one, while the practice involving animals is not."

Natural though this line of argument is, I do not think it goes any way toward justifying the differential treatment of the animals and humans in question. For on what grounds might it be claimed that the humans, but not the animals, have an equal natural right to be spared undeserved pain? Well, it cannot be...that all and only human beings have this right because all and only humans reason, make free choices or have a concept of their identity. These grounds will not justify the ascription of rights to all humans because some humans-infants and the severely mentally defective, for example-do not meet these conditions. Moreover, even if these conditions did form the grounds for the possession of rights; and even if it were true that all human beings met them; it still would not follow that *only* human beings have them. For on what grounds, precisely, might it be claimed that no animals can reason, make free choices or form a concept of themselves? What one would want here are detailed analyses of these operative concepts together with rationally compelling empirical data and other arguments which support the view that all non-human animals are deficient in these respects. It would be the height of prejudice merely to assume that man is unique in being able to reason, etc. To the extent that these beliefs are not examined in the light of what we know about animals and animal intelligence, the supposition that *only* human beings have these capacities is just that—a supposition, and one that could hardly bear the moral weight placed upon it by the differential treatment of animals and humans.

Nor will it do to argue that all and only human beings can use a language, and that this is why they can have the right in question while animals cannot. For even if it were true that all and only human beings can use a language, there would be no reason to believe that the possession of this capacity could have anything whatever to do with the possession of this right. For there is neither a logical nor an empirical connection between being able to use a language, on the one hand, and, on the other, being able to experience undeserved pain.

How, then, might we justify the ascription of an equal natural right to be spared undeserved pain to all human beings? This is not easy to say, and all I can do here is indicate what seems to me to be the most plausible line or argument in this regard....

Two things, at least, are reasonably clear. First, if the right in question is a *natural* right, then it cannot be one that is conferred upon one human being by other human beings; in particular, it cannot be a right that the governments or their laws can grant to or, for that matter, withhold from their subjects. Second, if the natural right in question is supposed to be one that belongs *equally* to all human beings, it cannot be a right which some human beings can acquire by doing something that other humans are unable to do; it must be a right, in other words, that all human beings have, to an equal extent, just because they are human beings. It is because of this second requirement that most proposed grounds for the right in question fail. For, given that there are some human beings who cannot, say, reason, or speak, or make free choices, it could not be the case that all humans have an equal right to be spared undeserved pain because all humans can reason, speak or make free choices. Any plausible argument for ascribing this right equally to all human beings, therefore, must invoke a basis that applies equally to all beings who are human.

Now, there is one argument for ascribing this natural right equally to all humans which has a degree of plausibility the others lack. This is the argument that begins with the claim that humans *can* have natural rights because humans *do* have interests. The word 'interests' here is used to cover such items as...liking-disliking, loving-hating, hoping-fearing, desiring-avoiding. As it is used in the present context, 'interests' is used to refer to what Perry calls "a certain class of acts or states which have the common characteristic of *being for or against*."...Although we may speak of a car as "needing some gas," we do not think that the car can have a right to the gas; and we do not think this because cars are not the kind of being that can have interests—that can *feel* the need to have gas or

desire to have it. In the case of human beings, however, we do experience desires and needs; we do have a connative life that includes the "acts or states" mentioned above; and it would seem to be because we do have such interests that we are the kind of being that can have rights.

A critic might object to this by saying that not all human beings have interests, from which it would follow that not all human beings can have rights, if a necessary condition of having rights is that one have interests. I do not find this criticism very persuasive. For it does seem to be the case that, when we are confronted with individuals who never have and never will manifest any interests whatsoever—where, that is, there is no reason to believe that they experience needs or wants, affection or aversion, hopes or fears, as in the case of those individuals who "vegetate"—...we have good reason to withhold the rubric "human being," despite the fact that they are the off-spring of human parents. To be a subject of interests, in short, does appear to be a necessary condition of being human.

...Even if this much is true, it does not follow that we have any rights; all that follows is that we *can* have them. So,..."Assuming that we can have rights, do we have any? In particular, do we all have the equal natural right to be spared undeserved pain?" The most plausible basis for supposing that we do would...have to show the following.

First, it would have to show that, in the absence of any wrong doing on the part of any individual human being, A, in terms of which it might be judged that A deserves to be punished—that is, that A deserves to be made to suffer pain—no one human being is any more deserving of being made to experience pain than is any other. Thus, to cause an innocent human being undeserved pain, on this account, will be to treat him *unjustly*; it is to cause a human being to suffer an evil, in the form of pain, which he does not deserve.

Second, the most plausible argument...would have to show that there is a necessary connection between injustice and rights, such that, if it is true that a person has been treated unjustly, it follows that one of his rights has been violated. At least for a sub-set of our duties, in other words, a correlation between duties and rights would have to be established, so that, though it will not always follow from the fact that I have a duty to do something (say, act benevolently) that someone has a corresponding right to demand that I act in this way toward him, this entailment will hold true in some cases....

Thus, assuming that all human beings are the kind of being that can have rights; and assuming that to cause any human being undeserved pain is to treat him unjustly; and assuming, finally, that anytime we treat a person unjustly we violate one of his rights; then it could be inferred that to cause a human being undeserved pain is to violate his natural right to be spared undeserved pain. And it could also be argued that this is a right which all human beings have, to an equal extent, just because they are human beings....

On this basis, then, it might be argued that all human beings have an equal right to be spared undeserved pain. Whether such an argument would succeed, I cannot say. All that I can say is, first, that it has a degree of plausibility that the other arguments lack, and, second, that precisely the same line of reasoning can be used in support of the contention that animals have an equal natural right to be spared undeserved pain. For animals, too, are the kind of being who have interests; we have no reason to believe, that is, that the contents of their conscious life are matters of uniform indifference to them; on the contrary, we have every reason to believe that there are many things toward which they are..."for or against"; unlike cars, they have needs, for example, which we have every reason to believe that they experience the desire to fulfill. Moreover, if it is unjust to cause a human being undeserved pain,...then it must also be unjust to cause an innocent animal undeserved pain. If it be objected that it is not possible to act unjustly toward animals, though it is possible to do so toward humans, then, once again, what we should demand is some justification of this contention; what we should want to know is just what there is that is characteristic of all human beings, and is absent from all other animals, that makes it possible to treat the former, but not the latter, unjustly. In the absence of such an explanation, I think we have every reason to suppose that restricting the concepts of just and unjust treatment to human beings is a prejudice.

If, then, the most plausible basis for attributing an equal natural right to be spared undeserved pain to all human beings turns on the idea that it is unjust to cause pain to an undeserving human being, then, given that it is unjust to do this to an innocent animal, it likewise would follow that animals have an equal natural right to be spared undeserved pain.

A critic will respond that all that this argument could show is that, among themselves, each animal has an equal natural right to be spared undeserved pain. What this argument could not show, this critic will contend, is that any animal could have a right that is equal to the right that any human being has to be spared undeserved pain. I do not think this criticism is justified. For assuming that the grounds for ascribing the right in question are the same for humans and animals, I do not understand how it can be logically inferred that humans possess this right to a greater extent than do animals. Unless or until we are given some morally relevant difference that characterizes all humans, but no animals,—a difference, that is, on the basis of which we could justifiably allege that our right to be spared undeserved pain is greater than the right that belongs to animals,—unless or until we are given such a difference I think reason compels us to aver that, if humans have this right, to an equal extent; for the reasons given, then animals have this right also, and have it to an extent that is equal to that in which humans possess it.

Now, none of this, even if its correct, establishes that animals (or humans) have an equal natural right to be spared undeserved pain. For my arguments in the preceding are arguments *about* arguments for and against the ascription or withholding of this right to humans and animals; they are not intended to show that humans or animals do or do not have this right. What I have argued, however, provides a sufficient basis to respond to the thesis that it is because human beings have an equal natural right to be spared undeserved pain, while animals do not, that we can be justified in treating them differently. What I have argued is that, at least in view of the arguments considered here, there is no good reason to believe this. For the grounds that might be invoked for denying that animals have this right—for example, that they cannot reason or make free choices—would also show that some humans do not have this right either, whereas what appear to be the most plausible grounds on which to rest the claim that all humans have this right are grounds which would equally well support the claim that animals do too....

Two objections should be addressed before proceeding. The first declares that animals cannot have rights because they lack the capacity to *claim* them. Now, this objection seems to be a variant of the view that animals cannot have rights because they cannot speak, and, like this more general view, this one too will not withstand a moment's serious reflection. For there are many human beings who cannot speak or claim their rights—tiny infants, for example....Thus, if a human being can possess this (or any other right) without being able to demand it, it cannot be reasonable to require that animals be able to do so, if they are to possess this (or any other) right. The second objection is different. It declares that the attribution of rights to animals leads to absurdity. For if, say, a lamb has the natural right to be spared undeserved pain, then the wolf, who devours it unmercifully, without the benefit of anaesthetic, should be said to violate the lamb's right. This, it is alleged, is absurd, and so, then, is the attribution of rights to animals. Well, absurd it may be to say that the wolf violates the lamb's right. But even supposing that it is, nothing said here implies that such deeds on the part of the wolf violate the lamb's rights. For the lamb can have rights only against those beings who are capable of taking the interests of the lamb into account and trying to determine, on the basis of its interests, as well as other relevant considerations, what, morally speaking, ought to be done. In other words, the only kind of being against which another being can have rights is a being that can be held to be morally responsible for its actions. Thus, the lamb can have rights against, say, most adult human beings. But a wolf, I think it would be agreed, is not capable of making decisions from the moral point of view; nor is a wolf the kind of being that can be held morally responsible; neither, then, can it make sense to say that the lamb has any rights against the wolf. This situation has its counterpart in human affairs. The severely mentally feeble, for example, lack the requisite powers to act morally; thus, *they* cannot be expected to recognize our rights, nor can *they* be said to violate our rights, even if, for example, they should happen to cause us undeserved pain. For as they are not the kind of being that can be held responsible for what they do, neither can they be said to violate anyone's rights by what they do.

Of course, even if it is true that animals and humans have an equal natural right to be spared undeserved pain, it would not follow that it is always wrong to cause them undeserved pain. For a right may always be overridden by more stringent moral demands. Thus, even if we assume that both human beings and animals have an equal natural right to be spared undeserved pain, questions can arise concerning when we would be justified in engaging in or supporting practices that cause undeserved pain to either humans or animals. Now, I have already suggested that we would not approve of engaging in or supporting practices which cause undeserved pain to some human beings merely on the grounds that these practices bring about an amount of pleasure equal to or slightly in excess of the amount of pain these humans are made to suffer. And I think that, if someone believes that human beings have an equal natural right to be spared undeserved pain, one of the reasons he would give for disapproving of these practices is that they would violate this right of their's. For to cause a human being pain simply on the basis that it will give others an equivalent amount of pleasure, or an amount of pleasure slightly in excess of the amount of pain involved, is not to show that he deserves to suffer anymore than anyone else, and it is not to go any way toward justifying, therefore, overriding his equal right not to suffer undeserved pain....

Accordingly, if we would object to the practice in question, when it involves the treatment of human beings, on the grounds that this right of their's is being violated, and assuming that we are unable to cite any grounds that would justify the claim that all humans but no animals have this right, then we must, if we are to be consistent, condemn any similar practice, for the same reasons, when it involves the treatment of animals.

But there is, of course, a third type of case to be considered. This is the case where the amount of undeserved pain caused by a practice is *greatly* exceeded by the amount of pleasure the practice brings about. And the question we must ask is whether, under these circumstances, the practice could be morally justified....A case might be made for the position that such a practice could be justified, if the undeserved pain involved is of a very trivial variety. Imagine, that is, that the world was such that, by inflicting a very slight, momentary, undeserved pain on animals, the human population, or a large segment of it, would experience an incredible amount of long lasting pleasure. Then, I think, we might submit that, though it might be better if the world allowed us to get this incredible pleasure without causing the animals the pain in question, still, the pain they experience is so slight and lasts for such a very short time that, despite the fact that it is undeserved, the vast amount of good that is brought about more than compensates for their very modest suffering. We might argue...that, even if animals do have a right to be spared undeserved pain, their right would be justifiably overridden in a situation such as this....

There are two points I want to make. The first is that, if such a practice is justified in the case where those who suffer are animals and those who secure the pleasure are humans, then, given the soundness of my argument up to now, and assuming that no one is able to show that there is a morally relevant difference between all humans and all animals, the same would be true of a practice where *both* those who suffer *and* those who secure the pleasure are humans. And, of course, the same thing would be true, given the conditions I have just stated, of a practice where those who receive the pain are humans and those who secure the pleasure are *animals*!

But the second thing I would say...is that...what is highly relevant to the conditional vegetarian's defense...is the case where the undeserved pain we are talking about is not trivial—where beings are made to suffer intense or long lasting pain, both physical and psychological. Imagine, then, that we have a practice that causes a given amount of non-trivial and undeserved pain for some human beings; and imagine, further, that this practice brings about an amount of pleasure greatly in excess of the pain these humans are made to suffer. Would we suppose that this practice was justified, simply on the ground that the pleasure greatly exceeded the pain? I do not think we would. For even if we happen to be of the opinion that inflicting undeserved, trivial pain might be justified in this way, I do not think we would be inclined to suppose that causing undeserved, non-trivial pain can be. I think we would be inclined to submit here, as in the earlier cases, that the equal right of humans not to suffer undeserved pain, assuming we have this right, is being unjustifiably overridden. But I also think that, if this is our considered opinion in this case, then, in the absence of any

morally relevant difference that exists between the humans and animals in question, we could not consistently render a different judgment if the practice in question caused non-trivial, undeserved pain to the animals. Certainly none of the arguments considered earlier succeeds in providing us with a credible basis on which to rest the belief that humans have a greater claim to an equal right to be spared undeserved pain than do animals....

Let us first take note of the fact that animals who are raised to be eaten by human beings very often are made to suffer. Nor is it simply that they suffer only when they are being shipped to the slaughter house or actually being slaughtered. For what is happening is this: The human appetite for meat has become so great that new methods of raising animals have come into being. Called intensive rearing methods, these methods seek to insure that the largest amount of meat can be produced in the shortest amount of time with the least possible expense. In ever increasing numbers, animals are being subjected to the rigors of these methods. Many are being forced to live in incredibly crowded conditions. Moreover, as a result of these methods, the natural desires of many animals often are being frustrated. In short, both in terms of the physical pain these animals must endure, and in terms of the psychological pain that attends the frustration of their natural inclinations, there can be no reasonable doubt that animals who are raised according to intensive rearing methods experience much non-trivial, undeserved pain. Add to this the gruesome realities of "humane" slaughter and we have, I think, an amount and intensity of suffering that can, with propriety, be called "great."

To the extent, therefore, that we eat the flesh of animals that have been raised under such circumstances, we help create the demand for meat that farmers who use intensive rearing methods endeavor to satisfy. Thus, to the extent that it is a known fact that such methods will bring about much undeserved, non-trivial pain, on the part of the animals raised according to these methods, anyone who purchases meat that is a product of these methods...is causally implicated in a practice which causes pain that is both non-trivial and undeserved for the animals in question. On this point too, I think there can be no doubt.

It is on these grounds that the conditional vegetarian can base at least part of his moral opposition to eating meat. First, he can point out that the onus of justification is always on anyone who supports a practice that is known to inflict non-trivial, undeserved pain on a sentient creature to show that, in doing so, he is not doing anything wrong. And he can point out, furthermore, that the onus of justification is always on those who support a practice that causes a sentient creature non-trivial, undeserved pain to show that, in doing so, the sentient creature's right to be spared this pain is not being violated....The conditional vegetarian...can rationally demand that those who lead a life contrary to his show how it is that *their* way of life can be morally justified, just as we are all rationally entitled to demand that those who are causally implicated in a practice that causes non-trivial, undeserved pain to human beings must show how it is that the practice, and their role in it, is not immoral. Contrary to the habit of thought which supposes that it is the vegetarian who is on the defensive and who must labor to show how his "eccentric" way of life can even remotely be defended by rational means, it is the non-vegetarian whose way of life stands in need of rational justification. Indeed, the vegetarian can, if I am right, make an even stronger claim than this....He can maintain that unless or until someone does succeed in showing how the undeserved, non-trivial pain animals experience as a result of intensive rearing methods is not gratuitous and does not violate the rights of the animals in question, then...the vegetarian is justified in believing that, and acting as if, it is wrong to eat meat, if by doing so we contribute to the intensive rearing of animals and, with this, to the great pain they must inevitably suffer. And the basis on which he can take this stand is the same one that vegetarians and non-vegetarians alike can and should take in the case of a practice that caused great undeserved pain to human beings—namely, that we are justified in believing that, and acting as if, such a practice is immoral unless or until it can be shown that it is not.

...The vegetarian...can point out that though those who contribute to the suffering of animals by purchasing meat in the usual way might conceivably be able to justify their buying and eating habits, they cannot do this by arguing that the non-trivial, undeserved pain these animals experience is a small price to pay for the variety and amount of human pleasure or other intrinsic goods brought into being by treating animals as we do. Such a 'justification' will not work...anymore than will the 'justification' that it is alright to cause non-trivial, undeserved pain to human beings so long as other human beings are able thereby to secure an abundant crop of pleasures or other intrinsic goods from the garden of earthly delights.

...There are...two further objections that might be raised, both of which, I think, uncover important limitations....The first is that a meat eater might be able to escape the thrust of my argument by the simple expedient of buying meat from farms where the animals are not raised according to intensive rearing methods, a difficult, but not impossible task, at the present time. For despite the widespread use of these methods, it remains true that there are farms where animals are raised in clean, comfortable quarters, and where the pain they experience is the natural result of the exigencies of animal existence....Or one might secure one's meat by hunting. And it is true, I think, that, judging from what some vegetarians have said, such expedients would escape the net of their moral condemnation, provided the animals were killed "humanely"....However, I think...this...would be conceding more than he should. For it is not merely considerations about the pain that an animal may feel that should form the moral basis of vegetarianism. It is also the fact that animals are routinely killed, whether "humanely" or not. Of course, nothing that I have said...goes anyway toward justifying this contention,...which is why I think my argument up to this point is deficient in an important respect. This is a deficiency I hope to remedy....

My argument [now]...turns on considerations about the natural "right to life" that we humans are sometimes said uniquely to possess, and to possess to an equal degree....What I will try to show is that arguments that might be used in defense of the claim that all human beings have this natural right, to an equal extent, would also show that animals are possessors of it, whereas arguments that might be used to show that animals do not have this right would also show that not all human beings do either....

Let us begin, then, with the idea that all humans possess an equal natural right to life,...one that we cannot acquire or have granted to us, and one that we all are supposed to have just because we are human beings. On what basis, then, might it be alleged that all and only human beings possess this right to an equal extent? Well, a number of familiar possibilities come immediately to mind. It might be argued that all and only human beings have an equal right to life because either (a) all and only human beings have the capacity to reason, or (b) all and only human beings have the capacity to make free choices, or (c) all and only human beings have a concept of "self," or (d) all and only human beings have all or some combination of the previously mentioned capacities. And it is easy to imagine how someone might argue that, since animals do not have any of these capacities, *they* do not possess a right to life, least of all one that is equal to the one possessed by humans....

It is not clear, first, that no non-human animals satisfy any one (or all) of these conditions, and, second, it is reasonably clear that not all human beings satisfy them. The severely mentally feeble, for example, fail to satisfy them. Accordingly, *if* we want to insist that they have a right to life, then we cannot also maintain that they have it because they satisfy one or another of these conditions. Thus, *if* we want to insist that they have an equal right to life, despite their failure to satisfy these conditions, we cannot consistently maintain that animals, because they fail to satisfy these conditions, therefore lack this right.

Another possible ground is that of sentience, by which I understand the capacity to experience pleasure and pain. But this view, too, must encounter a familiar difficulty—namely, that it could not justify restricting the right *only* to human beings.

What clearly is needed, then, if we are to present any plausible argument for the view that all and only human beings have an equal natural right to life, is a basis for this right that is invariant and equal in the case of all human beings and only in their case. It is against this backdrop...that the...view...arises...that the life of every human being has "intrinsic worth"—that, in Kant's terms, each of us exists as "an end in himself"—*and* that this intrinsic worth which belongs *only* to human beings, is shared *equally* by all. "Thus," it might be alleged, "it is because of the equal intrinsic worth of all human beings that we all have an equal right to life."

This view, I think, has a degree of plausibility which those previously discussed lack. For by saying that the worth that is supposed to attach to a being just because he or she is human is intrinsic, and that it is because of this that we all have an equal natural right to life,...rules out the possibility that one human being might give this right to or withhold it from another. It would appear, therefore, that this view could make sense of the alleged *naturalness* of the right in question. Moreover, by resting the equal right to life on the idea of the equal intrinsic worth of all human beings, this view may succeed, where the others have failed, in accounting for the alleged *equality* of this right.

Despite these apparent advantages, however, the view under consideration must face certain difficulties. One difficulty lies in specifying just what it is supposed to mean to say that the life of every human being is "intrinsically worthwhile." Now, it cannot mean that "each and every human being has a natural right to life." For the idea that the life of each and every human being has intrinsic worth was introduced in the first place to provide a basis for saying that each and every human being has an equal right to life. Accordingly, if, say, "Jones' life is intrinsically worthwhile" ends up meaning "Jones has an equal right to life," then the claim that the life of each and every individual is equally worthwhile, judged intrinsically, cannot be construed as a *basis* for saying that each and every human being has an equal right to life. For the two claims would mean the same thing, and one claim can never be construed as being the basis for another, if they both mean the same.

But a second and, for our purposes, more important difficulty is this: On what grounds is it being alleged that each and every human being, and only human beings, are intrinsically worthwhile? Just what is there, in other words, about being human, and only about being human, that underlies this ascription of unique worth? Well; one possible answer here is that there isn't "anything" that underlies this worth. The worth in question, in short, just belongs to anyone who is human, and only to those who are. It is a worth that we simply recognize or intuit, whenever we carefully examine that complex of ideas we have before our minds when we think of the idea, "human being." I find this view unsatisfactory, both because it would seem to commit us to an ontology of value that is very difficult to defend, and because I, for one, even after the most scrupulous examination I can manage, fail to intuit the unique worth in question. I do not know how to prove that the view in question is mistaken in a few swift strokes, however. All I can do is point out the historic precedents of certain groups of human beings who have claimed to "intuit" a special worth belonging to their group and not to others within the human family, and say that it is good to remember that alluding to a special, intuitive way of "knowing" such things could only serve the purpose of giving an air of intellectual respectability to unreasoned prejudices. And, further, I can only register here my own suspicion that the same is true in this case, though to a much wider extent. For I think that falling into talk about the "intuition of the unique intrinsic worth of being human" would be the last recourse of men who, having found no good reason to believe that human beings have an unique intrinsic worth, would go on believing that they do anyhow.

Short of having recourse to intuition, then, we can expect those who believe that human beings uniquely possess intrinsic worth to tell us what there is about being human, in virtue of which this worth is possessed. The difficulty here, however, as can be anticipated, is that some familiar problems are going to raise their tiresome heads. For shall we say that it is the fact that humans can speak, or reason, or make free choices, or form a concept of their own identity that underlies this worth? These suggestions will not work here, anymore than they have before. For there are some beings who are human who cannot do these things, and there very well may be some beings who are not human who can. None of these capacities, therefore, could do the job of providing the basis for a kind of worth that all humans and only humans are supposed to possess.

But suppose we try to unpack this notion of intrinsic worth in a slightly different way. Suppose we say that the reasons we have for saying that all and only human beings exist as ends in themselves are, first, that every human being has various positive interests, such as desires, goals, hopes, preferences and the like, the satisfaction or realization of which brings intrinsic value to their lives, in the form of intrinsically valuable experiences; and, second, that the intrinsic value brought to the life of any one man, by the satisfaction of his desires or the realization of his goals, is just as good,

judged in itself, as the intrinsic value brought to the life of any other man by the satisfaction or realization of those comparable desires and goals he happens to have. In this sense, then, all men are equal, and it is because of this equality among all men, it might be alleged, that each man has as much right as any other to seek to satisfy his desires and realize his goals, so long, at least, that, in doing so, he does not violate the rights of any other human being. "Now, since," this line of argument continues, "no one can seek to satisfy his desires or realize his goals if he is dead, and in view of the fact that every man has as much right as any other to seek to satisfy his desires and realize his goals, then to take the life of any human being will always be *prima facie* to violate a right which he shares equally with all other human beings—namely, his right to life."

What shall we make of this argument? I am uncertain whether it can withstand careful scrutiny. Whether it can or not, however, is not a matter I feel compelled to try to decide here....Of the arguments considered here, this one has a degree of plausibility the others lack....

At the same time, however,...I believe that, whatever plausibility this argument might have in this connection, it would also have in connection with the claim that animals, too, have an equal natural right to life.

For, once again, it seems clear that animals have positive interests, the satisfaction or realization of which would appear to be just as intrinsically worthwhile, judged in themselves, as the satisfaction or realization of any comparable interest a human being might have. True, the interests animals have may be of a comparatively low-grade, when we compare them to, say, the contemplative interests of Aristotle's virtuous man. But the same is true of many human beings: their interests may be largely restricted to food and drink, with occasional bursts of sympathy for a few. Yet we would not say that such a man has less of a right to life than another, assuming that all men have an equal right to life. Neither, then, can we say that animals, because of their "base" interests, have any less of a right to life.

One way to avoid this conclusion and, at the same time, to challenge part of the argument...is to deny that animals have interests. But on what basis might this denial rest? A by now familiar basis is that animals cannot speak; they cannot use words to formulate or express anything; thus, they cannot have an interest in anything. But this objection obviously assumes that only those beings who are able to use words to formulate or express something can have interests, and this, even ignoring the possibility that at least some animals might be able to do this, seems implausible. For we do not suppose that infants, for example, have to learn to use a language before they can have any interests. Moreover, the behavior of animals certainly seems to attest to the fact that they not only can, but that they actually do have interests. Their behavior presents us with many cases of preferential choice and goal directed action, in the face of which, and in the absence of any rationally compelling argument to the contrary, it seems both arbitrary and prejudicial to deny the presence of interests in them.

The most plausible argument for the view that humans have an equal natural right to life, therefore, seems to provide an equally plausible justification for the view that animals have this right also. But just as in saying that men and animals have an equal right to be spared undeserved pain, so here, too, we would not imply that the right in question can never be overridden. For there may arise circumstances in which an individual's right to life could be outweighed by other more pressing moral demands, and where, therefore, we would be justified in taking the life of the individual in question. But even a moment's reflection will reveal that we would not condone a practice which involved the routine slaughter of human beings simply on the grounds that it brought about this or that amount of pleasure, or this or that amount of intrinsically good experiences for others, no matter how great the amount of good hypothesized. For to take the lives of individuals, for this reason, is manifestly not to recognize that their life is just as worthwhile as anybody else's, or that they have just as much right to life as others do. Nor need any of this involve considerations about the amount of pain that is caused the persons whose lives are taken. Let us suppose that these persons are killed painlessly; that still would not alter the fact that they have been treated wrongly and that the practice in question is immoral....The same is true of any practice involving the slaughter of animals, and we have, therefore, grounds for responding to the...objection that since the only thing wrong

with the way animals are treated in the course of being raised and slaughtered is that they are caused a lot of undeserved pain, the thing to do is to desensitize them so that they don't feel anything. What we can see now, however, is that the undeserved pain animals feel is not the only morally relevant consideration; it is also the fact that they are killed that must be taken into account.

Similarly, to attempt to avoid the force of my argument for conditional vegetarianism by buying meat from farms that do not practice intensive rearing methods or by hunting and killing animals oneself...will not meet the total challenge vegetarians can place before their meat eating friends. For the animals slaughtered on even the most otherwise idyllic farms, as well as those shot in the wild, are just as much killed, and just as much dead, as the animals slaughtered under the most ruthless of conditions....

Once again, therefore, the onus of justification lies, not on the shoulders of those who are vegetarians, but on the shoulders of those who are not....It is the non-vegetarian who must show us how he can be justified in eating meat, when he knows that, in order to do so, an animal has had to be killed. It is the non-vegetarian who must show us how his manner of life does not contribute to practices which systematically ignore the right to life which animals possess, if humans are supposed to possess it on the basis of the most plausible argument considered here. And it is the non-vegetarian who must do all this while being fully cognizant of the fact that he cannot defend his way of life merely by summing up the intrinsic goods—the delicious taste of meat, for example—that come into being as a result of the slaughter of animals....

This is not to say that practices that involve taking the lives of animals cannot possibly be justified. In some cases, perhaps, they can be....What we would have to show...I think, in order seriously to consider approving of such a practice, is (1) that such a practice would prevent, reduce or eliminate a much greater amount of evil, including the evil that attaches to the taking of the life of a being who has as much claim as any other to an equal natural right to life; (2) that, realistically speaking, there is no other way to bring about these consequences; and (3) that we have very good reason to believe that these consequences will, in fact, obtain. Now, perhaps there are some cases in which these conditions are satisfied. For example, perhaps they are satisfied in the case of the eskimo's killing of animals and in the case of having a restricted hunting season for such animals as deer. But to say that this is (or may be) true of *some* cases is not to say that it is true of all, and it will remain the task of the non-vegetarian to show that what is true in these cases, assuming that it is true, is also true of any practice that involves killing animals which, by his actions, he supports.

Two final objections deserve to be considered before ending. The first is that, even assuming that what I have said is true of *some* nonhuman animals, it does not follow that it is true of *all* of them. For the arguments given have turned on the thesis that it is only beings who have interests who can have rights, and it is quite possible that, though some animals have interests, not all of them do. I think this objection is both relevant and very difficult to answer adequately. The problem it raises is how we can know when a given being has interests. The assumption I have made throughout is that this is an empirical question, to be answered on the basis of reasoning by analogy—that, roughly speaking, beings who are very similar to us, both in terms of physiology and in terms of non-verbal behavior, are, like us, beings who have interests. The difficulty lies in knowing how far this analogy can be pushed. Certain animals, I think, present us with paradigms for the application of this reasoning—the primates, for example. In the case of others, however, the situation is less clear, and in the case of some, such as the protozoa, it is very grey indeed. There are, I think, at least two possible ways of responding to this difficulty. The first is to concede that there are some beings who are ordinarily classified as animals who do not have interests and who cannot, therefore, possess rights. The second is to insist that all those beings who are ordinarily classified as animals do have interests and can have rights. I am inclined to think that the former of these two alternatives is the correct one, though I cannot defend this judgment here. And thus I think that the arguments I have presented do not, by themselves, justify the thesis that *all* animals have interests and can, therefore, possess rights....For the cases where we would, with good reason, doubt whether an animal has interests—for example, whether protozoa do—are cases which

are, I think, irrelevant to the moral status of vegetarianism. The question of the obligatoriness of vegetarianism, in other words, can arise only if and when the animals we eat are the kind of beings who have interests. Whatever reasonable doubts we may have about which animals do and which do not have interests do not apply, I think, to those animals that are raised according to intensive rearing methods or are routinely killed, painlessly or not, preparatory to our eating them. Thus, to have it pointed out that there are or may be some animals who do not have interests does not in any way modify the obligation not to support practices that cause death or non-trivial, undeserved pain to those animals that do.

Finally, a critic will object that there are no natural rights, not even natural rights possessed by humans. "Thus," he will conclude, "no animals have natural rights either and the backbone of your argument is broken." This objection raises problems too large for me to consider here, and I must content myself, in closing, with the following two remarks. First, I have not argued that either human beings or animals do have natural rights; what I have argued, rather, is that what seem to me to be the most plausible arguments for the view that all humans possess the natural rights I have discussed can be used to show that animals possess these rights also. Thus, if it should turn out that there is no good reason to believe that we humans have any natural rights, it certainly would follow that my argument would lose some of its force. Even so, however, this would not alter the principal logical points I have endeavored to make.

But, second, even if it should turn out that there are no natural rights, that would not put an end to many of the problems discussed here. For even if we do not possess natural rights, we would still object to practices that caused non-trivial, undeserved pain for some human beings if their 'justification' was that they brought about this or that amount of pleasure or other forms of intrinsic good for this or that number of people; and we would still object to any practice that involved the killing of human beings, even if killed painlessly, if the practice was supposed to be justified in the same way. But this being so, what clearly would be needed, if we cease to invoke the idea of rights, is some explanation of why practices which are not right, when they involve the treatment of people, can be right (or at least permissible) when they involve the treatment of animals. What clearly would be needed, in short, is what we have found to be needed and wanting all along—namely, the specification of some morally relevant feature of being human which is possessed by *all* human beings and *only* by those beings who are human. Unless or until some such feature can be pointed out, I do not see how the differential treatment of humans and animals can be rationally defended, natural rights or no.

Earth and Other Ethics

Christopher D. Stone

Issues regarding the moral and legal status of "things" other than individual normal persons crop up all the time. In New York recently, parents of a severely deformed and retarded newborn infant, "Baby Jane Doe," decided against life-prolonging surgery. A New York attorney responded with an effort to sue on its behalf as guardian. Can a defective newborn have "rights" assertable against its parents? Can a fetus have rights? A robot? Can we have obligations to the unborn? The furor over President Reagan's trip to lay a wreath at Kolmeshoehe Cemetery in Bitburg, where forty-nine Nazi SS members lie buried, rekindled old controversies about collective and group responsibility. What does it mean not for an individual, but for a *people* or a *nation*—or, for that matter, a *corporation*—to be (in morals) "to blame" or (in law) "guilty"?

The best evidence of the increasing significance of these unconventional "things" are the several bodies of literature one finds growing up around them. There is an animal rights literature, a fetus (including abortion) literature, a future-generations literature, an environmental literature, a cultural literature, and so on.…

Once begun, such an inquiry bores to the very bedrock of law and morals. Orthodox legal and moral theories provide nonhumans only a limited accounting, one that generally makes the claim on behalf of the thing directly dependent upon human interests. This is particularly so when we turn to things like rivers that (unlike whales) have no interests or preferences of their own. Hence, the more expansively one seeks to make a moral-legal accounting, the more critically we have to probe orthodox legal and moral philosophy.…

The conventional approach to ethics is to put forward a single coherent body of principles, such as utilitarianism's greatest good of the greatest number, and to demonstrate how it guides us through all moral dilemmas more satisfactorily than does its rivals. This conventional view of the ethicist's mission, which I call Moral Monism, has far-reaching implications for moral discourse. First, it is very much either-or. The writer typically proposes that there is a single key: life, or the capacity to feel pain, or the powers of reason, or something else. Those things that possess the key property count morally—all equally, and all in the same way. Those things that lack it are utterly irrelevant, except as resources for the benefit of those things that do count. Moreover, Monism implies that in arguing for, say, the preservation of a species, we have to appeal to the same principles that we would invoke in determining the punishment of terrorists or the obligations to one's kin.

From *Earth and Other Ethics* (New York: Harper & Row, Publishers, 1987). Reprinted by permission of the publisher.

These ambitions of Monism, to unify all ethics within a solitary framework capable of yielding the One Right Answer to all our quandaries, strike me as unattainable. First, the Monist's mission collides with the fact that morality involves not one, but several distinguishable *activities*—choosing courses of conduct, praising and blaming actors, and evaluating institutions, to mention three. Second, there is the variety of *things* whose considerateness commands some intuitive appeal: normal persons in a common moral community, persons remote in time and space, embryos and fetuses, nations and nightingales, beautiful things and sacred things. Trying to force into a single framework all these diverse moral activities as they touch on all these diverse entities seems fruitless. Worse, it imposes strictures on thought that stifle the emergence of more valid approaches. The alternative conception I will propound—what I call Moral Pluralism—invites us to conceive moral activities as partitioned into several distinct frameworks, each governed by distinct principles and logical texture. We do not try to force the analysis of good character into the same framework as for good acts; nor are our obligations to the spatially and temporally remote subject to exactly the same rules that relate us to our kin, on the one hand, or to species, on the other. The frameworks for each of these analyses are distinguishable in their respective capacities to produce a single right (or wrong) answer, and in the strictness of the judgments they render. In some domains we can speak in terms of what is mandatory. In other domains, perhaps those that encompass butterflies and "lower" life, our judgments are limited to what is morally permissive, or, more loosely, what is simply "more welcome." Under the view proposed here, there is some shift in the aims and ambitions of moral philosophy; a shift, too, in how practical dilemmas are defined, attacked, carried to solution, and justified. Most important, it holds, I believe, implications as to the sorts of persons we aim to become, the relations we build, and the world we will leave as legacy....

Our received ways of defining and handling legal and moral problems grew out of relationships among ordinary normal persons living in a collective society. I will refer to these persons as Persons—with a capital *P*. My term *Persons* is less extensive that the biologist's *homo sapiens*. *Per-*

sons is limited to normal adult human beings who, possessing full human faculties and living as neighbors in time and space, are capable of knitting the bonds of a common community. My definition of *Person* excludes, for example, humans who have not yet been born, those who live on the other side of the world, and those afflicted with such a serious defect that their capacity to form social bonds is impaired. All these are persons, of course, and worthy of our concern. But they are not the Persons who have been the focal concern of ordinary law and morals.

The use of a single term, *Persons*, does not mean that there has been a single, stable conception of "personhood" through history. In every era there have been contesting notions of what a person is, or could become, and the prevailing view has left its stamp on our thought....

The whole texture of conventional law and morals is dominated by the fact that many potential conflicts can be forestalled by assigning Persons claims and rights which they can then assert, waive, or trade to mutual benefit.

Some accounting has had to be made for creatures who did not fit the Persons mold—who were not normal persons in a common community, but were too conspicuous to be ignored entirely. These unconventional entities, or "Nonpersons" as I shall call them, ranged from natural persons of "special" sorts (including infants, lunatics, and the unborn) to such nonhumans as animals, the dead, and various sorts of aggregate or corporate bodies: nations, tribes, municipalities, business organizations, and universities.

The lands over which the U.S. government has dominion include the submerged bed of the Alaskan Beaufort Sea. The Department of Interior has proposed to lease the acreage to oil corporations for purposes of exploiting oil and gas that may underlie the region. To carry out exploratory drilling (and, certainly, in order to support development if commercial reserves should be discovered) drilling platforms will have to be constructed in the path that the bowhead whale, an endangered species, uses to reach its sole known spawning ground. Oil spills could have disastrous effects on their survival. Also, early-stage oil exploration often involves dynamiting (the explosions' echoes are used to map geophysical structures), and there is evidence that the procedures could destroy the whales' hearing, and thus their ability to navigate and survive. To make the matter more complex, if the whales successfully avoid these hazards by adjusting to a course that takes them somewhat to the north of their present route, they will be out of the range of a native tribe, the Inupiat Indians, who have long hunted the bowhead, a custom they claim to be integral to the maintenance of their culture.

Let me survey for a moment the various *sorts of conflicts* that appear to arise from this situation....First, there are conflicts of *Natural Persons versus Natural Persons*. The interests of the contemporary Indians, who want the bowhead to be undisturbed (except by themselves) are at odds with domestic consumers of petroleum products who have an interest in a secure source of petroleum products, and even stand to gain some relief, as taxpayers, from the government's oil-lease revenues. Observe that while this conflict has some elements that suit it to an ordinary Persons model of analysis, it lacks others....The petroleum consumers are widely separated both culturally and geographically from the Indians. It is not evident to what extent we all share a single "moral community."

There are also conflicts of *Natural Persons versus Corporations*. The native Americans are at odds both with the U.S. Department of Interior (a public agency) and with the oil companies (private corporate bodies) that wish to participate in the lease sale. There are *Corporations versus Corporations*. The village of Kaktovik, a municipal corporation, aligned in court against ARCO, an oil company, with the National Wildlife Federation, a nonprofit corporation, appearing as intervenor.

There is, in addition, a highly charged set-off of *Nation-States versus Nation-States*. The United States, as a nation member of the world body, is signatory to an International Whaling Convention (IWC). Other signatories include Russia and Japan, who have long been under U.S. pressure to reduce their whaling. Now, in the bowhead controversy, Russia and Japan have rejoined that if the United States is to honor *its* treaty obligations under the IWC, it must crack down on the Inupiat's "harvest" of bowheads or be subject to charges of hypocrisy on whale conservation and see its world leadership on the issue erode. Hence, on the plane of world bodies, the United States is in conflict with Japan and Russia.

There are, as well, conflicts of *Natural Persons versus Animals*, the whales being in jeopardy both from the Indians, who would kill them deliberately, and the consumers of oil products, who would jeopardize them indirectly to satisfy what economists call their "higher preferences."

We might consider, too, *Animals versus Animals*, since the decline of the bowhead would confer a benefit on the krill that the bowhead consumes....

Even beyond these conflicts among contemporaries, there are other colorable interests to examine, which might also be said to provide the basis for other conflicts over time. First, there is the Indian tribe or even culture to account for, by which I mean to indicate not merely the interests of this Indian or that, but the value of a community freighted with ways of life that transcend and survive particular lives. Second, there are analogous problems of species to consider. The survival of a species of *whale*, presents separate questions from the survival of any individual whale. In fact, foresters and zoo keepers face such conflicts regularly. To preserve an endangered species, there may be no viable alternative but to cull out or pen in individual members. The individual (in this illustration, the whale) has intelligence and can experience pleasure and pain—has, in short, several of the properties of a natural person, at least in degree. But a species—in this regard, like a corporation—*itself* lacks these properties, has neither sentience nor even substance, and thus to talk of the interests or claims of a species raises some of the same conundrums as when we speak of the interests or claims of a corporation, tribe, or culture per se.

There are, as well, future interests to consider. Our present actions—draining domestic oil reserves, eliminating or altering the Indian culture, infringing the population of bowhead whales—are going to influence the resources that the future generations have available to them, their recreational opportunities, even their tastes.

These future generations' problems are,...incredibly complex. We do not know (1) who—what sorts of or how many people—will be living in the distant future; (2) what consequences our present actions, such as the depletion of oil, will have on them in view of their alternatives; or even (3) what their preferences will be, assuming that we are committed to respect their preferences in some degree. For all we know, our descendants will be content to while away their time playing the progeny of Pac Man, and will consider us, their ancestors, at best quaint for having derived pleasure from the idea of there *being* whales and wild lions that almost none of us ever actually went off to see.

And, finally, there is some constituency for the affected habitat, or something even more encompassing, such as the whole ecological balance or the whole earth....

Implicit in all I have written thus far there runs a major question of *care* and *respect*. What are the things we ought to care about and respect, and in what ways should that attitude be manifested? Our two principal institutions for sorting out and implementing these concerns—morals and law—have been dominated, conventionally, by a Persons orientation. Therefore, increasing regard for Nonpersons requires us to consider how suited our received ways of normative analysis are to resolve or even guide us through the evolving problems of contemporary concern. In what ways, and with what justification, might Nonpersons be accounted for in moral thought and legal rules?...

The nature of a thing's *legal status*, and, in particular, the relationship between its legal status and its moral status, can be clarified if we confront at the start two popular misconceptions. The first mistake is to suppose that all questions of *legal status* can be conflated into questions of *legal rights*. That is, people tend to identify the question "Can some entity be accorded legal recognition?" with "Can (or does) the entity have a legal right?" In fact, the motive for recognizing something as a legal person may have nothing to do with *its* legal rights. For example, the courts may give a stillborn fetus the status of "person" in order to fulfill a technical prerequisite for the parents to file a malpractice case against the doctors. Giving the fetus its independent legal status is designed to secure the legal rights of the parents, not those of the fetus.

This first misconception is commonly compounded by a second error. This is the view that the only basis on which we can support according a thing a legal right (or other legal recognition) is if we can show it has something like its own moral right, underneath....

Let me begin here by placing *legal rights-holding* in perspective. The short of it is that having a legal right is one way to provide something a concern-manifesting legal recognition. But it is not

the only way. When the law criminalizes dog beating it institutionalizes concern for dogs. It does so, however, by creating a prospective liability for the dog beater, who is made answerable to public prosecutors at their discretion. In no accepted sense does such a statute create a "right" in the dog. The same principle is at work in legislation establishing animal sanctuaries, and laws that compel cattle transporters to provide minimally "humane" standards at the risk of losing their certificate. The law is enlisted in an effort to protect Nonpersons, but legal rights are not required. The federal government recently issued regulations requiring fishermen who accidentally land sea turtles on their decks to give them artificial respiration. The technique is set out in detail. But the term *turtle's rights* is never mentioned. Nor need it be. The turtles are provided a measure of legal protection by creating enforceable legal duties *in regard to* them, duties enforceable by others, presumably the Commerce Department and Coast Guard. In like vein, no one is doubting that we could create comparable duties in regard to things indisputably devoid of interests; for example, we can imagine a law making it a misdemeanor to deface some special rock, such as Mount Rushmore. Nor are relations built on duties the only alternative to those built on rights. We could give an algae colony an immunity from governmental action, say, from the draining of a stream for a federal works project.

This should remind us that while allocating rights is a fundamental way of operationalizing legal concern,...such concern can be implemented through a broad range of arrangements, not all of which can be forced into the classic "rights-holding," or even "duties-bearing," mold. Therefore, let me introduce as the more comprehensive notion *legal considerateness*. A terse operational definition would look like this. Consider a lake. The lake is considerate within a legal system if the system's rules have as their immediate object to affect (as to preserve) some condition of the lake. The law's operation would turn on proof that the lake is not in the condition that the law requires, without any further need to demonstrate anyone else's interests in or claims touching the lake.

We can illustrate by reference to a lake which is being polluted by a factory. Under conventional law, the pollution of the lake can be restrained at some human's behest (call him Jones) if Jones can show that he has a legally protectable interest in the lake. Jones might prove that the lake is on his land, or that, as owner of lakeside property, he has a right to the water in a condition suited for his domestic or agricultural use. Changes in the state of the lake—for example, its degradation—are relevant to Jones's proof, but his case cannot stop with the proof of such changes. As plaintiff, he has to prove that he has some right in respect of the lake's condition, which right the factory is infringing. Damages, if any, go to Jones. If the court awards him an injunction, it is *his* injunction; Jones has the liberty to sit down with the factory owners and negotiate an agreement not to enforce it, to let the pollution restart—if the factory owners make an offer that is *to Jones's advantage.*

Contrast that system to one in which the rules empower a suit to be brought against the factory in the name not of Jones, but of the lake, through a guardian or trustee. The factory's liability is established on the showing that without justification, it degraded the lake from one condition, which is lawful, to another, which is not.

In the first system described, the lake is not legally considerate. It has no protection that is not wholly parasitic upon the rights of some person ready and willing to assert them. In the latter system, it is the lake that is considerate, not the person empowered to assert claims on its behalf....

We can simply conceptualize considerateness into two broad categories: *legal advantage* (typified by holding a legal right) and *legal disadvantage* (typified by bearing a legal duty)....

At this point, someone is bound to object that all this talk about "positioning" a Nonperson in a position of Advantage or of Disadvantage simply slides over the most serious problem. In regard to legislation touching some Nonpersons—as when we criminalize dog beating, for example—few would deny we are acting for the dog's benefit, *really* advantaging it. But one cannot so plausibly characterize an arrangement that nestles the lake in the protective custody of a guardian as being "for the lake's 'benefit' " in any familiar sense of "benefit." We have simply plugged the lake into the legal system roughly in the place that a person might occupy, to a person's advantage; but it is a place that can be of no advantage to the lake, only to people. The same may be said of whatever we might do concerning many Nonpersons, from ants and aquifers to zoophytes and zygotes. Because they have no self-conscious interests in their own fates (as distinct from our interests in them), it is unclear how notions of Advantage and Disadvantage apply....

To examine the general problem, we best concentrate on the most implausible of my Nonperson clients, thereby confronting the most fundamental objections. What space is there in law and morals, what toehold even, for the subset of Nonpersons I will call "Things"—utterly disinterested entities devoid of feelings or interests except in the most impoverished or even metaphorical sense?

There are various classes of these disinterested Things. There are man-made inanimates exemplified by artworks and artificial intelligence. There are Things that were not always so disinterested—corpses—and Things with the potential to be otherwise—embryos and fetuses. There are trees and algae which, while without self-consciousness and preferences, are nonetheless living organisms with biological requirements. There are what we discern as functional systems, but not systems that conform to the boundaries of any organism; for example, the hydrologic cycle. Habitats are of this sort. That is, while the habitat may include higher animals, we may find ourselves wishing to speak for some value not reducible to the sum of the values of the habitat's parts, the various things that the habitat sustains in relation. There are several sorts of natural and conventional membership sets already mentioned: species, tribes, nations, corporations. We might for completeness' sake keep in mind such "things" as in the happenstance of our language are rendered as qualities, for example, the quality of the light in the Arizona desert at sunset. Finally, there are events that might be of legal and moral concern, such as the flooding of the Nile.

Whatever might motivate and justify the lawmakers to try to make some such Thing legally considerate, how can we coherently account for an entity that has no welfare? We can imagine our interlocutor putting it this way. "All right," he says, "let us suppose that somewhere in the text that follows, you will be able to demonstrate at least some rational basis that could motivate us to devise legal rules in which a Thing—a lake, say—is made legally considerate, as you use the term. We will even agree to provide it a court-appointed guardian empowered to get up in court and 'take on' polluters in the lake's name. But now comes the tough part. The lake itself being utterly indifferent to whether it is clear and full of fish or muddy and lifeless, when the guardian for the river gets up to speak, *what is he or she supposed to say?*"

My answer will sound, I am afraid, a bit anticlimactic. As in any situation in which a legal guardian is empowered to speak for a ward, what the guardian says will depend upon what the legal rules touching on the ward provide. By definition a Thing can neither be benefited nor detrimented in the ordinary sense, so that the rules cannot orient to its best interests in the way some rules of child custody enlist "the best interests of the child."

What we should be asking, then, is this: What states of a disinterested entity (a Thing), of necessity unrooted in its own interests or welfare or preferences, are available for the law to embody in legal rules, and what would be the implications of so embodying them?

To examine what sort of legally defined Advantages might be conferred on a Thing, and with what implications, let us begin by considering a system that took as its target preserving the lake's intactness. The lawmakers could provide stiff criminal penalties for anyone who polluted the lake in the least degree. They could fortify this "advantaging" by assimilating the lake into the civil-liability rules in a way that approximated constituting the lake a rights holder with guardian. Specifically, the law could provide that in case someone violated established effluent standards, altering the state of the lake, a complaint could be instituted in the name of the lake, as party plaintiff, against the polluter....This suit could be initiated and maintained—as suits are maintained as a matter of course for infants, the senile, and corporations—by a lawyer authorized to represent it, by *ad hoc* court appointment, or otherwise. Assuming that the guardian had to show damages, the law could simply provide that the lake's legal damages were to be measured by the costs of making the lake "whole" in the sense of restoring the lake to the condition it would have been in had its "legal right" to intactness not been violated. That is, if the defendant's liability were established (if the upstream plant were found to have violated the applicable standards), it would have to pay into a trust fund, for the repair of the river, funds adequate to cover

such items as aeration, restocking with fish and aquatic plants, filtering, and dredging.

If anyone considers this farfetched, note that the federal courts have allowed such a suit to be brought in the name of the Byram River (the river that forms part of the interstate boundary between southern Connecticut and New York) against the village of Port Chester, which had been polluting it. And it is certainly plausible that some recent and important federal legislation, including the Federal Water Pollution Control Act (FWPCA) and the Comprehensive Environmental Response, Compensation, and Liability Act of 1980 (CERCLA), will be construed as authorizing comparable results....

Commonwealth of Puerto Rico v. *SS Zue Colocotroni* is a striking illustration. In *Zue Colocotroni*, an oil tanker by that name was allowed by its owners to deteriorate into an unseaworthy condition, to be launched without proper charts, and to be manned, as the courts put it, by a "hopelessly lost" and "incompetent crew." The ship ran aground off Puerto Rico, spilling thousands of tons of crude oil. Puerto Rico, as trustee for its resources, submitted an estimate of damage to an area around a twenty-acre mangrove swamp. The major item was for a decline of 4,605,486 organisms per acre. "This means," the district court said, "92,109,720 marine animals were killed," largely sand crabs, segmented worms, and the like. Trying to get a handle on damages (the court's own can of segmented worms), the judge wrote:

The uncontradicted evidence establishes that there is a ready market with reference to biological supply laboratories, thus allowing a reliable calculation of the cost of replacing these organisms. The lowest possible replacement cost figure is $.06 per animal, with many species selling from $1.00 to $4.50 per individual. Accepting the lowest replacement cost, and attaching damages only to the lost marine animals in the West Mangrove area, we find the damages caused by Defendants to amount to $5,526,584.20.

Let me make clear that I am not claiming that each and every Nonperson could (much less should) be put in each and every position the law has carved out for Persons. There is, at the least, a threshold question of intelligibility, policy aside. For each arrangement, we have to ask, could *that* entity be fitted coherently into *that* legal provision? It would make no sense to accord a tree the right to sit on a jury, for example, or to make a will. But surely a tree could be the beneficiary of a will. And decisions to cut one down, even by its private owner, could be made subject to administrative review (some cities now do this)....

The basic point I want to carry forward is this. As concerns the positioning of Things in law, the range of options we can coherently implement is much wider than is commonly recognized. However, to say that any particular arrangement is coherent is not to say that it is *wise*, much less morally right or morally welcome. We could prosecute and execute the insane, but it would strain the moral fabric of the law. Indeed, each of the many options has costs that are easy to identify: the inflexibility that comes of assigning entitlements that will be practically inalienable, the added court burden, and perhaps even the erosion of judicial credibility should judges be regarded as subordinating identifiable human interests on behalf of a constituency that could not care one way or the other....Supposing that we *could* intelligibly adjust the legal system to provide various Nonpersons recognition in the law—that is, fit them into the legal framework through an assignment of Advantage and Disadvantage—why *ought* we to do so? What would an argument in favor of such laws look like? And, more broadly, on what basis might Nonpersons be accounted for, not merely in law, but in moral thought generally?

These, the moral questions, are, as I have already intimated, harder than the legal ones. And of these none seems more intractable than the ontological conundrum. By reference to what principles are we to carve up the world into those things that count, and those that don't? It is well known that in some conditions the survival of a herd may require the "thinning out" of individual members. If we take herds rather than individual animals as our moral unit, then presumably the "thinning" is all right. On the other hand, if the individual counts, but not the herds, then thinning is harder to defend. Hence, are *individuals* morally favored, or *herds*?...

As we saw,...it is an all too common mistake to suppose that all questions of legal considerateness boil down to questions of legal rights....There is an analogous error to confront: to suppose that the only basis for maintaining that X (someone or something) has a legal right is to demonstrate that

X has a moral right, as it were, underneath. Here, too, there is a fragment of truth on which the mistaken generalization rests. Some legal rights associated with ordinary humans—including some of the most fundamental, such as freedom of speech and of worship—relate to strong claims of moral right that were championed long before the constitutional provisions were enacted to secure them. With such an image in mind there is a temptation, when considering whether an animal or tree or future human should have a legal right (or other Advantage), to suppose that it requires proof of some independent and prior moral right.

But this is simply not so. One perfectly plausible moral basis for making Nonpersons legally considerate, even to the point of according them something approximating "legal rights," is where doing so is calculated to advance the welfare of humans. Such an argument can be carried through quite apart from any independent moral right that the Nonperson can be shown to have, and, indeed, quite apart from whether it is even of any independent moral interest.

Corporations, for example, are not Persons. Yet, they are fitted into law by assigning them legal, even constitutional, rights. General Motors can sue, be sued, and raise "its" rights to be free from unreasonable searches and seizures. This is a practice that has the support of persons who would not argue that corporations are themselves moral agents to which moral rights and duties can be ascribed. To *justify* positioning corporations as holders of legal rights (and bearers of legal liabilities), one need go no further than show that a regime in which corporations are so positioned is preferable in terms of the beneficial consequences of the resulting system for contemporary humans.

On a like basis, we can support the legal personification of many Nonpersons (e.g., granting them standing in court) because it is the most sensible way of promoting our normally recognized ends, without ever deciding whether the Nonperson deserves any independent moral rights. If the preservation of a species is of commercial benefit to us, one way to fortify that benefit is to appoint for the species a guardian. A legislature, averse to the risk of toxic wastes on humans, might be well disposed to create a guardian-enforced right in bodies of water to enjoin toxic-induced changes in their status quo, at a threshold before an irreversible hazard to humans has become provable. This would be a system in which some Things were made *legally* considerate. But it does not presuppose their being *morally* considerate. To supply moral warrant for the arrangement, one need not look beyond a sheerly conventional utilitarian calculus.

Similarly, someone who was persuaded that among basic human moral rights was the right to a clean environment could well support the assignment of environmental legal rights for the environment as means of securing the moral rights of Persons. In fact, in much of Anglo-American legal history a stream's "natural flow" was as protected from interference as any environmentalist might have wished; the protection stemmed, however, not from any moral claim on behalf of the stream but from what were conceived to be the "natural rights" of the riparian (streamside) landowner.

The reader may be tempted to respond, "Then we are talking about the legal rights of humans, not those of rivers." Not necessarily. Remember that even if the judge or legislature is animated solely by a concern for human welfare, the elements which the guardian is required to prove in court in a particular case need not include actual or potential damage *to humans*. On the contrary, we are assuming that the legal rule will authorize claims on behalf of the river when changes *in the river* exceed a certain standard. Under such a system, the direct interest—what would govern the lawyers' and judges' attention—would be evidence bearing on the river: whether it was being "damaged" in the legally defined sense under that standard. There would be no call to prove any hazard to humans, or any infringement of a human's rights, if the rule did not so provide.

Most people, I expect, are prepared to deal in those terms, and to reform legal and social arrangements to the extent they demonstrably inure to the benefit of contemporary (or, slightly more problematically, future) humans.

The falling out occurs when someone proposes going one step further. What happens when we are being asked to spare wilderness areas, rivers, species, and whatnot and thus to forego timber, living space, and chemicals, not from consideration of our interests as we ordinarily understand them, but from consideration of *something else*? The objection is not just that such sacrifices are unwarrant-

able. More severely, it is common to feel that a moral argument aimed at justifying sacrifices from consideration (somehow) of nonhumans, in particular of things devoid of interests, is not even intelligible. There is no "something else." (One Canadian writer, criticizing my views in *Trees*, paraphrases Gertrude Stein against me: "When you get there, there's no *their* there." "The only stone which could be of moral concern and hence deserving of legal rights," the critic gibes, "is one like Christopher."

The objection might be put this way. A moral dilemma grows out of, and operates to resolve, conflicts. All conflicts are conflicts of interest. We might have conflicts of interest among ourselves *in regard to* a particular river. This means that we would conserve a certain state of the river to the point, but not beyond the point, warranted by our collective interests *in it*. But the river itself has no independent interests. In our discussion of law, recall, it was possible to sidestep the river's lack of real independent interest by presuming that the lawmaking body would merely mandate whatever was to be the river's legally protected state. Legal interests and legal harms are what the law provides them to be. But when we step back to put ourselves in the position of lawmakers and ask what considerations we might mull to arrive at any environment-conserving standards, there is a corresponding question that definitions cannot stifle: How, not in legal fiction but in credible fact, can any legal position we put the river in make *it* better or worse off? The implication, it will be said, is that any apparent conflict between us and rivers is illusory.

Whatever truth there be to the claim that Things lack interests, it is also misleading. Of course, to speak of a moral dilemma presupposes interests, even some conflict: one interest that tugs one way and one interest that tugs another. That much is inherent in "dilemma." But there is no reason why the conflict cannot be a conflict within a single person, the moral agent faced with a decision. The "conflicting interests"—so far as that is required—may be one's own. Indeed, if morals are to be intelligible, it is imperative that our talk about interests (and "preferences" and "utility") allows for a conception of conflict between what we take our interests to be *before* carrying through a moral analysis, and what we take our interests to be *after*.

To illustrate, imagine Jones, who in the course of driving on his way to a business meeting sees along the roadside the baby that—as in its typical command appearances in the ethics readers—is about to drown in six inches of water. Jones's initial inclination is to hurry past, for if he stops he will forgo a favorable deal. But then Jones considers certain other things, including the value of the human life expiring in the water, the prospective parental grief, and the community's legitimate expectations. He saves the child.

How shall we analyze Jones's decision in terms of his interests? In some perfectly defensible sense of the term, we would be warranted to say that his "interest" was to save the baby, or that to do so was what he preferred or was of more utility to him. But if we elect those manners of speaking, we obscure the very process we are trying to illuminate: how moral reasoning contributes to amend our initial preferences into (and this is what finally matters) our morally reflective, more enlightened ones. To preserve the distinction, we do better to say that Jones recognized as his *initial* or *utility preference* signing the contract (sacrificing the child). But on reflection from a moral viewpoint about what he ought to do, Jones reached a *morally corrected preference* to save the child (forgoing the contract).

That distinction is vital if we are to make any sense of a nonhomocentric morality. Specifically, several writers espouse a "deep ecology" viewpoint that somehow values the environment beyond its value to us. But if such an ethic is to get off the ground, how does one even state its ambition coherently?

Return to the question of damming a wild river. Ultimately, the preferences the decision reflects will be our own, not the river's. That much is true, trivially. Only persons—certainly not rivers or fish—prefer. But the real issue is how our preferences will be arrived at. Surely anyone who considers the damming of a river will want to calculate the river's utility to us. Presumably that would involve, first, an estimate of the consumption and use values of the river in each alternative state. How do the revenues that damming would garner through electricity and irrigation compare to the loss of revenues from impeding barge traffic? Next, we would uncontroversially add a "shadow price" to account for the fact that the river has values to us that do not show up in actual market-price transactions, in lost traffic tolls, and so on.

The concept of shadow price is worth a moment's reflection. The general idea is this. In comparing the social value of two ordinary commodities, such as a loaf of bread and a can of paint, the relative price people will pay gives us a fair expression of the products' relative worth. If the bread commands a dollar and the paint sells for eight, then presumptively one more gallon of paint is worth more to society than one more loaf of bread. But we can make that judgment because the benefit from the bread and paint is limited to consumers to whom the products can be packaged and, as it were, auctioned off. But when it comes to valuing the social benefits of the river, the technique of "packaging and pricing" just will not work. I cannot enjoy the bread unless I pay for it. Many of the benefits of a river, however, are so far-reaching and diffuse that not all those who benefit can be excluded from, and therefore forced to pay for, the benefits each derives. I cannot feasibly be charged for the pleasure I get from the river just through driving by and looking at it. Hence, the concept of shadow price may be enlisted to give us a closer approximation to the river's real utility. It aggregates what people *would* pay in dollar terms to preserve such benefits if they were honestly to reveal their preferences and *could* be made to pay for them. No one evaluating the damming of a wild river would dispute the relevance of taking such an allowance for shadow cost into account.

To clarify what *is* in dispute, let us call the conventional shadow price of the economist the "base shadow price" to distinguish it from what I will call the "morally corrected shadow price." The market value plus the base shadow price measure what I referred to as utility preferences, for example, all value that would be ascribed to the river other than through conscious moral reflection. The "morally corrected shadow price" refers to the utility preferences adjusted as a consequence of moral reflection. It expresses the value which on some moral view we *ought to* be entering into our analyses, whether that value is conventionally recognized by most people or not.

Granted, by recasting the issue in these terms we do not provide an answer. But at least it gives a handle on what an easily clouded discussion is, or ought to be, about. Let us continue with the hardest case, that of a mere Thing. Is there any moral argument touching upon a Thing that can support modifying our utility preferences, specifically, so that a social arrangement not warranted by utility (because we would be sacrificing "too much") might yet be warranted by some morally corrected evaluation? To hold that there is such a revalued "price" for an object is what I mean by calling the object *morally considerate*. To illustrate the dilemma of "deep ecology" in these terms, imagine a state governor whose staff has done a cost-benefit analysis of the damming project. His staff has accounted for all of the beneficial interests we have *in* the river. They have calculated that we stand to benefit so much from the electricity. They have offset those gains with what is lost in boating and fishing. A dollar value is even allowed for lost scenic value. "On that basis," the governor says, "damming the river pencils out to be in our interests. Still, I want to do what's right. So I am prepared to think through my preferences further, to 'morally correct them,' as you say. But on what basis ought we to give up our benefits to preserve the river? Once we have summed up our interests *in it*, there is nothing else to add to the ledger."

The governor may concede that where we are considering relations with ordinary Persons, we may find ourselves amending our original dispositions by adopting a corrective moral viewpoint. But, the governor will maintain, that is possible because Persons, we all agree, are morally considerate. Persons have interests and preferences. We can adopt their standpoint and judge what is for their "good." He may even concede that some such a corrective analysis would warrant modifying our treatment of higher animals such as nonhuman primates and whales. They, too, may be morally considerate. But no such modification of thought processes touching the river is appropriate or even conceivable. "It may be possible to make a Thing *legally* considerate through legal fiction," he will say. "But there is no moral legerdemain through which you can make them really considerate."

How do we respond? We can grant, at the start, that Things, and indeed most Nonpersons, lack any number of properties deemed morally significant in the literature. They have not the capacity to understand what is happening to them, the power to frame a plan of life, to exercise moral choice,

and so on. A person whose initial inclination is to steal can be persuaded not to steal because stealing is the wrong thing to do. Such a dialogue is out of the question with Nonpersons, which is why rampaging rivers and lions may do harm, but they cannot do wrong. All this can be expressed by conceding that, unlike Persons, Nonpersons are not *moral agents* holding preferences that are correctable by ethical reasoning. But it is a long leap from the fact that Persons are the only audience of moral discourse, and therefore the only prospective obligors, to the inference that only Persons can be obligees or have other moral significance. It is not, let me grant, an utterly irrational leap. But to make it, one must lay as a ramp some additional premise, such as that we have no obligation to behave morally except toward those things capable of responding toward us in kind. Some philosophers, who trace all obligation to self-interest, tend to give reciprocity such a foundational role....

We commonly not only regard it as commendable, but speak of obligations to make sacrifices in favor of those who are in no position to reciprocate, such as the comatose, the dead (is there nothing to be said for Antigone?), and anonymous victims of wars we conduct in distant lands. In sum, there is no reason to accept the premise that being a moral agent, or obligor, is a prerequisite of being a moral patient or obligee.

The skeptic who concedes the obligor-obligee distinction, and who recognizes that being a moral agent is not a prerequisite for being morally considerate, may put before us a second barrier: to be considerate, a thing must be, at the least, a holder of moral rights....

What it takes to be a rights holder—remains a subject of considerable dispute. But most of the literature appears to assume that having (or "taking") interests of some sort is necessary. Things, by definition, do not take an interest in their wellbeing, if they have one. Therefore, it can be argued that when it comes to revising our inclinations touching Things, the route most familiar to contemporary moral philosophy, that via a discourse about rights, appears to be blocked....

My own view is that to speak of the moral (as opposed to legal) rights of a tree or river is not appropriate. But however one comes out on the rights question, it is not dispositive of the issue here, which goes not to rights but to moral considerateness. Just as...not all legal considerateness can be boiled down to legal rights, so, too, not all moral considerateness can be expressed in terms of moral rights. Consider the conventional good Samaritan dilemma: We need not reach the question whether the child in jeopardy has a right to the passerby's rescue, or even whether the passerby has a duty to the child, in order to say that it would be *morally commendable* for the passerby to rescue the child, or that the passerby would be *advancing some good.*

Similarly, to support the welfare system, one need not argue that the poor have some sort of moral right to welfare, although it is sometimes put that way. The welfare laws may be defended as good, as morally welcome, on the grounds that they conduce to the betterment of the whole society, or rightly recognize the considerateness of the destitute. On a parity of reasoning, to support placing a Thing in a certain legal position one is not required to prove that it has a moral right to be so situated. There is support for the arrangement if it is morally better so to amend the law, that is, if we can demonstrate that the amendment would advance some good.

This places our skeptic in a third, fallback position. He must say this: Even if we substitute some broader notion of good for rights as the key to moral evaluation, we have not detached ourselves from *interests.* Any moral revision of our thinking still requires an accounting of the interests of the things on whose behalf our disposition is to be revised—else, wherein lies the "good" in sacrificing our more obvious desires? If we discern some good in improving the lot of the poor, even at some sacrifice of general welfare, it is because we can identify some human interests that have been advanced. On the other hand, if we are asked to make a collective sacrifice in consideration of a river and are told to exclude from our thoughts any consideration of the interests of Persons affected thereby, where is the "good" in it to be found? Indeed, when we move to the realm of Things what are we being asked to think *about*? As Joel Feinberg puts the challenge, "[A] being without interests has no 'behalf' to act in, and no 'sake' to act for." But even if one agrees, does this mean that in evaluating actions affecting their condition, there is no "right" and "wrong," no "morally better," that is not fully explicable in terms of human utility and human

rights? Are there no intermediate foundational possibilities?

The question, then, is not, "Can a mere Thing have rights?" The question is, "Can a Thing be morally considerate?"...An entity—for example, a river—is morally considerate if in deciding what we ought to do, its condition enters into our reflections, not exclusively as an instrument to the pleasures of Persons. We are assuming, as moral philosophers often do, the vantage point of a hypothetical impartial, morally enlightened observer of events and character. The hypothetical observer's verdicts of right and wrong, just and unjust, permissible and impermissible are not fully determined by what is welfare maximizing, or what the majority of persons (at their contemporary stage of enlightenment and prejudice) happen conventionally to approve of. But even then the puzzle remains: when the independent observer reflects, not about our interests and welfare, but about the river, what does she think about? The challenge is to devise a coherent moral viewpoint from whose vantage reflections that account for a Thing serve to reevaluate decisions reached on the basis of ordinary Person-dominated welfare considerations alone....

Pluralism conceives the realm of morals to be partitioned into several planes. The planes are intellectual frameworks that support the analysis and solution of particular moral problems, roughly in the way that algebra and geometry provide frameworks for the problems to which they are respectively suited. Each plane is composed of two fundamental elements. First, there is an ontological commitment, that is to say, a foundational judgment as to which things are to be recognized and dealt with.

To illustrate, in doing plane geometry we make an ontological commitment to a world that consists of points, lines, and angles. Solid geometry posits a less flat citizenry of spheres and cubes and their surfaces. Arithmetic posits numbers. In the same vein, each moral plane embeds its own posits as to what things are to be deemed morally considerate within that framework. In some planes it is essentially sentient creatures whose interests count. In others it is Persons, species, or nation-states. But (the Pluralist maintains) just as the rules of solid geometry are not the rules of arithmetic, so the rules that govern our relations with animals are not the same rules that govern the relations among corporate bodies.

Thus there is for each plane a second element, what I call its governance—essentially the rules that apply. In the various geometries, the governance is the system of postulates, axioms, theorems, and corollaries that determines the range of questions that can be asked about the points, lines, and planes, the strategy of their analysis, and the quality and substance of the solutions. In the context of our inquiry, the governance for each moral plane is the body of rules, principles, and so on, to which that version of the world is subject.

A concrete illustration of where I am coming from—and heading—may be helpful. Under recent law, all federally funded institutions using live animals for research are required to establish review procedures to assure that the animals are being treated in a "humane" fashion. As the programs have developed, there has been increased vigilance to avoid the infliction of pain on the animals; but there is not the same reluctance to impose death. For example, if an animal awakening from an invasive procedure faces any prospect of continuing pain, it is almost certain to be sacrificed: "put out of its misery." By contrast, in dealing with a convalescing human who is unable to consent, we are ordinarily prepared to impose a regimen that entails considerable suffering if we believe there to be the faintest possibility of salvaging further life (even further pain-racked life). The exceptions, if any, are almost always where the human has become a (we say "vegetable" but we mean) lower animal, a Nonperson.

I presume that these distinctions have little appeal to a Monist. The moral world comprises one group of morally relevant entities ("rights-holders") all treated the same way ("equally"). Either animals don't count, so that we can use them for our benefit without constraint; or they do count, and have the same rights as we do. The implication of the either-or choice may be to dismiss the animal entirely. As one defender of animal experimentation [Carl Cohen] has recently argued,

If all forms of animal life...must be treated equally, and if therefore...the pains of a rodent count equally with the pains of a human, we are forced to conclude (1) that neither humans nor rodents possess rights, or (2) that rodents possess all the rights that humans possess.

Unsurprisingly, this chain of reasoning leads the author to conclude that animals have no rights.

Pluralism is an attempt to view the situation in a less binary, more flexible manner. The Pluralist is in no way surprised to find us being at once more considerate of animals' pain than of their lives, and of Persons' lives than of their pain. Both animals and Persons are considerate, but our relations with each are separately fabricated. With animals, it appears that those charged with making actual (nonphilosophic) decisions have adopted something close to a pure utilitarianism. That is, in selecting between courses of animal-affecting conduct, society is increasingly committed to minimize their pain. In dealings among Persons, we also seek to minimize pain; but we blend into our judgments an additional, sometimes conflicting consideration, what a Kantian would call respect-for-persons. What we have here, in the terminology presently being examined, are two separate worlds (Persons and animals) across which separate rules (moral governances) are in operation. People and rodents both experience pain, a morally salient fact that is accounted for by each of the two standard institutional review committees, those for humans and those for animal subjects. The respective committees decide—they invoke distinct governance considerations—when life is to be taken. Our duties toward rodents are shaped by doubts (which should remain open to examination) that a rodent forms self-conscious, detailed plans about the future. By contrast, normal *homo sapiens* project a life rich with goals, dreams, aims and far-reaching intentions.

To grasp the ontological element of Moral Pluralism, the notion that different moralities are based on different versions of the world's salient qualities, an analogy to mapping, albeit rough and incomplete, provides an instructive starting point.

Perhaps the most striking characteristic of mapping is that for a single terrain we can plot many maps, depending upon our interests. Consider the United States as a map subject. There are road maps, political maps, weather maps, topographical maps, soil maps, maps of populations, manufacture, and mineral deposits. Each map presents its own salient features in a coherent way, depending upon the anticipated interests of travelers, politicians, or mineral explorers. Most of them conform in some common, dominant features—the national boundaries and perhaps some major reference points, such as the seacoasts. Great Lakes, and principal rivers. But each of the maps also etches in, eliminates, or accentuates those variables that respond to *its* questions: average climatic conditions, altitude, roadside services. There is no one map that is right for all the things we want to do with maps, nor is one map, the topology map, more valid than another, the demographic. Indeed, we do not regard them, because of their variances, as inconsistent. We may in fact choose to overlay maps, that is, combine salient features. The hiker may want a map that combines the altitudinal isobars of a topographical map with the rain data of a climate map and the paths of a trail map.

In considering the analogy to morals, one principal parallel has already been intimated: the possibility that moral discourse can be partitioned into different domains depending upon the entities subject to like consideration, or the moral activity in which we are engaged.

What mapping offers ethics is a model for grasping how Pluralism might be conceived, that is, how morals might be partitioned into coherent subgroupings for definition and analysis. Unstructured, the ethical world, no less than the physical, presents itself as (in William James's phrase) "a blooming, buzzing confusion." The other extreme, a single, unified Monism, may be equally unsatisfactory for its own reasons. In between lies the alternative of groupings, systematic gatherings of diverse data, along the lines of maps. One set of mappings might accord with the type of activity in question, for example, whether our concern is prescribing action or evaluating character. Another set may divide according to type of entity....For some analyses, dominated by considerations of pain, one wants to map all sentient creatures affected. Another plane might map abstractions such as corporations, nations, species, tribes, cultures. These are entities to which "pain" and "harm" as it is understood in familiar Person discourse do not apply, and which can therefore receive an independent accounting only by reference to their own special principles and pleadings....

Take the question of whether we are warranted in putting limits on the Inupiat's traditional bowhead hunt. One way to attack the question is to posit individuals as the morally salient entities (individual Indians, individual whales, individual non-Indian Americans) and hash it out within the classic utilitarian framework....In that framework, we would decide what was right by aggregating welfares (or combining preferences) in some way that gave equal weight to each person's pleasures or desires....We would aggregate the utility gains to all those who benefit from increases in oil reserves and diplomatic maneuverability (roughly 200 million Americans) and subtract the utility losses to the several thousand Indians and their supporters. Even if the benefits of oil development to each non-Indian are individually insignificant, their weight in the aggregate will easily dominate in the final analysis. The calculations would not change appreciably if we included future generations in the universe of affected people....By most plausible measures, the benefits to the present-plus-future beneficiaries would still swamp the losses to the considerably smaller universe of present-plus-future tribe members.

Of course, it is for just this reason—to resist such a swamping of their interests—that the Native American groups, in common with other minorities, characteristically avoid tying moral choices to aggregated utility calculations. The math will always favor the majority. The conventional alternative is to ground claims in an individual-rights discourse....Specifically, an Indian will assert that the moral claim each tribe member has to retaining his cultural heritage is vital enough to be elevated to the status of a right, and therefore exempt from the counterbalancing of utilities that characterizes the utility planes. In discussions of law, this position ordinarily emerges as an assertion of the rights of individual Indians under the First Amendment or the American Indian Religious Freedom Act. One problem with adopting that strategy, however, is that each Indian's claimed right is destined to be met by a countervailing claim of right by the other side: the "property right" the rest of us have to lease the public lands for public benefit, perhaps even our First Amendment right to travel, an interest furthered by plentiful supplies of gasoline. Hence, for the Indians, a battle...carried out in the language of individualized-rights discourse, may carry the day in some cases, but in others is likely to be inconclusive or unsuccessful.

Is it possible that another strategy would have been more successful, one that drew attention to a plane that was predicated on the moral salience of Membership Entities? In the bowhead illustration, the idea would be to take an argument for nondevelopment of the Beaufort region based on claims of individual Indians, and supplement it by claims of independent duties owed to, or rights of, the Indian tribe or nation or culture. The coherence of such an argument depends upon identifying a value in groupness or community, and a way of talking about that value that transcends the interests of and toward the individuals. With the conflict so cast, the claims would not be a mere "summing" of the claims of individual Indians, and hence would not fairly be met by a summing of individual claims from the other side. They would have to be met, if at all, on their own plane by claims of the appropriate kind and weight....

9   Discrimination

In the context of social and political philosophy "discrimination," in the pejorative sense, refers to the practice of unequal political treatment of individuals on the basis of their religion, race, gender, or ethnic origin—for example, not allowing women or blacks to attend certain schools. Historically, there have been many issues relating to the problem of discrimination. For example, philosophers in the past have wondered whether there is any legitimate basis on which one group of people can treat members of another group within the same society in a systematically less favorable manner. Perhaps, as both Plato and Aristotle thought, there are naturally superior and inferior groups of people; if that is so, then perhaps the naturally superior have the right and the obligation to rule the naturally inferior. Perhaps, as many people have thought and some continue to think, there are naturally different *roles* assigned to different groups of people, men and women, for example, which legitimately require and sanction fundamentally different political treatment (men but not women being allowed to vote, to own property, hold public office, and so on). Much of the history of modern political thought in the Western world has been the gradual working out of the consequences of the distinctly modern notion that all people are in some sense "created equal," and are, as a matter of fact, fairly equal in actual abilities, at least so far as political considerations are concerned.

Needless to say, many individuals today continue to feel secretly, "in their hearts," that they, as a group, are superior to others and tend wherever possible to act as though they were. But there is no longer any respectable body of opinion to support those feelings and so they remain largely unconscious and unsupported, at least in scientific and philosophical circles.

The issue relating to discrimination which *has* become philosophically controversial in recent years is the question of what is known as "affirmative action," "preferential treatment," "reverse discrimination," "set asides," or "quotas." Assuming that everyone in a society is politically equal and therefore entitled to complete equality of opportunity regarding schools, jobs, housing, running for public office, and so on, and even assuming that all overt discrimination against individuals of traditionally despised minorities were removed in *fact* as well as in *theory*, most of the preferred positions in the society would still, for many years, continue to go to men, rather than women, whites rather than blacks or Hispanics, even though white males account for less than half the total population. Why? Simply because in the past white men tended to receive better training and psychological encouragement and so now have a considerable head start on women and minorities.

Of course, many discriminatory practices still exist in the United States and elsewhere. Even after removing laws which prohibit women or blacks from voting or attending certain schools or holding certain offices, those who must select successful applicants to such positions continue to prefer white males and so continue to award them the privileged positions. But suppose we could somehow get round this—suppose, for example, all applications were received anonymously, without photograph or handwriting, so that those who must decide among applicants could not tell who was male, female, white, or nonwhite. The process might now seem completely fair. Applicants would be accepted or rejected solely on the basis of their proven merit (grades, SAT scores, and so on). But, assuming for the moment that white males make up 38 percent of the total population, when the results came in, we might find, for example, that 76 percent of the successful applicants were white males, twice their proportion of the total population. How could this happen? The white males were better qualified. Why? Is it because they are as a group naturally superior? Or is it because they attended better schools, got more encouragement at home, and so on? And if so, why was *that*? Because in the past women and blacks were not allowed or encouraged to enter such professions and therefore to train for and to mentally prepare for them. Is this fair? Are we *still* (even in our idealized scenario) discriminating against women and minorities?

The question therefore arises whether justice demands something *more* be done than the removal of existing discriminatory practices, that is, whether in addition to removing existing statutory bans on blacks, Hispanics, and women, as well as existing practices which favor white men, justice demands a more *positive* effort to give a boost, in effect, to those who were held back in the past? Of course, we cannot admit completely unqualified applicants, but among those who are minimally or adequately qualified to do the work, or be successful in the school, should we allot, or "set aside," a certain percentage of positions to minorities (say, 12 percent black and 14 percent Hispanic) which reflects their proportion of the total population, even if some of these applicants are less qualified than some of the white males we thereby have to reject? Is that fair?

Most social and political questions can be analysed in one of two ways—either from the utilitarian perspective of what will produce the most desirable consequences or from the point of view of justice, of simply doing what is right, regardless of the consequences. Many would agree that from a utilitarian perspective it would be highly desirable to have better representation by women and minorities in such socially prestigious positions as doctors, lawyers, university professors, top executives, government officials, and so on. This would provide highly useful role models for younger members of such minorities (black teachers inspiring black youngsters to go into teaching, for example) and a better insight into the problems of minorities (women police officers interviewing rape victims, for example, or a Hispanic school official discussing with a Hispanic student reasons for staying in school).

On the negative side of the utilitarian calculus are the increased negative perceptions white males might have of women and minorities and the negative self-perceptions minorities are apt to have of themselves as a result of preferential treatment. The white male who lost out to a black applicant and the white male already at work where a minority has been hired, as well as the minority worker herself may feel that the applicant did not *deserve* to get the job, may not be qualified for the job, and therefore cannot do the job well. This can lead to resentment which in turn can translate into lack of on-the-job cooperation and support from fellow workers and therefore poor job performance, ending finally in possibly lower self-esteem for the newly hired minority worker. These are some of the positive and negative considerations from a utilitarian perspective.

But, despite the utilitarian outcome, is the practice of preferential treatment fair or just? One argument for affirmative action is that justice demands compensation for injustices in the past. If blacks are less able to compete in today's highly competitive world because they were held back in the past, and if, by the same token, whites were given a head start over members of other groups by superior schooling, societal values, family wealth, and social connections, then justice would seem to demand compensating the black applicant at the expense of the white applicant. But is it fair to award social goods on the basis of past injustices of which the *particular* applicants in question have not been guilty? Why should I be penalized for the sins of my father, grandfather, or great-grandfather who may have discriminated against your father, grandfather, or great-grandfather?

The arguments *against* the fairness or justice of preferential treatment, therefore, tend to look at the question from the point of view of the *individuals* involved. Given this particular black candidate and this particular white candidate, they argue, justice requires that after compensating either or both of these individuals for injustices done to them in the past, we must hire the most qualified of the two, white or black. We must not discriminate against this particular black candidate just because she is black, nor must we practice "reverse discrimination" against this particular white candidate just because he is white. Arguments *supporting* the fairness or justice of preferential treatment tend to move the argument away from the question of the rights of *individuals* to that of the rights of *groups*. Whatever my particular family history, I enjoy and have enjoyed benefits simply by being white or else I suffer and have suffered penalties simply by being black.

But does it make any sense to speak of the rights of *groups* of people, that is, over and above the rights of the individuals who make up those groups? Traditionally, philosophers have tended to consider that only individual people had rights, but some philosophers today argue that we can only understand and effectively deal with the ethnic tensions in Iraq, Israel, South Africa, the former Yugoslavia, Armenia, Romania, or Cambodia by acknowledging the legitimate rights of *groups*, that is, ethnic minorities, to a measure of autonomy and self-determination, that is, their right to life, liberty, and the pursuit of happiness *as groups*.

READINGS

James Fishkin of the University of Texas argues that preferential programs are unfair and unjust because they do not target the right people. It is unjust, he argues, to award social goods on the basis of past injustices of which the particular applicants in question have been neither guilty nor victims. In the famous *Bakke* case, in which a slightly better qualified white applicant to a University of California medical school was rejected in favor of a less qualified black applicant, Fishkin points out that the black applicant actually had had *better* educational opportunities than the white applicant. Furthermore, he argues, even if we agree in general that American whites as a group are responsible for the lower life prospects of blacks as a group, it doesn't follow that the ancestors of a particular white applicant were responsible for past injustices to blacks, nor that the ancestors of a particular black applicant suffered from those same injustices. It might turn out, for example, that the particular black applicant is a recent immigrant from Nigeria (whose relatives were not enslaved or discriminated against) while the white applicant is a recent immigrant from Norway (whose relatives did not enslave or discriminate against blacks). Finally, Fishkin argues, whatever the historical causes of the present advantages for whites and disadvantages for nonwhites, removing these advantages would be unjustly intrusive into the private lives of individual families. Unless the state is prepared to prevent affluent, educated white families from giving their children advantages within the home, such as books, computers, encouragement, and help with homework, inequalities in the life prospects of white and nonwhite children cannot be entirely removed, and that to remove those in-home advantages would be far too repressive of individual freedoms to ever be politically acceptable, at least in the United States.

Defending the justice of preferential treatment, Glenn Loury of the John F. Kennedy School of Government at Harvard University shifts the argument from the question of the rights of *individuals* to the rights of *groups*. Whatever my particular family history, he argues, I enjoy and have enjoyed benefits simply by being white, or suffer and have suffered penalties simply by being black. After all, in most cases, racial preference and discrimination are rather impersonal. The black family is not kept out of a white neighborhood because of anything peculiar to them but simply and only because of their membership in a larger group—just because they are black. Similarly, benefits resulting from living in an affluent middle-class, mostly white neighborhood are not conferred on individuals because of their individual talents or personality traits but simply because of their membership in a group—because they happen to be white.

Albert Mosley, professor of philosophy at Ohio University, defends affirmative action against some of its recent critics. He argues that even if the ancestors of today's blacks were not discriminated against in the past and even if the ancestors of today's whites were not the perpetrators of such discrimination, today's blacks are nonetheless at a disadvantage vis-à-vis today's whites. One writer has recently dramatized this point by asking black students how much money it would be worth to them to be turned instantly white and by asking white students how much money it would be worth to them *not* to be suddenly turned black. The extremely high sums of money offered on both sides of this imaginary scenario represent in a rough way the value or benefit of being white in our society no matter what your ancestors did to blacks (and the penalty for being black in this society no matter where your ancestors came from).

Mosley also argues that although affirmative action programs may fail on occasion to "target" the right people, as James Fishkin has pointed out, it is as accurate and fair as any public policy can be in its practical application. To be administratively practical, he argues, any public policy must specify identifiable groups of people which are statistically similar, but whose membership admit of exceptions. Voting is limited to those 18 or older because, while there are obviously some individuals younger than 18 capable of voting responsibly and some older than 18 who are not, *most* people under 18 are not capable and *most* people 18 or over are capable of voter responsibility. As Mosley points out, any voting legislation must specify *some* age, and no specification of age can eliminate entirely the problems of "targeting" the wrong individual. Suppose we tried to test each individual to see whether he or she is mature enough to vote or drive a car. Clearly, practical considerations prohibit such a practice. The conclusion Mosley draws is that any unfairness related to such statistical averaging is an integral part of the legislative process and not something peculiar to legislation relating to affirmative action. Besides, as Mosley points out, there are also good utilitarian reasons for adopting affirmative action programs.

Elizabeth Wolgast, a philosopher at California State University, Hayward, examines the question of sexism, or gender discrimination. She argues against the traditional egalitarian liberal position that gender discrimination should be understood as the injustice of treating women differently from men, or, put another way, that ending discrimination would be to treat women exactly like men. Aristotle said that justice consists in treating equals the same and unequals differently. Wolgast argues against some liberals that since women are *not* like men in crucial respects, they should *not* be treated exactly the same as men but rather with equal *consideration* in light of important differences between the sexes. Of course, egalitarian liberals are aware that men and women are different, but they argue that these differences are morally irrelevant for questions of social justice. Differences between men and women, these liberals argue, are no more morally or politically important than the difference between people who have blue eyes and those who are brown-eyed. According to the egalitarian position, only social and cultural conventions can make it possible to unjustly institutionalize differential treatment of blue-eyed and brown-eyed people. And by analogy, the argument goes, only unjust social conventions account for unequal treatment of men and women, for example, not allowing women into the military.

Wolgast disagrees, arguing that there are fundamental, culturally universal differences between men and women which justify different social and political treatment. So far, she argues, only women can give birth. Therefore, only a woman can know for sure that she is the child's parent. Giving birth to the child makes it harder for her to avoid her parenting responsibilities, as opposed to the biological father who may not know he is the father, or may successfully deny it even if he suspects he is, or may run away to avoid parental responsibility. Knowing this from an early age, Wolgast argues, cannot help but shape young women's sense of themselves and how they are different from men. They will have fundamentally different attitudes, for example, toward becoming pregnant and will typically be more cautious than a man concerning the long-term suitability of a mate. In addition, as long as most women are physically weaker than most men and as long as men are more likely to attempt to rape women than women are to attack men and as long as society considers the stigma of casual sexual contact greater for women than for men, the problem of rape will be different for women than for men. She argues it will not therefore be simply a matter of alterable, misguided social and historical convention for parents to be more reluctant for their daughter to hitchhike across the country alone than for their son to do so. Where differences between men and women are irrelevant, they should be treated equally—equal pay for equal kinds of work, for example. But where gender differences are *not* irrelevant, equality for women may involve *un*equal treatment—maternity leave for women but not for men, for example.

"Liberty versus Equal Opportunity"

James S. Fishkin

Liberalism has often been viewed as a continuing dialogue about the relative priorities between liberty and equality. When the version of equality under discussion requires equalization of outcomes, it is easy to see how the two ideals might conflict. But when the version of equality requires only equalization of opportunities, the conflict has been treated as greatly muted since the principle of equality seems so meager in its implications. However, when one looks carefully at various versions of equal opportunity and various versions of liberty, the conflict between them is, in fact, both dramatic and inescapable. Each version of the conflict poses hard choices which defy any *systematic* pattern granting priority to one of these basic values over the other. In this essay, I will flesh out and argue for this picture of fundamental conflict, and then turn to some more general issues about the kinds of answers we should expect to the basic questions of liberal theory.

I will explore the conflicts between liberty and equal opportunity by focusing on three positions,

From *Equal Opportunity*, Ellen Frankel Paul, *et al.*, eds. (Oxford: Basil Blackwell, 1987).
Reprinted by permission of *Social Philosophy and Policy*.

each of which can be considered in terms of its corresponding account of liberty and equal opportunity....I will term the three positions Laissez Faire, Meritocracy, and Strong Equality. While these labels are in some respects arbitrary, the positions they represent will turn out, I believe, to be familiar ones even though they travel under various banners.

A good recent example of the laissez-faire position is the one Nozick takes in *Anarchy, State, and Utopia*. One of the more provocative examples in the book compares decisions to marry with decisions by prospective employers and employees:

Suppose there are twenty-six women and twenty-six men each wanting to be married. For each sex, all of that sex agree on the same ranking of the twenty-six members of the opposite sex in terms of desirability as marriage partners: call them A to Z and A' to Z' respectively in decreasing preferential order. A and A' voluntarily choose to get married....When B and B' marry, their choices are not made nonvoluntary merely by the fact that there is something else they each would rather do....This contraction of the range of options continues down the line until we come to Z and Z', who each face a choice between marrying the other or remaining unmarried.

Nozick explicitly develops his account of liberty in market exchanges on analogy with these mating decisions:

Similar considerations apply to market exchanges between workers and owners of capital. Z is faced with working or starving; the choices and actions of all other persons do not add up to providing Z with some other options....Does Z choose to work voluntarily?...Z does choose voluntarily if the other individuals A through Y each acted voluntarily and within their rights.

In both the market and the mating cases, "A person's choice among differing degrees of unpalatable alternatives is not rendered nonvoluntary by the fact that others voluntarily chose and acted within their rights in a way that did not provide him with a more palatable alternative." Others acting within their rights cannot, on this view, do me harm. If we think of harm in the core negative-liberty sense of people individually or collectively being able to do as they please so long as they do not harm or violate the rights of others (with rights

violations being construed as harms for these purposes), then one can easily subsume both the right to marry and the right to get a job within the same conception of liberty and the same conception of justice. Nozick's slogan "From each as they choose, to each as they are chosen" works perfectly for the selection of mates under modern conditions. Nozick's extension of it to the market means only that the welfare state and other redistributional devices seem objectionable because they would prohibit capitalist acts between consenting adults.

Because A and A' are fully within their rights to marry, we do not think of their action as harming B and B' even though it does, obviously, limit their options. So far, the analogy between mating and employment retains some plausibility. However, there is also a crucial disanalogy, at least from the perspective of any advocate of equal opportunity.

In modern, secular, Western moral culture, we commonly think that members of the same ethnic group, race, or religion can, *if they choose*, select mates only from the same ethnic group, race, or religion. In fact, we commonly think they can marry more or less whomever they like. Those who would like to marry others who are similar in those respects are fully within their rights to do so; those who have other views are free to follow them as well.

In the job market, by contrast, if employers hire only members of the same ethnic group, race, or religion, we commonly view that not as an exercise of liberty but, rather, as an act of blatant discrimination. The laissez-faire view includes Lockean rights but not the right to equal consideration in the job market within the bench mark for relevant harms....Another way of making this point is to say that negative liberty is completely unfettered in both the private and public spheres on the laissez-faire view (completely unfettered in that so long as no one is harmed in the relevant sense, people may do as they please in both areas)....The two spheres are treated in the same way. But treating them in the same way trivializes equal opportunity in the job market because it eliminates any basis for complaints against discrimination and sheer arbitrariness. For this reason, the bench mark on harm compatible with meritocratic notions of equal opportunity can be thought of as the same as the laissez-faire notion—except for the incorporation of an additional right defining relevant harms, the right to equal consideration of one's qualifications in the job market.

Now it might be argued in defense of the laissez-faire view that rational employers will not discriminate; they will not hire less "qualified" people merely on the basis of irrelevant factors such as race, ethnicity, or religion. They will not do so because it will cost them something in terms of efficiency, productivity, or the like. There are two replies worth noting briefly. First, the rational behavior of economic actors is a theoretical idealization which some firms and some people approximate under some conditions, but fall far short of in others. There is no reason to assume that departures from rationality of this sort will not occur. Furthermore, within the laissez-faire theory, these actors are within their rights to be irrational, just as any prospective couple about to make an unwise decision to marry would also be within its rights to be irrational. (If, say, they were on any objective assessment really incompatible, they would still be within their rights to get married if they wished to do so.)

Second, statistical discrimination will, in fact, be rational for economic actors under some conditions. If members of a given group generally perform badly, then firms may decide to forgo the decision costs of individual evaluation and substitute group membership as a fairly reliable proxy for whatever individual factors they would have tested. If they do, they will be right most of the time, but at the cost of some serious injustices (in the meritocratic sense) to some individuals. Discrimination can be economically rational. The self-interest of economic actors is not sufficient protection if nondiscrimination is an important goal.

The second position,...meritocracy, is designed to rule out discrimination. Roughly, this position entails that there should be widespread procedural fairness in the evaluation of qualifications for positions. Qualifications must be job-relevant for the positions to be filled, and they must represent actual efforts of the individual, not merely group membership (shared, arbitrary native characteristics).

On the meritocratic position, an additional right has been added to the standard Lockean rights for determining the bench mark for harm. If I am discriminated against, then I am harmed in the sense that my right to equal consideration of my qualifications has been violated. This addition represents a sharp departure from the kind of negative liberty we presume in the private sphere. If Jane prefers John to Joseph as a mate, Joseph does not have grounds for complaint that his qualifications were not given equal consideration. Jane's preference is decisive, regardless of her reasons. But if Company X prefers John to Joseph as an employee, Joseph would have grounds for complaint if he could show that, because of his race or religion, a less qualified person (John) was hired instead. Under meritocracy, negative liberty is not unfettered in the public sphere as it is in the private, while under laissez faire, the two spheres are treated in the same way.

From the standpoint of advocates of strong equality, meritocracy does not go far enough. I believe its limitations are nicely captured by an example which I adopt from Bernard Williams. Imagine a warrior society, one which, from generation to generation, has been dominated by a warrior class. At some point, advocates of equal opportunity are granted a reform. From now on, new membership in the warrior class will be determined by a competition which tests warrior skills. A procedurally fair competition is instituted, but the children of the present warriors triumph overwhelmingly. To make it simple, let us assume that children from the other classes are virtually on the verge of starvation, and children from the warrior class have been exceedingly well-nourished. Hence, in the warrior's competition we might imagine three-hundred pound Sumo wrestlers vanquishing ninety pound weaklings. While this competition is procedurally fair in that, we will assume, it really does select the best warriors, it does not embody an adequate ideal of equal opportunity. The Sumo wrestlers have been permitted to develop their talents under such favorable conditions, while the weaklings have developed theirs under such unfavorable conditions, that measuring the results of such overwhelmingly predictable (and manipulable) causal processes does not represent an equal opportunity for the less advantaged to compete. The causal conditions under which they prepare for the competition deny them an effective opportunity. This criticism holds despite the fact that, on meritocratic grounds, the competition may operate perfectly so as to select the best warriors— as those warriors have developed under such unequal conditions.

A principle which captures the injustice embodied in the warrior society is the criterion of equal life chances. According to this principle, I should not be able to enter a hospital ward of newborn infants and predict what strata they will eventually reach merely on the basis of their arbitrary native characteristics such as race, sex, ethnic origin, or family background. To the extent that I can reliably make such predictions about a society, it is subject to a serious kind of inequality of opportunity. Obviously, inequality of life chances would be compatible with strictly meritocratic assignment. The warrior society scenario, where family background perfectly predicts success in the competition, illustrates how one sort of equal opportunity is entirely separable from the other. By contrast, the position I label "Strong Equality"...is committed to both forms—meritocratic assignment and, in addition, equality of life chances.

The difficulty with strong equality is that it is only realizable at an even more severe cost in liberty than that required for meritocracy. A clue as to the issues at stake can be found in the restriction of negative liberty by strong equality, not only in the public sphere but also in the private sphere....The liberty at stake in the private sphere turns out to be the autonomy of the family—the liberty of families, acting consensually, to benefit their children.

When family autonomy is combined with the two demanding components of equal opportunity considered thus far—meritocratic assignment and equal life chances—a pattern of conflicting and difficult choices emerges, a kind of dilemma with three corners which I term a "trilemma." It is a trilemma because realization of any two of these principles can realistically be expected to preclude the third. This pattern of conflict applies even under the most optimistic scenarios of ideal theory. If equal opportunity is to provide a coherent ideal which we should aspire to implement, then certain hard choices need to be faced....

The trilemma of equal opportunity can be sketched quickly. Let us assume favorable and realistic conditions—only moderate scarcity, and good faith efforts at strict compliance with the principles we propose (both in the present and in the relevant recent past). However, to be realistic, let us also assume background conditions of inequality, both social and economic. The issue of equal opportunity—the rationing of chances for

favored positions—would be beside the point if there were no favored positions, i.e., if there were strict equality of result throughout the society. Every modern developed country, whether capitalist or socialist, has substantially unequal payoffs to positions. The issue of equal opportunity within liberal theory is *how* people get assigned to those positions—by which I mean both their *prospects* for assignment and the *method* of assignment (whether, for example, meritocratic procedures are employed guaranteeing equal consideration of relevant claims).

The trilemma consists in a forced choice among three principles.

Merit: There should be widespread procedural fairness in the evaluation of qualifications for positions.

Equality of Life Chances: The prospects of children for eventual positions in the society should not vary in any systematic and significant manner with their arbitrary native characteristics.

The Autonomy of the Family: Consensual relations within a given family governing the development of its children should not be coercively interfered with except to ensure for the children the essential prerequisites for adult participation in the society.

Given background conditions of inequality, implementing any two of these principles can reasonably be expected to preclude the third. For example, implementing the first and third undermines the second. The autonomy of the family protects the process whereby advantaged families differentially contribute to the development of their children. Given background conditions of inequality, children from the higher strata will have been systematically subjected to developmental opportunities which can reliably be expected to give them an advantage in the process of meritocratic competition. Under these conditions, the principle of merit—applied to talents as they have developed under such unequal conditions—becomes a mechanism for generating unequal life chances. Hence, the difficulty with the meritocratic option...is the denial of equal life chances.

Suppose one were to keep the autonomy of the family in place but attempt to equalize life chances. Fulfilling the second and third principles would require sacrifice of the first. Given background conditions of inequality, the differential developmental influences just mentioned will produce disproportionate talents and other qualifications among children in the higher strata. If they must be assigned to positions so as to equalize life chances, then they must be assigned regardless of these differential claims. Some process of "reverse discrimination" in favor of those from disadvantaged backgrounds would have to be applied systematically throughout the society if life chances were to be equalized (while also maintaining family autonomy). Hence, the difficulty with the second option,...which I have labeled reverse discrimination, is the cost in merit.

Suppose one were to attempt to equalize life chances while maintaining the system of meritocratic assignment. Given background conditions of inequality, it is the autonomy of families that protects the process by which advantaged families differentially influence the development of talents and other qualifications in their children. Only if this process were interfered with in a systematic manner could both the principles of merit and of equal life chances be achieved. Perhaps a massive system of collectivized child rearing could be devised. Or perhaps a compulsory schooling system could be devised so as to even out home-inspired developmental advantages and prevent families from making any *differential* investments in human capital in their children, either through formal or informal processes. In any case, achieving both merit and equal life chances would require a systematic sacrifice in family autonomy. Hence, the difficulty with the third scenario, the strong equality position,...is the sacrifice in family autonomy.

Implementation of any two of these principles precludes the third. While inevitable conflicts might be tolerated by systematic theorists in the nonideal world, these conflicts arise within ideal theory. This argument is directed at the aspiration to develop a rigorous solution even if it is limited to the ideal theory case. Given only moderate scarcity and strict compliance with the principles chosen, and given that there is no aftermath of injustice from the immediate past, we are applying these principles in our thought experiment to the best conditions that could realistically be imagined for a modern, large-scale society.

Of course, liberalism has long been regarded as an amalgam of liberty and equality. And liberals and libertarians have long been fearful of the sacrifices in liberty that would be required to achieve equality of result. Equality of opportunity, by contrast, has been regarded as a weakly reformist, tame principle which avoids such disturbing conflicts. However, even under the best conditions, it raises stark conflicts with the one area of liberty which touches most of our lives most directly. Once we take account of the family, equal opportunity is an extraordinarily radical principle, and achieving it would require sacrifices in liberty which most of us would regard as grossly illiberal.

The force of the trilemma argument depends on there being independent support for each of the principles. Merit makes a claim to procedural fairness. However, as Brian Barry has argued, procedural fairness is a thin value without what he calls "background fairness," and background fairness would be achieved by equality of life chances. Family autonomy can be rationalized within a broader private sphere of liberty, it protects the liberty of families, acting consensually, to benefit their children through developmental influences. The principle leaves plenty of room for the state to intervene when some sacrifice in the essential interests of the child is in question or when consensual relations within the family have broken down (raising issues of child placement or children's rights). Without the core area of liberty defined by this narrow principle, the family would be unrecognizably different.

Hence, these principles are not demanding by themselves; they are demanding in combination. Each of the trilemma scenarios which fully implements two of the principles leads to drastic sacrifice of the third. To blithely assume that we can realize all three is to produce an incoherent scenario for equal opportunity, even under ideal conditions.

One reasonable, but unsystematic response to this pattern of conflict would be to trade off small increments of each principle without full realization of any. But this is to live without a systematic solution. The aspiration fueling the reconstruction of liberal theory has been that some single solution in clear focus can be defined for ideal conditions, and then policy can be organized so as to approach this vision asymptotically. But if trade-offs are inevitable, even for ideal theory, then we have ideals without an ideal, conflicting principles without a unifying vision.

My position is, first, that equal opportunity is a prime case for this result; second, that despite the lack of a systematic solution for ideal theory, there are significant policy prescriptions which can be derived without solving the priority relations among these principles; and third, that the lack of a systematic solution exemplifies the special difficulties facing liberalism in our contemporary culture.

Having sketched the first point, let us turn to the second: the issue of policy implications. There are two kinds of policy implications we can evaluate without having to solve the problem of priority relations among these three principles for ideal theory—without, in other words, employing the model of an asymptotic aspiration to a single unified and coherent ideal which we should, as best we can, approach through partial realization. The first kind of policy implication involves cases in which we can achieve a major *improvement* in the realization of one of these values without a major loss in any of the others (or in any other new values which the proposal impinges upon). The second kind of policy implication involves cases in which a proposal would impose a major *loss* in one of these values without any comparable gain in any of the other values (or in any new values which the proposal impinges upon).

The first kind of policy implication is exemplified by all those things we could do to improve equality of life chances, family autonomy, or meritocratic assignment. In the U.S. for example, we are far from the possibility frontier in achieving any of these values and, in some cases, we have moved further away rather than closer in recent years. We blithely tolerate the perpetuation of an urban underclass; a whole generation of urban youth is growing up with blighted life chances and with few opportunities to make it into the mainstream economy, and with few policy initiatives now focused on their problem. Family autonomy is protected for middle-class families, but poor families have far greater difficulty in forming and maintaining themselves intact. By neglecting job prospects among the poor, the…administration has also affected the incentives for family formation, as well as the ability of poor families to provide essential prerequisites for child development and socialization. We are also far from achieving meritocratic assignment. Discrimination persists against blacks, Hispanics, women, and other minorities, including homosexuals. There is no justification for tolerating job discrimination on the

basis of arbitrary factors which are irrelevant to the roles in question. In other words, despite…talk of protecting "the family" and of creating an "opportunity society,"…policies have promoted middle-class families and middle-class opportunities at the expense of the disadvantaged.

The second kind of policy implication is exemplified by the major quick fix for the first set of problems—preferential treatment based *merely* on arbitrary native characteristics. When it is applied in competitive meritocratic contexts, this policy yields a major sacrifice in one of our values, meritocratic assignment, without a significant gain in either of the others. The difficulty is that preferential treatment, when it is based merely on arbitrary native characteristics, is mistargeted as a policy which could have any effect on equality of life chances. It is mistargeted because, in competitive meritocratic contexts (e.g., admissions to graduate and professional schools) there are strong institutional pressures to accept the most qualified applicants with the specified arbitrary native characteristics. Just as family background provides disproportionate opportunities to develop qualifications among advantaged white children, it does so among relatively advantaged minority children. This policy only serves to widen the gap between the urban underclass and the black middle class—despite the fact that it is typically justified as special consideration for those who are from disadvantaged backgrounds.

My objection does not apply to policies which apply preferential treatment to those who are actually from disadvantaged backgrounds. In that case, meritocratic assignment is sacrificed for a gain in equal life chances. Rather, my objection applies to programs which are applied *merely* on the basis of arbitrary native characteristics, so as to reward the most qualified members of the group (who will, as a statistical matter, tend to come from its more advantaged portions). Hence, the irony of the De Funis and Bakke cases. De Funis, a Sephardic Jew from a relatively poor background, was not admitted to the University of Washington Law School while most of the minority students admitted on the basis of preferential treatment were, apparently, from more advantaged backgrounds (or, at least, were the children of black professionals). On the other hand, the program at the University of California at Davis which the Court struck down in the Bakke case was unusual for having procedures in place to direct special consideration to those who actually came from economically disadvantaged backgrounds. Theoretically, the program which the Court struck down in *Bakke* was defensible within our framework, while the program on which it avoided making a decision in *De Funis* (providing preferential treatment for race as such) would not be.

We should mention one persistent counterargument to this conclusion about preferential treatment. Preferential treatment based merely on race (or on other arbitrary native characteristics) is sometimes supported not as a remedy for developmental disadvantages in the present, but as a form of *compensation* for injustices in the past. However, the mistargeting objection has force here as well, but with additional complications.

First, the list of groups which were historically victims of discrimination is much broader than the groups now demanding compensation. Consistent pursuit of this argument would produce a host of other ethnic claims—Irish, Polish, and Italian, Catholic as well as Jewish, in addition to the more familiar arguments made on behalf of Hispanics, Native Americans, and Orientals. This proliferation is not fanciful. The Anti-Defamation League discovered one American law school which had no less than sixteen racial and ethnic categories for admissions classifications.

Second, the very notion of compensation raises conceptual challenges—unacknowledged by its proponents—when it is applied to this kind of problem. An individual X is supposed to be compensated by returning him to the level of well-being he would have reached had some identifiable injustice in the past (against his forebears) not occurred. In tracing back through the generations, however, it soon becomes clear that X would usually not now exist were it not for the historical injustice. If we try to imagine the world which would have existed had the historical injustices not occurred, we cannot return X to the level he would have reached, because he would not have reached any level at all. For example, let us take the well-documented case of Kunta Kinte. If Kunta Kinte, Alex Haley's ancestor in *Roots*, had not been brutally kidnapped and sold as a slave, there is no likelihood that the author of *Roots* would have come

to exist in the twentieth century. The mating and reproduction of each generation, in turn, depends on a host of contingencies. If the chain were to have been broken at any point, by a parent, grandparent, or great-grandparent, we would get a different result in this generation. If it were not for the initial injustice, Kunta Kinte's descendants might well have been native Africans, perhaps residents today of Juffure (Kunta Kinte's village in West Africa).

Hence, we cannot employ the straightforward notion of compensation (returning people to the level they would have reached had the injustice not occurred) when the injustice spans several generations. Perhaps some compelling version of the argument might be created which confronts this difficulty. Rather than deny this possibility I wish merely to claim that such an argument, if it were developed, should, at the least, accept my objection to mistargeting.

Compensation is not compatible with the mistargeting which results from preferential treatment applied *merely* to racial categories in competitive meritocratic contexts. Compensation cannot plausibly mean benefiting some blacks (who may be already well-off) for earlier injustices to *other* blacks—particularly when those who do *not*, by and large, benefit from the compensatory argument (the urban underclass) are experiencing extremely disadvantaged conditions. To take a provocative analogy, would it not have been outrageous if the German government, after World War II, had paid "compensation" to well-off American Jews, ignoring the orphans and other direct victims of the Holocaust? It would not have been compensation to benefit Jews indiscriminately or, even worse, to benefit disproportionately those who were untouched by the injustices at issue. For this reason, I conclude that the compensation argument does not alter the general conclusion about preferential treatment reached earlier. When it is directed at those who are themselves from disadvantaged backgrounds, it is admissible within our framework, for then the gain in equal life chances may balance the loss in strictly meritocratic assignment. But when, in competitive meritocratic contexts, it is applied merely on the basis of arbitrary native characteristics, then we have grounds for objecting to it.

"Why Should We Care About Group Inequality?"

Glenn C. Loury

This essay is about the ethical propriety and practical efficacy of a range of policy undertakings which, in the last twenty years, has come to be referred to as "affirmative action." These policies have been contentious and problematic, and a variety of arguments have been advanced in their support. Here I try to close a gap, as I see it, in this "literature of justification" which has grown up around the practice of preferential treatment.

It may seem fatuous in the extreme to raise as a serious matter, in the contemporary United States, the question "Why should we care about group inequality?" Is not the historical and moral imperative of such concern self-evident? Must not those who value the pursuit of justice be intensely concerned about economic disparities among groups of persons? The most obvious answer to the title question would seem, then, to be: "We should care because such inequality is the external manifestation of the oppression of individuals on the basis of their group identity."

Yet, this response, upon examination, is not entirely adequate. Why should the mere existence of group disparities evidence the oppressive treatment of individuals? There is little support in the historical record for the notion that, in the absence of oppression based upon group membership, all socially relevant aggregates of persons would achieve roughly the same distribution of economic rewards. Indeed, to hold this view is to deny the economic relevance of historically determined and culturally reinforced beliefs, values, interests, and attitudes which constitute the defining features of distinct ethnicities. Distinct cultures will necessarily produce distinct patterns of interest and work among their adherents. And while this need not be an argument against egalitarianism, since distinct interests and different work need not receive different remuneration, it does serve to shift our focus from disparities among groups *per se* to disparities in the rewards to the different types of activities toward which various groups' members incline.

In fact, there is a subtle logical problem which haunts the idea of equality among groups. To the extent that the arguments for equal group results presuppose the continued existence of general inequality, they end up (merely) demanding an equality *between groups* of a given amount of inequality *within groups*. They leave us with the question: Why is inequality among individuals of the same group acceptable when inequality between the groups is not? Indeed, there is "group inequality" whenever there is inequality—one need only take those at the bottom to constitute a "group." This is precisely what a radical, class analysis of society does. The unanswered question here is why the ethnic-racial-sexual identification of "group" should take precedence over all others. It is a question usually avoided in popular discussions of the need to equalize group disparities.

It is, of course, possible to hold that the very existence of distinct beliefs, values, interests, and so forth in distinct groups is evidence of oppression. And it is surely true that one major consequence of domination is to alter the conception of self held by the dominated. Women are socialized into the acceptance as natural or desirable of roles which undermine their competitive position in the world of work. Minorities, so this argument goes, do not aspire to those professions in which there are presently few persons like themselves to serve as role models, to illustrate that the opportunity for success is really there. In this view group disparities evidence oppression even when arising most

From "Why Should We Care About Group Inequality?" *Equal Opportunity*, Ellen Frankel Paul, Fred D. Miller, Jr., Jeffrey Paul, and John Ahreus, eds. (Oxford: Basil Blockwell, 1987). Reprinted by permission of the publisher.

immediately out of differences in "tastes" among persons, since those differences are themselves due to oppression.

But this argument, if it were valid, would prove too much. The differentiating effect of oppression has sometimes worked to make a group of persons *more* effective in economic competition. And the differences of belief and values among various groups sometimes reflect centuries of historical development, in lands far removed from that which they currently occupy. If group differences in beliefs and values bearing on economic achievement are the fruit of oppression, then why not also those group differences in cultural style so much celebrated by cultural pluralists? If, to put the matter in simplistic but illuminating terms, poor academic performance among black students reflects "oppression," why then should not outstanding athletic performance stem from the same source? We remain, then, with the question: when does group inequality constitute a moral problem and what may appropriately be done about it?

In contemporary American society such disparities are often taken to constitute a moral problem, and occasion a public policy response. The use of racial preferences in education, employment, or even politics is a frequent policy response. This has been controversial; courts and philosophers have sought to define the circumstances under which such preferences might legitimately be employed. Recently, both in the courts and in public discourse, questions have been raised about the legitimacy of government efforts on behalf of women, blacks, and other racial minorities. Some of these questions strike deeply at the philosophical foundation of preferential policies.

It is a tenet of long standing in American liberalism that the use by the state of ascriptive personal characteristics as a basis for discriminating among individuals, whether that discrimination be in their favor or to their disadvantage, is wrong. Such practice stigmatizes the individuals involved and reinforces private inclinations to make invidious distinctions based upon the same ascriptive characteristics. The antidiscrimination principle, codified in so many statutes and court rulings of recent decades, is founded upon such a world view. Martin King put it well when he said: "I have a dream that my four little children will one day live in a nation where they will not be judged by the color of their skin, but by the content of their character." Plaintiffs' attorneys in the landmark *Brown* cases, in oral argument before the Supreme Court, made similar representations when urging the Court to overturn the "separate but equal" doctrine. Civil rights advocates in the legislature, when working for the passage of the Civil Rights Act of 1964, offered extensive assurances that they sought only to enforce on the private sector such restrictions in their business practices as were consistent with assuring colorblind hiring and promotion standards. Throughout this early history of the civil rights revolution, the classical liberal principle of aversion to the use of racial (or religious or sexual) classification was adhered to by the advocates of change. And this antidiscrimination principle has a noble intellectual pedigree, harking back to the Enlightenment-era challenge to hereditary authority, and reflected in the "anonymity axiom" of modern social choice theory.

Yet, in a historically remarkable transformation this position of the liberal political community in our country has dramatically changed. Today, King's dream that race might one day become an insignificant category in American civic life seems naively utopian. It is no small irony that, a mere two decades after King's moving oration, the passionate evocation in public debate of his "colorblind" ideal is for many an indication of a limited commitment to the goal of racial justice. The recalcitrant persistence of group disparity in the face of formal equality of opportunity has forced many liberals to look to race-conscious public action as the only viable remedy.

However, unlike the earlier antidiscrimination principle, this more recent practice of color-conscious state action rests on rather less firm philosophical ground. The key court decisions supporting it are, in the main, closely divided ones. The arguments encountered in support of the practice in the ordinary political discourse of the nation seem, at least to this listener, to be more tortured and less compelling than those put forward on behalf of the colorblind principle. Typically, these arguments take the form of demonstrating the invalidity of the notion that positions should be distributed according to the nebulous criterion of "merit," followed by a set of unsupported empirical claims regarding the benefits sure to flow from a more equal distribution of positions among groups.

There is, for example, a tendency in these arguments to obscure the distinction between group-conscious state actions whose main purpose is to prevent overt, but undetectable, private discrimination, and those whose principal aim is to increase the representation of protected groups without any implication that their "underrepresentation" evidences illegal private behavior. The first set of policies, call them "enforcement-oriented," though requiring use by the state of what may be imperfect (i.e., color-conscious) means, aim to eliminate private practices and procedures which themselves violate the antidiscrimination principle. (They may be likened to the use of statistical market share data by antitrust authorities when seeking to determine whether a firm has engaged in illegal, but unobservable, business practices.) The second type of policies, call them "result-oriented," concern themselves with the outcome of private actions which may be wholly unobjectionable, but which occur in the face of unacceptable *de facto* racial disparities. The two types of policies cannot be rationalized in the same manner. A coherent theory of the practice of affirmative action, it would seem, must be able to distinguish among them. How, if at all, can the "result-oriented" use of racial categories by the state be justified?

I want to make here what might be called a "minimalist's" argument for departure from the colorblind standard. My purpose will be, in the first instance, to establish that a plausible specification of how multi-ethnic societies actually function will lead to the conclusions that *social justice is not consistent with a blanket prohibition on the use of group categories as a basis for state action*. In making this argument I will rely on an intellectual tradition long familiar to economics—one which justifies departures from *laissez faire* when, due to some sort of market failure, the outcomes of private actions are socially undesirable. The market failure to which I refer, it will be seen, rests upon the very social behavior which induces there to exist, as a permanent, structural matter, distinct racial and ethnic groups among which inequality might arise in the first place.

My approach to this problem will be to inquire whether, in theory, we should expect the continued application of racially neutral procedures to lead eventually to an outcome no longer reflective of our history of discrimination. If the answer to this query were negative, then adherence to a policy of equal opportunity alone would condemn those whose rights had historically been violated (and their progeny) to suffer indefinitely from what most would regard as ethically illegitimate acts. Since, presumably, this would be an ethically unacceptable state of affairs, a (weak) case for intervention would thereby be made. My point is that there are reasons to believe that the consequences of apparently innocuous and ubiquitous social behaviors are such as to systematically and intrinsically pass on from one generation to the next that group inequality originally engendered by historical discrimination.

Thus, I propose that we take certain aspects of the dynamic performance of an unrestrained market economy as a standard in evaluating the ethical legitimacy of affirmative action. The choice between public policy limited to what Douglas Rae has called "prospect-regarding equality of opportunity" or extended to some sort of color-conscious intervention, I submit, should depend upon the extent to which we are confident of the ability of markets naturally to erode historically generated differences in status between groups. I suggest, in other words, that one part of this puzzle can be resolved if we seek to identify precisely what it is about *laissez faire* which leads us to expect (as supporters of affirmative action typically do) that even in the absence of ongoing economic discrimination, genuine equality might not be attained without special state actions.

Imagine an economic model in which persons compete for jobs on competitive labor markets, where job assignments are made under conditions of equal opportunity, based solely on an individual's productive characteristics, and in which the markets for jobs operate without regard to individuals' ascriptive characteristics. Suppose, however, that the individual's acquisition of productive characteristics is favorably influenced by the economic success of the individual's parents. That is, and this is key, the notion of equal opportunity does not extend to the realm of social backgrounds, and differences in background are permitted to affect a person's access to training resources. This is much like the world in which we live. Persons begin life with endowments of what might be called "social capital," nontransferable advantages of birth which are conveyed by parental behaviors bearing on later-life productivity.

In such a world, the deleterious consequences of past discrimination for (say) a racial minority are reflected in the fact that minority young people have, on the average, less favorable parental influences on their skill-acquisition processes.

Further, imagine that families group themselves together into social clusters, or local "communities," and that certain "local public goods" important to subsequent individual productivity are provided uniformly to young people of the same community. These "local public goods" may be very general in nature. One thinks naturally of public education, but also important might be peer influences which shape the development of personal character, contacts which generate information about the world of work, and friendship networks which evolve among persons situated in the same or closely related "communities." What is critical is that these community "goods" (or, possibly, "bads") be provided *internally* to the social clusters in question, and that outsiders be excluded from the consumption of such goods. What I am calling here "communities" are to represent the private, voluntary associational behaviors common to all societies, in which persons choose their companions, often on the basis of common ethnicity, religion, or economic class. Since access to these "communities" could depend on parents' social status, this provides another avenue by which parental background influences offsprings' achievement—another source of social capital.

In order to pose the question most sharply, I assume that all individuals have identical preferences with respect to economic choices, and that an identical distribution of innate aptitudes characterizes each generation of majority and minority workers. Thus, in the absence of any historical economic discrimination, and notwithstanding the tendency for persons to cluster socially, we should expect that the economic status of minority and majority group members would be equal, on average. I want now to inquire whether, in this idealized world, the competitive labor market would function in such a way as eventually to eliminate any initial differences in the average status of the two groups which historical discrimination might have produced.

One can investigate this question by writing down a mathematical representation of this idealized world. It can be shown that the results obtained depend upon whether only family income, or both family income and race, influence the set of social clusters—i.e., "communities"—to which a family may belong. When persons in society discriminate in their choice of associates on the basis of economic class, but not ethnic group, one can show (with a few additional, technical assumptions) that equal opportunity as defined here always leads (eventually) to an equal distribution of outcomes between the groups. However, when there is social segregation in associational behavior along group as well as class lines, then it is not generally true that historically generated differences between the groups attenuate in the face of racially neutral procedures. Examples may be constructed in which group inequality persists indefinitely, even though no underlying group differences in tastes or abilities exist.

This happens because, when there is some racial segregation among communities—that is, when race operates as a basis of social discrimination, though not economic discrimination—the process by which status is transfered across generations does not work in the same way for minority and majority families. *The inequality of family circumstances generated by historical economic discrimination is exacerbated by differential access to the benefits of those quasi-public resources available only in the affiliational clusters which I have called communities.* A kind of negative intragroup "externality" is exerted, through local public goods provision, by the (relatively more numerous) lower income minority families on higher income minority families of the same communities. (Or, if you prefer, a positive intragroup externality is exerted by the relatively more numerous higher income majority families on the lower income majority families of the same communities.) And, because in a world of some social segregation the group composition of one's community depends in part on the choices of one's neighbors, this effect cannot be completely avoided by an individual's actions. As a consequence, the ability of equal opportunity to bring about equal results is impaired by the desire of majority and minority families to share communities with their own kind. This social clustering of the groups is, of course, an essential feature of a multi-ethnic society such as ours. Indeed, in its absence, there would not be selective mating by racial groups, and in short order (2–3 generations) the "problem" of group inequality would be submerged by wholesale miscegenation.

This discussion suggests that, as a general matter, we cannot expect *laissez faire* to produce equality of result between equally endowed social groups if these groups have experienced differential treatment in the past, and if among the channels through which parents pass on status to their children are included the social clustering of individuals along group-exclusive lines. On this argument, state action which is cognizant of groups is *legitimated* by the claim that, in its absence, the consequences of historical wrongs could be with us for the ages. It is *necessitated* by the fact that individuals, in the course of their private social intercourse, engage in racial distinctions which have material consequences. These distinctions are reflected in this model by what I referred to as the "choice of community"—with whom to spend one's time, in what neighborhoods to live, among which children to encourage one's offspring to play, to what set of clubs and friendship networks to belong, and with what sort of person to encourage one's children to mate. Such decisions, in our law and in our ethics, lie beyond the reach of the antidiscrimination mandate. They are private matters which, though susceptible to influence and moral suasion about the tolerance of diversity and the like, are not thought to constitute the proper subject of judicial or legislative decree. Freedom to act on the prejudices and discriminations which induce each of us to seek our identities with and to make our lives among a specific, restricted set of our fellows, are for many if not most Americans among those inalienable rights to life, liberty, and the pursuit of happiness enshrined in our Declaration of Independence.

There are two points I wish to stress about this "minimalist's" argument. First, it rests quite specifically on a conception of group differences in the transmission of status across generations, and thus points to those state interventions which are intended to neutralize such disparities. That is, racial preference is not defended here in the abstract, as a generalized remedy for racial inequality or repayment for past wrong. Rather, a specific mechanism which passes on from past to present to future the consequences of wrongful acts has been explicated. It is to neutralize *that* mechanism that "taking color into account" is legitimated.

And, I would argue, any alternative justification for racial preference should be similarly grounded on an explicit delineation of the "fine structure" of social life which causes the need for such extraordinary state action to arise. The simple evocation of "two hundred years of slavery" or of "past discrimination against minorities and women" does not begin to meet this standard. For the question remains: what specifically have been the consequences of past deeds which require for their reversal the employment of racial classification? The attainment of equal educational opportunities through race-conscious public policy provides a good example. Racial criteria used in the siting or allocation of public housing units would be another. But those racial preferences which confer benefits upon minority group members who do not suffer background related impediments to their mobility (e.g., minority business set-asides) could only be rationalized in this way if it could be demonstrated that the recipients' connection to their less fortunate fellows was such as to insure a sufficiently large beneficial spillover effect on the social mobility of the poor. This is a difficult empirical test for many current practices to meet.

Moreover, other remedies, not dependent on race-conscious action, but intended severely to reduce for all citizens the differential advantages due to poor social background (such as early childhood education, employment programs for disadvantaged urban youths, or publicly financed assistance in the acquisition of higher education) might also be sufficient to avoid the perpetuation of past racial wrongs. In other words, the type of argument which the late Justice William O. Douglas made in his *De Funis* dissent, which acknowledges the legitimacy of taking social background into account when making admissions decisions at a public law school, but nonetheless rejects explicit racial considerations, might well suffice to meet the concerns raised here. Again, it becomes an empirical question, resolved by inquiry into the explicit mechanisms of social mobility, on which the legitimacy of explicitly racial intervention would turn.

The second, perhaps more important point is that, in addition to providing a rationale for extraordinary state action intended to limit the degree of group inequality, the underlying behavioral premises of this model suggest that there are *limits* on what one can hope to achieve through the use of racial classification by the state. As noted above, our political and philosophical traditions are such that the reach of civil rights laws will be insufficient to eliminate all socially and economically relevant discriminatory behavior. That is, we are evidently not willing to undertake the degree of intrusion into the intimate associational choices of individuals which an equalizing redistribution of social capital would require.

Indeed, there are enormously important contractual relationships into which people enter, as a result of which their social and economic status is profoundly affected, but among which racial discrimination is routinely practiced. Choice of marital partner is but the most obvious. People discriminate here by race with a vengeance. A black woman, for example, does not have an opportunity equal to that of a white woman to become the wife of a given white man. And though this inequality in opportunity cuts both ways, since white men are on the whole better-off financially than blacks, one could imagine calculating the monetary damages to black women of this kind of racial discrimination. A class action suit might be brought on their behalf, alleging harm based upon invidious racial discrimination by white men! That such a notion strikes most people as absurd is mere testimony for the fact that we all basically accept the legitimacy of the practice of racial discrimination in the intimate, personal sphere.

The point, though, is much more general than love and marriage. While we seek to maintain integration through race conscious allocation of public housing units, it is clear that such practices cannot prevent disgruntled residents from moving away when the racial composition of their neighborhood changes contrary to their liking. And while racial school assignments may be needed, it is also clear that busing for desegregation cannot prevent unhappy parents (those who can afford it!) from sending their children to private schools or moving to another, more ethnically homogenous district. How intrusive we choose to be in restricting such responses is ultimately a political question, though it would seem that elimination altogether of this kind of discrimination would not be a reasonable possibility in this society. Application of the nondiscrimination mandate has, in practice, been restricted to the domain of impersonal, public, and economic transactions (employment, credit, housing, voting rights) but has not been allowed to interfere much with personal, private, and intimately social intercourse.

Moreover, it seems likely that the state's use of racial classification will generally be insufficient to overcome the economic consequences of this private discriminatory practice. For the fact that such exclusive social "clubs" do form along group lines has important economic consequences. There is an extensive literature in economics and sociology which documents the importance of family and community background as factors influencing a child's latter success. Much evidence suggests that the social and economic benefits deriving from privileged access to the "right" communities cannot be easily offset through the state's use of racial classification.

Having offered a rationale for departure from the "colorblind" standard, one could ask at this point whether there are not unsound rationales for worrying about group inequality which have been offered in our public debates. I think this is decidedly so. As political theorists have long recognized, more is required in the achievement and maintenance of a just society than the writing of a philosophical treatise or a constitution which upholds essential principles of liberty and equality. It is also necessary to secure, as a practical matter, the means through which such principles might be lived by and followed in the everyday life of the policy. In a pluralist society such as ours, where distinctions of race and religion are deep and widespread, this is not a trivial matter. I would venture that at this historical juncture, a sincere commitment in our government to reducing racial inequality is a necessary element of what is needed to establish a just political community in the United States. But this concern is not, by itself, sufficient to that task.

Indeed, certain features of our public discourse over the legitimacy of racial preferences undermine the maintenance of this kind of community. For example, affirmative action represents to many blacks not merely needed public action in the face of past wrong, but rather a just recompense for that wrong. The distinction is vital. For many, affirmative action finds its essential rationale in an interpretation of history—i.e., in an ideology: that blacks have been wronged by American society in such a way that justice now demands they receive special consideration as a matter of right. This is to be contrasted with the means-end calculus which I have offered above as justification for the practice. This reparations argument, however, immediately raises the question: Why do the wrongs of this particular group and not those of others deserve recompense? This can be a poisonous question for the politics of a pluralistic democracy.

There is, of course, a favored answer to this question: slavery. But this answer does not really satisfy anyone—black or white. For no amount of recounting the unique sufferings attendant to the slave experience makes plain why a middle-class black should be offered an educational opportunity which is being denied to a lower-class white. It is manifestly the case that many Americans are descended from forebearers who had, indeed, suffered discrimination and mistreatment at the hands of hostile majorities both here and in their native lands. Yet, and here is the crucial point, these Americans on the whole have no claim to the public acknowledgement and ratification of their past suffering as do blacks under affirmative action. The institution of this policy, rationalized in this specific way, therefore implicitly confers special *public* status on the historic injustices faced by its beneficiary groups, and hence devalues, implicitly, the injustices endured by others.

The public character of this process of acknowledgement and ratification is central to my argument. We are a democratic, ethnically heterogeneous polity. Racial preferences become issues in local, state, and national elections; they are the topic of debate in corporate board rooms and university faculty meetings; their adoption and maintenance requires public consensus, notwithstanding the role that judicial decree has played in their propagation. Therefore, the public consensus requisite to the broad use of such preferences results, *de facto*, in the complicity of every American in a symbolic recognition of extraordinary societal guilt and culpability regarding the plight of a particular group of citizens. Failure to embrace the consensus in favor of such practice invites the charge of insensitivity to the wrongs of the past or, indeed, the accusation of racism.

But perhaps most important, the public discourse around racial preference inevitably leads to comparisons among the sufferings of different groups—an exercise in what one might call "comparative victimology." Was the anti-Asian sentiment in the western states culminating in the Japanese interments during World War II "worse" than the discrimination against blacks? Were the restrictions and attendant poverty faced by Irish immigrants to Northeast cities a century ago "worse" than those confronting black migrants to those same cities some decades later? And ultimately, was the Holocaust a more profound evil than chattel slavery?

Such questions are, of course, unanswerable, if for no other reason than that they require us to compare degrees of suffering and extents of moral outrage as experienced internally, subjectively, privately, by different peoples. There is no neutral vantage, no Archimedian point, from which to take up such a comparison. We cannot expect that the normal means of argument and persuasion will reconcile divergent perceptions among ethnic groups about the relative moral affront which history has forced upon them. We must not, therefore, permit such disputes to arise, if we are to maintain an environment of comity among groups in this ethnically diverse society. Yet some critics of affirmative action can be heard to say "Our suffering has been as great"; and some defenders of racial quotas for blacks have become "…tired of hearing about the Holocaust."

These are enormously sensitive matters, going to the heart of how various groups in our society define their collective identities. James Baldwin, writing in the late 1960s on this subject, in the face of Jewish objections to the use of quotas in New York City, declared what many blacks believe: "One does not wish to be told by an American Jew that his suffering is as great as the American Negro's suffering. It isn't, and one knows it isn't from the very tone in which he assures you that it is." And when, in 1979, Jesse Jackson visited Yad Vashem, the Holocaust memorial in Jerusalem, he deeply offended many Jews with what he may have considered a conciliatory remark—that he now better understood "…the persecution complex of many Jewish people that almost invariably makes them overreact to their own suffering, because it is so great." By forcing into the open such comparative judgments concerning what amount to sacred historical meanings for the respective groups, the public rationalization of racial preference as payment for the wrongs of the past has fostered deeper, less easily assuaged divisions than could ever have been produced by a "mere" conflict of material interests.

So the legitimation of racial preference is not simply a matter of whether *blacks* think our ancestors' brutalization under slavery exceeded—in its inhumanity, its scale, its violence—the evil of Hitler's ovens. By involving judgments arrived at through democratic process, racially preferential treatment expresses the collective priorities of the nation as a whole. The special place of blacks in the practice of affirmative action is, therefore, doomed to be controversial, and in the end—should it become a permanent institution and should its application continue to favor blacks of comfortable social backgrounds over whites of more modest circumstances—unacceptable to a majority of Americans. Individual citizens—be they Catholics, Jews, Armenians, blacks, or other—will, of course, understand it as an important responsibility to ensure that their children are imbued with a keen sense of the wrongs done to their group in the past. It is important for many Americans to keep alive in the memory of successive generations what their ancestors endured; this is crucial to their knowing, fully, who they are. It is, however, another matter entirely when one group of citizens requires all others to share such a private understanding—when, as a matter of proper social etiquette, it is required that all others share a sense of guilt about the wrongs a particular group has endured.

There is something tenuous, and ultimately pathetic, about the position of blacks in this regard. Do not recoil here at the use of the word "pathetic"; that, after all, is what this is all about—evoking the pity, and the guilt, of whites. But, for that very reason, the practice is inconsistent with the goal of freedom and equality for blacks. One cannot be the equal of those whose pity or guilt one actively seeks. By framing the matter thus, the petitioner gives to those being petitioned an awesome power. He who has the capacity to grant your freedom evidently has the ability to take it away—you are therefore dependent upon his magnanimity.

How long can blacks continue to evoke the "slavery was terrible, and it was your fault" rhetoric and still suppose that dignity and equality can be had thereby? Is it not fantastic to suppose that the oppressor, whom strident racial advocates take

such joy in denouncing, would in the interest of decency, upon hearing the extent of his crimes, decide to grant the claimants their every demand? The direct sociological role of the slave experience in explaining the current problem seems to be quite limited. The evocation of slavery in our contemporary discourse has little to do with sociology, or with historical causation. Its main effect is moral. It uses the slave experience in order to establish culpability.

Yet the question remains: Why should others—the vast majority of whom have ancestors who arrived here after the emancipation, or who fought against the institution of slavery, or who endured profound discriminations of their own—permit themselves to be morally blackmailed with such rhetoric? How long can the failures of the present among black Americans be excused and explained by reference to the wrongs of the past? Would not one expect that, in due course, non-black Americans would become inured to the entreaties of the black who explains teenage motherhood, urban crime, and low SAT scores with the observation that blacks have been in bondage for 400 years. When pummelled with this rhetoric nowadays, most whites sit in silence. Dare we ask: What does that silence mean? (And, indeed, what does the constant repetition of this litany do to blacks themselves?) Must not, after some point, there begin to be resentment, contempt, and disdain for a group of people which sees itself in such terms? Consider the contradictions: Blacks seek general recognition of their accomplishments in the past, and yet must insist upon the extent to which their ancestors were reduced to helplessness. Blacks must emphasize that they live in a nation which has never respected their humanity, yet expect that by so doing, their fellow countrymen will be moved to come to their assistance....

I would like to explore some of the deleterious side-effects which can issue from the use of color-conscious methods in the public or private sectors. There is the danger that reliance on affirmative action to achieve minority or female representation in highly prestigious positions can have a decidedly negative impact on the esteem of the groups, because it can lead to the general presumption that members of the beneficiary groups would not be able to qualify for such positions without the help of special preference.

If, in an employment situation, say, it is known that racial classification is in use, so that differential selection criteria are employed for the hiring of different racial groups, and if it is known that the quality of performance on the job depends on how one did on the criteria of selection, then it is a rational statistical inference, absent further information, to impute a lower expected quality of job performance to persons of the race which was preferentially favored in selection. Using racial classification in selection for employment creates objective incentives for customers, co-workers, and so forth, to take race into account after the employment decision has been made. Selection by race makes race "informative" in the post-selection environment.

In what kind of environments is such an "informational externality" likely to be important? Precisely when it is difficult to obtain objective and accurate readings on a person's productivity, and when that unknown productivity is of significance to those sharing the employment environment with the preferentially selected employee. For example, in a "team production" situation (like a professional partnership, or among students forming study groups), where output is the result of the effort of several individuals, though each individual's contribution cannot be separately identified, the willingness of workers to participate in "teams" containing those suspected of having been preferentially selected will be less than it would have been if the same criteria of selection had been used for all employees.

Also, when the employment carries prestige and honor, because it represents an unusual accomplishment of which very few individuals are capable (an appointment to a top university faculty, for example), the use of preferential selection will undermine the ability of those preferred to garner for themselves the honorary, as distinct from pecuniary, benefits associated with the employment. (And this is true even for individuals who do not themselves require the preference.) If, for example, Nobel prizes in physics were awarded with the idea in mind that each continent should be periodically represented, it would be widely suspected (by those insufficiently informed to make independent judgements in such matters, and that includes nearly everyone) that a physicist from Africa who won the award had not made as significant a con-

tribution to the science as one from Europe, even if the objective scientific merit of the African's contribution were as great. If Law Review appointments at a prestigious law school were made to insure appropriate group balance, it could become impossible for students belonging to the preferred groups to earn honor available to others, no matter how great their individual talents....

Further illustration of the kind of unintended consequence which should be taken much more seriously by proponents of affirmative action, combining both the "team production" and the "honor" effects, comes from the world of corporate management. Many of those charged with the responsibility of managing large companies in the U.S. economy today are quite concerned with the state of their minority hiring efforts. The advent of affirmative action masks some serious, continuing disparities in the rates at which blacks, Hispanics, and women are penetrating the very highest ranks of power and control within these institutions. While equal opportunity could be said to be working tolerably well at the entry and middle level positions, it has proven exceedingly difficult for these "newcomers" to advance to the upper echelons of their organizations. The problem is so widespread that a name has been invented for it—the "plateau-ing phenomenon."

Increasingly, able and ambitious young women and blacks talk of taking the entrepreneurial route to business success, feeling stymied by their inability to get on the "fast track" of rapid promotion to positions of genuine power within their companies. Wall Street brokerage and law firms, though increasing the number of young black associates in their ranks, still have very few black partners and virtually no senior or managing partners. Though many large companies now have their complement of minority vice-presidents and staff personnel (especially in the governmental relations and equal opportunity areas), they remain with very few minorities at the rank of senior vice-president or higher, and with a paucity of nonwhites in those authoritative line positions where the companies' profits and future leaders are made.

The failure of women and minorities to penetrate the highest levels of the organization involves factors beyond the raw competence of the individuals involved. While people differ in their abilities, no one today suggests that there do not exist blacks or women with the aptitude and dedication to succeed at the highest levels in the corporate world. The fact that so very few of them do succeed suggests that, in addition to old-fashioned racism, the problem may well stem from subtle aspects of interpersonal relations within companies. When a company determines to increase the numbers of women and minorities in its management ranks, the normal way of proceeding is to make the recruitment and retention of such persons an organizational goal, and to evaluate the performance of those with authority to hire, in part, by the extent to which they succeed in advancing this goal. That is, the company encourages its personnel decision makers to use racial (or gender) classification in addition to other employment screens. This practice of goal setting is done with an explicitness and seriousness which, of course, varies from company to company. Yet, the inevitable result is to confer some advantage upon minority and women employees in the competition for entry and mid-level positions in the company. Even when such preferential treatment is avoided by management, the perception among white male employees, in this era of constant focus on the need to increase minority and female participation, is likely to be that the "newcomers" are getting some kind of break which is not available to them.

In addition, minority or female employees may be hired or promoted into jobs for which they are not ready; better qualified nonminority personnel may, from time to time, be passed over for promotion. Here too, nonfavored employees will often *perceive* that mistakes of this sort are being made, even when in fact they are not. Resentments and jealousies are likely to arise. Charges of "reverse discrimination" will, in all probability, be mumbled more or less quietly among white men who sense themselves disadvantaged. It only takes one or two "disasters," in terms of minority appointments which do not work out, to reinforce already existing prejudices and convince many in the organization that all minority managers are suspect. *The use of racial or sexual employment goals is therefore likely to alter the way in which minority or women managers are viewed by their white male subordinates and superiors.*

And even though most minority employees may measure up to, or even exceed, the standards of performance which others in the firm must meet, the presence of just a few who do not casts an aura of suspicion over the others. Such uncertainty about so-called "affirmative action hires"—those who, it is suspected, would not have their jobs if they were not minority or female—may only reflect the prejudice or bigotry of their co-workers. But, and this is crucial, to the extent that the suspicion is widely held, it can work to undermine the objective effectiveness of the minority manager.

Given that competition for advancement from the lower rungs of the corporate ladder is sure to be keen, there is a natural tendency for those not benefiting from the organization's equal opportunity goals to see the progress of minorities or women as due in great part to affirmative action. If, to illustrate, four white men and one woman are competing for a position which ultimately is awarded to the woman, all four male employees may harbor the suspicion that *they* were unfairly passed over in the interest of meeting diversity goals, when in fact this supposition must be false for at least three of them who would not have been promoted in any case. When, as happens in many companies, the attainment of equal opportunity goals is seen as something which occurs only at the expense of productivity—as a price to be paid for doing business in the inner city, or to "keep the feds off our backs"—then these suspicions are given tacit confirmation by the organization's very approach to the problem of diversity.

Thus, the use of racial classification can entail serious costs. It can, if not properly and carefully administered, create or promote a general perception that those minorities or women who benefit from the firm's interest in increasing diversity are somehow less qualified than others competing for the same positions. And this general perception, when widely held, whether well-founded or merely a reflection of prejudice, can work to limit the degree of success and long-term career prospects of minority and female managers. For it is plausible to hold that in such a managerial environment, the productivity of an individual is not merely determined by the individual's knowledge, business judgment, industry, or vision. It depends as well on the ability of the manager to induce the cooperation, motivation, trust, and confidence of those whom he or she must lead. It depends, in other words, on the extent to which the manager can command the *respect* of his or her colleagues and subordinates.

This observation illustrates the fact that general suspicion of the competence of minority or female managerial personnel can become a self-fulfilling prophecy. When the bottom-line performance of a manager depends on his or her ability to motivate others, and when those who are to be motivated begin with a lack of confidence in the ability of the manager, then even the most technically competent, hard-working individual may fail to induce top performance in his or her people. And the fact that top performance is not achieved only serves to confirm the belief of those who doubted the manager's competence in the first place.

This self-reinforcing cycle of negative expectations is likely to be a particularly significant problem in the higher-level and line, as distinct from lower-level and staff, positions in an organization. Here an individual's contribution to company profitability depends heavily upon leadership and interpersonal qualities, securing the confidence and trust of peers, motivating subordinates to achieve up to their potential. Managerial performance at this level depends rather less on individual, technical skills. That is, whether or not one becomes really "good" at these jobs is determined, in part, by how "good" others believe one can be.

Another critical factor at this level of an organization is self-confidence. This, too, may be undermined by the use of racial classification. Among the questions most frequently asked by minority personnel about to assume a post of unusual responsibility is: "Would I have been offered this position if I had not been a black (or woman, or...)?" Most people in such a situation want to be reassured that their achievement has been earned and is not based simply on the organizational requirement of diversity. And not only that, they want their prospective associates and subordinates to be assured of this as well. When appointments are being made partly on a racial or sexual basis, the inevitable result is to weaken the extent to which the recipients can confidently assert, if only to themselves, that they are as good as their achievements would seem to suggest. A genuinely outstanding person who rises quickly to the mid-level of an organization without ever knowing for sure whether or not this career advance would have taken place in the absence of affirmative action may not approach the job with the same degree of self-assurance as otherwise would be the case. And

this absence of the full measure of confidence which the person's abilities would have otherwise produced can make the difference between success and failure in the upper managerial ranks.

All of these potentially detrimental effects which I associate with the use of preferential treatment of non-white and female employees within an enterprise are reinforced by the general discussion of racial and sexual inequality in our society. The constant attention to numerical imbalances in the numbers of blacks vs. whites, or women vs. men, who have achieved a particular rank in the corporate sector, in addition to placing what may be entirely warranted pressure on individual companies, serves to remind people—black and white, male and female—of the fact that such preferences are a part of their work environment. In order to defend affirmative action in the political arena, its advocates often seem to argue that almost no blacks or women could reach the highest levels of achievement without the aid of special pressures. Yet, this tactic runs the risk of establishing the presumption that all blacks or women, whether directly or indirectly, are indebted to civil rights activity for their achievements. And this presumption may reinforce general suspicion about minority or female competence which already exists.

None of this should be construed as an expression of doubt about the desirability of vigorously promoting diversity in corporate management, or elsewhere in American society. What seems crucial is that, in light of the pitfalls discussed above, the process of achieving diversity be *managed* with care, mindful of the dangers inherent in the situation. What is involved with affirmative action is not simply the *rights* of individuals, as many lawyers are given to argue, but also the *prudence* of particular means used to advance their interests. The "plateau" phenomenon, where able young minority or female managers find themselves unable to advance to the top ranks of their companies, undoubtedly reflects factors beyond those I have discussed. But it is the consensus judgment of personnel managers with whom I have talked that these factors are involved in many cases. In particular, it seems quite probable that general distrust of the capabilities of minority and female managers will accompany and reinforce old-fashioned racist or sexist aversion to having "outsiders" join the "old boys network" of those holding real power within the organization. Such suspicions can, where occasionally validated by experience, provide the perfect excuse for preexisting prejudices. These prejudices are not merely "bad" behaviors which should be sanctioned. They are a part of the environment in which these policies operate and may determine their success or failure....

The debate over affirmative action has been too much left to lawyers and philosophers, and has too little engaged the interests of economists, sociologists, political scientists, and psychologists. It is as if for this policy, unlike all others, we could determine *a priori* the wisdom of its application in all instances—as if its practice were either "right" or "wrong," never simply "prudent" or "unwise." If I accomplish anything here, I hope it is to impress upon the reader the ambiguity and complexity of this issue, to make him see that there is in this area the opportunity to do much good, but also the risk of doing much harm. The impassioned pursuit of justice, untempered by respect for a reasoned evaluation of the consequences of our efforts, is not obviously an advance over indifference.

"In Defense of Affirmative Action"

Albert Mosley

Racism is an ideology that classifies individual human beings in terms of their belonging to inferior or superior races, and offers reasons as to why individuals of the superior race are always justified in receiving preferential treatment over members of the inferior race.

Racism justified holding Africans as a form of property which could be and was exploited at a much higher rate than were European immigrants. It was thus an essential element in the early development of American Capitalism, and initially was given a theological basis: Africans had been cursed with a black skin because of the transgressions of their progenitor Ham against his father Noah. It is alleged that Ham fornicated on the ark against the injunctions of Noah, and that Ham moreover looked at Noah naked, against the laws of the old testament. As a result, Ham, and the progeny of Ham, were cursed with the mark of blackness, and condemned to slavery as "servant of servants".

With the rise of Darwinian theory, the theological basis of racism was replaced with a more scientific one, namely that Africans were that subspecies of human beings closest to the apes, and were destined to domination and eventual extinction by the more evolved Europeans. Intelligence tests were introduced as a means of proving that different groups could be ordered from lowest to highest in terms of the average IQ for each group. These tests were considered scientific proof of African American (AA) intellectual inferiority, and their (AA) inability to benefit from educational and employment opportunities available to European Americans (EAs). As recently as 1972 Nobel Prize Laureate William Shockley put it:

Nature has color coded groups of individuals so that statistically reliable predictions of their adaptability to intellectually rewarding and effective lives can easily be made and profitably be used by the pragmatic man-in-the-street.

Thus, even after the abolishment of slavery, the ideology of racism justified denying African Americans (AAs) opportunities available to European Americans (EAs). It fostered an attitude that made preferential treatment for Europeans seem natural and necessary.

The manifest effect of racism consisted in denying individual African Americans (AAs) specific available opportunities, as when a particular slave was punished for attempting to learn to read. Or, after slavery, when an employer refused to hire a particular AA because of race. But the latent effect was to dissuade AAs as a group from attempting to cultivate skills and exploit opportunities available to EAs. Thus, the punishment of a particular slave for attempting to learn to read discouraged other slaves from attempting to learn. And the rejection of one AA because of race discouraged other AAs from applying for similar opportunities. All racist acts carried the message that any other AA might be treated as a particular AA had been treated. Recognizing this, most AAs planned their lives accordingly and did not seek opportunities reserved for EAs.

The Emancipation Proclamation abolished slavery, and the 13th amendment to the constitution made it illegal throughout the US and its territories. The 14th amendment to the constitution made it unconstitutional for any state to deny any individual the equal protection of the law. Despite these developments racism continued under the guise of offering equal opportunities in separate domains, while in fact offering inferior facilities to AAs and superior ones to EAs.

In *Brown* vs. *Board of Education* the Supreme Court rejected the doctrine of separate but equal as contrary to the 14th amendment. This meant that all governmentally supported statues and practices denying AAs opportunities that were available to EAs became suspect as unconstitutional, and could be challenged in the federal courts. The Civil Right's Movement of the 50s and 60s galvanized attitudes against practices that discriminated against AAs on the basis of racial supremacy. By extension, belief in the inherent inferiority of certain gender, religious, and physical qualities was also rejected, and the courts were given broad powers to ensure that practices based on such beliefs would not continue.

But racism and its effects remain: many EAs continue to believe that AAs are not competent for intellectually challenging positions, many AAs remain hesitant to seek such positions, and those who do seek such positions are often ill prepared for them. Because racist practices had been widely supported by private and governmental agencies, only when legal sanctions made such practices too costly to engage in were those agencies prepared to seriously alter their practices.

Affirmative action is a policy first ordered by Roosevelt in the early 1940s to inform AAs of opportunities in the armed services and in private industry that were formerly closed to them. Such policies were reaffirmed during the 1960s and afterwards, their aim being to actively (1) inform Americans that many formerly accepted forms of discrimination (on the basis of race, gender, or physical handicap) were illegal, (2) encourage groups disadvantaged by that discrimination to seek previously denied opportunities, and (3) require agencies to initiate programs designed to prevent injuries caused by discriminatory practices from being carried into the future.

It is in carrying out (3) that serious problems have arisen for the policy of affirmative action. For ceasing to discriminate on the basis of beliefs of racial superiority does nothing to redress the harm already done by the practice of such beliefs, harm that will perpetuate itself unless addressed.

Imagine a race where some racers have been assigned a heavy weight to carry because they belong to a particular group. Because of this handicap the average runner with weights will lag behind the average runner without weights, but some runners with weights will come out ahead of some runners without weights. Now suppose someone waves a magic wand and the weights are lifted from the backs of all runners. If the two groups of runners are equal in ability, the mean difference between the weighted and the unweighted group ceases to expand, but those who suffered from the earlier discrimination will never catch up. If this is a race where parents who are ahead are able to hand the baton to their children, there is no equalization of the race even across generations. The race can be made fair only if everyone is forced to stop and begin again at the same starting line, if those without weights are forced to carry weights until the differences in average group-performances disappear, or if those who have been handicapped in the past are given special privileges until they catch up.

Since it is not possible to stop the economy and redistribute human and physical capital equally, the only real choice is between handicapping those who benefited from the previous handicaps and giving special treatment to those who were hurt by the previous handicaps.

In preferential treatment affirmative action policies for AAs, race is a factor, like merit, that is used to justify awarding educational, employment, political, and capital development opportunities. The most controversial cases of this form of preferential treatment occur when an AA candidate is chosen over a better qualified EA candidate for a position in which race has no relationship to productive performance in that position. So called "backward looking" justifications of preferential treatment construe it as a means of making restitution to AAs for the injuries they have sustained as a result of slavery, segregation, and other racist practices. On the other hand, "forward looking" justifications of preferential treatment construe it as a means of guaranteeing equal opportunity in the future by providing AAs with the means to compensate for the handicaps imposed by racist practices. Both forms of justification recognize that special measures are required to block the perpetuation of racist injuries.

From the point of view of "backward looking" justifications, preferential treatment in affirmative action programs is a form of corrective justice, where paradigmatically the harm-doer is to make restitution to the harmed so that the harmed person is restored to the position he would have attained but for the injury. And the costs are to be borne by the party causing the injury. Thus, If x was intentionally or negligently injured by y, and x suffered income and equity losses of d amount, then it is not enough that y be restrained from continuing to injure x. For y might comply, yet continue to enjoy his ill gotten gains, while x continues to suffer his past losses. Clearly, x ought to be awarded damages from y such that x is brought to the point where x would have been, had it not been for the injuries caused by y. Ideally, y would also be deprived of the advantages of having injured x.

Analogously, suppose Ms. AA was refused a job by agency C because of racist practices by the agency. Then it is not enough for the agency to cease thereafter to engage in such practices. Rather, Ms. AA ought to be rewarded the position she would have had were it not for the racist practices, as well as the income she would have received in that position. We may extend this case in the following way: Suppose agency C has a history of refusing employment to AAs, and that each of the qualified AAs it has refused employment to in the past is awarded the positions they would have had, plus back benefits. Does this correct for all the injuries C has caused? Clearly

not, for it ignores the latent effect of C's actions. Many other AAs would have been dissuaded from applying for positions they qualified for because of C's policies, and many others may have been dissuaded from acquiring competitive qualifications, reasoning that they would be refused on the basis of race no matter what their qualifications. Typical evidence of such latent effects is when the percentage of AAs in C's workforce is substantially below the percentage of qualified AAs in the available labor pool. To correct for this latent injury, C might be required to hire qualified AAs until their percentage in its workforce equals their percentage in the pool of qualified candidates. When, in order to accomplish this, C must hire AAs from the qualified pool who are less qualified than some EAs who are not hired, then such AAs are the recipient of preferential treatment and those EAs that would have been hired purely on the basis of merit are the "victims" of affirmative action.

Citing such cases, some have argued that affirmative action is simply a way of giving preference to AAs purely on the basis of race, and is equally as immoral as racist restrictions which gave preference to EAs purely on the basis of race. Quotas, timetables, and goals, it is argued, are little more than a form of "reverse racial discrimination," and should be considered as repugnant as racist forms of preferential treatment.

This point of view mistakenly identifies *preferential treatment as a form of racist practice* (PTR) with *preferential treatment as a form of affirmative action* (PTA). But it is important to see clearly that they are not identical. The latter, PTA, is the use of race as a factor in awarding coveted positions for the purpose of eradicating the injuries of racism. It is not a form of "reverse racism," in which AAs are the superior race and EAs are the inferior race. This is not to deny that forms of reverse racism have been proposed. For instance, the Black Muslims of Elijah Muhammad taught that AAs were spiritually superior to EAs, and that AAs should be given five states in the south in which they would be recognized as a sovereign people, ruling themselves as American Indians rule themselves within their designated areas. Within such an area, AAs might have been given preference over EAs, based on the belief in AA superiority.

This would have been a form of "reverse racism" or "reverse racial discrimination." But affirmative action preferential treatment (PTA) is meant only to correct for injuries done by racism. It has no justification based on belief in the inherent superiority of the group to be given preference. On the contrary, its justification is that the group given preference has been wrongly injured, and must be given the special considerations required to repair the injuries.

Preferential treatment affirmative action (PTA) is often more difficult to understand in cases where a particular AA may never have lived under slavery and segregation, and a particular EA may never have discriminated against AAs. Yet the AA is given preference over the EA.

Many EA males charge that, as a result of PTA, they are being denied benefits they deserve and that they are not being treated equally. The basis of the feeling of resentment among EA males is the fact that they are often more qualified for a position than the person to whom it is awarded, and believe that if x is the most qualified person for position p, then x deserves to be awarded position p. But it is important to see that a person might be awarded a position not only because of what the person has done, but equally because of what may have been done to the person.

Suppose Mr. x should have gotten a position in the past that he was illegally denied, and the court has ordered that Mr. x be given preference in the next position available. If Mr. y is more qualified than Mr. x for that next position, but it nonetheless is awarded to Mr. x as restitution, Mr. y is not justified in feeling resentment. While Mr. y deserves the position because of what he has done in preparing himself to merit the position, Mr. x deserves the position because of what was done to him that precluded his getting a similar position in the past. Both have competing claims on the position. And if, in the situation, Mr. x's claim is judged to be most cogent, then Mr. y may resent not getting the position, but y's claim to the position is not as strong as x's claim.

Y understandably feels disappointment when he has made the achievement of the position an important objective of his life, has prepared himself to meet all the qualifications for the position, merits the position in the sense of showing highest promise of being most productive in the position, and yet is not awarded the position. But merit is only one of many considerations used to award such positions, and if

some other consideration outweighs merit in the situation, then Y is not justified in receiving the position. I have already argued that the need to make restitution to X might be one such consideration. Another might revolve around honesty and trustworthiness. Thus, a more qualified candidate might not be awarded a position because he is found to be less trustworthy than a less qualified candidate who is awarded the position.

Similarly, if it is found that a certain level of preparation is superfluous, then an individual has no right to feel that achievement of that level of preparation ought to make him deserve the position. Thus, consider the case of Mr. EA, who has prepared himself to meet the literacy requirements for voting in a particular locality, and indeed meets the requirements of being able to interpret the articles and amendments of the constitution. Mr. EA might resent the fact that Mr. AA is now able to qualify to vote without having to meet those standards. But if those standards had little or no relationship to making reasoned judgements on current issues in the political arena, then they were superfluous, and should not influence whether Mr. AA is allowed to participate in the political process. Mr. EA might feel resentment, but his resentment is unwarranted.

Another criticism that is often leveled at affirmative action is that, in so far as it is a restitution for the injuries of racism, it does little for those AAs who are worse off. Especially for those AAs who do not have the motivation or opportunity to gain even minimal qualifications, providing opportunities may be of little help. This, however, is nothing peculiar to AA poverty in America. Throughout the world, many of those who have no hope of doing better in life have accommodated themselves to poverty. Typically, their resources are too meager to be expended in ventures that offer little opportunity of success. Given their precarious circumstances, it is understandable for some to adapt behavior that accommodates their poverty.

Racist and sexist restrictions, drug addiction, ill health, illiteracy, large family responsibilities, and lack of opportunities are conditions that incline individuals to accept an accommodation to poverty. Neither anti-discrimination legislation nor preferential treatment policies are effective remedies for those who have lost hope. Economist John Kenneth Galbraith argues that development programs that have been aimed primarily at those who lack motivation have failed at alarming rates. But where development programs have targeted groups with higher aspiration levels, they have succeeded at correspondingly higher rates.

This does not mean that affirmative action programs are totally useless as aids to those who are most worse off. If those who accept preferential treatment serve as role models for others with the motivation to acquire the necessary skills, then many AAs among the worse off might be encouraged to invest the effort needed to acquire skills necessary for professional positions, knowing that such positions are indeed open to them. But it is important to acknowledge that many who are worse off may be that way for reasons beyond what affirmative action can repair.

A similar criticism of affirmative action preferential treatment policies is that they only help those in the group who are best off, and hence who have been harmed least by racism. As Alan Goldman puts it,

Since hiring within the preferred group still depends upon relative qualifications and hence upon past opportunities for acquiring qualifications, there is in fact an inverse ratio established between past discrimination and present benefits, so that those who benefit most from the program, those who actually obtain jobs, are those who deserve to least.

However, the claim that "those who benefit most from the program...are those who deserve to least" contains the hidden assumption that those who have obtained the minimal qualifications required by affirmative action programs are those who have been hurt least by racist practices. It is likely, however, that those AAs who were winners of the natural lottery in intelligence and motivation were most harmed by racist practices. This can be illustrated if we contrast slaves with an IQ of 80 or less and slaves with an IQ of 120 or more. The slave with an IQ of 160 would be deprived of many more opportunities relative to his capabilities and would be more likely to chance punishment in order to exercise his capabilities than would the slave of IQ 60. Conversely, the illiterate AA with an IQ of 60 might be able to realize many more of his life objectives under slavery than might an educated AA with an IQ of 160. Even under segregation, the

more skills an AA acquired, the higher the rate at which he was exploited. Thus, in 1959, of workers with less than eight years of education, whites made 27 percent more than blacks. But of workers with more than 4 years of college, whites made 62 percent more than blacks. It appears that the better off one was in terms of intelligence and motivation, the worse off one probably was under the restrictions of slavery and segregation.

Certainly even in the best of times there will be some who are worse off. And in the worst of times there will be some who benefit. What then of those AAs who may have benefited under slavery and segregation? Should they be allowed to benefit also from affirmative action? And what of EAs who may have been injured as a result of slavery and segregation? Should they be required to relinquish benefits under affirmative action?

Glenn Loury puts this objection to affirmative action preferential treatment quite succinctly:

...no amount of recounting the unique sufferings attendant to the slave experience makes plain why a middle-class black should be offered an educational opportunity which is being denied to a lower-class white.

Cases in which middle class AAs are given preferential treatment over lower class EAs seem to suggest that something is seriously wrong with preferential treatment as affirmative action.

There is certainly something morally outrageous about such possibilities. Most importantly, they alert us that race should not be a sufficient condition for receiving preferential treatment affirmative action. Indeed, if race was a sufficient condition for preferential treatment, then affirmative action would be virtually indistinguishable from a form of racism.

Consider, for instance, a qualified AA that applies to agency C. Even if C is committed to preferential treatment affirmative action, C might justifiably decline to hire this AA if he has a record of having been dismissed from the last five jobs he has held for theft. Just as there are considerations other than merit that are important in awarding sought after positions, so there are considerations other than race that are important in awarding PT affirmative action positions.

As with a racist act, the award of a PT affirmative action position has both manifest effects (prestige, salary, training, etc.) to a particular individual, and latent effects to AAs as a group. Appointing a minimally qualified and motivated AA to a highly skilled and competitive position might have negative effects at both the manifest and the latent levels. This illustrates again that just as there may be many valid reasons for not choosing the particular person who is most qualified for a position, so there may be many valid reasons for not choosing a particular qualified AA to fill a PT affirmative action position.

Loury's example is posed between a middle-class black and a lower-class white, each competing for a position not both can be awarded. Resolution of such a case should depend on the circumstances, recognizing that the choice will have both manifest and latent effects, and that race should not be a sufficient condition for PT affirmative action.

The manifest aim of preferential treatment affirmative action is to improve the situation of an individual that has suffered the injuries of racism. The latent aim is to encourage other AAs to seek such positions. But there are circumstances in which it might be necessary to maximize the latent effect even though the manifest effect is minimized, and vice versus. Thus, if a particular AA has not been injured by racism, and would not be injured if he were not awarded the position in question, it still might be possible to maximize the encouragement to others by awarding that position to that AA.

Consider the following scenario: Tom Huxtable was a slave working in a mortuary, and after slavery, because the EA funeral home would not service AAs, Tom established the Huxtable Funeral Home. Because of segregation, the Huxtables had no competition from the larger EA funeral homes, and the Huxtable family flourished. The Huxtables were able to afford private tutors for their children, and they received excellent educations. Marvin Huxtable applies to law school but, despite his advantages, his qualifications (LSAT, GPE, etc.) are not as good as those of John Chainsaw, a poor appalachian white male who was the first in his family to ever get a college education. Should Huxtable be awarded the position?

I believe it depends on the circumstances of the situation. If Huxtable is the first AA to apply to the particular law school in question, the latent effect

of admitting him might be so great as to justify admitting him over John Chainsaw. (Let us not forget that there may be other EAs that John Chainsaw ought to be admitted ahead of.) But if the law school has already established a reputation of admitting AAs, the latent effect of admitting Marvin might be minimal. And given the minimal manifest effect of admitting him (he already has his mortuary license), it might be justified in admitting John Chainsaw instead.

Being American of African descent is a good indicator that one has been injured as a result of racism. And being American of European descent is a good indicator that one has benefited from racism. These indicators define groups around which policies are designed. But the purpose of the policy and the groups defined to realize the policy may not provide a perfect fit. The group of all those injured by racism is not identical to the group of all AAs, and the group of all those benefited by racism is not identical to the group of all EAs. This misfit, however, is not a problem peculiar to the administration of affirmative action policies.

In most states, an individual must be 16 or older in order to get a drivers license. The rationale for this is that those under 16 tend to drive less safely and to have more accidents than those over 16. But there is no perfect fit between those under 16 and those who would not drive safely. There are some 16 year olds who would be perfectly safe drivers. And there are many over 16 who are irresponsible drivers.

Just as most states offer drivers licenses to qualified citizens over 16, so affirmative action preferential treatment may be offered to qualified AAs. And just as the citizen over 16 may nonetheless not be mature enough to drive, so the AA awarded a position under affirmative action preferential treatment might not have been injured by racism nor might he encourage other AAs to such positions. On the other hand, an EA might be rejected who was injured by racism and who would have been an effective spokesperson against racism. Unfortunately, this might happen. But it would be an unintended consequence of affirmative action, like the friendly fire victims of a just war. Though procedures should be designed to minimize such occurrences, such possibilities may occur. When they occur, they should not be made to exemplify the policy.

There may be cases in which the effect of affirmative action may be more important for the group than for the individual receiving it. An individual may have not been injured by racism, or may have other options not available to his competitors. Yet, if the latent effect is great enough, his receiving the position might be justifiable nonetheless. This kind of focus on group needs and rights, as opposed to the needs and rights of individuals, has been the topic of much controversy.

Many have argued that we should focus on individuals who have been injured, and ignore their group affiliation. No matter how one is injured, it is argued, if the injury handicaps one in the pursuit of a meaningful life, and one does not deserve that injury, then one ought to be compensated to the extent that one can pursue ones interests. Instead of affirmative action for those who have been injured by racism, why not affirmative action for those who have been undeservedly injured. Shouldn't undeserved needs be met, at least to the point where a person is not impoverished as a result of those needs? As Richard Cohen writes,

If economic need, not race, became the basis for what we now call affirmative action, most Americans would not object. Whites, too, could be helped as, indeed, they should be. After all, poor is poor, although a disproportionate number of them are black.

There is no need to exalt restitution over welfare. But even given a policy to raise everyone above the poverty level, a perspective on the distribution of income and wealth between groups remains important. Lester Thurow states,

Suppose...that society decided to eliminate poverty (as officially defined) using a negative income tax with a 50% marginal tax rate. Such a policy would significantly alter the distribution of income across individuals, but the median income of black households would still be just 59% of that of white households—precisely what it is now without a public policy aimed at eliminating poverty. Would we be willing to say that economic equity had been achieved since poverty had been eliminated?

The problem is that the elimination of poverty would do nothing to correct for the injuries of racism above the floor of poverty. A policy that concentrated on providing entry level jobs for the poor would not address the underrepresentation of AAs as lawyers, doctors, professors, managers, entrepreneurs, financiers, etc. Yet denying such positions to AAs was the express aim of racist practices. Restricted access to such opportunities was meant to ensure an under representation of AAs at every level except the lowest. Racist acts were directed primarily at AAs as a group, and only secondarily at AAs as specific individuals. Without PTA, the disproportionate impact of impoverishment on AAs can be expected to perpetuate itself.

So far I have attempted to defend affirmative action against many of the objections that have been raised against it. It is, I believe, also important to attempt to indicate its limits. In opposing the Kantian and Consequentalist views that there are certain duties that always take precedence, W. D. Ross gives a number of *prima facie* duties that we have, duties that on occasion will conflict and shift in terms of priority. These include the duty of fidelity (keeping your promise), of gratitude (helping those who help you), of benefience (produce as much good as possible), of non-maleficence (do no harm to others), of justice (oppose distributions not based on merit), as well as of reparation (repair wrongful injuries) and charity (help those who are in need). Ross's objective was to show that neither the duty to tell the truth nor the duty to produce as much as possible would in every case be the most important duty we have to fulfill. In a particular situation, then, race might be more important than merit because the duty to repair wrongful injuries takes priority over the duty to be most productive.

But the same considerations apply to the duty to provide reparation. For reparation may conflict with other duties and, in certain circumstances, may be superceded by them. When repaying a debt requires denying basic necessities to my family, then my duties of fidelity conflict with my duty to keep my promise, and the latter will probably be pre-empted. Likewise, we should also recognize that when EAs feel that restoring AAs injured by an unjust past threatens their ability to provide themselves with "basic necessities" in the present, then reparations may well be challenged.

William Julius Wilson...suggests that resentment towards affirmative action preferential programs is proportional to the probability of an EA candidate receiving a similar position elsewhere.

The more positions there are available, the less keen is the competition for similar positions. When unemployment is low and jobs are plentiful, affirmative action programs are likely to generate least resentment. But when unemployment is high and jobs are scarce, there will be more resentment of PT affirmative action because the probability of obtaining a similar position is lower. Wilson thus argues that our goal should be to advance a full employment political agenda that would ally blacks with poor whites and other disadvantaged groups.

In one sense, Wilson is correct in stressing that AAs should not be so inward looking that they fail to appreciate the tenuous circumstances of others, who are marginal for no such grandiose causes as slavery and segregation. Though the EA poor may have no such excuses for their situations, their situation may be just as or even more desperate nonetheless.

It may be that duties of restitution have their greatest sway under conditions of high productivity, and have least sway in times of low productivity. Those who defend PT affirmative action may need to recognize that when others feel threatened,

they are less likely to be beneficent; and that under certain circumstances, it would be inappropriate to demand that an old injury be redressed. Those who advocate PT affirmative action must consider when it would be appropriate to compromise and rally around more compelling social duties.

An advocate of PT affirmative action is not compelled to deny the importance of aid to the least well off. Tradeoffs to other worthy causes will often be necessary. But the injury of racism should not be forgotten, and should be alleviated. Even when the manifest effect of specific benefits is relinquished, the latent message that AAs are inherently incompetent must be confronted and opposed.

AAs should insist on a proportionate distribution of those positions that are available, while recognizing that duties of reparation may conflict with other social duties. There may be times when it is more important to maximize efficiency than to repay past debts. And there may be times when, instead of asking why AAs are receiving less than EAs, it is more important to ask why there are fewer opportunities available for everyone, and why the rich get richer while the poor get poorer.

Equality and the Rights of Women

Elizabeth H. Wolgast

Equality is the key to arguments for many kinds of rights and against many kinds of injustices—against slavery, despotism, economic exploitation, the subjection of women, racial oppression. It is not surprising then that arguments for women's rights turn on the notion of equality. But it is wonderful that one idea can serve so many causes. Does it always work the same, for instance, in regard to

race and sex? And particularly, what does equality mean when applied to men and women?

If people were all alike there would be no question about their equality. Thus the claim of human equality is often linked with the assertion of human similarity. The philosopher John Locke, for instance, said that there is "nothing more evident than that creatures of the same species and rank, promis-

From *Equality and the Rights of Women* (Ithaca, NY: Cornell University Press, 1980). Reprinted by permission of the publisher.

cuously born to all the same advantages of nature and the use of the same faculties, should also be equal one amongst another without subordination or subjection." Insofar as they are similar in birth and faculties they should be equal in society.

From the equality of men it is natural to infer the equality of their principal rights. "Equals must be equal in rights," one scholar expressed it. If men are equal, then none is privileged by nature, and their rights, like the men themselves, should be similar.

These ways of reasoning are very familiar in discussions of racial equality. Differences of race such as skin color and hair texture are superficial, it is argued; in the important respects the races are similar and therefore equal. To distinguish between the rights of one group and the rights of another when the only differences are these unimportant ones seems patently unjust. So an argument for racial equality based on similarity is tantamount to an argument for equal rights regardless of race.

Women's rights are commonly argued on the same lines. The first step is the assertion of their similarity with men, and the last step is the claim that they should have equal rights. The nineteenth-century philosopher John Stuart Mill argued in this way, long before most philosophers addressed the problem. "There is no natural inequality between the sexes," he claimed, "except perhaps in bodily strength." Women can be thought of as weak men. Now strength by itself is not a good ground for distinguishing among people's rights. Mill infers, "If nature has not made men and women unequal, still less ought the law to make them so." As in the case of race, similarity dictates similar treatment. "Men and women ought to be perfectly co-equal," and "a woman ought not to be dependent on a man, more than a man on a woman, except so far as their affections make them so."

If women are like men except perhaps for strength, the argument for sexual equality would be even more powerful than that for racial equality; for with race the differences are several and determined by heredity, while women and men may have the same genetic components and transmit the same ones. If strength alone differentiated women from men, sex equality would be perfectly apparent.

But of course women are not weak men, and Mill is not deceived. Women are talented like men and have imagination, determination, drive, and other capacities the same as men; but they are different in ways other than strength. Sometimes Mill acknowledges differences, even stresses their importance. He thinks that, while a woman should be able to support herself, "in the natural course of events she will not," but her husband will support them both. "It will be for the happiness of both that her occupation should rather be to "adorn and beautify" their lives. At the same time her commitment to the home is a large one....Women should conform to an inflexible set of demands by household and family. Their role does not stem from their weakness—that wouldn't make sense. The real reason for women having this role is that they are the "opposite" sex and the ones to have children. That "coequality" Mill advocates turns out to be a "natural arrangement" with man and wife "each being absolute in the executive branch of their own department." What happened to the equality nature provided? It was not so clear after all.

Mill is more convincing when he speaks of the particular virtues in which the sexes differ. Women have their distinctive contribution to make, he says: they bring depth to issues where men bring breadth; they are practical where men are theoretical; they introduce sentiment where it is needed and would otherwise be lacking; and of course women are especially apt in the care and training of children. To extol these characteristics of women, Mill must put aside that similarity which first supported equality of rights; but here his respect for women is unequivocal and plain.

In sum, Mill is ambivalent about the similarity of the sexes. On the one hand he argues as if women were weak men, on the other, that they have their distinctive and important virtues. On the one hand he espouses legal equality; on the other he endorses a conventional dependent role for married women.

If Mill's claim for sexual equality rested entirely on similarity, it would seem that that equality is in jeopardy. But he has another defense ready. There is, he says, "an a priori assumption...in favour of freedom and impartiality...[and] the law should be no respecter of persons, but should treat all alike, save where dissimilarity of treatment is required by positive reasons." Similar treatment is right by presumption, and dissimilar treatment will always need positive justification. The argument from similarity was unnecessary then. But what kind of reason would justify differences of treatment? Mill doesn't say.

An argument for sex equality deriving from similarity is one that stresses the ways in which men and women are alike. But of course they are not exactly alike or there would not be a problem in the first place. It becomes necessary to make some such statement as: they are alike in all *important* respects, just as people of different races are importantly alike and only trivially different. But now it is necessary to consider whether differences of sex really are trivial.

In the case of race it seems clear that skin color and hair and features are unimportant, being superficial. They are mere physical marks. Can one say the same about the differences of sex? That is not so clear.

There is also a danger in using the argument from similarity, namely that, while it is meant to justify treating people alike, it implies that if people were importantly different they might need to be treated differently. So by implication it allows differences between individuals to justify *unequal* rights. This feature shows the importance for this kind of reasoning of maintaining that differences of sex are really trivial, for if they are not shown to be so, the argument can work against equality of rights.

Consider this argument: Sex, like skin color and other features of race, is a merely biological characteristic. It is an aspect of a person's physical composition like the chemical constituents of cells, and has nothing to do with the person as a moral entity. The sex of a person, like these other characteristics, should have no influence on how she or he is treated. I call this the "mere biology" argument.

It is true that skin color is an unimportant difference and should not affect a person's rights. But it is not unimportant *for the reason that it is biological.* The difference between men and apes is merely biological too, as is the difference between men and fishes; yet these differences rightly lead to different treatment. Who says we must treat all biological forms alike? Indeed, among humans some biological differences justify differences of treatment, as helping a blind person and caring for a baby clearly show. The "mere biology" argument is therefore a bad one.

How can it be argued that sex is an unimportant difference? We can see the issue more clearly through a form of sex egalitarianism more sophisticated and modern than Mill's. Richard Wasser-

strom, a philosopher and lawyer, argues that the good society would give no more recognition to sex or racial differences than we presently give to eye color. "Eye color is an irrelevant category" he argues, "nobody cares what color people's eyes are; it is not an important cultural fact; nothing turns on what eye color you have." No laws or institutions distinguish between persons by eye color, nor do even personal decisions turn on it. The same would hold, in the good society, of racial and sexual differences. The good society would be "assimilationist" with respect to race and sex just as our society is with respect to eye color.

Race and sex and eye color would all be viewed in the same way if our society were just. All three kinds of difference are biological, natural; but among them sex is "deeper," he concedes, and seems to have greater social implications:

> What opponents of assimilationism seize upon is that sexual difference appears to be a naturally occurring category of obvious and inevitable social relevance in a way, or to a degree, which race is not....An analysis of the social realities reveals that it is the socially created sexual differences which tend in fact to matter the most. It is sex-role differentiation, not gender per se, that makes men and women as different as they are from each other.

It is the way we recognize sex differences in socially created sex roles that gives them their great importance. If we stopped such artificial forms of recognition, we would see that the underlying difference of sex, like that of race, is trivial. Even though it is a naturally occurring difference, that in itself does not justify a social distinction, a distinction in roles. The principle difference of sex is social, not biological. And so sex is analogous to race: the difference allows for assimilation, given a change in laws, in institutions, and in social mores. Although there will still *be* a sexual difference, it will not make a difference.

To compare sex and race in this way implies that reproductive differences and reproduction itself should not much affect our social arrangements: "There appear to be very few, if any, respects in which the ineradicable, naturally occurring differences between males and females *must* be taken into account," Wasserstrom says. The differences can just be ignored. But how do we ignore the reproductive differences? They are not many or very important, he argues, given the present state of medical knowledge:

> Sexual intercourse is not necessary, for artificial insemination is available. Neither marriage nor the family is required for conception or child rearing. Given the present state of medical knowledge and the natural realities of female pregnancy, it is difficult to see why any important institutional or interpersonal arrangements must take the existing gender difference of *in utero* pregnancy into account.

When you consider how many differences can be compensated for by medical innovations, there is only the nine months of *in utero* pregnancy left. And why should that make very much difference? Wasserstrom thinks it shouldn't. The sexes should be treated the same. Here is a variation of the "mere biology" argument, a "mere pregnancy" argument.

In the good society there is sex equality: that is a primary consideration. For treating similar people the same would seem inherently just. If therefore it is within our means to make people more similar, through science and medicine, that course has much to recommend it; for with equality the goodness of society is assured. "Even though there are biological differences between men and women by nature, this fact does not determine the question of what the good society can and should make of these differences," Wasserstrom writes. We don't need to be guided by nature; we can use our intelligence to control, adjust, and compensate for the differences nature produces.

Wasserstrom is not, like Mill, guided by existing similarities but is committed to create similarities wherever possible. Equality of the sexes is an ideal, an ideal of justice, and it requires similarities to exist. The good society, then, will create the similarities to go with its ideal, and that means it will create conditions under which its citizens will be, in all important ways, sexually similar.

I will not stop to consider whether this ideal is a pleasant or attractive one, for I want to ask the question: Is it true that merely biological differences of sex should not influence a good society?

Part of the egalitarian view expressed most commonly is the idea that biological differences of sex can be separated from social roles. Then the question is raised whether different sex roles, which are social artifacts, are desirable. Put this way, it is difficult to see why the roles should be very different. But it is not clear that the biological differences and the social ones *are* so distinct and separate.

Take the one fact, mentioned by Wasserstrom as unalterable at present, that women bear children after a period of pregnancy. From this one fact of *in utero* pregnancy one consequence directly follows: a woman does not normally have occasion to wonder whether the baby she bears is hers. She does not wonder if she or someone else is the mother. The father stands in a different relation to his child at the outset; his position is logically more distant, depending on inferences a mother need not make. And it is possible that he may doubt and, doubting, even fail to acknowledge a child that is in fact his, while it is difficult to imagine a mother in just that position—to imagine her bearing a child and then wondering whose it can be.

It is easy to imagine confusion about babies in the context of a modern hospital nursery, of course, but what I call attention to is a deeper and inherent asymmetry in parenthood, one that does not stem from institutions but from reproduction itself. As parents mothers have a primary place, one that cannot be occupied by a father.

This fact in turn has consequences. From the fact that mothers are primary parents it is clear that in general a mother is the more easily identifiable of a child's parents. This is important because a child is a very dependent creature and dependent for a very long time. Someone must have responsibility for it, and most generally that responsibility is given to parents. So now, in assigning responsibility for a child, it is simpler and less equivocal to assign the responsibility to a mother than to a father. This is so because doubts can be raised about his parenthood that have no analogue for hers.

From the mere fact of the way children are born, then, there are consequences important to society. Society, in its need to recognize someone as responsible for a child, rightly makes use of this fact of reproduction, the *in utero* pregnancy, so it can identify one parent with reasonable certainty.

I am assuming that parents are responsible for their children. However, this need not be part of the morality of a society, though it is part of the morality of most, and certainly part of ours. If this assumption is not made, the consequences would be different, depending on how society construes the relation of parent and child and places responsibility for the young. But it seems plausible that there will be some connection between parenthood and responsibility, and this connection will reflect the fact that mothers are primary parents.

That mothers are primary parents affects not only laws and institutions but also the way women look at their lives. The potential of pregnancy and motherhood are present from the time girls reach adolescence, and are part of a young female's life and thought in a way they cannot be for a male. She needs to consider parenthood's connection with her behavior, and this influences her options. It would be surprising if it did not also affect her relations with males, sharpening her sense of their polarity, arousing concern about the durability and stability of her relationships with them. In such ways the merely biological fact of *in utero* pregnancy comes to give different coloring to the sexual identity of males and females, laying the groundwork for some sex roles.

Nor is this all. In a society where paternal responsibility is recognized and valued, there is a need to identify males as fathers. Thus an institution that makes formal identification of fathers, such as marriage, becomes important. As a child has two biological parents, so it comes to have two parents in society, within a social structure. And it would be surprising if some mores involving chastity and fidelity did not arise as well. In this way the merely biological facts of reproduction will tend to influence both the form of society and its customs, even though the details of that influence will vary. Societies are not all formed alike; other influences are at work as well. My point is that the fact of *in utero* pregnancy will have some consequences connected with the asymmetry of parenthood. Wasserstrom complains that society "mistakenly leads many persons to the view that women are both naturally and necessarily better suited than men to be assigned the primary responsibilities of child rearing." If he had said "better situated," the observation he attributes to society would be profoundly right. The maternal role *is* more closely connected to parental responsibility than the paternal one, and neither talents nor conditioning nor tastes enter into it.

Suppose a society chooses not to acknowledge the asymmetry of parenthood. How would it do this? Would it assign equal responsibility to both parents? But what about the cases in which the father of an infant is unknown? It has a father, unless he is since deceased; but knowing this is no help. And what of the cases in which a mother refuses to acknowledge any father, is the child not then exclusively hers? In Hawthorne's *The Scarlet Letter*, Hester Prynne's Pearl is *hers*, although both she and the Reverend Dimmesdale know he is the father. How would the good society make that parenting equal?

I do not mean at all that fathers are less tender, less devoted, or less responsible than mothers, that parental solicitude and devotion are women's prerogatives. *That* kind of "sex role" is not implied by the primary parenthood of mothers. What is meant is that asymmetries of parenthood are neither small nor trivial. And because of this they will have asymmetrical effects on other aspects of a person's life, some only indirectly related to parenthood. In this sense of "sex role," it is difficult to understand how sex roles could be abolished or made alike. Would one have to ignore the asymmetries of reproduction? But that would be a pretense.

Since the parental roles are asymmetrical, a natural consequence is some asymmetry in the attitudes of young men and young women regarding both reproduction and sex. The same behavior, sexual intercourse for instance, will have different significance for each. A society that gives structure to these differences, that provides a context into which both genders are expected to fit, will thereby provide for differences in sex roles. A great deal may be embroidered here in the way of stereotypes, rituals, myths, and mores. But what I shall mean by sex roles is a minimal set of differences, differences in attitude and behavior and in life outlook, stemming from the asymmetries of reproduction and framed by a social context.

The answer to Wasserstrom then evolves: The biological differences of men and women do not determine what a good society should make of them, but a good society should take them into account, and probably must do so. In order to justify ignoring the asymmetries that characterize human reproduction, that form of reproduction would have to be drastically changed.

So long as babies develop *in utero* and not, for example, in bottles, parenthood will be an asymmetrical business. A good society will no more ignore it than it will ignore the fact that humans start out as babies and do not live forever.

Wasserstrom's next step may be the proposal that reproduction be changed so as to be more symmetrical, for example, by developing fetuses in the laboratory and delivering them at term to two symmetrically related parents. In this situation a child would have no primary parent; on both sides recognition of parenthood would depend on a similar inference. It is difficult to see that from either the child's point of view or society's this loss of a primary parent would be an improvement.

Sex equality does not always take such a radical form as Wasserstrom gives it. The feminist philosopher Alison Jaggar, for instance, adopts a more moderate position:

> A sexually egalitarian society is one in which virtually no public recognition is given to the fact that there is a physiological sex difference between persons. This is not to say that the different reproductive function of each sex should be unacknowledged in such a society nor that there should be no physicians specializing in female and male complaints, etc. But it is to say that, except in this sort of context, the question whether someone is female or male should have no significance.

There will be "virtually" no public recognition of physiological sex differences—this is difficult to understand in concrete terms. There will be medical specialists in male and female complaints; there will presumably be maternity facilities; there will presumably be some provisions for infants of unwed mothers. Are not these all forms of "public recognition"? And don't they work asymmetrically with regard to the sexes? Perhaps Jagger means to exclude issues connected with parenthood from her general rule, so that these asymmetries can be publicly recognized. Such things as maternity leaves and child support for unwed mothers would then qualify for public recognition. What would not qualify would be matters in respect to which women and men *should not* be treated differently in the first place. If this is the gist of her view, then it is substantially like mine. The question is why it should be called "egalitarian."

In Wasserstrom's ideal, people will regard one another, even in personal matters, without distinguishing the sexes. We don't distinguish between people on the basis of eye color: "so the normal,

typical adult in this kind of nonsexist society would be indifferent to the sexual, physiological differences of other persons for all interpersonal relationships. Bisexuality, not heterosexuality or homosexuality, would be the norm." In order for the sexes to be really equal, he reasons, we need to treat them alike even in personal and private ways. For if there are sex distinctions regularly made in private, they will be echoed somehow in the public sphere, and this means there will be a sex-differentiated form of society. This cure for sexual injustice is extreme: what is required here is a society of individuals who behave and are treated as if they were sexually alike. It requires an androgynous society.

Sex equality based on the similarity of the sexes as advocated by Wasserstrom, will lead to an assimilationist form of society, for insofar as people are similar, similar treatment of them will be justified, and the assimilationist society treats everyone alike. It ignores sex differences just as it ignores racial ones, and for the same reason—because they are unimportant. By this reasoning a nonassimilationist form of society will necessarily be unjust....

In restricting us sex roles are wrong. Through them "involuntarily assumed restraints have been imposed on the most central factors concerning the way one will shape and live one's life." But sex roles in the narrow sense I mean them are reflections of restrictions; they do not create restrictions or impose them. Rather the restrictions come from the way human reproduction works and the kinds of responsibilities it entails in the framework of a real human society. It is hard to speak of the restrictions being imposed, just as it is hard to think of the character of human vision imposing restrictions on us. We cannot see what is behind our heads at any given moment; that is frustrating and certainly limits our freedom, restricting what we can do, be, or become. But one wouldn't for that reason call the visual system "wrong." Living in a society involves restrictions too, and so does being born to particular parents, in a particular place, in this century. These things too affect "the most central factors concerning the way one will shape and live one's life." But from what point of view can we term them "wrong"? We do not have an abstract viewpoint from which to measure the "wrongness" of such accidents.

Our difficulty with the assimilationist ideal has two sides: On the one, it seems to be based on human similarity, on the triviality of sex differences. But, as I argue, there is much reason to reject this and much justification for recognizing some form of sex roles. On the other hand, the assimilationist ideal seems to commit one to *creating* similarities, through medical and social measures, as if the ideal did not rest on anything, but were self-evident. If all sex roles are wrong, then only a unisex form of society will be just. But we are not unisex creatures; we are not androgynous or hermaphroditic. So assimilationism seems an inappropriate ideal, at least for human beings.

Having sex roles is natural to us and not the creation of society. As Midgley says, maternal instinct is not reducible to "cultural conditioning by the women's magazines." If equality were adopted as an ideal, a massive effort at conditioning would be necessary to make us think like androgynous creatures with similar sex roles and sexual natures and so to fit that form of society. It is the androgynous role that is artificial, the product of a fictitious view of human nature. Instead of encouraging freedom and autonomy, the assimilationist society would thus restrict us to an androgynous form of life. It is a kind of Procrustean bed.

Sex is a deeper phenomenon than race, Wasserstrom concedes. Its differences are more pervasive, more securely built into our institutions and practices. Nevertheless, he believes sex can be treated along the same lines as race, without qualitative adjustments. Lumping race and sex together is also common where there is talk of "group discrimination" and programs to combat it. But the cases are not alike.

One way to see the difference is to consider the way "assimilation" applies in the two cases. It is conceivable that, with less strictness in our mores, the races would come eventually to be assimilated to one. Differences in color and physiognomy would be so muted as to count only as individual ones, on a par with eye color. There is the possibility of real, genetic assimilation in the case of race. But with sex this is obviously not possible, and even if it were, we would have to think hard whether we wanted it. To allow equality to determine the character of our species seems to show a wrong order of things.

Equality based on similarity is connected to the Aristotelian dictum that we should treat likes alike and unlikes differently. But which cases are alike and which different? The answer is not simple. In the matter of race we generally say the cases are alike; in the case of sex this is not at all obvious. The difference of sex is genetically nonassimilable and besides it is difficult to ignore. Perhaps Aristotle's rule should lead us to conclude that with sex the cases require different treatment.

Where similarity is a consideration, racial arguments and sexual ones need to be separated. A person's racial characteristics are not usually correlated with special concerns differentiating racial groups, while many of women's most important concerns, for instance those connected with pregnancy, are distinctive to women as a group. The fair treatment of the two sexes cannot be assumed to consist in the "assimilation" of their rights.

Less compelling is the fact that sex differences have a lot to do with our enjoyment of human relationships. Could we treat the sexes alike as Wasserstrom proposes? We normally respond differently to members of the opposite sex than to members of our own. Even putting sexual attraction aside, we still have different relations to members of different sexes. With members of our sex, we have and anticipate having, a good deal in common. To a child we say, "When I was a little girl..." (if we are women) with the implication that we lack the same identification with boys. While with members of the opposite sex we perceive contrasts and divergent points of view, for some areas of common experience are lacking. Understanding those other perspectives is often a tenuous matter, ignorance and mystery being the conditions it must work against; but it is also one that fascinates, challenges, delights, and amuses us.

Wasserstrom could respond that these differences are mostly the creation of society, and that the position I suggest amounts to an endorsement of present sex roles and stereotypes. This is not intended. What I propose is rather that biology differentiates us in ways that will have some implications for differentiated sex roles. It is not a "solution" to such differentiation to suggest that everyone have the same roles or pretend to have them. The feminist social critic Dorothy Dinnerstein argues in *The Mermaid and the Minotaur* that "gender symbiosis" is a neurotic condition that needs correcting. Although I agree with many of her observations about sex roles in our society and the need for changes, I am arguing that asymmetry will persist in some form or other, that the implications of biology are pervasive. The idea that, under propitious conditions, sex differences can be flattened out or "nullified" does not seem either necessary or attractive. Nor is it clearly possible. It may be no more possible for us to treat people of different sexes alike than it is for us to treat a baby as an adult, or an elderly man as a youth. Some differences cannot be discounted.

Our commitment to equality is deep. It goes back at least to Aristotle, who, though he was not egalitarian in our sense, defined justice as "a kind of equality." The problem is how to translate this. On one side the philosopher Hugo Bedau insists that all forms of equality "involve sameness, in the same sense of 'same.' That is why they are equalities." On the other side David Thomson claims that "the idea of equality has nothing to do with uniformity. To recognize that men are all equally individual human beings involves no desire or need to treat them uniformly in any ways other than those in which they clearly have a moral claim to be treated alike." Equality can be detached from similarity, according to this, and from equal treatment as well....

The claim that handicapped people have an "equal right" to access to public buildings is sometimes given as the justification for installing wheelchair ramps. Using equal rights in this way implies that handicapped persons are being denied a right, that their right to access is being thwarted and violated. But this way of putting things is misleading. When there are no ramps, the lame and handicapped are not being singled out for discrimination, or sorted out where their distinctive features should be ignored. Just the contrary: their special needs are *not* being remarked. They have an equal right to enter buildings (no one keeps them out); but they are unable to exercise it. What they need is a right to special entrances, allowing them to exercise their equal right of access.

Another case: it is sometimes argued that children with learning handicaps have an "equal right" to education and therefore should have special school facilities. This sounds strange to start with. Such schools relate to special needs; they are schools that normal children might not profit from.

We are not discriminating against abnormal children, singling them out for lesser treatment, when we have regular schools. The argument for special education should rather be that there is a specific *need* for it, a gap to be filled if these children are to get some education. The absence of special programs may constitute a kind of injustice but it is not a form of discrimination.

We are reminded in these cases of Bedau's observation that it is popular to characterize any arrangement one approves of as "egalitarian." It is as if an argument for equal rights were regarded as a superior form of argument, to be used even where special rights are wanted and without regard for its appropriateness. Likewise, discrimination, strictly understood, occurs in a context where differential treatment of people is wrong. To charge discrimination, then, is to charge that people are being sorted out when they are not supposed to be— where Justice should be blind. It makes sense only against a background of equal rights.

Straightening out this terminology, while it may clarify our thinking, does not settle any difficult questions about where people may be justly sorted out and where not. For instance, it is considered unfair to sort out applicants for jobs by their sex: men have won the right to be employed as attendants on airliners, to be telephone operators and secretaries; women in their turn have won the right to be telephone linesmen, construction workers, truck drivers, and members of the crew on Navy ships. To exclude applicants from these jobs because of their sex is considered sex discrimination and so inherently unfair: that is the law's position. But nothing forbids sorting people out in a variety of other ways: by geographical location, by intelligence, by attractiveness and personal charm, by congeniality, by family or institutional connection. No law prohibits these ways of screening applicants. So the question arises: Can sorting people out by such means have some of the same results as sex discrimination? While skin color, for example, may be counted a superficial difference, many other characteristics, even some that may be related to race, are not. And when we open these characteristics to question, it is not clear how equality of rights should work.

Minority groups sometimes argue for an "equal right" to positions of status and prominence and training in desirable professions, medicine and law notably. It is argued that the absence of minority members in these professions shows discrimination against the minority groups. But disparate numbers do not prove there is discrimination, for there is no equal right here being violated. There may be unfairness built into the tests or the criteria for admission may be misapplied, but there is no "equal right" of applicants to be admitted to such schools. Here the nature of the wrong is misidentified.

A remedy often sanctioned for correcting an imbalance of racial representation among lawyers and doctors is the institution of racial quotas for the admission of applicants into training for these professions. But quotas raise new questions in the context of equal rights, provoking the charge that they constitute "reverse discrimination," which is to say, a wrong of exactly the same nature as the one they are supposed to correct. The issue is almost hopelessly muddy. As Ronald Dworkin points out in commenting on the Bakke case, admission to medical school has always taken a variety of personal characteristics into account, not only scores and grades. There may have been racial prejudice expressed in making these decisions; but since there is no equal right to admission, even given certain test scores, there is not discrimination when people are denied admission on the basis of their individual characteristics.

One thing that may be needed for fairness is a shift in the criteria used for acceptance. To make race a positive consideration in the selection process is a change in the use of factors, but it is not a change in the nature of the process. I am among those who find the Supreme Court's decision confusing, not least because the social policy that justified affirmative selection programs has no connection with equal rights so far as I can see. Its justification is of a different kind.

The free use of the terms "discrimination" and "reverse discrimination" are side effects of our use of "equality" to describe a broad range of situations, and of our preference for "equal rights" when arguing against injustice. When we want to call some practice unfair, we say it is discriminatory, just as when we want to call something fair we say it shows equality of treatment. What is needed is a clearer understanding of these terms and more care in their use; then it will be evident that there can be racial injustice without discrimination and racial justice without equality....

The sense in which planks can be equal, and baskets of apples and pieces of cake, I call strict equality. It always involves a measure. But there is another kind of equality that pertains only to creatures in society, and this notion, though vague, is worth discussing. It is the sense in which people can be said to meet as equals and associate on equal terms. I will call this kind of equality the notion of "peers."...

The similarity necessary for peership changes from case to case and is difficult to specify. It can be grasped best, perhaps, by noticing some of the relationships where it is lacking. Many human relationships, as Aristotle recognized, are not those of equals, for example, the relations of parent and child, ruler and subject, master and servant. In these, the parties are dissimilar and stand asymmetrically to one another. In Aristotle's view the virtues of these relationships are different from those in the friendship of equals and not so valuable. Although one can say that parent and child have the "same interest," that is, the welfare and education of the child, this is very different from the similarity that characterizes two travelers, both wishing to get to their destination. The roles, if we want to use that term, are very different in one case, but alike in the other. The sense in which peers are similar is linked therefore to the condition of symmetry. Only in symmetrical relations will people meet as peers.

I use "peer" then to mean a relation between people with similar interests who associate and stand symmetrically to one another. As Aristotle says, comrades-at-arms are often related this way; so are children at play, especially when their ages and backgrounds are similar; while an elderly person and a youth cannot be peers, nor can a teacher and a student. It seems evident to Aristotle that neither can a husband and a wife....

Non-peer relations in my sense do not imply a difference in social status or class. Parents and their children are normally of the same class, and often so are doctor and patient, teacher and student, employer (in our society) and employee; though master and servant are commonly not. What determines peership is the way the parties stand, in their independence, similarities, and symmetry with respect to one another. For instance, two opera buffs or two scientists, two old people or two children, may relate to one another as peers regardless of their economic and social backgrounds.

In Aristotle's view, I remarked, a husband and wife could not possibly have the kind of friendship relating peers. The reason is that they are dissimilar in nature, and have different interests in their relationship. Since the relationship of husband and wife is, normally, asymmetrical, it will be usual in my sense too that husbands and wives are not peers. This description means no more than that the conditions of their relationship do not satisfy the conditions necessary for peership. And this fact derives both from the difference in conditions of life for the two sexes, and from the fact that sexual asymmetry or complementarity is an essential ingredient in the relationship. It is not just accidental or fortuitous that husbands and wives are usually of different sexes; that is part of the nature of the bond. Given this interpretation, I do not find anything pernicious in the conclusion that married people are often not united in a peer relation. After all, the sexes *are* different and those differences, some generated by roles in reproduction, have consequences for our perspectives. A union of individuals of opposite sexes which functions to raise children will necessarily contain asymmetries while childbearing concerns them. And this entails that the union is not, in that phase at least, one of peers.

Perhaps this needs further explaining. Given that a peer relation stems from independence, similarities, and symmetry, one can object that some couples *are* similar in just the kinds of features that would make us call them peers, were they of the same sex, both males or both females. Does sex alone prohibit their standing as peers? Peership works on different dimensions and admits of degrees. Such a relationship may share many characteristics with a peer relationship, and therefore might well be classed with them. A homosexual pair may be related as peers even though some dependency and subdued asymmetries characterize their relationship. As dependency, differences, and asymmetries become more pronounced, however, the peer relation turns into a non-peer one. To say that marriages with a function of childbearing involve non-peer relations is only to say that ordinarily the conditions for peership can't exist here.

It is not to say that the relation may not ever *become* one of peers. As the children of a marriage grow up and depart, and the attitudes and interests of a couple grow more similar—as they often do—something approaching peership often develops. There is no conceptual difficulty in this, just as there is none in the fact that elderly women in some tribes, well past childbearing and child-rearing, sometimes hold a position similar to the males and become, in that phase of life, their peers. As people's lives change, so do their relationships....

If we introduce my sense of peer into the proposition that men are equal, we get a result that is patently false. All humans *cannot* be peers. There could not be a society with only peer relations and without non-peer ones. Even the simplest society must have a variety of asymmetrical relations, husbands and wives, parents and children, a chief and a citizenry, and so on. A society of peers would not be a whole human society. It might be a band of hunters, or a group of women, or children of the same age at play, or a council of elders. A weird effect in William Golding's *Lord of the Flies* is that the entire community is of males who are roughly peers. But a real society cannot be made up of individuals having only peer relations. To be composed of peers, it would have to be more than androgynous—it would have to be perfectly homogenized.

The character of non-peer relations is often unclear to us. A child may complain to its parents that it is not being treated as an equal, meaning that they are not treating it as a peer. That's right, and the reason is that parents and children *aren't* peers. Nor has a parent a choice about the relation; the fact of parenthood generates asymmetry. Again, students sometimes protest that they are not treated as equals, meaning that they are not treated as peers. Why shouldn't they be? Are they inferior? Their logic is moving, but the fact is they are not treated as peers because they are not peers. Put differently, for them to be treated as peers would vitiate the teacher-student relation; one cannot have both things together.

Often what is wanted when these protests are made is an appropriate form of respect. When that is the case, why not ask for respect in its own name?

Sometimes when women demand equality with their husbands, what seems to be wanted is peership with them. But this demand is difficult to interpret. If peership is to be possible, the conditions for it must be present: independence, similarity, and symmetry. If they are absent, the demand for peership is an impossible one.

Yet it may be objected that what is needed in the way of feminine equality is just those conditions that would make peership possible, conditions making peership between men and women a more general and common relationship. This means that women should be independent, have the same interests as men, and stand symmetrically in relation to them, for these are the relevant conditions. To the degree that these conditions are fulfilled, there *can* be something resembling a peer relation. For instance, there is something close to peership in childless marriages where both parties are engrossed in careers, and also in some marriages after children are grown. These are not conditions to be demanded, nor does a *right* to them make sense. But where asymmetries enter, reproduction being the most prominent, peership departs. Therefore in those phases of marriage where reproduction and the rearing of children are principal functions, there will be asymmetries preventing husbands and wives from being peers.

Rather than understand a demand for equality as one for peership, we may often better understand it as a demand for respect. It does not help to say "equal respect," notice, unless equality is definable. And where the parties are importantly different, equality of respect may be indefinable, like the equality of oranges and corn and that of dogs and cats.

To be treated as incompetent or irresponsible or has having only a childlike character is humiliating. No man would treat his peer that way. So it seems plausible that a wife needs just that role from which respect and dignity will follow, which is to say, she seems to need to be his peer. But that role may not fit her. Nor is it necessary for respect. Respect may rather need to be demanded in appropriate forms and in its own name....

It is unclear that dominance ordering gives us a measure of anything except the ability to become dominant, either in the male or female sphere. But while dominance ordering does not signify inequalities among individuals, not important ones, it does signify non-peer relations. Where individuals are related to one another by a dominance relation, it follows that they do not stand as peers.

It is very tempting therefore to argue that non-peer relations are essentially forms of dominance relations. The teacher has dominance over the student, it might be said, the doctor has dominance over the patient, the parent over the child. By analogy, the relation of husband and wife can be thought of as one where the stronger is dominant over the weaker.

To say this, however, is to read dominance into relations where that makes no sense. From the fact that a relation is non-peer, it does not follow that dominance is involved. Examples show that dominance often isn't. The relation of a teacher and student is not founded on a competition for dominance which, fortuitously, the teacher always wins. Neither is a doctor's position dependent on the ability to dominate. Indeed, that is incongruous: why would one expect *care* from someone in that position? And if parental authority signified only dominance, we would have to suppose that only quite aggressive individuals could satisfy the parental role. Finally, it is absurd to suppose that a female usually accepts a long-term bond with a male because he has literally conquered her (although this "cave-man" myth is sometimes taken seriously). Why would she accept such terms? Males of many species on the contrary work hard at winning the female of their choice, striving to impress and attract her, using all their skills and masculine assets. Among some primates, where there is no bonding to speak of, this characteristic is naturally less prominent. Courting and bonding go together. That males may become overbearing and autocratic is undeniable. That their success in dominating a would-be mate forms the basis of a long-term bond is ludicrous.

I construe "dominance relations," following Wilson, in a way that connects with human struggles for ascendancy, and so with the notion of status that grows out of them. If one were to construe dominance differently, so that the dominant male is primarily a protective and nurturing figure, then there would be greater similarity between dominance relations and non-peer relations in my sense. Furthermore the notion of "status" associated with dominance would be different. It is not quite so obvious under such a characterization where such alpha males are found in modern human communities.

Peership and dominance, although they are not linked as simple alternatives, are importantly related. And our preference for peer relations as the model for just relations in society has this connection at its root. It can be explained in this way: Although the non-peer relations of teaching and parenting and doctoring are important for a good society, they contain built-in hazards. Each of them is highly susceptible of abuse. Moreover, these abuses—parental abuse of a child, a doctor's abuse of a patient, a husband's abuse of his wife—are morally terribly offensive. Why is this? It is not, as it first might seem, that the offense is connected with dominance by one over the other. For if dominance were integral to the relations, they would not have the character they have: we would never let a doctor anaesthetize us, or take our lawyer's advice, or assume that our parent had our welfare at heart. No: what characterizes these relations is the trust that one party places in another. And it is this trust which makes the opportunity for abuse. The doctor, for instance, has charge of the medicine given a patient; how easy to do harm from this position! And parents receive great trust from their children; how easy that makes it for them to do harm! And it is likewise easy for a trusted husband to harm his wife; simple too for her to harm him. Trust makes these harms possible.

To identify these harms with abuses of power would be wrong. We do not feel the same kind of revulsion for one man beating another where both are competing for ascendancy. That is quite different from a husband's beating his wife, or a parent's beating a child; our revulsion at these springs from the trust which forms their background. The roles of doctor, parent, teacher, husband, wife involve trust so essentially that abuse of that trust is offensive in a way that no mere exertion of power can be. A parent who violates the trust entailed by having young children, we sometimes say, is no parent; the doctor who mistreats a patient is no doctor. Abuses of trust vitiate the very roles. And the harm that may be done here is deeper and more painful than any harm one peer can do another.

Peer relations are free of these hazards. While a slaveowner is responsible for his slaves, and a lord may be responsible for his vassals, freemen are not responsible for one another. The hazards of trust are absent, and it is perhaps for this reason that we prefer peership relations among people in a community. Why introduce the potential for abuse of trust where it is unnecessary?

I think *this* point is sometimes meant by the claim that men are equal and should be treated that way. It means they should not stand in relations of trust and responsibility where those relations can be avoided. Aristotle said that it is in relations between equals that we find justice among men. While the meaning of this remark was not clear at first, it can now be given an explanation; Justice can characterize peer relations as it cannot characterize most important non-peer ones. The mistreatment of a child by its parent is not simply unjust: it is morally reprehensible. To speak of justice and injustice in this context is inadequate. The issue is too deep for that. Aristotle said that justice does not apply within a family except by analogy with relations between equals, nor does it apply strictly to a man's relations with his slaves. He can be understood to mean that in those contexts the terms of paternal responsibility, affection, and care are more appropriate. Exactly this, it might be said, shows the chief wrong of slavery: it denies relations of justice between adults, creating great dependency where there need be none, and thus undermines the dignity of the slave's position.

Relations of justice are on a different level from relations of trust. To the latter, moral language is appropriate, and claims to rights have a curious ring—a child's "rights" vis-à-vis its parents, for instance, or a wife's vis-à-vis her husband. While with regard to justice, rights and contracts and predictable rules are not only appropriate but central. In dealing with one's peers, one should be able to anticipate, by means of laws and institutions, what will count as respectful and fair behavior.

In considering the rights women aspire to, this distinction is useful. For while rights are important in regard to the work place and dealings with institutions and laws, they can only indirectly affect the non-peer relations in which women stand, the most important being their relations with their husbands on the one hand and their children on the other. Wrongs that are present in these relations are more intractable than the others and harder to redress. They cannot be reached by an appeal to equality or equal rights, but need a searching understanding of the relationships themselves, our expectations of them and the roles that custom connects with them. Such relations need to be acknowledged as special ones, essential to and characteristic of a society, embodying its morality in ways that relations of justice cannot. They are deeper than peer relations, more perilous, and have a claim to moral priority....

10　Economic Justice

The central question of economic justice brings to a head the division between the "libertarian liberals," who uphold the right of the individual to be free from governmental interference, especially as regards the right to use and dispose of private property, and the "egalitarian liberals," who believe in the right of every individual to full self-development, along with the means necessary to such self-development, including adequate food, shelter, clothing, education, and health care. The first is a kind of "negative" freedom *from* outside interference, to be left alone to do pretty much as one pleases. All the state has to do in order to protect *these* rights and freedoms is *not* to interfere and to *prevent* others from interfering. The second is the more "positive" freedom to *have* a job, adequate housing, enough to eat, decent education, minimal health care, and so on, in which case the state has to do far more to redistribute the wealth of the society as a whole in order to pay for all these necessities.

Obviously these two notions of rights and freedoms are bound to clash. To provide everyone with adequate food, shelter, education, and health care, we must take more from the wealthy members of the society in order to meet the needs of those less well-off. But this means that "egalitarian" rights and freedoms are always at the expense of "libertarian" rights and freedoms. Since a cardinal "libertarian" right is the right to accumulate private property, any system of taxation for the purpose of economic redistribution will seem unfair and unjust from a libertarian point of view. But if, on the other hand, the libertarian right to accumulate (and keep) private property is inviolable, then the poorer members of the society will be forever barred from receiving the "egalitarian" rights and freedoms to which they might be entitled, and this is equally unfair and unjust from the "egalitarian" perspective. Do individuals have a *right* and are they *entitled* to keep as much wealth as they are able to acquire by honest means? Or do individuals have a right and are they entitled to receive a more equal share of the basic necessities of life (such as food, shelter, medical care, etc.) in order to develop as autonomous human beings? If the answer is yes to *both*, how are we to balance the two? These are questions which occur *within* a given society and also between individuals of *different* societies. What rights and obligations exist among U. S. citizens, for example, and what rights and obligations obtain between Americans and those living outside the United States?

READINGS

The first two readings, by Garrett Hardin, professor emeritus of biology and human ecology at the University of California, Santa Barbara, and Peter Singer, professor of philosophy at Monash University in Australia and director of the Center for Human Bioethics, an animal rights organization, present this dilemma in the starkest and broadest terms possible. Thousands of people around the world starve to death every day, while in the rest of the world there is an overabundance of food. Everyone agrees that human suffering is wrong, but do we have a moral obligation to do something about it? Singer argues that we do; Hardin argues that we do not.

From a utilitarian perspective, Singer argues, it is immoral not to do whatever one can to increase the happiness and well-being of everyone. From a strictly moral (i.e., utilitarian) point of view, Singer argues this means that I ought to share my wealth with suffering humanity down to the point where I also begin to suffer adversely. Assuming I earn $40,000 a year and need only $20,000 to live reasonably well, then, according to Singer I am morally obligated, by the utilitarian principle, to give the remaining $20,000 to help relieve the millions of starving people around the world.

Hardin argues that it is counterproductive for everyone to share a limited amount of resources to the point where all are suffering equally. While it might seem fair to divide a pizza equally among six people, what good would it do to divide the pizza equally among six hundred people? Given the limited resources in the world and the enormous numbers of people around the world living below the poverty line, a program such as the one advocated by Singer would simply bankrupt the world, Hardin argues, siphoning off much needed capital for scientific, industrial, and technological development necessary for improving the general well-being of human beings. It also discourages, according to Hardin, more realistic attempts at population control and making those less well-off more self-sufficient, and so on. It would not make anyone happy or well-off, he argues; indeed, it would make many reasonably well-off individuals miserable without noticeably improving the lives of others. And by encouraging the romantically simplistic and overly optimistic view that world hunger can be overcome by greater generosity on the part of more affluent individuals, Hardin concludes, Singer's prescription undermines more serious and realistic efforts to solve these difficult international problems.

A. M. Honoré, law fellow emeritus at All Souls College, Oxford University, questions the libertarian assumption that everyone has a natural right to keep whatever wealth they have honestly acquired. This is the tradition in *some* societies, Honoré argues, especially in modern industrial societies, but not in *all*. In many societies tradition requires that everyone *share* what they have found, killed, or grown. If that is so, Honoré concludes, the onus is on libertarians to give reasons *why* wealthy individuals are entitled to keep what they have earned.

Ronald Dworkin, philosopher of law at University College, Oxford University, and at New York University, helps us to understand more clearly the tension within liberalism between what we are calling the libertarian liberal's staunch belief in private property and the right of the individual to be free of governmental interference and the egalitarian liberal's equally firm belief in the right of every person to the means to equal dignity and respect and the prospect of leading a life of one's own choosing.

Thomas Nagel, professor of philosophy at New York University, sees this tension not as the clash between two equally firmly held ideologies but as between the force of selfishness on the one hand and a sense of fairness on the other. In Nagel's view libertarian liberalism is little more than a transparent rationalization for the selfish desire of the "haves" to keep what they have. When we stop to *think* about it, Nagel argues, we can see that this is unfair and unjust, but egoistic self-interest is such a powerful *psychological* motivation, it unfortunately tends to overwhelm our *moral* sense of justice and fair play toward the "have-nots." But why, we might wonder, is the libertarian's position any more of a rationalization than that of the egalitarian, which could just as well be portrayed as a sub rosa device of unsuccessful "have-nots" to get from others what they could not or would not earn for themselves? It follows from Nagel's pessimistic position that true justice can never be achieved. The most that can be hoped for is a compromise whereby the rich are allowed to remain relatively wealthy but taxed sufficiently to bring the least advantaged up to a minimal "floor."

"The Case Against Helping the Poor"

Garrett Hardin

Environmentalists use the metaphor of the earth as a "spaceship" in trying to persuade countries, industries and people to stop wasting and polluting our natural resources. Since we all share life on this planet, they argue, no single person or institution has the right to destroy, waste, or use more than a fair share of its resources.

But does everyone on earth have an equal right to an equal share of its resources? The spaceship metaphor can be dangerous when used by misguided idealists to justify suicidal policies for sharing our resources through uncontrolled immigration and foreign aid. In their enthusiastic but unrealistic generosity, they confuse the ethics of a spaceship with those of a lifeboat.

A true spaceship would have to be under the control of a captain, since no ship could possibly survive if its course were determined by committee. Spaceship Earth certainly has no captain; the United Nations is merely a toothless tiger, with little power to enforce any policy upon its bickering members.

If we divide the world crudely into rich nations and poor nations, two thirds of them are desperately poor, and only one third comparatively rich, with the United States the wealthiest of all. Metaphorically each rich nation can be seen as a lifeboat full of comparatively rich people. In the ocean outside each lifeboat swim the poor of the world, who would like to get in, or at least to share some of the wealth. What should the lifeboat passengers do?

First, we must recognize the limited capacity of any lifeboat. For example, a nation's land has a limited capacity to support a population and as the current energy crisis has shown us, in some ways we have already exceeded the carrying capacity of our land.

So here we sit, say fifty people in our lifeboat. To be generous, let us assume it has room for ten more, making a total capacity of sixty. Suppose the fifty of us in the lifeboat see 100 others swimming in the water outside, begging for admission to our boat or for handouts. We have several options: we may be tempted to try to live by the Christian ideal of being "our brother's keeper," or by the Marxist ideal of "to each according to his needs." Since the needs of all in the water are the same, and since they can all be seen as "our brothers," we could take them all into our boat, making a total of 150 in a boat designed for sixty. The boat swamps,

From "Lifeboat Ethics: The Case Against Helping the Poor," *Psychology Today*, (Sept. 1974). Reprinted by permission of the publisher.

everyone drowns. Complete justice, complete catastrophe.

Since the boat has an unused excess capacity of ten more passengers, we could admit just ten more to it. But which ten do we let in? How do we choose? Do we pick the best ten, the neediest ten, "first come, first served"? And what do we say to the ninety we exclude? If we do let an extra ten into our lifeboat, we will have lost our "safety factor," an engineering principle of critical importance. For example, if we don't leave room for excess capacity as a safety factor in our country's agriculture, a new plant disease or a bad change in the weather could have disastrous consequences.

Suppose we decide to preserve our small safety factor and admit no more to the lifeboat. Our survival is then possible, although we shall have to be constantly on guard against boarding parties.

While this last solution clearly offers the only means of our survival, it is morally abhorrent to many people. Some say they feel guilty about their good luck. My reply is simple: "Get out and yield your place to others." This may solve the problem of the guilt-ridden person's conscience, but it does not change the ethics of the lifeboat. The needy person to whom the guilt-ridden person yields his place will not himself feel guilty about his good luck. If he did, he would not climb aboard. The net result of conscience-stricken people giving up their unjustly held seats is the elimination of that sort of conscience from the lifeboat.

This is the basic metaphor within which we must work out our solutions. Let us now enrich the image, step by step, with substantive additions from the real world, a world that must solve real and pressing problems of overpopulation and hunger.

The harsh ethics of the lifeboat become even harsher when we consider the reproductive differences between the rich nations and the poor nations. The people inside the lifeboats are doubling in numbers every eighty-seven years; those swimming around outside are doubling, on the average, every thirty-five years, more than twice as fast as the rich. And since the world's resources are dwindling, the difference in prosperity between the rich and the poor can only increase....

But, one could argue, this discussion assumes that current population trends will continue, and they may not. Quite so. Most likely the rate of population increase will decline much faster in the U.S. than it will in the other countries, and there does not seem to be much we can do about it. In sharing with "each according to his needs," we must recognize that needs are determined by population size, which is determined by the rate of reproduction, which at present is regarded as a sovereign right of every nation, poor or not. This being so, the philanthropic load created by the sharing ethic of the spaceship can only increase....

The fundamental error of spaceship ethics, and the sharing it requires, is that it leads to what I call "the tragedy of the commons." Under a system of private property, the men who own property recognize their responsibility to care for it, for if they don't they will eventually suffer. A farmer, for instance, will allow no more cattle in a pasture than its carrying capacity justifies. If he overloads it, erosion sets in, weeds take over, and he loses the use of the pasture.

If a pasture becomes a commons open to all, the right of each to use it may not be matched by a corresponding responsibility to protect it. Asking everyone to use it with discretion will hardly do, for the considerate herdsman who refrains from overloading the commons suffers more than a selfish one who says his needs are greater. If everyone would restrain himself, all would be well: but it takes only one less than everyone to ruin a system of voluntary restraint. In a crowded world of less than perfect human beings, mutual ruin is inevitable if there are no controls. This is the tragedy of the commons.

One of the major tasks of education today should be the creation of such an acute awareness of the dangers of the commons that people will recognize its many varieties. For example, the air and water have become polluted because they are treated as commons. Further growth in the population or percapita conversion of natural resources into pollutants will only make the problem worse. The same holds true for the fish of the oceans. Fishing fleets have nearly disappeared in many parts of the world, technological improvements in the art of fishing are hastening the day of complete ruin. Only the replacement of the system of the commons with a responsible system of control will save the land, air, water and oceanic fisheries.

On the average, poor countries undergo a 2.5 percent increase in population each year: rich countries, about 0.8 percent. Only rich countries have anything in the way of food reserves set aside, and even they do not have as much as they should. Poor countries have none. If poor countries received no food from the outside, the rate of their population growth would be periodically checked by crop failures and famines. But if they can always draw on a world food bank in time of need, their population can continue to grow unchecked, and so will their "need" for aid. In the short run, a world food bank may diminish that need, but in the long run it actually increases the need without limit.

Without some system of worldwide food sharing, the proportion of people in the rich and poor nations might eventually stabilize. The overpopulated poor countries would decrease in numbers, while the rich countries that had room for more people would increase. But with a well-meaning system of sharing, such as a world food bank, the growth differential between the rich and the poor countries will not only persist, it will increase. Because of the higher rate of population growth in the poor countries of the world, 88 percent of today's children are born poor, and only 12 percent rich. Year by year the ratio becomes worse, as the fast-reproducing poor outnumber the slow-reproducing rich.

A world food bank is thus a commons in disguise. People will have more motivation to draw from it than to add to any common store. The less provident and less able will multiply at the expense of the abler and more provident, bringing eventual ruin upon all who share in the commons. Besides, any system of "sharing" that amounts to foreign aid from the rich nations to the poor nations will carry the taint of charity, which will contribute little to the world peace so devoutly desired by those who support the idea of a world food bank.

As past U.S. foreign-aid programs have amply and depressingly demonstrated, international charity frequently inspires mistrust and antagonism rather than gratitude on the part of the recipient nation. The modern approach to foreign aid stresses the export of technology and advice, rather than money and food. As an ancient Chinese proverb goes: "Give a man a fish and he will eat for a day; teach him how to fish and he will eat for the rest of his days." Acting on this advice, the Rockefeller and Ford Foundations have financed a number of programs for improving agriculture in the hungry nations. Known as the "Green Revolution," these programs have led to the development of "miracle rice" and "miracle wheat," new strains that offer bigger harvests and greater resistance to crop damage. Norman Borlaug, the Nobel Prize winning agronomist who, supported by the Rockefeller Foundation, developed "miracle wheat," is one of the most prominent advocates of a world food bank.

Whether or not the Green Revolution can increase food production as much as its champions claim is a debatable but possibly irrelevant point. Those who support this well-intended humanitarian effort should first consider some of the fundamentals of human ecology. Ironically, one man who did was the late Alan Gregg, a vice president of the Rockefeller Foundation....He expressed strong doubts about the wisdom of such attempts to increase food production. He likened the growth and spread of humanity over the surface of the earth to the spread of cancer in the human body, remarking that "cancerous growths demand food; but, as far as I know, they have never been cured by getting it."

Every human born constitutes a draft on all aspects of the environment: food, air, water, forests, beaches, wildlife, scenery and solitude. Food can, perhaps, be significantly increased to meet a growing demand. But what about clean beaches, unspoiled forests, and solitude? If we satisfy a growing population's need for food, we necessarily decrease its per capita supply of the other resources needed by men.

India...already puts a huge load on a relatively impoverished environment. The country's forests are now only a small fraction of what they were three centuries ago, and floods and erosion continually destroy the insufficient farmland that remains. Every one...added to India's population puts an additional burden on the environment, and increases the economic and social costs of crowding. However humanitarian our intent, every Indian life saved through medical or nutritional assistance from abroad diminishes the quality of life for those who remain, and for subsequent generations....Will future generations of Indians thank us for hastening the destruction of their environment? Will our good intentions be sufficient excuse for the consequences of our actions?

My final example of a commons in action is one for which the public has the least desire for rational discussion—immigration. Anyone who publicly questions the wisdom of current U.S. immigration policy is promptly charged with bigotry, prejudice, ethnocentrism, chauvinism, isolationism or self-ishness. Rather than encounter such accusations, one would rather talk about other matters, leaving immigration policy to wallow in the crosscurrents of special interests that take no account of the good of the whole, or the interests of posterity.

Perhaps we still feel guilty about things we said in the past. Two generations ago the popular press frequently referred to Dagos, Wops, Polacks, Chinks and Krauts, in articles about how America was being "overrun" by foreigners of supposedly inferior genetic stock. But because the implied inferiority of foreigners was used then as justification for keeping them out, people now assume that restrictive policies could only be based on such misguided notions. There are other grounds....

Considering the growing use of birth-control devices, the potential effect of educational campaigns by such organizations as Planned Parenthood Federation of America and Zero Population Growth, and the influence of inflation and the housing shortage, the fertility rate of American women may decline so much that immigration could account for all the yearly increase in population. Should we not at least ask if that is what we want?

For the sake of those who worry about whether the "quality" of the average immigrant compares favorably with the quality of the average resident, let us assume that immigrants and nativeborn citizens are of exactly equal quality, however one defines that term. We will focus here only on quantity; and since our conclusions will depend on nothing else, all charges of bigotry and chauvinism become irrelevant.

World food banks *move food to the people*, hastening the exhaustion of the environment of the poor countries. Unrestricted immigration, on the other hand, *moves people to the food*, thus speeding up the destruction of the environment of the rich countries. We can easily understand why poor people should want to make this latter transfer, but why should rich hosts encourage it?

As in the case of foreign-aid programs, immigration receives support from selfish interests and humanitarian impulses. The primary selfish interest in unimpeded immigration is the desire of employers for cheap labor, particularly in industries and trades that offer degrading work. In the past, one wave of foreigners after another was brought into the U.S. to work at wretched jobs for wretched wages....The interests of the employers of cheap labor mesh well with the guilty silence of the country's liberal intelligentsia. White Anglo-Saxon Protestants are particularly reluctant to call for a closing of the doors to immigration for fear of being called bigots.

But not all countries have such reluctant leadership. Most educated Hawaiians, for example, are keenly aware of the limits of their environment, particularly in terms of population growth. There is only so much room on the islands, and the islanders know it. To Hawaiians, immigrants from the other forty-nine states present as great a threat as those from other nations. At a...meeting of Hawaiian government officials in Honolulu, I had the ironic delight of hearing a speaker, who like most of his audience was of Japanese ancestry, ask how the country might practically and constitutionally close its doors to further immigration. One member of the audience countered: "How can we shut the doors now? We have many friends and relatives in Japan that we'd like to bring here some day so that they can enjoy Hawaii too." The Japanese-American speaker smiled sympathetically and answered: "Yes, but we have children now, and someday we'll have grandchildren too. We can bring more people here from Japan only by giving away some of the land that we hope to pass on to our grandchildren some day. What right do we have to do that?"

At this point, I can hear U.S. liberals asking: "How can you justify slamming the door once you're inside? You say that immigrants should be kept out. But aren't we all immigrants, or the descendants of immigrants? If we insist on staying, must we not admit all others?" Our craving for intellectual order leads us to seek and prefer symmetrical rules and morals: a single rule for me and everybody else; the same rule yesterday, today, and tomorrow. Justice, we feel, should not change with time and place.

We Americans of non-Indian ancestry can look upon ourselves as the descendants of thieves who are guilty morally, if not legally, of stealing this land from its Indian owners. Should we then give back the land to the now living American descendants of those Indians? However morally or logically sound this proposal may be, I, for one, am unwilling to live by it and I know no one else who is. Besides, the logical consequence would be absurd. Suppose that, intoxicated with a sense of pure justice, we should decide to turn our land over to the Indians. Since all our wealth has also been derived from the land, wouldn't we be morally obliged to give that back to the Indians too?

Clearly, the concept of pure justice produces an infinite regression to absurdity. Centuries ago, wise men invented statutes of limitations to justify the rejection of such pure justice, in the interest of preventing continual disorder. The law zealously defends property rights, but only relatively recent property rights. Drawing a line after an arbitrary time has elapsed may be unjust, but the alternatives are worse.

We are all the descendants of thieves, and the world's resources are inequitably distributed. But we must begin the journey to tomorrow from the point where we are today. We cannot remake the past. We cannot safely divide the wealth equitably among all peoples so long as people reproduce at different rates. To do so would guarantee that our grandchildren, and everyone else's grandchildren, would have only a ruined world to inhabit.

To be generous with one's own possessions is quite different from being generous with those of posterity. We should call this point to the attention of those who, from a commendable love of justice and equality, would institute a system of the commons, either in the form of a world food bank, or of unrestricted immigration. We must convince them if we wish to save at least some parts of the world from environmental ruin.

Without a true world government to control reproduction and the use of available resources, the sharing ethic of the spaceship is impossible. For the foreseeable future, our survival demands that we govern our actions by the ethics of a lifeboat, harsh though they may be. Posterity will be satisfied with nothing less.

"The Famine Relief Argument"

Peter Singer

Robert McNamara...has suggested the term absolute poverty. The poverty we are familiar with in industrialized nations is relative poverty—meaning that some citizens are poor, relative to the wealth enjoyed by their neighbours. People living in relative poverty in Australia might be quite comfortably off by comparison with old-age pensioners in Britain, and British old-age pensioners are not poor in comparison with the poverty that exists in Mali or Ethiopia. Absolute poverty, on the other hand, is poverty by any standard. In McNamara's words:

Poverty at the absolute level...is life at the very margin of existence.

The absolute poor are severely deprived human beings struggling to survive in a set of squalid and degraded circumstances almost beyond the power of our sophisticated imaginations and privileged circumstances to conceive.

Compared to those fortunate enough to live in developed countries individuals in the poorest nations have

An infant mortality rate eight times higher
A life expectancy one-third lower
An adult literacy rate 60% less

From *Practical Ethics* (Cambridge: Cambridge University Press, 1979). Reprinted by permission of the publisher.

A nutritional level, for one out of every two in the population, below acceptable standards; and for millions of infants, less protein than is sufficient to permit optimum development of the brain.

And McNamara has summed up absolute poverty as:

a condition of life so characterized by malnutrition, illiteracy, disease, squalid surroundings, high infant mortality and low life expectancy as to be beneath any reasonable definition of human decency.

Absolute poverty is, as McNamara has said, responsible for the loss of countless lives, especially among infants and young children. When absolute poverty does not cause death it still causes misery of a kind not often seen in the affluent nations. Malnutrition in young children stunts both physical and mental development. It has been estimated that the health, growth and learning capacity of nearly half the young children in developing countries are affected by malnutrition. Millions of people on poor diets suffer from deficiency diseases, like goitre, or blindness caused by a lack of vitamin A. The food value of what the poor eat is further reduced by parasites such as hookworm and ringworm, which are endemic in conditions of poor sanitation and health education.

Death and disease apart, absolute poverty remains a miserable condition of life, with inadequate food, shelter, clothing, sanitation, health services and education....Absolute poverty is probably the principal cause of human misery today.

This is the background situation, the situation that prevails on our planet all the time. It does not make headlines. People died from malnutrition and related diseases yesterday, and more will die tomorrow. The occasional droughts, cyclones, earthquakes and floods that take the lives of tens of thousands in one place and at one time are more newsworthy. They add greatly to the total amount of human suffering; but it is wrong to assume that when there are no major calamities reported, all is well.

The problem is not that the world cannot produce enough to feed and shelter its people. People in the poor countries consume, on average, 400 lbs of grain a year, while North Americans average more than 2000 lbs. The difference is caused by the fact that in the rich countries we feed most of our grain to animals, converting it into meat, milk and eggs. Because this is an inefficient process, wasting up to 95% of the food value of the animal feed, people in rich countries are responsible for the consumption of far more food than those in poor countries who eat few animal products. If we stopped feeding animals on grains, soybeans and fishmeal the amount of food saved would—if distributed to those who need it—be more than enough to end hunger throughout the world.

These facts about animal food do not mean that we can easily solve the world food problem by cutting down on animal products, but they show that the problem is essentially one of distribution rather than production. The world does produce enough food. Moreover the poorer nations themselves could produce far more if they made more use of improved agricultural techniques.

So why are people hungry? Poor people cannot afford to buy grain grown by American farmers. Poor farmers cannot afford to buy improved seeds, or fertilizers, or the machinery needed for drilling wells and pumping water. Only by transferring some of the wealth of the developed nations to the poor of the underdeveloped nations can the situation be changed.

That this wealth exists is clear. Against the picture of absolute poverty that McNamara has painted, one might pose a picture of 'absolute affluence'. Those who are absolutely affluent are not necessarily affluent by comparison with their neighbours, but they are affluent by any reasonable definition of human needs. This means that they have more income than they need to provide themselves adequately with all the basic necessities of life. After buying food, shelter, clothing, necessary health services and education, the absolutely affluent are still able to spend money on luxuries. The absolutely affluent choose their food for the pleasures of the palate, not to stop hunger; they buy new clothes to look fashionable, not to keep warm; they move house to be in a better neighbourhood or have a play room for the children, not to keep out the rain; and after all this there is still money to spend on books and records, colour television, and overseas holidays.

At this stage I am making no ethical judgments about absolute affluence, merely pointing out that it exists. Its defining characteristic is a significant amount of income above the level necessary to provide for the basic human needs of oneself and one's dependents. By this standard Western Europe, North America, Japan, Australia, New Zealand and the oil-rich Middle Eastern states are all absolutely affluent, and so are many, if not all, of their citizens....To quote McNamara once more:

The average citizen of a developed country enjoys wealth beyond the wildest dreams of the one billion people in countries with per capita incomes under $200...

These, therefore, are the countries—and individuals—who have wealth which they could, without threatening their own basic welfare, transfer to the absolutely poor.

At present, very little is being transferred. Members of the Organization of Petroleum Exporting Countries lead the way, giving an average of 2.1% of their Gross National Product. Apart from them, only Sweden. The Netherlands and Norway have reached the modest UN target of 0.7% of GNP. Britain gives 0.38% of its GNP in official development assistance and a small additional amount in unofficial aid from voluntary organizations. The total comes to less than £1 per month per person, and compares with 5.5% of GNP spent on alcohol, and 3% on tobacco. Other, even wealthier nations, give still less: Germany gives 0.27%, the United States 0.22% and Japan 0.21%.

If these are the facts, we cannot avoid concluding that by not giving more than we do, people in rich countries are allowing those in poor countries to suffer from absolute poverty, with consequent malnutrition, ill health and death. This is not a conclusion which applies only to governments. It applies to each absolutely affluent individual, for each of us has the opportunity to do something about the situation; for instance, to give our time or money to voluntary organizations like Oxfam, War on Want, Freedom From Hunger, and so on. If, then, allowing someone to die is not intrinsically different from killing someone, it would seem that we are all murderers.

Is this verdict too harsh? Many will reject it as self-evidently absurd. They would sooner take it as showing that allowing to die cannot be equivalent to killing than as showing that living in an affluent style without contributing to Oxfam is ethically

equivalent to going over to India and shooting a few peasants. And no doubt, put as bluntly as that, the verdict *is* too harsh.

These are several significant differences between spending money on luxuries instead of using it to save lives, and deliberately shooting people.

First, the motivation will normally be different. Those who deliberately shoot others go out of their way to kill; they presumably want their victims dead, from malice, sadism, or some equally unpleasant motive. A person who buys a colour television set presumably wants to watch television in colour—not in itself a terrible thing. At worst, spending money on luxuries instead of giving it away indicates selfishness and indifference to the sufferings of others, characteristics which may be understandable but are not comparable with actual malice or similar motives.

Second, it is not difficult for most of us to act in accordance with a rule against killing people: it is, on the other hand, very difficult to obey a rule which commands us to save all the lives we can. To live a comfortable, or even luxurious life it is not necessary to kill anyone; but it is necessary to allow some to die whom we might have saved, for the money that we need to live comfortably could have been given away. Thus the duty to avoid killing is much easier to discharge completely than the duty to save. Saving every life we could would mean cutting our standard of living down to the bare essentials needed to keep us alive. To discharge this duty completely would require a degree of moral heroism utterly different from what is required by mere avoidance of killing.

A third difference is the greater certainty of the outcome of shooting when compared with not giving aid. If I point a loaded gun at someone and pull the trigger, it is virtually certain that the person will be injured, if not killed; whereas the money that I could give might be spent on a project than turns out to be unsuccessful and helps no one.

Fourth, when people are shot there are identifiable individuals who have been harmed. We can point to them and to their grieving families. When I buy my colour television, I cannot know who my money would have saved if I had given it away. In a time of famine I may see dead bodies and grieving families on my new television, and I might not doubt that my money would have saved some of them; even then it is impossible to point to a body and say that had I not bought the set, that person would have survived.

Fifth, it might be said that the plight of the hungry is not my doing, and so I cannot be held responsible for it. The starving would have been starving if I had never existed. If I kill, however, I am responsible for my victims' deaths, for those people would not have died if I had not killed them....

Do the five differences not only explain, but also justify, our attitudes? Let us consider them one by one:

1. Take the lack of an identifiable victim first. Suppose that I am a travelling salesman, selling tinned food, and I learn that a batch of tins contains a contaminant, the known effect of which when consumed is to double the risk that the consumer will die from stomach cancer. Suppose I continue to sell the tins. My decision may have no identifiable victims. Some of those who eat the food will die from cancer. The proportion of consumers dying in this way will be twice that of the community at large, but which among the consumers died because they ate what I sold, and which would have contracted the disease anyway? It is impossible to tell; but surely this impossibility makes my decision no less reprehensible than it would have been had the contaminant had more readily detectable, though equally fatal, effects.

2. The lack of certainty that by giving money I could save a life does reduce the wrongness of not giving, by comparison with deliberate killing; but it is insufficient to show that not giving is acceptable conduct. The motorist who speeds through pedestrian crossings, heedless of anyone who might be on them, is not a murderer. She may never actually hit a pedestrian; yet what she does is very wrong indeed.

3. The notion of responsibility for acts rather than omissions is more puzzling. On the one hand we feel ourselves to be under a greater obligation to help those whose misfortunes we have caused. (It is for this reason that advocates of overseas aid often argue that Western nations have created the poverty of Third World nations, through forms of economic exploitation which go back to the colonial system.) On the other hand any consequentialist would insist that we are responsible for all the consequences of our actions, and if a consequence of my spending money on a luxury item is that someone dies, I am responsible for that death. It is true that the person would have died even if I had never existed, but what is the relevance of that? The fact is that I do exist, and the consequentialist will say that our responsibilities

derive from the world as it is, not as it might have been.

One way of making sense of the non-consequentialist view of responsibility is by basing it on a theory of rights of the kind proposed by John Locke or, more recently, Robert Nozick. If everyone has a right to life, and this right is a right *against* others who might threaten my life, but not a right *to* assistance from others when my life is in danger, then we can understand the feeling that we are responsible for acting to kill but not for omitting to save. The former violates the rights of others, the latter does not.

Should we accept such a theory of rights? If we build up our theory of rights by imagining, as Locke and Nozick do, individuals living independently from each other in a 'state of nature', it may seem natural to adopt a conception of rights in which as long as each leaves the other alone, no rights are violated. I might, on this view, quite properly have maintained my independent existence if I had wished to do so. So if I do not make you any worse off than you would have been if I had had nothing at all to do with you, how can I have violated your rights? But why start from such an unhistorical, abstract and ultimately inexplicable idea as an independent individual? We now know that our ancestors were social beings long before they were human beings, and could not have developed the abilities and capacities of human beings if they had not been social beings first. In any case we are not, now, isolated individuals. If we consider people living together in a community, it is less easy to assume that rights must be restricted to rights against interference. We might, instead, adopt the view that taking rights to life seriously is incompatible with standing by and watching people die when one could easily save them.

4. What of the difference in motivation? That a person does not positively wish for the death of another lessens the severity of the blame she deserves; but not by as much as our present attitudes to giving aid suggest. The behaviour of the speeding motorist is again comparable, for such motorists usually have no desire at all to kill anyone. They merely enjoy speeding and are indifferent to the consequences. Despite their lack of malice, those who kill with cars deserve not only blame but also severe punishment.

5. Finally, the fact that to avoid killing people is normally not difficult, whereas to save all one possibly could save is heroic, must make an important difference to our attitude to failure to do what the respective principles demand. Not to kill is a minimum standard of acceptable conduct we can require of everyone; to save all one possibly could is not something that can realistically be required, especially not

in societies accustomed to giving as little as ours do. Given the generally accepted standards, people who give, say, £100 a year to Oxfam are more aptly praised for above average generosity than blamed for giving less than they might. The appropriateness of praise and blame is, however, a separate issue from the rightness or wrongness of actions. The former evaluates the agent: the latter evaluates the action. Perhaps people who give £100 really ought to give at least £1,000, but to blame them for not giving more could be counterproductive. It might make them feel that what is required is too demanding, and if one is going to be blamed anyway, one might as well not give anything at all.

(That an ethic which put saving all one possibly can on the same footing as not killing would be an ethic for saints or heroes should not lead us to assume that the alternative must be an ethic which makes it obligatory not to kill, but puts us under no obligation to save anyone. There are positions in between these extremes, as we shall soon see.)

To summarize our discussion of the five differences which normally exist between killing and allowing to die, in the context of absolute poverty and overseas aid. The lack of an identifiable victim is of no moral significance, though it may play an important role in explaining our attitudes. The idea that we are directly responsible for those we kill, but not for those we do not help, depends on a questionable notion of responsibility, and may need to be based on a controversial theory of rights. Differences in certainty and motivation are ethically significant, and show that not aiding the poor is not to be condemned as murdering them; it could, however, be on a par with killing someone as a result of reckless driving, which is serious enough. Finally the difficulty of completely discharging the duty of saving all one possibly can makes it inappropriate to blame those who fall short of this target as we blame those who kill; but this does not show that the act itself is less serious. Nor does it indicate anything about those who, far from saving all they possibly can, make no effort to save anyone.

These conclusions suggest a new approach. Instead of attempting to deal with the contrast between affluence and poverty by comparing not saving with deliberate killing, let us consider afresh whether we have an obligation to assist those whose lives are in danger, and if so, how this obligation applies to the present world situation.

The argument for an obligation to assist. The path from the library at my university to the Humanities lecture theatre passes a shallow ornamental pond. Suppose that on my way to give a lecture I notice that a small child has fallen in and is in danger of drowning. Would anyone deny that I ought to wade in and pull the child out? This will mean getting my clothes muddy, and either cancelling my lecture or delaying it until I can find something dry to change into; but compared with the avoidable death of a child this is insignificant.

A plausible principle that would support the judgment that I ought to pull the child out is this: if it is in our power to prevent something very bad happening, without thereby sacrificing anything of comparable moral significance, we ought to do it. This principle seems uncontroversial. It will obviously win the assent of consequentialists; but non-consequentialists should accept it too, because the injunction to prevent what is bad applies only when nothing comparably significant is at stake. Thus the principle cannot lead to the kinds of actions of which non-consequentialists strongly disapprove—serious violations of individual rights, injustice, broken promises, and so on. If a non-consequentialist regards any of these as comparable in moral significance to the bad thing that is to be prevented, he will automatically regard the principle as not applying in those cases in which the bad thing can only be prevented by violating rights, doing injustice, breaking promises, or whatever else is at stake. Most non-consequentialists hold that we ought to prevent what is bad and promote what is good. Their dispute with consequentialists lies in their insistence that this is not the sole ultimate ethical principle: that it is *an* ethical principle is not denied by any plausible ethical theory.

Nevertheless the uncontroversial appearance of the principle that we ought to prevent what is bad when we can do so without sacrificing anything of comparable moral significance is deceptive. If it were taken seriously and acted upon, our lives and our world would be fundamentally changed. For the principle applies, not just to rare situations in which one can save a child from a pond, but to the everyday situation in which we can assist those living in absolute poverty. In saying this I assume that absolute poverty, with its hunger and malnutrition, lack of shelter, illiteracy, disease, high infant mortality and low life expectancy, is a bad thing. And I assume that it is within the power of the affluent to reduce absolute poverty, without sacrificing anything of comparable moral significance. If these two assumptions and the principle we have been discussing are correct, we have an obligation to help those in absolute poverty which is no less strong than our obligation to rescue a drowning child from a pond. Not to help would be wrong, whether or not it is intrinsically equivalent to killing. Helping is not, as conventionally thought, a charitable act which it is praiseworthy to do, but not wrong to omit; it is something that everyone ought to do.

This is the argument for an obligation to assist. Set out more formally, it would look like this.

FIRST PREMISE: If we can prevent something bad without sacrificing anything of comparable significance, we ought to do it.
SECOND PREMISE: Absolute poverty is bad.
THIRD PREMISE: There is some absolute poverty we can prevent without sacrificing anything of comparable moral significance.
CONCLUSION: We ought to prevent some absolute poverty

The first premise is the substantive moral premise on which the argument rests, and I have tried to show that it can be accepted by people who hold a variety of ethical positions.

The second premise is unlikely to be challenged. Absolute poverty is, as McNamara put it, 'beneath any reasonable definition of human decency' and it would be hard to find a plausible ethical view which did not regard it as a bad thing.

The third premise is more controversial, even though it is cautiously framed. It claims only that some absolute poverty can be prevented without the sacrifice of anything of comparable moral significance. It thus avoids the objection that any aid I can give is just 'drops in the ocean' for the point is not whether my personal contribution will make any noticeable impression on world poverty as a whole (of course it won't) but whether it will prevent some poverty. This is all the argument needs to sustain its conclusion, since the second premise says that any absolute poverty is bad, and not merely the total amount of absolute poverty. If without sacrificing anything of comparable moral

significance we can provide just one family with the means to raise itself out of absolute poverty, the third premise is vindicated.

I have left the notion of moral significance unexamined in order to show that the argument does not depend on any specific values or ethical principles. I think the third premise is true for most people living in industrialized nations, on any defensible view of what is morally significant. Our affluence means that we have income we can dispose of without giving up the basic necessities of life, and we can use this income to reduce absolute poverty. Just how much we will think ourselves obliged to give up will depend on what we consider to be of comparable moral significance to the poverty we could prevent: colour television, stylish clothes, expensive dinners, a sophisticated stereo system, overseas holidays, a (second?) car, a larger house, private schools for our children....For a utilitarian, none of these is likely to be of comparable significance to the reduction of absolute poverty; and those who are not utilitarians surely must, if they subscribe to the principle of universalizability, accept that at least *some* of these things are of far less moral significance than the absolute poverty that could be prevented by the money they cost. So the third premise seems to be true on any plausible ethical view—although the precise amount of absolute poverty that can be prevented before anything of moral significance is sacrificed will vary according to the ethical view one accepts....

Property rights. Do people have a right to private property, a right which contradicts the view that they are under an obligation to give some of their wealth away to those in absolute poverty? According to some theories of rights (for instance, Robert Nozick's) provided one has acquired one's property without the use of unjust means like force and fraud, one may be entitled to enormous wealth while others starve. This individualistic conception of rights is in contrast to other views, like the early Christian doctrine to be found in the works of Thomas Aquinas, which holds that since property exists for the satisfaction of human needs, 'whatever a man has in superabundance is owed, of natural right, to the poor for their sustenance'. A socialist would also, of course, see wealth as belonging to the community rather than the individual, while utilitarians, whether socialist or not, would be prepared to override property rights to prevent great evils.

Does the argument for an obligation to assist others therefore presuppose one of these other theories of property rights, and not an individualistic theory like Nozick's? Not necessarily. A theory of property rights can insist on our *right* to retain wealth without pronouncing on whether the rich *ought* to give to the poor. Nozick, for example, rejects the use of compulsory means like taxation to redistribute income, but suggests that we can achieve the ends we deem morally desirable by voluntary means. So Nozick would reject the claim that rich people have an 'obligation' to give to the poor, in so far as this implies that the poor have a right to our aid, but might accept that giving is something we ought to do and failing to give, though within one's rights, is wrong—for rights is not all there is to ethics.

The argument for an obligation to assist can survive, with only minor modifications, even if we accept an individualistic theory of property rights. In any case, however, I do not think we should accept such a theory. It leaves too much to chance to be an acceptable ethical view. For instance, those whose forefathers happened to inhabit some sandy wastes around the Persian Gulf are now fabulously wealthy, because oil lay under those sands; while those whose forefathers settled on better land south of the Sahara live in absolute poverty, because of drought and bad harvests. Can this distribution be acceptable from an impartial point of view? If we imagine ourselves about to begin life as a citizen of either Kuwait or Chad— but we do not know which—would we accept the principle that citizens of Kuwait are under no obligation to assist people living in Chad?

Population and the ethics of triage. Perhaps the most serious objection to the argument that we have an obligation to assist is that since the major cause of absolute poverty is overpopulation, helping those now in poverty will only ensure that yet more people are born to live in poverty in the future.

In its most extreme form, this objection is taken to show that we should adopt a policy of 'triage'. The term comes from medical policies adopted in wartime. With too few doctors to cope with all the casualties, the wounded were divided into three categories: those who would probably survive without medical assistance, those who might survive if they received assistance, but otherwise probably would not, and those who even with medical assistance probably would not survive. Only those in the middle category were given medical assistance. The idea, of course, was to use limited medical resources as effectively as possible. For those in the first category, medical treatment was not strictly necessary; for those in the third category, it was likely to be useless. It has been suggested that we should apply the same policies to countries, according to their prospects of becoming self-sustaining. We would not aid countries which even without our help will soon be able to feed their populations. We would not aid countries which, even with our help, will not be able to limit their population to a level they can feed. We would aid those countries where our help might make the difference between success and failure in bringing food and population into balance.

Advocates of this theory are understandably reluctant to give a complete list of the countries they would place into the 'hopeless' category; but Bangladesh is often cited as an example. Adopting the policy of triage would, then, mean cutting off assistance to Bangladesh and allowing famine, disease and natural disasters to reduce the population of that country…to the level at which it can provide adequately for all.

In support of this view Garrett Hardin has offered a metaphor: we in the rich nations are like the occupants of a crowded lifeboat adrift in a sea full of drowning people. If we try to save the drowning by bringing them aboard our boat will be overloaded and we shall all drown. Since it is better that some survive than none, we should leave the others to drown. In the world today, according to Hardin, 'lifeboat ethics' apply. The rich should leave the poor to starve, for otherwise the poor will drag the rich down with them.

Against this view, some writers have argued that over-population is a myth. The world produces ample food to feed its population, and could, according to some estimates, feed ten times as many. People are hungry not because there are too many but because of inequitable land distribution, the manipulation of Third World economies by the developed nations, wastage of food in the West, and so on.

Putting aside the controversial issue of the extent to which food production might one day be increased, it is true, as we have already seen, that the world now produces enough to feed its inhabitants—the amount lost by being fed to animals itself being enough to meet existing grain shortages. Nevertheless population growth cannot be ignored. Bangladesh could, with land reform and using better techniques, feed its present population of 80 million; but by the year 2000, according to World Bank estimates, its population will be 146 million. The enormous effort that will have to go into feeding an extra 66 million people, all added to the population within a quarter of a century, means that Bangladesh must develop at full speed to stay where she is....

What will happen then? Population cannot grow indefinitely. It will be checked by a decline in birth rates or a rise in death rates. Those who advocate triage are proposing that we allow the population growth of some countries to be checked by a rise in death rates—that is, by increased malnutrition, and related diseases; by widespread famines; by increased infant mortality; and by epidemics of infectious diseases.

The consequences of triage on this scale are so horrible that we are inclined to reject it without further argument. How could we sit by our television sets, watching millions starve while we do nothing? Would not that be the end of all notions of human equality and respect for human life? Don't people have a right to our assistance, irrespective of the consequences?

Anyone whose initial reaction to triage was not one of repugnance would be an unpleasant sort of person. Yet initial reactions based on strong feelings are not always reliable guides. Advocates of triage are rightly concerned with the long-term consequences of our actions. They say that helping the poor and starving now merely ensures more poor and starving in the future. When our capacity to help is finally unable to cope—as one day it must be—the suffering will be greater than it would be if we stopped helping now. If this is correct, there is nothing we can do to prevent absolute starvation and poverty, in the long run, and so we have no obligation to assist. Nor does it seem reasonable to hold that under these circumstances people have a right to our assistance. If we do accept such a right, irrespective of the consequences, we are saying that, in Hardin's metaphor, we would continue to

haul the drowning into our lifeboat until the boat sank and we all drowned.

If triage is to be rejected it must be tackled on its own ground, within the framework of consequentialist ethics. Here it is vulnerable. Any consequentialist ethics must take probability of outcome into account. A course of action that will certainly produce some benefit is to be preferred to an alternative course that may lead to a slightly larger benefit, but is equally likely to result in no benefit at all. Only if the greater magnitude of the uncertain benefit outweighs its uncertainty should we choose it. Better one certain unit of benefit than a 10% chance of 5 units; but better a 50% chance of 3 units than a single certain unit. The same principle applies when we are trying to avoid evils.

The policy of triage involves a certain, very great evil: population control by famine and disease. Tens of millions would die slowly. Hundreds of millions would continue to live in absolute poverty, at the very margin of existence. Against this prospect, advocates of the policy place a possible evil which is greater still: the same process of famine and disease, taking place in, say, fifty years time, when the world's population may be three times its present level, and the number who will die from famine, or struggle on in absolute poverty, will be that much greater. The question is: how probable is this forecast that continued assistance now will lead to greater disasters in the future?

Forecasts of population growth are notoriously fallible, and theories about the factors which affect it remain speculative. One theory, at least as plausible as any other, is that countries pass through a 'demographic transition' as their standard of living rises. When people are very poor and have no access to modern medicine their fertility is high, but population is kept in check by high death rates. The introduction of sanitation, modern medical techniques and other improvements reduces the death rate, but initially has little effect on the birth rate. Then population grows rapidly. Most poor countries are now in this phase. If standards of living continue to rise, however, couples begin to realize that to have the same number of children surviving to maturity as in the past, they do not need to give birth to as many children as their parents did. The need for children to provide economic support in old age diminishes. Improved education and the emancipation and employment of women also reduce the birthrate, and so population growth begins to level off. Most rich nations have reached this stage, and their populations are growing only very slowly.

If this theory is right, there is an alternative to the disasters accepted as inevitable by supporters of triage. We can assist poor countries to raise the living standards of the poorest members of their population. We can encourage the governments of these countries to enact land reform measures, improve education, and liberate women from a purely child-bearing role. We can also help other countries to make contraception and sterilization widely available. There is a fair chance that these measures will hasten the onset of the demographic transition and bring population growth down to a manageable level. Success cannot be guaranteed; but the evidence that improved economic security and education reduce population growth is strong enough to make triage ethically unacceptable. We cannot allow millions to die from starvation and disease when there is a reasonable probability that population can be brought under control without such horrors.

Population growth is therefore not a reason against giving overseas aid, although it should make us think about the kind of aid to give. Instead of food handouts, it may be better to give aid that hastens the demographic transition. This may mean agricultural assistance for the rural poor, or assistance with education, or the provision of contraceptive services. Whatever kind of aid proves most effective in specific circumstances, the obligation to assist is not reduced.

One awkward question remains. What should we do about a poor and already overpopulated country which, for religious or nationalistic reasons, restricts the use of contraceptives and refuses to slow its population growth? Should we nevertheless offer development assistance? Or should we make our offer conditional on effective steps being taken to reduce the birthrate? To the latter course, some would object that putting conditions on aid is an attempt to impose our own ideas on independent sovereign nations. So it is—but is this imposition unjustifiable? If the argument for an obligation to assist is sound, we have an obligation to reduce absolute poverty: but we have no obligation to make sacrifices that, to the best of our knowledge, have no prospect of reducing poverty

in the long run. Hence we have no obligation to assist countries whose governments have policies which will make our aid ineffective. This could be very harsh on poor citizens of these countries—for they may have no say in the government's policies—but we will help more people in the long run by using our resources where they are most effective. (The same principles may apply, incidentally, to countries that refuse to take other steps that could make assistance effective—like refusing to reform systems of land holding that impose intolerable burdens on poor tenant farmers.)...

Too high a standard? The final objection to the argument for an obligation to assist is that it sets a standard so high that none but a saint could attain it. How many people can we really expect to give away everything not comparable in moral significance to the poverty their donation could relieve? For most of us, with commonsense views about what is of moral significance, this would mean a life of real austerity. Might it not be counter-productive to demand so much? Might not people say: 'As I can't do what is morally required anyway, I won't bother to give at all.' If, however, we were to set a more realistic standard, people might make a genuine effort to reach it. Thus setting a lower standard might actually result in more aid being given.

It is important to get the status of this objection clear. Its accuracy as a prediction of human behaviour is quite compatible with the argument that we are obliged to give to the point at which by giving more we sacrifice something of comparable moral significance. What would follow from the objection is that public advocacy of this standard of giving is undesirable. It would mean that in order to do the maximum to reduce absolute poverty, we should advocate a standard lower than the amount we think people really ought to give. Of course we ourselves—those of us who accept the original argument, with its higher standard—would know that we ought to do more than we publicly propose people ought to do, and we might actually give more than we urge others to give. There is no inconsistency here, since in both our private and our public behaviour we are trying to do what will most reduce absolute poverty.

For a consequentialist, this apparent conflict between public and private morality is always a possibility, and not in itself an indication that the underlying principle is wrong. The consequences of a principle are one thing, the consequences of publicly advocating it another.

Is it true that the standard set by our argument is so high as to be counterproductive? There is not much evidence to go by, but discussions of the argument, with students and others have led me to think it might be. On the other hand the conventionally accepted standard—a few coins in a collection tin when one is waved under your nose—is obviously far too low. What level should we advocate? Any figure will be arbitrary, but there may be something to be said for a round percentage of one's income like, say, 10%—more than a token donation, yet not so high as to be beyond all but saints. (This figure has the additional advantage of being reminiscent of the ancient tithe, or tenth, which was traditionally given to the church, whose responsibilities included care of the poor in one's local community. Perhaps the idea can be revived and applied to the global community.) Some families, of course, will find 10% a considerable strain on their finances. Others may be able to give more without difficulty. No figure should be advocated as a rigid minimum or maximum; but it seems safe to advocate that those earning average or above average incomes in affluent societies, unless they have an unusually large number of dependents or other special needs, ought to give a tenth of their income to reducing absolute poverty. By any reasonable ethical standards this is the minimum we ought to do, and we do wrong if we do less.

"Property, Title and Redistribution"

Tony Honoré

This discussion paper is concerned with the relationship between the institution of private property and the notion of economic equality. Is it inconsistent, or morally obtuse to recognize the value of the institution and at the same time to argue that each member of a society is entitled to an equal or approximately equal standard of living? I shall be particularly concerned with the argument of R. *Nozick*, in *Anarchy, State and Utopia* to the effect that under a system of "just entitlements" such as he specifies there is no room to admit that the state has the right or duty to redistribute benefits so as to secure an equal or more equal spread, because "the particular rights over things fill the space of rights, leaving no room for general rights to be in a certain material condition". Though *Nozick's* "just entitlements" are not confined to titles to property I shall so confine myself. Rights of a more personal character could in theory be the subjects of redistribution and indeed *Nozick* discusses the case for transplanting organs from A to B in order to correct physical maldistribution of parts of the body. Fascinating as such speculations may be,...the moral objections to the invasion of people's bodies for whatever purpose are much stronger than they are when what is proposed is to tax or, in some cases, to expropriate. Nor can one concede the argument that the redistribution of part of what A has earned to B goes beyond the invasion of property rights and amounts to a system of forced labour by which A is compelled to work part of his day for B, so that redistribution of property is really an invasion of the status and freedom of the person taxed or expropriated. This is no more compelling than the Marxist argument that a wageearner whose surplus product is appropriated

From "Property, Title and Redistribution," *Equality and Freedom: Past, Present and Future*, Carl Wellman, ed. (Wiesbaden: Franz Steiner Verlag GMBH, 1977). Reprinted by permission of the publisher.

by the employer is a sort of wageslave. The objection to this is not that the income-earner freely works under a system in which he knows that part of what he produces will be appropriated by his employer or transferred to other people by means of taxes. He may have no choice, if he is to earn a living, but to accept a system which he dislikes. The argument is open to attack rather because it rests on the morally questionable view that a person is entitled to keep exclusively and indefinitely for himself whatever he makes or produces. This would be true of a man working in complete isolation; no serious argument has been advanced to show that it is true of a social being.

Nozick's argument depends on accepting this questionable view. Against those who favour a principle of social justice by which things are to be distributed according to need, desert, the principle of equal claims or the like, he argues that the just allocation is the historically justifiable one. This can be ascertained, in relation to any given item of property, by asking whether the holder acquired it by a just title or derived his title justly from another who so held it, either originally or by derivation from such a just acquirer. Consequently just distribution depends on just acquisition and transfer, and redistribution is confined to those instances in which the original acquisition or the subsequent transmission of the property was unjust.

All therefore turns on what count as just principles of acquisition and transfer of title. According to *Nozick*—

1. a person who acquires a holding in accordance with the principle of justice in acquisition is entitled to that holding
2. a person who acquires a holding in accordance with the principle of justice in transfer from some one else entitled to the holding is entitled to the holding
3. no one is entitled to a holding except by (repeated) applications of 1 and 2.

The complete principle of distributive justice would say simply that a distribution is just if everyone is entitled to the holdings they possess under the distribution.

What is presupposed by this set of rules for tracing title is apparently only that the principles of acquisition and transfer should be morally respectable. For acquisition something like *Locke*'s theory of property is understood. Transfers in a free society will be consensual. But that is only the appearance. What *Nozick* additionally presupposes, without seeking to justify, is that the interest acquired and transmitted is the ownership of property as conceived in western society on the model of Roman law. He is assuming, first, that the acquirer obtains an exclusive right to the thing acquired, that he is entitled, having cleared the land, made the tool etc. to deny access and use to everyone else. Secondly he is supposing that the right acquired is of indefinite duration. The man who has made the clearing can remain there for his lifetime. He is not obliged to move on after so many years, and leave the fruits of his labour to another, nor does he lose his right by leaving. Thirdly the right is supposed to be transmissible inter vivos and on death, so that it can be sold, given inherited, mortgaged and the like again without limit of time. Under such a system of property law, of course, the initial acquisition is decisive. Once A has cleared the land his neighbours, friends, associates and, if it comes to that, his family are obliged to look on while he enjoys and transmits his 'entitlement' to whomsoever he chooses, irrespective of the fact that in a wider context they, along with him, form part of a single group which is dedicated, among other objects, to the preservation of all. This system of property law, whatever its economic merits, is not self-evidently just. If the interest acquired (western type ownership) is greater than can be morally justified, then however just the methods by which A acquires the thing in question and transfers it to X, the distribution of property under which the thing is allocated to X is not thereby saved from criticism. Indeed, quite the contrary. If the interest awarded to owners under the system is greater than can reasonably be justified on moral, as opposed to economic grounds, any distribution of property will be inherently unjust. Hence the intervention of the state will be needed if justice is to be done.

There is no doubt that the *Nozick* rules about just acquisition, transfer and distribution reproduce in outline western systems of property law based on the liberal conception of ownership. According to these notions, ownership is a permanent, exclusive and transmissible interest in property. But this type of property system is neither the only conceivable system, nor the easiest to justify from a moral point of view, nor does it predominate in those societies which are closest to a 'state of nature'.

In so far as the *Nozick* principles are meant to reproduce western property law they are incomplete in that they omit provision for lapse of title and for compulsory acquisition. Lapse of title is not perhaps of great moral importance, but it is worth noting that legal rules about limitation of actions and prescription embody the idea that an owner who neglects his property may be deprived of it. The acquirer (squatter or the like) obtains it by a sort of private expropriation. More important is expropriation by the state or public authority. It is not at all clear why the parts of western property law favourable to the private owner should be reproduced in the system of entitlements to the exclusion of those which favour the claims of the community. The latter, after all, balance the former. The individualistic bias of property law is corrected by the admission of state claims to tax and expropriate.

Aside from the omission of rules about lapse and compulsory acquisition one may note that *Nozick's* principles rest on the assumption that whether a justification exists for acquiring or transferring property can be decided in abstraction from the historical and social context. A just acquisition in 1066 or 1620 remains a just root of title in 1975. If this were really so one would have to say either that the acquisition of slaves is seen in retrospect always to have been unjust and that the state would have been justified in intervening in a slave-owning society to correct the injustice, or that the descendants of slave-owners are entitled to own the descendants of freed slaves. So with colonies, *mutatis mutandis*. Are we to say that as a result of the post-war movement to free colonies we now see that the acquisition of colonies, apparently valid at the time in international law and morality, was always wrong and that the international society would have been justified, had it been so minded, in intervening even in the nineteenth century to free the existing colonies and prevent further acquisitions. If so, how can we be sure that there are not equally unjustified forms of property ownership in present-day society which in fact justify state intervention in a redistributive sense? And how can we be sure in any future society that these objectionable forms of acquisition are not present? In which case, outside Utopia, the thesis advanced by *Nozick* has no application. But if the acquisition of slaves and colonies was initially just, surely some provision should be made in his system for the redistribution of entitlements when the moral basis on which they originally rested has become eviscerated. These instances would count morally as cases of lapse of title owing to changing views of right and wrong. Legally they would furnish examples of just expropriation. There would have to be a further exception in *Nozick*'s system to cater for changing conditions of fact. Suppose, apart from any question of the justification for colonies, that in the nineteenth century Metropolitania occupied a deserted tract which it proceeded to colonize, building roads and irrigating the land. As a result a numerous indigenous population crowded in from the neighbouring areas. These people now claim to be free and to decide their own destinies. Whether or not colonization is in general thought a permissible form of 'entitlement' the changed situation must surely change one's moral evaluation of Metropolitania's title to the formerly deserted tract. So with the Mayflowerite who bagged a large stretch of unoccupied land in 1620. If the situation is now that irrespective of title the tracts in question are occupied by people who have nowhere else to live surely the moral basis of the title of the Mayflowerite's successors must at least be open to debate. Once there was more than enough to go round, now there is not. And is the case very different if the thousands without property instead of occupying the colonies or tracts in question crowd the periphery and make claims on the unused resources inside? All this is intended to make the simple point that it is obtuse to suppose that the justification for acquiring or transmitting property could be settled once and for all at the date of acquisition or transfer. Legally it may be so, subject to the rules of lapse and expropriation. This is because of the need to frame rules of law in such a way as to ensure certainly of title. They are meant however to be applied in a context in which social and moral criticism may be directed against their operation and in which their defects may be corrected by legislation or similar means. Apart from positive law, can it seriously be maintained that the rules about what constitutes a just acquisition or transfer both express unchanging verities and in their application to the facts of a given acquisition or transfer, are exempt from reassessment in the light of changed circumstances?

Systems of property law which diverge from the orthodox western type based on liberal conceptions of ownership are conceivable, morally defensible and have actually obtained in certain societies. To begin with the conceivable, let us take an imaginary case. Suppose that, in a 'state of nature' a group of people live near a river and subsist on fish, which they catch by hand and berries. There is great difficulty in catching fish by hand. Berries are however fairly plentiful. There are bits of metal lying around and I discover how to make one of them into a fish hook. With this invention I quadruple my catch of fish. My neighbours cannot discover the knack and I decline to tell them. They press me to lend them the fish hook or to give them lessons in acquiring the technique. I have however acquired western notions of property law and Lockean ideas about entitlement. I point out that I have a just title to the fish hook, since according to *Nozick's* version of *Locke* they are no worse off as a result of my invention. I am therefore entitled to the exclusive, permanent and transmissible use of the fish hook. My neighbours may try their hands at finding out how to make one, of course, but if they fail they may look forward to eating berries and from time to time a bit of fish while I and those persons whom I choose to invite to a meal propose to enjoy ourselves with daily delicacies. If they object that this is unfair I shall point out (though the relevance is not obvious) that they are not actually starving. Nor am I monopolizing materials. There are other pieces of metal lying around. They are no worse off than they were before or than they would have been without my find [in fact they *are* worse off, relatively to me]. As to the parrot cry that they protect me and my family from marauders, wild animals and the like, so that I ought to share my good fortune with them, I reply that they have not grasped what is implied by a system of just entitlements. Are they saying that I am not entitled to the fishhook?

One of my brighter neighbours might well answer me as follows

I do not deny that you have a right to the fishhook. As you say you made it and you invented the system of using it to catch fish. But it does not follow that, as you assert, your right to it is exclusive, permanent and trans-

missible. Your views seem to be coloured by reading books about sophisticated societies. In those societies men are dedicated to increasing production, come what may, and in order to achieve that they accept institutions which to us seem very unfair. We are simple people used to sharing our fortunes and misfortunes. We recognize that you have a right to the fishhook but not that the right has the unlimited content which you assign to it. You ought to allow each of us to use it in turn. Naturally as the maker and inventor you are entitled to a greater share in the use than the rest of us individually, and if you like to call that share 'ownership' we shall not object. But please stop looking up the definition of 'ownership' in foreign books. These notions will only disrupt our way of life.

The point my neighbour is making is that a system of private property can be inherently distributive. In the system envisaged there is an "owner" in the sense of a person whose right to the use of the thing is greater than that of others, who has a residual claim if others do not want to use the thing, and in whom powers of management will be vested. He will be responsible for lending the fishhook out, it will be returned to him each evening, he will keep it in repair. But these powers of use, management and reversion fall short of western conception of ownership. In such a system the redistributive power of the state will be unnecessary unless the members of the group fail to keep the rules. For the rules themselves ensure an even distribution of property, subject to the recognition of desert and choice—a recognition which is not allowed to subvert the principle of sharing.

Is the projected system of property law obviously unjust? How does it compare with western notions of ownership? From the point of view of justice, though perhaps not of economic efficiency, it seems to compare rather favourably. It is designed to give effect to the interdependence of the members of the group and to recognize overtly that they cannot survive in isolation. It rejects the notion that I do no harm to a member of my group if as a result of my effort I am better off, and he is no worse off than he would otherwise be. That notion, which is common to the outlook of *Nozick* and *Rawls*, however much they otherwise differ, rests on the assumption that a person who is *comparatively* worse off is not worse off. But he is, and the precise wrong he suffers is that of being treated as an unequal by the more fortunate member or members of the group.

The fruits of an invention which raises production have therefore, in the projected system, to be shared, either by a system of compulsory loan or, in a weaker version, by a system of surplus sharing, under which what an owner has in excess of his needs or is not using must be made available to other members of his group.

The sort of system envisaged is unlikely to survive the division of labour, viz. specialisation. The members of the group other than the inventor are likely to feel that he can fish better than they and that they would do well to get him to fish for them. But then they must pay him. At first perhaps the payment is a fraction of the catch. Later the inventor is bemused by the idea that he is entitled to the whole product of his invention. So he argues that his neighbours owe him the whole of his catch and, if they want any of it, must pay in some other way, as by repairing his hut. As he has possession on his side his views may prevail. We slide insensibly, therefore, from a participatory to an exclusive system of property law, and it is difficult to keep alive, in a society of economic specialisation, the notion that each participates in a common enterprise. The remedy for this is not, or is only to a minor extent, a return to rotatory labour. It is rather that the community as a whole, the state, must act as the surrogate of the participatory principles. The inventor of the fishhook will have to be taxed. In that way the economic advantages of specialisation can be combined with a just, or juster distribution of the benefits derived from it. The tax will be used to give the other members of the group benefits corresponding to their former rights to use the fishhook.

There is no point in attempting to work out in detail what a participatory system of property law would be like. The idea is easy to grasp. If such a system is morally sound, then it follows that in a western-type system the intervention of the state, so far from being, as *Nozick* thinks, ruled out except in peripheral instances, (initially unjust acquisitions, subsequently unjust transfers) is essential in order to achieve justice in distribution. Whether one says that this is because in a western-type system all the holdings are unjust (because they are holdings of an unjust sort of property interest) or that they were initially just but that their

permanent retention cannot be justified, is debatable: the former seems more appealing. In any event either *Nozick's* conclusion is empty because the premises are never fulfilled, or if the premises are fulfilled, they do not lead to the conclusion to which they seem to lead.

If it is accepted that the sort of property system described is conceivable and morally defensible that is sufficient to rebut the argument which denies a redistributive function to the state. It is not irrelevant, however, to draw attention to the fact that among the variety of property arrangements found in simple societies there are some which approximate to the distributive arrangement outlined. Among other things this will serve to rebut any argument that I am relying on a gimmicky obligatory principle of transfer. A convenient outline of the variety of such property systems is to be found in *M. J. Herskowitz'* work. They are of course multifold: apart from arrangements which resemble the western institution of ownership there are to be found types of group (e.g., family or clan) ownership, public ownership, rotating individual use (e.g., of fishing grounds) and also the sort of arrangement here envisaged, namely what may be called private ownership subject to compulsory loan or sharing....

There are also examples of what I have termed surplus sharing, which give effect to the principle that what a person has in excess of his needs, or is not using must be made available to other members of the group....

These examples show that there is nothing unnatural about distributive property arrangements in a simple society. The mechanism, or one of the possible mechanisms by which such arrangements are secured, is that of what it seems preferable to call private ownership subject to a trust or a duty to permit sharing. The 'ownership' is not of course ownership of the classical western type, but neither is it 'primitive communism'. Its essential feature is that the titles to acquisition are much the same as in modern societies—finding, invention, occupation, making and the like—and the types of transfer—sale, gift, inheritance—are not necessarily dissimilar, but the type of interest acquired and transmitted is different. The principle of sharing is written into the delineation of interests of property.

There is no special reason to think that our moral consciousness is superior to that of simple societies. So if compulsory sharing commends itself to some of them it should not be dismissed out of hand for societies in which the division of labour has made those simple arrangements out of date: but in these, gives the weakened social cohesion which the division of labour introduces, the communal authority (the state) is needed to see that sharing takes place.

"Why Liberals Should Care About Equality"

Ronald Dworkin

Though liberalism is often discussed as a single political theory, there are in fact two basic forms of liberalism and the distinction between them is of great importance. Both argue against the legal enforcement of private morality—both argue against the Moral Majority's views of homosexuality and abortion, for example—and both argue for greater sexual, political, and economic equality. But they disagree about which of these two traditional liberal values is fundamental and which derivative. Liberalism based on neutrality takes as fundamental the idea that government must not take sides on moral issues, and it supports only such egalitarian measures as can be shown to be the result of that principle. Liberalism based on equality takes as fundamental that government treat its citizens as equals, and insists on moral neutrality only to the degree that equality requires it.

The difference between these two versions of liberalism is crucial because both the content and appeal of liberal theory depends on which of these two values is understood to be its proper ground. Liberalism based on neutrality finds its most natural defense in some form of moral skepticism, and this makes it vulnerable to the charge that liberalism is a negative theory for uncommitted people. Moreover it offers no effective argument against utilitarian and other contemporary justifications for economic inequality, and therefore provides no philosophical support for those who are appalled

at the Reagan administration's economic program. Liberalism based on equality suffers from neither of these defects. It rests on a positive commitment to an egalitarian morality and provides, in that morality, a firm contrast to the economics of privilege.

In this essay I shall set out what I believe are the main principles of liberalism based on equality. This form of liberalism insists that government must treat people as equals in the following sense. It must impose no sacrifice or constraint on any citizen in virtue of an argument that the citizen could not accept without abandoning his sense of his equal worth. This abstract principle requires liberals to oppose the moralism of the New Right, because no self-respecting person who believes that a particular way to live is most valuable for him can accept that this way of life is base or degrading. No self-respecting atheist can agree that a community in which religion is mandatory is for that reason finer, and no one who is homosexual that the eradication of homosexuality makes the community purer.

So liberalism as based on equality justifies the traditional liberal principle that government should not enforce private morality of this sort. But it has an economic as well as a social dimension. It insists on an economic system in which no citizen has less than an equal share of the community's resources just in order that others may have more of what he

From *A Matter of Principle* (Cambridge, MA: Harvard University Press, 1985). Reprinted by permission of the publisher.

lacks. I do not mean that liberalism insists on what is often called "equality of result," that is, that citizens must each have the same wealth at every moment of their lives. A government bent on the latter ideal must constantly redistribute wealth, eliminating whatever inequalities in wealth are produced by market transactions. But this would be to devote *unequal* resources to different lives. Suppose that two people have very different bank accounts, in the middle of their careers, because one decided not to work, or not to work at the most lucrative job he could have found, while the other single-mindedly worked for gain. Or because one was willing to assume especially demanding or responsible work, for example, which the other declined. Or because one took larger risks which might have been disastrous but which were in fact successful, while the other invested conservatively. The principle that people must be treated as equals provides no good reason for redistribution in these circumstances; on the contrary, it provides a good reason *against* it.

For treating people as equals requires that each be permitted to use, for the projects to which he devotes his life, no more than an equal share of the resources available for all, and we cannot compute how much any person has consumed, on balance, without taking into account the resources he has contributed as well as those he has taken from the economy. The choices people make about work and leisure and investment have an impact on the resources of the community as a whole, and this impact must be reflected in the calculation equality demands. If one person chooses work that contributes less to other people's lives than different work he might have chosen, then, although this might well have been the right choice for him, given his personal goals, he has nevertheless added less to the resources available for others, and this must be taken into account in the egalitarian calculation. If one person chooses to invest in a productive enterprise rather than spend his funds at once, and if his investment is successful because it increases the stock of goods or services other people actually want, without coercing anyone, his choice has added more to social resources than the choice of someone who did not invest, and this, too, must be reflected in any calculation of whether he has, on balance, taken more than his share.

This explains, I think, why liberals have in the past been drawn to the idea of a market as a method of allocating resources. An efficient market for investment, labor, and goods works as a kind of auction in which the cost to someone of what he consumes, by way of goods and leisure, and the value of what he adds, through his productive labor or decisions, is fixed by the amount his use of some resource costs others, or his contributions benefit them, in each case measured by their willingness to pay for it. Indeed, if the world were very different from what it is, a liberal could accept the results of an efficient market as *defining* equal shares of community resources. If people start with equal amounts of wealth, and have roughly equal levels of raw skill, then a market allocation would ensure that no one could properly complain that he had less than others, over his whole life. He could have had the same as they if he had made the decisions to consume, save, or work that they did.

But in the real world people do not start their lives on equal terms; some begin with marked advantages of family wealth or of formal and informal education. Others suffer because their race is despised. Luck plays a further and sometimes devastating part in deciding who gains or keeps jobs everyone wants. Quite apart from these plain inequities, people are not equal in raw skill or intelligence or other native capacities; on the contrary, they differ greatly, through no choice of their own, in the various capacities that the market tends to reward. So some people who are perfectly willing, even anxious, to make exactly the choices about work and consumption and savings that other people make end up with fewer resources, and no plausible theory of equality can accept this as fair. This is the defect of the ideal fraudulently called "equality of opportunity": fraudulent because in a market economy people do not have equal opportunity who are less able to produce what others want.

So a liberal cannot, after all, accept the market results as defining equal shares. His theory of economic justice must be complex, because he accepts two principles which are difficult to hold in the administration of a dynamic economy. The first requires that people have, at any point in their lives, different amounts of wealth insofar as the genuine choices they have made have been more or less expensive or beneficial to the community, measured by what other people want for their lives. The market seems indispensable to this principle.

The second requires that people not have different amounts of wealth just because they have different inherent capacities to produce what others want, or are differently favored by chance. This means that market allocations must be corrected in order to bring some people closer to the share of resources they would have had but for these various differences of initial advantage, luck, and inherent capacity.

Obviously any practical program claiming to respect both these principles will work imperfectly and will inevitably involve speculation, compromise, and arbitrary lines in the face of ignorance. For it is impossible to discover, even in principle, exactly which aspects of any person's economic position flow from his choices and which from advantages or disadvantages that were not matters of choice; and even if we could make this determination for particular people, one by one, it would be impossible to develop a tax system for the nation as a whole that would leave the first in place and repair only the second. There is therefore no such thing as the perfectly just program of redistribution. We must be content to choose whatever programs we believe bring us closer to the complex and unattainable ideal of equality, all things considered, than the available alternatives, and be ready constantly to reexamine that conclusion when new evidence or new programs are proposed.

Nevertheless, in spite of the complexity of that ideal, it may sometimes be apparent that a society falls far short of any plausible interpretation of its requirements. It is, I think, apparent that the United States falls far short now. A substantial minority of Americans are chronically unemployed or earn wages below any realistic "poverty line" or are handicapped in various ways or burdened with special needs; and most of these people would do the work necessary to earn a decent living if they had the opportunity and capacity. Equality of resources would require more rather than less redistribution than we now offer.

This does not mean, of course, that we should continue past liberal programs, however inefficient these have proved to be, or even that we should insist on "targeted" programs of the sort some liberals have favored—that is, programs that aim to provide a particular opportunity or resource, like education or medicine, to those who need it. Perhaps a more general form of transfer, like a negative income tax, would prove on balance more efficient and fairer, in spite of the difficulties in such schemes. And whatever devices are chosen for bringing distribution closer to equality of resources, some aid undoubtedly goes to those who have avoided rather than sought jobs. This is to be regretted, because it offends one of the two principles that together make up equality of resources. But we come closer to that ideal by tolerating this inequity than by denying aid to the far greater number who would work if they could. If equality of resources were our only goal, therefore, we could hardly justify the present retreat from redistributive welfare programs.

We must therefore consider a further and more difficult question. Must liberals insist on equality of resources no matter what the cost to the national economy as a whole? It is far from obvious that treating people as equals forbids any deviation from equality of resources for any reason whatsoever. On the contrary, people with a lively sense of their own equal worth, and pride in their own convictions, can nevertheless accept certain grounds for carrying special burdens for the sake of the community as a whole. In a defensive war, for example, we expect those who are capable of military service to assume a vastly greater share of danger than others. Nor is inequality permissible only in emergencies when the survival of the community is at stake. We might think it proper, for example, for the government to devote special resources to the training of exceptionally talented artists or musicians, beyond what the market would pay for the services these artists produce, even though this reduces the share others have. We accept this not because we think that the life of an artist is inherently more valuable than other lives, but because a community with a lively cultural tradition provides an environment within which citizens may live more imaginatively, and in which they might take pride. Liberalism need not be insensitive to these and similar virtues of community. The question becomes not whether any deviation is permitted, but what reasons for deviation are consistent with equal concern and respect.

That question is now pressing for this reason. Many economists believe that reducing economic inequality through redistribution is damaging to the general economy and, in the long run, self-defeating. Welfare programs, it is said, are inflationary, and the tax system necessary to support them depresses incentive and therefore production. The economy, it is claimed, can be restimulated only by reducing taxes and adopting other programs that will, in the short run, produce high unemployment and otherwise cause special damage to those already at the bottom of the economy. But this damage will only be temporary. For a more dynamic economy will produce prosperity, and this will in the end provide more jobs and more money for the handicapped and others truly needy.

Each of these propositions is doubtful, and they may well all be wrong. But suppose we were to accept them. Do they make a case for ignoring those in the economic cellar now? The argument would be unanswerable, of course, if *everyone* who lost because of stringent policies now would actually be better off in the long run. But though this is often suggested in careless supply-side rhetoric, it is absurd. People laid off for several years, with no effective retraining, are very unlikely to recoup their losses later, particularly if their psychological losses are counted. Children denied adequate nutrition or any effective chance of higher education will suffer permanent loss even if the economy follows the most optimistic path of recovery. Some of those who are denied jobs and welfare now, particularly the elderly, will in any case not live long enough to share in that recovery, however general it turns out to be.

So the currently popular argument, that we must reduce benefits now in order to achieve general prosperity later, is simply a piece of utilitarianism, which attempts to justify irreversible losses to a minority in order to achieve gains for the large majority....But this denies the principle fundamental to liberalism based on equality, the principle that people must be treated with equal concern. It asks some people to accept lives of great poverty and despair, with no prospect of a useful future, just in order that the great bulk of the community may have a more ample measure of what they are forever denied. Perhaps people can be forced into this position. But they cannot accept it consistently with a full recognition of their independence, and their right to equal concern on the part of their government.

But suppose the case for [policy]…is put differently, by calling attention to the distinct social dangers of continuing or expanding past programs of redistribution. We might imagine two arguments of this sort. The first calls attention to the damage inflation does, not simply to the spending power, savings, and prospects of the majority, as individuals, but also to the public environment in which all citizens must live and in which all might take either pride or shame. As society becomes poorer, because production falls and wealth decays, it loses a variety of features we cherish. Its culture fails, its order declines, its system of criminal and civil justice becomes less accurate and less fair; in these and other ways it steadily recedes from our conception of a good society. The decline cannot be arrested by further taxation to support these public goods, for that will only shrink production further and accelerate the decline. According to this argument, those who lose by programs designed to halt inflation and reinvigorate the economy are called upon to make a sacrifice, not just in order to benefit others privately, but out of a sense of loyalty to the public institutions of their own society.

The second argument is different because it calls attention to the interests of future generations. It asks us to suppose that if we are zealous for equality now, we will so depress the wealth of the community that future Americans will be even less well off than the very poor are now. Future Americans will have no more, perhaps, than the citizens of economically depressed third world countries in the present world. The second argument comes to this: the present poor are asked to sacrifice in favor of their fellow citizens now, in order to prevent a much greater injustice, to many more citizens, later.

Neither of these two arguments plainly violates the liberal's axiomatic principle of equal concern and respect. Each can be offered to people who take pride in their equal worth and in the value of their convictions. But only in certain circumstances. Both arguments, though in different ways, appeal to the idea that each citizen is a member of a community, and that he can find, in the fate of that community, a reason for special burdens he can accept with honor rather than degradation. This is appropriate only when that community offers him, at a minimum, the opportunity to develop and lead a life he can regard as valuable both to himself and to it.

We must distinguish, that is, between passive and active membership in a community. Totalitarian regimes suppose that anyone who is present in their community, and so is amenable to its political force, is a member of the community from whom sacrifice might fairly be asked in the name of that community's greatness and future. Treating people as equals requires a more active conception of membership. If people are asked to sacrifice for their community, they must be offered some reason why the community which benefits from that sacrifice is their community; there must be some reason why, for example, the unemployed blacks of Detroit should take more interest in either the public virtue or the future generations of Michigan than they do in those of Mali.

We must ask in what circumstances someone with the proper sense of his own independence and equal worth can take pride in a community as being his community, and two conditions, at least, seem necessary to this. He can take pride in its present attractiveness—in the richness of its culture, the justice of its institutions, the imagination of its education—only if his life is one that in some way draws on and contributes to these public virtues. He can identify himself with the future of the community and accept present deprivation as sacrifice rather than tyranny, only if he has some power to help determine the shape of that future, and only if the promised prosperity will provide at least equal benefit to the smaller, more immediate communities for which he feels special responsibilities, for example, his family, his descendants, and, if the society is one that has made this important to him, his race.

These seem minimal conditions, but they are nevertheless exigent. Together they impose serious restraints on any policy that denies any group of citizens, however small or politically negligible, the equal resources that equal concern would otherwise grant them. Of course no feasible program can provide every citizen with a life valuable in his own eyes. But these constraints set a limit to what a government that respects equality may deliberately choose when other choices are available. People must not be condemned, unless this is unavoidable, to lives in which they are effectively denied any active part in the political, economic, and cultural life of the community. So if economic policy contemplates an increase in unemployment, it must also contemplate generous public provision for retraining or public employment. The children

of the poor must not be stinted of education or otherwise locked into positions at the bottom of society. Otherwise their parents' loyalty to them acts not as a bridge but as a bar to any identification with the future these parents are meant to cherish.

If this is right, then it suggests an order of priorities which any retrenchment in welfare programs should follow. Programs like food stamps, Aid to Families with Dependent Children, and those using federal funds to make higher education available for the poor are the last programs that should be curtailed, or (what amounts to the same thing) remitted to the states through some "new federalism." If "targeted" programs like these are thought to be too expensive, or too inefficient, then government must show how alternative plans or programs will restore the promise of participation in the future that these programs offered. In any case, cutbacks in the overall level of welfare provided to the poor should be accompanied by efforts to improve the social integration and political participation of blacks and other minorities who suffer most, in order to assure them a more prominent role in the community for which they sacrifice. Reductions in welfare should not be joined to any general retreat from affirmative action and other civil rights programs, or to any effort to repeal or resist improvements in the Voting Rights Act. That is why the economic and social programs so far proposed or enacted by the present administration seem so mean-spirited and cynical. Taken together, they would reduce rather than enlarge the political participation and social mobility of the class from which they demand the greatest sacrifice.

These observations offer only rough guidelines to the necessary conditions for asking people to sacrifice equal resources for the sake of their community. Different people will interpret these guidelines differently, and disagree about when they have been violated. But they may nevertheless serve as the beginning of an overdue development of liberal theory. During the long period of liberal ascendancy, from the New Deal through the 1960s, liberals felt confident that the immediate reduction of poverty was in every way good for the larger community. Social justice would, in Lyndon Johnson's phrase, make the society great. Liberals thus avoided the question of what liberalism requires when prosperity is threatened rather than enhanced by justice. They offered no coherent and feasible account of what might be called economic rights for hard times: the floor beneath which people cannot be allowed to drop for the greater good.

If liberals remember the counsel of equal concern, they will construct such a theory now, by pointing to the minimal grounds on which people with self-respect can be expected to regard a community as their community, and to regard its future as in any sense their future. If government pushes people below the level at which they can help shape the community and draw value from it for their own lives, or if it holds out a bright future in which their own children are promised only second-class lives, then it forfeits the only premise on which its conduct might be justified.

We need not accept the gloomy predictions of the New Right economists that our future will be jeopardized if we try to provide everyone with the means to lead a life with choice and value, or if we continue to accept mobility as an absolute priority and try to provide appropriate higher education for everyone qualified. But if these gloomy predictions were sound, we should simply have to tailor our ambitions for the future accordingly. For society's obligation runs first to its living citizens. If our government can provide an attractive future only through present injustice—only by forcing some citizens to sacrifice in the name of a community from which they are in every sense excluded—then the rest of us should disown that future, however attractive, because we should not regard it as our future either.

Equality and Partiality

Thomas Nagel

This essay deals with what I believe to be the central problem of political theory. Rather than proposing a solution to it, I shall try to explain what it is, and why a solution is so difficult to achieve. This result need not be thought of pessimistically, since the recognition of a serious obstacle is always a necessary condition of progress, and I believe there is hope that in the future, political and social institutions may develop which continue our unsteady progress toward moral equality, without ignoring the stubborn realities of human nature.

My belief is not just that all social and political arrangements so far devised are unsatisfactory. That might be due to the failure of all actual systems to realize an ideal that we should all recognize as correct. But there is a deeper problem—not merely practical, but theoretical: We do not yet possess an acceptable political ideal, for reasons which belong to moral and political philosophy. The unsolved problem is the familiar one of reconciling the standpoint of the collectivity with the standpoint of the individual; but I want to approach it not primarily as a question about the relation between the individual and society, but in essence as a question about each individual's relation to himself. This reflects a conviction that ethics, and the ethical basis of political theory, have to be understood as arising from a division in each individual between two standpoints, the personal and the impersonal. The latter represents the claims of the collectivity and gives them their force for each individual. If it did not exist, there would be no morality, only the clash, compromise, and occasional convergence of individual perspectives. It

From *Equality and Partiality* (Oxford: Oxford University Press, 1991). Reprinted by permission of the publisher and the author.

is because a human being does not occupy only his own point of view that each of us is susceptible to the claims of others through private and public morality.

Any social arrangement governing the relations among individuals, or between the individual and the collective, depends on a corresponding balance of forces within the self—its image in microcosm. That image is the relation, for each individual, between the personal and impersonal standpoints, on which the social arrangement depends and which it requires of us. If an arrangement is to claim the support of those living under it—if it is to claim legitimacy, in other words—then it must rely on or call into existence some form of reasonable integration of the elements of their naturally divided selves. The division is rough, and spans a great deal of subordinate complexity, but I believe it is indispensable in thinking about the subject.

The hardest problems of political theory are conflicts within the individual, and no external solution will be adequate which does not deal with them at their source. The impersonal standpoint in each of us produces, I shall claim, a powerful demand for universal impartiality and equality, while the personal standpoint gives rise to individualistic motives and requirements which present obstacles to the pursuit and realization of such ideals. The recognition that this is true of everyone then presents the impersonal standpoint with further questions about what is required to treat such persons with equal regard, and this in turn presents the individual with further conflict.

The same problems arise with respect to the morality of personal conduct, but I shall argue that their treatment must be extended to political theory, where the relations of mutual support or conflict between political institutions and individual motivation are all-important. It emerges that a harmonious combination of an acceptable political ideal and acceptable standards of personal morality is very hard to come by. Another way of putting the problem, therefore, is this: When we try to discover reasonable moral standards for the conduct of individuals and then try to integrate them with fair standards for the assessment of social and political institutions, there seems no satisfactory way of fitting the two together. They respond to opposing pressures which cause them to break apart.

To a considerable extent, political institutions and their theoretical justifications try to externalize the demands of the impersonal standpoint. But they have to be staffed and supported and brought to life by individuals for whom the impersonal standpoint coexists with the personal, and this has to be reflected in their design. My claim is that the problem of designing institutions that do justice to the equal importance of all persons, without making unacceptable demands on individuals, has not been solved—and that this is so partly because for our world the problem of the right relation between the personal and impersonal standpoints within each individual has not been solved.

Most people feel this on reflection. We live in a world of spiritually sickening economic and social inequality, a world whose progress toward the acknowledgment of common standards of toleration, individual liberty and human development has been depressingly slow and unsteady. There are sometimes dramatic improvements, and recent events in Eastern Europe must give pause to all those, like myself, who in response to the dominant events of this century have cultivated a defensive pessimism about the prospects of humanity. But we really do not know how to live together. The professed willingness of civilized persons to slaughter each other by the millions in a nuclear war now appears to be subsiding, as the conflicts of political conviction which fueled it lose their sharpness. But even in the developed world, and certainly in the world taken as a whole, the problems which generated the great political and moral rift between democratic capitalism and authoritarian communism have not been solved by the utter competitive failure of the latter.

Communism may have been defeated in Europe, and we may live to celebrate its fall in Asia as well, but that does not mean that democratic capitalism is the last word in human social arrangements. At this historical moment it is worth remembering that communism owes its existence in part to an ideal of equality which remains appealing however great the crimes committed and the economic disasters produced in its name. Democratic societies have not found a way to contend with that ideal: it is a problem for the old democracies of the West, and it will be a very serious problem for the emerging democracies which succeed the collapse of communism in Eastern

Europe, and perhaps elsewhere. Political philosophy is not going to transform this situation, but it has its role, for some of the apparently practical problems of political life have theoretical and moral sources. Moral convictions drive political choices, and the absence of moral agreement, if severe, can be far more divisive than a mere conflict of interests. Anyone who is inclined to doubt the connection of political theory with reality cannot hold out against the events now unfolding; moral and theoretical battles are being fought across the globe, sometimes with real tanks.

One should think of political theory as an enterprise of discovery—the discovery of human possibilities whose coming to actuality is encouraged and assisted by the discovery itself. That is certainly how most of the traditional figures of political theory have seen it. They were in the business of imagining the moral future, with the hope of contributing to its realization. But this inevitably carries the risk of utopianism, and that problem is an important aspect of our subject.

A theory is utopian in the pejorative sense if it describes a form of collective life that humans, or most humans, could not lead and could not come to be able to lead through any feasible process of social and mental development. It may have value as a possibility for a few people, or as an admirable but unattainable ideal for others. But it cannot be offered as a general solution to the main question of political theory: How should we live together in society?

Worse still, when what is described is not in fact motivationally possible, the illusion of its possibility may motivate people nevertheless to try to institute it, with results that are quite different. Societies are constantly trying to beat people into shape because they stubbornly fail to conform to some preconceived pattern of human possibility. Political theory is in this sense an empirical discipline whose hypotheses give hostages to the future, and whose experiments can be very costly.

But while the avoidance of utopianism is important, it is no more important than the avoidance of hard-nosed realism, its diametrical opposite. To be sure, a theory that offers new possibilities must be aware of the danger that they may be purely imaginary. The real nature of humans and human motivation always has to be an essential part of the subject: Pessimism is always in order, and we have

been given ample reason to fear human nature. But we shouldn't be too tied down by limits derived from the baseness of actual motives or by excessive pessimism about the possibility of human improvement. It is important to try to imagine the next step, even before we have come close to implementing the best conceptions already available.

In this enterprise the use of moral intuition is inevitable, and should not be regretted. To trust our intuitions, particularly those that tell us something is wrong even though we don't know exactly what would be right, we need only believe that our moral understanding extends farther than our capacity to spell out the principles which underlie it. Intuition can be corrupted by custom, self-interest, or commitment to a theory, but it need not be, and often a person's intuitions will provide him with evidence that his own moral theory is missing something, or that the arrangements he has been brought up to find natural are really unjust. Intuitive dissatisfaction is an essential resource in political theory. It can tell us that something is wrong, without necessarily telling us how to fix it. It is a reasonable response to even the most ideal versions of current political practice, and I believe it is the correct response also at the level of theory: It tells us, not surprisingly, that we have not yet arrived at the truth. In that way it can help us to cultivate a healthy dissatisfaction with the familiar, without falling into utopianism of the uncritical sort.

I believe that the clash of personal and impersonal standpoints is one of the most pressing problems revealed in this way. If we cannot, through moral theory and institutional design, reconcile an impartial concern for everyone with a view of how each individual can reasonably be expected to live, then we cannot hope to defend the general acceptability of any political order. These problems of integration come with our humanity, and we cannot expect them ever to disappear. But the attempt to deal with them has to be part of any political theory that can claim to be realistic.

What makes this task so difficult is that our ultimate aim in political theory should be to approach as nearly as possible to unanimity, at some level, in support of the basic framework of those political institutions which are maintained by force and into which we are born. Such a claim may seem extravagant or unintelligible, since lack of unanimity is the essence of politics; but I shall try to defend it, and to explain how it is related to Kantian ethics and to the hypothetical contractualism which is its political expression.

The pure ideal of political legitimacy is that the use of state power should be capable of being *authorized* by each citizen—not in direct detail but through acceptance of the principles, institutions, and procedures which determine how that power will be used. This requires the possibility of unanimous agreement at some sufficiently high level, for if there are citizens who can legitimately object to the way state power is used against them or in their name, the state is not legitimate. To accept such unanimity as an ideal while respecting the complex realities of human motivation and practical reason is inevitably frustrating, but in my conception that is what presents political theory with its task. We must try both to give the condition a morally sensible interpretation and to see how far actual institutions might go toward meeting it.

It is a task which cannot be postponed till the millenium, when conflicts have disappeared and all share a common goal. The secular form of that seductive and dangerous vision, which condemns the aim of even idealized agreement under existing circumstances, and insists on struggle and the pursuit of victory so long as there are classes whose interests conflict, has been Marx's most conspicuous moral legacy to the world. Harmony is reserved for a future which will be achieved only by eschewing harmony for political war between irreconcilable interests in the present.

This view should be rejected, and the pursuit of human equality decisively separated from it. The aim of idealized agreement has a role at all stages in the pursuit of an improved human condition, even if full justice is far away. Force will always be necessary if that aim is not widely enough shared, but it is a disaster to exclude the aim from political morality until history has proceeded by other means to that mythical terminus at which it will be effortlessly achieved.

I want to consider what transformations of motive might make possible the realization of a more egalitarian social ideal. Given the inextinguishable appeal of egalitarianism and its enormous failures, together with the political and economic upheavals which they generate, this is an unavoidable question. Such an ideal could be sustained only if it were pervasively internalized. While institutions must play an important role in creating social and economic equality, they cannot sustain it unless they come to express what enough people feel.

Transformations in the tolerance of inequality can occur. In the United States, during my lifetime, and in other Western countries, there has been such a change in attitudes toward overt racial and sexual discrimination. (The change with respect to religious discrimination began a bit earlier.)...

This is not true of social attitudes to economic inequality, except with regard to extreme poverty. Those who win out in the competitive economy or as a result of the inheritance of wealth and social position tend simply to count themselves lucky, or deserving—certainly not, in most cases, as the recipients of ill-gotten gains, or gains whose origins make them disreputable. More people in our culture may feel this queasiness about inherited benefits than about earned benefits resulting from their productivity, but most, I suspect, feel it strongly about neither. The way the chips fall in a competitive economy where equality of opportunity is not blocked by traditional forms of discrimination may seem illegitimate to the losers, but to the winners and potential winners, it generally does not. Those with highly marketable skills rarely feel that their earnings are tainted, or that the difference between their standard of living and that of the average unskilled laborer is dishonorable.

In part this may reflect a belief that there is external justification for those inequalities, but it also indicates that for the most part prevailing opinion finds nothing prima facie wrong with them. Their beneficiaries feel on the whole entitled to count themselves fortunate in the natural abilities and social and educational opportunities which, suitably employed, have resulted in competitive advantage, and consequent rewards. Others are less lucky, but that's life. By contrast, the corresponding attitude toward the advantages of membership in a dominant race or sex is no longer respectable.

The creation of stable egalitarian institutions in a developed economy would require a change in these attitudes. Perhaps changed institutions can bring about the change in attitudes or perhaps they cannot; at any rate they will not survive unless they do. Not only the victims but the beneficiaries of socioeconomic inequality would have to come to regard such benefits with suspicion. But what change of this sort is possible? The question cannot really be treated separately from a consideration of the institutions in which equality might be embodied....

First of all, an egalitarian system would have to completely forget the idea, still popular in certain quarters, that the root of social injustice is exploitation—in the sense of a failure to reward people in accordance with their productive contribution or the true value of their labor. The defense of equality requires that rewards *not* depend on productive contribution, and in particular that some people receive much more of the social product than they contribute.

People's productive contributions are so unequal that the mere avoidance of exploitation would allow great inequalities of economic condition. I assume no one believes in the labor theory of value any more; but just for the record, it is clear that the value of a product is not a function of the amount of labor that went into it. It is the other way around: The value of someone's labor is a function of its contribution to the creation of a product, together with the value of the product. In a factory that manufactures telephones, for example, the subtraction of the designers of the telephones and the production process would cause the productive value of the labor of the factory workers to plummet, roughly, to what they could produce in a pre-industrial economy, whereas the subtraction of an equal number of laborers from the factory would reduce its productivity only slightly by slowing down the rate at which it could produce telephones.

Second, the pursuit of equality requires abandonment of the idea that there is a morally fundamental distinction, in regard to the socioeconomic framework which controls people's life prospects, between what the state does and what it merely allows. There are other areas of state action, impinging on individual rights, in which this distinction retains its moral significance, and of course it will continue to do so at the level of individual morality. But with regard to income, wealth, social position, health, education, and perhaps other things, it is essential that the society should be regarded by its members as responsible for how things are, if different feasible policies and institutions would result in their being different. And if the society is responsible, they are responsible through it, for it is their agent.

This is an extremely important issue, and one on which current community opinion is unclear. But I believe there is still significant attachment to the idea that certain aspects of the economic system are "natural," and do not have to be justified: Only when government interferes with them is it responsible for the results, and then the question of the justifiability of its policies can be raised. Libertarianism is a radical version of this view, but in less clear form it has considerable influence on more mainstream public opinion. Its decisive abandonment would be a major transformation of the common moral consciousness....

The acceptance of a serious egalitarian ideal would have to appeal to a notion of negative responsibility, on the part of the society, for failing to arrange things differently in ways that it could. If it is possible for people to be economically rewarded more equally under another arrangement, then maintenance of a system which allows rewards to be proportional to productivity would have to be regarded as a social choice to permit rewards to depend substantially on differences in natural talent, education, and background. Noninterference requires justification as much as interference does: *Every* arrangement has to be justified by comparison with every other real possibility, and if egalitarian impartiality has a substantial role in justification of this kind, then significant arguments on the other side will be needed to defend arrangements which permit large inequalities to develop as a consequence of their unimpeded operation.

A laissez-faire system, despite its name, has no special status as a "natural" process for whose results government is not responsible. In deciding to enforce only the rights which make such a system possible, the state makes a choice, and if there is a viable alternative, then it has chosen an arrangement which rewards those with greater productive capacity (and their heirs) at the expense of those with less—not in the sense that the latter are being deprived of some of the value of their labor, but in the sense that they are being deprived of what they could have under an alternative arrangement. The state, and therefore its citizens, are responsible for this result.

The sense that benefits not provided, which could be provided, are being *withheld* from the poor, will seem unnatural only if one rejects the assumption of negative responsibility. Of course if a more equal arrangement is chosen, then it is just as true that benefits are being withheld from the better off, which they would otherwise receive. But in an egalitarian view, this withholding may be justified by the priority of needs of those worse off. Whether it is or not depends on the arguments in the other direction.

In this respect, as I have said, political theory is different from the ethics of individual conduct. There, negative responsibility is much less significant: In a decent society, an individual who devotes most of his energies to the pursuit of his own life is not plausibly accused of withholding from others all the benefits he might provide for them instead. But the society itself must consider all systems of allocation prima facie equally eligible, since it has no "life of its own" to lead, apart from the way it arranges the collective life of its members. In deciding among alternatives, the importance of letting individuals lead their own lives must be weighed along with egalitarian values. But if, even in light of all that, the distribution of rewards is too strongly proportional to the natural or social accidents of birth, then the society must be regarded as having chosen to permit the distribution of benefits on morally irrelevant grounds. There is no default position that doesn't have to be justified because it is not chosen. Any way in which the society arranges things, any system it enforces, from laissez-faire to socialism, represents a choice which must be justified by comparison with the other viable alternatives.

This contrasts with the Lockean view that government constitutes an interference in the natural moral relations between individuals, which should be allowed to continue unless they threaten to break down without institutional support. In the view I am expressing, the existence of a legal order backed by government coercion is not in question: The only question is what it should do, and preserving the conditions for individual moral relations is only one of the tasks it makes sense to assign to it. It represents the ideal of a collectively held point of view of its members, and this ideal includes an impartial egalitarian element.

So if a society permits some people to become much richer than others and to pass this wealth on to their children, that is what it is doing—in a sense that is what we are all doing—and we have to ask the question whether the alternative arrangements

in which these kinds of inequality would be less would be still more objectionable in other ways.

Let me now move to a more detailed discussion of the change in attitudes toward the causes of inequality that would be needed to overcome the resistance to an egalitarian system. We can distinguish three sources of socioeconomic inequality (inequality, from now on), which raise questions of social justice and to which attitudes can easily be different, and a fourth which in itself is relatively unproblematic.

The first is intentional discrimination of the traditional kind: racial, sexual, religious, ethnic. The remedy for this is negative equality of opportunity, or positions open to qualifications (including acquired qualifications such as education).

The second is hereditary advantage both in the possession of resources and in access to the means of obtaining qualifications for open competitive positions. The remedy for this is not so clear, because so long as children grow up in families, they will inevitably benefit or suffer from the advantages or disadvantages of their parents, even if inheritance of property at death is considerably restricted. But some of the effects with respect to access to the kind of background and training which enhance qualifications can be softened by public support for child care, education, and the like. I shall call this *positive* equality of opportunity, to distinguish it from the negative equality of opportunity which results from the mere absence of discrimination. (Rawls calls it fair equality of opportunity, and describes it as the attempt to ensure that those with the same natural abilities will have the same chances in life.)

The third source is the variation in natural abilities themselves, or what Rawls calls the natural lottery....

Let me refer to these three sources of inequality respectively as *Discrimination, Class*, and *Talent*....I am concerned here with the character and legitimacy of differences in our attitudes toward these three sources of inequality. Finally let me add to the catalogue, for completeness and for purposes of contrast, a fourth important source of inequality, somewhat different from the others, which without further explanation I shall call *Effort*....

These four factors can vary independently, though they are often correlated in one way or another, and can also interact causally. Discrimination, class, and talent may influence effort; discrimination, talent, and effort in one generation may influence class in the next. And all of them have their effects on inequality only through the operation of an articulated social system which includes different positions or roles, with different opportunities, advantages, and disadvantages attached to them.

It is clear that effort will always make a difference, but the range of possible outcomes over which effort will determine the result, and the rough functional relation between effort and outcome, is fixed in advance for each person by the combined effects of discrimination pro or con, the class into which he is born, his natural talents, and the existing social structure. Our judgment of the social structure will depend on our attitude toward the way it permits these causes of inequality to operate.

In the order given, the four causes form a natural progression, from external to internal. While all of them affect an individual's sense of who he is, they do not all originate with him.

Deliberate discrimination is a force completely outside the victim, imposed on him by others. Of course it is likely to have internal psychological effects which compound the resulting inequality; but in itself it is not a feature of the victim at all, but a fact about how others treat him.

Class is also environmental but is transmitted to the individual by his family, a kind of native socioeconomic habitat deriving from his most intimate personal relations in virtue of their relation to the rest of society. It is the product not primarily of deliberate imposition by outsiders, but of innumerable personal choices in a competitive economy of families, which constantly generate stratification as a cumulative effect. Class can itself be a target of deliberate discrimination as well, though when this is systematic, with prohibitions on social mobility and intermarriage, it comes closer to a caste system. But even when it is a pure by-product of the operation of an economic system which permits social mobility, the class to which a person is born and bred is entirely the result of causes external to him: He himself contributes nothing to it.

Talent, as I am using the term, is innate, though its development and value depend on the other factors. (I shall usually speak of *ability* when I wish to refer to realized talent.) It is strongly internal to the individual, more an aspect of what he is in himself than either discrimination or class, though of course it generates material advantages only through his interaction with others.

Effort, finally, being a manifestation of the will, is the most personal or internal factor, and uniquely suitable to be regarded as the individual's personal responsibility....

The egalitarian ideal is particularly concerned with equality in advantages and disadvantages for which the recipients are not responsible....

The essence of this moral conception is equality of *treatment* rather than impartial concern for wellbeing. It applies to inequalities generated by the social system, rather than to inequalities in general. A society that permits significant inequalities among its members, in advantages and disadvantages for which they are not responsible, will be perceived as failing to treat them equally: it distinguishes in its treatment of them along morally arbitrary lines.

Let us now consider the four factors listed above from this point of view. By the standard of responsibility it would seem that only the last, effort (to the extent that it is independent of the others), should be immune from suspicion as a legitimate cause of variation in social condition. Yet there is a tendency to treat the other three factors as morally different from one another as well, with discrimination being most objectionable and talent least. Let us consider why this is so.

Discrimination is clearly the worst in one way: It involves deliberate imposition of disadvantages on some by others—unequal treatment in a strong sense—whereas class and talent produce advantages and disadvantages through the normal operation of a competitive economy populated by participants with normal human sentiments. Still, class and talent are not the individual's responsibility, even though they are not other people's responsibility in the way that deliberate discrimination is. This gives us a three-way classification: (1) causes for which others are responsible (discrimination), (2) causes for which no one is specifically responsible, only "the system" (class and talent), and (3) causes for which the individual himself is responsible (effort).

Now it would be possible to take either of two clear-cut positions with respect to this classification: (a) that only the first sort of cause is morally objectionable, or (b) that only the third sort of cause is morally unobjectionable. But either of these positions would mean taking causes of type (2) as morally similar, either all unobjectionable or all objectionable. Yet many people, rightly or wrongly, perceive a morally significant difference between inequalities in advantages due to class and inequalities in advantages due to talent. While neither is generally condemned, there is more uneasiness about the first than there is about the second.

This can be seen from some of the reactions to Rawls's position on the moral arbitrariness of the natural lottery. Some readers of *A Theory of Justice* who are in favor of fair equality of opportunity as a way of limiting the influence of class on life prospects will nevertheless draw the line at the difference principle, with its implied denial of the intrinsic legitimacy of advantages derived from the employment of marketable talents. This is not just a reaction to a work of philosophy, but the manifestation of a moral attitude common in modern societies, which shows up in standard liberal politics.

I think the personal-impersonal conflict can help us to understand the appeal of this contrast, and more generally to understand why the four causes are naturally seen as forming a progression, of increasing moral acceptability. The responsibility of the "victim" is not the only factor determining our response: The entire motivational situation is relevant.

Let me say something about class before going on to talent. Discrimination is the product of a bad motive, prejudice, and there is nothing to be said for it. But class depends on the special interest people take in their relatives, especially their children. There is no possibility of abolishing this interest, and no sane person would wish to do so. The only real possibility, for those of egalitarian sympathies, is to limit its scope of operation and the magnitude of its consequences. So long as people come in families, the approach to fair equality of opportunity can only be partial. The psychological aspect of the problem is the usual one: What division between personal and impersonal motives can be accepted by normal and reasonable human beings, with the support of an appropriate institutional setting?...

If we add...a public effort to provide fair or positive equality of opportunity, the personal-impersonal division is moved over a few notches, but the division remains. The stability of such a system requires a general sense that large competitive advantages resulting from exclusive access to higher education, for example, due to the accident that one's parents were well-to-do, are somehow tainted. Here again while the resentment of the losers is important, the uneasiness of the winners plays an important role in generating enough support for an egalitarian policy to prevent political revolt against its costs to them.

Yet even if such persons support the public provision of education and health care for all, in order to ensure everyone a fair start in life and a chance to develop those abilities which qualify for access to desirable positions, they will not stop favoring their children in their more personal choices. If they have the resources, they will continue to offer whatever extra advantages they can, by paying for superior education, by direct cultural enrichment, and by various forms of financial support. While these things are good in themselves, they also aim to give the child a competitive edge. This motivational split defines a familiar modern liberal mentality. I realize it attracts a certain amount of scorn, but that is quite unwarranted, for it is simply another example of the partition of motives which pervades morality.

Public institutional support for positive equality of opportunity does not abolish inequalities due to class, because it does not abolish the operation of family preference in the personal sphere, but merely seeks to limit it to that sphere. Operating there, it inevitably continues to have broader social effects because public institutions alone do not determine opportunities. Stratification is enhanced by the tendency of persons to marry within their socioeconomic class, and it is not diminished by social mobility between classes from one generation to the next. Social mobility is compatible with great inequality and it does nothing for those who stay put.

Any attempt to go beyond a certain point in eliminating the effects of class so long as there *are* classes will run up against strong and natural human resistance, which will inevitably invade the political sphere. Attempts to redraw the personal-impersonal boundary through institutional redesign, by making privately purchased education illegal, for example, are likely to generate fierce opposition. This is a controversial issue, but I do not think such resistance can be simply discounted. It would stem not only from concern over the waste of possibilities, but from the feeling that a legitimate expression of familial preference was being blocked....

In short, even the standard forms of remedy to class-caused inequalities do not depend on the position that all inequalities due to class are morally unacceptable. A personal core remains protected, and this core has large social consequences, though its scope remains a matter for argument and institutional definition. Only a totalitarian government could even attempt to abolish classes, and even then it would be unlikely to succeed.

It would not be unrealistic to hope for a change in attitude toward the inheritance of wealth, so that the privilege of endowing one's children with independent means was no longer regarded as the kind of expression of family feeling with which the state should not interfere. It might even be possible to design a system of estate and gift taxes without the loopholes that usually plague such efforts. It would be a big change, but not unthinkable, if people ceased to regard it as a reason for someone to be rich that his parents were rich. But this would not make a serious dent in the effects of class, because differences in parental income and personally acquired wealth are enough by themselves to generate large competitive distinctions among children prior to the time that inheritance becomes an issue. So long as there are substantial inequalities in income there will be substantial inequalities due to class, barring some unimaginable evaporation or pathological inhibition of natural family sentiment.

A major cause of inequalities in income is variation in talent, and there we see the problem of how to draw the personal-impersonal division in an even more acute form. For some reason it appears to be harder to internalize the sense that advantages derived from the exercise of talent are in themselves morally suspect, on the ground that the talent itself is a matter of luck. Lucky or not, it seems too intimate an aspect of the individual, too tied up with the pursuit of life itself, for this attitude to sit comfortably. The fact that differences in talent are not themselves socially created may also play a role. This resistance seems to me unreasonable, but it is certainly there. Perhaps because

everyone can imagine having been switched in the cradle, it is easy to think, about the members of a deprived class, "There but for the grace of God go I." But one's natural talents are not so easily switched, and that hinders the moral imagination.

It is true, of course, that your talents are an intimate part of you, and that any attempt by the state to prevent you from exercising and developing them would be intolerable. Like beauty, talent and excellence also attract recognition, admiration, and gratitude, and such responses are among the natural rewards of human life. But the economic rewards which some talents are able to command, if properly developed, are another story. They cannot be said to be merited just because the recognition of excellence on which they are based is merited. To try to sever the connection between talent and admiration would be wrong. But to sever the connection between talent and income, if it could be done, would be fine. Those with useful talents do not naturally deserve more material benefits than those who lack them.

The problem would be different if there were an institutional vehicle, as we have seen for other causes of inequality, to limit the effects of talent to a personal domain while blocking its consequences in a more public institutional setting which could then be governed by egalitarian principles. But that is just what is impossible for this case, unlike the case of class. One cannot realistically block the direct employment of talent to gain advantages in the public or semi-public sphere, as one can block nepotism and bribery. To do that one would have to abolish competition. Measures to block the influence of discrimination and class, by contrast, expand competition. In fact the aim of profiting from the exercise of talent is of utmost importance in the public sphere, and needs encouragement, not discouragement.

The advantages due to talent are not handed out as a reward for high scores on tests: They come as the result of demand for scarce resources in a competitive labor market. And the preservation of some form of labor market, with economic incentives, seems indispensible enough to provide an "external" justification for the differential rewards it generates. But if it is in operation, then people have to work for those rewards, employing their talents where the market reveals they are most in demand, and realizing economic and social gains when they succeed. The lives of people who work are pervaded by attempts to profit from their abilities in this way. I do not mean here to invoke the spectre of that mythical creature, rational economic man. We all know that other motives are essential for the success of cooperative enterprises and that the exercise of a productive skill can itself be a source of real satisfaction. But economic incentives that generate inequalities also play a very significant role.

Any attempt to limit the inequalities due to talent without abolishing the labor market must take the indirect form of progressive and redistributive taxation. But this is quite different from limiting the effects of talent to a special, personal domain. Work is acutely personal, as well as public. So the motives of personal advancement and impersonal egalitarianism come into conflict very directly here. An egalitarian in a competitive economy is expected to strive for precisely those advantages which he simultaneously wants to limit.

If we follow the pattern of discrimination and class, wide support for an egalitarian policy with regard to talent would require that those who can profit from superior talent through the economic system should come to feel that such advantages are tainted, even though it is recognized that they must be allowed for reasons of efficiency. But with what coherent set of attitudes are egalitarians supposed to embrace these motives simultaneously? As acquisitive individuals they must force their socially conscientious selves to permit talent-dependent rewards as the unavoidable price of productivity, efficiency, and growth. As participants in the system they are expected, indeed encouraged, to pursue those advantages, but as citizens they are expected to allow them only reluctantly: They must regard it as legitimate and natural to want them, but in another light not legitimate to have them....

The motivational problem for committed egalitarians in all this is that the egalitarian sense of fairness must make us regard as unfortunate those very inequalities which as economic actors we are bent on getting the benefit of, which our acquisitive demands make necessary, and which therefore are required for the benefit of the worse off. An economically competitive egalitarian with the appropriate partition of motives is supposed to reflect, as he signs the astronomical check for his three-star

meal, that although it's a shame that business talent such as his should command such rewards while others are scraping by, there is no help for it, since he and his peers have to be allowed to earn this kind of money if the economy is to function properly. A most unfortunate situation, really, but how lucky for him!

The motivational situation would be less peculiar if an egalitarian system were imposed from outside, and personal acquisitive motives were free to operate within it. But if the maintenance of any such system is a political choice, which the participants are expected to accept, they will have to juggle two conflicting attitudes toward their competitive gains and losses, trying to maximize their take from what they regard as a morally questionable source.

There are really two problems here, one having to do with incentives in the operation of an ostensibly egalitarian system, the other having to do with its stability and political support. The first problem is that the application of any serious egalitarian standard, such as the difference principle, involves a choice among different *unequal* systems, and the available options will be determined not only by technological and material facts, but by motivational ones. So long as personal motives are permitted to determine individual economic choices, the inequalities that the difference principle must tolerate will be determined by fundamentally anti-egalitarian factors.

The second problem is that it is difficult to combine, in a morally coherent outlook, the attitude toward inequalities due to talent which generates support for an egalitarian system with the attitude toward the employment of their own talents appropriate for individuals operating within it. The first attitude is that such inequalities are unfair and morally suspect, whereas the second attitude is that one is entitled to try to get as much out of the system as one can.

While such a division of motives is not self-contradictory, it is not strictly intelligible. The essential problem is that while we know roughly what is appealing in the way of political and personal ideals, we cannot devise a political morality and a personal morality that fit together satisfactorily. The two pull in opposite directions because they respond to different demands, and the conflicts are too direct to be solved through a division of labor between social institutions and individual conduct. So the combination of egalitarian public values and inegalitarian personal aims to which we are forced by motivational logic simply lacks the character of an integrated moral outlook. The egalitarian sentiment of unfairness will tend to clash with the sense of entitlement to pursue one's own aims, and the acquisitiveness licensed by the latter will tend to erode support for the egalitarian system at the political level among those with higher earning power. It is not like the case of people playing a fiercely competitive sport under strict rules—when support for the rules is guaranteed by the fact that without them winning is meaningless....

In light of these observations, the prospect of limiting social inequality to the goods for which their possessors are responsible seems remote....

The psychological difficulties of combining political egalitarianism with personal acquisitiveness are clear. But the substitution of other personal motives will not work either. People can of course be motivated to work hard at something they are interested in for its own sake, and sometimes this will yield a product which others also want. But it is a romantic fantasy to imagine the world run on such a basis. We cannot all be creative artists, research scientists, or professional athletes. It wouldn't even be enough if everyone was strongly motivated to do his job well. Each of the hundreds or thousands of parts that go into a washing machine or a truck or a ball-bearing factory has to be designed and manufactured by people motivated by economically expressed demand. They are not going to do it as a form of self-expression, and even if they wanted nothing better than to contribute to the well-being of mankind, this would not tell them what exactly to make in their semiconductor plant.

Benevolence is not enough. Even love of semiconductors is not enough. Among those who have to think of new things to do and new and more efficient ways to do them, there seems no substitute for the market as a source of information, and the most effective motive for responding to that information is a strong investment of personal ambition and desire for success in productive activities that will pay off. It is hard to do without people who work hard and exercise their ingenuity for gain and competitive success; yet in a stable egalitarian society they would have to combine this with a desire to live under a system which made it as difficult as possible for them to achieve these goals.

Some restrictions, because of their limited character, combine easily with an ethos of the pursuit of profit. The prevention of negative externalities, through the control of pollution for example, can exclude certain means to economic advantage without requiring a change in the basic motive. Admittedly we find limited enthusiasm for such regulation from those whose profits are reduced by it, but the point is that there is in principle no motivational difficulty about the partition of motives which would permit support for such boundaries around the domain of legitimate acquisitive activity. It is analogous to the rule against nepotism, which limits the ways one can benefit one's relatives, without requiring any basic change in the wish to do so. Another example is anti-trust regulation, which establishes the framework for competition. An impersonal motive in support of the framework can coexist with the personal motives of gain that operate within it, and that would, if left to themselves, lead to violations of the framework. The sense of the participants' common interest in establishing such rules also plays a role in these cases.

Acquisitiveness is motivationally compatible with the desire to provide at public expense a social minimum of some kind, for those who lose out badly in the competitive economy. This might be set at various levels, depending on the wealth of the society. But a decent social minimum is very different from an egalitarian policy. It does not require for its support a general suspicion of inequalities due to class or talent—all it requires is the sense that there are certain things no one should have to suffer through no fault of his own, if they can be prevented without too much cost. Here again the necessary partition of motives is clearly feasible, with acquisitiveness proceeding within a system of moderately redistributive taxation.

The trouble with stronger forms of egalitarianism, from a motivational point of view, is that they require too exclusive a reliance on egalitarian impartiality for support of the economic framework, and too complete an insulation of politics from personal motives. They require some as yet unimagined change either in the motivation of economic actors or in the design of economic systems, or both, which will support the incentives and generate the information needed for productive efficiency without at the same time generating large inequalities. The upshot of the discussion so far is that even if the principle of negative responsibility is widely accepted as regards the society's relation to the life chances conferred by its socioeconomic structure, there are serious obstacles to the additional changes in the pattern of personal and interpersonal motives which would be needed both to generate unanimous support by reasonable persons for a system which tried radically to reduce inequalities due to class and talent—and to make such a system work. If all this is true, then those who are attached to egalitarian ideals seem to be left with two options. Either they can lower their sights and aim for a partial approach to those ideals, through changes falling within the limits imposed by the present general character of human motives and the consequences of their interaction. Or they can hope for a more radical transformation of attitudes which, together with institutional changes, would lead to a much fuller realization of socioeconomic equality, while nevertheless leaving a personal sphere free for the expression of a reconstituted individuality.

The first option, a plainly nonutopian possibility which has considerable appeal in its own right and which is a natural fallback position from strong egalitarianism, would be a development of the already existing uneasiness about severe poverty in relatively wealthy societies into a much stronger insistence on a high social minimum, with healthy, comfortable, decent conditions of life and self-respect for everyone. This would be in addition to fair equality of opportunity, so that even those unable to command good incomes in a competitive economy would be guaranteed a decent standard of living.

Such an attitude need not be linked to any discomfort about inequalities above this level. Of course the social minimum would have to be financed by progressive taxation, used to support social services and a negative income tax (which would most effectively express the underlying idea if it were automatically added to wages just as positive income tax is automatically withheld from wages). This would have the effect of reducing the spread of disposable income above the social minimum; but the change of attitude I am imagining

would not include a desire for such reduction for its own sake. And it would also, most importantly, not include any uneasiness of conscience on the part of those who are far above the social minimum. Essentially it would abandon the idea of unfairness according to which all socially generated inequalities are suspect unless vindicated by a suitable condition of responsibility. Provided the minimum is set sufficiently high, individuals with competitive advantages would have no reluctance to pursue and enjoy affluence for themselves and their families. Therefore this attitude would do nothing to damp down the acquisitive motives that drive a competitive economy. There would be the task of designing social provision and a negative income tax so as not to destroy incentives among those being subsidized up to the social minimum; but that problem should be soluble. So long as it is possible to maintain a significant positive correlation between work and income, a guaranteed base will not prevent most people from working, since most people want more than they have.

This is essentially the point of view behind contemporary social democracy, which has never been politically significant in the United States, and seems to be in retreat in Europe, but which may have a future. If such an attitude became entrenched in a modern society, it would not support an egalitarian system and would not hinder the formation of classes, nor would it support unqualified application of the difference principle, since the priority of gains to the worse off would cease once they reached the social minimum. But it would mean that the society put every effort into combating the worst aspects of inequality—poverty and severe relative deprivation. While it would imply a rejection of the idea that those with competitive advantages were not entitled thereby to gain economically, it would likewise reject the idea that all anyone was entitled to was what he could command in the labor market. Something like the right of everyone to a decent standard of living, provided this is economically feasible, would be accorded priority in the economic organization of the society.

This is hardly an unworthy goal, and it may be that nothing beyond it can be seriously pursued until this much has been achieved and has become so well entrenched that it is considered the natural order of things: Then it will be time to complain that it is not yet good enough. But those who hope for something more in the long run must consider the second option—a psychological and institutional transformation which would permit innovation and cooperative production without generating substantial inequalities of reward.

In relation to the present state of things this is unavoidably an exercise of utopian imagination; but the change of attitude that suggests itself, one which would be far more egalitarian and more in line with the traditional ideals of socialism, is the development of a general reluctance on the part of members of the society to be conspicuously better off than others, either in standard of living as measured by consumption or in social advantages—and a corresponding disapproval of those who try to make themselves significantly better off in these ways. The reluctance would have to extend to special advantages for one's family as well.

This would not mean a takeover of all motives by the impersonal standpoint. Impartiality and egalitarianism would apply to the social structure, but not to private life, and individuals would be expected to devote their energies and their personal resources to the pursuit of happiness and the benefit of their families. But they would not be strongly motivated to get ahead of others—in fact the reverse: Their concern would be to reduce gaps between others and themselves, wherever in the socioeconomic spectrum they found themselves. If they were near the bottom, moving ahead would be the goal; if they were near the top, they would want less, and more for others. What I am imagining is not a general outbreak of asceticism. People would still want material comforts, good food, and vacations in Italy; but they would not feel right about having these things if other members of their society could not afford them.

It may be thought that this change is psychologically too bizarre to be worth considering, but I do not think it is out of the question. It might conceivably come about as the result of a long development, in which the attachment to equality extended to wider and wider areas of life, producing an intergenerational shift in people's sense of what they were entitled to, which would reduce resistance. But I grant that such a thing is highly unlikely, even over the very long run.

Apart from the issue of its psychological possibility, however, this change would not be enough by itself to create egalitarian prosperity. Something else would have to happen to fill the gap in incentives to economic activity that would open up if economic competitiveness disappeared from the scene. The desire to have more, but not more than others, seems very difficult to harness as an incentive for productive effort. If the acquisitive impulse disappears among those with the strongest potential competitive advantages, other incentives must replace it or else a market economy will slow down, cease to innovate, and cease to improve its per capita productivity, on which everyone's welfare depends....

My conclusion, as before, is that a strongly egalitarian society populated by reasonably normal people is difficult to imagine and in any case psychologically and politically out of reach, and that a more real possibility lies in the first alternative. Intolerance of severe poverty at least receives lip service in most liberal societies, and it ought to be possible to develop it into insistence on a higher and higher social minimum, until it becomes intolerable in a rich society if anyone does not have a decent standard of living and a fair opportunity to go as far as his natural talents will take him above that.

Even this would be an extraordinary transformation, but it would be compatible with great inequalities and a strong class structure which the absence of obstacles to social mobility would do nothing to destroy. I therefore think it is not a result we can be content with. Rather, it illustrates the difficulty of bringing together personal and impersonal standpoints and encourages the belief that an acceptable combination of individual and political morality remains to be invented.

11 Nationalism and International Relations

Most discussions in social and political philosophy concern the relation of individual citizens to the nation-state of which they are members. What rights and obligations do the citizens have *vis à vis* the state? What rights and obligations does the state have *vis à vis* its citizens? Another set of interesting and important questions arise when we ask a similar question about the relation of individual nation-states to one another?

What is the basis for deciding how nations ought to treat each other? The actions and policies of one state can affect the well-being of others. Should behavior be guided only by self-interest or should international relations be grounded on moral principle? What is the status of international law? How and who can or should enforce it? When, if ever, is war between nation-states morally justified, and under what conditions? When, if ever, is it morally justifiable to break a treaty one nation has made with another? When, if ever, is it morally justifiable for one nation to interfere in the internal affairs of another nation? Despite wide areas of disagreement, the fundamental principle of national sovereignty, the right of a state to control its own internal affairs free of outside interference by other sovereign states, has been accepted. This is the root of the idea that states are entitled to defend themselves against hostile acts or outside interference.

For the most part, however, even though it has always been considered wrong for one nation to interfere in the affairs of another, in actual practice this and other standards of international conduct have always been overridden by demands of national self-interest. The problem has always been the lack of any consistent mechanism for sanctioning failure to adhere to agreed upon principles of international conduct. As Hobbes and other social contractarians pointed out, the best example of the "state of nature" is the set of relations which often exist among nation-states. Despite pious declarations of limitations on the conduct of war and adherence to international treaties, the behavior of most nations has always been largely self-serving—each keeps promises only as long as they are thought to serve its own interests; each refrains from banned military practices until national self-interest requires their use. Even the principle of sovereignty ("Thou shalt not invade thy neighbor's territory, or interfere in his affairs") is followed only as long as it is consistent with national self-interest. In short, because of the lack of a consistent international will to compel compliance with international law, normative standards usually have not operated at the international level.

An exploration of the foreign policy of the United States reveals a pattern of adherence to self-interest rather than moral concern. The United States intervened in the internal affairs of Iraq (whose actions endangered our oil supply) to protect the rights of the Kurds but does not intervene on their behalf against our ally, Turkey, even though internal Turkish policy also endangers the Kurds.

The power of the United Nations to police the actions of nations has grown in the last 20 to 30 years, but during this period the ability to exert international pressure on individual nation-states was severely limited by the cold war divisions within the U.N. itself which split the international family of nations into two radically opposed groups—the wealthy, developed capitalist democracies of Europe and North America and their Third World allies, on the one side, and the Communist bloc countries and their alliance of poor, Third World developing nations on the other. Since each had the power to block the international efforts of the other, the result was decades of standoff.

Today, however, with the collapse of communism virtually everywhere and the consequent end of the cold war, we are witnessing what may be the emergence of an international body increasingly willing and able to act as a superstate to police the world and to force otherwise sovereign nation-states to protect the civil and minority and environmental rights of their citizens. Just as individual states of the United States long argued for their "states' rights," as protected by the U.S. Constitution, so independent sovereign nation-states insist on their right to do as they see fit within their borders. The general tendency within the United States has been a steady diminution of states' rights in favor of the broader federal protection of nationally uniform rights of individuals, and it may be that we are witnessing today the beginning of an irreversible trend toward the steady erosion of sovereign rights of nation-states in favor of a more internationally uniform policy of civil rights and the rights of minorities. When U.S. southern states' policy of Jim Crow discrimination against African Americans was determined by the rest of the nation as putting southern African Americans at an unjustified disadvantage, federal guidelines were introduced which gradually superseded and overturned the policies of the Jim Crow states. In much the same way an international consensus may be building toward a universal standard of treatment of persons and of minority groups within individual nation-states. Should this happen, nations which violate those standards may have their sovereignty superseded and overridden by international pressure. And finally, just as the erosion of states rights within the United States had the eventual effect of undermining the importance of the each of the 50 states as a political unit, so in a similar way the "new world order," as some are optimistically calling it, might have the effect of diminishing the role and even the need of the nation-state as the primary unit of international politics. If the rights of individuals to immigrate wherever they want (and are invited) are protected and if the rights of minorities to self-determination and autonomy are respected, what rightful power is left to the nation-state to bind, forcibly if necessary, different individuals and different ethnic groups into a single nation-state? Perhaps, as we see happening in the former Yugoslavia and countries of the former Soviet Union, each ethnic group will eventually become its own autonomous political unit, with scores of such units making up a greater Europe, hundreds more comprising subSaharan Africa, and so on.

While we cannot predict the eventual outcome of these momentous contemporary developments, the issue of whether international bodies or other nations ever have a *right* to override national sovereignty is a continuing philosophical debate. There are many possible justifications for such interference. Should nations acting alone or in concert intervene in Brazil to protect the remaining rain forest? in India to prevent the sale of child brides? in China to stop slave labor? in Bosnia to protect the Muslims? Or do nation-states have the sovereign right to do as they please? The answer depends on whether there is a universally valid set of moral, legal principles which *could* legitimately override any regional or ethnic differences. What if ethical and political values are relative to the particular group in question? Suppose a group of cattle tenders historically sees itself as superior to and with a natural right to rule and suppress a minority of traditional farmers living in its midst? Or suppose a group strongly believes in its divine mission to strictly segregate the sexes or races or castes? Of course, this would be contrary to the principles governing the majority of nation-states, but do these states have the right to impose their moral and legal code on others? Perhaps we feel that every group has the right to self-determination but only if that self-determination does not include actions which violate standards widely held elsewhere. "You are free to govern yourselves but only if you do so according to our guidelines."

These questions take on increased importance because everywhere in the world today we see the emergence or the reemergence of ethnic minorities demanding and struggling for their right to self determination. What is the origin of this seemingly intense and powerful source of group loyalty and identification, and what is its relation to our sense of ourselves as individuals and as members of nation-states and international bodies? From Plato to Rousseau to Hegel and Marx to twentieth-century totalitarian dictatorships of the right and the left, we have seen the emphasis in Western political thought on the priority of the state over the individual. Part of the foundation for this profound feeling for the "whole" of which each of us is only a "part" is the complex phenomenon known as "nationalism." There are many ways in which each of us can identify ourselves—sometimes in very particular terms (for example, as a distinctly unique individual person), sometimes in extremely broad terms (for example, as a member of the human species, or still more broadly, as a living creature), but more often we find ourselves somewhere in between these extremes, identifying ourselves as a man or a woman, as young or old, as black or white, as educated or illiterate, and so on. But one of the most pervasive ways in which people have identified themselves for thousands of years is by their membership in a particular ethnic group—as Serbian, Croatian, Kurd, or Armenian. Such identity is sometimes based on biological factors, such as race, but more often it is based on cultural factors such as a common history, customs, or language which members of a group perceive as crucial to their sense of themselves, as essentially defining who they are.

One of the ways in which people feel a sense of group identity is on the basis of a shared religion. The conflict of Protestants and Roman Catholics in Northern Ireland and between Hindus and Muslims in India are obvious examples. In the current conflict among the Serbs, Croats and Bosnians, religion is one, but only one, factor creating tension—the Serbs are Greek Orthodox Christians, the Croats are Roman Catholic Christians, and the Bosnians are Muslims. Although the separation of church and state has been an important part of European and North American policy for centuries, there is a long tradition in most parts of the world, including Europe until the eighteenth century and continuing in some parts of the world today, in which church and state are *identified*; in other words, those in which the state is governed on religious grounds. This is true of some Catholic countries; it is a goal of some forms of Jewish Zionism; and it is the ideal form of the historical Islamic state.

Whether bound together by a sense of race, language, history or religion, ethnic groups often demand self-determination and that generally means, ideally, the creation of a nation-state made up entirely of members who share this particular identity. But in actual fact the boundaries of political entities in the world were drawn by geopolitical forces, and so they are already made up of people of different identities. Iraq, for example, is composed of Sunni Muslims, Shiite Muslims, and Kurds in the north. Kurds also form a minority nationality in other countries, such as Turkey. The problem is what to do with minority groups when either they or the surrounding majority ethnic group demands self-determination. One solution is what has recently been called "ethnic cleansing." In 1992 Serbians in former Yugoslavia began to "ethnically cleanse" areas in which they formed a majority, or even a significant minority, by killing or forcing out all non-Serbs, many of whose families had lived in that area for generations. Other examples include Germany's ethnic cleansing of Jews and Gypsies, Indonesia's ethnic cleansing of Chinese, and East Africa's ethnic cleansing of Asian Indians. Another solution is to allow the minority to remain within its borders but in a diminished capacity as "second-class citizens," as were the Jews in seventeenth-century Germany, blacks in the Jim Crow U.S. south, Zoroastrians in Iran, Gypsies in Romania, Palestinians in Kuwait, or Koreans in Japan. Other solutions include attempts to assimilate the minority groups into the majority ethnic nationality. If the Kurds would adopt Turkish or Iraqi names, customs, and language, they would eventually become indistinguishable from Turks or Iraqis. But the Kurds may not *want* to assimilate; they may demand their own self-determination, insisting that they either be allowed to form their own nation-state or at least be given some measure of autonomy within Turkey and Iraq. And even if the minority *want* to assimilate, the majority ethnic group may not *allow* them to assimilate, as the Germans rejected the attempts of German Jews in the nineteenth and early twentieth centuries to assimilate into German culture.

The readings in this last chapter concern the relations which ought to obtain among the international community of nation-states and the status of ethnic minorities within nation-states.

READINGS

Vernon Van Dyke, emeritus professor of political science at the University of Iowa, argues for the extension of the concept of rights to include *groups* of people and not just individuals. In the broad liberal tradition, only individual human beings have been thought to have rights since only they have interests and can press claims. If groups of people cannot be said to have interests and to press claims over and above the interests and claims of the individuals which make up such groups, then the traditional liberal argument is, groups cannot be said to have rights. On the contrary, Van Dyke develops the argument that we do indeed commonly speak of states having obligations, rights, and of their making claims against other states.

More important, Van Dyke tries to extend this customary usage beyond states to ethnic communities. The right of an ethnic community to preserve its cultural heritage, he argues, cannot be reduced to the rights of the individuals involved to practice their cultural heritage as they choose. For example, the right of a particular Native American group to speak its own language requires more than the right and freedom of each member of that group to speak its native tongue in private gatherings if they so choose. It also requires that the state not require young Indians to speak English in school and, moreover, that the state offer instruction in their Native American language. Without these more positive measures the Native American language could well be forgotten and lost, even though no one is expressly forbidden to speak it. More controversially, perhaps, some American courts have recently upheld a ban endorsed by some African American groups forbidding adoption of African American children by white adoptive parents on the grounds that raising black children in white families undermines African American culture and thereby harms African Americans as a group—even though this may be the wishes of all the individuals most immediately involved. This is precisely why, Van Dyke argues, ethnic groups routinely demand the protection of group, and not just individual, rights.

Aleksandras Shtromas, a Lithuanian-American professor of political science and law at Hillsdale College in Michigan, analyzes the various ways in which modern nation-states are bound to limit their sovereignty in response to various pressures in the post–cold war era.

Poorer nations will *voluntarily* reliquish sovereignty in order to attract foreign investment and technical aid for modernization. In the absence of cold war tensions between competing superpowers, multinational consensus may be reached forcing individual nation-states to conform to an international standard of human rights, thus *involuntarily* giving up sovereignty in the treatment of their ethnic minorities, for example. Historically, the boundaries of many nation-states were artificially drawn to include within one country different, often hostile, ethnic minorities, while other ethnic groups were artificially divided among different countries. Where each nation-state is understood to have rightful sovereignty over all its citizens, it is possible for governments to mistreat some of their ethnic minorities with impunity. Shtromas argues that this sovereign right is now being challenged and limited by a growing international consensus backed up increasingly by a willingness to use international force to limit that sovereignty in order to protect the rights of individuals and ethnic minorities.

In their reading, Avishai Margalit, philosophy professor at Hebrew University, Jerusalem, and Joseph Raz, professor of law in All Souls College, Oxford University, explore the legitimate bases for the claims of ethnic nationalities to self-determination. Since those claims often conflict, as in the case of the claims of the Israelis and the Palestinians to the same territory, the grounds for such claims must be assessed and prioritized. Of all the different ways in which groups of people feel a sense of identity and belonging, from supporting a particular football team to having a common culture, including language and history, which deserve the most consideration and carry the most weight? Only when this assessment has been made, they argue, can we begin to rationally arbitrate the competing claims of different ethnic groups to self-determination.

In the selections from *Islam and Revolution* by Imam Khomeini (1900–1989), the late spiritual and political head of state of Iran, we see a defense of the Islamic state in the modern world. Because such a religiously controlled state restricts the freedom of religious dissenters, for example, atheists, Christians, Jews, Zoroastrians, and the behavior even of Muslims, most of us in the West remain very unsympathetic to the idea of an Islamic, or indeed any religious, state. It may seem to us backward and intolerant. But it is important to understand the powerful political forces in the Islamic world today struggling to achieve a fundamentalist Islamic state of the sort Khomeini describes. Part of the widespread enthusiasm for Islamic fundamentalism today is not so much religious fervor as it is the desire to throw off the remaining vestiges of Western cultural and economic domination and to reassert Islamic pride, strength, dignity, and respect.

Jeffrey Crawford, philosophy professor of Central State University of Ohio, addresses the precise degree to which African Americans want to and are allowed to assimilate into mainstream American culture and the precise degree to which they want to and are allowed to maintain a separate cultural identity. Similar problems confront Hispanic Americans and Native Americans. Should the majority, white American culture insist on "English only" as the medium of instruction in our schools, for example, and must that English be limited to "proper," that is, "white American English"?

Elizabeth Smith and Gene Blocker, of the philosophy department at Ohio University, explore the challenges of rethinking international relations with the end of the cold war. On the one hand, increased international cooperation seems to suggest the possibility of a world government diminishing the absolute sovereignty of nation-states. On the other hand, the end of the cold war appears to have unleashed bottled-up ethnic tensions around the world which threaten to partition the world into smaller and smaller ethnic groupings. What precisely is or ought to be the relationships among the individual, the ethnic "nationality," the nation-state, and the international body of the United Nations?

"Collective Entities and Moral Rights"

Vernon Van Dyke

Those who espouse traditional liberal-democratic thought—whom I will call *liberals*, however conservative or progressive they may be—have problems in dealing with collective entities. Their ideology focuses on the individual. They are protective and solicitous of the individual, seeking conditions that make for individual self-fulfillment. In bills of rights and, more recently, in various international documents such as the covenants on human rights, they have secured the spelling out of rights for individuals and are making the promotion of these rights (or some of them) a major issue in the world.

But liberals and their historic doctrine neglect collective entities. They assert the rights of individuals against the state and, thus, in a sense admit that the state exists with obligations, but, at the same time, they fear that this is an instance of reification and tend to dissolve the state into the persons who hold public office. Some liberals acknowledge that nations and peoples exist, and champion the idea of self-determination for them, but they tend to think of a nation or people not as a collective entity but as an aggregation of individuals. Liberals are naturally pleased with the requirement of the Charter of the United Nations that members shall promote human rights "without distinction as to race, sex, language, or religion," but are in a quandary over the proper response to groups identified by race, language, or religion that want differential treatment in order to preserve characteristics that they cherish.

Although the existence of a liberal dilemma is fairly obvious, I will include evidence of it in what follows. My more important aim, however, is to contribute toward a solution. The solution, like the dilemma itself, is fairly obvious, being intimated in much current practice. The solution lies in recognizing that certain kinds of collective entities exist, just as individuals do—perhaps not tangibly but not transcendentally either; that these collective entities have moral rights that are distinct from the rights of individual members; and that the frequent cases of conflict between the rights of individuals and the rights of collective entities, and between the rights of different collective entities, must be handled through a balancing process in which judgments are made about the relative urgency and importance of the various claims. Approximately the same standards can be employed in making these judgments as are already employed in connection with conflicts between the rights of individuals and the rights of states.

The argument that certain kinds of collective entities have both legal and moral rights calls for the definition of crucial terms. By collective entities I mean groups that exist as units and not simply as aggregations of individuals. I call them units and not persons to avoid any intimation that they may be organic. I assume that they exist in the same sense that corporations do, it being understood that a corporation is an entity that has rights and obligations distinct from those of individual stockholders. The corporation is conceded rights mainly so that it can serve the interests of stockholders, but the rights do not come from the stockholders and cannot be reduced to the rights of stockholders. They are original to the corporation.

The types of collective entities I have in mind are restricted in number. I am not speaking generally of interest groups. This is not an inquiry into the question of whether interest groups have rights. Rather, the collective entities that I have in mind are sovereign states, nations or peoples, and ethnic (including racial) communities. All of these terms have some vagueness about them, which suggests

From "Collective Entities and Moral Rights: Problems in Liberal-Democratic Thought," *The Journal of Politics*, vol. 44 (1982). Reprinted by permission of the publisher.

problems in the argument; but problems also attend the principle that individual persons have rights, for it is not always clear what organisms count as persons.

By a legal right I mean a claim or an entitlement that a government is bound to uphold and does seek to uphold, at least on occasion. (If the appeal is to international law, the obligation must be accepted by more than one government.) By a moral right I mean a claim or entitlement that ought to be honored if justice is to be done or the good promoted, regardless of the attitudes and actions of any government.

The sources or bases of legal rights are so generally agreed upon that nothing need be said on the subject here, but disagreement exists concerning the sources or bases of moral rights. I accept what I take to be the dominant liberal view, that moral rights reflect a conception of human interests and needs: some interests and needs are so important that they should be said to give rise to rights. In other words, it is to be presumed (the presumption being rebuttable) that human beings have those rights that are essential to the pursuit of their most basic interests and the satisfaction of their most basic needs. The view is reflected in various works, for example, in Taking Rights Seriously by Dworkin. The individual, according to Dworkin, has a right to pursue his interests and goals in the absence of good reason to the contrary:

> Individuals have rights when, for some reason, a collective goal is not a sufficient justification for denying them what they wish, as individuals, to have or to do, or not a sufficient justification for imposing some loss or injury upon them....The basic idea of a right-based theory is that distinct individuals have interests that they are entitled to protect if they so wish....In most cases, when we say that someone has a "right" to do something, we imply that it would be wrong to interfere with his doing it, or at least that some special grounds are needed for justifying any interference.

The conception suggests two sorts of comments. In the first place, assuming that the object is to satisfy the interests and needs of individuals, it does not necessarily follow that the associated rights should go to individuals. Where the right should be located is a matter of practicality; and in some instances it is best, if not essential, to locate it in a collective unit. So far as legal rights are concerned, it is clear that this often happens, and I will argue that it ought to be acknowledged with respect to some moral rights as well. In the second place, the liberal theory raises the question whether some interests and needs cannot be better conceived as collective rather than individual. If so, the same logic that leads from interests and needs to rights for individuals also leads to rights for collective entities.

The sovereign state is the most obvious illustration of a collective entity with rights. Sovereign states are persons in international law, and as such have legal rights. On this point everyone is agreed. The related point, which is perhaps more likely to be challenged, is that the rights of states are in many instances original to it, not derived from individuals. When the state imposes taxes, breaks up a monopoly, requires attendance at school, or conscripts a person and sends him into battle, it is not exercising rights taken over from individuals, for they never had such rights. Moreover, such rights could not reasonably be reduced to individual rights; they are necessarily and unavoidably the rights of a collective entity. Further, it is unsound to attribute such rights to "persons in public authority," as some do. To be sure, persons in public authority make the decisions and do the acting, for the state is not an organic entity that can itself decide or act. Moreover, persons in public authority may deserve personal credit for what they do, or be held personally culpable, as at Nuremberg. But whatever their personal accountability, the principal on whose behalf they act is also accountable. The rights exercised, and the obligations assumed, go with the office held, and not with the person. When Germany paid reparations after World War I, the money came out of the treasury of the state, not out of the pockets of those who made decisions on its behalf.

Acceptance of the state as a unit possessing legal rights does not necessarily entail its acceptance as a unit with moral rights. Ernest Barker demonstrates this, holding that "...in the moral world there are no group persons...." Once the state is incorporated, it has legal rights, but up to that moment, according to Barker, no group exists that has collective moral rights. Moreover, even after the state is organized, it should not be regarded as a moral person, for that would invite étatisme and "a philosophy of the total and engulfing State whose will is the peace—and the tomb of its members."

Though the danger that Barker fears may be real, his position is untenable. It is illogical to hold, for example, that the people of a colony, who collectively acquire legal rights the moment they are granted independence, have no collective moral claim up to that moment. Moreover, whatever the law may be, states are always facing issues in the moral realm—for example, in connection with plans for the use of nuclear weapons. The General Assembly of the United Nations obviously regards states as entities that should observe moral standards, as it indicated when it adopted the Universal Declaration of Human Rights. If bad consequences might flow from accepting the state as an entity with moral rights and obligations, even worse consequences might flow from any other course.

If the case is good for saying that states have moral rights and obligations, the same is true of nations and peoples. They are everywhere said to have the right of self-determination, and the Covenant on Civil and Political Rights is worth citing on the question of whether the right belongs to a collective entity or to individuals. The Covenant includes an article on minorities, the statement being that "persons belonging to...minorities" shall not be denied certain rights. The clear intent is to avoid giving minorities any basis for a claim of a collective right. But no such intent appears in connection with the assertion of the right of self-determination. This right is attributed to "all peoples" as such, not to persons belonging to peoples. Further, the General Assembly describes the possible outcomes of an exercise of self-determination as "the establishment of a sovereign and independent state, the free association or integration with an independent state, or the emergence into any other political status freely determined by a people"—language that does not suggest a reference to the rights of individual persons.

I am aware of assertions that the right of a people to self-determination is somehow an individual right, but such assertions have no reasonable basis that I can see. For example, a note in the *Yale Law Journal* says that "...in its broad meaning self-determination must be viewed as the basic right of an individual to form his own associations in order to maximize his preferred interests." But the author of that statement does not tell us how he leaps from the right of persons to freedom of association to the right of a people to independent sovereignty. Freedom of association does not imply for each individual the right to choose the sovereignty under which to live, and if individuals lack the right of choice they cannot delegate it. To repeat the statement already made: if individuals have any right in connection with self-determination, it is to participate in the decision of the group. The right belongs to the group, and it is the fate of the group that is determined.

Dov Ronen reflects a view similar to that in the Yale Law Journal when he says that "...the 'self' in self-determination is the singular, individual being and not any aggregation of human beings." Now I grant that one of the interests basic to the right is that of individuals. The individual has an interest in being grouped with his own kind for purposes of government—an interest in being governed by those who share his values, who accord him respect, and who fully accept him as an equal human being. But, as already pointed out, the fact that the interest is that of individuals does not necessarily mean that the related right goes to individuals. This does not follow either as a matter of logic or as a matter of practicality. Sometimes an interest of individuals can be best served, or only served, by allocating the related right to a group, and this is the case with self-determination. One of the reasons why some governments objected to the inclusion of the article on self-determination in the Covenants was that self-determination is for collectivities whereas the Covenants enumerated rights for individuals.

Perhaps simply as an elaboration of the meaning of self-determination, the General Conference of UNESCO asserts and assumes "the right of all countries and peoples to preserve their culture...." Similarly, a Declaration of the World Conference to Combat Racism and Racial Discrimination endorses "the right of indigenous peoples to maintain their traditional structure of economy and culture, including their language...." Such statements cannot reasonably be construed to affirm an individual right. It makes sense to speak of a right to preserve a culture only if the right is attributed to the cultural group as a whole. Further, it would be ridiculous to say that the right of a country or people to preserve its culture is the right of "persons in public authority." It is the right of a collective entity.

Where a country or people is sovereign, the right to preserve a culture is a legal right; at least, sovereign states are free to adopt laws designed to preserve a culture—laws having to do with education, for example. But surely in asserting the right of indigenous and other peoples to preserve their culture, the General Conference was not making legal pronouncements. Rather, it was proclaiming the existence of moral rights.

In addition to states and nations or peoples, ethnic communities in a number of countries have legal rights. Some of them are identified by religion, and claim freedom of religion. That freedom is not simply freedom for individuals. It is not the right of an individual to go into a closet and worship alone. It is a communal right, and it includes the right (widely recognized) to maintain the community. In the province of Alberta, Canada, schools are organized on a religious basis, with the minority religious community entitled to establish its own schools and impose a school tax on its members. In West Germany the main churches are formally accepted as corporate bodies under public law, authorized to tax their members, with government collecting the tax. Even in the individualistic United States the right to maintain the religious community is held to override the obligation to send children to school beyond a certain point. Many other such illustrations could be cited. I do not contend that a moral right lies behind every legal right, nor that the specific arrangements existing in Alberta or elsewhere are the only possible ways of satisfying a moral claim. But the generalization is surely valid that some kind of a claim of moral right lies behind decisions to grant legal rights to religious communities.

Comparable statements apply to ethnic communities identified mainly by language. If they want to maintain their identity, as they usually do, they are likely to demand (or insist on the preservation of) certain rights. In Switzerland, the linguistic communities are by custom conceded the right of territorial integrity; communes do not switch from one language to another regardless of the movement of people. Similarly, in Switzerland the linguistic communities are by custom assured of representation in the Federal Council. In Belgium,

these same rights for linguistic communities are written into the constitution. The constitution explicitly says that the country consists of three cultural communities, and goes on to say that "each community enjoys the powers invested in it." Moreover, powers are in fact invested. Further, the Belgian cabinet must be made up of an equal number of French-speaking and Dutch-speaking ministers, and the law requires that a just equilibrium (interpreted as parity) must be maintained between the two principal communities in the civil service. Clearly, these provisions do not grant rights to individuals. By implication, they concede rights to the linguistic communities as entities. And it is clear that the legal arrangements followed the acceptance of a moral claim.

Some ethnic communities are identified as indigenous, which implies that their members differ in a number of ways from members of the dominant society; they are likely to differ in language, in religion, in race, in level of development, and, most generally, in culture. The liberal's dilemma with respect to them is especially acute. If he sticks to his principles, he treats them severally as individuals, respecting their individual rights. But all history shows that the indigenous are as a rule not capable of upholding either their rights or their interests in free and open individualistic competition with those who are more advanced. Thus, the liberal, moved by humane concerns, has to favor some kind of a special, protective regime for them—perhaps establishing territorial reserves from which others are excluded. But this is contrary to liberal doctrine, which is at least integrationist if not assimilationist; permanent communalism is unacceptable. And so the liberal is torn. What he usually does is to say that the special measures for the indigenous are transitory, pending developments that permit integration. But if independence is impractical, permanent communalism may be exactly what the indigenous want.

The liberal dilemma with respect to the indigenous is illustrated by ambiguities and contradictions in policies of the United States toward the American Indians. The reference is to policies for which liberals might plausibly offer an intellectual and moral defense, and not to acts of despoliation and genocide that are obviously indefensible. The kind of problem I have in mind did not arise as long as "the Indian nations" were clearly "distinct, independent political communities, retaining their original natural rights...." But after Congress forbade the conclusion of any further treaties with Indians (in 1871) and, above all, after it conferred citizenship on the Indians, liberals could only squirm. On the one hand, both their ideology and other considerations impelled them to want "to break up reservations, destroy tribal relations, settle Indians on their own homesteads, incorporate them into the national life, and deal with them not as nations or tribes or bands but as individual citizens." On the other hand, they faced and still face the fact that many Indians do not want to be integrated into mainstream society. The outlook is expressed in the manifesto of the Indians who made the Longest Walk (1978): "How do we convince the U.S. government to simply leave us alone to live according to our ways of life?...We have the right to educate our children to our ways of life....We have the right to be a people. These are inherent rights....Our fight today is to survive as a people." The trouble is that the liberal has no place in his theory for peoples as distinct political units within the state. Individuals are the units, and when individuals are divided up for governmental purposes, it must be on a territorial basis and not on the basis of ethnic differences. Of course, sometimes ethnic communities are geographically concentrated, so territorial divisions may also be ethnic; but the liberal must say that it is geography, not ethnicity, that counts.

The same dilemma that American liberals face with respect to the Indians shows up in the Indigenous and Tribal Populations Convention. The convention euphemistically speaks of conditions that prevent indigenous peoples "from enjoying the benefits of the general laws of the country to which they belong," and says that so long as such conditions persist "special measures shall be adopted for the protection of [their] institutions, persons, property, and labor." They are to be "allowed to retain their own customs and institutions." At the same time, "the primary objective...shall be the fostering of individual dignity, and the advancement of individual usefulness and initiative," and "progressive integration" must be the goal. There seems to be no place in the liberal's thought for the possibility that an indigenous population might want to preserve its distinctive identity indefinitely. The Fijians, the Malays, the Maoris, and all other indigenous peoples are to be "integrated" whether they wish this or not.

Ethnic communities and nations or parts of nations are sometimes identified as minorities, and problems about them further illustrate the liberal's dilemma. The individualism of the liberal makes him quite willing to insist that members of minorities shall enjoy equal rights with other inhabitants and other citizens, and shall not be victims of discrimination. This is what international arrangements for minorities ordinarily provide, as in the minority treaties after World War I. Similarly, as noted already, the Covenant on Civil and Political Rights includes an article designed to protect "persons belonging to...minorities." The Covenant makes a gesture in the direction of acknowledging a group right in speaking of the possibility that these persons may want to act "in community with the other members of their own group," but an individual right of voluntary association or cooperation is not always enough. Minorities find it difficult, for example, to finance their own schools through voluntary contributions, especially when their members also have to pay taxes to support public schools, and they sometimes want the power to tax and otherwise to act as corporate entities. But this means political recognition and status, challenging the idea of national unity and suggesting a state within the state, and from this liberals draw back. Focusing on concerns at the level of the individual and the level of the state, they have no answer to the question of how to provide for those conditions of human well-being that can be promoted effectively only through corporate organizations operating at an intermediate level.

Ethnic communities are sometimes identified by race and want to preserve a racial identity. This is true above all today of the Whites of South Africa, and it leads to special problems. The special problems stem from the fact that insistence on the preservation of a racial identity has been associated historically with ideas of superiority and inferiority, and with privilege for the dominant rather than with concessions to the weak. As a matter of general principle, I see no reason why ethnic communities identified by race should not have rights just like other kinds of ethnic communities, but imputations of inferiority and the deliberate accentuation of advantage for those already strong are intolerable.

In the preceding section I have cited numerous illustrations of collective entities with rights without identifying standards for differentiating between them and other groupings that lack rights. Now the standards should be identified, lest it be thought that a Pandora's box has been opened from which all sorts of groupings might spring, demanding rights. Identifying them should be regarded more as a work of analysis than of imagination, the aim being to discover the standards intimated by the practices followed. The eight standards listed below are the result. They give valuable guidance, but do not eliminate the need for ad hoc judgments.

1. A group has a stronger claim the more it is a self-conscious entity with a desire to preserve itself. There ought to be a sense of belonging together, a we/they sense, a sense of solidarity vis-à-vis outsiders, a sense of sharing a common heritage and a common destiny, distinct from the heritage and destiny of others.

2. A group has a stronger claim the more evident it is that it has a reasonable chance to preserve itself. The characteristics referred to above should be stable and enduring, and the group should be of sufficient size to make long-term survival possible. If the group clearly seems destined to remain a "permanent and distinct" constituent of a plural society, the case becomes very strong.

3. A group has a stronger claim the clearer are the tests or criteria of membership, permitting all to know who are members and who are not. It may or may not be possible for a person to transfer membership from one group to another. Where it is possible, the person attempting the transfer must meet whatever conditions the receiving group fixes. Among the tests or criteria are race, language, religion, citizenship, and, more generally, adherence to a given set of cultural norms and social mores.

4. A group has a stronger claim the more significant it is in the lives of its members and the more the members tend to "identify themselves—explain who they are—by reference to their membership." Although a group may have great significance in the lives of its members if it is distinguished by only one characteristic, the chance of this is increased if it is distinguished by several—for example, not only by race but also by cultural characteristics such as language and religion. The claim is especially strong if the group serves as a major socializing agency, shaping the personalities and values of the members, and when not only their identity but also their well-being and their pride depend at least in part on their membership.

5. A group has a stronger claim the more important the rights that it seeks or ought to have are to the interests of its members, and the less costly or burdensome the grant of the rights is to others.

6. A group has a stronger claim the more clearly and effectively it is organized to act and to assume responsibilities. Formal organization, however, should not be regarded as imperative. Many a group—many a people—has succeeded in establishing its claim through the more or less spontaneous and uncoordinated actions of individual members.

7. A group has a stronger claim the more firmly established is the tradition of treating it as a group. By definition, groups with legal status as corporate entities have established their legal claim, however good their moral claim may be. And groups that historically have been victims of discrimination have a prescriptive basis for any claim they choose to make for continued differential treatment designed to advance them toward the equal enjoyment of human rights.

8. A group has a stronger claim the more clearly the status and rights that it seeks can be granted compatibly with the equality principle. The central requirements of that principle are that those affected get equal consideration, that like cases be treated in like manner, that the purpose pursued in differentiating between groups be legitimate, and that differences in treatment be justified by relevant differences and be proportionate to them.

These standards permit varying degrees of decisiveness in judging whether a group is entitled to status and rights, but they do not suggest any great proliferation of the kinds of groups to be recognized. In truth, I do not see that any kinds qualify other than those I have been discussing. What are commonly described as interest groups are clearly excluded. The question whether social classes might qualify is troublesome, but I would argue that their claims—and particularly those that are likely to be associated with an upper or privileged class—are rendered doubtful by the first standard and are ruled out by the third, fourth, fifth, and eighth.

The eighth standard—the equality principle— calls for comment. It requires that like cases be treated in like manner. First, I would argue that "like cases" may include those of groups as well as those of individuals. Thus, if the grant of a certain status and a certain set of rights to one group means that like groups cannot have a like status and a like set of rights, then the requirement of the equality principle is not met. No group in a plural society, for example, could be conceded monopoly control over government.

Second, given the need to consider whether like cases are treated in like manner, comparisons are necessary, and this requires a choice of the universe within which the comparisons should be made. When it is a question of a right under a constitution or law, the universe includes those in the relevant jurisdiction. Or, to put it more broadly, when it is a question of a right vis-à-vis an authoritative actor, the universe includes those to whom the authority extends. This principle is applicable even in connection with rights assured by treaty, such as those assured in the Covenant on Economic, Social, and Cultural Rights. In binding the parties to recognize the right of everyone to education, for example, and to guarantee that the right is exercised without discrimination, the Covenant is assuming comparisons within the national framework. If a person in Ecuador has educational opportunities inferior to those available to a person in England, no violation of the legal right to equal treatment occurs. Whether the same proposition holds with respect to moral rather than legal rights is a question. Moral rights are supposed to be general and universal, and in the long run the proposition that people in Ecuador should be treated equally with those in England is surely the ideal. Even now it makes a difference whether the inferior treatment of people in Ecuador results from deliberate choices of the government there or from the exigencies of relevant circumstances, such as a scarcity of necessary resources in Ecuador as compared to England. On the one hand, not even a moral right exists to what is impossible or impracticable. On the other hand, given the equality principle, the question is whether those receiving inferior treatment may not have a just claim to some kind of international action—for example, a transfer of resources—designed to advance them toward equality of treatment according to an international standard.

The third comment on the equality principle overlaps with the second. It is that different standards are employed around the world in interpreting the principle, and that caution is indicated in any attempt to say what it means. The situation is illustrated in the field of voting and political representation. I take for granted Article 25 of the Covenant on Civil and Political Rights, providing that every citizen shall have the right to equal suffrage

in genuine, free elections, but the article does not say how voters are to be grouped for electoral purposes—whether territorially or communally. Although every vote is no doubt to count as one in a numerical sense, the requirement of "equal" suffrage may or may not mean that the votes must have equal weight or value. Even the meaning of equal weight or value is uncertain. In the United States we compute the weight or value of votes in terms of the total population of electoral districts, but some other countries do it in terms of the number of eligible or actual voters. Further, granting that precise equality is unachievable, countries vary widely in the deviations that they permit, deviations of up to one-third being not at all uncommon.

The problem of the relationship between the equality principle and rules relating to voting and representation is complicated still more if practices at the international level are considered. There the general rule is one state/one vote despite egregious differences in the populations of the states casting the votes. In the Security Council the rule is supplemented by another: that the five permanent members have a veto whereas the other ten do not. In the World Bank voting is adjusted to the relative amounts of capital that the different member countries contribute. For the European parliament, it turns out that Luxembourg gets one member for every 60,000 persons in its population, Ireland one for every 220,000, Italy one for every 700,000, and West Germany one for every 760,000.

I have not seen a careful study of the relationship between these various practices and the equality principle. Perhaps the conclusion to be drawn is simply that the principle is frequently violated, but this would assume a meaning for the principle that others might not share. Moreover, some of the seeming departures can be explained in terms of other principles. For example, the principle is widely, though not universally, accepted that special concessions should be made to the weak, which may be the full explanation of the seeming "overrepresentation" of the weaker countries in the European parliament. Similarly, the principle is good that the voting power and influence of any unit should be more or less proportionate to its importance to the functioning of the system of which it is a part, or to its ability to defy or disrupt the system. Gross disparities between voting power and other kinds of power are dangerous to any system, for those with the other kinds of power will be tempted to use it instead of relying on a voting system that only brings defeat.

In calling attention to problems with the equality principle, I do not mean to attack the principle. I leave it as the eighth standard, as stated above. But neither the eighth nor any of the other standards is stated in unconditional terms. The statement is that the claims of intermediate groups will be stronger the more clearly or fully they meet the standards.

A substantial consensus has developed on the rights that individuals should have, but no comparable consensus exists on rights for groups intermediate between the individual and the state. And even where seeming consensus exists, as in connection with the right of peoples to self-determination and to preserve their culture, the language employed is vague. I see no general solution to this problem. Groups and the circumstance in which they find themselves differ so much that any acceptable code of group rights would have to be stated in quite general terms, leaving considerable room for ad hoc judgment. Given this situation, my argument is simply that there ought to be greater readiness to adopt special measures that respond to the legitimate claims of ethnic communities. Criteria for judging the strength of such claims have been stated above. The following are among the special measures to consider:

1. The granting of self-determination. The right of a state to its integrity and to choose a centralized governmental structure should not always be held to override the right of ethnic communities within the state to choose secession or some degree of autonomy.
2. The acceptance of some form of political communalism, assuring ethnic communities of reasonable representation in the legislative, executive, and judicial branches of government, including the civil and military services. An exclusive focus on the individual is not appropriate where the fate and fortunes of distinctive communities are at stake.
3. The adoption of other arrangements designed to enable ethnic communities to preserve their identity. In the case of communities that are territorially concentrated, the arrangements might authorize them to bar outsiders as property owners or permanent residents. Where at all feasible, they might authorize minorities

to operate their own schools, with tax support. And in appropriate ways they should assure that minority languages are protected and used.
4. Affirmative action. Though preferential treatment is unacceptable when its purpose is to preserve or promote special privilege for those already advanced and advantaged, as in South Africa, it should be employed when necessary to undo the effects of any past discrimination or to promote the equal enjoyment of human rights.

The course of action proposed involves problems that might as well be acknowledged. The right of self-determination is potentially explosive, and if given full rein might well transform the political map of the world. It might produce a large number of additional mini-states, breaking up existing states in the process, or it might produce civil wars as minorities try to secede; and it might force the decentralization of states whose international boundaries remain unquestioned. To accept communalism in any state would be to give up hope of assimilation or fusion and implicitly to emphasize social cleavages, perhaps even to encourage the emergence of new collectivities that demand status and rights. The record of communalism in Ceylon and India under the British is generally deplored, and communalism obviously has failed to solve the problems of Cyprus and Lebanon. In South Africa its distinctive application has been calamitous. Special measures designed to enable a minority to preserve its culture, and most particularly its language, would present problems too, for they would seem to militate against the development and preservation of unity within the state. Finally, problems relating to fairness to individuals in the more advanced communities obviously attend affirmative action on behalf of those in other communities.

A problem of a different sort relates to the impact on the rights of individuals of the proposed recognition of the rights of groups. Obviously, the impact might be entirely negative. The rights of individuals would no doubt be put in jeopardy. Where a conflict arises between the right of one person and the right of a group, the right of the group might always be held to prevail. Not only would this have practical significance for the fate of individuals, but it would mean that the proposals made here, instead of helping to solve a problem in liberal-democratic thought, would lead to the abandonment of a central feature of that thought—the stress on the freedom and rights of the individual.

The problems sketched in the above two paragraphs are real and are not to be dismissed. Nevertheless, considerations going in the opposite direction need to be taken into account too. Where is it written that the continued unity and even the peace of every existing state is the paramount value? Suppose that one nation or people within a state is dominant, and uses government mainly for its own advantage, consigning another nation or people or ethnic community to second-class status and governing oppressively. Suppose that those who emphasize unity and seek homogeneity are in effect taking the view that certain minorities simply do not count, or are demanding that the minorities abandon their language and their culture and take on the language and culture of the dominant community. Suppose that the dominant community magnanimously extends equal treatment to individuals in a minority, safe in the knowledge that the minority is too small to obtain representation in government. Suppose that the weaker people or the weaker ethnic community is indigenous and is threatened by an immigrant people that is more advanced, as in Fiji, Malaysia, New Zealand, and some other countries. Suppose that, even if social harmony is threatened by granting status and rights to a nation or a people or an ethnic community within the state, it is also threatened by a refusal of status and rights. After all, Northern Ireland has not achieved peace by insisting on individualism and by pretending that the population is homogeneous; and if the kind of communalism tried in Cyprus and Lebanon has not worked, this does not prove that individualism and majority rule would have worked better. A sizeable number of states in addition to those mentioned immediately above follow policies of the sort proposed here, whether on the basis of formal enactment or informal practice, including Belgium, Canada, Finland, India, West Germany, Switzerland, the USSR, and Zimbabwe. Even the individualistic United States follows such policies in limited measure—for example, in connection with the Indians and the indigenous inhabitants of American Samoa. How long Zimbabwe will continue its special measures for the Whites remains to be seen, but the others can be expected to continue their policies indefinitely and perhaps to extend them.

Liberal political theory has been based on implausible assumptions. Hobbes and Locke had no basis for assuming that individuals were the only significant units, or the crucial units, in the state of nature. And John Rawls has nothing but his imagination to go on in assuming that those in the "original position" are individuals who speak only for themselves and their immediate relatives. Had Hobbes and Locke conceived the state of nature in a plausibly different way, their theories would have been different, and so would the theories of Rawls if he had assigned those in the original position plausibly different roles. After all, it is highly unlikely that individuals in a state of nature or in an original position would be the only units that count, or that they would speak only for themselves and their relatives. Individuals are not self-sufficient. Everything we know suggests that in a state of nature, or in an original position, they would be joined not only in families but also in other collectivities of various kinds. They would be joined in groups identified by race, language, or religion, by social custom and convention, or more broadly by culture. They would make up tribes or communities or peoples. The development of their personalities and talents, their philosophies of life, and perhaps their very existence would depend on the community of which they are a part. Given these assumptions, it is incredible that in a state of nature or in an original position they would be concerned only with individuals. They also surely would be concerned about the community on which so much depends, and on its relationships both with individuals and with other communities. And these concerns surely would affect the terms of the contract reached and the nature of the rules adopted.

It would be wrong to say that all liberal political theorists, or all who write about political theory, focus on individuals to the exclusion of any examination of the role and the claims of groups, but surely anyone who goes over the relevant literature must be struck by pronounced tendencies going in this direction. Rawls illustrates the point. Dworkin, in the statement quoted earlier, grants a role to collective "goals," and in a brief footnote he says that "...a political theory that counts special groups, like racial groups, as having some corporate standing within the community may therefore speak of group rights"; but this is only a glance in the direction of a subject that deserves much fuller attention. Actually, to stress individualism in a democracy and to ignore or neglect the claims of groups is to fight the battle of any ethnic community that happens to be in a majority. Those in a majority community can insist on individualism and the nondiscriminatory treatment of individuals, and can decry any differentiation based on race, language, or religion, knowing that this formula assures their dominance. If the less numerous ethnic communities are to preserve their identity and their culture, and even if they are simply to be assured of a fair consideration of their interests, it may well be imperative to grant them special rights as collective entities.

"The Future World Order"

Aleksandras Shtromas

In the contemporary "interdependent world," national sovereignty in its classical absolute meaning remains an entirely valid concept. This is so despite the otherwise logically persuasive reasoning to the contrary by integration and convergence theorists....

Most of the "normal" modern nation-states, the major ones less and the minor ones more, are bound to limit their sovereignty, sometimes quite substantially, by the nature of goals they are setting themselves to achieve, and by the mere fact of their involvement in international economic and political structures. A typical Third World country that is setting itself the goal of rapid industrial development, in competing for foreign investment, is bound to offer the potential investors the most attractive terms and conditions; once established in such a country, the multinationals or other powerful investor-companies inevitably start wielding substantial influence on the state in which they operate, and the sheer possibility of their disinvestment forces the host-states to do the investors' bidding, whether they like it or not. Similar is the situation of the states which, when seeking outside credits or loans, have to accept the conditions attached to them. In the second half of the 1970's, the British Labor government, for example, in exchange for a substantial loan

bailing Britain out of serious economic trouble, agreed to accept the creditor International Monetary Fund's conditions which included severe cuts on the government's public spending and other measures that went against the grain of the very principles to which the British Labor Party was firmly committed. Also, each international treaty or covenant is in substance a limitation by the participating nation-states of their absolute sovereignty on issues, and to the extent determined in the respective treaties and covenants.

In all these cases, however, such self-limitation of sovereignty is voluntary. A truly sovereign state, if it is prepared to bear the economic and political consequences of such an act, can willfully break all its international commitments and resume full and absolute sovereignty at any moment. This is what Iran under Khomeini had done, and Albania under Enver Hoxja did even three times until her complete independence from any outside power was firmly established. Even Panama, which is usually regarded as a virtual semicolony of the USA, under General Noriega, blatantly defied the authority of that dominant power and managed to get away with it. To put an end to this defiance, the US had to resort to direct military intervention in Panama. It follows from the above that, in "our interdependent

From "The Future World Order and the Right of Nations to Self-Determination and Sovereignty," *International Journal on World Peace*, vol. 7 (1990). Reprinted by permission of the publisher.

world," sovereignty can still be used to its full absolute extent practically by every independent nation-state, however minor and seemingly dependent on outside powers and forces it may seem to be. Only a few nation-states, however, are prepared to use the potential of absolute sovereignty to its full extent. These are in the first place the ideocratic (communist or Islamic), "narcocratic" (as Panama under Noriega had been), and racially discriminating (in the first place, South Africa) states which are not prepared to sacrifice for fullfledged participation in the present world order the ways in which they operate and, in defending them, have to make use of their unfettered sovereign rights. Most other states, those which intend to serve the pragmatically, not ideologically-dogmatically, defined interests of their respective societies, and which are also ready to comply with at least the minimal standards of internationally acceptable behavior, would willingly engage in all kinds of international joint activities and organizations which demand certain limitations of their sovereignty. These states, together with a number of international bodies in which they, or some sections of their societies independently of them, participate, constitute the foundation of the present world order....

A global commonwealth of free and democratic nations should not undermine the principle of national sovereignty by assuming superior legislative powers or by subordinating to itself through global bureaucracies any national political and administrative institutions. The global commonwealth should in the first place establish its exclusive authority over issues and areas that are outside the domain of national sovereignty, and that naturally belong to the sovereignty of mankind as a whole. The issues and areas which the international law treats at present as those of "equal opportunity" for all nations are, of course, the *first* to come under full and exclusive sovereignty of mankind embodied in the institutions of the global commonwealth. Among them are, for example, the world ocean and the international seabed with their resources, the outer space, and the international territories, such as Antarctica.

Secondly, the global commonwealth should take full authority over the issues and areas that, at present, are inadequately handled by various weak international agencies, acting sometimes in concurrence, but more often in competition or even in confrontation with the much more powerful nation-states pursuing their own particular self-interests. Among such issues and areas are economic aid and development, inclusive of the whole task of bridging the North-South divide; protection from, and relief in the cases of, famine, epidemics, natural calamities, and other disasters; assistance to, and resettlement of, the refugees; etc.

Thirdly, the global commonwealth should be endowed with supreme authority, inclusive of coordination of efforts by nation-states and non-governmental organizations, over such naturally global issues as the protection of the natural environment and solution of other problems related to human ecology; development, management, and regulation of safety standards in the fields of nuclear, laser, and solar energy; development and management of global communication and information networks; regulation and management of demographic problems (e.g., of rational use of manpower resources); international policing efforts and combating globally spread crime (e.g., terrorism and drug trafficking); and coordination of, and supervision over, some globally vital areas of research, in the first place in the fields of genetics, cerebral biology, combat of killer diseases (cancer, AIDS, etc.), organ transplants, advanced energetics (inclusive of the development of new and alternative sources of energy), and information technology.

Fourthly, the global commonwealth should also establish a World Bank, emitting global currency (which should be set as a standard for national currencies) and concerned with prevention or, if this failed, curing of financial crises.

None of the above functions of the global commonwealth would in any way interfere with the national sovereignty of the member-states. On the contrary, the execution of the global commonwealth of the sovereignty of mankind in the naturally global areas listed above should greatly assist the member-states in carrying out their sovereign authority to a much fuller extent and in an optimally effective manner.

A voluntary agreement of free and democratic nations about establishing a global commonwealth will nevertheless have to involve the delegation by the founding member-states to this commonwealth of supreme power in certain areas and on certain issues. The whole arrangement about establishing a global commonwealth would have very little meaning if it would not endow the established global institutions with some sovereign rights overriding the sovereign rights of the member-states. International security and protection of human rights are perhaps the most important areas in which national sovereignty would have to be curtailed and supreme authority submitted to the global commonwealth.

Any viable world order system crowned by a global commonwealth, in order practically to ensure international security, would have to endow the newly established institutions of global authority with the following functions at least:

a. Exclusive control over all weapons of mass destruction.
b. Prevention of all armed conflicts with the ultimate right of military interference in order to stop armed struggle.
   (Both these functions imply the necessity for the global commonwealth to possess a military force superior to the combined military forces of several most powerful member-states.)
c. International arbitration and, when necessary, adjudication to settle conflicts between member-states.
   (This function implies the acceptance by all member-states of an elaborate World Code of Laws, according to which international conflicts are to be settled, and of a functioning system of global justice passing authoritative and enforceable judgments on such conflicts by applying that Code of Laws.)
d. Supervision over the implementation or, if necessary, enforcement of the conflict-settling decisions made by organs of global justice.

Similarly, in the area of human rights, the global commonwealth would have to be endowed with supreme authority of supervision over the application of a universally adopted World Code on Human Rights (such a code in an embryonic form already exists in the form of the Universal Declaration of Human Rights and the two supplementary covenants, one on civil and political rights and the other on social, economic, and cultural rights), instituting for this purpose within its structure a special World Court on Human Rights to serve as the highest body of judicial authority in cases involving violations of the World Code of Human Rights.

An agreement of this kind would severely limit the sovereign rights of member-states. They would lose in such an arrangement the right of going to war or using any other violent or coercive means against other states in the pursuit of their interests in the international sphere—a right which is considered to be the ultimate expression of the state's sovereignty and the surrendering of which is perceived as being tantamount to the surrender of national sovereignty itself. Even more severely, it infringes upon national sovereignty and the member-states' duty to submit themselves to a supranational system of justice, not only in their relations with other states, but also in the ways they treat their own citizens, to say nothing about the member-states having to accept interference of a supranational military force into any armed struggle they may be engaging in.

There is, however, nothing unprecedentedly novel in the states' self-limitation of their national sovereignty. By entering into international treaties and covenants, the states constantly limit their sovereign rights also in the above mentioned respects and, when such treaties and covenants are duly ratified by them, the provisions of these treaties and covenants acquire in the hierarchy of the states' laws a supreme status—even the provisions of the states' constitutional law have to be subordinated to the provisions of the ratified international laws and brought into concordance with them.

Analogous procedures would be applied to the arrangements instituting a global commonwealth. Before any of the World Codes would become legally valid for the member-states, they would have to be ratified by those states and made a part of their national legal system. The same goes for all the other provisions related to the institution of the global commonwealth, which could not be put in any other form, but that of international treaties or covenants.

As is the case with every other international treaty or covenant, states participating in a treaty-based global commonwealth will retain their right freely to terminate their association with it and thus to restore their full sovereignty whenever they choose to do so. Furthermore, the expulsion from the commonwealth (and thus restitution of full sovereignty) will be the ultimate sanction the commonwealth could apply to member-states refusing to obey the decisions of its judicial institutions.

The decisions of the World Courts would also be the only ones that the states entering into the global commonwealth would have to undertake to obey unconditionally and that would thus be binding on them. All other decisions of global institutions, before being implemented in the domain controlled by a member-state, would have to receive an explicit agreement of that state. Concrete decisions of global institutions, such, for example, as those on building pollution control centers or establishing energy-testing sites on a member-state's territory, would require as a prerequisite a contract between the global institution making the decision and the member-state agreeing to have this decision implemented on its territory. The decisions of global institutions establishing general normatives, in order to become laws applicable in the domain controlled by member-states, would have to receive proper ratification by the respective competent authorities of these states.

The legislation passed by the global commonwealth, even if it is on issues over which the commonwealth has exclusive authority, should not be made directly and automatically applicable in the domains controlled by member-states, as this is at present the case in most of the extant federal states (e.g., the USA). Before any new norms of global legislation (for example, amendments to the World Codes of Laws) could be applied to a member-state, that member-state would have to pass these norms into laws itself first, thus making them—with appropriate corrections, exclusions, and amendments—its own law. The law would then have to be applied by the member-state, or, within its jurisdiction, by the World Courts, too, in the version in which it was passed by that particular state. This is to say that even in a global commonwealth, supranational legislation, and other kinds of legal and political decision-making affecting a member-state, could become legally valid in that state only after they have become the laws or decisions of that member-state itself.

Such distribution of decision-making authority is probably the only way harmoniously to combine national sovereignty with the sovereignty of mankind. As long as the last word in legislation and decision-making generally belongs not to the global or any supranational but to national author-

ity, national sovereignty, however self-limited by any supranational arrangements it may be, remains a valid and practical concept. It is rather indicative in this respect that the first radical step taken by the Baltic republics of the USSR to reassert their national sovereignty, without breaking away from the Soviet Union completely, consisted in the passing by the respective supreme soviets of these republics of constitutional amendments, according to which All-Union laws become valid in the republic only after they have been explicitly approved by the republican legislature, and in the form in which the republican legislator had passed them.

The viability of a global commonwealth based on such loose ties between its constituent parts, and with so much weight put on preservation within its boundaries of the traditionally divisive national sovereignty, depends mainly on the ability of the member-states of this commonwealth generally to agree about the basic principles and laws on which it is to be founded....There are several conditions to be attached to the creation of a global commonwealth if it is to implement a genuinely peaceful world order: (a) the recognition of equal human rights for all individuals and nations of the world must be its basic principle; (b) a voluntary consensus of all nations, with no element of imposition or coercion within it, must be the source of its creation; (c) a negotiating procedure leading to a common agreement must be adapted for the elaboration of the Commonwealth's constitution and basic laws.

Only if these conditions are fulfilled, can the states forming a global commonwealth see in it, not an impediment on, but an unqualified advantage for, successful pursuit and enhancement of their particular national interests. Even the clauses concerning the globalization of military security, which seem so substantially limiting sovereign rights of the member-states in using their military power for the achievement of otherwise unobtainable national goals, would work out as a great advantage for the large majority of weaker nations which would be thus, on the one hand, protected by the global commonwealth from attacks and assaults of stronger nations and, on the other, enabled to achieve their legitimate national goals by means of international arbitration or adjudication, exercised in accordance with generally agreed principles and rules of international justice.

A global commonwealth, the universal foundation for which is provided by liberal-democratic principles, and which therefore has to accord to all individuals and nations equal human rights, would present most modern states, not only the ideocracies and autocracies, with some difficult problems.

The first such problem is related to multinationalism and multiracism of a great number of so-called nation-states. Such states are either underrepresentative minority states, like South Africa and Ethiopia, or misrepresentative majority states, like Russia, Turkey, Romania, Sri Lanka, and Spain; or incoherently heterogeneous states like Belgium, India, Sudan, Lebanon, and Afghanistan. Under any regime, these established states would be reluctant to recognize the equal right of all their constituent nations to self-determination and sovereignty and face, as a result, radical territorial restructuring or even disintegration.

It is true that liberal-democratic states are much better equipped to deal with the problems of multinationalism than are their nondemocratic counterparts; and the more developed and entrenched the liberal democratic order in a state is, the easier it is to arrive in it at a mutually agreeable solution of these problems. Belgium represents here, perhaps, a typical example. The unceasing struggle between the Flemings and the Walloons was tearing the Belgian state apart for many decades. The Flemings were fighting for a separate Flemish state, while the Walloons resisted them and some, in desperation, even strove to merge their part of Belgium with France.

In the conditions of a developed liberal-democratic order, various views on Belgium's future were openly debated, tested in elections, and otherwise probed and tossed with by political parties, linguistic and cultural societies, and other similar bodies. As a result, both feuding parties realized that, because of the indivisibility of Brussels, a Flemish city with a Walloon majority, Belgium's nations will have to stick together, retaining Belgium as their common state. Thanks again to the country's entrenched liberal and democratic traditions and procedures, a new constitutional settlement providing for a fairer coexistence of the two nations in one state has been devised. This settlement divided Belgium into three separate autonomous regions of Flanders, Wallonia, and Brussels. In July 1989, the final stitches were put to the transformation of Belgium into a full-fledged federal state consisting of the two separate national territorial communities with the binational capital becoming a third autonomous zone existing alongside the two main federated entities. It goes without saying that this settlement could not satisfy all Belgians, and that it indeed contains a number of flaws and shortcomings. But it doubtlessly represented a very significant step forward in the solution of Belgium's intranational problems which liberal democracy will surely be able gradually to improve, correct, and develop further in order to achieve as wide a consensus as possible.

After being transformed into a liberal democracy, Spain has also positively responded to the demands and grievances of its non-Castilians. The non-Castilian provinces were granted a large degree of autonomy and self-government which, not only the largely assimilated Andalusians and Galicians, but also the acutely nationalistic Catalonians accepted as for the time being satisfying their basic, if not all, demands. The Catalonians may still foster aspirations of full independence from Spain, but at the moment they clearly decided to concentrate on the usage of their newly acquired autonomy for consolidating and organizing themselves as a nation within the Spanish state. The Basques follow in the Catalonians' footsteps. If, under Franco, many Basques supported the radical national resistance organization ETA and approved of its militancy, now, under the conditions of liberal democracy, ETA's underground guerrilla forces increasingly find themselves in an isolated position. The majority of Basques did not stop being separatist—in this sense, their position is identical to that of ETA's—but, believing that now their separatist goals could be advanced and ultimately achieved by nonviolent political means, they roundly reject ETA's terrorist activities and increasingly refuse to back its clandestine paramilitary organizations. No wonder, then, that lately we hear less and less about ETA's terrorist attacks and its other violent wonts.

Democratic institutions and procedures also assured a peaceful solution within the Canadian state of the Quebec problem. De Gaulle's slogan, *Vive le Quebec libre*, has been realized by a series of reforms of the Canadian federal system and the introduction of bilingualism on the All-Union level. Quebec is now indeed practically free, although it remains a part of Canada.

In a global commonwealth, however, the relative satisfaction of stateless nations with their place and status within a larger nation-state may change. Entities like Quebec or Catalonia could opt for a direct association with the global commonwealth and prefer to drop their present state associations, which would prevent them from doing so. Liberal-democratic institutions of the member-states and the global commonwealth itself should be able to assure a positive solution even of such problems, despite the inertial commitment of every state, however liberal and democratic, to preserve its territorial integrity and to resist separatism of any kind.

The problem of multinationalism is much more complex and acute in nondemocratic countries and in the countries which, like India or the Philippines, could be classified as liberal democracies, but which were transformed into modern states as historically formed regional entities rather than nations, and thus have never been, and are not, nation-states in the classically European sense of this word. The rapidly developing process of national differentiation, which has spread far beyond Europe and at present embraces the entire world, made, however, such a historically and culturally defined regional basis for the formation of a modern state outmoded. With progressing modernization (or, which is one and the same thing, Westernization) of traditional societies in Asia, their old broad regional identities, based on either a common religion (India, Pakistan) or a dominant culture (China), are eroding quite fast, giving way to national identities that fortify in those states splintering tendencies and lead to their ultimate partition into a number of proper nation-states. In black Africa, on the other hand, the traditional tribal entities are growing and consolidating into proper national entities, too, which spells the necessity of radical reorganization in a not too distant future of most black African states whose identity is now based mainly on their colonial legacy and thus lacks an organic societal basis. Although then unsuccessful, the attempts in 1966–1970 to create the Ibo nation-state, Biafra, and thus to split Nigeria on ethnic grounds, emit to this effect a powerful signal indeed.

The integrity of those multinational states which came into existence before the national identities of peoples living in them were either properly formed, or started playing a predominant role, is already now visibly threatened. The Tamil struggle for separation from the Singhalese-dominated state of Sri Lanka, and the Sikhs' striving for the establishment of their separate state in the Indian province of Punjab, are just two examples of the explosive tendencies within these states. The common Muslim identity of the peoples of Pakistan was unable to prevent the splitting away from the Urdus and other smaller nations living in the western part of the country of the Bengalis situated in the country's eastern part who, with India's help, managed to establish in 1972 their separate nation state, Bangladesh. There are signs that the Hindu Bengalis of India increasingly identify themselves with the Muslim Bangladesh, tossing with the idea of splitting away from India and uniting the whole Bengali nation across the religious barriers in one separate nation-state. India's ploy to weaken Pakistan is thus turning nowadays increasingly against India herself, threatening her territorial integrity.

There are stateless nations in Asia whose territory is occupied by several states and who fight against all these states for their national independence. The Kurds are one such nation. Over 20,000,000 of them occupy a compact territory which is divided between five separate states— Turkey, the Caucasian area of the Soviet Union, Syria, Iraq, and Iran. Another such nation is the Baluchis living in Iran, Pakistan, India's Punjab, the southern part of the Asian USSR, and Afghanistan. There are also the Pathans living on both sides of the border between Afghanistan and Pakistan and a number of other similarly situated stateless nations.

There are no true nation-states in the whole of black Africa. Most black African states, as mentioned above, are heirs of former colonial entities, with their borders artificially cutting across many homogeneous tribal areas. Ethiopia, Africa's traditionally independent state, has always been, and remains, an empire of the Amharas who (together with the southern Tigres, acculturated by the Amharas) are otherwise known as the Abyssinian nation, which comprises only about a quarter of Ethiopia's population. For the last several decades, under both the Emperor Haile Selassie and the present communist regime of Colonel Menghistu, Ethiopia has been ravaged by a war of independence that the Eritreans and the Northern Tigres are conducting against Addis-Adaba, the capital of the Amharan (or Abyssinian) Empire.

Acute national conflicts which were for decades simmering under the monolithic surface of the communist world are also now coming out into the open and becoming visible. They powerfully call into question the validity of the state unity of many a communist state, starting with the Soviet Union itself. Only under liberal democracy, the search for the solution of the national conflicts besieging the multinational communist states could be properly instituted. The communist system is ideologically and politically too inflexible even to begin such a search....

It goes without saying that, as long as national strifes and conflicts continue to abound, the global commonwealth will be hardly able properly to fulfil its task of creating and safeguarding a peaceful and just world order system. For such a world order system to emerge and consolidate, it is necessary not only to found it on universally accepted liberal-democratic principles, but also effectively to apply these principles for achieving fair distribution of national sovereignty among all territorial nations of the world. A fair distribution of national sovereignty could not be achieved, however, without the present states going through thorough processes of fission: the USSR, Yugoslavia, Nigeria, and most other "structurally" multinational states would be the prime objects of such fission; fusion (Germany and Korea are the most obvious cases for it); and reshufflement (such, for example, as would be necessary between Ethiopia and Somalia for solving the Ogaden problem; between the USSR and Iran to bring into existence an integral Azeri state; among the five states housing the Kurds in order to form a sovereign Kurdistan; and between Spain and France for the sake of establishing a free Basque state, to say nothing of most black African states and many other states without a proper national identity throughout the world). It is in initiating and managing these extremely difficult processes that the global commonwealth, and especially its institutions of international justice, will have to assume prime responsibility.

It was...Immanuel Kant who convincingly demonstrated that only equal independence of every nation, big or small, from any other nation can provide an adequate foundation for a perpetually peaceful world order. Defining the independence of all nations as a preliminary condition for perpetual peace, Kant formulated it in the following maxim: "No nation, be it large or small, may be acquired by another nation by inheritance, exchange, purchase, or gift," let alone by conquest or coercion. A global commonwealth, built upon a universally accepted liberal democratic foundation, would be bound to make this Kantian idea its own, which is to say that the liberal-democratic right of every nation to self-determination and sovereignty will have to be included into the commonwealth's constitution as its principal element. Equally, the states entering the global commonwealth would have to pledge themselves to obey the moral and legal normatives which ensure for each nation a real possibility to become a separate state related to the global commonwealth either directly or through a voluntary association with other states, and which, consequently, deny each nation equally the right to include or contain within its sovereign realm another nation against its will. Only after these normatives are universally adopted and subsequently developed into a set of legal provisions incorporated into a World Code of Laws, could the global commonwealth begin effectively to preside over the process of restructuring the world's political map in concordance with the thus formulated first principles of international justice.

Under the circumstances of an established global commonwealth capable of guaranteeing effective military security to all nations and states, Israel would have to drop its objections to the establishment of a separate Palestinian state. The United Nations Security Council Resolution 242 could thus be at last practically implemented and a lasting, though in the beginning uneasy, peaceful settlement between Arabs and Jews in the Middle East begin to evolve.

The problem of granting national sovereignty to stateless nations which, as a result of foreign rule, became minorities in their own lands is more complex. The general principle which the global commonwealth should adopt for such anomalous cases is recognition of the inalienable right of each nation to be in sovereign possession of its historic homeland and capital city, whatever the arithmetic correlations in the ethnic composition of that homeland's or city's population may be. In this respect, the indigenous Fijians, who lost the majority in Fiji to immigrant Indians (43 percent of Fiji's population are native Fijians, whereas 51 percent immigrant Indians), were right in forcefully asserting their political supremacy in the country, although in order to do so they had to resort to a military coup.

The dispute between the Abkhazes and Georgians over sovereign rights in Abkhazia should be resolved in a similar fashion, that is, in favor of the Abkhazes, although they are a 17 percent minority in their own republic where the Georgians constitute 41 percent of the population (16.5 percent of Abkhazia's population are Russians, 15 percent are Armenians, and the rest belong to a few smaller ethnic minorities). The main reason for according the minority Abkhazes sovereign rights in Abkhazia is the fact that they do not have any other homeland but Abkhazia, whereas the Georgians, Russians, and Armenians living there have their own historic homelands outside Abkhazia. The same principle must also be applied to the Crimean Tatars, a people forcefully deported from their historic homeland in the Crimean peninsula, but aspiring to return and settle there as a minority nation that is, however, endowed with sovereign rights in the place which is their sole historic homeland. It is on similar grounds that the Jews rightfully reclaimed, and took, sovereignty over their historic homeland of Israel. In the Lithuanian-Polish dispute over Lithuania's capital city Vilnius which Poland had occupied in 1920 under the pretext that Poles constituted there a compact majority, the Lithuanians were right and the Poles were wrong, for without Vilnius, the sole and only capital city that the Lithuanian nation has, Lithuania's statehood would lose its historical continuity and proper integrity, while for the Poles Vilnius is just another provincial town on the margins of the Polish state whose being within or outside Poland does not affect the fate of the Polish nation in any substantial way.

In some cases, the territory of the historic homeland of a nation that has become there a minority could be divided between the indigenous and immigrant nations to the satisfaction of both. The enormous territory of Kazakhstan, where the native Kazakhs comprise only 36 percent of the population, has a solid Kazakh majority only in the Gur'ev, Kzyl-Orda, Ural'sk, and Chimkent provinces of the republic. These four provinces, together with Kazakhstan's capital city Alma-Ata, the Alma-Ata province, and the rest of the south-eastern Kazakhstan, could be consolidated into a viable nucleus of the Kazakh nation-state's proper territory, whereas the territories of northern Kazakhstan, where there are very few Kazakhs and the Slavs (Russians, Ukrainians, and Byelorussians) fully predominate, could be joined with Russia. The scarcely populated areas of present central and southwestern Kazakhstan could be then justly—that is, in accordance with the ethnic composition of the local rural population—apportioned to either Kazakhstan or Russia.

In each case, when a new nation-state is created, there are bound to remain on its territory significant numbers of people belonging to other nations and ethnic groups. These groups should get not simply equal rights but be granted, additionally, an extensive array of specific rights ensuring their full national-cultural autonomy. The protection of equal rights of all nationalities comprising a nation state, and of those nationalities' specific rights ensuring their full national-cultural autonomy, will be another important area for the global commonwealth to deal with. The standards and norms determining the commonwealth's activities in these areas should be unambiguously set by the World Code on Human Rights ratified by all member-states.

Precise legal standards should also be set for the global commonwealth to handle irredentist claims that foster enmity among many a nation. These standards should be based on the following principle: insofar as a nation is in possession of its own homeland and an established capital city within it, that nation can claim only such territories not presently in its possession in which that nation at the time of claiming constitutes a compact majority, and, conversely, no nation can refuse to cede sovereignty over provinces in which a different nation constitutes a compact majority. Purely historical claims to territory, except claims to historic homelands and capital cities by nations which lost them because of genocidal policies towards them of foreign rulers, should thus not be considered valid. In that respect, the Albanian claim to sovereignty over the presently Serbian province of Kosovo-Metohia, where the Albanians are the overwhelming majority, should be considered valid. The facts that at an early point in history Kosovo was the heartland of Serbia, and that 600 years ago the battle fought there, at Kosovo Polje, by the Serbs against the Ottoman Turks, decided the fate of Serbian statehood for many a century, should not be considered as justifying Serbian retention of sovereignty over Kosovo-Metohia. The two nations disputing sovereignty over Kosovo-Metohia have their established homelands outside that province and therefore their dispute over it should be resolved in favor of the nation which constitutes the majority of the disputed province's population, that is, in favor of Albanians. It goes, of course, without saying that Albania's sovereignty over Kosovo-Metohia should not adversely affect any civil, political, or cultural rights of the Serbian minority or prevent the Serbians from gathering, whenever they choose and in as great numbers as they wish, at Kosovo Polje to celebrate the anniversaries of their famous defeat there at the hands of the Ottoman Turks. Equally, if the Finns were to claim Leningrad (and historically they could do so even with regard to Moscow) or the Lithuanians claimed East Prussia, very few would have doubts about dismissing these claims outrightly in spite of their perfect historical justification. In the same way, the Hungarians have no valid claim to Transylvania, where the majority is Romanian, although historically Transylvania was an integral part of Hungary and at times even played the role of the pivotal heartland of that country. To be sure, the complaints about the harsh treatment by the Romanian state of the 2,000,000 strong Hungarian minority in Transylvania are fully justified. However, the gross violations on Romania's part of the Hungarians' human rights do not in any way invalidate Romania's sovereignty over Transylvania. These violations only called into question Ceausescu's government's overall ability to comply with international standards set for a state's treatment of its citizens and minority groups but could not justify claims for exemption of a territory containing a larger number of oppressed minorities from the sovereign authority of the Romanian nation-state. The anti-Ceausescu revolution in Romania was actually ignited by the Romanian authorities' brutal treatment of the Hungarians living in the Transylvania city of Timisoara. The fact that the ethnic Romanians in Bucharest rose against Ceausescu's regime in protest against the massacre of their Hungarian cocitizens of that city, and in defense of human rights of all Romanian citizens independently of their ethnic origins,

bodes well for the elimination in post-Ceausescu Romania of the discrimination suffered by the Hungarian minority under Ceausescu.

In many respects the case of Northern Ireland is analogous to the Transylvanian case. The Protestant majority's identity there is firmly British and therefore any attempt to transfer sovereignty over Ulster from the UK to the Irish Republic would represent an intolerable violation of that majority's basic rights. The fact that this majority discriminates against the Catholic minority, and that the British government is not doing enough to remedy the situation, represents a case of minorities' human rights, but in no way can it affect the situation with regard to sovereignty, let alone justify its transfer. Even less problematic in this respect is British sovereignty over the Falkland Islands where the population is entirely British and thus the Argentinian claim to sovereignty over the Malvinas, however correct the Argentinian reading of history may be, has no validity whatsoever.

According to the same standards, Armenians have a fully justifiable claim to Nagorno-Karabakh (Artsak), where theirs is an 80 percent majority, but not to Nakhichevan which, although historically an Armenian territory, too, is now mainly populated by the Azeris. The Armenians, because of that, do not even start claiming Nakhichevan, while the Azeris blatantly continue to cling to Nagorno-Karabakh, which neither historically nor demographically had ever been a part of Azerbaijan. The right in the Armenian-Azeri dispute is thus entirely on the Armenians' side. The Armenians would also be right to claim from Turkey the Ararat Valley, which is an indivisible part of the Armenian homeland containing the main spiritual center and supreme symbol of Armenia's nationhood, the holy Mountain of Ararat itself. Before 1921, when Lenin's Soviet Russian government ceded the Ararat Valley to Turkey, it was densely populated by Armenians; now it is scarcely populated at all, as if waiting to join Armenia again.

Contrary to beliefs of many students of world politics, the establishment on liberal-democratic principles of a global commonwealth does not necessarily either extinguish or even substantially erode the principle of national sovereignty, nor would it inevitably abolish the liberal-democratic right of all nations to self-determination and sovereignty. The idea of such a commonwealth is not to undermine but rather to amend and enhance national sovereignty by institutionalizing the sovereignty of mankind with the view of serving common interests of all nations and coordinating their mutual endeavors. The global institutions could be instrumental in providing for: fair and equal distribution of national sovereignty among the nations of the world, inviolable security of all member-states, just and peaceful solutions of international conflicts, and a better and more effective exploitation in the interests of all nations of mankind's common resources. The possibility for each nation to realize its full potential and exercise on equal grounds its right to self-determination and sovereignty would be enormously advanced by such a global arrangement.

"National Self-Determination"

Avishai Margalit and Joseph Raz

The core content of the claim to be examined is that there is a right to determine whether a certain territory shall become, or remain, a separate state (and possibly also whether it should enjoy autonomy within a larger state). The idea of national self-determination or (as we shall refer to it in order to avoid confusion) the idea of self-government encompasses much more....Assuming that self-determination as enjoyed by groups, what groups qualify? Given that the right is normally attributed to peoples or nations, it is tempting to give that as the answer and concentrate on characterizing "peoples" or "nations." The drawbacks of this approach are two: it assumes too much and it poses problems that may not require a solution.

It is far from clear that peoples or nations rather than tribes, ethnic groups, linguistic, religious, or geographical groups are the relevant reference group. What is it that makes peoples particularly suited to self-determination?...It may be useful to take nations and peoples as the obvious candidates for the right. We need not worry about their defining characteristics. But we may gain insight by comparing them with groups, e.g., the fiction-reading public, or Tottenham Football Club supporters, which obviously do not enjoy such a right. Reflection on such examples suggests six characteristics that in combination are relevant to a case for self-determination.

1. The group has a common character and a common culture that encompass many, varied and important aspects of life, a culture that defines or marks a variety of forms or styles of life, types of activities, occupations, pursuits, and relationships. With national groups we expect to find national cuisines, distinctive architectural styles, a common language, distinctive literary and artistic traditions, national music, customs, dress, ceremonies and holidays, etc. None of these is necessary. They are but typical examples of the features that characterize peoples and other groups that are serious candidates for the right to self-determination. They have pervasive cultures, and their identity is determined at least in part by their culture. They possess cultural traditions that penetrate beyond a single or a few areas of human life, and display themselves in a whole range of areas, including many which are of great importance for the well-being of individuals.

2. The correlative of the first feature is that people growing up among members of the group will acquire the group culture, will be marked by

From "National Self-Determination," *The Journal of Philosophy*, vol. 87 (1990). Reprinted by permission of the publisher.

its character. Their tastes and their options will be affected by that culture to a significant degree. The types of careers open to one, the leisure activities one learned to appreciate and is therefore able to choose from, the customs and habits that define and color relations with strangers and with friends, patterns of expectations and attitudes between spouses and among other members of the family, features of lifestyles with which one is capable of empathizing and for which one may therefore develop a taste—all these will be marked by the group culture....

As one would expect, the tie does not necessarily extend to all members of the group, and failure of socialization is not the only reason. The group culture affects those who grow up among its members, be they members or not. But to say this is no more than to point to various anomalies and dilemmas that may arise. Most people live in groups of these kinds, so that those who belong to none are denied full access to the opportunities that are shaped in part by the group's culture. They are made to feel estranged and their chances to have a rewarding life are seriously damaged. The same is true of people who grow up among members of a group so that they absorb its culture, but are then denied access to it because they are denied full membership of the group.

Nothing in the above presupposes that groups of the kind we are exploring are geographically concentrated, let alone that their members are the only inhabitants of any region. Rather, by drawing on the transmission of the group culture through the socialization of the young, these comments emphasize the historical nature of the groups with which we are concerned. Given that they are identified by a common culture, at least in part, they also share a history, for it is through a shared history that cultures develop and are transmitted.

3. Membership in the group is, in part, a matter of mutual recognition. Typically, one belongs to such groups if, among other conditions, one is recognized by other members of the group as belonging to it. The other conditions (which may be the accident of birth or the sharing of the group culture, etc.) are normally the grounds cited as reasons for such recognition. But those who meet those other conditions and are yet rejected by the group are at best marginal or problematic members of it. The groups concerned are not formal institutionalized groups, with formal procedures of admission. Membership in them is a matter of informal acknowledgement of belonging by others generally, and by other members specifically. The fiction-reading public fails our previous tests. It is not identified by its sharing a wide-ranging pervasive culture. It also fails the third test. To belong to the fiction-reading public all we have to do is to read fiction. It does not matter whether others recognize us as fiction-reading.

4. The third feature prepares the way for, and usually goes hand in hand with, the importance of membership for one's self-identification. Consider the fiction-reading public again. It is a historically significant group. Historians may study the evolution of the fiction-reading public, how it spread from women to men, from one class to others, from reading aloud in small groups to silent reading, from reliance on libraries to book buying, etc.; how it is regarded as important to one's qualification as a cultured person in one country, but not in another; how it furnishes a common topic of conversation in some classes but not in others; how belonging to the group is a mark of political awareness in some countries, while being a sign of escapist retreat from social concerns in another.

Such studies will show, however, that it is only in some societies that the existence of these features of the fiction-reading public is widely known. For the most part, one can belong to the group without being aware that one is a typical reader, that one's profile is that of most readers. Sometimes this is a result of a mistaken group image's being current in that society. Our concern is rather with those cases where the society lacks any very distinct image of that group. This indicates that, in such societies, membership of that group does not have a highly visible social profile. It is not one of the facts by which people pigeonhole each other. One need not be aware who, among people one knows, friends, acquaintances, shopkeepers one patronizes, one's doctor, etc., shares the habit. In such societies, membership of the fiction-reading public is not highly visible, that is, it is not one of the things one will normally know about people one has contact with, one of the things that identify "who they are." But it happens in some countries that membership of the reading public becomes a highly visible mark of belonging to a social group, to the intelligentsia, etc. In such countries, talk of the recently published novel becomes a means of mutual recognition.

One of the most significant facts differentiating various football cultures is whether they are cultures of self-recognition: whether identification as a fan or supporter of this club or that is one of the features that are among the main markers of people in the society. The same is true of occupational groups. In some countries, membership is highly visible and is among the primary means of pigeon-holing people, of establishing "who they are"; in others, it is not.

Our concern is with groups, membership of which has a high social profile, that is, groups, membership of which is one of the primary facts by which people are identified, and which form expectations as to what they are like, groups, membership of which is one of the primary clues for people generally in interpreting the conduct of others. Since our perceptions of ourselves are in large measure determined by how we expect others to perceive us, it follows that membership of such groups is an important identifying feature for each about himself. These are groups, members of which are aware of their membership and typically regard it as an important clue in understanding who they are, in interpreting their actions and reactions, in understanding their tastes and their manner.

5. Membership is a matter of belonging, not of achievement. One does not have to prove oneself, or to excel in anything, in order to belong and to be accepted as a full member. To the extent that membership normally involves recognition by others as a member, that recognition is not conditional on meeting qualifications that indicate any accomplishment....Although accomplishments play their role in people's sense of their own identity, it would seem that at the most fundamental level our sense of our own identity depends on criteria of belonging rather than on those of accomplishment. Secure identification at that level is particularly important to one's well-being.

6. The groups concerned are not small face-to-face groups, members of which are generally known to all other members. They are anonymous groups where mutual recognition is secured by the possession of general characteristics. The exclusion of small groups from consideration is not merely ad hoc. Small groups that are based on personal familiarity of all with all are markedly different in the character of their relationships and interactions from anonymous groups. For example, given the importance of mutual recognition to members of these groups, they tend to develop conventional means of identification, such as the use of symbolic objects, participation in group ceremonies, special group manners, or special vocabulary, which help quickly to identify who is "one of us" and who is not.

The various features we listed do not entail each other but they tend to go together. It is not surprising that groups with pervasive cultures will be important in determining the main options and opportunities of their members, or that they will become focal points of identification, etc. The way things are in our world, just about everyone belongs to such a group, and not necessarily to one only. Membership is not exclusive and many people belong to several groups that answer to our description. Some of them are rather like national groups, e.g., tribes or ethnic groups. Others are very different. Some religious groups meet our conditions, as do social classes, and some racial groups. Not all religions or racial groups did develop rich and pervasive cultures. But some did and those qualify....

The defining properties of the groups we identified are of two kinds. On the one hand, they pick out groups with pervasive cultures; on the other, they focus on groups, membership of which is important to one's self-identity. This combination makes such groups suitable candidates for self-rule. Let us call groups manifesting the six features *encompassing groups*. Individuals find in them a culture which shapes to a large degree their tastes and opportunities, and which provides an anchor for their self-identification and the safety of effortless secure belonging.

Individual well-being depends on the successful pursuit of worthwhile goals and relationships. Goals and relationships are culturally determined. Being social animals means not merely that the means for the satisfaction of people's goals are more readily available within society. More crucially it means that those goals themselves are (when one reaches beyond what is strictly necessary for biological survival) the creatures of society, the products of culture. Family relations, all other social relations between people, careers, leisure activities, the arts, sciences, and other obvious products of "high culture" are the fruits of society. They all depend for their existence on the sharing of patterns of expectations, on traditions preserving implicit knowledge of how to do what, of tacit conventions regarding what is part of this or that enterprise and what is not, what is appropriate and what is not, what is valuable and what is not. Familiarity with a culture determines the boundaries of the imaginable. Sharing in a culture, being part of it, determines the limits of the feasible.

It may be no more than a brute fact that our world is organized in a large measure around groups with pervasive cultures. But it is a fact with far-reaching consequences. It means, in the first place, that membership of such groups is of great importance to individual well-being, for it greatly affects one's opportunities, one's ability to engage in the relationships and pursuits marked by the culture. Secondly, it means that the prosperity of the culture is important to the well-being of its members. If the culture is decaying, or if it is persecuted or discriminated against, the options and opportunities open to its members will shrink, become less attractive, and their pursuit less likely to be successful.

It may be no more than a brute fact that people's sense of their own identity is bound up with their sense of belonging to encompassing groups and that their self-respect is affected by the esteem in which these groups are held. But these facts, too, have important consequences. They mean that individual dignity and self-respect require that the groups, membership of which contributes to one's sense of identity, be generally respected and not be made a subject of ridicule, hatred, discrimination, or persecution....The case for holding the prosperity of encompassing groups as vital for the prosperity of their members is a powerful one. Group interests cannot be reduced to individual interests. It makes sense to talk of a group's prospering or declining, of actions and policies as serving the group's interest or of harming it, without having to cash this in terms of individual interests. The group may flourish if its culture prospers, but this need not mean that the lot of its members or of anyone else has improved. It is in the interest of the group to be held in high regard by others, but it does not follow that, if an American moon landing increases the world's admiration for the United States, Americans necessarily benefit from this. Group

interests are conceptually connected to the interests of their members but such connections are nonreductive and generally indirect. For example, it is possible that what enhances the interest of the group provides opportunities for improvement for its members, or that it increases the chance that they will benefit.

This relative independence of group interest is compatible with the view that informs this article: that the moral importance of the group's interest depends on its value to individuals. A large decline in the fortunes of the group may, e.g., be of little consequence to its members. There is no a priori way of correlating group interest with that of its members or of other individuals. It depends on the circumstances of different groups at different times. One clear consequence of the fact that the moral significance of a group's interest is in its service to individuals is the fact that it will depend, in part, on the size of the group. The fortunes of a larger group may be material to the well-being of a larger number of people. Other things being equal, numbers matter.

Does the interest of members in the prosperity of the group establish a right to self-determination? Certainly not, at least not yet, not without further argument. For one thing we have yet to see any connection between the prosperity of encompassing groups and their political independence. The easiest connection to establish under certain conditions is an instrumental one. Sometimes the prosperity of the group and its self-respect are aided by, sometimes they may be impossible to secure without, the group's enjoying political sovereignty over its own affairs. Sovereignty enables the group to conduct its own affairs in a way conducive to its prosperity. There is no need to elaborate the point. It depends on historical conditions. Hence the prominence of a history of persecution in most debates concerning self-determination. But a history of persecution is neither a necessary nor a sufficient condition for the instrumental case for self-government. It is not a necessary condition, because persecution is not the only reason why the groups may suffer without independence. Suffering can be the result of neglect or ignorance of or indifference to the prosperity of a minority group by the majority. Such attitudes may be so well entrenched that there is no realistic prospect of changing them.

Persecution is not a sufficient condition, for there may be other ways to fight and overcome persecution and because whatever the advantages of independence it may, in the circumstances, lead to economic decline, cultural decay, or social disorder, which only make their members worse off. Besides, as mentioned above, pernicious groups may not deserve protection, especially if it will help them to pursue repressive practices with impunity. Finally, there are the interests of nonmembers to be considered. In short, the instrumental argument (as well as others) for self-government is sensitive to counterarguments pointing to its drawbacks, its cost in terms of human well-being, possible violations of human rights, etc.

We shall return to these issues below. First, let us consider the claim that the instrumental argument trivializes the case for self-government by overlooking its intrinsic value. Of the various arguments for the intrinsic value of self-government which have been and can be advanced, we examine one which seems the most promising.

The argument is based on an extension of individual autonomy or of self-expression (if that is regarded as independently valuable). The argument unravels in stages: (1) people's membership of encompassing groups is an important aspect of their personality, and their well-being depends on giving it full expression; (2) expression of membership essentially includes manifestation of membership in the open, public life of the community; (3) this requires expressing one's membership in political activities within the community. The political is an essential arena of community life, and consequently of individual well-being; (4) therefore, self-government is inherently valuable, it is required to provide the group with a political dimension.

The first premise is unexceptionable. So is the second, though an ambiguity might be detected in the way it is often understood. Two elements need separating. First, given the importance of membership to one's well-being, it is vital that the dignity of the group be preserved. This depends, in part, on public manifestations of respect for the group and its culture, and on the absence of ridicule of the group, etc., from the public life of the society of which one is a member. One should not have to identify with or feel loyalty to a group that denigrates an encompassing group to which one belongs. Indeed, one should not have to live in an environment in which such attitudes are part of the common culture. Second, an aspect of well-being is an ability to express publicly one's identification with the group and to participate openly in its public culture. An encompassing group is centered on mutual recognition and is inevitably a group with a public culture. One cannot enjoy the benefits of membership without participation in its public culture, without public participation in its culture.

Both elements are of great importance. Both indicate the vital role played by public manifestations of group culture and group membership among the conditions of individual well-being. To the extent that a person's well-being is bound up with his identity as a member of an encompassing group it has an important public dimension. But that dimension is not necessarily political in the conventional narrow sense of the term. Even where it is, its political expression does not require a political organization whose boundaries coincide with those of the group. One may be politically active in a multinational, multicultural polity....

Nothing in the instrumentalist and pragmatic nature of our approach should be allowed to disguise its sensitivity to subjective elements, its responsiveness to the perceptions and sensibilities of the people concerned. To a considerable extent, what matters is how well people feel in their environment: Do they feel at home in it or are they alienated from it? Do they feel respected or humiliated? etc. This leads to a delicate balance between "objective" factors and subjective perceptions....But...up to a point in matters of respect, identification, and dignity, subjective responses, justified or not, are the ultimate reality so far as the well-being of those who have them is concerned.

It may seem that the case for self-government establishes a right to self-determination. That is, it establishes the reasons for the right sort of group, an encompassing group, to determine that a territory shall be self-governing. But things are not that simple. The case for self-government shows that sometimes, under certain conditions, it is best that the political unit be roughly an encompassing group. A group's right to self-determination is its right to determine that a territory be self-governing, regardless of whether the case for self-government, based on its benefits, is established or not. In other words, the right to self-determination answers the question 'who is to decide?', not 'what is the best decision?'. In exercising the right, the group should act responsibly in light of all the considerations we mentioned so far. It should, in particular, consider not only the interests of its members but those of others who may be affected by its decision. But if it has the right to decide, its decision is binding even if it is wrong, even if the case for self-government is not made....

The problem is that the case for self-government is hedged by considerations of the interest of people other than members of the groups, and by the other interests of members of the groups, i.e., other than their interests as members of the groups. These include their fundamental individual interests which should be respected, e.g., by a group whose culture oppresses women or racial minorities. These considerations raise the question whether encompassing groups are the most suitable bodies to decide about the case for self-government. Can they be entrusted with the decision in a matter in which their group interests are in conflict with other interests of members of the group as well as with the interests of other people? At the very least this suggests that the right must be qualified and hedged to protect other interests.

More fundamental still is the question of how the right of self-determination fits within our general conception of democratic decision making. We are used to a two-level structure of argument concerning social issues, such as just taxation, the provision of public education, etc. First, we explore the principles that should govern the matter at issue. Second, we devise a form of democratic procedure for determining what shall be done. The first level answers the question 'what should be done?'. The second responds to the question 'who should decide?'.

On a simple majoritarian view, the issue of self-government seems to defy a democratic decision procedure. The question is 'what is the relevant democratic unit?' and that question cannot be democratically decided, at least not entirely so. In fact, of course, we are not simple majoritarians. We adopt a whole range of democratic procedures such as constitution-making privileged majorities, ordinary legislative processes, plebiscites, administrative processes, and decisions by special agencies under conditions of public accountability and indirect democratic control. We match various democratic processes with various social and political

problems. This means that there is no universal democratic formula serving as the universal answer to 'who decides?' questions. Rather, we operate a mixed principled-democratic system in which principles, whose credentials do not derive entirely from their democratic backing, determine what form of a democratic procedure is suited for what problem. Within this mixed principled-democratic framework, the right to self-determination fits as just another qualified democratic process suited to its object.

What are the principles involved? It is tempting to see here a principle giving the part veto over the issue of membership in a larger whole. To form a new political unit, or to remain part of an existing one, all component parts should agree. To break up a political unit, or to foil the creation of a new one, all that is required is the will of the group that wants to secede or to stay out. This principle derives its appeal from its voluntaristic aura. It seems to regard the justification of all political units as based on consent. But this is an undesirable illusion. It is undesirable since, as was explained above regarding encompassing groups, the more important human groupings need to be based on shared history, and on criteria of nonvoluntaristic (or at least not wholly contractarian) membership to have the value that they have. The principle presents no more than an illusion of a contractarian principle since it refers to groups, not to individuals. But the whole contractarian ethos derives its appeal from the claim that each individual's consent is a condition of the legitimacy of political units. Beyond all that, the principle simply begs the question that it is meant to answer, namely, what are the parts? Which groupings have the veto and which do not? Can the group of all the people whose surnames begin with a 'g' and end with an 'e' count for these purposes? Do they have the veto on membership in a larger political unit?

The right to self-determination derives from the value of membership in encompassing groups. It is a group right, deriving from the value of a collective good, and as such opposed in spirit to contractarian-individualistic approaches to politics or to individual well-being. It rests on an appreciation of the great importance that membership in and identification with encompassing groups has in the life of individuals, and the importance of the prosperity and self-respect of such groups to the well-being of their members. That importance makes it reasonable to let the encompassing group that forms a substantial majority in a territory have the right to determine whether that territory shall form an independent state in order to protect the culture and self-respect of the group, provided that the new state is likely to respect the fundamental interests of its inhabitants, and provided that measures are adopted to prevent its creation from gravely damaging the just interests of other countries. This statement of the argument for the right requires elaboration.

(1) The argument is an instrumental one. It says, essentially, that members of a group are best placed to judge whether their group's prosperity will be jeopardized if it does not enjoy political independence. It is in keeping with the view that, even though participation in politics may have intrinsic value to individuals, the shape and boundaries of political units are to be determined by their service to individual well-being, i.e., by their instrumental value. In our world, encompassing groups that do not enjoy self-government are not infrequently persecuted, despised, or neglected. Given the importance of their prosperity and self-respect to the well-being of their members, it seems reasonable to entrust their members with the right to determine whether the groups should be self-governing. They may sacrifice their economic or other interests for the sake of group self-respect and prosperity. But such a sacrifice is, given the circumstances of this world, often not unreasonable.

One may ask why should such matters not be entrusted to international adjudication by an international court, or some other international agency. Instead of groups' having a right to self-determination which makes them judges in their own cause, the case for a group's becoming self-governing should be entrusted to the judgment of an impartial tribunal. This would have been a far superior solution to the question 'who is to decide?' Unfortunately, there simply does not exist any international machinery of enforcement that can be relied upon in preference to a right of self-determination as the right of self-help, nor is there any prospect of one coming into existence in the near future. In the present structure of international relations, the most promising arrangement is one that recognizes group rights to self-determination and entrusts international bodies with the duty to help bring about its realization, and to see to it

that the limits and preconditions of the right are observed (these are enumerated in the points two to five below).

(2) The right belongs to the group. But how should it be exercised? Not necessarily by a simple majority vote. Given the long-term and irreversible nature of the decision (remember that while independence is up to the group, merger or union is not), the wish for a state must be shared by an overwhelming majority, reflecting deep-seated beliefs and feelings of an enduring nature, and not mere temporary popularity. The precise institutional requirements for the exercise of the right are issues that transcend the topic of this paper. They are liable to vary with the circumstances of different national and ethnic groups. Whatever they are they should reflect the above principle.

(3) The right is over a territory. This simply reflects the territorial organization of our political world. The requirement that the group be a substantial majority of the territory stems from further considerations aimed at balancing the interest in self-government against the interests of nonmembers. First, it is designed to ensure that self-government for a territory does not generate a problem as great as it is meant to solve, by ensuring that the independence will not generate a large-scale new minority problem. That risk cannot be altogether avoided. As was remarked before, numbers count in the end....

Do historical ties make a difference? Not to the right if voluntarily abandoned. Suppose that the group was unjustly removed from the country. In that case, the general principle of restitution applies, and the group has a right to self-determination and control over the territory it was expelled from, subject to the general principle of prescription. Prescription protects the interests of the current inhabitants. It is based on several deep-seated concerns. It is meant to prevent the revival of abandoned claims, and to protect those who are not personally to blame from having their life unsettled by claims of ancient wrongs, on the ground that their case now is as good as that of the wronged people or their descendants. Prescription, therefore, may lose the expelled group the right even though its members continue to suffer the effects of the past wrong. Their interest is a consideration to be borne in mind in decisions concerning immigration policies, and the like, but because of prescription they lost the right to self-determination. The outcome is not up to them to decide.

(4) The right is conditional on its being exercised for the right reasons, i.e., to secure conditions necessary for the prosperity and self-respect of the group. This is a major protection against abuse. Katanga cannot claim a right to self-determination as a way of securing its exclusive control over uranium mines within its territory. This condition does not negate the nature of a right. The group is still entrusted with the right to decide, and its decision is binding even if wrong, even if the case for self-government does not obtain, provided the reasons that motivate the group's decision are of the right kind.

(5) Finally, there are the two broad safeguards on which the exercise of the right is conditional. First, that the group is likely to respect the basic rights of its inhabitants, so that its establishment will do good rather than add to the ills of this world. Secondly, since the establishment of the new state may fundamentally endanger the interests of inhabitants of other countries, its exercise is conditional on measures being taken to prevent or minimize the occurrence of substantial damage of this kind. Such measures, which will vary greatly from case to case, include free-trade agreements, port facilities, granting of air routes, demilitarization of certain regions, etc.

Two kinds of interests do not call for special protection. One is the interest of a people to regard themselves as part of a larger rather than a smaller grouping or country. The English may have an interest in being part of Great Britain, rather than mere Englanders. But that interest can be justly satisfied only with the willing co-operation of, e.g.,

the Scots. If the other conditions for Scottish independence are met, this interest of the English should not stand in its way. Secondly, unjust economic gains, the product of colonial or other form of exploitation of one group by another, may be denied to the exploiting group without hesitation or compensation (barring arrangements for a transitory period). But where secession and independence will gravely affect other and legitimate interests of other countries, such interests should be protected by creating free-trade zones, demilitarized areas, etc.

(6) A right in one person is sufficient ground to hold some other person(s) to be under a duty. What duties arise out of the right to self-determination? How is this matter to be settled? As the previous discussion makes clear, the right of self-determination is instrumentally justified, as the method of implementing the case for self-government, which itself is based on the fact that in many circumstances self-government is necessary for the prosperity and dignity of encompassing groups. Hence, in fixing the limits of the right, one has to bear in mind the existing system of international politics, and show that, given other elements in that system, certain duties can be derived from the right to self-determination, whereas others cannot. The first and most important duty arising out of the right is the duty not to impede the exercise of the right, i.e., not to impede groups in their attempts to decide whether appropriate territories should be independent, so long as they do so within the limits of the right. This duty affects in practice first and foremost the state that governs the territory concerned and its inhabitants....

Islam and Revolution

Imam Khomeini

A body of laws alone is not sufficient for a society to be reformed. In order for law to ensure the reform and happiness of man, there must be an executive power and an executor. For this reason, God Almighty, in addition to revealing a body of law (i.e., the ordinances of the *shari'a*), has laid down a particular form of government together with executive and administrative institutions.

The Most Noble Messenger (peace and blessings be upon him) headed the executive and administrative institutions of Muslim society. In addition to conveying the revelation and expounding and interpreting the articles of faith and the ordinances and institutions of Islam, he undertook the implementation of law and the establishment of the ordinances of Islam, thereby bringing into being the Islamic state. He did not content himself with the promulgation of law; rather, he implemented it at the same time, cutting off hands and administering lashings and stonings. After the Most Noble Messenger, his successor had the same duty and function. When the Prophet appointed a successor, it was not for the purpose of expounding articles of faith and law; it was for the implementation of law and the execution of God's ordinances. It was this function—the execution of law and the establishment of Islamic institutions—that made the appointment of a successor such an important matter that the Prophet would have failed to fulfill his mission if he had neglected it. For after the Prophet, the Muslims still needed someone to execute laws and establish the institutions of Islam in society, so that they might attain happiness in this world and the hereafter.

By their very nature, in fact, law and social institutions require the existence of an executor. It has always and everywhere been the case that legislation alone has little benefit: legislation by itself cannot assure the well-being of man. After the establishment of legislation, an executive power must come into being, a power that implements the laws and the verdicts given by the courts, thus allowing people to benefit from the laws and the just sentences the courts deliver. Islam has therefore established an executive power in the same way that it has brought laws into being. The person who holds this executive power is known as the *vali amr*.[1]

The Sunna[2] and path of the Prophet constitute a proof of the necessity for establishing government....

It is self-evident that the necessity for enactment of the law, which necessitated the formation of a government by the Prophet (upon whom be peace), was not confined or restricted to his time, but continues after his departure from this world. According to one of the noble verses of the Qur'an, the ordinances of Islam are not limited with respect to time or place; they are permanent and must be enacted until the end of time. They were not revealed merely for the time of the Prophet, only to be abandoned thereafter, with retribution and the penal code of Islam no longer to be enacted, or the taxes prescribed by Islam no longer collected, and the defense of the lands and people of Islam suspended. The claim that the laws of Islam may remain in abeyance or are restricted to a particular time or place is contrary to the essential credal bases of Islam. Since the enactment of laws, then, is necessary after the departure of the Prophet from this world, and indeed, will remain so until the end of time, the formation of a government and the establishment of executive and administrative organs are also necessary. Without the formation of a government and the establishment of such organs to ensure that through enactment of the law, all activities of the individual take place in

From *Islam and Revolution*, Hamid Algar, trans. and ed. (Berkeley, CA: Mizan Press, 1981). Reprinted by permission of the publisher.

the framework of a just system, chaos and anarchy will prevail and social, intellectual, and moral corruption will arise. The only way to prevent the emergence of anarchy and disorder and to protect society from corruption is to form a government and thus impart order to all the affairs of the country.

Both reason and divine law, then, demonstrate the necessity in our time for what was necessary during the lifetime of the Prophet and the age of the Commander of the Faithful, Ali ibn Abi Talib (peace be upon them)—namely the formation of a government and the establishment of executive and administrative organs....

The nature and character of Islamic law and the divine ordinances of the *shari'a* furnish additional proof of the necessity for establishing government, for they indicate that the laws were laid down for the purpose of creating a state and administering the political, economic, and cultural affairs of society.

First, the laws of the *shari'a* embrace a diverse body of laws and regulations, which amounts to a complete social system. In this system of laws, all the needs of man have been met: his dealings with his neighbors, fellow citizens, and clan, as well as children and relatives; the concerns of private and marital life; regulations concerning war and peace and intercourse with other nations; penal and commercial law; and regulations pertaining to trade and agriculture. Islamic law contains provisions relating to the preliminaries of marriage and the form in which it should be contracted, and others relating to the development of the embryo in the womb and what food the parents should eat at the time of conception. It further stipulates the duties that are incumbent upon them while the infant is being suckled, and specifies how the child should be reared, and how the husband and the wife should relate to each other and to their children. Islam provides laws and instructions for all of these matters, aiming, as it does, to produce integrated and virtuous human beings who are walking embodiments of the law, or to put it differently, the law's voluntary and instinctive executors. It is obvious, then, how much care Islam devotes to government and the political and economic relations of society, with the goal of creating conditions conducive to the production of morally upright and virtuous human beings.

The Glorious Qur'an and the Sunna contain all the laws and ordinances man needs in order to attain happiness and the perfection of his state....

The taxes Islam levies and the form of budget it has established are not merely for the sake of providing subsistence to the poor or feeding the indigent among the descendants of the Prophet (peace and blessings be upon him); they are also intended to make possible the establishment of a great government and to assure its essential expenditures.

For example, *khums* is a huge source of income that accrues to the treasury and represents one item in the budget. According to our Shi'i school of thought, *khums* is to be levied in an equitable manner on all agricultural and commercial profits and all natural resources whether above or below the ground—in short, on all forms of wealth and income. It applies equally to the green-grocer with his stall outside this mosque and to the shipping or mining magnate. They must all pay one-fifth of their surplus income, after customary expenses are deducted, to the Islamic ruler so that it enters the treasury. It is obvious that such a huge income serves the purpose of administering the Islamic state and meeting all its financial needs. If we were to calculate one-fifth of the surplus income of all the Muslim countries (or of the whole world, should it enter the fold of Islam), it would become fully apparent that the purpose for the imposition of such a tax is not merely the upkeep of the *sayyids*[3] or the religious scholars, but on the contrary, something far more significant—namely, meeting the financial needs of the great organs and institutions of government. If an Islamic government is achieved, it will have to be administered on the basis of the taxes that Islam has established....The provision of such a huge budget must obviously be for the purpose of forming a government and administering the Islamic lands. It was established with the aim of providing for the needs of the people, for public services relating to health, education, defense, and economic development. Further, in accordance with the procedures laid down by Islam for the collection, preservation, and expenditure of this income, all forms of usurpation and embezzlement of public wealth have been forbidden, so that the head of state and all those entrusted with responsibility for conducting public affairs (i.e., members of the government) have no privileges over the ordinary citizen in benefiting from the public income and wealth; all have an equal share.

The ordinances pertaining to preservation of the Islamic order and defense of the territorial integrity and the independence of the Islamic *umma*[4] also demanded the formation of a government. An example is the command: "Prepare against them whatever force you can muster and horses tethered" (Qur'an, 8:60), which enjoins the preparation of as much armed defensive force as possible and orders the Muslims to be always on the alert and at the ready, even in time of peace.

If the Muslims had acted in accordance with this command and, after forming a government, made the necessary extensive preparations to be in a state of full readiness for war, a handful of Jews would never have dared to occupy our lands,...without the people's being capable of making an immediate response. All this has resulted from the failure of the Muslims to fulfill their duty of executing God's law and setting up a righteous and respectable government. If the rulers of the Muslim countries truly represented the believers and enacted God's ordinances, they would set aside their petty differences, abandon their subversive and divisive activities, and join together like the fingers of one hand. Then a handful of wretched Jews (the agents of America, Britain, and other foreign powers) would never have been able to accomplish what they have, no matter how much support they enjoyed from America and Britain. All this has happened because of the incompetence of those who rule over the Muslims....

After the death of the Most Noble Messenger (peace and blessings be upon him), the obstinate enemies of the faith...did not permit the Islamic state to attain stability....They did not allow a form of government to exist that was pleasing to God, Exalted and Almighty, and to his Most Noble Messenger. They transformed the entire basis of government, and their policies were, for the most part, contradictory to Islam....The form of government was thoroughly perverted by being transformed into a monarchy, like those of the kings of Iran, the emperors of Rome, and the pharaohs of Egypt. For the most part, this non-Islamic form of government has persisted to the present day, as we can see.

Both law and reason require that we not permit governments to retain this non-Islamic or anti-Islamic character. The proofs are clear. First, the existence of a non-Islamic political order necessarily results in the non-implementation of the Islamic political order. Then, all non-Islamic systems of government are the systems of *kufr*,[5] since the ruler in each case is an instance of *taghut*,[6] and it is our duty to remove from the life of Muslim society all traces of *kufr* and destroy them. It is also our duty to create a favorable social environment for the education of believing and virtuous individuals, an environment that is in total contradiction with that produced by the rule of *taghut* and illegitimate power. The social environment created by *taghut* and *shirk*[7] invariably brings about corruption such as you can now observe in Iran, the corruption termed "corruption on earth." This corruption must be swept away, and its instigators punished for their deeds...

A believing, pious, just individual cannot possibly exist in a socio-political environment of this nature and still maintain his faith and righteous conduct. He is faced with two choices: either he commits acts that amount to *kufr* and contradict righteousness, or in order not to commit such acts and not to submit to the orders and commands of the *taghut*, the just individual opposes him and struggles against him in order to destroy the environment of corruption. We have in reality, then, no choice but to destroy those systems of government that are corrupt in themselves and also entail the corruption of others, and to overthrow all treacherous, corrupt, oppressive, and criminal regimes.

This is a duty that all Muslims must fulfill, in every one of the Muslim countries, in order to achieve the triumphant political revolution of Islam.

We see, too, that together, the imperialists and the tyrannical self-seeking rulers have divided the Islamic homeland. They have separated the various segments of the Islamic *umma* from each other and artificially created separate nations. There once existed the great Ottoman State, and that, too, the imperialists divided. Russia, Britain, Austria, and other imperialist powers united, and through wars against the Ottomans, each came to occupy or absorb into its sphere of influence part of the Ottoman realm. It is true that most of the Ottoman rulers were incompetent, that some of them were corrupt, and that they followed a monarchical system. Nonetheless, the existence of the Ottoman State represented a threat to the imperialists. It was always possible that righteous individuals might rise up among the people and, with their assistance, seize control of the state, thus putting an end to imperialism by mobilizing the unified resources of the nation. Therefore, after numerous prior wars, the imperialists at the end of World War I divided the Ottoman State, creating in its territories about ten or fifteen petty states....

In order to assure the unity of the Islamic *umma*, in order to liberate the Islamic homeland from occupation and penetration by the imperialists and their puppet governments, it is imperative that we establish a government. In order to attain the unity and freedom of the Muslim peoples, we must overthrow the oppressive governments installed by the imperialists and bring into existence an Islamic government of justice that will be in the service of the people....

Through the political agents they have placed in power over the people, the imperialists have also imposed on us an unjust economic order, and thereby divided our people into two groups: oppressors and oppressed. Hundreds of millions of Muslims are hungry and deprived of all form of health care and education, while minorities comprised of the wealthy and powerful live a life of indulgence, licentiousness, and corruption. The hungry and deprived have constantly struggled to free themselves from the oppression of their plundering overlords, and their struggle continues to this day. But their way is blocked by the ruling minorities and the oppressive governmental structures they head. It is our duty to save the oppressed and deprived. It is our duty to be a helper to the oppressed and an enemy to the oppressor. This is nothing other than the duty that the Commander of the Faithful (upon whom be peace) entrusted to his two great offspring in his celebrated testament: "Be an enemy to the oppressor and a helper to the oppressed."

The scholars of Islam have a duty to struggle against all attempts by the oppressors to establish a monopoly over the sources of wealth or to make illicit use of them. They must not allow the masses to remain hungry and deprived while plundering oppressors usurp the sources of wealth and live in opulence....

How can we stay silent and idle today when we see that a band of traitors and usurpers, the agents of foreign powers, have appropriated the wealth and the fruits of labor of hundreds of millions of

Muslims—thanks to the support of their masters and through the power of the bayonet—granting the Muslims not the least right to prosperity? It is the duty of Islamic scholars and all Muslims to put an end to this system of oppression and, for the sake of the well-being of hundreds of millions of human beings, to overthrow these oppressive governments and form an Islamic government.

I will now paraphrase [a passage from Imam Riza[8]]: If someone should ask you, "Why has God, the All-Wise, appointed holders of authority and commanded you to obey them?" you should answer him as follows: "He has done so for various causes and reasons. One is that men have been set upon a certain well-defined path and commanded not to stray from it, nor to transgress against the established limits and norms, for if they were to stray, they would fall prey to corruption. Now men would not be able to keep to their ordained path and to enact God's laws unless a trustworthy and protective individual (or power) were appointed over them with responsibility for this matter, to prevent them from stepping outside the sphere of the licit and transgressing against the rights of others. If no such restraining individual or power were appointed, nobody would voluntarily abandon any pleasure or interest of his own that might result in harm or corruption to others; everybody would engage in oppressing and harming others for the sake of their own pleasures and interests.

"Another reason and cause is this: we do not see a single group, nation, or religious community that has ever been able to exist without an individual entrusted with the maintenance of its laws and institutions—in short, a head or a leader; for such a person is essential for fulfilling the affairs of religion and the world. It is not permissible, therefore, according to divine wisdom, that God should leave men, His creatures, without a leader and guide, for He knows well that they depend on the existence of such a person for their own survival and perpetuation. It is under his leadership that they fight against their enemies, divide the public income among themselves, perform Friday and congregational prayer, and foreshorten the arms of the transgressors who would encroach on the rights of the oppressed.

"Another proof and cause is this: were God not to appoint an Imam over men to maintain law and order, to serve the people faithfully as a vigilant trustee, religion would fall victim to obsolescence and decay. Its rites and institutions would vanish; the customs and ordinances of Islam would be transformed or even deformed. Heretical innovators would add things to religion and atheists and unbelievers would subtract things from it, presenting it to the Muslims in an inaccurate manner. For we see that men are prey to defects; they are not perfect and must needs strive after perfection. Moreover, they disagree with each other, having varying inclinations and discordant states. If God, therefore, had not appointed over men one who would maintain order and law and protect the revelation brought by the Prophet, in the manner we have described, men would fall prey to corruption; the institutions, laws, customs, and ordinances of Islam would be transformed; and faith and its content would be completely changed, resulting in the corruption of all humanity."...

In the past we did not act in concert and unanimity in order to establish proper government and overthrow treacherous and corrupt rulers. Some people were apathetic and reluctant even to discuss the theory of Islamic government, and some went so far as to praise oppressive rulers. It is for this reason that we find ourselves in the present state. The influence and sovereignty of Islam in society have declined; the nation of Islam has fallen victim to division and weakness; the laws of Islam have remained in abeyance and been subjected to change and modification; and the imperialists have propagated foreign laws and alien culture among the Muslims through their agents for the sake of their evil purposes, causing people to be infatuated with the West. It was our lack of a leader, a guardian, and our lack of institutions of leadership that made all this possible. We need righteous and proper organs of government; that much is self-evident.

Islamic government does not correspond to any of the existing forms of government. For example, it is not a tyranny, where the head of state can deal arbitrarily with the property and lives of the people, making use of them as he wills, putting to death anyone he wishes, and enriching anyone he wishes by granting landed estates and distributing the property and holdings of the people. The Most Noble Messenger (peace be upon him), the Commander of the Faithful (peace be upon him), and the other caliphs did not have such powers. Islamic government is neither tyrannical nor absolute, but constitutional. It is not constitutional in the current

sense of the word, i.e., based on the approval of laws in accordance with the opinion of the majority. It is constitutional in the sense that the rulers are subject to a certain set of conditions in governing and administering the country, conditions that are set forth in the Noble Qur'an and the Sunna of the Most Noble Messenger. It is the laws and ordinances of Islam comprising this set of conditions that must be observed and practiced. Islamic government may therefore be defined as the rule of divine law over men.

The fundamental difference between Islamic government, on the one hand, and constitutional monarchies and republics, on the other, is this: whereas the representatives of the people or the monarch in such regimes engage in legislation, in Islam the legislative power and competence to establish laws belongs exclusively to God Almighty. The Sacred Legislator of Islam is the sole legislative power. No one has the right to legislate and no law may be executed except the law of the Divine Legislator. It is for this reason that in an Islamic government, a simple planning body takes the place of the legislative assembly that is one of the three branches of government. This body draws up programs for the different ministries in the light of the ordinances of Islam and thereby determines how public services are to be provided across the country....

Islamic government is a government of law. In this form of government, sovereignty belongs to God alone and law is His decree and command. The law of Islam, divine command, has absolute authority over all individuals and the Islamic government. Everyone, including the Most Noble Messenger (peace be upon him) and his successors, is subject to law and will remain so for all eternity—the law that has been revealed by God, Almighty and Exalted, and expounded by the tongue of the Qur'an and the Most Noble Messenger....

Islamic government is not a form of monarchy, especially not an imperial system. In that type of government, the rulers are empowered over the property and persons of those they rule and may dispose of them entirely as they wish. Islam has not the slightest connection with this form and method of government. For this reason we find that in Islamic government, unlike monarchical and imperial regimes, there is not the slightest trace of vast palaces, opulent buildings, servants and retainers, private equerries, adjutants to the heir apparent, and all the other appurtenances of monarchy that consume as much as half of the national budget. You all know how the Prophet lived, the Prophet who was the head of the Islamic state and its ruler....

The qualifications essential for the ruler derive directly from the nature and form of Islamic government. In addition to general qualifications like intelligence and administrative ability, there are two other essential qualifications: knowledge of the law and justice....

Since Islamic government is a government of law, knowledge of the law is necessary for the ruler, as has been laid down in tradition. Indeed such knowledge is necessary not only for the ruler, but also for anyone holding a post or exercising some government function. The ruler, however, must surpass all others in knowledge. In laying claim to the Imamate, our Imams also argued that the ruler must be more learned than everyone else....The sole matters relevant to rule, those that were mentioned and discussed in the time of the Most Noble Messenger (upon whom be peace) and our Imams (upon whom be peace) and were, in addition, unanimously accepted by the Muslims, are: (1) the knowledgeability of the ruler or caliph, i.e., his knowledge of the provisions and ordinances of Islam; and (2) his justice, i.e., his excellence in belief and morals.

Reason also dictates the necessity for these qualities, because Islamic government is a government of law, not the arbitrary rule of an individual over the people or the domination of a group of individuals over the whole people. If the ruler is unacquainted with the contents of the law, he is not fit to rule; for if he follows the legal pronouncements of others, his power to govern will be impaired, but if, on the other hand, he does not follow such guidance, he will be unable to rule correctly and implement the laws of Islam....

If the ruler is not just in granting the Muslims their rights, he will not conduct himself equitably in levying taxes and spending them correctly and in implementing the penal code. It becomes possible then for his assistants, helpers, and confidants to impose their will on society, diverting the public treasury to personal and frivolous use....

The two qualities of knowledge of the law and justice are present in countless *fuqaha*[9] of the present age. If they would come together, they could establish a government of universal justice in the world.

If a worthy individual possessing these two qualities arises and establishes a government, he will possess the same authority as the Most Noble Messenger (upon whom be peace and blessings) in the administration of society, and it will be the duty of all people to obey him....

The authority that the Prophet and the Imam had in establishing a government, executing laws, and administering affairs exists also for the *faqih*. But the *fuqaha* do not have absolute authority in the sense of having authority over all other *fuqaha* of their own time, being able to appoint or dismiss them. There is no hierarchy ranking one *faqih* higher than another or endowing one with more authority than another.

Now that this much has been demonstrated, it is necessary that the *fuqaha* proceed, collectively or individually, to establish a government in order to implement the laws of Islam and protect its territory. If this task falls within the capabilities of a single person, he has personally incumbent upon him the duty to fulfill it; otherwise, it is a duty that devolves upon the *fuqaha* as a whole. Even if it is impossible to fulfill the task, the authority vested in the *fuqaha* is not voided, because it has been vested in them by God. If they can, they must collect taxes, such as *zakat*, *khums*, and *kharaj*, spend them for the welfare of the Muslims, and also enact the penalties of the law. The fact that we are presently unable to establish a complete and comprehensive form of government does not mean that we should sit idle. Instead, we should perform, to whatever extent we can, the tasks that are needed by the Muslims and that pertain to the functions an Islamic government must assume....It is evident, then, that to assume the function of government is to acquire a means and not a spiritual station, for if government were a spiritual station, nobody would be able to either usurp it or abandon it. Government and the exercise of command acquire value only when they become the means for implementing the law of Islam and establishing the just Islamic order; then the person in charge of government may also earn some additional virtue and merit.

Some people, whose eyes have been dazzled by the things of this world, imagine that leadership and government represented in themselves dignity and high station for the Imams, so that if others come to exercise power, the world will collapse. Now the Soviet ruler, the British Prime Minister, and the American President all exercise power, and they are all unbelievers. They are unbelievers, but they have political power and influence, which they use to execute anti-human laws and policies for the sake of their own interests.

It is the duty of the Imams and the just *fuqaha* to use government institutions to execute divine law, establish the just Islamic order, and serve mankind. Government in itself represents nothing but pain and trouble for them, but what are they to do? They have been given a duty, a mission to fulfill; the governance of the *faqih* is nothing but the performance of a duty....

The meaning of the statement of the Imam that the *fuqaha* are the fortresses of Islam is that they have a duty to protect Islam and that they must do whatever is necessary to fulfill that duty. It is one of their most important duties and, moreover, an absolute duty, not a conditional one. It is an issue to which the *fuqaha* of Islam must pay particular attention. The religious teaching institution must give due thought to the matter and equip itself with the means and strength necessary to protect Islam in the fullest possible sense, just as the Most Noble Messenger and the Imams (peace be upon them) were the guardians of Islam, protecting its beliefs, laws, and institutions in the most comprehensive manner.

We have abandoned almost all aspects of our duty, restricting ourselves to passing on, from one generation to the next, certain parts of Islamic law and discussing them among ourselves. Many of the ordinances of Islam have virtually become part of the occult sciences, and Islam itself has become a stranger; only its name has survived.

All the penal provisions of Islam, which represent the best penal code ever devised for humanity, have been completely forgotten; nothing but their name has survived. As for the Qur'anic verses stipulating penalties and sanctions, "Nothing remains of them but their recitation." For example, we recite the verse: "Administer to the adulterer and the adultress a hundred lashes each" (24:2), but we do not know what to do when confronted with a case of adultery. We merely recite the verse in order to improve the quality of our recitation and to give each sound its full value. The actual situation prevailing in our society, the present state of the Islamic community, the prevalence of lewdness and corruption, the protection and support extended by our governments to adultery—none of this concerns us! It is enough that we understand what penalties have been provided for the adulterer and the adultress without attempting to secure their implementation or otherwise struggling against the existence of adultery in our society!...

Law is actually the ruler; the security of all is guaranteed by the law, and law is their refuge. Muslims and the people in general are free within the limits laid down by the law; when they are acting in accordance with the provisions of the law, no one has the right to tell them, "Sit here," or "Go there." An Islamic government does not resemble states where the people are deprived of all security and everyone sits at home trembling for fear of a sudden raid or attack by the agents of the state....

Verily God commands you to return trusts to their owners, and to act with justice when you rule among men. Verily God counsels you thus, and God is all-hearing, all-seeing. O you who believe, obey God and obey the Messenger and the holders of authority from among you [i.e., those entrusted with leadership and government]. When you dispute with each other concerning a thing, refer it to God and His Messenger; if you believe in God and the Last Day, this will be best for you and the result, most beneficial. (Qur'an 4:58–59)

Now it has been established that since all the concerns of religion constitute a divine trust, a trust that must be vested in its rightful possessors, a part of the trust must inevitably be government. Thus, in accordance with this verse, the conduct of all governmental affairs must be based on the criteria of justice, or to put it differently, on the law of Islam and the ordinances of the *shari'a*. The judge may not issue an incorrect verdict—i.e., one based on some illegitimate, non-Islamic code—nor may the judicial procedure he follows or the law on which he bases his verdict be non-Islamic and therefore invalid. For example, when those engaged in planning the affairs of the country draw up a fiscal program for the nation, they must not impose unjust taxes on peasants working publicly owned lands, reducing them to wretchedness and destroying the land and agriculture as a whole through the burden of excessive taxation. If the executive branch of government wishes to implement the juridical ordinances of the law and its penal provisions, they must not go beyond the limits of the law by inflicting extra lashes upon the offender or abusing him....

It is the duty of all of us to overthrow the *taghut*: i.e., the illegitimate political powers that now rule the entire Islamic world. The governmental apparatus of tyrannical and anti-popular regimes must be replaced by institutions serving the public good and administered according to Islamic law. In this way, an Islamic government will gradually come into existence. In the Qur'an, God Almighty has forbidden men to obey the *taghut*—illegitimate regimes— and encouraged them to rise up against kings, just as He commanded Moses to rebel. There are a number of traditions encouraging people to fight against oppressors and those who wish to pervert religion. The Imams (upon whom be peace), joined by their followers, the Shi'a, have always fought against tyrannical governments and illegitimate regimes, as one can easily see by examining their biographies and way of life. Most of the time they were subject to the pressures of tyrannical and oppressive rulers, and were compelled to observe *taqiya*[10] out of extreme fear—not fear for themselves, of course, but fear for their religion, as is evident from an examination of the relevant traditions. Tyrannical rulers, for their part, stood in terror of the Imams. They were aware that if they gave the Imams the slightest opportunity, they would rebel and deprive them of their life, which was synonymous with pleasure-seeking and licentiousness....

The Imams (upon whom be peace) not only fought against tyrannical rulers, oppressive governments, and corrupt courts themselves; they also summoned the Muslims to wage *jihad* against those enemies....

The Muslims will be able to live in security and tranquillity and preserve their faith and morals only when they enjoy the protection of a government based on justice and law, a government whose form, administrative system, and laws have been laid down by Islam. It is our duty now to implement and put into practice the plan of government established by Islam. I hope that by presenting the system of government and the political and social principles of Islam to broad segments of humanity, we will create a strong new current of thought and a powerful popular movement that will result in the establishment of an Islamic government.

O God, foreshorten the arms of the oppressors that are stretched out against the lands of the Muslims and root out all traitors to Islam and the Islamic countries. Awaken the heads of the Muslim states from their deep sleep so that they may exert themselves on behalf of their people's interests and renounce divisiveness and the quest for personal gain. Grant that the younger generation studying in the religious colleges and the universities may struggle to reach the sacred aims of Islam and strive together, with ranks united, first, to deliver the Islamic countries from the clutches of imperialism and its vile agents, and then to defend them. Grant that the *fuqaha* and the scholars may strive to guide and enlighten the minds of the people, to convey the sacred aims of Islam to all Muslims, particularly the younger generation, and to struggle for the establishment of an Islamic government. From You is success, and there is neither recourse nor strength except in God, the Exalted, the Sublime.

NOTES

1. *Azan*: the call to prayer.
2. *Vali amr*: "the one who holds authority," a term derived from Qur'an. 4:59: "O you who believe! Obey God, and obey the Messenger and the holders of authority (uli'lamr) from among you."
3. *Sayyids*: the descendants of the Prophet through his daughter Fatima and son-in-law 'Ali, the first of the Twelve Imams.
4. *Umma*: the entire Islamic community, without territorial or ethnic distinction.

5. *Kufr*: the rejection of divine guidance; the antithesis of Islam.
6. *Taghut*: one who surpasses all bounds in his despotism and tyranny and claims the prerogatives of divinity for himself, whether explicitly or implicitly.
7. *Shirk*: the assignment of partners to God, either by believing in a multiplicity of gods, or by assigning divine attributes and prerogatives to other-than-God.

8. Imam Riza: eighth of the Twelve Imams, born in 148/765 and died in 203/817 in Tus (Mashhad). According to Shi'i belief, he was poisoned by the Abbasid caliph Ma'mun, who had appointed him as his successor at first, but then grew fearful of the wide following he commanded (see p. 148). His shrine in Mashhad is one of the principal centers of pilgrimage and religious learning in Iran.

9. *Faqih*: one learned in the principles and ordinances of Islamic law, or more generally, in all aspects of the faith; plural, *Fuqaha.*

10. Taqiya: prudential dissimulation of one's true beliefs under conditions of acute danger, a practice based on Qur'an, 3:28.

African American Separatism and Integration In Historical Perspective

Jeffrey Crawford

The so-called American Negro group...while it is in no sense absolutely set off physically from its fellow Americans, has nevertheless a strong, hereditary cultural unity born of slavery, of common suffering, prolonged proscription, and curtailment of political and civil rights....Prolonged policies of segregation and discrimination have involuntarily welded the mass almost into a nation within a nation.

W. E. B. DuBois (1947)

Introduction

As the renowned African American social scientist and activist, W. E. B. DuBois (1868–1963), observed, African American identity developed under conditions imposed upon the group from the outside. The experiences "of slavery, of common suffering, prolonged proscription, and curtailment of political and civil rights," ensured that group identity would develop in complex ways. For even as Africans in America resisted white domination, their circumstances demanded that they borrow, adapt and use central aspects of their oppressor's cultures.

Thus, while all culture is complex, the cultural experience of African Americans, as of any oppressed people, has additional dimensions of complexity. Beyond the usual interactions of the educated elite and the folk, there have also been the interactions between the Black inside and a white outside, each with its own elites and folks. The cultural grammar of the Black inside has roots in West Africa, but African Americans, like European Americans, have spoken a vocabulary that derives partly from ancient Palestine, from Greece, Rome and the Enlightenment. Yet there are differences, differences demanded by the history of systematic oppression and exploitation to which DuBois referred. Black people in America have had to know both themselves and the white outside, simply to survive. Whites, as a group, have been able to take much more for granted, because they have held a predominance of power.

One expression of the complexity of African American culture is the emergence and development of tendencies toward both separatism and integration. Each tendency has a long history and

This paper owes much to the thought and writing of Vincent Harding.

has played significant roles in promoting the interests of African Americans in what Vincent Harding called "this strangely promised land."

No single cause divides integration and separatism, but a central distinction does exist between them. Separatists have stressed the need for *independence* from whites, while integrationists have stressed the *interdependence* of the races. Still, Martin Luther King, Jr., an integrationist among integrationists, urged African Americans to work fervently for group identity, claiming that "integration" within the race was a necessary condition for integration between the races. W. E. B. DuBois, on the other hand, always acknowledged racial interdependence, even when in his most separatist period he advocated using social separatism to build a cooperative Black economy within competitive America.

Viewing separatism and integration as systems of concepts and precepts, will not reveal much about the historical processes out of which each has grown nor the needs each has served. It is more helpful to see integration and separatism as sometimes conflicting, but also complementary, strategies for the development of that "almost…nation within a nation" of which DuBois wrote. Viewed as alternative strategies for group uplift, the motivation for each tendency is clearly seen to grow out of the social, cultural and economic needs of the group, and how those needs have been shaped by historical circumstances. By viewing separatism and integration as "time and space bound," i.e., as development strategies aimed at meeting group needs within specific historical and institutional settings, the forms each has taken can be better understood and the likely continued influence of each tendency on America and the world can be better illuminated.

We first explore the tension between integration and separatism by considering Martin Luther King, Jr., and Malcolm X. The second section finds a precedent for the interplay between King and Malcolm in the relationship of Frederick Douglass and Martin Delany in the mid-1800s. The third section investigates how religion has shaped African American identity and how a central appeal of some forms of separatism has been a rejection of Christianity. The final section looks at the period since the civil rights movement of the 1960s to see how both integration and separatism continue to develop and interact.

King and Malcolm

Assessing the progress between the 1954 *Brown* vs. *Board of Education* decision and the Voting Rights Act of 1965, Martin Luther King, Jr. (1929–1968) raised a number of questions. Why had urban riots become a regular summer event? Why was there a "white backlash" against racial progress? Why were some declaring the civil rights movement to be a myth? And why were there increasing calls for Black Power and separatism? King's answer to these questions is revealing.

For King, the civil rights movement had two phases. The first was a struggle for legal equality and for African Americans to be treated with some degree of decency. King argued that this first phase ended with the passage of the Voting Rights Act of 1965. The second, and more problematic, phase was a struggle for substantive economic, social and political equality. According to King, a majority of white Americans may have been comfortable with the goals of the first phase, but the goals of the second phase were another matter. White Americans generally agreed that "the Negro should be spared the lash of brutality," but few whites had ever been committed to a racially egalitarian society in which African Americans held as much economic and political power as whites, proportionate to their numbers.

King's analysis had clear implications for separatism. If whites at best were uncommitted to substantive equality for Blacks, and at worst opposed it, then it would be irrational and counterproductive to work with them in the struggle for equality. Thus, some form of separatism seemed to be a virtual logical consequence of King's analysis. It is revealing to see how King avoided that consequence.

As with virtually every position he took, King argued on both practical and moral grounds, attempting to show how morality and practicality converged. Essentially King's practical argument was that separatism would not work because a minority organized solely for its own purposes could not effect changes sufficient to achieve economic, social and political equality. This practical argument was bolstered by King's moral vision which saw human beings as irrevocably interconnected and interdependent. The moral challenge for King was to achieve a social order in which the equal moral worth of all human persons would be recognized and matched by substantively equal opportunities and status. An essential part of this struggle, King believed, was the creative power of undeserved suffering. Those who suffered undeservedly for righteousness sake—in this case mostly African Americans—were the leading historical force in a difficult, yet redemptive, task that could save America and show a troubled world a way out of its problems. Jesus, rather than being an impractical idealist, was a practical realist, because his theology of love, forgiveness and redemptive suffering, promised real solutions to the age-old problems of poverty, war and oppression.

King saw America as facing a dilemma, the two horns of which were racism and democracy. King's moral vision, which for him provided the only sure and final practical solutions to social problems, led him to believe that the dilemma could be resolved in favor of democracy. He expressed this vision when he recounted a scene at the Montgomery airport as several thousand demonstrators waited for planes.

As I stood with them and saw white and Negro, nuns and priests, ministers and rabbis, labor organizers, lawyers, doctors, housemaids and shopworkers brimming with vitality and enjoying a rare comradeship, I knew I was seeing a microcosm of the mankind of the future in this moment of luminous and genuine brotherhood.

King was concerned not just with desegregation, but with true integration based on a profound and challenging moral vision. His moral vision implied not just progress and improvement for Black people: it implied social transformation. In seeing the fate of the Black "nation within" as tied to a greater, providential destiny, King drew on a deeply rooted theme of African American culture. For King the uplift of his people was a first step toward a larger destiny in which America could help show all the peoples of the world how to take strength from their diversity and live together peacefully in our "world house."

King spoke as an American, but also as a leader of the African American group and in terms significantly unique to that group. During his time he epitomized the integrationist tendency and integrationist leadership. His voice and vision were particularly well suited to the first phase of the movement, the southern based struggle to end legalized segregation and achieve some degree of dignity and respect. For many southern Blacks, King articulated their deepest knowledge of who they were, of their ability to confront their oppressors and to overcome. For many Americans, and for people throughout the world, King expressed their fondest hopes for justice and peace.

A different voice may have been better suited to the mood and experience of many African Americans in the urban North and West. There were no racial laws in Los Angeles or New York, but inequality was just as pervasive as in the South. Thus, outside the South, the first and second phases of the struggle, the fight for dignity and for substantive equality, were more closely linked. For many African Americans in the urban centers of the North and West, the voice and vision of Malcolm X (1925–1965) did what King's did in the South.

Malcolm agreed with the fundamentals of King's explanation of the white backlash and growing Black frustration: whites were opposed to substantive economic, political and social equality for African Americans. Unlike King, however, Malcolm accepted the consequences of this analysis: since whites were hostile to substantive equality for African Americans, it made no sense to work with them.

Where the rhetoric of the Southern civil rights movement was primarily moral and spiritual, Malcolm's rhetoric was primarily political. He rejected the notion that undeserved suffering had a redemptive and transformative power, arguing that Black people had a duty, not just a right, to defend themselves against violence. Malcolm advocated a just war theory in which African people in America, and around the world, had a right to revolutionary action because their fundamental human rights were being systematically violated. His argument that revolutions are justified when people's rights are systematically violated, and when peaceful means to redress their grievances have failed, are reminiscent of John Locke's (1632–1704) *Second Treatise Of Government* and the American Declaration of Independence. For Malcolm, the civil rights movement had provided ample evidence that substantive equality would not be achieved without at least the threat of force. He argued that in America, as elsewhere around the world and throughout history, it was perfectly legitimate to struggle for social, political and economic equality by any means necessary.

Malcolm identified American democracy as white nationalism, i.e., as government of, by and for white people, and prescribed Black Nationalism as the appropriate response. Within the United States Black people should control the economic, political and social lives of their communities. Internationally, people of color should join together to end white supremacy everywhere. Thus, even as King saw an international dimension for the Black struggle in America, so did Malcolm, though through somewhat different eyes. Ultimately for both men, African Americans achieving their legitimate goals in the United States implied some form of social transformation, both here and throughout the world.

King and Malcolm were complex men and this brief account necessarily misses the dynamic changes each made in response to his expanding experience and the turbulent times each helped to shape. While Malcolm never discounted racism as a major factor in Black oppression, he ultimately rejected the notion that whites were inherently devilish. Instead he came to see capitalism as a devilish system and the racism which permeated American institutions as helping to support capitalism. This change led him to invite contributions from whites and to seek a relationship with some largely white socialist political groups he saw as most egalitarian and progressive.

Malcolm did not, however, give up the idea that Black unity must precede Black-white unity and he continued to stress the necessity of African people organizing independently for their own purposes. His emphasis on racial solidarity led him to reach out even to mainline Black civil rights leaders he formerly had attacked, saying

The problem facing our people here in America is bigger than all the personal or organizational differences. Therefore, as leaders, we must stop worrying about the threat that we seem to think we pose to each other's personal prestige, and concentrate our united efforts toward solving the unending hurt that is being done daily to our people here in America.

This attempt to bridge the gap between integration and separatism indicates how the two tendencies interact with and reinforce each other. In a speech Malcolm gave in Selma, Alabama, in 1965 he called upon whites to listen to King and support Black voting rights, implying that if they did not deal with King, they would have to deal with him and others like him.

If Malcolm was a man in transition when he was killed, so was King. Turning increasingly to the struggle for economic, political and social equality, King became more aware of the economic basis of oppression and the difficulties of making capitalism socially responsible. His vision of social transformation and social justice led him to oppose U.S. involvement in Vietnam and to support sanitation workers in Memphis. As had Malcolm, King began to focus increasingly on the interconnections between the oppression of poor people in America and around the world.

Martin Luther King, Jr., and Malcolm X have come to symbolize two different responses to being Black in America: Martin the integrationist and Malcolm the separatist, the former a healer and pacifier, the latter a warrior. This picture is an oversimplification, of course, for each sought both to heal and to confront. Such an oversimplification is dangerous, for it suggests that one man had *the* right approach, while the other's was wrong and should be rejected. Rather than rejecting either, it would seem more fruitful to understand the bases of each approach and why each continues to have a strong appeal. Thus viewed, separatism and integration can be seen as complementary positions, each challenging, but also strengthening, the other. Indeed, each tendency seems an essential part of how African people have dealt with life in America. The historical background of separatism and integration certainly supports such a conclusion.

Integration and Separatism through the Civil War

Frederick Douglass (1818–1895) and Martin Delany (1812–1885) came of age when traditions of protest, resistance, and accommodation were already well established. An account of the background of these traditions is helpful to understand these men and the creative interplay between them.

As in the twentieth century, it is too simple to say that nineteenth century separatism was "radical," while integration was "conservative." Often separatists did not challenge the cultural, economic or social status quo. For some the goal was not to change the *status quo*, but to escape from it. Also, many separatists, especially among the educated, had imbibed elements of the prevailing racism and cultural chauvinism, including negative views of Africa.

A positive assessment of Europe, particularly England, and an endorsement of Christianity as the true religion, informed both emigrationism and civilizationism, two major nineteenth century separatist tendencies. Emigrationism held that the races should separate, Africans leaving America to build an independent nation or nations. Civilizationism held that "Europeanized" Africans should bring the benefits of Western culture, including Christianity, both to the African continent and to those trapped in slavery in America.

Emigrationism and civilizationism were natural allies, emigrationists often seeing their mission as a civilizing one. Some even worked with the essentially white African Colonization Society, a group condemned by most white and Black abolitionists because it was organized partly by slaveholders to rid America of free Black people and the problems they presented. The following excerpt from an appeal by Robert Breckinridge to the Maryland State Colonization Society in 1838 is telling.

The moment one city, one single city of free civilized Christian blacks, is placed near the equator, on the western coast of Africa, then the mighty prize is won! From that instant, the whole problem in all its complexity and vastness as to the black race, is solved. The slavetrade dies, the civilization and conversion of Africa is fixed; the destiny of the race of Ham is redeemed; the equatorial region of the earth reclaimed; and the human race itself launched into a new and glorious career, of which all the triumphs of the past afford no parallel.

Doubtless Breckinridge outdid himself, but no hyperbole was intended. Civilizationist ideas also influenced many Black and white abolitionists who were not emigrationists. To be educated in America in the mid-1800s meant to be Christian (by values, if not confession), Western, and often Anglo-philic. The prevailing values of the day were victorian, stressing chastity, hard work, self-control, frugality and prudence. Abolitionists generally held these values, as did most educated European Americans.

Leading American intellectuals such as Emerson, Thoreau and Whitman challenged these values without necessarily rejecting them, but such cultural countercurrents lacked appeal to the Black intelligensia. Departing from the mainstream of Euro-American norms was not seen as an effective strategy for a group trying to prove its acceptability in the face of continual denial. The prevailing consciousness among the Black elite was that African people in America and beyond needed more, not less, civilization. The task of the elite was to achieve a high level of civilization for themselves, thus disproving a central racist myth about Black capability, and then to provide enlightened leadership to the benighted masses held in slavery in America, or left in savagery in Africa.

To leave the account here, however, would distort the picture, for many African Americans did offer radical challenges to the values, norms and practices of white America, and rebellions such as that led by Nat Turner in 1831 were a clear rejection of any notions of white superiority. Two works published in 1829 explicitly challenged the dominance and values of European culture: Robert Alexander Young's *Ethiopian Manifesto* and David Walker's *Appeal*.

Both Young and Walker thought African people shared a divinely ordained destiny as agents of God's retribution against the white nation for its sinful practice of slavery. They urged captives to resist slavery by all effective means, including armed revolt, and both authors chastised their enslaved brothers and sisters for complicity in allowing slavery to continue. Young's and Walker's apocalyptic ethiopianism, which saw those who had been last becoming first, was a radical critique of white superiority. This critique is deeply embedded in Black American religion and will be explored further in the next section.

Strong integrationist tendencies were also well established by the early 19th century. Such tendencies were expressed in what the contemporary African American historian Vincent Harding calls The Great Tradition of Black Protest, the mainline of Black moral and political rhetoric that challenged America to be true to its founding ideals of freedom and justice for all. The center of The Great Tradition was integrationist and Frederick Douglass stood at that center.

Douglass, and others in The Great Tradition, accepted America as their current and future home and claimed citizenship by right of the labor and suffering of their people. In working for their own uplift and the redemption of the whole nation, it was necessary and proper to cooperate with whites of good will. Ultimately, the children of Europe and of Africa could learn to live and work together in the general society, even as they had learned to do in the abolitionist movement. Behind the processes and crises of the day, history revealed a providential plan: the emergence of a higher level of morality, justice and social development in America that could provide a model for the rest of the world. Extending The Great Tradition forward into the 1960s, it is clear that Martin Luther King Jr., was the heir of Frederick Douglass.

As King would later, Douglass stressed the interdependence of the races, taking as a "settled point that the destiny of the colored man is bound up with that of the white people of the country." Douglass' stress on interdependence was aimed partly at Black people who were ambivalent on this very point, but he spoke to whites also, and he did not mean to comfort them. He asserted that African people in America belong to the country and that "to imagine we shall ever be eradicated is absurd and ridiculous." Therefore, the question for white

philosophers and statesmen ought to be, what principles should dictate the policy of the [nation] toward us? We shall neither die out, nor be driven out; but shall go with [whites], either as a testimony against them, or as an evidence in their favor throughout their generations. We are on their hands and clearly must remain there forever.

The strength of The Great Tradition has always been its dual appeal to the reality that Black people were not going to go away and to the possibility of a "color blind" society that would be morally just. Yet, part of the strength of this dual appeal has also been part of its weakness. The rhetorical and moral force of The Tradition has spoken to the hope that a racist nation would solve the problem of its own racism. This hope has always been problematic. As King would point out more than a century later, even when the legal structure of racial oppression ended, white Americans never acted forcefully in support of full equality for Black people. Integra-

tionist strategies for development have had the appeal of Douglass' demographic sobriety on their side but the intransigence of racism and indifference against them. Separatism has exploited this intransigence and indifference.

If Douglass was at the center of The Great Tradition, Martin Delany was outside it, or perhaps at its outer edges. Delany asserted that "no people can be free who themselves do not constitute an essential part of the *ruling element* of the country in which they live." And it was clear to Delany that whites were not about to let Black people become an essential part of that ruling element. Freedom, therefore, implied emigration.

Delany urged African people around the world to unite immediately to preserve and develop themselves. Aware of the political nationalism current in Europe and among Americans in their recent annexation of large areas of Mexico (1845), Delany argued that each great racial group was responsible for its own expansion, consolidation and well-being. African people needed to take charge of their own destiny without depending on white benevolence.

Though his phraseology differed somewhat from Malcolm X's, Delany's view was essentially that American democracy was white nationalism. He counseled African people to adopt the actions and standards of their oppressors, rather than being fooled by what Malcolm would call the oppressor's "hypocritical tricknology." If one side of Douglass' sword was meant to cut the consciences of whites, one side of Delany's was meant to prick the pride of Blacks. He asked

Have we not now sufficient intelligence among us to understand our actual condition, and determine for ourselves what is best to be done? If we have not now, we never shall have, and should at once cease prating about our equality, capacity, and all that.

Like David Walker before him, Delany argued that the problem in America was not just the slave states of the South, but the federal government and the whole white nation. His arguments took on added force when the earlier fugitive slave laws— the first passed within a year of the ratification of the Constitution—were updated in the Fugitive Slave Act of 1850. The Act strengthened federal support for slavery, effectively broadening the power of whites in general to harrass Blacks. The passage of the Act added urgency to emigrationist activities, including the highly pragmatic strategy of extending the tracks of the underground railroad to Canada. Though the figures are a matter of debate, one researcher has claimed that between 1850 and the outbreak of the Civil War in 1861, fifteen to twenty thousand people took that extended ride.

The Fugitive Slave Act had a radicalizing effect. Douglass and Delany, who had worked together on *The North Star* for some years, now split apart. Some of Douglass' most strident rhetoric came after the Act was passed, including his 4th of July address in 1852, arguably his harshest condemnation of American moral hypocrisy. For a brief period, Douglass even looked into emigration as an alternative to integration.

The stormy period of the 1850s ended when the Civil War broke out in 1861. After the Emancipation officially sanctioned the use of Black troops, a national group of recruiters was formed, including both Douglass and Delany. The War's manifest power to change conditions effectively undercut, at least for a time, arguments against involvement in the affairs of the nation.

The War was seen as providential, a partial realization of the judgment Walker and Young had prophesied. Separatists and integrationsits were pulled together into the same deep and swift waters. Thus, even as Martin and Malcolm were forced to explore the tensions between them, and the tendencies they represented, Douglass and Delany found some common ground. The Civil War, though many of its promises went unrealized, brought African Americans together in new ways and under new circumstances. One version of "The Battle Hymn of the Republic" sung by Black troops included the following verse, indicative of the new circumstances.

We are done with hoeing cotton,
We are done with hoeing corn.
We are colored Yankee soldiers,
As sure as you are born.
When Massa hears us shouting,
He will think 'tis Gabriel's horn,
As we go marching on.

Emigrationism did not disappear, but the War and its aftermath lessened the urgency to escape and brought new opportunities for social, economic and political development within the United States. The African American experience had entered a new phase in which the overriding concern was not ending or escaping slavery, but raising the masses who had been held in slavery. The twentieth century American historian Eugene Geneovese claims that when the free Black troops who sang their own version of "The Battle Hymn" met the slaves of the countryside, they could see "a black nation at its genesis."

Religion and the Roots of Identity

Whether or not genesis of the Black nation lies in the Civil War, Genovese identifies one of the main differences between African Americans and other American groups. While other groups arrived in America with a national identity intact and have been relatively free to maintain that identity or reject it, African Americans have forged their identity here. African American identity may be based on significant African cultural carryovers, but Africans did not form a people when they were brought to this country. Rather, they have become a people through coping with the conditions they have faced here. This difference from other groups is part of why African Americans are the creative source of so much that is distinctive not just of them, but of America as a whole.

Another distinction between African Americans and other groups is the sense that their destiny is central to the destiny of America and even the world. We have seen that this sense of destiny has taken various forms, from the apocalyptic ethiopianism of Young and Walker, which stressed divine retribution, to the integrationist vision of King, which stressed divine redemption. Vincent Harding expressed a belief in the centrality of African American destiny to America as follows:

and what now is our destiny, and this nation's future, if these costly black dreams of freedom, long nurtured in the fires of persecution are broken and bastardized— or meanly forgotten—in a ruthless and unprincipled process of Americanization?

To better understand these two differences between African Americans and other American groups it will be helpful to look more closely at religion.

Harding points out that among the African peoples whose histories were "jammed together" in America were Muslims who knew the stories of the captive people who followed a certain Moses. Whether from Muslim or Christian sources, the appeal of the Moses story is clear: an oppressed people could be delivered through divine intervention. The God of Moses was seen as a God of justice, acting on behalf of the oppressed and against the oppressor. Ideas of divine deliverance and divine judgment are so deeply embedded in African American religious consciousness that they appear both in the United Negro Improvement Association of the Black nationalist Marcus Garvey (1887–1940) which was Christian and in the Nation of Islam, which rejected Christianity.

The implications of the Moses story extend beyond God's punishment of the oppressor, however, to His prescription for His people and how they must build a nation. In the story, the people could not keep faith both with God and with Pharoah, so God commanded Moses to demand that Pharoah let His people leave Egypt so they could worship Him appropriately. The story encodes the painful, tortuous and dynamic mechanisms of nation building, placing shared suffering at the heart of this process. Because they suffered together under Pharoah's oppression, Abraham's people were more a nation when they left Egypt than when they arrived.

As indicated in the quotation from DuBois at the beginning of this paper, African American identity has emerged from broadly similar conditions of suffering and resistance. The appeal of the Moses story, therefore, comes not only from the promise that an oppressed people may achieve freedom, but also from lessons about the bases of kinship and how identity develops and is shaped. A sense of identity may grow from experiences of shared suffering and resistance, but the process is not straightforward. Backsliding is common, there being no shortage of golden calves, and keeping the faith is always problematic. The experience of African people in America matches the cultural grammar of the Moses story on many levels, from promises and covenants, kept and broken, to the need to separate so that a people's destiny may be realized.

If the mythos of African American Christianity is somewhat distinct—and it is only *somewhat* distinct—from that of white Christianity, its institutional history differs more sharply. Formally, a separation may be seen by the 1770s, and as early as 1787 Richard Allen (1760–1831) and other African Christians had formed the Free African Society, a precursor to the breakaway African Methodist Episcopal Church. But before the formal separation of Allen and others, slave preachers had held sway at secret and forbidden meetings of the "invisible institution" since the early 1700s. They forged a Christianity that spoke directly, and in its own idiom, to the peculiar condition of African people in America.

The African American historian of religion Gayraud Wilmore argues that the theology of this earliest of Black churches was based on the African belief that "both the individual and the community had a continuous involvement with the spirit world in the practical affairs of daily life." Wilmore sees Black religion in America from its beginning as having a "radical programmatic secularity" as well as a "pervasive feeling" about the deeply spiritual nature of historical experience. African American forms of worship, such as call and response, are evidence of African influences on African American Christianity. So are the histories of the slave revolts. For instance, as Gabriel and Martin Prosser organized their 1800 slave revolt, they sought the help of native-born Africans with reputations for prophecy, despite the fact that Martin was a Christian preacher.

The Black church, then, before its official founding and recognition began as a community living out a shared historical destiny based on deep spiritual roots. These roots were related to, but also separate from, those of European Americans. Further, both the mythos and institutional forms of Black religion in America had strong elements which supported political separatism. Finally, much of the creative power of African American culture which has shaped the rest of America, including the musical traditions of spirituals, blues and jazz, grew out of traditions of worship and celebration first established in the Black church.

The religion of the slaves in the South, however, was not, and could not have been, uniformly radical. Christianity embodies significant theological tendencies toward accomodation, forgiveness, and social conservatism, and the Christianity among the slaves often drew on these tendencies. Quite naturally, the white slaveholders reinforced the conservative dimensions of Christianity. Their ability to organize culture to suit their needs, while not absolute, still exerted a powerful influence on Black people to accomodate to a system that was brutal and demeaning, but that promised eternal rewards and to which temporal resistance was very costly. Genovese sees the conservative essence of Christianity on two levels: first, it forged a bond between master and servant because both were children of the same God and members of the same religious body; second, it stressed individual rather than collective salvation. Thus, even as Christianity established a common basis in faith for Black identity, and powerful institutional and theological bases for individual dignity, it weakened some separatist tendencies of that identity.

The accomodationist aspects of Christianity partially explain the appeal of separatist movements that have opposed Christianity. The Moorish Science movement, led by Noble Drew Ali, was an early twentieth-century example. Moorish Science was essentially a religious movement which stressed that African Americans should reject Christianity and rediscover their true identity as Moors or Asiatics. The Nation of Islam, or Black Muslim movement, beginning in the 1930s and continuing until today, is in many ways the ideological heir of Moorish Science. Specifically, the Nation argues that because Christianity is the religion of their oppressors Black people should reject it and reidentify with their Afroasiatic origins.

The Nation of Islam has had a significant impact on popular consciousness, promoting positive views of Africa and greater identification with, and pride in, African culture. Malcolm X was an important force in promoting these shifts in consciousness and, as a spokesman for the Nation, one part of his critique was directed at white versions of history that overlooked the important contributions African people have made to world civilization. Even the attractiveness of orthodox Islam to some African Americans is partly due to the perception that Islam was established in Africa before Christianity and does not have as problematic a history there.

In contrast to Moorish Science and the Nation of Islam, Marcus Garvey's United Negro Improvement Association, which flourished in the early 1920s, did not reject Christianity. Garvey's brand of Christianity, however, was not integrationist, but accepted race separation as a virtue sanctioned both by God and Nature. Garvey saw the religious and political leaders of white Christian nations as creating God in their own images, and he founded the African Orthodox Church partly to promote Black images of the Madonna and Child and the worship of a Black Christ. Thus, though Garvey did not reject Christianity, his reinterpretation of it allowed his movement to tap some of the same rejectionist energy as Moorish Science and the Nation. Garvey's major appeal was in the urban North, which is precisely where the Nation of Islam, and particularly Malcolm X, were to have their greatest impact. This fact, among others, has led the African American social scientist C. Eric Lincoln to conclude that the Nation is the ideological heir of Moorish Science, but the organizational heir of Garvey.

Moorish Science, Garveyism and the Nation of Islam were part of a broader twentieth-century movement away from the African civilizationism of the nineteenth century. This movement away from civilizationism is supported by cultural developments outside the African American community, including the growth of moral and cultural relativism, Freud's challenge to puritan and victorian standards of sexual morality, and Jung's embrace of traditional cultures as sources of meaning. Modern European art borrowed freely from African sources around the turn of the century, even as colonialism gained a lock on Africa. In America, folk and popular culture, including jazz and blues, spread to a white audience and loosened the hold of European high culture on American standards of taste. The Harlem Renaissance of the 1920s reflected white ambivalence about race and Black American and Carribean culture provided dynamic alternatives to what some saw as stale and stilted white culture. Finally, two devastating world wars raised questions about European cultural superiority, and by the late 1940s significant numbers of European and Euro-American intellectuals were in revolt against their own cultures and systems of meaning. Existentialism, and the growth of Marxism, are two examples of this revolt. Thus, even as civilizationist ideas were increasingly rejected by African Americans in the twentieth century, the broader culture became somewhat more open to different and more positive images of Africa and African people.

Integration and Separatism Today

Where do things stand today? What progress has been made toward the full economic, social and political equality which King identified as the goal of the second phase of the civil rights movement? What forms have separatism and integration taken recently? These are among the issues explored in this final section.

As noted earlier, Martin Luther King identified two phases of the civil rights movement. The first phase was a struggle to end legalized segregation. The second phase sought to achieve full economic, social and political equality with whites. This has not happened, although there has been a significant growth of the African American middle class and Black people are more fully represented throughout society than at any previous time. Virtually all the historical varieties of integration and separatism have found some contemporary expression. Over all the African American ideological landscape is richer than ever, and Black people are represented within the camps of traditional American conservatism and liberalism, in a continuation of traditional civil rights organizations such as King's Southern Christian Leadership Conference and the NAACP, as well as in a significant growth of orthodox Islam and a revival of the Nation of Islam.

The diversification of the group has taken place within a single irreversible set of economic developments that help explain why the Black middle class has expanded while there has also been a growth of the Black underclass. Over the last thirty years in the most economically developed countries (the United States, Western Europe and Japan) industrial and assembly jobs increasingly have either been exported to less developed countries or automated out of existence. The developed economies have become information driven and their workforces have become increasingly college educated. The shrinking of the industrial job base in the U.S. means that stable high wage industrial jobs which attracted millions of African Americans to the North and West since the 1940s have been replaced by low wage

service sector jobs. Two adults working forty hours per week at five dollars per hour for fifty weeks will make twenty thousand dollars which puts a family of four below the poverty line.

These structural changes have led to an absolute increase in poverty, an increase which has affected all ethnic groups, but which has had a particularly great impact on African Americans. The Black middle class has approximately doubled, due partly to the expansion of the knowledge sector of the economy and the increased educational and other opportunities opened up by the civil rights movement. At the same time African Americans without college training or technical skills, those who would have filled industrial jobs had there been any to fill, have gone wanting. One result has been increasing class differentiation and alienation of the Black middle class from the Black poor.

The last thirty years have clarified several issues for those who have made it to the middle class, while also raising some new issues. Even in integrating increasingly into the economic mainstream, African Americans have not in general given up their group identification. Virtually every professional and occupational organization has within it a separately organized African American section, from the American Philosophical Society to the Fraternal Order of Police. This suggests that the primary goal of integration for most African Americans was not to assimilate culturally, but to increase their opportunities for education and to get a fair shot at job positions for which they were qualified. Still, it should be clear that American society is so far from being color blind that separate organizational structures within mainstream institutions are the better part of prudence.

A further indication that African Americans are interested in maintaining cultural distinctness is that after experiencing declining enrollments in the 1970s and 1980s enrollment at African American colleges and universities has been increasing. Middle class African Americans are choosing to send their children to Black schools for a variety of reasons, including a widespread sense that these schools, even in cases in which most of the faculty is white, do a better job of graduating students who are well equipped to serve both themselves and the group.

The last thirty years have also raised some new issues. In many areas of the country other minorities outnumber African Americans. Increasing immigration from South and Central America, the Middle East and from Asia, present new economic and cultural dynamics. Tensions over jobs and opportunities now often arise between Blacks and other minorities, rather than between Blacks and whites. Another dimension of the changing demographics of America is that the traditional majority, European Americans, will soon be a minority, outnumbered by all the other minorities put together. What such developments imply for African Americans and for separatism and integration is not clear. What is clear is that traditional assumptions about "race relations" in America may need to be rethought. The shift in the late 1980s from *Black* or *Afro-American* to *African American* may be a partial response to the emerging conditions mentioned above. The readiness with which the term has taken hold suggests that many African Americans see themselves as a group among other groups of hyphenated Americans who are rightfully proud of their cultural roots outside America.

The following thumb-nail sketches of three ways of thinking about group identity suggest some of the current diversity of African American thought on issues of separatism and integration.

Afrocentrism puts revaluation of and reidentification with Africa at the center of a cultural ideology of renewal and uplift. Current "Afrocentrism" is heir to what in the 1960s became known as "cultural nationalism," one of whose central tenets is that ethnicity takes precedence over class and economic issues in understanding and organizing to change social conditions. History, for many Afrocentrists, has been a history of culture and race conflict, more than a history of class conflict.

Most broadly Afrocentrism is intended by scholars such as Molefi Asante, Chairperson of African American Studies at Temple University, to designate a world view which places Africa and African people at the center of study and concern. Following the work of the Senegalese scholar, Cheikh Anta Diop, Asante argues that the founders of the civilization which flowered 5,000 years ago in Egypt were culturally and racially African. The great civilization of Egypt is seen as the archetypal African culture and as the basis for much that made ancient Greece what it was. Asante postulates an "African Cultural System" which stands behind Egypt, but is also revealed in Egypt, and which is embodied in virtually all other African cultures, including the cultures of African people in North and South America. He sees the elucidation and practicing of this African Cultural System as a process of group reconstruction and renewal. Afrocentrism is so far from the civilizationism of the nineteenth century that it seeks the value basis for its proposed reconstruction in Africa, not in the West.

A central project of Afrocentrism that is reflected in political battles going on today is a critique of the current K-12 and university curriculum on the basis that it is "Eurocentric." Afrocentrists argue that the curriculum gives white students an advantage over Black students, because it reinforces positive views of all things European, but downgrades all things African. Thus, while the current curriculum is intelligible and motivating to whites, it turns African American students off. The argument continues that the development and introduction of curricula which are based on the African Cultural System will enhance the academic performance of Black youth. Of course this is an empirical claim which may turn out to be true or not. Regardless of the efficacy of Afrocentric curricula, it is clear that the aim is to reach out to the Black poor and help students in schools and communities which are often seen as, and often are, dysfunctional. Other aspects of Afrocentrism, from psychology to sociology and history have a similar focus on group uplift and empowerment.

It remains to be seen how this Afrocentric variation on cultural identity and group reconstruction will develop in an increasingly ethnically diverse America. One possibility would be to promote a multi-cultural model of the institutions; another would be to foster increasingly separate directions. It seems likely that varieties of Afrocentrism will go both ways.

The thought of Albert Murray, novelist, professor and jazz critic, contrasts sharply with Afrocentrism. He acknowledges that American society is economically and politically unequal, but argues that it has been and continues to be one of the most culturally open societies in the world. Taking African American music as a guiding analytic metaphor, Murray sees America as a cultural explosion characterized by improvization on themes drawn from around the world, as well as grown right here. Murray sees culture as far too dynamic to be captured in projects like Asante's. Since America is already relatively open and democratic, the goal should be to make it more so.

It is counterproductive from Murray's perspective for African Americans to ground their values in the African past because to do so diverts attention from the exploits of African people in America. Interpreting the underground railroad as "an extension of the American quest for democracy brought to its highest level of epic heroism," he cites Harriet Tubman and Frederick Douglass as "adequate historical as well as mythological documentation for all that really matters" in the establishment of a Black national identity. He argues further that being culturally American already implies whites accepting themselves as part-Black, for culturally Americans are "part Yankee, part backwoodsman and Indian—and part Negro!"

After pointing out that America is much more biologically and culturally mixed than is often admitted, Murray proposes getting on with the business of learning to play the American games of power politics and economics. He puts forward a critique of the Great Tradition of Black Protest reminiscent of Martin Delany, ("Negro leaders, spokesmen, and even social technicians...have been addressing...moral issues and not the actualities of local, state, and national power"), and predicts that as more Black leaders

become more deeply...involved with the practical requirements of government in action and hence more personally familiar with the chord structure and progression of official maneuvers, the extension of the riff-style into politics is inevitable.

Murray represents an optimistic view of America and of all the cultural strains still in the mix here. Culture has no end point, for Murray. It is found, and created, in the living. His brand of integrationism, which does not exclude voting as a racial block, seems particularly well suited to an America which is becoming increasingly ethnically diverse and in which African Americans will continue to need the flexibility to play off others.

Manning Marable, an historian and political scientist at the University of Colorado at Boulder, argues that the three main tendencies of integration, emigration and the building of separate institutions within America all continue to be viable responses to the conditions African Americans have faced. For Marable each of these three responses grows out of concrete historical conditions and group needs. Access to mainstream institutions, repatriation to Africa and independent and separate institutions within America all are legitimate goals and should be supported. Marable's broader vision of America is of an egalitarian "Multi-cultural Democracy," in which African Americans and other ethnic minorities, as well as gays and lesbians, poor people, feminists, environmentalists, peace activists and working people in general can form a majoritarian movement toward common goals while maintaining their own traditions of thought and culture. Only through such a movement, Marable argues, can the persistent problems of racism and poverty be effectively overcome.

Marable represents a continuing tradition of African American social and political thought that draws on the ideas of the German social philosopher Karl Marx (1818–1883). Marable's analysis, in contrast to much Afrocentrist thought, stresses the class basis of African American oppression and sees the primary motive of racist ideology as the facilitation of labor exploitation. Yet Marable's brand of democratic socialism recognizes the importance of culture in shaping consciousness and he acknowledges and attempts to accomodate the diversity of American and of African American culture within his theory of social transformation. By stressing the legitimacy of both integration and separatism, he seeks to make a strength out of diversity and sees his approach as expanding on the common ground Malcolm X and Martin Luther King had begun to find late in their careers.

As these brief accounts of Asante, Murray and Marable suggest African American intellectuals continue to grapple with issues of integration and separatism from a number of different perspectives and within dynamically changing circumstances. Of course, the big picture, within the academy and beyond, is more varied and dynamic than can be described here.

A final development of the last decades that needs to be looked at is the significant increase in the number of African American elected officials. Accompanying this increase has been the maintenance of some old alliances and the weakening of others. Black elected officials are overwhelmingly affiliated with the Democratic party, reflecting that the traditional alliance of white liberals and African American civil rights leaders is holding firm, at least for the present. The long-standing Black-Jewish alliance appears to be weakening, however. A number of reasons may be cited for the strains in the relationship, but at least one is that to be seen as credible by their constituencies it has become increasingly necessary for Black political leaders to demonstrate their independence. Another reason is that international politics has become a much more important element in Black political thinking and there is a general identification of Israel as a settler nation with disturbing similarities to South Africa and the U.S.

Still, coalition building, if it includes promoting an agenda aimed specifically at meeting the needs of African Americans, continues as a viable political option, as was shown by Jesse Jackson's role in the Rainbow Coalition. Lest one think the Rainbow died with Jackson's presidential bid in 1988, the 1992 Democratic Convention, and the Clinton administration, while abandoning the Rainbow's rhetoric of dispossession, effectively coopted its vision of a government that looks like America, and in politics cooptation is the sincerest form of flattery.

A potential downside to these political developments is that the recent increase in Black elected officials came about partly through reapportionment to create majority Black voting districts. In many of these districts, however, fully twenty five percent of the population is below the poverty line, approximately twice the national average. How such stark economic realities will play themselves out politically is hard to predict. What is certain is that variations on the past themes of integration and separatism will continue.

It seems clear that rather than going away, the African American strains of American culture are continuing to elaborate themselves, to insinuate themselves into, and yet distinguish themselves from, the mainstream and thus, to transform the mainstream. In this process, the phenomenon of African Americans borrowing and experimenting with, accepting, rejecting, transforming and using, playing off of and signifying on cultural elements from the rest of America, and the world, continues.

Concluding Thoughts

Part of the Enlightenment heritage of America is the view that all human beings, regardless of different racial and ethnic backgrounds, should be able to live together and solve their mutual problems according to broad and universal principles. After all, as citizens of the world who endorse such principles, we should see the world through similar eyes. Such a perspective supports integrationist tendencies, but is problematic on several counts. It ignores the fact that "citizens of the world" often act as if their particular cultural eyes were the only ones through which the world can be correctly seen, the only ones through which universal principles can be properly understood. Where great inequalities, injustices and insecurities have persisted over centuries, it is naive to expect people to break with their perceived brothers and sisters, and rush to embrace their perceived enemies, regardless of universal principles.

Inequality, injustice and insecurity may be seen as negative roots of separatism, but separatism has positive roots as well. Its positive roots are the ways of life and cultural traditions which give purpose and meaning to life. Such traditions do not persist unless they are cared for and transmitted from generation to generation. This transmission goes on in a number of ways, but centers around birth communities, starting with families and reaching out to others who are perceived as sharing experience and meaning. In the context of such communities we become human persons and learn the fine texture of wit, taste and style that also gives meaning to life, just as broad and universal principles do.

Nations, and nations within nations, do need to recognize and adhere to universal principles of justice and morality. Yet adherance to such principles need not imply a single set of cultural standards or values. If, for Americans, "citizen of the world" can come to imply a right to cultural self-determination, and a recognition of the value of cultural diversity, then perhaps we can help a marvelously diverse world live together in both fruitful harmony and tension.

"Nationalism, Nation-State, and the United Nations"

Elizabeth Smith and H. Gene Blocker

In the days since the collapse of the Berlin Wall we have seen unparalleled changes in international political alignments. The relative stability of the Cold War era has ended and given rise to a period of transition so swift and widespread that cartographers are unable to redraw maps quickly enough to reflect the ongoing changes. These sorts of transitions have occurred repeatedly in the past after the collapse of expansionist empires. The last major resorting occurred after World War II when the demise of the Japanese empire and the end of European colonialism resulted in major realignments in Asia and Africa. Nonetheless, three factors make the current situation unique. First, all but the most isolated persons today can themselves witness the explosion of events as they transpire on live television. Hence it is possible, indeed necessary, to reflect on unfolding events in one locale in the context of what is occurring elsewhere. Second, it appears at the moment that there are no powerful states ready and willing to force their own preferences on others in order to enhance their position and power. What might emerge is a world-wide negotiation about how fairness and equity in political alignments can be achieved. International pressure, perhaps even military force, might be used to foster an outcome in the best interests of the concerned parties. Third, in reflecting on the forces that pull peoples together or that push them apart, we are forced to rethink those issues which underlie political unions and which, nevertheless, we do not understand very well.

On the one hand, it seems that we are moving toward "one world." No nation has its own economy any more since all economic systems are integrated. At the 1968 Democratic convention, demonstrators shouted, "the whole world is watching," as police brutalized the crowd. It probably wasn't true then. But when the troops marched into TianAnMen Square in Beijing and when Yeltsin defended his White House, the world *was* watching. We have an unprecedented sharing of culture, arts, and experiences. Increasingly we rely upon alliances or the United Nations to mediate international disputes and to enforce international policy. The popular culture reflects this vision of the future by depicting on *Star Trek* an Interstellar federation of peaceful nations operating in concert and welcoming the admission of even the Klingons, and by depicting in *Alien Nation*, the West Coast integrating into its fabric a whole nation of aliens.

But, on the other hand, despite this romantic and hopeful vision of the future, we are also confronted with ongoing bloody and seemingly intractible ethnic tensions in Northern Ireland, South Africa, the former Yugoslavia, India, and in the former nations of the Soviet Union and the Soviet Bloc countries of eastern Europe. The 1992 riots in Los Angeles tell us that an integration of the Blacks, Hispanics, Koreans, etc. living in the United States has not yet been achieved.

What is occuring is primarily a political reordering which shifts attention away from the super powers and relations among them as the primary focus of importance, to concentrations of groupings of people both larger and smaller than the traditional nation-state. On the one hand, there is a growing consensus that we ought to have geopolitical cooperation and exercise of power at the multi-national world level, perhaps through the United Nations, and, on the other hand, at the opposite end of the spectrum, a growing resurgence of demands for autonomy and "self-determination" by a proliferating number of smaller, ethnic and other minorities. Developments at these two seemingly opposite levels are nonetheless intimately related to one another in the sense that there is increasing concern about minorities being persecuted by the nation-states within which they currently exist. The sovereignty of Iraq might be abridged in favor of Kurdish rights; the sovereignty of Serbia is being challenged in favor of the rights of Bosnians and Croats. Ethnic and racial groups within South Africa, Kuwait, and Israel also demand protection and a measure of self-determination.

Clearly the most obvious reason for this shift of attention and concentration of power is the end of the Cold War. So long as the United States and its allies were locked in a nuclear standoff with the Soviet Union and its allies, no larger world political power could have much impact on these issues. At the same time, so long as the superpowers were deadlocked, there was no alternative but to respect the sovereignty of the superpower nation-states and their nation-state allies and client states, with the result that individual nation-states were free to suppress ancient claims of their ethnic minorities to self-determination. Apart from the inability of each superpower to interfere in the internal affairs of the other (and their allies and client states), there was also the presumption that in the noble language of the enlightenment, ethnic, racial and religious group solidarity had come to be seen as a politically irrelevant consideration.

Before the eighteenth century, people were accustomed to identify themselves as members of rather small groups, and then extended their community to larger groups such as Croatians, Lithuanians, Kurds, Protestants, Arabs, Jews, Black or White. Identification with ethnic and religious groups led to much petty but bloody conflict among people. But once it was claimed, in the enlightenment declarations about the universal and inalienable rights of man, that we are all primarily human beings, sharing equally with every other human being a common and proud "one world" humanity, it was hoped that all the petty, narrow-minded factionalism of the past would gradually fade away. We now see that presumption to have been an illusion, an overly optimistic dream which has now faded. This is a bitter disappointment to political liberals and those influenced by the enlightenment ideal that all humanity has one common nature.

Historically, "nationalism" was defined in terms of universal human rights in a way which made it seem that ethnic, tribal, racial, and linguistic identities were unimportant. In France and in America at the end of the eighteenth century, the foundations of government, legitimizing modern nation-states, was discussed in enlightened terms

of the rights which every human being posseses simply by virtue of being a human being—irrespective of whether that human being is a man or a woman, black or white, slave or free, Croatian or Serbian, Protestant or Roman Catholic, Christian or Jew, Yoruba or Ibo. Nonetheless, the subtext presupposed that the ideal nation-state was in fact an ethnically and culturally identical people forming themselves into a nation-state. The failure to recognize this subtext has had very serious consequences which are only now being realized.

Nationalism can be understood more broadly to mean the subjective perception of a group of people that they are united, or joined together in any one of several nonlegal, nonpolitical senses of group identity—on the basis of language, ethnicity, religion, race, culture, history or some combination of these. As such it is not a political or legal grouping but one which is primarily perceptual and in that sense "mythological." In this sense, "national" self-identity need not be based on biological or historical fact. An American who is 25% black and 75% white, is considered, both by black Americans and by white Americans, to be black. The Jewish ancestry of many European Jews may go back no further in history than the sixteenth or seventeenth century, and may in fact have no biological or family historical ties to the ancient Hebrews of Solomon's time. Another aspect of this subjective, "mythological," perceptual aspect of nationalism is the implication that how one sees oneself depends to a large extent on how *others* see us. So long as European Jews in early nineteenth century Germany (during the Napoleanic regime) who took German names, sincerely converted to Christianity, and culturally assimilated in every way to German culture were still perceived as Jews, to that extent the "reformed" assimilationists were forced to see *themselves* as Jews first and Germans second, if at all. And to the extent that black Americans are perceived by white Americans as a separate community, they tend to perceive themselves as blacks first.

In its present, modern form nationalism arose during the latter part of the eighteenth century. Connected at first with the French revolution, it defined a new concept of the modern nation-state—that of a group of people, a nation, demanding to be a state. In its original context the problem was simply one of changing the form of government of a group of people already existing in some sense as a political unit (e.g., France under a monarchy) which would better reflect the aspirations of "the people" (the "nation").

But here we must distinguish between the biological, anthropological *phenomenon* of nationalism and the emergence of the *concept* of "nationalism" as a key term in political discussions. The first is as old as human kind; the second as recent as the late eighteenth century. As Aristotle points out, "man is a social animal." But this means more than the fact that human beings want and need to live together in social communities. It also means that human beings tend to identify themselves with the particular cultural group of which they are members and to regard people of other cultural groups as alien, "others." For example, the word which many Native American and traditional African groups use to refer to themselves simply means "the people." This is the biological and anthropological root of the *phenomenon* of ethnic nationality. Man is biologically a pack animal and just as nature restricts the size of a wolf pack to a number that can be sustained by the prey available to the pack, so it may be that under some conditions human "packs" must also be exclusive. Whatever mechanism allows us to bond with each other also may be unconsciously at work in dividing us without our understanding it.

On the other hand, as a term used in historical, political and sociological contexts, the *concept* of "nationalism" in its earliest phase is linked with eighteenth century enlightenment ideas of the universal rights of man and with democracy as a superior form of government of "the people," by "the people" and for "the people." This idea developed first in Europe where, historically, groups which had shared for hundreds of years some cultural, linguistic sense of identity were already living, more or less, in contiguous geographical areas which were already recognized, more or less, as autonomous or semi-autonomous regions. An important preliminary stage on the road to the modern nation-state was the development of a centralized monarchy in Britain and France at the end of the Middle Ages which succeeded in wresting control from competing princes to consolidate a centralized national government.

The paradigm case was that of France where a culturally defined people living in a contiguous geographical area which had long been centrally governed by a monarch demanded in the eighteenth century that they should rule themselves. Other cases fall progressively away from this paradigm. German, and less obviously so, Italian speaking peoples, for example, like the French, sought a political unity to coincide with their cultural and linguistic sense of identity. But *unlike* the French this involved more than simply changing the form of government by revolutionary means. It also required constituting a new regional, political unit—creating out of many smaller principalities a modern Germany and a modern Italy—a political unity which already existed in the case of France. Later this idea was expanded still further to include people who perceived themselves as united in some nonpolitical sense but who were *not* politically organized within geographical borders, or who had no recent history, however checkered, of political independence—European Jews, Black Americans, Slavs, Kurds, Armenians, etc.

It is important to realize that although the language of the French Revolution was expressed in the universalist, enlightenment concepts of the "universal rights of man," what was intended was the self-determination of French-speaking, Roman Catholic, culturally and historically Gallic peoples—it was *not* meant to include Gypsies, Jews, or North African arabs who might be living within the geographical boundaries of France. Naturally, such a vague and imprecise and largely unconscious notion could admit of very large grey areas. In general it was not clear precisely how many or which combinations of "nationalist" features would qualify an outsider for membership into the "nation." Arabs and Jews who spoke French, adopted French customs, had converted to Catholicism for several generations could assimilate to membership in the French nation. Despite the universalist language of the enlightenment, the subtext is a demand that the French people ("ethnic nationality" as we are using the term) be self-governing, that they by right form a nation-state, that that "nation" should become a state.

Similarly in the American Declaration of Independence—did "all men" include women, as Abigail Adams asked her husband, did it include African slaves or American Indians—would it later come to include free Blacks, Chinese and later Japanese workers, Hispanics living within its territories? Admittedly, because of its pattern of settlement, the American "nation" was defined somewhat more broadly to include Europeans of English, German, French, or Dutch ethnic origins, but, although no one took the trouble to spell out explicitly who was included and who was excluded, it pretty clearly did not include non-Europeans and only marginally and begrudgingly, at least at first, Southern Europeans and Jews—unless, as in the case of French assimilation mentioned above, they could assimilate by speaking English, adopting Anglo-Saxon customs, though they were *not* required, because of our peculiar traditions of religious freedom, to convert to Protestantism. Different "nations" have different standards and different senses of tolerance for the assimilation of outsiders. French language, culture and religion are crucial; German biology and history are important; while in America race has proved the biggest barrier to full assimilation.

To some extent, therefore, the "nation" creates the "state" in the sense that an ethnic nationality demands to be a state. But to some extent it is also true that the "state" creates the "nation." Obviously the larger the population and the geographical area involved, the more differences there will be among "the people" thus joined together. They may all speak the same language but have somewhat different customs, or religious beliefs, and historical and economic histories. "Nation-building" will then be a matter of creating a greater sense of solidarity among all the people living within the state, to create of the state a "nation." Nonetheless, despite such flexibility in defining "group membership," historically there have been some groups which are excluded from full membership—Gypsies, Jews, freed African slaves, conquered indigenous groups, such as American Indians. And these groups are excluded despite the universalist language of the eighteenth century "declaration of the rights of man" which might seem to include *everyone.* When Martin Luther King, in his "I have a dream" speech, said that "America had defaulted on the promisory note that all men would be granted the unalienable rights of life, liberty, and the pursuit of happiness," he was harking back, as Lincoln had done earlier in his Gettysburg address, not to the Constitution, but to Jefferson's Declaration of Independence.

It was not that Thomas Jefferson failed to see the contradiction between slavery and the universal rights of all men; indeed he was keenly aware of that contradiction. Jefferson shared a confusion with other enlightenment thinkers between the claim that (1) each *nation,* each *ethnic group* had the right of self-determination and that each bona fide member of that "ethnic nationality" shared equally basic rights (which Jefferson *et al.* supported) and (2) the very different claim that each person, of whatever racial or ethnic origin, who happened to be living within the same geographical boundaries had equal rights within the same nation-state (which Jefferson *et al.* did *not* intend).

The key question which was not fully or consciously addressed then or now is precisely who belongs to the "nation." Who are "the people"? It is like membership in a club. Certain people belong and share equally rights and responsibilities of membership. Others may be invited to join, but still others are excluded and do not share in the rights, privileges and responsibilities of full membership. Because of the universalist language of the eighteenth century in which these rights were discussed, along with the failure to consider explicitly the "nationalist" requirements for "membership," confusions persist, including the false expectation that everyone living within the geographical boundaries are automatically included in "we the people," when in fact some are included and some are excluded.

We should not be surprised, therefore, that this hidden subtext begins to surface today in the rise of ethnic tensions in eastern Europe and the countries of the former Soviet Union. So long as some political communities, such as the United States, Canada and Australia, seemed to be thriving as "melting pots" harmonizing a rich palette of races, religions and ethnic groups, and so long as the Soviet Union succeeded in blocking and strangling ethnic demands by its imposition of a socialist ideal which transcended and superceded all ethnic and religious rivalries, the dream of "the melting pot" seemed for many decades a reality. Now we seriously question that dream. What does or should provide the basis for inclusion into a political community? Should the Serbs bond with the Croats in one nation or become two? Can the Hindus and Muslims live together as one country? Can the blacks, Hispanics, Koreans and whites "all get along" in Los Angeles?

Western Europeans were understandably pleased to hear their Eastern European neighbors embracing the rationalist/universalist language of the universal rights of man in defending their declarations of independence from Communist totalitarianism, but these same Westerners were soon disappointed to find the actual implementation of those "rights" quickly degenerating into the bloody ethnic conflict we are witnessing today known as "ethnic cleansing." Like America and France in the eighteenth century, Germany and Italy in the nineteenth century, so today, the Hungarians, Rumanians, Lithuanians, Armenians, Croats, Serbs express their demand for ethnic autonomy and self-determination in the universalist language of the universal rights of man. We are only surprised because we are only now, more than 200 years later, beginning to realize the deep ambiguity and conceptual confusions surrounding the enlightenment ideal of the rights of man.

Supposing that slavery is wrong because it violates the universal rights of men, does it follow (in the United States after 1865) that freed slaves should therefore become full citizens of the nation-state in which they were enslaved? Though the language of the Declaration of Independence makes it sound as though the answer to the one question must be the same as the answer to the other, they were in fact seen as two quite separate questions in the intended subtext of the document. This is why the question of the right to own slaves, however difficult, was much easier to answer in the United States than the very different and more vexing question, still not fully answered, of what status freed Africans should have—should they be returned to Africa, could they be made a permanent underclass of servants enjoying some but not all rights of citizenship (in the program of the Jim Crow south)—or failing to answer these questions satisfactorily, should they simply remain slaves as the lesser of two evils? For many otherwise intelligent southerners, the biggest problem with freeing the slaves was the prospect that they would thereby become part of the nation-state. Even abolitionists favored barring immigration of Africans and other non-Causasians. They thought slavery was wrong but they did not thereby intend a racially, culturally, ethnically mixed nation. And so the dilemma. If slavery is wrong then the slaves must be freed, but then what? Because of the deep

conceptual confusion we have been discussing, this question remains unresolved. The Civil Rights movement of the 1950s can be seen as the latest in a long line of attempts, including Lincoln's "Gettysburg Address," and Martin Luther Kings' "I have a dream speech," moving slowly and hesitatingly toward a recognition that the only solution is full integration of African Americans into the nation, that is, into mainstream American life. But the outcome of that struggle is today far from clear. Similarly, Chinese who came to the United States on work contracts (to build the rail roads) had certain rights as "legal aliens" but were denied full rights of citizenship for over a hundred years. In much the same way third and fourth generation Koreans living in Japan do not enjoy full rights of Japanese citizenship, nor Palestinians in Kuwait, to mention only a few such cases.

Many, perhaps a majority, of Americans still believe deeply but unconsciously that while those of African, Chinese, Hispanic and Native American descent live and will continue to live in the United States, they do not form an integral part of the American "nation," and in that sense America is Eurocentric and racist. We still consider our historical roots to be primarily European. We may concede that African Americans should study their African cultural roots, Chinese Americans their Asian roots, Hispanic Americans their Hispanic roots, Native Americans their Amerindian roots, but we don't see this as *our* American national roots—or, at best, we have some vague sense of a nation made up of many nations, so we can see African culture contributing to one of the subsidiary nations which make up the larger composite nation. But we, who are white, don't identify with these non-European contributions—with Chinese philosophy, Jewish history, American Indian customs, for example, or African art, even when they have shaped the nation we have become. Arguably, contemporary Americans are more like American Indians than Puritans. Just as the Germans, after Bismarck, recognized that although the Gypsies and Jews were living among them and would probably continue to do so, they nonetheless did not belong to the German nation-state (though they might have some rights), and as today Germans, French and British ponder the status of Turks, Africans, West Indians, Indians and Pakistanis living and working in their country, so many Americans continue to believe, secretly, that because Africans, Chinese, Hispanics and Native Americans did not come (were not "invited") to this country in order to become citizens and members of the American nation, they therefore still do not fully constitute a part of the American "nation" (though they have some rights and ought not be enslaved or mistreated).

Nationalism, then, in its most general sense is the perception which a group of people has of itself as possessing some sort of nonpolitical identity—ethnic, historical, linguistic, cultural, religious, racial—who demand "self-determination" in the sense of a supposed right to construct a political state which coincides with the nation (or at least some measure of autonomy within a larger state composed of other "nationalities"). American Indians, for example, did not originally have a concept of themselves as an "Indian nation" but as bands which had varying relationships with other bands, forming tribal groups which in turn entered into relationships with each other. In a similar way, Africans did not perceive themselves as a single group until they saw that Europeans so regarded them, and began to join together in a united front against the white European invaders. In the early nineteenth century many European ethnic minorities enthusiastically embraced the new conception of nationalism and made it part of the rhetoric of their demands for autonomy and self-determination. It was not until the twentieth century (when, unfortunately, it was too late for many of them) that African and Native American groups began to express their demands for autonomy and self-determination in the European language of "nationalism."

For ethnic nationalities living among other people within existing states, unable or unwilling to assimilate to the larger nation in which they find themselves, nationalism becomes a call for separatism—that this ethnic minority should form its own state, or at least some measure of autonomy within the geographical boundaries of the existing multinational state. For nationalities widely scattered in many different countries (e.g., the Jews) nationalism becomes either a mystical sense of an immaterial nation without a state, or else the demand for some land (in Palestine or South America, for example) in which to form their own nation-state. For the *majority* living within established geographical and political boundaries within which

are smaller minority "nationalities," nationalism can become the demand that the minority nationalities either assimilate, leave or be killed in what is now known as "ethnic cleansing," or else lose the rights of *full* citizenship ("the Jewish problem" in early twentieth century Germany, the problem of second generation Palestinians living in Kuwait, or third generation Koreans in Japan, or Muslims living in Bosnia and other parts of former Yugoslavia). For more or less fully constituted, "ideal" nation-states (those in which there is an identity of one nation, one state) nationalism can become an expansionist demand to spread their supposedly superior culture to other countries in other parts of the world—e.g., Nazi Germany, nineteenth century Imperialism, whether of the USA variety, or the French and English colonial type.

Colonialism is at once a kind of nationalism (expansionist, militarist type) and at the same time it creates artificial states without a sense of nationhood. States of Africa carved up by European colonial powers at the end of the nineteenth century joined together different ethnic, tribal groups into colonial states and divided other ethnic, tribal groups into different colonial states—so, for example, Nigeria is composed of dozens of different ethnic groups, some of whose tribal members (e.g., Yoruba) live beyond the borders of Nigeria in neighboring French-speaking Benin Republic. What identity these people have (first simply as "Africans" and then as "Nigerians") came largely from the white European colonial rulers. Only with the arrival of the Europeans did the Africans begin to see and think of themselves *as* "Africans"—not just as racially distinct but also as culturally distinct and, from the European colonial point of view, generally inferior to white European culture. From the European point of view, the aim of colonialism was in part an expression of nationalism, as the "white man's burden" to bring civilization to "primitive," mostly nonwhite peoples. And it was only through the European colonial powers that African peoples later came to think of themselves as Nigerians, Ghanaians, and so on. African "nationalism" was primarily the desire of people who now saw themselves as "African" for freedom from an alien colonial, European power. It was only the historical accident that they had been divided into various "countries" that this nationalist sense had to be directed to freeing each country, one by one, from various European colonial powers—French, English, Portuguese, German, Belgium, Spanish and Italian. Nationalism in Africa now expresses itself most often in the armed struggle for ethnic, tribal supremacy, or at least, autonomy.

There is no single solution to such a range of complex problems. Certainly we need to respect the right of groups to self-determination. If, as seems to be the case, group identification is so important to so many individuals' sense of self and self-esteem and value, then group rights would seem to follow from our more familiar notion of individual rights. Group rights would appear to be an extension of the individual's right to full self development. In other words, we must add to individual rights the notion of group rights, allowing the deeply felt desire of many "nationalities" to achieve a measure of autonomy and self-determination. This could take various forms, short of but including the ideal of each nationality becoming an independent nation-state—for example, regional autonomy, multiple language usage, respect for different religions and religious customs and holidays, perhaps even fixed group representation, or, as in Lebanon, rotation of government offices attached to specific ethnic nationalities. Sovereignty is thereby severely restricted since states cannot be allowed to oppress rights of groups living therein. If this is to be seen as a positive rather than negative development, a case needs to be made for defending international law and order even where it opposes national sovereignty at the nation-state level, whether in Iraq, Somalia, or the former Yugoslavia.

In other cases, however, in West Africa, for example, and other regions of the world which have only a recent history of political organization at the nation-state level, we need to encourage nation-building and multinational cooperation, speeding the evolution *away from* ethnic nationalism at the tribal level, experimenting with various forms of multinational unification around *political* principles rather than ethnic, racial, linguistic, religious and other (ancient) cultural forms of identity. Without organization at the nation-state level, it is hard to imagine a collection of ethnic minorities having sufficient technological, industrial, communications facilities and infrastructure to be able to participate effectively, as an equal, in the modern world. After several "false starts" toward democratic modernization during the colonial and

neo-colonial periods, the end of the Cold War marks the beginning of an optimistic sense throughout West Africa of a "second chance" at democracy which will *accelerate* the movement toward the formation of viable nation-states in that region.

Regions of the world where we could more easily imagine a move away from the nation-state as the preferred political grouping are those in which nation-states have evolved to the point of effective regional cooperation, such as seems to be happening in Europe, and is perhaps beginning to take place in North America and the Americas more generally. Even so, nation-states will probably continue to be important for some time to come, though in a somewhat diminished capacity. In some cases this will involve greater access of all minorities to assimilation to full citizenship in the larger nation-state (invitation to full membership). But in other cases it means a greater tolerance for diversity of different ethnic nationalities within a single nation-state. This last alternative implies a synthesis of "integration" and "separation"—integrating all individuals of all ethnic nationalities into the *political* and *economic* life of the nation-state, but also encouraging a degree of *cultural* and *ethnic* diversity (of language, custom, religion, music, taste, etc.). In the United States, for example, this might involve Hispanics speaking Spanish, listening to Hispanic radio, watching Hispanic TV programs and films, studying Hispanic history and culture, and so on; AfricanAmericans learning more about African and African American history and culture, and so on, with members of all ethnic groups participating fully in the middle-class "American dream" economically and professionally.

Another goal of "multiculturalism" is to embrace African, Chinese, Native American, etc. cultural contributions—not just for African Americans, Chinese Americans, Native Americans, respectively, but for *all* (and particularly for white) Americans. This is the sense of multicultural education which would emphasize nation-building, ethnic integration rather than ethnic separation, encouraging the idea, for example, that jazz is not a "black music" but an American music; "California Zen" is not a Chinese or Japanese religion but now an American religion; Mexican-American, Chinese-American food is American cuisine; and that American Indian traditions should become traditions for all Americans. African and Native American history, for example, would be taught to white students as well as African and Native American students. This would be a difficult and distant goal since these efforts will antagonize those who *do not* identify with these traditions, and who see integration of diverse cultures as the loss of their own cultural identity. Whichever way we go, how can we work to respect the rights not only of individuals but of groups when they may conflict with each other?

Similar problems of balancing integration and separation occur whenever and wherever minority groups living among a majority people were not "invited" to live there as citizens enjoying full rights of citizenship. American Indians and the Hispanics of the southwest did not "invite" Europeans to live within their geographical boundaries, nor did Europeans "invite," until much later, American Indians to become citizens of the United States. Chinese were invited to the United States (and to many other countries as well) initially only on work permits, not to become citizens. Other immigrants in similar circumstances were Asian Indians in Africa, Chinese in Indonesia, Koreans in Japan, Turkish workers in Germany, or Palestinian workers in Kuwait. In the past, groups suffering religious and other forms of persecution, such as Jews and Gypsies, were allowed to live in restricted areas, "ghettos," within certain countries, e.g., Germany, as an invited minority, but were *not* allowed the rights of full citizenship. The problem occurs with the passage of time—does the fourth generation descendant of Korean, Indian, Chinese, Palestinian, etc. worker, Jew, or Gypsy, operate under the same contractual agreement which their forefathers consented to fifty, a hundred or two hundred years ago? At what point does it become unrealistic to regard these minorities as "aliens" who are expected eventually to return "home"? If they have been allowed to stay, there would appear to be an implied consent that they can eventually become citizens. And if so, then they must be allowed full rights of citizenship. If this is *not* the intention, host countries should regularly and periodically update worker permits (and where the workers are no longer needed, discontinue the worker permit, thereby requiring the individuals to return to their home countries). Then it would be clear that they are *not* citizens, but temporary guest

workers, remaining at the pleasure of the host country for renewable five-year contract periods, for example, as long as they are needed. It does not seem fair after four or five generations (during which time nothing was said or done about their immigration status) either to insist that they go "home" or to be allowed to remain without the rights of full citizenship.

But if the minority group has been granted full citizenship rights, it seems only reasonable to allow them the choice of whether and to what extent to assimilate into the cultural life of the majority community. To grant them citizenship but not allow them to culturally assimilate is, in effect, a contradiction, since to actually enjoy many of the rights of citizenship individuals must be able to interact as equals with the mainstream, majority culture. This is why allowing country clubs to exclude blacks restricts African Americans' opportunity to enjoy their full rights as citizens. If blacks must eat in black restaurants, attend black schools, sleep in black hotels, live in black neighborhoods, they cannot fully participate in the economic and cultural life of the country. Similarly, if important business and political decisions are made through country club "networking," excluding blacks is a restriction of the enjoyment of their full rights, including economic rights, as citizens. Of course, this may restrict the individual rights and freedoms of those in the majority (white) culture who do not want to associate with blacks. But here we must weigh the relative injustice of forcing hotel or restaurant owners to serve patrons they do not wish to associate with against the injustice of restricting full access of African Americans to the economic and cultural life of the country. The same principle would seem to apply to restricting or segregating admission to schools, businesses, neighborhoods, and even country clubs.

One might wonder how it can be fair to demand that the majority *allow* the minority to culturally assimilate but *not require* the minority to assimilate culturally to the majority even if the minority don't want to. The answer is that "success" in the nation-state, as defined by the majority culture, depends on success *within* the majority culture which can only be accomplished by assimilation *into* the majority culture. Preventing minorities from assimilating works to the great disadvantage of members of the minority culture who *want* to be "successful" by the standards of the majority culture, whereas it is hard to see how the refusal of a minority to fully assimilate culturally could greatly affect the "success" of members of the mainstream majority culture in an adverse way. Some may object that members of the majority culture *prefer* to be culturally "pure" and that, however questionable or abhorrent we may find their reasons, they have the *right* to require cultural assimilation by outsiders as the only way to remain as culturally "pure" as they can. But this "harm" of "offensiveness" must be weighed against the more obvious and overt harm to the alienated minority. If a member of a minority wants to be "successful" by the standards of the mainstream majority culture, then they must be allowed full access (equal opportunity) to do so. On the other hand, if a member of a minority (or indeed any individual) rejects the majority standards of "success," they should be free to do as they please so long as they do not "harm" others.

We have considered a number of solutions to the problem of reconciling ethnic identity with multi-ethnic cooperation. What determines what is the best solution in a particular situation? Primarily, it should be based on the "will of the people"— both as individuals and as members of groups with which individuals identify. If the individuals and groups which have been "invited" to become citizens want to assimilate, they must be allowed to do so by removing all barriers of discrimination, negative stereotypes, and so on. If individuals and groups insist on self-determination and political autonomy, this must be supported, either with full autonomy as independent nation-states or with some measure of regional autonomy. If individuals and groups want political integration and cultural separation, this too must be allowed and facilitated.

In the past, one of the strongest arguments *against* group rights, especially the right of an ethnic minority to secede from the larger nation-state, has been the practical necessity of forming a viable nation-state with enough and a wide enough range of natural resources to be relatively self-sufficient militarily and economically. But that argument seems to carry less weight today as we move toward multinational political and economic associations. Why can't Nunavut, the new selfgoverning Native American territory in northern Canada, function as a politically autonomous entity within an American (including North, Central and South American) military and economic multinational cooperative association? Certainly, there is little resistance today to the break-up of Eastern European nation-states into a multitude of tiny nationalistic states under the larger Pan-European umbrella. Perhaps in the future the greatest incentive for ethnic minorities to remain within a larger nation-state will simply be the convenience and economic efficiency of a single monetary unit, unified educational and professional standards, a common highway system, a common language, etc. But even that incentive may erode over time, especially in the new European union and even today in the informal US-Canadian-Mexican PanAmerican association which could function in many ways as a single nation (exchangability of money, porous borders, similar educational and professional standards, an interconnected highway system, mutual access to radio and television transmission, and so on.)

Index